PROPER

NOUN

Speller

UPDATED &
UP-TO-DATE
Over 40,000 Entries

HAFTEL PUBLISHERS

Compiled by Beverly Loeblein Ritter & Patricia Pooser Rhyne

HAFTEL PUBLISHERS
Springfield, New Jersey 07081
800-255-5040

ISBN # 0-938643-35-5

FOREWORD

This *Proper Noun Speller* will prove to be an invaluable reference for the correct spelling of proper nouns (names). This updated edition contains over 40,000 entries compiled from over 4,000 sources.

AMONG THE PROPER NOUNS INCLUDED ARE THE NAMES OF

PEOPLE

Artists	Scientists
Business leaders	Sports figures
Entertainers	Tribes
Fictional characters	Nationalities
Media figures	US leaders
Mythological figures	World leaders
Religious figures	Writers

PLACES

Cities	Mountains
Continents	Nations
Countries	Oceans
Deserts	Planets & stars
Famous attractions	Rivers
Lakes	States

THINGS

Books	Medicines
Brand names	Movies
Businesses	Newspapers
Court cases	Organizations
Current events	Paintings
Government agencies	Plays
Historical events	Religions
Historical periods	Scientific terms
Holidays	Songs
Languages	Space vehicles
Laws	Trademarks
Magazines	TV shows

BONUS

To make this the most useful and complete proper noun speller on the market, a brief description is included with most entries to further authenticate that this is the name you're looking for.

> Wolfe, Thomas (Clayton)(US writer; 1900-38)
> Wolfe, Tom (b. Thomas Kennerly Wolfe, Jr.)(US writer; 1931-)
> Wolff, Tobias (US writer; 1945-)
> Woolf, (Adeline) Virginia (Stephen)(Br. writer; 1882-1941)

INTRODUCTION

STYLE OF ENTRIES

Most entries include a brief description in addition to the actual name. The description chosen is that which is most inclusive or most well known. For example, an entertainer (ent.) may be an actor, singer, director, etc.; a novel may also be a film or play.

When appropriate, names are cross referenced.

> Whoopi Goldberg (b. Karen Johnson)(ent.; 1950-)
> Goldberg, Whoopi (b. Karen Johnson)(ent.; 1950-)

Proper nouns known by more than one name are further cross referenced.

> Clemens, Samuel Langhorne (pseud. Mark Twain)(US writer; 1835-1910)
> Mark Twain (aka Samuel Langhorne Clemens)(US writer; 1835-1910)
> Samuel Langhorne Clemens (pseud. Mark Twain)(US writer; 1835-1910)
> Twain, Mark (aka Samuel Langhorne Clemens)(US writer; 1835-1910)

Dates refer to the birth and death dates of people and the date of occurrence for events.

> Battle of the Bulge (WWII; 1944-45)

When giving day/month/year, dates other than the 1900s will be itemized.

> Black Tuesday (US stock market crash; 10/29/29)
> Black Friday (US finan. disasters; 9/24/1869 & 9/19/1873)

ACRONYMS

Acronyms are included in the body of the text.

ALPHABETIZATION

Alphabetization is letter by letter with the following qualifications.

Abbreviated designations such as St. and Mt. are alphabetized as though they were spelled out as Saint and Mount. Arabic numbers are alphabetized as though they were spelled out. Symbols such as & are alphabetized by what they represent (e.g., the word "and").

Roman numerals are alphabetized by the actual letters. Punctuation marks, titles such as Sir and Dr., and material in parentheses are ignored for purposes of alphabetization.

Entries with the same first word are listed together before any entries followed by a comma.

> Henry Ford (US bus./auto.; 1863-1947)
> Henry Ford, II (US bus./auto.; 1917-87)
> Henry James (US writer; 1843-1916)
> Henry VIII (king, Eng.; 1491-1547)
> Henry Winkler (ent.; 1945-)
> Henry, John (fict. chara., exceptional strength)
> Henry, Patrick (US pol./orator; 1736-99)
> Henry's law (gas in liquid)

SPELLING VARIATIONS

Because of country origins or phonetic translations, some names may have more than one correct spelling. In addition, often the most respected references differ on the preferred spelling of a proper noun.

When one spelling has been generally accepted by the majority of reference sources, only that spelling has been included. When variant spellings are common, those variations have also been included.

> Bosnia-Hercegovina (republic, Yug.)(also Bosnia-Herzegovina)

PRONUNCIATION MARKS

Pronunciation marks have been included for those entries which retain them when Anglicized. Whether you need to include these marks will depend on the nature of your work.

> Perón, Evita (b. Maria Eva Duarte)(Argentinian pol.; 1919-52)

TRADEMARKS (™ & ®)

The trademark symbol has been included when its use has been confirmed.

The symbol ™ is used to indicate all trademarks, whether the trademark is applied for (™) or registered (®). Trademarked items should be capitalized. The word(s) following is generally not capitalized unless it is part of the brand name or is a proper noun in its own right.

> Godiva™ chocolates
> Godiva Chocolatier (US bus.)

Whether you need to include the ™ symbol will depend on the nature of your work. However, all brand names and trademarks should be capitalized unless unusual capitalization is part of the actual trademark.

> pHisoDerm™

ITALICIZED NOUNS

The following have been italicized:

> Titles of books, magazines, newspapers;
> Names of films, plays, TV and radio shows;
> Names of paintings, sculptures, symphonies, songs, poems;
> Legal citations;
> Crewed ships, planes, spacecraft.

> *Proper Noun Speller*

HYPHENATING PROPER NOUNS

Simply stated, it is best not to hyphenate a name. When hyphenation is unavoidable, follow these few rules.

> Do not divide nouns of one syllable.
> Do not divide an acronym unless it has a natural division (e.g., AFL-CIO).
> Do not separate the title from the name.

ABBREVIATIONS USED IN THIS TEXT

adm.	admiral	DC	District of Columbia,
admin.	administrator		Washington DC
adv.	advertiser, advertising	DE	Delaware
Afghan.	Afghanistan, Afghan(i)	Den.	Denmark
Afr.	Africa(n)	dipl.	diplomat
agcy.	agency	dir.	director
agr.	agriculture, agriculturalist	Dom Rep.	Dominican Republic
AK	Alaska	drama.	dramatist
aka	also known as	E	east
AL	Alabama	ecol.	ecology, ecologist
Amer.	America(n)	econ.	economics, economist,
anthrop.	anthropologist, anthropology		economical
AR	Arkansas	educ.	educator, educational
arch.	architect(ure)	Eg.	Egypt(ian)
archaeol.	archaeologist	elec.	electronics, electrical
art.	artistic	emp.	emperor
assoc.	association	Eng.	England, English
astro.	astronaut	eng.	engineer
astrol.	astrology, astrologer	ent.	entertainer, entertainment
astron.	astronomy, astronomer		industry
Atl.	Atlantic Ocean	environ.	environment(al)(ist)
atty.	attorney	est.	established
Aus.	Austria(n)	ethnol.	ethnologist
Austl.	Australia(n)	Eur.	Europe(an)
auto.	automobile, automotive	expl.	explorer
AZ	Arizona	fict.	fictitious
b.	born	Fin.	Finnish, Finland
bacteriol.	bacteriologist	finan.	financial, financier
BC	before Christ	FL	Florida
biol.	biologist, biology	fl.	flourished
Br.	British, Britain	Flem.	Flemish
bro.	brother	Fr.	French, France
bus.	business	GA	Georgia
c	circa	gen.	general
c.	century	geol.	geologist, geology
CA	California	Ger.	German(y)
CAmer.	Central America	gov-gen.	governor-general
Can.	Canada, Canadian	gov.	governor
capt.	captain	govt.	government
Ch.	China, Chinese	Gr.	Greek, Greece
chanc.	chancellor	grp.	group
chara(s).	character(s)	Guat.	Guatemala
chem.	chemical, chemist, chemistry	HI	Hawaii
CO	Colorado	hist.	history, historian
Co.	Company	Hung.	Hungary, Hungarian
Col.	Colonel	IA	Iowa
comm.	communications	ID	Idaho
comp.	composer	IL	Illinois
compu.	computers	IN	Indiana
cond.	conductor	Inc.	Incorporated
cong.	congress	inv.	inventor
cos.	companies	Ir.	Ireland, Irish
cosmo.	cosmonaut	Isr.	Israel(i)
CT	Connecticut	It.	Italian, Italy
Czech.	Czechoslovakia(n)	Jap.	Japan(ese)
Dan.	Danish	Jew.	Jewish

jour.	journalist	photo.	photographer, photography
KS	Kansas	phys.	physician
KY	Kentucky	physiol.	physiologist
l.c.	lower case	physt.	physicist
LA	Louisiana	PM	prime minister
lang(s).	language(s)	Pol.	Poland, Polish
lit.	literature, literary	pol.	politician, political, politics
Lith.	Lithuania(n)	Port.	Portugal, Portuguese
MA	Massachusetts	pres.	president
mag.	magazine	prods.	products
math.	mathematics, mathematician	pseud.	pseudonym
MD	Maryland	psych.	psychiatrist, psychologist,
ME	Maine		psychoanalyst
med.	medical, medicine	publ.	publisher, publishing
meteorol.	meteorologist	rel.	religion, religious, religionist
MI	Michigan	RI	Rhode Island
mil.	military, militarist	Rus.	Russia(n)
MN	Minnesota	S Afr.	South Africa (area)
MO	Missouri	S	south
MS	Mississippi	SAfr.	South Africa(n)(country)
MT	Montana	SAmer.	South America(n)
myth.	mythical, mythology	SC	South Carolina
N	north	scien.	scientist
NAfr.	North Africa	Scot.	Scottish, Scotland
NAmer.	North America	SD	South Dakota
nat.	naturalist	Secy.	Secretary
nav.	navigator	seismol.	seismologist
NC	North Carolina	sociol.	sociology, sociologist
ND	North Dakota	Sp.	Spanish
NE	Nebraska	St.	Saint
neurol.	neurologist	Ste.	Sainte
neuropharmacol.		SViet.	South Vietnam
	neuropharmacologist	Swed.	Sweden, Swedish
NewZeal.	New Zealand	Switz.	Switzerland
NH	New Hampshire	sym.	symbol
NIre.	Northern Ireland	TN	Tennessee
NJ	New Jersey	trans.	transporataion
NM	New Mexico	Turk.	Turkey, Turkish
Nor.	Norway, Norwegian	TX	Texas
NV	Nevada	UAE	United Arab Emirates
NViet.	North Vietnam	UK	United Kingdom
NY	New York	US	United States
ofc.	office	USSR	United Soviet Socialist
OH	Ohio		Republic
OK	Oklahoma	UT	Utah
OR	Oregon	VA	Virginia
org.	organization, organized	VI	Virgin Islands
orig.	originally	Viet.	Vietnam(ese)
ornithol.	ornithologist	virol.	virologist
PA	Pennsylvania	VP	vice president
Pac.	Pacific Ocean	VT	Vermont
Pak.	Pakistan(i)	W	west
paleontol.	paleontologist	WA	Washington
pathol.	pathologist	WGer.	West Germany
Pers.	Persia, Persian	WI	Wisconsin
petro.	petroleum	WSamoa	Western Samoa
pharm.	pharmaceuticals,	WV	West Virginia
	pharmacology	WY	Wyoming
Phil.	Philippine(s)	Yug.	Yugoslavia(n)
phil.	philosopher, philosophy	zool.	zoologist

A

AA (Alcoholics Anonymous, American Airlines, Associate of Arts)

AAA (American Automobile Association)

AAA World (mag.)

Aachen, Germany (also Aix-la-Chapelle)

Aage Bohr (Dan. physt.; 1922-)

Aalborg, Denmark

AAMCO Transmission, Inc.

AAMCO™ transmissions

A(lan) A(lexander) Milne (Br. writer; 1882-1956)

A & P Food Stores (Great Atlantic & Pacific Tea Co.)

A & W Brands, Inc.

A & W™ root beer

Aare River (also Aar)(Switz.)

Aarhus, Denmark (also Arhus)

Aaron Brothers Art Marts, Inc.

Aaron Burr (ex-US VP; 1756-1836)

Aaron Copland (US comp.; 1900-90)

Aaron Montgomery Ward (US bus.; 1843-1913)

Aaron Spelling (ent.; 1928-)

Aaron, Hank (Henry)(baseball; 1934-)

Aaron, Tommy (baseball; 1939-84)

AARP (American Association of Retired Persons)

AARP Bulletin (mag.)

AAU (Amateur Athletic Union)

AAUW (American Association of University Women)

ABA (American Bar Association, American Booksellers Association)

Aba, Nigeria

Abacha, Sani (acting ruler, Nigeria)

Abadan, Iran

Abaddon (also Apollyon)(destroyer, hell)

Abba Eban, (Aubrey Solomon)(Isr. pol.; 1915-)

Abbado, Claudio (It. ent.; 1933-)

Abbas I ("the Great")(Pers. shah; c1557-1629)

Abbasid dynasty (Islamic ruling family; 750-1258)

Abbe, Cleveland (US meteor.; 1838-1916)

Abbeville Press, Inc.

Abbeville, France

Abbey Road (Beatles album)

Abbey Theatre (Ir.)

Abbie (Abbott H.) Hoffman (US pol. activist; 1936-89)

Abbot, Charles Greeley (US physt.; 1872-1973)

Abbott (slang, Nembutal™)

Abbott and Costello (ent.)

Abbott Laboratories (US bus.)

Abbott, Bud (ent.; 1895-1974)

Abbott, George (ent.; 1889-?)

Abbott, Lyman (US rel.; 1835-1922)

Abby Dalton (ent.; 1932-)

Abby, Dear (Abigail Van Buren)(b. Pauline Esther Friedman)(US advice columnist; 1918-)

ABC (Alcoholic Beverage Control Board)

ABC™ (American Broadcasting Co.)

ABC After School Special

ABC Information Radio

ABC News (TV show)

ABC Radio Network News

A. B. (Happy) Chandler (baseball; 1899-1991)

Abd al-Salam al Majali (PM, Jordan)

Abdel Nasser, Gamal (ex-pres., Eg.; 1918-70)

Abdel-Rahman, Sheik Omar (Muslim rel.; 1938-)

Abdesalam, Belaid (Algerian pol.; 1928-)

A. B. Dick Co.

Abdou Diouf (pres., Senegal; 1935-)

Abdou, Muhammad (PM, Comoros)

Abdoulaye Sekou Sow (PM, Mali)

Abdul Gayoom, (Maumoon)(pres., Maldives)

Abdul Hashim Mutalov (PM, Uzbekistan)

Abdul-Jabbar, Kareem (b. [Ferdinand] Lew[is] Alcindor, Jr.)(basketball; 1947-)

Abdul, Paula (ent.; 1962-)

Abdullah ibn Hussein (ex-king, Jordan; 1882-1951)

Abdullah, Muhammad ibn (Arab, founded Islam; c570-632)

Abdumalik Abulajanov (PM, Tajikistan)

Abdur Rahman Biswas (pres., Bangladesh)

Abe Burrows (US writer; 1910-85)

Abe Fortas (US jurist; 1910-82)

Abe Kobo (Jap. writer; 1924-93)

Abe Vigoda (ent.; 1921-)

Abeche, Chad

Abel (son of Adam & Eve)

Abel Janszoon Tasman (Dutch expl./nav.; 1603?-59)

Abel (Tendekayi) Muzorewa (Zimbabwean pol./rel.; 1925-)

Abelard, Pierre (or Peter)(Fr. phil.; 1079-1142)

Abeokuta, Nigeria

Abercrombie & Fitch (US bus.)

Aberdeen (Black) Angus cattle

Aberdeen Proving Ground, MD (mil.)

Aberdeen, MD, SD, WA

Aberdeen, Scotland

Abernathy Sport™ (clothing)

Abernathy, Ralph David (US rel./civil rights leader; 1926-90)

A. B. Guthrie (US writer; 1901-91)

Abhidhamma Pitaka (rel.)

Abidjan, Ivory Coast

Abie's Irish Rose (play)

Abigail (Smith) Adams (wife of ex-US pres.; 1744-1818)

Abigail Van Buren (Dear Abby)(b. Pauline
   Esther Friedman)(US advice columnist;
   1918-)
Abilene, TX
Abington Township v. Schempp (US law; 1963-)
Abisala, Aleksandras (Lith. pol.)
Abkhazi (Georgian republic)
Abkhazian (people, area)
ABM (antiballistic missile)
Abner Doubleday (US mil., possibly inv.
   baseball; 1819-93)
Abner, Li'l (fict. chara.)
Abner, Lum and
ABO system (blood classification)
A-bomb (atom bomb; slang, heroin/marijuana
   cigarette)
Abomey, Benin
Abominable Snowman (also l.c.)
Aboriginal Science Fiction
Aborigine, Australian (people)(also l.c.)
Abracadabra, Lady
Abraham & Straus/Jordan Marsh Co.
Abraham Lincoln (16th US pres.; 1809-65)
Abraham, F. Murray (ent.; 1939-)
Abraham, Plains of (Can.)
Abraham's bosom (heaven)
Abramovitz, Max (US arch.; 1908-)
Abrams v. U.S. (US law; 1919)
Abrams, Creighton (US gen.; 1914-74)
Abrahamson, Brecht v. (US law; 1993)
Abruzzi (region, It.)
Abruzzi e Molise, Italy
Abscam scandal (*Ab*dul/Arab *Scam*, US cong.,
   bribes; 1978-80)
Absessalem, Belnid (ex-PM, Algeria)
Absolut™ (vodka)
Abu Bakr (Islamic pol., 573-634)
Abu Dhabi (state, UAE)
Abu Said Omar Dourda (PM, Libya)
Abuja, Nigeria
Abulajanov, Abdumalik (PM, Tajikistan)
Aburdene, Patricia (US writer)
Abyssinia (now Ethiopia)
Abyssinian (cat)
Abzug, Bella (Savitzky)(US pol.; 1920-)
AC (alternating current)
A/C (air conditioning)
Ac (chem. sym., actinium)
Acacia Winery (US bus.)
Academy Awards (also Oscars)
Academy of Arts, Royal (Br. ; est. 1768)
Academy of Country Music Awards
Academy of Sciences, National (org. 1863)
Academy of St. Martin-in-the-Fields (music
   ensemble)
Academy of Television Arts and Sciences,
   National (NATAS, Emmy Awards)
Acadia (now Nova Scotia)

Acadia National Park (ME)
Acadian (people)
Acapulco gold (marijuanna)
Acapulco, Mexico
Acarigua, Venezuela
Acclaim™, Plymouth (auto.)
Accord™, Honda (auto.)
Accra, Ghana (also Akka)
Accutane™ (med.)
AC/DC (electrical current; slang, bisexual)
AC/DC (pop music)
Ace bandage™
Ace Hardware Corp.
Acevedo, California v. (US law; 1991)
Achates (fict. chara., *Aeneid*)
Acheron River ("River of Woe")(myth.)
Acheson, Dean (Gooderham)(US pol.; 1893-
   1971)
Achieva™, Oldsmobile (auto.)
Achille Lauro (hijacked It. cruise ship; 1984)
Achilles (hero of Homer's *Iliad*)
Achilles (or Achilles') heel
Achilles tendon
Achinese (also Atjehnese)(lang./people)
Achmed Sukarno (ex-pres., Indonesia; 1901-70)
Achtung (Ger., attention)
Achu, Simon Achidi (PM, Cameroon)
ACLU (American Civil Liberties Union)
A. C. Nielsen (US bus./ratings; 1897-1980)
A. C. Nielsen Co. (TV ratings)
Acoma, NM (Pueblo Indian village)
Aconcagua Mountain (Argentina)
Acre, Israel
Acrilan™ (acrylic fiber)
Acropolis, the (Athens, Gr.)
ACS (American Cancer Society)
Act™ (toothpaste)
act of Congress
act of God
Actifed™ (med.)
Actium, Battle of (Rome, 31 BC)
Actors' Equity Association (also AEA)
Acts of the Apostles (also the Acts)(rel.)
Acuff, Roy (Claxton)(ent.; 1903-1992)
Acura™, Honda (auto.)
Acura Integra™, Honda (auto.)
Acura Legend™, Honda (auto.)
Acura NSX™, Honda (auto.)
Acutrim™ (med.)
AD (or A.D.) (Anno Domoni, in the year of the
   Lord)
Adam (rel., 1st man)
Adam and Eve (rel.)
Adam Ant (ent.; 1954-)
Adam Clayton Powell, Jr. (US pol./rel.; 1908-72)
Adam Smith (Br. econ.; 1723-90)
Adam 12 (TV show)
Adam Walsh (football; 1902-85)

Adam Willis Wagnalls (US publ.; 1843-1924)
Adam, Prince Hans (head of state, Liechtenstein; 1945-)
Adami, Edward Fenech (PM, Malta; 1934-)
Adam's apple (med.)
Adam's needle (plant)
Adam's Rib (film; 1949)
Adams, Abigail (Smith)(wife of ex-US pres.; 1744-1818)
Adams, Alice (US writer; 1926-)
Adams, Ansel (US photo.; 1902-84)
Adams, Brooks (US hist.; 1848-1927)
Adams, Bryan (ent.; 1959-)
Adams, Don (ent.; 1926-)
Adams, Edie (ent.; 1929-)
Adams, Harriet S. (pseud. Carolyn Keene)(US writer; 1803-82)
Adams, Henry (US hist.; 1838-1911)
Adams, Joey (ent.; 1911-)
Adams, John (2nd US pres.; 1735-1826)
Adams, John Quincy (6th US pres.; 1767-1848)
Adams, Mason (ent.; 1919-)
Adams, Maud (Swed. ent.; 1945-)
Adams, Maude (b. Maude Kiskadden)(ent.; 1872-1953)
Adams, Samuel (US pol.; 1722-1803)
Adana, Turkey
Adapa (myth.)
Adapin™ (med.)
Adar (Jew. month)
Adar Sheni (Jew. month)
ADC (aide-de-camp)
Addams Family, The (TV show, film)
Addams, Charles (cartoonist; 1912-88)
Addams, Jane (US reformer; 1860-1935)
Adderley, Cannonball (Julian)(US jazz; 1928-75)
Adderly, Herbert A. (football; 1939-)
Addis Ababa, Ethiopia
Addison, Joseph (Br. writer; 1672-1719)
Addison's disease
Addressograph™
Addyston Pipe and Steel Co. v. U.S. (US law; 1899)
Ade, George (US writer/humorist; 1866-1944)
Adelaide, Australia
Adele Astaire (ent.)
Adelina Patti (It. opera; 1843-1919)
Aden, Gulf of (Yemen/Africa)
Aden, Yemen
Adenauer, Konrad (ex-chanc., WGer.; 1876-1967)
Adha, Eid ul- (Muslim festival)
Adidas™ (sportswear)
Adidas USA, Inc.
Adigranth (also Grunth, Grant Sahib, Granth)(rel.)
Adirondack chair

Adirondack Mountains (also the Adirondacks)(NY)
Adja (people)
Adjodhia, Jules (Suriname pol.)
Adlai E(wing) Stevenson (ex-US VP; 1835-1914)
Adlai E(wing) Stevenson, II (US pol./IL gov.; 1900-65)
Adlai E(wing) Stevenson, III (US pol.; 1930-)
Adler, Alfred (Aus. psych.; 1870-1937)
Adler, Felix (US phil.; 1851-1933)
Adler, Larry (Lawrence Cecil)(US musician; 1914-)
Adler, Luther (ent.; 1903-84)
Adler, Richard (US comp.; 1921-)
Adler, Stella (US acting teacher; 1901-92)
Adlerian psychotherapy
Admetus (mythical king of Thessaly)
Administration, Office of (US govt.)
Admiral™ (appliances)
Admiral of the Fleet
Admiralty mile
Admission Day (holiday, AZ/CA/NV)
Adnan Khashoggi
Ado-Ekiti, Nigeria
Adobe™ (compu. software)
Adobe Illustrator™ (compu.)
Adobe Photoshop™ (compu.)
Adobe Systems, Inc.
Adolf Eichmann (Aus./Ger. Nazi; 1906-62)
Adolf Erik Nordenskjöld, (Nils), Baron (Swed. expl.; 1832-1901)
Adolf Hitler (ex-chanc./fuhrer, Ger.; 1889-1945)
Adolf Ogi (pres., Switz.)
Adolfas Slezevicius (PM, Lith.)
Adolfo Suárez González (ex-PM, Sp.; 1933-)
Adolph Coors Co.
Adolph Green (US lyricist; 1915-)
Adolph Zukor (ent.; 1873-1976)
Adolphe Joseph Thomas Monticelli (Fr. artist; 1824-86)
Adolphe Menjou (ent.; 1890-1963)
Adolphus Busch (US bus.; 1839-1913)
Adolphus Washington Greely (US mil.; 1844-1935)
Adonai (also Adonoy)(Hebrew, God)
Adonis (myth.)
ADP (automatic data processing)(compu.)
Adrenalin™ (med.)
Adriaen van Ostade (Dutch artist; 1610-85)
Adriamycin™ (med.)
Adrian (also Hadrian)(Publius Aelius Hadrianus)(emp., Rome; 76-138)
Adrian (Cedric) Boult, Sir (Br. cond.; 1889-1983)
Adrian Dantley (basketball; 1956-)
Adriatic Sea (arm, Mediterranean)
Adrien Arpel (cosmetics)
Adrien Sibomana (ex-PM, Burundi)

Adrienne Vittadini (clothing)
Adulyadej, Bhumibol (aka Rama IX)(king, Thailand; 1927-)
Advance, Staten Island (NY newspaper)
Advanced Translations Technology, Inc.
Advantage Software (US bus.)
Advent (rel.)
Advent Christian Church
Advent Sunday (rel.)
Adventist, Seventh-Day (rel.)
Adventure Road (mag.)
Adventures of Pinocchio, The (C. Collodi fantasy)
Adventures of Sonic the Hedgehog (cartoon)
Adversary, the (the Devil)
Advertiser, Honolulu (HI newspaper)
Advertiser, Montgomery (AL newspaper)
Advertising Age (mag.)
Advil™ (med.)
Advocate, Baton Rouge (LA newspaper)
Adyebo, George Cosmas (PM, Uganda)
Aeaea (myth.)
Aegean civilization (Gr.)
Aegean Islands (Gr.)
Aegean Sea (arm, Mediterranean)
Aegeus (myth.)
Aegir (myth.)
Aegis (myth., shield)
A(lfred) E(dward) Housman (Br. poet; 1859-1936)
Aeneas (fict. chara., *Aeneid*)
Aeneid (Virgil epic poem)
Aeolian harp (19th c. wind instr.)(also l.c.)
Aeolus (myth.)
Aer Lingus (airline)
Aero Peru (airline)
Aeroflot (airline)
Aerolineas Argentinas (airline)
Aeromexico (airline)
Aeronautics and Space Administration, National (NASA)(US govt. agcy.; est. 1958)
Aerosmith (pop music)
Aerospace Corp.
Aerostar, Ford (auto.)
Aeschines (Gr. orator; 389-314 BC)
Aeschylus (Gr. drama.; 525-456 BC)
Aesculapius (myth.)
Aesir (myth.)
Aesop (Gr. fabler; c620-c560 BC)
Aesop's fables
Aetna Life & Casualty Co.
A(lfred) E(lton) Van Vogt (US writer; 1912-)
AF (air force, audio-frequency)
AFA (Air Force Academy)
Afar (lang./people)
AFB (air force base)
AFC (American Football Conference, automatic frequency control)

AFDC (Aid to Families with Dependent Children)
Afewerki, Isaias (pres., Eritrea)
Affleck, Francis (auto racing; 1951-85)
Afghan (also Afghani)(people)
Afghan hound (dog)
Afghan Mujahedeen (Islamic holy warriors)
Afghanistan (Republic of)(S central Aisa)
AFL (American Federation of Labor, American Football League)
AFL-CIO (American Federation of Labor & Congress of Industrial Organizations)
Afonso de Albuquerque (Port. mil.; 1453-1515)
A-frame (arch.)
Aframerican (also Afro-American)(people)
Afrasian (people)
Africa
Africa, South (Republic of)
Africa, South-West (now Namibia)
African (people)
African American
African cherry-orange
African daisy (plant)
African elephant
African gray (parrot)
African green monkey
African honeybee (also killer bee)
African lily (also lily-of-the-Nile)
African lion hound (also Rhodesian ridgeback)
African mahogany
African marigold (also Aztec marigold)
African Methodist Episcopal Church
African Methodist Episcopal Zion Church
African millet
African mongoose
African Plate (division of earth's crust)
African Queen (film; 1951)
African sleeping sickness (also African trypanosomiasis)
African Unity, Organization of (OAU)(est. 1963)
African violet
Africanism
Africanist
Afrikaans (lang.)
Afrikander (also Africander)(cattle)
Afrikaner (also Afrikaaner)(formerly Boer)(people)
Afrin™ (med.)
Afro (hairstyle)
Afro-American (also Aframerican)(people)
Afro-Caribbean (people)
Afro-Cuban (people, music)
Afroasiatic (also Afro-Asiatic)(langs.)
After Five™ (toiletries)
AFTRA (American Federation of Television and Radio Artists)
AG (adjutant general, attorney general)
Ag (chem. sym., silver)

Aga Khan IV (Islamic rel.; 1936-)
Agadir, Morocco
Agam, Yaacov (Isr. artist; 1928-)
Agamemnon (myth.)
Agana, Guam
Agapemone (Br. utopian community; 1849)
Agassi, Andre (tennis; 1970-)
Agassiz, (Jean) Louis (Rodolphe)(Swiss nat.;
    1807-73)
Agatha Christie, Dame (Br. writer; 1891-1976)
Agathocles (Sicilian pol.; 361-289 BC)
Age Discrimination in Employment Act (US
    hist.; 1967)
Age of Aquarius (also Aquarian Age)
Age of Enlightenment (18th c. Eur. movement)
Age of Metternich
Age of Reason (phil.)
Age of Reason, The (by Thomas Paine; 1794-96)
Age, Space (also l.c.)
Agee, James (US writer; 1909-55)
Agence France-Press (Eur. news org.; est. 1944)
Agent Orange (poison, herbicide/defoliant)
Ager, Milton (US comp.; 1893-1979)
Agesilaus II (Spartan king; 444?-360? BC)
Agfachrome (photo.)
Agfacolor (photo.)
Agfa-Gevaert (photo.)
Aggadah (also Aggada, Agada, Haggadah)(rel.)
Agincourt, Battle of (Eng./Fr.; 1415)
Agincourt, France
Agnes De Mille (US dancer/choreographer;
    1905-93)
Agnes Moorehead (ent.; 1906-74)
Agnes Nixon
Agnes of God (film; 1985)
Agnes, St. (Christian martyr; ?-304?)
Agnes's Eve, St. (young woman dream of future
    husband; 1/20)
Agnew, David Hayes (US phys.; 1818-92)
Agnew, Spiro T(heodore)(ex-US VP; 1918-)
Agni (myth.)
Agnon, Shmuel Yosef (b. Samuel Josef
    Czaczkes)(Isr. writer; 1888-1970)
Agnus Dei (Latin, Lamb of God)
Agonistes, Samson (by J. Milton)
Agostinho Antonio Neto (ex-pres., Angola; 1922-
    79)
Agostino Carracci (It. artist; 1557-1602)
Agra, India
Agree™
Agricola, Gnaeus Julius (Roman mil./pol.; AD
    37-93)
Agriculture Organization, Food and (FAO)(UN
    agcy.)
Agriculture, Department of (US govt.)
Agrippa, Herod (Julius Agrippa)(king, Judea;
    c10 BC-AD 44)
Agrippa, Marcus Vipsanius (Roman mil./pol.;

63-12 BC)
Agrippina, the Elder (Roman matron; 13? BC-
    AD 33)
Agrippina, the Younger (Roman empress; AD
    15?-59)
Agua Caliente Race Track
Aguascalientes, Mexico
Aguecheek, Sir Andrew (fict. chara., *Twelfth
    Night*)
Aguinaldo, Emilio (Phil. revolutionary; 1869-
    1964)
Agulhas Cape, Africa
Agulhas Current (also Mozambique Current)
Ahab (Isr. king; c875-854 BC)
Ahab, Captain (fict. chara., *Moby Dick*)
A-head (slang, habitual amphetamine user)
Aherne, Brian (ent.; 1902-86)
Ahmad al-Jaber al-Sabah, Sheik Jaber al-
    (emir, Kuwait; 1928-)
Ahmad Jamal (US jazz)
Ahmad Rashad (football)
Ahmadal-Samarrai (PM, Iraq)
Ahmadzai Najibullah (Afghan. pol.; 1947-)
Ahmanson & Co., H. F. (S&L assoc.)
Ahmanson Theater (Los Angeles)
Ahmed I (Turk. sultan; 1589-1617)
Ahmed II (Turk. sultan; 1642-95)
Ahmed III (Turk. sultan; 1673-1736)
Ahmedabad, India (also Ahmadabad)
Aho, Esko (PM, Fin.; 1954-)
A horizon (geol.)
Ahtna (AK Indians)(also Ahtena or Atna)
Ahura Mazda (also Ormuzd, Ormazd)(rel.)
Ahvaz, Iran (also Ahwaz)
AI (artificial intelligence)(compu.)
Aida (opera by Verdi)
Aidan Quinn (ent.; 1959-)
Aidid, Muhammad Farad (Somali gen.)
AIDS (Acquired Immune Deficiency Syndrome)
AIDS-related complex (ARC)(med.)
AIDS-related virus (ARV)(med.)
Aiello, Danny (ent.; 1933-)
Aikawa, Japan
Aiken, Conrad Potter (US writer; 1889-1973)
Aiken, Howard H. (US math.; 1900-73)
Aiken, Joan (US writer)
Aikman, Troy (football; 1966-)
Ailey, Alvin (ent.; 1931-89)
AIM (American Indian Movement)
Aim™ (toothpaste)
Aimee Semple McPherson (US rel.; 1890-1944)
Aimee, Anouk (Fr. ent.; 1932-)
Ain't Misbehavin' (play)
Ainsworth, William Harrison (Br. writer; 1805-
    82)
Ainu (people)
Air Canada (airline)
Air Express™

Air Express International Corp.
Air Force Academy, U.S. (Colorado Springs CO)(est. 1954)
Air Force Cross
Air Force Magazine
Air Force One (US pres. plane)
Air Force Times (mag.)
Air Force, Department of the (US govt.)
Air Force, U.S. (US mil.)
Air France (airline)
Air India (airline)
Air Jamaica (airline)
Air Malta (airline)
Air Medal
Air New Zealand (airline)
Air Sedona (airline)
Air Supply (pop music)
Air Wisconsin, Inc. (airline)
Airbus™ (trans.)
Airedale terrier (dog)
Airplane! (film; 1980)
Airplane II: The Sequel (film; 1982)
Airport (film; 1970)
Airport '77 (film; 1977)
Airwick™ (air freshener)
Airwick Stick Ups™ (air freshener)
Aisha (chief wife of Mohammed; 611-678)
Aisne River (Fr.)
Aiwa™ (cassette)
Aix-en-Provence, France
Aix-la-Chapelle, Germany (also Aachen)
Ajaccio, Corsica
Ajax (myth.)
Ajax™ (cleanser)
A(nthony) J(oseph) Foyt (auto racing; 1935-)
Ajman (state, UAE)
A(lan) J(ohn) P(ercivale) Taylor (Br. hist.; 1906-89)
AK (Alaska)
AKA (or aka)(also known as)
Akai™ (stereo)
Akaka, Daniel Kahikina (US cong.; 1924-)
Akan (lang./people)
Akayev, Askar (pres., Kyrgyzstan)
Akbar Mizoyev (Tajikistan pol.)
Akbar the Great (Mogul emp. of India; 1542-1605)
AKC (American Kennel Club)
Ake v. Oklahoma (US law; 1985)
Akeley, Carl Ethan (US nat./sculptor; 1864-1926)
AK-47 (assault rifle)
Akhenaton (also Ikhnaton, Amenhotep IV)(king/pharaoh, Eg.; 14th c. BC)
Akhmedov, Khan (Turkmenistan pol.)
Akiba ben Joseph (Jew. rel.; AD 50?-132)
Akihito, Emperor (emp., Jap.; 1933-)
Akim Tamiroff (ent.; 1899-1972)

Akins, Claude (ent.; 1918-)
Akira Kurosawa (Jap. ent.; 1910-)
Akita (dog)
Akita, Japan
Akkadian (lang./people)
Akranes, Iceland
Akron Beacon Journal (OH newspaper)
Akron Center for Reproductive Health, Ohio v. (US law; 1983)
Akron, OH
Akureyri, Iceland
Akutagawa Ryunosuke (Jap. writer; 1892-1927)
AL (Alabama, American Legion)
Al (chem. sym., aluminum)
Al Capone (Alphonse, "Scarface")(US gangster; 1899-47)
Al Capp (Alfred Gerald Caplin)(cartoonist, *Li'l Abner*; 1909-79)
Al Cohn (US jazz; 1925-88)
Al Cowlings (US news)
Al(fonse M.) D'Amato (US cong.; 1937-)
Al Dubin (US lyricist; 1891-1945)
Al Fatah (also al-Fatah)(PLO guerrilla group)
Al Freeman, Jr. (ent.; 1934-)
Al Green (ent.; 1946-)
Al Hirschfeld (cartoonist; 1903-)
Al Hirt (ent.; 1922-)
Al Jarreau (ent.; 1940-)
Al Jizah, Egypt (also Gîza or El Gîza)
Al Jizah, Great Pyramids of (also Gîza or El Gîza)(Eg.)
Al Jolson (b. Asa Yoelson)(ent.; 1886-1950)
Al Joyner
Al(bert) Kaline (baseball; 1934-)
Al Lopez (baseball; 1908-)
Al McGuire (ent.; 1931-)
Al Michaels (ent.; 1944-)
Al Molinaro (ent.; 1919-)
Al Oerter (discus thrower; 1936-)
Al(berto) Pacino (ent.; 1940-)
Al Shean (ent.)
Al Simmons (baseball; 1902-56)
Al Unser (auto racing; 1939-)
Al Yankovic, Weird
ALA (American Library Association)
Alabama (AL)
Alabama River (AL/GA)
Aladdin (film)
Aladdin (myth.)
al-Adha, 'Id (Islamic festival)
al-Ahmad al-Jaber al-Sabah, Sheik Jaber (emir, Kuwait; 1928-)
Alain Robbe-Grillet (Fr. writer; 1922-)
Alain-René Lesage (Fr. writer; 1668-1747)
Alamanni (also Alemanni)(Ger. tribes; 3rd-5th c.)
Alameda Naval Air Station (CA)
Alameda, CA

Alamine™ (med.)
Alamo™ (car rental)
Alamo, the (TX)
Alamogordo, NM
Alan Alda (ent.; 1936-)
Alan Alexander Milne ("A.A.")(Br. writer; 1882-1956)
Alan Ameche (football; 1933-88)
Alan Arkin (ent.; 1934-)
Alan Autry (ent.; 1952-)
Alan Bates (ent.; 1934-)
Alan B(artlett) Shepard, Jr. (astro.; 1923-)
Alan Greenspan (Chair/US Fed. Reserve Sys.; 1926-)
Alan Hale (ent.; 1892-1950)
Alan Hale, Jr. (ent.; 1919-90)
Alan Hovhaness (US comp.; 1911-)
Alan Jay Lerner (US lyricist; 1918-86)
Alan King (ent.; 1927-)
Alan K. Simpson (US cong.; 1931-)
Alan Ladd (ent.; 1913-64)
Alan L(aVern) Bean (astro.; 1932-)
Alan Menken (US comp.; 1950-)
Alan Parsons (ent.)
Alan Parsons Project (pop music)
Alan Rachins (ent.; 1947-)
Alan Thicke (ent.; 1947-)
Alan Young (ent.; 1919-)
Al-Anon (alcoholism support grp.)
Alar™ (pesticide)
Alarcón, Pedro Antonio de (Sp. writer/pol.; 1833-91)
Alaric (Visigoth king; c370-410)
Alaska (AK)
Alaska Airlines (airline)
Alaska Highway (also Alaskan, Alcan Highway)
Alaska Purchase (also Seward's Folly/folly)(1867)
Alaska Range (AK mountains)
Alaska Standard Time
Alaska, baked
Alaskan king crab
Alaskan malamute (dog)
Alaskan Pipeline, Trans- (oil transport; 1977-)
al-Assad, Hafez (pres., Syria; 1930-)
Alassane Ouattara (PM, Ivory Coast)
al-Attas, Haidar Abu Bakr (PM, Yemen; 1939-)
Alba, Duke of (also Alva; Fernando Alvarez de Toledo)(Sp. gen./pol.; 1508-82)
Alba, Italy (also Alba Longa)
Alban Berg (Aus. comp.; 1885-1935)
Albania (Republic of)(SE Eur.)
Albanian (lang./people)
Albans, Council of St. (Br. hist.)
Albany Congress (US hist.; 1754)
Albany Convention (Amer. colonies; 1754)
Albany Marine Corps Logistics Base (GA)
Albany Times-Union (NY newspaper)

Albany, Austria
Albany, CA, GA, NY, OR
al-Bashir, Omar Hassan (PM, Sudan; 1944?-)
Albee, Edward (US writer; 1928-)
Albemarle, Duke of (George Monck)(Br. mil./pol.; 1608-70)
Alben William Barkley (ex-US VP; 1877-1956)
Alberghetti, Anna Maria (It./US ent.; 1936-)
Albers, Josef (US artist; 1888-1976)
Albert A(rnold) Gore, Jr. (US VP; 1948-)
Albert A(braham) Michelson (US physt.; 1852-1931)
Albert Bierstadt (US artist; 1830-1902)
Albert Brooks (ent.; 1947-)
Albert Bruce Sabin (US phys./biol.; 1906-93)
Albert Camus (Fr. writer; 1913-60)
Albert Claude (Belgium biol.; 1899-1983)
Albert Dekker (ent.; 1905-68)
Albert Einstein (Ger./US physt.; 1879-1955)
Albert Finney (ent.; 1936-)
Albert Gallatin (US pol.; 1761-1849)
Albert (Léon) Gleizes (Fr. artist; 1881-1953)
Albert II (king, Belgium)
Albert Kahn (US arch.; 1869-1942)
Albert King (US jazz; 1923-92)
Albert Lasker (US bus.; 1880-1952)
Albert Museum, Victoria & (London)
Albert Nipon (clothing)
Albert Pickham Ryder (US artist; 1847-1917)
Albert Reynolds (PM, Ir.; 1932-)
Albert Schweitzer, Dr. (Ger. phys./phil./rel.; 1875-1965)
Albert Shanker
Albert (Goodwill) Spalding (baseball; 1850-1915)
Albert Speer (Ger. arch./Nazi pol.; 1905-81)
Albert the Great, St. (also St. Albertus Magnus)(Ger. rel.; 1193-1280)
Albert von Tilzer (US comp.; 1878-1956)
Albert Warner (ent.; 1884-1967)
Albert Zafy (pres., Madagascar; 1927?-)
Albert, Eddie (ent.; 1908-)
Albert, Fat (cartoon chara.)
Albert, Prince (Br., husband of Queen Victoria; 1819-61)
Albert, Prince (prince, Monaco)
Alberta (province, Can.)
Alberto™ (hair care)
Alberto-Culver Co.
Alberto Dahik (VP, Ecuador)
Alberto Fujimori (pres., Peru; 1938-)
Alberto Giacometti (It. sculptor; 1901-66)
Alberto Juantoreno (track; 1951-)
Alberto Salazar (track; 1958-)
Alberto Santos-Dumont (Fr. aviator; 1873-1932)
Alberto VO5™ (hair care)
Albertson, Jack (ent.; 1907-81)
Albertsons™ (food stores)

Albertson's, Inc.

Albertus Magnus, St. (also St. Albert the Great)(Ger. rel.; 1193-1280)

Albrecht Dürer (Ger. artist; 1471-1528)

Albright, Ivan Le Lorraine (US artist; 1897-1983)

Albright, Madeleine (US ambassador to UN; 1937-)

Albright, William Foxwell (US archaeol.; 1891-1971)

Albuquerque Journal (NM newspaper)

Albuquerque Living

Albuquerque Tribune (NM newspaper)

Albuquerque, Afonso de (Port. conquerer; 1453-1515)

Albuquerque, NM

Alcaeus (Gr. poet; c611-c580 BC)

Alcan Aluminum, Ltd.

Alcan Highway (also Alaska Highway, Alaskan)

Alcatraz Island (CA)

Alcatraz Prison ("The Rock")(CA)

Alcatraz, The Birdman of (film; 1962)

Alcestis (myth.)

Alcibiades (Gr. pol.; 450-404 BC)

Alcide De Gasperi (It. pol.; 1881-1954)

Alcindor, Lew(is), Jr. (aka Kareem Abdul-Jabbar)(basketball; 1947-)

Alcoa Corp. (Aluminum Co. of America)

Alcoholics Anonymous (also AA)

Alcoholism, National Council on (est. 1944)

Alcott, Amy (golf)

Alcott, (Amos) Bronson (US educ./phil.; 1799-1888)

Alcott, Louisa May (US writer; 1832-88)

Alcuin (also Flaccus Albinus Alcuinus, Ealhwine Flaccus, Alchuine, Albinus)(Br. scholar; 735-804)

Alcyone (also Halcyon or Halcyone)(astron.; myth.)

Alda, Alan (ent.; 1936-)

Alda, Robert (ent.; 1914-86)

Aldebaran (also Alpha Tauri)(astron.)

Aldeburgh, Baron Britten of (aka Benjamin Britten)(Br. comp.; 1913-76)

Alder, Kurt (Ger. chem.; 1902-58)

Aldington, Richard (Br. poet; 1892-1962)

Aldo Moro (ex-PM, It.; 1916-78)

Aldo Ray (ent.; 1927-91)

Aldous Leonard Huxley (Br. writer; 1894-1963)

Aldrich, Henry (Br. rel./logician; 1647-1710)

Aldrich, Nelson Wilmarth (US finan./pol.; 1841-1915)

Aldrich, Thomas Bailey (US writer; 1836-1907)

Aldridge, Ira Frederick (ent.; 1804-67)

Aldrin, Edwin Eugene, Jr. ("Buzz")(astro.; 1930-)

Aldus™ (compu.)

Aldus Corp.

Aldus Freehand™ (compu.)

Aldus PageMaker™ (compu.)

Alec (Alexander Frederick) Douglas-Home, Sir (ex-PM, Br.; 1903-)

Alec Baldwin (ent.; 1958-)

Alec Guinness, Sir (ent.; 1914-)

Alec John Jeffreys (Br. geneticist; 1950-)

Alegre, Norberto Costa (PM, Saõ Tomé/Príncipe)

Aleichem, Shalom (or Sholom)(aka Solomon Rabinowitz)(Yiddish writer; 1859-1916)

Aleixandre, Vicente (Sp. poet; 1898-1984)

Aleksandr Aleksandrovich Blok (Rus. poet; 1880-1921)

Aleksandr (Feodorovich) Kerensky (Rus. pol.; 1881-1970)

Aleksandr Nikolaevich (Alexander II)(emp., Rus.; 1818-81)

Aleksandr Pavlovich (Alexander I)(emp., Rus.; 1777-1825)

Aleksandr (Sergeyevich) Pushkin (Rus. writer; 1799-1837)

Aleksandr Samsonov (Rus. mil.; 1859-1914)

Aleksandr S. Yakovlev (Rus. airplane designer; 1905-89)

Aleksandras Abisala (Lith. pol.)

Aleksei (Arkhipovich) Leonov (cosmo., 1st to walk in space; 1934-)

Aleksei Maksimovich Peshkov (pseud. Maxim Gorky [or Gorki])(Rus. writer; 1868-1936)

Aleksei Nikolaevich Kosygin (also Alexei Nikolaievich)(ex-PM, USSR; 1904-80)

Aleksei Yeliseyev (cosmo.; 1934-)

Alekseyev, Konstantin Sergeyevich (aka Konstantin Stanislavsky [or Stanislavski])(Rus. theater; 1863-1938)

A. Leland Stanford (US bus./finan.; 1824-93)

Alemanni (also Alamannic)(Ger. tribes; 3rd-5th c.)

Alençon lace (also point d'Alençon)

Aleppo grass (also Johnson grass, Means grass)

Aleppo, Syria

Alesana, Tofilau Eti (PM, WSamoa)

Alessandria, Italy

Alessandro Farnese (Pope Paul III)(It.; 1468-1549)

Alessandro (Gaspare) Scarlatti, (Pietro)(It. comp.; 1660-1725)

Alessandro Stradella (It. comp.; 1642-82)

Alessandro Volta, Count (It. physt.; 1745-1827)

Aleut (also Aleutian)(NAmer. Indians)

Aleut, Eskimo- (NAmer. Indians)

Aleutian Islands (N Pac.)

A level (Br. school, advanced level)

Alex Comfort (Br. phys./writer)

Alex Cord (ent.; 1931-)

Alex Haley (US writer; 1921-92)

Alex Karras (ent.; 1935-)

Alex Peter Delvecchio (hockey; 1931-)
Alex Raymond (cartoonist, *Flash Gordon, Jungle Jim*; 1909-56)
Alex Trebek (ent.; 1940-)
Alex Webster (football; 1931-)
Alexander & Alexander Services, Inc.
Alexander Archipenko (US sculptor; 1887-1964)
Alexander Borodin (Rus. comp.; 1833-87)
Alexander Calder (US sculptor; 1898-1976)
Alexander "Alec" (Frederick) Douglas-Home, Sir (ex-PM, Br.; 1903-)
Alexander Dubcek (Czech. pol.; 1921-92)
Alexander Fleming, Sir (Br. bacteriol.; 1881-1955)
Alexander Godunov (Rus./US ent.; 1949-)
Alexander Graham Bell (US inv., telephone; 1847-1922)
Alexander Hamilton (US pol.; 1755-1804)
Alexander I ("the Fierce")(king, Scot.; c1078-1124)
Alexander I (Aleksandr Pavlovich)(emp., Rus.; 1777-1825)
Alexander I (king, Epirus; ?-330 BC)
Alexander I (king, Yug.; 1888-1934)
Alexander I (prince, Bulgaria; 1857-93)
Alexander I Obrenovich (king, Serbia; 1876-1903)
Alexander II (Aleksandr Nikolaevich)(emp., Rus.; 1818-81)
Alexander II (king, Epirus; ?-242 BC)
Alexander II (king, Scot.; 1198-1249)
Alexander III (Aleksandr Aleksandrovich)(emp., Rus.; 1845-94)
Alexander III (Alexander the Great)(king, Macedonia; 356-323 BC)
Alexander III (king, Scot.; 1241-86)
Alexander III (Orlando Bandinelli)(pope; 1159-81)
Alexander (or Aleksandr) Isayevich Solzhenitsyn (Rus. writer; 1918-)
Alexander (or Aleksandr) Konstantinovich Glazunov (Rus. comp.; 1865-1936)
Alexander Mackenzie (ex-PM, Can.; 1822-92)
Alexander Mackenzie, Sir (Scot. expl.; 1764-1820)
Alexander Meiklejohn (US educ.; 1872-1964)
Alexander Meksi (PM, Albania)
Alexander M. Haig, Jr. (US gen./pol.; 1924-)
Alexander Nikolayevich Scriabin (Rus. comp.; 1872-1915)
Alexander Pope (Br. poet; 1688-1744)
Alexander Rutskoi (Rus. pol.)
Alexander (Nikolayevich) Scriabin (Rus. comp.; 1872-1915)
Alexander Selkirk (Scot. sailor; 1676-1721)
Alexander technique™ (med.)
Alexander the Great (Alexander III)(king, Macedonia; 356-323 BC)

Alexander Vasilievich Kolchak (Rus. adm.; 1875-1920)
Alexander VI (Rodrigo Borgia)(pope; 1431-1503)
Alexander von Humboldt, (Friedrich Heinrich), Baron (Ger. expl.; 1769-1859)
Alexander von Kluck (Ger. gen.; 1846-1934)
Alexander Woollcott (US writer; 1887-1943)
Alexander, brandy (also l.c.)(cocktail)
Alexander, Grover Cleveland (baseball; 1887-1950)
Alexander, Harold (Br. mil.; 1891-1969)
Alexander, Jane (ent.; 1939-)
Alexander, Jason (ent.; 1959-)
Alexandra Danilova (Rus. ballet; 1906-)
Alexandra Feodorovna (empress, Rus.; 1872-1918)
Alexandra Kollontai (Rus. mil./pol./writer; 1872-1952)
Alexandre Dumas (aka Dumas fils)(Fr. writer; 1824-95)
Alexandre Dumas (aka Dumas père)(Fr. writer; 1802-70)
Alexandre-Edmond Becquerel (Fr. physt.; 1820-91)
Alexandre Millerand (ex-pres., Fr.; 1859-1943)
Alexandria Women's Health Clinic, Bray v. (US law; 1993)
Alexandria, Egypt
Alexandria, LA, VA
Alexandria, Library of (Eg.)
Alexandrine (poetry style)
Alexandrine rat
Alexio, Dennis
Alexis Carrel (US phys.; 1873-1944)
Alexis (Charles Henri Maurice Clérel) de Tocqueville (Fr. hist.; 1805-59)
Alexis Emmanuel Chabrier (Fr. comp.; 1841-94)
Alexis Smith (ent.; 1921-)
Alf (TV show)
Alf(red Mossman) Landon (US pol.; 1887-1987)
Alfa Romeo™ (auto.)
Alfa Romeo™ Spider (auto.)
Alfardaws (Muslim paradise)
al-Fayumi, Saadia ben Joseph
Alfie (song)
Alfonso Bustamante (PM, Peru
Alfre Woodard (ent.; 1953-)
Alfred Adler (Aus psych.; 1870-1937)
Alfred A(braham) Knopf (US publ.; 1892-1984)
Alfred A. Knopf, Inc.
Alfred Bester (US writer; 1913-87)
Alfred Binet (Fr. psych.; 1857-1911)
Alfred B(ernhard) Nobel (Swed. chem./eng./finan.; 1833-96)
Alfred C. Fuller (US, bus./brushes; 1885-1973)
Alfred Charles Kinsey (US sociol./biol.; 1894-1956)
Alfred Damon Runyon (US writer; 1880-1946)

Alfred de Musset (Fr. writer; 1810-57)
Alfred Drake (ent.; 1914-)
Alfred Dreyfus (Fr. capt.; 1859-1935)
Alfred E. Neuman (fict. chara., *Mad* magazine)
Alfred E(manuel) Smith (NY gov.; 1873-1944)
Alfred (Joseph) Hitchcock, Sir (Br. writer/ent.; 1899-1980)
Alfred Hitchcock Hour, The (TV show)
Alfred Hitchcock Presents (TV show)
Alfred Hitchcock's Mystery Magazine
Alfred Krupp (Ger. armaments maker; 1812-87)
Alfred Krupp (Ger. armaments maker; 1907-67)
Alfred L(ouis) Kroeber (US anthrop.; 1876-1960)
Alfred Lord Tennyson (Br. poet; 1809-92)
Alfred Lunt (ent.; 1892-1977)
Alfred L(othar) Wegener (Ger. meteor.; 1880-1930)
Alfred M. Worden (astro.; 1932-)
Alfred North Whitehead (Br. phil./math.; 1861-1947)
Alfred Noyes (Br. poet; 1880-1958)
Alfred Pritchard Sloan (US bus.; 1875-1966)
Alfred Rosenberg (Ger. Nazi; 1893-1946)
Alfred Russel Wallace (Br. naturalist; 1823-1913)
Alfred Sisley (Fr. artist; 1840?-99)
Alfred Stieglitz (US photo.; 1864-1946)
Alfred the Great (king, Wessex; c848-c900)
Alfred von Tirpitz (Ger. mil.; 1849-1930)
Alfredo Cristiani (ex-pres., El Salvador; 1947-)
Alfredo Stroessner (ex-pres., Paraguay; 1912-)
Algeciras, Gibraltar
Alger Hiss (US pol.; 1904-)
Alger, Horatio, Jr. (US writer; 1832-99)
Algeria (Democratic and Popular Republic of)(NAfr.)
Algerian ivy (also Canary Island ivy)(plant)
Algernon (Charles) Swinburne (Br. poet; 1837-1909)
al Ghazali (Islamic phil.; 1058-1111)
Algiers, Algeria
Algiers, Battle of (Algeria/Fr.; 1954-62)
Algirdas Brazauskas (pres., Lith.)
Algol (also Beta Persei)(astron.)
Algonquian (langs.)
Algonquin (NAmer. Indians)
Algonquin Hotel (NYC)
al-Hairi, Rafiq (PM, Lebanon)
Alhaji Shehu Shagari (ex-pres., Nigeria; 1925-)
Alhambra (palace in Spain)
Alhambra, CA
Ali Abdullah Saleh (pres., Yemen)
Ali Akbar Hashemi Rafsanjani, Hojatolislam (pres., Iran; 1935-)
Ali Baba (fict. chara.)
Ali Baba and the Forty Thieves (fairy tale)
Ali Hassan Mwinyi (pres., Tanzania; 1925-)

Ali Jinnah, Muhammad (India/Pak. pol.; 1876-1948)
Ali Kafi (pres., Algeria; 1928-)
Ali Khamenei, Ayatollah Sayyed (rel. leader, Iran; 1940-)
Ali MacGraw (ent.; 1938-)
Ali Mahdi, Muhammad (ex-pres., Somalia)
Ali Pasha ("the Lion")(Turk. pol.; 1741-1822)
Ali Pasha, Mehmed Emin (Turk. pol.; 1815-71)
Ali Rakhmanov (acting pres., Tajikistan)
Ali Seybou (ex-pres., Niger; 1940-)
Ali, Hyder (also Haidar Ali)(Indian ruler/mil.; 1722-82)
Ali, Muhammad (also Mehemet Ali)(Eg. pol./ mil.; 1769-1849)
Ali, Muhammad (b. Cassius Clay, Jr.)(boxing; 1942-)
Ali, Zine el-Abidine Ben (pres., Tunisia; 1936-)
Alia Ramiz (ex-pres., Albania; 1925-)
Alia Royal Jordanian Airlines (airline)
Alice Adams (US writer; 1926-)
Alice B. Toklas (US writer; 1877-1967)
Alice Cooper (b. Vincent Furnier)(ent.; 1948-)
Alice Doesn't Live Here Anymore (film; 1974)
Alice Dunbar-Nelson
Alice Faye (ent.; 1912-)
Alice Ghostley (ent.; 1926-)
Alice Marble (tennis; 1913-90)
Alice Munro (Can. writer)
Alice Town, the Bahamas
Alice Walker (US writer; 1944-)
Alice, Bob & Carol & Ted & (film; 1969)
Alice's Restaurant (film; 1969)
Alien and Sedition Acts (US hist.; 1798)
Alien (film; 1979)
Aliens (film; 1986)
Alighieri, Dante (It. poet, *Divine Comedy*; 1265-1321)
Alija Izetbegovic (pres., Bosnia-Hercegovina)
A-line (clothing)
Alison Lurie (US writer; 1926-)
Alistair Cooke (Br./US jour.; 1908-)
Alitalia (airline)
Aliyev, Geidar (pres., Azerbaijan)
al-Jaber al-Sabah, Sheik Jaber al-Ahmad (emir, Kuwait; 1928-)
al-Jazair, Algeria
al-Jubayl, Saudi Arabia
Alka-Seltzer™ (med.)
Alka-Seltzer Plus™ (med.)
al-Khalifa, Sheik Isa bin Sulman (emir, Bahrain; 1933-)
al-Khalifa, Khalifa bin Sulman (PM, Bahrain; 1935-)
All About Eve (film; 1950)
All Creatures Great and Small (book, TV show)
All Fools' Day (also April Fools' Day)(April 1)
All-Hallows (also Hallowmas, All Saints'

Day)(rel.)
All in the Family (TV show)
All-Knowing (God)
All My Children (TV soap)
All Nippon Air (airline)
All Saints' Day (also Hallowmas, All-Hallows)(rel.)
All Souls' Day (rel.)
All-Star Game (baseball)
al-Ladhiqiyah, Syria
Allah (Islam God)
Allah akbar (rel.)
all-American
Allan Carr
Allan Dean Feuerbach (track; 1948-)
Allan Nevins (US hist./educ.; 1890-1971)
Allan Pinkerton (US detective; 1819-84)
Allante, Cadillac™ (auto.)
All-Bran™ (cereal)
Allegany, NY
Allegheny Mountains (PA)(also Alleghenies)
Allegheny National Forest (PA)
Allegheny River (PA)
Allegheny, PA
Allegra Kent (ent.; 1937-)
Allen Funt (ent.; 1914-)
Allen Ginsberg (US poet; 1926-)
Allen Ludden
Allen radiation belts, Van (regions surrounding earth)
Allen screw (constr.)
Allen wrench (constr.)
Allen, Debbie (ent.; 1950-)
Allen, Ethan (US Revolutionary War hero; 1738-89)
Allen, Dick (Richard Anthony)(baseball; 1942-)
Allen, Fred (ent.; 1894-1956)
Allen, George (football; 1918-90)
Allen, George F. (VA gov.)
Allen, Gracie (ent.; 1906-64)
Allen, Inc., Ethan
Allen, Joan (ent.; 1956-)
Allen, Karen (ent.; 1951-)
Allen, Marcus (football; 1960-)
Allen, Mel (ent.; 1913-)
Allen, Nancy (ent.; 1949-)
Allen, Steve (ent.; 1921-)
Allen, Tim (b. Timothy Allen Dick)(ent.)
Allen, Woody (b. Allen Stewart Konigsberg)(ent.; 1935-)
Allenby, Edmund (Br. mil.; 1861-1936)
Allentown Morning Call (PA newspaper)
Allentown, PA
Allergan™ (eye care)
Allergan Lens Plus™ (eye care)
Allergan, Inc.
Alley, Gasoline (comic strip)
Alley, Kirstie (ent.; 1955-)

Allhallowmas (also Allhallows, All Saints's Day)
Allhallowtide
Allied-Signal, Inc.
Allied Van Lines (US bus.)
Allies, the (of WW I, WW II, NATO)
Alliluyeva, Svetlana (Iosifovna)(daughter of J. Stalin; 1927-)
Allison Smith (ent.; 1969-)
Allison, Bobby (Robert Arthur)(auto racing; 1937-)
Allison, Fran (ent.; 1908-89)
Allman Brothers, the (pop music)
Allman, Gregg (ent.; 1947-)
Allman, Duane (ent.; 1947-71)
All-Pro (sports)
All's Well That Ends Well (Shakespeare comedy)
Allsburg, Chris Van (US writer/artist; 1949-)
Allston, Washington (US artist; 1779-1843)
Alltel Corp.
Ally Sheedy (ent.; 1962-)
Allyce Beasley (ent.; 1954-)
Allyson, June (ent.; 1917-)
ALM Antillean Airlines (airline)
Alma-Ata, Kazakhstan
Almaden™ (wine)
Almagest (by Ptolemy, 2nd c.)
al-Maktoum, Sheik Maktoum ibn Rashid (PM, UAE)
Almay™ (cosmetics)
Almay, Inc.
Almighty, the (God)
Almond Joy™ (candy)
al-Nahayan, Sheik Zaid bin Sultan (pres., UAE; 1918-)
al-Nimeiry, Gaafar Muhammad (ex-pres., Sudan; 1930-)
Aloha Airlines (airline)
Aloha Bowl (college football)
Aloha State (nickname, HI)
Alomar, Roberto (baseball; 1968-)
Alpert and The Tijuana Brass, Herb (pop music)
Alpert, Herb (ent.; 1935-)
Alpes, Rhône- (region, Fr.)
Alpha Aquilae (also Altair)(astron.)
Alpha Aurigae (also Capella)(astron.)
Alpha Beta Co. (Alpha Beta stores)
Alpha Bootis (also Arcturus)(astron.)
Alpha Canis Minoris (also Procyon)(astron.)
Alpha Carinae (also Canopus)(astron.)
Alpha Centauri (also Rigel Kentaurus)(astron.)
Alpha Keri™
Alpha Orionis (also Betelgeuse)(astron.)
Alpha Oumar Konare, (pres., Mali; 1946-)
Alpha Scorpii (also Antares)(astron.)
Alpha Tauri (also Aldebaran)(astron.)
Alpha-Bits™ (cereal)

Alphonse Bertillon (Fr. anthrop./criminol.; 1853-1914)
Alphonse de Lamartine (Fr. writer; 1790-1869)
Alphonse, King (mixed drink)
Alpine (cigarette)
Alpine (people)
Alpine skiing (sports)(also l.c.)
Alpo™
Alpo Petfoods, Inc.
Alps, Lunar (mountains, the moon)
Alps, the (mountains, It./Fr./Ger./Aus.)
al Qaiwain (or Qaywayn), Umm (state, UAE)
A(lfred) L(eslie) Rowse (Br. hist.; 1903-)
al-Sabah, Sheik Jaber al-Ahmad al-Jaber (emir, Kuwait; 1928-)
al-Sabah, Sheik Saad al-Abdullah al-Salim (PM, Kuwait
Alsace (Fr. wine region)
Alsace-Lorraine (region, Fr.)
al-Said, Qaboos bin Said (sultan/PM, Oman; 1940-)
al-Salim al-Sabah, Sheik Saad al-Abdullah (PM, Kuwait)
Alsatian (dog)
Alsatian (people)
Alsatian German (lang.)
Al-Solh, Rashid (ex-PM, Lebanon)
Alston, Walter (baseball; 1911-84)
Alstyne, Egbert van (US comp.; 1882-1951)
Altadena, CA
Altair (also Alpha Aquilae)(astron.)
Altamaha-Ocmulgee River (GA)
Altamira, Caves of (also Altamira caves)(Sp. paleolithic paintings)
Altamont, CA
Altamont (racetrack)(CA)
Altamonte Springs, FL
Altec™ (speaker)
Alternative Nation (TV show)
al-Thani, Sheik Khalifa ibn Hamad (emir, Qatar; 1932-)
Althea Gibson (tennis; 1927-)
Althing (Iceland parliament)
Altima™, Nissan (auto.)
Altima™ SE, Nissan (auto.)
Altman & Co., B.
Altman, Robert (ent.; 1925-)
Altman, Robert (US atty.)
Altman, Robert (US banker)
Alton, IL
Altoona, PA
Altus Air Force Base, OK (mil.)
Aluminum Co. of America (Alcoa Corp.)
Alundum™ (abrasive prods.)
Alurate™ (med.)
Alva, Duke of (also Alba, Fernando Alvarez de Toledo)(Sp. gen./pol.; 1508-82)
Alvarez, Luis Walter (US physt.; 1911-88)

Alvin Ailey (ent.; 1931-89)
Alvin & the Chipmunks (cartoon)
Alvin Dark (baseball; 1922-)
Alvin F. Poussaint (ent.; 1934-)
Alvin Toffler (US sociol./writer; 1928-)
Always™ (health)
Alworth, Lance (football; 1940-)
Alysheba (racehorse)
Alyssa Milano (ent.; 1972-)
Alzheimer's disease
AMA (American Medical Association)
Amadeo Avogadro (It. chem.; 1776-1856)
Amadeo P. Giannini (US, founded Bank of America; 1870-1949)
Amadeus (film; 1984)
Amadeus Quartet
Amadou Cheiffou (ex-PM, Niger)
Amadou Toumani Toure (ex-pres., Mali)
Amalekite (people)
Amalthea (Jupiter moon; myth.)
Amana Church Society
Amana™
Amana Refrigeration, Inc.
Amanda Blake (ent.; 1929-89)
Amanda Plummer (ent.; 1957-)
Amandine Aurore Lucie Dudevant (b. Dupin)(pseud. George Sand)(Fr. writer; 1804-76)
Amanita (fungus, usually poisonous)
Amarcord (film; 1974)
Amarillo Globe-Times (TX newspaper)
Amarillo News-Globe (TX newspaper)
Amarillo, TX
Amata Kabua (pres., Marshall Islands)
Amateur Athletic Union of the United States (AAU)
Amati, Andrea (It. violin maker; c1510-?)
Amati, Antonio (It. violin maker; 1555-1638)
Amati, Geronimo (It. violin maker, father of Nicolo; 1556-1630)
Amati, Geronimo (It. violin maker, son of Nicolo; 1649-1740)
Amati, Nicholo (It. violin maker; 1596-1684)
Amato, Guiliano (ex-PM, It.; 1938-)
Amazing Spider-Man, The (cartoon chara.)
Amazing Stories
Amazon (myth., female warriors)
Amazon River (SAmer.)
Amazonian Highway, Trans- (also Transamazonica)(Brazil; 1970-)
Ambersons, The Magnificent (B. Tarkington novel)
Ambler, Eric (Br. writer; 1909-)
Amboise, France
Ambroise, Thomas (Fr. comp.; 1811-96)
Ambrose Everett Burnside (US gen.; 1824-81)
Ambrose Gwinnett Bierce (US writer; 1842-1914)

Proper Noun Speller

Ambrose, St. (bishop of Milan; c340-397)
Ambrosian Library (It.)
AMC Gremlin (auto.)
Ameche, Alan (football; 1933-88)
Ameche, Don (ent.; 1908-93)
Amedeo Modigliani (It. artist; 1884-1920)
Amelia Bloomer (US reformer; 1818-94)
Amelia Earhart (US aviator; 1897-1937?)
Amelia Island (FL)
Amen (or Amon), Temple of (Karnak, Eg.; built 13th-20th c. BC)
Amen-Ra (also Amon-Ra)(Eg. myth.)
Amenhotep (also Amenophis)(four Eg. pharaohs)
Amenhotep I (Eg. pharaoh; fl. 1570 BC)
Amenhotep III (Eg. pharaoh; c1400 BC)
Amenhotep IV (also Ikhnaton, Akhenaton)(king/pharaoh, Eg.; 14th c. BC)
Amenti (myth., region of the dead)
Amerada Hess Corp.
Amerasian (also Amer-Asian)
America
America West Airlines™
America, Captain (cartoon chara.)
America, Inc., Audi of
America, Latin (S & central Amer.)
America, North
America, South
America, Voice of (US broadcasting service)
Americaine™ (med.)
American (people)
American Airlines™
American Airlines, Inc.
American Artist (mag.)
American Association of University Women (AAUW)
American Ballet Theater
American Bandstand™ (pop music)
American Banking Association number (ABA number)
American Bar Association
American Bar Association Journal
American Beauty rose
American beech (tree)
American Book Review
American Brands, Inc.
American Broadcasting Cos., Inc. (Capital Cities-ABC, Inc.)(ABC™)
American Cage Bird (mag.)
American cheese
American Civil Liberties Union (ACLU)
American Civil War (also War of Secession, War Between the States)(1861-65)
American Comedy Awards, The
American Cyanamid Co.
American Demographics
American Dream/dream
American eagle

American elm (tree)
American English (also General American)
American Express™ card
American Express Co.
American Express Travelers Cheques™
American Federation of Labor and Congress of Industrial Organizations (AFL-CIO)
American Federation of Television and Radio Artists (AFTRA)
American Football Conference (AFC)
American foxhound (dog)
American Graffiti (film; 1973)
American Greetings Corp.
American Health (mag.)
American Heritage (mag.)
American Heritage Dictionary, The
American Heroes & Legends (cartoon)
American Home Products Corp.
American Homestyle (mag.)
American Honda Motor Co.
American Hunter (mag.)
American Indian (also Native American)(peoples)
American Indian Day
American Indian Movement
American Institute of Architects (AIA)
American Isuzu Motors, Inc.
American Journal (TV show)
American League of Professional Baseball Clubs
American Legion (mag.)
American Legion (war veterans org.)
American Legion Auxiliary (mag.)
American Library Association (ALA)
American lion
American Medical Association (AMA)
American Movie Classics (AMC)(cable TV)
American Museum of Natural History (NYC)
American National Red Cross (US relief agcy.; est. 1881)
American Oil Co. (Amoco Oil Co.)
American Opinion Bookstore
American Party of the U.S. (US pol.)
American Photo (mag.)
American pit bull terrier (also American Staffordshire terrier)(dog)
American Poetry Review (mag.)
American quarter horse
American Revolution (also Revolutionary War; 1776-83)
American Rifleman (mag.)
American saddle horse
American Samoa
American serviceberry (also Juneberry)(shrub)
American Sign Lang. (also Ameslan)
American Staffordshire terrier (also American pit bull terrier)(dog)
American Standard Code for Information

Interchange (ASCII)(compu.)
American Standard Version (of the Bible)
American Standards Association (ASA)(photo.)
American States, Organization of (OAS)(N/ central/S Amer.; est.; 1948)
American-Statesman, Austin (TX newspaper)
American Stock Exchange (AMEX, Amex)
American Stores Co.
American Telephone & Telegraph Co. (AT&T)
American Tobacco Co., The
American Tobacco Co., U.S. v. (US law; 1911)
American Tourister (US bus.)
American trotter (also Standardbred)(horse)
American War, Spanish-
American water spaniel (dog)
American West (west of Mississippi River)
American wirehair (cat)
American Woodworker (mag.)
American, Hispanic (also Hispano)(people)
Americana
Americanism
America's Cup (yacht racing)
America's Funniest Home Videos™ (TV show)
America's Most Wanted (TV show)
Americans With Disabilities Act (US hist.; 1990)
Americans, Jay and the (pop music)
Americo-Liberians (people)
Americus Vespucius (also Amerigo Vespucci)(It. nav./expl.; 1451?-1512)
Amerind (also Amerindian)(American Indian, dialects/langs.)
Amerindian (lang.)
Ameritech (utilities co.)
Ames Brothers, the (pop music)
Ames Department Stores, Inc.
Ames test (biochemistry)
Ames, Champion v. (also Lottery Case)(US law; 1903)
Ames, Ed (ent.; 1927-)
Ames, Leon (ent.; 1903-93)
Ameslan (also American Sign Language)
AMEX (or Amex)(American Stock Exchange)
Amhara (people)
Amharic (lang./people)
Amherst College (MA)
Amherst, Jeffrey, Baron (Br. gen.; 1717-97)
Amherst, MA, OH
Amherst, Nova Scotia, Canada
Amiens, France
Amiens, Treaty of (Br. & Fr./Sp./Batavia; 1802)
AmigaWorld
Amilcare Ponchielli (It. comp.; 1834-86)
Amin (Dada), Idi Oumee (ex-pres., Uganda; 1926-)
Amin Gemayel (ex-pres., Lebanon; 1942-)
Amin Tarif, Sheik (Islamic rel.; 1898-1993)
Amish (Mennonites, Dunkers, Plain

People)(rel.)
Amityville Horror, The (film/book)
Amityville, NY
Amman, Jordan (also Rabbath Ammon)
Ammens™ (health)
Ammianus (Roman hist.; c330-395 BC)
Ammon (also Amon)(king, Judah; 6th c BC)
Ammonite (people)
Amnesty International (human rights org.)
Amoco™
Amoco Oil Co. (American Oil Co.
Amon (or Ammon)(king, Judah; 6th c BC)
Amon (or Amen), Temple of (Karnak, Eg.; built 13th-20th c. BC)
Amon-Ra (also Amen-Ra)(Eg. myth.)
Amorite (lang./people)
Amory, Cleveland (US writer; 1917-)
Amos Alonzo Stagg (football; 1862-1965)
Amos Bronson Alcott (US educ./phil.; 1799-1888)
Amos Chocolate Chip Cookie, The Famous (US bus.)
Amos Sawyer (pres., Liberia)
Amos, John (ent.; 1942-)
Amoskaeg (textiles)
Amoxil™ (med.)
Ampère, André Marie (Fr. physt.; 1775-1836)
Ampère's law (or rule)(elect.)
Amphitrite (myth.)
AMR Corp
Amschel Mayer Rothschild (Ger. finan.; 1773-1855)
Amsterdam, Morey (ent.; 1914-)
Amsterdam, NY
Amsterdam, the Netherlands (or Holland)
Amtrak
Amu Darya (Oxus River)(cental Asia)
Amur grape (plant)
Amur River (E. Asia)
AMVETS (American Veterans of WWII, Korea, Vietnam)
Amway Corp.
Amy Alcott (golf)
Amy Carter (ex-US pres.'s daughter; 1967-)
Amy Fisher ("Long Island Lolita")(US news)
Amy Grant (ent.; 1960-)
Amy Irving (ent.; 1953-)
Amy Johnson, (Br. aviator; 1903-41)
Amy Lowell (US poet; 1874-1925)
Amy Madigan (ent.; 1957-)
Amy Tan (US writer)
Amy Vanderbilt (US writer/manners)
Amy Vanderbilt's Complete Book of Etiquette
Amytal™ (med.)
An Wang (Ch./US inv./bus.; 1920-90)
ANA (American Nurses Association)
Anabaptist (rel.)
Anacin™ (med.)

Anacreon (Gr. poet; c582-c485 BC)
Anadir (or Anadyr) Mountains (Siberia)
Anadir (or Anadyr) River (Siberia)
Anaheim, CA (Disneyland)
Anais Anais™ (cosmetics)
Anais Nin (US writer; 1903-77)
Analects (rel.)
Anand Panyarachun (ex-PM, Thailand; 1933-)
Anapurna (also Annapurna, Devi,
    Parvati)(myth.)
Anastas Mikoyan (USSR pol.; 1895-1978)
Anastasia (film; 1956)
Anastasia (Nikolaievna Romanov)(Rus. Grand
    Duchess; 1901-18)
Anastasio Somoza (Debayle)(ex-pres.,
    Nicaragua; 1925-80)
Anastasio Somoza (Garcia)(ex-pres., Nicaragua;
    1896-1956)
Anatole, France (Fr. writer; 1844-1924)
Anatolia (part of Turk.)
Anatolijs Gorbunov (ex-pres., Latvia)
Anatoly (Federovich) Dobrynin (Rus. dipl.;
    1919-)
Anatoly Berezovoy (cosmo.)
Anatoly Dobrynin
Anatoly Filipchenko (cosmo.; 1928-)
Anatoly Karpov (Rus., chess; 1951-)
Anaxagoras (Gr. phil.; c500-428 BC)
Anaximander (Gr. phil./astron.; 611-546 BC)
Anbesol™ (med.)
Anchorage Daily News (AK newspaper)
Anchorage News (AK newspaper)
Anchorage, AK
Ancient Mystic Order Rosae Crucis
    (AMORC)(order of Rosicrucian)(phil./rel.)
Ancren Riwle (monastic life rules; 13th c)
Andalusia (also Andalucia)(region, Sp.)
Andalusia, AL
Andalusian (horse)
Andalusian (people)
Andalusian, Blue (chicken)
Andaman Islands (India, Bay of Bengal)
Andaman Sea (part of Bay of Bengal)
Andamanese (also Andaman)(people)
Anders (Leonhard) Zorn (Swed. artist; 1860-
    1920)
Anders Celsius (Swed. astron.; 1701-44)
Anders, Jonas Angström (Swed. astrophyst.;
    1814-74)
Anders, William A. (astro.; 1933-)
Andersen™ (windows/doors)
Andersen Windows, Inc.
Andersen, Hans Christian (Dan. writer; 1805-
    75)
Anderson, Brad (cartoonist, *Marmaduke*; 1924-)
Anderson, (Gary) Donny (football; 1949-)
Anderson, Eddie "Rochester" (ent.; 1905-77)
Anderson, Harry (ent.; 1949-)

Anderson, IN, SC
Anderson, Jack (US jour.; 1922-)
Anderson, Dame Judith (ent.; 1898-1992)
Anderson, Ken (football; 1949-)
Anderson, Leroy (US comp.; 1908-75)
Anderson, Loni (ent.; 1946-)
Anderson, Lynn (ent.; 1947-)
Anderson, Marian (ent.; 1902-93)
Anderson, Maxwell (US writer; 1888-1959)
Anderson, Melissa Sue (ent.; 1962-)
Anderson, Richard (ent.; 1926-)
Anderson, Richard Dean (ent.; 1953-)
Anderson, Sherwood (US writer; 1876-1941)
Anderson, Sparky (George)(baseball; 1934-)
Andersonville National Cemetery (GA)
Andersonville Prison (GA)
Andersson, Bibi (Swed. ent.; 1935-)
Andes Mountains (SAmer.)
Andes, Christ of the (peace monument between
    Chile/Argentina)
Andie MacDowell (ent.; 1958-)
Andorra (Principality of)(Eur.)
Andorra la Vella, Andorra
Andorran (people)
Andre Agassi (tennis; 1970-)
André Breton (Fr. poet; 1896-1966)
Andre Cold Duck™ (champagne)
André Courréges (Fr. designer; 1923-)
Andre Dawson (baseball; 1954-)
André Gide (Fr. writer; 1869-1951)
André Kolingba (ex-pres., Central African
    Republic; 1936-)
Andre Kostelanetz (ent.; 1901-80)
André Malraux (Fr. writer; 1901-76)
André Marie Ampère (Fr. physt.; 1775-1836)
André Maurois (aka Emile Herzog)(Fr. writer;
    1885-1967)
André Milongo (ex-PM, Congo)
André (George) Previn (US cond./comp.; 1929-)
Andre the Giant (wrestling; 1946-92)
Andre, Carl (US sculptor; 1935-)
André, John, Major (Br. spy; 1751-80)
Andrea Amati (It. violin maker; c1510-?)
Andrea del Sarto (It. artist; 1486-1530)
Andrea del Verrocchio (b. Andrea di Michele di
    Francesco di Cioni)(It. artist; 1435-88)
Andrea della Robbia (It. sculptor; 1437-1528)
Andrea Doria (It. adm./pol.; 1466-1560)
Andrea Doria, S.S. (steamship; sank 1956)
Andrea Mantegna (It. artist; 1431-1506)
Andrea McArdle (ent.; 1963-)
Andrea Palladio (It. arch.; 1508-80)
Andrea Pisano (b. Andrea da Pontadera)(It.
    sculptor; c1290-c1349)
Andrea Sansovino (It. sculptor; 1460-1529)
Andreas (Bernhard Lyonel) Feininger (US
    photo.; 1906-)
Andreas (George) Papandreou (PM, Gr.; 1919-)

Andrei A. Gromyko (ex-pres., Rus.; 1909-89)
Andrei Chesnokov (tennis)
Andrei Dmitrievich Sakharov (Rus. physt.; 1921-89)
Andrei Sangheli (PM, Moldova)
Andrés Rodríguez (ex-pres., Paraguay; 1923-)
Andres Segovia (ent.; 1893-1987)
Andress, Ursula (Swiss ent.; 1936-)
Andretti, Mario (Gabriel)(auto racing; 1940-)
Andrew Aguecheek, Sir (fict. chara., *Twelfth Night*)
Andrew Bonar Law (Br. pol.; 1858-1923)
Andrew Carnegie (US bus./finan.; 1835-1919)
Andrew Dice Clay (b. Andrew Silverstein)(ent.)
Andrew Jackson ("Old Hickory")(7th US pres.; 1767-1845)
Andrew Jackson Young, Jr. (US dipl./pol.; 1932-)
Andrew Jerkins Co., The
Andrew Johnson (17th US pres.; 1808-75)
Andrew Lloyd Webber (Br. comp.; 1948-)
Andrew Marvell (Br. poet/satirist; 1621-78)
Andrew McCarthy (ent.; 1963-)
Andrew N(ewell) Wyeth (US artist; 1917-)
Andrew Stevens (ent.; 1955-)
Andrew Volstead (US pol.; 1860-1947)
Andrew William Mellon (US finan./bus.; 1855-1937)
Andrew Young (US pol./reformer; 1932-)
Andrew, Hurricane (FL/LA; 1992)
Andrew, Merry (slang, adv. chara.)
Andrew, Prince (Andrew Albert Christian Edward)(2nd son of Queen Elizabeth II; 1960-)
Andrew, St. (patron saint of Scot.)
Andrew's Cross/cross, St. (X-shaped cross)
Andrews Air Force Base, DC (mil.)
Andrews Sisters (Patty, Maxene, Laverne)(music)
Andrews, Archie (cartoon chara.)
Andrews, Dana (ent.; 1909-92)
Andrews, Julie (ent.; 1935-)
Andrews, Laverne (ent.; Andrew Sisters; 1913-67)
Andrews, Maxene (ent., Andrews Sisters; 1918-)
Andrews, Patty (ent., Andrews Sisters; 1920-)
Andrian G(rigorievich) Nikolayev (cosmo.; 1929-)
Andries Pretorius (SAfr. colonizer/mil.; 1799-1853)
Andrija Mohorovicic (Yug. physt.; 1857-1936)
Androcles (also Androclus)(myth., Roman slave, befriended lion)
Androcles (Gr. orator; 5th c BC)
Androcles and the Lion (by G. B. Shaw)
Andromache (myth.)
Andromache (Euripides play)
Andromeda (astron., chained lady; myth.)

Andromeda Strain (M. Crichton novel)
Andronicus, Titus (Shakespeare play)
Andropov, Yuri (ex-pres., Rus.; 1914-84)
Andros Town, the Bahamas
Andrus, Cecil D. (ID gov.; 1931-)
Andy (Andrew Aitken) Rooney (US TV jour.; 1919-)
Andy Capp (comic strip)
Andy Devine (ent.; 1905-77)
Andy Garcia (ent.; 1956-)
Andy Gibb (ent.; 1958-88)
Andy Griffith (ent.; 1926-)
Andy Griffith Show, The (TV show)
Andy Razaf (US lyricist; 1895-1973)
Andy Warhol (b. Andrew Warhola)(US artist; 1927-87)
Andy Williams (ent.; 1930-)
Andy, Raggedy Ann &
Aneerood Jugnauth (PM, Mauritius; 1930-)
Anegada (Br. Virgin Island)
Aneurin Bevan (Br. pol.; 1897-1960)
Angana, Guam
Angas (lang.)
Ange Patasse (pres., Central African Republic)
Angel Cordero (jockey; 1942-)
Angel Falls (Venezuela)(world's highest waterfall)
Angel Soft™ (paper prods.)
Angel Street (play)
Angela (Yvonne) Davis (US activist/Communist; 1944-)
Angela Lansbury (ent.; 1925-)
Angeleno (also Los Angeleno)(native of Los Angeles)
Angeles, Port (WA)
Angelico, Fra (It. artist; 1400-55)
Angelo Secchi (It. astron.; 1818-78)
Angelo Siciliano (aka Charles Atlas)(US body builder; 1894-1972)
Angelou, Maya (US writer; 1928-)
Angels, California (baseball team)
Angelus (prayer, bell)(also l.c.)
Angie Dickinson (ent.; 1931-)
Angkor Wat (also Vat)
Angkor, Cambodia
Anglais, creme (sauce)
Angle (Ger. tribes invaded Br., 5th c.)
Anglican Church (also Church of England)
Anglican Orthodox Church
Anglo-American
Anglo-Australian
Anglo-French
Anglo-Indian
Anglo-Saxon (also Old English)(lang.; c500-1050)
Anglo-Saxon (Ger. tribes invaded Br., 5th and 7th c.)
Anglo-Saxon Chronicle (Eng. hist.; 55 BC-AD

1154)
Anglophile
Anglophobia
Angola (People's Republic of)(SW Afr.)
Angolan (people)
Angora cat
Angora goat
Angora rabbit
Angora wool
Angström, Anders Jonas (Swed. physt.; 1814-
	74)
Anguilla, West Indies
Angus cattle, Red
Anh, Le Duc (pres., Viet.)
Anheuser Busch, August, Jr. (US bus.; 1899-
	1989)
Anheuser-Busch, Inc.
Aníbal Cavaco Silva (PM, Port.; 1939-)
Animal Farm (G. Orwell novel)
Animal House, National Lampoon's (film; 1978)
Animalia (biol.)
Animals, the (pop music)
Animals' Voice Magazine
Anita Baker (ent.; 1958-)
Anita Ekberg (Swed./US ent.; 1931-)
Anita Gillette (ent.; 1938-)
Anita Loos (US writer; 1893?-1981)
Anita O'Day (US jazz; 1919-)
Anjelica Huston (ent.; 1951-)
Anjou (region, Fr.)
Anjou pear
Anjou, House of (or Plantagenet)(Br. ruling
	family; 1154-1399)
Anjou, Margaret of (queen, Eng./wife of Henry
	VI; 1430-82)
Anka, Paul (Can./US comp./ent.; 1941-)
Ankara, Turkey
Ann & Andy, Raggedy
Ann Arbor, MI
Ann Beattie (US writer; 1947-)
Ann B. Davis (ent.; 1926-)
Ann Blyth (ent.; 1928-)
Ann doll, Raggedy
Ann Jillian (ent.; 1950-)
Ann Landers (Eppie Lederer)(b. Esther Pauline
	Friedman)(US advice columnist; 1918-)
Ann-Margret (ent.; 1941-)
Ann Miller (ent.; 1919-)
Ann (Ward) Radcliffe (Br. writer; 1764-1823)
Ann Reinking (ent.; 1950-)
Ann Richards (TX gov.; 1933-)
Ann Rutherford (ent.; 1920-)
Ann Rutledge (fiancée of Abraham Lincoln;
	1816-35)
Ann Sheridan (ent.; 1915-67)
Ann Sothern (ent.; 1909-)
Ann Taylor (designer)
Anna Freud (Aus./Br. psych.; 1895-1982)

Anna Held (ent.; 1873-1918)
Anna Karenina (L. Tolstoy novel)
Anna Magnani (ent.; 1908-73)
Anna Maria Alberghetti (It./US ent.; 1936-)
Anna Moffo (ent.; 1927-)
Anna Pavlova (Rus. ballet; 1885-1931)
Anna Quindlen (US jour.)
Anna Sewell (Br. writer; 1820-78)
Anna Sokolow (US dancer/choreographer;
	1915-)
Anna, Antonio (López) de Santa (ex-pres/gen.,
	Mex.; 1795?-1876)
Annana/Bone, Algeria
Annapolis Convention (US hist.; 1786)
Annapolis, MD
Annapurna (also Anapurna, Devi,
	Parvati)(myth.)
Annapurna (mountain, Himalayas, Nepal)
Anne Archer (ent.; 1950-)
Anne Bancroft (ent.; 1931-)
Anne Baxter (ent.; 1923-85)
Anne Boleyn (2nd wife of Henry VIII; 1507-36)
Anne (Dudley) Bradstreet (US poet, c1612-72)
Anne Brontë (aka Acton Bell)(Br. writer; 1820-
	49)
Anne Francis (ent.; 1930-)
Anne Frank (Ger./Jew. diarist; 1929-45)
Anne Harvey Sexton (US poet; 1928-74)
Anne Hathaway (wife of Shakespeare; 1557?-
	1623)
Anne Jackson (ent.; 1925-)
Anne Jeffreys (ent.; 1923-)
Anne Klein™
Anne Klein & Co.
Anne Klein Jewelry (US bus.)
Anne-Marie Johnson (ent.)
Anne Meara (ent.; 1929-)
Anne Murray (ent.; 1945-)
Anne of Austria (queen, Fr./mother of Louis
	XIV; 1601-66)
Anne of Brittany (queen, Fr.; 1477-1514)
Anne of Cleves (4th wife of Henry VIII; 1515-
	57)
Anne of Denmark (queen consort, James VI of
	Scot.; 1574-1619)
Anne Rice (US writer)
Anne Spencer (Morrow) Lindbergh (US writer/
	aviator; 1906-)
Anne style, Queen (arch./furn.; 1700-20)
Anne Tyler (US writer; 1941-)
Anne, Princess (Anne Elizabeth Alice
	Louise)(daughter of Queen Elizabeth II;
	1950-)
Anne, Queen (queen, Br./Ir.; 1665-1714)
Annemarie Moser Proell (skiing; 1953-)
Annenberg, Walter (US publ./finan.; 1908-)
Anne's lace, Queen (plant)
Anne's War, Queen (Br./Fr. in Amer.; 1702-13)

Annette Bening (ent.; 1958-)
Annette Funicello (ent.; 1942-)
Annette O'Toole (ent.; 1953-)
Annibale Carracci (It. artist; 1560-1609)
Annie (play)
Annie Besant (Br. theosophist; 1847-1933)
Annie Dillard (US writer)
Annie Get Your Gun (film; 1950)
Annie Hall (film; 1977)
Annie Oakley (Phoebe Mozee)(ent./
  sharpshooter; 1860-1926)
Annie Potts (ent.)
Annie, Little Orphan (fict. chara.)
Annie, Tugboat
anno Domini (also AD)(Latin, in the year of the
  Lord)
Annunciation (rel.)
Annunciation lily (also Madonna lily)
Annunzio Mantovani (ent.; 1905-80)
Another World (TV soap)
Anouk Aimee (Fr. ent.; 1932-)
Anschluss (Ger., union)
Ansel Adams (US photo.; 1902-84)
Anselm Feuerbach (Ger. artist; 1829-80)
Anselm, St. (archbishop of Canterbury; c1033-
  1109)
Anshar (myth.)
An-Shih, Wang (Ch. pol.; 1021-86)
Anspach, Susan (ent.; 1939-)
Ant, Adam (ent.; 1954-)
ANTA (American National Theatre and
  Academy)
Antabuse™ (med.)
Antaeus (myth.)
Antall, József (ex-PM, Hung.; 1932-)
Antananarivo, Madagascar
Antarctic Circle (South Pole)
Antarctic Peninsula (West Antarctica)
Antarctica (also Antarctic Continent)(South
  Pole)
Antares (also Alpha Scorpii)(astron.; myth.)
Anthony and the Imperials, Little (pop music)
Anthony Armstrong-Jones (Earl of
  Snowdon)(Br. photo.; 1930-)
Anthony Burgess (Br. writer/comp.; 1917-1993)
Anthony Comstock (US reformer; 1844-1915)
Anthony Eden, Sir (Earl of Avon)(ex-PM, Br.;
  1897-1977)
Anthony Edwards (ent.; 1962-)
Anthony Francisco (Tony)(ent.; 1928-)
Anthony Geary (ent.)
Anthony Gustav de Rothschild (Br. finan.;
  1887-1961)
Anthony Hopkins (ent.; 1937-)
Anthony Johnson (rowing; 1940-)
Anthony Lake (US Nat'l Security Adviser;
  1939-)
Anthony Lewis

Anthony Lukas, J.
Anthony M. Kennedy (US jurist; 1936-)
Anthony Newley (ent.; 1931-)
Anthony (Tony) Perkins (ent.; 1932-)
Anthony Quinn (ent.; 1915-)
Anthony "Fat Tony" Salerno (US Mafia; 1912-
  92)
Anthony Trollope (Br. writer; 1815-82)
Anthony van Dyck, Sir (Flem. artist; 1599-
  1641)
Anthony Wayne (Mad Anthony)(US gen.; 1745-
  96)
Anthony Zerbe (ent.; 1936-)
Anthony, Earl (bowling; 1938-)
Anthony, Piers
Anthony, St. (Eg., founded monasticism; c251-
  356)
Anthony, Susan B(rownell)(US reformer/
  suffragist; 1820-1906)
Anthony's Cross/cross, St. (T-shaped cross)
Anthony's fire, St. (skin disease)
Anti-Corn-Law League (Br. hist.; 1839)
Anti-Masonic Party (US pol. org.; 1827-1840)
Anti-Saloon League of America (US org.; 1895-)
anti-Semite
anti-Semitism
Antibes, France
Antichrist (opponent of Christ)
Antietam National Battlefield (MD)
Antietam, Battle of (US hist.; 1862)
Antigone (myth.)
Antigua and Barbuda (State of)
Antigua, Guatemala
Antilles, Greater (West Indies)(Cuba,
  Hispaniola, Jamaica, Puerto Rico)
Antilles, Lesser (West Indies)(Aruba,
  Netherlands Antilles, Trinidad and Tobago,
  Windward Islands, Leeward Islands)
Antilles, Netherlands (West Indies)
Antioch, CA
Antioch, Turkey (also Antakya)
Antiphon (Gr. speechwriter; c480-411 BC)
Antiques, The Magazine (mag.)
Antlia (astron., air pump)
Antofagasta, Chile
Antoine Cadillac (founded Detroit; 1658-1730)
Antoine-César Becquerel (Fr. physt.; 1788-
  1878)
Antoine (Marie Roger) de Saint-Exupery (Fr.
  writer/aviator; 1900-44)
Antoine-Henri Becquerel (Fr. physt.; 1852-
  1908)
Antoine Laurent Lavoisier (Fr. chem.; 1743-
  1794)
Antoine Pevsner (Fr. artist; 1886-1962)
Antoine Watteau (Fr. artist; 1684-1721)
Antoinette, Marie (queen, Fr./wife of Louis XVI;
  1755-93)

Anton Bruckner (Austl. comp.; 1824-96)

Anton (Pavlovich) Chekhov (Rus. writer; 1860-1904)

Anton Denikin (Rus. mil.; 1872-1947)

Anton Dvorak (also Antonin)(Czech. comp.; 1841-1904)

Anton (Grigoryevich) Rubinstein (Rus. pianist/comp.; 1829-94)

Anton van Leeuwenhoek (Dutch, father of microbiology; 1632-1723)

Anton, Susan (ent.; 1950-)

Antonia Fraser (Br. writer; 1932-)

Antonia Novello

Antonin Dvorak (also Anton)(Czech. comp.; 1841-1904)

Antonin Scalia (US jurist; 1936-)

Antoninus Pius (emp., Rome; AD 86-161)

Antonio Allegri da Correggio (It. artist; 1494-1534)

Antonio Amati (It. violin maker; 1555-1638)

Antonio de O(liveira) Salazar (ex-PM, Port.; 1899-1970)

Antonio (López) de Santa Anna (ex-pres/gen., Mex.; 1795?-1876)

Antonio dos Santos Ramalho Eanes (ex-pres., Port.; 1935-)

Antonio Gaudí (Sp. arch.; 1852-1926)

Antonio Mascarenhas Monteiro (pres., Cape Verde; 1944-)

Antonio Rossellino (It. sculptor; 1427-79)

Antonio Salieri (It. comp./cond.; 1750-1825)

Antonio Sant'Elia (It. arch.; 1888-1916)

Antonio (Lucio) Vivaldi (It. comp.; 1678-1741)

Antonius Stradivarius (also Antonio Stradivari)(It. violin maker; 1644-1737)

Antonius, Marcus (aka Mark Antony)(Roman gen.; 83?-30 BC)

Antonius, Marcus Aurelius (b. Marcus Annius Verus)(emp., Rome; 121-180)

Antony and Cleopatra (Shakespeare play)

Antony, Mark (aka Marcus Antonius)(Roman gen.; 83?-30 BC)

Antron™ (nylon)

Antsiranana, Madagascar

Antwerp (province, Belgium)

Antwerp, Belgium

Anu (myth.)

Anubis (myth.)

Anvers Island, Antarctica

Anwar (el-) Sadat (ex-pres., Eg.; 1918-81)

Anything But Love (TV show)

Anza, Juan Bautista de (Sp. expl.; 1735-88?)

Anzac Day (Austl. and New Zeal.)

A.1.™ Steak Sauce

AP (Associated Press)(US news org.; est. 1848)

APA (American Pharmaceutical Association, American Psychiatric Association, American Psychological Association)

Apache (NAmer. Indians)

Apalachicola National Forest (FL)

Apalachicola River (GA/FL)

Apalachicola, FL

APB (all-points bulletin)

APEC (Asia-Pacific Economic Cooperation Conference; 1989)

Apennine Mountains (It.)

Apgar score (med.)

Aphrodite (myth.)

API (American Petroleum Institute)

Apia, Western Samoa

Appling, Luke (baseball; 1907-90)

APO (Army and Air Force Post Office)

Apocalypse Now (film; 1979)

Apocalypse, the (also l.c.)

Apocrypha (also l.c.)(rel.)

Apollo (also Phoebus)(myth., sun god)

Apollo (US crewed space flights)

Apollo asteroid (astron.)

Apollo at Delphi, oracle of

Apollo Comedy Hour (TV show)

Apollo project (US space flight to moon, 7/20/69)

Apollo-Saturn (US crewed space flights)

Apollo Theater (Harlem, NYC)

Apollodorus (writer; myth.)

Apollonian (adj. = l.c.)

Apollonius of Perga (Gr. math.; c265-170 BC)

Apollonius of Rhodes (Gr. poet; c220-180 BC)

Apollonius of Tyana (Gr. phil.; 1st c AD)

Apollonius of Tyre (fict. Gr. hero)

Apollyon (also Abaddon)(destroyer, hell)

Apostles' Creed (rel.)

Apostolic Fathers (rel.)

Appalachia (eastern US)

Appalachia, VA

Appalachian Mountains (eastern US)

Appalachian Trail (ME to GA)

Appaloosa (horse)

Appenzell, Switzerland

Appian Way (ancient Roman highway)

Apple™

Apple Computer, Inc.

Apple Jacks™ (cereal)

Apple Macintosh™ (compu.)

Apple Newtons™ (cookies)

Apple Pan Dowdy, Shoo-Fly Pie & (song)

Appleby, John Francis (US inv.; 1840-1917)

Applegate, Christina (ent.; 1972-)

Applegate, Jesse (US pioneer/pol.; 1811-88)

Appleseed, Johnny (b. John Chapman)(US pioneer; 1774-1845)

Appleton, WI

Appomattox Court House National Historical Park (VA)

Appomattox, VA

Apra, Guam

April Fools' Day (also All Fools' Day)(April 1)

Aptidon, Hassan Gouled (pres., Djibouti; 1916-)

Apuleius, Lucius (Roman satirist/atty.; c124-c170 BC)

Apure River (Venezuela)

Apus (astron., bird of paradise)

APV (all-purpose vehicle)

Aqaba, Gulf of (Jordan)

Aqua-Lung™ (underwater apparatus)

Aqua Net™ (hair care)

Aqua Velva™ (toiletries)

Aquafresh™ (toothpaste)

Aquaman (cartoon chara.)

Aquarian Age (also Age of Aquarius)

Aquarium Fish (mag.)

Aquarius (zodiac, astron., water bearer)

Aquascutum™ (raincoat)

Aquila (astron., eagle)

Aquinas, St. Thomas ("the Angelic Doctor")(It. phil./rel.; 1225-74)

Aquino, Corazon (ex-pres., Phil.; 1933-)

Aquitaine (region, Fr.)

Aquitaine, Eleanor of (queen, Louis VII [Fr.] & Henry II [Eng.]; c1122-1204)

AR (Arkansas, army regulation)

Ar (chem. sym., argon)

Ara (astron., altar)

Ara Parseghian (football; 1923-)

Arab (lang./people)

Arab-Berber (people)

Arab Emirates (also United Arab Emirates)

Arab-Israeli Six-Day War (1967)

Arab-Israeli Wars (series of wars since 1948)

Arab League (govt.)

Arab League Day (Arab nations)

Arab Petroleum Exporting Countries, Organization of (OAPEC)(est.; 1968)

Arab, Omani (people)

Arabia (also Arabian Peninsula)

Arabia, (T[homas] E[dward]) Lawrence of (Br. mil.; 1888-1935)

Arabia, Lawrence of (film; 1962)

Arabian camel (dromedary, one hump)

Arabian Desert (Eg.)

Arabian Gulf (also Persian Gulf)(SW Asia)

Arabian horse

Arabian Nights' Entertainments, The (also *The Thousand and One Nights, Arabian Nights*)(myth.)

Arabian Sea (India/Arabia)

Arabic (lang.)

Arabic alphabet

Arabic numerals

Arable, Fern

Arachne (myth.)

Arafat, Yassir (also Yasser)(PLO Chairman; 1929-)

Aragon (region, Sp.)

Aragon, Catherine of (1st wife of Henry VIII; 1485-1536)

Araguaia River (Brazil)(also Araguaya)

Arak, Iran

Araks River (Turk.)

Aral Sea (was Lake Aral)(Kazakhstan/Uzbekistan)

Arallu (also Aralu)(ancient Babylonian world of the dead)

Aram Ilich (or Ill'yich) Khachaturian (Armenian comp.; 1903-78)

Aramaic (lang.)

Arapaho (NAmer. Indians)

Arapaho National Forest

Ararat, Mount (Turk.)(Noah's Ark landing)

Araucana chicken (also Easter egg chicken)

Araucanian (also Araucan)(Chile Indians)

Arawak (SAmer. Indians)

Arbitron ratings

Arbor Day

Arbuckle, Fatty (Roscoe)(ent.; 1887-1933)

Arbuthnot, John (Scot. phys./satirist; 1667-1735)

Arby's™

Arby's, Inc.

Arc de Triomphe (Arch of Triumph)(Paris)

Arc, St. Joan of (also Jeanne d'Arc, Maid of Orléans)(Fr. rel./mil.; 1412?-31)

Arcadia (ancient Gr. region)

Arcadia, CA, FL

Arcaro, Eddie (George Edward)(jockey; 1916-)

Arch Oboler

Arch of Constantine (Rome)

Arch of Titus (statue)

Archaeology (mag.)

Archangel Blue (now Russian Blue)(cat)

archangel Gabriel

archbishop of Canterbury (archbishop, Church of England)

Archeozoic era (also Archaeozoic)

Archer-Daniels-Midland (food prods.)

Archer, Anne (ent.; 1950-)

Archerd, Army

Arches National Park (UT)

Archibald Cox (US atty./Watergate; 1912-)

Archibald Joseph Cronin ("A.J.")(Br. phys./writer; 1896-1981)

Archibald MacLeish (US poet; 1892-1982)

Archibald M. Willard (US artist; 1836-1918)

Archibald (Percival) Wavell (Br. mil.; 1883-1950)

Archie (cartoon)

Archie Andrews (cartoon chara.)

Archie Bunker (fict. chara., *All in the Family*)

Archie Goodwin (fict. chara.)

Archie Moore (boxing; 1913-)

Archimedean (or Archimedes') screw (pump)

Archimedean water snail

Archimedes (Gr. math.; c287-212 BC)

Archimedes' (or Archimedean) screw (pump)

Archimedes' principle (physics)

Archipenko, Alexander (US sculptor; 1887-1964)

Architectural Digest (mag.)

Archives and Records Administration, National (NARA)(US govt. agcy.; est. 1984)

Archives, National (DC)

Arco Products, Inc.

Arcosanti community (AZ)(self-sufficient desert community)

Arctic Circle (North Pole)

Arctic Current (also Labrador Current)(cold ocean current)

Arctic Ocean (North Pole)

Arctic region (North Pole)

Arctic, the (North Pole)

Arcturus (or Alpha Bootis)(astron.)

Arden doctrine, Enoch (divorce)

Arden Co., Elizabeth

Arden, Elizabeth (US bus.; 1884-1966)

Arden™, Elizabeth (cosmetics)

Arden, Enoch (missing person presumed dead, but is alive)

Arden, Enoch (Tennyson poem)

Arden, Eve (ent.; 1908-90)

Ardenne, Champagne- (region, Fr.)

ARE (Arab Republic of Egypt, Association for Research & Enlightenment)

Are You Being Served (TV show)

Arequipa, Peru

Ares (myth., god of war)

Aretha Franklin (ent.; 1942-)

Arezzo, Italy

Argentina (also Argentine Republic)(SAmer.)

Argo (astron., ship)

Argo (myth., Jason's ship in quest of the Golden Fleece)

Argonauts (myth.)

Argonne Forest (Fr.)(also Argonne)

Argos (ancient Gr. city)

Argote, Luis de Gongora y (Sp. writer; 1561-1627)

Argus (myth.)

Argyle (diamond-shaped pattern)(also l.c.)

Argyll, Duke of (John D. S. Campbell)(ex-gov-gen,, Can.; 1845-1914)

Arhat (rel.)(also Arhant)

Arhus, Denmark (also Aarhus)

Ariadne (myth.)

Arica, Chile

Ariel (astron.)

Ariel Durant (US hist.; 1898-1981)

Ariel Sharon (Isr. pol./mil.; 1928-)

Aries (zodiac, astron., ram)

Arima, Trinidad

Aris-Isotoner™ (gloves)

Aristide Briand (ex-PM, Fr.; 1862-1932)

Aristide Maillol (Fr. sculptor; 1861-1944)

Aristide, Jean-Bertrand (deposed pres., Haiti; 1953-)

AristoCAT™ (CAT system)

Aristophanes (Gr. drama.; c448-380 BC)

Aristotelian logic (also Aristotelean)

Aristotelianism (phil.)

Aristotle (Gr. phil.; 384-322 BC)

Aristotle Socrates Onassis (Gr. bus.; 1900-75)

Arizona (AZ)

Arizona Daily Star (AZ, newspaper)

Arizona Highways (mag)

Arizona Republic (AZ newspaper)

Arizona v. Fulminate (US law; 1991)

Arizona, Miranda vs. (US law; 1966)

Ark of the Covenant (rel.)

Ark, Joan Van (ent.; 1943-)

Arkansas (AR)

Arkansas River (CO-LA)

Arkie™ (compu. game)

Arkin, Alan (ent.; 1934-)

Arkwright, Sir Richard (Br. inv.; 1732-92)

Arledge, Roone (US TV exec.; 1931-)

Arlen Specter, J. (US cong.; 1930-)

Arlen, Harold (US comp.; 1905-86)

Arlen, Richard (ent.; 1900-76)

Arlene Dahl (ent.; 1928-)

Arlene Francis (ent.; 1908-)

Arles, France

Arlington National Cemetery (VA)

Arlington, MA, NJ, TX, VA

Arliss, George (ent.; 1868-1946)

Arlo Guthrie (ent.; 1947-)

ARM (adjustable-rate mortgage)

A.R.M.™ (allergy relief medicine)(med.)

Armada, Spanish (Invincible Armada)(fleet of ships)

Armageddon (rel., final battle)

Armagh, County (NIre.)

Armagnac (brandy)

Armagnac (district, Fr.)

Armand Assante (ent.; 1949-)

Arm & Hammer™ (baking soda)

Armand Hammer (US bus.; 1898-1990)

Armand Jean du Plessis Richelieu, Duc de (Fr. cardinal/pol.; 1585-1642)

Armando Calderon Sol (pres., El Salvador; 1948-)

Armani, Giorgio (It. designer; 1935-)

Armbruster, Robert

Armed Forces Day

Armed Forces Radio

Armenia (Republic of)(formerly part of USSR)(W Asia)

Armenian (lang./people)

Armenian Church

Armetale™ (dinnerware)

Armistice Day (now Veterans Day)

Armor™ All cleaner
Armor All Corp.
Armour™ (meats)
Armour Swift-Eckrich (US bus.)
Armour, Philip D. (US bus.; 1832-1901)
Arms, College of (also Heralds' College)(Br. heraldry)
Armstrong-Jones, Anthony (Earl of Snowdon)(Br. photo.; 1930-)
Armstrong World Industries, Inc.
Armstrong, Henry (boxing; 1912-88)
Armstrong, Louis "Satchmo" (US jazz; 1900-71)
Armstrong, Neil A(lden)(astro., 1st to walk on moon; 1930-)
Army Air Forces
Army and Air Force Post Office (APO)
Army Corps of Engineers (US mil.)
Army Magazine
Army of the U.S. (also United States Army)
Army Times (mag.)
Army, Archerd
Army, Department of the (US govt.)
Army, Red (USSR army until 1946)
Army, Regular (US army maintained in both peace and war)
Army, U.S. (US mil.)
Arnaz, Desi (ent.; 1917-86)
Arnaz, Desi, Jr. (ent.; 1953-)
Arnaz, Lucie (ent.; 1951-)
Arne Carlson (MN gov.; 1934-)
Arness, James (ent.; 1923-)
Arnie Robinson (track; 1948-)
Arno, Peter (aka Curtis Arnoux Peters)(cartoonist, *New Yorker*; 1904-68)
Arnold Lucius Gesell (US psych./educ.; 1880-1961)
Arnold (Daniel) Palmer (golf; 1929-)
Arnold Rüütel (ex-pres., Estonia)
Arnold (Franz Walter) Schoenberg (Aus. comp.; 1874-1951)
Arnold Schwarzenegger (ent.; 1947-)
Arnold Stang (ent.; 1925-)
Arnold (Joseph) Toynbee (Br. hist.; 1889-1975)
Arnold, Benedict (US traitor; 1741-1801)
Arnold, Eddy (ent.; 1918-)
Arnold, Edward (ent.; 1890-1956)
Arnold, Hap (Henry)(US mil.; 1886-1950)
Arnold, Matthew (Br. poet/critic; 1822-88)
Arnold, Roseanne (Barr)(ent.; 1952-)
Aroostook War (US/Can.; 1838-39)
Arp, Jean (or Hans)(Fr. artist; 1887-1966)
Arpad Goncz (pres., Hung.; 1922-)
Arpel, Adrien (cosmetics)
Arpels, Inc., Van Cleef &
Arquette, Cliff (pseud. Charlie Weaver)(ent.; 1905-74)
Arquette, Rosanna (ent.; 1959-)
Arrau, Claudio (Chilean pianist; 1903-91)

Arrid™ (anti-perspirant)
Arrid Extra Dry™
Arrigo Boito (It. comp./writer; 1842-1918)
Arrindell, Clement Athelston (gov-gen., St. Kitts/Nevis
Arrowhead, Lake, CA
Arrowhead Drinking Water Co.
Arroyo, Martina (ent.; 1937-)
Arsenic and Old Lace (play; film, 1942)
Arsenio Hall (ent.; 1955-)
Arshile (Vosdanig Adoian) Gorky (US artist; 1905-48)
Art & Antiques (mag.)
Art Blakey (US jazz; 1919-90)
Art Buchwald (US columnist; 1925-)
Art Carney (ent.; 1918-)
Art Deco (also l.c.)
Art Garfunkel (ent.; 1942-)
Art in America (mag.)
Art Institute of Chicago
Art Linkletter (ent.; 1912-)
Art News
Art Nouveau (also l.c.)
Art Pepper (US jazz; 1925-82)
Art Rooney (football; 1901-88)
Art Sansom (cartoonist, *The Born Loser*; 1920-91)
Art Spiegelman (cartoonist; 1948-)
Art(hur) Tatum (US jazz; 1910-56)
Art Young (pol. cartoonist; 1866-1943)
Artagnan, Charles de Baatz d', Seigneur (fict. chara., *Three Musketeers*)
Arte Johnson (ent.; 1929-)
Artemia, Inc.
Artemis (myth.)
Artemis™ (toiletries)
Artemision (also Temple of Artemis at Ephesus)
Artful Dodger (fict. pickpocket, *Oliver Twist*)
Arthur (film; 1981)
Arthur Ashe (tennis; 1943-93)
Arthur C(harles) Clarke (Br. writer; 1917-)
Arthur (Holly) Compton (US physt.; 1892-1962)
Arthur Conan Doyle, Sir (Br. phys./writer, Sherlock Holmes; 1859-1930)
Arthur Davies (US artist; 1862-1928)
Arthur Dove (US artist; 1880-1946)
Arthur Fiedler (US cond.; 1894-1979)
Arthur Fonzerelli (also "the Fonz" or "Fonzie")(fict chara.)
Arthur Godfrey (ent.; 1903-83)
Arthur Godfrey and Friends (TV show)
Arthur Godfrey's Talent Scouts (TV show)
Arthur Hailey (US writer; 1920-)
Arthur Hays Sulzberger (US publ.; 1881-1968)
Arthur Hill (ent.; 1922-)
Arthur Honegger (Swiss comp.; 1892-1955)
Arthur H(endrick) Vandenberg (US pol.; 1884-1951)

Proper Noun Speller

Arthur James Balfour (ex-PM, Br.; 1848-1930)
Arthur Kennedy (ent.; 1914-90)
Arthur Kornberg (US chem.; 1918-)
Arthur Laffer (US econ.; 1940-)
Arthur Levitt, Jr. (Chair/SEC; 1931-)
Arthur Lewis, Sir (William)(Br. econ.; 1915-91)
Arthur "Harpo" Marx (ent.; 1888-1964)
Arthur Miller (US writer; 1915-)
Arthur M(eier) Schlesinger (US hist.; 1888-1965)
Arthur M(eier) Schlesinger, Jr. (US hist.; 1917-)
Arthur Murray (US dancer; 1896-1991)
Arthur Murray Dance Studios (US bus.)
Arthur Ochs Sulzberger (US publ.; 1926-)
Arthur Penn (ent.; 1922-)
Arthur Rimbaud, (Jean Nicolas)(Fr. poet; 1854-91)
Arthur Rubinstein (Pol./US pianist; 1887-1982)
Arthur Saint Clair (US gen.; 1736-1818)
Arthur Schopenhauer (Ger. phil.; 1788-1860)
Arthur Schwartz (US comp.; 1900-84)
Arthur S(eymour) Sullivan, Sir (Br. comp.; 1842-1900)
Arthur Thomas Quiller-Couch, Sir (aka "Q")(Br. writer; 1863-1944)
Arthur Travers Harris, Sir (Br. mil.; 1895-1984)
Arthur Treacher (ent.; 1894-1975)
Arthur Treacher's Fish & Chips (US bus.)
Arthur Wellesley (Duke of Wellington)(Br. mil.; 1769-1852)
Arthur, Bea (Beatrice)(ent.; 1926-)
Arthur, Chester A(lan)(21th US pres.; 1829-86)
Arthur, Jean (ent.; 1900-91)
Arthur, King (legendary Br. king, 6th c.)
Arthur, Port (Ontario, Can.)
Arthur, Port (TX)
Arthurian legend
Arthus' reaction/phenomenon (med.)
Articles of Confederation (US hist.; 1781)
Articles of War
Artie Shaw (US jazz; 1910-)
Artis Gilmore (basketball; 1949-)
Artist's Magazine
Arts & Entertainment Network (A&E)(cable TV)
Arts and Humanities, National Endowment on (or for) the (US govt. agcy.; est. 1965)
Arturo Toscanini (It. cond.; 1867-1957)
Artweek
Aruba (the Netherlands, Antilles)
Arutyunyan, Gagik (VP, Armenia)
Arvin Industries, Inc.
Aryan (langs.)
As (chem. sym., arsenic)
As the World Turns (TV soap)
As You Like It (Shakespeare play)
Asa Candler (U.S., founded Coca-Cola Co.; 1851-1929)

ASAP (as soon as possible)
Asbury Jukes, Southside Johnny and the (pop music)
Asbury Park Press (NJ newspaper)
Asbury Park, NJ
ASCAP (American Society of Composers, Authors, and Publishers)
Ascension (Br. island[s] in S Atl.)
Ascension Day (also Holy Thursday)(rel.)
A. Schulman (US bus.)
ASCII (American Standard Code for Information Interchange (compu.)
Ascot Heath (race course, Eng.)
Ascot races (Eng.)
Ascriptin™ (med.)
Asendin™ (med.)
Asgard (myth.)
Ashburner, Charles (US geol.; 1854-89)
Ashbury, Haight- (district, San Francisco)
Ashcan school (1908-14, art from city life)
Ashe, Arthur (tennis; 1943-93)
Asher Brown Durand (US artist; 1796-1886)
Asheville, NC
Ashford, Evelyn (tract & field; 1957-)
Ashkenazi (plural = Ashkenazim)(people)
Ashkenazy, Vladimir (Rus. pianist/cond.; 1937-)
Ashkhabad, Turkmenistan
Ashland Oil, Inc.
Ashland, KY, OH, OR, PA, WI
Ashley Montagu, (Montague Francis)(Br./US anthrop.; 1905-)
Ashley, Elizabeth (ent.; 1941-)
Ashley™, Ellen (clothing)
Ashley™, Laura
Ashley, Laura (Br. designer; 1926-85)
Ashley, Laura (US bus.)
Ashman, Howard (US lyricist; 1951-91)
ash-Shariqah (state, UAE)
Ash-Shaytan (rel., Satan)
Ashton-Tate Co.
Ashwander v. Tennessee Valley Authority (US law; 1936)
Ash Wednesday (rel.)
Asia
Asia Minor (ancient region, Turk.)(now Anatolia)
Asia-Pacific Economic Cooperation Conference (APEC; 1989)
Asia Week
Asiago (liqueur)
Asiago, Italy
Asian (people)
Asian-American
A-side (music, hit side)
Asimov, Isaac (US writer/sci-fi; 1920-92)
Asimov's Science Fiction Magazine, Isaac
Askar Akayev (pres., Kyrgyzstan)
ASL (American sign language)

Asmara, Ethiopia (also Asmera)

Asmodeus (an evil spirit)

Asner, Ed (ent.; 1929-)

ASPCA (American Society for the Prevention of Cruelty to Animals)

Aspen Music Festival

Aspen Music School

Aspen, CO

Aspercreme™ (med.)

Aspergum™ (med.)

Aspin, Les (ex-US Secy./Defense; 1938-)

Asquith, Herbert H. (ex-PM, Br.; 1852-1928)

Assab, Ethiopia

Assad, Hafez al- (pres., Syria; 1930-)

as-Salimiyah, Kuwait

Assama (Muslim paradise)

Assamese (lang.)

Assante, Armand (ent.; 1949-)

Assemblies of God (rel.)

Assiniboin (NAmer. Indians)

Assiniboine River (Can.)

Assiniboine, Mount (Can.)

Assisi, Italy

Assisi, St. Francis of (It. rel., founded Franciscans; 1182-1226)

Associated Press (AP)(US news org.; est. 1848)

Association for the Advancement of Colored People, National (NAACP)(org. 1909)

Association of Broadcast Employees and Technicians, National (also NABET)

Association of Broadcasters, National (also NAB)

Association of Intercollegiate Athletics, National (also NAIA)

Association of Manufacturers, National (NAM)(est. 1895)

Association of Radio and Television News Analysts (ARTNA)

Association of Television and Radio Announcers, National (also NATRA)

Association, the (pop music)

Assumption (rel.)

Assumption Day

Assur (myth.)

Assyria (ancient Asian empire)

Assyrian (lang.)

Assyrian art (17-7th c. BC)

AST (Atlantic Standard Time)

Astaire, Adele (ent.)

Astaire, Fred (ent.; 1899-1987)

Astarte (myth.)

Asti Spumante/spumante (wine)

Astin, John (ent.; 1930-)

Astin, Patty Duke (ent.; 1946-)

Astor, John Jacob (US bus.; 1763-1848)

Astor, John Jacob, 5th (US/Br. publ.; 1886-1971)

Astor, Mary (ent.; 1906-87)

Astoria Hotel, Waldorf- (NYC)

Astoria, OR

Astounding Science Fiction

Astrodome, the (Houston, TX)

Astrophysical Observatory, Special (USSR)

Astros, Houston (baseball team)

Astroturf™

Asturian (people)

Asturias (cheese)

Asturias (region, Sp.)

Asturias, Miguel Angel (Guat. writer/dipl.; 1899-1974)

Asunción, Paraguay

Aswan High Dam (Eg.)

Aswan, Egypt

Asylum/Nonesuch Records, Elektra/ (US bus.)

Atabrine™ (med.)

Atahualpa (last Incan emp.; c1502-33)

A T & T (American Telephone & Telegraph Co.)

Atari™ (compu.)

Atari, Inc.

Atatürk, Kemal (b. Mustafa Kemal Pasha)(ex-pres./dictator, Turk.; 1881-1938)

Atbara River (NE Afr.)

A. T. Cross Co.

A-Team (TV show)

Atef Sidqi (PM, Eg.)

Athanasius, St. (bishop of Alexandria; 298-373)

Atharva-Veda (rel.)

Athena (myth.)

Athena Nike, Temple of (Gr.)

Athena Parthenos, Temple of (also Parthenon, Gr.)

Athena, Pallas (myth.)

Athena, Temple of (Gr.)

Athenaeum (Athena temple[s])(also l.c.)

Athenaeus (Gr. scholar/writer; 3rd c. AD)

Athens, AL, GA, OH, PA, TN, TX

Athens, Greece

Athens, School of (by Raphael)

Athens, Timon of (by Shakespeare)

Atherton, Gertrude (Franklin Horn)(US writer; 1857-1948)

Atherton, William (ent.; 1947-)

Athletic Association, National Collegiate (NCAA)(est. 1906)

Athletic Union of the United States, Amateur (AAU)

Athletics, National Association of Intercollegiate (also NAIA)

Athletics, Oakland (also Oakland A's)(baseball team)

Ativan™ (med.)

Atjehnese (also Achinese)(lang./people)

Atkins, Chet (Chester)(ent.; 1924-)

Atkins. Tommy (slang, Br. army private)

Atkinson, (Justin) Brooks (US critic; 1894-1984)

Atkov, Oleg (cosmo.)

Atlanta Braves (baseball team)
Atlanta Constitution (GA newspaper)
Atlanta Falcons (football team)
Atlanta Hawks (basketball team)
Atlanta International Airport, Hartsfield (GA)
Atlanta Journal (GA newspaper)
Atlanta, GA
Atlantic & Pacific Tea Co., Great (A&P Food
   Stores)
Atlantic Beach, FL
Atlantic Charter (WWII, US/Br.)
Atlantic City Press (NJ newspaper)
Atlantic City, NJ
Atlantic Monthly, The (mag.)
Atlantic Ocean (also the Atlantic)
Atlantic Richfield Co.
Atlantic Standard Time
Atlantis (legendary continent)
Atlantis (US space shuttle)
Atlantis, New (utopia, Sir Francis Bacon)
Atlas (astron., myth.)
Atlas Mountains (NW Afr.)
Atlas, Charles (b. Angelo Siciliano)(US body
   builder; 1894-1972)
Atlas, Mercury- (US crewed space flights)
ATM (automatic teller machine)
Atman (World Soul, rel.)
Atna (AK Indians)(also Ahtena or Ahtna)
Atna River (also Copper River)(AK)
Atomic Age (usually l.c.)
Atonement, Day of (Yom Kippur)(rel.)
Atropos (myth.)
Attas, Haidar Abu Bakr al- (PM, Yemen; 1939-)
Attenborough, Sir Richard (ent.; 1923-)
Attends™ (undergarments)
Attic (lit., Gr.)
Attica (region, Gr.)
Attica, IN, NY
Attila the Hun ("Scourge of God")(King of the
   Huns; c406-453)
Attlee, Clement R(ichard)(ex-PM, Br.; 1883-
   1967)
ATV (all-terrain vehicle)
Atwater, Lee (Harvey Leroy)(US pol.; 1951-91)
Atwood, Margaret (Can. writer; 1939-)
Au (chem. sym., gold)
Auberjonois, Rene (ent.; 1940-)
Aubervilliers, France
Aubrey Solomon "Abba" Eban (Isr. pol.; 1915-)
Aubrey Vincent Beardsley (Br. artist; 1872-98)
Aubrey, John (Br. antiquarian; 1626-97)
Auburn, AL, CA, IN, MA, ME
Aubusson tapestry/rug
Aubusson, France
Auchincloss, Louis Stanton (US writer; 1917-)
Auckland, New Zealand
Auden, W. H. (Br. poet; 1907-73)
Audie Murphy (ent., war hero; 1924-71)

Audio (mag.)
Audio/Video Interiors (mag.)
Audi of America, Inc.
Audi™ (auto.)
Audi™ Cabriolet (auto.)
Audi™ 100CS (auto.)
Audi™ 100S (auto.)
Audi™ 100S Wagon (auto.)
Audi™ 90CS (auto.)
Audi™ 90S (auto.)
Audi Quattro™ (auto.)
Audrey Hepburn (ent.; 1929-73)
Audrey Meadows (ent.; 1924-)
Audrey Rose (film; 1977)
Audubon Society, National (environ. org.)
Audubon, John James (US artist, birds; 1785-
   1851)
Audubon's warbler (bird)
Auel, Jean M.
Auerbach, Red (Arnold)(basketball; 1917-)
auf Wiedersehen (Ger., good-bye, until we meet
   again)
Augean stables (mythical stables not cleaned
   for 30 years)
Auger effect (astron.)
Auger shower (cosmic ray shower)
Augmentin™ (med.)
Augsburg, Germany
August Anheuser Busch, Jr. (US bus.; 1899-
   1989)
August Belmont (US finan.; 1816-90)
August Macke (Ger. artist; 1887-1914)
August Strindberg (Johan)(Swed. writer; 1849-
   1912)
August von Wassermann (Ger. phys./bacteriol.;
   1866-1925)
August Wilhelm von Schlegel (Ger. writer;
   1767-1845)
August Wilson (US writer; 1945-)
Augusta Ada Byron (Lady Lovelace)(Br. math./
   inv., compu.; 1815-52)
Augusta Chronicle (GA newspaper)
Augusta Gregory, Lady (Ir. writer; 1852-1932)
Augusta Herald (GA newspaper)
Augusta, GA, KS, ME
Auguste Comte (Fr. phil.; 1798-1857)
Auguste Escoffier (Fr. chef/writer; 1847-1935)
Auguste (Marie) Lumière (Fr. inv.; 1862-1954)
Auguste Piccard (Swiss physt.; 1884-1962)
Auguste (René) Rodin, (François)(Fr. sculptor;
   1840-1917)
Augustin Eugene Scribe (Fr. writer; 1791-1861)
Augustin Fresnel (Fr. physt.; 1788-1827)
Augustine of Hippo, St. (rel.; 354-430)
Augustine, St. (1st archbishop of Canterbury;
   late 6th c.)
Augusto César Sandino (Nicaraguan mil.; 1893-
   1934)

Augusto Pinochet (Ugarte)(ex-pres., Chile; 1915-)

Augustus Saint-Gaudens (US artist; 1848-1907)

Augustus, Caesar (aka Gaius Julius Caesar Octavius)(1st Roman emp.; 63 BC-AD 14)

Aukland, New Zealand

Auld Lang Syne (song)

Aulus Gellius (Latin writer; c130-c165)

Aumont, John-Pierre (Fr. ent.; 1909-)

Aunt Emma (slang, morphine)

Aunt Jemima™ (food)

Aunt Jemima (offensive slang, black woman subservient to whites)

Aunt Sally (Br. slang, person set up as easy target)

Auntie Mame (film; 1958)

Aureomycin™ (med.)

Auriga (astron., charioteer)

Aurora (myth., goddess of dawn)

Aurora, CO, IL, IN, MO, NE

Auschwitz, Poland

Auslander (Ger., foreigner, outsider)

Ausseil, Jean (Monacan pol.)

Aussie™ (hair care)

Aussie (native of Austl.)

Austen Chamberlain (Br. pol.; 1863-1937)

Austen, Jane (Br. writer; 1775-1817)

Austin American-Statesman (TX newspaper)

Austin City Limits (TV show)

Austin v. U.S. (US law; 1993)

Austin, MN, TX

Austin, Patti (ent.; 1948-)

Austin, Stephen Fuller (Texas colonizer; 1793-1836)

Austin, Tracy (tennis; 1962-)

Australia (Commonwealth of)

Australia Day (Austl. holiday)

Australia, South (state, Austl.)

Australian (people)

Australian Aborigine (people)

Australian Airlines

Australian Alps

Australian Antarctic Territory

Australian ballot (voting method; used in US since 1888)

Australian Capital Territory (govt. headquarters)

Australian cattle dog (dog)

Australian crawl

Australian heeler (dog)

Australian kelpie (dog)

Australian rye grass

Australian shepherd (dog)

Australian terrier (dog)

Australopithecus (anthrop.)

Australorp (chicken)

Austria (Republic of)(Eur.)

Austria, Anne of (queen, Fr.; mother of Louis XIV; 1601-66)

Austria, Margaret of (regent, Netherlands; 1480-1530)

Austrian Airlines

Austrinius, Piscis (astron., southern fish)

Austronesian (also Malayo-Polynesian)(lang.)

Austro-Prussian War (also Seven Weeks' War)(Aus./Prussia; 1866)

Authorized Version (of the Bible)(also King James Version)

Autodesk™

Autodesk, Inc.

Autoharp™ (music)

Automat™

Automobile (mag.)

Automobile Workers of America, United (UAW)(union, est. 1935)

Automundo (mag.)

AutoWeek (mag.)

Autry, Alan (ent.; 1952-)

Autry, Gene (ent.; 1907-)

Auvergne (region, Fr.)

AV (audiovisual)

Av (also Ab)(Jew. month)

Ava Gardner (ent.; 1922-90)

Avalanche-Journal, Lubbock (TX newspaper)

Avalon (myth. utopia)

Avalon, CA, PA

Avalon, Frankie (ent.; 1939-)

Avanti Automotive Corp.

Ave Maria (also *Hail Mary*)(prayer)

Avedon, Richard (US photo.; 1923-)

Aveeno™

Avensa Airlines

Averback, Hy

Averell Harriman, (William)(US pol./dipl.; 1891-1986)

Averill, Earl (baseball; 1915-83)

Avernus (It. lake, myth. entrance to hell)

Averroe™ (clothing)

Averroes (Islamic phil.; 1126-98)

Avery Brooks (ent.)

Avery Dennison Corp.

Avery Label Systems (US bus.)

Avery Schreiber (ent.; 1935-)

Avery, Steve (baseball; 1970-)

Avery, Tex (cartoonist, *Bugs Bunny, Porky Pig, Daffy Duck*; 1908-80)

Avesta, Zend- (rel.)

Avia™

Avia Athletic Footwear (US bus.)

Aviation Week and Space Technology (mag.)

Avignon, France

Avis™

Avis Rent a Car System, Inc.

Avogadro, Amadeo (It. chem.; 1776-1856)

Avogadro's constant/hypothesis/law/number (chem.)

Avon Products, Inc.
Avonlea (TV show)
Awakening, the Great
AWOL (absent without leave)
Ax, Emmanuel (Rus. ent.; 1949-)
Axelrod, Julius (US neuropharmacol.; 1912-)
Axis (of WW II)
Axl Rose (ent.)
Axminster carpet
Axton, Hoyt (ent.; 1938-)
Ayatollah Ruhollah Khomenei (Iran, rel.; 1900-89)
Ayatollah Sayyed Ali Khamenei (Iran, rel.; 1940-)
Ayer, Francis W. (US adv.; 1848-1923)
Aykroyd, Dan (ent.; 1952-)
Aylesbury (duck)
Aylesbury, England
Aylwin Azócar, Patricio (pres., Chile; 1918-)
Aymara (lang./people)
Ayn Rand (US writer/phil.; 1905-82)
Ayres, Lew (ent.; 1908-)
Ayrshire (cattle)
Ayurveda (med., ancient)
AZ (Arizona)
Azazel (evil spirit, rel.)
Azerbaijan (Republic of)(formerly part of USSR)(W Asia)
Azerbaijani (lang./people)
Azeri (lang./people)
Azinger, Paul (golf
Aziz, Fahd ibn Abdul (King Fahd)(king, Saudi Arabia; 1922-)
Aziz, Faisal ibn Abdul (king/PM, Saudi Arabia; 1905-75)
Azlan Muhibuddin Shah, Rajah (king, Malaysia
Aznavour, Charles (Fr. ent.; 1924-)
Azócar, Patricio Aylwin (pres., Chile; 1918-)
Azores Islands (also the Azores)(mid-Atl.)
AZT (zidovudine or azidothymidine)(med.)
Aztec (Mex. Indians)
Aztec marigold (also African marigold)
Aztec two-step (also Montezuma's revenge)(traveler's diarrhea)
Azuza, CA
Az-Zarqa, Jordon
Azzedine Laraki (ex-PM, Morocco)

B

B (chem. sym., boron)
BA (Bachelor of Arts)
Ba (chem. sym., barium)
Baal (myth.)
Baal Shem-Tov (also Israel ben Eliezer)(Jew.
  rel.; c1700-60)
Baalbek, Lebanon (ruins of Temple of the Sun)
Ba'ath Party (Iraqi pol. party)
Baba and the Forty Thieves, Ali (fairy tale)
Baba Yaga (myth. monster, eats children)
Baba, Ali (fict. chara.)
Babangida, Ibrahim (ex-pres., Nigeria; 1941-)
Babashoff, Shirley (swimming; 1957-)
Babar the Elephant (fict. chara.)
Babbage, Charles (Br. math., inv., compu.;
  1792-1871)
Babbitt (S. Lewis novel)
Babbitt metal (used for bearings)
Babbitt, Bruce E. (US Secy./Interior; 1938-)
Babbitt, George F(ollansbee)(fict. chara.)
Babbitt, Harry
Babbitt, Milton Byron (US comp.; 1916-)
Babe (Mildred) Didrikson Zaharias (US athlete;
  1914-56)
Babe (Floyd Caves) Herman (baseball; 1903-87)
Babe (George Herman) Ruth (baseball; 1895-
  1948)
Babe Ruth league (baseball)
Babe the Blue Ox (Paul Bunyan's)(US folklore)
Babel, Isaac (Rus. writer; 1894-1941)
Babel, Tower of (Babylon, different languages)
Babes in Toyland (film; 1934)
Babes in Toyland (pop music)
Babi (or Babism)(now Baha'i, Baha'ism)(rel.)
Babrak Karmal (ex-pres., Afghan.; 1929-)
Baby Bells (slang, regional phone cos.)
Baby Doc (Jean-Claude Duvalier)(ex-pres.,
  Haiti; 1951-)
Baby Dodds (Warren)(US jazz; 1898-1959)
Baby Face Nelson (film; 1957)
Baby Jane?, Whatever Happened to (film; 1962)
Baby Jessica (US news)
Baby Magic™ (baby care prods.)
Baby Ruth™ (candy)
Baby Snooks (fict. chara., radio)
Babylon (ancient capital of Babylonia)
Babylon, Hanging Gardens of (1 of 7 Wonders of
  the World)
Babylonia (ancient country)
Babylonian captivity (Isr. hist., exile of the
  Jews)
Bacall, Lauren (ent.; 1924-)
Bacardi™ (rum)
Bacardi cocktail (mixed drink)

Baccarat, Inc.
Bacchanalia (ancient feasts)
Bacchus (also Dionysus)(myth.)
Baccio Bandinelli (It. sculptor; 1493-1560)
Bach, Catherine (ent.)
Bach, Johann Ambrosia (Ger. musician, father
  of J.S.; 1645-95)
Bach, Johann Christian (Ger. comp., son of J.S.;
  1735-82)
Bach, Johann Christoph Friedrich (Ger. comp.,
  bro. of J.S.; 1732-95)
Bach, Johann Sebastian (Ger. comp.; 1685-
  1750)
Bach, Johannes (or Hans)(Ger. musician, great-
  grandfather of J.S.; 1580-1626)
Bach, Karl (or Carl) Philipp Emanuel (Ger
  comp.; 1714-88)
Bach, P. D. Q. (aka Peter Schickele)(ent.)
Bach, Richard (US writer)
Bach, Wilhelm Friedemann (Ger. comp.; 1710-
  84)
Bacharach, Burt (US comp.; 1928-)
Bachelor of Arts (B.A.)
Bachelor of Fine Arts (B.F.A.)
Bachelor of Science (B.S.)
Back to the Future (film; 1985)
Back to the Future, Part II (film)
Back to the Future, Part III (film)
Backus, Jim (ent.; 1913-89)
Bacolod, Philippines
Bacon, Delia Salter (US writer; 1811-59)
Bacon, Francis (Br. artist; 1909-92)
Bacon, Sir Francis (Br. phil./pol.; 1561-1626)
Bacon, Henry (US arch.; 1866-1924)
Bacon, Kevin (ent.; 1958-)
Bacon, Nathaniel (US pol.; 1647-76)
Bacon, Roger (Br. phil./scien.; 1214-94)
Bacon's Rebellion (Nathaniel)(VA; 1676)
Bac-Os™
Bactine™ (med.)
Bactria (ancient Persian province)
Bactrian camel (2 humps)
Bad Lands (region, NE/SD)
Bad News Bears, The (film; 1976)
Badajoz, Spain
Badalona, Spain
Baden (former Ger. state)
Baden-Baden, Germany
Baden-Powell, Sir Robert (Br. gen., founded Boy
  Scouts; 1857-1941)
Baden-Württemberg (state, Ger.)
Badenov, Boris (fict. chara.)
Badenov, Natasha (or Fataly)(fict. chara.)
Bader Ginsburg, Ruth (US jurist; 1933-)
Badger State (nickname, WI)
Badlands National Park (SD)
Badran, Mudar (ex-PM, Jordan)
Baedeker, Karl (Ger. guidebook publ.; 1801-

1959)
Baer, Max (boxing; 1909-59)
Baez, Joan (ent.; 1941-)
Baffin Bay, Canada
Baffin Island, Northwest Territories, Canada
Baffin, William (Br. nav.; 1584-1622)
Bagehot, Walter (Br. econ./jour.; 1826-77)
Baggie™ (storage bags)
Baggins, Bilbo (fict. chara.)
Baggins, Frodo (fict. chara.)
Baghdad, Iraq (also Bagdad)
Baha'i (also Baha'ism, Bahai)(formerly Babi,
    Babism)(rel.)
Bahamas (Commonwealth of the)(islands, SE of
    FL)
Bahamas Air (airline)
Bahasa Indonesian (lang.)
Bahaullah (Mirza Husayn Ali)(Pers., founded
    Bahaism; 1817-92)
Bahía Blanca, Argentina
Bahia grass
Bahia, Brazil
Bahrain (State of)(also Bahrein)(SW Asia)
Bahraini (people)
Baia Mare, Romania
Baikal, Lake (also Baykal)(Russia)(deepest lake
    in the world)
Baikonur (Soviet launch site)
Bailey bridge (temporary, prefab bridge)
Bailey Circus, Barnum &
Bailey Circus, Ringling Brothers and Barnum
    &
Bailey Olter (pres., Micronesia)
Bailey, Beetle (comic strip)
Bailey, DeFord
Bailey, F(rancis) Lee (US atty.; 1933-)
Bailey, Mildred (US jazz; 1907-51)
Bailey, Nathan(iel)(Br. lexicographer; ?-1742)
Bailey, Old (London criminal court)
Bailey, Pearl (Mae)(US jazz; 1918-90)
Bain de Soleil™ (health)
Bain, Conrad (Can. ent.; 1923-)
Bainter, Fay (ent.; 1892-1968)
Baio, Scott (ent.; 1961-)
Bairam (rel. festival)
Baird, Bill (William Britton)(US puppeteer;
    1904-87)
Baird, John Logie ("Father of Television")(Scot.
    eng.; 1888-1946)
Baird, Zoë (US atty.)
Baiul, Oksana (figure skating; 1978-)
Baizerman, Saul
Baja California (state, Mex.)
Baja California Sur (state, Mex.)
Bajan (lang.)
baked Alaska (dessert)
Bakelite™ (1st synthetic plastic)
Bake-Off™ (cooking contest)

Baker v. Carr (US law; 1962)
Baker, Anita (ent.; 1958-)
Baker, Carroll (ent.; 1931-)
Baker, Chet (US jazz; 1929-88)
Baker, George (cartoonist, *The Sad Sack*; 1915-
    75)
Baker, James A., III (US pol.; 1930-)
Baker, Joe Don (ent.; 1936-)
Baker, Josephine (ent.; 1906-75)
Baker, Mark Linn- (ent.; 1953-)
Bakersfield Californian (CA newspaper)
Bakersfield, CA
Bakhtaran, Iran (formerly Kermanshah)
*Bakke, Regents of the University of California
    vs.* (US law; 1978)
Bakken, Jim (James Leroy)(football; 1940-)
Bakker, Jim (James Orsen)(US evang.; 1940-)
Bakker, Tammy Faye (LaValley)(ex-wife of Jim
    Bakker)
Bakongo (people)
Bakr, Abu (Islamic leader; 573-634)
Bakst, Léon (Rus. artist/designer; 1867-1924)
Baku, Azerbaijan
Bakula, Scott (ent.)
Bakunin, Mikhail (Rus. pol.; 1814-76)
Balaguer, Joaquín Ricardo (pres., Domi Rep.;
    1907-)
Balakirev, Mily Alexeyevich (Rus. comp.; 1837-
    1910)
Balanchine, George (US choreographer; 1904-
    83)
Balanta (people)
Balboa Heights, Panama
Balboa, CA
Balboa, Vasco Núñez de (Sp. expl., discovered
    Pac.; 1475-1519)
Baldassare, Castiglione (It. pol.; 1478-1529)
Balder (myth.)
Baldwin (apple)
Baldwin Park, CA
Baldwin, Alec (ent.; 1958-)
Baldwin, James (US writer; 1924-87)
Baldwin, James Mark (US psych.; 1861-1934)
Baldwin, William (ent.; 1963-)
Baleares (province, Sp.)
Balearic Islands (Mediterranean)
Balenciaga, Cristobal (Sp. designer; 1895-1972)
Balfe, Michael (William)(Ir. comp./ent.; 1808-
    70)
Balfour Declaration (national home for Jews in
    Palestine)
Balfour, Arthur James (ex-PM, Br.; 1848-1930)
Bali™ (clothing)
Bali (Indonesian island)
Bali Ha'i (song)
Balikpapan, Indonesia
Balinese (cat)
Balinese (lang.)

Balkan Mountains (Bulgaria)
Balkan Peninsula (SE Eur.)
Balkan States (also the Balkans)(countries
  occupying Balkan Peninsula)
Balkan Wars (1878-1913)
Balkhash, Lake (Kazakhstan)(salt)
Ball™ jar
Ball Brothers Glass (canning jars)
Ball Mason™ jar
Ball Park Franks™
Ball, Ernest (US comp.; 1878-1927)
Ball, George W(ildman)(US atty./banker/pol.;
  1909-)
Ball, Lucille (ent.; 1911-89)
Balla, Giacomo (It. artist; 1871?-1958)
Balladur, Édouard (PM, Fr.; 1929-)
Ballantine™
Ballantine Books (US bus.)
Ballarat, Victoria, Australia
Ballard, J(ames) G(raham)(Br. writer; 1930-)
Ballard, Kaye (ent.; 1926-)
Balleek ware
Ballesteros, Seve (golf; 1957-)
Ballet Folklórico de México
Ballet Russe de Monte Carlo
Ballington Booth (US, founded Volunteers of
  America; 1859-1940)
Bally Manufacturing Corp.
balm of Gilead (also balm-of-Gilead)
Balmer, Johann (Jakob)(Swiss math./physt.;
  1825-98)
Balmoral (clothing)
Balmoral Castle, Scotland
balsam of Peru (also Peru balsam)
Balsam, Martin (ent.; 1919-)
Balsas River (Mex.)
Balthazar (one of three Magi)
Baltic (lang./people)
Baltic Sea (N. Eur.)
Baltic States (Estonia, Latvia, Lith.)
Baltimore chop (baseball)
Baltimore Evening Sun (MD newspaper)
Baltimore method (real estate)
Baltimore oriole (bird)
Baltimore Orioles (baseball team)
Baltimore Sun (MD newspaper)
Baltimore, Barron v. (US law; 1833)
Baltimore, Lord (Sir George Calvert)(founded
  MD; 1606-75)
Baltimore, MD
Baltimore's Inner Harbor (MD)
B. Altman & Co.
Baluchi (lang./people)
Baluchistan region (SE Iran/SW Pak.)
Balzac, Honoré de (Fr. writer; 1799-1850)
Balzers, Liechtenstein
Bamako, Mali
Bamangwato (people)

Bamba, La (film; 1987)
Bamba, La (song)
Bambara (lang./people)
Bambi (fict. deer)
Bambi (film; 1942)
Bambi (F. Salten book)
Bamileke (people)
Ban™ Roll-On (anti-perspirant)
Banacek (TV show)
Banana Boat™ (health)
Banana Republic (US bus.)(l.c. when referring
  to countries)
Banana River (FL)
Bananas (film; 1971)
Banbury (Eng. market town)
Banbury cake (also Banbury bun)(pastry)
Banbury tart
Bancroft, Anne (ent.; 1931-)
Bancroft, George (ent.; 1882-1956)
Bancroft, George (US hist.; 1800-91)
Band-Aid™ (med.)
Banda (Indonesian islands)
Banda (people)
Banda Sea (Indonesia)
Banda, (Ngwazi) Hastings Kamuzu (pres.,
  Malawi; 1902-)
Bandar Seri Begawan, Brunei (formerly Brunei
  Town)
Bandaranaike, Sirimavo (ex-PM, Sri Lanka;
  1916-)
Bandaranaike, Solomon West Ridgeway Dias
  (ex-PM, Sri Lanka; 1899-1959)
B & B (bed and breakfast)
B and B (liqueur)
B & E (breaking and entering)
Bandinelli, Baccio (It. sculptor; 1493-1560)
Bandung, Java (Indonesia)(also Bandoeng)
Banff National Park (Can.)
Banff, Alberta, Canada
Banff, Scotland
Bangalore, India
Bangkok, Thailand
Bangla (also Bengali)(lang.)
Bangladesh (People's Republic of)(S Asia)
Bangor News (ME newspaper)
Bangor Submarine Base (WA)(mil.)
Bangor, ME
Bang's disease (of cattle)
Bangui, Central African Republic
Bangwaketse (people)
Banja, Bosnia-Hercegovina
Banjermasin, Indonesia
Banjul, Gambia
Bank of America
Bank of Credit and Commerce International
  (BCCI)(internat'l banking scandal; 1991)
Bank of England
Bankhead, Tallulah (ent.; 1902-68)

Bankruptcy Reform Act (US hist.; 1978)
Banks, Ernie (baseball; 1931-)
Banks, Jonathan (ent.; 1947-)
Ban-Lon™ (also Banlon™)(textile)
Banner, Nashville (TN newspaper)
Bannister, Sir Roger (Gilbert)(Brit, runner/
    phys.; 1929)
Bannon, Jack (ent.; 1940-)
Banon (cheese)
Banquet™
Banquet Foods Corp.
Banquo (fict. chara., *Macbeth*)
Bantam chicken (also l.c.)
Bantam Doubleday Dell Publishing Group, Inc.
Bantu (lang./people)
Banzai, Buckaroo (fict. chara.)
Bapounon (people)
Baptist (rel.)
Baptist Church
Bar Harbor, ME
Barabbas (Biblical thief)
Barbados (island, British West Indies)
Barbara A. Mikulski (US cong.; 1936-)
Barbara Ann Cochran (skiing; 1951-)
Barbara Bailey Kennelly (US cong.; 1936-)
Barbara Barrie (ent.; 1931-)
Barbara Bel Geddes (ent.; 1922-)
Barbara Bosson (ent.; 1939-)
Barbara Boxer (US cong.; 1940-)
Barbara (Pierce) Bush (wife of ex-US pres.;
    1925-)
Barbara Cook (ent.; 1927-)
Barbara Eden (ent.; 1934-)
Barbara Feldon (ent.; 1941-)
Barbara Frietchie (C. Fitch play)
Barbara Hale (ent.; 1922-)
Barbara Harris (ent.; 1935-)
Barbara Hershey (ent.; 1948-)
Barbara Hutton (US heiress; 1887-1979)
Barbara (Charline) Jordan (US atty./educ./pol.;
    1936-)
Barbara Mandrell (ent.; 1948-)
Barbara McClintock (US geneticist; 1902-92)
Barbara Roberts (OR gov.; 1936-)
Barbara Rush (ent.; 1930-)
Barbara Stanwyck (ent.; 1907-90)
Barbara W(ertheim) Tuchman (US writer/hist.;
    1912-89)
Barbara Walters (US TV jour.; 1931-)
Barbara Woodhouse (Br. dog trainer)
Barbarella (film; 1968)
Barbarosa (film; 1982)
Barbarossa (Frederick I, "Red Beard")(Holy
    Roman emp.; 1123-90)
Barbarossa I (aka Arouj)(Turk. pirate; 1473?-
    1518)
Barbarossa II (aka Khair ed-Din)(Turk. pirate;
    c1466-1546)

Barbary ape
Barbary Coast (NAfr.)
Barbary Coast (San Francisco)
Barbary horse
Barbary sheep
Barbary States (Afr.)
Barbasol™ (healthcare)
Barber of Seville, The (Beaumarchais play, G.
    Rossini opera)
Barber, Red (Walter)(ent.; 1908-92)
Barber, Samuel (US comp.; 1910-81)
Barbera (wine)
Barbera, Joe (cartoonist, *Tom & Jerry,
    Huckleberry Hound, Yogi Bear, Flintstones*;
    1911-)
Barbers Point Naval Air Station (HI)
Barbers Point, HI (also Kalaeloa Point)
Barbi Benton (US playmate)
Barbie (mag.)
Barbie™ doll
Barbie, Klaus (Ger. Nazi leader; 1913-91)
Barbirolli, Sir John (Br. cond.; 1899-1970)
Barbizon School (Fr. group of artists)
Barbizon, France
Barbour, John (Scot. poet; 1316?-95)
Barbra Streisand (ent.; 1942-)
Barbuda, Antigua and (State of)
Barcalounger™
Barcalounger Co.
Barcellona, Italy
Barcelona chair
Barcelona, Spain
Barclay Plager (hockey; 1941-88)
Bard of Avon (Shakespeare)
Bardeen, John (US physt.; 1908-91)
Bardi, Beatrice Portinari de' (inspiration for
    Dante's Beatrice; 1266-90)
Bardolino (wine)
Bardot, Brigitte (Fr. ent.; 1934-)
Barefoot in the Park (play)
Barenboim, Daniel (Isr. pianist/cond.; 1942-)
Barents Sea (part of Arctic Ocean)
Baretta (TV show)
Bari, Italy
Bariba (people)
Barkat Gourad Hamadou (PM, Djibouti)
Barker, Bob (ent.; 1923-)
Barkin, Ellen (ent.; 1955-)
Barkley, Alben William (ex-US VP; 1877-1956)
Barkley, Charles (basketball; 1963-)
Barksdale Air Force Base, LA
Barlach, Ernst (Heinrich)(Ger. sculptor/writer;
    1870-1938)
Barleycorn, John (personification of alcohol)
Barmecide (fict. chara., *Arabian Nights*)
Barmecide feast (false feast with empty dishes)
Barmecides (wealthy, powerful Persian family;
    fl. 752-803)

Barnabas, St. ("fellow laborer")
Barnard College (NYC)
Barnard Hughes (ent.; 1915-)
Barnard, Dr. Christiaan (SAfr. phys.,
     performed 1st human heart transplant;
     1922-)
Barnard, Henry (US educ.; 1811-1900)
Barnardo, Thomas (Br. reformer; 1845-1905)
Barnburners v. Hunkers (US pol.; mid 1800s)
Barnes & Noble™ Books
Barnes & Noble Bookstores, Inc.
Barnes & Noble, Inc.
Barns v. Glen Theater (US law; 1991)
Barnett Newman (US artist; 1905-70)
*Barnette, West Virginia State Board of
     Education v.* (US law; 1943)
Barnevelder (chicken)
Barney (TV dinosaur)
Barney & Friends (TV show)
Barney Bigard (US jazz; 1906-80)
Barney Frank (US cong.; 1940-)
Barney Google (cartoon)
Barney Kessel (US jazz; 1923-)
Barney Miller (TV show)
Barney (Berna Eli) Oldfield (auto racing; 1878-
     1946)
Barney Rubble (cartoon chara.)
Barnie's Coffee & Tea Co., Inc.
BarNone™ (candy)
Barnsley, England
Barnum & Bailey Circus
Barnum, P(hineas) T(aylor)(ent., circus; 1810-
     91)
Barolo (wine)
Baron Vaea (PM, Tonga)
Baroque (style of art/arch.)
Barquisimeto, Venezuela
Barr body (also sex chromatin)(med.)
Barr, Murray L. (Can. phys.; 1908-)
Barr (Arnold), Roseanne (ent.; 1952-)
Barranquilla, Colombia
Barré syndrome, Guillain-
Barre, MA, VT
Barred Rock (chicken)
Barrès, Maurice (Fr. writer/pol.; 1862-1923)
Barrett Browning, Elizabeth (Br. poet, wife of
     Robert; 1806-61)
Barrett, Rona (US gossip columnist)
Barricini/Loft's Candies, Inc.
Barrie Dunsmore
Barrie, Barbara (ent.; 1931-)
Barrie, Sir James M. (Br. writer; 1860-1937)
Barrie, Ontario, Canada
Barris, Chuck (ent.)
Barron v. Baltimore (US law; 1833)
Barron's Educational Series, Inc.
*Barron's National Business and Financial
     Weekly*

Barrow, Clyde (US criminal; 1900-34)
Barrow, Nita (gov-gen.; Barbados)
Barrow, Point, AK (northernmost point of US)
Barrow-in-Furness, England
Barry Bonds (baseball; 1964-)
Barry Bostwick (ent.; 1946-)
Barry Corbin (ent.; 1940-)
Barry Fitzgerald (ent.; 1888-1961)
Barry Levinson (ent.; 1932-)
Barry Lyndon (film; 1975)
Barry Manilow (ent.; 1946-)
Barry Mann (US comp.; 1939-)
Barry M(orris) Goldwater (US pol.; 1909-)
Barry M(orris) Goldwater, Jr. (US pol.; 1938-)
Barry Serafin (US TV jour.)
Barry Sullivan (ent.; 1912-)
Barry White (ent.; 1944-)
Barry, Dave (US writer/humorist; 1947-)
Barry, Madame (Jeanne Bécu) du (Comtesse,
     mistress, Louis XV; 1743-93)
Barry, Gene (ent.; 1919-)
Barry, John (US mil.; 1745-1803)
Barry, Philip (US writer; 1896-1949)
Barry, Rick (Richard)(basketball; 1944-)
Barry, Sy (cartoonist)
Barrymore, Diana (ent.; 1921-60)
Barrymore, Drew (ent.; 1975-)
Barrymore, Ethel (ent.; 1879-1959)
Barrymore, John (Blythe)(ent.; 1882-1942)
Barrymore, John Drew (ent.; 1932-)
Barrymore, Lionel (ent.; 1878-1954)
Barrymore, Maurice (ent.; 1848-1905)
Bars, Stars and (also Southern
     Cross)(Confederate flag)
Barstow Marine Corps Logistics Base (CA)
Barstow, CA
Bart(lett) Giamatti, (Angelo)(US educ./writer/
     baseball; 1938-89)
Bart Simpson (cartoon chara.)
Bart Starr (football; 1934-)
Barth, John (US writer; 1930-)
Barth, Karl (Swed. rel.; 1886-1968)
Barthes, Roland (Fr. critic; 1915-80)
Bartholdi, Frederic-Auguste (Fr. sculptor,
     designed Statue of Liberty; 1834-1904)
Bartholomeu Dias (also Diaz)(Port. expl.; c1450-
     1500)
Bartholomew, Freddie (ent.; 1925-92)
Bartholomew, St. (apostle)
Bartles & Jaymes™ (wine coolers)
Bartlett pear
Bartlett, John (US publ./editor, *Familiar
     Quotations*; 1820-1905)
Bartlett's *Familiar Quotations* (book)
Bartók, Béla (Hung. comp.; 1881-1945)
Bartoli, Cecilia (US opera; 1972-)
Bartolomé Esteban Murillo (Sp. artist; 1618-82)
Bartolommeo, Fra (It. artist; 1472-1517)

Proper Noun Speller

Bartolommeo, Michelozzo di (aka Michelozzo Michelozzi)(It. sculptor/arch.; 1396-1472)

Barton, Clara (U.S., founded American Red Cross; 1821-1912)

Barton™, Reed &

Barton Silversmiths, Reed & (US bus.)

Barton Yarborough

Barty, Billy (ent.; 1924-)

Baruch Spinoza (also Benedict de)(Dutch phil.; 1632-77)

Baruch, Bernard M. (US finan./pol.; 1870-1965)

Baryshnikov, Mikhail (Latvian/US dancer; 1948-)

Base Exchange™ (BX)

Baseball Clubs, American League of Professional

Baseball Digest (mag.)

Baseball Hall of Fame and Museum, National (est. 1939, Cooperstown, NY)

Basehart, Richard (ent.; 1914-84)

Basel, Switzerland

Basenji (dog)(also l.c.)

BASF Corp.

Bashir, Omar Hassan al- (PM, Sudan; 1944?-)

Bashkir (lang./people)

Bashö Matsuo (aka Matsuo Munefusa)(Jap. poet, haiku; 1644-94)

BASIC (Beginners' All-Purpose Symbolic Instruction Code)(compu.)

Basic English

Basie, Count (William)(US jazz; 1904-84)

Basil Rathbone (ent.; 1892-1967)

Basildon, England

Basinger, Kim (ent.; 1953-)

Baskerville (type style)

Baskerville, John (Br. typographer; 1706-75)

Baskervilles, The Hound of the (by A.C. Doyle)

Basket Maker Indian culture

Basketball Association, National (NBA)

Basketball Digest (mag.)

Baskin-Robbins™

Baskin-Robbins Ice Cream Co.

Basque (also Basque Provinces)(region, Sp.)

Basque (lang./people)

Basra, Iraq

Bass™ (shoes)

Bass Pro Shops, Inc.

Basse-Normandie (region, Fr.)

Basse-Terre, Guadeloupe

Basseterre, St. Kitts and Nevis

Bassey, Shirley (ent.; 1937-)

Bassett™

Bassett Furniture Industries, Inc.

Bastille Day (Fr.)

Bastille, the (former castle/prison, Paris)

Bastogne, Belgium

Basutoland (now called Lesotho)(SAfr.)

Bat (William Barclay) Masterson (US marshal; 1853-1921)

Bata, Equatorial Guinea

Bataan Death March (Phil.)

Bataan, Philippines

Batak Toda (lang.)

Batalla, Francesc Badia (covicar, Andorra)

Batangas, Luzon, Philippines

Bateke (people)

Bateman, Jason (ent.; 1969-)

Bateman, Justine (ent.; 1966-)

Bates, Alan (ent.; 1934-)

Bates, Katharine Lee (US poet/educ.; 1859-1929)

Bates, Kathy (ent.; 1948-)

Bath chair (type of wheelchair)

Bath, England

Bath, Order of the (Br. order of knighthood)

Bathinette™

Bathsheba (rel., wife of King David)

Batista y Zaldivar, Fulgencio (ex-dictator, Cuba; 1901-73)

Batiuk, Tom (cartoonist)

Batman (film, cartoon)

Baton Rouge Advocate (LA newspaper)

Baton Rouge, LA

Battambang, Cambodia

Battenberg cake

Battersea district (old London)

Battle Creek, MI

Battle of Actium (Rome, 31 BC)

Battle of Agincourt (Eng./Fr.; 1415)

Battle of Algiers (Algeria/Fr.; 1954-62)

Battle of Antietam (US hist.; 1862)

Battle of Brandywine (US hist.; 1777)

Battle of Britain (WWII air battle)

Battle(s) of Bull Run (US hist.; 1861 & 1862)

Battle of Bunker Hill (Breed's Hill)(US hist., MA; 1775)

Battle(s) of Cambrai (WWI; 1917)

Battle of Chancellorsville (US hist.; 1863)

Battle(s) of Chattanooga (US hist.; 1863)

Battle of Corregidor (WWII; 1942)

Battle of Dien Bien Phu (also Dienbienphu)(NViet.; 1954)

Battle of Edgehill (Eng.; 1642)

Battle of Fredericksburg (US hist.; 1862)

Battle of Gettysburg (US hist.; 1863)

Battle of Hastings (Br. hist.; 1066)

Battle of Iwo Jima (WWII; 1945)

Battle of Lexington (US hist.; 1775)

Battle of Marathon (Gr./Persia; 490 BC)

Battle of Monmouth (US hist.; 1778)

Battle of New Orleans (US/Br.; 1815)(Amer. Civil War; 1862)

Battle of Shiloh (also Pittsburg Landing)(US hist.; 1862)

Battle of the Bulge (WWII; 1944-45)

Battle of the Little Bighorn (also Custer's Last

Stand)(US/Sioux Indians; 1876)
Battle of the Wilderness (US hist.; 1864)
Battle of Tippecanoe (US hist.; 1811)
Battle of Trafalgar (Br./Fr.-Sp.; 1805)
Battle of Waterloo (Napoleon's defeat; 1815)
Battle, Kathleen (opera; 1948-)
Battles of Saratoga (US hist.; 1777)
Battlestar Galactica (film; 1979)
Batumi, Georgia
Bat-Yam, Israel
Baucus, Max (US cong.; 1941-)
Baudelaire, Charles Pierre (Fr. poet; 1821-67)
Baudouin, King (Belgium; 1930-93)
Bauer Expedition Outfitter, Eddie (US bus.)
Bauer, Hank (Henry)(baseball; 1922-)
Baugh, Sammy (Samuel Adrian)(football; 1914-)
Bauhaus (Ger. school of design)
Baule (lang./people)
Baum, L(yman) Frank (US writer; 1856-1919)
Baumer Candle Co., Inc., Will &
Baumeister, Willi (Ger. artist; 1889-1955)
Baumgarten's (US bus.)
Bausch & Lomb™ (vision care)
Bausch & Lomb, Inc.
Bavaria (state, Ger.)
Bavarian cream (dessert)
Bawoyeu, Jean Alingue (ex-PM, Chad)
Baxter International, Inc.
Baxter, Anne (ent.; 1923-85)
Baxter, Meredith (ent.; 1947-)
Bay City, MI, TX
Bay of Bengal (part of Indian Ocean)
Bay of Biscay (Fr./Sp.)
Bay of Fundy (N Atl., Can.)
Bay of Pigs (Cuban inlet, invasion)
Bay State (nickname, MA)
Baya (people)
Bayamón, Puerto Rico
Bayard Taylor, (James)(US jour.; 1825-78)
Bayer™ (med.)
Bayeux Tapestry (Fr., depicting Norman
    Conquest; created 11th c.)
Bayeux, France
Bayh, Evan (IN gov.; 1955-)
Bayi, Filbert (runner; 1953-)
Baykal, Lake (also Baikal)(Russia)(deepest lake
    in the world)
Baylor University (Waco, TX)
Baylor, Elgin (basketball; 1934-)
Bayonne Military Ocean Terminal (NJ)(mil.)
Bayonne, France
Bayonne, NJ
Bayou State (nickname, MS)
Bayreuth Wagner Festival (Bavaria, Ger.)
Bayreuth, Germany
Bazin, Marc (ex-PM, Haiti)
Baziotes, William (US artist; 1912-63)
Bazooka Joe™ (bubble gum)

BBC (British Broadcasting Corp.)
B. B. King (b. Riley B. King)(ent.; 1925-)
B-bomb (slang, benzedrine inhaler)
BC (before Christ, British Columbia)
BC (comic strip)
B complex (vitamin)
B. Cribari & Sons Winery (US bus.)
B. Dalton Bookseller (US bus.)
Be (chem. sym., beryllium)
Bea Arthur (Beatrice)(ent.; 1926-)
Bea Wain (ent.; 1917-)
Beach Boys, the (pop music)
Beacon Journal, Akron (OH newspaper)
Beal, John (ent.; 1909-)
Beale Air Force Base, CA (mil.)
Beam Brands Co., Jim
Beamon, Bob (jumper; 1946-)
Bean, Alan L(aVern)(astro.; 1932-)
Bean, Judge Roy (US frontier; 1825?-1903)
Bean, Inc., L. L.
Bean, Orson (ent.; 1928-)
Beanee Weenee™
Bear Bryant, (Paul)(football coach; 1913-83)
Bear Co., The Gummy
Bear Mountain(s)(NY & PA)
Bear, Smokey the (fict. chara.)
Bear, Yogi (cartoon)
Beard, Charles A. (US hist.; 1874-1948)
Beardsley gown (Br. gown; 19th c.)
Beardsley, Aubrey Vincent (Br. artist; 1872-98)
Bears, Chicago (football team)
Bear's Jellystone Park Camp-Resort, Yogi (US
    bus.)
Beasley, Allyce (ent.; 1954-)
Beast, Beauty and the (fairy tale, TV show, film)
Beastie Boys (pop music)
Beat Generation (also Beat
    movement)(beatniks; 1950s-60s)
Beat the Clock (TV show)
Beatitudes (Jesus' blessings, Sermon on the
    Mount)
Beatles, the (pop music)
Beaton, Sir Cecil (Br. photo.; 1904-80)
Beatrice "Bea" Arthur (ent.; 1926-)
Beatrice Cos., Inc.
Beatrice Lillie (ent.; 1894-1989)
Beatrice Portinari de' Bardi (inspiration for
    Dante's Beatrice; 1266-90)
Beatrice Straight (ent.; 1918-)
Beatrice Tanner (aka Mrs. Patrick
    Campbell)(ent.; 1865-1940)
Beatrice (Potter) Webb, (Martha)(Br. reformer/
    writer; 1858-1943)
Beatrice, Princess (daughter of Prince Andrew
    and Sarah; 1988-)
Beatrix (Wilhelmina Armgard)(queen, the
    Netherlands; 1938-)
Beatrix Potter, (Helen)(Br. writer/artist; 1866-

Proper Noun Speller

1943)

Beattie, Ann (US writer; 1947-)

Beatty, Clyde (ent.; 1904-65)

Beatty, Ned (ent.; 1937-)

Beatty, Warren (ent.; 1937-)

Beau Bassin, Mauritius

Beau Bridges (ent.; 1941-)

Beau (George Bryan) Brummell (Br. dandy; 1778-1840)

Beau Brummell (film; 1954)

Beau Brummell Ties (US bus.)

Beau Geste (film; 1939)

Beau (Richard) Nash (Br. dandy/gambler; 1674-1761)

Beaufort Marine Corps Air Station (SC)

Beaufort scale (wind velocity)

Beaufort Sea (part of the Arctic Ocean)

Beaufort, NC, SC

Beaujolais (wine)

Beaumarchais, Pierre Augustin Caron de (Fr. writer; 1732-99)

Beaumont Enterprise (TX newspaper)

Beaumont, TX

Beauport, Quebec, Canada

Beauregard, P(ierre) G(ustave) T(outant)(US gen.; 1818-93)

Beauty and the Beast (fairy tale, TV show, film)

Beauvoir, Simone de (Fr. writer; 1908-86)

Beaver Cleaver ("the Beaver")(fict. chara.)

Beaver Falls, PA

Beaverbrook, William Maxwell, Baron (aka Lord Beaverbrook)(Br. finan./pol.; 1879-1964)

Beaverton, OR

Beavis and Butt-Head (TV show)

Bebe Daniels (ent.; 1901-71)

Bebe Neuwirth (ent.)

B cell (med.)

Bechet, Sidney (US jazz; 1897-1959)

Bechuanaland (now Botswana)(SAfr.)

Beck, C. C. (cartoonist, *Captain Marvel*; 1910-89)

Beck, John (ent.; 1943-)

Becker, Boris (tennis; 1967-)

Becker, Paula Modersohn- (Ger. artist; 1867-1907)

Becket, St. Thomas à (Br. rel./pol.; 1118-70)

Beckett Baseball Card Monthly (mag.)

Beckett, Samuel (Ir. writer; 1906-89)

Becklin-Neugebauer object (astron.)

Beckmann, Max (Ger. artist; 1884-1950)

Beck's (beer)

Becky Sharp (fict. chara., *Vanity Fair*)

Becquerel rays (now gamma rays)

Becquerel, Alexandre-Edmond (Fr. physt.; 1820-91)

Becquerel, Antoine-César (Fr. physt.; 1788-1878)

Becquerel, Antoine-Henri (Fr. physt.; 1852-

1908)

Becton Dickinson Co.

Bede, St. ("the Venerable Bede")(Br. rel./hist.; c673-735)

Bedelia, Bonnie (ent.; 1948-)

Bedford-Stuyvesant (Brooklyn neighborhood)

Bedford, England (also Bedfordshire, Beds)

Bedford, IN, MA, OH, PA, TX, VA

Bedie, Henri Konan (pres., Ivory Coast)

Bedivere, Sir (Arthurian legend)

Bedlam (early Eng. mental hospital)

Bedlington terrier (dog)

Bedloe's Island (now Liberty Island)(NY)

Bedouin (or Beduin)(people)

Bedrich Smetana (Czech. comp.; 1824-84)

Bedtime for Bonzo (film; 1951)

Bee Gees, the (pop music)

Bee, Clair (basketball; 1896-1983)

Bee, Fresno (CA newspaper)

Bee, Modesto (CA newspaper)

Bee, Sacramento (CA newspaper)

Beebe, (Charles) William (US nat./expl./writer; 1877-1962)

Beecham, SmithKline (US bus.)

Beecham, Sir Thomas (Br. cond.; 1879-1961)

Beecher, Henry Ward (US rel./abolitionist; 1813-87)

Beech-Nut, Inc.

beef Bourguignonne

beef Stroganoff (also l.c.)

Beef Tonight™ (sauce)

beef Wellington

Beefaroni™

Beefeater (Br. Yeoman of the Guard)

Beefsteak Charlie's, Inc.

Beehive State (nickname, UT)

Beelzebub (Satan/a devil)

Beene, Geoffrey (US designer; 1927-)

Beerbohm, Sir Max (Br. critic/caricaturist; 1872-1956)

Beer-Nuts™

Beersheba, Israel

Beery, Noah (ent.; 1884-1946)

Beery, Noah, Jr. (ent.; 1913-)

Beery, Wallace (ent.; 1889-1949)

Beethoven, Ludwig van (Ger. comp.; 1770-1827)

Beetle Bailey (comic strip)

Beetlejuice (film; 1988)

Begin, Menachem (ex-PM, Isr.; 1913-92)

Begley, Ed (ent.; 1901-70)

Begley, Ed, Jr. (ent.; 1949-)

Begum Khaleda Zia (PM, Bangladesh; 1944-)

Behan, Brendan (Ir. writer; 1923-64)

Behrens, Peter (Ger. arch.; 1868-1940)

Behring, Emil von (Ger. bacteriol.; 1854-1917)

Behrman, S(amuel) N(athaniel)(US writer; 1893-1973)

Beiderbecke, Bix (Leon Bismarck)(US jazz;

1903-31)
Beijing duck (also Peking duck)
Beijing man (also Peking Man)(*Homo erectus*)
Beijing, China (formerly Peking)
Being There (film; 1979)
Beira, Mozambique
Beirut, Lebanon (also Beyrouth)
Beja (lang./people)
Bekaa Valley (Lebanon)
Bekins™
Bekins Van Lines Co.
Bel (myth.)
Bel Geddes, Barbara (ent.; 1922-)
Bel Geddes, Norman (US designer; 1893-1958)
Bel Paese™ (cheese)
Béla Bartók (Hung. comp.; 1881-1945)
Bela Karolyi (gymnastics)
Béla Kun (Hung. pol.; 1885-1938)
Bela Lugosi (ent.; 1882-1956)
Belafonte, Harry (ent.; 1927-)
Belaid Abdesalam (Algerian pol.; 1928-)
Belarus (people)
Belarus (Republic of)(formerly part of USSR)(E
    central Eur.)
Belasco, David (US writer/ent.; 1854-1931)
Belau (Republic of)(formerly Palau)(island,
    Micronesia)
Belch, Sir Toby (fict. chara., *Twelfth Night*)
Belem, Brazil
Belfast, Northern Ireland
Belgaum, India
Belgian (horse)
Belgian Congo (now Zaire)
Belgian endive
Belgian hare
Belgian Malinois (dog)
Belgian sheepdog (also Groenendael)(dog)
Belgian Tervuren (dog)
Belgium (Kingdom of)
Belgrade, Serbia
Belgrave Square (London)
Belgravia (district in London)
Belial (Satan, evil personified)
Believe It or Not!, Ripley's
Belinda Carlisle (ent.)
Belinda, Johnny (film; 1948)
Beliveau, Jean (hockey; 1931-)
Belize (formerly British Honduras)
Belize City, Belize
Bell & Howell™
Bell & Howell Co.
Bell Atlantic Corp.
Bell for Adano, A (film; 1945)
Bell Laboratories, Inc.
Bell, Alexander Graham (US inv., telephone;
    1847-1922)
Bell™, Bonne (cosmetics)
Bell, Grove City v. (US law; 1984)

Bell, Inc., Bonne
Bell, Ma (slang, AT&T)
Bell, Rickey (football; 1949-84)
Bella (Savitzky) Abzug (US pol.; 1920-)
Bellamy, Edward (US writer; 1850-98)
Bellamy, Ralph (ent.; 1904-91)
Bellatrix (astron.)
Belle Isle, Strait of (Labrador/Newfoundland)
Belle Starr (b. Myra Belle Shirley)(US outlaw;
    1848-89)
Belleek ware (porcelain)
Bellén, Sixto Durán (pres., Ecuador; 1921-)
Bellerophon (also Bellerophontes)(myth.)
Belleville, IL, KS, NJ
Belleville, Ontario, Canada
Bellevue Hospital (NYC)
Bellevue, KY, NE, OH, PA, WA
Bellflower, CA
Belli, Melvin (Mouron)(US atty.; 1907-)
Bellingham, MA, WA
Bellini, Gentile (It. artist; 1426-1507)
Bellini, Giovanni (It. artist; 1426-1516)
Bellini, Jacopo (It. artist; 1400-70)
Bellini, Vincenzo (It. comp.; 1801-35)
Bellisario, Donald P.
Bellow, Saul (US writer; 1915-)
Bellows, George Wesley (US artist; 1882-1925)
Bell's palsy (med.)
BellSouth Corp.
Belluschi, Pietro (US arch.; 1899-?)
Belmondo, Jean-Paul (Fr. ent.; 1933-)
Belmont Park, NY
Belmont Park Race Track
Belmont Stakes (racing)
Belmont, August (US finan.; 1816-90)
Belmont, CA, MA, NC
Belmonts, Dion and the (pop music)
Belmopan, Belize
Belnid Absessalem (ex-PM, Algeria)
Belo Horizonte, Brazil
Beloit, WI
Belorussia (also Byelorussia)(former USSR
    republic)
Belorussian (lang.)
Belouch (Pers. rug)
Belsen (Ger./Nazi concentration camp)
Belshazzar (rel.)
Beltone Electronics Corp.
Beltsy, Moldova
Belushi, James "Jim" (ent.; 1954-)
Belushi, John (ent.; 1949-82)
Belvedere, Mr. (TV show)
Belvoir, Fort, VA (mil.)
Belyayev, Pavel I. (cosmo.; 1925-70)
Beluga Caviar Imports & Exports (US bus.)
Belvedere Winery (US bus.)
Beman, Deane (golf; 1938-)
Bemba (lang./people)

Proper Noun Speller

Bembo (typeface)
Ben Ali, Zine el-Abidine (pres., Tunisia; 1936-)
Ben Blue (ent.; 1901-75)
Ben Bradlee (US publ.; 1921-)
Ben Crenshaw (golf; 1952-)
Ben Cross (ent.; 1947-)
Ben Franklin Stores (US bus.)
Ben-Gay™ (med.)
Ben Gazzara (ent.; 1930-)
Ben Grauer (ent.
Ben-Gurion, David (ex-PM, Isr.; 1886-1973)
Ben Hecht (US writer; 1894-1964)
Ben Hogan (golf; 1912-)
Ben Hur (film; 1959)
Ben Johnson (Can. runner)
Ben Johnson (ent.; 1918-)
Ben Jonson (Br. writer; 1572-1637)
ben Joseph, Saadia (Jew. phil./scholar; 882-942)
Ben Kingsley (ent.; 1943-)
Ben Murphy (ent.; 1942-)
Ben(jamin) Nelson, E. (NE gov.; 1941-)
Ben Nicholson (Br. artist; 1894-1982)
Ben Nighthorse Campbell (US cong.; 1933-)
Ben(jamin) Shahn (US artist; 1898-1969)
Ben Turpin (ent.; 1874-1940)
Ben Vereen (ent.; 1946-)
Ben Webster (US jazz; 1909-73)
Benadryl™ (med.)
Ben & Jerry's Homemade, Inc.
Benatar, Pat (ent.; 1953-)
Benay Venuta (ent.; 1911-)
Benazir Bhutto (PM, Pak.; 1953-)
Bench, Johnny (baseball; 1947-)
Benchley, Peter (US writer; 1940-)
Benchley, Robert (US writer/humorist; 1889-
   1945)
Bender Gestalt test (also Bender
   gestalt)(psych.)
Bendery, Moldova
Bendix Corp.
Bendix, William (ent.; 1906-64)
Benedetto Croce (It. phil.; 1866-1952)
Benedict Arnold (US traitor; 1741-1801)
Benedict de Spinoza (also Baruch)(Dutch phil.;
   1632-77)
Benedict, Dirk (ent.; 1945-)
Benedict, eggs (also l.c.)
Benedict, Ruth (US anthrop.; 1887-1948)
Benedict, St. (It., founded the Benedictines;
   c480-547)
Benedictine (liqueur)
Benedictine (order of monks/nuns)
Benes, Eduard (Czech. pol.; 1884-1948)
Benét, Stephen Vincent (US poet/novelist; 1898-
   1943)
Benetton™
Benetton (US bus.)
Benetton, Guiliana (It. designer; 1938-)

Benevolent and Protective Order of Elks
   (BPOE)(US society, founded 1868)
Bengal (former province, India)
Bengal light
Bengal tiger
Bengal, Bay of (part of Indian Ocean)
Bengali (lang./people)
Bengals, Cincinnati (football team)
Bengasi, Libya (also Benghazi)
Benglis, Lynda
Benguela Current
Benguela, Angola
Benihana of Tokyo (US bus.)
Benin (Republic of, formerly Dahomey)(W Afr.)
Bening, Annette (ent.; 1958-)
Benito (Pablo) Juárez (ex-pres., Mex.; 1806-72)
Benito Mussolini (aka *Il Duce*)(ex-PM, It.; 1883-
   1945)
Benjamin Britten (also Baron Britten of
   Aldeburgh)(Br. comp.; 1913-76)
Benjamin Disraeli (ex-PM/writer, Br.; 1804-81)
Benjamin F. Chavis, Rev. (US rel./head
   NAACP; 1948-)
Benjamin Franklin (US publ./writer/inv./dipl.;
   1706-90)
Benjamin Franklin Wade (US pol.; 1800-78)
Benjamin Harrison (23rd US pres.; 1833-1901)
Benjamin Harrison (US pol.; 1726?-91)
Benjamin Harrison, Fort, IN (mil.)
Benjamin Henry Latrobe (US arch.; 1764-1820)
Benjamin Lawson Hooks (US civil rights leader;
   1925-)
Benjamin Lincoln (US mil./pol.; 1722-1810)
Benjamin Moore & Co.
Benjamin Rush (US phys./writer; 1745-1813)
Benjamin "Bugsy" Siegel
Benjamin (McLane) Spock, Dr. (US phys./
   writer; 1903-)
Benjamin West (US artist; 1738-1820)
Benjamin, Private (film; 1980)
Benjamin, Richard (ent.; 1938-)
Benji (dog)
Benji (film; 1974)
Benji the Hunted (film; 1987)
Benji's Moist 'n Chunky™ (dog food)
Bennett Cerf (US editor/publ.; 1898-1971)
Bennett, Constance (ent.; 1904-65)
Bennett, Cornelius (football; 1966-)
Bennett, Joan (ent.; 1910-90)
Bennett, Robert (US cong.; 1933-)
Bennett, Tony (ent.; 1926-)
Bennie Moten (US jazz; 1894-1935)
Benning, Fort, GA (mil.)
Benny Carter (US jazz; 1907-)
Benny (Benjamin David) Goodman (US jazz;
   1909-86)
Benny Goodman Story, The (film; 1955)
Benny Hill (ent.; 1925-92)

Benny (Benjamin Leiner) Leonard (boxing; 1896-1947)
Benny, Jack (b. Benjamin Kubelsky)(ent.; 1894-1974)
Benoit Samuelson, Joan (Olympic marathon; 1957-)
Benrus Watch Co.
Benson, Ezra Taft (US pol.)
Benson, George (ent.; 1943-)
Benson, Robby (ent.; 1955-)
Benten (myth.)
Bentham, Jeremy (Br. rel.; 1748-1832)
Bentley Motors, Inc.
Benton Harbor, MI
Benton, Barbi (US playmate)
Benton, Thomas Hart (US artist; 1889-1975)
Benton, Thomas Hart (US pol.; 1782-1858)
Bentsen, Lloyd (US Secy./Treasury; 1921-)
Benvenuto Cellini (It. sculptor; 1500-71)
Benylin™ (med.)
Benz™, Mercedes- (auto.)
Benzedrex™ (med.)
Benzedrine™ (med.)
Beothuk (Can. Indian Tribe)
Beowulf (cartoon chara.)
Beowulf (epic poem; 8th c.)
Beradino, John (ent.; 1917-)
Berber (lang./people)
Berbera, Somalia
Berberati, Central African Republic
Berchtesgaden, Germany
Bercy (sauce)
Beregovoi, Georgi (or Georgy) T. (cosmo.; 1921-)
Bérégovoy, Pierre (ex-PM, Fr.; 1925-93)
Berenger, Tom (ent.; 1950-)
Berenice's Hair (astron.)
Berenices, Coma (astron., Berenice's hair)
Berenson, Bernard (or Bernhard)(US art critic; 1865-1959)
Berets, Green (also Special Forces)(US mil.)
Beretta™, Chevrolet Corsica/ (auto.)
Berezovoy, Anatoly (cosmo.)
Berg, Alban (Aus. comp.; 1885-1935)
Berg, Gertrude (ent.; 1899-1966)
Berg, Patty (Patricia Jane)(golf; 1918-)
Berg, Paul (US molecular biol.; 1926-)
Bergalis, Kimberly (US AIDS victim; 1968-91)
Bergdorf Goodman (store)
Bergen County Record (NJ newspaper)
Bergen, Candice (ent.; 1946-)
Bergen, Edgar (ent.; 1903-78)
Bergen, Norway
Bergen, Polly (ent.; 1930-)
Berger, Thomas (US writer; 1924-)
Bergerac (wine)
Bergerac, Cyrano de (Fr. poet/mil.; 1619-55)
Bergerac, Cyrano de (play)
Bergman, Ingmar (Swed. ent.; 1918-)

Bergman, Ingrid (ent.; 1915-82)
Bergson, Henri (Fr. phil.; 1859-1941)
Bergsonian/Bergsonism (phil.)
Bergstrom Air Force Base (TX)(mil.)
Beria, Lavrenti (USSR pol.; 1899-1953)
Berigan, Bunny (US jazz; 1909-42)
Bering Sea (N. Pac., Afr./Siberia)
Bering Strait (Alaska/Siberia)
Berisha, Sali (pres., Albania; 1944-)
Berke Breathed (cartoonist, *Bloom County*; 1957-)
Berkeleian/Berkeleianism (phil.)
Berkeley Laboratory, Lawrence (nuclear research, CA)
Berkeley, Busby (ent.; 1895-1976)
Berkeley, CA, MO
Berkeley, England
Berkeley, George (Ir. phil.; 1685-1753)
Berkley Publishing Corp.
Berkley, MI
Berkshire (county, Eng.)
Berkshire Music Festival (Tanglewood, MA)
Berkshire swine
Berkshires (also Berkshire Hills)(MA)
Berle, Milton ("Uncle Miltie")(ent.; 1908-)
Berlin (state, Ger.)
Berlin Wall (divided E/W Berlin; 1961-89)
Berlin, CT, NH, WI
Berlin, Germany
Berlin, Irving (US comp.; 1888-1989)
Berlinger, Warren (ent.; 1937-)
Berlioz, Louis Hector (Fr. comp.; 1803-69)
Berlitz Language Center
Berlusconi, Silvio (PM, It.)
Berman, Shelly (ent.; 1926-)
Bermuda
Bermuda bag (handbag)
Bermuda grass
Bermuda onion
Bermuda shorts
Bermuda Triangle (also Devil's Triangle)
Bern, Switzerland
Bernadette Peters (ent.; 1948-)
Bernadette, St. (aka Bernadette of Lourdes)(Fr.; 1844-79)
Bérnaise sauce (also l.c.)
Bernard A. De Voto (US hist.; 1897-1955)
Bernard (or Bernhard) Berenson (US art critic; 1865-1959)
Bernard Dowiyogo (pres., Nauru; 1946-)
Bernard Gimbel (US bus.; 1885-1966)
Bernard Howell Leach (Br. potter; 1887-1969)
Bernard Law Montgomery (Br. mil.; 1887-1976)
Bernard Lovell, Sir (Alfred Charles)(Br. astron.; 1931-)
Bernard Malamud (US writer; 1914-86)
Bernard Marcel Parent (hockey; 1945-)
Bernard M. Baruch (US finan./pol.; 1870-1965)

Bernard R. Maybeck (US arch.; 1862-1957)

Bernard Shaw, (George)(Ir. writer/critic; 1856-1950)

Bernard, Crystal (ent.)

Bernard, St. (dog)

Bernardi, Herschel (ent.; 1923-86)

Bernardo Bertolucci (It. ent.; 1940-)

Bernardo Rossellino (It. arch./sculptor; 1409-64)

Berne, Dr. Eric (US psych./writer; 1910-70)

Bernese Alps (also Bernese Oberland)(Switz.)

Bernese mountain dog

Bernhard H. Goetz (US news, shot NYC robbers)

Bernhard Riemann, (Georg Friedrich)(Ger. math.; 1826-66)

Bernhard von Bülow, Prince (ex-chanc., Ger.; 1849-1929)

Bernhard, Sandra (ent.; 1955-)

Bernhardt, Sarah (ent.; 1844-1923)

Bernie Kopell (ent.; 1933-)

Bernie Taupin (lyricist)

Bernina™

Bernina Sewing Machine Co., Inc.

Berning, Susan Maxwell (golf; 1941-)

Bernini, Giovanni Lorenzo (It. sculptor; 1598-1680)

Bernoulli effect (physics)

Bernoulli, Daniel (Swiss math.; 1700-82)

Bernoulli, Jakob (Swiss math./scien.; 1654-1705)

Bernoulli, Johann (Swiss math./scien.; 1667-1748)

Bernoulli's principle (law of averages)

Bernsen, Corbin (ent.; 1955-)

Bernstein Foods, Inc.

Bernstein, Carl (US jour.; 1944-)

Bernstein, Leonard (US comp./cond.; 1918-90)

Bernstein's™

Berov, Lyuben (PM, Bulgaria)

Berra, Yogi (Lawrence Peter)(baseball; 1925-)

Berry Gordy, Jr. (US bus./founded Motown)

Berry, Bertice (TV show)

Berry, Chuck (Charles)(ent.; 1926-)

Berry, Jim (cartoonist, *Berry's World*; 1932-)

Berry, Ken (ent.; 1933-)

Berry, Raymond (football; 1933-)

Berryman, John (US poet; 1914-72)

Berry's World (comic strip)

Bert Convy (ent.; 1934-91)

Bert Lahr (b. Irving Lahrheim)(ent.; 1895-1967)

Bert Lytell

Bert Parks (ent.; 1914-92)

Bertha Krupp (Ger. armaments maker; 1886-1957)

Bertha, Big (WWII Ger. cannon)

Berthe Morisot (Fr. artist; 1841-95)

Bertice Berry (TV show)

Bertillon system (criminology)

Bertillon, Alphonse (Fr. anthrop./criminol.; 1853-1914)

Bertinelli, Valerie (ent.; 1960-)

Bertolli™

Bertolli USA, Inc.

Bertolt Brecht (Ger. writer; 1898-1956)

Bertolucci, Bernardo (It. ent.; 1940-)

Bertram G. Goodhue (US arch.; 1869-1924)

Bertrand (Arthur William) Russell (Br. phil./math.; 1872-1970)

Berzelius, Jöns Jakob, Baron (Swed. chem.; 1779-1848)

Besançon, France (Roman ruins)

Besant, Annie (Br. theosophist; 1847-1933)

Bess Myerson

Bess (Wallace) Truman (wife of ex-US pres.; 1885-1982)

Bess, Porgy and (Gershwin operetta)

Bessemer process (steel)

Bessemer, Sir Henry (Br. eng.; 1813-98)

Besser, Joe (ent.; 1907-88)

Bessie Smith (US jazz; 1894-1937)

Best Foods™

Best Foods Baking Group (US bus.)

Best Little Whorehouse in Texas, The (play/film)

Bester, Alfred (US writer; 1913-87)

Beta fiber

Beta Orionis (also Rigel)(astron.)

Beta Persei (also Algol)(astron.)

Betamax™ (also Beta™)(video format)

Bete (people)

Betelgeuse (also Alpha Orionis)(astron.)

Bethe, Hans Albrecht (US physt.; 1906-)

Bethesda Naval Hospital (MD)

Bethesda, MD

Bethlehem Steel Corp.

Bethlehem, Jordan

Bethlehem, PA

Bethlehem, Star of

Bethlehem, Star-of- (plant)

Bethune, Mary McLeod (US educ./civil rights; 1875-1955)

Beti (lang.)

Betsy Palmer (ent.; 1929-)

Betsy (Elizabeth Earle) Rawls (golf; 1928-)

Betsy (Griscom) Ross (made 1st US flag; 1752-1836)

Betsy, The (film; 1978)

Bette Davis (ent.; 1908-89)

Bette Davis Eyes (song)

Bette Midler (ent.; 1945-)

Bettelheim, Bruno (Aus./US psych.; 1903-90)

Better Business Bureau

Better Homes and Gardens (mag.)

Better Homes & Gardens Books (US bus.)

Bettino Craxi (ex-PM, It.; 1934-)

Betty Boop (cartoon chara.)

Betty Broderick (US news)

Betty Buckley (ent.; 1947-)
Betty Comden (US lyricist/ent.; 1919-)
Betty Crocker™
Betty Ford (b. Elizabeth Bloomer Warren)(wife of ex-US pres.; 1918-)
Betty (Naomi Goldstein) Friedan (US feminist/writer; 1921-)
Betty (Elizabeth) Furness (US ent./consumer activist)
Betty Garrett (ent.; 1919-)
Betty Grable (ent.; 1916-73)
Betty Hutton (ent.; 1921-)
Betty White (ent.; 1922-)
Beulah Bondi (ent.; 1892-1981)
Beulah, Land of (*Pilgrim's Progress*)
Beuys, Joseph (Ger. sculptor/ent.; 1921-86)
Bevan, Aneurin (Br. pol.; 1897-1960)
Beverly Cleary (US writer; 1916-)
Beverly Crusher, Dr. (fict. chara., *Star Trek*)
Beverly D'Angelo (ent.; 1954-)
Beverly Garland (ent.; 1926-)
Beverly Hillbillies, The (TV show/film)
Beverly Hills, CA
Beverly Hills Cop (film; 1984)
Beverly Hills Cop II (film; 1987)
Beverly Hills Cop III (film; 1994)
Beverly Hills Hotel
Beverly Hills 90210 (TV show)
Beverly Sassoon (US bus.)
Beverly Sills (b. Belle Silverman)(US opera; 1929-)
Beverly, MA, NJ
Bevin, Ernest (Br. pol.; 1881-1951)
Bewitched (TV show)
Bexley (borough in London, Eng.)
Bexley, OH
Beyle, Marie Henri (aka Stendahl)(Fr. writer; 1783-1842)
Beyond Good and Evil (by F. Nietzsche)
Beyrouth, Lebanon (also Beirut)
Bezier curve (compu. graphics)
BFA (Bachelor of Fine Arts)
B. F. Goodrich™ (tires)
B. F. Goodrich Co.
B(urrhus) F(rederic) Skinner (US psych./writer; 1903-90)
BHA (synthetic antioxidant preservative)
Bhádgáon, Nepal
Bhagavad-Gita (also Gita)(rel.)
Bhagwan (aka Shree [or Osho] Rajneesh)(b. Chaadra Mohan Jain)(Indian rel.; 1931-90)
Bhaktapur, Nepal
Bhakti (rel.)
Bharat Natya (dance, India)
Bhavnagar, India (also Bhaunagar)
Bhili (lang.)
Bhiwandi, India
Bhojpuri (lang.)

Bhopal, India
B horizon (geol.)
Bhote (people)
BHT (synthetic antioxidant preservative)
Bhumibol Adulyadej (aka Rama IX)(king, Thailand; 1927-)
Bhutan (Kingdom of)
Bhutto, Benazir (PM, Pak.; 1953-)
Bhutto, Zulfikar Ali (ex-pres/PM, Pak.; 1928-79)
Bi (chem. sym., bismuth)
BIA (Bureau of Indian Affairs)
Biafra, Bight of (also Bight of Bonny)(bay, Afr.)
Biafra, Republic of (former republic)(Afr.)
Bialystok, Poland
Bianca Jagger (b. Bianca Peréz Morena de Macías)
Biarritz, France
Bibb lettuce
Bibi Andersson (Swed. ent.; 1935-)
Bible
Bible Belt
Bibliothèque Nationale (Fr. National Library, Paris)
Bic™ (pens, razors)
Bic Corp.
Bickford, Charles (ent.; 1889-1967)
Bicol (lang.)
BiCozene™ (med.)
Bicycle Guide (mag.)
Biddle, John (Br. rel.; 1615-62)
Biddle, Nicholas (US finan.; 1786-1844)
Biden, Joseph R., Jr. (US cong.; 1942-)
Biedermeier (style of art/furniture)
Biel, Switzerland (also Bienne)
Bielefeld, Germany
Bienne, Switzerland (also Biel)
Bienville, Jean Baptiste Le Moyne (Fr. colonial admin.; 1680-1768)
Bierce, Ambrose Gwinnett (US writer; 1842-1914)
Bierstadt, Albert (US artist; 1830-1902)
Bifrost (myth.)
Big Apple (nickname, NYC)
Big Bang theory (astron.)
Big Bear City, CA
Big Ben (London clock)
Big Bend National Park (TX)
Big Bertha (WWII Ger. cannon)
Big Bill Broonzy (US jazz; 1893-1958)
Big Bill (William Tatem) Tilden, Jr. (tennis; 1893-1953)
Big Bird (fict. chara., *Sesame Street*)
Big Board (New York Stock Exchange)
Big Bopper, the (b. J. P. "Jape" Richardson)(ent.)
Big Boy Restaurants (US bus.)
Big Brother (sociology)
Big Daddy (also l.c.)

Big Dipper (also Ursa Major)(astron.)
Big Foot (also Bigfoot or Sasquatch)
Big Joe Turner (ent.; 1911-85)
Big Rapids, MI
Big Rock Candy Mountain, The (W. Stegner novel)
Big Sid Catlett (US jazz; 1910-51)
Big Sur region (CA)
Big Sur River (CA)
Big Train (Walter Perry) Johnson (baseball; 1887-1946)
Big Valley, The (TV show)
Big, Mr. (pop music)
Big, Mr. (slang, man in charge)
Bigard, Barney (US jazz; 1906-80)
Bigelow™ (carpet)
Bigelow™ (tea)
Bigelow, Inc., Karastan-
Bighorn Mountains (WY)
Bighorn, Battle of the Little (also Custer's Last Stand)(US/Sioux Indians; 1876)
Bight of Biafra (also Bight of Bonny)(bay, Afr.)
Bihari (people)
Bijan (US bus.)
Bikenibeu Paeniu (ex-PM, Tuvalu)
Bikini Atoll (atomic bomb test site-1940s)
Biko, Stephen (b. Stephen Bantu)(SAfr. civil rights leader; 1946-77)
Bikol (lang.)
Bil Keane (cartoonist, *The Family Circus*; 1922-)
Bilbao, Spain
Bilbo Baggins (fict. chara.)
Bildt, Carl (PM, Swed.; 1949-)
Bildungsroman (lit.)
Bileka, Silvestre Siale (PM, Equatorial Guinea)
Biletnikoff, Frederick (football; 1943-)
Bilko, Sergeant (TV show)
Bill (William Britton) Baird (US puppeteer; 1904-87)
Bill Bixby (ent.; 1934-93)
Bill Blass™
Bill Blass (US designer; 1922-)
Bill (William Warren) Bradley (US cong./ basketball; 1943-)
Bill Broonzy, Big (US jazz; 1893-58)
Bill Burrud (ent.; 1925-90)
Bill (William Jefferson) Clinton (42nd US Pres.; 1946-)
Bill Cosby (ent.; 1937-)
Bill (William L.) Cullen (ent.; 1920-90)
Bill Dana (ent.; 1924-)
Bill Davison, Wild (US jazz; 1906-89)
Bill Durham (film; 1988)
Bill Evans (US jazz; 1929-80)
Bill Gates (US bus.)
Bill Haley (ent.; 1925-81)
Bill Haley and the Comets (pop music)

Bill Hanna (cartoonist, *Tom & Jerry, Huckleberry Hound, Yogi Bear, Flintstones*; 1910-)
Bill (William) Hartack, Jr. (jockey; 1932-)
Bill Hickok, Wild (b. James Butler Hickok)(US frontier; 1837-76)
Bill (William Orland) Kilmer (football; 1939-)
Bill Macy (ent.; 1922-)
Bill Madlock (baseball; 1951-)
Bill (William Henry) Mauldin (US writer/ cartoonist; 1921-)
Bill Moyers (US jour.; 1934-)
Bill Murray (ent.; 1950-)
Bill of Rights (1st 10 amendments, US Constitution)
Bill (William) Richardson (US cong.; 1947-)
Bill ("Bojangles") Robinson (US tap dancer; 1878-1949)
Bill Russell (basketball; 1934-)
Bill Russell (US jazz; 1905-92)
Bill Shoemaker (horse racing; 1931-)
Bill "Moose" Skowron (baseball; 1930-)
Bill (William Tatem) "Big Bill" Tilden, Jr. (tennis; 1893-1953)
Bill Walton (basketball; 1952-)
Bill Watterson (cartoonist, *Calvin and Hobbes*; 1958-)
Bill White
Bill, Buffalo (aka William F(rederick) Cody)(Amer. scout/ent.; 1846-1917)
Bill, Mr. (fict. chara.)
Bill, Pecos (legendary cowboy)
Billboard™ (mag.)
Billboard Music Awards
Billie Burke (ent.; 1885-1970)
Billie Holiday (b. Eleanora Fagan)(US jazz; 1915-59)
Billie Jean (Moffitt) King (tennis; 1943-)
Billings, Josh (b. Henry Wheeler Shaw)(US humorist; 1818-85)
Billings, MT
Billingsgate (London fish market, coarse lang.)
Billionaire Boys Club
Bills, Buffalo (football team)
Billy Barty (ent.; 1924-)
Billy Budd (H. Melville story)
Billy (William Aldon) Carter, III (US bro. of pres.; 1937-88)
Billy Casper (golf; 1931-)
Billy Crash Craddock (ent.; 1940-)
Billy Crystal (ent.; 1947-)
Billy DeBeck (cartoonist, *Barney Google*; 1890-1942)
Billy Dee Williams (ent.; 1937-)
Billy De Wolfe (ent.; 1907-74)
Billy Eckstine (ent.; 1914-93)
Billy (William Franklin) Graham, Rev. (US rel.; 1918-)

Billy Idol (ent.; 1955-)
Billy Jack (film; 1971)
Billy Joel (ent.; 1949-)
Billy (Alfred Manuel) Martin (baseball; 1928-89)
Billy Mitchell (US mil.; 1879-1936)
Billy Ocean (ent.; 1950-)
Billy Packer (ent.; 1940-)
Billy Preston (ent.; 1946-)
Billy Rose (ent.; 1899-1966)
Billy Sims (football; 1955-)
Billy Smith (hockey; 1950-)
Billy Sol Estes (US bus./scandal)
Billy Strayhorn (US jazz; 1915-67)
Billy (William Ashley) Sunday (US rel.; 1862-1935)
Billy Taylor (US jazz; 1921-)
Billy the Kid (aka William Henry Bonney)(US outlaw; 1859-81)
Billy (Samuel) Wilder (ent./writer; 1906-)
Biloxi (NAmer. Indians)
Biloxi Blues (film; 1988)
Biloxi, MS
Binaca™ (health)
Binding Corp., General (GBC)
Binet test, Stanford- (intelligence test)
Binet, Alfred (Fr. psych.; 1857-1911)
Bing cherry
Bing (Harry Lillis) Crosby (ent.; 1903-77)
Bing, Dave (basketball; 1943-)
Bing, Sir Rudolf (opera; 1902-)
Bingaman, Jeff (US cong.; 1943-)
Bingham, George Caleb (US artist; 1811-79)
Binghamton Press & Sun-Bulletin (NY newspaper)
Binghamton, NY
Bioko, Cristino Seriche (ex-PM, Equatorial Guinea)
Biondi, Matt (swimming; 1965-)
BioSphere 2 (BS2)(ecological test project)
BIP (*Books in Print* [Bowker])
Biphetamine™ (med.)
Biratnagar, Nepal
Birch Society, John (US pol.)
Bird Watchers Digest
Bird, Caroline (US writer)
Bird, Larry (basketball; 1956-)
Bird, Vere C(ornwall)(PM, Antigua and Barbuda
Birdie (George R.) Tebbetts (baseball; 1914-)
Birdman of Alcatraz, The (film; 1962)
Birdseye™ (frozen foods)
Birdseye, Clarence ("Bob")(US inv., frozen food; 1886-1956)
Birendra Bir Bikram Shah Dev (king, Nepal; 1945-)
Birganj, Nepal
Birgit Nilsson (Swed., opera; 1918-)

Birkavs, Valdis (PM, Latvia)
Birkenhead, England
Birkenstock™
Birkenstock Footprint Sandals, Inc.
Birkirkara, Malta
Birman (cat)
Birmingham News (AL newspaper)
Birmingham Post-Herald (AL newspaper)
Birmingham, AL, MI
Birmingham, England
Birnam Wood (Scot.)
Birney, David (ent.; 1939-)
Birney, James Gillespie (US reformer; 1792-1857)
Birobizhan (also Birobidjan)(Jew. settlement)
Birth of Venus, The (by Botticelli)
Biscay, Bay of (Fr./Sp.)
Biscayne Bay (Miami, FL)
Biscayne Boulevard (Miami, FL)
Biscayne National Park (FL)
Bishkek, Kyrgyzstan
Bishop, Elizabeth (US poet; 1911-79)
Bishop, Joey (ent.; 1918-)
Bislama (lang.)
Bismarck Archipelago (SW Pac. islands)
Bismarck, ND
Bismarck, Otto (Eduard Leopold) von, Prince ("Iron Chancellor")(ex-chanc., Ger.; 1815-98)
Bismarck, the (Ger. WWII battleship; sunk 1941)
Bisoglio, Val (ent.; 1926-)
Bisquick™
Bissau, Guinea- (Republic of)(W Afr.)
Bissau, Guinea-Bissau
Bissell™ (sweeper)
Bissell, Inc.
Bisset, Jacqueline (ent.; 1944-)
Bissinger's™
Bissinger's, Inc.
Biswas, Abdur Rahman (pres., Bangladesh)
Bitterroot Range (also Bitter Root Range)(ID/MT)
Bivar, Rodrigo Diaz de (also El Cid, el Campeador)(Sp. mil.; 1040-99)
Bix Beiderbecke, (Leon Bismarck)(US jazz; 1903-31)
Bixby, Bill (ent.; 1934-93)
Biya, Paul (pres., Cameroon; 1933-)
Biysk, Siberia (also Bisk, Biisk)
Biz™ (bleach)
Bizerte, Tunisia (also Bizerta)
Bizet, Georges (Fr. comp.; 1838-75)
Björn Borg (tennis; 1956-)
Bk (chem. sym., berkelium)
B(ernard) Kliban (cartoonist, cats; 1935-91)
Black & Decker™ (power tools)
Black & Decker Corp., The
Black and Tans (Br. troops; 1920-21)

Black Angus cattle (also Aberdeen Angus)
Black Audio Network (BAN)
Black Beauty (Anna Sewell novel/film)
Black Crowes, the (pop music)
Black Dahlia (Elizabeth Short)
Black Death (bubonic plague; 14th c)
Black Enterprise (mag.)
Black Entertainment Television (BET)(cable TV)
Black Forest (Ger.)
Black Forest cake
Black Friday (US finan. disasters; 9/24/1869 & 9/19/1873)
Black Hand (various pol. & criminal societies)
Black Hawk War (US hist.; 1831-32)
Black Hawk, Chief (Sauk Indians; 1767-1838)
Black Hawks, Chicago (hockey team)
Black Hills (SD/WY mountains)
Black Hole of Calcutta (prison cell; 1756)
Black Maria (patrol wagon)
Black Mass
Black Monday (US stockmarket crash; 10/19/87)
Black Mountains (SE US)
Black Muslims (also Nation of Islam)(rel.)
Black Panther Party (Black separatist group)
Black Prince, Edward the (Prince of Wales; 1330-76)
Black Russian (mixed drink)
Black Sabbath (pop music)
Black Sea (SE Eur.)
Black Tuesday (US stockmarket crash; 10/29/29)
Black Velvet™ (whiskey)
Black Watch (Br. Royal Highland regiment)
Black, Clint (ent.; 1962-)
Black, Hugo LaFayette (US jurist; 1886-1971)
Black, Karen (ent.; 1942-)
Black, Shirley Temple (US ent./dipl.; 1928-)
Blackbeard (Edward Teach)(also Thatch, Thach)(pirate; ?-1718)
Blackburn, Mount (AK)
Blackburnian warbler (bird)
Blackett, Patrick Maynard Stuart, Baron (Br. physt.; 1897-1974)
black-eyed Susan (plant)
Blackfoot (NAmer. Indians)
Blackfriars (Elizabethan playhouse, London)
Blackhawk (cartoon chara.)
Blackie, Boston (fict. detective)
Blackmun, Harry A(ndrew)(ex-US jurist; 1908-)
Blackpool, England
Blackstone, Harry, Jr. (ent.; 1934-)
Blackstone, Sir William (Br. jurist; 1723-80)
Blackwall hitch (knot)
Blackwater State (nickname, NE)
Blackwell, Elizabeth (1st US woman phys.; 1821-1910)
Blackwell, Mr.
Blackwell™, Crosse &
Blackwell Co., The Crosse &
Blackwood, Nina
Blaik, Earl H. (football; 1897-1989)
Blaine, James G(illespie)(US pol.; 1830-93)
Blaine, Vivian (ent.; 1921-)
Blair Brown (ent.; 1948-)
Blair Underwood (ent.)
Blair, Bonnie (speed skating)
Blair, Eric A(rthur)(pseud. George Orwell)(Br. writer; 1903-50)
Blair, Linda (ent.; 1959-)
Blaise Compaoré (pres., Burkina Faso; 1951-)
Blaise Pascal (Fr. phil./math.; 1623-62)
Blaize, Herbert (ex-PM, Grenada; 1918-1989)
Blake Edwards (ent.; 1922-)
Blake, Amanda (ent.; 1929-89)
Blake, Eubie (James Hubert)(US jazz pianist/comp.; 1883-1983)
Blake, Robert (ent.; 1933-)
Blake, Robert, Adm. (Br. mil.; 1599-1657)
Blake, William (Br. poet/artist; 1757-1827)
Blakey, Art (US jazz; 1919-90)
Blanc, (Jean Joseph Charles) Louis (Fr. socialist/hist.; 1811-82)
Blanc, Mel (ent.; 1908-89)
Blanc, Mont (Fr./It.)
Blanca Peak (CO)
Blanda, George (Frederick)(football; 1927-)
Blanding, Sarah G. (US educ.; 1899-1985)
Blandings Builds His Dream House, Mr. (film; 1948)
Blanton, Jimmy (US jazz; 1921-42)
Blantyre, Malawi
Blarney stone (Ir.)
Blass™, Bill
Blass, Bill (US designer; 1922-)
Blaue Reiter, der ("the blue Rider")(Ger. painters)
Blavatsky Hahn, Madame Helena Petrovna (Rus. theosophist; 1831-91)
Bledsoe, Tempestt (ent.; 1973-)
Blenheim spaniel (dog)
Blenheim, Germany
Blenkinsop rack (railroad)
Blériot, Louis (Fr. aviator; 1872-1936)
Blessed Sacrament (rel.)
Blessed Virgin (rel.)
Bligh, William (Br. capt., H.M.S. *Bounty*; 1754-1817)
Blimp, Colonel (fict. chara.)
Blind Faith (pop music)
Blind Lemon Jefferson (US jazz; 1897-1930)
Bliss, Fort, TX (mil.)
Blistex™ (med.)
Blistex, Inc.
Blistik™ (lip balm)

Blitzkrieg (also the Blitz)(Ger., lightning
  war)(also l.c.)
Blixen, Karen (pseud. Isak Dinesen)(Dan.
  writer; 1885-1962)
BLM (Bureau of Land Management)
Bloch, Ernest (Swiss/US comp.; 1880-1959)
Bloch, Felix (Swiss/US physt.; 1905-83)
Bloch, Konrad (Emil)(US chem.; 1912-)
Bloch, Ray (ent.)
Block, Herb(ert Lawrence)("Herblock")(pol.
  cartoonist; 1909-)
Block, Inc., H & R
Blockbuster Bowl (college football)
Blockbuster Video (US bus.)
Blocker, Dan (ent.; 1928-72)
Bloemfontein, South Africa
Blois, France
Blok, Aleksandr Aleksandrovich (Rus. poet;
  1880-1921)
Blondell, Gloria (ent.)
Blondell, Joan (ent.; 1909-79)
Blondie (pop music)
Blondie Bumstead (cartoon chara.)
Blood, Sweat, and Tears (pop music)
Bloodless Revolution (also English [or Glorious]
  Revolution)(Br. hist.; 1688-89)
Bloods and Crips (pop music)
Bloodworth-Thomason, Linda (ent.)
Bloody Mary (alcoholic drink)
Bloody Mary (also Mary Tudor, Mary I)(queen,
  Eng.; 1516-58)
Bloody Sunday (Rus. hist, 1905; NIre. hist.,
  1972)
Bloom County (comic strip)
Bloom, Claire (ent.; 1931-)
Bloomer, Amelia (US reformer; 1818-94)
Bloomfield, CT, IA, IN, NJ
Bloomfield, Leonard (US linguist; 1887-1949)
Bloomingdale's (also "Bloomies")(stores)
Bloomington, IL, IN, MN
Bloomsbury group (writers/artists, London)
Blossom Dearie (ent.)
Blow, Joe (also Joe Doakes)(average guy)
BLT (bacon, lettuce, and tomato)
Blücher, Gebhard von (Ger. gen.; 1742-1819)
Blue Andalusian (chicken)
Blue Angels, the (aviation)
Blue Bonnet™ (margarine)
Blue Book™ (auto.)
Blue Cross™ (med. insurance)
Blue Cross & Blue Shield Association (med.
  insurance)
Blue Ice™
Blue Jays, Toronto (baseball team)
Blue Mountains (Austl.)
Blue Nile (Ethiopia)
Blue Ridge Mountains (WV to GA)
Blue Shield™ (med. insurance)

Blue Suede Shoes (song)
Blue Swedish (duck)
Blue, Ben (ent.; 1901-75)
Blue, Vida (baseball; 1949-)
Bluebeard (legendary murderer of wives)
Blueberry Morning™ (cereal)
Bluegrass State (nickname, KY)
Blues Brother, The (film; 1980)
Blues, St. Louis (hockey team)
Blum, Léon (Fr. pol.; 1872-1950)
Blume in Love (film; 1973)
Blume, Judy (US writer; 1938-)
Bly, Nellie (Elizabeth Cochrane Seaman)(US
  jour./reformer; 1867-1922)
Blyth, Ann (ent.; 1928-)
Blythe Danner (ent.; 1944-)
Blytheville Air Force Base, AR (mil.)
Blytheville, AR
BMOC (big man on campus)
BMW™ (auto.)
BMW (Bayerische Motoren Werke)
BMW of North America, Inc. (US bus.)
BMW™ 325is (auto.)
B'nai B'rith (US Jew. org.)
BO (box office, branch office, body odor)
Bo Derek (ent.; 1956-)
Bo Diddley (b. Elias McDaniel)(ent.; 1928-)
Bo (Vincent) Jackson (baseball; 1962-)
Bo, Sierra Leone
Board of Education of Topeka, Kansas, Brown
  v. (US law; 1954)
Boas, Franz (US anthrop.; 1858-1942)
Boating (mag.)
Bob & Carol & Ted & Alice (film; 1969)
Bob Barker (ent.; 1923-)
Bob Beamon (jumper; 1946-)
Bob (Clarence) Birdseye (US inv., frozen food;
  1886-1956)
Bob Clampett (fict. chara.)
Bob Costas (ent.; 1952-)
Bob (Robert Joseph) Cousy (basketball; 1928-)
Bob Crane (ent.; 1928-78)
Bob Cratchit (fict. chara., *A Christmas Carol*)
Bob (George Robert) Crosby (ent.; 1913-93)
Bob Denver (ent.; 1935-)
Bob (Robert) Dole (US cong.; 1923-)
Bob Dylan (b. Robert Zimmerman)(US comp./
  ent.; 1941-)
Bob Elliott (ent.; 1923-)
Bob Eubanks
Bob Feller (baseball; 1918-)
Bob (Robert Prometheus) Fitzsimmons (boxing;
  1862-1917)
Bob Fosse (ent.; 1927-87)
Bob Geldof (ent.; 1954-)
Bob Gibson (baseball; 1935-)
Bob "Bobcat" Goldthwait (ent.; 1962-)
Bob (Robert) Graham (US cong.; 1936-)

Bob (Robert Allen) Griese (football; 1945-)

Bob (Robert James Lee) Hawke (ex-PM, Austl.; 1929-)

Bob Hope (b. Leslie Townes Hope)(ent.; 1903-)

Bob Hoskins (ent.; 1942-)

Bob Jamieson

Bob Keeshan (ent.; 1927-)

Bob Knight (basketball; 1940-)

Bob Mackie

Bob (Robert Nesta) Marley (ent.; 1945-81)

Bob (Robert) Martinez (US pol.; 1934-)

Bob Mathias (Olympic star; 1930-)

Bob McAdoo (basketball; 1951-)

Bob Merrill (US lyricist; 1921-)

Bob (Robert) Miller (NV gov.; 1945-)

Bob Montana (cartoonist, *Archie*; 1920-75)

Bob Newhart (ent.; 1929-)

Bob Newhart Show, The (TV show)

Bob (Robert William) Packwood (US cong.; 1932-)

Bob Pettit (basketball; 1932-)

Bob Prince (baseball announcer; 1917-85)

Bob Saget (ent.; 1956-)

Bob (Robert Lloyd) Seagren (pole vaulter; 1946-)

Bob Smith ("Buffalo Bob")(ent.; 1917-)

Bob Thaves (cartoonist, *Frank and Ernest*; 1924-)

Bob Uecker ("Mr. Baseball")(ent.; 1935-)

Bob Waterfield (football; 1921-83)

Bob Woodward (US jour.; 1943-)

Bobbies (Br. police officers)

Bobbitt, John Wayne (US news)

Bobbitt, Lorena (US news)

Bobbsey Twins, The (book series)

Bobby (Robert Arthur) Allison (auto racing; 1937-)

Bobby (Robert) Breen (ent.)

Bobby (Robert Earle) Clarke (hockey; 1949-)

Bobby Darin (ent.; 1936-73)

Bobby (Robert James) Fischer (US chess; 1943-)

Bobby Goldsboro (ent.; 1942-)

Bobby Hackett (US jazz; 1915-76)

Bobby (Robert Marvin) Hull (hockey; 1939-)

Bobby (Robert Tyre) Jones, Jr. (golf; 1902-71)

Bobby Layne (football; 1927-86)

Bobby McFerrin (ent.; 1950-)

Bobby (Robert Gordon) Orr (hockey; 1948-)

Bobby Rahal

Bobby Riggs (tennis)

Bobby Rydell (ent.; 1942-)

Bobby Seale (cofounded Black Panther Party)

Bobby Short (ent.; 1924-)

Bobby Unser (auto racing; 1934-)

Bobby Vinton (ent.; 1935-)

Bobcat (Bob) Goldthwait (ent.; 1962-)

Bobo-Dioulasso, Burkina Faso

Bobois, Roche- (US bus.)

Bobruisk, Belarus

Boca Raton, FL

Boccaccio, Giovanni (It. writer; 1313-75)

Boccherini, Luigi (It. comp.; 1743-1805)

Boccioni, Umberto (It. artist; 1882-1916)

Boch Tableware, Ltd., Villeroy &

Boch™, Villeroy &

Bochco, Steven (ent.; 1943-)

Bochum, Germany

Bock, Jerry (US comp.; 1928-)

Bode, Johann Elert (Ger. astron.; 1747-1826)

Bodenheim, Maxwell (US writer; 1892-1954)

Bode's law (astron.)

Bodhisattva (rel.)

Bodleian Library (Oxford Univ., Eng.)

Bodley, Sir Thomas (Br. scholar/dipl., founded Bodleian Library; 1545-1613)

Bodoni (type style)

Bodoni, Giambattista (It. printer/typographer; 1740-1813)

body English

Boehm, Sydney

Boehme, Jakob (Ger. theosophist; 1575-1624)

Boeing Company

Boer (now Afrikaner)(people)

Boer War (also South African War)(Boers/Br.; 1899-1902)

Boesky, Ivan F(rederick)(US stock market scandal; 1937-)

Boeslav I ("the Mighty")(king, Pol.; ?-1025)

Boeslav II ("the Bold")(king, Pol.; 1039?-83)

Boeslav III ("Wry-mouthed")(king, Pol.; 1086-1138)

Boeslav IV (king, Pol.; 1127-73)

Boeslav V ("the Chaste")(king, Pol.; 1221-79)

Boethius (Roman scholar; c480-524 BC)

Bofors Gun, The (film)

Bogarde, Dirk (ent.; 1920-)

Bogart, Humphrey ("Bogey")(ent.; 1899-1957)

Bogasian, Eric (ent.; 1953-)

Bogdanovich, Peter (ent.; 1939-)

Boggs, Dock (ent.)

Boggs, Wade (baseball; 1958-)

Bogor, Java (Indonesia)

Bogota, Colombia

Bogue, Merwyn (aka Ish Kabibble)(ent.; 1908-94)

Bohème, La (by Puccini)

Bohemia, Czechoslovakia

Bohemian (also l.c.)

Bohr theory (of atomic structure)

Bohr, Aage (Dan. physt.; 1922-)

Bohr, Niels Henrik David (Dan. physt.; 1885-1962)

Boigny, Félix Houphouët- (ex-pres., Ivory Coast; 1905-93)

Boitano, Brian (figure skating)

Bois Wines, Clos Du (US bus.)

Bois, W(illiam) E(dward) B(urghardt) Du (US educ./writer, NAACP; 1868-1963)
Boise Cascade Corp.
Boise, ID
Boito, Arrigo (It. comp./writer; 1842-1918)
Bojangles (Bill Robinson)(US tap dancer; 1878-1949)
Bokhara (Pers. rug)
Bold and the Beautiful (TV soap)
Bold, Philip the (Fr., duke, Burgundy; 1342-1404)
Bold, Philip the (Philip III)(king, Fr.; 1245-85)
Bolden, (Charles) Buddy (US jazz; 1868-1931)
Boléro (M. Ravel music)
Boleyn, Anne (2nd wife Henry VIII; 1507-36)
Bolger, Jim (James Brendan)(PM, NewZeal.; 1935-)
Bolger, Ray (ent.; 1904-87)
Bolingbroke, Henry of (Henry IV, king, Eng.; 1367-1413)
Bolivar, Simon ("El Libertador")(SAmer. pol.; 1783-1830)
Bolivia (Republic of)(central SAmer.)
Bolkiah, Muda Hassanal, Sultan (PM, Brunei)
Böll, Heinrich (Theodor)(Ger. writer; 1917-85)
Bolla Soave (It. wine)
Bolling Air Force Base, DC (mil.)
Bologna, Italy
Bolognese (art style)
Bolshevik (also bolshevik)(Rus. pol. party)
Bolshevik Revolution (Rus.; 1917)
Bolshevism (communist doctrine)
Bolshoi Ballet
Bolton, England
Boltzmann constant (physics, k)
Boltzmann, Ludwig (Aus. physt.; 1844-1906)
Bolzano, Italy
Boma, Zaire
Bombay duck (fish)
Bombay, India
Bombeck, Erma (US writer/humorist; 1927-)
BOMC (Book-of-the-Month Club)
b'Omer, Lag (rel.)
Bomu River (also Mbomu)(Africa)
Bon (Jap. holiday)
Bon Appétit (mag.)
Bon Jovi (pop music)
Bon Jovi, Jon (ent.; 1962-)
Bon, Simon Le (ent.; 1958-)
Bonaire, the Netherlands Antilles
Bonanza (TV show)
Bonaparte, Jerome (bro. of Napoleon, king, Westphalia; 1784-1860)
Bonaparte, Joseph (bro. of Napoleon, king, Naples/Spain; 1768-1844)
Bonaparte, Louis (bro. of Napoleon, king, Holland; 1778-1846)
Bonaparte, Lucien (bro. of Napoleon, prince, Canino; 1775-1840)
Bonaparte, Napoleon (Napoleon I, "the Little Corporal")(emp., Fr.; 1769-1821)
Bonapartism
Bonar Law, (Andrew)(Br. pol.; 1858-1923)
Bonaventure, St. (also Bonaventura)("the Seraphic Doctor")(It. rel./phil.; 1221-74)
Bond, Carrie Jacobs (US comp.; 1862-1946)
Bond, Christopher Samuel ("Kit")(US cong.; 1939-)
Bond, James (fict. spy)
Bond, James (ornithol.; 1900-89)
Bond, Julian (US reformer/pol.; 1940-)
Bond, Ward (ent.; 1903-60)
Bondi, Beulah (ent.; 1892-1981)
Bonds, Barry (baseball; 1964-)
Bonds, Gary "U.S." (ent.)
Bones, Mr. (slang)
Bonet, Lisa (ent.; 1967-)
Bongo, (Albert Bernard) Omar (pres., Gabon; 1935-)
Bonheur, Rosa (Maria Rosalie)(Fr. artist; 1822-99)
Boniface (name of nine popes)
Boniface, St. (Br. rel. in Ger.; 680-754)
Bonilla, Bobby (baseball; 1963-)
Bonin Islands (Pac.)
Bonior, David E. (US cong.; 1945-)
Bonjour Tristesse (F. Sagan novel)
Bonkers (cartoon)
Bonn, Germany
Bonnard, Pierre (Fr. artist; 1867-1947)
Bonne Bell™ (cosmetics)
Bonne Bell, Inc.
Bonneville Salt Flats (UT)
Bonneville, Pontiac™ (auto.)
Bonney, William Henry ("Billy the Kid")(US outlaw; 1859-81)
Bonnie and Clyde (film; 1967)
Bonnie Bedelia (ent.; 1948-)
Bonnie Blair (speed skating)
Bonnie Franklin (ent.; 1944-)
Bonnie Parker (US criminal; 1911-34)
Bonnie Prince Charles (or Charlie)(Charles Edward Stuart, aka the Young Pretender)(prince, Br.; 1720-88)
Bonnie Raitt (ent.; 1949-)
Bonny, Bight of (also Bight of Biafra)(bay, Afr.)
Bono, Sonny (ent./pol.; 1935-)
Bonwit Teller & Co.
Bonzo, Bedtime for (film; 1951)
Boog (John) Powell (baseball; 1941-)
Book Dealers World
Book of Books (Bible)
Book of Changes (also *I Ching*)(rel.)
Book of Common Prayer (Church of England)
Book of Job (rel.)
Book of Kells (rel.)

Book of Kings (rel.)
Book of Mormon (rel.)
Book of Proverbs (rel.)
Book of the Dead (Eg., rel.)
Book of the Dead, The Tibetan (rel.)
Book-of-the-Month Club™
Booke, Sorrell (ent.; 1930-)
Booker T and the MGs (pop music)
Booker T(aliaferro) Washington (US educ./
reformer; 1856-1915)
Books of Chronicles (rel.)
Boole, George (Br. math.; 1815-64)
Boolean algebra (math.)
Boom Boom (Bernie) Geoffrion (hockey; 1931-)
Boomer State (OK)
Boone Pickens, T.
Boone, Daniel (US pioneer; 1734-1820)
Boone, Debbie (ent.; 1956-)
Boone, Pat (ent.; 1934-)
Boone, Richard (ent.; 1917-81)
Boop, Betty (cartoon chara.)
Boosler, Elayne (ent.)
Boötes (astron., herdsmen)
Booth Tarkington, (Newton)(US writer; 1869-
1946)
Booth, Ballington (US, founded Volunteers of
Amer.; 1859-1940)
Booth, Edwin Thomas (US actor, brother of
John Wilkes; 1833-93)
Booth, Evangeline Cory (US, Salvation Army;
1865?-1950)
Booth, George (cartoonist, *New Yorker*; 1926-)
Booth, John Wilkes (US, assassinated Lincoln,
actor; 1838-65)
Booth, Junius Brutus (US actor, father of John
Wilkes; 1796-1852)
Booth, Shirley (ent.; 1907-92)
Booth, William ("General Booth")(Br., founded
Salvation Army; 1829-1912)
Boothe Luce, Clare (US drama./pol./dipl.; 1903-
87)
Boothia Peninsula (Can.)
Boothia, Gulf of (Arctic/N Can.)
Bootle, England
Bophuthatswana (S. Africa)
Bo-Peep, Little (fict. chara.)
Bopper, the Big (b. J. P. "Jape" Richardson)
(ent.)
BOQ (bachelor officers' quarters, base officers'
quarters)
Bora-Bora (French Polynesian islands)
Borah, William E. (US pol.; 1865-1940)
Borateem™ (laundry aid)
Bordeaux (Fr. wine region)
Bordeaux mixture (fungicide)
Bordeaux, France
Bordelaise (sauce)
Borden™ (dairy prods.)

Borden, Inc.
Borden, Lizzie A. (US, tried/acquitted of ax
murders; 1860-1927)
Border States (US Civil War, DE/MD/KY/MO)
Borders (region, Scot.)
Boren, David Lyle (US cong.; 1941-)
Borg, Björn (tennis; 1956-)
Borge, Victor (Dan./US ent./musician; 1909-)
Borges, Jorge Luis (Argentinean writer; 1900-
86)
Borghese Gallery (It.)
Borghese, Halston- (US bus.)
Borgia, Cesare (It. mil./pol.; 1476-1507)
Borgia, Lucrezia (It., Duchess of Ferrara; 1480-
1519)
Borglum, (John) Gutzon (US sculptor; 1871-
1941)
Borgnine, Ernest (ent.; 1917-)
Boris Badenov (fict. chara.)
Boris Becker (tennis; 1967-)
Boris B. Yegorov (cosmo.; 1937-)
Boris (Fëdorovich) Godunov (Rus. tsar; 1552-
1605)
Boris Karloff (William Henry Pratt)(ent.; 1887-
1969)
Boris (Leonidovich) Pasternak (Rus. writer;
1890-1960)
Boris V. Volyanov (cosmo.)
Boris (Nikolayevich) Yeltsin (pres., Rus.; 1931-)
Borman, Frank (astro.; 1928-)
Bormann, Martin (Ger. Nazi leader; 1900-45)
Born Loser, The (comic strip)
Born Yesterday (play/film)
Born, Max (Ger. physt.; 1882-1970)
Borneo (island, W Pac.)
Borodin, Alexander (Rus. comp.; 1833-87)
Boros, Julius (golf; 1920-)
Boross, Peter (PM, Hung.)
Bors, Sir (Arthurian knight)
Bosc (pear)
Bosch™
Bosch Corp., Robert
Bosch, Carl (or Karl)(Ger. chem.; 1874-1940)
Bosch, Hieronymous (Dutch artist; 1450-1516)
Bosco, Philip (ent.; 1930-)
Bose™ (stereo equip.)
Bose Corp., The
Bose, Sir Jagadis Chunder (Indian physt.; 1858-
1937)
Bose, Satyendranath (Indian physt./chem./
math.; 1894-1974)
Boskop (man, skull)
Bosley, Tom (ent.; 1927-)
Bosnia-Hercegovina (republic, Yug.)(also
Bosnia-Herzegovina)
Bosnian Muslims (people)
Bosnian Serbs (people)
Bosporus Strait (Turk.)

Boss Tweed (William M[arcy] Tweed)(US pol.; 1823-78)
Bossangoa, Central African Republic
Bosson, Barbara (ent.; 1939-)
Bossy, Mike (hockey; 1957-)
Bostic, Earl (ent.)
Boston bag (luggage)
Boston baked beans
Boston Bay
Boston Blackie (fict. detective)
Boston brown bread
Boston Bruins (hockey team)
Boston bull terrier (also Boston terrier)(dog)
Boston Celtics (basketball team)
Boston cream pie
Boston fern (plant)
Boston Globe (MA newspaper)
Boston Herald (MA newspaper)
Boston ivy (also Japanese Ivy)(plant)
Boston lettuce
Boston Massacre (US hist.; 3/5/1770)
Boston Museum of Fine Arts
Boston National Historical Park (MA)
Boston Pops Orchestra
Boston Red Sox (baseball team)
Boston rocker
Boston Tea Party (US hist.; 12/16/1773)
Boston terrier (also Boston bull terrier)(dog)
Boston, MA
Boston, Ralph (jumper; 1939-)
Bostonian
Bostitch Inc., Stanley-
Bostwick, Barry (ent.; 1946-)
Boswell, James (Scot. biographer; 1740-95)
Bosworth Field (Eng.)
Bosworth, Brian (football)
Botany Bay, Australia (early Br. penal colony)
Botany 500 (US bus.)
Botany wool (also botany)
Botha, Louis (ex-PM, SAfr.; 1863-1919)
Botha, Pieter W. (ex-pres., SAfr.; 1916-)
Bothnia, Gulf of (Swed./Fin.)
Botswana (Republic of)(formerly Bechuanaland)(central Afr.)
Botticelli, Sandro (It. artist; 1444-1510)
Bottoms, Timothy (ent.; 1951-)
Bottrop, Germany
Botts dots (auto.)
Bouaké, Ivory Coast
Bouar, Central African Republic
Boubacar, Sidi Mohamed Ould (PM, Mauritania)
Boucher, François (Fr. artist; 1703-70)
Bougainville Islands (S Pac.)
Bougainville, Louis-Antoine de (Fr. nav.; 1729-1811)
Bouillon, Godfrey of (also Godefroy de Bouillon) (Fr. crusader; c1060-1100)

Boulanger, Nadia (Fr. cond./educ.; 1887-1979)
Boulder City, NV
Boulder Dam (officially Hoover Dam)(between Nevada and Arizona)
Boulder, CO
Boulez, Pierre (Fr. comp./cond.; 1925-)
Boulogne-Billancourt, France (also Boulogne-sur-Seine)
Boulogne, France (also Boulogne-sur-Mer)
Boult, Sir Adrian (Cedric)(Br. cond.; 1889-1983)
Boulwareism (econ.)
Bountiful, Lady (fict. chara., *Beau's Strategem*)
Bountiful, UT
Bounty™ (paper towels)
Bounty, H.M.S. (ship; naval mutiny against Capt. Bligh)
Bounty, Mutiny on the (book/film)
Bourbon dynasty (France)
Bourbon Street (New Orleans)
Bourbonism (extreme political conservatism)
Bourdelle, Emile Antoine (Fr. artist; 1861-1929)
Bourdon(-tube) gauge (chem.)
Bourgeois, Léon Victor Auguste (Fr. pol.; 1851-1925)
Bourgeois, Louise (Fr./US sculptor; 1911-)
Bourgogne (region, Fr., formerly Burgundy)
Bourguignonne sauce
Bourguignonne, beef
Bourke-White, Margaret (US photo./writer; 1906-71)
Bournemouth, England
Bourque, Ray (hockey; 1960-)
Boursin (cheese)
Bouvier des Flandres (also bouvier)(dog)
Bovary, Madame (G. Flaubert novel)
Bovary, Madame Emma (fict. chara.)
Bow Church (also St. Mary-le-Bow Church)(London)
Bow, Clara (the "It Girl")(ent.; 1905-65)
Bowdler, Thomas (Shakespeare editor; 1754-1825)
Bowe, Riddick (boxing; 1967-)
Bowers v. Hardwick (US law; 1986)
Bowery Boys
Bowery, the (NYC)(cheap hotels, saloons, destitutes)
Bowes, Major Edward (ent.; 1874-1946)
Bowes' Original Amateur Hour, Major
Bowie Kent Kuhn (baseball; 1926-)
Bowie knife (also l.c.)
Bowie, David (ent.; 1947-)
Bowie, James "Jim" (US frontier; 1796-1836)
Bowker Co., R. R.
Bowles, Camilla Parker- (Br. news)
Bowling Green, KY, OH
Boxer Rebellion/Uprising (Ch.; 1898-1900)
Boxer, Barbara (US cong.; 1940-)
Boxing Day (Br. holiday)

Boxleitner, Bruce (ent.; 1950-)
Boy Blue, Little (nursery rhyme)
Boy George (ent.; 1961-)
Boy Scouts of America (founded 1910)
Boyardee™, Chef
Boycott, Charles C., Capt. (Br., boycotted by Ir. tenants; 1832-97)
Boyd, Guillermo Ford (VP, Panama)
Boyd, William (ent.; 1898-1972)
Boyer, Charles (ent.; 1899-1978)
Boykin spaniel (dog)
Boyle, Peter (ent.; 1933-)
Boyle, Robert (Br. physt./chem.; 1627-91)
Boyle's law (physics)
Boynton greeting cards
Boynton, Sandra (US bus.)
Boy's Town of the West (Hanna Boys Center) (CA)
Boys Town, NE
Boys' Life (mag.)
Boyz II Men (pop music)
Boz (pseud. of Charles Dickens)
Boz Scaggs (ent.; 1944-)
Bozcaada (Turk. island in Aegean Sea)
Bozeman Trail (to MT, gold fields; 1863-65)
Bozeman, John
Bozeman, MT
B/P (blood pressure)
BPD (also bpd)(barrells per day)
BPI (or bpi)(bytes per inch, bits per inch)
BPOE (Benevolent and Protective Order of Elks)
Br (chem. sym., bromine)
Brabant (province, Belgium)
Brabant Copper™ (cookware)
Bracco, Lorraine (ent.; 1955-)
Brace Jovanovich, Inc., Harcourt
Brach & Sons, E. J. (US bus.)
Brach's™ (candy)
Bracken, Eddie (ent.; 1920-)
Bracknell, Lady (fict. chara., *The Importance of Being Earnest*)
Brad Anderson (cartoonist, *Marmaduke*; 1924-)
Brad(ford) Park, (Douglas)(hockey; 1948-)
Bradbury, Ray (US writer/sci fi; 1920-)
Braddock, Edward (Br. gen. in Amer.; 1695-1755)
Bradenton, FL
Bradford Dillman (ent.; 1930-)
Bradford Exchange, Inc.
Bradford, England
Bradford, William (1st gov., Pilgrim colony; 1590-1657)
Bradlee, Ben (US newspaper exec.; 1921-)
Bradley Co., Milton
Bradley, Bill (William Warren)(US cong./ basketball; 1943-)
Bradley, Ed (US TV jour.; 1941-)

Bradley™, Milton-
Bradley, Omar Nelson (US gen.; 1893-1981)
Bradley, Tom (ex-mayor, Los Angeles, CA; 1917-)
Bradley, Truman
Bradshaw, Terry (football; 1948-)
Bradstreet Corp., Dun &
Bradstreet, Anne Dudley (US poet, c1612-72)
Brady Bill (gun control; 1993)
Brady Bunch (TV show)
Brady, James B. ("Diamond Jim")(US finan.; 1856-1917)
Brady, Mathew B. (US photo.; 1823?-96)
Braganza, Catherine of (Br. queen of Charles II; 1638-1705)
Bragg, Fort, NC (mil.)
Bragg, Sir William Henry (Br. physt.; 1862-1942)
Bragg, Sir William Lawrence (Br. physt.; 1890-1971)
Brahma (also Brahman)(cattle)
Brahma (chicken)
Brahma (rel.)
Brahman (also Brahmin)(rel.)
Brahmanism (rel.)
Brahmaputra River (Asia)
Brahms, Johannes (Ger. comp.; 1833-97)
Brahui (lang.)
Braila, Romania
Braille (writing system for the blind)
Braille Institute (Los Angeles)
Braille, Louis (Fr., blind inv. of Braille; 1809-52)
Brain Trust (FDR's advisers)
Braithwaite, Nicholas (PM, Grenada; 1925-)
Bram (Abraham) Stoker (Br. writer; 1847-1912)
Brampton, Ontario, Canada
Brancacci Chapel (Italy)
Branch Davidians (rel. cult)
Branch Rickey, (Wesley)(baseball; 1881-1965)
Brancusi, Constantin (Romanian artist; 1876-1957)
Brand, Vance (astro.; 1931-)
Brandauer, Klaus Maria (ent.)
Brandeis, Louis (Dembitz)(US jurist; 1856-1941)
Brandenburg (state, Ger.)
Brandenburg Concerto (by Johann Sebastian Bach)
Brandenburg Gate
Brandenburg, Germany
Brando, Marlon (ent.; 1924-)
Brandon De Wilde (ent.; 1942-72)
Brandon Tartikoff (ent.; 1949-)
Brandon, Manitoba, Canada
Brandt, Willy (Herbert Ernst Karl Frahm)(ex-chanc., WGer.; 1913-92)
brandy Alexander (also l.c.)(cocktail)

Brandywine, Battle of (US hist.; 1777)
Branestawm, Professor
Branford Marsalis (ent.; 1960-)
Braniff™ Airways
Branigan, Laura (ent.)
Branko Crvenkovski (PM, Macedonia)
Branson, MO
Branstad, Terry E. (IA gov.; 1946-)
Brantford, Ontario, Canada
Braque, Georges (Fr. artist; 1882-1963)
Brasilia, Brazil
Brasov, Romania
Brasselle, Keefe (ent.)
Brasseur, Isabelle (figure skating; 1971-)
Brathwaite, Chris (track; 1949-84)
Bratislava, Czechoslovakia
Brattain, Walter Houser (US physt./inv.; 1902-87)
Brattleboro, VT
Bratwurst (also l.c.)(sausage)
Braun, Carol Moseley- (US cong.; 1947-)
Braun, Eva (mistress of Adolph Hitler; 1910-45)
Braun principle, Le Chatelier- (also Le Chatelier['s] p.)(chem.)
Braun, Werner (or Wernher) von (Ger./US eng.; 1912-77)
Braunschweig, Germany (also Brunswick)
Braunschweiger (also braunschweiger)(sausage)
Braun™
Braun Corp.
Braun, Inc.
Brave New World (A. Huxley novel)
Braves, Atlanta (baseball team)
Bray v. Alexandria Women's Health Clinic (US law; 1993)
Brazauskas, Algirdas (pres., Lith.)
Brazil (Federative Republic of)(SAmer.)
Brazil nut (tree/nut)
Brazzaville, Congo
Brazzi, Rossano (It. ent.; 1916-)
Brea Tar Pits, La (fossils, CA)
Breaker Morant (film; 1979)
Breakfast at Tiffany's (film; 1961)
Breakstone Sugar Creek Foods (US bus.)
Breakstone's™ (dairy prods.)
Bream, Julian (Alexander)(ent.; 1933-)
Breasted, James Henry (US archaeol.; 1865-1935)
Breathalyzer™ (alcohol level)
Breathed, Berke (cartoonist, Bloom County; 1957-)
Breathless Mahoney (fict. chara., Dick Tracy)
Breaux, John B. (US cong.; 1944-)
Brecht v. Abrahamson (US law; 1993)
Brecht, Bertolt (Ger. writer; 1898-1956)
Breckinridge, John C(abell)(ex-US VP/gen; 1821-75)

Breck™ (hair care)
Breck™, Miss (hair care)
Breeders' Cup (racing)
Breed's Hill (Battle of Bunker Hill)(US hist., MA; 1775)
Breen, Bobby (Robert)(ent.)
Bremen (state, Ger.)
Bremen, Germany
Bremerhaven, Germany
Bremerton, WA
Brenda Lee (ent.; 1944-)
Brenda Starr (comic strip)
Brenda Vaccaro (ent.; 1939-)
Brendan Behan (Ir. writer; 1923-64)
Brennan, Eileen (ent.; 1935-)
Brennan, Walter (ent.; 1894-1974)
Brennan, William J(oseph), Jr. (US jurist; 1906-)
Brenner Pass (in Alps, Aus./It.)
Brenner, David (ent.; 1945-)
Brennschluss (astron.)
Brent Musburger (ent.; 1939-)
Brent Scowcroft (US pol.; 1925-)
Brent, George (ent.; 1904-79)
Brentano's Bookstore
Brentwood, CA, MO, PA
Brer Fox (fict. chara., Uncle Remus)
Brer Rabbit (fict. chara., Uncle Remus)
Brer Rabbit™ molasses
Brereton C. Jones (KY gov.; 1939-)
Breslin, Jimmy (US writer; 1930-)
Brest, Belarus
Brest, France
Bret Harte, (Francis)(US writer; 1839-1902)
Bret Maverick (fict chara.; Maverick)
Bret Saberhagen (baseball; 1964-)
Bretagne, France (also Brittany)
Breton (headwear, lace)
Breton (lang.)
Breton, André (Fr. poet; 1896-1966)
Brett Butler (ent.)
Brett Hull (hockey; 1964-)
Brett, George (baseball; 1953-)
Breuer chair (tubular steel)
Breuer, Marcel (US arch.; 1902-81)
Brewer, Teresa (ent.; 1931-)
Brewers, Milwaukee (baseball team)
Brewster chair
Brewster, Punky (fict. chara.)
Brewster, William (Br., Pilgrim leader; 1567-1644)
Breyer, Stephen (US jurist; 1939-)
Breyers™ ice cream
Brezhnev, Leonid Ilyich (ex-pres., USSR; 1906-82)
Brian Aherne (ent.; 1902-86)
Brian Boitano (figure skating)
Brian Bosworth (football)

Brian Dennehy (ent.; 1938-)
Brian De Palma (ent.; 1940)
Brian Donlevy (ent.; 1889-1972)
Brian Epstein (ent.; 1935-67)
Brian Gottfried (tennis; 1952-)
Brian Holland (US comp.; 1941-)
Brian Keith (ent.; 1921-)
Brian Mulroney (ex-PM, Can.; 1939-)
Brian Orser (figure skating)
Brian Spencer (hockey; 1949-88)
Brian Stuart Goodell (swimming; 1959-)
Brian Wilson (ent.; 1942-)
Briand Pact, Kellogg- (also Kellogg Peace Pact)(US/Fr.; 1927)
Briand, Aristide (ex-PM, Fr.; 1862-1932)
Briar Cliff College (IA)
Briard (dog)
Brice, Fanny (b. Fannie Borach)(ent.; 1891-1951)
Brick, NJ
Bride of Frankenstein (film; 1935)
Bride's (mag.)
Bridge of San Luis Rey, The (film; 1944)
Bridge on the River Kwai, The (film; 1957)
Bridgeport Marine Corps Mountain Warfare Training Center (CA)
Bridgeport Post (CT newspaper)
Bridgeport, AL, CT, IL, OH, PA, TX
Bridger-Teton National Forest
Bridges of Madison County, The (R. J. Waller novel)
Bridges, Beau (ent.; 1941-)
Bridges, Harry (Alfred Renton Bridges)(US labor leader; 1901-90)
Bridges, Jeff (ent.; 1949-)
Bridges, Lloyd (ent.; 1913-)
Bridgestone Tire Co. Ltd.
Bridgeton, NJ
Bridgetown, Barbados
Brie (cheese)
Brigadoon (film; 1954)
Brighton Beach Memories (film; 1986)
Brigitte Nielsen (ent.)
Briggs & Stratton™
Briggs & Stratton Corp.
Briggs, Clare (cartoonist, *Mr. & Mrs.*; 1875-1930)
Brigham Young (US rel./Mormon; 1801-77)
Brigham Young University (UT)
Brighton Beach Memoirs (play)
Brighton, CO
Brighton, England
Brighton, Victoria, Australia
Bright's disease
Brigitte Bardot (Fr. ent.; 1934-)
Brillo™ pad
Brill's disease
Brimley, Wilford (ent.; 1934-)

Brindisi, Italy
Brinell hardness test (metal)
Brinell, Johann August (Swed. eng.; 1849-1925)
Bringing Up Father (comic strip)
Brinker, or the Silver Skates, Hans (children's book)
Brinkley, Christie (US model; 1953-)
Brinkley, David (US TV jour.; 1920-)
Brink's armored car
Brisbane, Queensland, Australia
Bristol Bay (AK)
Bristol board (cardboard)
Bristol Channel (Eng.)
Bristol, CT, PA, RI, TN, VA
Bristol, England
Bristol-Myers Squibb Co.
Britain, Battle of (WWII air battle)
Britain, Great (Eng., Scot., and Wales, part of the UK)
Britannia (poetic for Great Britain)
Briticism (also Britishism)(linguistics)
British (people)
British Airways™
British Antarctic Territory
British Broadcasting Corporation (BCC)(TV)
British Columbia (province, Can.)
British East India Company (trade; 1600-1873)
British Empire
British English
British Guiana (now Guyana)
British Honduras (now Belize)
British Indian Ocean Territory
British Hong Kong
British Isles
British Knights™
British Knights (US bus.)
British Museum (London)
British North America Act (Can.; 1867)
British Somaliland (now part of Somalia)
British thermal unit (BTU, B.T.U., Btu, B.t.u.)(physics)
British Virgin Islands (West Indies)
British West Indies
Britisher (also Brit or Briton)(native of Br.)
BritRail Pass
Britt Ekland (Swed./US ent.; 1942-)
Brittany spaniel (dog)
Brittany, Anne of (queen, Fr.; 1477-1514)
Brittany, France
Britten, Benjamin (also Baron Britten of Aldeburgh)(Br. comp.; 1913-76)
Brix scale (chem., sugar content)
Brno, Czechoslovakia
Broadcast Employees and Technicians, National Association of (also NABET)
Broadcasters, National Association of (also NAB)
Broadcasting Company, National (also NBC)

Broad Home Corp., Kaufman and
Broadway (major NYC avenue; theater district, "the Great White Way")
Broadway Danny Rose (film; 1984)
Broadway Joe (aka Joe [Joseph William] Namath)(football; 1943-)
Broadway, Off (also off Broadway)(theater)
Broadway, Off Off (also off off Broadway)(theater)
Brobdingnag (fict. land of giants, *Gulliver's Travels*)
Brock Candy Co.
Brock Peters (ent.; 1927-)
Brock, Lou(is Clark)(baseball; 1939-)
Brocklin, Norm Van (football; 1926-83)
Brockton, MA
Broderick Crawford (ent.; 1911-86)
Broderick, Betty (US news)
Broderick, Matthew (ent.; 1962-)
Brodie, The Prime of Miss Jean (film; 1969)
Brodsky, Joseph (US writer; 1940-)
Broglie, Louis de (Fr. physt.; 1893-1987)
Brokaw, Tom (US TV jour.; 1940-)
Broken Arrow, OK
Brokopondo, Suriname
Brolin, James (ent.; 1940-)
Bromo-Seltzer™ (med.)
Brompton('s) cocktail/mixture (med.)
Bronco Eddie Bauer, Ford (auto.)
Bronco XL, Ford (auto.)
Bronco XLT, Ford (auto.)
Bronco, Ford (auto.)
Broncos, Denver (football team)
Bronica™
Bronica (US bus.)
Bronislaw Malinowski (Pol. anthrop.; 1884-1942)
Bronko (Bronislaw) Nagurski (football; 1908-90)
Bronson Alcott, Amos (US educ./phil.; 1799-1888)
Bronson Pinchot (ent.; 1959-)
Bronson, Charles (ent.; 1922-)
Brontë sisters (Anne, Charlotte, Emily)
Brontë, Anne (aka Acton Bell)(Br. writer; 1820-49)
Brontë, Charlotte (aka Currer Bell)(Br. writer; 1816-55)
Brontë, Emily (aka Ellis Bell)(Br. writer; 1818-48)
Bronx (borough, NYC)
Bronx cheer (also raspberry)
Bronx cocktail (mixed drink)
Bronx Zoo (NYC)
Bronze Age (anthrop.)
Bronze Star Medal (Bronze Star)
Brook Farm (MA community; 1841-47)
Brooke Shields (ent.; 1965-)
Brooke, Edward William (US pol.; 1919-)

Brooke, Rupert (Br. poet; 1887-1915)
Brookhaven National Laboratory (atomic energy, Long Island NY)
Brookings Institution (econ. org.; DC)
Brookline, MA
Brooklyn (borough, NYC)
Brooklyn Bridge (NYC)
Brooklyn Coast Guard Air Station
Brooklyn, NY, OH
Brooks Adams (US hist.; 1848-1927)
Brooks Atkinson (Justin)(US critic; 1894-1984)
Brooks Brothers
Brooks Robinson (baseball; 1937-)
Brooks, Albert (ent.; 1947-)
Brooks, Avery (ent.)
Brooks, Garth (ent.; 1956-)
Brooks, Gwendolyn (US writer; 1917-)
Brooks, Mel (b. Melvin Kaminsky)(ent.; 1926-)
Brooks, Van Wyck (US hist.; 1886-1963)
Broom Hilda (comic strip)
Broonzy, Big Bill (US jazz; 1893-1958)
Brosnan, Pierce (ent.; 1953-)
Brotherly Love, City of (Philadelphia)
Brothers Grimm (wrote/collected folk tales)
Brothers Karamazov, The (Dostoevsky novel)
Brothers, Dr. Joyce (US psych.; 1928-)
Brothers, Marx (Chico, Harpo, Groucho, Gummo, Zeppo)
Brothers, The Mills (pop music)
Brougham™, Cadillac (auto.)
Brougham™, Cadillac Fleetwood™ (auto.)
Brown & Co., Inc., Little,
Brown & Williamson Tobacco Corp.
Brown Apparel, Inc., Buster
Brown Group, Inc.
Brown Swiss (cattle)
Brown v. Board of Education of Topeka, Kansas (US law; 1954)
Brown, Blair (ent.; 1948-)
Brown, Buster (cartoon chara.)
Brown, Buster (shoes, collar)
Brown, Charlie (fict. chara., *Peanuts*)
Brown, Christy (Ir. writer/artist; 1932-81)
Brown, Clifford (US jazz; 1930-56)
Brown, Edmund Gerald "Jerry," Jr. (ex-gov., CA; 1938-)
Brown, Edmund Gerald "Pat", Sr. (ex-gov., CA; 1905-)
Brown, Ford Madox (Br. artist; 1821-93)
Brown, Hank (US cong.; 1940-)
Brown, Helen Gurley (US editor/writer; 1922-)
Brown, James (ent.; 1928-)
Brown, Jesse (US Secy./Veteran Affairs; 1944-)
Brown, Jimmy (James Nathaniel)(football/ent.; 1936-)
Brown, Joe E. (ent.; 1892-1973)
Brown, John (US abolitionist; 1800-59)
Brown, Larry (football; 1947-)

Brown, Lee P. (Dir./Ofc. Drug Control; 1937-)
Brown, Les (ent.; 1912-)
Brown, Murphy (fict. chara.)
Brown, Murphy (TV show)
Brown, Nacio Herb (US comp.; 1896-1964)
Brown, Pat (Edmund Gerald), Sr. (ex-gov., CA; 1905-)
Brown, Paul (football coach; 1908-91)
Brown, Rap (b. Hubert Gerald Brown)(US activist; 1943-)
Brown, Ray (US jazz; 1926-)
Brown, Robert (Scot. botanist; 1773-1858)
Brown, Ron(ald Harmon)(US Secy./Commerce; 1941-)
Browne belt, Sam (mil. sword belt)
Browne, Dik (cartoonist, *Hi & Lois, Hagar the Horrible*; 1917-89)
Browne, Jackson (ent.)
Browne, Roscoe Lee (ent.; 1925-)
Browner, Carol M. (Head/EPA; 1955-)
brown-eyed Susan (plant)
Brown-Forman, Inc.
Brownian movement/motion (particles in fluid)
Brownie points
Browning automatic rifle/machine gun
Browning, Elizabeth Barrett (Br. poet, wife of Robert; 1806-61)
Browning, John M(oses)(US inv.; 1955-1926)
Browning, Kurt (figure skating; 1967-)
Browning, Robert (Br. poet, husband of Elizabeth; 1812-89)
Browns Ferry (nuclear power station, AL)
Browns, Cleveland (football team)
Brownsville, FL, PA, TN, TX
Broyhill™
Broyhill Furniture Industries, Inc.
Brubaker (film; 1980)
Brubeck, Dave (David Warren)(US jazz; 1920-)
Bruce Boxleitner (ent.; 1950-)
Bruce Dern (ent.; 1936-)
Bruce E. Babbitt (US Secy./Interior; 1938-)
Bruce Furniss (swimming; 1957-)
Bruce G. Sundlun (RI gov.; 1920-)
Bruce Jenner (US track/TV jour.; 1949-)
Bruce King (NM gov.; 1924-)
Bruce Lee (ent./martial arts; 1940-73)
Bruce Springsteen (ent.; 1949-)
Bruce Wayne (ent.)
Bruce Weitz (ent.; 1943-)
Bruce Willis (ent.; 1955-)
Bruce Winery, David (US bus.)
Bruce, Lenny (ent.; 1926-66)
Bruce, Nigel (ent.; 1895-1953)
Brücke, die (Ger. art movement)
Bruckner, Anton (Austl. comp.; 1824-96)
Brudenell, James Thomas (7th Earl of Cardigan)(Br. mil./pol., cardigan sweater; 1797-1868)

Brueghel, Jan (also Breughel)(aka the "Velvet Bruegel")(Flem. artist; 1568-1625)
Brueghel, Pieter, the Elder (also Breughel)(aka "Peasant Bruegel")(Flem. artist; 1525-69)
Brueghel, Pieter, the Younger (also Breughel)(aka "Hell Bruegel")(Flem. artist; 1564-1638)
Bruges, Belgium
Bruhl, Lucien Lévy- (Fr. phil.; 1857-1939)
Bruins, Boston (hockey team)
Brumel, Valeri (jumper; 1942-)
Brummell Ties, Beau (US bus.)
Brummell, Beau (George Bryan)(Br. dandy; 1778-1840)
Brummell, Beau (film; 1954)
Brundtland, Gro Harlem (PM, Nor.; 1939-)
Brunei (State of)(also Brunei Darussalam)(NW Borneo)
Brunei, Sultan of (Muda Hassanal Bolkiah Mu'izzaddin Waddaulah)
Brunelleschi, Filippo (It. arch.; 1377-1446)
Brunhart, Hans (premier, Liechtenstein)
Brunner, Emil (Swed. rel.; 1889-1966)
Bruno Bettelheim (Aus./US psych.; 1903-90)
Bruno Kirby (ent.; 1949-)
Bruno, Giordano (It. phil.; 1548-1600)
Brunswick black (color, varnish)
Brunswick Corp.
Brunswick green (color)
Brunswick Naval Air Station (ME)
Brunswick stew
Brunswick, Caroline of (Br. queen of George IV; 1768-1821)
Brunswick, GA, ME, MD, OH
Brunswick, Germany
Brussels carpet
Brussels griffon (dog)
Brussels lace
Brussels sprout(s)(vegetable)
Brussels, Belgium
Brut™, Fabergé (cologne)
Brut 33™ (cologne)
Brutus, Marcus Junius (Roman pol., Caesar assassin; c78-42 BC)
Bryan Adams (ent.; 1959-)
Bryan Trottier (hockey; 1956-)
Bryan, OH, TX
Bryan, Richard H. (US cong.; 1937-)
Bryan, William Jennings (US pol./orator; 1860-1925)
Bryant Gumbel (US TV jour.; 1948-)
Bryant, Bear (Paul)(football coach; 1913-83)
Bryant, Inc., Lane
Bryant, Rosalyn Evette (track; 1956-)
Bryant, William Cullen (US poet/jour.; 1794-1878)
Bryce Canyon National Park (UT)
Brylcreem™ (hair care)

Bryn Mawr College (PA)
Bryn Mawr, PA
Brynmawr, Wales
Brynner, Yul (ent.; 1915-85)
Bryophyta (plant classification)
Bryson, Peabo (ent.)
B school (business school)
BS (Bachelor of Science)
BSA (Boy Scouts of America)
B-side (music)
BTU (also BTU, Btu, B.t.u.)(Br. thermal unit)
Bubba (Charles Aaron) Smith (football; 1945-)
Bubble Yum™ (gum)
Bubble™, Mr. (bubble bath)
Buber, Martin (Isr. phil.; 1878-1965)
Bubi (lang./people)
Bucaramanga, Columbia
Buccaneers, Tampa Bay (football team)
Bucephalus (war horse of Alexander the Great)
Buchanan, James (15th US pres.; 1791-1868)
Buchanan, Liberia
Buchanan, Patrick J. (US pol. commentator; 1938-)
Bucharest, Romania
Buchenwald (Ger. concentration camp)
Bucher, Lloyd M., Commander (US mil.)
Buchner funnel (chem.)
Buchner, Eduard (Ger. chem.; 1860-1917)
Buchwald, Art (US columnist; 1925-)
Buck Clayton (US jazz; 1911-)
Buck Owens (ent.; 1929-)
Buck Rogers (fict. chara.)
Buck Rogers in the 21st Century (film; 1979)
Buck, Pearl S(ydenstricker)(US writer; 1892-1973)
Buckaroo Banzai (fict. chara.)
Bucket, Charlie
Buckeye State (nickname, OH)
Buckingham Palace (London, home of royal family)
Buckingham, England
Buckingham, Quebec, Canada
Buckinghamshire (county, Eng.)
Buckley v. Fitzsimmons (US law; 1993)
Buckley, Betty (ent.; 1947-)
Buckley, William F., Jr. (US editor/writer; 1925-)
Bucknell University (PA)
Bucks County Courier-Times (PA newspaper)
Bucks, Milwaukee (basketball team)
Bud Abbott (ent.; 1895-1974)
Bud Collyer
Bud Fisher (cartoonist, *Mutt & Jeff*; 1884-1954)
Bud Powell (US jazz; 1924-66)
Bud Wilkinson (football; 1916-)
Bud Yorkin (ent.)
Budapest, Hungary
Budd, Billy (H. Melville story)

Budd, Zola (SAfr. athlete; 1966-)
Buddha (Gautama Siddhartha)(Indian phil., founded Buddhism; c563-c483 BC)
Buddhism (rel.)
Buddhism, Lama(istic)(rel.)
Buddhism, Mahayana (rel.)
Buddhism, Theravada (rel.)
Buddhism, Tibetan
Buddhism, Zen (rel.)
Buddhist (rel.)
Buddig & Co., Carl
Buddig™, Carl (meats)
Buddy Bolden, (Charles)(US jazz; 1868-1931)
Buddy De Franco (US jazz; 1933-)
Buddy De Sylva (US lyricist; 1895-1950)
Buddy Ebsen (ent.; 1908-)
Buddy Hackett (ent.; 1924-)
Buddy Holly (ent.; 1936-59)
Buddy Holly and the Crickets (pop music)
Buddy Rich (US jazz; 1917-87)
Budge, Don (tennis; 1915-)
Budget™
Budget Rent A Car Corp.
Budgetel Inns (US bus.)
Budweiser™ (beer)
Buehler Vineyards (US bus.)
Buena Park, CA
Buena Vista Pictures
Buena Vista Winery (US bus.)
Buenadventura, Colombia
Bueno, Maria (tennis; 1939-)
Buenos Aires, Argentina
Buf-Puf™
Buff (goose)
Buffalo Bill (William Frederick) Cody (US scout/ent.; 1846-1917)
Buffalo Bills (football team)
Buffalo Bob Smith (ent.; 1917-)
Buffalo China (chinaware)
Buffalo News (NY newspaper)
Buffalo Sabres (hockey team)
Buffalo Spree Magazine
Buffalo Springfield (pop music)
Buffalo, NY
Bufferin™ (med.)
Buffett, Jimmy (ent.)
Bugatti (auto.)
Bugatti EB110 (auto.)
Bugatti, Ettore (It. designer; 1881-1947)
Bugatti, Jean (It. designer; 1909-39)
Bugis (lang.)
Bugs Bunny (cartoon chara.)
Bugs Bunny & Looney Tunes Magazine (mag.)
Bugs (George) Moran (US gangster)
Bugsy Malone Story, The (film; 1976)
Bugsy (Benjamin) Siegel
Buick™ (auto.)
Buick™ Century (auto.)

Buick™ LeSabre (auto.)
Buick™ Park Avenue (auto.)
Buick™ Reatta (auto.)
Buick Riviera™ (auto.)
Buick™ Skylark (auto.)
Buick Starfire™ (auto.)
Buick, David Dunbar (US bus./auto.; 1854-1929)
Building Design Journal (mag.)
Buji (lang.)
Bujold, Genevieve (ent.; 1942-)
Bujumbura, Burundi
Bukavu, Zaire
Bukhara, Uzbekistan
Bukharin, Nikolai (USSR pol.; 1888-1938)
Bulawayo, Zimbabwe
Bulfinch, Charles (US arch.; 1763-1844)
Bulfinch's Mythology
Bulgakov, Mikhail (Rus. writer; 1891-1940)
Bulganin, Nikolai A(leksandrovich)(ex-PM USSR; 1895-1975)
Bulgaria (Republic of)(SE Eur.)
Bulgarian (lang./people)
Bulgarian Orthodox (rel.)
Bulge, Battle of the (WWII; 1944-45)
Bull Frog™ (healthcare)
Bull Moose Party (US pol.; 1912-17)
Bull Run, Battle(s) of (US hist.; 1861 & 1862)
Bull, John (Br. comp.; 1562-1628)
Bull, John (pamphlets)(Br. hist.; 1712)
Bull, John (synonym for Eng. people)
Bullets, Washington (basketball team)
Bullion State (nickname, MO)
Bullitt, William C. (US dipl.; 1891-1967)
Bullock's (US bus.)
Bulls, Chicago (basketball team)
Bullwinkle (cartoon)
Bully Hill (US bus.)
Bulova Corp.
Bülow, Bernhard von, Prince (ex-chanc., Ger.; 1849-1929)
Bulow, Claus von (US news)
Bulow, Sunny (Martha) von (US news)
Bumble Bee™
Bumble Bee Seafoods (US bus.)
Bumbry, Grace (ent.; 1937-)
Bumpers, Dale (US cong.; 1925-)
Bumstead, Blondie (cartoon chara.)
Bumstead, Dagwood (cartoon chara.)
Bunche, Ralph J. (US dipl.; 1904-71)
Bundesrat (Ger. govt.)
Bundt™ (pan)
Bundy, Ted (US serial killer; ?-1989)
Bunk Johnson (US jazz; 1879-1949)
Bunker Hill (Boston, MA)
Bunker Hill, Battle of (Breed's Hill)(US hist., MA; 1775)
Bunker, Archie (fict. chara., *All in the Family*)

Bunny Berigan (US jazz; 1909-42)
Bunny Lake is Missing (film; 1965)
Bunny, Bugs (cartoon chara.)
Bunsen burner (chem.)
Bunsen, Robert W. (Ger. chem./inv., Bunsen burner; 1811-99)
Bunshaft, Gordon (US arch.; 1909-90)
Bunyan, John (Br. writer/rel.; 1628-88)
Bunyan, Paul (& Babe the Blue Ox)(fict. lumberjack)
Buonarroti, Michelangelo (It. artist/poet; 1475-1564)
Burbage, Richard (Br. Shakespearean actor; 1567-1619)
Burbank, CA
Burbank, Luther (US horticulturist; 1849-1926)
Burberry™ (raincoat)
Bureau of Customs and Excise (Br.)
Bureau of Indian Affairs (BIA)(US govt. agcy.; est. 1849)
Bureau of Standards, National (NBS)(US govt. agcy.; est. 1901)
Buren, Abigail Van (Dear Abby)(b. Pauline Esther Friedman)(US advice columnist; 1918-)
Buren, Martin Van (8th US pres.; 1782-1862)
Burgas, Bulgaria
Burger King™
Burger King Corp.
Burger, Warren Earl (US jurist; 1907-)
Burgess Meredith (ent.; 1908-)
Burgess Shale Site (fossils, Can.)
Burgess, Anthony (Br. writer/comp.; 1917-1993)
Burghers of Calais (by Rodin)
Burghoff, Gary (ent.; 1940-)
Burgoyne, John (Br. gen./writer; 1722-92)
Burgundy (Fr. wine region)
Burgundy (region, Fr., now Bourgogne)
Burgundy, Mary of (heiress of Charles the Bold; 1457-82)
Burhanuddin Rabbani (pres., Afghan.; 1940-)
Burke, Billie (ent.; 1885-1970)
Burke, Delta (ent.; 1956-)
Burke, Edmund (Ir./Br. pol.; 1729-97)
Burke, Johnny (US lyricist; 1908-84)
Burke, Martha Jane (Calamity Jane)(US frontier; c1852-1903)
Burkina Faso (People's Democratic Republic of)(formerly Upper Volta)(W Afr.)
Burkitt, Denis (Br. phys./rel.; 1911-93)
Burkitt's lymphoma (med.)
Burl Ives (Icle Ivanhoe)(ent.; 1909-)
Burlington Coat Factory Warehouse Corp.
Burlington Free Press
Burlington Industries, Inc.
Burlington, IA, MA, NC, NJ, VT, WI
Burlington, Ontario, Canada
Burma (now Myanmar)

Burma Road (Ch.)
Burma Shave signs
Burman (people)
Burmese (cat)
Burmese (lang./people)
Burnaby, British Columbia, Canada
Burne Hogarth (cartoonist, *Tarzan*; 1911-)
Burne-Jones, Edward (Br. artist; 1833-98)
Burnett, Carol (ent.; 1933-)
Burnham Lambert, Drexel (US stock market scandal)
Burnham, Daniel H. (US arch.; 1846-1912)
Burns, Conrad (US cong.; 1935-)
Burns, George (b. Nathan Birnbaum)(ent.; 1896-)
Burns, Robert (Scot. poet; 1759-96)
Burnside, Ambrose Everett (US gen.; 1824-81)
Burpee™ (seeds/plants)
Burpee Co., W. Atlee
Burpee, David (US horticulturist; 1893-1980)
Burr, Aaron (ex-US VP; 1756-1836)
Burr, Raymond (ent.; 1917-93)
Burroughs Corp.
Burroughs, Edgar Rice (US writer; 1875-1950)
Burrows, Abe (US writer; 1910-85)
Burrows, Darren E. (ent.; 1966-)
Burrud, Bill (ent.; 1925-90)
Bursa, Turkey
Burstyn, Ellen (ent.; 1932-)
Burt Bacharach (US comp.; 1928-)
Burt(on Stephen) Lancaster (ent.; 1913-)
Burt Reynolds (ent.; 1936-)
Burt Wolf (US chef/writer)
Burt Young (ent.; 1940-)
Burton Lane (US comp.; 1912-)
Burton, LeVar (or Levar)(ent.; 1957-)
Burton, Michael (swimming; 1947-)
Burton, Richard (b. Richard Walter Jenkins)(ent.; 1925-84)
Burton, Sir Richard Francis (Br. expl.; 1821-90)
Burundi (Republic of)(central Afr.)
Bururi, Burundi
Busby Berkeley (ent.; 1895-1976)
Buscaglia, Leo F.
Busch™ (beer)
Busch, Adolphus (US bus.; 1839-1913)
Busch, August Anheuser, Jr. (US bus.; 1899-1989)
Busch, Inc., Anheuser-
Busey, Gary (ent.; 1944-)
Busfield, Timothy (ent.; 1957-)
Bush, Barbara (Pierce)(wife of ex-US pres.; 1925-)
Bush, George Herbert Walker (41st US pres.; 1924-)
Bush, Vannevar (US eng.; 1890-1974)
Bushman, Francis X. (ent.; 1883-1966)
Bushmiller, Ernie (cartoonist, *Nancy*; 1905-82)

Bushnell™
Bushnell Associates (US bus.)
Busignani, Patricia (captain-regent; San Marino)
Business Administration, Small (SBA)(US govt. agcy.; est. 1953)
Business Week (mag.)
Busoni, Ferruccio (It. comp.; 1866-1924)
Buspar™ (med.)
Bustamante, Alfonso (PM, Peru)
Buster Brown (cartoon chara.)
Buster Brown (shoes, collar)
Buster Brown Apparel, Inc.
Buster Crabbe (ent./swimmer; 1908-83)
Buster (Joseph Frank) Keaton (ent.; 1895-1966)
Buster Poindexter (ent.)
Butisol Sodium™ (med.)
Butare, Rwanda
Butch and Sundance: The Early Days (film; 1979)
Butch Cassidy and the Sundance Kid (film; 1969)
Butchart Gardens (Can.)
Butcher's Blend™ (dog food)
Butkus, Dick (Richard Marvin)(football/ent.; 1942-)
Butler™ (health)
Butler Derrick (US cong.; 1936-)
Butler, Brett (ent.)
Butler, Nicholas Murray (US educ.; 1862-1947)
Butler, Rhett (fict. chara., *Gone With the Wind*)
Butler, Samuel (Br. writer; 1835-1902)
Butler, U.S. v. (US law; 1936)
Buttafuoco, Joey (US news)
Butte, MT
Butterfield & Butterfield
Butterfinger™ (candy)
Butterflies Are Free (play/film)
Butterfly McQueen (ent.; 1911-)
Butterick Co., The
Butterick patterns
Butterick, Ebenezer (US inv./tailor; 1826-1903)
Butterworth's™, Mrs.
Butt-Head, Beavis and (TV show)
Button, Dick (Richard)(figure skating/ent.; 1929-)
Buttons, Red (ent.; 1919-)
Buttram, Pat (ent.)
Buxtehude, Dietrich (Dan. comp.; 1637-1707)
Buyoya, Pierre, Maj. (ex-pres., Burundi; 1949?-)
Buzz Aldrin (Edwin Eugene, Jr)(astro.; 1930-)
Buzzards Bay, MA (also Buzzard's Bay)
Buzzi, Ruth (ent.; 1936-)
BVD™
B.V.D. Co., Inc., The
BVM (Blessed Virgin Mary)
BX (base exchange)
Byambasuren, Dashiyn (ex-PM, Mongolia)

Proper Noun Speller

Byas, Don (US jazz; 1912-72)
Bydgoszcz, Poland
Byelorussia (also Belorussia)(former USSR
   republic)
Byelorussian (lang./people)
Byington, Spring (ent.; 1893-1971)
Bykovsky, Valéry F. (cosmo.; 1934-)
Bynum Winery, Davis (US bus.)
BYO (bring your own)
Byrd, Richard E., Adm. (US expl.; 1888-1957)
Byrd, Robert Carlyle (US cong.; 1917-)
Byrd, William (Br. comp.; 1543-1623)
Byrds, the (pop music)
Byrnes, Edd "Kookie" (ent.)
Byron Leslie Dorgan (US cong.; 1942-)
Byron Nelson (golf; 1911-)
Byron R(aymond) White ("Whizzer")(US jurist;
   1917-)
Byron, Augusta Ada (Lady Lovelace)(Br. math./
   inv., compu.; 1815-52)
Byron, George Gordon, Lord (Br. poet; 1788-
   1824)
Byronic (literature)
Byte (mag.)
Byzantine (style, arch./art/music)
Byzantine Church (also Orthodox Church)(rel.)
Byzantine Empire (390-1453)
Byzantium (later called Constantinople, now
   Istanbul)

C

C (chem. sym., carbon)
CA (California)
Ca (chem. sym., calcium)
Caaguazú, Paraguay
Caan, James (ent.; 1939-)
CAB (Civil Aeronautics Board)(US govt.)
Cab Calloway (ent.; 1907-)
Cabaret (play; film, 1972)
Cabbage Patch dolls
Cabell, James Laurence (US phys.; 1813-89)
Cabernet Sauvignon (grape, wine)
Cable News Network (CNN)(cable TV)
Cabot Lodge, Henry (US pol.; 1850-1924)
Cabot Lodge, Henry, Jr. (US jour./pol.; 1902-85)
Cabot, John (also Giovanni Caboto)(It. nav.;
   1450-98)ø
Cabot, Sebastian (ent.; 1918-77)
Cabot, Sebastian (It. nav./expl.; 1474-1557)
Caboto, Giovanni (also John Cabot)(It. nav.;
   1450-98)
Cabrini, Mother (also St. Frances Xavier
   Cabrini)(US rel./reformer; 1850-1917)
Cabrio™, Volkswagen (auto.)ø
Cabriolet, Audi™ (auto.)
Caciocavallo (cheese)
CACM (Central American Common Market)
Cactus Flower (play/film)
CAD (computer-aided design)
Cadbury™ (candy)
Cadbury Corp., Peter Paul
Caddo (NAmer. Indians)
Caddylak Systems, Inc.
Cadillac™ (auto.)
Cadillac™ Allante (auto.)
Cadillac Brougham™ (auto.)
Cadillac de Ville™ (auto.)
Cadillac™ Eldorado (auto.)
Cadillac Fleetwood™ (auto.)
Cadillac Fleetwood™ Brougham™ (auto.)
Cadillac™ Seville (auto.)
Cadillac, Antoine (founded Detroit; 1658-1730)
Cádiz, Spain
Caelum (astron., chisel)
Caenozoic era (also Cenozoic)(65 million years
   ago to present)
Caerphilly (cheese)
Caesar Augustus (aka Gaius Julius Caesar
   Octavius)(1st Roman emp.; 63 BC-AD 14)
Caesar salad
Caesar, Gaius (aka Caligula)(Roman emp.; AD
   12-41)
Caesar, Germanicus (Roman gen.; 15 BC-AD
   19)
Caesar, Julius (Gaius Julius)(Roman gen.; 100-

44 BC)
Caesar, Julius (Shakespeare play)
Caesar, Sid (ent.; 1922-)
Caesar's Palace (Las Vegas NV hotel/casino)
Caesar's World, Inc.
Cage aux Folles, La (play; film, 1978)
Cage aux Folles II, La (film; 1981)
Cage aux Folles 3: The Wedding, La (film; 1986)
Cage, John (Milton)(US comp.; 1912-92)
Cage, Nicholas (ent.; 1964-)
Cagney & Lacey (TV show)
Cagney, James (ent.; 1899-1986)
Cahn, Sammy (b. Samuel Cohen)(US lyricist;
   1913-93)
Caicos Islands, Turks and (Br. West Indies)
Cain (1st son of Adam and Eve, murdered Abel)
Cain, James M(allahan)(US writer; 1892-1977)
Caine Mutiny, The (H. Wouk novel)
Caine, Michael (ent.; 1933-)
Cairns, Queensland, Australia
Cairo Museum
Cairo, Egypt
Cairo, The Purple Rose of (film; 1985)
Caius (also Gaius)(Roman jurist; 2nd c. AD)
Caius, St. (also Gaius)(pope; ?-296)
Cajun (people)
Cajun music
Cakebread Cellars (US bus.)
Cal(eb) Yarborough, (William)(auto racing;
   1939-)
Calabar, Nigeria
Caladryl™ (med.)
Calafia Winer (US bus.)
Calais, France
Calais, Oldsmobile (auto.)
Calamity Jane (aka Martha Jane Burke)(US
   frontier; c1852-1903)
Calan™ (med.)
Calcutta!, Oh! (play)
Calcutta, India
Caldecott Medal/Award (children's lit.)
Caldecott, Randolph (Br. artist; 1846-86)
Calder, Alexander (US sculptor; 1898-1976)
Calderón Fournier, Rafael Angel (pres., Costa
   Rica; 1949-)
Calderón Guardia, Rafael Angel (ex-pres., Costa
   Rica; 1900-71)
Calderon Sol, Armando (pres., El Salvador;
   1948-)
Caldwell, Erskine (US writer; 1903-87)
Caldwell, Sarah (ent.; 1924-)
Caledonia (type style)
Calgary Flames (hockey team)
Calgary, Alberta, Canada
Calgon™ water softener
Calhern, Louis (ent.; 1895-1956)
Calhoun, John C. (ex-US VP; 1782-1850)
Calhoun, Rory (ent.; 1923-)

Cali, Colombia
Caliban (fict. chara., *Tempest*)
California (CA)
California Angels (baseball team)
California condor (bird)
California current (cold ocean current)
California Raisin Bowl (college football)
California sunshine (slang, LSD)
California v. Acevedo (US law; 1991)
California, Gulf of (CA/Mex.)
California, Whitney v. (US law; 1927)
Californian, Bakersfield (CA newspaper)
Caligula (aka Gaius Caesar)(Roman emp.; 12-
    41 AD)
Calisher, Hortense (US writer; 1911-)
Callaghan, James (ex-PM, Br.; 1912-)
Callao, Peru
Callas, Charlie (ent)
Callas, Maria (ent.; 1923-77)
Callaway™
Callaway Carpets (US bus.)
Callaway Vineyard & Winery (US bus.)
Callejas, Rafael Leonardo (pres., Honduras;
    1943-)
Caller-Times, Corpus Christi (TX newspaper)
Caller, Corpus Christi (TX newspaper)
Callicrates (Gr. arch.; 5th c. BC)
Callimachus (Gr. poet; c305-240 BC)
Calliope (myth.)
Callisto (myth.; Jupiter moon)
Callot, Jacques (Fr. engraver; 1592?-1635)
Calloway, Cab (ent.; 1907-)
Calphalon™ (cookware)
Calpurnia (Caesar's 3rd wife; 1st c. BC)
Calvados (liqueur)(also l.c.)
Calvary (rel.)
Calvert, Sir George (aka Lord
    Baltimore)(founded MD; 1606-75)
Calvin and Hobbes (comic strip)
Calvin Coolidge (30th US pres.; 1872-1933)
Calvin cycle (photosynthesis)
Calvin Klein™
Calvin Klein (US designer; 1942-)
Calvin Klein Cosmetics Corp.
Calvin Klein, Ltd.
Calvin Murphy (basketball; 1948-)
Calvin Peete (golf; 1943-)
Calvin Trillin (US writer; 1935-)
Calvin, John (Fr. rel.; 1509-64)
Calvinism (rel.)
Calypso (J. Cousteau's ship)
Calypso (myth., sea nymph)
CAM (computer-aided manufacturing)
Cam red (red, Cambodian marijuana)
Camaguey, Cuba
Camero™, Chevrolet (auto.)
Camaro Z28™, Chevrolet (auto.)
Cambodia (State of)(SE Asia)

Cambodian (people)
Cambrai, Battle(s) of (WWI; 1917)
Cambrai, Treaty of (Rome/Fr.; 1529)
Cambrian period (570-500 million years ago)
Cambridge Platform (MA rel. statement; 1648)
Cambridge University (Eng.)
Cambridge, England
Cambridge, Godfrey (ent.; 1933-76)
Cambridge, MA, MD, OH
Camden Courier-Post (NJ newspaper)
Camden, AR, ME, NJ, SC
Camelopardalis (astron., giraffe)
Camelot (film; 1967)
Camelot (King Arthur's utopia)
Camembert cheese
Cameron Mitchell (ent.; 1918-)
Cameron, Candace (ent.)
Cameron, Kirk (ent.; 1970-)
Cameroon (Republic of)((W Afr.)
Camilla Parker-Bowles (Br. news)
Camille (Dumas novel)
Camille Flammarion (Fr. astron.; 1842-1925)
Camille Guérin (Fr. bacteriol.; 1872-1961)
Camille (Jacob) Pissarro (Fr. artist; 1830-1903)
Camille Saint-Saëns (Charles)(Fr. comp.; 1835-
    1921)
Camillo Benso Cavour (It. pol.; 1810-61)
Camillo Golgi (It. biol.; 1843-1926)
Camp Butler Marine Corps Base (Okinawa)
Camp David Accords/Agreements (Isr./Eg., Isr./
    Palestine)
Camp David, MD (official country home of US
    pres.)
Camp Fire members (formerly Camp Fire girls)
Camp Lejeune Marine Corps Base (NC)
Camp Pendleton Marine Corps Base (CA)
Camp Sea Food Co., Inc., Van
Camp, Rosemary De (ent.; 1910-)
Camp, Walter (football; 1859-1925)
Campaign of Vicksburg (US hist.; 1862-63)
Campanella, Joseph (ent.; 1927-)
Campanella, Roy (baseball; 1921-93)
Campari U.S.A., Inc.
Campbell Conference (hockey)
Campbell Soup Co.
Campbell, Ben Nighthorse (US cong.; 1933-)
Campbell, Carroll A., Jr. (SC gov.; 1940-)
Campbell, Earl (football; 1955-)
Campbell, Glen (ent.; 1936-)
Campbell, John D. S. (Duke of Argyll)(ex-gov/
    gen, Can.; 1845-1914)
Campbell, Joseph (US mythologist/folklorist;
    1904-87)
Campbell, Khaki (duck)
Campbell, Kim (ex-PM, Can.)
Campbell, Patrick, Mrs. (aka Beatrice Tanner)
    (ent.; 1865-1940)
Campbell's™

Campeador, el (also El Cid, Rodrigo Diaz de
    Bivar)(Sp. mil.; 1040-99)
Campeche, Mexico
Campho-Phenique™ (med.)
Campine (chicken)
Camry, Toyota (auto.)
Camry DX, Toyota (auto.)
Camry LE, Toyota (auto.)
Camry SE, Toyota (auto.)
Camry Wagon, Toyota (auto.)
Camry XLE, Toyota (auto.)
Camus, Albert (Fr. writer; 1913-60)
Canaan, Promised Land of (rel.)
Canada
Canada Company (for colonization of S. Can.;
    org. 1825)
Canada Day (formerly Dominion Day)
Canada Dry™ (soft drink)
Canada First movement
Canada goose
Canada jay
Canada lily
Canada lynx
Canada mayflower
Canada thistle (plant)
Canadian (or Laurentian) Plateau/Shield (also
    Precambrian Shield)(Can.)
Canadian (people)
Canadian Airlines
Canadian bacon
Canadian Broadcasting Corp. (CBC)
Canadian English
Canadian Football League (CFL)
Canadian French
Canadian Press (Can. news org.)
Canadian Shield (also Laurentian Plateau)
Canadian whiskey
Canadiens, Montreal (hockey team)
Canal Zone, Panama (CAmer.)
Canaletto (b. Giovanni Antonio Canale)(It.
    artist; 1697-1768)
Canary Island ivy (also Algerian ivy)(plant)
Canary Islands (also Canaries)(NW coast of
    Afr.)
Canaveral, Cape (FL)(Kennedy Space Center)
Canberra, Australia
Cancer (zodiac, astron., crab)
Cancer, Tropic of (H. Miller novel)
Cancer, tropic of (23°27' N of equator)
Cancun, Mexico
Candice Bergen (ent.; 1946-)
Candid Camera (TV show)
Candida (G. B. Shaw comedy)
Candida (genus)
Candida albicans (med.)
Candide (Voltaire satire)
Candido Jacuzzi (It./US eng./inv.; 1903-86)
Candie's™

Candie's Socks (US bus.)
Candlemas (also Candlemas Day)(rel.)
Candler, Asa (U.S., founded Coca-Cola Co.;
    1851-1929)
Candlestick Park (San Francisco, CA)
C & R Clothiers, Inc.
C & W (country & western)
Candy, John (ent.; 1950-94)
Canes Venatici (astron., hunting dogs)
Caniff, Milton (cartoonist, *Terry & the Pirates,
    Steve Canyon*; 1907-88)
Canis Major (astron., great dog, inc. the Dog
    Star, Sirius)
Canis Minor (astron., little [or lesser] dog)
Cannabis indica (marijuana plant)
Cannabis sativa (marijuana plant)
Canned Heat (pop music)
Cannell, Stephen J. (ent.; 1942-)
Cannery Row (film)
Cannes Film Festival (Cannes, Fr.)
Cannes, France
Cannon™ (linens)
Cannon Air Force Base, NM (mil.)
Cannon Beach, OR
Cannon, Dyan (ent.; 1937-)
Cannon, Inc., Fieldcrest-
Cannonball (Julian) Adderley (US jazz; 1928-
    75)
Cannonball Express (Casey Jones' train)
Canon™ (elec.)
Canon USA, Inc.
Canopus (also Alpha Carinae)(astron.)
Canova, Judy (ent.)
Canseco, Jose (baseball; 1964-)
Canterbury bells (also Campanula)(flowering
    plant)
Canterbury Tales, The (by Chaucer)
Canterbury, archbishop of (archbishop, Church
    of England)
Canterbury, England
Canticle for Leibowitz, A
Canticles (also Canticle of Canticles, Song of
    Solomon, Song of Songs)
Cantinflas (b. Mario Moreno)(Mex. ent.; 1912-
    1993)
Canton (crepe, enamel)
Canton Repository (OH newspaper)
Canton, China (also Guangzhou or Kuang-chou)
Canton, CT, IL, MA, MS, NC, NY, OH, SD
Cantonese (lang./people)
Cantonese food
Cantor, Eddie (ent.; 1892-1964)
Cantrell, Lana (ent.; 1943-)
Canuck (slang, Fr. Canadian)
Canucks, Vancouver (hockey team)
Canyon de Chelly National Monument
    (AZ)(cliff-dweller ruins)
Canyon, Steve (comic strip)

Canyonlands National Park (UT)
CAP (Civil Air Patrol)
Cap-Haïtien, Haiti
Capac, Manco (legendary Inca ruler)
Cape Breton Islands (Nova Scotia)
Cape buffalo
Cape Canaveral, FL (Kennedy Space Center)
Cape Charles Air Force Station, VA (mil.)
Cape Charles, VA
Cape Cod cottage
Cape Cod Times (MA newspaper)
Cape Cod, MA
Cape Codder (mixed drink)
Cape Fear, NC
Cape fox
Cape gooseberry (plant)
Cape Guardafui (also Ras Asir)(cape, Somalia)
Cape Hatteras, NC
Cape Henlopen, DE
Cape Horn (SAmer.)
Cape May Coast Guard Air Station (NJ)
Cape May, NJ
Cape of Good Hope (SAfr)
Cape Province (SAfr)
Cape Town, South Africa
Cape Verde (Republic of)(E Atl.)
Capella (also Alpha Aurigae)(astron.)
Capelli & Company (TV show)
Caperton, Gaston (WV gov.; 1940-)
Capetown, South Africa (also Cape Town, Kaapstad)
Capezio™
Capezio (US bus.)
Capital Cities-ABC, Inc. (American Broadcasting Cos., Inc., ABC)
Capital Times, Madison (WI newspaper)
Capitals, Washington (hockey team)
Capitol Center (Landover, MD)
Capitol Hill (also Capitol, the Hill)(US Congress)
Capitol Reef National Park (UT)
Capitol, the (US Capitol building)
Capitoline Hill (ancient Roman temple)
Cap'n Crunch™ (cereal)
Cap'n Crunch's Crunch Berries™ (cereal)
Capone, Al (Alphonse, "Scarface")(US gangster; 1899-47)
Caponi, Donna Maria (golf; 1945-)
Capote, Truman (US writer; 1924-84)
Capoten™ (med.)
Capp, Al (Alfred Gerald Caplin)(cartoonist, *Li'l Abner*; 1909-79)
Capp, Andy (comic strip)
Cappelletti, Gino (football; 1934-)
Capra, Frank (ent.; 1897-1991)
Capri (cigarettes)
Capri pants
Capri, Italy

Capriati, Jennifer (tennis; 1976-)
Caprice, Chevrolet™ (auto.)
Capricorn (also Capricornus)(astron., goat)
Capricorn, Tropic of (H. Miller novel)
Capricorn, tropic of (23°27' S of equator)
Captain Ahab (fict. chara., *Moby Dick*)
Captain America (cartoon chara.)
Captain & Tennille (Daryl & Toni)(pop music)
Captain Horatio Hornblower (film; 1951)
Captain Kangaroo (fict. chara.)
Captain (William) Kidd (Scot. pirate; 1645?-1701)
Captain Marvel (cartoon chara.)
Captain Midnight (cartoon chara.)
Captain Planet (TV show)
Captain Queeg (fict. chara., *The Caine Mutiny*)
Captiva Island, FL
Capucine (b. Germaine Lefebvre)(Fr. ent.; 1933-90)
Capulet and Montague families (*Romeo and Juliet*)
Capulet, Juliet (fict. chara., *Romeo and Juliet*)
Car and Driver (mag.)
Car Audio and Electronics (mag.)
Cara, Irene (ent.; 1959-)
Caracalla (Marcus Aurelius Bassianus)(emp., Rome; 188-217)
Caracas, Venezuela
Caravaggio, Michelangelo da (It. artist; 1573-1610)
Caravan, Dodge (auto.)
Caray, Harry
Carbondale, IL, PA
Carboniferous period (345-280 million years ago)
Carborundum™ (hard artificial compound)
Cárdenas, Lázaro (ex-pres., Mex.; 1895-1970)
Cárdenas, Victor Hugo (VP, Bolivia
Cardiff by the Sea, CA
Cardiff, Wales
Cardigan, Earl of (James Thomas Brudenell (Br. mil./pol., cardigan sweater; 1797-1868)
Cardin, Pierre (Fr. designer; 1922-)
Cardinal de Richelieu ("red eminence")(Fr. pol.; 1585-1642)
Cardinale, Claudia (ent.)
Cardinals, Phoenix (football team)
Cardinals, St. Louis (baseball team)
Cardizem™ (med.)
CARE (Cooperative for American Relief Everywhere, Inc.)
Care Bears™
Care Bears (cartoon)
Care Bears Adventures in Wonderland, The (film; 1987)
Care Bears Movie II: A New Generation (film; 1986)
Care Bears Movie, The (film; 1985)

Carefree™ (panty shields)
Caress™ (soap)
Carew, Rod(ney Cline)(baseball; 1945-)
Carew, Thomas (Br. poet; 1595?-?)
Carey, Macdonald (ent.; 1913-)
Carey, Mariah (ent.; 1970-)
Carhartt™ (clothes)
Carhartt, Inc.
Carib (people, lang.)
Caribbean Community and Common Market
   (CARICOM)
Caribbean Sea
Caribbean Travel & Life (mag.)
Carillo, Leo
Carina (astron., ship's keel)
Carl Andre (US sculptor; 1935-)
Carl August Nielsen (Dan. comp.; 1865-1931)
Carl Bernstein (US jour.; 1944-)
Carl Bildt (PM, Swed.; 1949-)
Carl (or Karl) Bosch (Ger. chem.; 1874-1940)
Carl Buddig™ (meats)
Carl Buddig & Co.
Carl Czerny (also Karl)(Aus. pianist; 1791-
   1857)
Carl E. Mundy, Jr. (US gen.)
Carl Ethan Akeley (US nat./sculptor; 1864-
   1926)
Carl (or Karl) Friedrich Gauss (Ger. math.;
   1777-1855)
Carl Furillo (baseball; 1922-89)
Carl Gustaf Emil von Mannerheim, Baron (Fin.
   gen./pol.; 1867-1951)
Carl Gustav Jung (Swiss psych.; 1875-1961)
Carl Hubbell (baseball; 1903-88)
Carl Icahn
Carl(eton) Lewis, (Frederick)(track; 1961-)
Carl Maria (Friedrich Ernst) von Weber, Baron
   (Ger. comp.; 1786-1826)
Carl M. Levin (US cong.; 1934-)
Carl Orff (Ger. comp.; 1895-1982)
Carl Perkins (ent.; 1932-)
Carl (or Karl) Philipp Emanuel Bach (Ger.
   comp.; 1714-88)
Carl Reiner (ent.; 1922-)
Carl R(ansom) Rogers (US psych.; 1902-87)
Carl Ruggles (US comp.; 1876-1971)
Carl (Edward) Sagan (US astron./writer; 1934-)
Carl (August) Sandburg (US poet; 1878-1967)
Carl Schurz (Ger./US pol.; 1829-1906)
Carl Seashore (US psych.; 1866-1949)
Carl Spaatz (US mil.; 1891-1974)
Carl von Clausewitz (also Karl)(Ger. mil./
   writer; 1780-1831)
Carl XVI Gustaf (king, Swed.; 1946-)
Carl Yastrzemski (baseball; 1939-)
Carla Hills
Carlene Carter (ent.)
Carlene Watkins (ent.; 1952-)

Carlin Glynn
Carlin, George (ent.; 1937-)
Carlisle Tire & Rubber Co.
Carlisle Barracks, PA (mil.)
Carlisle, Belinda (ent.)
Carlisle, England
Carlisle, James (gov-gen.; Antigua/Barbuda)
Carlisle, Kitty (ent.; 1915-)
Carlisle, PA
Carlo Azeglio Ciampi (ex-PM, It.)
Carlo Carra (It. artist; 1881-1966)
Carlo Ponti (It. ent.; 1913-)
Carlo Rossi™ (wine)
Carlo Rossi Vineyards (US bus.)
Carlo Rubbia (It. physt.; 1934-)
Carlo Sforza, Conte (It. pol./dipl.; 1873-1952)
Carlos A. Morales Troncoso (VP, Dom Rep.)
Carlos Andrés Pérez (ex-pres., Venezuela;
   1922-)
Carlos Castaneda (US anthrop./writer; 1925-)
Carlos Chávez (Mex. comp.; 1899-1978)
Carlos I (king, Port.; 1863-1908)
Carlos I, Juan (king, Spain; 1938-)
Carlos (Saul) Menem (pres., Argentina; 1935-)
Carlos Salinas de Gortari (pres., Mex.; 1949-)
Carlos Santana (ent.; 1947-)
Carlos Veiga (PM, Cape Verde)
Carlos, Don (F. von Schiller play, Verdi opera)
Carlos, Don (prince, Spain; 1545-68)
Carlos, John (sprinter; 1945-)
Carlot Korman, Maxine (PM, Vanatu)
Carl's Jr.™
Carlsbad Caverns National Park (NM)
Carlsbad, CA, NM
Carlsberg (beer)
Carlson, Arne (MN gov.; 1934-)
Carlton (cigarettes)
Carlton E. Morse
Carlton, Steve(n Norman)(baseball; 1944-)
Carlucci, Frank (US pol.; 1930-)
Carly Simon (ent.; 1945-)
Carlyle, Thomas (Scot. hist.; 1795-1881)
Carmarthen, Wales
Carmel, CA (also Carmel-by-the-Sea)
Carmel, Mount
Carmel, NY
Carmelite order ("White Friars")
Carmen (opera)
Carmen Dragon
Carmen McRae (ent.)
Carmen Miranda (ent.; 1913-55)
Carmen Sandiego (TV show)
Carmen, Eric (ent.; 1949-)
Carmichael, Hoagy (Hoagland Howard)(US
   comp.; 1899-1981)
Carnahan, Mel (MO gov.)
Carnap, Rudolph (US phil.; 1891-1970)
Carnation Co.

Carnegie Corp. of New York (philanthropic agcy. est. 1911)
Carnegie Hall (NYC concert hall)
Carnegie-Mellon University (PA)
Carnegie Steel Co.
Carnegie, Andrew (US bus./finan.; 1835-1919)
Carnegie, Dale (US writer/educ.; 1888-1955)
Carner, Joanne Gunderson (golf; 1939-)
Carnera, Primo (boxing; 1907-67)
Carneros Creek Winery (US bus.)
Carney, Art (ent.; 1918-)
Carney, Harry (US jazz; 1910-74)
Carnival Cruise Lines, Inc.
Carnock, Erskine of (aka John Erskine)(Scot. writer, law; 1695-1768)
Carol & Ted & Alice, Bob & (film; 1969)
Carol Burnett (ent.; 1933-)
Carol Channing (ent.; 1923-)
Carol Kane (ent.; 1952-)
Carol Lawrence (ent.; 1934-)
Carol Leifer (ent.; 1956-)
Carol Mann (golf; 1941-)
Carol M. Browner (Head/EPA; 1955-)
Carol Moseley-Braun (US cong.; 1947-)
Carol Reed, Sir (ent.; 1906-76)
Carole King (US comp./ent.; 1942-)
Carole Landis (ent.; 1919-48)
Carole Lombard (b. Jane Alice Peters)(ent.; 1909-42)
Carolina horse nettle (plant)
Carolina Panthers (football team)
Caroline affair (US steamer sank by Can.; 1837)
Caroline Bird (US writer)
Caroline Kennedy Schlossberg (US atty., daughter of JFK; 1957-)
Caroline of Brunswick (queen of George IV; 1768-1821)
Caroline, Princess (princess, Monaco)
Carolingian dynasty (Frankish, Fr./Ger.; c800-987)
Carolyn Jones (ent.; 1933-83)
Carolyn Keene (aka Harriet S. Adams)(US writer; 1803-82)
Carolyne Roehm
Caron, Leslie (Fr./US ent.; 1931-)
Carousel (film; 1956)
Carpathian Mountains (central Eur.)
Carpenter, Karen (ent.; 1950-83)
Carpenter, M(alcolm) Scott (astro.; 1925-)
Carpenters, The (pop music)
Carper, Tom (DE gov.)
Carpeteria™
Carpeteria (US bus.)
Carpio, Ramiro de León (pres., Guat.)
Carr, Allan
Carr, Baker v. (US law; 1962)
Carr, Gerald P(aul)(astro.; 1932-)
Carr, Vikki (ent.; 1941-)

Carra, Carlo (It. artist; 1881-1966)
Carracci, Agostino (It. artist; 1557-1602)
Carracci, Annibale (It. artist; 1560-1609)
Carracci, Lodovico (or Ludovico)(It. artist; 1555-1619)
Carradine, David (ent.; 1936-)
Carradine, John (ent.; 1906-88)
Carradine, Keith (ent.; 1949-)
Carré, John le (b. David Cornwell)(Br. writer; 1931-)
Carrel, Alexis (Fr. phys.; 1873-1944)
Carreras, José (Sp. tenor; 1947-)
Carrickmacross (lace)
Carrie (film; 1976)
Carrie Chapman Catt (US suffragist; 1859-1947)
Carrie Fisher (ent.; 1956-)
Carrie Jacobs Bond (US comp.; 1862-1946)
Carrie (Amelia Moore) Nation (US temperance leader; 1846-1911)
Carrie Snodgrass (ent.; 1946-)
Carroll A. Campbell, Jr. (SC gov.; 1940-)
Carroll Baker (ent.; 1931-)
Carroll Naish, J. (ent.; 1900-73)
Carroll O'Connor (ent.; 1924-)
Carroll, Diahann (ent.; 1935-)
Carroll, Leo G. (ent.; 1892-1972)
Carroll, Lewis (aka Charles Dodgson)(Br. writer/math.; 1832-98)
Carroll, Pat (ent.; 1927-)
Carrol's Vanities, Earl
Carruthers, Kitty (figure skating)
Carruthers, Peter (figure skating)
Cars, the (pop music)
Carson City, NV
Carson (Smith) McCullers (US writer; 1917-67)
Carson, CA
Carson, Jack (ent.; 1910-63)
Carson, Johnny (ent.; 1925-)
Carson, Kit (Christopher)(US frontier; 1809-68)
Carson, Rachel (Louise)(US writer/biol.; 1907-64)
Carswell Air Force Base (TX)(mil.)
Cartagena, Columbia
Cartagena, Spain
Carte, Richard D'Oyly (Br. opera; 1844-1901)
Car-Temps™ (car rental)
Carter Hawley Hale Stores, Inc.
Carter-Wallace, Inc.
Carter, Amy (daughter of ex-US pres.; 1967-)
Carter, Benny (US jazz; 1907-)
Carter, Billy (William Aldon), III (US bro. of ex-pres.; 1937-88)
Carter, Dixie (ent.; 1939-)
Carter, Howard (Br. archaeol.; 1873-1939)
Carter, Jack (ent.; 1923-)
Carter, Jimmy (James Earl, Jr.)(39th US pres.; 1924-)

Carter, Joe (baseball; 1960-)
Carter, June (ent.; 1929-)
Carter, Lynda (ent.; 1951-)
Carter, Maybelle "Mother" (ent.; 1909-78)
Carter, Nick (fict. detective)
Carter, Ron (US jazz; 1937-)
Carter, Rosalynn (wife of US pres.; 1927-)
Cartesian coordinates (geometry)
Cartesianism (Descartes phil.)
Carthage (ancient city, NAfr.)
Carthage, IL, MO, NY
Cartier™ (jewelry)
Cartier, Inc.
Caruso, Enrico (It. tenor; 1873-1921)
Carvel Ice Cream Stores (US bus.)
Carvel, Tom (Ger./US bus.; 1908-90)
Carver chair
Carver, George Washington (US botanist/chem.;
    1860?-1943)
Carvey, Dana (ent.; 1955-)
Cary Grant (b. Archibald Leach)(ent.; 1904-86)
Caryatids, Porch of the (Gr., female figures
    used for columns)
Caryl Chessman ("Red Light Bandit")(US
    rapist; ?-1960)
Caryn Kadavy
Casa Grande, AZ (prehistoric ruins)
Casablanca™
Casablanca (film; 1942)
Casablanca Conference (Roosevelt/Churchill;
    1943)
Casablance Fan Co.
Casablanca, Morocco
Casals, Pablo (Sp. musician; 1876-1973)
Casals, Rosemary (tennis; 1948-)
Casanova (film)
Casanova, Giovanni Jacopo (also Casanova de
    Seingalt)(It. adventurer; 1725-98)
Casbah, the (also Kasbah)
Cascade™ (dish detergent)
Cascade Range (mountains, OR/WA)
Cascade, Seychelles
Casey (John Luther) Jones (US railroad eng.;
    1864-1900)
Casey Kasem (ent.; 1933-)
Casey Siemaszko
Casey (Charles) Stengel (baseball; 1891-1975)
Casey Tibbs
Casey, Robert (PA gov.; 1932-)
Casey, William J. (ex-dir./FBI; 1914-87)
Cash, Johnny (ent.; 1932-)
Cash, Rosanne (ent.; 1955-)
Cashmere (also Kashmir)(goat)
Casimir (or Kasimir) Malevich (Rus. artist;
    1878-1935)
Casimir Oye-Mba (PM, Gabon)
Casio™
Casio, Inc.

Caslon (type style)
Caslon, William (Br. typographer; 1692-1766)
Caspar (one of the Magi)
Caspar David Friedrich (Ger. artist; 1774-1840)
Caspar Milquetoast (cartoon chara.)
Casper the Friendly Ghost (cartoon chara.)
Caspar "Cap" W(illard) Weinberger (US pol.;
    1917-)
Casper, Billy (golf; 1931-)
Casper, WY
Caspian Sea (SE Eur./W Asia)
Caspian, Prince (by C.S. Lewis)
Cass Elliot (ent.; 1941-74)
Cass Gilbert (US arch.; 1859-1934)
Cass, Peggy (ent.; 1924-)
Cassam Uteem (pres., Mauritius)
Cassandra (myth.)
Cassandra Peterson (aka Elvira)(ent.; 1951-)
Cassatt, Mary (US artist; 1845-1926)
Cassavetes, John (ent.; 1929-89)
Cassegrain (or Cassegrainian) reflector/
    telescope (astron.)
Cassel brown (also Vandyke brown, Cassel
    earth)(color)
Cassel yellow (color)
Cassidy and the Sundance Kid, Butch (film;
    1969)
Cassidy, David (ent.; 1950-)
Cassidy, Hopalong (fict. chara.)
Cassidy, Hopalong (TV show)
Cassidy, Joanna (ent.)
Cassini (space probe to Saturn)
Cassini, Giovanni Domenico (It./Fr. astron.;
    1625-1712)
Cassini, Inc., Oleg
Cassini, Oleg (US designer; 1913-)
Cassiopeia (astron., queen; myth.)
Cassius Clay, Jr. (aka Muhammad Ali)(boxing;
    1942-)
Cassius, Gaius (Roman leader of conspiracy
    against Caesar; ?-42 BC)
Castaneda, Carlos (US anthrop./writer; 1925-)
Casterbridge, The Mayor of (T. Hardy novel)
Castiglione Baldassare (It. pol.; 1478-1529)
Castile (region, Sp.)
Castile, Eleanor of (queen, Eng.; c1245-90)
Castilian (lang./people)
Castilian brown (color)
Castilian red (color)
Castle Air Force Base, CA (mil.)
Castle, Irene (Foote)(US dancer; 1893-1969)
Castle, Vernon (US dancer; 1887-1918)
Castlereagh, Robert (Br. pol.; 1769-1822)
Castor and Pollux (astron., myth., Gemini/
    twins)
Castries, St. Lucia
Castro Convertibles (US bus.)
Castro Ruíz, Fidel (pres., Cuba; 1927-)

Castroism (pol.)
Casual Corner™ (clothing)
Caswell-Massey Co., Ltd.
CAT (computer-aided translation/transcription)
Cat Ballou (film; 1965)
Cat Fancy (mag.)
CAT scan (med.)
Cat Stevens (ent.; 1948-)
Catacombs, the (subterranean burial chambers, ancient Rome)
Catalan (lang./people)
Catalina™ (sportswear)
Catalina Island, CA (also Catalina, Santa Catalina)
Catalonia (region, Sp.)
Catania, Italy
Catawba (NAmer. Indians)
Catawba River (NC/SC)
Catcher in the Rye, The (J.D. Salinger novel)
Catch-22 (Joseph Heller novel)
Caterpillar Tractor Co.
Cates, Phoebe (ent.)
Catfish (Jim) Hunter (baseball; 1946-)
Cathay Pacific Airways (airline)
Cathedral of St. John the Divine (NYC)
Cather, Willa (US writer; 1876-1947)
Catherine Bach (ent.)
Catherine de' Medici (queen, Fr./wife of Henry II; 1518-89)
Catherine Deneuve (Fr. ent.; 1943-)
Catherine Howard (5th wife of Henry VIII; 1520?-42)
Catherine I (Rus. empress, wife of Peter the Great; 1684-1727)
Catherine II (Rus. empress, Catherine the Great; 1729-96)
Catherine of Aragon (1st wife of Henry VIII; 1585-36)
Catherine of Braganza, (Br., queen of Charles II; 1638-1705)
Catherine of Siena, St. (It. mystic; 1347-80)
Catherine Parr (6th wife of Henry VIII; 1512-48)
Catherine the Great (Rus. empress, Catherine II; 1729-96)
Catherine Tizard (gov.-gen., NewZeal.)
Catholic (rel.)
Catholic Apostolic Church
Catholic Church
Catholic Church, Roman (also Church of Rome)
Catholic Emancipation Act (Br.; 1829)
Catholic Epistles (rel.)
Catholic Foreign Mission Society of America (also Maryknoll Missioners)(rel.)
Catholic Reformation (also Counter Reformation)(Eur. rel./hist.; 16th-17th c.)
Catholic, Roman (rel.)
Catholicism (also Roman Catholicism)(rel.)

Cathy (comic strip)
Cathy Guisewite (cartoonist, *Cathy*; 1950-)
Cathy Rigby (gymnast)
Catilina (Lucius Sergius)(also Catiline)(Roman pol.; c108-62 BC)
Catlett, Sidney ("Big Sid")(US jazz; 1910-51)
Catlin, George (US artist; 1796-1872)
Cato the Elder (also Cato the Censor, Marcus Porcius Cato)(Roman pol.; 234-149 BC)
Cats (mag.)
Cats (play)
Catskills (also Catskill Mountains)(NY)
Catt, Carrie Chapman (US suffragist; 1859-1947)
Catullus (Gaius Catullus)(Roman poet; c84-43 BC)
Caucasoid (also Caucasian)(one of three major races of humans)
Caulfield, Joan (ent.; 1922-91)
Caulkins, Tracy (swimming; 1963-)
Cauthen, Steve (jockey)
cavalier King Charles spaniel (dog)
Cavalier, Chevrolet™ (auto.)
Cavaliers, Cleveland (basketball team)
Cavendish, Henry (Br. chem./physt.; 1731-1810)
Caves of Altamira (also Altamira caves)(Sp. paleolithic paintings)
Cavett, Dick (ent.; 1936-)
Cavour, Camillo Benso (It. pol.; 1810-61)
Caxton, William (1st English printer; c1422-91)
Cayenne, French Guiana
Cayman Airways
Cayman Islands (Br. West Indies)
Caymus Vineyards, Inc.
Cayuga (NAmer. Indians)
Cayuga duck
Cayuga Lake (NY)
CB radio
CBC (Canadian Broadcasting Corp.)
CBS Evening News With Dan Rather, The (TV show)
CBS News (TV show)
CBS Records (US bus.)
CBS Sunday Night Movie (TV show)
CBS, Inc. (Columbia Broadcasting System)
C. C. Beck (cartoonist, *Captain Marvel*; 1910-89)
CCC (Civilian Conservation Corps)
CCR (Certified Court Reporter)
CCU (coronary care unit)
Cd (chem. sym., cadmium)
CD (certificate of deposit, civil defense, compact disk)
CDC (Centers for Disease Control)
CD-ROM (Compact Disk-Read Only Memory)(compu.)
CE (chemical engineer, civil engineer)
Ce (chem. sym., cerium)

Ceausescu, Nicolae (ex-pres., Romania; 1918-89)
Cebu, Philippines
Cebuano (lang.)
Cecchetti method (ballet)
Cecchetti, Enrico (ballet; 1850-1928)
Cecil B. De Mille (ent.; 1881-1959)
Cecil Beaton, Sir (Br. photo.; 1904-80)
Cecil D. Andrus (ID gov.; 1931-)
Cecil Day Lewis (Ir. poet; 1904-72)
Cecil (John) Rhodes (Br./SAfr. pol., est. Rhodes scholarships; 1853-1902)
Cecil Taylor (US jazz; 1933-)
Cecilia Bartoli (US opera; 1972-)
Cecilia Helena Payne-Gaposchkin (Br./US astron.; 1900-79)
Ceclor™ (med.)
Cecropia moth (silkworm)
Cecrops (myth.)
Cedar Falls, IA
Cedar Rapids Gazette Post (IA newspaper)
Cedar Rapids, IA
Cedars-Sinai Medical Center
Cédras, Lieut. Gen. Raoul (Haitian mil.)
Cedric Hardwicke, Sir (ent.; 1893-1964)
CEEB (College Entrance Examination Board)
Celanese™ (yarn, fabric)
Celebes (now Sulawesi)(Indonesian island)
Celeste Holm (ent.; 1919-)
Celestial City (from *Pilgrim's Progress*)
Celestial Seasonings™
Celestial Seasonings, Inc.
Celestine I, St. (pope; ?-432)
Celestine II, St. (Guido del Castello)(pope; ?-1144)
Celestine III, St. (Giacinto Bobone)(It. pope; 1106?-98)
Celestine IV, St. (Gofredo Castiglioni)(It. pope; ?-1241)
Celestine V, St. (Pietro di Murrone [or Morone])(pope; 1215-96)
Celica, Toyota (auto.)
Cellini, Benvenuto (It. sculptor; 1500-71)
Celotex™ (constr.)
Celsius (also Centigrade)(temperature scale)
Celsius, Anders (Swed. astron.; 1701-44)
Celt (people)
Celtic (lang./people)
Celtic art
Celtic Church
Celtic cross
Celtic Renaissance (also Irish Literary Renaissance, Irish Revival)(lit.)
Celtic Sea (UK)
Celtics, Boston (basketball team)
Cenozoic era (65 million years ago to present)
Centauri, Alpha (also Rigel Kentaurus)(astron.)
Centauri, Proxima (astron.)

Centaurus (astron., centaur [half man/half horse])
Centennial State (nickname, CO)
Centers for Disease Control and Prevention (CDC)
Centigrade (also Celsius)(temperature scale)
Central African Republic
Central America
Central American Common Market (CACM)
Central American States, Organization of (ODECA)(est. 1951/1962)
Central Asian Republics (Kazakhstan, Kyrgyzstan, Tajikistan, and Turkmenistan; Uzbekistan)
Central Highlands
Central Intelligence Agency (CIA)(US govt.)
Central Islip, NY
Central Powers (of WW I)
Central Standard Time (also Central Time)
Centre (region, Fr.)
Centrex™
Centrex Corp.
Centris, Macintosh™ (compu.)
Centrum™ (med.)
Centrum Products Co.
Centrum, Jr. ™ (med.)
Century (type style)
Century 21™
Century 21 Real Estate Corp.
Century, Buick™ (auto.)
CEO (chief executive officer)
Cepacol™ (med.)
Cepastat™ (med.)
Cepheid variable(s)(astron.)
Cepheus (astron., king)
Cerberus (myth., 3-headed guard dog)
Cerdic, House of (Br. ruling family; 827-1016, 1042-66)
Cerenkov radiation
Ceres (astron., myth.)
Ceres, CA
Cerf, Bennett (US editor/publ.; 1898-1971)
Cernan, Eugene A(ndrew)(astro.; 1934-)
Cerro Tololo Inter-American Observatory (Chile)
Cervantes Saavedra, Miguel de (Sp. writer; 1547-1616)
César Auguste Franck (Belg. comp.; 1822-90)
Cesar Chavez (US labor leader; 1927-93)
César Gaviria Trujillo (pres., Colombia; 1947-)
Cesar Romero (ent.; 1907-)
Cesare Borgia (It. mil./pol.; 1476-1507)
Cessna™
Cessna Aircraft Co.
Cetinje, Montenegro (Yug.)
Cetus (astron., whale)
C. Everett Koop (ex-US surgeon gen.; 1916-)
Ceylon (now Sri Lanka)

Ceylon tea (tree)
Cézanne, Paul (Fr. artist; 1839-1906)
Cf (chem. sym., californium)
CFI (cost, freight, and insurance)
CFTC (Commodity Futures Trading
    Commission)
CG (coast guard)
Ch'in dynasty (also Qin)(Ch.; 221-206 BC)
Chablis (wine)
Chablis, France
Chabrier, Alexis Emmanuel (Fr. comp.; 1841-
    94)
Chaco (province, Argentina)
Chaco Culture National Historical Park
    (NM)(formerly Chaco Canyon National
    Monument)
Chad (Republic of)(N Afr.)
Chad Everett (ent.; 1936-)
Chad, Lake (Nigeria)
*Chadha, Immigration and Naturalization
    Service v.* (US law; 1983)
Chadwick, Florence (US swimmer; 1918-)
Chadwick, Sir James (Br. physt.; 1891-1974)
Chadwick's of Boston, Ltd™ (clothing)
Chafee, John H. (US cong.; 1922-)
Chaffee, Fort, AR (mil.)
Chagall, Marc (Fr. artist; 1887-1985)
Chagas' disease
Chaim Gross (US artist; 1904-91)
Chaim Herzog (ex-pres., Isr.; 1918-)
Chaim Potok (US writer; 1929-)
Chaim Soutine (Fr. artist; 1893-1943)
Chaim Weizmann (ex-pres., Isr.; 1874-1952)
Chairman Mao (also Mao Tse-tung, Mao
    Zedong)(Ch. leader; 1893-1976)
Chaka Khan (ent.; 1953-)
Chakma (lang.)
Chakrabarty, Diamond v. (US law; 1980)
Chalcedon, Council of (rel.)
Chaldea (part of Babylonia)
Chaldean (ancient people)
Challenger (Br. oceanic expedition; 1872-76)
Challenger (US space shuttle)
Challenger space shuttle disaster (1/28/86)
Cham (people)
Chamaeleon (astron., chameleon)
Chamberlain, (Joseph) Austen (Br. pol.; 1863-
    1937)
Chamberlain, Joseph (Br. pol.; 1836-1914)
Chamberlain, (Arthur) Neville (ex-PM, Brit;
    1869-1940)
Chamberlain, Richard (ent.; 1935-)
Chamberlain, Wilt (Norman)(Wilt the
    Stilt)(basketball; 1936-)
Chambers, Sir William (Br. arch.; 1723-96)
Chamorro (lang.)
Chamorro, Violeta Barrios de (pres., Nicaragua;
    1939-)

Champagne (Fr. wine region)
Champagne-Ardenne (region, Fr.)
Champaign, IL
Champion™ (spark plug)
Champion International Corp.
Champion v. Ames (also Lottery Case)(US law;
    1903)
Champion, Gower (US dancer; 1921-80)
Champion, Marge (US dancer; 1923-)
Champlain, Lake (NY/VT/Can.)
Champlain, Samuel de (Fr. expl.; c1567-1635)
Champollion, Jean François (Fr. archaeol.;
    1790-1832)
Champs Élysées (Paris avenue)
Chan Chan ruins (Peru)
Chan, Charlie (fict. detective)
Chan, Dennis
Chan, Lien (premier; Taiwan
Chancellor of the Exchequer (Br. govt.)
Chancellor, John (US TV jour.; 1927-)
Chancellorsville, Battle of (US hist.; 1863)
Chancellorsville, VA
Chandler Pavilion, Dorothy (Los Angeles)
Chandler period (also Chandler
    wobble)(oscillation of earth's axis)
Chandler, A. B. (Happy)(baseball; 1899-1991)
Chandler, Jeff (ent.; 1918-61)
Chandler, Raymond (US writer; 1888-1959)
Chandler, Spud (baseball; 1907-90)
Chandrasekhar limit (astron., physics)
Chanel, Gabrielle "Coco" (Fr. designer; 1883-
    1971)
Chanel, Inc.
Chaney, Lon (ent.; 1883-1930)
Chaney, Lon, Jr. (ent.; 1905-73)
Chang Jiang River (also Yangtze Kiang)(Ch.)
Chang, Lee Hoi (PM; SKorea)
Chang, Michael (tennis; 1972-)
Changchiakow, China (also Zhangjiakou)
Changchun, China (formerly Hsinking)
Changes, Book of (also *I Ching*)
Changing Times (mag.)
Changsha, China
Chanin, Irwin (US arch.; 1892-1988)
Channel Islands (English Channel)
Channel Islands National Park, CA
Channel Tunnel (also Chunnel)(tunnel joining
    Eng./Fr.)
Channing, Carol (ent.; 1923-)
Channing, Edward (US hist.; 1856-1931)
Channing, Stockard (ent.; 1944-)
Channing, William Ellery (US rel.; 1780-1842)
Chanson de Roland (Fr. epic poem, *Song of
    Roland*)
Chantilly lace
Chantilly, crème (sauce)
Chantilly, France
Chanukah (also Hanukkah)(rel.)

Chanute Air Force Base, IL (mil.)
Chaos (myth.)
Chap Stick™ (med.)
Chapelle Winery, Inc., Ste.
Chapin, Harry (ent.; 1942-81)
Chaplin, Charlie (Sir Charles Spencer)(ent.; 1889-1977)
Chaplin, Geraldine (ent.; 1944-)
Chapman, John (aka Johnny Appleseed)(US pioneer; 1774-1845)
Chapman, Tracy (ent.; 1964-)
Chapot, Frank (equestrian; 1934-)
Chappaquiddick bridge (site of Ted Kennedy/ Mary Jo Kopechne accident; 1969)
Chappaquiddick Island, MA
Chapter 11 (of US Bankruptcy Code)
Chapultepec, Mexico
Charbray (cattle)
Charcot, Jean M. (Fr. phys.; 1825-93)
Chardin, Jean-Baptiste-Siméon (Fr. artist; 1699-1779)
Chardonnay (grape, wine)
Chardzhov, Turkmenistan
Charge of the Light Brigade (battle, Crimean War)
Charge of the Light Brigade (poem)
Charger, Dodge (auto.)
Chargers, San Diego (football team)
Charing Cross (London railroad terminal)
Charisse, Cyd (ent.; 1921-)
Charlemagne (also Charles the Great, Charles I)(Holy Roman Emperor; 742-814)
Charlene Tilton
Charleroi, Belgium
Charles A. Beard (US hist.; 1874-1948)
Charles Addams (cartoonist; 1912-88)
Charles A(ugustus) Lindbergh (US aviator; 1902-74)
Charles Arthur Floyd ("Pretty Boy")(US bank robber; 1901-34)
Charles Ashburner (US geol.; 1854-89)
Charles Atlas (aka Angelo Siciliano)(US body builder; 1894-1972)
Charles Augustin de Coulomb (Fr. physt.; 1736-1806)
Charles Aznavour (Fr. ent.; 1924-)
Charles Babbage (Br. math., inv. precursor of modern compu.; 1792-1871)
Charles Barkley (basketball; 1963-)
Charles Bickford (ent.; 1889-1967)
Charles Bolden ("Buddy")(US jazz; 1868-1931)
Charles Boyer (ent.; 1899-1978)
Charles Bronson (ent.; 1922-)
Charles Bulfinch (US arch.; 1763-1844)
Charles Camille Saint-Saëns (Fr. comp.; 1835-1921)
Charles C. Boycott, Capt. (Br., boycotted by Ir. tenants; 1832-97)

Charles Chips (US bus.)
Charles Coburn (ent.; 1877-1961)
Charles Conrad, Jr. (astro.; 1930-)
Charles Cornwallis (Br. gen./pol.; 1738-1805)
Charles Cotesworth Pinckney (US pol.; 1746-1825)
Charles Crocker (US railroad/finan.; 1822-88)
Charles Curtis (ex-US VP; 1860-1936)
Charles Dana Gibson (US artist; 1867-1944)
Charles de Baatz d'Artagnan, Seigneur (fict. chara., *Three Musketeers*)
Charles de Gaulle (ex-pres., Fr.; 1890-1970)
Charles (Maurice) de Talleyrand(-Périgord)(Fr. pol.; 1754-1838)
Charles (John Huffam) Dickens ("Boz")(Br. writer; 1812-70)
Charles Dodgson (pseud. Lewis Carroll)(Br. writer/math.; 1832-98)
Charles Durning (ent.; 1923-)
Charles Eames (US arch./designer; 1907-78)
Charles Édouard Jeanneret (aka Le Corbusier)(Fr. arch./artist; 1887-1965)
Charles Edward Stuart (aka the Young Pretender, Bonnie Prince Charles [or Charlie])(prince, Br.; 1720-88)
Charles E. Greene (sprinter; 1945-)
Charles Elton (Br. ecol.; 1900-91)
Charles E. Merrill (US finan.; 1885-1956)
Charles Ernest Grassley (US cong.; 1933-)
Charles Evers, (James)(US civil rights leader; 1922-)
Charles Farrell (ent.; 1902-90)
Charles F(ollen) McKim (US arch.; 1847-1909)
Charles Fourier (Fr. social scien.; 1772-1837)
Charles Francis Richter (US seismol.; 1900-85)
Charles François Gounod (Fr. comp.; 1818-93)
Charles Frederick Menninger (US psych.; 1862-1953)
Charles Frohman (US theater; 1860-1915)
Charles Fuller (US writer; 1939-)
Charles G. Dawes (US pol./banker; 1865-1951)
Charles G(eorge) Gordon, (Br. mil.; 1833-85)
Charles Goodyear (US inv.; 1800-60)
Charles Greeley Abbot (US physt.; 1872-1973)
Charles Grodin (ent.; 1935-)
Charles Haid (ent.; 1944-)
Charles Hard Townes (US physt.; 1915-)
Charles Haughey (ex-PM, Ir.; 1925-)
Charles H. Goren (US contract bridge authority; 1901-91)
Charles Hickcox (swimming; 1947-)
Charles I (aka Charles the Great, Charlemagne)(Holy Roman emp.; 742-814)
Charles I (king, Br./Ir.; 1600-49)
Charles II (aka Charles the Bald)(Holy Roman emp.; 823-877)
Charles II (king, Br./Ir.; 1630-85)
Charles II (king, Sp.; 1661-1700)

Charles III (aka Charles the Fat)(Holy Roman emp.; 839-888)

Charles III (aka Charles the Simple)(king, Fr.; 893-922)

Charles III (king, Sp.; 1716-88)

Charles IV (aka Charles the Fair)(king, Fr.; 1294-1328)

Charles IV (Holy Roman emp.; 1316-78)

Charles IV (king, Sp.; 1748-1819)

Charles (Edward) Ives (US comp.; 1874-1954)

Charles IX (king, Fr.; 1550-74)

Charles IX (king, Swed.; 1550-1611)

Charles Joseph "Joe" Clark (ex-PM, Can.; 1939-)

Charles H. Keating, III (US bank scandal)

Charles H. Keating, Jr. (US bank scandal)

Charles Krug Winery (US bus.)

Charles Kuralt (US TV jour.; 1934-)

Charles Lamb ("Elia")(Br. writer; 1775-1834)

Charles Lang Freer (US bus./art collector; 1856-1919)

Charles Laughton (ent.; 1899-1962)

Charles' law (also Gay-Lussac's law)(thermodynamics)

Charles Lewis Tiffany (US bus.; 1912-1902)

Charles Louis Montesquieu (Fr. phil.; 1689-1755)

Charles Manson (US, mass murderer; 1934-)

Charles McGraw

Charles M. Duke (astro.)

Charles Messier (Fr. astron.; 1730-1817)

Charles Mingus (US jazz; 1922-79)

Charles M. McKim (US arch.; 1920-)

Charles M. Russell (US arch.; 1866-1926)

Charles M(ichael) Schwab (US bus.; 1862-1939)

Charles M(onroe) Schulz (cartoonist, *Peanuts*; 1922-)

Charles Nelson Reilly (ent.; 1931-)

Charles O. Finley (athlete; 1918-)

Charles of the Ritz Group, Ltd.

Charles Pasarell (tennis; 1944-)

Charles Pathé (Fr. bus./films; 1863-1957)

Charles Perrault (Fr. writer; 1628-1703)

Charles Pierre Baudelaire (Fr. poet; 1821-67)

Charles Pinckney (US pol.; 1757-1824)

Charles P(roteus) Steinmetz (Ger./US eng.; 1865-1923)

Charles Rangel (US pol.; 1930-)

Charles Rennie Mackintosh (Scot. arch.; 1868-1928)

Charles Ringling (US circus; 1863-1926)

Charles River Bridge v. Warren Bridge (US law; 1837)

Charles Robert Darwin (Br. scien.; 1809-82)

Charles Robinson (ent.)

Charles Robinson (US pol.; 1818-94)

Charles "Charlie" Ruggles (ent.; 1886-1970)

Charles R. Walgreen (US bus.; 1873-1939)

Charles Scribner, Jr. (US publ.)

Charles Scribner, Sr. (US publ.)

Charles Scribner's Sons (US bus.)

Charles S(anders) Peirce (US physt./phil.; 1839-1914)

Charles S. Robb (US cong.; 1939-)

Charles Sheeler (US artist; 1883-1965)

Charles (Scott) Sherrington, Sir (Br. physiol.; 1857-1952)

Charles spaniel, King (dog)

Charles "Casey" Stengel (baseball; 1891-1975)

Charles Stewart Parnell (Ir. pol.; 1846-91)

Charles Strouse (US comp.; 1928-)

Charles Sumner (US pol.; 1811-74)

Charles T(aze) Russell (US, rel./Jehovah's Witnesses; 1852-1916)

Charles the Great (also Charlemagne, Charles I)(Holy Roman emp.; 742-814)

Charles Town, WV

Charles Townshend (Br. pol., Townshend Acts; 1725-67)

Charles Townshend, Viscount ("Turnip")(Br. pol./agr.; 1675-1738)

Charles V (aka the Wise)(king, Fr.; 1337-80)

Charles V (Holy Roman emperor; 1500-58)

Charles Van Doren (US educ./TV scandal)

Charles VI (aka the Mad, the Well-Beloved)(king, Fr.; 1368-1422)

Charles VI (Holy Roman emperor; 1685-1740)

Charles VII (Holy Roman emperor; 1697-1745)

Charles VII (king, Fr.; 1403-61)

Charles VIII (king, Fr.; 1470-98)

Charles VIII (king, Swed.; 1408-70)

Charles W. Colson (US pol./Watergate; 1931-)

Charles W. Fairbanks (US VP; 1852-1918)

Charles "Cootie" Williams (US jazz; 1908-85)

Charles Wilson Peale (US artist; 1741-1827)

Charles X (king, Fr.; 1757-1836)

Charles X (king, Swed.; 1622-60)

Charles XI (king, Swed.; 1655-97)

Charles XII (king, Swed.; 1682-1718)

Charles XIII (king, Swed./Nor.; 1748-1818)

Charles XIV (John Baptiste Jules)(king, Swed./Nor.; 1763-1844)

Charles XV (king, Swed./Nor.; 1826-72)

Charles (or Charlie), Bonnie Prince (Charles Edward Stuart, aka the Young Pretender)(prince, Br.; 1720-88)

Charles, Jacques (Alexandre César)(Fr. physt.; 1746-1823)

Charles, Lake, LA

Charles, Mary Eugenia (PM, Dominica; 1919-)

Charles, Prince (Charles Philip Arthur George, Prince of Wales)(eldest son of Queen Elizabeth II; 1948-)

Charles, Ray (ent.; 1930-)

Charlesbourg, Quebec, Canada

Charleston (dance)

Charleston Air Force Base, SC (mil.)
Charleston Gazette (WV newspaper)
Charleston Gazette-Mail (WV newspaper)
Charleston Mail (WV newspaper)
Charleston Naval Shipyard (SC)
Charleston Naval Station (SC)
Charleston Naval Weapons Station (SC)
Charleston Post & Courier (SC newspaper)
Charleston, IL, MO, SC, WV
Charlie Brown (fict. chara., *Peanuts*)
Charlie Bucket
Charlie Callas (ent.)
Charlie Chan (fict. detective)
Charlie Chaplin (Sir Charles Spencer)(ent.;
    1889-1977)
Charlie Christian (US jazz; 1919-42)
Charlie Daniels (ent.; 1936-)
Charlie Gehringer (baseball; 1903-)
Charlie Jones (ent.; 1930-)
Charlie "Bird" Parker (b. Charles Christopher
    Parker, Jr.)(US jazz; 1920-55)
Charlie Pride (ent.; 1939-)
Charlie Rich (ent.; 1932-)
Charlie (Charles) Ruggles (ent.; 1886-1970)
Charlie Sheen (ent.; 1965-)
Charlie Spivak
Charlie Weaver (aka Cliff Arquette)(ent.; 1905-
    74)
Charlie, Checkpoint (East/West Berlin)
Charlie, Mr. (Black slang, white man)
Charlie's Angels (TV show)
Charlie's, Inc., Beefsteak
Charlotte Amalie, St. Thomas, VI
Charlotte Brontë (aka Currer Bell)(Br. writer;
    1816-55)
Charlotte Corday d'Armont (Fr. patriot; 1768-
    93)
Charlotte Hornets (basketball team)
*Charlotte-Mecklenburg County Board of
    Education, Swann v.* (US law; 1971)
Charlotte Observer (NC newspaper)
Charlotte Rae (ent.; 1926-)
Charlotte, Hush...Hush, Sweet (film; 1965)
Charlotte, NC
Charlottesville, VA
Charlotte's Web (children's book)
Charlottetown, Prince Edward Island, Canada
Charlton Heston (ent.; 1924-)
Charmin™ (bath tissue)
Charming, Prince
Charo (Sp./US ent.; 1951-)
Charolais (also Charolaise)(cattle)
Charon (myth.)
Charpentier, Gustave (Fr. comp.; 1860-1956)
Chartres Cathedral (Fr., cathedral of Notre
    Dame)
Chartres, France
Chartreuse™ (liqueur)

Charybdis (also modern-Galofalo, Garofalo)
Charybdis, Scylla and (myth.)
Chase Manhattan Bank
Chase Manhattan Corp.
Chase Smith, Margaret (US pol.; 1897-)
Chase, Chevy (ent.; 1943-)
Chase, Ilka (US writer/ent.; 1905-?)
Chase, Salmon P. (US jurist; 1808-73)
Chasid (also Hasid, Hassid)(rel.)
Chasidism (also Hasidism)(rel.)
Chast, Roz (cartoonist, *New Yorker*; 1954-)
Chateaubriand (steak)
Chateaubriand, François René (Fr. writer;
    1768-1848)
Chateauguay, Quebec, Canada
Chateau Haut-Brion (Fr. wine)
Chateau Lafite-Rothschild (Fr. wine)
Chateau Latour (Fr. wine)
Chateau Leoville-Las-Cases (Fr. wine)
Chateau Margaux (Fr. wine)
Chateau Montelena Winery (US bus.)
Chateau Montrose (Fr. wine)
Chateau Petrus (Fr. wine)
Chateau Souverain (US bus.)
Chateau St. Jean, Inc.
Chateau Ste. Michelle Vintners (US bus.)
Chatelaine (mag.)
Chatelier('s) principle, Le (also Le Chatelier-
    Braun p.)(chem.)
Chatham Islands (S Pac.)
Chatham, England
Chatham, Ontario, Canada
Chattahoochee River (GA/AL/FL)
Chattahoochee, FL
Chattanooga Choo Choo (song)
Chattanooga News-Free Press (TN newspaper)
Chattanooga Times (TN newspaper)
Chattanooga, Battle(s) of (US hist.; 1863)
Chattanooga, TN
Chatterley, Lady Constance (fict. chara.)
Chatterley's Lover, Lady (D.H. Lawrence novel)
Chatterton, Thomas (Br. poet; 1752-70)
Chaucer, Geoffrey (Br. poet; c 1340-1400)
Chaudry, Fazal Elahi (ex-pres., Pak.; 1904-88)
Chauncey Olcott (US comp./ent.; 1860-1932)
Chausson, Ernest (Fr. comp.; 1855-99)
Chautauqua movement (US adult educ.)
Chautauqua, NY
Chavannes, Pierre Cecile Puvis de (Fr. artist;
    1824-98)
Chavez, Carlos (Mex. comp.; 1899-1978)
Chávez, Cesar (US labor leader; 1927-93)
Chavis, Benjamin F., Rev. (US rel./head
    NAACP; 1948-)
Chavez, Julio Cesar (boxing; 1962-)
Chayefsky, Paddy (US writer; 1923-81)
Che (Ernesto) Guevara (SAmer. mil.; 1928-67)
Cheapside district (London, Eng.)

Checker™ cab
Checker Motors Corp.
Checker, Chubby (ent.; 1941-)
Checkpoint Charlie (East/West Berlin)
Cheddar cheese (also cheddar)
Cheddar, England
Cheddi (Berrat) Jagan (pres., Guyana; 1918-)
Cheech & Chong (entertainers)
Cheech Marin (ent.; 1946-)
Cheetah Systems (US bus.)
Cheektowaga, NY
Cheer™ (detergent)
Cheerios™ (cereal)
Cheers (TV show)
Cheese Nips™
Chee-tos™ (chips)
Cheever, John (US writer; 1912-82)
Cheever, Susan (US writer)
Cheez Doodles™
Cheez-It™ (crackers)
Chef Boyardee™
Cheiffou, Amadou (ex-PM, Niger)
Chekhov, Anton (Pavlovich)(Rus. writer; 1860-1904)
Chekiang (also Zhejiang)(province, Ch.)
Chellean (early humans)
Chelsea Clinton (daughter of US pres.; 1970-)
Chelsea Quinn Yarbro
Chelsea, Kensington and (London borough)
Chelsea, MA, ME
Cheltenham (type style)
Chelyabinsk, Siberia
Chem-Dry™ (carpet cleaning)
Chem-Dry (US bus.)
Chemistry, Nobel Prize for
Chemnitz, Germany (formerly Karl-Marx-Stadt)
Chemomyrdin, Viktor S. (PM, Rus.)
Chen Ning Yang (Ch./US physt.; 1922-)
Cheney, Richard B. (US pol.; 1941-)
Chengchow, China (also Zhengzhou)
Chengdu, China (also Chengtu)
Chenin Blanc (grape, wine)(also l.c.)
Chennault, Claire Lee (US gen.; 1890-1958)
Cheong, Ong Teng (pres., Singapore
Cheops (or Khufu), Great Pyramid of (Eg.)
Cher (b. Cherilyn Sirkisian)(ent.; 1946-)
Cherbourg, France
Chernenko, Konstantin (ex-pres., USSR; 1911-85)
Chernobyl, Ukraine (nuclear accident; 1986)
Cherokee (NAmer. Indians)
Cherokee, Jeep™ Grand (auto.)
Cherokee rose (plant)
Cherry Heering
Cherry Hill, NJ
Cherry Orchard, The (play by Chekhov)
Cherry Point Marine Corps Air Station (NC)

Cheryl Ladd (ent.; 1951-)
Cheryl Tiegs (model/ent.; 1947-)
Chesapeake and Ohio Canal National Historical Park (MD/WV/DC)
Chesapeake Bay (MD, VA)
Chesapeake Bay retriever (dog)
Chesapeake Beach, MD
Chesapeake, USS
Chesapeake, VA
Chesebrough-Ponds™ (toiletries)
Chesebrough-Ponds, Inc.
Cheshire (cheese)
Cheshire (county, Eng.)
Cheshire cat
Chesnokov, Andrei (tennis)
Chessman, Caryl ("Red Light Bandit")(US rapist; ?-1960)
Chester A(lan) Arthur (21th US pres.; 1829-86)
Chester Gould (cartoonist, *Dick Tracy*; 1900-85)
Chester W(illiam) Nimitz (US adm.; 1885-1966)
Chesterfield, Lord Philip (4th Earl of Chesterfield, Philip Dormer Stanhope)(Br. writer/pol.; 1694-1773)
Chet (Chester) Atkins (ent.; 1924-)
Chet Baker (US jazz; 1929-88)
Chet Huntley (US TV jour.; 1912-74)
Chevalier, Maurice (ent.; 1888-72)
Chevette, Chevrolet™ (auto.)
Cheviot Hills (Scot./Eng.)
Cheviot sheep (Scot./Br./Austl.)
Cheviot, OH
Chevret (cheese)
Chevrolet™ (auto.)
Chevrolet Camero™ (auto.)
Chevrolet Caprice™ (auto.)
Chevrolet Cavalier™ (auto.)
Chevrolet Chevette™ (auto.)
Chevrolet Corsica/Beretta™ (auto.)
Chevrolet Corvette™ (auto.)
Chevrolet Geo Prizm™ (auto.)
Chevrolet Lumina™ (auto.)
Chevrolet S-Blazer™ (auto.)
Chevrolet Vega™ (auto.)
Chevron™
Chevron Corp.
Chevy™ (auto.)
Chevy Chase (ent.; 1943-)
Chevy Chase, MD
Chevy Cheyenne™ (auto.)
Chevy Lumina™ (auto.)
Chevy Silverado™ (auto.)
Chevy Sportside™ (auto.)
Chevy S-Blazer™ (auto.)
Chewa (lang./people)
Cheyenne Mountain Complex (CO)
Cheyenne River (WY)
Cheyenne™, Chevy (auto.)
Cheyenne, WY

Cheyne-Stokes respiration (med.)
Chiang Ching (also Jiang Qing)(Ch. pol./widow of Mao Zedong; 1914-91)
Chiang Kai-shek (also Chiang Chung-cheng)(ex-pres., Nationalist China; 1887-1975)
Chiang Kai-shek, Madame (b. Soong Mei-ling)(Ch. lecturer/writer; 1898-?)
Chiangmai, Thailand
Chianti (region, It.)
Chianti (wine)
Chiba, Japan
Chic Young (cartoonist, *Blondie*; 1901-73)
Chicago (pop music)
Chicago Bears (football team)
Chicago Black Hawks (hockey team)
Chicago Board of Trade
Chicago Bulls (basketball team)
Chicago Cubs (baseball team)
Chicago Eight, the (US hist.; 1968)
Chicago Fire (also l.c.)(1871)
Chicago Herald (IL newspaper)
Chicago Loop (also "The Loop")(highway)
Chicago Sun-Times (IL newspaper)
Chicago Tribune (IL newspaper)
Chicago White Sox (baseball team)
Chicago, Art Institute of
Chicago, IL
Chicano (Mex.-Amer.)
Chichen Itzá (ancient Mayan ruins)
Chick Corea (US jazz; 1941-)
Chick Webb (US jazz; 1902-39)
Chickadee, My Little (film)
Chickasaw (horse)
Chickasaw (NAmer. Indians)
chicken Kiev
Chicken Little (fict. chara.)
chicken Marengo (food)
Chicken of the Sea™ (tuna)
chicken Tetrazzini (food)
Chicken Tonight™ (sauce)
Chiclayo, Peru
Chico (Leonard) Marx (ent.; 1886-1961)
Chico (Filho Francisco) Mendes (Brazilian environ./labor leader; 1944-88)
Chico (Glenn) Resch (hockey; 1948-)
Chico San™ (rice cakes)
Chico, CA
Chief Black Hawk (Sauk Indians; 1767-1838)
Chief Cochise (Apache Indians; 1812?-74)
Chief Cornplanter (Seneca Indians, half-white, aided Br. in Amer. Rev.; c1740-1836)
Chief Crazy Horse (Sioux Indians, Little Bighorn; 1842-77)
Chief Executive (US pres. title)
Chief Joseph (Nez Percé Indians; c1840-1904)
Chief Justice of the United States (US Supreme Court)

Chief (Joseph) Leabua Jonathan (ex-PM, Lesotho; 1914-87)
Chief Little Turtle (Michikinikwa)(Miami Indians; 1752?-1812)
Chief Mangas Coloradas (Apache Indians; c1797-1863)
Chief Massasoit (Wampanoag Indians, peace treaty with Pilgrims; c1590-1661)
Chief of Naval Operations (US mil.)
Chief Osceola (Seminole Indians; 1800?-38)
Chief Pontiac (Ottawa Indians; c1720-69)
Chief Red Cloud (Sioux Indians; 1822-1909)
Chief Seattle (also Seatlh)(Suquamish Indians; c1790-1866)
Chief Sequoya (aka George Guess)(Cherokee Indians, scholar; c1766-1843)
Chief Sitting Bull (Tatanka Yotanka)(Sioux Indians; c1831-90)
Chief Tecumseh (also Tecumtha)(Shawnee Indians; 1768-1813)
Chiefs, Kansas City (football team)
Chiesa, Vivienne Della (ent.; 1920-)
Chihuahua (dog)
Chihuahua, Mexico
Child (mag.)
Child Life (mag.)
Child, Julia (US chef/writer; 1912-)
Childe Hassam (US artist; 1859-1935)
Children of a Lesser God (film; 1986)
Children's Crusade (Fr-Ger./Jerusalem; 1212)
Children's Fund, United Nations (UNICEF)(formerly United Nations International Children's Emergency Fund)(est. 1946)
Chile (Republic of)(SAmer.)
Chiles, Lawton (FL gov.; 1930-)
Chill Wills (ent.; 1903-78)
Chillicothe, MO, OH
Chilliwack, British Columbia, Canada
Chilly Willy (cartoon chara.)
Chiluba (also Luba-Lulua)(lang.)
Chiluba, Frederick (pres., Zambia; 1943-)
Chin dynasty, Eastern (Ch.; 317-420)
Chin dynasty, Later (Ch.; 1115-1234)
Chin dynasty, Western (Ch.; 265-316)
Chin, Tiffany
China (People's Republic of)(mainland China)
China (Republic of)(Nationalist China)
China aster (flower)
China Beach (TV show)
China grass (fiber)
China grasscloth
China hibiscus (plant)
China Lake Naval Weapons Center (CA)
China oil
China rose (plant)
China Sea (also South China Sea)(off SE Asia)
China silk

China Syndrome, The (film; 1979)
China tree
China White (slang for heroin)
China, Great Wall of
China, Red (People's Republic of China)
Chinaglia, Giorgio (soccer; 1947-)
Chinaman
Chinatown
Chinatown (film; 1974)
Chincoteague (pony)
Chincoteague, VA
Chine, crepe de (fabric)
Chinese (goose)
Chinese (lang./people)
Chinese art
Chinese cabbage/celery
Chinese checkers (game)
Chinese chestnut
Chinese date (tree)
Chinese Empire
Chinese gooseberry (also kiwi)(fruit)
Chinese ink (also India ink)
Chinese lantern (also Japanese lantern)
Chinese lantern (plant)
Chinese molasses (slang, opium)
Chinese New Year
Chinese parsley (coriander)
Chinese puzzle
Chinese red (color)
Chinese-restaurant syndrome
Chinese Revolution (1911 & 1949)
Chinese Shar-Pei (dog)
Chinese white (color)
Chinese wisteria (plant)
Ching dynasty (also Manchu)(Ch.; 1644-1912)
Ching, Chiang (also Jiang Qing)(Ch. pol./widow
    of Mao Zedong; 1914-91)
Ching, I (also Book of Changes)(rel.)
Ching, Tao-te (rel.)
Chinock (helicopter)
Chinon™ (movie equip.)
Chinon America, Inc.
Chinook (NAmer. Indians)
Chinook salmon
Chinook State (nickname, WA)
Chip Hanauer (boat racing)
Chipata, Zambia
Chipewyan (NAmer. Indians)
Chipmunks, Alvin & the (cartoon)
Chip 'N' Dale, The Adventures of (TV show)
Chippendale chair
Chippendale style
Chippendale, Thomas (Br. furniture designer;
    c1718-79)
Chippewa (also Ojibwa)(NAmer. Indians)
Chippewa Falls, WI
Chippewa National Forest
CHiPs (TV show)

Chips Ahoy!™ (cookies)
Chips, Goodbye, Mr. (film; 1939)
Chirac, Jacques (ex-PM, Fr.; 1932-)
Chirico, Giorgio de (It. artist; 1888-1978)
Chisholm Trail (cattle drives)
Chisholm v. Georgia (US law; 1793)
Chisholm, MN
Chisholm, Shirley (Anita St. Hill)(US pol.;
    1924-)
Chisinau, Moldova (also Kishinev)
Chissano, Joaquim Alberto (pres., Mozambique;
    1939-)
Chita Rivera (ent.; 1933-)
Chittagong, Bangladesh
Chitty Chitty Bang Bang (film; 1968)
Chivas Regal (scotch)
Chloë, Daphnis and (Gr. romance)
Chloraseptic™ (med.)
Chloris (myth.)
Chloromycetin™ (med.)
Chlorophyta (green algae phylum)
Chlor-Trimeton™ (med.)
Chocolatier (mag.)
Choctaw (NAmer. Indians)
Choice Hotels International (US bus.)
Chomsky, Norm (US linguist; 1928-)
Chondokyo (rel.)
Chong, Cheech & (ent.)
Chong, Rae Dawn (ent.; 1961-)
Chong, Tommy (Thomas)(ent.; 1938-)
Chongjin, North Korea
Chongqing, China (also Chungking)
Chop, Lamb (S. Lewis puppet)
Chopin, Frédéric (Pol. comp.; 1810-49)
Chopsticks (also The Celebrated Chop Waltz)(by
    A. de Lulli)
C horizon (geol.)
Chorus Line, A (play)
Chorzow, Poland
Chosen People (also l.c.)(rel.)
Chou dynasty (Ch. hist.; 1122-255 BC)
Chou En-Lai (also Zhou Enlai)(ex-PM, Ch.;
    1898-1976)
Chouteau, Jean Pierre (US pioneer/fur trader;
    1758-1849)
Chouteau, Rene Auguste (US pioneer/fur
    trader; 1749-1829)
Choybalsan, Mongolia
Chretién, (Joseph Jacques) Jean (PM, Can.;
    1934-)
Chris Brathwaite (track; 1949-84)
Chris-Craft™
Chris Craft Boats (US bus.)
Chris Evert-Lloyd (tennis; 1954-)
Chris Lemmon (ent.)
Chris Schenkel (ent.; 1923-)
Chris Van Allsburg (US writer/artist; 1949-)
Christ of the Andes (peace monument between

Chile/Argentina)

Christ, Jesus (known as Jeshua ben Joseph to contemporaries)

Christ, Vicar of (pope)

Christ, Yellow (by Gauguin)

Christa McAuliffe (US educ., *Challenger*; 1948-86)

Christchurch, England

Christchurch, New Zealand

Christendom (rel.)

Christhood

Christiaan Barnard, Dr. (SAfr. phys., performed 1st human heart transplant; 1922-)

Christian (rel.)

Christian Broadcasting Network (CBN)

Christian Brothers™ (brandy)

Christian Brothers religious order (also Brother of the Christian Schools)

Christian Dior (Fr. designer; 1905-57)

Christian Dior Perfumes Corp.

Christian Doppler (Aus. physt.; 1803-53)

Christian Endeavor Societies (rel.)

Christian Era

Christian Huygens (or Huyghens)(Dutch math./physt./astron.; 1629-95)

Christian I (king, Den.; 1426-48)

Christian IV (king, Den./Nor.; 1577-1648)

Christian IX (king, Den.; 1818-1906)

Christian name (first [baptismal] name)

Christian Science (also Church of Christ, Scientist)

Christian Science Monitor (Christian Science newspaper)

Christian VIII (king, Den.; 1786-1848)

Christian X (king, Den./Iceland; 1870-1947

Christian, Charlie (US jazz; 1919-42)

Christian, Judeo- (beliefs, traditions)

Christianity (rel.)

Christians and Jews, National Conference of (est. 1928)

Christiansted, St. Croix

Christie Ann Hefner (US publ.)

Christie Brinkley (US model; 1953-)

Christie, Agatha, Dame (Br. writer; 1891-1976)

Christie, Julie (ent.; 1940-)

Christie's (auction)

Christina (queen, Swed.; 1626-89)

Christina Applegate (ent.; 1972-)

Christina Onassis (Gr. heiress; 1951-88)

Christina Pickles

Christina (Georgina) Rossetti (Br. poet; 1830-94)

Christina Stead (Austl. writer; 1903-83)

Christina's World (A. Wyeth painting)

Christine Ebersole

Christine Jorgensen (1st sex-change operation; 1927-89)

Christine Lahti (ent.; 1950-)

Christmas (also Noel, Xmas)(rel.)

Christmas cactus (flowering plant)

Christmas Carol, A (C. Dickens novel)

Christmas club (type of savings account)

Christmas Day (12/25)

Christmas Eve (12/24)

Christmas fern (plant)

Christmas Island (also Gilbert Islands)(site of nuclear testing, Pac.)

Christmas Island (Indian Ocean)

Christmas rose (plant)

Christmas tree

Christmas tree (slang for Tuinal™)

Christmasberry

Christmastide

Christmastime

Christo (Christo Javacheff)(Bulgarian artist; 1935-)

Christology (rel.)

Christoph W(illibald) von Gluck (Ger. comp.; 1714-87)

Christopher Columbus (It./Sp. nav.; 1451-1506)

Christopher Dean (figure skating)

Christopher Fry (Br. writer; 1907-)

Christopher Grant LaFarge (US arch.; 1862-1938)

Christopher (William Bradshaw) Isherwood (Br. writer; 1904-86)

Christopher J. Dodd (US cong.; 1944-)

Christopher Lee (aka Lee Yuen Kam)(ent.; 1922-)

Christopher Lloyd (ent.; 1938-)

Christopher Marlowe (Br. writer; 1564-93)

Christopher (Darlington) Morley (US writer/editor; 1890-1957)

Christopher-Nevis, St. (Federation of)(also St. Kitts-Nevis)(West Indies)

Christopher Plummer (ent.; 1927-)

Christopher Reeve (ent.; 1952-)

Christopher Robin (fict. chara, *Winnie-the-Pooh*)

Christopher Samuel Bond ("Kit")(US cong.; 1939-)

Christopher Walken (ent.; 1943-)

Christopher Wren, Sir (Br. arch.; 1632-1723)

Christopher, St. (patron saint of travelers)

Christopher, Warren (US Secy./State; 1925-)

Christopher, William (ent.; 1932-)

Christy Brown (Ir. writer/artist; 1932-81)

Christy (Christopher) Mathewson (baseball; 1880-1925)

Christy, Edwin P. (ent.; 1815-62)

Christy's Minstrels (music)

Chronicle of Higher Education

Chronicle, Augusta (GA newspaper)

Chronicle, Houston (TX newspaper)

Chronicle, San Francisco (CA newspaper)

Chronicles, Books of (rel.)
Chrysler (auto.)
Chrysler Concorde (auto.)
Chrysler Corp.
Chrysler Dodge/Plymouth Neon (auto.)
Chrysler Jeep™ Grand Cherokee (auto.)
Chrysler Jeep™ Grand Cherokee Laredo (auto.)
Chrysler LH sedan (auto.)
Chrysler New Yorker (auto.)
Chrysler-Plymouth Fifth Avenue (auto.)
Chrysler-Plymouth Imperial (auto.)
Chrysler-Plymouth Le Baron (auto.)
Chrysler-Plymouth New Yorker (auto.)
Chrysler Town & County (auto.)
Chrysler, Walter P(ercy)(US bus./auto.; 1875-
   1940)
Chrysophyta (phylum)
Chuan Leekpai (PM, Thailand)
Chubby Checker (ent.; 1941-)
Chuck Barris (ent.)
Chuck (Charles) Berry (ent.; 1926-)
Chuck Connors (ent.; 1921-92)
Chuck Jones (cartoonist, *Bugs Bunny, Porky
   Pig, Daffy Duck*; 1905?-)
Chuck Mangione (ent.; 1940-)
Chuck Noll (football; 1931-)
Chuck Norris (ent.; 1940-)
Chuck (Charles) Scarborough
Chuck Wagon™ (dog food)
Chuck Woolery (ent.)
Chuck (Charles Elwood) Yeager, Col. (US
   aviator; 1923-)
Chula Vista, CA
Chun Doo Hwan (ex-pres., SKorea; 1931-)
Chung King™ (foods)
Chung King Corp.
Chung Won Shik (ex-PM, SKorea)
Chung, Connie (US TV jour.; 1946-)
Chung, Eye to Eye With Connie (TV show)
Chungking, China (also Chongqing)
Chunky Soup™
Chunnel (tunnel joining Eng./Fr.)
Church of Christ (also Christian Science/
   Scientist)
Church of England (also Anglican Church)
Church of God
Church of Jesus Christ of the Latter-Day Saints
   (also Latter-Day Saints, Mormon Church)
Church of Rome (also Roman Catholic Church)
Church of Scientology (rel.)
Church of Scotland
Church of the Brethren (also Dunkers)
Church of the New Jerusalem (also
   Swedenborgians)
Church of Tonga
Church Rock (NM)(nuclear accident; 1979)
Church, Frederic (US artist; 1826-1900)
Churches of Christ in the United States of

America, National Council of the (est. 1950)
Churchill, Baroness Clementine Spencer- (wife
   of ex-Br. PM; 1885-1977
Churchill, Jennie (Br., mother of Winston;
   1854-1921)
Churchill, John (aka Duke of Marlborough)(Br.
   mil.; 1650-1722)
Churchill, Manitoba, Canada
Churchill, Randolph (Henry Spencer), Lord (Br.
   pol., father of Winston; 1849-95)
Churchill, Sarah (Br., duchess of Marlboro;
   1660-1744)
Churchill, Sir Winston (Leonard Spencer)(ex-
   PM, Br.; 1874-1965)
Churchill, Winston (US writer; 1871-1947)
Church's Fried Chicken, Inc.
Chuvash (lang./people)
Chyngyshev, Tursenbek (PM, Kyrgyzstan)
CIA (Central Intelligence Agency)
Ciampi, Carlo Azeglio (ex-PM, It.)
Ciano, Galeazzo (It. pol.; 1903-44)
Ciba Consumer Pharmaceuticals (US bus.)
Cibola, Seven Cities of (utopia)
Cicely Tyson (ent.; 1933-)
Cicero, Marcus Tullius ("Tully")(Roman orator/
   writer/pol.; 106-43 BC)
Cid, El (also el Campeador, Rodrigo Diaz de
   Bivar)(Sp. mil.; 1040-99)
Ciera, Oldsmobile (auto.)
Cilea, Francesco (It. comp.; 1866-1950)
Ciller, Tansu (PM, Turk.)
Cimabue, Giovanni (It. artist; 1240-1302)
Cimarosa, Domenico (It. comp.; 1749-1801)
Cimarron™ (CAT system)
Cimarron, Territory of (now Oklahoma
   panhandle)
Cimino, Michael (US ent.; 1943-)
Cimmerians (myth. people, lived in darkness)
C in C (commander in chief)
Cincinnati Bengals (football team)
Cincinnati Enquirer (OH newspaper)
Cincinnati Post (OH newspaper)
Cincinnati Reds (baseball team)
Cincinnati, OH
Cinco de Mayo (Mex. holiday)
Cinderella (fairy tale)
Cindy Crawford (US model; 1966-)
Cindy Nelson (skiing; 1955-)
Cindy Pickett (ent.; 1947-)
Cindy Williams (ent.; 1947-)
Cinema Corp., General
CinemaScope™ (wide screen)
Cinemax (MAX)(cable TV)
Cineplex™
Cineplex Odeon Theaters
Cinerama™ (wide screen)
CineTellFilms
Cinzano USA, Inc.

Cipro™ (med.)
Circassia (region, Russia)
Circassian (people)
Circassian walnut (wood of the English walnut
tree)
Circe (myth.)
Circinus (astron., compasses)
Circle K™ (store)
Circle K Corp.
Circuit City Stores, Inc.
Circus Flaminius (Roman circus)
Circus Maximus (ancient Roman circus)
Circus, Circus Enterprises, Inc.
Cisco Kid (fict. chara.)
Cisneros, Henry (US Secy./HUD; 1947-)
CITES (Convention on International Trade in
Endangered Species)
Citgo Petroleum (US bus.)
Citibank™
Citicorp™
Citicorp Diners Club (US bus.)
Citium, Zeno of (Gr. phil.; late 4th early 3rd c.
BC)
Citizen Kane (film; 1941)
Citizen Watch Co. of America
Citizens Band (CB)(radio)
Citrucel™ (med.)
Citrus Bowl (college football)
City Lights (film)
City of Brotherly Love (Philadelphia)
City of David (also Jerusalem, Bethlehem)
City of God (heaven)
City of God, The (Latin, De Civitate Dei)(by St.
Augustine)
City of Light (Paris)
City of Seven Hills (Rome)
Ciudad Bolivar, Venezuela
Ciudad Guzman, Mexico
Ciudad Juarez, Mexico
Ciudad Rodrigo, Spain
Ciudad Trujillo, Santo Domingo
Civic, Honda™ (auto.)
Civil Aeronautics Board (CAB)(US govt.)
Civil Rights Act, the (US hist.; 1875, 1964)
Civil War, American (also War of Secession,
War Between the States)(1861-65)
Civil War, English (1642-47)
Civil War, Spanish (1936-39)
Civilian Conservation Corps (CCC)(US govt.;
1933-42)
Civitan International (service club)
C. J. Van Houten & Zoon, Inc.
Cl (chem. sym.,.chlorine)
Clabber Girl™ (baking powder)
Claes (Thure) Oldenburg (US artist; 1929-)
Claiborne Pell (US cong.; 1918-)
Claiborne, Craig (US writer/food; 1920-)
Claiborne, Inc., Liz

Claiborne™, Liz (clothing)
Claiborne, Liz (US designer; 1929-)
Clair Bee (basketball; 1896-1983)
Clair de Lune (by Debussy)
Clair, Arthur Saint (US gen.; 1736-1818)
Claire Bloom (ent.; 1931-)
Claire Lee Chennault (US gen.; 1890-1958)
Claire Trevor (ent.; 1909-)
Clairol™ (hair care)
Clairol, Inc.
Clamato™ (juice)
Clampett, Bob (fict. chara.)
Clampett, Elly May (fict. chara.)
Clampett, Jed (fict. chara.)
Clampett, Jethro (fict. chara.)
Clancy, Tom (Ir. ent.; 1923-90)
Clancy, Tom (US writer; 1947-)
Clapton, Eric (ent.; 1945-)
Clara Barton (U.S., founded American Red
Cross; 1821-1912)
Clara Bow (the "It Girl")(ent.; 1905-65)
Clara Josephine (Wieck) Schumann (Ger.
pianist; 1819-96)
Clare (county, Ir.)
Clare Boothe Luce (US drama./dipl./pol.; 1903-
87)
Clare Briggs (cartoonist, *Mr. & Mrs.*; 1875-
1930)
Clarence Birdseye ("Bob")(US inv., frozen food;
1886-1956)
Clarence (Seward) Darrow (US atty./writer;
1857-1938)
Clarence Day, Jr. (US writer; 1874-1935)
Clarence Kelley
Clarence (Augustus) Seignoret (pres.,
Dominica)
Clarence "Pinetop" Smith (US jazz; 1904-29)
Clarence S. Stein (US arch.; 1882-1975)
Clarence Thomas (US jurist; 1948-)
Clarendon (also l.c.)(type style)
Clarion™ (cosmetics)
Clarion-Ledger, Jackson (MS newspaper)
Clarion, Ltd.
Clark Clifford (US pol.; 1906-)
Clark Corp., Kimberly-
Clark Expedition, Lewis and (St. Louis to Pac.;
1804-06)
Clark Gable, (William)(ent.; 1901-60)
Clark National Historical Park, George Rogers
(IN)
Clark National Park, Lake (AK)
Clark, Charles Joseph "Joe" (ex-PM, Can.;
1939-)
Clark, Dane (ent.; 1913-)
Clark, Dick (ent.; 1929-)
Clark, George Rogers (US mil.; 1752-1818)
Clark, Inc., Coats &
Clark, Joe (Charles Joseph)(ex-PM, Can.; 1939-)

Clark, Mark (US gen.; 1896-1984)
Clark, Mary Higgins (US writer; 1931-)
Clark, Petula (ent.; 1932-)
Clark, Roy (ent.; 1933-)
Clark, Susan (ent.; 1940-)
Clark, Will (baseball; 1964-)
Clarke, Arthur C(harles)(Br. sci-fi writer; 1917-)
Clarke, Bobby (Robert Earle)(hockey; 1949-)
Clarke, Kenny (US jazz; 1914-85)
Clarksville, AR, IN, TN, TX
Clash, the (pop music)
Classic, U.S. v. (US law; 1941)
Classicism (style, art/music/lit.)
Claude Akins (ent.; 1918-)
Claude Dauphin
Claude Debussy (Fr. comp.; 1862-1918)
Claude Garamond (Fr. typographer; c1480-1561)
Claude glass (photo.)
Claude Lévi-Strauss (Fr. anthrop.; 1908-1990)
Claude Lorrain (Fr. artist; 1600-82)
Claude Monet (Fr. artist; 1840-1926)
Claude Pepper (US pol.; 1901-89)
Claude Rains (ent.; 1890-1967)
Claude (Henri de Rouvoy) Saint-Simon, Comte de (Fr. phil.; 1760-1825)
Claude, Albert (Belgium biol.; 1899-1983)
Claudette Colbert (Fr./US ent.; 1903-)
Claudia Cardinale (ent.)
Claudia "Lady Bird" (Alta Taylor) Johnson (wife of ex-US pres.; 1912-)
Claudia Kolb (swimming; 1949-)
Claudian (Roman poet; c370-c404 BC)
Claudio Abbado (It. ent.; 1933-)
Claudio Arrau (Chilean pianist; 1903-91)
Claudio (Giovanni Antonio) Monteverdi (It. comp.; 1567-1643)
Claudius I (Tiberius Claudius Drusus Nero Germanicus)(emp., Rome; 10 BC-AD 54)
Claudius Nero (Caesar) Tiberius (emp., Rome; 42 BC-AD 37)
Claus von Bulow (US news)
Claus, Santa (also St. Nicholas, Kriss Kringle)
Clausen, Zorach v. (US law; 1952)
Clausewitz, Karl von (Ger. mil.; 1780-1831)
Claussen™
Claussen Pickle Co.
Clavell, James (Br./US writer; 1924-)
Clay, Andrew Dice (b. Andrew Silverstein)(ent.)
Clay, Cassius, Jr. (aka Muhammad Ali)(boxing; 1942-)
Clay, Henry (also Great Compromiser, Great Pacificator)(US pol.; 1777-1852)
Clay, Lucius D. (US gen.; 1897-1978)
Clayburgh, Jill (ent.; 1944-)
Claymation™ (animated clay figures)
Clayton Antitrust Act (US hist.; 1914)

Clayton Homes (manufactured homes)
Clayton Moore (ent.; 1908-)
Clayton, Buck (US jazz; 1911-)
Clean & Clear™ (cosmetics)
Clean™, Mr. (cleaner)
Clean, Mr. (slang, scandal free)
Clear Eyes™ (med.)
Clearasil™ (skincare)
Clearly Canadian™
Clearly Canadian Beverage Corp. (US/Can. bus.)
Clearwater, FL
Cleary, Beverly (US writer; 1916-)
Cleaver, Beaver ("the Beaver")(fict. chara.)
Cleaver, Eldridge (US activist/writer; 1935-)
Cleavon Little (ent.; 1939-92)
Cleef & Arpels, Inc., Van
Cleef, Lee Van (ent.; 1925-89)
Cleese, John (ent.; 1939-)
Clemenceau, Georges (ex-PM, Fr.; 1841-1929)
Clemens W(enzel) L(othar) Metternich (Prince von Metternich)(ex-chanc., Aus.; 1773-1859)
Clemens, Roger (baseball; 1962-)
Clemens, Samuel Langhorne (pseud. Mark Twain)(US writer; 1835-1910)
Clement (name of 14 popes)
Clement Athelston Arrindell (gov-gen., St. Kitts/Nevis
Clement C(lark) Moore (US poet/educ.; 1779-1863)
Clement R(ichard) Attlee (ex-PM, Br.; 1883-1967)
Clement Studebaker (US bus.; 1831-1901)
Clement VII (pope; 1478-1534)
Clement Vineyards, St. (US bus.)
Clemente, Roberto (baseball; 1934-72)
Clementine Spencer-Churchill, Baroness (wife of ex-Br. PM; 1885-1977
Cleo Laine (ent.; 1927-)
Cleopatra (queen, Eg.; c68-30 BC)
Cleopatra, Antony and (Shakespeare play)
Cleopatra's Needle(s)(Eg. obelisks in NYC and London)
Clerides, Glafcos (pres., Cyprus; 1919-)
Cleveland Abbe (US meteor.; 1838-1916)
Cleveland Amory (US writer; 1917-)
Cleveland bay (horse)
Cleveland Browns (football team)
Cleveland Cavaliers (basketball team)
Cleveland Indians (baseball team)
Cleveland Plain Dealer (OH newspaper)
Cleveland, Abbe
Cleveland, Grover (22nd & 24th US pres.; 1837-1908)
Cleveland, MS, OH, OK, TN
Cleves, Anne of (4th wife of Henry VIII; 1515-57)
Cliburn, Van (Harvey Lavan Cliburn, Jr.)(ent.;

1934-)
Cliff Arquette (pseud. Charlie Weaver)(ent.; 1905-74)
Cliff Robertson (ent.; 1925-)
Clifford Brown (US jazz; 1930-56)
Clifford Darling (gov-gen., Bahamas)
Clifford Odets (US writer; 1906-63)
Clifford, Clark (US pol.; 1906-)
Cliffs Notes, Inc.
Clift, Montgomery (ent.; 1920-66)
Clifton Davis (ent.; 1945-)
Clifton Fadiman (US writer/editor; 1904-)
Clifton Webb (ent.; 1891-1966)
Clifton, AZ, NJ
Cline, Patsy (ent.; 1932-63)
Cling Free™ (fabric softener)
Clingman's Dome (Great Smoky Mts.)
Clinique™ (skincare)
Clinique Laboratories, Inc.
Clint Black (ent.; 1962-)
Clint Eastwood (ent.; 1930-)
Clinton, Bill (William Jefferson)(42nd US pres.; 1946-)
Clinton, Chelsea (daughter of US pres.; 1970-)
Clinton, DeWitt (US pol.; 1769-1828)
Clinton, George (ex-US VP; 1739-1812)
Clinton, Henry (Br. mil.; 1738-95)
Clinton, Hillary Rodham (US atty.; wife of US pres.; 1947-)
Clinton, Roger (half-brother of US pres.)
Clio (myth.)
Clio (TV ad award)
Clippers, Los Angeles (basketball team)
Clive, Robert (Br. leader in India; 1725-74)
Clockwork Orange, A (film; 1971)
Cloisters, the (NYC)(museum of medieval art)
Clooney, Rosemary (ent.; 1928-)
Clootie (also Cloot, Cloots)(Satan)
Cloris Leachman (ent.; 1926-)
Clorox™ bleach
Clorox Co., The
Clos Du Bois Wines (US bus.)
Clos du Val Wine Co., Ltd., The
Close Encounters of the Third Kind (film; 1977)
Close-Up™ (toothpaste)
Close, Glenn (ent.; 1947-)
Clotho (myth.)
Cloud, Chief Red (Sioux Indians; 1822-1909)
Clovis, NM
Club Med™ (travel)
Cluj-Napoca, Romania
CLVS (Certified Legal Video Specialist)
Clyde Barrow (US criminal; 1900-34)
Clyde Beatty (ent.; 1904-65)
Clyde McPhatter (ent.)
Clyde, Bonnie and (film; 1967)
Clyde, Bonnie and (US criminals)
Clydesdale (horse)

Clydesdale terrier (dog)
Clytemnestra (myth.)
CM (Certificate of Merit)
CMRS (Certified Manager of Reporting Services)
CNN International (cable TV)
Cnossos (also Knossos)(ruins, palace, Crete)
C-note (also C)(hundred dollar bill)
CO (Colorado)
Co (chem. sym., cobalt)
Coach (TV show)
Coachman Industries, Inc.
Coalinga, CA
Coast Guard Academy, U.S. (New London, CT)(est. 1876)
Coast Guard, U.S. (US mil.)
Coasters, the (pop music)
Coats & Clark, Inc.
Coats, Daniel R. (US cong.; 1943-)
Cobb, Lee J. (ent.; 1911-76)
Cobb, Ty(rus Raymond)(baseball; 1886-1961)
COBE (Cosmic Background Explorer)(US satellite)
COBOL (common business-oriented lang.)(compu.)
Coburg-Gotha, House of Saxe- (Br. ruling family; 1901-10)
Coburn, Charles (ent.; 1877-1961)
Coburn, James (ent.; 1928-)
Coca, Imogene (ent.; 1908-)
Coca-Cola™
Coca-Cola Co., The
Cocacolonize/Cocacolonization (US trade/ cultural influence on foreign countries)
Cochabamba, Bolivia
Cochin-China chicken (also Cochin-China fowl, cochin)
Cochin-China, South Vietnam
Cochise, Chief (Apache Indians; 1812?-74)
Cochran, Barbara Ann (skiing; 1951-)
Cochran, Eddie (ent.)
Cochran, Marilyn (skiing; 1950-)
Cochran, Robert (skiing; 1951-)
Cochran, Thad (US cong.; 1937-)
Cock Robbin
Cockaigne (also Cockayne)(myth. utopia)
Cockcroft, John D. (Br. physt.; 1897-1967)
Cocker, Joe (John Robert)(ent.; 1944-)
Coco Chanel, (Gabrielle)(Fr. designer; 1883-1971)
Coco, James (ent.)
Cocoa Beach, FL
Cocoa Krispies™ (cereal)
Cocoa Pebbles™ (cereal)
Cocoa Puffs™ (cereal)
Coconino National Forest
Coconut Grove (area, Los Angeles)
Coconut Grove, FL

Cocoon (film; 1985)
Cocos Islands (also Keeling Islands)(Indian Ocean)
Cocteau, Jean (Fr. writer/artist; 1889-1963)
COD (cash [or collect] on delivery, certificate of death)
Code Napoléon (also Napoleonic Code)(Fr. law)
Cody, William F(rederick) "Buffalo Bill" (US scout/ent.; 1846-1917)
Coe, Sebastian (Newbold)(track; 1956-)
Coeur d'Alene (NAmer. Indians)
Coeur d'Alene, ID
Coeur d'Alene National Forest (ID)
Coffee™, Mr.
Cogburn, Rooster (film; 1975)
Cognac (also l.c.)(brandy)
Cognac, France
Cohan, George M(ichael)(US comp; 1878-1942)
Cohen, Mickey
Cohen, William S. (US cong.; 1940-)
Cohn, Al (US jazz; 1925-88)
Cohn, Myron (ent.; 1902-86)
Coimbra, Portugal
Cointreau™ (liqueur)
Coke™
Cola Co., Pepsi-
Colavito, Rocky (Rocco Domenico)(baseball; 1933-)
Colbert, Claudette (Fr./US ent.; 1903-)
Colbert, Jean Baptiste (Fr. pol.; 1619-83)
Cold War (US/USSR; 1945-90)
Coldstream Guards (Br. mil., formerly Monck's Regiment)
Coldwell Banker™ Real Estate
Cole of California™ (sportswear)
Cole of California, Inc.
Cole Porter (US comp.; 1893-1964)
Cole(man) Younger, (Thomas)(US outlaw; 1844-1916)
Cole, Cozy (US jazz; 1909-81)
Cole, Gary (ent.; 1957-)
Cole, Nat "King" (ent.; 1919-65)
Cole, Natalie (ent.; 1950-)
Cole, Olivia (ent.; 1942-)
Cole, Thomas (US artist; 1801-48)
Coleman Hawkins (US jazz; 1904-69)
Coleman Young (Detroit mayor; 1918-)
Coleman, Cy (US comp.; 1929-)
Coleman, Dabney (ent.; 1932-)
Coleman, Derrick (basketball; 1967-)
Coleman, Gary (ent.; 1968-)
Coleman, Ornette (US jazz; 1930-)
Coleraine, Northern Ireland
Coleridge-Taylor, Samuel (Br. comp.; 1875-1912)
Coleridge, Samuel Taylor (Br. poet; 1772-1834)
Colette, Sidonie Gabrielle (Fr. writer; 1873-1954)

Colfax, Schuyler (ex-US VP; 1823-85)
Colgate™
Colgate-Palmolive Co.
Colgate, William (US bus.; 1783-1857)
Colin Davis (Br. cond.; 1927-)
Colin L(uther) Powell, Gen. (ex-chair., Joint Chiefs of Staff; 1937-)
Colleen Dewhurst (ent; 1926-1991)
Colleen McCullough (Austl. writer
College Entrance Examination Board (CEEB)
College of Arms (also Heralds' College)(Br. heraldry)
College of Cardinals (also Sacred College of Cardinals)(rel.)
College of William and Mary (VA)
College Park, GA, MD
College Station, Texas
Collegiate Athletic Association, National (NCAA)(est. 1906)
Collins, Fort (CO)(city)
Collins, Herrera v. (US law; 1993)
Collins, Jackie (US writer)
Collins, Joan (ent.; 1933-)
Collins, Judy (ent.; 1939-)
Collins, Michael (astro.; 1930-)
Collins, Pauline (ent.; 1940-)
Collins, Phil (ent.; 1951-)
Collins, Tom (mixed drink)
Collis Potter Huntington (US bus.; 1821-1900)
Collyer, Bud
Colman, Ronald (ent.; 1891-1958)
Cologne brown (color)
Cologne Cathedral
Cologne, eau de
Cologne, Germany (also Köln)
Coloma, CA
Colombia (Republic of)(SAmer.)
Colombian gold (slang, South American marijuana)
Colombo, Sri Lanka
Colón, Panama
Colonel Blimp (fict. chara.)
Colonel Sanders (US bus./chicken)
Colonial architecture
Colonial Dames of America
Colonial Homes (mag.)
Colonial National Historical Park (VA)
Colonial Penn Insurance Co.
Colonies, Thirteen (original US states)
Colonus, Oedipus at (by Sophocles)
Colony, Lost (VA settlement; disappeared 1591)
Color Key™ (graphic design)
Coloradas, Chief Mangas (Apache Indians; c1797-1863)
Colorado (CO)
Colorado potato beetle
Colorado River (Argentina)
Colorado River (SW US)

Colorado River (TX)
Colorado Rockies (baseball team)
Colorado Springs Gazette Telegraph (CO
   newspaper)
Colorado Springs, CO
Colosseum of Rome (site of mock battles &
   Christian sacrifices)
Colossians, Epistle to the (rel.)
Colossus of Memnon, (ancient Eg. statue)
Colossus of Rhodes (statue of Apollo; fell in 224
   BC)
Colón, Panama
Colson, Charles W. (US pol./Watergate; 1931-)
Colt™ (revolver)
Colt, Samuel (US gunsmith; 1814-62)
Coltrane, John (US jazz; 1926-67)
Colts, Indianapolis (football team)
Columba (also Columba Noae)(astron., dove)
Columbia (US space shuttle, 1st to orbit &
   return to Earth)
Columbia Broadcasting System (CBS)
Columbia Pictures (US film co.)
Columbia River (Can.)
Columbia State (SC newspaper)
Columbia University (NYC)
Columbia, District of (Washington, DC, US
   capital)
Columbia, MD, MO, MS, PA, SC, TN
Columbian Order of NYC (also Tammany
   Society)
Columbo (TV show)
Columbo, Mrs. (TV show)
Columbo, Russ (ent.; 1908-34)
Columbus Day (formerly Discovery
   Day)(October 12)
Columbus Dispatch (OH newspaper)
Columbus, Christopher (It./Sp. nav.; 1451-1506)
Columbus, GA, IN, KS, MS, NE, OH, TX, WI
Columbus, Knights of (rel. org.)
Coma Berenices (astron., Berenice's hair)
Coma cluster (astron.)
Comanche (NAmer. Indians)
Comaneci, Nadia (gymnast; 1961-)
Comden, Betty (US lyricist/ent.; 1919-)
Comedy Central (COM)(cable TV)
Comedy of Errors, The (Shakespeare play)
Comet™ (cleanser)
Comets, Bill Haley and the (pop music)
Comédie Française (Fr. national theater)
Comfort, Alex (Br. phys./writer
Comice (pear)
Coming to America (film)
Comintern (Third Communist International)
Commager, Henry Steele (US hist./educ.; 1902-)
Commerce Commission,-Interstate (ICC)(US
   govt. agcy.)
Commerce, Department of (US govt.)
Commercialware™ (cookware)

Commerical Appeal, Memphis (TN newspaper)
Commish, The (TV show)
Commodity Credit Corporation
   (CCC)(agriculture)
Commodore™ (compu.)
Commodore International, Ltd.
Common Market (EEC)(also European
   Economic Community, est. 1957)
Common Prayer, Book of (Church of England)
Common Sense (by Thomas Paine; 1776)
Common Sense™ Oat Bran (cereal)
Commons, House of (Br. & Can. parliaments)
Commons, John R. (US econ./hist.; 1862-1945)
Commonwealth Day (Br. holiday)
Commonwealth of Independent States
   (CIS)(informal successor body to the USSR)
Commonwealth of Nations
Commonwealth, the (voluntary assoc. of past &
   present British Empire countries)
Communion, Holy (also Eucharist, Lord's
   Supper)(rel.)
Communism (usually l.c.)
Communism Peak (also Pik
   Kommunizma)(formerly Mount Garmo,
   Mount Stalin)(Tajikisyan)
Communist Manifesto (by K. Marx/F. Engels)
Communist Party (pol.)
Como, Perry (ent.; 1912-)
Comorian (also Comoran)(people)
Comoros (Federal Islamic Republic of
   the)(Indian Ocean)
Compaoré, Blaise (pres., Burkina Faso; 1951-)
Compaq™
Compaq Computer Corp.
Compazine™
Compoboard™ (constr.)
Composite column (arch.)
Compound W™
Compromise of 1850 (US hist. re: slaves)
Compromiser, Great (also Great
   Pacificator)(Henry Clay)(US pol.; 1777-1852)
Compton effect (also Compton-Debye effect)(x-
   rays)
Compton, Arthur (Holly)(US physt.; 1892-1962)
Compton, John (George Melvin)(PM, St. Lucia
CompuServe™ (compu.)
Compute (mag.)
Computer Chronicles (TV show)
Computer Graphics World
Computer Shopper (mag.)
Computerland™
Computerland Corp.
Computerworld
Comsat™ (*communications satellite*)
Comstock Lode (gold/silver vein, NV)
Comstock, Anthony (US reformer; 1844-1915)
Comstock, Henry T(omkins) P. (US, Comstock
   Lode)

Comstockery (censorship of arts)
Comte, Auguste (Fr. phil.; 1798-1857)
Comtrex™ (med.)
Comus (also Komos)(myth.)
ConAgra, Inc.
Conair™ (appliances)
Conair Corp.
Conakry, Guinea
Conan Doyle, Sir Arthur (Br. phys./writer; 1859-1930)
Conan O'Brien (ent.)
Conan the Adventurer (TV show)
Conan the Barbarian (film; 1982)
Conan the Destroyer (film; 1984)
Concepción, Chile
Conchata Ferrell (ent.; 1943-)
Concord (grape/wine)
Concord coach (trans.)
Concord Naval Weapons Station (CA)
Concord, CA, MA, NC, NH
Concorde, Chrysler (auto.)
Concorde, Place de la (building/museum, Paris)
Concorde™, the (supersonic jet)
Conde Nast (US publ.)
Conde Nast Traveler (mag.)
Condon, Eddie (US jazz; 1904-73)
Conduct Medal, Distinguished (mil.)
Cone Mills Corp.
Conecuh National Forest
Coneheads, the (fict. charas.)
Conestoga (NAmer. Indians)
Conestoga wagon (horse drawn, covered)
Coney Island (NYC)
Confederate Memorial Day
Confederate note (econ.)
Confederate States of America (also Confederacy)(US hist.; 1861-65)
Confederation, Articles of (US hist.; 1781)
Conference of Christians and Jews, National (est. 1928)
Conference on Environment and Development, United Nations (Earth Summit)(June 1992)
Conference on Trade and Development, United Nations (UNCTAD)(est. 1964)
Confessions of Nat Turner, The (W. Styron book)
Confucianism (also called Confucian, Confucius)(philosophy/rel.)
Confucianist (rel.)
Confucius (Ch., founded Confucianism; 551-479 BC)
Cong, Vo Chi (ex-pres., Viet.)
Congo (Republic of the)(W central Afr.)
Congo red
Congo River (also Zaire River)(Afr.)
Congo snake (also l.c.)
Congo, Niger- (langs.)
Congoleum™

Congoleum Corp.
Congregational Church
Congregationalism (rel.)
Congress (of the U.S.)(US govt.)
Congress of Industrial Organizations (US labor org.)
Congress of Racial Equality (CORE)(US civil-rights org.)
Congress of Vienna (Eur. hist.; 1814-15)
Congress, Library of (DC)
Congressional Medal of Honor (also Medal of Honor)(mil.)
Congressional Record (US Congress proceedings)
Congreve, William (Br. writer; 1670-1729)
Conigliaro, Tony (baseball; 1945-90)
Connally, John B. (ex-gov., TX; 1917-93)
Connecticut (CT)
Connecticut General Life Insurance Co.
Connecticut Wits (also Hartford Wits)(18th c US lit. grp.)
Connecticut Yankee in King Arthur's Court, A (Mark Twain novel)
Connecticut, Griswold v. (US law; 1965)
Connell, Evan S. (US writer; 1924-)
Connemara pony
Conner, Nadine (ent.; 1913-)
Connery, Sean (Scot./US ent.; 1930-)
Connick, Harry, Jr. (ent.; 1967-)
Connie Chung (US TV jour.; 1946-)
Connie Chung, Eye to Eye With (TV show)
Connie Francis (ent.; 1938-)
Connie Mack (b. Cornelius McGillicuddy)(baseball; 1862-1956)
Connie Mack III (US cong.; 1940-)
Connie Sellecca (ent.; 1955-)
Connie Stevens (ent.; 1938-)
Conniff Orchestra, Ray
Conniff, Ray (ent.; 1916-)
Connolly, Maureen ("Little Mo")(tennis; 1934-69)
Connors, Chuck (ent.; 1921-92)
Connors, Jimmy (James Scott)(tennis; 1952-)
Connors, Mike (ent.; 1925-)
Conoco, Inc.
Conrad (Potter) Aiken (US writer; 1889-1973)
Conrad Bain (Can. ent.; 1923-)
Conrad Burns (US cong.; 1935-)
Conrad I (king, Ger.; ?-918)
Conrad II (king, Ger., Holy Roman emp.; c990-1039)
Conrad III (king, Ger.; 1093-1152)
Conrad IV (king, Ger.; 1228-54)
Conrad Janis (ent.; 1928-)
Conrad Nagel (ent.; 1896-1970)
Conrad N(icholson) Hilton (US bus./hotels; 1888-1979)
Conrad Potter Aiken (US writer; 1889-1973)

Conrad V (also Conradin)(king, Ger.; 1252-68)
Conrad, Charles, Jr. (astro.; 1930-)
Conrad, Joseph (Br. writer; 1857-1924)
Conrad, Kent (US cong.; 1948-)
Conrad, Paul (pol. cartoonist; 1924-)
Conrad, Robert (ent.; 1935-)
Conrad, William (ent.; 1920-)
Conried, Hans (ent.; 1917-82)
Conroy, Pat (US writer; 1945-)
Conservative Judaism (rel.)
Conservative Party (UK pol.)
Conservative Party (US pol.)
Conservative Party, Progressive- (Can. pol.)
Constable, John (Br. artist; 1776-1837)
Constance Bennett (ent.; 1904-65)
Constance Cummings (ent.; 1910-)
Constance Talmadge (ent.)
Constanta, Romania
Constantin Brancusi (Romanian artist; 1876-1957)
Constantine I (aka Constantine the Great)(emp., Rome; 306-337)
Constantine I (king, Gr.; 1868-1923)
Constantine II (deposed king, Gr.; 1940-)
Constantine Karamanlis (pres., Gr.; 1907-)
Constantine Mitsotakis (ex-PM, Gr.; 1918-)
Constantine the Great (aka Constantine I)(emp., Rome; 306-337)
Constantine, Arch of (Rome)
Constantine, Michael (ent.; 1927-)
Constantinople (formerly Byzantium, now Istanbul)
Constitution (of the U.S.)(ratified 1787)
Constitution State (nickname, CT)
Constitution, Atlanta (GA newspaper)
Constitution, The (*"Old Ironsides"*)(US naval ship)
Constitutional Convention (US hist.; 1787)
Consumer Guide™ (book)
Consumer Price Index
Consumer Reports (mag.)
Consumer Reports Buying Guide (book)
Consumers Digest (mag.)
Consumers Union (US consumers' org.; est. 1936)
Contac™ (med.)
Contadina™
Contadina Foods (US bus.)
Conte Alessandro Volta (It. physt.; 1745-1827)
Conté™ (art crayon)
Conte Lansana (pres., Guinea; 1945?-)
Conté, Richard (ent.; 1911-75)
Conti, Tom (Scot. ent.; 1941-)
Continental Airlines, Inc.
Continental Congress (US hist.; 1774-89)
Continental Divide (also the Great Divide)(the Rockies)
Continental™, Lincoln-Mercury (auto.)

Contras, the (Central Amer. guerrilla force; 1979-90)
Control Data Corp.
Convention on International Trade in Endangered Species (CITES)
Convy, Bert (ent.; 1934-91)
Conway Twitty (ent.; 1933-93)
Conway, Tim (ent.; 1933-)
Coogan, Jackie (ent.; 1914-84)
Cook Islands (Polynesian)
Cook, Barbara (ent.; 1927-)
Cook, James, Capt. (Br. nav./expl.; 1728-79)
Cook, Jay (US finan.; 1821-1905)
Cook, Robin (writer)
Cook, Thomas (Br. travel agent; 1808-92)
Cooke, Alistair (Br./US jour.; 1908-)
Cooke, Howard (gov-gen.; Jamaica
Cooke, Sam (ent.; 1935-64)
Cookie Monster (fict. chara.)
Cookin' USA (TV show)
Cooking Light (mag.)
Cook's tour (travel)
Cool Hand Luke (film; 1967)
Cool, L. L. (pop music)
Cool, Mr. (slang)
Cooley, Spade (ent.)
Coolidge, Calvin (30th US pres.; 1872-1933)
Coolidge, Rita (ent.; 1945-)
Cooney, Gerry (boxing)
Cooney, Joan Ganz (ent.; 1929-)
Coonts, Stephen (US writer)
Cooper-Hewitt Museum (Smithsonian, DC)
Cooper Industries, Inc.
Cooper Tire & Rubber Co.
Cooper, Alice (b. Vincent Furnier)(ent.; 1948-)
Cooper, Gary (ent.; 1901-62)
Cooper, Jackie (ent.; 1921-)
Cooper, James Fenimore (US writer; 1789-1851)
Cooper, L(eroy) Gordon, Jr. (astro.; 1927-)
Cooper, Peter (US bus.; 1791-1883)
Cooperstown, NY (baseball)
Coors™ (beer)
Coors Co., Adolph
Coos Bay (OR)
Cootie (Charles) Williams (US jazz; 1908-85)
Coowescoowe (aka John Ross)(Cherokee Indian chief; 1790-1866)
Copas, Lloyd "Cowboy" (ent.)
Copco, Inc.
Copeland, Kenneth
Copenhagen, Denmark
Copernican physics
Copernican system (movement of solar system)
Copernicus, Nicholas (or Nicolaus)(Pol. astron.; 1473-1543)
Copland, Aaron (US comp.; 1900-90)
Copley, John Singleton (US artist; 1738-1815)

Copper Age (anthrop.)
Copper Bowl (college football)
Copper River (also Atna River)(AK)
Copperfield, David (C. Dickens novel)
Copperfield, David (ent.; 1956-)
Copperheads (northerners opposing Civil War)
Coppertone™ (health)
Coppélia (ballet by Délibes)
Coppola, Francis Ford (ent.; 1939-)
Copt (people)
Coptic (lang.)
Coptic Christian (rel.)
coquilles St. Jacques (scallop dish)
Coral Gables, FL
Coral Sea (Pac. /NE Austl.)
Coral Sea Islands Territory (Austl.)
Corazon Aquino (ex-pres., Phil.; 1933-)
Corbett, James "Gentleman Jim" (boxing; 1866-1933)
Corbin™ (clothing)
Corbin Bernsen (ent.; 1955-)
Corbin, Barry (ent.; 1940-)
Corbin, Ltd.
Corbusier, Le (aka Charles Édouard Jeanneret)(Fr. arch./artist; 1887-1965)
Corby Group, The (US bus.)
Corby, Ellen (ent.; 1913-)
Cord, Alex (ent.; 1931-)
Corday d'Armont, (Marie Anne) Charlotte (Fr. patriot; 1768-93)
Cordell Hull (US pol.; 1871-1955)
Cordero, Angel (jockey; 1942-)
Cordilleras, the (mountain range, S/CAmer.)
Córdoba, Argentina
Córdoba, Francisco Fernandez de (also Cordova)(Sp. expl.; 1475?-1526)
Córdoba, Mexico
Córdoba, Spain (also Cordova)
Cordobés, El (Manuel Benitez Pérez)(Sp. matador; 1936?-)
Cordova, AK
Cordovan (leather)
CORE (Congress of Racial Equality)
Corea, Chick (US jazz; 1941-)
Coretta Scott King (US civil rights; 1927-)
Corey, Jeff (ent.; 1914-)
Corey, Wendell (ent.; 1914-68)
Corfu (Gr. island)
Corian™ (countertop)
Coricidin™ (med.)
Coricidin 'D'™ (med.)
Corinth, Greece
Corinth, Lovis (Ger. artist; 1858-1925)
Corinth, MS, NY
Corinthian column/order (arch. column)
Corinthians, Epistles to the (rel.)
Corinto, Nicaragua
Coriolanus (Shakespeare play)

Coriolanus, Gaius (or Gnaeus) **Marcius** (Roman hero; 5th c)
Coriolis (effect/force/acceleration)(Earth's rotation)
Cork (county, Ir.)
Cork, Ireland
Corn Belt (agriculture)
Corn Chex™ (cereal)
Corn Flakes™ (cereal)
Corn Laws (Br., regulating grain trade)
Corn Pops™ (cereal)
Corn Silk™ (cosmetics)
Cornel Wilde (ent; 1915-89)
Cornelia Otis Skinner (US writer/ent.; 1901-79)
Cornelius McGillicuddy (aka Connie Mack)(baseball; 1862-1956)
Cornelius Nepos (Roman hist.; c100-c25 BC)
Cornelius Tacitus, (Publius)(Roman hist.; c55-c120)
Cornelius Vanderbilt (US bus./finan.; 1794-1877)
Cornelius Vanderbilt (US bus./finan.; 1843-99)
Cornell MacNeil (ent.; 1922-)
Cornell University (NY)
Cornell, Ezra (US, bus.; 1807-74)
Cornell, Katharine (ent.; 1893-1974)
Corner Brook, Newfoundland
Cornhusker State (nickname, NE)
Corning Fiberglas Corp., Owens-
Corning, Erastus (US finan.; 1794-1872)
Corning, Inc.
Corning, NY
Cornish (lang.)
Cornish hen
Cornish pasty
Cornish Rex (cat)
Cornishman
Cornishwoman
Cornplanter, Chief (Seneca Indians, half-white, aided Br. in Amer. Rev.; c1740-1836)
Cornwall and Isles of Scilly (county, Eng.)
Cornwall, Ontario, Canada
Cornwallis, Charles (Br. gen./pol.; 1738-1805)
Cornwell, David (pseud. John le Carré)(Br. writer; 1931-)
Corolla, Toyota (auto.)
Corona Australis (astron., southern crown)
Corona Borealis (astron., northern crown)
Coronado Naval Amphibious Base (CA)
Coronado, Francisco Vásquez de (Sp. expl.; c1510-54)
Coronel Oviedo, Paraguay
Coronet™ (paper prods.)
Corot, Jean-Baptiste-Camille (Fr. artist; 1796-1875)
Corozal, Belize
Corporal, Little (Napoleon Bonaparte)
Corporation for Public Broadcasting (CPB)

Corps of Engineers, Army (US mil.)
Corpus Christi Caller (TX newspaper)
Corpus Christi Caller-Times (TX newspaper)
Corpus Christi day (Catholic festival)
Corpus Christi, TX
Corrado™, Volkswagen (auto.)
Corrado™ SLC, Volkswagen (auto.)
Correctol™ (med.)
Correggio, Antonio Allegri da (It. artist; 1494-1534)
Corregidor Island (Phil.)
Corregidor, Battle of (WWII; 1942)
Corriedale sheep
Corsica (Fr. island, Mediterranean)
Corsica/Beretta™, Chevrolet (auto.)
Cortaid™ (med.)
Cortizone-10™ (med.)
Cortez, Hernando (or Ferdinand)(also Cortés)(Sp. expl.; 1485-1547)
Corvette™, Chevrolet (auto.)
Corvus (astron., crow)
Coryell, John (US writer; 1927-)
COS (cash on shipment)
Cosa Nostra (US secret org. crime assoc.)
Cosby Show, The (TV show)
Cosby, Bill (ent.; 1937-)
Cosell, Howard (US sportscaster; 1920-)
Cosenza, Italy
Cosgrave, Liam (ex-PM, Ir.; 1920-)
Cosgrave, William Thomas (Ir. pol.; 1880-1965)
Cosmic Background Explorer (COBE)(US satellite)
Cosimo de' Medici (It. pol.; 1389-1464)
Cosimo de' Medici I (It., Duke of Florence; 1519-74)
Cosmopolitan (mag.)
Cosmos (Soviet satellites)
Cossack (people)
Costa Brava, Spain
Costa del Sol, Spain
Costa Mesa, CA
Costa Rica (Republic of)(CAmer.)
Costas, Bob (ent.; 1952-)
Costello, Abbott and (ent.)
Costello, Elvis (Declan McManus)(ent.; 1954-)
Costello, Lou (ent.; 1906-59)
Costner, Kevin (ent.; 1955-)
Côte d'Azur (Fr. Riviera)
Cote d'Ivorie (also Ivory Coast)
Côtes du Rhône (Fr. wine region)
Coton de Tulear (dog)
Cotonou, Benin
Cotswold Hills, England (also Cotswolds)
Cotswold sheep
Cotten, Joseph (ent.; 1905-)
Cotti, Flavio (ex-pres., Switz.)
Cottian Alps (It./Fr.)
Cotton Bowl (college football)

Cotton Mather (US rel.; 1663-1728)
Cotton State (nickname, AL)
Cotton, John (Br./US rel.; 1584-1652)
Cotton, King (US hist., early 19th c)
Coty™ (cosmetics)
Coty (US bus.)
Couch, Sir Arthur Thomas Quiller- (aka "Q")(Br. writer; 1863-1944)
Cougar, Lincoln-Mercury (auto.)
Coulomb, Charles Augustin de (Fr. physt.; 1736-1806)
Coulomb's law (elec.)
Coumadin™ (med.)
Council of Chalcedon (rel.)
Council of Economic Advisers (US govt.)
Council of Europe
Council of Lyons
Council(s) of Nicaea (also Nicene Council)(rel.; 325)
Council of Pisa (Roman Catholic Church; 1409)
Council of St. Albans (Br. hist.)
Council of the Churches of Christ in the United States of America, National (est. 1950)
Council of Trent (rel. hist.; 1545-63)
Council on Alcoholism, National (org. 1944)
Council on Environmental Quality (US govt.)
Count Basie (William)(US jazz; 1904-84)
Count Dracula (vampire based on Vlad Tepes, the Impaler)
Count Duckula (cartoon)
Count of Monte Cristo (by Dumas)
Countee Cullen (US poet; 1903-46)
Counter Reformation (also Catholic Reformation)(Eur. rel./hist.; 16th-17th c.)
Country America (mag.)
Country Home (mag.)
Country Living (mag.)
Country Music Association Awards, The
Country Music Awards, Academy of
Country of the Gillikins
County Armagh (NIre.)
County Cork (Ir.)
County Kerry (Ir.)
County Tipperary (Ir.)
Couples, Fred (golf; 1959-)
Courant, Hartford (CT newspaper)
Courbet, Gustave (Fr. artist; 1819-77)
Couric, Katherine "Katie" (US TV jour.; 1957-)
Courier-Journal, Louisville (KY newspaper)
Courier-Post, Camden (NJ newspaper)
Courier-Times, Bucks County (PA newspaper)
Courier, Evansville (IN newspaper)
Courier, Jim (tennis; 1970-)
Cournoyer, Yvan Serge (hockey; 1943-)
Courréges, André (Fr. designer; 1923-)
Court of Arbitration, Permanent (internat'l court; est. 1899)
Court of International Justice, United Nations

Proper Noun Speller

Permanent (also World Court)(est. 1945)
Court of St. James (Br. royal court)
Court of Star Chamber (Br. hist.; 1487-1641)
Court Reporters Association, National (NCRA)
Court, Margaret Smith (tennis; 1942-)
Courtenay, Robert of (Constantinople emp.; 13th c.)
Courtenay, Tom (ent.; 1937-)
Courtois, Jean-Pierre (covicar, Andorra)
Courvoisier™ (cognac)
Cousin, Cousine (film;1975)
Cousins, Norman (US editor/writer; 1912-90)
Cousteau, Jacques Yves (Fr. oceanographer; 1910-)
Cousy, Bob (Robert Joseph)(basketball; 1928-)
Covenant, Ark of the (rel.)
Covent Garden (London)
Coventry, Earl of (card game)
Coventry, England
Cover Girl™ (cosmetics)
Coverdell, Paul (US cong.; 1939-)
Coverly, Sir Roger de (dance)
Covington, GA, IN, KY, LA, TN, VA
Coward, Sir Noel (Br. writer/comp.; 1899-1973)
Cowboy (Lloyd) Copas (ent.)
Cowboys, Dallas (football team)
Cowlings, Al (US news)
Cowper, William (Br. judge; 1665?-1723)
Cowper, William (Br. phys.; 1666-1709)
Cowper, William (Br. poet; 1731-1800)
Cowper's glands (med.)
Cox, Archibald (US atty./Watergate; 1912-)
Cox, Ronny (ent.; 1938-)
Cox, Tricia (Patricia) Nixon (daughter of ex-US pres.; 1946-)
Cox, Wally (ent.; 1924-73)
Coyote State (nickname, SD)
Cozumel, Mexico
Cozy Cole (US jazz; 1909-81)
CP (command post, Communist Party)
CPA (certified public accountant)
CPC International, Inc.
CPI (consumer price index)
C(lement) P(hilibert) Leo Delibes (Fr. comp.; 1836-91)
CPO (chief petty officer)
CPR (cardiopulmonary resuscitation)
C(harles) P(ercy) Snow, Baron (Br. writer/physt.; 1905-80)
CPU (central processing unit)(compu.)
Cr (chem. sym., chromium)
Crab Nebula (astron.)
Crabbe, Buster (ent./swimmer; 1908-83)
Crabtree & Evelyn™ (toiletries)
Crabtree & Evelyn, Ltd.
Crabtree, Lotta (ent.; 1847-1924)
Cracker Jack (US bus.)
Cracker Jacks™ (snack)

Cracklin' Oat Bran™ (cereal)
Craddock, Billy "Crash" (ent.; 1940-)
Crafts (mag.)
Craftsman™ (tools)
Craig Claiborne (US writer/food; 1920-)
Craig L. Morton (football; 1943-)
Craig T. Nelson (ent.; 1946-)
Craig Weight Loss Centers, Jenny (US bus.)
Craig, Larry (US cong.; 1945-)
Crain, Jeanne (ent.; 1925-)
Crain's New York Business (mag.)
Craiova, Romania
Cram, Ralph Adams (US arch.; 1863-1942)
Cranberries, the (pop music)
Crane Co.
Crane, Bob (ent.; 1928-78)
Crane, (Harold) Hart (US poet; 1899-1932)
Crane, Ichabod (fict. chara., *Legend of Sleepy Hollow*)
Crane, Stephen (US writer; 1871-1900)
Cranmer, Thomas (Br. rel./writer; 1489-1556)
Cranston, RI
Crash Craddock, Billy (ent.; 1940-)
Crassus, Marcus Licinius (Roman gen.; c108-53 BC)
Cratchit, Bob (fict. chara., *A Christmas Carol*)
Cratchit, Tiny Tim (fict. chara., *A Christmas Carol*)
Crate & Barrel™ (housewares)
Crate & Barrel (US bus.)
Crater (astron., cup)
Crater Lake National Park (OR)
Crater Mound (AZ)(also Meteor Crater)
Cratinus (Gr. drama.; 520-421 BC)
C ration
Craven, Wes
Crawford, Broderick (ent.; 1911-86)
Crawford, Cindy (US model; 1966-)
Crawford, Joan (ent.; 1908-77)
Craxi, Bettino (ex-PM, It.; 1934-)
Cray™
Cray Research, Inc.
Crayola™ (crayons)
Crazy Eights (also Wild Eights)(card game)
Crazy Guggenheim (aka Frank Fontaine)(ent.; 1920-78)
Crazy Horse, Chief (Sioux Indians, Little Bighorn; 1842-77)
Cream (pop music)
Cream of Wheat™ (cereal)
Creamette™ (pasta)
Creamette Co., The
Creation (rel.)
Creative Forces (also All That Is, Divine Mind, God)
Creator, the (God)
Cree (NAmer. Indians)
Creedence Clearwater Revival (pop music)

Creek (NAmer. Indians)
Creighton Abrams (US gen.; 1914-74)
crema Danica (cheese)
creme Anglais (sauce)
crème Chantilly (sauce)
Cremona (province in Lombardy, It.)
Crenna, Richard (ent.; 1926-)
Crenshaw (melon)
Crenshaw, Ben (golf; 1952-)
Creole (langs., peoples)
Creole, Haitian (lang.)
Creole, Jamaican (lang.)
crepe de Chine (fabric)
crepes Suzette (also l.c.)
Crescent Wrench™ (constr.)
Crescent, Red (functioning as Red Cross in
    Muslim countries)
Cressida, Troilus and (Shakespeare play)
Cresson, Edith (ex-PM, Fr.; 1934-)
Crest™ (toothpaste)
Cretaceous period (136-65 million years ago)
Cretan dittany (plant)
Crete (Gr. island)
Crews, Harry (US writer; 1935-)
CRI (Certified Reporting Instructor)
Cribari (wine)
Cribari & Sons Winery, B.
Crichton, Michael (US writer; 1942-)
Crichton, Robert (US writer; 1925-93)
Crick model, Watson- (3-D structure of DNA)
Crick, Francis H(arry) C(ompton)(Br. physt.;
    1916-)
Cricket Lighters (US bus.)
Crickets, Buddy Holly and the (pop music)
Crime and Punishment (Dostoevski novel)
Crimea (peninsula on the Black Sea)
Crimean War (Turk./Rus.; 1853-56)
Crimes and Misdemeanors (film)
Crippen, Robert L. (astro.; 1937-)
Cripple Creek, CO (gold mining)
Cripps, Sir Stafford (Br. pol.; 1889-1952)
Crips, Bloods and (pop music)
Crisco™ (vegetable shortening)
Crispix™ (cereal)
Crist, Judith (US writer; 1922-)
Cristiani, Alfredo (ex-pres., El Salvador; 1947-)
Cristino Seriche Bioko (ex-PM, Equatorial
    Guinea)
Cristobal Balenciaga (Sp. designer; 1895-1972)
Cristobal, Panama
Cristy Lane (ent.; 1940-)
Crito (by Plato)
Crito (Gr. phil.; 5th c BC)
Crittenden Compromise (plan to avert US Civil
    War)
Cro-Magnon (prehistoric human)
Croat (people)
Croatia (republic. Yug.)

Croatian (people)
Croatian, Serbo- (lang.)
Croce, Benedetto (It. phil.; 1866-1952)
Croce, Jim (ent.; 1942-73)
Crochet World (mag.)
Crocker™, Betty
Crocker, Charles (US railroad/finan.; 1822-88)
Crockett, Davy (David)(US frontier/pol.; 1786-
    1836)
Crockpot™ (cooking)
Crocodile Dundee (film; 1986)
Crocodile Dundee II (film; 1988)
Croesus (king, Lydia, noted for great wealth;
    c560-c546 BC)
Croesus (very rich person)
Crohn's disease
Croix de Guerre (Fr. mil. award)
Cromwell Current (also Equatorial
    Countercurrent)
Cromwell, Oliver (Br. gen./pol.; 1599-1658)
Cronin, A(rchibald) J(oseph)(Br. phys./writer;
    1896-1981)
Cronin, Joe (baseball exec.; 1906-84)
Cronkite, Walter (US TV jour.; 1916-)
Cronus (also Kronos)(myth.)
Cronyn, Hume (ent.; 1911-)
Crook and Chase (TV show)
Crookes tube (cathode rays)
Crookes, Sir William (Br. physt./chem.; 1832-
    1919)
Crosby, Bing (Harry Lillis)(ent.; 1903-77)
Crosby, Bob (George Robert)(ent.; 1913-93)
Crosby, David (ent.; 1941-)
Crosby, Stills & Nash (pop music)
Crosby, Stills, Nash & Young (pop music)
Crosman™ air gun
Crosman Corp.
Cross Co., A. T.
Cross Creek (film; 1983)
cross of Lorraine
cross the Rubicon (take an irrevocable step)
Cross, American National Red (US relief agcy.;
    est. 1881)
Cross, Ben (ent.; 1947-)
Cross, Red (internat'l relief agcy.; est. 1864)
Crosse & Blackwell™
Crosse & Blackwell Co., The
Crossfire (TV show)
Crothers, Scatman (ent.; 1910-86)
Crouse, Lindsay (ent.; 1948-)
Crouse, Russel (US writer; 1893-1966)
Crow (NAmer. Indians)
Crow laws, Jim (US hist., pro-segregation; pre-
    1960s)
Crow, Jim (racial discrimination)(also l.c.)
Crowell, Rodney (ent.; 1950-)
Crowley, John (US writer; 1942-)
Crowley, Patricia (ent.)

Crown Books (US bus.)
Crown Royal™ (whiskey)
Crown, Cork & Seal (US bus.)
CRR (Certified Real-Time Reporter)
CRT (cathode ray tube)(compu.)
Crucifixion, the (rel.)
Cruel, Peter the (king, Castile/León; 1334-69)
Cruella DeVille (fict. chara., *101 Dalmatians*)
Cruikshank, George (Br. artist; 1792-1878)
Cruise, Tom (b. Thomas Cruise Mapother, IV)(ent.; 1962-)
Cruising World (mag.)
Crumb, Robert (cartoonist, underground; 1943-)
Crunch 'n Munch™
Crusade, Children's (Fr./Ger. v. Jerusalem; 1212)
Crusades, the (rel. wars; 11th-13th c)
Crusher, Dr. Beverly (fict. chara., *Star Trek*)
Crusher, Ensign Wesley (fict. chara., *Star Trek*)
Crusoe, Robinson (D. Defoe novel)
Crux (astron., cross)
Cruyff, Johan (soccer; 1947-)
Crvenkovski, Branko (PM, Macedonia)
Cryptophyta (phylum, biology)
Crystal Bernard (ent.)
Crystal Brands, Inc.
Crystal Gayle (ent.; 1951-)
Crystal Light™
Crystal Palace (London)
Crystal, Billy (ent.; 1947-)
Crystals, the (pop music)
C-section (med.)
C(ecil) S(cott) Forester (Br. writer; 1899-1966)
C(live) S(taples) Lewis ("Clive Hamilton")(Br. writer; 1898-1963)
Csonka, Larry (Lawrence Richard)(football; 1946-)
C-SPAN (CSP)(cable TV)
CSR (Certified Shorthand Reporter)
CST (Central Standard Time)
CT (Connecticut)
C. Thomas Howell (ent.; 1966-)
C3P0 (fict. chara., *Star Wars*)
C-type (photo.)
Cub Scouts (also l.c.)
Cuba (Republic of)(Caribbean Sea)
Cuba libre (mixed drink)
Cuban heel (footwear)
Cuban missile crisis (1962)
Cuban royal palm
Cuban sandwich
Cubism (art movement)(also l.c.)
Cubs, Chicago (baseball team)
Cuckoo's Nest, One Flew Over the (film; 1975)
Cuéllar, Javier Pérez de (Peruvian/UN dipl.; 1920-)
Cuenca, Ecuador
Cuenca, Spain

Cuernavaca, Mexico
Cuervo Gold™ (tequila)
Cuervo™, Jose (tequila)
Cugat, Xavier (Sp./US cond.; 1920-90)
Cuisenaire™ rod (colored rods used to teach arithmetic)
Cuisinart™
Cuisinart, Inc.
Cujo (S. King novel)
Cukor, George (ent.; 1899-1983)
Culbro Corp.
Culkin, Macaulay (ent.; 1980-)
Cullen, Bill (William L.)(ent.; 1920-90)
Cullen, Countee (US poet; 1903-46)
Culligan™ (water conditioner)
Culligan International, Inc.
Cullum, John (ent.; 1930-)
Culp, Robert (ent.; 1930-)
Cultural Revolution (Ch.; 1966-69)
Cumberland Gap National Historical Park (KY/TN/VA)
Cumberland Plateau/Mountains (part of Appalachians, VA/KY/TN/GA/AL)
Cumberland River (KY/TN)
Cumberland Road (MD to IL)
Cumberland, MD, RI
Cumbria (county, Eng.)
Cummings, Constance (ent.; 1910-)
Cummings, Edward Estlin (pseud. e.e. cummings)(US poet; 1894-1962)
Cummings, Robert (ent.; 1908-90)
Cunard Line (ships)
Cunard, Samuel (Can., trans-Atl. navigation; 1787-1865)
Cunningham, Merce (US dancer/choreographer; 1919-)
Cunningham, Randall (football; 1963-)
Cunningham, R. Walter (astro.; 1932-)
Cuomo, Mario M(atthew)(NY gov.; 1932-)
Cupid (myth., god of love)
Curaçao (island, the Netherlands Antilles)
Curad (bandage)
Curepipe, Mauritius
Curia Romana (papal govt.)
Curie point/temperature)(chem.)
Curie, Frédéric Joliot- (Fr. physt.; 1900-58)
Curie, Irène Joliot- (Fr. physt.; 1897-1956)
Curie, Madame Marie (Fr. physt., radium; 1867-1934)
Curie, Pierre (Fr. physt., radium; 1859-1906)
Curie's law
Curie-Weiss law
Curitiba, Brazil
Curly Howard (b. Jerome Horwitz)(ent.; 1903-52)
Current Affair (TV show)
Current Affair: Extra (TV show)
Currier & Ives (US lithography)

Currier, Nathaniel (US lithographer; 1813-88)
Curry, John Steuart (US artist; 1897-1946)
Curt Gowdy (ent.; 1919-)
Curt Jurgens (ent.)
Curtin, Jane (ent.; 1947-)
Curtis Arnoux Peters (aka Peter Arno)(cartoonist, *New Yorker*; 1904-68)
Curtis Industries, Helene
Curtis (Emerson) LeMay (US gen.; 1906-90)
Curtis-Mathes Corp.
Curtis Mayfield (ent.; 1942-)
Curtis Strange (golf)
Curtis, Charles (ex-US VP; 1860-1936)
Curtis, Jamie Lee (ent.; 1958-)
Curtis, Keene (ent.; 1923-)
Curtis, Tony (ent.; 1925-)
Curtiss, Glenn Hammond (US aviator/inv.; 1878-1930)
Curzon, George Nathaniel (Marquis Kedleston of Curzon)(Br. leader in India; 1859-1925)
Cusack, Joan (ent.; 1962-)
Cusack, John (ent.; 1966-)
Cushing, Harvey Williams (US phys.; 1869-1939)
Cushing, Peter (ent.; 1913-)
Cushing's disease (also Cushing's syndrome)(med.)
Custer, George A(rmstrong)(US gen., Little Bighorn; 1839-76)
Custer, SD
Custer's Last Stand (also Battle of the Little Bighorn)(US/Sioux Indians; 1876)
Customs and Excise, Bureau of (Br.)
Cutex™
Cutlass Supreme, Oldsmobile (auto.)
Cut-Rite™ (wax paper)
Cutty Sark™
Cuxhaven, Germany
Cuyahoga Falls, OH
Cuzco, Peru (Incan ruins)
CWO (cash with order, chief warrant officer)
Cy (Denton True) Young (baseball; 1867-1955)
Cy Coleman (US comp.; 1929-)
Cy Young Award (baseball)
Cybele (myth.)
Cybill Shepherd (ent.; 1949-)
Cyclades Islands (Gr., Aegean Sea)
Cycle™ (dog food)
Cycle™ Plan, The (dog food)
Cyclone™ (fence)
Cyclops (myth.; plural = Cyclopes)
Cyd Charisse (ent.; 1921-)
Cygnus (astron., swan)
Cymbeline (king, Br; 1st c. AD)
Cymbeline (Shakespeare play)
Cymric (also Kymric)(Celtic langs.)
Cyndi Lauper (ent.; 1953-)
Cynicism (phil.)

Cynthia Gregory (ent.; 1946-)
Cynthia Ozick (US writer; 1928-)
Cynthia Weil (US comp.; 1937-)
Cynthia Woodhead (swimming; 1964-)
Cypress Gardens, FL
Cypress, CA
Cyprian, St. (rel. in Africa; ?-258)
Cypriot (people)
Cyprus (Republic of)(south, Gr.; north, Turk.)
Cyrano de Bergerac (Fr. poet/mil.; 1619-55)
Cyrano de Bergerac (play)
Cyrenaic (phil.; 4th c BC)
Cyril Ritchard (ent.; 1898-1977)
Cyrillic alphabet
Cyrus (Hall) McCormick (US inv.; 1809-84)
Cyrus R(oberts) Vance (US pol.; 1917-)
Cyrus West Field (US finan., 1st Atl. cable; 1819-92)
Czech (lang./people)
Czechoslovak Airlines
Czechoslovakia (now Czech and Slovakia)(central Eur.)
Czerny, Karl (Aus. pianist; 1791-1857)
Czestochowa, Poland

D

DA (district attorney)
da Caravaggio, Michelangelo (It. artist; 1573-1610)
da Correggio, Antonio Allegri (It. artist; 1494-1534)
da Gama, Vasco (Port. nav.; c1460-1524)
da Palestrina, Giovanni P(ierluigi)(It. comp.; c1525-94)
Da Silva, Howard (ent.; 1909-86)
da Vinci, Leonardo (It. artist/scien.; 1452-1519)
Dabney Coleman (ent.; 1932-)
Dacca, Bangladesh (also Dhaka)
Dachau, Germany (concentration camp)
Dacron™ (polyester fiber)
Dada (also Dadaism)(art./lit. movement)
Daedalus (myth.)
Daffy Duck (cartoon chara.)
Dafoe, Willem (ent.; 1955-)
Dag (Hjalmar Agne Carl) Hammarskjöld (Swed., UN secy gen.; 1905-61)
Dagenhart, Hammer v. (US law; 1918)
Dagomba, Moshi- (people)
Daguerre, Louis Jacques Mande (Fr. photo.; 1789-1851)
Dagwood Bumstead (cartoon chara.)
Dagwood sandwich
Dahik, Alberto (VP, Ecuador)_
Dahl, Arlene (ent.; 1928-)
Dahl, Roald (Br./US writer; 1916-90)
Dahlia, Black (Elizabeth Short)
Dahmer, Jeffrey (US serial killer)
Dahomey (now Benin)
Daikoku (myth.)
Dailey, Dan (ent.; 1914-78)
Dailey, Janet (US writer; 1944-)
Daily Mirror (Br. newspaper)
Daily News, Anchorage (AK newspaper)
Daily News, Los Angeles (CA newspaper)
Daily News, New York (NY newspaper)
Daily News, Philadelphia (PA newspaper)
Daily Oklahoman, Oklahoma City (OK newspaper)
Daimier, Gottlieb (Ger. eng./inv.; 1834-1900)
Daio, Daniel Lima dos Santos (ex-PM, São Tomé/Príncipe)
Dairy Queen/Brazier
Daisetz Teitaro Suzuki (Jap. rel.; 1870-1966)
Daisy Duck (cartoon chara.)
Daisy Miller (H. James novel)
Daisy, Driving Miss (film; 1989)
Dakar, Senegal
Dakota (also Sioux)(NAmer. Indians)
Dakota, Dodge (auto.)
Daladier, Édouard (Fr. pol.; 1884-1970)

Dalai Lama (b. Tenzin Gyatso)(Tibetan rel.; 1935-)
Dalai Lama (spiritual leader of Tibetan Buddhism)
Dale Bumpers (US cong.; 1925-)
Dale Carnegie (US writer/educ.; 1888-1955)
Dale Evans (ent.; 1912-)
Dale Messick (cartoonist, *Brenda Starr*; 1906-)
Dale Murphy (football; 1956-)
Dale Robertson (ent.; 1923-)
d'Alençon, point (also Alençon lace)
Daley, Richard Joseph (ex-mayor, Chicago; 1902-76)
Daley, Richard M. (Chicago mayor; 1942-)
Dali, Salvador (Sp. artist; 1904-89)
Dalkon Shield™ (med.)
Dallas (TV show)
Dallas Cowboys (football team)
Dallas-Fort Worth International Airport (TX)
Dallas Mavericks (basketball team)
Dallas Morning News (TX newspaper)
Dallas, George M. (ex-US VP; 1792-1864)
Dallas, OR, TX
Dallas, Stella (film; 1937)
Dalles, The, OR
Dalmane™ (med.)
Dalmatian (dog)
Dalmatians, 101
Daloa, Ivory Coast
Dalton Bookseller, B. (US bus.)
Dalton, Abby (ent.; 1932-)
Dalton, John (Br. chem./physt.; 1766-1844)
Dalton, Timothy (ent.; 1944-)
Daltonism (red/green color blindness)
Dalton's law (of partial pressures)(chem.)
Daly, Chuck (basketball; 1930-)
Daly, John (golf; 1966-)
Daly, John Charles, Jr. (ent./TV news exec.; 1914-91)
Daly, Marcus (US bus.; 1841-1900)
Daly, Timothy (ent.; 1958-)
Daly, Tyne (ent.; 1947-)
Damara (people)
Damascus steel (also l.c.)
Damascus, Syria
D'Amato, Al(fonse M.)(US cong.; 1937-)
Dameron, Tadd (US jazz; 1917-65)
Damian, St. Peter (It. rel.; 1007-72)
Damien: Omen II (film; 1978)
Damietta, Egypt
Dammam, Saudi Arabia
Damme, Jean-Claude Van (ent.)
Damocles (myth.)
Damocles, Sword/sword of
Damon and Pythias (myth., loyal friendship)
Damon Runyon, (Alfred)(US writer/jour.; 1880-1946)
Damon Wayans (ent.; 1960-)

Damone, Vic (ent.; 1928-)
Dan Aykroyd (ent.; 1952-)
Dan Blocker (ent.; 1928-72)
Dan Dailey (ent.; 1914-78)
D & B (Dun & Bradstreet)
D & C (dilatation and curettage)
Dan Duryea (ent.; 1907-68)
Dan Fogelberg (ent.; 1951-)
Dan Gable (wrestling; 1945-)
Dan Marino (football; 1961-)
Dan McGrew, The Shooting of (R.W. Service
   ballad)
Dan O'Herlihy (ent.; 1919-)
Dan(forth) Quayle, (James)(ex-US VP; 1947-)
Dan Rather (US TV jour.; 1931-)
Dan Rather, The CBS Evening News With (TV
   show)
Dan(iel) Rostenkowski (US cong.; 1928-)
Dan Rowan (ent.; 1922-87)
Dan, Steely (pop music)
Dana Andrews (ent.; 1909-1992)
Dana Carvey (ent.; 1955-)
Dana Corp.
Dana Delany (ent.; 1957-)
Dana, Bill (ent.; 1924-)
Danang, Vietnam
Danann, Tuatha Dé (myth.)
Danbury Hatters Case (*Loewe v. Lawler*)(US
   law; 1908)
Danbury, CT
Dance (mag.)
Dance Theater of Harlem
Dancer, Stanley (harness racing; 1927-)
Dances With Wolves (film)
Dancin' (play)
Dandie Dinmont terrier (dog)
Dandridge, Dorothy (ent.; 1923-65)
Dandridge, Ruby
Dane (people)
Dane Clark (ent.; 1913-)
Dane, Great (dog)
Danforth, John Claggett (US cong.; 1936-)
D'Angelo, Beverly (ent.; 1954-)
Danger Cave (UT)
Dangerfield, Rodney (ent.; 1922-)
Dangriga, Belize
Danica, crema (cheese)
Daniel (rel.)
Daniel arap Moi (pres., Kenya; 1924-)
Daniel Barenboim (Isr. pianist/cond.; 1942-)
Daniel Bernoulli (Swiss math.; 1700-82)
Daniel Boone (US pioneer; 1734-1820)
Daniel Chester French (US artist; 1850-1931)
Daniel D. Tompkins (ex-US VP; 1774-1825)
Daniel Day-Lewis (ent.; 1957-)
Daniel Defoe (Br. writer; 1660-1731)
Daniel Frohman (US writer/ent.; 1851-1940)
Daniel Guggenheim (US finan./bus.; 1856-1930)

Daniel H. Burnham (US arch.; 1846-1912)
Daniel J. Travanti (ent.; 1940-)
Daniel K. Inouye (US cong.; 1924-)
Daniel Kahikina Akaka (US cong.; 1924-)
Daniel Lima dos Santos Daio (ex-PM, São
   Tomé/Príncipe)
Daniel Morgan (US mil.; 1736-1802)
Daniel O'Connell ("the Liberator")(Ir. pol.;
   1775-1847)
Daniel Ortega Saavedra, (José)(ex-pres.,
   Nicaragua; 1945-)
Daniel Patrick Moynihan (US cong.; 1927-)
Daniel R. Coats (US cong.; 1943-)
Daniel S. Goldin (Head/NASA; 1940-)
Daniel Schorr (US jour.; 1916-)
Daniel Shays (US mil./pol.; 1747?-1825)
Daniel Webster (US orator/pol.; 1782-1852)
Daniel Distillery, Jack (US bus.)
Daniela Silivas
Daniell cell (elec.)
Daniell, Harry (ent.; 1894-1963)
Daniell, John Frederic (Br. chem.; 1790-1845)
Danielle Steel (writer)
Daniels, Bebe (ent.; 1901-71)
Daniels, Charlie (ent.; 1936-)
Daniels, Jeff (ent.; 1955-)
Daniels, William (ent.; 1927-)_
Danilova, Alexandra (Rus. ballet; 1906-)
Danish (lang.)
Danish blue (cheese)
Danish East India Company (trade; 1729-1801)
Danish ham
Danish pastry
Dannay, Frederick (pseud. Ellery Queen)(US
   writer; 1905-82)
Danner, Blythe (ent.; 1944-)
Dannon™ yogurt
Dannon Co., Inc., The
D'Annunzio, Gabriele (It. writer; 1863-1938)
Danny Aiello (ent.; 1933-)
Danny and the Juniors (pop music)
Danny DeVito (ent. 1944-)
Danny Ferguson (US news)
Danny Glover (ent.; 1947-)
Danny Kaye (ent.; 1913-87)
Danny Rose, Broadway (film; 1984)
Danny Thomas (ent.; 1912-91)
Danny Thomas Show, The (TV show)
Danny Wood (ent.; 1969-)
Dansk International Designs, Ltd.
Danskin, Inc.
Danson, Ted (ent.; 1947-)
Dante (Alighieri)(It. poet, *Divine Comedy*; 1265-
   1321)
Dante (or Savonarola) chair
Dante Gabriel Rossetti (Br. poet/artist; 1828-82)
Dante's Inferno (*Divine Comedy*)
Dantès Edmund (fict. chara., *Count of Monte*

Proper Noun Speller

Cristo)
Dantine, Helmut
Dantley, Adrian (basketball; 1956-)
Danton, Georges (Fr. mil.; 1759-94)
Danube River (Eur.)
Danville, VA
Danza, Tony (ent.; 1950-)
Danzig, Poland (also Gdansk)
Dao, Lee Tsung (Ch. physt.; 1926-)
Daphne (myth.)
Daphne Du Maurier (Br. writer; 1907-89)
Daphne Maxwell Reid
Daphnis and Chloë (Gr. romance)
DAR (Daughters of the American Revolution)
Dar es Salaam, Tanzania
Darby and Joan (fict. happy, elderly, married couple)
D'Arby, Terence Trent (ent.; 1962-)
Darby Lumber Co., U.S. v. (US law; 1941)
Darby, Kim (ent.; 1948-)
d'Arc, Jeanne (also St. Joan of Arc or Maid of Orléans)(Fr. rel./mil.; 1412?-31)
Dardanelles (Turk. strait)(formerly Hellespont)
Dare, Virginia (1st Eng. child born in Amer.; 1587-?)
Darhan, Mongolia
Dari (lang.)
Dari Persian (lang.)
Darin, Bobby (ent.; 1936-73)
Darius I ("the Great")(king, Persia; c558-486 BC)
Darius Milhaud (Fr. comp.; 1892-1974)
Darjeeling tea
Darjeeling, India
Dark Ages (c476-13th c of the Middle Ages)
Dark Continent (old name for Africa)
Dark, Alvin (baseball; 1922-)
Darkness, Prince of (the Devil)
Darley Arabian (horse)
Darling children (Wendy, John, Michael)(*Peter Pan*)
Darling River, Australia (also Range-Aus)
Darling, Clifford (gov-gen., Bahamas)
Darling, Jay N. ("Ding")(pol. cartoonist; 1876-1962)
d'Armont, (Marie Anne) Charlotte Corday (Fr. patriot; 1768-93)
Darnell, Linda (ent.; 1921-65)
Darrell Pace (archery; 1956-)
Darren E. Burrows (ent.; 1966-)
Darren McGavin (ent.; 1922-)
Darren Stephens (fict. chara., *Bewitched*)
Darrow, Clarence (Seward)(US atty./writer; 1857-1938)
Darryl F(rancis) Zanuck (ent.; 1902-79)
Darryl Strawberry (baseball; 1962-)
d'Artagnan, Charles de Baatz, Seigneur (fict. chara., *Three Musketeers*)

Darth Vader (fict. chara., *Star Wars*)
D'Arthur, Le Morte (by T. Malory)
Dartmoor pony
Dartmoor Prison (Eng.)
Dartmoor sheep
Dartmouth College Case (*Trustees of Dartmouth College v. Woodward*)(US law; 1819)
Dartmouth, Nova Scotia, Canada
Darvocet-N™ (med.)
Darvon™ (med.)
Darvon-N™ (med.)
Darwin, Australia
Darwin, Charles Robert (Br. scien.; 1809-82)
Darwinism (also Darwin's theory)(evolution)
Darwinism, neo- (evolution theory)
Darwinism, Social/social (sociol.)
Daryl F. Gates (US news)
Daryl Hall (ent.; 1948-)
Daryl Hannah (ent.; 1961-)
Daryle Lamonica (football; 1941-)
Das Kapital (by Karl Marx)
Daschle, Thomas Andrew (US cong.; 1947-)
Dashiell Hammett, (Samuel)(US writer; 1894-1961)
Dashiyn Byambasuren (ex-PM, Mongolia)
Dash™, Mrs. (seasoning)
Data General Corp.
Data, Lt. Commander (*Star Trek*)
DataTimes (compu.)
Dateline NBC (TV show)
Daugavpils, Latvia
Daugherty, Brad (basketball; 1965-)
Daughters of the American Revolution (D.A.R.)(org. 1890)
Daumier, Honoré (Fr. artist; 1808-79)
Dauphin, Claude
Dauphin, the (title of eldest son of Fr. king until 1830)
Daulton, Darren (baseball; 1962-)
Davao, Philippines
Dave Barry (US writer/humorist; 1947-)
Dave Bing (basketball; 1943-)
Dave Brubeck (David Warren)(US jazz; 1920-)
Dave DeBusschere (basketball; 1940-)
Dave Garroway (TV host)
Dave Robinson (basketball; 1965-)
Dave Tough (US jazz; 1908-48)
Dave Winfield (baseball; 1951-)
Dave, Sam and (pop music)
Davenport Quad City Times (IA newspaper)
Davenport, IA
Davenport, Lacey (fict. chara., *Doonesbury*)
Davenport, Willie (track; 1943-)
Dave's World (TV show)
David (Donatello sculpture)
David (king, Isr.; c1060-970 BC)
David (Michelangelo sculpture)

David Alfaro Siqueiros (Mex. artist; 1896-1974)
David and Goliath (rel.)
David Aykroyd (ent.)
David Belasco (US writer/ent.; 1854-1931)
David Ben-Gurion (ex-PM, Isr.; 1886-1973)
David Birney (ent.; 1939-)
David Bowie (ent.; 1947-)
David Brenner (ent.; 1945-)
David Brinkley (US TV jour.; 1920-)
David Bruce Winery (US bus.)
David Burpee (US horticulturist; 1893-1980)
David Carradine (ent.; 1936-)
David Cassidy (ent.; 1950-)
David Copperfield (C. Dickens novel)
David Copperfield (ent.; 1956-)
David Cornwell (pseud. John le Carré)(Br. writer; 1931-)
David Crockett ("Davy")(US frontier/pol.; 1786-1836)
David Crosby (ent.; 1941-)
David Dinkins (ex-mayor, NYC; 1927-)
David Doyle (ent.; 1929-)
David Du Bose Gaillard (US mil./eng.; 1859-1913)
David Dubinsky (US labor leader; 1892-1982)
David Duke (US pol.; 1950-)
David Dukes (ent.; 1945-)
David Dunbar Buick (US bus./auto.; 1854-1929)
David E. Bonior (US cong.; 1945-)
David Eddings
David Farragut (US adm.; 1801-70)
David Faustino (ent.; 1974-)
David F. Durenberger (US cong.; 1934-)
David Friedkin
David Frost (ent.; 1939-)
David Garrick (ent.; 1717-79)
David Gergen (US pol.)
David Graham (golf; 1946-)
David Groh (ent.; 1941-)
David Halberstam (writer; 1934-)
David Hampton Pryor (US cong.; 1934-)
David Hartman (ent.; 1935-)
David Hasselhoff (ent.; 1952-)
David Hayes™
David Hayes Agnew (US phys.; 1818-92)
David Hilbert (Ger. math.; 1862-1943)
David Hockney (Br. artist; 1937-)
David Hollis™ (clothing)
David Horowitz (writer)
David H(ackett) Souter (US jurist; 1939-)
David Hume (Scot. phil./hist.; 1711-76)
David I (king, Scot.; 1084-1153)
David II (king, Scot.; 1324-72)
David Jack (gov-gen., St. Vincent/Grenadines)
David James Wottle (runner; 1950-)
David Janssen (ent.; 1930-80)
David J. Stern (basketball; 1942-)
David Keith (ent.; 1954-)

David Koresh (US cult leader; ?-1993)
David (Russell) Lange (ex-PM, NewZeal.; 1942-)
David Lean, Sir (ent.; 1908-91)
David Lee Roth (ent.; 1955-)
David Letterman (ent.; 1947-)
David Letterman, Late Night With (TV show)
David Levine (cartoonist; 1926-)
David Livingstone, Dr. (Scot. rel./expl. in Afr.; 1813-73)
David Lloyd George (ex-PM, Br.; 1863-1945)
David L. Wolper (ent.)
David L. Wolper Productions
David Lyle Boren (US cong.; 1941-)
David Lynch (ent.; 1946-)
David Malcolm Storey (Br. writer; 1933-)
David Mamet (US writer; 1947-)
David McCallum (ent.; 1933-)
David Merrick (ent.; 1912-)
David Niven (ent.; 1909-83)
David Oddsson (PM, Iceland)
David Ogden Stiers (ent.; 1942-)
David Ogilvy (US writer/adv.)
David O(liver) Selznick (ent.; 1902-65)
David Rabe (US writer; 1940-)
David Ricardo (Br. econ.; 1772-1823)
David Riesman (US sociol./writer; 1909-)
David Rittenhouse (US astron./inv.; 1732-96)
David Rockefeller (US finan.; 1915-)
David Rose (US comp.; 1910-90)
David Ross Locke (aka Petroleum V[esuvius] Nasby)(US humorist; 1833-88)
David R. Scott (astro.)
David Sarnoff (US TV pioneer, NBC; 1891-1971)
David (Roland) Smith (US sculptor; 1906-65)
David Soul (ent.; 1943-)
David Susskind (US ent.; 1920-)
David Thompson (basketball; 1954-)
David Walters (OK gov.; 1951-)
David Wayne (ent.; 1914-)
David, City of (also Jerusalem, Bethlehem)
David, Hal (US lyricist; 1921-)
David, Inc., Harry &
David, Jacques Louis (Fr. artist; 1748-1825)
David, Mogan (or Magen)(also Star of David)(6 points, Jew. symbol)
David™, Mogen (kosher foods)
David™, Mogen (wine)
David, Panama
David, Star of (also Magen [or Mogan] David)(6 points, Jew. symbol)
Davidians, Branch (rel. cult)
Davidson, Inc., Harley
Davidson, John (ent.; 1941-)
Davies, Arthur (US artist; 1862-1928)
Davies, Peter Maxwell (Br. comp./cond.; 1934-)
Davis & Co., Parke,
Davis Bynum Winery (US bus.)

Davis Cup (tennis)
Davis Group, Spencer (pop music)
Davis, Al (football; 1929-)
Davis, Angela (Yvonne)(US activist/Communist; 1944-)
Davis, Ann B. (ent.; 1926-)
Davis, Bette (ent.; 1908-89)
Davis, Clifton (ent.; 1945-)
Davis, Colin (Br. cond.; 1927-)
Davis, Eddie "Lockjaw" (US jazz; 1921-86)
Davis, Geena (ent.; 1957-)
Davis, Jefferson (US pol./confederate pres,; 1808-89)
Davis, Jim (cartoonist, *Garfield*; 1945-)
Davis, Mac (ent.; 1956-)
Davis, Miles (US jazz; 1926-91)
Davis, Ossie (ent.; 1917-)
Davis, Sammy, Jr. (ent.; 1925-90)
Davis, Skeeter (ent.)
Davis-Monthan Air Force Base, AZ (mil.)
Davison, Wild Bill (US jazz; 1906-89)
Davy Crockett (David)(US frontier/pol.; 1786-1836)
Davy Jones (personification of sea)
Davy Jones's locker (ocean bottom; grave of those who die at sea)
Davy, Sir Humphry (Br. chem.; 1778-1829)
Daw Books, Inc.
Daw, Margery
Dawber, Pam (ent.; 1951-)
Dawda Kairaba Jawara, Sir (pres., Gambia; 1924-)
Dawes plan (Ger. war debts, WWI)
Dawes, Charles G. (US pol./banker; 1865-1951)
Dawn, Tony Orlando and (pop music)
Dawnn Lewis (ent.; 1960-)
Dawson, Andre (baseball; 1954-)
Dawson, Leonard Ray (football; 1935-)
Dawson, Richard (ent.; 1932-)
Dawson, Yukon, Canada
Day-Glo™ (graphic design)
Day-Glo Color Corp.
Day Lewis, Cecil (Ir. poet; 1904-72)
Day-Lewis, Daniel (ent.; 1957-)
Day of Atonement (Yom Kippur)(rel.)
Day of the Jackal, The (film; 1973)
Day, Clarence, Jr. (US writer; 1874-1935)
Day, Dennis (ent.; 1917-88)
Day, Doris (ent.; 1924-)
Day, Dorothy (US reformer; 1897-1980)
Dayan, Moshe (Isr. pol./gen.; 1915-81)
Days Inns of America (US bus.)
Days of Our Lives (TV soap)
Dayton News (OH newspaper)
Dayton, OH
Daytona Beach News-Journal (FL newspaper)
Daytona Beach, FL
Daytona International Speedway (FL)

Daytona, Dodge (auto.)
DBA (also d/b/a)(doing business as)
DC (direct current, District of Columbia)
d-Con™ (pest control)
D-Con Co., Inc., The
D-Day (WW II, invasion of Normandy; 6/6/44)
DDC (Dewey Decimal System)
DDS (Doctor of Dental Surgery)
DDT (dichlorodiphenyltrichloroethane)
DE (Delaware)
DEA (Drug Enforcement Administration)
de Alarcón, Pedro Antonio (Sp. writer/pol.; 1833-91)
de Albuquerque, Afonso (Port. conquerer; 1453-1515)
de Anza, Juan Bautista (Sp. expl.; 1735-88?)
de Balboa, Vasco Núñez (Sp. expl., discovered Pac.; 1475-1519)
de Balzac, Honoré (Fr. writer; 1799-1850)
de' Bardi, Beatrice Portinari (inspiration for Dante's Beatrice; 1266-90)
de Beaumarchais, Pierre Augustin Caron (Fr. writer; 1732-99)
de Beauvoir, Simone (Fr. writer; 1908-86)
de Bergerac, Cyrano (Fr. poet/mil.; 1619-55)
de Bergerac, Cyrano (play)
de Bivar, Rodrigo Diaz (also El Cid, el Campeador)(Sp. mil.; 1040-99)
de Bougainville, Louis-Antoine (Fr. nav.; 1729-1811)
de Broglie equation
de Broglie principle (physics)
de Broglie wave/wavelength
de Broglie, Louis (Fr. physt.; 1893-1987)
de Broglie's hypothesis (chem.)
De Camp, Rosemary (ent.; 1910-)
de Cervantes Saavedra, Miguel (Sp. writer; 1547-1616)
de Chamorro, Violeta Barrios (pres., Nicaragua; 1939-)
de Champlain, Samuel (Fr. expl.; c1567-1635)
de Chavannes, Pierre Cecile Puvis (Fr. artist; 1824-98)
de Chirico, Giorgio (It. artist; 1888-1978)
de Córdoba, Francisco Fernandez (Sp. expl.; 1475?-1526)
de Coronado, Francisco Vásquez (Sp. expl.; c1510-54)
de Coulomb, Charles Augustin (Fr. physt.; 1736-1806)
de Coverly, Sir Roger (dance)
de Cuéllar, Javier Pérez (Peruvian/UN dipl.; 1920-)
Dé Danann, Tuatha (myth.)
de Falla, Manuel (Sp. comp.; 1876-1946)
de Fermat, Pierre (Fr. math.; 1601-65)
de Forest, Lee (US inv., radio/sound films/TV; 1873-1961)

De Franco, Buddy (US jazz; 1933-)
de Frontenac, Louis (Fr./Can. gov.; 1620-98)
De Gasperi, Alcide (It. pol.; 1881-1954)
de Gaulle, Charles (ex-pres., Fr.; 1890-1970)
de Givenchy, Hubert (Fr. designer; 1927-)
de Gortari, Carlos Salinas (pres., Mex.; 1949-)
de Graaf, Regnier (Dutch phys.; 1641-73)
de Graaff generator, Van (also electrostatic generator)
de Graaff, Robert Jemison Van (US physt.; 1901-67)
de Greiff, Monica
De Havilland, Olivia (ent.; 1916-)
de Kamp's Frozen Foods, Van (US bus.)
de Klerk, Frederik W(illem)(ex-pres., SAfr; 1936-)
de Kooning, Willem (US artist; 1904-)
de Lafayette, Marquis (aka Marie Joseph Gilbert de Motier Lafayette)(Fr. mil./pol.; 1757-1834)
de la Mare, Walter (Br. poet; 1873-1956)
de Lamartine, Alphonse (Fr. writer; 1790-1869)
de la Renta, Ltd., Oscar
de la Renta, Oscar (US designer; 1932-)
De Laurentiis, Dino (It. ent.; 1919-)
De La Warr, Thomas West, Baron (also Delaware)(US colonial leader; 1577-1618)
de León, (Juan) Ponce (Sp. expl.; c1460-1521)
de Lesseps, Ferdinand, Vicomte (Fr. dipl./eng.; 1805-94)
De Lorean™ car
De Lorean, John (US bus./auto.; 1925-)
de Lozada, Gonzalo Sánchez (pres., Bolivia)
de Maupassant, (Henri René Albert) Guy (Fr. writer; 1850-93)
de' Medici, Catherine (queen, Fr./wife of Henry II; 1518-89)
de' Medici, Cosimo I (It., Duke of Florence; 1519-74)
de' Medici, Lorenzo ("the Magnificent")(It. poet/pol.; 1449-92)
de' Medici, Marie (queen, Fr./wife of Henry IV; 1573-1642)
de' Medici, Piero (It. pol.; 1416-69)
de Mello, Fernando Collor (ex-pres., Brazil; 1949-)
De Mille, Agnes (US dancer/choreographer; 1905-93)
De Mille, Cecil B. (ent.; 1881-1959)
de Milo, Venus (also *Venus of Melos, Aphrodite of Melos*)(Gr. statue; c.200 BC)
de Montaigne, Michel (Eyquem)(Fr. writer; 1533-92)
de Montcalm (-Gozon), Louis (-Joseph)(Fr. mil.; 1712-59)
De Mornay, Rebecca (ent.; 1962-)
de Musset, Alfred (Fr. writer; 1810-57)
de Nemours & Co., E. I. du Pont

de Nemours, E(leuthere) I. du Pont (US bus.; 1771-1834)
De Niro, Robert (ent.; 1943-)
De Palma, Brian (ent.; 1940)
de Paul, St. Vincent (Fr. rel.; c1581-1660)
de Perón, Eva Duarte ("Evita")(ex-pres., Argentina; 1919-52)
de Perón, Maria Estela ("Isabel") Martínez (ex-pres., Argentina; 1931-)
de Pompadour, Marquise (aka Jeanne Antoinette Poisson Le Normant d'Étioles)(mistress of Louis XV, Fr.; 1721-64)
de Richelieu, Cardinal ("red eminence")(Fr. pol.; 1585-1642)
de Rivera, José (US sculptor; 1904-85)
de Ronsard, Pierre (Fr. poet; 1524-85)
de Rothschild, Anthony Gustav (Br. finan.; 1887-1961)
de Rothschild, Lionel (Br. finan.; 1882-1942)
de Rothschild, Lionel, Baron (Br. pol./finan.; 1808-79)
de Sade, Marquis (Donatien)(Fr. mil./writer; 1740-1814)
de Saint-Exupery, Antoine (Marie Roger)(Fr. writer/aviator; 1900-44)
de Santa Anna, Antonio (ex-pres/gen., Mex.; 1795?-1876)
de Saussure, Ferdinand (Swiss linguist; 1857-1913)
de Seingalt, Casanova (also Giovanni Jacopo Casanova)(It. adventurer; 1725-98)
De Sica, Vittorio (ent.; 1901-74)
de Soto, Hernando (or Fernando)(Sp. expl.; c1496-1542)
de Spinoza, Benedict (also Baruch)(Dutch phil.; 1632-77)
de Stijl (Dutch art, early 20th c.)
De Sylva, Buddy (US lyricist; 1895-1950)
de Talleyrand(-Périgord), Charles (Maurice)(Fr. pol.; 1754-1838)
de Tocqueville, Alexis (Charles Henri Maurice Clérel)(Fr. hist.; 1805-59)
de Toulouse-Lautrec, Henri (Marie Raymond)(Fr. artist; 1864-1901)
de Valera, Eamon (ex-PM/pres., Ir.; 1882-1975)
De Varona, Donna
de Vega (Carpio), Lope (Félix)(Sp. writer; 1562-1635)
de Vlaminck, Maurice (Fr. artist; 1876-1958)
de Ville™, Cadillac (auto.)
De Vol, Frank
De Voto, Bernard A. (US hist.; 1897-1955)
de Young Memorial Museum, M. H. (San Francisco)
De Vries, Hugo (Dutch botanist; 1848-1935)
De Vries, Peter (US writer; 1910-93)
De Wilde, Brandon (ent.; 1942-72)
De Wolfe, Billy (ent.; 1907-74)

Deacon (David) Jones (football; 1938-)
Dead-End Kids
Dead Poets Society (film)
Dead Sea (Isr./Jordan)
Dead Sea Scrolls (ancient writings; c150 BC-AD 68)
Dead, Book of the (Eg., rel.)
Dead, The Tibetan Book of the (rel.)
Deadwood, SD
Dean (Gooderham) Acheson (US pol.; 1893-1971)
Dean Jagger (ent.; 1903-91)
Dean Jones (ent.; 1935-)
Dean Martin (ent.; 1917-)
Dean R. Koontz (US writer)
Dean Rusk, (David)(US pol.; 1909-)
Dean Smith (basketball; 1931-)
Dean Stockwell (ent.; 1936-)
Dean Witter Reynolds, Inc.
Dean Young (cartoonist)
Dean, Christopher (figure skating)
Dean, Dizzy (Jay Hanna)(baseball; 1911-74)
Dean, Howard (VT gov.; 1948-)
Dean, James (ent.; 1931-55)
Dean, Jimmy (ent.; 1928-)
Dean, Morton
Deane Beman (golf; 1938-)
Deanna Durbin (ent.; 1921-)
Dean™, Jimmy (sausage)
Dean Meat Co., Jimmy
Dear Abby (Abigail Van Buren)(b. Pauline Esther Friedman)(US advice columnist; 1918-)
Dear John letter
Dearborn Heights, MI
Dearborn, MI
Dearie, Blossom (ent.)
Death Valley (CA/NV)
Death Valley National Monument (CA/NV)
Deathtrap (play)
Deauville, France
DeBakey, Michael Ellis (US phys.; 1908-)
Debbie Allen (ent.; 1950-)
Debbie Boone (ent.; 1956-)
Debbie Gibson (ent.; 1970-)
Debbie Reynolds (ent.; 1932-)
DeBeck, Billy (cartoonist, *Barney Google*; 1890-1942)
Debi Thomas (figure skating)
Deborah Harry (ent.; 1945-)
Deborah Kerr (ent.; 1921-)
Deborah Meyer (swimming; 1952-)
Deborah Norville (US TV jour.; 1958-)
Deborah Raffin
Debra Winger (ent.; 1955-)
Debrecen, Hungary
Debs Garms (baseball; 1908-84)
Debs, Eugene V. (US labor leader; 1855-1926)

Debs, In re (US law; 1895)
DeBusschere, Dave (basketball; 1940-)
Debussy, (Achille) Claude (Fr. comp.; 1862-1918)
Déby, Idriss (pres., Chad; 1955?-)
Decalog(ue)(also Ten Commandments)(rel.)
Decalogue Books, Inc.
Decameron, The (Boccaccio tales)
DeCarlo, Yvonne (ent.; 1922-)
Decatur, AL, IL, GA
Decatur, Stephen (US mil.; 1779-1820)
Decca Records, Inc.
Deccan (region, India)
December Bride (TV show)
Decker™, Black & (power tools)
Decker Corp., The Black &
Decker Slaney, Mary (US runner; 1958-)
Decker (or Dekker), Thomas (Br. writer; 1572?-1632?)
Declaration of Independence (US; July 4, 1776)
Declaration of Rights (Br.)
DeConcini, Dennis (US cong.; 1937-)
Decoration Day (now Memorial Day)
DeCordova, Fred(erick)(US TV exec.; 1910-)
DeCorsia, Ted
Dee, Frances (ent.; 1907-)
Dee, Ruby (ent.; 1924-)
Dee, Sandra (ent.; 1942-)
Deems Taylor (US comp.; 1885-1966)
Deep Sea Drilling Project
Deep South
Deep Throat (Watergate informant)
Deer Hunter, The (film; 1978)
Deere & Co.
Def Leppard (pop music)
Defense Electronics (mag.)
Defense, Department of (DOD)(US govt.)
Defoe, Daniel (Br. writer; 1660-1731)
DeFord Bailey
Defore, Don (ent.; 1917-)
DeForest Kelley (ent.; 1920-)
Dégas, (Hilaire Germain) Edgar (Fr. artist; 1834-1917)
Dehaene, Jean-Luc (PM, Belgium; 1940-)
DeHaven, Gloria (ent.; 1925-)
Dehiwala-Mount Lavinia, Sri Lanka
Dei gratia (Latin, by the grace of God)
Dei, Agnus (Latin, Lamb of God)
Deidre Hall (ent.; 1948-)
Deimos (Mars moon)
Deity (in ref. to God)
Deke (Donald Kent) Slayton (astro.; 1924-93)
Dekker, Albert (ent.; 1905-68)
Dekker, Thomas (also Decker)(Br. writer; 1572?-1632?)
Del Coronado Hotel (CA)
Del Insko (harness racing; 1931-)
Del Mar, CA

Del Monte™
Del Monte Corp.
Del Monte Foods (US bus.)
Del Rey™ Books
Del Rio, Dolores (ent.; 1908-83)
del Sarto, Andrea (It. artist; 1486-1530)
Del Shannon (ent.; 1940-90)
del Verrocchio, Andrea (b. Andrea di Michele di
    Francesco di Cioni)(It. artist; 1435-88)
Del Webb Hotels (US bus.)
Del Williams (football; 1945-84)
Delacorte, George T. (US publ.; 1893-1991)
Delacroix, Eugene (Fr. artist; 1789-1863)
Delaney Amendment (banned carcinogenic food
    additives)
Delany, Dana (ent.; 1957-)
Delaroche, Paul (Fr. hist./artist; 1797-1856)
Delaware (DE)
Delaware (grape)
Delaware (NAmer. Indians)(also Lenni Lenape)
Delaware River (NY/PA/NJ/DE)
Delaware, Thomas West, Baron (also De La
    Warr)(US colonial leader; 1577-1618)
Delbruck, Max (US biol.; 1907-81)
Delft, Netherlands
Delhi, India
Delia Salter Bacon (US writer; 1811-59)
Delibes, C(lement) P(hilibert) Leo (Fr. comp.;
    1836-91)
Delicious (apple), Golden
Delicious (apple), Red
Delilah, Samson & (rel.)
Delius, Frederick (Br. comp.; 1862-1934)
Deliverance (film; 1972)
Dell Computer Corp.
Dell Publishing Group, Inc., Bantam,
    Doubleday
Della Chiesa, Vivienne (ent.; 1920-)
della Francesca, Piero (It. artist; c1415-92)
Della Reese (ent.; 1931-)
della Robbia, Andrea (It. sculptor; 1437-1528)
della Robbia, Luca (It. artist; 1400-82)
Dello Joio, Norman (US comp.; 1913-)
Delmonico steak
Delos Island (Aegean Sea)
Delphi, Greece
Delphi, Oracle of (also Delphic oracle)(noted for
    ambiguous answers)
Delphi, oracle of Apollo at
Delphinus (astron., dolphin)
Delray Beach, FL
Delsarte method/system (calisthenics)
Delta™
Delta Air Lines, Inc.
Delta Burke (ent.; 1956-)
Delta Connection™, The (airline)
Delta 88, Oldsmobile (auto.)
Delta Force (mil.)

Delta Plan
Delta team (mil.)
Deluge, the (also the Flood)(rel.)
DeLuise, Dom (ent.; 1933-)
DeLuise, Peter
Delvaux, Paul (Belgian artist; 1897-)
Delvecchio, Alex Peter (hockey; 1931-)
Demarest, William (ent.; 1892-1983)
Demaret, Jim (golf; 1910-83)
Demerol™ (med.)
Demeter (myth.)
Demetrius I (Demetrius Poliorcetes)(king,
    Macedonia; c337-283 BC)
Demi Moore (ent.; 1962-)
Demirel, Suleyman (PM, Turk.; 1924-)
Demme, Jonathan (ent.; 1944-)
Democracy, National Endowment for (US pol.
    agcy.)
Democrat (politics)
Democrat & Chronicle, Rochester (NY
    newspaper)
Democrat-Gazette, Little Rock (AR newspaper)
Democrat, Tallahassee (FL newspaper)
Democratic Party (US pol.)
Democratic Party, New (NDP)(Can. pol.)
Democratic Party, Social (Br. pol.; 1981-90)
Democrats, Social (US pol. party)
Democrats, Social and Liberal (Br. pol. party)
Democritus ("the Laughing Philosopher")(Gr.
    phil.; c460-370 BC)
Demond Wilson (ent.; 1946-)
Demosthenes (Gr. orator/pol.; 384-322 BC)
Demotic Greek (lang.)
Dempsey, Jack (William Harrison)(boxing;
    1895-1983)
Denali National Park (formerly Mount
    McKinley National Park)(AK)
Dene (people)
Deneb (also Alpha Cygni)(astron.)
Deneuve, Catherine (Fr. ent.; 1943-)
Deng Xiaoping (also Teng Hsiao-ping)(Ch. pol.;
    1904-)
Denikin, Anton (Rus. mil.; 1872-1947)
Denis Burkitt (Br. phys./rel.; 1911-93)
Denis Charles Potvin (hockey; 1953-)
Denis Diderot (Fr. phil.; 1713-84)
Denis Sassou-Nguesso (ex-pres., Congo; 1943-)
Denise Levertov (Br./US poet; 1923-)
Denise Nicholas (ent.; 1944-)
Denison, TX
Denmark (Kingdom of)(N Eur.)
Denmark Strait (Greenland/Iceland)
Denmark, Anne of (Queen consort, James VI of
    Scot.; 1574-1619)
Dennehy, Brian (ent.; 1938-)
Dennis Alexio
Dennis Chan
Dennis Day (ent.; 1917-88)

Dennis DeConcini (US cong.; 1937-)
Dennis et al v. U.S. (US law; 1951)
Dennis Franz (ent.; 1944-)
Dennis Gabor (Br. inv., holography; 1900-70)
Dennis Hopper (ent.; 1936-)
Dennis James (ent.; 1917-)
Dennis McLain (baseball; 1944-)
Dennis Miller (ent.; 1953-)
Dennis Morgan (ent.; 1910-)
Dennis O'Keefe (ent.; 1908-68)
Dennis Quaid (ent.; 1954-)
Dennis Ralston (tennis; 1942-)
Dennis the Menace (comic strip)
Dennis Weaver (ent.; 1924-)
Dennis, Sandy (ent.; 1937-92)
Dennison Corp., Avery
Dennison Manufacturing Co.
Denny, Reginald (US news)
Denny, Reginald (ent.; 1891-1967)
Denny's, Inc.
Denon™ (audio)
Denon America, Inc.
Denorex™ (med.)
Dentyne™ (gum)
Denver boot (car tire clamp)
Denver Broncos (football team)
Denver Nuggets (basketball team)
Denver Post (CO newspaper)
Denver Pyle (ent.; 1920-)
Denver Rocky Mountain News (CO newspaper)
Denver, Bob (ent.; 1935-)
Denver, CO
Denver, John (ent.; 1943-)
Denzel Washington (ent.; 1954-)
Deo volente (Latin, God willing)
Dep™ (hair care)
Department of Agriculture (US govt.)
Department of Commerce (US govt.)
Department of Defense (DOD)(US govt.)
Department of Education (US govt.)
Department of Energy (US govt.)
Department of Health and Human Services
    (HHS)(US govt.)
Department of Housing and Urban
    Development (HUD)(US govt.)
Department of Justice (DOJ)(US govt.)
Department of Labor (DOL)(US govt.)
Department of State (US govt.)
Department of the Air Force (US mil.)
Department of the Army (US mil.)
Department of the Interior (US govt.)
Department of the Navy (US mil.)
Department of the Treasury (US govt.)
Department of Transportation (DOT)(US govt.)
Department of Veterans Affairs (US govt.)
Department of War (US govt.)
DePauw University (IN)
Depo-Provera™ (med.)

Depp, Johnny (ent.; 1963-)
Depression glass
Depression, the Great (US hist.; 1930s)
der Blaue Reiter (*"the blue Rider"*)(Ger.
    painters)
der Fuhrer (also *Fuehrer*)(title adopted by
    Hitler)
der Post, Laurens (Jan) Van (SAfr. writer;
    1906-)
der Rohe, Ludwig Mies van (US arch.; 1886-
    1969)
Der Spiegel (*The Mirror,* Ger. news magazine)
der Weyden, Rogier van (Flem. artist; c1400-64)
Derby (cheese)
Derby (horse races)
Derby, England
Derbyshire (county, Eng.)
Derbyshire chair (also Yorkshire chair)
Derek Jacobi (ent.; 1938-)
Derek, Bo (ent.; 1956-)
Derek, John (ent.; 1926-)
Deringer pistol
Deringer, Henry (US gunsmith; 19th c.)
DeRita, Joe (b. Joseph Wardell)(ent.; 1909-93)
DermaFlex™ (med.)
Dermarest™ (med.)
Dermocaine™ (med.)
Dern, Bruce (ent.; 1936-)
Dern, Laura (ent.; 1967-)
Derrel's law
Derrick, Butler (US cong.; 1936-)
Derry (county, NIre.)
Derry, Northern Ireland (formerly
    Londonderry)
Des Moines Register (IA newspaper)
Des Moines, IA
Descartes, René (Fr. phil.; 1596-1650)
Deschutes National Forest
Deschutes River (OR)
Desdemona (fict. chara., *Othello*)
Desenex™ (med.)
Desert Culture (anthrop.)
Desert Shield, Operation (Gulf War; 1990-91)
Desert Storm, Operation (Gulf War; 1991)
Desi Arnaz (ent.; 1917-86)
Desi Arnaz, Jr. (ent.; 1953-)
Desiderius Erasmus (Dutch scholar; c1466-
    1536)
Designing Women (TV show)
Desilu Productions (film co.)
Desitin™ (med.)
Desmond Hoyte, Hugh (ex-pres., Guyana)
Desmond Morris (Br. writer; 1928-)
Desmond (Mpilo) Tutu (SAfr. rel.; 1931-)
Desmond, Paul (US jazz; 1924-77)
Desperately Seeking Susan (film; 1985)
Dessau, Germany
Dessau, Paul (Ger. comp; 1894-1979)

d'Estaing, Valéry Giscard (ex-pres., Fr.; 1926-)
d'Étioles, Jeanne Antoinette Poisson Le
    Normant (Marquise de Pompadour)(mistress
    of Louis XV, Fr.; 1721-64)
Detrick, Fort (MD)(mil.)
Detroit Arsenal (MI)(mil.)
Detroit Free Press (MI newspaper)
Detroit Lions (football team)
Detroit Metropolitan Wayne County Airport
    (MI)
Detroit News (MI newspaper)
Detroit News & Free Press (MI newspaper)
Detroit Pistons (basketball team)
Detroit Red Wings (hockey team)
Detroit Tigers (baseball team)
Detroit, MI
Deukmejian, George (ex-gov., CA; 1928-)
Deuteronomy (rel.)
Deutsche mark (also Deutschemark)
Deutschland (Ger. name for Germany)
Dev, Birendra Bir Bikram Shah (king, Nepal;
    1945-)
Devanagari (also Nagari)(alphabetic script)
Devane, William (ent.; 1937-)
Development Program, United Nations (UNDP)
    (est. 1965)
Devens, Fort, MA (mil.)
Devereux, Robert (Earl of Essex)(Br. mil./pol.;
    1567-1601)
Devers, Gail (track; 1966-)
Devi (also Anapurna, Annapurna, Parvati)
    (myth.)
DeVicenzo, Roberto (golf; 1923-)
Devil, the
DeVille, Cruella (fict. chara., *101 Dalmatians*)
Devil's Island (former penal colony, Fr. Guiana)
Devil's Triangle (also Bermuda Triangle)
Devils, New Jersey (hockey team)
Devine, Andy (ent.; 1905-77)
DeVito, Danny (ent. 1944-)
Devon (also Devonshire)(county, Eng.)
Devon cattle
Devon(shire) cream
Devon sheep
Devonian period (395-345 million years ago)
Devonshire (also Devon)(county, Eng.)
Dewar flask/vessel (thermos)
Dewar, Sir James (Scot. chem/physt.; 1842-
    1923)
Dewey decimal system (library classification)
Dewey, George (US adm.; 1837-1917)
Dewey, John (US phil./educ.; 1859-1952)
Dewey, Melvil (US librarian; 1851-1931)
Dewey, Thomas E(dmund)(ex-gov., NY; 1902-
    71)
Dewhurst, Colleen (ent; 1926-1991)
DeWitt Clinton (US pol.; 1769-1828)
DeWitt Wallace (US publ.; 1889-1981)

DeWitt, Joyce (ent.; 1949-)
DeWolf Hopper (ent.; 1858-1935)
Dexatrim™ (med.)
Dexedrine™ (med.)
Dexter Gordon (US jazz; 1923-90)
Dey, Susan (ent.; 1952-)
DFC (Distinguished Flying Cross)
Dhaka, Bangladesh (also Dacca)
Dhamma (rel.)
Dhammapada (rel. work)
D(avid) H(erbert) Lawrence (Br. writer; 1885-
    1930)
DI (drill instructor)
Di-Gel™ (med.)
di Lampedusa, Giuseppe (Tomasi)(It. writer;
    1896-1957)
di Sant' Angelo, Giorgio
di Suvero, Mark (US artist; 1933-)
DiaBeta™ (med.)
Diabetes Self-Management
Diabinese™ (med.)
Diaghilev, Sergei (Pavlovich)(Rus. ballet; 1872-
    1929)
Diahann Carroll (ent.; 1935-)
Dial Corp., Greyhound-
Dial Corp., The (dial™)
Dial One service (comm.)
Dial Magazine
Dialog (compu. database)
Diamond Head, Honolulu
Diamond Jim Brady (US finan.; 1856-1917)
Diamond Star (auto.)
Diamond State (nickname, DE)
Diamond v. Chakrabarty (US law; 1980)
Diamond, Neil (US comp./ent.; 1941-)
Diamond, Selma (ent.; 1920-85)
Dian Fossey (US zool., gorillas; 1932-85)
Diana (myth.)
Diana Barrymore (ent.; 1921-60)
Diana English
Diana Gregory
Diana Hyland
Diana Lynn (ent.; 1926-71)
Diana Muldaur (ent.; 1938-)
Diana Nyad
Diana Rigg (ent.; 1938-)
Diana Ross (ent.; 1944-)
Diana Vreeland (Fr./US editor/designer; 1903-
    89)
Diana, Princess (Princess of Wales, Lady Diana
    Spencer; 1961-)
Diane English
Diane Keaton (ent.; 1946-)
Diane Ladd (ent.; 1932-)
Diane Lane (ent.; 1963-)
Diane Sawyer (US TV jour.; 1945-)
Diane von Furstenberg (US bus.)
Diane von Furstenberg Importing Co.

Diane, steak
Dianetics (Scientology therapy, L. Ron Hubbard)
Dianne Feinstein (US cong.; 1933-)
Dianne Wiest (ent.; 1948-)
Dias, Bartholomeu (also Diaz)(Port. expl.; c1450-1500)
Diaspora (dispersal of Jews outside Isr.)
Diba, Farah
Dibbs, Edward George (tennis; 1951-)
Dick (Richard Anthony) Allen (baseball; 1942-)
Dick (Richard) Button (figure skating, ent.; 1929-)
Dick Butkus (Richard Marvin)(football/ent.; 1942-)
Dick Cavett (ent.; 1936-)
Dick Clark (ent.; 1929-)
Dick Co., A. B.
Dick Ebersol (ent.)
Dick Enberg
Dick (Richard) Fosbury (jumper; 1947-)
Dick Francis (Br. writer/jockey; 1920-)
Dick Gregory (ent.; 1932-)
Dick Haymes (ent.)
Dick Howser (baseball; 1937-87)
Dick Martin (ent.; 1923-)
Dick Moores (cartoonist, *Gasoline Alley*; 1909-86)
Dick Powell (ent.; 1904-63)
Dick Sargent (ent.)
Dick Schaap (US TV sports jour.)
Dick (Francis Richard) Scobee (astro., *Challenger*; 1939-86)
Dick Smothers (ent.; 1939-)
Dick Tracy (fict. chara.)
Dick (Richard) Turpin (Br. highwayman; 1706-39)
Dick Van Dyke (ent.; 1925-)
Dick Van Dyke Show, The (TV show)
Dick Van Patten (ent.; 1928-)
Dick Vitale (ent.; 1940-)
Dick Wakefield (baseball; 1921-85)
Dick Williams (baseball; 1929-)
Dick York (ent.; 1929-92)
Dick, Moby (H. Melville novel)
Dickens, Charles (John Huffam)("Boz")(Br. writer; 1812-70)
Dickens, Little Jimmy (ent.)
Dickenson, Vic (US jazz; 1906-84)
Dickerson, Eric (football; 1960-)
Dickerson, Minnesota v. (US law; 1993)
Dickinson, Angie (ent.; 1931-)
Dickinson, Emily (US poet; 1830-86)
Dictaphone™
Dictaphone Corp.
Dictator, The Great (film)
Dictograph™
Dictograph Products, Inc.

Diddley, Bo (b. Elias McDaniel)(ent.; 1928-)
Diderot, Denis (Fr. phil.; 1713-84)
Didier Ratsiraka (ex-pres., Madagascar; 1936-)
Didion, Joan (US writer; 1934-)
Dido (myth.)
Didot point system (printing)
Didot, François (Ambrose)(Fr. printer; 1730-1804)
die Brücke (Ger. art movement)
Die Fledermaus (Strauss operetta)
Die Hard 2 (film)
Die Walküre (Wagner opera)
Diebenkorn, Richard (US artist; 1922-93)
Diebold, Inc.
Diefenbaker, John George (ex-PM, Can.; 1895-1979)
Diego Rivera (Mex. artist; 1886-1957)
Diego (Rodríguez de Silva y) Velázquez (Sp. artist; 1599-1660)
Diem, Ngo Dinh (ex-pres., SViet.; 1901-63)
Dien Bien Phu, Battle of (also Dienbienphu) (NViet.; 1954)
Dien Bien Phu, Vietnam (also Dienbienphu)
Dieppe lace
Dieppe, France
Diesel, Rudolf (Ger. eng.; 1858-1913)
Diet Coke™
Diet of Worms (rel. hist.; 1521)
Diet Pepsi™
Diet 7UP™
Dietrich Buxtehude (Dan. comp.; 1637-1707)
Dietrich, Marlene (b. Maria Magdalene von Losch)(ent.; 1901-92)
Dietz, Howard (US lyricist.; 1896-1983)
Dietz, James W. (rowing; 1949-)
Dieu et mon droit (motto, Br. royalty, God and my right)
Digger Indians (tribes who dig roots for food)
Diggers (Br. hist.; 1649-60)
Digges, Dudley (ent.; 1879-1947)
Digital Equipment Corp.
Digory Ketterley
Dijon mustard
Dijon, France
Dik Browne (cartoonist, *Hi & Lois, Hagar the Horrible*; 1917-89)
Dikhil, Djibouti
Dilantin™ (med.)
Dilaudid™ (med.)
Dillard Department Stores, Inc.
Dillard, Annie (US writer)
Dillard's (stores)
Diller, Phyllis (ent.; 1917-)
Dillinger, John (US bank robber/murderer; 1902?-34)
Dillman, Bradford (ent.; 1930-)
Dillon, Matt (ent.; 1964-)
Dillon, Matt, Marshal (fict. chara., *Gunsmoke*)

DiMaggio, Dom (baseball; 1917-)
DiMaggio, Joe (baseball; 1914-)
Dimetane™ (med.)
Dimetapp™ (med.)
Dimitri Shostakovich (Rus. comp.; 1906-75)
Dimitri Tiomkin (Rus./US comp.; 1899-)
Dimitrov, Filip (ex-PM, Bulgaria)
Dimitrov, Georgi (ex-PM, Bulgaria; 1882-1949)
Dimli (lang.)
Din, Gunga (film; 1939)
Dina Merrill (ent.; 1925-)
Dinah Manoff (ent.; 1958-)
Dinah Shore (ent.; 1917-94)
Dinah Washington (ent.; 1924-63)
d'Indy, (Paul Marie Théodore) Vincent (Fr.
  comp.; 1851-1931)
Dine, Jim (US artist; 1935-)
Diners Club™ credit card
Diners Club International (US bus.)
Diners Club, Citicorp (US bus.)
Diners Club, Inc.
Dinesen, Isak (aka Karen Blixen)(Dan. writer;
  1885-1962)
Ding Dong School (TV show)
Dingiri Banda Wijetunge (pres., Sri Lanka)
Dinka (lang./people)
Dinkins, David (ex-mayor, NYC; 1927-)
Dino De Laurentiis, (It. ent.; 1919-)
Dinty Moore™ (stew)
Diocletian window (also Palladian window)
Diodorus (Gr. hist.; 1st c. BC)
Diogenes (Gr. phil.; 4th c. BC)
Diola (people)
Diomedes (myth.)
Dion and the Belmonts (pop music)
Dione (Saturn moon)(myth.)
Dionne quintuplets
Dionne Warwick (ent.; 1941-)
Dionne, Marcel (hockey; 1951-)
Dionysius Longinus (Gr. critic; 1st c. AD)
Dionysius, the Elder (Gr. mil.; 432-367 BC)
Dionysius, the Younger (Gr. mil.; c390-344 BC)
Dionysus (myth.)
Dior Perfumes Corp., Christian
Dior, Christian (Fr. designer; 1905-57)
Diouf, Abdou (pres., Senegal; 1935-)
Diphedryl™ (med.)
Dippity-do™ (hair care)
Dippity-Do It (US bus.)
Dire Dawa, Ethiopia
Dire Straits (pop music)
Directoire (arch. style)
Dirk Benedict (ent.; 1945-)
Dirk Bogarde (ent.; 1920-)
Dirk Kempthorne (US cong.; 1951-)
Dirks, Rudolph (cartoonist, *Katzenjammer Kids*;
  · 1877-1968)
Dirksen, Everett M. (US pol./orator; 1896-1969)

Dirty Harry (film; 1971)
Dis (also Dis Pater)(myth.)
Disabilities Act, Americans With (US hist.;
  1990)
Disarmament Conference
Disciples of Christ (also The Christian Church)
Disciples, Twelve
Discover (mag.)
Discovery (US space shuttle)
Discovery Channel, The (DSC)(cable TV)
Discovery Day (now Columbus Day)(October 12)
Disease Control and Prevention, Centers for
  (CDC)
Dismal Swamp, VA/NC
Disney Adventures (mag.)
Disney Channel, The (DIS)(cable TV)
Disney Co., The Walt
Disney-MGM Studios Theme Park
Disney World (FL)
Disney, Walt(er) Elias (US bus./ent.; 1901-66)
Disneyland™ (CA)
Dispatch, Columbus (OH newspaper)
Dispatch, York (PA newspaper)
Disraeli, Benjamin (ex-PM/writer, Br.; 1804-81)
Distinguished Conduct Medal (mil.)
Distinguished Flying Cross (mil.)
Distinguished Service Cross (mil.)
Distinguished Service Medal (mil.)
Distinguished Service Order (Br. mil.)
District of Columbia (Washington, DC, US
  capital)
District, Lake (region, Eng.)
Distrito Federal, Mexico (also Federal District)
Ditka, Mike (football; 1939-)
Ditko, Steve (cartoonist, *Spider-Man*; 1927-)
Ditmars, Ivan
Ditmars, Raymond (US zool., writer; 1876-1942)
Ditto machine™
Divehi (lang.)
Divide, Continental (also the Great Divide)(the
  Rockies)
Divine Comedy, The (by Dante)
Divine Father (God)
Divine Light Mission (rel.)
Divine Liturgy (rel.)
Divine Mind (rel.)
Divine Mother (rel.)
Divine Office (also Liturgy of the Hours)(rel.)
Divine, Major M. J. (also Father Divine)(b.
  George Baker)(US rel.; 1882-1965)
Divinity, the
Divorce Court (TV show)
Diwali (Hindu rel. festival)
Dix, Dorothea (US educ./reformer; 1802-87)
Dix, Fort, NJ (mil.)
Dix, Otto (Ger. artist; 1891-1969)
Dixie (song)
Dixie Carter (ent.; 1939-)

Dixie™ cup
Dixie Stores, Inc., Winn-
Dixiecrat (politics)
Dixieland (music)
Dixon, U.S. v. (US law; 1993)
Dizzy Dean (Jay Hanna)(US baseball; 1911-74)
Dizzy (John Birks) Gillespie (US jazz; 1917-93)
DJ (disc jockey)
Djakarta, Indonesia (also Jakarta)
Django Reinhardt (US jazz; 1910-53)
Djerma (people)
DJI (Dow-Jones Industrials)
DJIA (Dow-Jones Industrial Average)
Djibouti (Republic of)(E Afr.)
Djibouti, Djibouti
D.J. Jazzy Jeff & the Fresh Prince (pop music)
Djohar, Said Muhammad (pres., Comoros
Djurgarden (parkland, Stockholm)
Dlamini, Obed (ex-PM, Swaziland)
DLO (dead letter office)
Dmitry (Dmitriyevich) Shostakovich (Rus.
  comp.; 1906-75)
DMSO (dimethylsulfoxide [colorless liquid])
DMV (Department of Motor Vehicles)
DMZ (demilitarized zone)
DNA (deoxyribonucleic acid)
Dnepr River (also Dnieper)(Rus./Ukraine)
Dnepropetrovsk, Ukraine
Dnieper River (also Dnepr)(Rus./Ukraine)
Dniester River (also Dnestr)(Ukraine)
DO (Doctor of Osteopathy)
DOA (dead on arrival)
Doakes, Joe (also Joe Blow)(average guy)
Doan's™ pills (med.)
DOB (date of birth)
Dobbins Air Force Base, GA (mil.)
Doberman pinscher (dog)
Dobie Gillis (fict. chara.)
Dobrynin, Anatoly
Dobro™ (music)
Dobrovolsky, Georgi (or Georgy) T. (cosmo.;
  1928-71)
Dobson, Kevin (ent.; 1944-)
Doc Holliday, John (US frontier)
Doc (Jerome) Pomus (US comp.; 1925-91)
Doc Severinsen (ent.; 1927-)
Doc, Baby (Jean-Claude Duvalier)(ex-pres.,
  Haiti; 1951-)
Doc, Papa (François Duvalier)(ex-pres., Haiti;
  1907-71)
Dock Boggs (ent.)
Dockers™ (clothing)
Doctor of Juridical Science (also S.J.D.,
  Scientiae Juridicae Doctor)
Doctor of Laws (also LL.D., Legum Doctor)
Doctor of Letters (also D. Litt., Doctor
  Litterarum)
Doctor of Medicine (also M.D., Medicinae
  Doctor)
Doctor of Philosophy (also Ph.D., doctorate)
Doctor of Science (also Sc.D., Scientiae Doctor)
Doctor of Theology (also D.Th., D.Theol.)
Doctor Zhivago (B. Pasternak novel)
Doctorow, E(dgar) L(awrence)(US writer; 1931-)
DOD (Department of Defense)(US govt.)
Dodd, Christopher J. (US cong.; 1944-)
Dodd, Mead & Co., Inc.
Dodds, Johnny (US jazz; 1892-1940)
Dodds, Warren "Baby" (US jazz; 1898-1959)
Dodecanese Islands (Aegean Sea)
Dodge (auto.)
Dodge Caravan (auto.)
Dodge Charger (auto.)
Dodge City, KS
Dodge Dakota (auto.)
Dodge Daytona (auto.)
Dodge Dynasty (auto.)
Dodge Grand Caravan ES (auto.)
Dodge Intrepid (auto.)
Dodge Omni (auto.)
Dodge/Plymouth Neon, Chrysler's (auto.)
Dodge RAM (auto.)
Dodge RAM Van (auto.)
Dodge Shadow (auto.)
Dodge Spirit (auto.)
Dodge Viper (auto.)
Dodge, Mary Abigail (pseud. Gail Hamilton)(US
  writer; 1833-96)
Dodge, Mary Elizabeth Mapes (US writer/
  editor; 1831-1905)
Dodgem (carnival bumper cars)
Dodger Stadium (Los Angeles)
Dodgers, Los Angeles (baseball team)
Dodgson, Charles (pseud. Lewis Carroll)(Br.
  writer/math.; 1832-98)
Dodoma, Tanzania
Dody Goodman (ent.)
Doe, Jane (unidentified or "any" woman)
Doe, John (unidentified or "any" man)
Doesburg, Theo van (Dutch artist/writer; 1883-
  1931)
Doeskin Products (US bus.)
Dog Day Afternoon (film; 1975)
Dog Fancy (mag.)
Dog Star (astron., part of Canis Major [or Great
  Dog])
Dog World (mag.)
Dog, Great (astron., Canis Major, includes the
  Dog Star, Sirius)
Dogpatch, U.S.A.
Dogri (lang.)
Doha, Qatar
Doherty, Shannen (ent.)
Dohnányi, Ernst (or Ernö) von (Hung. pianist/
  comp.; 1877-1960)
Doister, Ralph Roister (Nicholas Udall comedy)

DOJ (Department of Justice)(US govt.)
DOL (Department of Labor)(US govt.)
Dolby™ sound system
Dolby Laboratories, Inc.
Dolce Vita, La (film; 1960)
Dolcetto (wine)
Dole™
Dole Foods Co.
Dole, Bob (Robert)(US cong.; 1923-)
Dole, Elizabeth (US pol.; 1936-)
Dole, Sanford B. (ex-gov., HI; 1844-1921)
Dollar General Corp.
Dollar Rent-A-Car Systems, Inc.
Dolley (Payne Todd) Madison (wife of ex-US
    pres.; 1768-1849)
Dollfuss, Engelbert (ex-chanc. Aus.; 1892-1934)
Doll's House (H. Ibsen play)
Dolly Parton (ent.; 1946-)
Dolly Varden (clothing style)
Dolly Varden (fict. chara.)
Dolly Varden trout (colorful fish)
Dolophine™ (narcotic)
Dolores Del Rio (ent.; 1908-83)
Dolph Lundgren (ent.)
Dolphins, Miami (football team)
Dolphy, Eric (US jazz; 1928-64)
Dom DeLuise (ent.; 1933-)
Dom DiMaggio (baseball; 1917-)
Dom(inic) Mintoff (ex-PM, Malta; 1916-)
Dom Pérignon, Curvée (champagne)
Dome of the Rock (Jerusalem)
Domenici, Pete V. (US cong.; 1932-)
Domenico Cimarosa (It. comp.; 1749-1801)
Domenico Scarlatti, (Giuseppe)(It. comp.; 1685-
    1757)
Domesday Book (also Doomsday Book)(Br. Wm
    the Conqueror land surveys)
Domestic Policy Council (US govt.)
Domingo, Placido (Sp. tenor; 1941-)
Dominic, St. (Sp. rel, founded Dominican order;
    1170-1221)
Dominica (Commonwealth of)
Dominican order (Catholic friars)
Dominican Republic (West Indies)
Dominick Dunne
Dominion Day (now Canada Day)
Dominique (also Dominick) chicken
Domino, Fats (Antoine)(ent.; 1928-)
Domino's Pizza™
Domino's Pizza, Inc.
Dominquin, Luis Miquel (Sp. matador; 1926-)
Dominus (God)
Dominus vobiscum (Latin, the Lord be with
    you)
Domoni, Comoros
Don (Sp. & It. male title)
Don Adams (ent.; 1926-)
Don Ameche (ent.; 1908-1993)

Don Budge (tennis; 1915-)
Don Byas (US jazz; 1912-72)
Don Carlos (F. von Schiller play, Verdi opera)
Don Carlos (prince, Spain; 1545-68)
Don Defore (ent.; 1917-)
Don Drysdale (baseball; 1937-93)
Don Everly (ent.; 1937-)
Don Giovanni (by Mozart)
Don Giovanni (Don Juan)(Sp. legend)
Don Henley (ent.; 1947-)
Don Ho (ent.; 1930-)
Don Hudson (football; 1913-)
Don Johnson (ent.; 1949-)
Don Juan (Don Giovanni)(Sp. legend)
Don Knotts (ent.; 1924-)
Don Martin (cartoonist, *Mad* magazine; 1931-)
Don Mattingly (baseball; 1961-)
Don Michael Paul
Don Murray (ent.; 1929-)
Don Quixote de la Mancha (by Cervantes)
Don Redman (US jazz; 1900-64)
Don Rickles (ent.; 1926-)
Don(ald Francis) Shula (football; 1930-)
Don(ald Howard) Sutton (baseball; 1945-)
Dona (also Doña)(Sp. female title)
Donahue, Elinor (ent.)
Donahue, Phil (ent.; 1935-)
Donahue, Phil (TV show)
Donahue, Troy (ent.; 1936-)
Donald Duck (cartoon chara.)
Donald E(dward) Newhouse
Donald E. Westlake (US writer; 1933-)
Donald Hutson (football; 1913-)
Donald J. Trump (US bus.; 1946-)
Donald Kent "Deke" Slayton (astro.; 1924-93)
Donald Lee Nickles (US cong.; 1948-)
Donald Moffat (ent.; 1930-)
Donald O'Connor (ent.; 1925-)
Donald P. Bellisario
Donald Schollander (swimming; 1946-)
Donald Sutherland (ent.; 1934-)
Donald W. Riegle, Jr. (US cong.; 1938-)
Donald's Quack Attack (TV show)
Donaldson, Sam (US TV jour.; 1934-)
Donaldson, Walter (US comp.; 1893-1947)
Donatello (It. sculptor; 1386-1466)
Donatien Alphonse François, Comte de Sade
    (Marquis de Sade)(Fr. mil./writer; 1740-1814)
Donegal (county, Ir.)
Donegal tweed (fabric)
Donegal, Ireland
Donegan (railroad slang)
Donen, Stanley (ent.; 1924-)
Donetsk, Ukraine
Dong (lang.)
Dong, Pham Van (ex-PM, NViet.; 1906-)
Donizetti, Gaetano (It. comp.; 1797-1848)
Donlevy, Brian (ent.; 1889-1972)

Donn F. Eisele (astro.; 1930-87)
Donna De Varona
Donna Douglas (ent.)
Donna E. Shalala (US Secy./HHS; 1941-)
Donna Fargo (ent.; 1945-)
Donna Karan (US designer; 1948-)
Donna McKechnie (ent.; 1942-)
Donna Maria Caponi (golf; 1945-)
Donna Mills (ent.; 1942-)
Donna Reed (ent.; 1921-86)
Donna Reed Show, The (TV show)
Donna Rice (US news; 1958-)
Donna Summer (ent.; 1948-)
Donne, John (Br. poet; 1573-1631)
Donnelley & Sons, R. R. (US bus.)
Donner Party (CA; 1846-47)
Donner Pass, CA
Donnie Wahlberg (ent.; 1969-)
Donny Anderson, (Gary)(football; 1949-)
Donny Osmond (ent.; 1958-)
Donovan, William Joseph ("Wild Bill")(US mil.; 1883-1959)
Doobie Brothers (also the Doobies)(pop music)
Doodles Weaver
Doody, Howdy (fict. chara.)
Doogie Howser, M.D. (TV show)
Doohan, James R. (Scotty on *Star Trek*)
Dooley, Thomas A. (US phys.; 1927-61)
Dooley, Tom (song)
Doolittle, Dr. (fict. chara.)
Doolittle, Dr. (film; 1967)
Doolittle, Eliza (fict. chara., *Pygmalion*)
Doolittle, Hilda ("HD")(US poet; 1886-1961)
Doolittle, James Harold (US aviator; 1896-93)
Doomsday Book (also Domesday Book)(Br. Wm the Conqueror land surveys)
Doone, Lorna (R.D. Blackmore novel)
Doonesbury (comic strip)
Doors, the (pop music)
Doppelgänger (Ger., phantom double)
Doppler effect (physics)(sound/light waves)
Doppler shift (astron.)
Doppler, Christian (Aus. physt.; 1803-53)
Dorado (astron., goldfish)
Dorcas society (church women who help poor)
Dore Schary (US writer/ent./reformer; 1905-80)
Doré, Gustave (Fr. artist; 1832-83)
Doren, Charles Van (US educ./TV scandal)
Doren, Mamie Van (ent.; 1933-)
Dorgan, Byron Leslie (US cong.; 1942-)
Doria, Andrea (It. adm./pol.; 1466-1560)
Dorian Gray, The Picture of (O. Wilde novel)
Dorian Harewood (ent.; 1951-)
Dorians (ancient Gk. division/people)
Doric (also Doric order)(arch. column)
Do-Right, Dudley, Mountie (fict. chara.)
Doris Day (ent.; 1924-)
Doris Duke (US finan.; 1913-93)

Doris (May Taylor) Lessing (Br. writer; 1919-)
Doris Roberts (ent.; 1929-)
Dorking chicken (Br., 5 toes instead of 4)
Dorland's Medical Dictionary
Dormouse, the (fict. chara.)
Dorothea Dix (US educ./reformer; 1802-87)
Dorothea Lange (US photo.; 1895-1965)
Dorothy (fict. chara., *Wizard of Oz*)
Dorothy bag (handbag)
Dorothy Chandler Pavilion (Los Angeles)
Dorothy Dandridge (ent.; 1923-65)
Dorothy Day (US reformer; 1897-1980)
Dorothy Fields (US lyricist; 1905-74)
Dorothy Gish (ent.; 1898-1968)
Dorothy Gray Cosmetics, Ltd.
Dorothy (Stuart) Hamill (figure skating; 1956-)
Dorothy Kilgallen (US columnist/ent.)
Dorothy Kirsten (US opera; 1919-92)
Dorothy Lamour (ent.; 1914-)
Dorothy Loudon (ent.; 1933-)
Dorothy L(eigh) Sayers (Br. writer; 1893-1957)
Dorothy Malone (ent.; 1925-)
Dorothy McGuire (ent.; 1919-)
Dorothy (Rothschild) Parker (US writer; 1893-1967)
Dorothy Sarnoff (ent.; 1917-)
Dorothy Wordsworth (Br. writer; 1771-1855)
Dorset (county, Eng.)(also Dorsetshire)
Dorset Horn (sheep)
Dorsett, Tony (football; 1954-)
Dorsey, Jimmy (US cond.; 1904-57)
Dorsey, Tommy (US cond.; 1905-56)
Dortmund, Germany
Dory, John (fish)
DOS (disk operating system)(compu.)
Dos Equis XX™ (beer)
Dos Passos, John (US writer; 1896-1970)
dos Santos Daio, Daniel Lima (ex-PM, São Tomé/Príncipe)
dos Santos, José Eduardo (pres., Angola; 1942-)
Dostoyevsky, Fyodor (also Dostoevsky)(Rus. writer; 1821-81)
DOT (Department of Transportation)(US govt.)
Dothan, AL
Dottie West (ent.; 1932-91)
Dou, Gerard (also Dow or Douw)(Dutch artist; 1613-75)
Douala, Cameroon (also Duala)
Douay Bible (also Douay Version)
Double Dutch
Doubleday & Co., Inc.
Doubleday Book Club™
Doubleday Book Shop
Doubleday Dell Publishing Group, Inc., Bantam
Doubleday, Abner (US mil., possibly inv. baseball; 1819-93)
Doubleday, Frank Nelson (US publ.; 1862-1934)
Doubtfire, Mrs. (film)

doubting Thomas
Doug Henning (ent.; 1947-)
Doug McClure (ent.; 1935-)
Douglas Corp., McDonnell
Douglas debates, Lincoln- (US hist.; 1858)
Douglas Edwards (US TV jour.; 1917-90)
Douglas Fairbanks, Jr. (ent.; 1909-)
Douglas Fairbanks, Sr. (ent.; 1883-1939)
Douglas fir (tree)
Douglas Haig (Br. mil.; 1861-1928)
Douglas MacArthur (US gen.; 1880-1964)
Douglas pine (tree)
Douglas spruce (tree)
Douglas Wilder, L(awrence)(ex-gov., VA; 1931-)
Douglas, Donna (ent.)
Douglas, Kirk (b. Issur Danielovich
    Demsky)(ent.; 1916-)
Douglas, Melvyn (ent.; 1901-81)
Douglas, Michael (ent.; 1944-)
Douglas, Paul (ent.; 1907-59)
Douglas, Stephen A. (US pol./orator; 1813-61)
Douglas, William O(rville)(US jurist; 1898-
    1980)
Douglas-Home, Sir Alexander "Alec" Frederick
    (ex-PM, Br.; 1903-)
Douglass, Frederick (US abolitionist, ex-slave;
    1817-95)
Dourda, Abu Said Omar (PM, Libya)
Douw, Gerard (also Dou or Dow)(Dutch artist;
    1613-75)
Dove, Arthur (US artist; 1880-1946)
Dove, Rita (US poet)
Dover Air Force Base, DE (mil.)
Dover sole (fish)
Dover, DE, NH, NJ, OH, TN
Dover, England
Dover, Strait of (Eng./Fr.)
Dovre™ wood stove
Dovre, Inc.
Dow Chemical Co., The
Dow Jones & Co.
Dow Jones Average™ (NY Stock Exchange
    index)
Dow Jones Index
Dow Jones News/Retrieval (compu. database)
Dow, Gerard (also Dou or Douw)(Dutch artist;
    1613-75)
Dow, Herbert H(enry)(US bus./chem.; 1866-
    1930)
Dowding, Hugh C. (Br. mil.; 1883-1970)
Dowiyogo, Bernard (pres., Nauru; 1946-)
Down (county, NIre)
Down East (mag.)
Down, Leslie-Ann (ent.; 1954-)
Downey, Morton
Downey, Morton, Jr.
Downey, Robert, Jr. (ent.; 1965-)
Downing Street (London, site of Br. govt.)

Down's (or Down) syndrome (med.)
Downs, Hugh (ent.; 1921-)
Downy™ (clothes softener)
Downyflake™ (waffles)
Doxology, the (rel.)
Doxsee Food Corp.
Doyle, Sir Arthur Conan (Br. phys./writer,
    Sherlock Holmes; 1859-1930)
Doyle, David (ent.; 1929-)
D'Oyly Carte Opera Company (Birmingham,
    Eng.)
D'Oyly Carte, Richard (Br. opera; 1844-1901)
Dozier, Lamont (US comp.; 1941-)
DP (dew point)
Dr. Doolittle (fict. chara.)
Dr. Doolittle (film; 1967)
Dr. Faustus (The Tragical History of Dr.
    Faustus)(Marlowe)
Dr. Frankenstein (fict. chara.)
Dr. Jekyll and Mr. Hyde, The Strange Case of
    (by R.L. Stevenson)
Dr. Kildare (TV show)
Dr. No (film; 1962)
Dr Pepper™
Dr Pepper/Seven-Up Cos.
Dr. Quinn, Medicine Woman (TV show)
Dr. Scholl's™
Dr. Seuss (aka Theodore Seuss Geisel)(US
    writer/artist; 1904-91)
Dr. Strangelove: or, How I Learned to Stop
    Worrying and Love the Bomb (film; 1964)
Dr. Watson (fict. chara. w/Sherlock Holmes)
Drabble, Margaret (Br. writer; 1939-)
Drackett Products Co.
Draco (astron., dragon)
Draco (Gr. pol.; 7th c. BC)
Draconian laws (severe; 7th c. BC)
Dracula (film; 1931, 1979)
Dracula, Count (vampire based on Vlad Tepes,
    the Impaler)
Dragon, Carmen
Dragons™, Dungeons & (compu. game)
Dragnet (TV show)
Draize test (Rabbit's eye test)
Drake, Alfred (ent.; 1914-)
Drake, Sir Francis (Br. expl.; c1545-96)
Drake, Larry (ent.)
Drake, Stan (cartoonist)
Dramamine™ (med.)
Dramamine II™ (med.)
Drambuie™ (liqueur)
Drang, Sturm und (Storm and Stress)(Ger. lit.;
    18th c.)
Drano™
Draper, Ruth (ent.; 1889-1956)
Dravidian (lang./people)
Dream On (TV show)
Dreamgirls (play)

Proper Noun Speller

Drechsler, Heike
Dred Scott (US slave; 1795?-1858)
Dred Scott Case/Decision (US law, pro-slavery; 1856-57)
D region
Dreiser, Theodore (US writer; 1871-1945)
D-ring (also D ring)(clothing closure)
Dresden china/porceline/ware (also Meissen)
Dresden, Germany
Dresser Industries
Dresser, Louise (ent.; 1881-1965)
Dressler, Marie (ent.; 1869-1934)
Drew Barrymore (ent.; 1975-)
Drew Pearson (US jour.; 1897-1969)
Drew, Ellen (ent.; 1915-)
Drew, John, Mrs. (ent.; 1820-97)
Drew, Nancy (fict. chara.)
Drexel Burnham Lambert (US stock market scandal)
Drexler, Clyde (basketball; 1962-)
Dreyer's™
Dreyer's Grand Ice Cream, Inc.
Dreyfus Affair
Dreyfus Corp., The
Dreyfus, Alfred (Fr. capt.; 1859-1935)
Dreyfus, Julia Louis- (ent.; 1961-)
Dreyfuss, Richard (ent.; 1947-)
Drifters, the (pop music)
Drinkwater, Terry
Dristan™ (med.)
Driving Miss Daisy (film; 1989)
Drixoral™ (med.)
Drnovsek, Janez (PM, Slovenia)
Drogheda, Ireland
Drood, Edwin (fict. chara., C. Dickens)
Droste™ (chocolate)
Droste USA, Ltd.
Drottningholm (palaces in Swed.)
Dru, Joanne (ent.; 1923-)
Drucker, Mort (cartoonist, *Mad* magazine; 1929-)
Drug Administration, Food and (FDA)(US govt. agcy.)
Drug Control Policy, Office of National (US govt.)
Drug Emporium (US bus.)
Drum, Fort (NY)(mil.)
Drummondville, Quebec, Canada
Drumstick™ (ice cream)
Drumstick Co.
Drury Lane theatre (London)
Druse (also Druze)(rel.)
Druten, John (William) Van (US writer; 1901-57)
Dry Ice™
Dry Ice Corp. of America
Dryden Flight Research Center (CA)
Dryden, John (Br. writer; 1631-1700)

Dryden, John Fairchild (US bus./pol.; 1839-1911)
Dryden, Kenneth (hockey; 1947-)
Dryer, Fred (ent.; 1946-)
Drysdale, Don (baseball; 1937-93)
DSC (Distinguished Service Cross)
DSM (Distinguished Service Metal)
DSO (Distinguished Service Order)
DST (daylight-saving time)
DT's (delirium tremens)
du Barry, Madame (Jeanne Bécu)(Comtesse, mistress, Louis XV; 1743-93)
Du Bois Wines, Clos (US bus.)
Du Bois, W(illiam) E(dward) B(urghardt)(US educ./writer, NAACP; 1868-1963)
Du Maurier, Daphne (Br. writer; 1907-89)
Du Pont™ chemicals
Du Pont Circle (DC traffic circle)
du Pont de Nemours & Co. E. I.
du Pont de Nemours, E(leuthere) I. (US bus.; 1771-1834)
Du Pont™ fibers
du Pont Pharmaceuticals (US bus.)
du Pont, Henry (US bus.; 1812-89)
du Pont, Henry Algernon (US mil./pol.; 1838-1926)
du Pont, Henry (Belin)(US bus.; 1899-1970)
Du Pont, Pierre Samuel (Fr. econ./pol.; 1739-1817)
du Pont, Pierre Samuel (US bus.; 1870-?)
du Pont, Samuel Francis (US mil.; 1803-65)
du Pont, Thomas Coleman (US bus./pol.; 1863-1930)
du Val Wine Co., Ltd., The Clos
Dual Alliance
Dual Entente (Fr./Rus. alliance; 1893-1917)
Duala, Cameroon (also Douala)
Duane Allman (ent.; 1947-71)
Duane Hanson (US sculptor; 1925-)
Duarte, José Napoleon (ex-pres., El Salvador; 1925-90)
Dubai (state, UAE)
Dubavy, United Arab Emirates
Dubcek, Alexander (Czech. pol.; 1921-92)
Dubin, Al (US lyricist; 1891-1945)
Dubinsky, David (US labor leader; 1892-1982)
Dublin, Ireland
Dubonnet™ (wine)
DuBose Heyward (US lyricist; 1885-1940)
Dubrovnik, Croatia
Dubuffet, Jean (Fr. artist; 1902-85)
Dubuque, IA
Duce, Il (aka Benito Mussolini)(ex-PM, It.; 1883-1945)
Duchamp, Marcel (Fr. artist; 1887-1968)
Duchamp-Villon, Raymond (Fr. artist; 1876-1918)
Duchin, Eddy (ent.; 1909-51)

Duck Soup (film; 1933)
Duck, Daffy (cartoon chara.)
Duck, Daisy (cartoon chara.)
Duck, Donald (cartoon chara.)
Dudelange, Luxembourg
Dudevant, Amandine Aurore Lucie (b. Dupin)(pseud. George Sand)(Fr. writer; 1804-76)
Dudley Digges (ent.; 1879-1947)
Dudley Do-Right, Mountie (fict. chara.)
Dudley Moore (ent.; 1935-)
Duel in the Sun (film; 1946)
Duff, Howard (ent.; 1914-90)
Duffy, Julia (ent.; 1951-)
Duffy, Patrick (ent. 1949-)
Dufour, Val (ent.; 1927-)
Dufy, Raoul (Fr. artist; 1877-1953)
DUI (driving under the influence)
Duisburg, Germany (formerly Duisburg-Hamborn)
Dukakis, Kitty (Katharine)(wife of ex-MA gov.)
Dukakis, Michael S. (ex-gov., MA; 1933-)
Dukakis, Olympia (ent.; 1931-)
Dukas, Paul (Fr. comp.; 1865-1935)
Duke Astin, Patty (ent.; 1946-)
Duke Ellington (Edward Kennedy)(US comp./US jazz; 1899-1974)
Duke Kahanamoku (Olympic swimmer; 1890-1968)
Duke of Alba (also Alva, Fernando Alvarez de Toledo)(Sp. pol.; 1508-82)
Duke of Albemarle (George Monck)(Br. mil./pol.; 1608-70)
Duke of Argyll (John D. S. Campbell)(ex-gov-gen., Can.; 1845-1914)
Duke of Edinburgh, (Philip Mountbatten, Lt., Prince of the UK and NIre.; 1921-)
Duke of Marlborough (John Churchill)(Br. mil.; 1650-1722)
Duke of Paducah (aka Whitey [Edward Charles] Ford)(baseball; 1928-)
Duke of Wellington (Arthur Wellesley)(Br. mil.; 1769-1852)
Duke of Windsor (Edward VIII)(abdicated Br. throne; 1894-1972)
Duke (Edwin) Snider (baseball; 1926-)
Duke University (NC)
Duke, Charles M. (astro.)
Duke, David (US pol.; 1950-)
Duke, Doris (US finan.; 1913-93)
Duke, James (US bus.; 1856-1925)
Duke, the (nickname, John Wayne)
Duke, Vernon (US comp.; 1903-69)
Dukes, David (ent.; 1945-)
Dukham, Qatar
Dukhobors (people)
Dulcolax™ (laxative)
Dullea, Keir (ent.; 1936-)

Dulles International Airport (DC/VA)
Dulles, John Foster (US pol.; 1888-1959)
Duluth News-Tribune (MN newspaper)
Duluth, MN
Dumas, Alexandre (aka Dumas fils)(Fr. writer; 1824-95)
Dumas, Alexandre (aka Dumas peré)(Fr. writer; 1802-70)
Dumbarton Oaks (estate in Washington DC)
Dumbbell Nebula/nebula (astron.)
Dumbo's Circus (TV show)
Dumont, Alberto Santos- (Fr. aviator; 1873-1932)
Dumpster™ (refuse container)
Dun & Bradstreet Corp.
Dunaway, Faye (ent.; 1941-)
Dunbar-Nelson, Alice
Duncan Phyfe (Scot./US furniture maker; c1768-1854)
Duncan, Isadora (US dancer; 1878-1927)
Duncan, Sandy (ent.; 1946-)
Dundalk, MD
Dundee, Scotland
Dunedin, New Zealand
Dunem, Fernando Jose de Franca Dias van (ex-PM, Angola)
Dungeness crab
Dungeons & Dragons™ (compu. game)
Dunham, Katherine (ent.; 1910-)
Dunkers (also Church of the Brethren, Amish, Mennonites, Plain People)(rel.)
Dunkin' Donuts™
Dunkin' Donuts of America, Inc.
Dunkirk, France
Dunkirk, IN, NY
Dunlap, Inc., Grosset &
Dunlop (cheese)
Dunlop Sports Corp.
Dunlop Tire Corp.
Dunn, James (ent.; 1905-67)
Dunne, Dominick
Dunne, Griffin (ent.; 1955-)
Dunne, Irene (ent.; 1898-1990)
Dunne, John Gregory (US writer; 1932-)
Dun's (mag.)
Dunsinane (hill in Scot.)
Dunsmore, Barrie
Dupont, Jacques (minister/state, Monaco)
Duracell™ (batteries)
Duracell Co. USA, The
Durán Bellén, Sixto (pres., Ecuador; 1921-)
Duran Duran (pop music)
Duran, Roberto (boxing; 1951-)
Durand, Asher Brown (US artist; 1796-1886)
Durango, Mexico
Durant, Ariel (US hist.; 1898-1981)
Durant, Thomas C. (US bus./finan.; 1820-85)
Durant, Will (US hist.; 1885-1981)

Durant, William C. (US bus., GM; 1861-1947)
Durante, Jimmy (James Francis)(ent.; 1893-1980)
Durban, South Africa
D'Urbervilles, Tess of the (T. Hardy novel)
Durbin, Deanna (ent.; 1921-)
Durenberger, David F. (US cong.; 1934-)
Dürer, Albrecht (Ger. artist; 1471-1528)
Durga (Hindu goddess)
Durham (county, Eng.)
Durham, Bill (film; 1988)
Durham, England
Durham, NC, NH
Durkee™
Durkee French Foods (US bus.)
Durkheim, Emile (Fr. sociol.; 1858-1917)
Durning, Charles (ent.; 1923-)
Durocher, Leo (baseball; 1906-91)
Durr, Francois (tennis; 1942-)
Durrell, Lawrence (Br. writer; 1912-90)
Durres, Albania
Durward Kirby (ent.; 1912-)
Duryea, Dan (ent.; 1907-68)
Duse, Eleonora (ent.; 1858-1924)
Dushanbe, Tajikistan
Dussault, Nancy (ent.; 1936-)
Düsseldorf, Germany
Dust Bowl (KS/OK/TX/NM/CO)
Dustin Hoffman (ent.; 1937-)
Dustin Nguyen
Dusty Springfield (ent.; 1939-)
Dutch (lang./people)
Dutch Belted cattle
Dutch bob (hair style)
Dutch Borneo (now Kalimantan)
Dutch cap (headwear)
Dutch door
Dutch East India Company (trade; 1602-1798)
Dutch East Indies (now Indonesia)
Dutch elm disease
Dutch Guiana (now Suriname)
Dutch oven
Dutch Reformed Church
Dutch treat (share expenses)
Dutch uncle
Dutch West India Co. (1621-1794)
Dutch-Flemish (lang.)
Dutchman's-breeches (plant)
Dutchman's-pipe (plant)
Dutton, E(dward) P(ayson)(US publ.; 1831-1923)
Duvalier, François (aka Papa Doc)(ex-pres., Haiti; 1907-71)
Duvalier, Jean-Claude (aka Baby Doc)(ex-pres., Haiti; 1951-)
Duvall, Robert (ent.; 1931-)
Duvall, Shelley (ent.; 1949-)
Duvall's Bedtime Stories, Shelley (TV show)

DVM (Doctor of Veterinary Medicine)
Dvorak, Anton (also Antonin)(Czech. comp.; 1841-1904)
Dweezil Zappa (ent.)
DWI (driving while intoxicated)
Dwight D(avid) Eisenhower (34th US pres.; 1890-1969)
Dwight Edwin Stones (track; 1953-)
Dwight Gooden (baseball; 1964-)
Dwight Hemion
D(avid) W(ark) Griffith (ent.; 1875-1948)
Dwight Lyman Moody (US rel.; 1837-99)
Dwight Yoakam (ent.)
Dy (chem. sym., dysprosium)
Dyan Cannon (ent.; 1937-)
Dyazide™ (med.)
Dyck, Sir Anthony van (Flem. artist; 1599-1641)
Dyerma (lang.)
Dyke Show, Dick Van (TV show)
Dyke, Dick Van (ent.; 1925-)
Dyke, Jerry Van (ent.; 1931-)
Dykstra, Lenny (baseball; 1963-)
Dylan (Marlais) Thomas (Welsh poet; 1914-53)
Dylan, Bob (b. Robert Zimmerman)(US comp./ent.; 1941-)
Dynasty, Dodge (auto.)
Dynel™
Dysart, Richard (ent.; 1929-)
Dzongkha (lang.)

E

Ea (Babylonian god)
Eadweard Muybridge (aka Edward James Muggeridge)(US photo.; 1830-1904)
Eagle (auto.)
Eagle™ (potato chips)
Eagle Vision TSi (auto.)
Eagle, Reading (PA newspaper)
Eagle, Wichita (KS newspaper)
Eagles, Philadelphia (football team)
Eagles, the (pop music)
Eakins, Thomas (US artist; 1844-1916)
Eames (chair)
Eames, Charles (US arch./designer; 1907-78)
Eamon de Valera (ex-PM/pres., Ir.; 1882-1975)
E & J Gallo Winery (US bus.)
Eanes, Antonio dos Santos Ramalho (ex-pres., Port.; 1935-)
Earhart, Amelia (Mary)(US aviator; 1897-1937?)
Earl Anthony (bowling; 1938-)
Earl Averill (baseball; 1915-83)
Earl Bostic (ent.)
Earl Campbell (football; 1955-)
Earl Carrol's Vanities
Earl Grey (tea)
Earl "Fatha" Hines (US jazz; 1905-83)
Earl H. Blaik (football; 1897-1989)
Earl Holliman (ent.; 1928-)
Earl Morrall (football; 1934-)
Earl of Albemarle (George Monk [also Monck])(Br. mil./pol.; 1608-70)
Earl of Cardigan (James Thomas Brudenell (Br. mil./pol., cardigan sweater; 1797-1868)
Earl of Coventry (card game)
Earl of Essex (Robert Devereux)(Br. mil./pol.; 1566-1601)
Earl of Sandwich (John Montagu)(Br. pol.; 1718-92)
Earl of Shaftesbury (A. A. Cooper)(Br. reformer; 1801-85)
Earl of Southhampton (Henry Wriothesley)(Br., 3rd
Earl Scheib™ (auto painting)
Earl Scheib, Inc.
Earl Scruggs (ent.; 1924-)
Earl Warren (US jurist; 1891-1974)
Earl Weaver (baseball; 1930-)
Earle Hyman (ent.; 1926-)
Early Modern English (lang.; c1550-1700)
Early, Jubal Anderson (US gen.; 1816-94)
Earp, Wyatt (Berry Stapp)(US frontier; 1848-1929)
Earth (planet)(also l.c.)
Earth Journal (mag.)

Earth Summit (UN Conference on Environment and Development)(June 1992)
Earth, Wind, and Fire (pop music)
Eartha Kitt (ent.; 1928-)
Earthly Delights, Garden of (Bosch)
Earthwatch
Ease Sport™ (clothing)
East Berlin (now part of united Berlin, Ger.)
East China Sea (also Dong Hai)
East Flanders (province, Belgium)
East Germany (now part of united Germany)
East Goths (also Ostrogoths)(ancient Germans)
East India Company, British (trade; 1600-1873)
East India Company, Danish (trade; 1729-1801)
East India Company, Dutch (trade; 1602-1798)
East India Company, French (trade; 1664-1794)
East Indian (people)
East Indies (formerly SE Asia, now only Malay Archipelago)
East Lansing, MI
East London, South Africa
East Lynne, or The Elopement (E.P. Wood novel)
East of Eden (John Steinbeck novel)
East Orange, NJ
East Pakistan (now Bangladesh)
East Sussex (county, Eng.)
Easter (rel. holiday)
Easter egg
Easter Island (also Rapa Nui)(S Pac.)
Easter lily
Easter Rebellion (also Easter Rising)(Ir.; 1916)
Eastern Conference (basketball)
Eastern Hamitic (people)
Eastern Hemisphere
Eastern Orthodox Church (also Orthodox Eastern Church)(rel.)
Eastern Standard Time
Eastern Tsin (or Chin) dynasty (Ch.; 317-420)
Easterner
Eastertide
Eastman Kodak Co.
Eastman, George (US inv./photo.; 1854-1932)
Easton, Sheena (ent.; 1959-)
Eastwick, The Witches of (film; 1987)
Eastwood, Clint (ent.; 1930-)
Easy-Off™ (oven cleaner)
Easy Rider (film; 1969)
Easy Street
Eating Raoul (film; 1982)
Eating Well (mag.)
Eaton Corp.
Eaton Paper Co.
eau de Cologne
Eban, Aubrey Solomon "Abba" (Isr. pol.; 1915-)
Ebbets Field
Ebenezer Butterick (US inv./tailor; 1826-1903)
Ebenezer Scrooge (fict. chara., *A Christmas*

Carol)
Eber, José (hairstylist)
Ebersol, Dick (ent.)
Ebersole, Christine
Ebert, Friedrich (Ger. pol.; 1871-1925)
Ebert, Roger (US critic; 1942-)
Ebert, Siskel & (US critics)
Ebing, Richard von Krafft-, Baron (Ger. phys.;
    1840-1902)
Ebony (mag.)
Ebony Man (mag.)
Ebsen, Buddy (ent.; 1908-)
E(lwyn) B(rooks) White (US writer; 1899-1985)
EC (European Community)(pol./econ. alliance)
Ecclesiastes (rel.)
ECG (electrocardiogram)
Echlin, Inc.
Echo (myth.)
Echo (US space satellite)
Eckerd™ (drug stores)
Eckersley, Dennis (baseball; 1954-)
E. C. Knight Co., U.S. v. (US law; 1895)
Eckrich™ meats
Eckrich, Armour Swift- (US bus.)
Eckstine, Billy (ent.; 1914-93)
Eclipse (CAT system)
Economic Advisers, Council of (US govt.)
Economic Community of West African States
    (ECOWAS)(est. 1975)
Economic Cooperation and Development,
    Organization for (OECD)(internat'l; est.
    1961)
Economic Policy Council (US govt.)
Economic World
Ecotrin™ (med.)
Ecuador (Republic of)(SAmer.)
Ecuatoriana Airlines
Ecumedia News Service
Ed Ames (ent.; 1927-)
Ed Asner (ent.; 1929-)
Ed Begley (ent.; 1901-70)
Ed Begley, Jr. (ent.; 1949-)
Ed Bradley (US TV jour.; 1941-)
Ed Flanders (ent.; 1934-)
Ed Gallagher (ent.)
Ed Giacomin (hockey; 1939-)
Ed Harris (ent.; 1950-)
Ed Herlihy
Ed "Too Tall" Jones
Ed Lauter (ent.; 1940-)
Ed Marinaro
Ed McMahon (ent.; 1923-)
Ed(win Corley) Moses (US track; 1955-)
Ed Nelson (ent.; 1928-)
Ed O'Neill (ent.; 1946-)
Ed(ward Vincent) Sullivan (ent.; 1902-74)
Ed Sullivan Show, The (TV show)
Ed Wynn (ent.; 1886-1966)

Ed, Mr. (fict. horse)
EDA (Economic Development Administration)
Edam cheese
Edam, Netherlands
Edberg, Stefan (tennis; 1966-)
Edd "Kookie" Byrnes (ent.)
Edd Roush (baseball; 1893-1988)
Edd, Fred (US lyricist; 1936-)
Edda (also *Prose Edda*)(Icelandic folk tales)
Eddie Albert (ent.; 1908-)
Eddie "Rochester" Anderson (ent.; 1905-77)
Eddie (George Edward) Arcaro (jockey; 1916-)
Eddie Bauer Expedition Outfitter (US bus.)
Eddie Bracken (ent.; 1920-)
Eddie Cantor (ent.; 1892-1964)
Eddie Cochran (ent.)
Eddie Condon (US jazz; 1904-73)
Eddie "Lockjaw" Davis (US jazz; 1921-86)
Eddie Fisher (ent.; 1928-)
Eddie Foy (ent.; 1857-1928)
Eddie Heywood (US jazz; 1916-89)
Eddie Holland (US comp.; 1939-)
Eddie Lopat (baseball; 1918-92)
Eddie Mathews (baseball; 1931-)
Eddie Merckx ("the Cannibal")(Belgian cyclist;
    1945-)
Eddie Murphy (ent.; 1961-)
Eddie Rabbitt (ent.; 1941-)
Eddie (Edward Vernon) Rickenbacker, Capt.
    (US aviator; 1890-1973)
Eddie Shore (hockey; 1902-85)
Eddie Van Halen (ent.; 1957-)
Eddings, David
Eddy Arnold (ent.; 1918-)
Eddy Duchin (ent.; 1909-51)
Eddy, Mary Baker (US, founder Christian
    Science; 1821-1910)
Eddy, Nelson (ent.; 1901-67)
Ede, Nigeria
Edelman, Herb (ent.; 1933-)
Edelpilzkäse (cheese)
Eden, Sir Anthony (Earl of Avon)(ex-PM, Br.;
    1897-1977)
Eden, Barbara (ent.; 1934-)
Eden, Garden of (rel.)
Eden, Villa Mt. (US bus.)
Ederle, Gertrude (swimming; 1906-)
Edgar Allan Poe (US writer; 1809-49)
Edgar Bergen (ent.; 1903-78)
Edgar Dégas (Fr. artist; 1834-1917)
Edgar D. Mitchell (astro.)
Edgar (Albert) Guest (US writer; 1881-1959)
Edgar Lee Masters (US writer; 1869-1950)
Edgar Rice Burroughs (US writer; 1875-1950)
Edgar the Peaceful (king, Eng.; 944-975)
Edgar, Jim (IL gov.; 1946-)
Edgehill, Battle of (Eng.; 1642)
Edict of Nantes (Fr. hist.; 1598)

Edie Adams (ent.; 1929-)
Edie McClurg (ent.; 1951-)
Edinburg, IN, TX
Edinburgh fog (dessert)
Edinburgh, Duke of (Philip Mountbatten, Lt.,
   Prince of the UK and NIre.)
Edinburgh, Scotland
Edison Co., McGraw-
Edison effect (physics)
Edison, NJ
Edison, Thomas Alva (US inv.; 1847-1931)
Edith Cresson (ex-PM, Fr.; 1934-)
Edith Evans, Dame (ent.; 1888-1976)
Edith Hamilton (Ger./US educ./writer; 1867-
   1963)
Edith Head (US designer; 1898?-1981)
Edith Piaf (b. Edith Giovanna Gassion)(Fr. ent.;
   1915-63)
Edith Sitwell, Dame (Br. writer; 1887-1964)
Edith (Newbold Jones) Wharton (US writer;
   1862-1937)
Edmond O'Brien (ent.; 1915-85)
Edmond Rostand (Fr. writer; 1868-1918)
Edmond, OK
Edmonton Oilers (hockey team)
Edmonton, Alberta, Canada
Edmund Allenby (Br. mil.; 1861-1936)
Edmund Burke (Ir./Br. pol.; 1729-97)
Edmund Dantès (fict. chara., *Count of Monte
   Cristo*)
Edmund Gerald "Jerry," Brown, Jr. (ex-gov.,
   CA; 1938-)
Edmund Gerald "Pat" Brown, Sr. (ex-gov., CA;
   1905-)
Edmund Gwenn (ent.; 1875-1959)
Edmund Halley (Br. astron.; 1656-1742)
Edmund Husserl (Ger. phil.; 1859-1938)
Edmund II ("Ironside")(king, Eng.; c989-1016)
Edmund Kean (ent.; 1787-1833)
Edmund Muskie (US pol.; 1914-)
Edmund P. Hillary, Sir (NewZeal. expl., Mt.
   Everest; 1919-)
Edmund (Jennings) Randolph (US atty.; 1753-
   1813)
Edmund Ruffin (US agriculturist; 1794-1865)
Edmund Spenser (Br. poet; 1552-99)
Edmund Wilson (US writer/critic; 1895-1972)
Edna Ferber (US writer; 1887-1968)
Edna St. Vincent Millay (US poet; 1892-1950)
Edna Valley Vineyard (US bus.)
Edo (lang.)
Édouard Balladur (PM, Fr..; 1929-)
Édouard Daladier (Fr. pol.; 1884-1970)
Édouard Frank (ex-PM, Central African
   Republic)
Édouard Herriot (ex-PM/pres., Fr.; 1872-1957)
Édouard Lalo, (Victor Antoine)(Fr. comp.; 1823-
   92)

Édouard Manet (Fr. artist; 1832-83)
Édouard Vuillard, (Jean)(Fr. artist; 1868-1940)
Edsel (Bryant) Ford (US bus./auto.; 1893-1943)
Edsel™, Ford (auto.)
EDT (Eastern Daylight Time)
EDTA (crystalline solid used as food
   preservative)
Eduard A. Shevardnadze (pres., Georgia; 1928-)
Eduard Benes (Czech. pol.; 1884-1948)
Eduard Buchner (Ger. chem.; 1860-1917)
Eduardo Paolozzi (Br. sculptor; 1924-)
Educating Rita (film; 1983)
Education Association of the United States,
   National (NEA)(est. 1906)
Education Testing Service
Education, Department of (US govt.)
Educational Broadcasting Corp.
Educational, Scientific, and Cultural
   Organization, United Nations (UNESCO)
   (est. 1945)
Edvard (Hagerup) Grieg (Nor. comp.; 1843-
   1907)
Edvard Munch (Nor. artist; 1863-1944)
Edward Albee (US writer; 1928-)
Edward Arnold (ent.; 1890-1956)
Edward Bellamy (US writer; 1850-98)
Edward Bennett Williams (US atty.; 1920-88)
Edward Bowes, Major (ent.; 1874-1946)
Edward Braddock (Br. gen. in Amer.; 1695-
   1755)
Edward Burne-Jones (Br. artist; 1833-98)
Edward Channing (US hist.; 1856-1931)
Edward Charles "Whitey" Ford ("Duke of
   Paducah")(baseball; 1928-)
Edward Charles Pickering (US astron./physt.;
   1846-1919)
Edward Durell Stone (US arch.; 1902-75)
Edward Eggleston (US writer; 1837-1902)
Edward (William) Elgar, Sir (Br. comp.; 1857-
   1934)
Edward Estlin Cummings (pseud. e.e.
   cummings)(US poet; 1894-1962)
Edward Everett Hale (US writer/rel.; 1822-
   1909)
Edward Everett Horton (ent.; 1886-1970)
Edward Fenech Adami (PM, Malta; 1934-)
Edward Fitzgerald (Br. poet; 1809-83)
Edward George Dibbs (tennis; 1951-)
Edward G. Gibson (astro.)
Edward Gibbon (Br. hist.; 1737-94)
Edward G. Robinson (ent.; 1893-1973)
Edward (Richard George) Heath (ex-PM, Br.;
   1916-)
Edward Herrmann (ent.; 1943-)
Edward H(enry) Harriman (US bus.; 1848-
   1909)
Edward Hicks (US artist; 1780-1849)
Edward Hopper (US artist; 1882-1967)

Edward H(iggins) White, II (astro., 1st Amer. to walk in space; 1930-67)
Edward I (king, Eng.; 1239-1307)
Edward II (king, Eng.; 1284-1327)
Edward III (king, Eng.; 1312-77)
Edward IV (king, Eng.; 1442-83)
Edward James Olmos (ent.; 1947-)
Edward Jenner (Br. phys., smallpox vaccine; 1749-1823)
Edward J(ames) "Ted" Hughes (Br. poet; 1930-)
Edward (Irving) Koch (ex-mayor, NYC; 1924-)
Edward Koren (cartoonist; *New Yorker*; 1935-)
Edward Lawrie Tatum (US chem.; 1909-75)
Edward Lear (Br. artist/humorist; 1812-88)
Edward McDowell (US comp.; 1861-1908)
Edward M. House (US dipl.; 1858-1938)
Edward M(oore) "Ted" Kennedy (US cong.; 1932-)
Edward Mulhare (ent.; 1923-)
Edward O. Wilson (US zool.; 1929-)
Edward R(oscoe) Murrow (US TV jour.; 1908-65)
Edward R. Stettinius, Jr. (US bus./pol.; 1900-49)
Edward Sapir (Ger./US anthrop.; 1884-1939)
Edward (Wyllis) Scripps (US publ.; 1854-1926)
Edward Steichen (US photo.; 1879-1973)
Edward Stratemeyer (US writer; 1862-1930)
Edward Teach (also Thatch, Thach; Blackbeard)(pirate; ?-1718)
Edward Teller, Dr. (US physt., A-bomb/H-bomb; 1908-)
Edward the Black Prince (Prince of Wales; 1330-76)
Edward the Confessor (king, Eng.; 1003-66)
Edward the Elder (king, W Saxons; c870-924)
Edward the Martyr (king, Eng.; c963-978
Edward T. Schafer (ND gov.)
Edward V (king, Eng.; 1470-83)
Edward Vernon "Eddie" Rickenbacker, Capt. (US aviator; 1890-1973)
Edward VI (king, Eng.; 1537-53)
Edward VII (king, Br.; 1841-1910)
Edward VIII, Duke of Windsor (abdicated Br. throne; 1894-1972)
Edward William Brooke (US pol.; 1919-)
Edward Woodward (ent.; 1930-)
Edward, Prince (Edward Anthony Richard Louis, Prince of the UK)(3rd son of Queen Elizabeth II; 1964-)
Edwards Air Force Base, CA (mil.)
Edwards, Anthony (ent.; 1962-)
Edwards, Blake (ent.; 1922-)
Edwards, Douglas (US TV jour.; 1917-90)
Edwards, Edwin (LA gov.; 1927-)
Edwards, Gus (US comp.; 1879-1945)
Edwards, Jonathan (US rel.; 1703-58)
Edwards, Ralph (ent.; 1913-)

Edwards, Sherman (US comp.; 1919-81)
Edwin Arlington Robinson (US poet; 1869-1935)
Edwin Drood (fict. chara., C. Dickens)
Edwin Edwards (LA gov.; 1927-)
Edwin Eugene "Buzz" Aldrin, Jr. (astro.; 1930-)
Edwin (Herbert) Land (US inv., Polaroid Land camera; 1910-91)
Edwin Meese, III (US pol.; 1931-)
Edwin M(cMasters) Stanton (US mil./pol.; 1814-69)
Edwin Newman (US writer)
Edwin P. Christy (ent.; 1815-62)
Edwin P(owell) Hubble (US astron.; 1889-1953)
Edwin Thomas Booth (US actor, bro. of John Wilkes; 1833-93)
EEC (European Economic Community)(also Common Market, est. 1957)
e. e. cummings (b. Edward Estlin Cummings)(US poet; 1894-1962)
EEG (electroencephalogram)
EEOC (Equal Employment Opportunity Commission)
Eero Saarinen (US arch.; 1910-61)
Eeyore (fict. chara., *Winnie-the-Pooh*)
Effect of Gamma Rays on Man-in-the-Moon Marigolds, The (film; 1972)
Efferdent™ (health)
Efik (lang.)
Efrem Zimbalist, Jr. (ent.; 1923-)
Efrem Zimbalist, Sr. (US violinist/comp.; 1889-1985)
EFT (electronic fund transfer)
EFTA (European Free Trade Association)(est. 1960)
Egbert van Alstyne (US comp.; 1882-1951)
Eggleston, Edward (US writer; 1837-1902)
Eggo™ (waffles)
eggs Benedict (also l.c.)
Eglin Air Force Base, FL (mil.)
E. G. Marshall (ent.; 1910)
Egon Schiele (Aus. artist; 1890-1918)
Egypt (Arab Republic of)(NE Afr.)
Egyptair (airline)
Egyptian (lang./people)
Egyptian archeology
Egyptian architecture (mainly ancient Egypt)
Egyptian art (mainly ancient Egypt)
Egyptian Mau (cat)
Egyptology (study of ancient Eqypt)
Ehrenburg, Ilya G. (Rus. writer; 1891-1967)
Ehrlich, Paul (Ger. bacteriol.; 1854-1915)
Ehrlichman, John Daniel (US pol./Watergate; 1925-)
Eichhorn, Lisa (ent.; 1952-)
Eichmann, Adolf (Aus./Ger. Nazi; 1906-62)
Eid ul-Adha (Muslim festival)
Eid ul-Fitr (Muslim festival)
E. I. du Pont de Nemours & Co.

E(leuthere) I. du Pont de Nemours (US bus.; 1771-1834)

Eielson Air Force Base, AK (mil.)

Eiffel Tower (Paris, Fr.)

Eiffel, (Alexandre) Gustave (Fr. eng.; 1832-1923)

Eight Immortals (myth.)

Eight, the (group of US artists, Ashcan school)

Eightfold Path (rel.)

Eikenberry, Jill (ent.; 1947-)

Eilat, Israel (also Elath)

Eileen Brennan (ent.; 1935-)

Eileen Farrell (ent.; 1920-)

Eileen Heckart (ent.; 1919-)

Eindhoven, the Netherlands (or Holland)

Eine kleine Nachtmusik (by Mozart)

Einstein, Albert (Ger./US physt.; 1879-1955)

Eire (Republic of Ireland)(NW Eur.)

Eisaku Sato (ex-PM, Jap.; 1901-75)

Eisele, Donn F. (astro.; 1930-87)

Eisenhower, Dwight D(avid)(34th US pres.; 1890-1969)

Eisenhower, Julie Nixon (daughter of ex-US pres.; 1948-)

Eisenhower, Mamie (Doud)(wife of ex-US pres.; 1896-1979)

Eisler, Lloyd (figure skating; 1964-)

Eisner, Michael (US bus.; 1942-)

E. J. Brach & Sons (US bus.)

E. J. Gitano (US bus.)

Ejup Ganic (VP, Bosnia-Hercegovina)

Ekaterinburg (formerly Sverdlovsk)

Ekberg, Anita (Swed./US ent.; 1931-)

Ekco™

EKCO Housewares, Inc.

EKG (electrocardiogram)

Ekland, Britt (Swed./US ent.; 1942-)

el-Abidine Ben Ali, Zine (pres., Tunisia; 1936-)

El Al Israel Airlines

El Bluff, Nicaragua

El Cajon, CA

El Camino Real

El Cid (also el Campeador, Rodrigo Diaz de Bivar)(Sp. mil.; 1040-99)

El Cid (film; 1961)

El Cordobés (Manuel Benitez Pérez)(Sp. matador; 1936?-)

El Djazair, Algeria

El Dorado (fabled city of gold)

El Dorado, AR, KS

El Gîza, Egypt (also Gîza or Al Jizah)

El Gîza, Great Pyramids of (also Gîza or Al Jizah)(Eg.)

El Greco (aka Domenikos Theotocopoulos)(Sp. artist; 1541-1614)

El Mansura, Egypt (also Mansura)

El Monte, CA

El Niño (warm ocean current)

El Paso Herald-Post (TX newspaper)

El Paso Times (TX newspaper)

El Paso, TX

el-Sadat, Anwar (also Anwar Sadat)(ex-pres., Eg.; 1918-81)

El Salvador (Republic of)(CAmer.)

Elaine Malbin (ent.; 1932-)

Elaine May (ent.; 1932-)

Elaine Stritch (ent.; 1926-)

Elaine Zayak (US figure skating; 1965-)

Elam, Jack (ent.; 1916-)

Elantra, Hyundai (auto.)

Elantra GLS, Hyundai (auto.)

Elath, Israel (also Eilat)

Elavil™ (med.)

E layer (also Kennelly-Heaviside layer)(in lower regions, ionosphere)

Elayne Boosler (ent.)

Elba Island (Mediterranean Sea)

Elbasan, Albania

Elbe River (Ger.)

Elbert H. Gary (US steel exec.; 1846-1927)

Elbridge Gerry (ex-US VP, gerrymander; 1744-1814)

Elburz Mountain (Eur.)

Elder, Lee (golf; 1934-)

Elderhostel™ (econ. accommodations for elderly)

Elder Beerman Stores

Elders, Dr. Joycelyn (US surgeon gen.; 1937-)

E(dgar) L(awrence) Doctorow (US writer; 1931-)

Eldon Industries, Inc.

Eldorado, Cadillac™ (auto.)

Eldorado, IL, OK

Eldridge Cleaver (US activist/writer; 1935-)

Eldridge, Roy (US jazz; 1911-89)

Elea, Zeno of (Gr. phil./math.; c490-430 BC)

Eleanor Holmes Norton (US pol.; 1937-)

Eleanor of Aquitaine (queen, Louis VII [Fr.] & Henry II [Eng.]; c1122-1204)

Eleanor of Castile (queen, Eng.; c1245-90)

Eleanor Parker (ent.; 1922-)

Eleanor Powell (ent.; 1912-82)

Eleanor Roosevelt, (Anna)(wife of US pres., UN dipl.; 1884-1962)

Eleaticism (Gr. phil.;6th & 5th c BC)

Election Day (US)

Electra (myth.)

Electra (type style)

Electra complex (psych.)

Electra-Park Avenue, Buick™ (auto.)

Electric Co., General

Electric Light Orchestra

Electrolux (US bus.)

Electrolux™ vacuum

Electronic Data Systems Corp.

Electronic Realty Associates, Inc.

Elektra/Asylum/Nonesuch Records (US bus.)

Eleonora Duse (ent.; 1858-1924)
Elephant Man, the (B. Pomerance play)
Elephant Man, the (b. John Merrick)(?-1890)
Eleusinian Mysteries (rel.)
Eleutherios Venizelos (Gr. pol.; 1864-1936)
Elgar, Sir Edward (William)(Br. comp.; 1857-1934)
Elgin™
Elgin Baylor (basketball; 1934-)
Elgin marbles (ancient Gr. sculptures)
Elgin, IL
Elgin Watch International (US bus.)
Eli Lilly & Company
Eli Wallach (ent.; 1915-)
Eli Whitney (US inv./bus.; 1765-1825)
Elia Kazan (ent.; 1909-)
Elias Howe (US inv., sewing machine; 1819-67)
Elias Hrawi (pres., Lebanon; 1926-)
Elias Ramaema, Col. (Lesotho, mil.)
Elias Sarkis (ex-pres., Lebanon)
Elías, Jorge Serrano (ex-pres., Guat.)
Elias, St. Mount (mountain, AK/Can.)
Elie(zer) Wiesel (US writer/reformer; 1928-)
Eliel Saarinen, (Gottlieb)(US arch.; 1873-1950)
Eliezer, Israel ben (also Baal Shem-Tov)(Jew. rel.; c1700-60)
Elihu Root (US atty./pol.; 1845-1937)
Elihu Yale (US bus./finan.; 1649-1721)
Elijah (prophet; 9th c. BC)
Elijah Muhammad (b. Elijah Poole)(US rel.; 1897-1975)
Elinor Donahue (ent.)
Elinor Wylie (US poet; 1885-1928)
Eliot Janeway (US econ.; 1913-93)
Eliot, George (aka Mary Ann [or Marian] Evans)(Br. writer; 1819-80)
Eliot, T(homas) S(terns)(US/Br. poet; 1888-1965)
Eliott Ness (US FBI agent; 1902-57)
Eliphalet Remington (US inv./bus.; 1793-1861)
Elisabeth Kübler-Ross (Swiss/US phys./writer; 1926-)
Elisabeth Schwarzkopf (Ger. opera; 1915-)
Elisha (Graves) Otis (US inv., elevator; 1811-61)
Eliza Doolittle (fict. chara., *Pygmalion*)
Elizabeth (empress, Rus.; 1709-62)
Elizabeth Ann (Bayley) Seton, St. (also Mother Seton)(US rel.; 1774-1821)
Elizabeth Arden™ (cosmetics)
Elizabeth Arden (US bus.; 1884-1966)
Elizabeth Arden Co.
Elizabeth Ashley (ent.; 1941-)
Elizabeth Barrett Browning (Br. poet, wife of Robert; 1806-61)
Elizabeth Bishop (US poet; 1911-79)
Elizabeth Blackwell (1st US woman phys.; 1821-1910)

Elizabeth Cady Stanton (US suffragist; 1815-1902)
Elizabeth Dole (US pol.; 1936-)
Elizabeth I (queen, Eng.; 1533-1603)
Elizabeth II (Elizabeth Alexandra Mary Windsor)(queen, Eng./UK; 1926-)
Elizabeth Janeway (US writer)
Elizabeth "Sister" Kenny (Austl. nurse; 1886-1952)
Elizabeth McGovern (ent.; 1961-)
Elizabeth Montgomery (ent.; 1933-)
Elizabeth Perkins (ent.; 1961-)
Elizabeth P. Peabody (US educ.; 1804-94)
Elizabeth (Rosemond) Taylor (ent.; 1932-)
Elizabeth Wilson (ent.; 1925-)
Elizabeth, NJ
Elizabethan architecture/style
Elizabethan literature (1558-1603)
Elizabethan sonnet
Elizabethton, TN
Elizabethtown, KY, NY, PA
Elizondo, Hector (ent.; 1936-)
Elk (member, BPOE)
Elkay™
Elkay Products Co., Inc.
Elke Sommer (ent.; 1940-)
Elkhart, IN
Elkin, Stanley (US writer; 1930-)
Elko, NV
Elks (mag.)
Elks, Benevolent and Protective Order of (BPOE)(US society, founded 1868)
Elkton, MD
Ella Fitzgerald (US jazz; 1918-)
Ella Raines (ent.)
Ella Tambussi Grasso (US pol.; 1919-81)
Ella Wheeler Wilcox (US poet; 1850-1919)
Elle (mag.)
Elle Decor (mag.)
Ellen Ashley™ (clothing)
Ellen Barkin (ent.; 1955-)
Ellen Burstyn (ent.; 1932-)
Ellen Corby (ent.; 1913-)
Ellen Drew (ent.; 1915-)
Ellen (Alicia) Terry, Dame (ent.; 1847-1928)
Ellen (Kean) Tree (ent.; 1806-80)
Ellen Winery, Glen (US bus.)
Ellen, Vera- (ent.; 1926-81)
Ellerbee, Linda
Ellery Queen (pseud. for US writers: Frederick Dannay, 1905-82; Manfred B. Lee, 1905-71)
Ellery Queen (TV show)
Ellery Queen's Mystery Magazine
Ellington, Duke (Edward Kennedy)(US comp./ US jazz; 1899-1974)
Elliot, Cass (ent.; 1941-74)
Elliot, Sam (ent.; 1944-)
Elliott Gould (ent.; 1938-)

Elliott, Bob (ent.; 1923-)
Elliott, Sumner Locke
Ellis Island (NY Harbor)
Ellis Rabb (ent.; 1930-)
Ellis, (Henry) Havelock (Br. psych.; 1859-1939)
Ellis™, Perry
Ellis, Perry (US designer)
Ellis Sportswear, Inc., Perry
Ellison, Harlan (US writer)
Ellison, Ralph (US writer; 1914-)
Ellroy, James
Ellsworth Air Force Base, SD (mil.)
Elly May Clampett (fict. chara.)
Elman, Mischa (ent.; 1891-67)
Elman, Ziggy
Elmendorf Air Force Base, AK (mil.)
Elmer (Leopold) Rice (US writer; 1892-1967)
Elmer Ambrose Sperry (US eng./inv.; 1860-
    1930)
Elmer Fudd (fict. chara.)
Elmer Gantry (S. Lewis novel)
Elmer's™ (glue)
Elmer's Adhesives (US bus.)
Elmira Minita Gordon, Dame (gov-gen., Belize)
Elmira, NY
Elmo Zumwalt, III (US adm.)
Elmore Leonard (US writer; 1925-)
Elmo's fire/light, St. (visible electrical
    discharge)
Eloah (God)
Elohim (God)
Elopement, East Lynne, or The (E.P. Wood
    novel)
Elsa Lanchester (ent.; 1902-82)
Elsa Schiaparelli (Fr. designer; 1890-1973)
Elsinore, Denmark (also Helsingor)
Elston Howard (baseball; 1929-80)
Elton (Hercules) John (b. Reginald Kenneth
    Dwight)(ent.; 1947-)
Elton, Charles (Br. ecol.; 1900-91)
Elul (Jew. month)
Elvin Hayes (basketball; 1945-)
Elvin Jones (US jazz; 1927-)
Elvira (aka Cassandra Peterson)(ent.; 1951-)
Elvis (Aron) Presley (ent.; 1935-77)
Elvis Costello (Declan McManus)(ent.; 1954-)
Elway, John (football; 1960-)
Elyria, OH
Elysée Palace (Fr. pres. residence)
Elysian Fields (also Elysium)(also Elysian
    fields)(myth. heaven)
Elzie C. Segar (cartoonist, *Popeye*; 1894-1938)
E-mail (also electronic mail)(also l.c.)(compu./
    comm.)
Emancipation Proclamation (freed Southern
    slaves; 1862)
Emanuel Leutze (US artist; 1816-68)
Emanuel Swedenborg (Swed. phil./mystic; 1688-

1772)
Embargo Act of 1807 (US hist., limit trade)
Embassy Suites, Inc.
Embden (goose)
EMCOF (European Monetary Cooperation
    Fund)(econ.)
Emerald Isle (Ir.)
Emeraude™ (perfume)
Emergency Broadcast System (radio)
Emerson™
Emerson Electric Co.
Emerson Fittipaldi (auto racing)
Emerson, Lake and Palmer (pop music)
Emerson, Ralph Waldo (US writer/phil.; 1803-
    82)
Emerson, Roy (tennis; 1936-)
Emery™
Emery Air Freight Corp.
E(dward) M(organ) Forster (Br. writer; 1879-
    1970)
Emil Brunner (Swed. rel.; 1889-1966)
Emil Erlenmeyer (Ger. chem.; 1825-1909)
Emil Hermann Fischer (Ger. chem.; 1852-1919)
Emil Nolde (b. Emil Hansen)(Ger. artist; 1867-
    1956)
Emil von Behring (Ger. bacteriol.; 1854-1917)
Emile Antoine Bourdelle (Fr. artist; 1861-1929)
Emile Durkheim (Fr. sociol.; 1858-1917)
Emile Herzog (pseud. André Maurois)(Fr.
    writer; 1885-1967)
Emile Jonassaint (pres., Haiti; 1914-)
Émile (Édouard Charles Antoine) Zola (Fr.
    writer; 1840-1902)
Emiliano Zapata (Mex. mil./agr.; c1879-1919)
Emilio Aguinaldo (Phil. revolutionary; 1869-
    1964)
Emilio Estevez (ent. 1962-)
Emilio Guglielmo Winery (US bus.)
Emilio Pucci (It. designer; 1914-92)
Emilio Pucci Perfumes International, Inc.
Emily Brontë (aka Ellis Bell)(Br. writer; 1818-
    48)
Emily Dickinson (US poet; 1830-86)
Emily Lloyd (ent.; 1970-)
Emily (Price) Post (US writer, social etiquette;
    1873?-1960)
Eminence, Your (title)
Emma Bovary, Madame (fict. chara.)
Emma Goldman (Rus./US reformer; 1869-1940)
Emma Hamilton, Lady (b. Amy Lyon)(Br. lady;
    1765?-1815)
Emma Lazarus (US poet; 1849-87)
Emma Peel
Emma Samms (ent.; 1960-)
Emma Thompson (ent.; 1959-)
Emma (Hart) Willard (US educ.; 1787-1870)
Emmanuel Ax (Rus. ent.; 1949-)
Emmanuel Lewis (ent.; 1971-)

Proper Noun Speller

Emmeline (Goulden) Pankhurst (Br. suffragist; 1858-1928)
Emmenthaler (cheese)
Emmett Kelly, (Leo)(US clown; 1898-1979)
Emmy Awards
Emmylou Harris (ent.; 1947-)
Empedocles (Gr. phil.; c490-430 BC)
Empire architecture/style (fl. 1804-15)
Empire State (nickname, NY)
Empire State Building (NYC, built 1931)
Empire State of the South (nickname, GA)
Empire Strikes Back, The (film; 1980)
Empirin™ (med.)
Empty Nest (TV show)
EMS (European Monetary System)(est. 1979)
EMU (European Monetary Union)(econ.)
En-Lai, Chou (also Zhou Enlai)(ex-PM, Ch.; 1898-1976)
Enberg, Dick
Encarnación, Paraguay
Enceladus (Saturn moon)(myth.)
Encyclopaedia Britannica
Encyclopedism (also Encyclopaedism)(also l.c.)(phil.)
Endara, Guillermo (pres., Panama; 1936-)
Endeavor (US space shuttle)
Ender, Kornelia (swimming; 1958-)
Enderby Land (region, Antarctica)
Enders, John F. (US virol.; 1897-1985)
Endless Vacation (mag.)
Endowment for Democracy, National (US pol. agcy.)
Endowment on (or for) the Arts and Humanities, National (US govt. agcy.; est. 1965)
Endust™
Endymion (myth.)
Energy, Department of (US govt.)
Enesco (or Enescu), Georges (Romanian cond./ comp.; 1881-1955)
Enfield rifle (also Lee-Enfield rifle)
Engelbert Dollfuss (ex-chanc. Aus.; 1892-1934)
Engelbert Humperdinck (ent.; 1936-)
Engelbert Humperdinck (Ger. comp.; 1854-1921)
Engels, Friedrich (Ger. pol. writer; 1820-95)
Energizer™ (battery, bunny)
Engineers, Army Corps of (US mil.)
England (largest part of Great Britain and the UK)
England Air Force Base, LA (mil.)
England, Church of (also Anglican Church)
Engler, John (MI gov.; 1948-)
English (lang./people)
English (type style)
English bulldog (dog)
English Channel (Eng./Fr.)
English Civil War (1642-47)

English cocker spaniel (dog)
English foxhound (dog)
English Game, Old (chicken)
English horn (instrument)
English ivy (plant)
English law (legal system)
English Leather™ (toiletries)
English muffin
English Revolution (also Bloodless [or Glorious] Revolution)(Br. hist.; 1688-89)
English Revolution (Eng. hist.; 1640-60)
English rye grass
English saddle
English setter (dog)
English sheepdog, Old
English shepherd (dog)
English sonnet (Shakespearean sonnet)
English sparrow (house sparrow)
English springer spaniel (dog)
English toy spaniel (dog)
English walnut (tree)
English, Diana
English, Early Modern (lang.; c1550-1700)
English, Late Modern (lang.; c1700-present)
English, Middle (lang.; c1050-1550)
English, Old (also Anglo-Saxon)(lang.; c500-1050)
English, Old (type style)
Englishman
Englishwoman
Englund, Robert (ent.; 1948-)
Enid, OK
Enigma (WWII decoder)
Eniwetok atoll (nuclear bonb tests, W Pac.)
Enkidu (myth.)
Enlai, Zhou (also Chou En-Lai)(ex-PM, Ch.; 1898-1976)
Enlightenment, Age of (18th c. Eur. movement)
Enlil (myth.)
Ennio Morricone (It. comp.; 1928-)
Enniskillen, Northern Ireland
Ennius (Latin poet; 239-170 BC)
Enoch (rel.)
Enoch Arden (missing person presumed dead, but is alive)
Enoch Arden (Tennyson poem)
Enoch Arden doctrine (divorce)
Enoch Derant Lakoue (PM, Central African Republic)
Enovid™ (med.)
Enquirer, Cincinnati (OH newspaper)
Enrico Caruso (It. tenor; 1873-1921)
Enrico Cecchetti (ballet; 1850-1928)
Enrico Fermi (It. physt.; 1901-54)
Enriquez, Rene (ent.; 1932-90)
Ensenada, Mexico
Ensor, James, Baron (Belgian artist; 1860-1949)

Entebbe, Uganda
Entente Cordiale (Br./Fr.; 1904)
Enterprise™
Enterprise™ Rent-A-Car (US bus.)
Enterprise, Beaumont (TX newspaper)
Entertainment Tonight (TV show)
Entertainment Weekly (mag.)
Entrepreneur (mag.)
Entrepreneurial Women (mag.)
Enugu, Nigeria
Environmental Protection Agency (EPA)(US govt.)
Environmental Quality, Council on (US govt.)
Enzo Ferrari (It. bus./auto.; 1898-1988)
Eocene epoch (54-38 million years ago)
Eolithic Age (also l.c.)
Eos (myth.)
EPA (Environmental Protection Agency)(US govt.)
Epaminondas (Gr. mil./pol.; 418?-362 BC)
E(dward) P(ayson) Dutton (US publ.; 1831-1923)
Ephesians, Epistle to the (rel.)
Ephesus, Temple of Artemis at (also Artemision)
Epic of Gilgames (myth.)
Epicharmus (Gr. drama.; c530-440 BC)
Epictetus (Gr. phil.; c55-c135 BC)
Epicureanism (phil.)
Epicurus (Gr. phil.; 341-270 BC)
Epiphany (rel.)
Epirus (region, Gr.)
Episcopal Church
Episcopalian (rel.)
Epistle of James (rel.)
Epistle to the Colossians (rel.)
Epistle to the Ephesians (rel.)
Epistles to the Corinthians (rel.)
EPI Products (US bus.)
Epoisses (cheese)
Eppie Lederer (aka Ann Landers)(b. Esther Pauline Friedman)(US advice columnist; 1918-)
Epsom Downs (Br. racetrack)
Epsom salts (med.)
Epsom, England
Epson™ (compu.)
Epson America, Inc.
Epstein-Barr virus (EBV)(med.)
Epstein, Brian (ent.; 1935-67)
Epstein, Jacob (Br. sculptor; 1880-1959)
Epstein's disease/nephrosis/pearls/syndrome (med.)
Equal™ (sweetener)
Equal Employment Opportunity Commission
Equal Rights Amendment
Equality State (nickname, WY)
Equanil™ (med.)

Equatorial Countercurrent
Equatorial Current
Equatorial Guinea (Republic of)(formerly Spanish Guinea)(W Afr.)
Equitable Life Assurance Society of the United States
Equuleus (astron., little horse)
Equus (P. Shaffer play)
Er (chem. sym., erbium)
ERA (Equal Rights Amendment)
ERA™ (detergent)
Erasistratus (Gr. phys.; 3rd c. BC)
Erasmus, Desiderius (Dutch scholar; c1466-1536)
Erastianism (rel.)
Erastus Corning (US finan.; 1794-1872)
Eratosthenes (Gr. geographer/math.; c276-194 BC)
Erb's palsy (med.)
Erebus (myth., darkness)
Erebus, Mount (volcano, Antarctica)
Erechtheum (Gr. temple, Acropolis)
Erector Set™ (building toy)
E region (lower ionosphere region)
Erewhon (S. Butler novel)
Erhard, Ludwig (ex-chanc., WGer.; 1897-1977)
Eric A(rthur) Blair (pseud. George Orwell)(Br. writer; 1903-50)
Eric Ambler (Br. writer; 1909-)
Eric Berne, Dr. (US psych./writer; 1910-70)
Eric Bogasian (ent.; 1953-)
Eric Carmen (ent.; 1949-)
Eric Clapton (ent.; 1945-)
Eric Dickerson (football; 1960-)
Eric Dolphy (US jazz; 1928-64)
Eric Heiden (speed skating; 1958-)
Eric (Honeywood) Partridge (Br. lexicographer; 1894-1979)
Eric Roberts (ent.; 1956-)
Eric Sevareid (US TV jour.; 1913-92)
Eric Stoltz (ent.; 1961-)
Eric the Red (Norse expl., Greenland; 940-1010)
Erica (Mann) Jong (US writer; 1942-)
Erich Fromm (Ger. psych.; 1900-80)
Erich Leinsdorf (ent.; 1912-)
Erich Maria Remarque (Ger./US writer; 1898-1970)
Erich Segal (US writer; 1937-)
Erich Von Stroheim (ent.; 1885-1957)
Ericsson, Leif (Norse expl.; c.1000)
Eridanus (astron., river)
Erie (NAmer. Indians)
Erie Canal (NY)
Erie News (PA newspaper)
Erie Times (PA newspaper)
Erie, Lake (NY/OH/PA/Can.)
Erie, PA
Erik Estrada (ent.; 1949-)

Proper Noun Speller

Erik Menendez (US news)
Erik (Alfred Leslie) Satie (Fr. comp.; 1866-1925)
Erika Slezak (ent.; 1946-)
Erin (also Ireland)
Erin Gray
Eris (myth.)
Eritrea (province, Ethiopia)
Erle Stanley Gardner (US writer; 1889-1970)
Erlenmeyer flask (chem.)
Erlenmeyer, Emil (Ger. chem.; 1825-1909)
Erma Bombeck (US writer/humorist; 1927-)
Ermanno Wolf-Ferrari (It. comp.; 1876-1948)
Ernest Ball (US comp.; 1878-1927)
Ernest Bevin (Br. pol.; 1881-1951)
Ernest Bloch (Swiss/US comp.; 1880-1959)
Ernest Borgnine (ent.; 1917-)
Ernest Chausson (Fr. comp.; 1855-99)
Ernest F. Hollings (US cong.; 1922-)
Ernest Gallo (US winemaker)
Ernest (Heinrich) Haeckel (Ger. zool.; 1834-1919)
Ernest (Miller) Hemingway (US writer; 1899-1961)
Ernest J(oseph) King (US mil.; 1878-1956)
Ernest O(rlando) Lawrence (US physt.; 1901-58)
Ernest "Ernie" Pyle (US jour.; 1900-45)
Ernest Rutherford, Baron (Br. physt.; 1871-1937)
Ernest (Henry) Shackleton, Sir (Br. expl.; 1874-1922)
Ernest Solvay (Belgian chem.; 1838-1922)
Ernest Truex (ent.; 1890-1973)
Ernest Tubb (ent.)
Ernest, Frank and (comic strip)
Ernestine Schumann-Heink (ent.; 1861-1936)
Ernesto "Che" Guevara (SAmer. mil.; 1928-67)
Ernie Banks (baseball; 1931-)
Ernie Bushmiller (cartoonist, *Nancy*; 1905-82)
Ernie Ford, Tennessee (ent.; 1919-91)
Ernie Kovacs (ent.; 1919-62)
Ernie Nevers (football; 1903-76)
Ernie (Ernest) Pyle (US jour.; 1900-45)
Erno Rubik (Hung. arch. 1944-)
Ernst & Young, Inc.
Ernst (Heinrich) Barlach (Ger. sculptor/writer; 1870-1938)
Ernst Kaltenbrunner (Aus. Nazi; 1901-46)
Ernst Lubitsch (Ger. ent.; 1892-1947)
Ernst Mach (Aus. physt./psych./phil.; 1838-1916)
Ernst Röhm (Ger. Nazi; 1887-1934)
Ernst (or Ernö) von Dohnányi (Hung. pianist/comp.; 1877-1960)
Ernst, Max (Ger. artist; 1891-1976)
Eros (astron.)
Eros (myth., god of love)
Errol Flynn (ent.; 1909-59)

Erroll Garner (US jazz; 1921-77)
Ershad, Hussain Mohammad (ex-pres., Bangladesh; 1930-)
Erskine Caldwell (US writer; 1903-87)
Erskine Lloyd Sandiford (PM, Barbados; 1937-)
Erskine of Carnock (aka John Erskine)(Scot. writer, law; 1695-1768)
Erté (Romain de Tirtoff)(Rus. designer; 1893-1990)
Ervin, Sam, Jr. (US pol.; 1896-1985)
Erving, Julius "Dr J" (basketball; 1950-)
Erwin Rommel (aka "Desert Fox")(Ger. gen. in NAfr.; 1891-1944)
Erwin Schrödinger (Ger. physt.; 1887-1961)
Es (chem. sym., einsteinium)
ESA (Eur. Space Agency)(est. 1975)
Esa-Pekka Salonen
Esbjerg, Denmark
Escher, M(aurits) C(ornelis)(Dutch artist; 1902-72)
Escoffier, (Georges) Auguste (Fr. chef/writer; 1847-1935)
Escondido, CA
Escort, Ford (auto.)
Esdraelon Plain (also Plain of Jezreel)(Isr.)
Esfahan, Iran
Eskimo (people)
Eskimo dog (dog)
Eskimo Pie™
Eskimo Pie Corp.
Eskimo-Aleut (NAmer. Indians)
Eskisehir, Turkey
Esko Aho (PM, Fin.; 1954-)
ESP (extrasensory perception)
Esperanto (artificial internat'l lang.)
Espinosa, Nino (baseball; 1953-88)
ESPN (cable TV)
Esposito, Phil(ip Anthony)(hockey; 1942-)
Esprit™ (clothing)
Espy, Mike (US Secy./Agriculture; 1953-)
Esquimalt, British Columbia, Canada
Esquire (mag.)
Esquivel, Manuel (PM, Belize; 1940-)
Essen, Germany
Essence (mag.)
Essene (rel.)
Essex (county, Eng.)
Essex, CT, MD, VT
Essex, Earl of (Robert Devereux)(Br. mil./pol.; 1566-1601)
Essex, Ontario, Canada
Estée Lauder™ (cosmetics)
Estée Lauder, Inc.
Estefan, Gloria (ent.; 1958-)
Estelle Getty (ent.; 1924-)
Estelle Parsons (ent.; 1927-)
Estenssoro, Victor Paz (ex-pres., Bolivia; 1907-)
Estes Kefauver, (Carey)(US pol.; 1903-63)

Estes, Billy Sol (US bus./scandal)
Estevez, Emilio (ent.; 1962-)
Esther Ralston (ent.; 1902-)
Esther Rolle (ent.; 1933-)
Esther Williams (ent./swimming; 1923-)
Estonia (Republic of)(formerly part of the
    USSR)(N Eur.)
Estonian (lang./people)
Estrada, Erik (ent.; 1949-)
Estrada, Joseph (VP, Phil.)
Estrada Winery, Joe P. (US bus.)
Estwing hammer
ETA (estimated time of arrival)
Etah, Greenland
Etah, India
ETD (estimated time of departure)
Eteocles (myth., Seven against Thebes)
Ethan Allen (US Revolutionary War hero; 1738-
    89)
Ethan Allen, Inc.
Ethan Frome (E. Wharton novel)
Ethel Barrymore (ent.; 1879-1959)
Ethel Kennedy (wife of ex-US senator)
Ethel Merman (ent.; 1908-84)
Ethel (Greenglass) Rosenberg (US, executed for
    treason; 1915-53)
Ethel Smyth, Dame (Br. comp.; 1858-1944)
Ethel Waters (ent.; 1900-77)
Ethelred II ("the Unready")(king, Eng.; c968-
    1016)
Ethiopia (People's Democratic Republic
    of)(formerly Abyssinia)(E Afr.)
Ethiopian (lang./people)
Ethyl Corp.
Etienne Tshisekedi (premier, Zaire)
Etna, Mount (volcano, Sicily)
Etobicoke, Ontario, Canada
Eton collar (clothing)
Eton College (Br. public school)
Eton jacket
Eton, England
Etrafon™ (med.)
Etruria (now Tuscany and W. Umbria)
Etruscan (ancient civilization; fl. 7th-5th c BC)
E.T.: The Extra-Terrestrial (film; 1982)
Etting, Ruth (ent.)
Ettore Bugatti (It. designer; 1881-1947)
Ettore Maserati (It. bus./auto.; 1894-1990)
Eu (chem. sym., europium)
Eubanks, Bob
Eubie Blake, (James Hubert)(US jazz pianist/
    comp.; 1883-1983)
Euboea (Gr. island)
Eucharist (also Holy Communion, Lord's
    Supper)(rel.)
Euclid (Gr. math.; c330-c260 BC)
Euclidean geometry (math.)
Eudora Welty (US writer; 1909-)

Euell Gibbons
Eugene A(ndrew) Cernan (astro.; 1934-)
Eugene Delacroix (Fr. artist; 1789-1863)
Eugene Fodor (US travel guide writer; 1906-91)
Eugène Ionesco (Fr. writer; 1912-)
Eugene J. Keogh (US pol.; 1907-)
Eugene Loring (dancer/choreographer)
Eugene (Joseph) McCarthy (US pol.; 1916-)
Eugene (Gladstone) O'Neill (US writer; 1888-
    1953)
Eugene Ormandy (US cond.; 1899-1985)
Eugene Register-Guard (OR newspaper)
Eugene Roche (ent.; 1928-)
Eugène Scribe, (Augustin)(Fr. writer; 1791-
    1861)
Eugene V. Debs (US labor leader; 1855-1926)
Eugene, OR
Eugenia Charles, (Mary)(PM, Dominica; 1919-)
Eugénie, Empress (Comtesse de Teba, wife of
    Napoleon III; 1826-1920)
Eugénie, Marie Ignace Augustine de Montijo
    (empress, Fr.; 1826-1920)
Eugenie, Princess (daughter of Prince Andrew
    and Sarah; 1990-)
Eugenio Montale (It. poet; 1896-1981)
Eulenspiegel, Till (Ger. legend/practical jokes;
    14th c.,)
Euler, Leonhard (Swiss math./physt.; 1707-83)
Euler's diagram (logic)
Euler's formula/phi-function (math.)
Eumenides (myth.)
Eunice Kennedy Shriver (US, wife of pol.;
    1921-)
Euphrates River (Turk.)
Eurailpass
Eurasia
Eurasian (people)
Eurasian Plate
Eurotom (European Atomic Energy
    Commission)(est. 1957)
Eureka™ (vacuum cleaner)
Eureka, CA, KS, UT
Eureka Co., The
Euripides (Gr. drama.; c484-406 BC)
Eurobond (econ.)
Euroclydon wind
Eurocurrency (also Euromoney)
Eurodollar (econ.)
Europa (Jupiter moon, myth.)
Europe
Europe, Council of
European (people)
European Atomic Energy Commission
    (Eurotom)(est. 1957)
European Community (EC)(pol./econ. alliance)
European Court of Justice (court of EC)
European Economic Community (EEC)(also
    Common Market, est. 1957)

European Free Trade Association (EFTA)(est. 1960)
European Monetary Cooperation Fund (EMCOF)(econ.)
European Monetary System (EMS)(est. 1979)
European Monetary Union (EMU)(econ.)
European Parliament (EC parliament)
European Recovery Program (also Marshall Plan)(after WWII)
European Space Agency (ESA)(est. 1975)
European Telecommunications Satellite Organization (Eutelsat)
Eurotom (European Atomic Energy Commission)(est. 1957)
EuroVan™, Volkswagen (auto.)
Eurydice (myth.)
Eurythmics, the (pop music)
Eustis, Fort, VA (mil.)
Eutelsat (European Telecommunications Satellite Organization)
Euterpe (myth., muse of music)
Eva Braun (mistress of Adolph Hitler; 1910-45)
Eva Evdokimova
Eva Gabor (ent.; 1921-)
Eva Le Gallienne (ent.; 1899-91)
Eva Marie Saint (ent.; 1924-)
Eva "Evita" Perón (b. Maria Eva Duarte)(Argentinian pol.; 1919-52)
Eva Tanguay (ent.; 1878-1947)
Evan Bayh (IN gov.; 1955-)
Evan Mecham (ex-gov, AZ)
Evan Picone™
Evan-Picone, Inc.
Evan S. Connell (US writer; 1924-)
Evander Holyfield (boxing; 1962-)
Evangel (rel.)
Evangelical (rel.)
Evangelical Alliance (Christian assoc.; est. 1846)
Evangelical Lutheran Church
Evangeline Cory Booth (US, Salvation Army; 1865?-1950)
Evangelist (rel.)
Evans, Bill (US jazz; 1929-80)
Evans, Dale (ent.; 1912-)
Evans, Edith, Dame (ent.; 1888-1976)
Evans, Gil (US jazz; 1912-88)
Evans, Greg (cartoonist)
Evans, Janet (swimming; 1971-)
Evans, Lee (runner; 1947-)
Evans, Linda (ent.; 1942-)
Evans, Mary Ann (or Marian)(pseud. George Eliot)(Br. writer; 1819-80)
Evans, Maurice (ent.; 1901-89)
Evans, Robert (ent.; 1930-)
Evans, Ronald E. (astro.)
Evanston, IL, WY
Evansville Courier (IN newspaper)

Evansville Press (IN newspaper)
Evansville, IN
Evdokimova, Eva
Eve (rel., 1st woman)
Eve Arden (ent.; 1908-90)
Eve, Adam and (rel.)
Eve, All About (film; 1950)
Eve, The Three Faces of (film; 1957)
Evel (Robert Craig) Knievel (US daredevil; 1938-)
Evelyn (Arthur St. John) Waugh (Br. writer; 1903-66)
Evelyn Ashford (track & field; 1957-)
Evelyn Keyes (ent.)
Evelyn Wood Reading Dynamics (US bus.)
Evelyn Wood™ speed-reading method
Evelyn™, Crabtree & (toiletries)
Evelyn, Ltd., Crabtree &
Evenflo™ (baby bottle)
Evening at the Improv (TV show)
Evening Shade (TV show)
Evening Sun, Baltimore (MD newspaper)
Evensong (also l.c.)(evening prayer)
Eveready™ (battery)
Everest, Mount (highest mountain, Himalayas)
Everett Koop, C. (ex-US surgeon gen.; 1916-)
Everett M. Dirksen (US pol./orator; 1896-1969)
Everett, Chad (ent.; 1936-)
Everett, MA, WA
Everglades (S FL)
Everglades National Park (FL)
Evergreen State (nickname, WA)
Everly Brothers, the (pop music)
Everly, Don (ent.; 1937-)
Everly, Phil (ent.; 1938-)
Evers, (James) Charles (US civil rights leader; 1922-)
Evers, Medgar (Wiley)(US civil rights leader; 1925-63)
Evert-Lloyd, Chris (tennis; 1954-)
Everyman (Eng. play; 15th c.)
Evian™
Evian Waters of France (US bus.)
Evigan, Greg (ent.; 1953-)
Evinrude™ (boat/engine)
Evita (play)
Evita Perón (b. Maria Eva Duarte)(Argentinian pol.; 1919-52)
Evonne Goolagong (Cawley)(tennis; 1951-)
Evyan Perfumes, Inc.
Ewbank, Weeb (football; 1907-)
Ewe (lang./people)
Ewell, Tom (ent.; 1909-)
Ewing, J. R. (fict. chara., *Dallas*)
Ewing, Patrick (basketball; 1962-)
Ewok (fict. chara., *Star Wars*)
Ewry, Ray (Olympics; 1873-1937)
E. W. Scripps Co.

Ex parte McCardle (US law; 1869)
Ex parte Merryman (US law; 1861)
Ex parte Milligan (US law; 1866)
Examiner, San Francisco (CA newspaper)
Excalibur (Arthurian magic sword)
Excalibur (film; 1981)
Excedrin™ (med.)
Excedrin PM™ (med.)
Excel GL, Hyundai (auto.)
Excel GS, Hyundai (auto.)
Excel, Hyundai (auto.)
Excel, Microsoft™ (compu.)
Excellency, Your (title)
Excelsior State (nickname, NY)
Exchange Rate Mechanism (ERM)(European
    Community)
Exchequer, Chancellor of the (Br. finance
    minister)
Executive Female (mag.)
Exercycle™
Exercycle Corp.
Exeter, CA, NH, PA
Exeter, England
Ex-Lax™ (med.)
Exodus (L. Uris novel)
Exodus (rel., Israelites deliverance from Eg.)
Exon, J. James (US cong.; 1921-)
Exorcist, The (W.P. Blatty novel)
Exorcist II: The Heretic (film; 1977)
Explorer (mag.)
Explorer (US space satellite)
Explorer, Ford (auto.)
Expos, Montreal (baseball team)
Express Mail™ (USPS service)
Express News, San Antonio (TX newspaper)
Expressionism (art/lit.)
Exupery, Antoine (Marie Roger) de, Saint- (Fr.
    writer/aviator; 1900-44)
Exxon™
Exxon Corp.
Exxon Valdez (US tanker, oil spill; 1989)
Eyadéma, Gnassingbe (pres., Togo; 1937-)
Eyck, Hubert (or Huybrecht) van (Flem. artist;
    1366-1426)
Eyck, Jan van (Flem. artist; 1380-1441)
Eydie Gorme (ent.; 1932-)
Eye to Eye With Connie Chung (TV show)
E. Y. "Yip" Harburg (US lyricist; 1898-1981)
Eyre, Jane (C. Brontë novel)
Eyre, Lake (Austl.)
Eysenck, Hans Jurgen (Br. psych.; 1916-)
Ezekiel (also Ezechiel)(rel.)
Ezer Weizman (pres., Isr.; 1924-)
Ezio Pinza (ent.; 1892-1957)
Ezra Cornell (U.S., bus.; 1807-74)
Ezra Loomis Pound (US poet; 1885-1972)
Ezra Taft Benson (US pol.)

F

F (chem. sym., fluorine)
FAA (Federal Aviation Administration)(DOT
    agcy.)
Fabares, Shelley (ent.; 1942-)
Fabergé Brut™
Faberge Co. (Fabergé)
Fabergé egg
Fabergé, Peter Carl (Rus. jeweler; 1846-1920)
Fabian (Forte)(ent.; 1943-)
Fabian Society (Br. socialist org.)
Fabianism (pol.)
Fabio (model)
Fabius Maximus Verrucosus, Quintus
    ("Cunctator")(Roman pol./mil.; 275-03 BC)
Fabius, Laurent (ex-PM, Fr.; 1946-)
Fabray, Nanette (ent.; 1920-)
Face the Nation (TV show)
Factor & Co., Max
Factor™, Max (cosmetics)
Factor, Max (US bus.; 1877-?)
Facts of Life (TV show)
Fadiman, Clifton (US writer/editor; 1904-)
Faeroe Islands (also Faroe)(N Atl.)
Fafnir (myth.)
Fagatogo, American Samoa
Fagin (fict. chara., *Oliver Twist*, crim., fence)
Fahd (ibn Abdul Aziz al-Saud)(king, Saudi
    Arabia; 1922-)
Fahrenheit 451 (R. Bradbury novel)
Fahrenheit scale (temperature)
Fahrenheit, Gabriel D(aniel)(Ger. physt.; 1686-
    1736)
Fain, Sammy (US comp.; 1902-89)
Fair Deal (Pres. Truman policy)
Fair Labor Standards Act (also Wages and
    Hours Act; 1938)
Fair, Philip the (Philip IV)(king, Fr.; 1268-1314)
Fairbanks, AK
Fairbanks, Charles W. (ex-US VP; 1852-1918)
Fairbanks, Douglas, Jr. (ent.; 1909-)
Fairbanks, Douglas, Sr. (ent.; 1883-1939)
Fairchild Air Force Base, WA (mil.)
Fairchild Corp.
Fairchild, Morgan (ent.; 1950-)
Faircloth, Lauch (US cong.; 1928-)
Fairfax, VA
Fairweather, Mount (AK)
Faisal I (also Feisal I)(ex-king, Iraq; 1885-1933)
Faisal ibn Abdul Aziz (ex-king/PM, Saudi
    Arabia; 1905-75)
Faisal II (also Feisal I)(ex-king, Iraq; 1935-58)
Faisalabad, Pakistan
Falana, Lolo (ent.; 1946-)
Falasha (people)

Falcons, Atlanta (football team)
Faldo, Nick (golf; 1957-)
Falk, Lee (cartoonist)
Falk, Peter (ent.; 1927-)
Falkenburg, Jinx
Falkland Islands (Br., S Atl.)
Falklands War (Argentina/Br.; 1982)
Fall of the House of Usher, The (E.A. Poe short
    story)
Fall River, MA
Falla, Manuel de (Sp. comp.; 1876-1946)
Falling Water (also Kaufman house)(F.L.
    Wright house)
Fallon, NV
Fallon Naval Air Station (NV)
Fallopian tube(s)(med.)
Falstaff, Sir John (fict. chara., Shakespeare)
Faludi, Susan (US writer)
Falwell, Jerry, Rev. (US rel.; 1933-)
Famagusta, Cyprus (Turk.)
Fame Bowl, Hall of (college football)
Fame, Hall of (NY)(erected 1990)
Familiar Quotations, Bartlett's (book)
Family Affair (TV show)
Family Channel, The (FAM)(cable TV)
Family Circle (mag.)
Family Circus, The (comic strip)
Family Feud (TV show)
Family Handyman, The (mag.)
Family Matters (TV show)
Family Stone, Sly and the (pop music)
Family Ties (TV show)
FamilyFun (mag.)
Famous Amos Chocolate Chip Cookie, The (US
    bus.)
Fang (lang./people)
Fangio, Juan (auto racing; 1911-)
Fannie (Frances) Farmer (ent.; 1914-70)
Fannie (Merritt) Farmer (US chef/educ./writer;
    1857-1915)
Fannie Mae (also Federal National Mortgage
    Association, FNMA)
Fanny Brice (b. Fannie Borach)(ent.; 1891-
    1951)
Fanny (Francis Anne) Kemble (Br. writer/ent.;
    1809-93)
Fantasia (film; 1940)
Fantastic Four, The (cartoon charas.)
Fantastic Sam's Family Haircutters (US bus.)
Fantastik™ (cleaner)
Fantasy Island (TV show)
Fantin-Latour, (Ignace) Henri (Joseph
    Théodore)(Fr. artist; 1836-1904)
FAO (Food and Agriculture Organization)(UN
    agcy.)
F.A.O. Schwarz Imports, Ltd.
Far East (all of Asia E of the Indian subconti-
    nent)

Far Niente Winery (US bus.)
Far Side, The (cartoon)
Farad Aidid, Muhammad (Somali gen.)
Faraday cage (shield)
Faraday, Michael (Br. chem./physt; 1791-1867)
Faraday's constant (elec.)
Faraday's laws (elec.)
Farah Diba
Farah, Inc.
Farberware, Inc.
Farentino, James (ent.; 1938-)
Farge, John La (US artist; 1835-1910)
Fargo & Co., Wells
Fargo, Donna (ent.; 1945-)
Fargo, ND
Fargo, William George (US bus.; 1818-81)
Farley Granger (ent.; 1925-)
Farm Journal
Farmer, Fannie (Frances)(ent.; 1914-70)
Farmer, Fannie (Merritt)(US chef/educ./writer; 1857-1915)
Farmer's Almanac, The
Farmer's Loan and Trust Co., Pollock v. (US law; 1895)
Farmington, CT, ME, MI, MO, NH, NM
Farnese Palace (Rome)
Farnese, Alessandro (Pope Paul III)(It.; 1468-1549)
Farnsworth, Philo T. (US physt./TV pioneer; 1906-71)
Faro, Portugal
Faroe Islands (also Faeroe)(N Atl.)
Faroese (lang.)
Farooq Leghari (pres., Pak.)
Farouk I (king, Eg.; 1920-65)
Farr, Jamie (ent.; 1934-)
Farragut, David (US adm.; 1801-70)
Farrah Aidid, Mohammed (Somali gen.)
Farrah Fawcett (ent.; 1947-)
Farrakhan, Louis (Islam/US rel.)
Farrar, Geraldine (ent.; 1882-1967)
Farrar, Straus & Girous, Inc.
Farrell, Charles (ent.; 1902-90)
Farrell, Eileen (ent.; 1920-)
Farrell, James T(homas)(US writer; 1904-79)
Farrell, Mike (ent.; 1939-)
Farrow, Mia (ent.; 1945-)
Fars (province, Iran)
Farsi (lang.)
Fassbinder, Rainer Werner (Ger. ent.; 1946-82)
Fasteeth™ (med.)
FasText™ (text entry system)
Fast Times at Ridgemont High (film; 1982)
Fat Boy's Bar-B-Q (US bus.)
Fat Albert (cartoon chara.)
Fat City
Fata Morgana (Arthurian)
Fatah, Al (also al-Fatah)(PLO guerrilla group)

Fatal Attraction (film)
Fate (mag.)
Fates, three (Clotho, Lachesis, Atropos)(myth.)
Father (God)
Father Divine (also Major M. J. Divine)(b. George Baker)(US rel.; 1882-1965)
Father Dowling Mysteries (TV show)
Father Time
Father, Life With (play/film)
Father's Day (3rd Sunday in June)
Fatiha (rel.)
Fátima (fict. chara., *Arabian Nights*)
Fátima (wife of Ali, daughter of Mohammed; 606?-632)
Fátima, Miracle of
Fátima, Portugal
Fatman, Jake & the (TV show)
Fats (Antoine) Domino (ent.; 1928-)
Fats (Theodore) Navarro (US jazz; 1923-50)
Fats (Thomas Wright) Waller (US comp./jazz; 1904-43)
Fatty (Roscoe) Arbuckle (ent.; 1887-1933)
Faulkner, William (US writer; 1897-1962)
Fauntleroy suit, Little Lord
Fauntleroy, Little Lord (book by F. H. Burnett)
Faunus (myth.)
Fauré, Gabriel (Fr. comp.; 1845-1924)
Faust (by Goethe)
Faust (legendary magician, sold his soul to the Devil)
Faust (or Faustus), Johann (Ger. fortuneteller/magician; 1480?-1540?)
Faustin Twagiramungu (PM, Rwanda)
Faustino, David (ent.; 1974-)
Faustus, Doctor (also *The Tragical of Doctor Faustus*)(by C. Marlowe)
Fauves, Les (also l.c.)(Fauvist artists)
Fauvism (also l.c.)(style of painting)
Fauvist (also l.c.)(grp. of Fr. artists)
Fawcett Books (US bus.)
Fawcett, Farrah (ent.; 1947-)
Fawkes Day, Guy (Br.)
Fawkes, Guy (Br. conspirator; 1570-1606)
Fawlty Towers (TV show)
Fawn Hall (US news)
Fay Bainter (ent.; 1892-1968)
Fay Separates, Leslie (US bus.)
Fay Wray (ent.; 1907-)
Fay, Inc., Leslie
Fay, Morgan le (also Morgain le Fay)(King Arthur's fairy sister)
Fayard Nicholas (ent.; 1914-)
Faye Dunaway (ent.; 1941-)
Faye Wattleton (US reformer; 1943-)
Faye, Alice (ent.; 1912-)
Fayette, Marie Madeleine Pioche de la Vergne La (Comtesse de La Fayette)(Fr. writer; 1634-93)

Fayetteville Observer-Times (NC newspaper)
Fayetteville, AR, NC, TN
Fayumi, Saadia ben Joseph al-
Fazal Elahi Chaudry (ex-pres., Pak.; 1904-88)
Fazio, Vic (US cong.; 1942-)
FBI (Federal Bureau of Investigation)(DOJ agcy.)
FCC (Federal Communications Commission) (US govt. agcy.)
FDA (Food and Drug Administration)(US govt. agcy.)
FDIC (Federal Deposit Insurance Corporation) (banking)
February Revolution (Fr.; 1848)
February Revolution (Russian Revolution; 1917)
Fedders Corp.
Federal Aviation Administration (FAA)(DOT agcy.)
Federal Bureau of Investigation (FBI)(DOJ agcy.)
Federal Communications Commission (FCC)(US govt. agcy.)
Federal Constitutional Convention
Federal Deposit Insurance Corporation (FDIC)(banking)
Federal Express™
Federal Express Corp.
Federal Home Loan Mortgage Corporation (FHLMC, Freddie Mac)
Federal Insurance Contributions Act (FICA)
Federal Land Bank(s)(US govt.)
Federal National Mortgage Association (FNMA, Fannie Mae)
Federal Reserve Bank
Federal Reserve note
Federal Reserve System (also the "Fed")(US banking)
Federal Trade Commission (FTC)(US govt. agcy.)
Federalist (US pol. party; late 1700s)
Federated Department Stores, Inc.
Federated Malay States
Federico Fellini (It. ent. ; 1920-93)
Federico Pena (US Secy./Trans.; 1947-)
Fehling, Hermann (Ger. chem.; 1812-85)
Fehling's test/solution (sugar)
Feiffer, Jules (cartoonist; 1929-)
Fein, Sinn (Ir. pol. party)
Feingold, Russell (US cong.; 1953-)
Feininger, Andreas (Bernhard Lyonel)(US photo.; 1906-)
Feininger, Lyonel (Charles Adrian)(US artist; 1871-1956)
Feinstein, Dianne (US cong.; 1933-)
Feisal I (also Faisal I)(king, Iraq; 1885-1933)
Feisal II (also Faisal II)(king, Iraq; 1935-58)
Felber, Réne (ex-pres., Switz.)

Feldene™ (med.)
Feldman, Marty (ent.; 1933-82)
Feldon, Barbara (ent.; 1941-)
Feldshuh, Tovah (ent.; 1952-)
Feliciano, Jose (ent.; 1945-)
Felipe González Márquez (PM, Spain; 1942-)
Felix Adler (US phil.; 1851-1933)
Felix Bloch (Swiss/US physt.; 1905-83)
Felix Frankfurter (US jurist; 1882-1965)
Félix Houphouët-Boigny (ex-pres., Ivory Coast; 1905-93)
Felix Mendelssohn (-Bartholdy), (Jakob Ludwig)(Ger. comp.; 1809-47)
Felix Salten (b. Siegmund Salzman)(Aus. writer; 1869-1945)
Felix Wankel (Ger., inv.; 1902-88)
Fell, Norman (ent. 1924-)
Feller, Bob (baseball; 1918-)
Fellini, Federico (It. ent. ; 1920-93)
Fellowes Manufacturing Co.
Feltsman, Vladimir (Rus. pianist; 1952-)
Feminist Majority Foundation
Femiron™ (med.)
Fenech Adami, Edward (PM, Malta; 1934-)
Fenian movement (Ir./Amer. ; 1858-67)
Fenland (also the Fens)(fertile agricultural area, Eng.)
Fenneman, George
Fenway Park (Boston)
Fenwick, Millicent (US pol.; 1900-92)
Feoktistov, Konstantin P. (cosmo.)
Ferber, Edna (US writer; 1887-1968)
Ferde Grofe (US comp.; 1892-1972)
Ferdinand (king, Bulgaria; 1861-1948)
Ferdinand Cortés (or Hernando)(also Cortez)(Sp. expl.; 1485-1547)
Ferdinand de Lesseps, Vicomte (Fr. dipl./eng.; 1805-94)
Ferdinand de Saussure (Swiss linguist; 1857-1913)
Ferdinand E(dralin) Marcos (ex-pres., Phil.; 1917-89)
Ferdinand Foch (Fr. mil.; 1851-1929)
Ferdinand I (Ferdinand the Great)(king, Castile; c1016-65)
Ferdinand II (Holy Roman emp.; 1578-1637)
Ferdinand III (Holy Roman emp.; 1608-57)
Ferdinand Magellan (Port. nav.; c1480-1521)
Ferdinand Porsche (Ger. eng./auto.; 1875-1951)
Ferdinand the Great (Ferdinand I)(king, Castile; c1016-65)
Ferdinand V (king, Castile; 1452-1516)
Ferdinand von Zeppelin, Graf (or Count)(Ger. mil./aeronaut; 1838-1917)
Ferdinand, Franz (or Francis)(archduke, Aus.; 1863-1914)
Ferenc Molnár (Hung. writer; 1878-1952)
Ferenc Nagy (ex-PM, Hung.; 1903-)

Ferghana, Uzbekistan
Fergie (Sarah Margaret) Ferguson (Br., Duchess of York; 1959-)
Ferguson Arthur Jenkins (baseball; 1943-)
Ferguson, Danny (US news)
Ferguson, Inc., Massey-
Ferguson, Maynard (ent.)
Ferguson, Plessy v. (US law; 1896)
Ferguson, Sarah Margaret "Fergie" (Br., Duchess of York; 1959-)
Ferlin Husky
Ferlinghetti, Lawrence (US writer/publ.; 1919-)
Fermanagh (county, NIre.)
Fermat, Pierre de (Fr. math.; 1601-65)
Fermi, Enrico (It. physt.; 1901-54)
Fermilab (Fermi National Accelerator Lab.)
Fern Arable
Fernand Leger (Fr. artist; 1881-1955)
Fernando Collor de Mello (ex-pres., Brazil; 1949-)
Fernando Jose de Franca Dias van Dunem (ex-PM, Angola)
Fernando Lamas (ent.; 1915-82)
Fernando Valenzuela (baseball; 1960-)
Ferrante & Teicher (US piano duo)
Ferrari™ (auto.)
Ferrari North America (US bus.)
Ferrari, Enzo (It. bus./auto.; 1898-1988)
Ferrari, Ermanno Wolf- (It. comp.; 1876-1948)
Ferraris, Galileo (It. physt./eng.; 1847-97)
Ferraro, Geraldine (US pol./1st major US female VP candidate; 1935-)
Ferrell, Conchata (ent.; 1943-)
Ferrer, Jose (ent.; 1912-92)
Ferrer, Mel (ent.; 1917-)
Ferri, Alessandra
Ferrigno, Lou (ent.)
Ferris wheel
Ferris, George Washington Gale (US eng./inv.; 1859-96)
Ferruccio Busoni (It. comp.; 1866-1924)
Ferruccio Lamborghini (It. bus.; 1917-93)
Fertile Crescent (Middle East)
Fess Parker (ent.; 1925-)
Festus Mogae (VP, Botswana)
Fetchit, Stepin (ent.; 1898-1985)
Fetzer Vineyards (US bus.)
Feuerbach, Allan Dean (track; 1948-)
Feuerbach, Anselm (Ger. artist; 1829-80)
Feynman, Richard (Phillips)(US physt.; 1918-88)
Fez, Morocco (also Fès)
FFA (Future Farmers of America)
FHA (Farmers Home Administration, Federal Housing Administration)
FHLMC (also Federal Home Loan Mortgage Corporation, Freddie Mac)
FHMA (Federal Home Mortgage Corp. [Freddie Mac])Fianarantsoa, Madagascar
Fianna (also Fians)(Ir. hist.; 2nd-3rd c)
Fianna Fáil (Irish pol. party; 20th c)
Fians (also Fianna)(Ir. hist.; 2nd-3rd c)
Fiat USA, Inc.
Fibber McGee and Molly (radio comedy)
Fiberglas™ (constr.)
Fibonacci numbers/sequence (math.)
Fibonacci, Leonardo (It. math.; c1175-c1250)
Fibranne™
Fibreboard Corp.
FICA (Federal Insurance Contributions Act)
Fichte, Johann (Ger. phil.; 1762-1814)
Fiddler on the Roof (play)
Fidel Castro Ruíz (pres., Cuba; 1927-)
Fidel V. Ramos (pres., Phil.; 1928-)
Fidèle Moungar (PM, Chad)
Fidelism (also Fidelismo)
Fiedler, Arthur (US cond.; 1894-1979)
Fiedler, John (ent.; 1925-)
Field & Stream (mag.)
Field, Cyrus West (US finan., 1st Atl. cable; 1819-92)
Field, Marshall (US merchant; 1834-1906)
Field, Sally (ent.; 1946-)
Fieldcrest-Cannon, Inc.
Fielder, Cecil (baseball; 1963-)
Fielding, Henry (Br. writer; 1707-54)
Fields, Dorothy (US lyricist; 1905-74)
Fields, Gracie (ent.; 1898-1979)
Fields, Inc., Mrs.
Fields, Totie (ent.; 1931-78)
Fields, W. C. (b. William Claude Dukenfield)(US ent.; 1880-1946)
Fiesta Bowl (college football)
Fiesta ware
Fife (region, Scot.)
Fife Smytington (AZ gov.; 1945-)
FIFO (first in, first out)
Fifth Avenue, Chrysler-Plymouth (auto.)
Fifty-four-forty or Fight (US hist.)
Fig Newtons™
Fiji (Republic of)(SW Pac.)
Fijian (lang./people)
Filbert Bayi (runner; 1953-)
Filene's department store (Boston)
Filho, Oscar Niemeyer Soares (Brazilian arch.; 1907-)
Filip Dimitrov (ex-PM, Bulgaria)
Filipchenko, Anatoly (cosmo.; 1928-)
Filipino (also Pilipino)(lang.)
Filipino (people)
Filippo Brunelleschi (It. arch.; 1377-1446)
Filippo (or Filippino) Lippi (It. artist; 1457-1504)
Filippo Lippi, (Fra)(It. artist; 1406-69)
Filippo, Fra Lippi (It. artist; 1406-69)
Fillmore, Millard (13th US pres.; 1800-74)

Final/Last Judgment (rel.)
Final Solution (Nazi annihilation policy)
Finance Committee, Senate (US govt.)
Financial World (mag.)
Finch, Peter (ent.; 1916-77)
Finder™ (compu.)
Fine, Larry (b. Louis Feinberg)(ent.; 1902-75)
Finesse™ (hair care)
Fingal's Cave (by Mendelssohn)
Fingal's Cave (Scot.)
Finger Lakes region (NY)
Finian's Rainbow (film; 1968)
Finland (Republic of)(N Eur.)
Finland, Gulf of (arm of Baltic Sea)
Finlandia
Finley, Charles O. (athlete; 1918-)
Finn, Huckleberry (fict. chara., Mark Twain)
Finn, Huckleberry (M. Twain novel)
Finn, Mickey (drugged drink)
Finnair (airline)
Finnbogadóttir, Vigdís (pres., Iceland; 1930-)
Finney, Albert (ent.; 1936-)
Finney, Joan (KS gov.; 1925-)
Finnish (lang./people)
Finnish War, Russo- (Rus./Fin.; 1939-40)
Finno-Ugric (family of langs.)
Finns (people)
Fiorello (Henry) La Guardia (ex-mayor, NYC; 1882-1947)
Firebird, Pontiac™ (auto.)
Firebird, The (by Stravinsky)
Firestone™
Firestone Tire & Rubber Co.
Firestone, Harvey (Samuel)(US bus.; 1868-1938)
Firing Line (TV show)
First Cause (rel.)
First Legal Tender Case (*Hepburn v. Griswold*)(US law; 1870)
First Reich (Holy Roman Empire; 962-1806)
First State (nickname, DE)
First Temple (rel.)
First Triumvirate (ancient Rome ruling board)
First World War (also World War I, WWI)(1914-18)
Firth of Forth (also Firth of Forth Bridge)(Scot., arm of North Sea)
Firth, Peter (ent.; 1953-)
Fischer™ (skis)
Fischer, Bobby (Robert James)(US chess; 1943-)
Fischer, Emil Hermann (Ger. chem.; 1852-1919)
Fischer, Hans (Ger. chem.; 1881-1945)
Fish, Hamilton (US pol.; 1808-93)
Fish, Hamilton, III (US pol.; 1899-1991)
Fish, Hamilton, Jr. (US cong.; 1926-)
Fishburne, Larry (ent.; 1962-)
Fisher™ (nuts)
Fisher Nut Co.

Fisher-Price™
Fisher-Price Toys (US bus.)
Fisher USA Corp., Sanyo
Fisher, Amy ("Long Island Lolita")(US news)
Fisher, Bud (cartoonist, *Mutt & Jeff*; 1884-1954)
Fisher, Carrie (ent.; 1956-)
Fisher, Eddie (ent.; 1928-)
Fisher, Fred (US comp.; 1875-1942)
Fisher, Ham (US cartoonist, *Joe Palooka*; 1900-55)
Fisher, Irving (US econ.; 1867-1947)
Fisher, Mary Frances Kennedy (M.F.K.)(US writer; 1909-92)
Fiske, John (US hist.; 1842-1901)
Fiske, Minnie Maddern (ent.; 1865-1932)
Fitch, Abercrombie & (US bus.)
Fitch, John (US inv.; 1743-98)
Fitchburg, MA
Fitr, Eid ul- (Muslim festival)
Fittipaldi, Emerson (auto racing)
Fitzgerald, Barry (ent.; 1888-1961)
Fitzgerald, Edward (Br. poet; 1809-83)
Fitzgerald, Ella (US jazz; 1918-)
Fitzgerald, F(rancis) Scott (Key)(US writer; 1896-1940)
Fitzgerald, Geraldine (Ir./US ent.; 1913-)
FitzRoy (James Henry) Somerset Raglan, Baron (Br. gen., raglan sleeve; 1788-1855)
Fitzsimmons Army Medical Center (CO)(mil.)
Fitzsimmons, Bob (Robert Prometheus)(boxing; 1862-1917)
Fitzsimmons, Buckley v. (US law; 1993)
Fitzwater, Marlin (US pol.; 1942-)
Five Civilized Tribes/Nations
Five Dynasties
Five Dynasties and Ten Kingdoms
Five Satins, the (pop music)
Five-Year Plan (USSR hist., Stalin)
Fixit, Mr. (slang)
Fixx, James "Jim" S. (US runner)
F. Korbel & Brothers, Inc.
FL (Florida)
Flaccus Albinus Alcuinus (also Alcuin, Ealhwine Flaccus, Alchuine, Albinus)(Br. scholar; 735-804)
Flack, Roberta (ent.; 1939-)
Flag Day (unofficial holiday)
Flagg, James Montgomery (US cartoonist, Uncle Sam; 1877-1960)
Flagler, Henry M(orrison)(US finan.; 1830-1913)
Flagstaff, AZ
Flaherty, Robert (ent.; 1884-1951)
Flame Glow™ (toiletries)
Flames, Calgary (hockey team)
Flamingo Kid, The (film; 1984)
Flammarion, Camille (Fr. astron.; 1842-1925)

Flanders field
Flanders, Ed (ent.; 1934-)
Flanders, The Fortunes and Misfortunes of the Famous Moll (D. Defoe)
Flannagan, John Bernard (US sculptor; 1895-1942)
Flannery O'Connor, (Mary)(US writer; 1925-64)
Flash Gordon (comic strip)
Flash, Jumpin' Jack (film; 1986)
Flash, Jumpin' Jack (song)
Flat Earth Research Society International
Flathead (also Salish)(NAmer. Indians)
Flatt, Lester (Raymond)(ent.; 1914-79)
Flaubert, Gustave (Fr. writer; 1821-80)
Flavio Cotti (ex-pres., Switz.)
Flavius Sabinus Vespasianus (aka Titus)(Roman emp.; AD 39-81)
F(rancis) Lee Bailey (US atty.; 1933-)
Fleet™ enema
Fleet Street (London, publishing)
Fleet, Jo Van (ent.; 1922-)
Fleetwood™ Brougham™, Cadillac (auto.)
Fleetwood Enterprises, Inc.
Fleetwood Mac (pop music)
Fleetwood™, Cadillac (auto.)
Fleischer, Max (US cartoonist, *Betty Boop, Popeye*; 1883-1972)
Fleischmann's Yeast, Inc.
Fleiss, Heidi (US news)
Fleming (people)
Fleming, Sir Alexander (Br. bacteriol.; 1881-1955)
Fleming, Ian (Lancaster)(Br. writer ; 1908-64)
Fleming, Peggy (Gale)(figure skating; 1948-)
Fleming, Rhonda (ent.; 1923-)
Flemish (lang./people)
Flemish architecture
Flemish art
Flensburg, Germany
Fletcher Henderson (US jazz; 1898-1952)
Fletcher v. Peck (US law; 1810)
Fletcher, Jessica (fict. chara., *Murder, She Wrote*)
Fletcher, Louise (ent.; 1936-)
Flickertail State (nickname, ND)
Flim Flam Man, The (film; 1967)
Flinders Petrie, Sir (William Matthew)(Br. archaeol.; 1853-1942)
Flint Journal (MI newspaper)
Flint, MI
Flintstone, Fred (cartoon chara.)
Flintstones™ vitamins
Flintstones, The (cartoon, film)
Flip Wilson (ent.; 1933-)
Flippen, Jay C. (ent. 1900-71)
Flipper (TV show)
Flip-Top™ (cigarette box)
Flo Jo (Florence Griffith) Joyner (sprinter; 1959-)
Flo(renz) Ziegfeld (ent.; 1869-1932)
Flood, the (also the Deluge)(rel.)
Flora (myth.)
Florence Chadwick (US swimmer; 1918-)
Florence fennel (also finocchio)(herb)
Florence Griffith Joyner ("Flo Jo")(track; 1959-)
Florence Henderson (ent.; 1934-)
Florence Nightingale (Br., founded modern nursing; 1820-1910)
Florence, AL, CO, SC
Florence, Italy (also Firenze)
Florida (FL)
Florida Keys (FL)
Florida Marlins (baseball team)
Florio, James J. (NJ gov.; 1937-)
Florists' Transworld Delivery (FTD™)
Florsheim™
Florsheim Shoe Co., The
Flotow, Friedrich von (Ger. comp.; 1812-83)
Floyd Caves (Babe) Herman (baseball; 1903-87)
Floyd Douglas Little (football; 1942-)
Floyd Patterson (boxing; 1935-)
Floyd, Charles Arthur ("Pretty Boy")(US bank robber; 1901-34)
Floyd, Pink (pop music)
Floyd, Pretty Boy (Charles Arthur)(US bank robber; 1901-34)
Floyd, Ray (golf; 1942-)
FLSA (Fair Labor Standards Act)
Flushing Meadow, NY (tennis center)
Flushing, NY
Fly, The (cartoon chara.)
Fly, The (film; 1958, 1986)
Fly, The Human (cartoon chara.)
Flyers, Philadelphia (hockey team)
Flying (mag.)
Flying Cross, Distinguished (mil.)
Flying Dutchman (legendary mariner)
Flying Fortress (B-17 bomber)
Flying Tiger Line
Flying Tigers
Flying Wallendas
Flynn, Errol (ent.; 1909-59)
FMC Corp.
F. Murray Abraham (ent.; 1939-)
FNMA (also Federal National Mortgage Association [Fannie Mae])
FO (foreign office)
Foch, Ferdinand (Fr. mil.; 1851-1929)
Foch, Nina (ent.; 1924-)
Fodor, Eugene (US travel guide writer; 1906-91)
Fodor's Travel Guides (US bus.)
FOE (Fraternal Order of Eagles)(FoE, Friends of the Earth [Br. environ. grp., est. 1971])
Fogarty, Tom (ent.; 1942-90)
Fogelberg, Dan (ent.; 1951-)

Proper Noun Speller

Fogg Art Museum (Harvard Univ.)
Foghorn Leghorn (cartoon chara.)
Fokin, Vitold (Ukrainian pol.)
Foley catheter (med.)
Foley, Red (ent.; 1910-68)
Foley, Thomas S. (US cong.; 1929-)
Foley's department store
Folger Shakespeare Library (DC)
Folgers™
Folger Coffee Co., The
Folgers™ Coffee Singles™
Folies-Bergère (Paris music hall)
Folkestone, England
Follett Publishing Co.
Follett, Ken(neth Martin)(Br. writer; 1949-)
Follette, Robert Marion La (ex-gov., WI; 1855-1925)
Follette, Robert Marion La, Jr. (US pol./publ., WI; 1895-1953)
Folsom culture (anthrop., NM)
Folsom Prison (CA)
Fon (lang./people)
Foncard™ (comm.)
Fonda, Bridget (ent.)
Fonda, Henry (ent.; 1905-82)
Fonda, Jane (ent.; 1937-)
Fonda, Peter (ent.; 1939-)
Fontaine, Frank (aka Crazy Guggenheim)(ent.; 1920-78)
Fontaine, Jean de la (Fr. poet; 1621-95)
Fontaine, Joan (ent.; 1917-)
Fontainebleau school (Fr., art)
Fontainebleau, France
Fontainebleau, palace at
Fontanne, Lynn (ent.; 1887-1983)
Fonteyn, Margot, Dame (ballet; 1919-91)
Fontvieille, Monaco
Fonzerelli, Arthur (also "the Fonz" or "Fonzie") (fict chara.)
Food and Agriculture Organization (FAO)(UN agcy.)
Food and Drug Act, Pure (US hist.; 1906)
Food and Drug Administration (FDA)(US govt. agcy.)
Food & Wine (mag.)
Foods USA, General (US bus.)
Football Foundation and Hall of Fame, National (NFFHF)(est. 1947)
Football League, National (NFL)
For Better or Worse (comic strip)
Forbes (mag.)
Forbes, Malcolm (US publ.; 1919-90)
Forbidden City (Peking, Ch.)
Ford C. Frick (baseball; 1894-1978)
Ford (auto.)
Ford Aerostar (auto.)
Ford Bronco (auto.)
Ford Edsel™ (auto.)

Ford Escort (auto.)
Ford Explorer (auto.)
Ford Pinto (auto.)
Ford Foundation
Ford Madox Brown (Br. artist; 1821-93)
Ford Madox Ford (b. Ford Herman Heuffer)(Br. writer; 1873-1939)
Ford Mercury Villager (auto.)
Ford Mondeo (auto.)
Ford Motor Co.
Ford Mustang (auto.)
Ford Probe GT (auto.)
Ford Ranger (auto.)
Ford Taurus (auto.)
Ford Tempo (auto.)
Ford Thunderbird (T-Bird)(auto.)
Ford, Betty (b. Elizabeth Bloomer Warren)(wife of ex-US pres.; 1918-)
Ford, Edsel (Bryant)(US bus./auto.; 1893-1943)
Ford, Gerald R(udolph)(b. Leslie Lynch King, Jr.)(38th US pres.; 1913-)
Ford, Glenn (ent.; 1916-)
Ford, Harrison (ent.; 1942-)
Ford, Henry (US bus./auto.; 1863-1947)
Ford, Henry, II (US bus./auto.; 1917-87)
Ford, Les Paul & Mary (ent.)
Ford, Mary (ent.; 1928-77)
Ford, Tennessee Ernie (ent.; 1919-91)
Ford, Wendell Hampton (US cong.; 1924-)
Ford, Whitey (Edward Charles)("Duke of Paducah")(baseball; 1928-)
Fordham University (NYC)
Fordham University Press (US bus.)
Fordice, Kirk (MS gov.; 1934-)
Ford's Theater
Forego (champion horse)
Foreign Legion (mil.)
Foreign Wars of the United States, Veterans of (VFW)(est. 1899)
Foreman, George (boxing; 1949-)
Forest Hills, NY
Forest Lawn Memorial Park (Glendale, CA)
Forest, Lake, IL
Forest, Lee de (US inv., radio/sound films/TV; 1873-1961)
Forester, C(ecil) S(cott)(Br. writer; 1899-1966)
Forman, Milos (Czech. ent.; 1932-)
Formby, Inc., Thompson &
Formby's™
Formfit Rogers™
Formfit Rogers (US bus.)
Formica™
Formica Corp.
Formosa (now Taiwan)
Formosa Strait (now Taiwan Strait)
Formosan (people)
Formula 409™ (cleaner)
Fornax (astron., furnace)

Forrest E(dward) Mars
Forrest Tucker (ent.; 1919-86)
Forrest, Nathan Bedford (US gen.; 1821-77)
Forrest, Steve (ent.; 1924-)
Forrestal, James V(incent)(ex-secy/navy/
   defense; 1892-1949)
Forster, E(dward) M(organ)(Br. writer; 1879-
   1970)
Forstner bit (constr.)
Forsyth, Frederick (Br. writer; 1938-)
Forsythe, John (ent.; 1918-)
Fort Belvoir, VA (mil.)
Fort Benning, GA (mil.)
Fort Bliss, TX (mil.)
Fort Bragg, CA (city)
Fort Bragg, NC (mil.)
Fort Chaffee (AR)(mil.)
Fort Collins, CO (city)
Fort-de-France, Martinique
Fort Detrick (MD)(mil.)
Fort Devens, MA (mil.)
Fort Dix, NJ (mil.)
Fort Drum (NY)(mil.)
Fort Eustis, VA (mil.)
Fort George G. Meade (MD) (mil.)
Fort Gillern (GA)(mil.)
Fort Gordon, GA (mil.)
Fort Hamilton, NY (mil.)
Fort (Benjamin) Harrison, IN (mil.)
Fort Hood, TX (mil.)
Fort (Sam) Houston, TX (mil.)
Fort Huachuca, AZ (mil.)
Fort Hunter Liggett (CA)(mil.)
Fort Irwin, CA (mil.)
Fort Jackson, SC (mil.)
Fort Knox, KY (mil., gold depository)
Fort Laramie (WY)
Fort Laramie National Historic Site (WY)
Fort Lauderdale News (FL newspaper)
Fort Lauderdale Sun-Sentinel (FL newspaper)
Fort Lauderdale, FL (city)
Fort Leavenworth, KS (mil.)
Fort Lee, NJ (city)
Fort Lee, VA (mil.)
Fort Leonard Wood, MO (mil.)
Fort McClellan, AL (mil.)
Fort McCoy (WI)
Fort McHenry (MD)(*Star Spangled Banner*)
Fort (Lesley J.) McNair (DC) (mil.)
Fort McPherson, GA (mil.)
Fort (George G.) Meade (MD) (mil.)
Fort Monmouth, NJ (mil.)
Fort Monroe, VA (mil.)
Fort Myer, VA (mil.)
Fort Myers News-Press (FL newspaper)
Fort Myers, FL (city)
Fort Ord, CA (mil.)
Fort Pierce, FL (city)

Fort Polk, LA (mil.)
Fort Richardson, AK (mil.)
Fort Riley, KS (mil.)
Fort Ritchie, MD (mil.)
Fort Rucker, AL (mil.)
Fort Sam Houston, TX (mil.)
Fort Shafter, HI (mil.)
Fort Sheridan, IL (mil.)
Fort Sill, OK (mil.)
Fort Smith, AR (city)
Fort Story, VA (mil.)
Fort Sumter, SC (fort)
Fort Ticonderoga, NY (fort)
Fort Wainwright (AK)(mil.)
Fort Walton Beach, FL (city)
Fort Wayne Journal-Gazette (IN newspaper)
Fort Wayne News-Sentinel (IN newspaper)
Fort Wayne, IN (city)
Fort Worth International Airport, Dallas- (TX)
Fort Worth Star-Telegram (TX newspaper)
Fort Worth, TX (city)
Fort Yukon, AK (city)
Fortaleza, Brazil
Fortas, Abe (US jurist; 1910-82)
Forth River (Scot.)
FORTRAN (formula translator)(compu. lang.)
Fortrel™ (fabric)
Fortune (mag.)
Fortune 500 (500 largest publicly-owned US
   indust. cos.)
48 Hours (TV show)
Forty Hours (rel.)
49ers, San Francisco (football team)
42rd Street (play/movie)
Fosbury flop (track & field)
Fosbury, Dick (Richard)(jumper; 1947-)
Foscavir™ (med.)
Fosdick, Harry Emerson (US rel./writer; 1878-
   1969)
Fosse, Bob (ent.; 1927-87)
Fossey, Dian (US zool., gorillas; 1932-85)
Foster Parents Plan, Inc.
Foster, Hal (US cartoonist; *Tarzan, Prince
   Valiant*; 1892-1982)
Foster, Jodie (ent.; 1962-)
Foster, Meg
Foster, Preston (ent.; 1901-70)
Foster, Stephen Collins (US comp.; 1826-64)
Foster, Vincent, Jr. (US pol.; ?-1993)
Fotomat™
Fotomat Corp.
Foulah (also Fulah)(people)
Founding Fathers (Constitutional Convention
   delegates)
Fountain of Youth (fabled fountain)
Four Aces, The (pop music)
Four Corners (point where 4 states meet, AZ/
   UT/CO/NM)

Four Freedoms of FDR (of speech, of worship, from want, from fear; 1941)

Four-H Club (4-H)(agriculture)

Four Horsemen of the Apocalypse

Four Lads, The (pop music)

Four Noble Truths (Buddhism)

Four Seasons Hotel (NYC)

Four Seasons Solar Products, Corp.

Four Seasons, the (pop music)

Four Tops, the (pop music)

Four Wheeler (mag.)

Fourier, Charles (Fr. social scien.; 1772-1837)

Fourier, Jean B(aptiste) J(oseph)(Fr. math.; 1768-1830)

Fourierism (social phil.)

Fournier, Rafael Angel Calderón (pres., Costa Rica; 1949-)

Fourth of July (also July Fourth, Independence Day)

Fowles, John (Br. writer; 1926-)

Fox (NAmer. Indians)

Fox Broadcasting Company

Fox Channel (FX)(cable TV)

Fox Film Co., 20th Century-

Fox Indians, Sac (or Sauk) and

Fox Record Corp., 20th Century-

Fox, Brer (fict. chara., *Uncle Remus*)

Fox, George (Br. rel.; 1624-91)

Fox, James (ent.; 1939-)

Fox, Katherine (Can./US spiritualist)

Fox, Margaret (Can./US spiritualist; 1833-93)

Fox, Michael J. (ent.; 1961-)

Fox, Nellie (Jacob Nelson)(baseball; 1927-75)

Foxworth, Robert (ent.; 1941-)

Foxx, Jimmy (James Emory)(baseball; 1907-67)

Foxx, Redd (ent.; 1922-91)

Foy, Eddie (ent.; 1857-1928)

Foyt, A(nthony) J(oseph)(auto racing; 1935-)

Fozzie Bear (muppet)

FPC (Federal Power Commission)

FPO (U.S. Navy Fleet Post Office)

Fr (chem. sym., francium)

Fra Angelico (It. artist; 1400-55)

Fra Bartolommeo (It. artist; 1472-1517)

Fra Filippo Lippi (It. artist; 1406-69)

Fraggle Rock (cartoon)

Fragonard, Jean Honoré (Fr. artist; 1732-1806)

Fraktur (type style)

Framingham, MA

Frampton, Peter (ent.; 1950-)

Fran & Ollie, Kukla, (TV show)

Fran Allison (ent.; 1908-89)

Fran(cis Asbury) Tarkenton (football; 1940-)

Francaise, Comédie (Fr. national theater)

France (French Republic)(Eur.)

France-Albert René (pres., Seychelles; 1935-)

France Besançon (Roman ruins)

France, Anatole (Fr. writer; 1844-1924)

France, Tour de (Fr. bicycle race)

France-Press, Agence (Eur. news org.; est. 1944)

Frances "Fanny" Anne Kemble (Br. writer/ent.; 1809-93)

Frances Dee (ent.; 1907-)

Frances E(lizabeth Caroline) Willard (US educ./reformer; 1839-98)

Frances "Fannie" Farmer (ent.; 1914-70)

Frances Langford (ent.; 1913-)

Frances Perkins (US sociol.; 1882-1965)

Frances Sternhagen (ent.; 1930-)

Frances Xavier Cabrini, St. (also Mother Cabrini)(US rel./reformer; 1850-1917)

Francesc Badia Batalla (covicar, Andorra)

Francesca, Piero della (It. artist; c1415-92)

Francesco Cilea (It. comp.; 1866-1950)

Francesco Guicciardini (It. hist.; 1483-1540)

Francesco Petrarca (It. poet; 1304-74)

Francesco Sforza (It. pol.; 1401-66)

Franche-Comté (region, Fr.)

Franchi, Sergio (ent.; 1933-90)

Franchot Tone (ent.; 1903-68)

Francie Larrieu (track; 1952-)

Francine Pascal

Francis Affleck (auto racing; 1951-85)

Francis Bacon (Br. artist; 1909-92)

Francis Bacon, Sir (Br. phil./pol.; 1561-1626)

Francis Billy Hilly (PM, Solomon Islands)

Francis Drake, Sir (Br. expl.; c1545-96)

Francis E(verett) Townsend (US phys./reformer; 1867-1960)

Francis (or Franz) Ferdinand (archduke, Aus.; 1863-1914)

Francis Ford Coppola (ent.; 1939-)

Francis H(arry) C(ompton) Crick (Br. physt.; 1916-)

Francis I (king, Fr.; 1492-1547)

Francis II (Holy Roman emp.; 1768-1835)

Francis II (king, Fr.; 1544-60)

Francis (or Franz) Joseph (Aus./Hung., emp.; 1830-1916)

Francis Lear (US publ.; 1923-)

Francis Lightfoot Lee (US pol.; 1734-97)

Francis L. Sullivan (ent.; 1903-56)

Francis Marion ("the Swamp Fox")(US mil./pol. c1732-95)

Francis of Assisi, St. (It. rel., founded Franciscans; 1182-1226)

Francis Parkman (US hist.; 1823-93)

Francis (Jean Marcel) Poulenc (Fr. comp.; 1899-1963)

Francis Quarles (Br. poet; 1592-1644)

Francis Richard "Dick" Scobee (astro., *Challenger*; 1939-86)

Francis Scott Key (US atty., wrote *The Star Spangled Banner*; 1780-1843)

Francis W. Ayer (US adv.; 1848-1923)

Francis X. Bushman (ent.; 1883-1966)

Francis Xavier, St. (Francisco Javier)("the Apostle of the Indies")(Sp. rel.; 1506-52)

Francis, Anne (ent.; 1930-)

Francis, Arlene (ent.; 1908-)

Francis, Connie (ent.; 1938-)

Francis, Dick (Br. writer/jockey; 1920-)

Francis, Emile (hockey; 1926-)

Franciscan order (of friars)

Franciscan Vineyards (US bus.)

Francisco (José) de Goya y Lucientes (Sp. artist; 1746-1828)

Francisco Fernandez de Córdoba (also Cordova)(Sp. expl.; 1475?-1526)

Francisco Franco, Generalissimo (dictator, Sp.; 1892-1975)

Francisco Macías Nguema (ex-pres., Equatorial Guinea; 1924-79)

Francisco Pizarro (Sp. mil./expl.; 1475?-1541)

Francisco Vásquez de Coronado (Sp. expl.; c1510-54)

Francisco, Tony (Anthony)(ent.; 1928-)

Franciscus, James (ent.; 1934-91)

Francisque Ravony (PM, Madagascar)

Francistown, Botswana

Franck, César Auguste (Belg. comp.; 1822-90)

Franck, James (Ger./US physt.; 1882-1964)

Franco-American™ (foods)

Franco Harris (football; 1950-)

Franco Zeffirelli (ent.; 1923-)

Franco, Buddy De (US jazz; 1933-)

Franco, Generalissimo Francisco (dictator, Sp.; 1892-1975)

Franco, Itamar (pres., Brazil; 1930-)

Franco-Prussian War (also Franco-German War)(Fr./Ger.-Prussia; 1870-71)

François Boucher (Fr. artist; 1703-70)

François (Ambrose) Didot (Fr. printer; 1730-1804)

Francois Durr (tennis; 1942-)

François Duvalier (aka Papa Doc)(ex-pres., Haiti; 1907-71)

François Girardon (Fr. sculptor; 1628-1715)

François La Rochefoucauld, Duc de (Fr. writer; 1613-80)

François Mansard (or Mansart), (Nicolas)(Fr. arch.; 1598-1666)

François Mauriac (Fr. writer; 1885-1970)

François Mitterrand (pres., Fr.; 1916-)

François Quesnay (Fr. econ.; 1694-1774)

François Rabelais (Fr. writer; 1495-1553)

François René Chateaubriand (Fr. writer; 1768-1848)

François Rochefoucauld, Duc de La (Fr. writer; 1613-80)

François Toussaint L'Ouverture (Haitian pol.; c1744-1803)

François Truffaut (Fr. ent.; 1932-84)

François Villon (Fr. poet; 1431-63?)

François, Donatien Alphonse, Comte de Sade (Marquis de Sade)(Fr. mil./writer; 1740-1814)

Françoise Sagan (b. Françoise Quoirez)(Fr. writer; 1935-)

Francophile

Francophobe

François (Fr. form of Francis)

Franjo Greguric (ex-PM, Croatia)

Franjo Tudjman (pres., Croatia; 1922-)

Frank (ancient people; 3rd-9th c.)

Frank and Ernest (comic strip)

Frank B(illings) Kellogg (US pol.; 1856-1937)

Frank B. Kelso, II, (US adm.)

Frank Borman (astro.; 1928-)

Frank Capra (ent.; 1897-1991)

Frank Carlucci (US pol.; 1930-)

Frank Chapot (equestrian; 1934-)

Frank De Vol

Frank Ernest Gannett (US newspaper publ.; 1876-?)

Frank Fontaine (aka Crazy Guggenheim)(ent.; 1920-78)

Frank Gifford (ent./football; 1930-)

Frank Gilroy (US writer; 1925-)

Frank Gorshin (ent.; 1934-)

Frank G. Slaughter (US writer

Frank H. Murkowski (US cong.; 1933-)

Frank James (US outlaw)

Frank King (cartoonist; *Gasoline Alley*; 1883-1969)

Frank Kupka

Frank Langella (ent.; 1940-)

Frank Lloyd Wright (US arch.; 1867-1959)

Frank Loesser (US comp.; 1910-69)

Frank Lorenzo

Frank Lovejoy (ent.; 1912-62)

Frank (Francis William) Mahovlich (hockey; 1938-)

Frank McCloskey (US cong.; 1939-)

Frank Nelson Doubleday (US publ.; 1862-1934)

Frank Norris (US writer; 1870-1902)

Frank Oz (Muppet puppeteer; 1944-)

Frank Reynolds (US jour.; 1923-83)

Frank Rich

Frank Rizzo (ex-mayor, Phila.; 1921-91)

Frank R. Lautenberg (US cong.; 1924-)

Frank Robinson (baseball; 1935-)

Frank Rosollino (US jazz; 1926-78)

Frank Selke (hockey; 1893-1985)

Frank Shorter (runner; 1947-)

Frank (Francis Albert) Sinatra (ent.; 1915-)

Frank Stella (US artist; 1936-)

Frank (Francis Richard) Stockton (US writer; 1834-1902)

Frank Tuttle

Frank Viola (baseball; 1960-)

Frank Willard (cartoonist, *Moon Mullins*; 1893-

1958)
Frank W. Taussig (US econ./educ.; 1859-1940)
Frank W(infield) Woolworth (US bus.; 1852-1919)
Frank Yerby (US writer; 1916-92)
Frank Zappa (ent.; 1940-1993)
Frank, Anne (Ger./Jew. diarist; 1929-45)
Frank, Barney (US cong.; 1940-)
Frank, Édouard (ex-PM, Central African Republic)
Frankenheimer, John (ent.; 1930-)
Frankenstein (by Mary Shelley)
Frankenstein (film; 1931)
Frankenstein Meets the Wolf Man (film; 1943)
Frankenstein, Bride of (film; 1935)
Frankenstein, Dr. (fict. chara.)
Frankenstein, House of (film; 1944)
Frankenstein, The Revenge of (film; 1958)
Frankenstein, Young (film; 1974)
Frankenthaler, Helen (US artist; 1928-)
Frankfort, IN, KY, NY
Frankfurt, Germany
Frankfurt-am-Main, Germany
Frankfurter, Felix (US jurist; 1882-1965)
Frankie Avalon (ent.; 1939-)
Frankie Laine (ent.; 1913-)
Frankie Lymon (ent.)
Frankie Valli (ent.; 1937-)
Franklin D(elano) Roosevelt (FDR)(32nd US pres.; 1882-1945)
Franklin D(elano) Roosevelt, Jr. (US pol.; 1914-88)
Franklin Gothic (type style)
Franklin Pierce (14th US pres.; 1804-69)
Franklin Stores, Ben (US bus.)
Franklin stove
Franklin, Aretha (ent.; 1942-)
Franklin, Benjamin (US publ./writer/inv./dipl.; 1706-90)
Franklin, Bonnie (ent.; 1944-)
Franklin, Joe (ent.; 1929-)
Frann, Mary (ent.; 1943-)
Frans Hals (Dutch artist; c1580-1666)
Frans Snyders (Flem. artist; 1579-1657)
Frantisek Kupka (Czech. artist; 1871-1957)
Franz Boas (US anthrop.; 1858-1942)
Franz (or Francis) Ferdinand (archduke, Aus.; 1863-1914)
Franz (or Francis) Joseph (Aus./Hung. emp.; 1830-1916)
Franz Joseph Haydn (Aus. comp.; 1732-1809)
Franz Joseph II (ruler, Liechtenstein; 1906-89)
Franz Joseph Strauss (WGer. pol.; 1915-88)
Franz Kafka (Ger. writer; 1889-1961)
Franz Lehar (Hung. comp.; 1870-1948)
Franz Liszt (Hung. comp.; 1811-86)
Franz Marc (Ger. artist; 1880-1916)
Franz (or Friedrich Anton) Mesmer (Ger. phys.; 1734-1815)
Franz (Peter) Schubert (Aus. comp.; 1797-1828)
Franz von Papen (Ger. pol.; 1879-1969)
Franz Vranitzky (chanc., Aus.; 1937-)
Franz Waxman
Franz Xaver Gabelsberger (Ger. stenographer; 1789-1849)
Franz, Dennis (ent.; 1944-)
Franzia Brothers Winery (US bus.)
Frascati (wine)
Frasch process (sulfur extraction)
Fraser River (British Columbia, Can.)
Fraser, Antonia (Br. writer; 1932-)
Fratianne, Linda (figure skating; 1960-)
Frau (Ger., married woman)
Fräulein (Ger., unmarried woman)
Fraunhofer lines/spectrum (dark lines of the sun)
Fraunhofer, Joseph von (Ger. optician/physt.; 1787-1826)
Frawley, William (ent.; 1887-1966)
Frazier, Joe (boxing; 1944-)
Frazier, Walt (basketball; 1945-)
Freberg, Stan
Fred Allen (ent.; 1894-1956)
Fred & Barney (cartoon)
Fred Astaire (ent.; 1899-1987)
Fred(erick) DeCordova (US TV exec.; 1910-)
Fred Dryer (ent.; 1946-)
Fred Edd (US lyricist; 1936-)
Fred Fisher (US comp.; 1875-1942)
Fred Flintstone (cartoon chara.)
Fred Gwynne (ent.; 1926-93)
Fred Lasswell (cartoonist)
Fred Lawrence Whipple (US astron.; 1906-)
Fred Lawrence Whipple Observatory (AZ)
Fred MacMurray (ent.; 1908-91)
Fred M. Waring (US cond., designed Waring blender; 1900-84)
Fred Rogers (ent.; 1928-)
Fred Savage (ent.; 1976-)
Fred Shero (hockey; 1945-90)
Fred Silverman (ent.)
Fred Timakata (pres., Vanuatu)
Fred Ward (ent.; 1943-)
Fred W(allace) Haise, Jr. (astro.; 1933-)
Fred(erick) Zinnermann (ent.; 1907-)
Freddie Bartholomew (ent.; 1925-92)
Freddie Mac (also FHLMC, Federal Home Loan Mortgage Corporation)
Freddie Prinze (ent.; 1954-77)
Frederic-Auguste Bartholdi (Fr. sculptor, designed Statue of Liberty; 1834-1904)
Frederic Chopin (Pol. comp.; 1810-49)
Frederic Church (US artist; 1826-1900)
Frederic Eugene Ives (US inv.; 1856-1937)
Frederic Joliot-Curie (Fr. physt.; 1900-58)
Frederic Michael Lynn (baseball; 1952-)

Frederic Mistral (Fr. poet; 1830-1914)
Frederic Remington (US artist; 1861-1909)
Frederica Von Stade (ent.; 1945-)
Frederick & Nelson department store
Frederick Biletnikoff (football; 1943-)
Frederick Burr Opper (cartoonist, *Happy Hooligan*; 1857-1937)
Frederick Chiluba (pres., Zambia; 1943-)
Frederick Dannay (pseud. Ellery Queen)(US writer; 1905-82)
Frederick Delius (Br. comp.; 1862-1934)
Frederick Douglass (US abolitionist, ex-slave; 1817-95)
Frederick Forsyth (Br. writer; 1938-)
Frederick I (Barbarossa, "Red Beard")(Holy Roman emp.; 1123-90)
Frederick II ("Frederick the Great")(king, Prussia; 1712-86)
Frederick II ("the Wonder of the World")(Holy Roman emp.; 1194-1250)
Frederick III (king, Prussia; emp., Ger.; 1831-88)
Frederick IX (king, Den.; 1899-1972)
Frederick J(ackson) Turner (US hist./educ.; 1861-1932)
Frederick Loewe (US comp.; 1901-88)
Frederick L(aw) Olmsted (US landscaper; 1822-1903)
Frederick North (ex-PM, Br.; 1732-92)
Frederick Sanger (Br. chem.; 1918-)
Frederick Soddy (Br. chem.; 1877-1956)
Frederick the Great (Frederick II)(king, Prussia; 1712-86)
Frederick V ("the Winter King")(king, Bohemia for one winter; 1596-1632)
Frederick William I (king, Prussia; 1688-1740)
Frederick William II (king, Prussia; 1744-97)
Frederick William III (king, Prussia; 1770-1840)
Frederick William IV (king, Prussia; 1795-1861)
Frederick Winslow Taylor (US inv.; 1856-1915)
Frederick, Pauline (US radio/TV jour.; 1918-90)
Frederick's of Hollywood, Inc.
Fredericksburg, Battle of (US hist.; 1862)
Fredericksburg, TX, VA
Fredericktown, MO
Fredericton, New Brunswick, Canada
Frederik Pohl (US writer, sci-fi; 1919-)
Frederik W(illem) de Klerk (ex-pres., SAfr; 1936-)
Fredric March (ent.; 1897-1975)
Free Church of Tonga (rel.)
Free Press, Detroit (MI newspaper)
Free-Soil (pol. party)
Free State (nickname, MD)
Free Wesleyan (rel.)
Freebies (mag.)
Freed, James Ingo (US arch.)

Freedom Bowl (college football)
Freedom of Information Act
Freedom, Presidential Medal of (US, highest civilian honor)
Freeh, Louis (dir., FBI)
Freehand™, Aldus (compu.)
Freeman™
Freeman (Amos) Gosden (ent.; 1899-1982)
Freeman, Al, Jr. (ent.; 1934-)
Freeman, Morgan (ent.; 1937-)
Freemark Abbey Winery (US bus.)
Freemason (member, fraternal organization)
Freemasonry (Freemason phil.)
Freeport, IL, ME, NY, PA, TX
Freeport, the Bahamas
Freer Gallery of Art (Smithsonian, DC)
Freer, Charles Lang (US bus./art collector; 1856-1919)
Freetown, Sierra Leone
Frege, Friedrich Ludwig Gottlob (Ger. phil.; 1848-1925)
Freiburg, Germany
Freixenet (champagne)
Freixenet USA (US bus.)
Fremont, CA, NE
Fremont, John Charles (US mil.; 1813-90)
French (lang./people)
French Alpine (goat)
French and Indian War (NAmer./Br.; 1754-63)
French bed
French braid (hairstyle)
French bread
French bulldog (dog)
French Canadian
French coach horse
French connection (mixed drink)
French Creole (lang.)
French cuff (clothing)
French curve (drafting instrument)
French doors
French dressing
French East India Company (trade; 1664-1794)
French endive
French Equatorial Africa (former county)
French fries
French Guiana (SAmer.)
French heel (footwear)
French horn (musical inst.)
French kiss
French knot (also Fr. twist)(hairstyle)
French leave
French letter (slang, condom)
French patois (lang.)
French Polynesia (S Pac.)
French provincial/Provincial style
French Revolution (Fr. hist.; 1789-99)
French Revolutionary calendar
French Riviera

Proper Noun Speller

French roll
French seam (clothing)
French Sudan (now Republic of Mali)(NW Afr.)
French telephone
French toast
French twist (also Fr. knot)(hairstyle)
French West Africa (Senegal, Mauritania,
    Sudan, Burkina Faso, Guinea, Niger, Ivory
    Coast, Benin)
French windows
French, Daniel Chester (US artist; 1850-1931)
French, Norman (lang.)
Frenchman
French's™ Dijon mustard
Frenchwoman
Freon™
Fresh Prince, D.J. Jazzy Jeff & the (pop music)
Fresh Start™ (detergent)
Fresh Step™ (cat litter)
Fresnel™ lens (lighthouses)
Fresnel, Augustin (Fr. physt.; 1788-1827)
Fresno Bee (CA newspaper)
Fresno, CA
Freud, Anna (Aus./Br., founder of child
    psychoanalysis; 1895-1982)
Freud, Sigmund (Aus. phys., founder of
    psychoanalysis; 1856-1939)
Freudian slip
Frey (also Freyr)(myth.)
Freya (also Frigga)(myth.)
Friar John (fict. chara., *Gargantua, Pantagruel*)
Friar Tuck (fict. chara., *Robin Hood*)
Friars Club
Frick Collection (art museum, NYC)
Frick Winery (US bus.)
Frick, Ford C. (baseball; 1894-1978)
Frick, Henry Clay (US bus.; 1849-1919)
Friday, girl/man
Fridtjof Nansen (Nor. expl; 1861-1930)
Friedan, Betty (Naomi Goldstein)(US feminist/
    writer; 1921-)
Friedkin, David
Friedkin, William (ent.; 1939-)
Friedman, Milton (US econ.; 1912-)
Friedman, Pauline Esther (pseud. Abigail Van
    Buren, "Dear Abby")(US advice columnist;
    1918-)
Friedrich Alfred Krupp (Ger. armaments
    maker; 1854-1902)
Friedrich Anton (or Franz) Mesmer (Ger. phys.;
    1734-1815)
Friedrich Ebert (Ger. pol.; 1871-1925)
Friedrich Engels (Ger. pol. writer; 1820-95)
Friedrich Froebel (Ger. educ.. orig. kindergar-
    ten; 1782-1852)
Friedrich Hund
Friedrich Krupp, (Ger. armaments maker;
    1787-1826)

Friedrich Ludwig Gottlob Frege (Ger. phil.;
    1848-1925)
Friedrich (Ernst Daniel) Schleiermacher (Ger.
    rel.; 1768-1834)
Friedrich von Flotow (Ger. comp.; 1812-83)
Friedrich von Schiller, (Johann Christoph)(Ger.
    writer/hist.; 1759-1805)
Friedrich von Schlegel (Ger. phil./writer; 1772-
    1829)
Friedrich Wilhelm Joseph von Schelling (Ger.
    phil.; 1775-1854)
Friedrich Wilhelm Nietzsche (Ger. phil.; 1844-
    1900)
Friedrich Wilhelm (Ludolf Gerhard Augustin)
    von Steuben, Baron (Prussian/US gen.; 1730-
    94)
Friedrich, Caspar David (Ger. artist; 1774-
    1840)
Friendly Ice Cream Corp.
Friendly Islands (also Tonga)(SW Pac.)
Friends of the Earth (FoE, FOE)(Br. environ.
    grp., est. 1971)
Friends, Society of (also Quakers)(rel.)
Friendship 7 (US spacecraft)
Frietchie, Barbara (Clyde Fitch play)
Frigga (also Freya)(myth.)
Frigid Zone (also l.c.)
Frigidaire™ (appliances)
Frigidaire Co.
Frigo Cheese Corp.
Friml, Rudolf (US comp.; 1879-1972)
Frisbee™ (game disk)
Frisco
Frisco Kid, The (film; 1979)
Frisian (lang.)
Friskies™ (cat food)
Friskies Buffet™ (cat food)
Friskies Petcare Co.
Frito-Lay, Inc.
Frito Lay's™ (chips)
Fritos™ (chips)
Fritz Haber (Ger. chem.; 1868-1934)
Fritz Kreisler (Aus. comp.; 1875-1962)
Fritz Lang (Aus. ent.; 1890-1976)
Fritz the Cat (film; 1972)
Fritz Weaver (ent.; 1926-)
Frizzle chicken
Frobisher, Sir Martin (Br. nav./expl.; 1535-94)
Frodo Baggins (fict. chara.)
Froebel, Friedrich (Ger. educ., orig. kindergar-
    ten; 1782-1852)
Frog's Leap Winery (US bus.)
Frohman, Charles (US theater; 1860-1915)
Frohman, Daniel (US writer/ent.; 1851-1940)
Froman, Jane (ent.)
Frome, Ethan (E. Wharton novel)
Fromm, Erich (Ger. psych.; 1900-80)
Fromme, Squeaky (Lynette)(US, shot Pres.

Ford)
Frontenac, Louis de (Fr./Can. gov.; 1620-98)
Frookie Cookie™
Frookie, R. W. (US bus.)
Froot Loops™ (cereal)
Frost, David (ent.; 1939-)
Frost, Jack (personification of frost)
Frost, Robert (Lee)(US poet; 1874-1963)
Frosted Flakes™ (cereal)
Frosted Mini-Wheats™ (cereal)
Frosted Wheat Bites™ (cereal)
FRS (Federal Reserve System)
Fructuoso Rivera, (José)(ex-pres., Uruguay;
     1784-1854)
Fruehauf Trailer Corp (US bus.)
Frugal Gourmet (TV show)
Fruit Of The Loom™
Fruit of the Loom, Inc.
Fruity Pebbles™ (cereal)
Fry, Christopher (Br. writer; 1907-)
FS (forest service)
F(rancis) Scott (Key) Fitzgerald (US writer;
     1896-1940)
FTC (Federal Trade Commission)(US govt.
     agcy.)
FTD™ (Florists' Transworld Delivery)
F Troop (TV show)
Fu Hsing (myth.)
Fu Manchu (fict. criminal)
Fu, Tu (Ch. poet; 710-770)
Fuad I (king, Eg.; 1868-1936)
Fuchs, Klaus (Emil Julius)(Ger. spy; 1911-88)
Fudd, Elmer (fict. chara.)
Fudgsicle™
Fugger, Jakob (Jakob the Rich)(Ger. banker;
     1459-1525)
Fuhrer, der (also *Fuehrer*)(title adopted by
     Hitler)
Fujairah (state, UAE)
Fuji Electric Co., Ltd.
Fuji film™
Fuji Photo Film USA, Inc.
Fuji, Japan
Fuji, Mount (also Fujiyama)(Jap. dormant
     volcano)
Fujian (also Fukien)(province, Ch.)
Fujicolor™
Fujimori, Alberto (pres., Peru; 1938-)
Fujiyama (also Mount Fuji)(Jap. volcano)
Fukien (also Fujian)(province, Ch.)
Fukuoka, Japan
Fula (lang./people)
Fulakunda (lang.)
Fulani (lang./people)
Fulbright Act (scholarships)
Fulbright, J(ames) William (US pol.; 1905-)
Fulgencio Batista y Zaldivar (ex-dictator, Cuba;
     1901-73)

Full House (TV show)
Fuller Brush Co., The
Fuller Brush man
Fuller, Alfred C. (US, bus./brushes; 1885-1973)
Fuller, Charles (US writer; 1939-)
Fuller, Margaret (US writer/reformer; 1810-50)
Fuller, Melville Weston (US jurist; 1833-1910)
Fuller, R(ichard) Buckminster (US eng./arch.;
     1895-1983)
Fullerton, CA
Fullilove v. Klutznick (US law; 1980)
Fulminate, Arizona v. (US law; 1991)
Fulton Fish Market
Fulton J(ohn) Sheen, Bishop (US rel./writer/
     educ.; 1895-1979)
Fulton, Robert (US gunsmith/artist/eng./inv.
     steamship; 1745-1815)
Fumimaro Konoe, Prince (ex-PM, Jap.; 1891-
     1946)
Funafuti, Tuvalu
Funchal, Madeira
Functionalism (arch./design)
Fundy, Bay of (N Atl., Can.)
Funicello, Annette (ent.; 1942-)
Funk & Wagnalls Corp.
Funkadelic, Parliament- (pop music)
Funky Winkerbean (comic strip)
Funny Girl (play)
Funt, Allen (ent.; 1914-)
Furies (also the Erinyes)(myth.)
Furillo, Carl (baseball; 1922-89)
Furness, Betty (Elizabeth)(US ent./consumer
     activist)
Furniss, Bruce (swimming; 1957-)
Furstenberg, Diane von (US bus.)
Furstenberg Importing Co., Diane von
Futuna Islands, Wallis and (SW Pac.)
Futura (type style)
Future Farmers of America (FFA)
Futurism (art./lit. movement; 1909-14)
Futurist
Fuzzbuster™
Fuzzy Zoeller (golf)
F(riedrich) W(ilhelm Plumpe) Murnau (Ger.
     ent.; 1889-1931)
F. W. Woolworth Co.
FYA (for your attention)
FYI (for your information)
Fyodor Dostoyevsky (or Dostoevsky)(Rus.
     writer; 1821-81)

#

GA (Georgia)

Ga (chem. sym., gallium)

Ga (people)

Ga-Adangme (lang.)

Gaafar Muhammad al-Nimeiry (ex-pres., Sudan; 1930-)

Gabby (George) Hayes (ent.; 1885-1969)

Gabel, Martin

Gabelsberger, Franz Xaver (Ger. stenographer; 1789-1849)

Gable, (William) Clark (ent.; 1901-60)

Gable, Dan (wrestling; 1945-)

Gabler, Hedda (H. Ibsen play)

Gabo, Naum (b. Naum Pevsner)(US sculptor; 1890-1977)

Gabon (Gabonese Republic)(central Afr.)

Gabor, Dennis (Br. inv., holography; 1900-70)

Gabor, Eva (ent.; 1921-)

Gabor, Zsa Zsa (ent.; ?-)

Gaborone, Botswana

Gabriel (rel., archangel)

Gabriel D(aniel) Fahrenheit (Ger. physt.; 1686-1736)

Gabriel Fauré (Fr. comp.; 1845-1924)

Gabriel Kaplan

Gabriel, Jacques Ange (Fr. arch.; 1689?-1782)

Gabriel, John (ent.; 1931-)

Gabriel, Peter (ent.; 1950-)

Gabriel, Roman (football; 1940-)

Gabriela Mistral (aka Lucilla Godoy de Alcayaga)(Chilean poet; 1889-1957)

Gabriela Sabatini (tennis)

Gabriele D'Annunzio (It. writer; 1863-1938)

Gabrielle Chanel ("Coco")(Fr. designer; 1883-1971)

Gad (rel.)

Gaddafi (or Khadafy, Khaddhafi, Qaddafi), Moammar (or Moamer al, Muammar al)(pres., Libya; 1942-)

Gaddis, William (US writer; 1922-)

Gadsden Purchase (AZ/NM; 1853)

Gadsden, AL

Gadsden, James (US mil./dipl.; 1788-1858)

Gaea (also Ge)(myth.)

Gaelic (lang.)

Gaetano Donizetti (It. comp.; 1797-1848)

Gagarin, Yuri A(lexeyevich)(cosmo.; 1st to orbit earth; 1934-68)

Gage, Thomas (Br. gen./colonial gov.; 1721-87)

Gagik Arutyunyan (VP, Armenia)

Gahan Wilson (US cartoonist; 1930-)

Gail Godwin (US writer; 1937-)

Gail Goodrich (basketball; 1943-)

Gail Hamilton (aka Mary Abigail Dodge)(US writer; 1833-96)

Gail Russell (ent.; 1924-61)

Gail Sheehy (US writer)

Gail, Max (ent.; 1943-)

Gaillard Cut (section of Panama Canal)

Gaillard, David Du Bose (US mil./eng.; 1859-1913)

Gaillard, Slim

Gaines, William M. (US publ.; 1922-92)

Gainesville Sun (FL newspaper)

Gainesville, FL, GA, TX, VA

Gainsborough, Thomas (Br. artist; 1727-88)

Gaitskell, Hugh (Br. pol.; 1906-63)

Gaius (also Caius)(Roman jurist; 2nd c. AD)

Gaius (or Gnaeus) Marcius Coriolanus (Roman hero; 5th c)

Gaius Caesar (aka Caligula)(Roman emp.; AD 12-41)

Gaius Cassius Longinus (Roman leader, conspired against Caesar; ?-42 BC)

Gaius Julius Caesar Octavius (aka Caesar Augustus)(1st Roman emp.; 63 BC-AD 14)

Gaius Lucilius (Roman poet; c180-c102 BC)

Gaius Petronius ("Arbiter Elegantiae")(Roman writer; ?-AD 66)

Gaius, St. (also Caius)(pope; ?-296)

Galactica, Battlestar (film; 1979)

Galahad, Sir (Arthurian knight)

Galanos, James (US designer; 1925-)

Galápagos Islands (also Archipiélago de Colón)(Pac.)

Galatea (Pygmalion's statue)(myth.)

Galati, Romania

Galatians (rel.)

Galbraith, John Kenneth (US/Can. econ.; 1908-)

Gale Gordon (ent.; 1906-)

Gale Sayers (football; 1943-)

Gale Storm (ent.; 1922-)

Gale, Zona (US writer; 1874-1938)

Galeazzo Ciano (It. pol.; 1903-44)

Galeazzo Maria Sforza (It. pol.; 1444-76)

Galen (Gr. phys./writer; c129-199)

Galicia (region, Sp.)

Galician (lang./people)

Galilean satellites (astron.)

Galilean telescope (astron.)

Galilee (region, Isr.)

Galilee, Man of (Jesus)

Galilee, Sea of (also Lake Tiberias)(Isr.)

Galilei, Galileo (It. astron./physt./math.; 1564-1642)

Galileo (US uncrewed space probe)

Galileo Ferraris (It. physt./eng.; 1847-97)

Galileo Galilei (It. astron./physt./nath.; 1564-1642)

Galla (lang./people)

Gallagher™ (clothing)

Gallagher & (Al) Shean, (Ed)(ent.)

Gallagher, Ed (ent.)
Gallagher, Michael Donald (skiing; 1941-)
Gallatin, Albert (US pol.; 1761-1849)
Gallaudet, Thomas (Hopkins)(US educ. for the deaf; 1787-1851)
Gallaudet, Thomas (US rel./educ. for the deaf; 1822-1902)
Galle, Sri Lanka
Gallery Magazine
Galliano™ (liqueur)
Gallic Wars
Gallico, Paul (William)(US writer; 1897-1976)
Gallienne, Eva Le (ent.; 1899-91)
Gallienne, Richard Le (US/Br. writer; 1866-1947)
Gallo™
Gallo Winery, E & J (US bus.)
Gallo, Ernest (US winemaker)
Gallo, Julio (US winemaker; 1910-93)
Gallo, Robert Charles (US scien.; 1937-)
Galloping Gourmet (aka Graham Kerr)(US chef)
Galloway (district, SW Scot.)
Galloway cattle
Gallup poll
Gallup, George (Horace)(US jour./statistician; 1901-84)
Gallup, NM
Galoob™ (toys)
Galoob, Inc., Lewis
Galsworthy, John (Br. writer; 1867-1933)
Galt, John (fict. chara.; *Atlas Shrugged*)
Galt, John (Scot. writer; 1779-1839)
Galtieri, Leopoldo (ex-pres., Argentina; 1926-)
Galvani, Luigi (It. phys./physt.; 1737-98)
Galveston, TX
Galway (county, Ir.)
Galway, James (Ir./US ent.; 1939-)
Gama, Vasco da (Port. nav.; c1460-1524)
Gamal Abdel Nasser (ex-pres., Eq.; 1918-70)
Gamay (wine, grape)
Gambetta, Léon (Fr. pol.; 1838-82)
Gambia (Republic of)(W Afr.)
Gambia River (W Afr.)
Gamble Co., Procter &
Gambling Times
Game (chicken)
Game Show Channel, The (cable TV)
Gammelost (cheese)
Gamsakhurdia, Zviad (ex-pres., Georgia)
Gan (lang.)
Ganda (also Luganda)(lang.)
Gandhi, Indira (b. Nehru)(ex-PM, India; 1917-84)
Gandhi, Mahatma (Mohandas Karamchand)(Indian pol./pacifist; 1869-1948)
Gandhi, Rajiv (ex-PM, India; 1944-91)
Ganesha (myth.)

Ganges River (also Ganga)(India/Bangladesh)
Ganic, Ejup (VP, Bosnia-Hercegovina)
Ganilau, Ratu Sir Penaia (pres., Fiji; 1918-)
Gann, Paul (US reformer; 1912-89)
Gannett Co., Inc.
Gannett, Frank Ernest (US publ.; 1876-?)
Gansu (also Kansu)(province, Ch.)
Gant, Ron (baseball; 1965-)
Gantry, Elmer (S. Lewis novel)
Ganymede (Jupiter moon; myth.)
GAO (Government Accounting Office)
Gap Stores, Inc., The
Gaposchkin, Cecilia Helena Payne- (Br./US astron.; 1900-79)
Garagiola, Joe (ent.; 1926-)
Garamond (type style)
Garamond, Claude (Fr. typographer; c1480-1561)
Garand (or M-1) rifle (semiautomatic)
Garbage (mag.)
Garbo, Greta (b. Greta Lovisa Gustafsson)(ent.; 1905-90)
Garcia v. San Antonio Metropolitan Transit Authority (US law; 1985)
Garcia, Andy (ent.; 1956-)
Garden Design (mag.)
Garden Grove, CA
Garden of Earthly Delights (by Bosch)
Garden of Eden (also Paradise)(rel.)
Garden of Gethsemane (rel.)
Garden of Irem (myth.)
Garden State (NJ)
Garden, The Victory (TV show)
Gardena, CA
Gardenia, Vincent (ent.; 1921-92)
Gardiner, Reginald
Gardner, Ava (ent.; 1922-90)
Gardner, Erle Stanley (US writer; 1889-1970)
Garfield (comic strip)
Garfield, James A(bram)(20th US pres.; 1831-81)
Garfield, John (ent.; 1913-52)
Garfunkel, Art (ent.; 1942-)
Garfunkel, Simon and (pop music)
Gargantua (F. Rabelais satire)
Gargas, William C. (US phys.; 1854-1920)
Garibaldi, Giuseppe (aka Peppino)(It. mil.; 1879-1950)
Garibaldi, Giuseppe (It. mil.; 1807-82)
Garland, Beverly (ent.; 1926-)
Garland, Judy (b. Frances Gumm)(ent.; 1922-69)
Garland, Red (US jazz; 1923-1984)
Garland, TX
Garms, Debs (baseball; 1908-84)
Garner, Erroll (US jazz; 1921-77)
Garner, James (ent.; 1928-)
Garner, John Nance (ex-US VP; 1868-1967)

Garnet Hill, Inc.
Garoua, Cameroon
Garp, The World According to (J. Irving novel)
Garr, Teri (ent.; 1945-)
Garret A(ugustus) Hobart (ex-US VP; 1844-99)
Garrett, Betty (ent.; 1919-)
Garrett, Pat(rick Floyd), Sheriff (US sheriff, shot "Billy the Kid"; 1850-1908)
Garrick Utley
Garrick, David (ent.; 1717-79)
Garriott, Owen K. (US physt./astro.; 1930-)
Garrison Keillor (US humorist/writer; 1942-)
Garrison, Jim (US atty.; 1922-92)
Garrison, William Lloyd (US reformer; 1805-79)
Garrison, Zina
Garroway, Dave (TV host)
Garry Moore (ent.; 1915-93)
Garry Shandling (ent.; 1949-)
Garry Trudeau (Can./US cartoonist, *Doonesbury*; 1948-)
Garson, Greer (ent.; 1908-)
Garter, Order of the (Br., knighthood)
Garth Brooks (ent.; 1956-)
Garuda Indonesia Airways (airline)
Garvey, Marcus (Jamaican/US reformer; 1887-1940)
Garvey, Steve (baseball; 1948-)
Gary "U.S." Bonds (ent.)
Gary Burghoff (ent.; 1940-)
Gary Busey (ent.; 1944-)
Gary Cole (ent.; 1957-)
Gary Coleman (ent.; 1968-)
Gary Cooper (ent.; 1901-62)
Gary Francis Powers (US mil.)
Gary Hall (swimming; 1951-)
Gary (or Garry) Kasparov (Rus., chess; 1963-)
Gary Larson (US cartoonist, *The Far Side*; 1950-)
Gary Morton
Gary Player (golf; 1935-)
Gary Post-Tribune (IN newspaper)
Gary Puckett and the Union Gap (pop music)
Gary Sandy (ent.; 1945-)
Gary, Elbert H. (US bus.; 1846-1927)
Gary, IN
Gascony (region, Fr.)
Gasoline Alley (comic strip)
Gasperi, Alcide De (It. pol.; 1881-1954)
Gasset, Jose Ortega y (Sp. phil.; 1883-1955)
Gassman, Vittorio (ent.; 1922-)
Gaston Caperton (WV gov.; 1940-)
Gaston Lachaise (US sculptor; 1882-1935)
Gastonia, NC
Gas-X™ (med.)
Gates of Paradise (by Ghiberti)
Gates of the Artic National Park (AK)
Gates Rubber Co., The
Gates, Bill (US bus.)

Gates, Daryl F. (US news)
Gates, Horatio (US gen.; 1728-1806)
Gates, Robert M. (CIA Director; 1943-)
Gateway Bookstore (US bus.)
Gatlin Brothers, The (pop music)
Gatlin, Larry (ent.; 1948-)
Gatling gun (early machine gun)
Gatling, Richard (Jordan)(US inv.; 1818-1903)
Gator Bowl (college football)
Gatorade™
Gatsby, Jay (fict. chara., *The Great Gatsby*)
Gatsby, The Great (F.S. Fitzgerald novel)
GATT (General Agreement on Tariffs and Trade)(UN org.)
Gauche, Rive (also Left Bank)(Paris)
Gaudí, Antonio (Sp. arch.; 1852-1926)
Gauguin, (Eugène Henri) Paul (Fr. artist; 1848-1903)
Gaul (ancient Fr./Belgium, people)
Gaulle, Charles de (ex-pres., Fr.; 1890-1970)
Gault, In re (US law; 1967)
Gault, Willie (football; 1960-)
Gaunt, John of (Br. pol.; 1340-99)
Gauss, Carl (or Karl) Friedrich (Ger. math.; 1777-1855)
Gaussian curve (also normal curve, probability curve)(a bell curve)
Gaussian distribution (also normal distribution)
Gaussian image (also Gaussian image point)
Gaussian integer
Gautama (Buddha) Siddhartha (Indian phil., founded Buddhism; c563-c483 BC)
Gavin MacLeod (ent.; 1930-)
Gaviria Trujilo, César (pres., Colombia; 1947-)
Gawain, Sir (Arthurian knight)
Gay, John (Br. writer; 1685-1732)
Gay-Lussac, Joseph (Louis)(Fr. chem./physt.; 1778-1850)
Gay-Lussac's law (also Charles' law)(thermodynamics)
Gaye, Marvin (ent.; 1939-84)
Gayle, Crystal (ent.; 1951-)
Gaylord Perry (baseball; 1938-)
Gaynor, Janet (ent.; 1906-84)
Gaynor, Mitzi (ent.; 1930-)
Gayoom, (Maumoon) Abdul (pres., Maldives)
Gaza Strip (on Mediterranean Sea)(occupied by Isr.; 1967)
Gazette Journal, Reno (NV newspaper)
Gazette-Mail, Charleston (WV newspaper)
Gazette Post, Cedar Rapids (IA newspaper)
Gazette Telegraph, Colorado Springs (CO newspaper)
Gazette, Charleston (WV newspaper)
Gazette, Kalamazoo (MI newspaper)
Gazette, Phoenix (AZ newspaper)
Gazette, Texarkana (AR newspaper)
Gazzara, Ben (ent.; 1930-)

GD (Great Britain)
GCT (Greenwich Conservatory Time)
Gd (chem. sym., gadolinium)
Gdansk, Poland (also Danzig)
Gdynia, Poland
Ge (also Gaea)(myth.)
Ge (chem. sym., germanium)
Geary, Anthony
Geb (rel.)
Gebaur Air Force Base, Richards- (MO)
Gebel-Williams, Gunther
Gebhard von Blücher (Ger. gen.; 1742-1819)
GED (general equivalency diploma [high
    school])
Geddes, Barbara Bel (ent.; 1922-)
Geddes, Norman Bel (US designer; 1893-1958)
Geena Davis (ent.; 1957-)
Geer, Will (ent.; 1902-78)
Gehenna (hell)
Gehrig, (Henry) Lou(is)(baseball; 1903-41)
Gehrig's disease, Lou (med.)
Gehringer, Charlie (baseball; 1903-)
GEICO Corp.
Geidar Aliyev (pres., Azerbaijan)
Geiger(-Müller) counter (detects radiation)
Geiger(-Müller) tube
Geiger, Hans (Ger. physt.; 1882-1945)
Geingob, Hage (PM, Namibia)
Geisel, Theodore Seuss (pseud. Dr. Seuss)(US
    writer/artist; 1904-91)
Geissler pump (air pump)
Geissler tube (elect.)
Geissler, Heinrich (Ger. inv./glassblower; 1814-
    79)
Gelderland (also Guelders)(province,
    Netherlands)
Geldof, Bob (ent.; 1954-)
Gell-Mann, Murray (US physt.; 1929-)
Geller, Uri
Gellius, Aulus (Latin writer; c130-c165)
Gelsenkirchen, Germany
Gelsey Kirkland (ent.; 1953-)
Gem State (nickname, ID)
Gemayel, Amin (ex-pres., Lebanon; 1942-)
Gemeinschaft and Gesellschaft (Ger.,
    community and association)
Gemini (A. Innaurato play)
Gemini (US crewed space flights)
Gemini (zodiac; astron., twins)
Gemini-Titan (US crewed space flights)
Geminids (also Geminid)(meteor shower,
    c December 13)
Gemütlichkeit (also Gemuetlichkeit)(Ger., good-
    natured)
Gena Rowlands (ent.; 1934-)
Gencorp (US bus.)
Gene Autry (ent.; 1907-)
Gene Barry (ent.; 1919-)

Gene Hackman (ent.; 1930-)
Gene Kelly (ent.; 1912-)
Gene Krupa (US jazz; 1909-73)
Gene Littler (golf; 1930-)
Gene Lockhart (ent.; 1891-1957)
Gene Raymond (ent.; 1908-)
Gene (Eugene Wesley) Roddenberry (writer/
    producer, *Star Trek*; 1921-91)
Gene Saks (ent.; 1921-)
Gene Sarazen (golf; 1902)
Gene Shalit (US critic)
Gene Simmons (ent.; 1949-)
Gene Siskel (US critic; 1946-)
Gene Tierney (ent.; 1920-91)
Gene Tunney (b. James Joseph Tunney)(boxing;
    1898-1978)
Gene Vincent (ent.; 1935-71)
Gene Wilder (ent.; 1935-)
General Accounting Office (GAO)(US govt.)
General Agreement on Tariffs and Trade
    (GATT)(UN org.)
General Assembly (UN)
General Binding Corp. (GBC)
General Cinema Corp.
General Dynamics Corp.
General Electric Co.
General Foods™
General Foods™ International Coffees
General Foods USA (US bus.)
General Hospital (TV soap)
General Mills™
General Mills, Inc.
General Motors™
General Motors Corp. (GM Corp.)
General Nutrition Corp. (GNC)
General Tire™
General Tire, Inc.
Generra™
Generra Sportswear (US bus.)
Genesco, Inc.
Genesis (pop music)
Genesis (rel., 1st book of the Bible)
Genet, Jean (Fr. writer; 1911-86)
Geneva bands (clerical neckwear)
Geneva Conference (US/Br./Jap.; 1927)
Geneva Convention(s)(treatment of war
    wounded and POWs; 1864, 1868, 1906, 1929,
    1949, 1977)
Geneva gown (clerical wear)
Geneva Protocol (arbitration of internat'l
    disputes; 1924)(agreement to prohibit
    chemical warfare; 1974)
Geneva, AL, IL, NY, OH)
Geneva, Lake of (also Lake Leman)(Switz./Fr.)
Geneva, Switzerland
Genevieve Bujold (ent.; 1942-)
Genghis Khan (also Jenghiz, Chinghiz Khan,
    Temujin)(Mongol conqueror; c1167-1227)

GEnie (compu. database)
Genie™ remote control
Genie Co., The
Genji (also Minamoto)(Jap. hist.; 1192-1219)
Genoa salami
Genoa, Italy
Genovese, Vito (US Mafia; 1898-1969)
Genscher, Hans-Dietrich (Ger. pol.; 1927-)
Gentile Bellini (It. artist; 1426-1507)
Gentile, Giovanni (It. phil./educ.; 1875-1944)
Gentleman Jim (James) Corbett (boxing; 1866-
1933)
Geo™, Chevrolet (auto.)
Geo Metro™, Chevrolet (auto.)
Geo Prizm™, Chevrolet (auto.)
Geo Tracker™, Chevrolet (auto.)
Geoffrey Beene (US designer; 1927-)
Geoffrey Chaucer (Br. poet; c 1340-1400)
Geoffrey of Monmouth (Br. writer/chronicler;
c1100-54)
Geoffrion, Boom Boom (Bernie)(hockey; 1931-)
Geographic Society, National (est. 1888)
Geological Survey, U.S. (US agcy.)
Georg (Simon) Ohm (Ger. physt.; 1789-1854)
Georg Philipp Telemann (Ger. comp.; 1681-
1767)
Georg Solti, Sir (Br. cond.; 1912-)
Georg W(ilhelm Friedrich) Hegel (Ger. phil.;
1770-1831)
George Abbott (ent.; 1889-?)
George A(rmstrong) Custer (US gen., Little
Bighorn; 1839-76)
George Ade (US writer/humorist; 1866-1944)
George A. Hormel & Co.
George Air Force Base, CA (mil.)
George Allen (football; 1918-90)
George Arliss (ent.; 1868-1946)
George Baker (cartoonist, *The Sad Sack*; 1915-
75)
George Balanchine (US choreographer; 1904-
83)
George Bancroft (ent.; 1882-1956)
George Bancroft (US hist.; 1800-91)
George Benson (ent.; 1943-)
George Berkeley (Ir. phil.; 1685-1753)
George Bernard Shaw (Ir. writer/critic; 1856-
1950)
George (Frederick) Blanda (football; 1927-)
George B(rinton) McClellan (US gen.; 1826-85)
George Boole (Br. math.; 1815-64)
George Booth (cartoonist, *New Yorker*; 1926-)
George Brent (ent.; 1904-79)
George Brett (baseball; 1953-)
George Browne Post (US arch.; 1837-1913)
George Burns (b. Nathan Birnbaum)(ent.;
1896-)
George Caleb Bingham (US artist; 1811-79)
George Calvert, Sir (aka Lord

Baltimore)(founded MD; 1606-75)
George Carlin (ent.; 1937-)
George Catlin (US artist; 1796-1872)
George Clinton (ex-US VP; 1739-1812)
George C(atlett) Marshall (US gen.; 1880-1959)
George C(ampbell) Scott (ent.; 1927-)
George Cosmas Adyebo (PM, Uganda)
George C(orley) Wallace (ex-gov., AL; 1919-)
George Cruikshank (Br. artist; 1792-1878)
George Cukor (ent.; 1899-1983)
George Deukmejian (ex-gov., CA; 1928-)
George Dewey (US adm.; 1837-1917)
George Eastman (US inv./photo.; 1854-1932)
George Eliot (aka Mary Ann [or Marian]
Evans)(Br. writer; 1819-80)
George E. Moore (Br. phil.; 1873-1958)
George E(dward) Pickett (US gen.; 1825-75)
George F. Allen (VA gov.)
George F(ollansbee) Babbitt (fict. chara.)
George Fenneman
George Foot Moore (US rel.; 1851-1931)
George Foreman (boxing; 1948-)
George Foster Peabody Radio and Television
Awards
George Fox (Br. rel.; 1624-91)
George Frederic Watts (Br. artist; 1817-1904)
George Frederick (also Georg Friedrich) Handel
(Ger./Br. comp.; 1685-1759)
George (Horace) Gallup (US jour./statistician;
1901-84)
George Gaylord Simpson (US paleontol.; 1902-
84)
George Gershwin (US comp.; 1898-1937)
George Gervin (basketball; 1952-)
George Gobel (ent.; 1921-91)
George Gordon Byron, Lord (Br. poet; 1788-
1824)
George Grenville (ex-PM, Br.; 1712-70)
George Grizzard (ent.; 1928-)
George (Stanley) Halas (football; 1895-1983)
George Hamilton (ent.; 1939-)
George Harrison (ent.; 1943-)
George Hearn (ent.; 1935-)
George Hepplewhite (Br. furniture designer; ?-
1786)
George Herbert Walker Bush (41st US pres.;
1924-)
George Herman "Babe" Ruth (baseball; 1895-
1948)
George Herriman (US cartoonist, *Krazy Kat*;
1881-1944)
George H. Meade (US phil.; 1863-1931)
George H(enry) Thomas (US mil.; 1816-70)
George I (Christian William Ferdinand
Adolphus George)(king, Gr.; 1845-1913)
George I (George Louis)(king, Br./Ir.; 1660-
1727)
George II (George Augustus)(king, Br.; 1683-

1760)

George II (king, Gr.; 1890-1947)

George III (George William Frederick)(king, Br./Ir.; 1738-1820)

George Inness (US artist; 1825-94)

George IV (George Augustus Frederick)(king, Br./Ir.; 1762-1830)

George Jean Nathan (US writer; 1882-1958)

George Jessel (ent.; 1898-1981)

George J. Mitchell (US cong.; 1933-)

George Jones (ent.; 1931-)

George Kennedy (ent.; 1925-)

George Lepping (gov-gen.; Solomon Islands)

George L. Murphy, (US ent./pol.; 1902-92)

George (Benjamin) Luks (US artist; 1867-1933)

George Macaulay Trevelyan (Br. hist.; 1876-1962)

George Macready (ent.; 1909-73)

George Mason (US pol.; 1725-92)

George McManus (US cartoonist, *Bringing Up Father*; 1884-1954)

George M(ichael) Cohan (US comp; 1878-1942)

George M. Dallas (ex-US VP; 1792-1864)

George (Gordon) Meade (US gen.; 1815-72)

George Meany (US labor leader; 1894-1980)

George Meredith (Br. writer; 1828-1909)

George Michael (ent. 1963-)

George Mikan (basketball; 1924-)

George Monck (Duke of Albemarle)(Br. mil./pol.; 1608-70)

George Moore (Ir. writer; 1852-1933)

George "Bugs" Moran (gang killed in St. Valentine's Day massacre)

George Nathaniel Curzon (Marquis Kedleston of Curzon)(Br. leader in India; 1859-1925)

George Orwell (aka Eric A[rthur] Blair)(Br. writer; 1903-50)

George Papadopoulos (ex-pres., Gr.; 1919-)

George Papandreou (ex-PM, Gr.; 1888-1968)

George Peabody (US bus./finan.; 1795-1869)

George Peppard (ent.; 1928-94)

George Plimpton (US writer; 1927-)

George (Cadle) Price (ex-PM, Belize; 1919-)

George Price (US cartoonist, *New Yorker*; 1901-)

George P(ratt) Shultz (US pol. ; 1920-)

George Raft (ent.; 1895-1980)

George Reeves (ent.; 1914-59)

George Rogers Clark (US mil.; 1752-1818)

George Rogers Clark National Historical Park (IN)

George Romney (Br. artist; 1734-1802)

George Romney (US pol./bus.; 1907-)

George Roy Hill (ent.; 1922-)

George Russell (US jazz; 1923-)

George Saitoti (VP, Kenya)

George Sand (aka Amandine Aurore Lucie Dupin)(Fr. writer; 1804-76)

George Sanders (ent.; 1906-72)

George Santayana (Sp./US writer/phil.; 1863-1952)

George Schaefer

George Schlatter (ent.)

George Segal (ent.; 1934-)

George Segal (US sculptor; 1924-)

George Shearing (US jazz; 1919-)

George Simmel (Ger. sociol./phil.; 1858-1918)

George S. Irving (ent.; 1922-)

George (Harold) Sisler (baseball; 1893-1973)

George S(imon) Kaufman (US writer; 1889-1961)

George S(tanley) McGovern (US pol.; 1922-)

George S. Mickelson (ex-gov., SD; 1941-93)

George S(mith) Patton (US gen.; 1885-1945)

George (Michael) Steinbrenner, III (US bus./baseball; 1930-)

George Strait (ent.; 1952-)

George Stubbs (Br. artist; 1724-1806)

George Szell (US cond.; 1897-1970)

George Takei (ent.)

George T. Delacorte (US publ.; 1893-1991)

George Town, the Bahamas

George Townshend, Marquis (Br. mil.; 1724-1807)

George (Otto) Trevelyan, Sir (Br. hist.; 1838-1928)

George V (George Frederick Ernest Albert)(king, Br.; 1865-1936)

George Vassilou (ex-pres., Cyprus; 1931-)

George VI (Albert Frederick Arthur George)(king, Br.; 1895-1952)

George Voinovich (OH gov.; 1936-)

George Washington (1st US pres.; 1732-99)

George Washington Carver (US botanist/chem.; 1860?-1943)

George Washington Gale Ferris (US eng./inv.; 1859-96)

George Washington University (DC)

George W(ildman) Ball (US atty./banker/pol.; 1909-)

George Weiss (baseball exec.; 1895-1972)

George Wendt (ent.; 1948-)

George Wesley Bellows (US artist; 1882-1925)

George Westinghouse (US bus.; 1846-1914)

George W(ashington) Goethals (US mil./eng.; 1858-1928)

George Wilbur Peck (US writer; 1840-1916)

George Will (US jour.; 1941-)

George William Norris (US pol.; 1861-1944)

George W. Lucas, Jr. (ent.; 1944-)

George Wythe (US jurist; 1726-1806)

George, Boy (ent.; 1961-)

George, David Lloyd (ex-PM, Br.; 1863-1945)

George, St. (by Donatello)

George, St. (patron saint of Eng., legendary dragon slayer; ?-c303)

Georges Bizet (Fr. comp.; 1838-75)

Georges Braque (Fr. artist; 1882-1963)
Georges Clemenceau (ex-PM, Fr.; 1841-1929)
Georges Danton (Fr. mil.; 1759-94)
Georges Edouard Lemaître (Belgium astron.; 1894-1966)
Georges Enesco (or Enescu)(Romanian cond./ comp.; 1881-1955)
Georges (Jean Raymond) Pompidou (ex-pres., Fr.; 1911-74)
Georges (Henri) Rouault (Fr. artist; 1871-1958)
Georges Seurat (Fr. artist; 1859-91)
Georgetown (area in DC)
Georgetown University (DC)
Georgetown, Gambia
Georgetown, Guyana
Georgetown, KY, SC
Georgetown, Malaysia (also Penang)
Georgette crepe (fabric)
Georgi Dimitrov (ex-PM, Bulgaria; 1882-1949)
Georgi (Valentinovich) Plekhanov (Rus. phil., "Father of Russian Marxism"; 1857-1918)
Georgi S. Shonin (cosmo.)
Georgi (or Georgy) T. Beregovoi (cosmo.; 1921-)
Georgi (or Georgy) T. Dobrovolsky (cosmo.; 1928-71)
Georgi (Konstantinovich) Zhukov (USSR mil.; 1895-1974)
Georgia (GA)
Georgia (Republic of)(formerly part of the USSR)(SE Eur.)
Georgia O'Keeffe (US artist; 1887-1986)
Georgia on my Mind (song)
Georgia-Pacific Corp.
Georgia, Chisholm v. (US law; 1793)
Georgian (lang./people)
Georgian style (arch.)
Georgy Girl (film; 1966)
Gephardt, Richard A. (US cong.; 1941-)
Geradus (or Gerhardus) Mercator (aka Gerhard Kremer)(Flem. geographer; 1512-94)
Gerald Grosvenor
Gerald McRaney (ent.; 1948-)
Gerald P(aul) Carr (astro.; 1932-)
Gerald R(udolph) Ford (b. Leslie Lynch King, Jr.)(38th US pres.; 1913-)
Geraldine Chaplin (ent.; 1944-)
Geraldine Farrar (ent.; 1882-1967)
Geraldine Ferraro (US pol./1st major female VP candidate; 1935-)
Geraldine Fitzgerald (Ir./US ent.; 1913-)
Geraldine Page (ent.; 1924-87)
Geraldo (TV show)
Geraldo Rivera (ent.; 1943-)
Gerard Swope (US bus./econ.; 1872-1957)
Gerber™ (baby prods.)
Gerber Products Co.
Gere, Richard (ent.; 1949-)
Gergen, David (US pol.)

Gerhard Henrik Armauer Hansen (Nor. phys.; 1841-1912)
Gerhardus (or Geradus) Mercator (aka Gerhard Kremer)(Flem. geographer; 1512-94)
Geritol™
Germaine Greer (Austl. writer/feminist; 1939-)
German (lang./people)
German coach horse
German measles (rubella)
German shepherd (also Alsatian, German police dog)(dog)
German shorthaired pointer (dog)
German silver (silvery alloy of nickel/copper/ zinc)
German wirehaired pointer (dog)
Germanic languages
Germanic law
Germanic religion
Germanicus Caesar (Roman gen.; 15 BC-AD 19)
Germanophile
Germanophobe
Germantown (carriage)
Germany (Federal Republic of)(formerly East and West Germany)(Eur.)
Germiston, South Africa
Geronimo (Chiricahua Apache chief; 1829-1909)
Geronimo Amati (It. violin maker, father of Nicolo; 1556-1630)
Geronimo Amati (It. violin maker, son of Nicolo; 1649-1740)
Geronimo, OK
Gerry Cooney (boxing)
Gerry Goffin (US lyricist; 1939-)
Gerry Mulligan (US jazz; 1927-)
Gerry, Elbridge (ex-US VP, gerrymander; 1744-1814)
Gershwin, George (US comp.; 1898-1937)
Gershwin, Ira (US lyricist; 1896-1983)
Gertrude Atherton (Franklin Horn)(US writer; 1857-1948)
Gertrude Berg (ent.; 1899-1966)
Gertrude Ederle (swimmer; 1906-)
Gertrude Lawrence (ent.; 1898-1952)
Gertrude "Ma" Rainey (US jazz; 1886-1939)
Gertrude Stein (US writer; 1874-1946)
Gerulaitis, Vitas (tennis; 1954-)
Gervin, George (basketball; 1952-)
Gesamtkunstwerk (Ger., performing arts)
Gesell, Arnold Lucius (US psych./educ.; 1880-1961)
Gesellschaft, Gemeinschaft and (Ger., community, association)
Gestalt (Ger., unified whole)(usually l.c.)
Gestalt psychology/therapy (also l.c.)
Gestalt test, Bender (also Bender gestalt)(psych.)
Gestapo (Ger. Nazi secret police)
Geste, Beau (film; 1939)

Gesundheit (Ger., good health to you)(also l.c.)
Get Smart (TV show)
Gethsemane cheese (also Trappist cheese)
Gethsemane, Garden of (rel.)
Getty Petroleum Corp.
Getty, Estelle (ent.; 1924-)
Getty, J(ean) Paul (US bus.; 1892-1976)
Gettysburg Address (by Pres. Lincoln; 11/19/63)
Gettysburg military campaign
Gettysburg National Military Park (PA)
Gettysburg, Battle of (US hist.; 1863)
Gettysburg, PA
Getz, Stan(ley)(US jazz; 1927-91)
Gewürztraminer (wine)
Geyser Peak Winery (US bus.)
G-force (gravity force)
G. Gordon Liddy (US pol./Watergate)
Ghalib, Umar Arteh (ex-PM, Somalia)
Ghana (Republic of)(W Afr.)
Ghazali, al (Islamic phil.; 1058-1111)
Ghent Altarpiece (by J. van Eyck)
Ghent, Belgium
Ghent, Treaty of (US/Br.; 1814)
Gherman (or Herman) S(tepanovich) Titov
    (cosmo.; 1935-)
Ghibellines (It. pol.; 12th-15th c.)
Ghiberti, Lorenzo (It. sculptor; 1378-1455)
Ghirardelli™
Ghirardelli Chocolate Co.
Ghirardelli Square (San Francisco)
Ghost (film; 1992)
Ghost and Mrs. Muir, The (film; 1947)
Ghost Rider (cartoon chara.)
Ghostbusters (film; 1984)
Ghostbusters II (film)
Ghostley, Alice (ent.; 1926-)
Ghulam Ishaq Khan (ex-pres., Pak.)
GI (gastrointestinal, government issue)
GI Bill
GI Joe (US soldier)
Giacometti, Alberto (It. sculptor; 1901-66)
Giacomin, Ed (hockey; 1939-)
Giacomo Balla (It. artist; 1871?-1958)
Giacomo Meyerbeer (b. Jakob Liebmann
    Beer)(Ger. comp.; 1791-1864)
Giacomo (Antonio Domenico Michele Secondo
    Maria) Puccini (It. comp.; 1858-1924)
Giamatti, (Angelo) Bart(lett)(US educ./writer/
    baseball; 1938-89)
Giambattista Bodoni (It. printer/typographer;
    1740-1813)
Giancana, Sam "Momo" (US gangster; 1908-75)
Gian-Carlo Menotti (It./US comp.; 1911-)
Giannini, Amadeo P. (US, founded Bank of
    America; 1870-1949)
Giant Food, Inc.
Giants, New York (football team)
Giants, San Francisco (baseball team)

Gibb, Andy (ent.; 1958-88)
Gibbon, Edward (Br. hist.; 1737-94)
Gibbons v. Ogden (US law; 1924)
Gibbons, Euell
Gibbons, Leeza (ent.)
Gibbons, Orlando (Br. comp.; 1583-1625)
Gibbs free energy (also Gibbs function,
    thermodynamic potential)
Gibbs, Josiah W(illard)(US physt./chem.; 1839-
    1903)
Gibbs, Marla (ent.; 1931-)
Gibraltar (Br. dependency, S Sp.)
Gibraltar, Rock of (S coast Sp.)
Gibralter, Strait of (NAfr./Sp.)
Gibran, Kahlil (Lebanese writer/mystic/artist;
    1883-1931)
Gibson (cocktail)
Gibson girl
Gibson, Althea (tennis; 1927-)
Gibson, Bob (baseball; 1935-)
Gibson, Charles Dana (US artist; 1867-1944)
Gibson, Debbie (ent.; 1970-)
Gibson, Edward G. (astro.)
Gibson, Henry (ent.; 1935-)
Gibson, Hoot (ent.; 1892-1962)
Gibson, Kirk
Gibson, Mel (ent.; 1956-)
Gide, André (Fr. writer; 1869-1951)
Gideon(s) Bible
Gideon v. Wainwright (US law; 1963)
Gideon Welles (US pol./jour.; 1802-78)
Gideons International, The
Gidget (film; 1959)
Gielgud, Sir (Arthur) John (ent.; 1904-)
Giffard, Henri (Fr. inv.; 1825-82)
Gifford, Frank (ent./football; 1930-)
Gifford, Kathie Lee (ent.)
Gig Young (ent.; 1913-78)
Gigantes (myth.)
Gigi (film; 1958)
GIGO (garbage in, garbage out)
Gil Evans (US jazz; 1912-88)
Gil Hodges (baseball; 1924-72)
Gil Lamb (ent.; 1906-)
Gila monster (poisonous lizard)
Gilaki (lang.)
Gilbert & Sullivan (created comic operas)
Gilbert (Hovey) Grosvenor (US geographer/
    writer/editor; 1875-1966)
Gilbert Islands (now Kiribati)(central Pac.)
Gilbert M. Grosvenor (US publ.)
Gilbert Roland (ent.; 1905-)
Gilbert (Charles) Stuart (US artist; 1755-1828)
Gilbert, Cass (US arch.; 1859-1934)
Gilbert, Melissa (ent.; 1964-)
Gilbert, Rod(rique)(hockey; 1941-)
Gilbert, Sir William (Br. physt./phys.; 1540-
    1603)

Gilbert, Sir W(illiam) S(chwenck)(Br. writer; 1836-1911)
Gilbertese (lang.)
Gilbey's International (US bus.)
Gilda Marx™
Gilda Marx Swimwear (US bus.)
Gilda Radner (ent.; 1946-89)
Giles system, Wade- (Eng. representation of Ch.)
Giles, Warren (baseball exec.; 1896-1979)
Gilgamesh (myth.)
Gilgamesh, Epic of (myth.)
Gillern, Fort (GA)(mil.)
Gillespie, Dizzy (John Birks)(US jazz; 1917-93)
Gillette™
Gillette Co., The
Gillette, Anita (ent.; 1938-)
Gillette, King Camp (US bus., razor; 1855-1932)
Gilley, Mickey (ent.; 1936-)
Gilligan's Island (TV show)
Gillikins, Country of the
Gillis, Dobie (fict. chara.)
Gillooly, Jeff (US news)
Gilmore, Artis (basketball; 1949-)
Gilroy, Frank (US writer; 1925-)
Gimbel, Bernard (US bus.; 1885-1966)
Gimbel, Inc., J.
Gina Lollobrigida (It. ent.; 1927-)
Ginger Rogers (ent.; 1911-)
Gingold, Hermione (ent.; 1897-1987)
Gingrich, Newt(on Leroy)(US cong.; 1943-)
Ginnie Mae (also Government National Mortgage Association, GNMA)
Gino Cappelletti (football; 1934-)
Gino Severini (It. artist; 1883-1966)
Ginsberg, Allen (US poet; 1926?-)
Ginsburg, Ruth Bader (US jurist; 1933-)
Ginty, Robert (ent.; 1948-)
Ginza (district, Tokyo)
Gioacchino (Antonio) Rossini (It comp.; 1792-1868)
Gioconda, La (aka *Mona Lisa*)(da Vinci painting)
Giordano Bruno (It. phil.; 1548-1600)
Giordano, Umberto (It. comp.; 1867-1948)
Giorgio Armani (designer)
Giorgio Beverly Hills™
Giorgio Beverly Hills (US bus.)
Giorgio Chinaglia (soccer; 1947-)
Giorgio de Chirico (It. artist; 1888-1978)
Giorgio di Sant'Angelo
Giorgione (del Castelfranco)(It. artist; c1475-1510)
Giotto (di Bondone)(It. artist; 1267-1337)
Giotto (space probe)
Giovanni Battista Tiepolo (It. artist; 1696-1770)
Giovanni Bellini (It. artist; 1426-1516)
Giovanni Boccaccio (It. writer; 1313-75)

Giovanni Caboto (also John Cabot)(It. nav.; 1450-98)
Giovanni Cimabue (It. artist; 1240-1302)
Giovanni Domenico Cassini (It./Fr. astron.; 1625-1712)
Giovanni Gentile (It. phil./educ.; 1875-1944)
Giovanni Jacopo Casanova (also Casanova de Seingalt)(It. adventurer; 1725-98)
Giovanni Lorenzo Bernini (It. sculptor; 1598-1680)
Giovanni P(ierluigi) da Palestrina (It. comp.; c1525-94)
Giovanni Pisano (It. artist; c1250-c1314)
Giovanni (Virginio) Schiaparelli (It. astron.; 1835-1910)
Giovanni (Battista) Vico (It. hist./phil.; 1668-1744)
Giovanni, Don (by Mozart)
Giovanni, Don (Don Juan)(Sp. legend)
Girard, Stephen (US finan.; 1750-1831)
Girardon, Francois (Fr. sculptor; 1628-1715)
Giraudoux, Jean (Fr. writer/dipl.; 1882-1944)
Girija Prasad Koirala (PM, Nepal; 1925-)
Girl Guides (Br.)
Girl Scouts (US)
girl/man Friday
Girolamo Savonarola (It. rel./reformer; 1452-98)
Girondin (also Girondist)(Fr. hist.)
Giscard d'Estaing, Valéry (ex-pres., Fr.; 1926-)
Gisele MacKenzie (ent.)
Giselle (Coralli, Perrot, Adam ballet)
Gish, Dorothy (ent.; 1898-1968)
Gish, Lillian (ent.; 1895-1993)
Gita (also Bhagavad-Gita)(rel.)
Gitano™
Gitano, E. J. (US bus.)
Gitega, Burundi
Gitlow v. New York (US law; 1925-)
Giuliani, Rudolph W. (NYC mayor)
Guiliano Amato, (ex-PM, Italy; 1938-)
Giuseppe (Tomasi) di Lampedusa, (It. writer; 1896-1957)
Giuseppe Garibaldi (aka Peppino)(It. mil.; 1879-1950)
Giussepe Mazzini (It. reformer; 1805-72)
Giuseppe (Fortunino Francesco) Verdi (It. comp.; 1813-1901)
Givenchy, Hubert de (Fr. designer; 1927-)
Givens, Robin (ent.; 1964-)
Giverny, France
Gîza, Egypt (also El Gîza or Al Jizah)
Gîza, Great Pyramids of (also El Gîza or Al Jizah)(Eg.)
Gjetost (cheese)
Glace Bay, Nova Scotia, Canada
Glacier Bay National Park (AK)
Glacier National Park (MT)
Glackens, William (James)(US artist; 1870-

1938)
Glad™ Cling Wrap
Glad-Lock™ (plastic bags)
Gladsheim (myth.)
Gladstone bag (luggage)
Gladstone, William E(wart)(ex-PM, Br.; 1809-98)
Gladys Knight (ent.; 1944-)
Gladys Knight & the Pips (pop music)
Gladys Swarthout (US opera; 1904-69)
Glafcos Clerides (pres., Cyprus; 1919-)
Glamour (mag.)
Glance, Harvey (track; 1957-)
Glaser, Paul Michael (ent.; 1942-)
Glasgow, Scotland
Glass Menagerie, The (T. Williams play)
Glass Plus™ (cleaner)
Glass, Ron (ent.)
Glastonbury chair
Glastonbury, England
Glauber's salt (med.)
Glavine, Tom (baseball; 1966-)
Glazunov, Alexander (or Aleksandr) Konstantinovich (Rus. comp.; 1865-1936)
Gleason, Jackie (Herbert John)(ent.; 1916-87)
Gleason, James (ent.; 1886-1959)
Gleem™ (toothpaste)
Gleizes, Albert (Léon)(Fr. artist; 1881-1953)
Glen Campbell (ent.; 1936-)
Glen Canyon Dam (AZ)
Glen Ellen Winery (US bus.)
Glen Theater, Barns v. (US law; 1991)
Glenda Jackson (ent.; 1936-)
Glendale, AZ, CA
Glenlivet™ scotch
Glenn Close (ent.; 1947-)
Glenn Ford (ent.; 1916-)
Glenn (Herbert) Gould (Can. comp.; 1932-82)
Glenn Hammond Curtiss (US aviator/inv.; 1878-1930)
Glenn Miller (US jazz; 1904-44)
Glenn Miller Story, The (film; 1954)
Glenn T(heodore) Seaborg, Dr. (US chem./chair, AEC; 1912-)
Glenn Yarborough (ent.; 1930-)
Glenn, John H(erschel), Jr. (US cong./astro.; 1921-)
Glenn, Scott (ent.; 1942-)
Glenview Naval Air Station (IL)
Gless, Sharon (ent.; 1943-)
Glidden™ paint
Glidden Co., The
Gligorov, Kiro (pres., Macedonia)
Glinka, Mikhail Ivanovitch (Rus. comp.; 1804-57)
Globe (mag.)
Globe & Mail, Toronto (Can. newspaper)
Globe Theatre (London, Shakespeare; fl. 16th-17th c.)
Globe, Boston (MA newspaper)
Globe-Times, Amarillo (TX newspaper)
Globetrotters, Harlem (basketball team; founded 1927)
Gloria Blondell (ent.)
Gloria DeHaven (ent.; 1925-)
Gloria Estefan (ent.; 1958-)
Gloria Grahame (ent.; 1925-81)
Gloria in Excelsis Deo (also great[er] doxology)(rel.)
Gloria Loring (ent.; 1946-)
Gloria Marshall Figure Salon (US bus.)
Gloria Steinem (US jour./feminist; 1934-)
Gloria Swanson (ent.; 1899-1983)
Gloria Vanderbilt™ (perfume/clothing)
Gloria Vanderbilt (US bus.)
Glorious Revolution (also English [or Bloodless] Revolution)(Br. hist.; 1688-89)
Gloucester (also Gloucestershire)(county, Eng.)
Gloucester (cheese)
Gloucester, England
Gloucester, MA
Gloucestershire (also Gloucester)(county, Eng.)
Glover, Danny (ent.; 1947-)
Gluck, Christoph W(illibald) von (Ger. comp.; 1714-87)
Glucotrol™ (med.)
Glyndebourne Opera Festival (Eng.)
Glynis Johns (ent.; 1923-)
Glynn, Carlin
GM (general manager)
GM™ (auto.)
GM Corp. (General Motors Corp.)
GM Heavy Truck Corp., Volvo
GMAC™ (auto.)
G-man (FBI agent)
GMC Truck (US bus.)
GMT (Greenwich Mean Time)
Gnaeus Julius Agricola (Roman mil./pol.; AD 37-93)
Gnaeus (or Gaius) Marcius Coriolanus (Roman hero; 5th c)
Gnassingbe Eyadéma (pres., Togo; 1937-)
Gnosticism (rel.)
GNP (gross national product)
Go-Jo™
Go-Jo Industries, Inc.
Go Kart™
Gobel, George (ent.; 1921-91)
Gobi Desert (Mongolia/Ch.)
God (the supreme being)
God Almighty (God)
God City of (heaven)
God the Father (God)
God the Son (Jesus Christ)
God, Kingdom of (heaven)
God, Lamb of (Jesus)

God, man of (saint, clergy, priest, etc.)
God, Mother of (rel.)
God, Party of (also Hezbollah)(rel./mil.)
God, The City of (Latin, *De Civitate Dei*)(by St. Augustine)
God, the Word of
Godard, Jean-Luc (Fr. ent.; 1930-)
Goddard Space Flight Center (MD)
Goddard, Paulette (ent.; 1905-90)
Goddard, Robert H. (US physt., father of modern rocketry; 1882-1945)
Godden, (Margaret) Rumer (Br. writer; 1907-)
Goddess, The Great (also The Great Mother)(rel.)
Gödel's incompleteness theorem (math.)
Godey, Louis Antoine (US publ.; 1804-78)
Godey's Lady's Book (1st US women's magazine)
Godfather, The (M. Puzo novel)
Godfather's Pizza (US bus.)
Godfrey Cambridge (ent.; 1933-76)
Godfrey of Bouillon (also Godefroy de Bouillon)(Fr. crusader; c1060-1100)
Godfrey, Arthur (ent.; 1903-83)
Godhavn, Greenland
Godhead (rel.)
Godiva™ chocolates
Godiva Chocolatier (US bus.)
Godiva, Lady (Br. noblewoman ; c1040-80)
Godmanis, Ivars (ex-PM, Latvia)
Godot, Waiting for (S. Beckett play)
Godoy, Virgilio (VP, Nicaragua)
God's acre (cemetery)
God's Little Acre (E. Caldwell novel)
Godspell (play)
Godthaab, Greenland (also Godthåb)
Godunov, Alexander (Rus./US ent.; 1949-)
Godunov, Boris (Fëdorovich)(Rus. tsar; 1552-1605)
Godwin, Gail (US writer; 1937-)
Godzilla (film; 1985)
Goebbels, (Paul) Joseph (Ger. Nazi propagandist; 1897-1945)
Goering (or Göring), Hermann Wilhelm (Ger. Nazi; 1893-1946)
Goethals, George W(ashington)(US mil./eng.; 1858-1928)
Goethe, Johann Wolfgang von (Ger. writer/phil.; 1749-1852)
Goetz, Bernhard H. (US news, shot NYC robbers)
Gog and Magog (rel.)
Gogh, Vincent van (Dutch artist; 1853-90)
Gogo (lang.)
Gogol, Nikolai (Vasilievich)(Rus. writer; 1809-52)
Goh Chok Tong (PM, Singapore; 1941-)
Golan Heights (plateau on Isr./Syrian border)

Golconda (ruined city known for diamond cutting, India)
Gold Rush, The (film)
Gold Star Medal
Golda Meir (also Goldie Mabovitch, Goldie Myerson)(ex-PM, Isr.; 1898-1979)
Goldberg, Rube (complex/impractical inventions)
Goldberg, Rube (Reuben Lucius)(US cartoonist, *Boob McNutt*; 1883-1970)
Goldberg, Whoopi (b. Karen Johnson)(ent.; 1950-)
Goldblum, Jeff (ent.; 1952-)
Golden Age (Gr./Roman myth.)
Golden Age of Spain
Golden Ass, The (also *Metamorphoses*)(L. Apuleius novel)
Golden Books™
golden Cadillac (mixed drink)
Golden Delicious (apple)
Golden Dipt™ (marinade)
Golden Dipt Co.
Golden Fleece (myth., stolen by Jason and the Argonauts)
Golden Gate Bridge (San Francisco)
Golden Gate Park (San Francisco)
Golden Girls (TV show)
Golden Gloves (boxing)
Golden Horde, Empire of the
Golden Horn
Golden Rule
Golden Sebright bantam (chicken)
Golden State (nickname, CA)
Golden State Warriors (basketball team)
Golden Temple (Sikh temple, India)
Golden Years (TV show)
Goldfinger (film; 1964)
Goldie Hawn (ent.; 1945-)
Goldilocks (fict. chara.)
Goldin, Daniel S. (Head/NASA; 1940-)
Golding, William (Gerald)(US writer; 1912-93)
Goldman, Emma (Rus./US reformer; 1869-1940)
Goldman, William (US writer; 1931-)
Goldmark, Karl (Hung. comp.; 1830-1915)
Goldsboro, Bobby (ent.; 1942-)
Goldsboro, NC
Goldsmith, Oliver (Br./Ir. writer; 1730?-74)
GoldStar™
Goldstar Electronics International, Inc.
Goldthwait, Bob "Bobcat" (ent.; 1962-)
Goldwater, Barry M(orris)(US pol.; 1909-)
Goldwater, Barry M(orris), Jr. (US pol.; 1938-)
Goldwyn Girls (ent.)
Goldwyn, Samuel (b. Samuel Goldfish)(ent.; 1882-1974)
Golf (mag.)
Golf Digest (mag.)
Golf Illustrated (mag.)

Golf, Volkswagen™ (auto.)
Golgi apparatus/body (med.)
Golgi tendon organs (med.)
Golgi, Camillo (It. biol.; 1843-1926)
Golgotha (hill where Jesus was crucified)
Goliards (Eur. minstrels; 12th-13th c.)(also l.c.)
Goliath (Biblical giant)
Goliath, David and (rel.)
Golliwogg (also Golliwog)(grotesque doll)(also l.c.)
Gomel, Belarus
Gomer Pyle (fict. chara.)
Gomorrah, Sodom and (ancient cities destroyed for wickedness)
Gompers, Samuel (US labor leader; 1850-1924)
Gonaïves, Haiti
Goncz, Arpad (pres., Hung.; 1922-)
Gondi (lang.)
Gone With the Wind (M. Mitchell novel; film, 1939)
Goneril (*King Lear*)
Gongora y Argote, Luis de (Sp. writer; 1561-1627)
Gongorism (lit. style)
González Márquez, Felipe (PM, Spain; 1942-)
González, Adolfo Suárez (ex-PM, Sp.; 1933-)
Gonzalez, Juan (baseball; 1969-)
Gonzalez, Pancho (Richard Alonzo)(tennis; 1928-)
Gonzalo Sánchez de Lozada (pres., Bolivia)
Gonzo journalism
Good Book, the (Bible)
Good Friday (rel., Friday before Easter)
Good Hope, Cape of (SAfr)
Good Housekeeping (mag.)
Good Humor™ (ice cream)
Good Humor™ bar
Good Humor™ man
Good Humor Corp., The
Good King Wenceslas (also *Wenceslaus*)(song)
Good King Wenceslaus (also St. Wenceslaus)
Good Morning (TV show)
Good Morning, America (TV show)
Good Neighbor Policy (govt.)
Good News™, Gillette (razor)
Good Samaritan
Good Seasons™ (salad dressing)
Good Shepherd (Jesus Christ)
Goodall, Jane (Br. animal behaviorist/writer; 1934-)
Goodbar, Looking for Mr. (film; 1977)
Goodbar™, Mr. (candy)
Goodbye Girl, The (film; 1977)
Goodbye, Columbus (P.Roth novel)
Goodbye, Mr. Chips (film; 1939)
Goodell, Brian Stuart (swimming; 1959-)
Gooden, Dwight (baseball; 1964-)
Goodfellow, Robin (also Puck, Hobgoblin)(fict.
chara, *A Midsummer Night's Dream*)
Goodhue, Bertram G. (US arch.; 1869-1924)
Goodman, Benny (Benjamin David)(US jazz; 1909-86)
Goodman Story, The Benny (film; 1955)
Goodman, Bergdorf (store)
Goodman, Dody (ent.)
Goodman, John (ent.; 1953-)
Goodrich™
Goodrich Co., B. F.
Goodrich Tire Co., Uniroyal
Goodrich, Gail (basketball; 1943-)
Goodson, Mark (ent.; 1915-92)
good-time Charlie
Goodwill Industries
Goodwin, Archie (fict. chara.)
Goodwrench™, Mr.
Goodyear™
Goodyear Tire & Rubber Co.
Goodyear, Charles (US inv.; 1800-60)
Goody™ (hair care)
Google, Barney (cartoon)
Goolagong (Cawley), Evonne (tennis; 1951-)
Goose and Grimm , Mother (comic strip)
Goose (Rich) Gossage (baseball; 1951-)
Goose Tales, Mother (fairy tales, C. Perrault)
Goose (Reece) Tatum (basketball)
Goose, Mother (fict. author of fairy tales)
GOP (Grand Old Party [Republican])
Gopher State (nickname, MN)
Gorbachev, Mikhail (Sergeyevich)(ex-pres.; Rus. 1931-)
Gorbachev, Raisa (Maksimova Titorenko)(wife of ex-Rus. pres./educ.; 1934-)
Gorbatko, Viktor V(asilyevich)(cosmo.; 1934-)
Gorbunov, Anatolijs (ex-pres., Latvia)
Gorcey, Leo (ent.; 1915-69)
Gordian knot (myth.)
Gordie (Gordon) Howe (hockey; 1928-)
Gordon Bunshaft (US arch.; 1909-90)
Gordon Cooper, L(eroy), Jr. (astro.; 1927-)
Gordon Jump (ent.; 1932-)
Gordon Liddy, G. (US pol./Watergate)
Gordon Lightfoot (ent.; 1938-)
Gordon MacRae (ent.; 1921-86)
Gordon R. Sullivan (US mil.)
Gordon setter (dog)
Gordon, Charles G(eorge)(Br. mil.; 1833-85)
Gordon, Dexter (US jazz; 1923-90)
Gordon, Flash (comic strip)
Gordon, Fort, GA (mil.)
Gordon, Gale (ent.; 1906-)
Gordon, Mack (Pol./US lyricist; 1905-59)
Gordon, Mary (US writer; 1949-)
Gordon, (Elmira) Minita, Dame (gov-gen., Belize)
Gordon, Richard F., Jr. (astro.)
Gordon, Ruth (ent.; 1896-1985)

Gordy, Berry, Jr. (US bus./founded Motown)
Gore Vidal (US writer/critic; 1925-)
Gore, Albert A(rnold), Jr. (US VP; 1948-)
Gore-Tex™ (fabric laminate)
Goren, Charles H. (US contract bridge
    authority; 1901-91)
Gorgon (myth.)
Gorgonzola cheese
Gorham™ (silverware)
Gorham (US bus.)
Gorilla, Magilla (cartoon)
Göring, Hermann Wilhelm (also Goering)(Ger.
    Nazi; 1893-1946)
Gorky Park (M.C. Smith novel)
Gorky, Arshile (Vosdanig Adoian)(US artist;
    1905-48)
Gorky (or Gorki), Maxim (aka Aleksei
    Maksimovich Peshkov)(Rus. writer; 1868-
    1936)
Gorky, Russia (now Nizhni-Novgorod)
Gorme, Eydie (ent.; 1932-)
Gorshin, Frank (ent.; 1934-)
Gortari, Carlos Salinas de (pres., Mex.; 1949-)
Gorton, Slade (US cong.; 1928-)
Gorton's™ (fish prods.)
Gosden, Freeman (Amos)(ent.; 1899-1982)
Goshen (Biblical fertile land)
Goshen, IN
Gospel(s)(rel.)
Gospels, Synoptic/synoptic
Gosport, England
Gossage, Goose (Rich)(baseball; 1951-)
Gossett, Louis, Jr. (ent.; 1936-)
Göteborg, Sweden
Goth (people)
Gotha, House of Saxe-Coburg- (Br. ruling
    family; 1901-10)
Gotham (nickname for NYC)
Gotham City (Batman's)
Gotham, England
Gothic (arch./art/lit.)(Eur.; 12th-15th c)
Gothic novel/romance
Gothic revival (arch.; 19th c)
Goths, East (also Ostrogoths)(ancient Germans)
Gotland (island, Baltic Sea)
Götterdämmerung (also Ragnarök)(myth.)
Gottfried Wilhelm von Leibnitz, Baron (Ger.
    phil./math; 1646-1716)
Gottfried, Brian (tennis; 1952-)
Gotthold (Ephraim) Lessing (Ger. writer; 1729-
    81)
Gotti, John
Gottlieb Daimier (Ger. eng./inv.; 1834-1900)
Gottschalk, Louis Moreau (US comp.; 1829-69)
Gottwald, Klement (Czech. pol.; 1896-1953)
Goucher College (MD)
Gouda (cheese)
Gouda, the Netherlands

Goudy (type style)
Gould, Chester (cartoonist, *Dick Tracy*; 1900-
    85)
Gould, Elliott (ent.; 1938-)
Gould, Glenn (Herbert)(Can. comp.; 1932-82)
Gould, Harold (ent.; 1923-)
Gould, Jay (US finan., railroad; 1836-92)
Gould, Morton (ent.; 1913-)
Gould, Stephen Jay (US paleontol./writer;
    1941-)
Goulet, Robert (ent.; 1933-)
Gounod, Charles François (Fr. comp.; 1818-93)
Gourmet (mag.)
Gourmet, Galloping (aka Graham Kerr)(US
    chef
Gouveja, U.S. v. (US law; 1984)
Gouverneur Morris (US pol./dipl.; 1752-1816)
Government National Mortgage Association
    (also Ginnie Mae, GNMA)
Government Printing Office (US govt. agcy.)
Gowdy, Curt (ent.; 1919-)
Gower Champion (US dancer; 1921-80)
Goya y Lucientes, Francisco (José) de (Sp.
    artist; 1746-1828)
GPO (general post office, Government Printing
    Office)
GQ (mag.)
Graaf, Regnier de (Dutch phys.; 1641-73)
Graaff generator, Van de (also electrostatic
    generator)
Graaff, Robert Jemison Van de (US physt.;
    1901-67)
Graafian follicle (med.)
Grable, Betty (ent.; 1916-73)
Grace & Co., W. R.
Grace Bumbry (ent.; 1937-)
Grace Jones (ent.; 1952-)
Grace (Patricia) Kelly (US actress; princess,
    Monaco; 1929-82)
Grace Metalious (US writer)
Grace Paley (US writer; 1922-)
Grace Slick (ent.; 1939-)
Grace Under Fire (TV show)
Grace, Princess (b. Grace Patricia Kelly)(US
    actress; princess, Monaco; 1929-82)
Grace, Your (title)
Graces (3 goddesses)(myth.)
Gracie Allen (ent.; 1906-64)
Gracie Fields (ent.; 1898-1979)
Graco™ (baby prods.)
Graf (Ger./Aus./Swed. title, a count)
Graf Zeppelin (Ger. airship)
Graf, Steffi (Stephanie Maria)(tennis; 1969-)
Graham Greene (Henry)(Br. writer; 1904-91)
Graham Kerr (aka Galloping Gourmet)(US
    chef)
Graham (Vivian) Sutherland (Br. artist; 1903-
    80)

Graham, Billy (William Franklin), Rev. (US rel.; 1918-)
Graham, Bob (Robert)(US cong.; 1936-)
Graham, David (golf; 1946-)
Graham, Katharine (US newspaper exec.; 1917-)
Graham, Martha (US dancer/choreographer; 1894-1991)
Graham, Otto (football; 1921-)
Graham, Sheilah (gossip columnist; 1904-88)
Graham, Thomas (Scot. chem.; 1805-69)
Graham, Virginia (ent.; 1912-)
Grahame, Gloria (ent.; 1925-81)
Grahame, Kenneth (Scot. writer; 1859-1932)
Graham's law (diffusion of gases)
Grail, the Holy (legendary cup used by Jesus at the Last Supper)
Gram Parsons (ent.)
Gram, Hans Christian Joachim (Dan. phys.; 1853-1938)
Gramercy Park (NYC)
Gramm, Phil (US cong.; 1942-)
Grammy Awards (music)
Gram's method (med.)
Gram's stain (med.)
Gran Quivira (utopia)
Granada, Nicaragua
Granada, Spain
Granby, Quebec, Canada
Grand Alliance (Fr. hist.; 1689, 1701)
Grand Am, Pontiac™ (auto.)
Grand Army of the Republic (G.A.R.)(US hist.; founded 1865)
Grand Canal (Ch.)
Grand Canyon National Park (AZ)
Grand Canyon State (nickname, AZ)
Grand Caravan ES, Dodge (auto.)
Grand Cherokee Laredo, Jeep™ (auto.)
Grand Cherokee, Jeep™ (auto.)
Grand Coulee Dam (WA)
Grand Duke Jean (pres., Luxembourg; 1921-)
Grand Forks Air Force Base, ND (mil.)
Grand Forks, ND
Grand Funk Railroad (pop music)
Grand Guignol (theater)
Grand Island, NE
Grand Junction, CO
Grand Marnier™ (liqueur)
Grand Old Party (GOP, Republican Party)
Grand Ole Opry
Grand Ole Opry Live (TV show)
Grand Prix (racing)
Grand Prix, Pontiac™ (auto.)
Grand Rapids Press (MI newspaper)
Grand Rapids, MI
Grand Slam (golf, tennis)
Grand Teton National Park (WY)
Grand Voyager LE, Plymouth (auto.)

Grandma Moses (b. Anna Mary Robertson)(US artist; 1860-1961)
Grandpa Jones (ent.; 1913-)
Grange (or Granger) Movement, the (US hist.,; 1867-c1878)
Grange, Red (Harold)(football; 1903-91)
Granger, Farley (ent.; 1925-)
Granger, (James) Stewart (ent.; 1913-93)
Granite State (nickname, NH)
Granny Smith (apple)
Granolith™ (concrete)
Grant Sahib (also Grunth, Granth, Adigranth)(rel.)
Grant Tinker (ent.; 1926-)
Grant Wood (US artist; 1891-1942)
Grant, Amy (ent.; 1960-)
Grant, Cary (b. Archibald Leach)(ent.; 1904-86)
Grant, Lee (ent.; 1929-)
Grant, Ulysses S(impson)(18th US pres.; 1822-85)
Granth (also Grunth, Grant Sahib, Adigranth)(rel.)
Granville, France
Grape-Nuts™ (cereal)
Grapes of Wrath, The (J. Steinbeck novel)
Graphic Arts Monthly (mag.)
Grappelli, Stephane (US jazz; 1908-)
Grass, Günter (Wilhelm)(Ger. writer/artist; 1927-)
Grassley, Charles Ernest (US cong.; 1933-)
Grasso, Ella Tambussi (US pol.; 1919-81)
Grateful Dead (pop music)
Grau, Shirley Ann (US writer; 1929-)
Grauer, Ben (ent.)
Graves (Fr. wine district)
Graves' disease
Graves, Peter (ent.; 1926-)
Graves, Robert (Ranke)(Br. writer/hist.; 1895-1985)
Gravy Train™ (dog food)
Gray Cosmetics, Ltd., Dorothy
Gray Lady (Amer. Red Cross volunteer)
Gray, Erin
Gray, Harold (US cartoonist, *Little Orphan Annie*; 1894-1968)
Gray, Linda (ent.; 1940-)
Gray, The Picture of Dorian (O. Wilde novel)
Gray, Thomas (Br. poet; 1716-71)
Grayson, Kathryn (ent.; 1922-)
Graz, Austria
Graziano, Rocky (Thomas Rocco Barbella)(1919-90)
Grease (play/film)
Great Atlantic & Pacific Tea Co. (A&P Food Stores)
Great Awakening, the
Great Barrier Reef (coral reefs/islands off E Austl.)

Great Basin (region, W US)
Great Basin National Park (NV)
Great Britain (Eng., Scot., and Wales; part of the UK)
Great Chefs of Chicago (TV show)
Great Chefs of New Orleans (TV show)
Great Chefs of New York (TV show)
Great Chefs of San Francisco (TV show)
Great Compromiser (also Great Pacificator)(Henry Clay)(US pol.; 1777-1852)
Great Dane (dog)
Great Depression, the (US hist.; 1930s)
Great Dictator, The (film)
Great Divide (also Continental Divide)(the Rockies)
Great Dog (astron., Canis Major, includes the Dog Star, Sirius)
Great Falls, MT
Great Gatsby, The (F.S. Fitzgerald novel)
Great Goddess, The (also The Great Mother)(rel.)
Great Lake State (nickname, MI)
Great Lakes Naval Training Center (IL)(mil)
Great Lakes, the (US/Can. border: Erie ,Huron, Michigan, Ontario, Superior)
Great Mosque of Samarra
Great Mother, The (also The Great Goddess)(rel.)
Great Ouse River (also Ouse)(Eng.)
Great Pacificator (also Great Compromiser)(Henry Clay)(US pol.; 1777-1852)
Great Plains region (E of Rockies: TX/OK/KS/ NE/SD/ND)
Great Pyramid of Khufu (or Cheops)(Eg.)
Great Pyramids of Gîza (also El Gîza or Al Jizah)(Eg.)
Great Pyrenees (dog)
Great Rift Valley (SW Asia/SE Afr.)
Great River Winery, Windsor Vineyards & (US bus.)
Great Salt Lake (UT)
Great Santini, The (film; 1980)
Great Schism (also the Schism of the West)(rel.)
Great Slave Lake (Northwest Territories, Can.)
Great Smoky Mountains (NC/TN)
Great Smoky Mountains National Park (NC/ TN)
Great Sphinx, the (Eg.; c2500 BC)
Great Turtle (myth.)
Great Wall (astron.)
Great Wall of China (1,450 miles; built 214 BC)
Great War (also World War I, First World War, War of the Nations)(1914-18)
Great White Way, the (Broadway theatre district)
Greater Antilles, West Indies (Cuba, Hispaniola, Jamaica, Puerto Rico)

Greater Pittsburgh International Airport (PA)
Greatest Show on Earth, The (film)
Greatest Show on Earth, The (P.T. Barnum's circus)
Grecian bend
Grecian profile
Greco, El (aka Domenikos Theotocopoulos)(Sp. artist; 1541-1614)
Greco, El (art style)
Greco-Roman wrestling
Greece (Hellenic Republic)(SE Eur.)
Greek (lang./people)
Greek Church (also Greek Orthodox Church)
Greek fire (ignites with water)
Greek gods/goddesses
Greek modes (music)
Greek Orthodox Church (also Greek Church)
Greek Revival (arch.)
Greeley, Horace (US publ./pol.; 1811-72)
Greely, Adolphus Washington (US mil.; 1844-1935)
Green Bay Packers (football team)
Green Bay Press-Gazette (WI newspaper)
Green Bay, WI
Green Berets (also Special Forces)(US mil.)
Green Giant™
Green Giant Co.
Green Lantern (cartoon chara.)
Green Mountain Boys (US mil.; late 1700s)
Green Mountain State (nickname, VT)
Green Party, International (pol.)
Green River (WY/UT)
Green River ordinance/law)(bans door-to-door selling)
Green, Adolph (US lyricist; 1915-)
Green, Al (ent.; 1946-)
Green, Gretna ("any" town for eloping couples)
Green, Hamilton (ex-PM, Guyana)
Green, Hetty (US finan., "witch of Wall Street"; 1834-1916)
Green, Hubert (golf; 1946-)
Green, William (US labor leader; 1873-1952)
Greenaway, Kate (Catherine)(Br. artist/writer; 1846-1901)
Greenback-Labor Party (US hist.; 1878-c1884)

Greenback Party (US hist.; 1875-78)
Greene, Charles E. (sprinter; 1945-)
Greene, (Henry) Graham (Br. writer; 1904-91)
Greene, "Mean" Joe (football; 1946-)
Greene, Lorne (ent.; 1915-87)
Greene, Michele (ent.)
Greene, Nathanael (US mil.; 1742-86)
Greene, Shecky (ent.; 1926-)
Greenland (also Kalaallit Nunaat)(island, N Atl.)
Greenlandic (lang.)
Greenough, Horatio (US sculptor; 1805-52)

Greenpeace (environ. grp.; founded 1971)
Greensboro News & Record (NC newspaper)
Greensboro, NC
Greensburg Tribune-Review (PA newspaper)
Greensburg, PA
Greenspan, Alan (Chair/US Fed Reserve Sys; 1926-)
Greenstreet, Sydney (ent.; 1879-1954)
Greenville News (SC newspaper)
Greenville Piedmont (SC newspaper)
Greenville, Liberia
Greenville, MS, NC, OH, SC, TX
Greenwich (London borough)
Greenwich Mean Time (GMT)(also Greenwich Time, coordinated universal time [UTC])
Greenwich meridian (0° longitude, Greenwich, London)
Greenwich Observatory, Royal (London)(also Old Royal Observatory)
Greenwich Village (NYC)
Greenwich Village Theatre (NYC)
Greenwich, CT
Greer Garson (ent.; 1908-)
Greer, Germaine (Austl. writer/feminist; 1939-)
Greg Evans (cartoonist)
Greg Evigan (ent.; 1953-)
Greg Gumbel (ent.; 1946-)
Greg LeMond (US cyclist; 1961-)
Greg(ory) Louganis (US diver; 1960-)
Greg Morris (ent.; 1934-)
Greg(ory) Norman (golf; 1955-)
Gregg Allman (ent.; 1947-)
Gregg, John Robert (inv. shorthand system; 1868-1948)
Gregg, Judd (US cong.; 1847-)
Gregg, William (US bus.; 1800-67)
Gregor J(ohann) Mendel (Aus. biol.; 1822-84)
Gregorian calendar
Gregorian chant (music, rel.)
Gregory Harrison (ent.; 1950-)
Gregory Hines (ent.; 1946-)
Gregory I, St. ("the Great")(It., pope; c540-604)
Gregory II, St. (It., pope; ?-731)
Gregory III, St. (Syrian, pope; ?-741)
Gregory Peck, (Eldred)(ent.; 1916-)
Gregory VII, St. (aka Hildebrand)(It., pope; c1023-85)
Gregory XIII (Ugo Buoncompagno)(It., pope; 1502-85)
Gregory, Lady Augusta (Ir. writer; 1852-1932)
Gregory, Cynthia (ent.; 1946-)
Gregory, Diana
Gregory, Dick (ent.; 1932-)
Gregory, James (ent.; 1911-)
Gregory, Lisa
Greguric, Franjo (ex-PM, Croatia)
Greiff, Monica de
Gremlin, AMC (auto.)

Gremlins (film; 1984)
Grenada, West Indies
Grenadines, St. Vincent and the (island nation)(West Indies)
Grendel (fict. chara., *Beowulf*)
Grenoble, France
Grenville, George (ex-PM, Br.; 1712-70)
Grenville, Grenada
Grenville (or Greynville), Sir Richard (Br. mil.; 1541-91)
Grenville, William Wyndham, Baron (Br. pol.; 1759-1834)
Gresham, OR
Gresham, Sir Thomas (Br. finan.; 1519?-79)
Gresham's law (econ.)
Greta Garbo (b. Greta Lovisa Gustafsson)(ent.; 1905-90)
Grete (Andersen) Waitz (runner; 1953-)
Gretel, Hänsel and (folktale)
Gretna Green ("any" town for eloping couples)
Gretna Green, Scotland (Scot./Eng. border town where couples eloped)
Gretzky, Wayne (hockey; 1961-)
Grey Cup (Can. football)
Grey Poupon™ (mustard)
Grey, Earl (tea)
Grey, Joel (ent.; 1932-)
Grey, Lady Jane (Dudley)(queen, Eng. [10 days]; 1537-54)
Grey, Zane (US writer; 1875-1939)
Greyhound™ bus
Greyhound-Dial Corp.
Greynville (or Grenville), Sir Richard (Br. mil.; 1541-91)
*Greystoke: The Legend of Tarzan, Lord of t*he Apes (film; 1984)
Greystoke, Lord (fict. chara., *Tarzan*)
Grieg, Edvard (Hagerup)(Nor. comp.; 1843-1907)
Grier, Roosevelt "Rosey" (ent./football; 1932-)
Griese, Bob (Robert Allen)(football; 1945-)
Griffey, Ken, Jr. (baseball; 1969-)
Griffin Act, Landrum- (US hist.; 1959)
Griffin Dunne (ent.; 1955-)
Griffin, Merv (ent.; 1925-)
Griffiss Air Force Base, NY (mil.)
Griffith Joyner, Florence ("Flo Jo")(track; 1959-)
Griffith Park (Los Angeles)
Griffith, Andy (ent.; 1926-)
Griffith, D(avid) W(ark)(ent.; 1875-1948)
Griffith, Hugh (ent.; 1912-80)
Griffith, Melanie (ent.; 1957-)
Grigori Efimovich Rasputin ("Rasputin")(Rus. rel.; c1865-1916)
Grigory Aleksandrovich Potemkin, Prince (Rus. pol.; 1739-91)
Grim Reaper
Grimes, Tammy (ent.; 1934-)

Grimm, Brothers (wrote/collected folk tales)
Grimm, Jakob (Ludwig Karl)(Ger. writer/
    linguist; 1785-1863)
Grimm, Mother Goose and (comic strip)
Grimm, Wilhelm (Karl)(Ger. writer/linguist;
    1786-1859)
Grimm's Fairy Tales (by the Brothers Grimm)
Grimm's law (linguistics)
Grimsby, England
Gris, Juan (b. José Vittoriano Gonzales)(Sp.
    artist; 1887-1927)
Griselda
Grisham, John (US writer; 1955-)
Grissom Air Force Base (IN)(mil.)
Grissom, Virgil I. "Gus" (astro.; 1926-67)
Griswold v. Connecticut (US law; 1965)
Griswold, Hepburn v. (US law; 1870)
Grizzard, George (ent.; 1928-)
Gro Harlem Brundtland (PM, Nor.; 1939-)
Grodin, Charles (ent.; 1935-)
Grodno, Belarus
Groebli, "Mr. Frick" (Werner)(ice skating;
    1915-)
Groenendael (also Belgian sheepdog)(dog)
Groening, Matt(hew Akbar)(US cartoonist, *The
    Simpsons*; 1954-)
Grofe, Ferde (US comp.; 1892-1972)
Groh, David (ent.; 1941-)
Grolier, Inc.
Gromyko, Andrei A. (ex-pres., Rus.; 1909-89)
Groningen (province, Netherlands)
Grooms, Red (Charles Roger)(US artist; 1937-)
Gropius, Walter (Adolf)(US arch.; 1883-1969)
Gross, Chaim (US artist; 1904-91)
Gross, Mary
Gross, Michael (ent.; 1947-)
Grosse Point, MI
Grosset & Dunlap, Inc.
Grosvenor, Gerald
Grosvenor, Gilbert (Hovey)(US geographer/
    writer/editor; 1875-1966)
Grosvenor, Gilbert M. (US publ.)
Groucho Marx, (Julius)(ent.; 1890-1977)
Groundhog Day (Feb. 2)
Group W. Productions
Grove City v. Bell (US law; 1984)
Grove, Lefty (Robert Moses)(baseball; 1900-75)
Grover Cleveland (22nd & 24th US pres.; 1837-
    1908)
Grover Cleveland Alexander (baseball; 1887-
    1950)
Growing Pains (TV show)
Groza, Lou (football; 1924-)
Grrravy™, Purina (dog food)
Grub Street (lit., London)
Grumbacher, Inc., M.
Grumman Corp.
Grundy (narrow-minded person)

Grundy, Mrs. (fict. chara., *Speed the Plough*)
Grünewald, Matthias (or Mathäus)(Ger. artist;
    1480-1528)
Grunth (also Granth, Grant Sahib,
    Adigranth)(rel.)
Grus (astron., crane)
Gruyère (district, Switz.)
Gruyère cheese
GSA (General Services Administration, Girl
    Scouts of America)
G spot (also G-spot, Grafenberg spot)
GST (Greenwich Sidereal Time)
Gstaad, Switzerland
G-string (also gee-string, gee string)
G-suit (also g-suit, G suit, anti-G
    suit)(antigravity suit)
GTE™
GTE Communications Systems, Inc.
GTE Corp.
Guadalajara, Mexico
Guadalajara, Spain
Guadalcanal Diary
Guadalcanal Island (SW Pac.)
Guadalupe Hidalgo, Treaty of (ended Mexican
    War; 1848)
Guadalupe Mountains National Park (TX)
Guadalupe Victoria (b. Manuel Félix
    Fernández)(1st pres., Mex.; 1789-1843)
Guadeloupe (West Indies)(Fr.)
Guam (US territory, W Pac.)
Guangdong (also Kwangtung)(province, Ch.)
Guangxi (also Kwangsi-Chuang)(region, Ch.)
Guangzhou, China (also Canton or Kuang-chou)
Guantánamo Bay (Cuba)
Guantánamo, Cuba
Guaraní (lang./people)
Guardafui, Cape (also Ras Asir)(cape, Somalia)
Guardia, Rafael Angel Calderón (ex-pres., Costa
    Rica; 1900-71)
Guardian (Br. newspaper)
Guardian Angels
Guardino, Harry (ent.; 1925-)
Guare, John (US writer; 1938-)
Guatemala (Republic of)(CAmer.)
Guatemala (City), Guatemala
Guatemalan (people)
Guayaquil, Ecuador
Guaymas, Mexico
Guaymi (Costa Rican Indians)
Gub Gub the pig
Gucci™
Gucci America, Inc.
Guderian, Heinz (Ger. gen.; 1888-1953)
Guelders (also Gelderland)(province,
    Netherlands)
Guelph, Ontario, Canada
Guelphs (It. pol.; 12th-15th c.)
Guérin, Camille (Fr. bacteriol.; 1872-1961)

Guerlain™
Guerlain, Inc.
Guernica (Picasso)
Guernica, Spain
Guernsey cattle
Guernsey, Isle of (island, English Channel)
Guerrero (state, Mex.)
Guess™ (jeans)
Guess? Inc.
Cucot Quarters, Inc
Guest, Edgar (Albert)(US writer; 1881-1959)
Guevara, Ernesto "Che" (SAmer. mil.; 1928-67)
Guggenheim Museum, Solomon R. (NYC)
Guggenheim, Crazy (aka Frank Fontaine)(ent.; 1920-78)
Guggenheim, Daniel (US bus./finan.; 1856-1930)
Guggenheim, Harry F. (US bus./finan.; 1890-?)
Guggenheim, Meyer (US bus./finan.; 1828-1905)
Guggenheim, Peggy (US finan.; 1898-1979)
Guggenheim, Simon (US bus./finan.; 1867-1941)
Guggenheim, Solomon R(obert)(US bus./finan.; 1861-1949)
Guglielmo Marconi (It. eng./inv., radio; 1874-1937)
Guglielmo Winery, Emilio (US bus.)
Guiana (SAmer., inc. Fr. Guiana/Guyana/Surinam)
Guiana, Dutch (now Suriname)
Guicciardini, Francesco (It. hist.; 1483-1540)
Guideposts (mag.)
Guidi (Masaccio), Tommaso (It. artist; 1401-28?)
Guiding Light (TV soap)
Guidry, Ronald Ames (baseball; 1950-)
Guildenstern (fict. chara., *Hamlet*)
Guildenstern, Rosencrantz & (T. Stoppard play)
Guiliana Benetton (It. designer; 1938-)
Guiliano Amato (ex-PM, Italy; 1938-)
Guilin, China (also Kweilin)
Guillain-Barré syndrome
Guillaume, Robert (ent.; 1937-)
Guillermo Endara (pres., Panama; 1936-)
Guillermo Ford Boyd (VP, Panama)
Guillermo Vilas (tennis; 1952-)
Guinea (Republic of)(W Afr.)
Guinea, Equatorial (Republic of)(formerly Spanish Guinea)(W central Afr.)
Guinea, Spanish (now Equatorial Guinea)
Guinea-Bissau (Republic of)(W Afr.)
Guinevere, Queen (King Arthur's wife, Sir Lancelot's love)
Guinier, Lani (US atty.)
Guinness Book of World Records
Guinness, Sir Alec (ent.; 1914-)
Guiscard, Robert (Robert de Hauteville)(Norman /It. mil.; c1015-85)

Guise, Mary of (queen to James V, Scot.; 1515-60)
Guisewite, Cathy (cartoonist, *Cathy*; 1950-)
Guiyang (also Kweiyang), China
Guizhou (also Kweichow)(province, Ch.)
Gujarat (also Gujerat)(state, India)
Gujarati (lang./people)
Gula (myth.)
GULAG (USSR prison system)(also gulag)
Gulbuddin Hekmatyar (PM, Afghan.)
Gulden's™ mustard
Gulf of Aden (Yemen/Africa)
Gulf of Aqaba (Jordan)
Gulf of Boothia (Arctic/N Can.)
Gulf of Bothnia (Swed./Fin.)
Gulf of California (CA/Mex.)
Gulf of Finland (arm of Baltic Sea)
Gulf of Lions
Gulf of Mexico (US/Mex.)
Gulf of Oman (Oman/Iran)
Gulf of Siam (or Thailand)
Gulf of Suez (Eg.)
Gulf of Tadjoura (Djibouti)
Gulf of Thailand (or Siam)
Gulf of Tonkin (also Tonkin Gulf)(Viet./Ch.)
Gulf Oil Corp.
Gulf States, Persian (Bahrain/Iran/Iraq/Kuwait/Oman/Qatar/Saudi Arabia/UAE)
Gulf States, U.S. (AL/FL/LA/MS/TX)
Gulf Stream (warm ocean current, Gulf of Mexico)
Gulf War (also Iran-Iraq War)(1980-88)
Gulf War (28 nations [inc. US]/Iraq; 1991)
Gulfport, FL, MS
Gullah (lang./people)
Gulliver's Travels (J. Swift satire)
Gulu, Uganda
Gumbel, Bryant (US TV commentator; 1948-)
Gumbel, Greg (ent.; 1946-)
Gummi Bears, The (cartoon)
Gummo Marx, (Milton)(ent.; 1893-1977)
Gummy Bear Co., The
Gump's store
Gunfight at the O.K. Corral (film; 1957)
Gunga Din (film; 1939)
Gunn effect
Gunn, Peter (TV show)
Gunnar (myth.)
Gunnar Myrdal (Swed. econ.; 1898-1987)
Gunpowder Plot (Br. hist.; 1605)
Guns 'N Roses (pop music)
Guns of Navarone, The (film; 1961)
Gunsmoke (TV show)
Gunter (Wilhelm) Grass (Ger. writer/artist; 1927-)
Gunter, Nancy Richey (tennis; 1942-)
Gunter's chain (surveyor's measure/chain)
Gunther Gebel-Williams

Gunther, John (US jour./writer; 1901-70)
Guntis Ulmanis (pres., Latvia)
Guofeng (or Kuo-feng), Hua (ex-PM, Ch.; 1920?-)
Guomindang (also Kuomintang)(Ch. pol. party)
Gupta (Indian dynasty/empire)
Gur languages
Gurkha (soldier, people)
Gurung (lang.)
Gus Edwards (US comp.; 1879-1945)
Gus (Virgil I.) Grissom (astro.; 1926-67)
Gus Kahn (US lyricist; 1886-1941)
Gush Emunim (Isr. pol. grp.; founded 1973)
Gusii (lang.)
Gustaf, Carl XVI (king, Swed.; 1946-)
Gustafsons Dairy, Inc.
Gustav (Theodore) Holst (Br. comp.; 1874-1934)
Gustav Klimt (Aus. artist; 1862-1918)
Gustav Mahler (Aus. comp.; 1860-1911)
Gustav Stresemann (ex-chanc., Ger.; 1878-1929)
Gustave Charpentier (Fr. comp.; 1860-1956)
Gustave Courbet (Fr. artist; 1819-77)
Gustave Doré (Fr. artist; 1832-83)
Gustave Eiffel, (Alexandre)(Fr. eng.; 1832-1923)
Gustave Flaubert (Fr. writer; 1821-80)
Gustave Moreau (Fr. artist; 1826-98)
Gustavo Thoeni (skiing; 1951-)
Gustavus I (Gustavus Vasa [or Eriksson])(king, Swed.; 1496-1560)
Gustavus II (Gustavus Adolphus)("Snow King," "Lion of the North")(king, Swed.; 1594-1632)
Gustavus III (king, Swed.; 1746-92)
Gustavus IV (Gustavus Adolphus)(king, Swed.; 1778-1837)
Gustavus Swift (US pioneer meat packer; 1839-1903)
Gustavus V (Gustaf)(king, Swed.; 1858-1950)
Gustavus VI (king, Swed.; 1882-?)
Gutenberg Bible (also Mazarin Bible)
Gutenberg, Johann (Ger. printer; c1400-68)
Guthrie, A. B. (US writer; 1901-91)
Guthrie, Arlo (ent.; 1947-)
Guthrie, Sir Tyrone (William)(Br. ent.; 1900-71)
Guthrie, Woody (Woodrow Wilson)(ent.; 1912-67)
Guttenberg, Steve (ent.; 1958-)
Gutzon Borglum, (John)(US sculptor; 1871-1941)
Guy de Maupassant, (Henri René Albert)(Fr. writer; 1850-93)
Guy Fawkes (Br. conspirator; 1570-1606)
Guy Fawkes Day (Br.)
Guy Kibbee (ent.; 1886-1956)
Guy Lafleur (hockey; 1951-)
Guy (Albert) Lombardo (ent.; 1902-77)
Guy Mollet (Fr. pol.; 1905-75)
Guy (Willy) Razanamasy (ex-PM, Madagascar)

Guy Williams (ent.; 1924-89)
Guy, Jasmine (ent.; 1964-)
Guyana (Cooperative Republic of)(formerly British Guiana)(SAmer.)
Guyana Airways (airline)
Guys and Dolls (play; film, 1955)
Gwaltney of Smithfield, Ltd.
Gwelo, Zimbabwe (also Gweru)
Gwen Verdon (ent.; 1925-)
Gwendolyn Brooks (US writer; 1917-)
Gwenn, Edmund (ent.; 1875-1959)
Gwent (county, Wales)
Gweru, Zimbabwe (also Gwelo)
Gwyn (or Gwynne), Nell (Eleanor)(ent.; 1651-87)
Gwynedd (county, Wales)
Gwynn, Tony (baseball; 1960-)
Gwynne, Fred (ent.; 1926-93)
Gyandzha, Azerbaijan
Gyne-Lotrimin™ (med.)
Gyne-Moistrin™ (med.)
Gynt, Peer (H. Ibsen play)
Gyo Obata (US arch.; 1923-)
Gypsy (people/lang.)(lang. also Romany)
Gypsy Rose Lee (b. Rose Louise Hovick)(ent.; 1914-70)

H

H (chem. sym., hydrogen)
Häagen-Dazs Co., Inc., The
Häagen-Dazs™ ice cream
Haarlem, the Netherlands
Haber process (chem.)
Haber, Fritz (Ger. chem.; 1868-1934)
Habib Thiam (PM, Senegal)
Habyarimana, Juvénal (ex-pres., Rwanda;
   1937-94
Hackensack Record (NJ newspaper)
Hackensack, NJ
Hackett, Bobby (US jazz; 1915-76)
Hackett, Buddy (ent.; 1924-)
Hackman, Gene (ent.; 1930-)
Hackney (horse)
Hadassah (Jew. org.)
Hades (myth., Hell)
Hadiyya (lang.)
Hadrian (also Adrian)(Publius Aelius
   Hadrianus)(emp., Rome; 76-138)
Hadrian's Wall (Roman hist.; 122-383)
Haeckel, Ernest (Heinrich)(Ger. zool.; 1834-
   1919)
Hafez al-Assad (pres., Syria; 1930-)
Haflinger (horse)
Haganah (Isr. army)
Hagar the Horrible (comic strip)
Hage Geingob (PM, Namibia)
Hagen, Germany
Hagen, Walter (golf; 1892-1969)
Hagerstown, MD
Haggadah (also *Haggada*)(rel.)
Haggar Co.
Haggar™ slacks
Haggard, Merle (ent.; 1937-)
Hagia Sophia (also Saint [or Santa]
   Sophia)(museum, Istanbul)
Hagiographa, the (also *Ketuvim, Ketubim*)(rel.)
Hagler, Marvelous Marvin (boxing; 1954-)
Hagman, Larry (ent.; 1931-)
Hague Conferences (internat'l; late 18th/early
   19th c.)
Hague Tribunal (also Permanent Court of
   Arbitration)(internat'l court)
Hague, (The), the Netherlands (or Holland)
Hahn, Madame Helena Petrovna Blavatsky
   (Rus. theosophist; 1831-91)
Hahn, Jessica (US news)
Hahn, Otto (Ger. chem.; 1879-1968)
Hai Duong, Vietnam
Haid, Charles (ent.; 1944-)
Haida (NAmer. Indians)
Haidar Abu Bakr al-Attas (PM, Yemen; 1939-)
Haidar (or Hyder) Ali (Indian ruler/mil.; 1722-

82)
Haifa, Israel
Haig, Alexander M., Jr. (US gen./pol.; 1924-)
Haig, Douglas (Br. mil.; 1861-1928)
Haight-Ashbury (district, San Francisco)
Hail Mary (also *Ave Maria*)(prayer)
Haile Mariam Mengistu (ex-pres., Ethiopia;
   1937-)
Haile Selassie (Ras [Prince] Tafari, "the Lion of
   Judah")(emp., Eth.; 1891-1975)
Hailey, Arthur (US writer; 1920-)
Hain Pure Food Co., Inc.
Hainaut (province, Belgium)
Haiphong, Vietnam
Hair (play; film, 1979)
Hairi, Rafiq al- (PM, Lebanon)
Haise, Fred W(allace), Jr. (astro.; 1933-)
Haiti (Republic of)(Caribbean Sea)
Haiti Trans Air (airline)
Haitian Centers Council, Sale v. (US law; 1993)
Haitian Creole (lang.)
Hakka (lang.)
Hal David (US lyricist.; 1921-)
Hal Foster (US cartoonist; *Tarzan, Prince
   Valiant*; 1892-1982)
Hal Holbrook (ent.; 1925-)
Hal Linden (ent.; 1931-)
Hal Roach (ent.; 1892-92)
Hal (Harold Brent) Wallis (ent.; 1899-1986)
Hal Williams (ent.; 1938-)
Halakhah (also Halakah, Halachah,
   Halacha)(Jew. law/tradition)
Halas, George (Stanley)(football; 1895-1983)
Halberstam, David (writer; 1934-)
Halcion™ (med.)
Halcyon (also Halcyone)(astrol., myth.)
Haldeman, H. R. "Bob" (US pol.; 1926-93)
Haldol™ (med.)
Hale Irwin (golf; 1945-)
Hale Stores, Inc., Carter Hawley
Hale, Alan (ent.; 1892-1950)
Hale, Alan, Jr. (ent.; 1919-90)
Hale, Barbara (ent.; 1922-)
Hale, Edward Everett (US writer/rel.; 1822-
   1909)
Hale, Nathan (US mil.,; 1755-76)
Haleakala National Park (HI)
Halen, Eddie Van (ent.; 1957-)
Haley and the Comets, Bill (pop music)
Haley, Alex (US writer; 1921-92)
Haley, Bill (ent.; 1925-81)
Haley, Jack (ent.; 1899-1979)
Haley's M-O™ (med.)
Half Moon Bay, CA
Half Price Books, Records, and Magazines
Haliburton, Thomas Chandler (pseud. Sam
   Slick)(Can. writer/judge/hist.; 1796-1865)
Halicarnassus (SW Asia Minor)

Halicarnassus, Mausoleum at (1 of 7 Wonders of the World)
Halifax, England
Halifax, Nova Scotia, Canada
Hall & Oates (pop music)
Hall of Fame (NY)(erected 1990)
Hall of Fame Bowl (college football)
Hall, Annie (film; 1977)
Hall, Arsenio (ent.; 1955-)
Hall, Daryl (ent.; 1948-)
Hall, Deidre (ent.; 1948-)
Hall, Fawn (US news)
Hall, Gary (swimming; 1951-)
Hall, Huntz (ent.; 1919-)
Hall, Monty (ent.; 1925-)
Hall, Peter (Reginald Frederick)(Br. theater; 1930-)
Hall, Tom T. (ent.; 1936-)
Halle, Germany (also Halleander Saale)
Halleander Saale, Germany (also Halle)
Halley, Edmund (Br. astron.; 1656-1742)
Halley's Comet (astron.)
Hallmark Cards, Inc.
Halloween (10/31)
Hallowmas (also All Saints' Day, All-Hallows)(rel.)
Hall's honeysuckle (plant)
Halls™ Mentho-Lyptus (med.)
Halpern, Steven
Hals, Frans (Dutch artist; c1580-1666)
Halsey, William F(rederick)(US mil.; 1882-1959)
Halston (Roy Halston Frowick)(US designer; 1932-90)
Halston™
Halston-Borghese (US bus.)
Ham Fisher (US cartoonist, *Joe Palooka*; 1900-55)
Hamadou, Barkat Gourad (PM, Djibouti
Hambletonian (horse, race)
Hamburg (chicken)
Hamburg (state, Ger.)
Hamburg, Germany
Hamburg, NY
Hamburger Helper™
Hamden, CT
Hamed Karoui (PM, Tunisia)
Hamel, Veronica (ent.; 1943-)
Hamill, Dorothy (Stuart)(figure skating; 1956-)
Hamill, Mark (ent.; 1951)
Hamilton Beach/Proctor-Silex, Inc.
Hamilton Fish (US pol.; 1808-93)
Hamilton Fish, III (US pol.; 1899-1991)
Hamilton Fish, Jr. (US cong.; 1926-)
Hamilton Green (ex-PM, Guyana)
Hamilton River (Can.)
Hamilton, Alexander (US pol.; 1755-1804)
Hamilton, Bermuda

Hamilton, Edith (Ger./US educ./writer; 1867-1963)
Hamilton, Lady Emma (b. Amy Lyon)(Br. lady; 1765?-1815)
Hamilton, Fort, NY (mil.)
Hamilton, Gail (aka Mary Abigail Dodge)(US writer; 1833-96)
Hamilton, George (ent.; 1939-)
Hamilton, Linda (ent.)
Hamilton, New Zealand
Hamilton, OH
Hamilton, Ontario, Canada
Hamilton, Scotland
Hamilton, Scott (figure skating; 1958-)
Hamites (people)
Hamitic (lang./people)
Hamitic, Nilo (lang.)
Hamito-Semitic (langs.)
Hamlet (Prince of Denmark)(Shakespeare play)
Hamlin, Hannibal (ex-US VP; 1809-91)
Hamlin, Harry (ent.; 1951-)
Hamlisch, Marvin (US comp.; 1944-)
Hamm Brewing Co.
Hamm, Germany
Hammacher, Schlemmer & Co., Inc.
Hammarskjöld, Dag (Hjalmar Agne Carl)(Swed., UN secy gen.; 1905-61)
Hammer v. Dagenhart (US law; 1918)
Hammer, Armand (US bus.; 1898-1990)
Hammer, M. C. (b. Stanley Kirk Burrell)(ent.; 1962-)
Hammer, Mike (fict. chara., Mickey Spillane)
Hammermill Paper Co.
Hammerstein, Oscar (ent.; 1847-1919)
Hammerstein, Oscar, II (US lyricist; 1895-1960)
Hammett, (Samuel) Dashiell (US writer; 1894-1961)
Hammond organ™
Hammond Organ Co.
Hammond, IN, LA
Hammond, Kathy (runner; 1951-)
Hamm's™
Hammurabi (also Hammurapi)(king, Babylonia; c20th c. BC)
Hammurabi Code (ancient law)
Hampshire (also Hampshire Down)(sheep)
Hampshire (also Hants)(county, Eng.)
Hampshire (hog)
Hampton Court (palace, London)
Hampton Court Conference (Br. hist.; 1604)
Hampton Institute (VA)
Hampton Roads Channel (VA/Chesapeake Bay)
Hampton, Lionel (US jazz; 1913-)
Hampton, VA
Han (people)
Han Chinese (people)
Han Cities, China (also Wuhan)
Han dynasty (Ch. hist.; 202 BC-AD 220)

Han River (Ch.)
Han Solo (fict. chara., *Star Wars*)
Hana Mandlikova (tennis; 1962-)
Hanafi (Islamic law)
Hanauer, Chip (boat racing)
Hanbali (Islamic law)
Hancock Bowl, John (college football)
Hancock Mutual Life Insurance Co., John
Hancock, Herbie (US jazz; 1940-)
Hancock, John (one's signature)
Hancock, John (US pol.; 1737-93)
Hand, Learned (Billings)(US jurist; 1872-1961)
Handel, George Frederick (also Georg
    Friedrich)(Ger./Br. comp.; 1685-1759)
Handi-Wrap™
H & R Block™ tax service
H & R Block, Inc.
Handy, W(illiam) C(hristopher)(US jazz; 1873-
    1958)
Hanes™
Hanes Hosiery, Inc.
Hanes Underwear (US bus.)
Hangchow, China (now Hangzhou)
Hanging Gardens of Babylon (1 of 7 Wonders of
    the World)
Hangtown Fry (oyster omelet)
Hangul (Korean alphabet)
Hangzhou, China (formerly Hangchow)
Hani (lang.)
Hanimex™ (movie equipment)
Hanimex USA, Inc.
Hank (Henry) Aaron (baseball; 1934-)
Hank (Henry) Bauer (baseball; 1922-)
Hank Brown (US cong.; 1940-)
Hank Ketcham (US cartoonist, *Dennis the
    Menace*; 1920-)
Hank Snow (ent.; 1914-)
Hank Williams (ent.; 1923-53)
Hank Williams, Jr. (ent.; 1939-)
Hanks, Tom (ent.; 1956-)
Hanna-Barbera Productions, Inc.
Hanna Boys center (Boys' Town of the
    West)(CA)
Hanna Suchocka (ex-PM, Pol.)
Hanna, Bill (cartoonist, *Tom & Jerry,
    Huckleberry Hound, Yogi Bear, Flintstones*;
    1910-)
Hannaford Brothers Co.
Hannah More (Br. writer; 1745-1833)
Hannah, Daryl (ent.; 1961-)
Hanni Wenzel
Hannibal (Carthaginian gen.; 247-182 BC)
Hannibal Hamlin (ex-US VP; 1809-91)
Hannibal, MO
Hanns Kornell Champagne Cellars (US bus.)
Hanoi, Vietnam
Hanover, Germany
Hanover, House of (Br. ruling family; 1714-

1901)
Hans Adam, Prince (head of state,
    Liechtenstein; 1945-)
Hans Albrecht Bethe (US physt.; 1906-)
Hans (or Jean) Arp (Fr. artist; 1887-1966)
Hans (or Johannes) Bach (Ger. musician, great-
    grandfather of J.S.; 1580-1626)
Hans Brinker, or the Silver Skates (children's
    book)
Hans Brunhart (premier, Liechtenstein
Hans Christian Andersen (Dan. writer; 1805-
    75)
Hans Christian Joachim Gram (Dan. phys.;
    1853-1938)
Hans Conried (ent.; 1917-82)
Hans-Dietrich Genscher (Ger. pol.; 1927-)
Hans Fischer (Ger. chem.; 1881-1945)
Hans Geiger (Ger. physt.; 1882-1945)
Hans Holbein, the Elder (Ger. artist; 1460-
    1524)
Hans Holbein, the Younger (Ger. artist; 1497-
    1543)
Hans Jurgen Eysenck (Br. psych.; 1916-)
Hans (Adolf) Krebs, Sir (Ger./Br. chem.; 1900-
    81)
Hans (Christian) Oersted (Dan. physt; 1777-
    1851)
Hans Sachs (Ger. writer; 1494-1576)
Hans Zinsser (US bacteriol.; 1878-1940)
Hansa League (also Hanseatic)(Ger. hist.)
Hansard (verbatim published reports of Br.
    Parliament)
Hansard, Luke (Br. Parliament reporter; 1752-
    1828)
Hansberry, Lorraine (US writer; 1930-65)
Hanscom Air Force Base (MA)
Hanseatic League (also Hansa)(Ger. hist.)
Hänsel and Gretel (folktale)
Hansen, Gerhard Henrik Armauer (Nor. phys.;
    1841-1912)
Hansen™, Sally (cosmetics)
Hansen, Sally (US bus.)
Hansen's disease (leprosy)
Hansom, J. A. (Br. arch., hansom cab; 1803-82)
Hanson, Duane (US sculptor; 1925-)
Hanson, Howard (US comp.; 1896-1981)
Hanukkah (also Chanukah)(rel.)
Hanuman (myth.)
Hanzell Vineyards (US bus.)
Hap (Henry) Arnold (US mil.; 1886-1950)
Happy (A. B.) Chandler (baseball; 1899-1991)
Happy Days (TV show)
Happy Hooligan (comic strip)
Happy Valley (utopia, S. Johnson)
Happy Valley-Goose Bay, Newfoundland,
    Canada
Hapsburg family (also Habsburg)(Eur./Ger.
    royal family)

Haq, Muhammad Zia ul- ("President Zia")(ex-pres., Pak.; 1924-88)

Har Gobind Khorana (India/US chem.; 1922-)

Harald V (also Harold)(king, Nor.; 1936-)

Harappa

Harare, Zimbabwe

Harbin, China (also Haerhpin, Pinkiang)

Harburg, (E. Y.) Yip (US lyricist; 1898-1981)

Harcourt Brace Jovanovich, Inc.

Harcourt, Port (Nigeria)

Hard Copy (TV show)

Hardaway, Anfernee (basketball; 1972-)

Hardaway, Tim (basketball; 1966-)

Hardee's™

Hardee's Food Systems, Inc.

Hardin, John Wesley (US outlaw; 1853-95)

Harding, Tonya (figure skating)

Harding, Warren G(amaliel)(29th US pres.; 1865-1923)

Hardwick, Bowers v. (US law; 1986)

Hardwicke, Sir Cedric (ent.; 1893-1964)

Hardy Boys (Joe & Frank)

Hardy, Laurel & (Stan & Oliver)(US comedy team)

Hardy, Oliver (ent.; 1892-1957)

Hardy, Thomas (Br. writer; 1840-1928)

Hardy-Weinberg principle/law/distribution (genetics)

Hare Krishna (rel.)

Harewood, Dorian (ent.; 1951-)

Hargreaves, James (Br. inv.; ?-1778)

Hari, Mata (b. Gertrud Margarete Zelle)(Dutch dancer, executed as spy by Fr.; 1876-1917)

Harijans (also Scheduled Castes, formerly Untouchables)(India)

Harkin, Thomas R. (US cong.; 1939-)

Harlan Ellison (US writer)

Harlan Fiske Stone (US jurist; 1872-1946)

Harlan Mathews (US cong.; 1927-)

Harlan, John Marshall (US jurist; 1833-1911)

Harlan, John Marshall (US jurist; 1899-1971)

Harlem (NYC)

Harlem Globetrotters (basketball team; founded 1927)

Harlem Renaissance (also Black Renaissance)(post-WWI)

Harlem River (NY)

Harlequin (comic chara.)(also l.c.)

Harlequin Enterprises, Ltd.

Harley-Davidson™ motorcycle

Harley Davidson, Inc.

Harlingen, TX

Harlow Shapley (US astron.; 1885-1972)

Harlow, Jean (b. Harlean Carpenter)(ent.; 1911-37)

Harman-Kardon™ stereo

Harman-Kardon, Inc.

Harmon Killebrew (baseball; 1936-)

Harmon, Mark (ent.; 1951-)

Harmonic Convergence (astron./astrol.)

Harmonicats, The (ent.)

Harold Alexander (Br. mil.; 1891-1969)

Harold and Maude (film)

Harold Arlen (US comp.; 1905-86)

Harold Gould (ent.; 1923-)

Harold "Red" Grange, (football; 1903-)

Harold Gray (US cartoonist, *Little Orphan Annie*; 1894-1968)

Harold Guy Hunt (AL gov.; 1933-)

Harold Lloyd (ent.; 1893-1971)

Harold Macmillan, (Maurice)(ex-PM, Br.; 1895-1987)

Harold Nicholas (ent.; 1924-)

Harold Pinter (Br. writer; 1930-)

Harold Ramis (ent.)

Harold Robbins (US writer; 1916-)

Harold Rome (US comp.; 1908-)

Harold Solomon (tennis; 1952-)

Harold (Edward) Stassen (US pol.; 1907-)

Harold V (also Harald)(king, Nor.; 1936-)

Harold Wilson, Sir (James)(ex-PM, Br.; 1916-)

Harper & Row Publishers, Inc.

Harper, Jessica (ent.; 1949-)

Harper, Tess (ent.; 1950-)

Harper, Valerie (ent.; 1940-)

Harper's Bazaar (mag.)

Harper's Magazine (mag.)

Harpers (or Harper's) Ferry (WV)

Harpers (or Harper's) Ferry National Historical Park (MD/WV)

Harpo Marx, (Arthur)(ent.; 1888-1964)

Harpy (myth.)

Harrelson, Woody (ent.; 1961-)

Harriet Beecher Stowe (US writer/abolitionist; 1811-96)

Harriet (Hilliard) Nelson (ent.; 1914-)

Harriet Nelson, Ozzie & (TV couple)

Harriet S. Adams (pseud. Carolyn Keene)(US writer; 1803-82)

Harriet Tubman (b. Araminta Ross)(US reformer; c1820-1913)

Harriman, (William) Averell (US pol./dipl.; 1891-1986)

Harriman, Edward H(enry)(US bus., railroad; 1848-1909)

Harrington, Michael (US reformer/writer; 1928-89)

Harrington, Pat, Jr. (ent.; 1929-)

Harris Poll

Harris Tweed™ (fabric)

Harris Wofford (US cong.; 1926-)

Harris, Sir Arthur Travers (Br. mil.; 1895-1984)

Harris, Barbara (ent.; 1935-)

Harris, Ed (ent.; 1950-)

Harris, Emmylou (ent.; 1947-)

Harris, Franco (football; 1950-)

Harris, Jean (Struven)(US educ., shot Dr. H. Tarnower)
Harris, Joel Chandler (US writer; 1848-1908)
Harris, Julie (ent.; 1925-)
Harris, Louis (US pollster/writer; 1921-)
Harris, Neil Patrick (ent.; 1973-)
Harris, Phil (ent.; 1904-)
Harris, Richard (ent.; 1933-)
Harris, Roy (US comp.; 1898-1979)
Harrisburg News (PA newspaper)
Harrisburg Patriot (PA newspaper)
Harrisburg, PA
Harrison Ford (ent.; 1942-)
Harrison H. Schmitt (astro.)
Harrison, Benjamin (23rd US pres.; 1833-1901)
Harrison, Benjamin (US pol.; 1726?-91)
Harrison, Fort (Benjamin), IN (mil.)
Harrison, George (ent.; 1943-)
Harrison, Gregory (ent.; 1950-)
Harrison, Peter (US arch.; 1716-75)
Harrison, Rex (Reginald Carey)(ent.; 1908-90)
Harrison, Wallace K. (US arch.; 1895-1981)
Harrison, William Henry (9th US pres.; 1773-1841)
Harrods store (London)
Harrow (London borough)
Harrow(-on-the-Hill)(London school; founded 1571)
Harry A(ndrew) Blackmun (ex-US jurist; 1908-)
Harry & David, Inc.
Harry Anderson (ent.; 1949-)
Harry Babbitt
Harry Belafonte (ent.; 1927-)
Harry Blackstone, Jr. (ent.; 1934-)
Harry Bridges, (Alfred Renton Bridges)(US labor leader; 1901-90)
Harry Caray
Harry Carney (US jazz; 1910-74)
Harry Chapin (ent.; 1942-81)
Harry Connick, Jr. (ent.; 1967-)
Harry Crews (US writer; 1935-)
Harry Daniell (ent.; 1894-1963)
Harry Dean Stanton (ent.; 1926-)
Harry Diamond Laboratories (MD)(mil.)
Harry Emerson Fosdick (US rel./writer; 1878-1969)
Harry F. Guggenheim (US finan./bus.; 1890-?)
Harry Guardino (ent.; 1925-)
Harry Hamlin (ent.; 1951-)
Harry Hershfield (US cartoonist, *Abie the Agent*; 1885-1974)
Harry Houdini (Erich Weiss)(US magician; 1874-1926)
Harry James (ent.; 1916-83)
Harry Morgan (ent.; 1915-)
Harry M. Reid (US cong.; 1922-)
Harry M(orris) Warner (ent.; 1881-1958)
Harry Reasoner (US TV jour.; 1923-91)

Harry Rono (track; 1952-)
Harry Ruby (US comp.; 1895-1974)
Harry Stack Sullivan (US psych.; 1892-1949)
Harry S Truman (33rd US pres.; 1884-1972)
Harry Thomason (ent.)
Harry von Tilzer (US comp.; 1872-1946)
Harry Von Zell (ent.; 1906-81)
Harry Warren (US comp.; 1893-1981)
Harry Winston (US bus./diamonds)
Harry Winston, Inc.
Harry, Deborah (ent.; 1945-)
Harsco Corp.
Hart Crane, (Harold)(US poet; 1899-1932)
Hart to Hart (TV show)
Hart, Johnny (US cartoonist, *BC, Wizard of Id*; 1931-)
Hart, Lorenz (US lyricist; 1895-1943)
Hart, Mary (ent.; 1951-)
Hart, Moss (US writer; 1904-61)
Hart, Rodgers & (comp./lyricist team)
Hart, William S(hakespeare)(ent.; 1870?-1946)
Hartack, Bill (William), Jr. (jockey; 1932-)
Harte, (Francis) Bret (US writer; 1839-1902)
Hartex, Leggett & Platt/ (US bus.)
Hartford Courant (CT newspaper)
Hartford Whalers (hockey team)
Hartford Wits (also Connecticut Wits)(18th c US lit. grp.)
Hartford, CT
Hartley Act, Taft (Labor-Management Relations Act of 1947)
Hartley, Mariette (ent.; 1940-)
Hartman, David (ent.; 1935-)
Hartman, Lisa (ent.; 1956-)
Hartsfield Atlanta International Airport (GA)
Haruki Murakami (Jap. writer; 1949-)
Harum, Procol (pop music)
Harunobu, Suzuki (Jap. artist; 1725-70)
Harvard Business Review
Harvard Magazine
Harvard University (MA)
Harvard, John (Br./US rel.; 1607-38)
Harvey (play/film)
Harvey (Samuel) Firestone (US bus.; 1868-1938)
Harvey Glance (track; 1957-)
Harvey Keitel (ent.; 1947-)
Harvey Korman (ent.; 1927-)
Harvey Kuenn (baseball; 1930-88)
Harvey Kurtzman (cartoonist, *Mad* magazine; 1925-93)
Harvey Milk (San Francisco pol., murdered)
Harvey Wallbanger (mixed drink)
Harvey Williams Cushing (US phys.; 1869-1939)
Harvey, Laurence (ent.; 1928-73)
Harvey, Paul (US news commentator; 1918-)
Harvey, William (Br. phys.; 1578-1657)

Harveys™ Bristol Cream
Harwood, Vanessa
Hasaniya Arabic (lang.)
Hasbro™ (toys)
Hasbro, Inc.
Hashanah, Rosh (High Holy Day, Yom Kippur, High Holiday)
Hashemi Rafsanjani, Hojatolisiam Ali Akbar (pres., Iran; 1934-)
Hashemite Kingdom of Jordan (SW Asia)
Hasid (also Hassid, Chasid)(rel.)
Hasidic movement (rel.)
Hasidism (also Chasidism)(rel.)
Hasmonaean (also Maccabee)(rel.)
Hassam, Childe (US artist; 1859-1935)
Hassan Gouled Aptidon (pres., Djibouti; 1916-)
Hassan II (king, Morocco; 1929-)
Hassanal Bolkiah, Muda, Sultan (PM, Brunei; 1946-)
Hassanali, Noor (Mohammed)(pres., Trinidad/Tobago)
Hassanya Arabic (lang.)
Hasselblad™ camera
Hasselblad, Inc., Victor
Hasselhoff, David (ent.; 1952-)
Hasso, Signe (Swed. ent.; 1910-)
Hastings Kamuzu Banda, (Ngwazi)(pres., Malawi; 1902-)
Hastings, Battle of (Br. hist.; 1066)
Hastings, England
Hastings, MN, NE
Hastings, Thomas (US arch.; 1860-1929)
Hatch Act (US hist.; 1939)
Hatch, Orrin Grant (US cong.; 1934-)
Hatfield, Mark O. (US cong.; 1922-)
Hatfield-McCoy Feud (opposite sides, Amer. Civil War)
Hathaway, Anne (wife of Shakespeare; 1557?-1623)
Hatlo, Jimmy (US cartoonist, *Little Iodine*; 1898-1963)
Hatshepsut (queen, Eg.; c1540-c1481 BC)
Hatteras, Cape (NC)
Hattie McDaniel (ent.; 1895-1952)
Hattiesburg, MS
Hau Pei-tsum (ex-PM, Taiwan)
Hauer, Rutger (Neth. ent.; 1944-)
Haughey, Charles (ex-PM, Ir.; 1925-)
Haughton, William (harness racing; 1923-86)
Hausa (lang./people)
Hausa States (NW Afr.)
Haute-Normandie (region, Fr.)
Hava Nagilah (Isr. dance/song)
Havana (cigar)
Havana brown (cat)
Havana, Cuba
Havarti (cheese)
Havasu City, Lake, AZ

Havatampa Co.
Have Gun, Will Travel (TV show)
Havel, Václav (pres./writer, Czech; 1936-)
Havelock Ellis, (Henry)(Br. psych.; 1859-1939)
Haver, June (ent.; 1926-)
Haverhill, MA
Havilland, Olivia De (ent.; 1916-)
Havlicek, John (basketball; 1940-)
Havoc, June (ent; 1916-)
Havre de Grace, MD
Hawaii (HI)
Hawaii Five-O (TV show)
Hawaii Volcanoes National Park (HI)
Hawaiian Airlines, Inc.
Hawaiian guitar
Hawaiian shirt
Hawaiian Punch™
Hawaiian Tropic™ (health)
Hawalli, Kuwait
Hawke, Bob (Robert James Lee)(ex-PM, Austl.; 1929-)
Hawken, Paul (US bus./writer)
Hawkes, John (US writer; 1925-)
Hawkeye State (nickname, IA)
Hawking, Stephen (William)(Br. physt./math./writer; 1942-)
Hawkins Day, Sadie
Hawkins, Coleman (US jazz; 1904-69)
Hawks, Atlanta (basketball team)
Hawley Hale Stores, Inc., Carter
Hawley-Smoot Tariff Act (US hist.; 1930)
Hawn, Goldie (ent.; 1945-)
Hawthorne, Nathaniel (US writer; 1804-64)
Hay, John (Milton)(US pol.; 1838-1905)
Haya (lang.)
Hayakawa, Sessue (ent.; 1890-1973)
Hayakawa, S(amuel) I(chiye)(US educ./pol./linguist; 1906-92)
Hayatou, Sadou (ex-PM, Cameroon)
Hayden Planetarium (NYC)
Hayden, Sterling (ent.)
Hayden, Tom (Thomas E.)(US pol.; 1941-)
Hayden, William George (gov-gen., Austl.)
Haydn, Franz Joseph (Aus. comp.; 1732-1809)
Hayes, Elvin (basketball; 1945-)
Hayes, Gabby (George)(ent.; 1885-1969)
Hayes (Brown McArthur), Helen (ent.; 1900-93)
Hayes, Isaac (ent.; 1942-)
Hayes, Peter Lind (ent.)
Hayes, Robert (ent.; 1947-)
Hayes, Rutherford B(irchard)(19th US pres.; 1822-93)
Hayes, Woody (football; 1913-87)
Hayley Mills (ent.)
Haymarket Square riot (Chicago; 1886)
Haymes, Dick (ent.)
Haynes, Roy (US jazz; 1926-)
Haynie, Sandra (golf; 1943-)

Hays, Wayne L. (US pol.; 1912-89)
Hayward, CA
Hayward, Susan (ent.; 1917-75)
Haywood, William Dudley (US labor leader; 1869-1928)
Hayworth, Rita (ent.; 1918-87)
Hazara (people)
Hazel (cartoon)
Hazel R. O'Leary (US Secy./Energy; 1937-)
H-bomb (hydrogen bomb)
HDL (high-density lipoprotein)
He (chem. sym., helium)
Head™
Head & Shoulders™ (hair care)
Head of the Class (TV show)
Head Sports, Inc.
Head Sports Wear, Inc.
Head Start, Project (educ.)
Head, Edith (US designer; 1898?-1981)
Headline News™ (CNN)
Headline News (TV show)
Headroom, Max (fict. chara.)
HeadStart™ (compu.)
Health (mag.)
Health and Human Services, Department of (HHS)(US govt.)
Health Care Financing Administration (HCFA) (US govt.)
Health-tex™ clothes
Health-Tex, Inc.
Health Valley™
Health Valley Natural Foods (US bus.)
Healthy Choice™ (food)
Healy, Ted (b. Charles Earnest Nash)(ent.; 1896-1937)
Heard, John (ent.; 1945-)
Hearn, George (ent.; 1935-)
Hearns, Thomas ("Hit Man")(boxing)
Hearst Castle (San Simeon, CA)
Hearst, Patty (Patricia)(US heiress, kidnapped/ imprisoned; 1954-)
Hearst, William Randolph (US publ.; 1863-1951)
Hearst, William Randolph, Jr. (US publ.; 1908-93)
Heart of Atlanta Motel, Inc. v. U.S. (US law; 1964)
Heart of Dixie (nickname, AL)
Heartbreakers, Tom Petty and the (pop music)
Hearts, Queen of
Heat of the Night (TV show)
Heat, Miami (basketball team)
Heath, Edward (Richard George)(ex-PM, Br.; 1916-)
Heathcliff (cartoon)
Heather Locklear (ent.; 1961-)
Heather O'Rourke (ent.; 1978-88)
Heatherton, Joey (ent.)

Heathrow Airport (London)
Heatilator™
Heatilator, Inc.
Heaven (rel.)
Heaven, King of (God)
Heaven, Kingdom of (heaven)
Heaven, Queen of (Virgin Mary)
Heaviside layer, (Kennelly)(also E layer)(in lower regions, ionosphere)
Hebe (myth., astron.)
Hebrew (lang./people)
Hebrew-Aramaic
Hebrew Bible/Scriptures (rel.)
Hebrew calendar (also Jewish calendar)
Hebrew National™ (meats)
Hebrew school (rel.)
Hebrides, Inner (islands, W Scot.)
Hebrides, New (now Vanuatu)
Hebrides, Outer (islands, W Scot.)
Hecate (myth.)
Hecatoncheires (myth.)
Hecht, Ben (US writer; 1894-1964)
Hecht's (department store)
Heckart, Eileen (ent.; 1919-)
Hector (myth.)
Hector (or Louis-Hector) Berlioz (Fr. comp.; 1803-69)
Hector Elizondo (ent.; 1936-)
Hecuba (myth., queen of Troy)
Hedda Gabler (H. Ibsen play)
Hedda Hopper (US columnist/ent.; 1890-1966)
Hedren, Tippi (ent.)
Hedrick Smith (US writer; 1933-)
Hedy Lamarr (ent.; 1913-)
Hee, Park Chung (ex-pres., SKorea; 1917-79)
Heep, Uriah (villain, *David Copperfield*)
Heflin, Howell Thomas (US cong.; 1921-)
Heflin, Van (ent.; 1910-71)
Hefner, Christie Ann (US publ.)
Hefner, Hugh (US publ.; 1926-)
Hefner, Kimberley (US, wife of Hugh H.)
Hefty™ Cinch Sak
Hegel, Georg W(ilhelm Friedrich)(Ger. phil.; 1770-1831)
Hegelian dialectic (phil.)
Hegira (rel.)
Heian period (Jap. hist.; 794-1185)
Heidegger, Martin (Ger. phil.; 1889-1976)
Heidelberg jaw (anthrop.)
Heidelberg man (anthrop.)
Heidelberg, Germany
Heiden, Eric (speed skating; 1958-)
Heidi (by J. Spyri)
Heidi Fleiss (US news)
Heidsieck, Inc., Piper-
Heidt, Horace
Heifetz, Jascha (Rus./US violinist; 1901-87)
Heigh-Ho (song, *Snow White and the Seven*

*Dwarf*s)
Heihachiro, Marquis Togo (Jap. mil.; 1847-1934)
Heike Drechsler
Heike monogatari (Jap. written hist.; 14th c.)
Heimlich maneuver (med.)
Heineken™ (beer)
Heink, Ernestine Schumann- (ent.; 1861-1936)
Heinlein, Robert A(nson)(US writer, sci-fi; 1907-88)
Heinrich (Theodor) Böll (Ger. writer; 1917-85)
Heinrich Geissler (Ger. inv./glassblower; 1814-79)
Heinrich (Rudolph) Hertz (Ger. physt.)
Heinrich Himmler (Ger. Nazi; 1900-45)
Heinrich Lenz (Estonian physt.; 1804-65)
Heinrich Muhlenberg (Ger. rel.; 1711-87)
Heinrich Schliemann (Ger. archaeol.; 1822-90)
Heinz™
Heinz Co., H. J.
Heinz Guderian (Ger. gen.; 1888-1953)
Heinz Pet Products Co.
Heinz, Henry J(ohn)(US food exec.; 1844-1919)
Heisei era (Japan)
Heisenberg uncertainty (or indeterminacy) principle
Heisenberg, Werner Carl (Ger. physt.; 1901-76)
Heisman Trophy (also Heisman Memorial Trophy)(football)
Heitor Villa-Lobos (Brazilian comp.; 1881-1959)
Heitz Wine Cellars (US bus.)
Hekmatyar, Gulbuddin (PM, Afghan.)
Helbros Watches (US bus.)
Held, Anna (ent.; 1873-1918)
Held, John, Jr. (US cartoonist; 1889-1958)
Helen (myth.)
Helen Brooke Taussig (US phys.; 1898-1986)
Helen Frankenthaler (US artist; 1928-)
Helen Gurley Brown (US editor/writer; 1922-)
Helen (Brown McArthur) Hayes (ent.; 1900-93)
Helen Hunt Jackson (pseud. H. H.)(US writer; 1830-85)
Helen (Adams) Keller (US writer/educ., blind/deaf; 1880-1968)
Helen (Clark) MacInnes (Scot. writer; 1907-85)
Helen Newington Wills (Moody)(tennis; 1906-)
Helen O'Connell (ent.; 1921-)
Helen of Troy (myth.)
Helen Reddy (ent.; 1941-)
Helen Slater (ent.; 1963-)
Helen Traubel (US opera; 1903-72)
Helen Vinson (ent.; 1907-)
Helena Modjeska (ent.; 1844-1909)
Helena Petrovna Blavatsky Hahn, Madame (Rus. theosophist; 1831-91)
Helena Rubinstein™ (cosmetics)
Helena Rubinstein (US bus.; 1871-1965)
Helena, MT

Helene Curtis™ (cosmetics)
Helene Curtis Industries
Heliopolis (ancient Eg. city)
Helios (myth.)
Helios space probe
Hellenic languages (also Greek)
Hellenic period (Gr.; 776-323 BC)
Hellenism (Gr. hist.)
Hellenist (Greek-like)
Hellenistic period (Gr.; 323-27 BC)
Heller, Joseph (US writer; 1923-)
Hellespont, the (now the Dardanelles)(strait, Eur./Asia)
Helling v. McKinney (US law; 1993)
Hellman, Lillian (Florence)(US writer; 1905-84)
Hello, Dolly (play/film)
Hell's Kitchen (NYC)
Hellzapoppin (play; film, 1941)
Helmholtz, Hermann (Ludwig Ferdinand) von (Ger. physt.; 1821-94)
Helmond, Katherine (ent.; 1934-)
Helmont, Jean Baptiste van (Belgian physt.; 1577-1644)
Helms, Jesse Alexander (US cong.; 1921-)
Helms, Richard (McGarrah)(US, CIA; 1913-)
Helmsley, Leona (US bus./hotel; c1920-)
Helmut Dantine
Helmut Kohl (Ger. chanc.; 1930-)
Helmut (Heinrich Waldemar) Schmidt (ex-chanc., WGer.; 1918-)
Helmuth von Moltke (Ger. mil.; 1800-91)
Héloïse (Fr., rel., Abelard's love; 1101-64)
Heloise (US writer; 1951-)
Helprin, Mark (US writer; 1947-)
Helsingör, Denmark (also Elsinore)
Helsinki Conference (internat'l mtg.; 1975)
Helsinki, Finland
Helvetica (type style)
Hemingway, Ernest (Miller)(US writer; 1899-1961)
Hemingway, Margaux (ent.; 1955-)
Hemingway, Mariel (ent.; 1961-)
Hemion, Dwight
Hemisphere, Eastern
Hemisphere, Northern
Hemisphere, Southern
Hemisphere, Western
Hemsley, Sherman (ent.; 1938-)
Hencken, John (swimming; 1954-)
Henderson, Fletcher (US jazz; 1898-1952)
Henderson, Florence (ent.; 1934-)
Henderson, NV
Henderson, Ray (US comp.; 1896-1970)
Henderson, Rickey (baseball; 1958-)
Henderson, Skitch (US cond.; 1918-)
Hendrick Terbrugghen (Dutch artist; 1588-1629)
Hendricks, Thomas A(ndrews)(ex-US VP; 1819-

85)

Hendrik F. Verwoerd (ex.pm, SAfr; 1901-66)
Hendrix, Jimi (James Marshall)(ent.; 1942-70)
Henie, Sonja (figure skating/ent.; 1912-69)
Henlein, Konrad (Ger. Nazi; 1898-1945)
Henley, Don (ent.; 1947-)
Henner, Marilu (ent.; 1952-)
Henning, Doug (ent.; 1947-)
Henny Youngman (ent.; 1906-)
Henredon™
Henredon Furniture Industries, Inc.
Henreid, Paul (ent.; 1908-92)
Henri Bergson (Fr. phil.; 1859-1941)
Henri (Marie Raymond) de Toulouse-Lautrec
    (Fr. artist; 1864-1901)
Henri (Joseph Théodore) Fantin-Latour,
    (Ignace)(Fr. artist; 1836-1904)
Henri Giffard (Fr. inv.; 1825-82)
Henri Konan Bedie (pres., Ivory Coast
Henri Laurens (Fr. sculptor; 1884-?)
Henri Matisse (Fr. artist; 1869-1954)
Henri Philippe Pétain (Fr. mil.; 1856-1951)
Henri Poincaré (Fr. math./physt.; 1854-1912)
Henri (Julien Félix) Rousseau ("Le
    Douanier")(Fr. artist; 1844-1910)
Henrietta Maria (queen, Eng.; 1609-69)
Henrik (Johan) Ibsen (Nor. writer; 1828-1906)
Henry "Hank" Aaron (baseball; 1934-)
Henry Adams (US hist.; 1838-1911)
Henry A(lfred) Kissinger, Dr. (US pol.; 1923-)
Henry Aldrich (fict. chara.)
Henry Algernon du Pont (US mil./pol.; 1838-
    1926)
Henry Armstrong (boxing; 1912-88)
Henry "Hap" Arnold (US mil.; 1886-1950)
Henry A(gard) Wallace (ex-US VP; 1888-1965)
Henry Bacon (US arch.; 1866-1924)
Henry Barnard (US educ.; 1811-1900)
Henry Bessemer, Sir (Br. eng.; 1813-98)
Henry Cabot Lodge (US pol.; 1850-1924)
Henry Cabot Lodge, Jr. (US jour./pol.; 1902-85)
Henry Cavendish (Br. chem./physt.; 1731-1810)
Henry Cisneros (US Secy./HUD; 1947-)
Henry Clay (also Great Compromiser, Great
    Pacificator)(US pol.; 1777-1852)
Henry Clay Frick (US bus.; 1849-1919)
Henry Clinton (Br. mil.; 1738-95)
Henry David Thoreau (US writer/phil./nat.;
    1817-62)
Henry Deringer (US gunsmith; 19th c.)
Henry du Pont (US bus.; 1812-89)
Henry (Belin) du Pont (US bus.; 1899-1970)
Henry E. Huntington Library and Art Gallery
    (CA)
Henry Engelhard Steinway (b. Steinweg)(US
    piano manufacturer; 1797-1871)
Henry Fielding (Br. writer; 1707-54)
Henry Fonda (ent.; 1905-82)

Henry Ford (US bus./auto.; 1863-1947)
Henry Ford, II (US bus./auto.; 1917-87)
Henry Gibson (ent.; 1935-)
Henry H. Richardson (US arch.; 1838-86)
Henry Hudson (Br. expl.; c1565-c1611)
Henry I ("the Fowler")(king, Ger.; c876-936)
Henry I ("the Scholar")(king, Eng.; 1068-1135)
Henry I (king, Fr.; 1008-60)
Henry II ("the Saint")(king, Ger./Holy Roman
    emp.; 973-1024)
Henry II (king, Eng.; 1133-89)
Henry II (king, Fr.; 1519-59)
Henry III (king, Eng.; 1207-72)
Henry III (king, Fr.; 1551-89)
Henry III ("the Black")(king, Ger./Holy Roman
    emp.; 1017-56)
Henry IV (Bolingbroke)(king, Eng.; 1367-1413)
Henry IV (king, Ger./Holy Roman emp.; 1050-
    1106)
Henry IV (Rom emp.; 1050-1106)
Henry IV ("the Great")(king, Fr.; 1553-1610)
Henry James (US writer; 1843-1916)
Henry J(ohn) Kaiser (US bus.; 1882-1967)
Henry John Temple Palmerson, Viscount (ex-
    PM, Br.; 1784-1865)
Henry Jones (ent.; 1912-)
Henry Laurens (US pol.; 1724-92)
Henry "Light-Horse Harry" Lee (Amer. gen.;
    1756-1818)
Henry L(ewis) Stimson (US pol.; 1867-1950)
Henry Mancini (US comp.; 1924-94)
Henry Martyn Robert (US eng., wrote Robert's
    Rules of Order; 1837-1923)
Henry M(orrison) Flagler (US finan.; 1830-
    1913)
Henry Miller (US writer; 1891-1980)
Henry Moore (Br. sculptor; 1898-1986)
Henry Morgan (ent.; 1915-)
Henry Morgan, Sir (Welsh buccaneer in Amer.;
    1635?-88)
Henry Morgenthau (US finan./dipl.; 1856-1946)
Henry Morgenthau, Jr. (US publ./pol.; 1891-
    1967)
Henry M(orton) Stanley, Sir (aka John
    Rowlands)(Br. jour./expl.; 1841-1904)
Henry Percy, Sir (aka Hotspur)(Br. mil.; 1366-
    1403)
Henry Purcell (Br. comp.; 1658?-95)
Henry R. Kravis
Henry Robinson Luce (US publ.; 1898-1967)
Henry Roth (US writer; 1906-)
Henry Royce, (Frederick)(Br. eng./Rolls-Royce;
    1863-1933)
Henry Steele Commager (US hist./educ.; 1902-)
Henry the Fowler (Henry I)(king, Ger.; c876-
    936)
Henry the Lion (Roman duke/mil.; 1129-95)
Henry the Navigator (Port. prince/nav.; 1394-

1460)

Henry T(omkins) P. Comstock (US, Comstock Lode)

Henry V (king, Eng.; 1387-1422)

Henry V (king, Ger./Holy Roman emp.; 1081-1125)

Henry VI (king, Eng./Fr.; 1421-71)

Henry VI (king, Ger./Holy Roman emp.; 1165-97)

Henry VII (Henry Tudor)(king, Eng.; 1457-1509)

Henry VII (of Luxemburg)(king, Ger./Holy Roman emp.; 1275?-1313)

Henry VIII (king, Eng.; 1491-1547)

Henry Villard (US bus.; 1835-1900)

Henry Wadsworth Longfellow (US poet; 1807-82)

Henry Ward Beecher (US rel./abolitionist; 1813-87)

Henry Wheeler Shaw (pseud. Josh Billings)(US humorist; 1818-85)

Henry Wilson (ex-US VP; 1812-75)

Henry Winkler (ent.; 1945-)

Henry Wriothesley (Earl of Southhampton)(Br. scholar; 1573-1624)

Henry, John (fict. chara., exceptional strength)

Henry, Joseph (US phys./inv.; 1797-1878)

Henry, O. (aka. William Sydney Porter)(US writer; 1862-1910)

Henry, Patrick (US pol./orator; 1736-99)

Henry, William (Br. chem.; 1774-1836)

Henry's law (gas in liquid)

Henson, Jim (James Maury)(US puppeteer/ Muppets; 1936-90)

Henze, Hans Werner (Ger. comp.; 1926-)

Hepburn v. Griswold (US law; 1870)

Hepburn, Audrey (ent.; 1929-93)

Hepburn, Katharine (ent.; 1907-)

Hephaestus (myth.)

Hepplewhite, George (Br. furniture designer; ?-1786)

Hera (myth.)

Heracles (also Hercules)(myth.)

Heraclitus ("the Obscure")(Gr. phil.; c535-c475 BC)

Heraclius (Byzantine emp.; c575-641)

Herald-American, Syracuse (NY newspaper)

Herald Examiner, Los Angeles (CA newspaper)

Herald-Journal, Syracuse (NY newspaper)

Herald-Leader, Lexington (KY newspaper)

Herald-Post, El Paso (TX newspaper)

Herald-Tribune, Sarasota (FL newspaper)

Herald, Augusta (GA newspaper)

Herald, Boston (MA newspaper)

Herald, Chicago (IL newspaper)

Herald, Miami (FL newspaper)

Heralds' College (also College of Arms)(Br. heraldry)

Herat, Afghanistan

Herb Alpert (ent.; 1935-)

Herb Alpert and The Tijuana Brass (pop music)

Herb(ert Lawrence) Block (aka Herblock)(US pol. cartoonist; 1909-)

Herb Edelman (ent.; 1933-)

Herb Kohl (US cong.; 1935-)

Herb Shriner (ent.)

Herbalife™

Herbalife International (US bus.)

Herbert A. Adderly, (football; 1939-)

Herbert Beerbohm Tree, Sir (ent.; 1853-1917)

Herbert Blaize (ex-PM, Grenada; 1918-1989)

Herbert C(lark) Hoover (31st US pres.; 1874-1964)

Herbert H. Asquith (ex-PM, Br.; 1852-1928)

Herbert H(enry) Dow (US bus./chem.; 1866-1930)

Herbert Marcuse (US phil.; 1898-1979)

Herbert Marshall (ent.; 1890-19676)

Herbert "Zeppo" Marx (ent.; 1901-79)

Herbert Spencer (Br. phil.; 1820-1903)

Herbert Tree, Sir (b. Herbert Beerbohm)(ent.; 1853-1917)

Herbert von Karajan (Aus. cond.; 1908-)

Herbert, Victor (Ir./US comp./cond.; 1859-1924)

Herbie Hancock (US jazz; 1940-)

Herbie Mann (US jazz; 1930-)

Herblock (aka Herbert [Lawrence] Block)(US pol. cartoonist; 1909-)

Herb-Ox™ (bouillon cubes)

Hercegovina, Bosnia- (republic. Yug.)(also Bosnia-Herzegovina)

Hercule Poirot (fict. detective, Agatha Christie)

Hercules (also Heracles)(myth.)

Hercules (astron.)

Hercules, Pillars of (rocks/entrance, Strait of Gibralter)

Herder, Johann G(ottfried von)(Ger. phil.; 1744-1803)

Hereford (cattle, hogs)

Hereford and Worcester (county, Eng.)

Herero (people)

Here's Lucy (TV show)

Heritage USA (rel., PTL)

Herlihy, Ed

Herman Jansen Knickerbocker (Dutch settler in NY; 1650?-1716?)

Herman Melville (US writer; 1819-91)

Herman Miller, Inc. (furniture)

Herman (or Gherman) S(tepanovich) Titov (cosmo.; 1935-)

Herman Tarnower (US phys., Scarsdale Diet; 1911-80)

Herman Wouk (US writer; 1915-)

Herman, Floyd Caves (Babe)(baseball; 1903-87)

Herman, Jerry (US comp.; 1932-)

Herman, Pee-Wee (aka Paul Rubens)(ent.;

1952-)
Herman, Woody (Woodrow)(US jazz; 1913-87)
Hermann Fehling (Ger. chem.; 1812-85)
Hermann Hesse (Ger. writer; 1877-1962)
Hermann Wilhelm Goering (or Göring)(Ger. Nazi; 1893-1946)
Hermaphroditus (myth.)
Hermes (myth.)
Hermione Gingold (ent.; 1897-1987)
Hermitage museum (Leningrad, USSR)
Hernandez, Keith (baseball; 1953-)
Hernando Cortés (or Ferdinand)(also Cortez)(Sp. expl.; 1485-1547)
Hernando (or Fernando) de Soto (Sp. expl.; c1496-1542)
Herndon v. Lowry (US law; 1937)
Herne, Germany
Hero and Leander (myth.)
Herod Agrippa I (b. Marcus Julius Agrippa)(king, Palestine; c10 BC-AD 44)
Herod Agrippa II (king, Chalcis; c40-93)
Herod Antipas (gov., Galilee; 21 BC-AD 39)
Herod the Great (king, Judea; 74-4 BC)
Herodotus (Gr. hist.; c484-420 BC)
Herrera v. Collins (US law; 1993)
Herrera, Luis Alberto Lacalle (pres. Uruguay; 1941-)
Herrera, Omar Torrijos (Panamanian gen./pol.; 1929-81)
Herriman, George (US cartoonist, *Krazy Kat*; 1881-1944)
Herriot, Édouard (ex-PM/pres., Fr.; 1872-1957)
Herriot, James (Br. writer)
Herrmann, Edward (ent.; 1943-)
Herschel Bernardi (ent.; 1923-86)
Herschel, Caroline Lucretia (Br. astron.; 1750-1848)
Herschel, John Frederick William (Br. astron.; 1792-1871)
Herschel, William (Br. astron.; 1738-1822)
Hershiser, Orel (baseball; 1958-)
Hersey, John (US writer; 1917-93)
Hershey Bar™
Hershey Chocolate USA (US bus.)
Hershey Foods Corp.
Hershey, Barbara (ent.; 1948-)
Hershey, Milton (Snavely)(US, bus./chocolate; 1857-1945)
Hershey, PA
Hershey's™ chocolate
Hershfield, Harry (US cartoonist, *Abie the Agent*; 1885-1974)
Hersholt, Jean
Hertfordshire (county, Eng.)
Hertz™ (car rental)
Hertz Corp.
Hertz, Heinrich (Ger. physt.; 1857-94)
Hertzog, James Barry Munnik (ex-PM, SAfr.;

1866-1942)
Hertzsprung-Russell diagram (astron.)
Herve Villechaize (ent.; 1943-93)
Herzegovina, Bosnia- (republic. Yug.)(also Bosnia-Hercegovina)
Herzi, Theodor (Aus. pol.; 1860-1904)
Herzog (S. Bellow novel)
Herzog, Chaim (ex-pres., Isr.; 1918-)
Herzog, Emile (pseud. André Maurois)(Fr. writer; 1885-1967)
Herzog, Werner (Ger. ent.; 1942-)
Heshvan (Jew. month)
Hesiod (Gr. poet; 8th c. BC)
Hesperides (myth.)
Hesperus, The Wreck of the (by. H.W. Longfellow)
Hess, (Walther Richard) Rudolf (Ger. Nazi; 1894-1987)
Hess, Victor Franz (Aus. physt.; 1883-?)
Hesse (state, Ger.)
Hesse, Hermann (Ger. writer; 1877-1962)
Hesseman, Howard (ent.; 1940-)
Hessian boots
Hessian troops (mercenaries, Amer. Rev.)
Hess's law (chem.)
Hestia (myth.)
Heston, Charlton (ent.; 1924-)
Hetty Green (US finan., "witch of Wall Street"; 1834-1916)
Heublein Fine Wine Group (US bus.)
Heublein, Inc.
Heusen Corp., Phillips-Van
Heusen, Jimmy (James) Van (US comp.; 1913-90)
HEW (Department of Health, Education, and Welfare)
Hewitt Museum, Cooper- (Smithsonian, DC)
Hewlett-Packard™
Hewlett-Packard Co. (HP)
Heydrich, Reinhard (Ger. Nazi; 1904-42)
Heyerdahl, Thor (Nor. expl./anthrop.; 1914-)
Heyward, DuBose (US writer/lyricist; 1885-1940)
Heywood, Eddie (US jazz; 1916-89)
Hezbollah (also Party of God)(rel./mil.)
HF (high frequency)
Hf (chem. sym., hafnium)
H. F. Ahmanson & Co. (S&L assoc.)
Hg (chem. sym., mercury)
H(erbert) G(eorge) Wells (Br. writer; 1866-1946)
HH (Her/His Highness)
H. H. (aka Helen Hunt Jackson)(US writer; 1830-85)
H(ector) H(ugh) Munro (pseud. Saki)(Br. writer; 1870-1916)
H-hour (mil., time of attack)
HHS (Department of Health and Human Services)(US govt.)

HI (Hawaii)
Hi & Lois (comic strip)
Hi-C™ (drink)
Hi Ho™ (crackers)
Hialeah Park Racetrack (FL)
Hialeah, FL
Hiawatha, Chief (NAmer. Indian/educ.; 16th c.)
Hiawatha, The Song of (Longfellow poem)
Hickam Air Force Base, HI (mil.)
Hickcox, Charles (swimming; 1947-)
Hickel, Wally (Walter J.)(AK gov.; 1919-)
Hickok, Wild Bill (James Butler)(US frontier/law; 1837-76)
Hickory Farms™
Hickory Farms, Inc.
Hickory, NC
Hicks, Edward (US artist; 1780-1849)
Hicks, St. Mary's Honor Center v. (US law; 1993)
Hidalgo (state, Mex.)
Hidalgo y Costilla, Miguel (Mex. rel.; 1753-1811)
Hidatsa Indians/lang.)
Hidden Valley™ (food)
Hide-A-Bed™
Hideki, Tojo (ex-PM, Jap.; 1884-1948)
Hieronymous Bosch (Dutch artist; 1450-1516)
Higby's Yogurt & Treat Shoppe, J. (US bus.)
Higginbotham, Jay C. (US jazz; 1906-73)
Higgins, William R. (US mil.)
Higgledy-Piggledy (play)
High Anxiety (film; 1977)
High Church
High German
High Holy Day (Rosh Hashanah, Yom Kippur, High Holiday)
High Mass (rel.)
High Noon (film; 1952)
High Point, NC (furniture)
High Renaissance
High Society (film; 1956)
High Times
Highland fling (Scot. dance)
Highland Park, MI
Highland Region (Scot.)
Highlands (Scot. area)
Highlights for Children (mag.)
Highness, Your (title)
Highway to Heaven (TV show)
Hijrah (also Hegira)(rel.)
Hilbert, David (Ger. math.; 1862-1943)
Hilda Doolittle ("HD")(US poet; 1886-1961)
Hilda, Broom (comic strip)
Hildegarde (ent,; 1906-)
Hildegarde Neff (ent.)
Hiligaynon, Panay- (lang.)
Hill Book Co., McGraw-
Hill Street Blues (TV show)

Hill Winery, William (US bus.)
Hill, Arthur (ent.; 1922-)
Hill, Benny (ent.; 1925-92)
Hill, George Roy (ent.; 1922-)
Hill, Inc., McGraw-
Hill, James J. (US bus.; 1838-1916)
Hill, Steven (ent.; 1922-)
Hill, the (also Capitol, Capitol Hill)(US Congress)
Hillary Rodham Clinton (US atty.; wife of US pres.; 1947-)
Hillary, Sir Edmund P(ercival)(NewZeal. expl., Mt. Everest; 1919-)
Hillel (Jew. rel./educ.; fl. 30 BC-AD 9)
Hillel Foundation
Hiller, Wendy, Dame (ent.; 1912-)
Hillerman, John (ent.; 1932-)
Hillman, Sidney (US labor leader; 1887-1946)
Hills Bros™
Hills Brothers Coffee, Inc.
Hills, Carla
Hillsborough, Grenada
Hillshire Farm™
Hillshire Farm Co.
Hilly, Francis Billy (PM, Solomon Islands)
Hilo, HI
Hilton Head Island, SC
Hilton Hotels Corp.
Hilton, Conrad N(icholson)(US bus./hotels; 1888-1979)
Himalayan (cat)
Himalayas (also Himalaya[n] Mountains)(India)
Himmler, Heinrich (Ger. Nazi; 1900-45)
Hinayana Buddhism (also Theravada Buddhism)(rel.)
Hinckley, John (Warnock), Jr. (US, shot R. Reagan; 1955-)
Hindemith, Paul (Ger./US comp.; 1895-1963)
Hindenburg (dirigible disaster)
Hindenburg, Paul (Ludwig Hans) von (Beneckendorf und)(ex-pres., Ger.; 1847-1932)
Hindenburg, Poland (also Zabrze)
Hindi (lang.)
Hinds, Samuel (PM, Guyana)
Hindu (people)
Hindu Kush Mountains (Asia)
Hinduism (rel.)
Hindustan ("land of the Hindus," India)
Hindustani (people/lang.)
Hines, Duncan (US travel writer/publ.; 1880-1959)
Hines, Earl "Fatha" (US jazz; 1905-83)
Hines, Gregory (ent.; 1946-)
Hines, James (sprinter; 1946-)
Hines, Jerome (ent.; 1921-)
Hingle, Pat (ent.; 1924-)

Hinton, S. E. (US writer; 1948-)
Hipparchus (Gr. astron.; c190-c120 BC)
Hipparcos (*high precision parallax collecting satellite*)(Eur. satellite; 1989)
Hippo, St. Augustine of (rel.; 354-430)
Hippocrates (Gr. phys.; c460-377 BC)
Hippocratic oath (med.)
Hippolyta (queen of Amazons)(myth.)
Hippolyte (Adolphe) Taine (Fr. hist.; 1828-93)
Hippolytus (myth.)
Hirabayashi v. U.S. (US law; 1943)
Hiram Powers (US sculptor; 1805-73)
Hiram Stevens Maxim, Sir (US/Br. inv.; 1840-1916)
Hiram Walker & Sons, Inc.
Hiraoka Kimitake (pseud. Mishima Yukio)(Jap. writer; 1925-70)
Hirobumi Ito, Prince (ex-PM, Jap.; 1841-1909)
Hirohito ("Showa")(emp., Jap.; 1902-89)
Hiroshima, Japan
Hirsch, Judd (ent.; 1935-)
Hirschfeld, Al (cartoonist; 1903-)
Hirshhorn Museum and Sculpture Garden (Smithsonian, DC)
Hirshhorn, Joseph (US bus./finan.)
Hirt, Al (ent.; 1922-)
Hismanal™ (med.)
Hispanic (mag.)
Hispanic American (also Hispano)(people)
Hispaniola, Greater Antilles (Haiti, Dom Rep.)
Hispano (also Hispanic American)(people)
Hiss, Alger (US pol.; 1904-)
Hitachi™
Hitachi Home Electronics America, Inc.
Hitachi-Maxell, Ltd.
Hitchcock Hour, The Alfred (TV show)
Hitchcock Presents, Alfred (TV show)
Hitchcock, Sir Alfred (Joseph)(ent.; 1899-1980)
Hitchcock's Mystery Magazine, Alfred
Hite, Shere (US writer; 1942-)
Hitler, Adolf (Schicklgruber)(*der Führer*)(ex-chanc./dictator, Ger.; 1889-1945)
Hittite (lang./people)
H. J. Heinz Co.
H(enry) L(ouis) Mencken (US writer/editor; 1880-1956)
HM (Her/His Majesty)
HMO (health maintenance organization)
HMS (Her/His Majesty's Service/Ship/Steamer)
H.M.S. *Bounty* (ship, naval mutiny against Capt. Bligh)
H.M.S. *Pinafore (or The Lass that Loved a Sailor)*(Gilbert/Sullivan opera)
Hnatyshyn, Ramon (gov-gen., Can.)
H. Norman Schwarzkopf (US gen.; 1934-)
Ho (chem. sym., holmium)
Ho (lang.)
Ho Chi Minh (b. Nguyen That Tan)(ex-pres.,

NViet; 1890-1969)
Ho Chi Minh City, Vietnam (formerly Saigon)
Ho Chi Minh Trail (Vietnam)
Ho, Don (ent.; 1930-)
Hoagy Carmichael (Hoagland Howard)(US comp.; 1899-1981)
Hoban, James (US arch.; 1762-1831)
Hobart, Australia
Hobart, Garret A(ugustus)(ex-US VP; 1844-99)
Hobbes, Calvin and (comic strip)
Hobbes, Thomas (Br. writer/phil.; 1588-1679)
Hobbit, The (by J.R.R. Tolkien)
Hobbs, NM
Hobby, Oveta Culp (US publ./pol.; 1905-)
Hobgoblin (also Robin Goodfellow, Puck)(fict. chara., *A Midsummer Night's Dream*)
Hobie Cat Co.
Hobson-Jobson (linguistics)
Hobson, Thomas (Br. bus.; 1544-1631)
Hobson's choice (take choice given or nothing)
Hockey League, National (also NHL)
Hockney, David (Br. artist; 1937-)
Hodges, Gil (baseball; 1924-72)
Hodges, Johnny (US jazz; 1906-71)
Hodgkin's disease
Hodiak, John (ent.; 1914-55)
Hódmezövásárhely, Hungary
Hoechst Celanese Corp.
Hoffa, Jimmy (James R(iddle)(US labor leader; 1913-75?)
Hoffa, Portland (ent.)
Hoffman, Abbie (Abbott)(US pol. activist; 1936-89)
Hoffman, Dustin (ent.; 1937-)
Hoffmann, The Tales of (Jacques Offenbach opera)
Hofmann, Hans (US artist; 1880-1966)
Hofstadter, Richard (US hist.; 1916-70)
Hofstadter, Robert (US physt.; 1915-90)
Hogan, Ben (golf; 1912-)
Hogan, Hulk (wrestling)
Hogan, Paul (ent.; 1939-)
Hogan's Heroes (TV show)
Hogarth, Burne (cartoonist, *Tarzan*; 1911-)
Hogarth, William (Br. artist; 1697-1764)
Hogg, James ("the Ettrick Shepherd")(Scot. poet; 1770-1835)
Hohhot, China
Hojatolislam Ali Akbar Hashemi Rafsanjani (pres., Iran; 1935-)
HoJo (Howard Johnson)
Hokinson, Helen (US cartoonist; 1900-49)
Hokkaido (Jap. island)
Hokusai, (Katsushika)(Jap. artist; 1760-1849)
Holbein, the Elder, Hans (Ger. artist; 1460-1524)
Holbein, the Younger, Hans (Ger. artist; 1497-1543)

Proper Noun Speller

Holbrook, Hal (ent.; 1925-)
Holden, William (ent.; 1918-81)
Holetown, Barbados
Holi (Hindu festival)
Holiday Bowl (college football)
Holiday Inn™
Holiday, Billie (b. Eleanora Fagan)(US jazz;
  1915-59)
Holiness, Your (title)
Holland (the Netherlands)
Holland, Brian (US comp.; 1941-)
Holland, Eddie (US comp.; 1939-)
Holland, MI
Hollander, Nicole (US cartoonist, *Sylvia*; 1939-)
Holliday, John "Doc " (US frontier)
Holliday, Judy (ent.; 1922-65)
Holliday, Polly (ent.; 1937-)
Holliman, Earl (ent.; 1928-)
Hollings, Ernest F. (US cong.; 1922-)
Hollis™, David (clothing)
Holloman Air Force Base, NM (mil.)
Holloway, Sterling (ent.; 1905-1992)
Holly Farm Foods, Inc.
Holly Hunter (ent.; 1958-)
Holly, Buddy (ent.; 1936-59)
Holly, Buddy and the Crickets (pop music)
Hollywood bed
Hollywood Park
Hollywood Reporter, The
Hollywood Squares (TV show)
Hollywood, CA, FL
Holm, Celeste (ent.; 1919-)
Holmes, Larry (boxing; 1949-)
Holmes, Oliver Wendell (US writer/phys.; 1809-
  94)
Holmes, Oliver Wendell, Jr. (US jurist; 1841-
  1935)
Holmes, Sherlock (fict. detective)
Holocaust Memorial Museum, United States
  (DC)
Holocaust, the (Nazi annihilation of Jews; 1933-
  45)
Holocene epoch (geological time, began 10,000
  years ago)
Holon, Israel
Holst, Gustav(us Theodore von)(Br. comp.;
  1874-1934)
Holstein(-Friesian) cattle
Holstein, Schleswig- (state, Ger.)
Holt, John (US educ./writer; 1924-85)
Holt, Tim (ent.; 1918-73)
Holtz, Lou (football; 1937-)
Holtzman technique (personality evaluation,
  inkblots)
Holy Alliance ("Christian Union of Charity,
  Peace, and Love")(Rus./Eur. hist.; 1815-1823)
Holy Ark
Holy Bible

Holy City
Holy Communion (also Eucharist, Lord's
  Supper)(rel.)
Holy Cross, AK
Holy Cross, Mount of the (CO)
Holy Father (Pope's title)
Holy Ghost (also Holy Spirit)(part of Christian
  Trinity)
Holy Grail, the (legendary cup used by Jesus at
  the Last Supper)
Holy Land (Isr.)
Holy Mother (also the Madonna, Mary, Our
  Lady, Virgin Mary)(rel.)
Holy One
Holy Roller (rel.)
Holy Roman Empire (Ger. empire; 962-1806)
Holy Saturday
Holy Scripture(s)(rel.)
Holy See (also See of Rome)(Vatican)
Holy Sepulcher (Jesus' tomb)
Holy Spirit (also Holy Ghost)(part of Christian
  Trinity)
Holy Thursday (also Ascension Day)(rel.)
Holy Trinity, the (also Trinity)(Father, Son,
  Holy Ghost/Spirit)(rel.)
Holy Week (week before Easter)
Holy Writ (Bible)
Holyfield, Evander (boxing; 1962-)
Holyoke, MA
Home (mag.)
Home Alone (film)
Home & Away (mag.)
Home Box Office (HBO)(cable TV)
Home Depot, Inc.
Home Improvement (TV show)
Home Mechanix (mag.)
Home Office Computing (mag.)
Home Rule (Irish/English)(DC)
Home, Sir Alexander "Alec" Frederick Douglas-
  (ex-PM, Br.; 1903-)
Home, William Douglas- (Br. writer)
Homefront (TV show)
Homeier, Skippy
Homelite (US bus.)
Homelite™ saw
Homer (Gr. poet; c850 BC)
Homer Simpson (cartoon chara.)
Homer & Jethro
Homer, Winslow (US artist; 1836-1910)
Homeric Hymns (wrongly attributed to Homer)
Homestead Act (US hist.; 1862)
Homestead Air Force Base, FL (mil.)
Homestead, FL, PA
Homo (anthrop.)
Homo erectus (anthrop.)
Homo habilis (anthrop.)
Homo sapiens (anthrop.)
Homoiousian (rel.)

Homoousian (rel.)
Homs, Syria
Hon Industries
Honda™ (auto.)
Honda Accord™ (auto.)
Honda Acura™ (auto.)
Honda™ Civic (auto.)
Honda Motor Co., American
Hondo, Solchiro (Jap. bus./auto.; 1907-91)
Honduras (Republic of)(CAmer.)
Honegger, Arthur (Fr. comp.; 1892-1955)
Honey Bunches of Oats™ (cereal)
Honey-Comb™ (cereal)
Honey Maid™ (crackers)
Honeymooners, The (TV show)
Honeywell, Inc.
Hong Kong (Br. colony, SE Ch.)
Honiara, Soloman Islands
Honokohau National Historical Park, Kaloko-
   (HI)
Honolulu Advertiser (HI newspaper)
Honolulu International Airpoty (HI)
Honolulu Star-Bulletin (HI newspaper)
Honolulu, HI
Honor, Legion of (Fr.)
Honor, Medal of (also Congressional Medal of
   Honor)(mil.)
Honor, Your (title)
Honorat, Jean-Jacques (ex-PM, Haiti)
Honoré Daumier (Fr. artist; 1808-79)
Honoré de Balzac (Fr. writer; 1799-1850)
Honoré Gabriel (Riqueti) Mirabeau, Comte de
   (Fr. pol.; 1749-91)
Honshu (Jap. island)
Honus Wagner, (John Peter)(baseball; 1867-
   1955)
Hood, Fort, TX (mil.)
Hood, Prince of Thieves, Robin (film)
Hood, Raymond (US arch.; 1881-1934)
Hood, Robin (legendary Eng. hero/outlaw; 13th-
   14th c.)
Hooke, Robert (Br. physt./inv.; 1635-1703)
Hooker, Joseph (US gen.; 1814-79)
Hooker, Sir Joseph Dalton (Br. botanist; 1817-
   1911)
Hooker, Thomas (US rel.; 1586-1647)
Hooke's law (of elasticity)
Hooks, Benjamin Lawson (US civil rights
   leader; 1925-)
Hooks, Jan (ent.; 1957-)
Hooks, Robert (ent.; 1937-)
Hooligan, Happy (comic strip)
Hooper (film; 1978)
Hoosier cabinet
Hoosier State (nickname, IN)
Hoot Gibson (ent.; 1892-1962)
Hoover Co., The
Hoover Dam (also Boulder Dam)(AZ/NV)

Hoover, Herbert C(lark)(31st US pres.; 1874-
   1964)
Hoover, J(ohn) Edgar (ex-dir., FBI; 1895-1972)
Hoover, William Henry (US bus./vacuum
   cleaner; 1849-1932)
Hopalong Cassidy (fict. chara.)
Hopalong Cassidy (TV show)
Hope Lange (ent.; 1931-)
Hope Town, the Bahamas
Hope, Bob (b. Leslie Townes Hope)(ent.; 1903-)
Hopi (NAmer. Indians)
Hopkins Hospital, Johns (Baltimore, MD)
Hopkins Observatory, Mount (now Fred
   Lawrence Whipple Observatory)(AZ)
Hopkins University, Johns (Baltimore, MD)
Hopkins, Anthony (ent.; 1937-)
Hopkins, Harry L. (US pol.; 1890-1946)
Hopkins, Johns (US bus./finan.; 1795-1873)
Hopkins, Mark (US educ./rel.; 1802-87)
Hopkins, Sam "Lightnin" (US jazz; 1912-82)
Hopkins, Samuel (US rel.; 1721-1803)
Hopkins, Telma (ent.; 1948-)
Hopkinsville, KY
Hopper, Dennis (ent.; 1936-)
Hopper, DeWolf (ent.; 1858-1935)
Hopper, Edward (US artist; 1882-1967)
Hopper, Hedda (US columnist/ent.; 1890-1966)
Horace (b. Quintus Horatius Flaccus)(Latin
   poet; 65-8 BC)
Horace Greeley (US publ./pol.; 1811-72)
Horace Heidt
Horace Mann (US pol./educ.; 1796-1859)
Horace Silver (US jazz; 1928-)
Horace (Horatio) Walpole (Earl of Oxford)(Br.
   writer; 1717-97)
Horatio Alger, Jr. (US writer; 1832-99)
Horatio Gates (US gen.; 1728-1806)
Horatio Greenough (US sculptor; 1805-52)
Horatio Hornblower, Captain (film; 1951)
Horatio H. Kitchener (Br. mil.; 1850-1916)
Horatio Hornblower, Capt. (fict. chara., C.S.
   Forester)
Horatio Nelson, Viscount (Br. admiral; 1758-
   1805)
Horchow™
Horizon Air Industries (airline)
Horizon, Plymouth (auto.)
Hormel™ (meats)
Hormel & Co., George A.
Hormel Corp.
Hormuz (also Ormuz)(island, Iran)
Hormuz (or Ormuz), Strait of (Iran)
Horn, Cape (Chile)
Hornblower, Captain Horatio (film; 1951)
Hornby, Leslie "Twiggy" (model; 1946-)
Horne, Lena (ent.; 1917-)
Horne, Marilyn (ent.; 1934-)
Horner, Little Jack (nursery rhyme)

Hornets, Charlotte (basketball team)
Horney, Karen Danielsen (Ger./US psych./ writer; 1885-1952)
Hornie (the Devil)
Hornsby, (Rajah) Rogers (baseball; 1896-1963)
Hornung, Paul (football; 1935-)
Horologium (astron., clock)
Horowitz, David (writer)
Horowitz, Vladimir (Rus./US pianist; 1904-89)
Horse Guards (Br.)
Horsehead Nebula (astron.)
Horsley, Lee (ent.; 1955-)
Hortense Calisher (US writer; 1911-)
Horton, Edward Everett (ent.; 1886-1970)
Horus (Eg. deity)
Hoskins, Bob (ent.; 1942-)
Hosni Mubarak (pres., Eqypt; 1928-)
Hosokawa, Morihiro (PM, Jap.)
Host International Corp.
Hot Lips Houlihan (fict. chara., *M*A*S*H*)
Hot Lips Page
Hot Rod (mag.)
Hot Springs National Park (AR)
Hot Wheels™ (toys)
Hotchner, A. E. (writer)
Hotel New Hampshire, The (J. Irving novel)
Hotpoint (US bus.)
Hotspur (aka Sir Henry Percy)(Br. mil.; 1366-1403)
Hottentot (also Khoikhoi)(people)
Hottentot's bread (plant)
Houdin, Eugène "Jean" Robert (Fr. magician; 1805-71)
Houdini, Harry (b. Erich Weiss)(US magician; 1874-1926)
Houghton Mifflin Co.
Houk, Ralph (baseball; 1919-)
Houlihan, Hot Lips (fict. chara., *M*A*S*H*)
Houma, LA
Hound of the Baskervilles, The (by A.C. Doyle)
Hound, Huckleberry (cartoon)
Houphouët-Boigny, Félix (ex-pres., Ivory Coast; 1905-93)
Hours, Book of (rel.)
Hours, Liturgy of the (also Divine Office)(rel.)
House Beautiful (mag.)
House Committee on Un-American Activities (HUAC)(US govt. comm.; 1938-75)
House of Almonds (US bus.)
House of Anjou (or Plantagenet)(Br. ruling family; 1154-1399)
House of Burgesses
House of Cerdic (Br. ruling family; 827-1016, 1042-66)
House of Commons (Br. & Can. parliaments)
House of Frankenstein (film; 1944)
House of Hanover (Br. ruling family; 1714-1901)

House of Lancaster (Br. ruling family; 1399-1461, 1470-71)
House of Lords (Br. parliament)
House of Normandy (Br. ruling family; 1066-1154)
House of Orange (Br. ruling family; 1689-1702)
House of Orange (royal family, Netherlands)
House(s) of Parliament (Br. govt.)
House of Plantagenet (or Anjou)(Br. ruling family; 1154-1399)
House of Representatives (US govt.)
House of Saxe-Coburg-Gotha (Br. ruling family; 1901-10)
House of Stuart (Br. ruling family; 1603-49, 1660-88, 1702-14)
House of the Skjoldungs of Denmark (Br. ruling family; 1016-42)
House of Tudor (Br. ruling family; 1485-1603)
House of Usher (film; 1960)
House of Usher, The Fall of the (E.A. Poe short story)
House of Windsor (Br. ruling family; 1910-present)
House of York (Br. ruling family; 1461-70, 1471-85)
House Un-American Activities Committee (HUAC)(US govt.; est. 1938)
House Ways and Means Committee (US govt.)
House, Edward M(andell)(US pol./dipl.; 1858-1938)
Houseman, John (ent.; 1902-88)
Housing and Urban Development, Department of (HUD)(US govt.)
Housman, A(lfred) E(dward)(Br. poet; 1859-1936)
Houston Astros (baseball team)
Houston Chronicle (TX newspaper)
Houston Intercontinental Airport (TX)
Houston Oilers (football team)
Houston Post (TX newspaper)
Houston Rockets (basketball team)
Houston, Fort Sam (TX)(mil.)
Houston, Sam(uel)(US gen./pol.; 1793-1863)
Houston, TX
Houston, Whitney (ent.; 1963-)
Houten & Zoon, Inc., C. J. Van
Houyhnhnm (fict. race of horses; *Gulliver's Travels*)
Hovercraft™
Hovhaness, Alan (US comp.; 1911-)
How to Succeed in Business Without Really Trying (play)
Howard Ashman (US lyricist; 1951-91)
Howard Carter (Br. archaeol..; 1873-1939)
Howard Cooke (gov-gen.; Jamaica
Howard Cosell (US sportscaster; 1920-)
Howard Da Silva (ent.; 1909-86)
Howard Dean (VT gov.; 1948-)

Howard Dietz (US lyricist.; 1896-1983)
Howard Duff (ent.; 1914-90)
Howard H. Aiken (US math.; 1900-73)
Howard Hanson (US comp.; 1896-1981)
Howard Hesseman (ent.; 1940-)
Howard (Robard) Hughes (US bus./ent./aviator; 1905-76)
Howard Johnson (US bus.; 1896-1972)
Howard Johnson Co. (US bus)
Howard Keel (ent.; 1917-)
Howard K. Smith (US TV jour.)
Howard M. Metzenbaum (US cong.; 1917-)
Howard Morris (ent.; 1925-)
Howard Nemerov (US writer; 1920-91)
Howard Rollins (ent.; 1950-)
Howard Stern (ent.; 1954-)
Howard University (DC)
Howard W. Hunter (US atty./rel.)
Howard, Catherine (5th wife of Henry VIII; 1520?-42)
Howard, Curly (b. Jerome Horwitz)(ent.; 1903-52)
Howard, Elston (baseball; 1929-80)
Howard, Jane (US writer)
Howard, Joe (ent.; 1867-1961)
Howard, Ken (ent.; 1944-)
Howard, Leslie (ent.; 1890-1943)
Howard, Melvin and (film. 1980)
Howard, Moe (b. Moses Horwitz)(ent.; 1897-1975)
Howard, Ron (ent.; 1953-)
Howard, Shemp (b. Samuel Horwitz)(ent.; 1895-1955)
Howard, Trevor (Wallace)(ent.; 1916-88)
Howdy Doody (fict. chara.)
Howdy Doody Show, The
Howe, Elias (US inv./sewing machine; 1819-67)
Howe, Gordie (Gordon)(hockey; 1928-)
Howe, Julia Ward (US reformer/writer; 1819-1910)
Howe, Richard, Earl (Br. mil.; 1726-99)
Howe, Samuel G(ridley)(US educ./reformer; 1801-76)
Howe, Sir William (Br. mil.; 1729-1814)
Howell Edmunds Jackson (US jurist; 1832-95)
Howell Thomas Heflin (US cong.; 1921-)
Howell, C. Thomas (ent.; 1966-)
Howell, Jim Lee (football; 1914-)
Howells, William Dean (US writer; 1837-1920)
Howes, Sally Ann (ent.; 1930-)
Howie Mandell (ent.; 1955-)
Howie Morenz (hockey; 1902-37)
Howser, Dick (baseball; 1937-87)
Howser, M.D., Doogie (TV show)
Hoyer, Steny Hamilton (US cong.; 1939-)
Hoyle, Edmund (Br. writer/card game rules; 1672-1769)
Hoyle, Fred(erick)(Br. astron./writer; 1915-)

Hoyt Axton (ent.; 1938-)
Hoyte, Hugh Desmond (ex-pres., Guyana)
HP (horse power)
H(oward) P(hillips) Lovecraft (US writer; 1890-1937)
HQ (headquarters)
HR (home run)
Hrawi, Elias (pres., Lebanon; 1926-)
H. R. "Bob" Haldeman (US pol.; 1926-93)
H. Ross Perot (US bus./pol.; 1930-)
HS (high school)
Hsia dynasty (also Xia)(Ch.; 2205-1766 BC)
Hsiao-ping, Teng (also Deng Xiaoping)(Ch. pol.; 1904-)
HTLV (human T-cell leukemia virus)
Hua Kuo-feng (or Guofeng)(ex-PM, Ch.; 1920?-)
HUAC (House Un-American Activities Committee)
Huachuca, Fort, AZ (mil.)
Huambo, Angola
Huang Hai (also Yellow Sea)(Ch./Korea)
Huang He (also Yellow River)(Ch.)
Hubbard, L(afayette) Ron(ald)(US writer/rel., Scientology; 1911-86)
Hubbard, Mother (fict. chara., nursery rhyme)
Hubbard, Mother (loose gown; railroad engine)
Hubbell, Carl (Owen)(baseball; 1903-88)
Hubble classification scheme (astron.)
Hubble Space Telescope (HST)(US/Eur. uncrewed space probe)
Hubble, Edwin P(owell)(US astron.; 1889-1953)
Hubble's constant (astron.)
Hubble's law (astron.)
Hubert (or Huybrecht) van Eyck (Flem. artist; 1366-1426)
Hubert de Givenchy (Fr. designer; 1927-)
Hubert Green (golf; 1946-)
Hubert H(oratio) Humphrey, (ex-US VP; 1911-78)
Hubert Ingraham (PM, Bahamas; 1947-)
Huckleberry Finn (fict. chara., Mark Twain)
Huckleberry Finn (M. Twain novel)
Huckleberry Hound (cartoon)
HUD (Department of Housing and Urban Development)(US govt.)
Hud (film; 1963)
Huddie "Leadbelly" Ledbetter (US jazz; 1888-1949)
Huddle House, Inc.
Hudibrastic verse (lit.)
Hudson Bay (Can.)
Hudson Bay™ blanket
Hudson River (NY)
Hudson River School (grp. of artists; early 19th c.)
Hudson, Don (football; 1913-)
Hudson, Henry (Br. expl.; c1565-c1611)
Hudson, Rock (b. Roy Scherer, Jr.)(ent.; 1925-

85)

Hudson's Bay Company (Can./NAmer. Indians, trade; founded 1670)

Hue, Vietnam

Huey Lewis (ent.; 1951-)

Huey Lewis and the News (pop music)

Huey P(ierce) Long ("the Kingfish")(ex-gov., LA; 1893-1935)

Huey P. Newton (US, cofounded Black Panthers; 1942-89)

Huff, Sam (Robert Lee)(football; 1934-)

Huffy Corp.

Huggies™ (diapers)

Hugh C. Dowding (Br. mil.; 1883-1970)

Hugh Desmond Hoyte (ex-pres., Guyana)

Hugh Downs (ent.; 1921-)

Hugh Gaitskell (Br. pol.; 1906-63)

Hugh Griffith (ent.; 1912-80)

Hugh Hefner (US publ.; 1926-)

Hugh Lofting (Br. writer; 1886-1947)

Hugh MacDiarmid (b. Christopher Murray Grieve)(Scot. poet; 1892-1978)

Hugh O'Brian (ent.; 1925-)

Hughes Aircraft Corp.

Hughes Markets, Inc.

Hughes, Barnard (ent.; 1915-)

Hughes, Edward J(ames) "Ted" (Br. poet; 1930-)

Hughes, Howard (Robard)(US bus./ent./aviator; 1905-76)

Hughes, John (Joseph)(US rel.; 1797-1864)

Hughes, Langston (US writer; 1902-67)

Hughes, Ted (Edward James)(Br. poet; 1930-)

Hugo De Vries (Dutch botanist; 1848-1935)

Hugo L(aFayette) Black (US jurist; 1886-1971)

Hugo Wolf (Aus. comp.; 1860-1903)

Hugo, Hurricane (E US; 1989)

Hugo, Victor (Marie)(Fr. writer; 1802-85)

Huguenots (rel.)

Hui (lang./people)

Huitzilopochtli (also Uitzilopochtli)(myth.)

Hula Hoop™

Hulce, Tom (ent.; 1953-)

Huldreich (or Ulrich) Zwingli (Swiss rel.; 1484-1531)

Hulk Hogan (wrestling)

Hulk, The Incredible (cartoon chara.)

Hull House (Chicago settlement house)

Hull, Bobby (hockey; 1939-)

Hull, Brett (hockey; 1964-)

Hull, Cordell (US pol.; 1871-1955)

Hull, England (officially Kingston-upon-Hull)

Hull, Isaac (US mil.; 1773-1843)

Hull, Josephine (ent.; 1886-1957)

Hull, Quebec, Canada

Hull, Robert Marvin "Bobby" (hockey; 1939-)

Human Fly, The (cartoon chara.)

Human Rights Day (UN)

Human Torch, The (cartoon chara.)

Humana, Inc.

Humbert I (king, It.; 1844-1900)

Humboldt Current (now Peru Current)(cold ocean current)

Humboldt, (Friedrich Heinrich) Alexander von, Baron (Ger. expl.; 1769-1859)

Hume Cronyn (ent.; 1911-)

Hume, David (Scot. phil./hist.; 1711-76)

Hummel figurines

Hummel, Johann Nepomuk (Ger. comp.; 1778-1837)

Humperdinck, Engelbert (ent.; 1936-)

Humperdinck, Engelbert (Ger. comp.; 1854-1921)

Humphrey Bogart ("Bogey")(ent.; 1899-1957)

Humphrey, Hubert H(oratio)(ex-US VP; 1911-78)

Humphry Davy, Sir (Br. chem.; 1778-1829)

Humpty Dumpty (fict. chara.)

Humpty Dumpty's (mag.)

Hun (ancient people)

Hun Sen (co-PM, Cambodia; 1950-)

Hun, Attila the ("Scourge of God")(king of the Huns; c406-453)

Hunan (province, Ch.)

Hunchback of Notre Dame, The (V. Hugo novel)

Hund, Friedrich

Hundred Days (FDR/Congress; 1933)

Hundred Flowers (Ch. hist.; 1957)

Hundred Years' War (also Hundred Years War)(Br./Fr.; 1337-1453)

Hund's rule (chem.)

Hungarian (lang./people)

Hungarian uprising (Hung. hist.; 1956)

Hungary (Republic of)(Eur.)

Hungnam, North Korea

Hungry Jack™ (pancake mix)

Hunkers, Barnburners v. (US pol.; mid 1800s)

Huns, the (people)

Hunsa (lang.)

Hunt-Wesson, Inc.

Hunt, Harold Guy (AL gov.; 1933-)

Hunt, H. L. (US bus./oil; 1889-1974)

Hunt, James B., Jr. (NC gov.)

Hunt, Linda (ent.; 1945-)

Hunt, Richard M(orris)(US arch.; 1827-95)

Hunter Army Airfield (GA)

Hunter Fans Co.

Hunter Liggett, Fort (CA)(mil.)

Hunter S. Thompson (US jour.; 1939-)

Hunter, Catfish (Jim)(baseball; 1946-)

Hunter, Holly (ent.; 1958-)

Hunter, Jeffrey (ent.; 1925-69)

Hunter, Kim (ent.; 1922-)

Hunter™, Reed (clothing)

Hunter, Ross (ent.; 1921-)

Hunter, Tab (ent.; 1931-)

Hunter's Lessee, Martin v. (US law; 1816)

Huntington Beach, CA
Huntington Library and Art Gallery, Henry E. (CA)
Huntington Park, CA
Huntington, Collis P(otter)(US bus.; 1821-1900)
Huntington, Henry E(dwards)(US bus.; 1850-1927)
Huntington, IN, WV
Huntington's chorea (med.)
Huntley, Chet (US TV jour.; 1912-74)
Huntley, Joni (track; 1956-)
Hunt's (ketchup)
Huntsville News (AL newspaper)
Huntsville Times (AL newspaper)
Huntsville, AL, TX
Huntz Hall (ent.; 1919-)
Huron (NAmer. Indians)
Huron-Manistee National Forest
Huron, Lake (MI/Can.)
Huron, Port (MI)
Hurricane Andrew (FL/LA; 1992)
Hurricane Hugo (E US; 1989)
Hurt, John (ent.; 1940)
Hurt, Mary Beth (ent.; 1946-)
Hurt, William (ent.; 1950-)
Husák, Gustav (ex-pres., Czech.; 1913-91)
Husayn, Bahaullah Ali Mirza (Pers., founded Baha'i faith; 1817-92)
Huseynov, Surat (PM, Azerbaijan)
Hush...Hush, Sweet Charlotte (film; 1965)
Hush Puppies™ (shoes)
Husky, Ferlin
Hussain Mohammad Ershad (ex-pres., Bangladesh; 1930-)
Hussein I (ibn Talal)(king, Jordan; 1935-)
Hussein, Abdullah ibn (ex-king, Jordan; 1882-1951)
Hussein, Kamil (or Kemal)(Eg. sultan; 1850?-1917)
Hussein (al-Tikriti), Saddam (pres., Iraq; 1937-)
Husserl, Edmund (Gustav Albercht)(Ger. phil.; 1859-1938)
Hussey, Olivia (ent.)
Hussey, Ruth (ent.; 1914-)
Hustler (mag.)
Huston, Anjelica (ent.; 1951-)
Huston, John (US ent./writer; 1906-87)
Huston, Walter (ent.; 1884-1950)
Hutchinson, Anne (Marbury)(US rel.; 1591-1643)
Hutchinson, Kathyrn Bailey "Kay" (US cong.; 1943-)
Hutchinson, KS
Hutson, Donald (football; 1913-)
Hutton, Barbara (US heiress; 1887-1979)
Hutton, Betty (ent.; 1921-)
Hutton, James (Scot. geol.; 1726-97)
Hutton, Timothy (ent.; 1960-)

Hutu (people)
Hutzler Manufacturing Co.
Huxley, Aldous (Leonard)(Br. writer; 1894-1963)
Huxley, Sir Julian (Br. biol.; 1887-1975)
Huxley, Thomas (Henry)(Br. phil./educ.; 1825-95)
Huybrecht (or Hubert) van Eyck (Flem. artist; 1366-1426)
Huygens (or Huyghens), Christian (Dutch math./physt./astron.; 1629-95)
Huygens eyepiece
Huygens principle
Hwan, Chun Doo (ex-pres., SKorea; 1931-)
Hwange, Zimbabwe
Hy Averback
Hyannis Port, MA (Kennedy Compound)
Hyatt Hotels Corp.
Hyde Park (London)
Hyde Park, NY
Hyde, Jekyll and (dual personality, one good/one evil)
Hyde, The Strange Case of Dr. Jekyll and Mr. (by R.L. Stevenson)
Hyder (or Haidar) Ali (Indian ruler/mil.; 1722-82)
Hyderabad, India
Hyderabad, Pakistan
Hydra (myth., astron., water snake [female])
Hydrox™ (cookies)
Hydrus (astron., water snake [male])
Hygieia (myth.)
Hyksos (ancient Eg. kings; 1680-1580 BC)
Hyland, Diana
Hylton v. U.S. (US law; 1796)
Hyman George Rickover, Adm. (US mil./A-bomb; 1900-86)
Hyman, Earle (ent.; 1926-)
Hymen (myth.)
Hyperion (astron.; myth.)
Hypnus (myth.)
Hyponex™ (agriculture)
Hyponex Corp.
Hyundai (auto.)
Hyundai Elantra (auto.)
Hyundai Excel (auto.)
Hyundai Motor America (US bus.)
Hyundai Scoupe (auto.)
Hyundai Sonata (auto.)

I

I (chem. sym., iodine)
IA (Iowa)
Iacocca, Lee A. (US auto exec.; 1924-)
Iago (fict. chara., *Othello*)
Ian (Lancaster) Fleming (Br. writer ; 1908-64)
Ian (Douglas) Smith (ex-PM, Rhodesia; 1919-)
Ian, Janis (ent.; 1951-)
IAS (indicated airspeed)
Ibadan, Nigeria
Ibadhi Moslem (rel.)
Iban (lang.)
Iberia (also Iberian Peninsula)(Sp./Port.)
Iberia (now Georgia)
Iberia Air Lines of Spain (airline)
Iberian (lang./people)
Iberian Peninsula (also Iberia)(Sp./Port.)
Ibiza (Balearic Island)
Ibizan hound (also Ibizan Podenco)
Iblis (rel., evil spirit)
IBM™
IBM Corp. (International Business Machines Corp.)
Ibn Saud (also Abdul-Azaz Ibn-Saud)(king, Saudi Arabia; 1880-1953)
Ibo (also Igbo)(lang./people)
Ibrahim Babangida (ex-pres., Nigeria; 1941-)
Ibsen, Henrik (Johan)(Nor. writer; 1828-1906)
Icahn, Carl
I Can't Believe It's Not Butter™
I Can't Believe It's Yogurt, Inc.
ICAO (International Civil Aviation Organization)
Icarus (astron.; myth.)
ICBM (intercontinental ballistic missile)
ICC (Interstate Commerce Commission)(US govt.)
Iceland (Republic of)(N Atl.)
Icelandair (airline)
Icelandic (lang.)
Ichabod Crane (fict. chara., *Legend of Sleepy Hollow*)
I'chaim (Hebrew, to your health)
I Ching (also *Book of Changes*)(rel.)
Ichiro Ozawa (Jap. writer)
ICU (intensive care unit)
ID (Idaho, identity document)
'Id al-Adha (Islamic festival)
Id, Wizard of (comic strip)
Ida Lupino (ent.; 1914-)
Ida Minerva Tarbell (US writer; 1857-1944)
Idaho (ID)
Idaho Falls, ID
Idaho Supreme Potatoes, Inc.
Ideals Publishing Co.

Ideas for Better Living
Ides (15th day of Mar., May, July, Oct.)(also l.c.)
Ides of March (3/15)
Idi Oumee Amin (Dada)(ex-pres., Uganda; 1926-)
Iditarod Trail Sled Dog Race
Idol, Billy (ent.; 1955-)
Idriss Déby (pres., Chad; 1955?-)
Ife, Nigeria
I formation (football)
IFR (instrument flight rules)
I. F. Stone (US jour.; 1908-89)
IG (inspector general)
Igbo (also Ibo)(lang./people)
Iggy Pop (pop music)
Iglesias, Julio (Sp./US ent.; 1943-)
Igloo™ cooler
Igloo Corp.
Ignace Henri (Joseph Théodore) Fantin-Latour, (Fr. artist; 1836-1904)
Ignace Jan Paderewski (ex-PM, Pol./comp.; 1860-1941)
Ignatius of Loyola, St. (aka (Iñigo de Oñez y Loyola)(Sp. rel.; 1491-1556)
Igor F(ederovich) Stravinsky (Rus./US comp.; 1882-1971)
Igor Kipnis
IGY (International Geophysical Year)
Ijaw (lang.)
Ike Turner (ent.; 1931-)
Ikhnaton (also Akhenaton, Amenhotep IV) (king/pharaoh, Eg.; 14th c. BC)
IL (Illinois)
Il Duce (aka Benito Mussolini)(ex-PM, It.; 1883-1945)
Il Tintoretto ("the little dyer")(b. Jacopo Robusti)(It. artist; 1518-94)
Il Trovatore (Verdi opera)
Ila, Nigeria
Ildebrando Pizzetti (It. comp./hist.; 1880-1968)
Ile-de-France (now Mauritius)
Ile-de-France (region, Fr.)
Ilesha, Nigeria
ILGWU (International Ladies Garment Workers Union)
Iliad (Homer epic poem)
Ilie Nastase (tennis; 1946-)
Iliescu, Ion (pres., Romania; 1930-)
Ilka Chase (US writer/ent.; 1905-?)
I'll Fly Away (TV show)
Illinois (IL)
Illinois (NAmer. Indians)
Illinois Tool Works, Inc.
Illinois, Inc., Owens-
Illinois, Munn v. (US law; 1877)
Illustrator™, Adobe (compu.)
ILO (International Labor Organization)
Ilocano (also Ilokano)(lang./people)

Iloilo, Philippines
Ilorin, Nigeria
I Love Lucy (TV show)
Ilya G. Ehrenburg (Rus. writer; 1891-1967)
I. Magnin (retail stores)
Imelda (Romualdez) Marcos (Phil. pol., wife of ex-pres; 1930-)
IMF (International Monetary Fund)
Imhotep (Eg. phys.; c2800 BC)
Immaculate Conception (rel.)
Immanuel (rel.)
Immanuel Kant (Ger. phys./phil.; 1724-1804)
Immelmann turn (airplace maneuver)
Immigration and Naturalization Service v. Chadha (US law; 1983)
Imodium A-D™ (med.)
Imogene Coca (ent.; 1908-)
Impe, Jack Van (TV show)
I(eoh) M(ing) Pei (US arch.; 1917-)
Imperial conference
Imperial Highness (title)
Imperial Majesty (title)
Imperial™ margarine
Imperial Valley, CA
Imperial, Chrysler-Plymouth (auto.)
Imperials, Little Anthony and the (pop music)
Importance of Being Earnest, The (Oscar Wilde comedy)
Impressionism (art movement; fl. 1860-c1900)
Imre Nagy (ex-PM, Hung.; c1895-1958)
IN (Indiana)
In God We Trust
In re Debs (US law; 1895)
In re Gault (US law; 1967)
In Search of... (TV show)
In the Heat of the Night (TV show)
Inauguration Day
Inc.™ (mag.)
Inca empire (Peru; fl. 1200-c1530)
Inchon, South Korea (formerly Chemulpo)
Income Opportunities
Increase Mather (US rel.; 1639-1723)
Incredible Hulk, The (cartoon chara.)
Independence Bowl (college football)
Independence Day (also Fourth of July, July 4th)
Independence Hall (Philadelphia, PA)
Independence National Historical Park (PA)
Independence, Declaration of (US; July 4, 1776)
Independence, KS, MO
Independent Order of Odd Fellows (fraternal society; est. 1918)
Inderal™ (med.)
Index Expurgatorius (rel.)
Index Librorum Prohibitorum (rel.)
India (Republic of)(S Asia)
India ink (also Chinese ink)
India-Pakistan wars

India paper
India-rubber tree
Indian (langs., peoples)
Indian Affairs, Bureau of (BIA)(US govt. agcy.; est. 1849)
Indian corn (grass)
Indian cress (plant)
Indian currant (also snowberry)(plant)
Indian fig (plant)
Indian hawthorn (plant)
Indian hemp (plant)
Indian mulberry (tree)
Indian Mutiny (also Sepoy Rebellion/ Mutiny)(India/Br.; 1857-58)
Indian Ocean (Afr./Austl.)
Indian paintbrush (plant)
Indian pipe (plant)
Indian pudding (dessert)
Indian red (color)
Indian strawberry (also mock strawberry)(plant)
Indian Territory (part of OK; 1829-1907)
Indian War, French and (NAmer./Br.; 1754-63)
Indian warrior (plant)
Indian yellow (color)
Indian, American (also Native American)(peoples)
Indiana (IN)
Indiana Jones (fict. chara.)
Indiana Jones and the Last Crusade (film)
Indiana Jones and the Temple of Doom (film; 1984)
Indiana Pacers (basketball team)
Indianapolis Colts (football team)
Indianapolis 500 (racing)
Indianapolis News (IN newspaper)
Indianapolis Star (IN newspaper)
Indianapolis, IN
Indians, Cleveland (baseball team)
Indic (also Indo-Aryan)(lang[s], people)
Indira Gandhi (b. Nehru)(ex-PM, India; 1917-84)
Individual Investor (mag.)
Individual Retirement Account (IRA)
Indo-Aryan languages (also Indo-European)
Indochina (now Cambodia, Laos, and Viet.)
Indochinese (langs., peoples)
Indo-European languages (also Indo-Aryan)
Indo-Germanic languages (now Indo-European)
Indo-Heriz (Pers. rug)
Indo-Iranian languages
Indonesia (Republic of)(SE Asia)
Indonesian (lang.)
Indonesian, Malay- (lang./people)
Indo-Tabriz (Pers. rug)
Indra (Hindu god)
Indus (astron., Indian)
Indus River (India)

Indus Valley civilization (India, c2500 BC)
Industrial Development Organization, United Nations (UNIDO)(est. 1966)
Industrial Recovery Act, National (NIRA)(US law; 1933)
Industrial Revolution (US/Eur. hist.; c1830-c1925)
Industrial Workers of the World (IWW, "Wobblies")(labor movement; 1905-1917)
Industrial World
Industry Week
Indy, (Paul Marie Théodore) Vincent d' (Fr. comp.; 1851-1931)
Infinite, the (also the Infinite Being)
Infiniti, Nissan™ (auto.)
Information Act, Freedom of
Information America (compu. database)
Information Week
InfoWorld
Inge, William (Motter)(US writer; 1913-73)
Inge, William (Ralph)(Br. rel.; 1860-1954)
Ingels, Marty
Ingemar Johansson (Swed. boxing)
Ingemar Stenmark (skiing; 1956-)
Inger Stevens (ent.; 1934-70)
Ingersoll-Rand Co.
Inglenook™ (wine)
Inglewood, CA
Ingmar Bergman (Swed. ent.; 1918-)
Ingraham, Hubert (PM, Bahamas; 1947-)
Ingres, Jean Auguste Dominique (Fr. artist; 1780-1867)
Ingrid Bergman (ent.; 1915-82)
Inigo Jones (Br. arch.; 1573-c1652)
Initial Teaching Alphabet (also augmented Roman)
Ink Spots, The (pop music)
Inkatha (SAfr. pol. org.; 1975-)
Inner Hebrides (islands, W Scot.)
Inner Mongolia (NE Ch.)
Inness, George (US artist; 1825-94)
Inns of Court (Br. law)
Innsbruck, Austria
Inouye, Daniel K. (US cong.; 1924-)
Inquirer, Philadelphia (PA newspaper)
Inquisition (rel.)
Inside Edition (TV show)
Inside Sports (mag.)
Inside Washington (TV show)
Insko, Del (harness racing; 1931-)
Inspector Gadget (cartoon)
Instamatic™ camera
Institute for Training and Research, United Nations (UNITAR)(est. 1963)
Institutes of Health, National (NIH)(US govt. agcy.; est. 1930)
Integra™, Honda Acura (auto.)
Integrated Services Digital Network

(ISDN)(internat'l telecommunications)
Intel™ (compu. chip)
Intel Corp.
IntelliCAT™ (CAT system)
Intelligencer-Journal, Lancaster (PA newspaper)
Intelsat (also INTELSAT, International Telecommunications Satellite)(comm.)
Interco, Inc.
Intercollegiate Athletics, National Association of (NAIA)
Interior, Department of the (US govt.)
Interlaken, Switzerland
Intermediate Nuclear Forces Treaty (US/USSR; 1987)
Internal Revenue Service (IRS)(US govt. agcy.; est. 1862)
International Bank for Reconstruction and Development (World Bank)(UN; est. 1945)
International Brotherhood of Teamsters, Chauffeurs, Warehousemen, and Helpers of America (Teamsters Union)(trade union; est. 1903)
International Business Machines Corp. (IBM Corp.)
International Court of Justice (also World Court)(UN; founded 1945)
International Criminal Police Organization (Interpol)
International Date Line (IDL)(180° longitude)
International Development Association (IDA)(UN; est. 1960)
International Green Party (US pol.)
International Harvester Co.
International Labour Organization (ILO)(UN; est. 1919)
International Monetary Fund (IMF)(UN; est. 1944)
International Paper Co.
International Phonetic Alphabet (also IPA)
International Standard Book Number (ISBN)
International Style (arch.)
International System of Units (also SI, Système Internationale d'Unités)
International Telephone and Telegraph Corp (ITT)
Internet (compu.)
Interpol (International Criminal Police Organization)
Interstate Commerce Commission (ICC)(US govt. agcy.)
Interview (mag.)
Intifada (Liberation Army of Palestine; founded 1987)
Intolerable Acts (US/Br. hist.; 1774)
Intracoastal Waterway (SE US)
Intrepid, Dodge (auto.)
Intuit (US bus.)

Inuit (lang./people)
Inuktitut (lang.)(also Inuktituut)
Invar™ (iron alloy)
Inverness, Scotland
Investor's Business Daily (mag.)
Invincible Armada (Spanish Armada)(fleet of
   ships; 1588)
Invitation Tournament, National
   (NIT)(basketball)
INXS (pop music)
Io (Jupiter moon; myth.)
Iodine, Little (comic strip)
Iolani Palace (HI)
Iolanthe (Gilbert and Sullivan)
Ion Iliescu (pres., Romania; 1930-)
Ionesco, Eugène (Fr. writer; 1912-)
Ionia (ancient Asia Minor)
Ionian (people)
Ionian Islands (Ionian/Mediterranean seas)
Ionian Sea (arm of Mediterranean)
Ionic™ (type style)
Ionic order (arch., lang.)
IOOF (Independent Order of Odd Fellows)
IOU (I owe you)
Iowa (IA)
Iowa City, IA
I Pagliacci (R. Leoncavallo opera)
Iphigene Ochs Sulzberger (US publ.; 1883-1990)
Ipoh, Malaysia
Ipswich, Australia
Ipswich, England
Ipswich, MA
IQ (intelligence quotient)
Iquique, Chile
Iquitos, Peru
Ir (chem. sym., iridium)
IRA (Individual Retirement Account)
IRA (Irish Republican Army)(mil.; est. 1919)
Ira Frederick Aldridge (ent.; 1804-67)
Ira Gershwin (US lyricist; 1896-1983)
Ira Levin (US writer; 1929-)
Iráklion, Greece
Iran (Islamic Republic of)(formerly Persia)(SW
   Asia)
Iran-Contra scandal (also Irangate)(US pol.
   scandal; 1987)
Iran-Iraq War (also Gulf War)(1980-88)
Irangate (also Iran-Contra scandal)(US pol.
   scandal; 1987)
Iranian (lang./people)
Iraq (Republic of)(SW Asia)
Iraq War , Iran- (also Gulf War)(1980-88)
Irbid, Jordan
IRBM (intermediate range ballistic missile)
Ireland (Republic of)(also Erie)(NW Eur.)
Ireland, Jill (ent.; 1936-90)
Ireland, John (ent.; 1914-92)
Ireland, Northern (part of the UK)

Ireland, Patricia (US, ex-pres. NOW; 1945-)
Irem, Garden of (myth.)
Irene Cara (ent.; 1959-)
Irene (Foote) Castle (US dancer; 1893-1969)
Irene Dunne (ent.; 1898-1990)
Irène Joliot-Curie (Fr. physt.; 1897-1956)
Irene Papas (ent.; 1926-)
Irene Ryan (ent.; 1903-73)
Irianese (people)
Iris (myth.)
Iris Murdoch (Br. writer; 1919-)
Irish (lang./people)
Irish coffee (mixed drink)
Irish Gaelic (lang.)
Irish harp (music)
Irish knit (sweater)
Irish Literary Renaissance (also Irish Revival,
   Celtic Renaissance)
Irish Mist (liqueur)
Irish Republican Army (IRA)(mil.; est. 1919)
Irish setter (dog)
Irish terrier (dog)
Irish water spaniel (dog)
Irish wolfhound (dog)
Irma La Douce (film; 1963)
Iron Age (c2000 BC to present)
Iron Chancellor (Prince Otto [Eduard Leopold]
   von Bismarck)(ex-chanc., Ger.; 1815-98)
Iron Cross, the (Ger. war medal)
Iron Curtain (imaginary boundary between
   capitalist/communist Eur.)
Iron Guard (Romanian hist.; 1930's)
Iron Maiden (rock group)
Iron, Ralph (aka Olive Schreiner)(SAfr. writer;
   1855-1920)
Irons, Jeremy (ent.; 1948-)
Ironsides, Old (*Constitution, The*)(US naval
   ship)
Iroquois (NAmer. Indians)
Iroquois Confederacy/League (NAmer. Indians)
Irrawaddy River (Myanmar/Burma)
IRS (Internal Revenue Service)
Irvin, Michael (football; 1966-)
Irvine, CA
Irving Berlin (US comp.; 1888-1989)
Irving Fisher (US econ.; 1867-1947)
Irving Stone (US writer; 1903-89)
Irving R. Levine (US TV jour.)
Irving (Grant) Thalberg (ent.; 1899-1936)
Irving Wallace (US writer; 1916-90)
Irving, Amy (ent.; 1953-)
Irving, George S. (ent.; 1922-)
Irving, John (US writer; 1942-)
Irving, TX
Irving, Washington (US writer/hist.; 1783-1859)
Irwin Chanin (US arch.; 1892-1988)
Irwin, Fort, CA (mil.)
Irwin, Hale (golf; 1945-)

Irwin, James B. (astro.; 1930-91)
Isa bin Sulman al-Khalifa, Sheik (emir, Bahrain; 1933-)
Isa Town, Bahrain
Isaac (rel.)
Isaac Asimov (US writer/sci-fi; 1920-92)
Isaac Asimov's Science Fiction Magazine
Isaac Babel (Rus. writer; 1894-1941)
Isaac B(ashevis) Singer (Pol./US writer; 1904-91)
Isaac Hayes (ent.; 1942-)
Isaac M(errit) Singer (US inv./sewing machine; 1811-75)
Isaac Newton, Sir (Br. physt./math., gravity; 1642-1727)
Isaac Pitman, Sir (Br., inv. shorthand system; 1813-97)
Isaac Stern (Rus. violinist; 1920-)
Isaacs, Susan
Isabel de Perón (b. Maria Estela Martínez)(ex-pres., Argentina; 1931-)
Isabel Sanford (ent.)
Isabella I ("the Catholic")(queen, Sp.; 1451-1504)
Isabella II (queen, Sp.; 1830-1904)
Isabella Rossellini (It. ent.; 1952-)
Isabelle Brasseur (figure skating; 1971-)
Isadora (film; 1969)
Isadora Duncan (US dancer; 1878-1927)
Isaiah (Hebrew prophet; 8th c. BC)
Isaias Afewerki (pres., Eritrea)
Isak Dinesen (aka Karen Blixen)(Dan. writer; 1885-1962)
Isamu Noguchi (Jap./US artist; 1904-88)
ISBN (International Standard Book Number)
Iscariot, Judas (betrayer of Jesus; ?-c28 BC)
Isenheim Altarpiece (Grünewald)
Iseult, Tristan and (also Tristam, Isolde)(Celtic legend)
Isfahan, Iran
Ish Kabibble (aka Merwyn Bogue)(ent.; 1908-94)
Isherwood, Christopher (William Bradshaw)(Br. writer; 1904-86)
Ishiguro, Kazuo (Jap./US writer; 1954-)
Ishihara('s) test (for color blindness)
Ishmael (rel.)
Ishmael Reed (US writer; 1938-)
Ishtar (film)
Ishtar (myth.)
Isiah Thomas (basketball; 1961-)
Isidor Isaac Rabi (US physt.; 1899-1988)
Isis (Eg. goddess)
Islam (rel.)
Islam A. Karimov (pres., Uzbekistan)
Islam, Nation of (also Black Muslims)(rel.)
Islamabad, Pakistan
Islamic Jihad (Islamic Holy War)(Middle East terrorist movement)
Islamic New Year's Day
Islamic Resistance Movement
Island of La Grande Jatte, A Sunday Afternoon on the (by Seurat)
Islanders, New York (hockey team)
Islands (mag.)
Isle of Guernsey (island, English Channel)
Isle of Man (island, Irish Sea)
Isle of Wight (island/county, Eng.)
Isle Royale National Park (MI)
Isles of Scilly, Cornwall and (county, Eng.)
islets of Langerhans (med.)
Isley Brothers, The (pop music)
Islip, NY
Ismail I (also Ismail Pasha)(ex-gov., Eg.; 1830-95)
Ismail I (shah, Persia; 1486-1524)
Isma'ili (rel.)
Ismailia, Egypt
Isocrates (Gr. orator; 436-338 BC)
Isolde, Tristan and (also Tristam, Iseult)(Celtic legend)
Isotoner™ (gloves/slippers)
I Spy (TV show)
Israel (State of)(SW Asia)
Israel ben Eliezer (also Baal Shem-Tov)(Jew. rel.; c1700-60)
Israel, Tribes of
Israeli (people)
Israeli Wars, Arab- (series of wars since 1948)
Israelite (people)
Issa (lang./people)
Issoufou, Mahamadou (PM, Niger)
Istanbul, Turkey (previously called Byzantium and Constantinople)
Isuzu Motors, Inc., American
Isuzu, Joe (fict. chara.)
Itaipu (dam, Brazil)
Italia (grape)
Italian (lang./people)
Italian aster (flowering plant)
Italian dressing
Italian greyhound (dog)
Italian ice (dessert)
Italian jasmine (plant)
Italian sausage
Italian sonnet (also Petrarchan sonnet)(lit.)
Italy (Republic of)(S Eur.)
Itamar Franco (pres., Brazil; 1930-)
ITAR-Tass (Rus. news org.)
Ithaca (Gr. island)
Ithaca, NY
ITO (International Trade Organization)
Ito, Hirobumi, Prince (ex-PM, Jap.; 1841-1909)
Ito, Midori (figure skating)
It's a Living (TV show)
It's A Mad, Mad, Mad, Mad World (film)

*Itsy Bitsy Teenie Weenie Yellow Polka Dot
	Bikini* (song)
ITT Corp.
Iturbi, Jose (Sp. cond.; 1895-1980)
Itzhak Perlman (Isr./US violinist; 1945-)
IUD (intrauterine device)
Ivan Ditmars
Ivan F(rederick) Boesky (US stock market
	scandal; 1937-)
Ivan III ("the Great")(ex-tsar, Muscovy; 1440-
	1505)
Ivan IV ("the Terrible")(ex-tsar, Muscovy; 1530-
	84)
Ivan Le Lorraine Albright (US artist; 1897-
	1983)
Ivan Lendl (tennis; 1960-)
Ivan Nagy
Ivan (Petrovich) Pavlov (Rus. physiol.; 1849-
	1936)
Ivan Tors
Ivan (Sergeievich) Turgenev (Rus. writer; 1818-
	83)
Ivana Trump (US, ex-wife of D. Trump)
Ivars Godmanis (ex-PM, Latvia)
I've Got a Secret (TV show)
Ives, Burl (Icle Ivanhoe)(ent.; 1909-)
Ives, Charles (Edward)(US comp.; 1874-1954)
Ives, Currier & (US lithography)
Ives, Frederic Eugene (US inv.; 1856-1937)
Ives, James (Merritt)(US lithographer; 1824-95)
Ives™, St. (toiletries)
Ivey, Judith (ent.; 1951-)
Ivory Coast (Republic of)(W Afr.)
Ivory Liquid™ (detergent)
Ivory Snow™ (soap)
Ivry-sur-Seine, France
Ivy League colleges (Brown/Columbia/Cornell/
	Dartmouth/Harvard/Pennsylvania/Princeton/
	Yale)
I Witness Video (TV show)
Iwo Jima (also U.S. Marine Corps War
	Memorial)(VA)
Iwo Jima (island, W Pac.)
Iwo Jima, Battle of (WWII; 1945)
Iwo, Nigeria
IWW (Industrial Workers of the World)
Ixion (myth.)
Ixtapa, Mexico
Iyar (also Iyyar)(Jew. month)
Izaak Walton (Br. writer; 1593-1683)
Izanagi and Izanami (Jap. myth.)
Izetbegovic, Alija (pres., Bosnia-Hercegovina)
Izmir, Turkey (formerly Smyrna)
Iznik, Turkey (formerly Nicaea)

J

JA (judge advocate)
Jabberwocky (L. Carroll poem)
Jaber al-Ahmad al-Jaber al-Sabah, Sheik (emir, Kuwait; 1928-)
Jack Albertson (ent.; 1907-81)
Jack Anderson (US jour.; 1922-)
Jack and Jill (nursery rhyme)
Jack and the Beanstalk (fairy tale)
Jack Bannon (ent.; 1940-)
Jack Benny (b. Benjamin Kubelsky)(ent.; 1894-1974)
Jack Carson (ent.; 1910-63)
Jack Carter (ent.; 1923-)
Jack Daniel Distillery (US bus.)
Jack Daniel's
Jack Dempsey, (William Harrison)(boxing; 1895-1983)
Jack Elam (ent.; 1916-)
Jack Flash, Jumpin' (film; 1986)
Jack Flash, Jumpin' (song)
Jack Frost (personification of frost)
Jack Haley (ent.; 1899-1979)
Jack Horner, Little (nursery rhyme)
Jack (John Arthur) Johnson (boxing; 1878-1946)
Jack Jones (ent.; 1938-)
Jack Kelly (ent.; 1927-92)
Jack Kemp (US pol.; 1935-)
Jack (John Fitzgerald) Kennedy, (35th US pres.; 1917-63)
Jack Kerouac, (Jean-Louis Lefris de)(US writer; 1923-69)
Jack Ketch (Br. slang, official hangman)
Jack Kevorkian (US phys.)
Jack Klugman (ent.; 1922-)
Jack Kramer (tennis; 1921-)
Jack LaLanne (US, fitness educ.)
Jack La Lanne Health Spas (US bus.)
Jack Lemmon (ent.; 1925-)
Jack Lescoulie
Jack (John Griffith) London (US writer; 1876-1916)
Jack Lord (ent.; 1922-)
Jack L(eonard) Warner (ent.; 1892-1978)
Jack (John) Lynch (ex-PM, Ir.; 1917-)
Jack McDowell (baseball; 1966-)
Jack Nicholson (ent.; 1937-)
Jack (William) Nicklaus (golf; 1940-)
Jack Norworth (US lyricist; 1879-1959)
Jack Oakie (ent.; 1903-78)
Jack Paar (ent.; 1918-)
Jack Palance (ent.; 1920-)
Jack R(obert) Lousma (astro.; 1936-)
Jack Rose (mixed drink)

Jack Ruby (US, murdered L.H. Oswald; 1911-67)
Jack Russell terrier (dog)
Jack Schaefer (US writer; 1908-91)
Jack (Harrison Hahen) Schmitt (US pol./astro.; 1935-)
Jack Sharkey (boxing)
Jack (Weldon John) Teagarden (US jazz; 1905-64)
Jack the Ripper (London murderer; 1888)
Jack Valenti (US writer; 1921-)
Jack Van Impe (TV show)
Jack Warden (ent.; 1920-)
Jack Webb (ent.; 1920-82)
Jack Weston (ent.; 1924-)
Jack Wrather
Jack Yellen (US lyricist; 1892-1991)
Jack, Billy (film; 1971)
Jack, David (gov.-gen., St. Vincent/Grenadines)
Jack, Union (Br. flag)(also l.c.)
Jack, Wolfman (disc jockey, *American Graffiti*)
Jackee (ent.; 1957-)
Jacket, Red (Sagoyewatha)(Seneca Indian leader; c1756-1830)
Jackie Collins (US writer)
Jackie Coogan (ent.; 1914-84)
Jackie (Herbert John) Gleason (ent.; 1916-87)
Jackie Gleason Show, The (TV show)
Jackie Joyner-Kersee (track; 1962-)
Jackie Mason (b. Yacov Moshe Maza)(ent.; 1931-)
Jackie (Jacqueline Lee Bouvier Kennedy) Onassis (US editor/photo.; wife of ex-US pres.; 1929-94)
Jackie Presser (US labor leader; 1927-88)
Jackie (John Roosevelt) Robinson (baseball; 1919-72)
Jackie Stewart (auto racing; 1939-)
Jackie Wilson (ent.)
Jack-in-the-pulpit (plant)
Jackson & Perkins™ (plants/seeds)
Jackson & Perkins Co.
Jackson Browne (pop music)
Jackson Clarion-Ledger (MS newspaper)
Jackson 5, the (pop music)
Jackson Hole National Monument (WY)
Jackson Pollock, (Paul)(US artist; 1912-56)
Jackson Winery, Kendall- (US bus.)
Jackson, Andrew ("Old Hickory")(7th US pres.; 1767-1845)
Jackson, Anne (ent.; 1925-)
Jackson, Bo (Vincent)(baseball; 1962-)
Jackson, Fort (SC)(mil.)
Jackson, Glenda (ent.; 1936-)
Jackson, Helen Hunt (pseud. H. H.)(US writer; 1830-85)
Jackson, Howell Edmunds (US jurist; 1832-95)
Jackson, Janet (ent.; 1966-)

Jackson, Jermaine (ent.; 1954-)
Jackson, Jesse (Louis), Rev. (US rel./pol.; 1941-)
Jackson, Kate (ent.; 1948-)
Jackson, Keith
Jackson, La Toya (ent.; 1956-)
Jackson, Mahalia (US jazz; 1911-72)
Jackson, MI, MS, TN, WY
Jackson, Michael (ent.; 1958-)
Jackson, Milt (US jazz; 1923-)
Jackson, Reggie (baseball; 1946-)
Jackson, Shirley (US writer; 1916-65)
Jackson, Stonewall (ent.)
Jackson, Stonewall (Thomas Jonathan)(US
    gen.; 1824-63)
Jackson, Victoria (ent.; 1959-)
Jacksonville Jaguars (football team)
Jacksonville Times-Union (FL newspaper)
Jacksonville, FL
Jaclyn Smith (ent.; 1947-)
Jacob (rel.)
Jacob Epstein (Br. sculptor; 1880-1959)
Jacob Javits (US pol.; 1904-86)
Jacob J. Shubert (US theater; 1880-1963)
Jacob Marley, the ghost of (fict. chara., *The
    Christmas Carol*)
Jacob Nena (VP, Micronesia)
Jacob (August) Riis (US reformer; 1849-1914)
Jacob (Isaackszoon) van Ruisdael (Dutch artist;
    c1628-82)
Jacobean style/literature (Br.; early 17th c.)
Jacobi, Derek (ent.; 1938-)
Jacobin (Fr. hist.; 1789-94)
Jacobite (Br. hist.; 1688-1746)
Jacobite Church (rel.)
Jacob's-ladder (plant)
Jacobs, Walter L. (US bus.; 1898-1985)
Jacopo Bellini (It. artist; 1400-70)
Jacopo Robusti (aka Tintoretto)(It. artist; 1518-
    94)
Jacopo Sansovino (It. sculptor; 1486-1570)
Jacqueline Bisset (ent.; 1944-)
Jacqueline "Jackie" Lee Bouvier Kennedy
    Onassis (US editor/photo.; wife of ex-US
    pres.; 1929-94)
Jacqueline Susann (US writer; 1921-74)
Jacques Ange Gabriel (Fr. arch.; 1689?-1782)
Jacques Callot (Fr. engraver; 1592?-1635)
Jacques (Alexandre César) Charles (Fr. physt.;
    1746-1823)
Jacques Chirac (ex-PM, Fr.; 1932-)
Jacques Dupont (minister/state, Monaco)
Jacques Étienne Montgolfier (Fr. hot-air
    balloonist; 1745-99)
Jacques-Joachim Yhombi-Opango (PM, Congo;
    1940-)
Jacques Lipchitz (US sculptor; 1891-1973)
Jacques Louis David (Fr. artist; 1748-1825)
Jacques Maritain (Fr. phil.; 1882-1973)

Jacques Marquette (Fr. expl./rel. in Amer.;
    1637-75)
Jacques Necker (Fr. pol.; 1732-1804)
Jacques (Levy) Offenbach (Fr. comp.; 1819-80)
Jacques Plante (hockey; 1929-86)
Jacques Santer (PM, Luxembourg; 1937-)
Jacques Villon (b. Gaston Duchamp)(Fr. artist;
    1875-1963)
Jacques Yves Cousteau (Fr. oceanographer;
    1910-)
Jacques, coquilles St. (scallop dish)
Jacuzzi™
Jacuzzi Whirlpool Bath (US bus.)
Jacuzzi, Candido (It./US eng./inv.; 1903-86)
Jaeckel, Richard (ent.; 1926-)
Jaffe, Sam (ent.; 1891-1984)
Jaffna, Sri Lanka
JAG (Judge Advocate General)
Jagadis Chunder Bose, Sir (Indian physt.; 1858-
    1937)
Jagan, Cheddi (Berrat)(pres., Guyana; 1918-)
Jagger, Bianca (b. Bianca Peréz Morena de
    Macías)
Jagger, Dean (ent.; 1903-91)
Jagger, Mick (Michael Phillip)(ent.; 1943-)
Jaguars, Jacksonville (football team)
J. A. Hansom (Br. arch., hansom cab; 1803-82)
Jahweh (also Jehovah, God)
Jaime Paz Zamora (ex-pres., Bolivia)
Jainism (rel.)
Jaipur, India
Jakarta, Indonesia (also Djakarta)
Jake & the Fatman (TV show)
Jake La Motta (boxing)
Jakes, John (William)(US writer; 1932-)
Jakob Bernoulli (Swiss math./scien.; 1654-1705)
Jakob Boehme (Ger. theosophist; 1575-1624)
Jakob Fugger (Jakob the Rich)(Ger. banker;
    1459-1525)
Jakob (Ludwig Karl) Grimm (Ger. writer/
    linguist; 1785-1863)
Jalalabad, Afghanistan
Jalisco (Mex. state)
Jamaica (island, Caribbean)
Jamaican Creole (lang.)
Jamal Warner, Malcolm- (ent.; 1970-)
Jamal, Ahmad (US jazz)
James A. Baker, III (US pol.; 1930-)
James A(bram) Garfield (20th US pres.; 1831-
    81)
James Agee (US writer; 1909-55)
James A. Lovell, Jr. (astro.; 1928-)
James A(lton) McDivitt (astro.; 1929-)
James A(lbert) Michener (US writer; 1907-)
James & the Shondells, Tommy (pop music)
James A(lbert) Pike, Bishop (US rel.; 1913-69)
James Arness (ent.; 1923-)
James Baldwin (US writer; 1924-87)

Proper Noun Speller

James B. Brady ("Diamond Jim")(US finan.; 1856-1917)

James "Jim" Belushi (ent.; 1954-)

James B. Hunt, Jr. (NC gov.)

James B. Irwin (astro.; 1930-91)

James "Jim" (Brendan) Bolger (PM, NewZeal.; 1935-)

James Bond (fict. spy)

James Bond (ornithol.; 1900-89)

James Boswell (Scot. biographer; 1740-95)

James "Jim" Bowie (US frontier; 1796-1836)

James Brolin (ent.; 1940-)

James Brown (ent.; 1928-)

James "Jimmy" (Nathaniel) Brown (football/ent.; 1936-)

James Browning Wyeth (US artist; 1946-)

James B. Sikking (ent.; 1934-)

James Buchanan (15th US pres.; 1791-1868)

James Caan (ent.; 1939-)

James Cagney (ent.; 1899-1986)

James Callaghan (ex-PM, Br.; 1912-)

James Carlisle (gov-gen.; Antigua and Barbuda)

James Chadwick, Sir (Br. physt.; 1891-1974)

James Clark Ross, Sir (Br. expl.; 1800-62)

James Clavell (Brit./US writer; 1924-)

James Coburn (ent.; 1928-)

James Coco (ent.)

James Cook, Capt. (Br. nav./expl.; 1728-79)

James "Gentleman Jim" Corbett (boxing; 1866-1933)

James C(ash) Penney (US bus.; 1875-1971)

James Dean (ent.; 1931-55)

James Dewar, Sir (Scot. chem/physt.; 1842-1923)

James Dewey Watson (US biol.; 1928-)

James Duke (US bus.; 1856-1925)

James Dunn (ent.; 1905-67)

James "Jimmy" Earl Carter, Jr. (39th US pres.; 1924-)

James Earl Jones (ent.; 1931-)

James Earl Ray (US, assassinated M.L. King; 1929-)

James Edmund Scripps (US publisher; 1835-1906)

James (Francis) Edward Stuart ("Old Pretender")(prince, Br.; 1688-1766)

James Ellroy

James Ensor, Baron (Belgian artist; 1860-1949)

James E(dward) Oglethorpe (Br. gen., founded Georgia; 1696-1785)

James E. Watt (Scot. eng./inv.; 1736-1819)

James Farentino (ent.; 1938-)

James Fenimore Cooper (US writer; 1789-1851)

James Fox (ent.; 1939-)

James Franciscus (ent.; 1934-91)

James Franck (Ger./US physt.; 1882-1964)

James Gadsden (US mil./dipl.; 1788-1858)

James Galanos (US designer; 1925-)

James Galway (Ir./US ent.; 1939-)

James Garner (ent.; 1928-)

James G(illespie) Blaine (US pol.; 1830-93)

James Gillespie Birney (US reformer; 1792-1857)

James Gleason (ent.; 1886-1959)

James Gregory (ent.; 1911-)

James G. Watt (US pol.)

James Hargreaves (Br. inv.; ?-1778)

James Harold Doolittle (US aviator; 1896-93)

James Henry Breasted (US archaeol.; 1865-1935)

James Herriot (Br. writer)

James Hines (sprinter; 1946-)

James Hogg ("the Ettrick Shepherd")(Scot. poet; 1770-1835)

James H. Robinson (US hist./educ.; 1863-1936)

James I ("the Conqueror")(king, Aragon; 1208-76)

James I (also James VI, Scot.)(king, Eng.; 1566-1625)

James I (king, Scot.; 1394-1437)

James II ("the Just")(king, Aragon; 1260-1327)

James II (also James VII, Scot.)(king, Eng.; 1633-1701)

James II (king, Scot.; 1430-60)

James III (aka James [Francis] Edward Stuart, Old Pretender)(Br. prince; 1688-1766)

James III (king, Scot.; 1451-88)

James Ingo Freed (US arch.)

James IV (king, Scot.; 1473-1513)

James J. Florio (NJ gov.; 1937-)

James J. Jeffries (boxing; 1875-1953)

James (Merritt) Ives (US lithographer; 1824-95)

James Jones (US writer; 1922-77)

James (Prescott) Joule (Br. physt.; 1818-89)

James Joyce (Ir. writer; 1882-1941)

James Kirke Paulding (US writer/pol.; 1778-1860)

James Knox Polk (11th US pres.; 1795-1849)

James Laurence Cabell (US phys.; 1813-89)

James Lee Witt (Dir./Fed. Emergency Mgmt. Agy.; 1944-)

James Levine (ent.; 1943-)

James L(awrence) Laughlin (US econ.; 1850-1933)

James Longstreet (US gen.; 1821-1904)

James MacArthur (ent.; 1937-)

James Madison (4th US pres.; 1751-1836)

James Mark Baldwin (US psych.; 1861-1934)

James Mason (ent.; 1909-84)

James M. Barrie, Sir (Br. writer; 1860-1937)

James M(allahan) Cain (US writer; 1892-1977)

James McGill (Can. trader/finan.; 1744-1813)

James (Abbott) McNeill Whistler (US artist; 1834-1903)

James Mill (Scot. phil.; 1773-1836)

James Mitchell (ent.; 1920-)

James Mitchell (PM, St. Vincent/Grenadines)
James M. Jeffords (US cong.; 1934-)
James Monroe (5th US pres.; 1758-1831)
James Montgomery Flagg (US cartoonist, Uncle Sam; 1877-1960)
James Naismith (Can., inv. basketball; 1861-1939)
James Naughton (ent.; 1946-)
James Noble (ent.; 1922)
James (Alvin) Palmer (baseball; 1945-)
James P. Johnson (US jazz; 1891-1955)
James P(rescott) Joule (Br. physt.; 1818-89)
James P(aul) Mitchell (US bus./pol.; 1902-?)
James Ralph Sasser (US cong.; 1936-)
James R. Doohan (Scotty on *Star Trek*)
James Renwick, Jr. (US arch.; 1818-95)
James (Barrett) Reston (US jour.; 1909-)
James R(iddle) "Jimmy" Hoffa (US labor leader; 1913-75?)
James River (VA)
James River Corp.
James Rothschild (Ger./Fr. finan.; 1792-1868)
James Russell Lowell (US poet/editor; 1819-91)
James "Jim" S. Fixx (US runner)
James Spader (ent.; 1960-)
James S(choolcraft) Sherman (ex-US VP; 1855-1912)
James Stephens (ent.; 1951-)
James Stephens (Ir. writer; 1882-1950)
James "Jimmy" Stewart (ent.; 1908-)
James Taylor (ent.; 1948-)
James T(homas) Farrell (US writer; 1904-79)
James T. Kirk, Capt. (fict. chara., *Star Trek*)
James Thomas Brudenell (7th Earl of Cardigan)(Br. mil./pol., cardigan sweater; 1797-1868)
James Thomson Shotwell (Can/US hist.; 1874-1965)
James (Grover) Thurber (US writer/humorist; 1894-1961)
James Tobin (US econ.; 1918-)
James V (king, Scot.; 1512-42)
James "Jimmy" Van Heusen, (US comp.; 1913-90)
James V(incent) Forrestal (ex-secy., navy/defense; 1892-1949)
James VI (also James I, Eng.)(king, Scot.; 1566-1625)
James VII (also James II, Eng.)(king, Scot.; 1633-1701)
James Walter Thompson (US bus.; 1847-1928)
James Warren "Jim" Jones (US/Guyana cult leader; 1931-78)
James W. Dietz (rowing; 1949-)
James Weldon Johnson (US writer, NAACP; 1871-1938)
James Whitcomb Riley (US poet; 1849-1916)
James Whitmore (ent.; 1921-)

James Wilson Morrice (Can. artist; 1865-1924)
James Woods (ent.; 1947-)
James Woolsey, R. (Director/CIA; 1941-)
James, Court of St. (Br. royal court)
James, Dennis (ent.; 1917-)
James, Epistle of (rel.)
James, Frank (US outlaw)
James, Harry (ent.; 1916-83)
James, Henry (US writer; 1843-1916)
James, Jesse (Woodson)(US outlaw; 1847-82)
James, Rick (ent.)
James, Stanislaus (gov-gen., St. Lucia)
James, William (US phil./psych.; 1842-1910)
Jameson Parker (ent.; 1947-)
Jamestown, ND, NY, VA
Jamie Farr (ent.; 1934-)
Jamie Lee Curtis (ent.; 1958-)
Jamieson, Bob
Jammu and Kashmir (state, India)
Jan Brueghel (also Breughel)(aka the "Velvet Bruegel")(Flem. artist; 1568-1625)
Jan C(hristian) Smuts (ex-PM, SAfr.; 1870-1950)
Jan H(endrik) Oort (Dutch astron.; 1900-92)
Jan Kodes (tennis; 1946-)
Jan (Garrigue) Masaryk (Czech. pol.; 1886-1948)
Jan-Michael Vincent (ent.; 1944-)
Jan Peerce (ent.; 1904-84)
Jan (Havickszoon) Steen (Dutch artist; 1626-79)
Jan Stenerud (football; 1942-)
Jan Swammerdam (Dutch biol./nat.; 1637-80)
Jan van Eyck (Flem. artist; 1385?-1441?)
Jan Vermeer (Dutch artist; 1632-75)
J&B (scotch)
Jane Addams (US reformer; 1860-1935)
Jane Alexander (ent.; 1939-)
Jane Austen (Br. writer; 1775-1817)
Jane Bryant Quinn
Jane Curtin (ent.; 1947-)
Jane Doe (unidentified or "any" woman)
Jane Eyre (Charlotte Brontë novel)
Jane Fonda (ent.; 1937-)
Jane Froman (ent.)
Jane Goodall (Br. animal behaviorist/writer; 1934-)
Jane (Dudley) Grey, Lady (queen, Eng. [10 days]; 1537-54)
Jane Howard (US writer)
Jane Pauley, (Margaret)(US TV jour.; 1950-)
Jane Powell (ent.; 1928-)
Jane Russell (ent.; 1921-)
Jane Seymour (ent.; 1951-)
Jane Seymour (queen, Eng., 3rd wife of Henry VIII; 1509?-37)
Jane Withers (ent.; 1926-)
Jane Wyatt (ent.; 1911-)
Jane Wyman (ent.; 1914-)

Jane, Calamity (b. Martha Jane Burke)(US frontier heroine; c1852-1903)
Jane?, Whatever Happened to Baby (film; 1962)
Janesville, WI
Janet Dailey (US writer; 1944-)
Janet D. Steiger (Chair/FTC; 1939-)
Janet Gaynor (ent.; 1906-84)
Janet Jackson (ent.; 1966-)
Janet Leigh (ent.; 1927-)
Janet Lynn (figure skating; 1953-)
Janet Margolin (ent.; 1943-)
Janet Reno (US atty. gen.; 1938-)
Janeway, Eliot (US econ.; 1913-93)
Janeway, Elizabeth (US writer)
Janez Drnovsek (PM, Slovenia)
Janice Merrill (track; 1962-)
Jani-King International, Inc.
Janine Turner (ent.; 1962-)
Janis Ian (ent.; 1951-)
Janis Joplin (ent.; 1943-70)
Janis Paige (ent.; 1922-)
Janis, Conrad (ent.; 1928-)
Janklow, William (SD gov.)
János Kádár, (ex-PM, Hung.; 1912-89)
Jansenism (rel.)
Janson (type style)
Janssen, David (ent.; 1930-80)
J. Anthony Lukas
Janus (astron., myth.)
Janus Book Publishers (US bus.)
Janus-faced (two-faced)
Japan (also Nippon)(NE Asia)
Japan Airlines
Japan, Sea of (Jap./Pac.)
Japanese (lang./people)
Japanese bantam (chicken)
Japanese beetle (insect)
Japanese Chin (formerly Japanese spaniel)(dog)
Japanese creeper (plant)
Japanese fleeceflower (plant)
Japanese garden
Japanese knotweed (also Mexican bamboo)(plant)
Japanese lawn grass (also Korean lawn grass)
Japanese spaniel (now Japanese Chin)(dog)
Japanese War, Russo- (Rus./Jap.; 1904-05)
Japanese War(s), Sino- (Jap./Ch.; 1894-95, 1931-45)
Japanese wisteria (plant)
Japlish (linguistics)
Jared Sparks (US hist./educ; 1789-1866)
J. Arlen Specter (US cong.; 1930-)
Jarlsberg™ (cheese)
Jaroslav Seifert (Czech. poet; 1902-86)
Jarreau, Al (ent.; 1940-)
Jarrett, Keith (US jazz; 1945-)
Jarriel, Tom (TV jour.)
Jaruzelski, Wojceich (ex-pres., Pol.; 1923-)

Jascha Heifetz (Rus./US violinist; 1901-87)
Jasmine Guy (ent.; 1964-)
Jason (myth.)
Jason Alexander (ent.; 1959-)
Jason Bateman (ent.; 1969-)
Jason Priestley (ent.; 1969-)
Jason Robards, Jr. (ent.; 1922-)
Jasper Johns (US artist; 1930-)
Jaspers, Karl (Ger. phil.; 1883-1969)
Jasray, Puntsagiyn (PM, Mongolia)
Jat (people)
Jataka (rel.)
Java man (fossil remains of *Homo erectus*)
Java, Indonesia
Javanese (lang./people)
Javier Pérez de Cuéllar (Peruvian/UN dipl.; 1920-)
Javits, Jacob (US pol.; 1904-86)
Jawaharlal Nehru (ex-PM, India; 1889-1964)
Jawara, Sir Dawda Kairaba (pres., Gambia; 1924-)
Jaworski, Leon (US atty.; 1905-82)
Jaws (P. Benchley novel, film)
Jaws of Life™ (auto.)
Jay and the Americans (pop music)
Jay C. Flippen (ent. 1900-71)
Jay Cook (US finan.; 1821-1905)
Jay Gatsby (fict. chara., *The Great Gatsby*)
Jay Gould (US finan., railroad; 1836-92)
Jay Leno (ent.; 1950-)
Jay McInerney
Jay N. Darling ("Ding")(pol. cartoonist; 1876-1962)
Jay Sandrich
Jay Silverheels (ent.)
Jay Silvester (discus thrower; 1937-)
Jay Thomas (ent.)
Jay, John (US jurist/dipl.; 1745-1829)
Jaycees (Junior Chambers of Commerce members)
Jayhawker State (KS)
Jaymes™, Bartles & (wine coolers)
Jayne Kennedy-Overton (ent.; 1951-)
Jayne Mansfield (ent.; 1932-67)
Jayne Meadows (ent.; 1920-)
Jayne Torvill (figure skating)
Jay's Treaty (US/Eng.; 1795)
Jazz, Utah (basketball team)
Jazzercise (US bus.)
Jazzy Jeff & the Fresh Prince, D.J. (pop music)
J. Bennett Johnston, Jr. (US cong.; 1932-)
J(ohn) B(oynton) Priestley (Br. writer; 1894-1984)
JC (Jesus Christ)
J. Carroll Naish (ent.; 1900-73)
J. C. Penney Co.
JD (Justice Department, juvenile delinquent)
JDL (Jewish Defense League)

J(ames) Danforth "Dan" Quayle, III (ex-US VP; 1947-)
J(erome) D(avid) Salinger (US writer; 1919-)
Jean Alingue Bawoyeu (ex-PM, Chad)
Jean Antoine Watteau (Fr. artist; 1684-1721)
Jean (or Hans) Arp (Fr. artist; 1887-1966)
Jean Arthur (ent.; 1900-91)
Jean Auguste Dominique Ingres (Fr. artist; 1780-1867)
Jean Ausseil (Monacan pol.)
Jean-Baptiste-Camille Corot (Fr. artist; 1796-1875)
Jean Baptiste Colbert (Fr. pol.; 1619-83)
Jean Baptiste Le Moyne Bienville (Fr. colonial administrator; 1680-1768)
Jean Baptiste Molière (Fr. writer; 1622-73)
Jean-Baptiste-Siméon Chardin (Fr. artist; 1699-1779)
Jean Beliveau (hockey; 1931-)
Jean-Bertrand Aristide (deposed pres., Haiti; 1953-)
Jean B(aptiste) J(oseph) Fourier (Fr. math.; 1768-1830)
Jean B(aptiste) Lamarck, (Fr. nat.; 1744-1829)
Jean Brodie, The Prime of Miss (film; 1969)
Jean Bugatti (It. designer; 1909-39)
Jean Chretién, (Joseph Jacques)(PM, Can.; 1934-)
Jean-Claude Duvalier (aka Baby Doc)(ex-pres., Haiti; 1951-)
Jean-Claude Killy (Fr. skier; 1943-)
Jean-Claude Van Damme (ent.)
Jean Cocteau (Fr. writer/artist; 1889-1963)
Jean de la Fontaine (Fr. poet; 1621-95)
Jean Dubuffet (Fr. artist; 1902-85)
Jean Félix Piccard (Swiss chem./eng.; 1884-1963)
Jean François Champollion (Fr. archaeol.; 1790-1832)
Jean François Millet (Fr. artist; 1814-75)
Jean Genet (Fr. writer; 1911-1986)
Jean Giraudoux (Fr. writer/dipl.; 1882-1944)
Jean Harlow (b. Harlean Carpenter)(ent.; 1911-37)
Jean (Struven) Harris (US educ., shot Dr. H. Tarnower)
Jean Hersholt
Jean Honore Fragonard (Fr. artist; 1732-1806)
Jean (Eugène Robert) Houdin (Fr. magician; 1805-71)
Jean-Jacques Honorat (ex-PM, Haiti)
Jean Jacques Rousseau (Fr. phil./writer; 1712-78)
Jean Kerr (US writer; 1923-)
Jean Lafitte (or Laffite)(Fr. mil./pirate; c1780-c1825)
Jean Laffite National Historical Park (LA)
Jean Louis Rodolphe Agassiz (Swiss nat.; 1807-73)
Jean-Luc Dehaene (PM, Belgium; 1940-)
Jean-Luc Godard (Fr. ent.; 1930-)
Jean-Luc Picard, Capt. (fict. chara., *Star Trek*)
Jean-Marie Le Pen (Fr. pol.; 1928-)
Jean Marsh (ent.; 1934-)
Jean M. Auel
Jean M. Charcot (Fr. phys.; 1825-93)
Jean Naté™ (toiletries)
Jean Naté, Inc.
Jean Parker (ent.; 1912-)
Jean-Paul Belmondo (Fr. ent.; 1933-)
Jean Paul Marat (Fr. pol.; 1743-93)
Jean Paul Riopelle (Can. artist; 1923-)
Jean-Paul Sartre (Fr. phil./writer; 1905-80)
Jean Philippe Rameau (Fr. comp.; 1683-1764)
Jean Picard (Fr. astron.; 1620-82)
Jean Pierre Chouteau (US pioneer/fur trader; 1758-1849)
Jean-Pierre Rampal (Fr. flutist; 1922-)
Jean (Baptiste) Racine (Fr. writer; 1639-99)
Jean Ratelle, (Joseph Gilbert Yvon)(hockey; 1953-)
Jean Renoir (Fr. ent./writer; 1894-1979)
Jean R. Yawkey (US bus./baseball; 1908-92)
Jean Seberg (ent.; 1938-79)
Jean (Julius Christian) Sibelius (Fin. comp.; 1865-1957)
Jean Simmons (ent.; 1929-)
Jean Stapleton (ent.; 1923-)
Jean Valjean (fict. chara., *Les Miserables*)
Jean, Grand Duke (pres., Luxembourg; 1921-)
Jean, Inc., Chateau St.)
Jeane (Jordan) Kirkpatrick (US pol./dipl.; 1926-)
Jeanette MacDonald (ent.; 1903-65)
Jeanne Antoinette Poisson Le Normant d'Étioles (Marquise de Pompadour)(mistress of Louis XV, Fr.; 1721-64)
Jeanne Bécu du Barry, Madame (Comtesse, mistress, Louis XV; 1743-93)
Jeanne Crain (ent.; 1925-)
Jeanne d'Arc (also St. Joan of Arc, Maid of Orléans)(Fr. rel./mil.; 1412?-31)
Jeanne Moreau (ent.; 1928-)
Jeanneret, Charles Édouard (aka Le Corbusier)(Fr. arch./artist; 1887-1965)
Jeannette Rankin (US pol.; 1880-1973)
Jeannie C. Riley (ent.; 1945-)
J(ames) E(well) B(rown) Stuart (US mil.; 1833-64)
Jeb Stuart Magruder (US pol./Watergate)
Jed Clampett (fict. chara.)
J(ohn) Edgar Hoover (ex-dir., FBI; 1895-1972)
Jedi, Return of the (film)
Jeep™ (auto)
Jeep™ Grand Cherokee, Chrysler (auto.)
Jeep™ Grand Cherokee Laredo, Chrysler

(auto.)
Jeep Wrangler (auto.)
Jeeves, the butler (fict. chara.)
Jeff & the Fresh Prince, D.J. Jazzy (pop music)
Jeff Bingaman (US cong.; 1943-)
Jeff Bridges (ent.; 1949-)
Jeff Chandler (ent.; 1918-61)
Jeff Corey (ent.; 1914-)
Jeff Daniels (ent.; 1955-)
Jeff Gillooly (US news)
Jeff Goldblum (ent.; 1952-)
Jeff MacNelly (cartoonist, *Shoe*; 1947-)
Jeff, Mutt & (comic strip)
Jeffers, (John) Robinson (US writer; 1887-1962)
Jefferson Airplane (pop music)
Jefferson City, MO
Jefferson Davis (US pol./confederate pres,;
    1808-89)
Jefferson Memorial, (Thomas)(DC)
Jefferson Starship (pop music)
Jefferson, Blind Lemon (US jazz; 1897-1930)
Jefferson, Thomas (3rd US pres.; 1743-1826)
Jeffersons, The (TV show)
Jeffires, Haywood (football; 1964-)
Jeffords, James M. (US cong.; 1934-)
Jeffrey Amherst, Baron (Br. gen.; 1717-97)
Jeffrey Dahmer (US serial killer)
Jeffrey Lynn (ent.; 1909-)
Jeffreys, Alec John (Br. geneticist; 1950-)
Jeffreys, Anne (ent.; 1923-)
Jeffries, James J. (boxing; 1875-1953)
Jehoshaphat (king, Judah; ?-851? BC)
Jehoshaphat, jumping
Jehovah (also Jahweh, God)
Jehovah's Witnesses (rel.)
Jehovah's Witnesses, Kingdom Hall of
Jekyll and Hyde (dual personality, one good/one
    evil)
Jekyll and Mr. Hyde, The Strange Case of Dr.
    (by R.L. Stevenson)
Jelgava, Latvia
Jell-O™
Jelly Roll Morton (b. Ferdinand Joseph La
    Menthe)(US jazz; 1885-1941)
Jellystone Park Camp-Resort, Yogi Bear's (US
    bus.)
Jemima Puddleduck
Jenkins' Art Workshop (TV show)
Jenkin's Ear, War of (Br./Sp.; 1739-41)
Jenkins, Fergusin Arthur (baseball; 1943-)
Jenkins, Snuffy
Jenn-Air™ (appliances)
Jenn-Air Corp.
Jenner, Bruce (US track/TV jour.; 1949-)
Jenner, Edward (Br. phys., smallpox vaccine;
    1749-1823)
Jenner, William (Br. phys.; 1815-98)
Jennie Churchill (mother of Winston; 1854-

1921)
Jennifer Capriati (tennis; 1976-)
Jennifer Jason Leigh (ent.; 1958-)
Jennifer Jones (ent.; 1919-)
Jennifer O'Neill (ent.; 1932-)
Jennings, Peter (US TV jour.; 1938-)
Jennings, Waylon (ent.; 1937-)
Jenny Craig Weight Loss Centers (US bus.)
Jenny Lind (Johanna Maria Lind Goldschmidt,
    "The Swedish Nightingale")(ent.; 1820-87)
Jeno's™ pizza
Jeno's, Inc.
Jeopardy (TV show)
Jeremiah (Hebrew prophet; 7th-6th c. BC)
Jeremy Bentham (Br. rel.; 1748-1832)
Jeremy Irons (ent.; 1948-)
Jergens™ (skin care)
Jergens Co., The Andrew
Jericho, Jordan (ancient walled city)
Jericho, NY
Jericho, rose of (plant)
Jermaine Jackson (ent.; 1954-)
Jeroboam I (king, Isr.; ?-912? BC)
Jeroboam II (king, Isr.; ?-744? BC)
Jerome Bonaparte (bro. of Napoleon, king,
    Westphalia; 1784-1860)
Jerome (David) Kern (US comp.; 1885-1945)
Jerome "Doc" Pomus (US comp.; 1925-91)
Jerome Robbins (US ballet; 1918-)
Jerry Bock (US comp.; 1928-)
Jerry Brown, (Edmund Gerald), Jr. (ex-gov.,
    CA; 1938-)
Jerry Falwell, Rev. (US rel.; 1933-)
Jerry Kramer (football; 1936-)
Jerry Lee Lewis (ent.; 1935-)
Jerry Leiber (US comp.; 1933-)
Jerry Lewis (b. Joseph Levitch)(ent.; 1926-)
Jerry Martin Koosman (baseball; 1942-)
Jerry Orbach (ent.; 1935-)
Jerry (John) Rawlings (pres., Ghana; 1947-)
Jerry Reed (ent.; 1937-)
Jerry Rice (football; 1962-)
Jerry Seinfeld (ent.; 1954-)
Jerry Siegel (cartoonist, *Superman*; 1914-)
Jerry Springer
Jerry Stiller (ent.; 1929-)
Jerry Vale (ent.; 1931-)
Jerry Van Dyke (ent.; 1931-)
Jerry West (basketball; 1938-)
Jerry, Tom and (cartoon)
Jerry, Tom and (cocktail)
Jerry's Homemade, Inc., Ben &
Jersey (cattle)
Jersey (island, English Channel)
Jersey City, NJ
Jersey Giant (chicken)
Jersey Joe Walcott (b. Arnold Raymond
    Cream)(boxing; 1914-)

Jerusalem artichoke (plant)
Jerusalem, Church of the New (also
    Swedenborgians)
Jerusalem, Israel
Jerusalem, Temple of (rel.)
Jerzy (Nikodem) Kosinski (or Kozinski)(Pol./US
    writer; 1933-91)
Jessamyn West (US writer; 1903-84)
Jesse Alexander Helms (US cong.; 1921-)
Jesse Applegate (US pioneer/pol.; 1811-88)
Jesse Brown (US Secy./Veteran Affairs; 1944-)
Jesse (Louis) Jackson, Rev. (US rel./pol.; 1941-)
Jesse (Woodson) James (US outlaw; 1847-82)
Jesse (James Cleveland) Owens (track; 1913-
    80)
Jesse White (ent.; 1919-)
Jessel, George (ent.; 1898-1981)
Jessica Fletcher (fict. chara., *Murder, She
    Wrote*)
Jessica Hahn (US news)
Jessica Harper (ent.; 1949-)
Jessica Lange (ent.; 1949-)
Jessica (Beth) Savitch (US TV jour.; 1947-83)
Jessica Tandy (ent.; 1909-)
Jessica Walter (ent.; 1944-)
Jessica, Baby (US news)
Jessye Norman (ent.; 1945-)
Jesuit (also Society of Christ)(rel.)
Jesus Christ (also Jesus, Christ Jesus, Jesus of
    Nazareth)(known as Jeshua ben Joseph to
    contemporaries)
Jesus freak
Jesus Christ, Vicar of (pope)
Jet (mag.)
Jet Propulsion Laboratory (JPL)(NASA
    installation; Pasadena, CA)
Jethro Clampett (fict. chara.)
Jethro Tull (Br. agr.; 1674-1741)
Jethro Tull (pop music)
Jets, New York (football team)
Jets, Winnipeg (hockey team)
Jetsons, The (cartoon)
Jett, Joan (ent.; 1960-)
Jetta, Volkswagen™ (auto.)
Jew (people)
Jewish (people, rel.)
Jewish calendar (also Hebrew calendar)
Jewison, Norman (ent.; 1926-)
Jewry (Jewish people)
Jew's harp (music)
Jews, National Conference of Christians and
    (est. 1928)
Jezebel (film; 1938)
Jezebel (rel.)
Jezek, Linda (swimming; 1960-)
Jezreel, Plain of (also Esdraelon Plain)(Isr.)
J. F. Kennedy International Airport (NY)
J. Fred Muggs (TV chimp; c1952)

J(ames) G(raham) Ballard (Br. writer; 1930-)
J. Gimbel, Inc.
Jheri Redding Products, Inc.
J. Higby's Yogurt & Treat Shoppe (US bus.)
Jhirmack™ (hair care)
Jiang Qing (also Chiang Ching)(Ch. pol./widow
    of Mao Zedong; 1914-91)
Jiang Zemin (pres., Ch.; 1926-)
Jiangsu (also Kiangsu)(province, Ch.)
Jiangxi (also Kiangsi)(province, Ch.)
Jidd Hafs, Bahrain
Jiddah, Saudi Arabia (also Jidda)
Jif™ peanut butter
Jiffy Lube (US bus.)
Jiggs, Maggie and (comic strip)
Jigme Singye Wangchuk (king, Bhutan
Jilin (also Kirin)(province, Ch.)
Jill Clayburgh (ent.; 1944-)
Jill Eikenberry (ent.; 1947-)
Jill Ireland (ent.; 1936-90)
Jill St. John (ent.; 1940-)
Jill Trenary
Jill, Jack and (nursery rhyme)
Jillian, Ann (ent.; 1950-)
Jillie Mack
Jim Backus (ent.; 1913-89)
Jim (James Leroy) Bakken (football; 1940-)
Jim (James Orsen) Bakker (US evang.; 1940-)
Jim Beam Brands Co.
Jim (James) Belushi (ent.; 1954-)
Jim Berry (cartoonist, *Berry's World*; 1932-)
Jim (James Brendan) Bolger (PM, NewZeal.;
    1935-)
Jim (James) Bowie (US frontier; 1796-1836)
Jim Brady, Diamond (US finan.; 1856-1917)
Jim Croce (ent.; 1942-73)
Jim Crow (racial discrimination)(also l.c.)
Jim Crow laws (US hist., pro-segregation; pre-
    1960's)
Jim Davis (cartoonist, *Garfield*; 1945-)
Jim Demaret (golf; 1910-83)
Jim Dine (US artist; 1935-)
Jim Edgar (IL gov.; 1946-)
Jim (James S.) Fixx (US runner)
Jim Garrison (US atty.; 1922-92)
Jim Guy Tucker (AR gov.)
Jim (James Maury) Henson (US puppeteer/
    Muppets; 1936-90)
Jim (James Warren) Jones (US/Guyana cult
    leader; 1931-78)
Jim Kaat (baseball; 1938-)
Jim Lee Howell (football; 1914-)
Jim Lehrer (US news jour.; 1934-)
Jim McKay (sports)
Jim Messina (ent.; 1947-)
Jim Montgomery (swimming; 1955-)
Jim Morrison (ent.; 1943-71)
Jim Nabors (ent.; 1933-)

Proper Noun Speller

Jim Nance (football; 1943-92)
Jim Palmer (baseball; 1945-)
Jim Perry (baseball; 1936-)
Jim Plunkett (football; 1947-)
Jim Reeves (ent.)
Jim Rice (baseball; 1953-)
Jim (James Ronald) Ryun (runner; 1947-)
Jim Stafford
Jim (James Francis) Thorpe (Olympics; 1888-1953)
Jim Walter Corp.
Jim, Jungle (comic strip)
Jima, Iwo (island, W Pac.)
Jimi (James Marshall) Hendrix (ent.; 1942-70)
Jimmie Lunceford (US jazz; 1902-47)
Jimmy Blanton (US jazz; 1921-42)
Jimmy Breslin (US writer; 1930-)
Jimmy (James Nathaniel) Brown (football/ent.; 1936-)
Jimmy Buffett (ent.)
Jimmy (James Earl) Carter, Jr. (39th US pres.; 1924-)
Jimmy (James Scott) Connors (tennis; 1952-)
Jimmy Dean (ent.; 1928-)
Jimmy Dean™ (sausage)
Jimmy Dean Meat Co.
Jimmy Dickens, Little (ent.)
Jimmy Dorsey (US cond.; 1904-57)
Jimmy (James Francis) Durante (ent.; 1893-1980)
Jimmy (James Emory) Foxx (baseball; 1907-67)
Jimmy Hatlo (US cartoonist, *Little Iodine*; 1898-1963)
Jimmy (James Riddle) Hoffa (US labor leader; 1913-75?)
Jimmy McHugh (US comp.; 1894-1969)
Jimmy McPartland (US jazz; 1907-)
Jimmy Rodgers (ent.; 1933-)
Jimmy Smits (ent.; 1955-)
Jimmy "the Greek" Snyder
Jimmy (James) Stewart (ent.; 1908-)
Jimmy Swaggart, Rev. (US rel.)
Jimmy (James) Van Heusen, (US comp.; 1913-90)
Jimmy (James John) Walker (ex-mayor, NYC; 1881-1946)
Jimmy Webb (US comp.; 1946-)
Jimmy Yancey (US jazz; 1894-1951)
Jinja, Uganda
Jinnah, Muhammad Ali (India/Pak. pol.; 1876-1948)
Jinsha Jiang River (Ch.)
Jinx Falkenburg
Jivaro (lang./people)
J. James Exon (US cong.; 1921-)
J. J. Johnson (US jazz; 1924-)
J(oseph) J(ohn) Thomson, Sir (Br. physt.; 1856-1940)

J(ames) J(oseph Jacques) Tissot (Fr. artist; 1836-1902)
J. Lohr Winery (US bus.)
J. L. Plum™ (clothing)
J. M. Smucker Co., The
J(oseph) M(allord) W(illiam) Turner (Br. artist; 1774-1851)
Jo Anne Worley (ent.)
Jo Jones (US jazz; 1911-85)
Jo Stafford (ent.; 1918-)
Jo Van Fleet (ent.; 1922-)
Joachim Murat (king, Naples; 1767-1815)
Joachim von Ribbentrop (Ger. Nazi pol.; 1893-1946)
Joachim Yhombi-Opango, Jacques- (PM, Congo; 1940-)
Joan Aiken (US writer)
Joan Allen (ent.; 1956-)
Joan Baez (ent.; 1941-)
Joan Bennett (ent.; 1910-90)
Joan Benoit Samuelson (Olympic marathon; 1957-)
Joan Blondell (ent.; 1909-79)
Joan Caulfield (ent.; 1922-91)
Joan Collins (ent.; 1933-)
Joan Crawford (ent.; 1908-77)
Joan Cusack (ent.; 1962-)
Joan Didion (US writer; 1934-)
Joan Finney (KS gov.; 1925-)
Joan Fontaine (ent.; 1917-)
Joan Ganz Cooney (ent.; 1929-)
Joan Jett (ent.; 1960-)
Joan Leslie (ent.; 1925-)
Joan Lunden (US TV jour.; 1950-)
Joan Miró (Sp. artist; 1893-1983)
Joan of Arc, St. (also Jeanne d'Arc, Maid of Orléans)(Fr. rel./mil.; 1412?-31)
Joan Rivers (ent.; 1933-)
Joan Sutherland (opera; 1926-)
Joan Van Ark (ent.; 1943-)
Joan, Darby and (fict. happy, elderly, married couple)
Joan, Pope (card game)
Joanna Cassidy (ent.)
Joanna Kerns (ent.; 1953-)
Joanne Dru (ent.; 1923-)
Joanne Gunderson Carner (golf; 1939-)
Joanne Woodward (ent.; 1930-)
João Bernardo Vieira (pres., Guinea-Bissau; 1939-)
Joaquim Alberto Chissano (pres., Mozambique; 1939-)
Joaquín Ricardo Balaguer (pres., Dom Rep.; 1907-)
Job Corps
Job, Book of (rel.)
JoBeth Williams (ent.; 1953-)
Jobs, Steve(n)(US bus./compu.; 1955-)

Job's-tears (grass)
Jocasta (myth.)
Jock Scot (or Scott)(fishing)
Jockey International, Inc.
Jockey shorts™ (underwear)
Jodhpur, India (also Marwar)
Jodie Foster (ent.; 1962-)
Jody Watley
Joe Barbera (cartoonist, *Tom & Jerry,*
    Huckleberry Hound, Yogi Bear, Flintstones;
    1911-)
Joe Besser (ent.; 1907-88)
Joe Blow (also Joe Doakes)(average guy)
Joe (Charles Joseph) Clark (ex-PM, Can.; 1939-)
Joe (John Robert) Cocker (ent.; 1944-)
Joe College (average college student)
Joe Cronin (baseball exec.; 1906-84)
Joe DeRita (b. Joseph Wardell)(ent.; 1909-93)
Joe DiMaggio (baseball; 1914-)
Joe Doakes (also Joe Blow)(average guy)
Joe Don Baker (ent.; 1936-)
Joe E. Brown (ent.; 1892-1973)
Joe E. Lewis (ent.; 1902-71)
Joe Franklin (ent.; 1929-)
Joe Frazier (boxing; 1944-)
Joe Garagiola (ent.; 1926-)
Joe Greene, "Mean" (football; 1946-)
Joe Howard (ent.; 1867-1961)
Joe Isuzu (fict. chara.)
Joe Jones, Philly (US jazz; 1923-85)
Joe Louis (b. Joseph Louis Barrow)(boxing;
    1914-81)
Joe Mantegna (ent.; 1947-)
Joe (Joseph Vincent) McCarthy (baseball; 1887-
    1978)
Joe McIntyre (ent.; 1972-)
Joe Miller (familiar joke/book of jokes)
Joe Montana (football; 1956-)
Joe (Leonard) Morgan (baseball; 1943-)
Joe Morton (ent.; 1947-)
Joe (Joseph William) Namath ("Broadway
    Joe")(football; 1943-)
Joe Palooka (comic strip)
Joe Pass (US jazz)
Joe Pesci (ent.; 1943-)
Joe P. Estrada Winery (US bus.)
Joe Piscopo (ent.; 1951-)
Joe Sewell (baseball; 1898-1990)
Joe Shuster (cartoonist, *Superman*; 1914-92)
Joe Slovo
Joe Spano (ent.; 1946-)
Joe Theismann (football; 1946-)
Joe Turner, Big (ent.; 1911-85)
Joe Venuti (US jazz; 1904-78)
Joe Walcott, Jersey (b. Arnold Raymond
    Cream)(boxing; 1914-)
Joe Williams (ent.; 1918-)
Joe, Broadway (aka Joe [Joseph William]

Namath)(football; 1943-)
Joel Chandler Harris (US writer; 1848-1908)
Joel Grey (ent.; 1932-)
Joel McCrea (ent.; 1905-90)
Joel Siegel
Joel, Billy (ent.; 1949-)
Joey Adams (ent.; 1911-)
Joey Bishop (ent.; 1918-)
Joey Buttafuoco (US news)
Joey Heatherton (ent.)
Joffre, Joseph (Jacques Césaire)(Fr. mil.; 1852-
    1931)
Joffrey Ballet
Joffrey, Robert (Abdullah Jaffa Bey Khan)(US
    ballet; 1930-88)
Johan Cruyff (soccer; 1947-)
Johann Ambrosia Bach (Ger. musician, father
    of J.S.; 1645-95)
Johann August Brinell (Swed. eng.; 1849-1925)
Johann (Jakob) Balmer (Swiss math./physt.;
    1825-98)
Johann Bernoulli (Swiss math./scien.; 1667-
    1748)
Johann Christian Bach (Ger. comp., son of J.S.;
    1735-82)
Johann Christoph Friedrich Bach (Ger. comp.,
    bro. of J.S.; 1732-95)
Johann David Wyss (Swiss writer; 1743-1818)
Johann Elert Bode (Ger. astron.; 1747-1826)
Johann Faust (also Faustus)(Ger. fortuneteller/
    magician; 1480?-1540?)
Johann Fichte (Ger. phil.; 1762-1814)
Johann Gutenberg (Ger. printer; c1400-68)
Johann Pachelbel (Ger. comp.; 1653-1706)
Johann Rudolf Wyss (Swiss writer; 1782-1830)
Johann Sebastian Bach (Ger. comp.; 1685-1750)
Johann Strauss (the Elder)(Aus.comp./cond.;
    1804-49)
Johann Strauss (the Younger)("The Waltz
    King")(Aus. comp.; 1825-99)
Johann Wolfgang von Goethe (Ger. writer/phil.;
    1749-1852)
Johanna Spyri (Swiss writer; 1827-1901)
Johannes (or Hans) Bach (Ger. musician, great-
    grandfather of J.S.; 1580-1626)
Johannes Brahms (Ger. comp.; 1833-97)
Johannes Evangelista Purkinje (Czech.
    physiol.; 1787-1869)
Johannes (or Johann) Kepler (Ger. astron./
    math.; 1571-1630)
Johannesburg, South Africa
Johannisberg Riesling (wine)
Johansson, Ingemar (Swed. boxing)
John Adams (2nd US pres.; 1735-1826)
John Alexander Macdonald, Sir (ex-PM, Can.;
    1815-91)
John Amos (ent.; 1942-)
John and Leeza (TV show)

John André, Major (Br. spy; 1751-80)
John Arbuthnot (Scot. phys./satirist; 1667-1735)
John Astin (ent.; 1930-)
John A(ugustus) Sutter (US pioneer, gold; 1803-80)
John Aubrey (Br. antiquarian; 1626-97)
John Barbirolli, Sir (Br. cond.; 1899-1970)
John Barbour (Scot. poet; 1316?-95)
John Bardeen (US physt.; 1908-91)
John Barleycorn (personification of alcohol)
John Barry (US mil.; 1745-1803)
John (Blythe) Barrymore (ent.; 1882-1942)
John Barth (US writer; 1930-)
John Bartlett (US publ./editor, *Familiar Quotations*; 1820-1905)
John Baskerville (Br. typographer; 1706-75)
John Bassett Moore (US jurist; 1860-1947)
John B. Breaux (US cong.; 1944-)
John B. Connally (ex-gov., TX; 1917-93)
John Beal (ent.; 1909-)
John Beck (ent.; 1943-)
John Belushi (ent.; 1949-82)
John Beradino (ent.; 1917-)
John Bernard Flannagan (US sculptor; 1895-1942)
John Berryman (US poet; 1914-72)
John Biddle (Br., rel.; 1615-62)
John Birch Society (politics)
John Bozeman
John Brown (US abolitionist; 1800-59)
John B(atterson) Stetson (US bus.; 1830-1906)
John B. Stetson Co.
John Bull (Br. comp.; 1562-1628)
John Bull (synonym for Eng. people)
John Bull pamphlets (Br. hist.; 1712)
John Bunyan (Br. writer/rel.; 1628-88)
John Burgoyne (Br. gen./writer; 1722-92)
John Cabell Breckinridge (ex-US VP/gen; 1821-75)
John Cabot (also Giovanni Caboto)(It. nav.; 1450-98)
John (Milton) Cage (US comp.; 1912-92)
John Calvin (Fr. rel.; 1509-64)
John Cameron Swayze (US TV jour.)
John Candy (ent.; 1950-94)
John Carlos (sprinter; 1945-)
John Carradine (ent.; 1906-88)
John Cassavetes (ent.; 1929-89)
John C. Calhoun (ex-US VP; 1782-1850)
John Chancellor (US TV jour.; 1927-)
John Chapman (aka Johnny Appleseed)(US pioneer; 1774-1845)
John Charles Daly, Jr. (ent./TV news exec.; 1914-91)
John Charles Frémont (US mil.; 1813-90)
John Cheever (US writer; 1912-82)
John Churchill (aka Duke of Marlborough)(Br. mil.; 1650-1722)

John Claggett Danforth (US cong.; 1936-)
John Cleese (ent.; 1939-)
John Coltrane (US jazz; 1926-67)
John (George Melvin) Compton (PM, St. Lucia)
John Constable (Br. artist; 1776-1837)
John Coryell (US writer; 1927-)
John Cotton (Br./US rel.; 1584-1652)
John Cougar Mellencamp
John Crowley (US writer; 1942-)
John Cullum (ent.; 1930-)
John Cusack (ent.; 1966-)
John Dalton (Br. chem./physt.; 1766-1844)
John Daniel Ehrlichman (US pol./Watergate; 1925-)
John Davidson (ent.; 1941-)
John D. Cockcroft (Br. physt.; 1897-1967)
John De Lorean (US bus./auto.; 1925-)
John Denver (ent.; 1943-)
John Derek (ent.; 1926-)
John Dewey (US phil./educ.; 1859-1952)
John Dillinger (US bank robber/murderer; 1902?-34)
John D. MacDonald (US writer; 1916-86)
John Doe (unidentified or "any" man)
John Donne (Br. poet; 1573-1631)
John Dory (fish)
John Dos Passos (US writer; 1896-1970)
John Drew Barrymore (ent.; 1932-)
John Drew, Mrs. (ent.; 1820-97)
John D(avison) Rockefeller (US bus./finan.; 1839-1937)
John D(avison) Rockefeller, III (US finan.; 1906-78)
John D(avison) "Jay" Rockefeller, IV (US cong.; 1937-)
John D(avison) Rockefeller, Jr. (US bus./finan.; 1874-1960)
John Dryden (Br. writer; 1631-1700)
John D. S. Campbell (Duke of Argyll)(ex-gov/gen, Can.; 1845-1914)
John Dudley Northumberland, Duke (Br. pol.; c1502-53)
John D. Waihee, III (HI gov.; 1946-)
John Edgar Wideman (US writer; 1941-)
John Engler (MI gov.; 1948-)
John Erskine ("Erskine of Carnock")(Scot. writer, law; 1695-1768)
John Fairchild Dryden (US bus./pol.; 1839-1911)
John Falstaff, Sir (fict. chara., Shakespeare)
John F. Enders (US virol.; 1897-1985)
John Fiedler (ent.; 1925-)
John Fiske (US hist.; 1842-1901)
John Fitch (US inv.; 1743-98)
John F(itzgerald) "Jack" Kennedy (35th US pres.; 1917-63)
John F. Kennedy Center for the Performing Arts (DC)

John F. Kennedy Space Center (FL)
John F. McWethy
John Forsythe (ent.; 1918-)
John Foster Dulles (US pol.; 1888-1959)
John Fowles (Br. writer; 1926-)
John F. Poindexter (US pol.)
John Francis Appleby (US inv.; 1840-1917)
John Frankenheimer (ent.; 1930-)
John Frederic Daniell (Br. chem.; 1790-1845)
John F(rench) Sloan (US artist; 1871-1951)
John Gabriel (ent.; 1931-)
John Galsworthy (Br. writer; 1867-1933)
John Galt (fict. chara.; *Atlas Shrugged*)
John Galt (Scot writer; 1779-1839)
John Garfield (ent.; 1913-52)
John Gay (Br. writer; 1685-1732)
John George Diefenbaker (ex-PM, Can.; 1895-1979)
John Gielgud, Sir (Arthur)(ent.; 1904-)
John Goodman (ent.; 1953-)
John Gotti
John Greenleaf Whittier (US poet/jour.; 1807-92)
John Gregory Dunne (US writer; 1932-)
John Grisham (US writer; 1955-)
John G. Tower (US pol.; 1926-91)
John Guare (US writer; 1938-)
John Gunther (US jour./writer; 1901-70)
John Hancock (one's signature)
John Hancock (US pol., Declaration of Independence; 1737-93)
John Hancock Bowl (college football)
John Hancock Mutual Life Insurance Co.
John Hanning Speke (Br. expl. in Afr.; 1827-64)
John Harvard (Br./US rel.; 1607-38)
John Havlicek (basketball; 1940-)
John Hawkes (US writer; 1925-)
John (Milton) Hay (US pol.; 1838-1905)
John Hay Whitney (US publ./finan.; 1905-82)
John H. Chafee (US cong.; 1922-)
John Heard (ent.; 1945-)
John Hencken (swimming; 1954-)
John Henry (fict. chara., exceptional strength)
John Hersey (US writer; 1917-93)
John H(erschel) Glenn, Jr. (US cong./astro.; 1921-)
John (Warnock) Hinckley, Jr. (US, shot R. Reagan; 1955-)
John H(enry) Newman, (Br. rel.; 1801-90)
John Hodiak (ent.; 1914-55)
John Houseman (ent.; 1902-88)
John H. Sununu (US pol.; 1939-)
John (Joseph) Hughes (US rel.; 1797-1864)
John Hunt Morgan (US confed. gen.; 1826-64)
John Ireland (ent.; 1914-92)
John Irving (US writer; 1942-)
John Jacob Astor (US bus.; 1763-1848)
John Jacob Astor, 5th (US/Br. publ.; 1886-1971)

John (William) Jakes (US writer; 1932-)
John James Audubon (US artist, birds; 1785-1851)
John Jay (US jurist/dipl.; 1745-1829)
John J(oseph) Pershing ("Blackjack")(US gen.; 1860-1948)
John Kander (US comp.; 1927-)
John Karlen (ent.; 1933-)
John Keats (Br. poet; 1795-1821)
John Kenneth Galbraith (US/Can. econ.; 1908-)
John Kerr (ent.; 1931-)
John Kerry (US cong.; 1943-)
John Ketch (Br. executioner; 1663?-86)
John Kinsella (swimming; 1952-)
John Knowles (US writer; 1926-)
John Knox (Scot. rel.; 1505-72)
John Labatt, Ltd.
John La Farge (US artist; 1835-1910)
John Landis (ent.; 1950-)
John Landis Mason (US inv.)
John Landy (runner; 1930-)
John Larroquette (ent.; 1947-)
John le Carré (b. David Cornwell)(Br. writer; 1931-)
John Lennon (Br. comp./ent.; 1940-80)
John Lewis (US jazz; 1920-)
John Lily (or Lyly, Lilly)(Br. writer; 1554?-1606)
John (Vliet) Lindsay (ex-mayor, NYC; 1921-)
John Lithgow (ent.; 1945-)
John L(lewellyn) Lewis (US labor leader; 1880-1969)
John Locke (Br. phil.; 1632-1704)
John Logie Baird ("Father of Television")(Scot. eng.; 1888-1946)
John Loudon McAdam (Scot. eng.; 1756-1836)
John Lovitz (ent.; 1957-)
John L(awrence) Sullivan (boxing; 1858-1918)
John L. Swigart, Jr. (astro.)
John Luther "Casey" Jones (US railroad eng.; 1864-1900)
John Lyly (or Lily, Lilly)(Br. writer; 1554?-1606)
John Mackey (football; 1941-)
John Madden (football/ent.; 1936-)
John Major (PM, Br.; 1943-)
John Malecela (PM, Tanzania)
John Malkovich (ent.; 1953-)
John Marin (US artist; 1870-1953)
John Marshall (US jurist; 1755-1835)
John Marshall Harlan (US jurist; 1833-1911)
John Marshall Harlan (US jurist; 1899-1971)
John Masefield (Br. poet; 1878-1967)
John Matuszak
John Maynard Keynes (Br. econ.; 1883-1946)
John Maynard Smith (Br. biol.; 1920-)
John M(oses) Browning (US inv.; 1955-1926)
John McAllister Schofield (US mil.; 1831-1906)

John (Patrick) McEnroe (tennis; 1959-)
John (Joseph) McGraw (baseball; 1873-1934)
John McIntire (ent.; 1907-91)
John McLean (US jurist; 1785-1861)
John Mellencamp (ent.)
John Mills (ent.; 1908-)
John Milton (Br. poet; 1608-74)
John Mitchell (US labor leader; 1870-1919)
John (Newton) Mitchell (US pol./Watergate;
   1913-88)
John Montagu (Earl of Sandwich)(Br. pol.;
   1718-92)
John Morrell™ (meats)
John Morrell & Co. (US bus.)
John Mortimer (Br. writer/atty.; 1923-)
John M(arlan) Poindexter (US adm.; 1936-)
John M(illington) Synge (Ir. writer; 1871-1909)
John Muir (US environ.; 1838-1914)
John Naber (swimming; 1956-)
John Nance Garner (ex-US VP; 1868-1967)
John Napier (Scot. math.; 1550-1617)
John Newbery (Br. publ.; 1713-67)
John Newcombe (tennis; 1943-)
John Oates (ent.; 1948-)
John (Joseph) O'Connor, Cardinal (US rel.;
   1920-)
John of Gaunt (Br. pol.; 1340-99)
John O'Hara (US writer; 1905-70)
John (James) Osborne (Br. writer; 1929-)
John (McAuley) Palmer (US gen./pol.; 1817-
   1900)
John Paul I (Albino Luciani)(It. pope; 1912-78)
John Paul II (b. Karol Wojtyla)(Pol. pope; 1920-)
John Paul Jones (US mil.; 1747-92)
John Paul Mitchell Systems (US bus.)
John Paul Stevens (US jurist; 1920-)
John Payne (ent.; 1912-89)
John Philip Sousa (US comp.; 1854-1932)
John-Pierre Aumont (Fr. ent.; 1909-)
John Portman (US arch.; 1934-)
John Pym (Br. pol.; 1583?-1643)
John Q. Public (average US citizen)
John Quincy Adams (6th US pres.; 1767-1848)
John Rae (Scot. expl.; 1813-93)
John Randolph (ent.; 1915-)
John Randolph (of Roanoke)(US pol.; 1773-
   1833)
John Ratzenberger (ent.; 1947-)
John Ray (Br. nat.; 1627-1705)
John Ritter (ent.; 1948-)
John R. Lewis (US cong.; 1940-)
John R. McKernan, Jr. (ME gov.; 1948-)
John Robert Gregg (inv. shorthand system;
   1868-1948)
John Rolfe (Br. colonist in VA, husband of
   Pocahontas; 1585-1622)
John Ross (aka Coowescoowe)(Cherokee Indian
   chief; 1790-1866)

John Ross, Sir (Br. expl.; 1777-1856)
John Rubinstein (ent.; 1946-)
John Russell (ex-PM, Br.; 1792-1878)
John Russell Pope (US arch.; 1874-1937)
John R. Wooden (basketball; 1910-)
John R. Wooden Award (basketball)
John Saxon (ent.; 1935-)
John Sayles (ent.; 1950-)
John Schneider (ent.; 1954-)
John Sculley (US bus.)
John Shea (ent.; 1949-)
John Sherman (US pol.; 1823-1900)
John Sholto Douglas Queensberry (Marquis of
   Queensberry; 1844-1900)
John Silver's Seafood Shoppes, Long (US bus.)
John Singer Sargent (US artist; 1856-1925)
John Singleton Copley (US artist; 1738-1815)
John Sirica (US judge; 1904-92)
John Slidell (US pol.; 1793-1871)
John Smith (Br. colonist in Amer., Pocahontas;
   1580-1631)
John Spencer (ent.; 1946-)
John Stamos (ent.; 1963-)
John Steed
John (Ernst) Steinbeck (US writer; 1902-68)
John Steuart Curry (US artist; 1897-1946)
John Stossel
John Stuart McCain (US cong.; 1936-)
John Stuart Mill (Br. phil./econ.; 1806-73)
John Sturges (ent.; 1910-92)
John Suckling, Sir (Br. poet; 1609-42)
John Sullivan (US mil./pol.; 1740-95)
John Swan (premier, Bermuda)
John Taliaferro Thompson (US mil./inv.; 1860-
   1940)
John Tenniel, Sir (Br. artist; 1820-1914)
John Tesh (ent.)
John the Baptist, St. (Judean rel.; c6 BC-AD 27)
John the Divine, Cathedral of St. (NYC)
John Travolta (ent.; 1954-)
John Trumbull (US artist; 1756-1843)
John Trumbull (US poet/atty.; 1750-1831)
John T(homas) Scopes (US educ./evolution;
   1901-70)
John (Napier) Turner (ex-PM, Can.; 1929-)
John Turturro (ent.; 1967-)
John Tyler (10th US pres.; 1790-1862)
John (Hoyer) Updike (US writer; 1932-)
John Vanderlyn (US artist; 1775-1852)
John (William) Van Druten (US writer; 1901-
   57)
John Wanamaker (US bus.; 1838-1922)
John Wanamaker, Inc.
John Wayne (b. Marion Michael Morrison, aka
   "the Duke")(ent.; 1907-79)
John Wayne Bobbitt (US news)
John Werner Kluge
John Wesley (Br. rel., founded Methodism;

1703-91)

John Wesley Hardin (US outlaw; 1853-95)

John Wesley Powell (US geol./ethnol.; 1834-1902)

John Wilkes Booth (US, assassinated Lincoln, actor; 1838-65)

John Williams (US comp./cond.; 1932-)

John Winthrop (Br./Amer., ex-gov., MA; 1588-1649)

John Winthrop (ex-gov., CT; 1606-76)

John (or Fitz-John) Winthrop (ex-gov., CT; 1638-1707)

John Winthrop (US astron./math./physt.; 1714-79)

John Witherspoon (US rel.; 1723-94)

John W. Warner (US cong.; 1927-)

John Wycliffe (Br. rel.; c1320-84)

John W(atts) Young (astro.; 1930-)

John XXII (Jacques d'Euse)(Fr., pope; 1249-1334)

John XXIII (Angelo Giuseppe Roncalli)(It., pope; 1881-1963)

John XXIII (It., [anti]pope; 1370?-1419)

John, Elton (Hercules)(b. Reginald Kenneth Dwight)(ent.; 1947-)

John, Friar (fict. chara., *Gargantua, Pantagruel*)

John, Little (fict. chara., *Robin Hood*)

John, Olivia Newton- (ent.; 1947-)

John, Prester (legendary priest-king; 12th-16th c.)

Johnnie Ray (ent.; 1927-90)

Johnnie Walker™ (whiskey)

Johnny and the Asbury Jukes, Southside (pop music)

Johnny Appleseed (b. John Chapman)(US pioneer; 1774-1845)

Johnny Belinda (film; 1948)

Johnny Bench (baseball; 1947-)

Johnny Burke (US lyricist; 1908-84)

Johnny Carson (ent.; 1925-)

Johnny Cash (ent.; 1932-)

Johnny-come-lately

Johnny Depp (ent.; 1963-)

Johnny Dodds (US jazz; 1892-1940)

Johnny Hart (US cartoonist, *BC, Wizard of Id*; 1931-)

Johnny Hodges (US jazz; 1906-71)

Johnny-jump-up

Johnny Longden (horse racing; 1907-)

Johnny Mathis (ent.; 1935-)

Johnny Mercer (US lyricist; 1909-76)

Johnny Miller (golf; 1947-)

Johnny-on-the-spot

Johnny Paycheck (ent.; 1941-)

Johnny Reb (Confederate soldier, southerner)

Johnny Rivers (ent.)

Johnny Rodriquez (ent.; 1951-)

Johnny Rutherford (auto racing; 1938-)

Johnny (John Constantine) Unitas (football; 1933-)

Johnny (Peter John) Weissmuller (US swimmer/ent.; 1903-84)

John's-bread, St. (herb/spice, tree)

Johns Hopkins Hospital (Baltimore, MD)

Johns Hopkins University (Baltimore, MD)

Johns, Glynis (ent.; 1923-)

Johns, Jasper (US artist; 1930-)

Johnson & Co., Mead

Johnson & Johnson™

Johnson & Johnson (US bus.)

Johnson & Son, Inc., S. C.

Johnson bar (railroad)

Johnson City, NY, TN

Johnson Co., Howard (US bus)

Johnson grass (also Aleppo grass, Means grass)

Johnson National Historical Park, Lyndon B. (TX)

Johnson Robb, Lynda Bird (daughter, US pres.; 1944-)

Johnson Space Center, Lyndon B. (TX)

Johnson, Amy (Br. aviator; 1903-41)

Johnson, Andrew (17th US pres.; 1808-75)

Johnson, Anne-Marie (ent.)

Johnson, Anthony (rowing; 1940-)

Johnson, Arte (ent.; 1929-)

Johnson, Ben (Can. runner)

Johnson, Ben (ent.; 1918-)

Johnson, Bunk (US jazz; 1879-1949)

Johnson, Don (ent.; 1949-)

Johnson, Howard (US bus.; 1896-1972)

Johnson, Jack (John Arthur)(boxing; 1878-1946)

Johnson, James P. (US jazz; 1891-1955)

Johnson, James Weldon (US writer, NAACP; 1871-1938)

Johnson, Jimmy (football; 1943-)

Johnson, J. J. (US jazz; 1924-)

Johnson, Kevin (basketball; 1966-)

Johnson, Lady Bird (b. Claudia Alta Taylor)(wife of ex-US pres.; 1912-)

Johnson, Larry (basketball; 1969-)

Johnson, Luci Baines (daughter, US pres.; 1947-)

Johnson, Lyndon Baines (36th US pres.; 1908-73)

Johnson, Magic (Earvin)(basketball; 1959-)

Johnson, Drs. Masters and (sexual behavior study)

Johnson, Philip C(ortelyou)(US arch.; 1906-)

Johnson, Rafer (decathlon; 1935-)

Johnson, Richard M(entor)(ex-US VP; 1780-1850)

Johnson, Samuel ("Dr. Johnson")(Br. lexicographer/writer; 1709-84)

Johnson, Samuel (US educ.; 1696-1772)

Johnson, Van (ent.; 1916-)

Johnson, Dr. Virginia E(shelman)(US psych., Masters & Johnson; 1925-)

Johnson, Walter (Perry) "Big Train" (baseball; 1887-1946)

Johnston, J. Bennett, Jr. (US cong.; 1932-)

Johnston, Joseph Eggleston (US/confed. gen.; 1807-91)

Johnston, Lynn (cartoonist; *For Better or Worse*; 1947-)

Johnstown flood (PA; 1889)

Johnstown, PA

Johor Baharu, Malaysia

Joint Chiefs of Staff (US govt.)

Joio, Norman Dello (US comp.; 1913-)

Joker's Wild (TV show)

Joliet Army Ammunition Plant (IL)

Joliet, IL

Joliet (or Jolliet), Louis (Fr./Can. expl.; 1645-1700)

Joliot-Curie, Frédéric (Fr. physt.; 1900-58)

Joliot-Curie, Irène (Fr. physt.; 1897-1956)

Jolly Roger (pirate flag)

Jolson, Al (b. Asa Yoelson)(ent.; 1886-1950)

Jomo Kenyatta (b. Kamau Ngengi)(ex-pres., Kenya; 1893?-1978)

Jon Bon Jovi (ent.; 1962-)

Jon Vickers (ent.; 1926-)

Jon Voight (ent.; 1938-)

Jonah (Hebrew prophet; 8th c. BC)

Jonas Angström Anders (Swed. astrophyst.; 1814-74)

Jonas (Edward) Salk (US phys./biol.; 1914-)

Jonas Savimbi (Angolan mil.; 1934-)

Jonassaint, Emile (pres., Haiti; 1914-)

Jonathan (apple)

Jonathan Banks (ent.; 1947-)

Jonathan Demme (ent.; 1944-)

Jonathan Edwards (US rel.; 1703-58)

Jonathan Knight (ent.; 1968-)

Jonathan Livingston Seagull (R. Bach novel)

Jonathan Logan, Inc.

Jonathan M(ayhew) Wainwright (US gen.; 1883-1953)

Jonathan Pryce (ent.; 1947-)

Jonathan Swift (b. Isaac Bickerstaff)(Br. writer; 1667-1745)

Jonathan Trumbull (US pol.; 1710-85)

Jonathan Winters (ent.; 1925-)

Jonathan, Chief (Joseph) Leabua (ex-PM, Lesotho; 1914-87)

Jones and Laughlin Steel Co., National Labor Relations Board v. (US law; 1937)

Jones and the Temple of Doom, Indiana (film; 1984)

Jones Computer Network (cable TV)

Jones Index, Dow

Jones News/Retrieval, Dow (compu. database)

Jones, Anthony Armstrong- (Earl of Snowdon)(Br. photo.; 1930-)

Jones, Bobby (golf; 1902-71)

Jones, Brereton C. (KY gov.; 1939-)

Jones, Carolyn (ent.; 1933-83)

Jones, Charlie (ent.; 1930-)

Jones, Chuck (cartoonist, *Bugs Bunny, Porky Pig, Daffy Duck*; 1905?-)

Jones, Davy (personification of sea)

Jones, Deacon (David)(football; 1938-)

Jones, Dean (ent.; 1935-)

Jones, Ed "Too Tall"

Jones, Edward Burne- (Br. artist; 1833-98)

Jones, Elvin (US jazz; 1927-)

Jones, George (ent.; 1931-)

Jones, Grace (ent.; 1952-)

Jones, Grandpa (ent.; 1913-)

Jones, Indiana (fict. chara.)

Jones, Inigo (Br. arch.; 1573-c1652)

Jones, Jack (ent.; 1938-)

Jones, James (US writer; 1922-77)

Jones, James Earl (ent.; 1931-)

Jones, Jennifer (ent.; 1919-)

Jones, Jim (James Warren)(US/Guyana cult leader; 1931-78)

Jones, Jo (US jazz; 1911-85)

Jones, John Luther "Casey" (US railroad eng.; 1864-1900)

Jones, John Paul (US mil.; 1747-92)

Jones, Mother (mag.)

Jones, Mother (Mary Harris Jones)(US labor leader; 1830-1930)

Jones, Philly Joe (US jazz; 1923-85)

Jones, Quincy (US jazz; 1933-)

Jones, Paula (US news)

Jones, Robert "Bobby" (Tyre), Jr. (golf; 1902-71)

Jones, Shirley (ent.; 1934-)

Jones, Spike (ent.; 1911-1965)

Jones, Thad (US jazz; 1923-86)

Jones, Tom (ent.; 1940-)

Jones, Tommy Lee (ent.; 1946-)

Jones's locker, Davy (ocean bottom; grave of those who die at sea)

Jonestown mass suicide (Guyana; 1978)

Jonestown, Guyana

Jong, Erica (Mann)(US writer; 1942-)

Joni Huntley (track; 1956-)

Joni Mitchell (b. Roberta Joan Anderson)(ent.; 1943-)

Jonny Quest (cartoon)

Jonquière, Quebec, Canada

Jöns Jakob Berzelius, Baron (Swed. chem.; 1779-1848)

Jonson, Ben (Br. writer; 1572-1637)

Jooss, Kurt (Ger. ballet; 1901-79)

Joplin, Janis (ent.; 1943-70)

Joplin, MO

Joplin, Scott (US jazz; 1868-1917)

Jordache™
Jordache Enterprises, Inc.
Jordan (Hashemite Kingdom of)(SW Asia)
Jordan almonds
Jordan Knight (ent.; 1970-)
Jordan Marsh Co., Abraham & Straus/
Jordan River (UT)
Jordan Vineyard & Winery (US bus.)
Jordan, Barbara (Charline)(US atty./educ./pol.;
   1936-)
Jordan, Michael "Mike" (basketball/baseball;
   1963-)
Jordan, Richard (ent.; 1938-)
Jordan, River (Pak.)
Jorge Luis Borges (Argentinean writer; 1900-
   86)
Jorge Serrano Elías (ex-pres., Guat.)
Jorgensen, Christine (1st sex-change operation;
   1927-89)
Jory, Victor (ent.; 1902-82)
José Canseco (baseball; 1964-)
José Carreras (Sp. tenor; 1947-)
José Clemente Orozco (Mex. artist; 1883-1949)
Jose Cuervo™ (tequila)
José de Rivera (US sculptor; 1904-85)
José Eber (hairstylist)
José Eduardo dos Santos (pres., Angola; 1942-)
José Feliciano (ent.; 1945-)
José Ferrer (ent. 1912-92)
José Francisco Merino (VP, El Salvador)
José Iturbi (Sp. cond.; 1895-1980)
José Limón (Mex./US dancer; 1908-72)
José Limón Dance Company
José Maria Olazabal (golf; 1966-)
José (Julian) Marti (Cuban pol./poet; 1853-95)
José Napoleon Duarte (ex-pres., El Salvador;
   1925-90)
José Ortega y Gasset (Sp. phil.; 1883-1955)
Josef Albers (US artist; 1888-1976)
Josef A. Pasternack (ent.; 1881-1940)
Josef Mengele, Dr. ("angel of death")(Ger. Nazi;
   ?-1979?)
Josef Strauss (Aus. comp.; 1827-70)
Josef Suk (Czech. comp.; 1874-1935)
Joseph (of Nazareth)(husband of the Virgin
   Mary)
Joseph Addison (Br. writer; 1672-1719)
Joseph A. Yablonski (US labor leader; ?-1969)
Joseph Banks Rhine (US psych.; 1895-1980)
Joseph Beuys (Ger. sculptor/ent.; 1921-86)
Joseph Bonaparte (bro. of Napoleon, king,
   Naples/Sp.; 1768-1844)
Joseph Brodsky (US writer; 1940-)
Joseph Campanella (ent.; 1927-)
Joseph Campbell (US mythologist/folklorist;
   1904-87)
Joseph Chamberlain (Br. pol.; 1836-1914)
Joseph Conrad (Br. writer; 1857-1924)

Joseph Cotten (ent.; 1905-)
Joseph Dalton Hooker, Sir (Br. botanist; 1817-
   1911)
Joseph Eggleston Johnston (US gen.; 1807-91)
Joseph E. Seagram & Sons, Inc.
Joseph Estrada (VP, Philippines)
Joseph (Louis) Gay-Lussac (Fr. chem./physt.;
   1778-1850)
Joseph Goebbels, (Paul)(Ger. Nazi
   propagandist; 1897-1945)
Joseph Hayne Rainey (US pol.; 1832-87)
Joseph Henry (US phys./inv.; 1797-1878)
Joseph Hirshhorn (US bus./finan.)
Joseph Hooker, (US gen.; 1814-79)
Joseph I. Lieberman (US cong.; 1942-)
Joseph (Jacques Césaire) Joffre (Fr. mil.; 1852-
   1931)
Joseph Kokou Koffigoh, (PM, Togo)
Joseph (Louis) Lagrange (Fr. astron./math.;
   1736-1813)
Joseph Lister, Baron (Br. phys./antiseptic
   surgery; 1827-1912)
Joseph L(eo) Mankiewicz (US ent./writer; 1909-
   93)
Joseph Meyer (US comp.; 1894-1987)
Joseph Michel Montgolfier (Fr. hot-air
   balloonist; 1740-1810)
Joseph Mollicone, Jr. (US bank scandal)
Joseph Papp (ent.; 1921-91)
Joseph Patrick Kennedy (US bus./dipl.; 1888-
   1969)
Joseph Patrick Kennedy, II (US cong.; 1952-)
Joseph Patrick Kennedy, Jr. (US mil./pol.;
   1915-44)
Joseph Phelps Vineyards (US bus.)
Joseph Pilsudski (Pol. dictator; 1867-1935)
Joseph P(eter) Kerwin (astro.; 1932-)
Joseph Priestley (Br. chem./writer; 1733-1804)
Joseph Pulitzer (US jour./publ./finan.; 1847-
   1911)
Joseph Pulitzer, Jr. (US publ.; 1913-93)
Joseph R. Biden, Jr. (US cong.; 1942-)
Joseph R(aymond) McCarthy (US pol.; 1908-57)
Joseph Robert Kerrey (US cong.; 1943-)
Joseph Schildkraut (ent.; 1895-1964)
Joseph (Alois) Schumpeter (US econ.; 1883-
   1950)
Joseph Smith (US rel./founded Mormons; 1805-
   44)
Joseph Stalin (b. Iosif Vissarionovich
   Dzhugashvili)(ex-dictator, USSR; 1879-1953)
Joseph Story (US jurist; 1779-1845)
Joseph von Fraunhofer (Ger. optician/physt.;
   1787-1826)
Joseph Wambaugh (US writer; 1937-)
Joseph Wapner, Judge (*People's Court*)
Joseph W(arren) Stilwell ("Vinegar Joe")(US
   gen.; 1883-1946)

Joseph, Akiba ben (Jew. rel. leader; AD 50?-132)

Joseph, Chief (Nez Percé Indians; c1840-1904)

Joseph, Franz (or Francis)(Aus./Hung., emp.; 1830-1916)

Joseph, Franz, II (ruler, Liechtenstein; 1906-89)

Joseph, Saadia ben (Jew. phil./scholar; 882-942)

Josephine (Marie Joséphe Rose Tascher de la Pagerie, Joséphine de Beauharnais)(empress, Fr., wife of Napoleon I; 1763-1814)

Josephine Baker (ent.; 1906-75)

Josephine Hull (ent.; 1886-1957)

Josey Wales, The Outlaw (film; 1976)

Josh Billings (b. Henry Wheeler Shaw)(US humorist; 1818-85)

Joshua (rel.)

Joshua Lederberg (US geneticist; 1925-)

Joshua Logan (US writer/ent.; 1908-88)

Joshua Nkomo (Zimbabwean pol.; 1917-)

Joshua Reynolds, Sir (Br. artist; 1723-92)

Joshua tree (tree)

Joshua Tree National Monument (CA)

Joshua Tree, CA

Josiah (king, Judah; ?-608? BC)

Josiah Royce (US phil.; 1855-1916)

Josiah Spode (Br. potter, father; 1733-97)

Josiah Spode (Br. potter, son; 1754-1827)

Josiah Wedgwood (Br. potter; 1730-95)

Josiah W(illard) Gibbs (US physt./chem.; 1839-1903)

Josip Broz Tito (ex-pres., Yug.; 1892-1980)

Jost van Dykes (Br. Virgin Island)

Jostens, Inc.

Jotul USA, Inc.

Jotul™ wood stove

Jotun (also Jotunn)(myth.)

Joule-Kelvin effect (temperature drop in gases)

Joule-Thomson effect (thermodynamics)

Joule, James P(rescott)(Br. physt.; 1818-89)

Joule's law (physics)

Jourdan, Louis (Fr. ent.; 1919-)

Journal-Bulletin, Providence (RI newspaper)

Journal-Gazette, Fort Wayne (IN newspaper)

Journal of Medicine, New England (mag.)

Journal Star, Peoria (IL newspaper)

Journal, Albuquerque (NM newspaper)

Journal, Atlanta (GA newspaper)

Journal, Flint (MI newspaper)

Journal, Lincoln (NE newspaper)

Journal, Milwaukee (WI newspaper)

Journal, Montgomery (AL newspaper)

Journal, Providence (RI newspaper)

Journal, Winston-Salem (NC newspaper)

Jovan™

Jovanovich, Inc., Harcourt Brace

Jovi, Jon Bon (ent.; 1962-)

Jovian planet (Jupiter/Saturn/Neptune/Uranus)

Joy of Cooking (cookbook)

Joyce Brothers, Dr. (US psych.; 1928-)

Joyce Carol Oates (US writer; 1938-)

Joyce Kilmer, (Alfred)(US poet; 1886-1918)

Joyce Randolph (ent. 1925-)

Joyce, James (Ir. writer; 1882-1941)

Joycelyn Elders, Dr. (US surgeon gen.; 1937-)

Joyner-Kersee, Jackie (track & field; 1962-)

Joyner, Al

Joyner, Florence Griffith ("Flo Jo")(track; 1959-)

József Antall (ex-PM, Hung.; 1932-)

JP (justice of the peace)

J(ean) Paul Getty (US bus.; 1892-1976)

J. Pedroncelli Winery (US bus.)

JPL (Jet Propulsion Laboratory)

J(ohn) P(ierpont) Morgan (US finan.; 1837-1913)

J(ames) Ramsay MacDonald (ex-PM, Br.; 1866-1937)

J. R. Ewing (fict. chara., *Dallas*)

J(ulius) Robert Oppenheimer (US physt., atomic bomb; 1904-67)

J(ohn) R(onald) R(euel) Tolkien (Br. writer/educ.; 1892-1973)

J(ames) Strom Thurmond (US cong.; 1902-)

J(ames) Thomas Talbot

Juan Bautista de Anza (Sp. expl.; 1735-88?)

Juan Carlos I (king, Spain; 1938-)

Juan Carlos Wasmosy (pres., Paraguay; 1942-)

Juan de Fuca, Strait of (also Juan de Fuca Strait)(WA/Can.)

Juan Domingo Perón (ex-pres., Argentina; 1895-1974)

Juan Fangio (auto racing; 1911-)

Juan Gris (b. José Vittoriano Gonzales)(Sp. artist; 1887-1927)

Juan Marichal (baseball; 1937-)

Juan Ponce de León (Sp. expl.; c1460-1521)

Juan, Don (Don Giovanni)(Sp. legend)

Juantoreno, Alberto (track; 1951-)

Juárez, Benito (Pablo)(ex-pres., Mex.; 1806-72)

Juba, Sudan

Juba River (E Afr.)

Jubal Anderson Early (US gen.; 1816-94)

Judaea, Palestine (also Judea, Judah)

Judah (also Judea, Judaea)(now part of Palestine)

Judaica (books, objects re: Jew. life/customs)

Judaism (rel.)

Judas hole (door peephole)

Judas Iscariot (betrayer of Jesus; ?-c28 BC)

Judas Priest (pop music)

Judas tree (tree)

Judd Gregg (US cong.; 1847-)

Judd Hirsch (ent.; 1935-)

Judd Nelson (ent.; 1959-)

Judd, Naomi (ent.; 1946-)

Judd, Wynonna (ent.; 1964-)

Judds, the (pop music)

Jude, St. (also St. Judas)(rel.; 1st c. AD)
Judea (also Judaea, Judah)(now part of Palestine)
Judeo-Christian (beliefs, traditions)
Judge Reinhold (ent.; 1956-)
Judge Roy Bean (US frontier; 1825?-1903)
Judgment Day (rel.)
Judith Anderson, Dame (ent.; 1898-1992)
Judith Crist (US writer; 1922-)
Judith Ivey (cnt.; 1951-)
Judith Krantz (US writer; 1928-)
Judith Light (ent.; 1950-)
Judy Blume (US writer; 1938-)
Judy Canova (ent.)
Judy Collins (ent.; 1939-)
Judy Garland (b. Frances Gumm)(ent.; 1922-69)
Judy Holliday (ent.; 1922-65)
Judy (Torluemke) Rankin (golf; 1945-)
Judy show, Punch-and- (Br. puppet show)
Jugendstil (art)(also l.c.)
Jugnauth, Aneerood (PM, Mauritius; 1930-)
Juha Widing (hockey; 1948-85)
Juilliard School of Music (NYC)
Jule Styne (Br./US comp.; 1905-)
Jules Adjodhia (Suriname pol.)
Jules Feiffer (cartoonist; 1929-)
Jules (Émile Frédéric) Massenet (Fr. comp.; 1842-1912)
Jules Mazarin (b. Giulo Mazarini)(Fr. rel./pol.; 1602-61)
Jules Verne (Fr. writer; 1828-1905)
Julia Child (US chef/writer; 1912-)
Julia Duffy (ent.; 1951-)
Julia Louis-Dreyfus (ent.; 1961-)
Julia Roberts (ent.; 1967-)
Julia Ward Howe (US reformer/writer; 1819-1910)
Julia, Raul (ent.; 1940-)
Julian "Cannonball" Adderley (US jazz; 1928-75)
Julian Bond (US reformer/pol.; 1940-)
Julian (Alexander) Bream (ent.; 1933-)
Julian calendar
Julian Day (astron.)
Julian Huxley, Sir (Br. biol.; 1887-1975)
Julian Lennon (ent.)
Julian (Seymour) Schwinger (US physt.; 1918-)
Juliana (ex-queen, Netherlands; 1909-)
Julie Andrews (ent.; 1935-)
Julie Christie (ent.; 1940-)
Julie Harris (ent.; 1925-)
Julie Kavner (ent.; 1951-)
Julie Kent (US dancer; 1971-)
Julie London (ent.; 1926-)
Julie Newmar (ent.)
Julie Nixon Eisenhower (daughter of ex-US pres.; 1948-)
Juliet Capulet (fict. chara., *Romeo and Juliet*)

Juliet Prowse (ent.)
Juliet, Romanoff and (film; 1961)
Juliet, Romeo and (Shakespeare play)
Juliette (Gordon) Low (US, founded Girl Scouts; 1860-1927)
Juliette Récamier (b. Jeanne Françoise Julie Adélaide Bernard)(Fr. society; 1777-1849)
Julio Gallo (US winemaker; 1910-93)
Julio Iglesias (Sp./US ent.; 1943-)
Julius Axelrod (US neuropharmacologist; 1912-)
Julius Boros (golf; 1920-)
Julius Caesar (Gaius Julius)(Roman gen.; 100-44 BC)
Julius Caesar (Shakespeare play)
Julius "Dr J" Erving (basketball; 1950-)
Julius La Rosa (ent.)
Julius "Groucho" Marx (ent.; 1890-1977)
Julius (Kambarage) Nyerere (ex-pres., Tanzania; 1922-)
Julius Rosenberg (US, executed for treason; 1918-53)
Julius Streicher (Ger. Nazi/publ.; 1885-1946)
July Fourth (also Fourth of July, Independence Day)
July Revolution (Fr.; 1830)
Jump, Gordon (ent.; 1932-)
Jumpin' Jack Flash (film; 1986)
Jumpin' Jack Flash (song)
jumping Jehoshaphat
June Allyson (ent.; 1917-)
June bug (also Junebug, May beetle)
June Carter (ent.; 1929-)
June Haver (ent.; 1926-)
June Havoc (ent; 1916-)
June Lockhart (ent.; 1925-)
June Valli
Juneau, AK
Juneberry (also American serviceberry)(shrub)
Jung, Carl Gustav (Swiss psych.; 1875-1961)
Jung, Kim Dae (SKorean pol.; 1924-)
Jungian psychology
Jungle Jim (comic strip)
Junior Scholastic (mag.)
Junípero, Miguel José Serra, Father (Sp. rel.; 1713-84)
Junius Brutus Booth (US actor, father of John Wilkes; 1796-1852)
Juno (astron.; myth.)
Junot, Philippe
Jupiter (also Jove)(myth.)
Jupiter (planet)
Jupiter, FL
Jurassic Park (book/film by M. Crichton)
Jurassic period (195-136 million years ago)
Jurgens, Curt (ent.)
Jurgensen, Sonny (football; 1934-)
Juridical Science, Doctor of (also S.J.D., Scientiae Juridicae Doctor)

Jurmala, Latvia
Jurong, Singapore
Just Cross Stitch (mag.)
Just My Size™
Justerini & Brooks, Ltd. (J&B)
Justice, David (baseball; 1966-)
Justice, Department of (DOJ)(US govt.)
Justin Martyr, St. (It. rel.; 100?-165)
Justine Bateman (ent.; 1966-)
Justinian Code (law)
Justinian I ("the Great")(Flavius Anicius [or
    Petrus Sabbatius] Justinianus)(emp.,
    Byzantine; 483-565)
Justus von Liebig, Baron (Ger. chem.; 1803-73)
Jute (people)
Juvenal (Roman satirist; c60-c127)
Juvénal Habyarimana (ex-pres., Rwanda; 1937-
    94)
Juventas (myth.)
JVC™ (elec.)
JVC Co. of America
J(ames) William Fulbright (US pol.; 1905-)
J. William Klime (US adm.)
JWP (Jewish Welfare Board)
JWV (Jewish War Veterans)

K

K (chem. sym., potassium)
K (kilobyte)(compu.)
Kaaawa, HI
Kaaba (also Ka'ba, Ka'bah, Ka'abah)(rel.)
Kaat, Jim (baseball; 1938-)
Kaba (also Kabah, Kaabah)(rel. bldg., Mecca)
Kabibble, Ish (aka Merwyn Bogue)(ent.; 1908-94)
Kabua, Amata (pres., Marshall Islands)
Kabuki (Jap. drama; 16th-18th c.)(also l.c.)
Kabul, Afghanistan
Kabwe, Zambia
Kabyle (lang./people)
Kádár, János (ex-PM, Hung.; 1912-89)
Kadavy, Caryn
Kaddish (rel.)
Kaduna, Nigeria
Kaédi, Mauritania
Kafi, Ali (pres., Algeria; 1928-)
Kafka, Franz (Ger. writer; 1889-1961)
Kafre (or Khafre), Pyramid of (Eg.)
Kahan, Meir (or Martin)(Jew. activist; 1932-90)
Kahanamoku, Duke (swimming; 1890-1968)
Kahlil Gibran (Lebanese writer/mystic/artist; 1883-1931)
Khalifa bin Sulman al-Khalifa (PM, Bahrain; 1935-)
Khalifa, Sheik Isa bin Sulman al-, (emir, Bahrain; 1933-)
Kahlúa™ (liqueur)
Kahn, Albert (US arch.; 1869-1942)
Kahn, Gus (US lyricist; 1886-1941)
Kahn, Louis (US arch.; 1901-74)
Kahn, Madeline (ent.; 1942-)
Kai Winding (US jazz; 1922-83)
Kai-shek, Chiang (also Chiang Chung-cheng)(ex-pres., Nationalist China; 1887-1975)
Kai-shek, Madame Chiang (b. Soong Mei-ling)(Ch. lecturer/writer; 1898-)
Kaifu Toshiki (ex-PM, Jap.; 1931-)
Kailua, HI
Kain, Karen
Kaiser (former title, Ger./Aus.)
Kaiser Aluminum & Chemical Corp.
Kaiser-Permanente Foundation (Kaiser Foundation Health Plan)
Kaiser-Permanente Medical Group
Kaiser, Henry J(ohn)(US bus.; 1882-1967)
Kakuei Tanaka (ex-PM, Jap.; 1918-93)
Kal Kan™ (pet food)
Kal Kan Foods, Inc.
Kalaallit Nunaat (also Greenland)(island, N Atl.)

Kalahari Desert (S Afr)
Kalakaua Ave., Honolulu, HI
Kalamazoo Gazette (MI newspaper)
Kalamazoo, MI
Kalanga (people)
Kalaupapa leper colony
Kalaupapa National Historic Park (HI)
Kali (myth.)
Kali-Yuga (rel.)
Kalimantan (province, Indonesia)
Kaline, Al(bert)(baseball; 1934-)
Kalki (rel.)
Kallikaks (fict. family name, sociological study)
Kaloko-Honokohau National Historical Park (HI)
Kaltenbrunner, Ernst (Aus. Nazi; 1901-46)
Kama Sutra (also Kamasutra)(Indian/Sanskrit treatise on love)
Kamakura (Jap. art; 13th-15th c)
Kamakura period
Kamakura shogunate
Kamakura, Japan
Kamasutra (also Kama Sutra)(Indian/Sanskrit treatise on love)
Kamba (lang./people)
Kamchatka (region, Siberia)
Kamchatka peninsula (NE Asia)
Kamehameha I (ex-king, Haw.; c1758-1819)
Kampala, Uganda
Kampgrounds of America (US bus.)
Kamp's Frozen Foods, Van de (US bus.)
Kampuchea (now State of Cambodia)
Kamuta Laatasi (PM, Tuvalu)
Kanaka (Hawaiian for native)
Kanaly, Steve (ent.; 1946-)
Kananga, Zaire
Kandahar, Afghanistan
Kander, John (US comp.; 1927-)
Kandinsky, Wassily (or Vasili, Vasily)(Rus. artist; 1866-1944)
Kandy, Sri Lanka
Kane, Carol (ent.; 1952-)
Kangaroo, Captain (fict. chara.)
Kaniksu National Forest
Kankakee (IL)
Kankan, Guinea
Kannada (lang.)
Kannon (also Kwannon)(rel.)
Kano (Jap. school of painters)
Kano, Nigeria
Kanpur, India
Kansas (KS)
Kansas City Chiefs (football team)
Kansas City Royals (baseball team)
Kansas City Star (MO newspaper)
Kansas City, KS, MO
Kansas-Nebraska Act/Bill (US hist.; 1854)
Kansu (also Gansu)(province, Ch.)

Kant, Immanuel (Ger. phil./phys.; 1724-1804)
Kantor, Mickey (US trade rep; 1939-)
Kanuri (lang.)
Kanuzi-Dongola (lang.)
Kaohsiung, Taiwan
Kaolack, Senegal
Kaopectate™ (med.)
Kaplan, Gabriel
Kaposi's sarcoma (med.)
Karabakh, Nagorno- (region, Azerbaijan)
Karachi, Pakistan
Karaganda, Kazakhstan
Karajan, Herbert von (Aus. cond.; 1908-)
Karakul (sheep)
Karamanlis, Constantine (pres., Gr.; 1907-)
Karamazov, The Brothers (Dostoevsky novel)
Karan, Donna (US designer; 1948-)
Karastan™ (carpet)
Karastan-Bigelow, Inc.
Karbe, Myanmar
Kardon™, Harman- (stereo)
Kardon, Inc., Harman-
Kareem Abdul-Jabbar (b. Ferdinand) Lew(is)
    Alcindor, Jr.)(basketball; 1947-)
Karen (lang./people)
Karen Allen (ent.; 1951-)
Karen Black (ent.; 1942-)
Karen Blixen (pseud. Isak Dinesen)(Dan.
    writer; 1885-1962)
Karen Carpenter (ent.; 1950-83)
Karen Kain
Karen Silkwood (US nuclear safety advocate)
Karen Young
Karenina, Anna (L. Tolstoy novel)
Kariba dam (Zimbabwe)
Kariba, Lake (Zimbabwe)
Karimov, Islam A. (pres., Uzbekistan)
Karl A(ugustus) Menninger (US psych.; 1893-
    1990)
Karl Baedeker (Ger. guidebook publ.; 1801-
    1959)
Karl Barth (Swed. rel.; 1886-1968)
Karl (or Carl) Bosch (Ger. chem.; 1874-1940)
Karl Czerny (Aus. pianist; 1791-1857)
Karl Goldmark (Hung. comp.; 1830-1915)
Karl Jaspers (Ger. phil.; 1883-1969)
Karl Malden (ent.; 1913-)
Karl Mannheim (Hung. sociol./hist.; 1893-1947)
Karl (Heinrich) Marx (Ger. phil.; 1818-83)
Karl-Marx-Stadt, Germany (now Chemnitz)
Karl Millöcker
Karl (or Carl) Philipp Emanuel Bach (Ger
    comp.; 1714-88)
Karl (Jay) Shapiro (US poet/editor; 1913-)
Karl von Clausewitz (Ger. mil.; 1780-1831)
Karl Wallenda (Ger. circus; 1905-78)
Karlen, John (ent.; 1933-)
Karlheinz Stockhausen (Ger. comp.; 1928-)

Karloff, Boris (William Henry Pratt)(ent.; 1887-
    1969)
Karlsruhe, Germany
Karmal, Babrak (ex-pres., Afghan.; 1929-)
Karnak, Egypt
Karnak, temples of (Eg., built 21st-1st c. BC)
Karo™ (syrup)
Karo-Dairi (lang.)
Karol Wojtyla (Pope John Paul II)(Pol. pope;
    1920-)
Karolyi, Bela (gymnastics)
Karoui, Hamed (PM, Tunisia)
Karpov, Anatoly (Rus., chess; 1951-)
Karras, Alex (ent.; 1935-)
Karsavina, Tamara (Rus. ballet; 1885-1978)
Kasdan, Lawrence (ent./writer; 1948-)
Kasem, Casey (ent.; 1933-)
Kashmir (also Cashmere)(goat)
Kashmir (area, Pak.)
Kashmir, Jammu and (state, India)
Kashmiri (lang.)
Kasimir (or Casimir) Malevich (Rus. artist;
    1878-1935)
Kaspar Schwenkfeld von Ossig (Ger. rel.; 1490-
    1561)
Kasparov, Gary (or Garry)(Rus., chess; 1963-)
Kassebaum, Nancy Landon (US cong.; 1932-)
Kassel, Germany
Kaszner, Kurt (ent.)
Kat Club, Kit- (also Kit-Cat)(London pol. grp.;
    1703-20)
Kat, Krazy (comic strip)
Katanga (now Shaba)
Katarina Witt (Ger. figure skating; 1965-)
Kate (Catherine) Greenaway (Br. artist/writer;
    1846-1901)
Kate Jackson (ent.; 1948-)
Kate Millett (US writer/feminist; 1934-)
Kate Mulgrew (ent.; 1955-)
Kate (Kathryn) Smith (ent.; 1909-86)
Katharine Cornell (ent.; 1893-1974)
Katharine "Kitty " Dukakis (wife of ex-MA gov.)
Katharine Graham (US publ.; 1917-)
Katharine Hepburn (ent.; 1907-)
Katharine Lee Bates (US poet/educ.; 1859-1929)
Käthe (Schmidt) Kollwitz (Ger. artist; 1867-
    1945)
Katherine Anne Porter (US writer; 1890-1980)
Katherine "Katie" Couric (TV commentator;
    1957-)
Katherine Dunham (ent.; 1910-)
Katherine Fox (Can./US spiritualist)
Katherine Mansfield (Br. writer; 1888-1923)
Katherine Ross (ent.; 1942-)
Kathie Lee Gifford (ent.)
Kathie Lee, Regis & (TV show)
Kathleen Battle (opera; 1948-)
Kathleen Nesbitt (ent.)

Kathleen (Thompson) Norris (US writer; 1880-1966)
Kathleen Sullivan (ent.)
Kathleen Turner (ent.; 1954-)
Kathleen Woodiwiss (writer)
Kathmandu, Nepal (also Katmandu)
Kathryn Grayson (ent.; 1922-)
Kathryn Kuhlman (faith healer)
Kathy Bates (ent.; 1948-)
Kathy Hammond (runner; 1951-)
Kathy Laverne McMillan (track; 1957-)
Kathy Whitworth (golf; 1939-)
Kathyrn Bailey "Kay" Hutchinson (US cong.; 1943-)
Kathryn Kuhlman (faith healer)
Katie (Katherine) Couric (TV commentator; 1957-)
Katmai National Park (AK)
Katmandu, Nepal (also Kathmandu)
Katowice, Poland
Katt, William (ent.)
Katyn Forest (Rus.)
Katzenjammer Kids (comic strip)
Kauai (island, HI)
Kauai, HI
Kaufman and Broad Home Corp.
Kaufman house (also Falling Water)(F.L.Wright house)
Kaufman, George S(imon)(US writer; 1889-1961)
Kaukauna™
Kaukauna Cheese (US bus.)
Kaunas, Lithuania
Kaunda, Kenneth (David)(ex-pres., Zambia; 1924-)
Kavango (people)
Kavner, Julie (ent.; 1951-)
Kawasaki™
Kawasaki disease
Kawasaki Heavy Industries Ltd.
Kawasaki Motors Corp.
Kawasaki Steel Corp.
Kawasaki, Japan
Kay-Bee Food Products, Inc.
Kay (Kathyrn Bailey) Hutchinson (US cong.; 1943-)
Kay Jewelers, Inc.
Kay Kendall (ent.; 1926-59)
Kay Kyser (US cond.)
Kay Kyser's Kollege of Musical Knowledge
Kay Swift (US comp.; 1908-93)
Kaye Ballard (ent.; 1926-)
Kaye, Danny (ent.; 1913-87)
Kaye, M. M.
Kaye, Stubby
Kayes, Mali
Kaypro™
Kaypro Corp.

Kayseri, Turkey
Kaysone Phomvihan (ex-PM, Laos; 1920-92)
Kazakh (lang./people)
Kazakhstan (Republic of)(formerly part of USSR)(central Asia)
Kazan, Elia (ent.; 1909-)
Kazan, Lainie (ent.; 1942-)
Kazan, Russia
Kazantzakis, Nikos (Gr. writer; 1883?-1957)
Kazuo Ishiguro (Jap./US writer; 1954-)
Kazvin, Iran (also Qazvin)
k. d. lang (ent.; 1961-)
Keach, Stacy (ent.; 1941-)
Kealakekua (Bay), HI
Kean, Edmund (ent.; 1787-1833)
Keane, Bil (cartoonist, *The Family Circus*; 1922-)
Keanu Reeves (ent.)
Kearney, NE
Kearny, NJ
Kearny, Philip (US mil.; 1814-62)
Kearny, Stephen (Watts)(US mil.; 1794-1848)
Keating, Paul (PM, Austl.; 1954-)
Keating, Charles H., III (US bank scandal)
Keating, Charles H., Jr. (US bank scandal)
Keaton, Buster (Joseph Frank)(ent.; 1895-1966)
Keaton, Diane (b. Diane Hall)(ent.; 1946-)
Keaton, Michael (ent.; 1951-)
Keats, John (Br. poet; 1795-1821)
Kebich, Vyacheslav F. (PM, Belarus)
Kecskemét, Hungary
Kedleston, Marquis Curzon of (b. George Nathaniel Curzon)(Br. leader in India; 1859-1925)
Kedron (also Kidron)(rel.)
Keds™ (shoes)
Keds Corp.
Keebler™
Keebler Co.
Keefe Brasselle (ent.)
Keeler, Ruby (ent.; 1909-93)
Keeling Islands (also Cocos Islands)(Indian Ocean)
Keelung, Taiwan
Keely Smith (ent.; 1935-)
Keenan Ivory Wayans (ent.; 1958-)
Keenan Winery, Robert (US bus.)
Keenan Wynn (ent.; 1916-86)
Keene Curtis (ent.; 1923-)
Keene, Carolyn (aka Harriet S. Adams)(US writer; 1803-82)
Keene, NH
Keeshan, Bob (ent.; 1927-)
Keesler Air Force Base, MS (mil.)
Kefauver, (Carey) Estes (US pol.; 1903-63)
Keillor, Garrison (US humorist/writer ; 1942-)
Keino, Kipchoge (runner; 1940-)
Keir Dullea (ent.; 1936-)

Keitel, Harvey (ent.; 1947-)
Keith Carradine (ent.; 1949-)
Keith Hernandez (baseball; 1953-)
Keith Jackson
Keith Jarrett (US jazz; 1945-)
Keith Richard (ent.; 1943-)
Keith, Brian (ent.; 1921-)
Keith, David (ent.; 1954-)
Keith, Minor C. (US bus.; 1848-1929)
Kelenjin (people)
Keller, Helen (Adams)(US writer/educ., blind/
    deaf; 1880-1968)
Kellerman, Sally (ent.; 1937-)
Kelley, Clarence
Kelley, DeForest (ent.; 1920-)
Kelley, Kitty
Kellogg-Briand Pact (also Kellogg Peace
    Pact)(US/Fr.; 1927)
Kellogg Co., The
Kellogg, Frank B(illings)(US pol.; 1856-1937)
Kellogg, Will K. (US bus.; 1860-1951)
Kellogg's™ (cereal)
Kells, Book of (rel.)
Kellwood Co.
Kelly Air Force Base, TX (mil.)
Kelly McGillis (ent.; 1957-)
Kelly Services, Inc.
Kelly, Emmett (Leo)(US clown; 1898-1979)
Kelly, Gene (ent.; 1912-)
Kelly, Grace (Patricia)(US actress; princess,
    Monaco; 1929-82)
Kelly, Jack (ent.; 1927-92)
Kelly, Jim (football; 1960-)
Kelly, Leroy (football; 1942-)
Kelly, Red (Leonard Patrick)(hockey; 1927-)
Kelly, Sharon Pratt (DC mayor)
Kelly, Walt (cartoonist, Pogo; 1913-73)
Kelso (champion horse)
Kelso, Frank B., II (US adm.)
Kelthane™ (pesticide)
Kelvin effect, Joule- (temperature drop in
    gases)
Kelvin scale (temperature)(also l.c.)
Kelvin, William Thomson, Lord (Br. physt./
    math.; 1824-1907)
Kelvinator™ (appliances)
Kelvinator, Inc.
Kemal Atatürk (also Mustafa Kemal Pasha)(ex-
    pres./dictator, Turk.; 1881-1938)
Kemble, Francis "Fanny" Anne (Br. writer/ent.;
    1809-93)
Kemp, Jack (US pol.; 1935-)
Kemp, Shawn (basketball; 1969-)
Kempis, Thomas à (Gr. rel.; c1380-1471)
Kempthorne, Dirk (US cong.; 1951-)
Ken Anderson (football; 1949-)
Ken Berry (ent.; 1933-)
Ken(neth Martin) Follett (Br. writer; 1949-)

Ken Kercheval (ent.; 1935-)
Ken Kesey (US writer; 1935-)
Ken Murray (ent.; 1903-88)
Ken Olin (ent.; 1954-)
Ken Rosewall (tennis; 1934-)
Ken Russell (ent.; 1927-)
Ken Wahl (ent. 1956-)
Kenai Fjords National Park (AK)
Kendal green (color, fabric)
Kendal sneck bent (fishing)
Kendall-Jackson Winery (US bus.)
Kendall, Kay (ent.; 1926-59)
Keneally, Thomas (Michael)(Austl. writer;
    1935-)
Kenema, Sierra Leone
Kenesaw Mountain Landis (US jurist/baseball
    exec.; 1866-1944)
Kenmore™ (appliances)
Kennebunkport, ME
Kennedy A(lphonse) Simmonds (PM, St. Kitts-
    Nevis)
Kennedy Center for the Performing Arts, John
    F. (DC)
Kennedy Compound (Hyannis Port, MA)
Kennedy International Airport, J. F. (NY)
Kennedy Onassis, Jacqueline "Jackie" Lee
    Bouvier (US editor/photo.; wife of ex-US
    pres.; 1929-94)
Kennedy-Overton, Jayne (ent.; 1951-)
Kennedy Schlossberg, Caroline (US atty.,
    daughter of JFK; 1957-)
Kennedy Shriver, Eunice (US, wife of pol.;
    1921-)
Kennedy Space Center, (John F.)(FL)
Kennedy, Anthony M. (US jurist; 1936-)
Kennedy, Arthur (ent.; 1914-90)
Kennedy, Edward M(oore) "Ted" (US cong.;
    1932-)
Kennedy, Ethel (wife of ex-US senator)
Kennedy, George (ent.; 1925-)
Kennedy, John F(itzgerald) "Jack" (35th US
    pres.; 1917-63)
Kennedy, Joseph Patrick (US bus./dipl.; 1888-
    1969)
Kennedy, Joseph Patrick, II (US cong.; 1952-)
Kennedy, Joseph Patrick, Jr. (US mil./pol.;
    1915-44)
Kennedy, Robert F(rancis)(US pol.; 1925-68)
Kennedy, Rose (mother of ex-US pres.; 1890-)
Kennedy, Ted (Edward Moore)(US cong.; 1932-)
Kennedy, William (US writer; 1928-)
Kennelly-Heaviside layer (also E layer)(in lower
    regions, ionosphere)
Kennelly, Barbara Bailey (US cong.; 1936-)
Kennerly, Thomas, Jr. (pseud. Tom Wolfe)(US
    writer; 1931-)
Kenneth Copeland
Kenneth Dryden (hockey; 1947-)

Kenneth Grahame (Scot. writer; 1859-1932)
Kenneth (David) Kaunda (ex-pres., Zambia; 1924-)
Kenneth Millar (pseud. Ross Macdonald)(US writer; 1915-)
Kenneth Noland (US artist; 1924-)
Kenneth R(oy) Thomson
Kenneth Stabler (football; 1945-)
Kenny Clarke (US jazz; 1914-85)
Kenny G (US jazz)
Kenny Loggins (ent.; 1947-)
Kenny Rogers (ent.; 1938-)
Kenny, Sister (Elizabeth)(Austl. nurse; 1886-1952)
Kenosha, WI
Kensington and Chelsea (London borough)
Kent (county, Eng.)
Kent Conrad (US cong.; 1948-)
Kent Family Chronicles (J. Jakes novels)
Kent, Allegra (ent.; 1937-)
Kent, Julie (US dancer; 1971-)
Kentaurus, Rigel (also Alpha Centauri)(astron.)
Kenton, Stan (US jazz; 1912-79)
Kentucky (KY)
Kentucky and Virginia Resolutions (US hist.; 1798)
Kentucky bluegrass (grass)
Kentucky coffee beans
Kentucky coffee tree
Kentucky Derby (horse racing)
Kentucky Fried Chicken™
Kentucky Fried Chicken Corp. (KFC Corp.)
Kentucky Fried Movie (film; 1977)
Kenwood Vineyards (US bus.)
Kenworth™
Kenworth Truck Co.
Kenya (Republic of)(E Afr)
Kenya Airlines
Kenya, Mount (also Kirinyaga)(extinct volcano)
Kenyatta, Jomo (b. Kamau Ngengi)(ex-pres., Kenya; 1893?-1978)
Keogh plan (econ.)
Keogh, Eugene J. (US pol.; 1907-)
Kepler telescope
Kepler, Johannes (or Johann)(Ger. astron./math.; 1571-1630)
Kepler's laws (planetary motion)
Kerala (state, India)
Kercheval, Ken (ent.; 1935-)
Kerensky, Aleksandr (Feodorovich)(Rus. pol.; 1881-1970)
Kerkorian, Kirk (ent./MGM)
Kermanshah (also Kirman, Kirmanshah)(Pers. rug)
Kermit the Frog (Muppet)
Kern, Jerome (David)(US comp.; 1885-1945)
Kerns, Joanna (ent.; 1953-)
Kerouac, Jack (Jean-Louis Lefris de)(US writer; 1923-69)
Kerr-McGee Corp.
Kerr, Deborah (ent.; 1921-)
Kerr, Graham (aka Galloping Gourmet)(US chef)
Kerr, Jean (US writer; 1923-)
Kerr, John (ent.; 1931-)
Kerr, Walter F. (US writer/critic; 1913-)
Kerrey, Joseph Robert (US cong.; 1943-)
Kerrigan, Nancy (figure skater; 1969-)
Kerry (county, Ir.)
Kerry blue terrier (dog)
Kerry, John (US cong.; 1943-)
Kersee, Jackie Joyner- (track; 1962-)
Kerwin, Joseph P(eter)(astro.; 1932-)
Kesey, Ken (US writer; 1935-)
Keshia Knight Pulliam (ent.; 1979)
Kessel, Barney (US jazz; 1923-)
Ketch, Jack (Br. slang, official hangman)
Ketch, John (Br. executioner; 1663?-86)
Ketcham, Hank (US cartoonist, *Dennis the Menace*; 1920-)
Ketchikan, AK
Kettering Institute for Cancer Research, Sloan-(NYC)
Ketterley, Digory
Kettle, Ma & Pa (fict. charas.)
Ketuvim (also *Ketubim, the Hagiographa*)(rel.)
Kevin Bacon (ent.; 1958-)
Kevin Costner (ent.; 1955-)
Kevin Dobson (ent.; 1944-)
Kevin Kline (ent.; 1947-)
Kevin McCarthy (ent.; 1914-)
Kevin Nealon (ent.; 1953-)
Kevin Roche (US arch.; 1922-)
Kevin Spacey (ent.; 1960-)
Kevorkian, Jack (US phys.)
Kew Gardens (Eng.)(also Royal Botanic Gardens)
Kew, England
Kewpie™ doll
Key Biscayne, FL
Key Largo, FL
Key lime pie
Key West Naval Air Station (FL)
Key West, FL
Key, Francis Scott (US atty., wrote *The Star Spangled Banner*; 1780-1843)
Key, Ted (cartoonist, *Hazel*; 1912-)
Keyes, Evelyn (ent.)
Keynes, John Maynard (Br. econ.; 1883-1946)
Keynesian economics
Keystone Kops (or Cops)
Keystone State (nickname, PA)
KFC Corp. (Kentucky Fried Chicken Corp.)
KGB (USSR secret police; disbanded 1991)
Khachaturian, Aram Ilich (or Ill'yich)(Armenian comp.; 1903-78)

Khadafy (or Khaddhafi, Qaddafi, Gaddafi),
Moammar (or Moamer al, Muammar
al)(pres., Libya; 1942-)
Khafre (or Kafre), Pyramid of (Eg.)
Khai, Phan Dinh (aka Le Duc Tho)(NViet pol.;
1911-90)
Khaki Campbell (duck)
Khaleda Zia, Begum (PM, Bangladesh; 1944-)
Khalifa bin Sulman al-Khalifa (PM, Bahrain
Khalifa ibn Hamad al-Thani, Sheik (emir,
Qatar; 1932-)
Khalifa, Sheik Isa bin Sulman al-, (emir,
Bahrain; 1933-)
Khalka (lang.)
Khalsa (rel.)
Khama, Seretse (ex-pres., Botswana; 1921-80)
Khamenei, Ayatollah Sayyed Ali (Iran rel.;
1940-)
Khamtai Siphandon (PM, Laos; 1925-)
Khan Akhmedov (Turkmenistan pol.)
Khan IV, Aga (Islamic rel.; 1936-)
Khan, Chaka (ent.; 1953-)
Khan, Genghis (also Jenghiz, Chinghiz Khan,
Temujin)(Mongol conqueror; c1167-1227)
Khan, Ghulam Ishaq (ex-pres., Pak.)
Khan, Kublai (also Kubla Khan)(Mongol/Ch.
emp.; 1216-94)
Khan, Liaquat Ali (ex-PM, Pak.; 1895-1951)
Khan, Princess Yasmin (Aga)
Khardungla Pass (India)
Kharkov, Ukraine
Khartoum, Sudan (also Khartum)
Khashoggi, Adnan
Khayyám, Omar (Persian poet/math.; c1028-
1122)
Khayyám, The Rubáiyát of Omar (book of
verses)
Khíos Island (Gr.)
Khirbet Qumran (Dead Sea Scrolls site)
Khmer (lang./people)
Khmer Empire (ancient Cambodia and Laos)
Khmer Republic (now Cambodia)
Khmer Rouge (Cambodian communist
movement)
Khodzhent, Tajikistan
Khoikhoi (lang./people)
Khoisan (langs.)
Khomenei, Ayatollah Ruhollah (Iran, rel.; 1900-
89)
Khorana, Har Gobind (India/US chem.; 1922-)
Khrunov, Yevgeny V(asilyevich)(cosmo.; 1933-)
Khrushchev, Nikita S(ergeyevich)(ex-premier,
USSR; 1894-1971)
Khufu (king, Eg.; c2600 BC)
Khufu (or Cheops), Great Pyramid of (Eg.)
Khulna, Bangladesh
Khyber Pass (also Khaibar Pass)(Pak./Afghan.)
Kiangsi (also Jiangxi)(province, Ch.)

Kiangsu (also Jiangsu)(province, Ch.)
Kibbee, Guy (ent.; 1886-1956)
Kibbles 'N Bits™ (pet food)
Kibbles And Chunks™ (pet food)
Kickapoo (NAmer. Indians)
Kid Ory (US jazz; 1886-1973)
Kid (or Kyd), Thomas (Br. writer; c1557-95)
Kidd, William (aka Captain Kidd)(Scot. pirate;
1645?-1701)
Kidder, Margot (ent.; 1948-)
Kidder, Peabody & Co., Inc.
Kidron (also Kedron)(rel.)
Kids in the Hall (TV show)
Kiefer Sutherland (ent.; 1966-)
Kiel, Germany
Kierkegaard, Sören (or Søren)(Dan. phil.; 1813-
55)
Kiet, Vọ Van (PM, Viet.)
Kiev, chicken
Kiev, Ukraine
Kigali, Rwanda
Kiichi Miyazawa (ex-PM, Jap.; 1919-)
Kikkoman International, Inc.
Kikkoman™ soy sauce
Kikuyu (lang./people)
Kilauea (volcanic crater, HI)
Kilbride, Percy (ent.; 1888-1964)
Kildare (county, Ir.)
Kildare, Dr. (TV show)
Kiley, Richard (ent.; 1922-)
Kilgallen, Dorothy (US columnist/ent.)
Kilimanjaro, Mount (Afr.)
Kilkenny (county, Ir.)
Kilkenny cats
Kilkenny, Ireland
Killarney, Lakes of (Ir.)
Killebrew, Harmon (baseball; 1936-)
Killeen, TX
Killian's Red™ (beer)
Killy, Jean-Claude (Fr. skier; 1943-)
Kilmer, Bill (William Orland)(football; 1939-)
Kilmer, (Alfred) Joyce (US poet; 1886-1918)
Kilroy was here (WWII saying)
Kim Basinger (ent.; 1953-)
Kim Campbell (ex-PM, Can.)
Kim Dae Jung (SKorean pol.; 1924-)
Kim Darby (ent.; 1948-)
Kim Il Sung (pres., NKorea; 1912-)
Kim Linehan (swimming; 1962-)
Kim Novak (ent.; 1933-)
Kim Stanley (ent.; 1925-)
Kim Young Sam (pres., SKorea; 1927-)
Kim Zimmer
Kimba Wood (US atty.)
Kimball International, Inc.
Kimball™ pianos
Kimberly Bergalis (US AIDS victim; 1968-91)
Kimberly-Clark Corp.

Kimberley Hefner (US, wife of Hugh H.)
Kimberly Mays (US news, switched at birth)
Kimbrough, Charles (ent.)
Kimbundu (lang./people)
Kimitake, Hiraoka (pseud. Mishima Yukio)(Jap. writer; 1925-70)
Kinco Manufacturing Co.
Kiner, Ralph (baseball; 1922-)
King Albert II (king, Belgium
King Alphonse (mixed drink)
King and I, The (play; film, 1956)
King Arthur (legendary Br. king, 6th c.)
King Azlan (Muhibuddin) Shah, (Rajah)(king, Malaysia
King Bhumibol Adulyadej (aka King Rama IX)(king, Thailand; 1927-)
King Birendra Bir Bikram Shah Dev (king, Nepal; 1945-)
King Camp Gillette (US bus./razor; 1855-1932)
King Carl XVI Gustaf (king, Swed.; 1946-)
King Charles spaniel (dog)
King Cotton (US hist., early 19th c)
king crab, Alaskan
King Fahd (ibn Abdul Aziz al-Saud)(king, Saudi Arabia; 1922-)
King Harald V (also Harold)(king, Nor.; 1936-)
King Hassan II (king, Morocco; 1929-)
King Hussein I (ibn Talal)(king, Jordan; 1935-)
King International, Inc., Jani-
King James Bible (also King James Version, Authorized Version)
King Juan Carlos I (king, Spain; 1938-)
King Kong (film; 1933, 1976)
King Lear (Shakespeare play)
King Letsie III (king, Lesotho)
King Ludd (also Lludd, Nudd, Ned Ludd)(Welsh legend)
King Menelaus (myth.)
King Midas (myth.)
King Minos (myth.)
King Mswati III (king, Swaziland; 1968-)
King Norodom Sihanouk (king, Cambodia; 1922-)
King of Heaven (God)
King of Kings/kings (God, Jesus)
King (Joseph) Oliver (US jazz; 1885-1938)
King Rama IX (b. Bhumibol Adulyadej)(king, Thailand; 1927-)
King Taufa'ahau Tupou IV (king, Tonga; 1918-)
King Tut (Tutankhamen)(king, Eg.; 1343-25 BC)
King (Wallis) Vidor (ent.; 1895-1982)
King Wenceslaus (also St. Wenceslas)(duke, Bohemia; 907-929)
King Wenceslas, Good (also *Wenceslaus*)(song)
King World Productions, Inc. (TV)
King, Alan (ent.; 1927-)
King, Albert (US jazz; 1923-92)

King, B. B. (b. Riley B. King)(ent.; 1925-)
King, Billie Jean (Moffitt)(tennis; 1943-)
King, Bruce (NM gov.; 1924-)
King, Carole (US comp./ent.; 1942-)
King, Coretta Scott (US civil rights; 1927-)
King, Ernest J(oseph)(US mil.; 1878-1956)
King, Frank (cartoonist; *Gasoline Alley*; 1883-1969)
King, Larry (ent.; 1933-)
King, Rev. Dr. Martin Luther, Jr. (US civil rights leader; 1929-68)
King, Pee Wee (US comp.)
King, Perry (ent.; 1948-)
King, Richard (US rancher; 1825-85)
King, Rodney (US news; 1965-)
King, Rufus (US pol.; 1755-1827)
King, Stephen (US writer; 1947-)
King, William Lyon Mackenzie (ex-PM, Can.; 1874-1950)
King, William R(ufus De Vane)(ex.US VP; 1786-1853)
Kingdom Hall of Jehovah's Witnesses (rel.)
Kingdom of God (heaven)
Kingdom of Heaven (heaven)
Kingdom, Middle (Eg. hist.; c2040-1670 BC)(Ch. term for China until 1912)
Kingdoms period, Three (Korean hist.; began 3rd c.)
Kingman, AZ
Kings Canyon National Park (CA)
King's (or Queen's) Bench (Br. law)
King's (or Queen's) Counsel (Br. law)
king's (or queen's) English (correct English)
Kings of the Orient, Three (also Wise Men of the East, Magi, Three Wise Men)(rel.)
Kings, Book of (rel.)
Kings, Los Angeles (hockey team)
Kings, Sacramento (basketball team)
Kingsley, Ben (ent.; 1943-)
Kingsport, TN
Kingston Trio (folk music)
Kingston-upon-Hull, England (also Hull)
Kingston, Jamaica
Kingston, Maxine Hong (US writer; 1940-)
Kingston, NY, PA
Kingston, Ontario, Canada
Kingstown, Saint Vincent and the Grenadines
Kingsville Naval Air Station (TX)
Kinigi, Sylvie (PM, Burundi)
Kinks, The (pop music)
Kinney Shoe Corp.
Kinsella, John (swimming; 1952-)
Kinsey Report (officially *Sexual Behavior in the Human Male/Female*, 2 books by A.C. Kinsey)
Kinsey scale (of sexual orientation)
Kinsey, Alfred Charles (US sociol./biol.; 1894-1956)

Kinshasa, Zaire (formerly Leopoldville)
Kinte, Kunta (fict. chara., *Roots*)
Kiowa (NAmer. Indians)
Kipchoge Keino (runner; 1940-)
Kipling, (Joseph) Rudyard (Br. writer; 1865-
    1936)
Kiplinger's Personal Finance (mag.)
Kipnis, Igor
Kippur, Yom (Day of Atonement)(rel.)
Kir (mixed drink)
Kir royale (mixed drink)
Kiraly, Karch (volleyball; 1960-)
Kirby Puckett (baseball; 1961-)
Kirby™ vacuum
Kirby, Bruno (ent.; 1949-)
Kirby, Durward (ent.; 1912-)
Kirghiz (people)
Kiribati (Republic of)(formerly Gilbert
    Islands)(central Pac.)
Kirin™
Kirin (also Jilin)(province, Ch.)
Kirin Brewery Co., Ltd.
Kirinyaga, Mount (also Kenya)(extinct volcano)
Kirk Cameron (ent.; 1970-)
Kirk Douglas (b. Issur Danielovich
    Demsky)(ent.; 1916-)
Kirk Fordice (MS gov.; 1934-)
Kirk Gibson
Kirk Kerkorian (ent./MGM)
Kirk, James T., Capt. (fict. chara., *Star Trek*)
Kirk-Stieff™
Kirk Stieff Co.
Kirkland, Gelsey (ballet; 1953-)
Kirkpatrick, Jeane (Jordan)(US pol./dipl.;
    1926-)
Kirksville, MO
Kirlian photography
Kirman (also Kirmanshah, Kermanshah)(Pers.
    rug)
Kiro Gligorov (pres., Macedonia)
Kirov Ballet
Kirov, Russia (now Vyatka)
Kirov, Sergei Mironovich (Rus. pol.; 1886-1934)
Kirsch™ blinds
Kirsch Co.
Kirsten, Dorothy (US opera; 1919-92)
Kirstie Alley (ent.; 1955-)
Kirtland Air Force Base, NM (mil.)
Kirundi (also Rundi)(lang.)
Kisangani, Zaire
Kisatchie National Forest
K. I. Sawyer Air Force Base (MI)
Kishinev, Moldova (also Chisinau)
Kislev (Jew. month)
Kismayu, Somalia
Kismet (play; film, 1944, 1955)
Kiss (pop music)
Kiss Me Kate (film; 1953)

Kiss of the Spider Woman (film; 1985)
Kissimmee, FL
Kissinger, Dr. Henry A(lfred)(US pol.; 1923-)
Kisumu, Kenya
Kiswahili (also Swahili)(lang.)
Kit Carson, (Christopher)(US frontier; 1809-68)
Kit Kat™ bar (candy)
Kit-Kat Club (also Kit-Cat)(London pol. grp.;
    1703-20)
Kitaj, Ron B. (US artist; 1932-)
Kitakyushu, Japan
Kitaro (New Age multiinstrumentalist)
Kitchen Cabinet (US hist., Pres. A. Jackson
    advisers; 1829-33)
KitchenAid™ (appliances)
Kitchenaid (US bus.)
Kitchener, Ontario, Canada
Kite, Tom (golf; 1949-)
Kitt Peak National Observatory (AZ)
Kitt, Eartha (ent.; 1928-)
Kitts-Nevis, St. (officially Federation of St.
    Christopher-Nevis)(West Indies)
Kitty Carlisle (ent.; 1915-)
Kitty Carruthers (figure skating)
Kitty (Katharine) Dukakis (wife of ex-MA gov.)
Kitty Hawk, NC
Kitty Kelley
Kitty Wells (ent.; 1919-)
Kituba (lang.)
Kitwe, Zambia
Kiwanis
Kix™ (cereal)
Kizim, Leonid (cosmo.)
KKK (Ku Klux Kan)
Klaipeda, Lithuania
Klamath Falls, OR
Klan, Ku Klux (also KKK, the Klan)(US racist
    society; founded 1866)
Klaus Barbie (Ger. Nazi leader; 1913-91)
Klaus (Emil Julius) Fuchs (Ger. spy; 1911-88)
Klaus Maria Brandauer
Klaus, Václav (PM, Czech; 1941-)
Klee, Paul (Swiss artist; 1879-1940)
Kleenex™
Klein & Co., Anne
Klein Cosmetics Corp., Calvin
Klein Jewelry, Anne (US bus.)
Klein™, Calvin
Klein, Calvin (US designer; 1942-)
Klein, Ltd., Calvin
Klein, Melanie (Aus. psych.; 1882-1960)
Klein, Robert (ent.; 1942-)
Klemens W. N. L. Metternich (Aus. pol.; 1773-
    1859)
Klement Gottwald (Czech. pol.; 1896-1953)
Klemperer, Otto (Ger. cond.; 1885-1973)
Klemperer, Werner (Ger. ent.; 1919-)
Klerk, Frederik W(illem) de (ex-pres., SAfr;

1936-)
Klestil, Thomas (pres., Austria; 1932-)
Kliban, B(ernard)(cartoonist, cats; 1935-91)
Klime, J. William (US adm.)
Klimt, Gustav (Aus. artist; 1862-1918)
Kline test (for syphilis)
Kline, Kevin (ent.; 1947-)
Klinefelter's syndrome (genetics)
Klingon (*Star Trek*)
KLM Royal Dutch Airlines
Klondike (region, Yukon, gold found 1896)
Klondike Gold Rush National Historical Park
  (AK/WA)
Klondike River
Kluck, Alexander von (Ger. gen.; 1846-1934)
Kluge, John Werner
Klugman, Jack (ent.; 1922-)
Kluszeewski, Ted (baseball; 1924-88)
Klute (film; 1971)
Klutznick, Fullilove v. (US law; 1980)
Kmart Corp.
Knesset (Isr. parliament)
Knickerbocker, Herman Jansen (Dutch settler
  in NY; 1650?-1716?)
Knickerbockers (Dutch settlers in NY)
Knicks, New York (basketball team)
Knievel, Evel (Robert Craig)(US daredevil;
  1938-)
Knievel, Robbie
Knight & the Pips, Gladys (pop music)
Knight-Ridder Finanical News
Knight-Ridder, Inc.
Knight, Bob (Robert Montgomery)(basketball;
  1940-)
Knight, Gladys (ent.; 1944-)
Knight, Jonathan (ent.; 1968-)
Knight, Jordan (ent.; 1970-)
Knight, Ted (ent.; 1923-86)
Knights of Columbus (rel. org.)
Knights of Labor (US labor org.; 1869-1917)
Knights of Pythias (US benevolent secret
  society; founded 1864)
Knights of the Round Table (legendary King
  Arthur knights)
Knights of the Temple of Solomon (also
  Templar)(rel./mil. order; 1119-1307)
Knights of the Teutonic Order (also Teutonic
  Knights)(Ger. mil./rel.; est. 1190)
Knights Templars (rel./mil. order; 1119-1307)
Knightsbridge (London)
Knokke-Heist, Belgium
Knopf, Inc., Alfred A.
Knopf, Alfred A(braham)(US publ.; 1892-1984)
Knorr Beeswax Products, Inc.
Knossos (also Cnossos)(ruins, palace, Crete)
Knott's Berry Farm (US bus.)
Knots Landing (TV show)
Knotts, Don (ent.; 1924-)

Know-Nothings (US pol. party; 1852-60)
Knowles, John (US writer; 1926-)
Knox™ gelatin
Knox, Fort, KY (mil., gold depository)
Knox, John (Scot. rel.; 1505-72)
Knoxville News-Sentinel (TN newspaper)
Knoxville, TN
Knud Johan Victor Rasmussen (Dan. expl.;
  1879-1933)
Knudsen™ (food)
Knudsen & Sons, Inc.
Knudsen Dairy Products (US bus.)
Knudsen, William S. (US bus.; 1879-1848)
Knute (Kenneth) Rockne (football; 1888-1931)
KO (knock out)
Koala Blue™ (sportswear)
Koala Blue, Inc.
Koala Springs™
Koala Springs International (US bus.)
Kobe beef (extremely tender)
Kobe, Japan
Kobo, Abe (Jap. writer; 1924-93)
Kobuk Valley National Park (AK)
Koch, Edward (Irving)(ex-mayor, NYC; 1924-)
Kodachrome™ (photo.)
Kodacolor™ (photo.)
Kodak™ (photo.)
Kodel™ (fabric)
Kodak Co., Eastman
Kodály, Zoltán (Hung. comp.; 1882-1967)
Kodamatic™ (photo.)
Kodel™ (polyester fiber)
Kodes, Jan (tennis; 1946-)
Kodiak bear
Kodiak Island (AK)
Koenig, Walter
Koffigoh, Joseph Kokou (PM, Togo)
Kohinoor diamond (also Koh-i-noor)
Kohl, Helmut (Ger. chanc.; 1930-)
Kohl, Herb (US cong.; 1935-)
Kohler™ (plumbing fixtures)
Kohoutek (comet; 1973-74)
Kohtla-Jarve, Estonia
Koidu, Sierra Leone
Koirala, Girija Prasad (PM, Nepal; 1925-)
Koivisto, Mauno (Henrik)(pres., Fin.; 1923-)
Kojak (TV show)
Kokomo, IN
Kokoschaka, Oscar (Aus. artist; 1886-1980)
Kol Nidre (rel.)
Kolb, Claudia (swimming; 1949-)
Kolchak, Alexander Vasilievich (Rus. adm.;
  1875-1920)
Kolingba, André (ex-pres., Central African
  Republic; 1936-)
Kollontai, Alexandra (Rus. mil./pol./writer;
  1872-1952)
Kollwitz, Käthe (Schmidt)(Ger. artist; 1867-

1945)

Komarov, Vladimir M(ikhalovich)(cosmo.; 1927-
67)

Kommunizma, Pik (also Communism
Peak)(formerly Mount Garmo, Mount
Stalin)(Tajikistan)

Komodo dragon (large lizard, Indonesia)

Komondor (dog)

Komos (also Comus)(myth.)

Kompong Som, Cambodia

Komsomol (communist org.)

Kon-Tiki (myth.)

Kon Tiki (T. Heyerdahl raft used to cross Pac.;
1947)

Konare, Alpha Oumar (pres., Mali; 1946-)

Kongo (lang.)

Konica™ (copier)

Konica USA, Inc.

Konitz, Lee (US jazz; 1927-)

Konkani (lang.)

Konoe, Fumimaro, Prince (ex-PM, Jap.; 1891-
1946)

Konrad Adenauer (ex-chanc., WGer.; 1876-
1967)

Konrad (Emil) Bloch (US chem.; 1912-)

Konstantin Chernenko (ex-pres., USSR; 1911-
85)

Konstantin P. Feoktistov (cosmo.)

Konstantin (Sergeivich) Stanislavsky (Rus. ent.;
1863-1938)

Kontic, Radoje (premier; Yug.)

Koo Stark (Br. news)

Kookie (Edd) Byrnes (ent.)

Kool-Aid™

Kooning, Willem de (US artist; 1904-)

Koontz, Dean R. (US writer)

Koop, C. Everett (ex-US surgeon gen.; 1916-)

Koosman, Jerry Martin (baseball; 1942-)

Kootenay National Park (Can.)

Kootenay River (also Kootenai)(Can.)

Kopechne, Mary Jo (US, died at
Chappaquiddick; 1941-69)

Kopell, Bernie (ent.; 1933-)

Koppel, Ted (US TV jour.; 1940-)

Kopy Kat Instant Kopy-Printing Centers (US
bus.)

Koran (also Quran)(rel.)

Korat (cat)

Korbel & Brothers, Inc., F.

Korbel™ champagne

Korbut, Olga (Soviet gymnast; 1955-)

Kordite™ (trash bags)

Korea Strait (S Korea/SW Jap.)

Korea, North (Democratic People's Republic of)
(E Asia)

Korea, South (Republic of Korea)(E Asia)

Korean (lang./people)

Korean Air (airline)

Korean lawn grass (also Japanese lawn grass)

Korean War (NKorea, Ch./SKorea, UN; 1950-
53)

Korematsu v. U.S. (US law; 1944)

Koren, Edward (cartoonist; *New Yorker*; 1935-)

Koresh, David (US cult leader; ?-1993)

Koret™

Koret North America (US bus.)

Korman, Harvey (ent.; 1927-)

Korman, Maxime Carlot (PM, Vanuatu)

Kornberg, Arthur (US chem.; 1918-)

Kornelia Ender (swimming; 1958-)

Kornell Champagne Cellars, Hanns (US bus.)

Korsakov, Nicolay (Andreyevich) Rimsky- (Rus.
comp.; 1844-1908)

Kosciusko, Mount (Austl.)

Kosinski (or Kozinski), Jerzy (Nikodem)(Pol./US
writer; 1933-91)

Kosovo (province, Serbia)

Kossuth, Lajos (Hung. pol./editor; 1802-94)

Kostelanetz, Andre (ent.; 1901-80)

Kosti, Sudan

Kosygin, Aleksei Nikolaevich (also Alexei
Nikolaievich)(ex-PM, USSR; 1904-80)

Kota Kinabalu, Malaysia

Kotex™ (healthcare)

Kotter, Welcome Back (TV show)

Kotto, Yaphet (ent.; 1937-)

Koudougou, Burkina Faso

Koufax, Sandy (Sanford)(baseball; 1935-)

Kourou River (French Guiana)

Kourou, French Guiana

Koussevitsky, Serge (Sergei
Alexandrovich)(Rus. cond.; 1874-1951)

Kovac, Michal (pres., Slovakia)

Kovacs, Ernie (ent.; 1919-62)

Kowloon, Hong Kong

Kozinski (or Kosinski), Jerzy (Nikodem)(Po./US
writer; 1933-91)

Kozlowski, Linda (ent.)

KozyKitten™ (cat food)

KP (kitchen police)

Kpalimé, Togo

Kr (chem. sym., krypton)

Krafft-Ebing, Richard von, Baron (Ger. phys.;
1840-1902)

Kraft™

Kraft General Foods, Inc.

Kraft, Inc.

Kragujevac, Serbia

Krakatoa (also Krakatau, Krakatao)(volcanic
island, Java/Sumatra)

Kraken (myth.)

Kraków, Poland (also Cracow)

Kraljevo, Yugoslavia

Kramer v. Kramer (film; 1979)

Kramer, Jack (tennis; 1921-)

Kramer, Jerry (football; 1936-)

Kramer, Stanley (ent.; 1913-)
Krantz, Judith (US writer; 1928-)
Kraprayoon, Suchinda (Thailand gen.)
Krasnovodsk, Turkmenistan
K ration (US mil. food rations)
Kravchuk, Leonid (pres., Ukraine; 1934-)
Kravis, Henry R.
Kravitz, Lenny (ent.)
Krazy Kat (comic strip)
Krazy Glue™
Krazy Glue, Inc.
Krebs cycle (food converted into energy)
Krebs, Sir Hans (Adolf)(Ger./Br. chem.; 1900-
    81)
Kreisler, Fritz (Aus. comp.; 1875-1962)
Kremer, Gerhard (aka Geradus [or Gerhardus]
    Mercator)(Flem. geographer; 1512-94)
Kremlin, the (former USSR govt.)(also l.c.)
Kremlinology (sociol.)
Kress, Samuel H. (US bus.; 1863-1955)
Kreutzer, Rodolphe (Fr. comp.; 1766-1831)
Kringle, Kriss (also Santa Claus, St. Nicholas)
Kris Kristofferson (ent.; 1936-)
Krishna (rel.)
Krishna, Hare (rel.)
Krispy Kreme Doughnut (US bus.)
Kriss Kringle (also Santa Claus, St. Nicholas)
Kristallnacht ("night of [broken] glass")(Nazi/
    Jew.; 11/9-10/38)
Kristi Yamaguchi (figure skating; 1971-)
Kristofferson, Kris (ent.; 1936-)
Kristy McNichol (ent.; 1962-)
Krivoi Rog, Ukraine
Kroc, Ray(mond A.)(US bus., founded
    McDonalds; 1902-84)
Kroch's & Brentano's
Kroeber, Alfred L(ouis)(US anthrop.; 1876-
    1960)
Kroger Co.
Krofft, Marty
Krofft, Sid
Kroft, Steve
Kronborg Castle (Hamlet's)
Kronos (also Cronus)(myth.)
Kropotkin, Piotr (or Pyotr, Peter)(Alekseevich),
    Prince (Rus. anarchist; 1842-1921)
Kru (lang./people)
Krug Winery, Charles (US bus.)
Kruger, Otto (ent.; 1885-1974)
Krugerrand (also l.c.)(SAfr. money)
Kruk, John (baseball; 1961-)
Krupa, Gene (US jazz; 1909-73)
Krupp von Bohlen und Halbach (Ger.
    armaments maker; 1870-1950)
Krupp, Alfred (Ger. armaments maker; 1812-
    87)
Krupp, Alfred (Ger. armaments maker; 1907-
    67)

Krupp, Bertha (Ger. armaments maker; 1886-
    1957)
Krupp, Friedrich (Ger. armaments maker;
    1787-1826)
Krupp, Friedrich Alfred Krupp (Ger.
    armaments maker; 1854-1902)
Krups™ (appliances)
Krups North America, Robert (US bus.)
Krypton (fict. planet)
Krzysztof Penderecki (Pol. comp.; 1933-)
Krzyzewski, Mike (basketball; 1947-)
KS (Kansas)
K. T. Oslin (ent.; 1942-)
Ku Klux Klan (also KKK, the Klan)(US racist
    society; founded 1866)
Ku Kluxer (Klan member)
Kuala Belait, Brunei
Kuala Lumpur, Malaysia
Kuang-chou, China (also Canton or Guangzhou)
Kuanyin (myth.)
Kubasov, Valery N(ikolayevich)(cosmo.; 1935-)
Kubera (myth.)
Kublai Khan (also Kubla Khan)(Mongol/Ch.
    emp.; 1216-94)
Kübler-Ross, Elisabeth (Swiss/US phys./writer;
    1926-)
Kubota™ riding mower
Kubrick, Stanley (ent.; 1928-)
Kucan, Milan (pres., Slovenia)
Kuching, Malaysia
Kudos™
Kuenn, Harvey (baseball; 1930-88)
Kufic (early Arabic alphabet)
Kuhlman, Kathryn (faith healer)
Kuhn, Bowie Kent (baseball; 1926-)
Kukla, Fran & Ollie (TV show)
Kulp, Nancy (ent.; 1921-91)
Kulyab, Tajikistan
Kumasi, Ghana
Kumayri, Armenia
Kumminost (cheese)
Kun, Béla (Hung. pol.; 1886-c1939)
Kung (people)
Kung Fu: The Legend Continues (TV show)
Kunming, China (formerly Yunnan)
Kunstler, William (US atty.; 1919-)
Kunta Kinte (fict. chara., *Roots*)
Kuo-feng (or Guofeng), Hua (ex-PM, Ch.;
    1920?-)
Kuomintang (also Guomindang)(Ch. pol. party)
Kupka, Frank
Kupka, Frantisek (Czech. artist; 1871-1957)
Kuralt, Charles (US TV jour.; 1934-)
Kurd (people)
Kurdish (lang.)
Kurdistan (Persian-style rug)
Kurdistan (region, SW Asia)
Kurgan-Tyube, Tajikistan

Kurosawa, Akira (Jap. ent.; 1910-)
Kurt Alder (Ger. chem.; 1902-58)
Kurt Browning (figure skating; 1967-)
Kurt Jooss (Ger. ballet; 1901-79)
Kurt Kaszner (ent.)
Kurt Lewin (US psych.; 1890-1947)
Kurt Masur (Ger. cond.; 1928-)
Kurt Russell (ent.; 1951-)
Kurt Schwitters (Ger. artist; 1887-1948)
Kurt von Schuschnigg (ex-chanc., Aus.; 1897-
   1977)
Kurt Vonnegut, Jr. (US writer; 1922-)
Kurt Waldheim (ex-pres., Aus./UN dipl.; 1918-)
Kurt (Julian) Weill (Ger./US comp.; 1900-50)
Kurtz, Swoosie (ent.; 1944-)
Kurtzman, Harvey (cartoonist, *Mad* magazine;
   1925-93)
Kutaisi, Georgia
Kutuzov, Mikhail (Larionovich)(Rus. mil.; 1745-
   1813)
Kuvasz (dog)(also l.c.)
Kuwait (State of)(SW Asia)
Kuwait, Kuwait (also Kuwait City)(formerly
   Qurein)
Kuwaiti (people)
Kuybyshev, Russia (now Samara)
Kwa (lang.)
Kwai, The Bridge on the River (film; 1957)
Kwajalein Island (Marshall Islands atoll)
Kwakiutl (NAmer. Indians)
Kwalik, Ted (Thaddeus John)(football; 1947-)
Kwame Nkrumah (ex-PM, Ghana; 1909-72)
Kwangchow, China (also Guangzhou, Canton)
Kwangchu, South Korea (also Kwangju)
Kwangju, South Korea (also Kwangchu)
Kwangsi-Chuang (also Guangxi)(region, Ch.)
Kwangtung (also Guangdong)(province, Ch.)
Kwannon (also Kannon)(rel.)
Kwanza (Afr.-Amer. festival)
Kwatah, Pakistan (also Quetta)
Kweichow (also Guizhou)(province, Ch.)
Kweilin, China (also Guilin)
Kweiyang (also Guiyang), China
Kwekwe, Zimbabwe (also Que Que)
Kwik-Kopy™
Kwik-Kopy Copy (US bus.)
KY (Kentucky)
K-Y™ jelly (med.)
Kyd (or Kid), Thomas (Br. writer; c1557-95)
Kyle MacLachlan (ent.; 1960-)
Kyle Rote (football; 1928-)
Kyodo News Agency (Jap. news org.)
Kyoto, Japan
Kyrenia, Cyprus
Kyrghiz (people)
Kyrgystan (Republic of)(formerly part of USSR)
   (central Asia)
Kyrgyz (lang.)

Kyrie (music/rel.)
Kyrie eleison (Lord have mercy)
Kyser, Kay (US cond.)
Kyser's, Kay Kollege of Musical Knowledge
Kyushu (Jap. island)
Kyzyl-Kiya, Kyrgyzstan

L

LA (Louisiana, Los Angeles)
La (chem. sym., lanthanum)
La Bamba (film; 1987)
La Bamba (song)
La Bohème (Puccini)
La Brea Tar Pits (fossils, CA)
La Cage aux Folles (play; film, 1978)
La Cage aux Folles II (film; 1981)
La Cage aux Folles 3: The Wedding (film; 1986)
La Ceiba, Honduras
La Choy™ Chinese foods
La Choy Food Products (US bus.)
La Condamine (area, Monaco)
La Crosse, WI
La Dolce Vita (film; 1960)
La Farge, John (US artist; 1835-1910)
La Fayette, Marie Madeleine Pioche de la
   Vergne (Comtesse de La Fayette)(Fr. writer;
   1634-93)
La Follette, Robert Marion (ex-gov., WI; 1855-
   1925)
La Follette, Robert Marion, Jr. (US pol./publ.,
   WI; 1895-1953)
La Gioconda (aka *Mona Lisa*)(da Vinci
   painting)
La Grange, Georgia
La Guaira, Venezuela
La Guardia Airport (NY)
La Guardia, Fiorello (Henry)(ex-mayor, NYC;
   1882-1947)
La Lanne Health Spas, Jack (US bus.)
La Leche League
La Mancha (district, Sp.)
La Mancha, Man of (play)
la Mare, Walter de (Br. poet; 1873-1956)
La Marseillaise, (Fr. anthem)
La Motta, Jake (boxing
La Paz™ (margarita mix)
La Paz Products (US bus.)
La Paz, Bolivia
La Paz, Mexico
La Plata, Argentina
La Quinta Motor Inns, Inc.
la Renta, Ltd., Oscar de
la Renta, Oscar de (US designer; 1932-)
La Rioja (region, Sp.)
La Rochefoucauld, François, Duc de (Fr. writer;
   1613-80)
La Rosa, Julius (ent.)
La Salle, (René) Robert Cavelier (aka Sieur de
   La Salle)(Fr. expl.; 1643-87)
La Salle, IL
La Salle, Quebec, Canada
La Scala (opera house, It.)

La Sueur™ (peas)
La Sylphide (ballet)
La Toya Jackson (ent.; 1956-)
La Traviata (G. Verdi opera)
La Victoria™
La Victoria Foods, Inc.
Laar, Mart (PM, Estonia
Laarne, Belgium
Laatasi, Kamuta (PM, Tuvalu)
Laban, Rudolf von (Hung. ballet; 1879-1958)
Labanotation (dance)
Labatt, Ltd., John
Labé, Guinea
LaBelle, Patti (ent.; 1944-)
Labor and Human Resources Committee (US
   govt.)
Labor Day (1st Monday in September)
Labor Party (Austl. pol.)
Labor Party, Greenback- (US hist.; 1878-c1884)
Labor Relations Act, National (NLRA)(US law;
   1935)
Labor Relations Board, National (NLRB)(US
   govt. agcy.; est. 1935)
Labor, Department of (DOL)(US govt.)
Labor, Knights of (US labor org.; 1869-1917)
Laborism
Labour Day (Br.)
Labour Party (Br. pol.)
Labrador (NE Can.)
Labrador Current (also Arctic Current)(cold
   ocean current)
Labrador retriever (dog)
Lacalle Herrera, Luis Alberto (pres. Uruguay;
   1941-)
Lacedaemon (also Sparta)(ancient Gr.)
Lacerta (astron., lizard)
Lacey Davenport (fict. chara., *Doonesbury*)
Lacey, Cagney & (TV show)
Lachaise, Gaston (US sculptor; 1882-1935)
Lachesis (myth.)
Lachine, Quebec, Canada
Lachryma Christi (It. wine, tear of Christ)
Lackawanna, NY
Lackland Air Force Base, TX (mil.)
LACSA Airline of Costa Rica
Lactaid™ (med.)
Ladd, Alan (ent.; 1913-64)
Ladd, Cheryl (ent.; 1951-)
Ladd, Diane (ent.; 1932-)
Ladies' Home Journal (mag.)
Lady Abracadabra
Lady Augusta Gregory (Ir. writer; 1852-1932)
Lady Baltimore cake
Lady Bird Johnson (b. Claudia Alta
   Taylor)(wife of ex-US pres.; 1912-)
Lady Bountiful (fict. chara., *Beaus' Strategem*)
Lady Bracknell (fict. chara., *The Importance of
   Being Earnest*)

Lady Chatterley's Lover (D.H. Lawrence novel)
Lady Day (Billie Holiday)
Lady Godiva (Br. noblewoman ; c1040-80)
Lady Jane (Dudley) Grey (queen, Eng. [10 days]; 1537-54)
Lady Lovelace (aka Augusta Ada Byron)(Br. math./inv., compu.; 1815-52)
Lady Luck (personification of luck)
Lady Macbeth (fict. chara., *Macbeth*)
Lady Macduff (fict. chara., *Macbeth*)
Lady Manhattan Co., The
Lady Mary (Wortley) Montagu (aka Mary Pierrepont)(Br. writer; 1689-1762)
Lady of Mercy, Order of Our (rel.)
Lady of Shalott (Tennyson poem)
Lady of the Lake, The (Arthurian chara.)
Lady of the Lake, The (by Sir Walter Scott)
Lady or the Tiger?, The (F.R. Stockton short story)
Lady, Gray (Amer. Red Cross volunteer)
Lady, Our (also the Madonna, Holy Mother, Mary, Virgin Mary)(rel.)
Lady's Circle (mag.)
Lae, Papua New Guinea
Laertes (fict. chara., *Hamlet*; myth.)
LaFarge, Christopher Grant (US arch.; 1862-1938)
Lafayette College (PA)
Lafayette, IN, LA
Lafayette, Marquis de (aka Marie Joseph Gilbert de Motier Lafayette)(Fr. mil./pol.; 1757-1834)
Laffer curve (econ.)
Laffer, Arthur (US econ.; 1940-)
Laffit Pincay, Jr. (jockey; 1946-)
Lafitte (or Laffite), Jean (Fr. mil./pirate; c1780-c1825)
Lafleur, Guy (hockey; 1951-)
LaFontaine, Pat (hockey; 1965-)
Lag b'Omer (rel.)
L. A. Gear™ (shoes)
L. A. Gear, Inc.
Lagos, Nigeria
Lagrange, Joseph (Louis)(Fr. astron./math.; 1736-1813)
Lagrangian points (in space)
Laguna Beach, CA
Lahore, Pakistan
Lahr, Bert (b. Irving Lahrheim)(ent.; 1895-1967)
Lahti, Christine (ent.; 1950-)
Lahti, Finland
Lailat ul-Barah (rel., "Night of Forgiveness")
Lailat ul-Isra Wal Mi'raj (rel.)
Lailat ul-Qadr (rel., "Night of Power")
Laine, Cleo (ent.; 1927-)
Laine, Frankie (ent.; 1913-)
Laing, R(onald) D(avid)(Scot. psych./writer; 1927-89)
Lainie Kazan (ent.; 1942-)
Lajos Kossuth (Hung. pol./editor; 1802-94)
Lake and Palmer Emerson (pop music)
Lake Arrowhead, CA
Lake Baikal (also Baykal)(Russia)(deepest lake in the world)
Lake Balkhash (Kazakhstan)(salt)
Lake Chad (Nigeria)
Lake Champlain (NY/VT/Can.)
Lake Charles, LA
Lake Clark National Park (AK)
Lake County Times (IN newspaper)
Lake District (region, Eng.)
Lake Erie (NY/OH/PA/Can.)
Lake Eyre (Austl.)
Lake Forest, IL
Lake Havasu City, AZ
Lake Kariba (Zimbabwe)
Lake Leman (also Lake of Geneva)(Switz./Fr.)
Lake Louise (Can.)
Lake Malawi (SE Afr.)
Lake Manitoba (Can.)
Lake Maracaibo (Venezuela)
Lake Mead (Hoover Dam, AZ/NV)
Lake Michigan (N central US)
Lake Natron (Tanzania)
Lake Nipigon (Ontario, Can.)
Lake Nipissing (Can.)
Lake Nyasa (now Lake Malawi)
Lake of Geneva (also Lake Leman)(Switz./Fr.)
Lake of the Ozarks (MO)
Lake of the Woods (Ontario, Can.)
Lake Okeechobee (FL)
Lake Onega (NW Russia)
Lake Onondaga (NY)
Lake Ontario (US/Can.)
Lake Oswego, OR
Lake Peipus (NE Eur.)
Lake Placid, NY
Lake Ponchartrain (LA)
Lake Powell (AZ/UT)
Lake Superior (US/Can.)
Lake Tahoe (CA/NV)
Lake Tanganyika (E Afr.)
Lake Titicaca (SAmer.)
Lake Victoria (Afr.)
Lake Windermere (Eng.)
Lake Winnebago (WI)
Lake Winnipeg (Can.)
Lake Wobegon (fict. town, G. Keillor)
Lake, Anthony (US Nat'l Security Adviser; 1939-)
Lake, Ricki
Lake, The Lady of the (Arthurian chara.)
Lake, The Lady of the (by Sir Walter Scott)
Lake, Veronica (ent.; 1919-73)
Lakeland Ledger (FL newspaper)

Lakeland terrier (dog)
Lakeland, FL
Lakenvelder (chicken)
Lakers, Los Angeles (basketball team)
Lakes of Killarney (Ir.)
Lakewood, OH
Lakoue, Enoch Derant (PM, Central African
    Republic)
Lakshmi (myth.)
Lal Bahadur Shastri (Shri)(ex-PM, India; 1904-
    66)
LaLanne, Jack (US, fitness educ.)
L .A. Law (TV show)
Lalique crystal
Lalique, René (Fr. designer; 1860-1945)
Lalitpur, Nepal (formerly Patan)
Lally column (constr.)
Lalo, (Victor Antoine) Édouard (Fr. comp.;
    1823-92)
Lam, Wilfredo (Cuban artist; 1902-82)
Lama(istic) Buddhism (rel.)
Lama, Dalai (b. Tenzin Gyatso)(Tibetan rel.;
    1935-)
Lama, Panchen (Tibetan rel.; 1939-89)
Lamaism (rel.)
Lamarck, Jean B(aptiste)(Fr. nat.; 1744-1829)
Lamarr, Hedy (ent.; 1913-)
Lamartine, Alphonse de (Fr. writer; 1790-1869)
Lamas, Fernando (ent.; 1915-82)
Lamas, Lorenzo (ent.; 1958-)
Lamaze method (childbirth)
Lamb Chop (S. Lewis puppet)
Lamb Chop's Play-Along (TV show)
Lamb of God (Jesus)
Lamb, Charles ("Elia")(Br. writer; 1775-1834)
Lamb, Gil (ent.; 1906-)
Lamb, Mary (Br. writer; 1764-1847)
Lambert Corp., Norton-
Lambert Co., Warner-
Lambert-St. Louis International Airport (MO)
Lambert, Drexel Burnham (US stock market
    scandal)
Lambeth walk (dance)
Lamborghini™ (auto.)
Lamborghini, Ferruccio (It. bus.; 1917-93)
Lambrusco (wine)
Lammas (rel.)
Lamonica, Daryle (football; 1941-)
Lamont Dozier (US comp.; 1941-)
Lamour, Dorothy (ent.; 1914-)
L'Amour, Louis (Dearborn)(US writer; 1908-88)
Lampedusa, Giuseppe (Tomasi) di (It. writer;
    1896-1957)
Lamrani, Mohammed Karim (PM, Morocco)
LAN (local area network)(compu.)
Lana Cantrell (ent.; 1943-)
Lana Turner (ent.; 1920-)
Lanai, HI

Lancashire (cheese)
Lancaster (also Lancashire)(county, Eng.)
Lancaster Intelligencer-Journal (PA newspaper)
Lancaster New Era (PA newspaper)
Lancaster News (PA newspaper)
Lancaster, Burt(on Stephen)(ent.; 1913-)
Lancaster, CA, NY, OH, PA, TX
Lancaster, House of (Br. ruling family; 1399-
    1461, 1470-71)
Lance Alworth (football; 1940-)
Lancelot (of the Lake)(Arthurian knight)
Lanchester, Elsa (ent.; 1902-82)
LanChile Airlines
Lancome (US bus.)
Lancôme cosmetics
Land Cruiser, Toyota (auto.)
Land O' Lakes™ (butter)
Land O' Lakes, Inc.
Land of Beulah (*Pilgrim's Progress*)
Land of Enchantment (nickname, NM)
Land of Lincoln (nickname, IL)
Land of Opportunity (nickname, AR)
Land of Oz
Land of the Leal (heaven)
land of Nod (myth. land of sleep)
Land Rover™ (auto.)
Land, Edwin (Herbert)(US inv., Polaroid Land
    camera; 1910-91)
Landau, Martin (ent.; 1934-)
Landers, Ann (Eppie Lederer)(b. Esther Pauline
    Friedman)(US advice columnist; 1918-)
Landis, Carole (ent.; 1919-48)
Landis, John (ent.; 1950-)
Landis, Kenesaw Mountain (US jurist/baseball
    exec.; 1866-1944)
Landon, Alf(red Mossman)(US pol.; 1887-1987)
Landon, Michael (ent.; 1936-91)
Landrum-Griffin Act (US hist.; 1959)
Landry, Tom (football; 1924-)
Land's End (cape, Eng.)
Lands' End™
Lands' End, Inc.
Landsat (US satellite)
Landsbergis, Vytautas (ex-pres., Lith.; 1932-)
Landy, John (runner; 1930-)
Lane Bryant, Inc.
Lane™ (furniture)
Lane Co., Inc., The
Lane Smith
Lane, Burton (US comp.; 1912-)
Lane, Cristy (ent.; 1940-)
Lane, Diane (ent.; 1963-)
Lane, Priscilla (ent.; 1917-)
Lanford Wilson (US writer; 1937-)
Lang, Fritz (Aus. ent.; 1890-1976)
lang, k. d. (ent.; 1961-)
Lang, Stephen (ent.; 1952-)
Lange, David (Russell)(ex-PM, NewZeal.; 1942-)

Lange, Dorothea (US photo.; 1895-1965)
Lange, Hope (ent.; 1931-)
Lange, Jessica (ent.; 1949-)
Langella, Frank (ent.; 1940-)
Langerhans, islets of (med.)
Langford, Frances (ent.; 1913-)
Langley Air Force Base, VA (mil.)
Langtry, Lillie ("the Jersey Lily")(b. Emily
    Charlotte le Breton)(Br. ent.; 1853-1929)
Lani Guinier (US atty.)
Lanier™ (bus. machines)
Lanier, Sidney (US poet; 1842-81)
Lanier Voice Products, Inc.
Lanne Health Spas, Jack La (US bus.)
Lanny McDonald (hockey; 1953-)
Lanoxin™ (med.)
Lansana, Conté (pres., Guinea; 1945?-)
Lansbury, Angela (ent.; 1925-)
Lansing State-Journal (MI newspaper)
Lansing, IL, MI
Lansing, Robert (ent.; 1928-)
Lansing, Robert (US atty./pol.; 1864-1928)
Lansing, Sherry Lee
Lanson, Snooky (ent.; 1914-90)
Lantz, Walter (cartoonist, *Woody Woodpecker*;
    1900-)
Lanza, Mario (opera; 1921-1959)
Lanzhou, China (also Lanchow)
Lao (lang./people)
Lao-Tzu (also Lao-tzu)(Ch. phil.; c570-490 BC)
Laocoön (myth.)
Laodamia (myth.)
Laodice (myth.)
Laomedon (myth.)
Laos (Lao People's Democratic Republic)(SE
    Asia)
Laotian (people)
Laplace, Pierre S(imon)(aka Marquis de
    Laplace)(Fr. astron./math.; 1749-1827)
Lapland (region, N Eur.)
Lapps (also Laplanders)(people)
Lapsang souchong tea
Laputa Island (fict. place, *Gulliver's Travels*)
Lar Lubovitch (US dance; 1945-)
Laraki, Azzedine (ex-PM, Morocco)
Laramie, Fort (WY)
Laramie, WY
LaRaza Unida Party (US pol.)
Lardner, Ring(gold Wilmer)(US writer; 1885-
    1933)
Laredo, Ruth (ent.; 1937-)
Laredo, TX
Lares (myth.)
Large Electron Positron Collider (LEP)(particle
    accelerator)
Large Magellanic Cloud (astron.)
Largo Entertainment
Largo, Key, FL

Larissa, Greece
Larkin, Barry (baseball; 1964-)
Larkin, Philip (Br. poet; 1922-85)
Larnaca, Cyprus
LaRouche, Lyndon H., Jr. (US pol./econ.; 1922-)
Larrieu, Francie (track; 1952-)
Larroquette, John (ent.; 1947-)
Larry (Lawrence Cecil) Adler (US musician;
    1914-)
Larry Bird (basketball; 1956-)
Larry Brown (football; 1947-)
Larry Craig (US cong.; 1945-)
Larry (Lawrence Richard) Csonka (football;
    1946-)
Larry Drake (ent.)
Larry Fine (b. Louis Feinberg)(ent.; 1902-75)
Larry Fishburne (ent.; 1962-)
Larry Gatlin (ent.; 1948-)
Larry Hagman (ent.; 1931-)
Larry Holmes (boxing; 1949-)
Larry King (ent.; 1933-)
Larry King Live (TV show)
Larry Mahan
Larry McMurtry, (Jeff)(US writer; 1936-)
Larry Pressler (US cong.; 1942-)
Larry Rivers (b. Vitzroch Loiza Grossberg)(US
    artist; 1923-)
Larry Robinson (hockey; 1951-)
Larry Sanders Show, The (TV show)
Larry Storch (ent.; 1923-)
Larson, Gary (US cartoonist, *The Far Side*;
    1950-)
Las Cruces, NM
Las Palmas (de Gran Canaria), Canary Islands
Las Vegas Airlines
Las Vegas Review-Journal (NV newspaper)
Las Vegas Sun (NV newspaper)
Las Vegas, NM, NV
Lascaux Cave (Fr., prehistoric wall paintings)
LaserWriter™ (compu. printer)
Lasix™ (med.)
Lasker, Albert (US bus.; 1880-1952)
Lasorda, Tommy (baseball/ent.; 1927-)
Lassa fever (med.)
Lasse Viren (track; 1949-)
Lassen Peak (also Mount Lassen)(CA volcano)
Lassen Volcanic National Park (CA)
Lasser, Louise (ent.; 1939-)
Lassie (dog)
Lassie (TV show)
Lassie Come Home (film; 1943)
Lassiter (film; 1984)
Lasswell, Fred (cartoonist)
Last Frontier (nickname, AK)
Last (or Final) Judgment (rel.)
Last of the Mohicans, The (J.F. Cooper novel)
Last Supper (rel.)
Last Supper, The (da Vinci)

Lastex™ (elastic fiber)
Latakia tobacco
Latakia, Syria
Late Modern English (lang.; c1700-present)
Late Night (TV show)
Late Night With David Letterman (TV show)
Later Tsin (or Chin) dynasty (also Chin)(Ch.; 936-46)
Lateran basilica (also Basilica of the Savior)(Rome)
Lateran Treaty(ies)(It./Vatican; 1929)
Latin (lang.)
Latin alphabet (also Roman alphabet)
Latin America (S & Central Amer.)
Latin cross
Latin school
Latino (slang)
Latour, (Ignace) Henri (Joseph Théodore) Fantin- (Fr. artist; 1836-1904)
Latrobe, Benjamin Henry (US arch.; 1764-1820)
Latter-Day Saints (also Church of Jesus Christ of the Latter-Day Saints, Mormon Church)(rel.)
Latvia (Republic of)(formerly part of USSR)(N Eur.)
Latvian (lang./people)
Lauch Faircloth (US cong.; 1928-)
Lauderdale, Fort, FL (city)
Lauder™, Estée (cosmetics)
Lauder, Inc., Estée
Laugh-In, Rowan and Martin's (TV show)
Laughlin Air Force Base, TX (mil.)
Laughlin, James L(awrence)(US econ.; 1850-1933)
Laughton, Charles (ent.; 1899-1962)
Laundromat™
Lauper, Cyndi (ent.; 1953-)
Laura Ashley™
Laura Ashley (Br. designer; 1925-85)
Laura Ashley (US bus.)
Laura Branigan (ent.)
Laura D'Andrea Tyson (Chair/Council Econ Advisers; 1947-)
Laura Dern (ent.; 1967-)
Laura Ingalls Wilder (US writer; 1867-1957)
Laurance S(pelman) Rockefeller (US bus./finan.; 1910-)
Laurel & Hardy (Stan & Oliver)(US comedy team)
Laurel, MS
Laurel, Stan (b. Arthur Stanley Jefferson)(ent.; 1890-1965)
Lauren Bacall (ent.; 1924-)
Lauren Leathergoods, Polo/Ralph (US bus.)
Laurent SA., Yves St.- (US bus.)
Lauren™, Ralph
Lauren, Ralph (US bus.)
Lauren, Ralph (b. Ralph Lifshitz)(US designer; 1939-)
Laurence Harvey (ent.; 1928-73)
Laurence Luckinbill (ent.; 1934-)
Laurence (Kerr) Olivier, Sir (ent.; 1907-89)
Laurence Sterne (Ir. writer; 1713-68)
Laurens (Jan) Van der Post (SAfr. writer; 1906-)
Laurens, Henri (Fr. sculptor; 1884-?)
Laurens, Henry (US pol.; 1724-92)
Laurent Fabius (ex-PM, Fr.; 1946-)
Laurent, Louis S(tephen) St. (ex-PM, Can.;1882-1973)
Laurent, Yves (Henri Donat Mathieu) Saint- (Fr. designer; 1936-)
Laurentian (or Canadian) Plateau/Shield (also Precambrian Shield)(Can.)
Laurentiis, Dino De (It. ent.; 1919-)
Laurie Metcalf (ent.; 1955-)
Laurie, Piper (ent.; 1932-)
Lauritz Melchior (ent.; 1890-1973)
Lauro, Achille (hijacked It. cruise ship; 1984)
Lausanne, Switzerland
Lautenberg, Frank R. (US cong.; 1924-)
Lauter, Ed (ent.; 1940-)
Lauti, Toaripi (gov-gen., Tuvalu)
Lautoka, Fiji
Lautrec, Henri (Marie Raymond) de Toulouse- (Fr. artist; 1864-1901)
Laval, Pierre (ex-PM, Fr.; 1883-1945)
Laval, Quebec, Canada
Laver, Rod(ney George)(tennis; 1938-)
Laverne & Shirley (TV show)
Laverne Andrews (ent.; Andrew Sisters; 1913-67)
Lavin, Linda (ent.; 1937-)
Lavoisier, Antoine Laurent (Fr. chem.; 1743-94)
Lavoris™ (mouthwash)
Lavrenti Beria (USSR pol.; 1899-1953)
Law & Order (TV show)
Law of Moses (rel.)
Law of the Twelve Tables (Roman law; est. 451-50 BC)
Law, (Andrew) Bonar (Br. pol.; 1858-1923)
LaWanda Page (ent.; 1920-)
Lawford, Peter (ent.; 1923-84)
Lawler, Loewe v. (US law; 1908)
Lawn-Boy (US bus.)
Lawrence Berkeley Laboratory (nuclear research, CA)
Lawrence Durrell (Br. writer; 1912-90)
Lawrence Ferlinghetti (US writer/publ.; 1919-)
Lawrence Kasdan (ent./writer; 1948-)
Lawrence Livermore Laboratory (nuclear research, CA)
Lawrence of Arabia (film; 1962)
Lawrence Sanders (US writer; 1920-)
Lawrence Spivak (ent.; 1900-)
Lawrence (Mervil) Tibbett (ent.; 1896-1960)

Proper Noun Speller

Lawrence Welk (US cond.; 1903-92)
Lawrence, Carol (ent.; 1934-)
Lawrence, D(avid) H(erbert)(Br. writer; 1885-1930)
Lawrence, Ernest O(rlando)(US physt.; 1901-58)
Lawrence, Gertrude (ent.; 1898-1952)
Lawrence, IN, KS, MA
Lawrence, Steve (ent.; 1935-)
Lawrence, T(homas) E(dward)(aka Lawrence of Arabia)(Br. mil.; 1888-1935)
Lawrence, Sir Thomas (Br. artist; 1769-1830)
Lawrence, Vicki (ent.; 1949-)
Lawry's™
Lawry's Foods, Inc.
Laws, Doctor of (also LL.D., Legum Doctor)
Lawton Chiles (FL gov.; 1930-)
Lawton, OK
Layne, Bobby (football; 1927-86)
Layne, Tamirat (PM, Ethiopia
Lázaro Cárdenas (ex-pres., Mex.; 1895-1970)
Lazarus (rel.)
Lazarus, Emma (US poet; 1849-87)
Lazarus, Mell (cartoonist, *Momma, Miss Peach*; 1929-)
La-Z-Boy™
La-Z-Boy Chair Co.
Lazio (region, It.)
LC (landing craft, Library of Congress)
LCD/LED (liquid crystal display/light-emitting diode)(compu.)
LCV (landing craft vehicle)
LDL (low-density lipoprotein)
L-dopa (med.)
Le Baron, Chrysler-Plymouth (auto.)
Le Bon, Simon (ent.; 1958-)
le Carré, John (b. David Cornwell)(Br. writer; 1931-)
Le Chatelier('s) principle (also Le Chatelier-Braun p.)(chem.)
Le Corbusier (aka Charles Édouard Jeanneret)(Fr. arch./artist; 1887-1965)
Le Creuset of America, Inc.
Le Duc Anh (pres., Viet.)
Le Duc Tho (aka Phan Dinh Khai)(NViet pol.; 1911-90)
le Fay, Morgan (also Morgain le Fay)(King Arthur's fairy sister)
Le Gallienne, Eva (ent.; 1899-91)
Le Gallienne, Richard (US/Br. writer; 1866-1947)
Le Havre, France
Le Journal de Montreal
Le Journal de Quebec
Le Mans, France (auto racing)
Le Marche (region, It.)
Le Misanthrope (Molière comedy)
Le Morte D'Arthur (by T. Malory)

Le Pen, Jean-Marie (Fr. pol.; 1928-)
Le Petit Trianon, (built for Mme de Pompadour by Louis XV)
Le Tartuffe (Molière comedy)
Lea & Perrins™
Lea & Perrins, Inc.
Lea Thompson (ent.; 1961-)
Leach, Bernard Howell (Br. potter; 1887-1969)
Leach, Robin (ent.; 1941-)
Leachman, Cloris (ent.; 1926-)
Leacock, Stephen (Butler)(Can. writer/humorist; 1868-1944)
Leadbelly (Huddie) Ledbetter (US jazz; 1888-1949)
League of Nations (internat'l govt. org.; 1920-)
League of Women Voters
Leahy, Patrick (US cong.; 1940-)
Leahy, William Daniel (US adm.; 1875-1959)
Leakey, Louis S(eymour) B(azett)(Br. archaeol..; 1903-72)
Leakey, Mary (Douglas)(Br. archaeol.; 1913-)
Leakey, Richard (Br. archaeol.; 1944-)
Leal, Land of the (heaven)
Lean Cuisine™, Stouffer's™
Lean, Sir David (Br. ent.; 1908-91)
Leaning Tower of Pisa (It.)
Lear jet™ (trans.)
Lear, Edward (Br. artist/humorist; 1812-88)
Lear, Francis (US publ.; 1923-)
Lear, King (Shakespeare play)
Lear, Norman (ent.; 1922-)
Learned (Billings) Hand (US jurist; 1872-1961)
Learned, Michael (ent.; 1939-)
Learning Channel, The (cable TV)
Leary, Timothy (US educ./writer; 1920-)
Leavenworth prison (KS)
Leavenworth, Fort, KS (mil.)
Leavenworth, KS
Leavitt, Mike (UT gov.)
Lebanon (Republic of)(W Asia)
Lebanon, PA
Lebedev, Valentin (Vitalyevich)(cosmo.; 1942-)
Lebensraum (Ger., expansion)
Lech Walesa (pres., Pol.; 1943-)
LED (light-emitting diode)(compu.)
Led Zeppelin (pop music)
Leda (myth.)
Ledbetter, Huddie "Leadbelly" (US jazz; 1888-1949)
Lederberg, Joshua (US geneticist; 1925-)
Lederer, Eppie (aka Ann Landers)(b. Esther Pauline Friedman)(US advice columnist; 1918-)
Ledger, Lakeland (FL newspaper)
Lee A. Iacocca (US bus./auto.; 1924-)
Lee and Yang (Ch. physicists)
Lee (Harvey Leroy) Atwater (US pol.; 1951-91)
Lee Corp., Sara

Lee de Forest (US inv., radio/sound films/TV; 1873-1961)
Lee Elder (golf; 1934-)
Lee-Enfield rifle (also Enfield rifle)
Lee Evans (runner; 1947-)
Lee Falk (cartoonist)
Lee Grant (ent.; 1929-)
Lee Harvey Oswald (assassinated JFK; 1939-63)
Lee Hoi Chang (PM; SKorea
Lee Horsley (ent.; 1955-)
Lee J. Cobb (ent.; 1911-76)
Lee™ jeans
Lee Konitz (US jazz; 1927-)
Lee Majors (ent.; 1940-)
Lee Marvin (ent.; 1924-87)
Lee P. Brown (Dir./Ofc. Drug Control; 1937-)
Lee Radziwill, Princess
Lee Remick (ent.; 1935-91)
Lee Salk (US psych.; 1927-92)
Lee Shepherd (auto racing; 1945-85)
Lee Shubert (US theater; 1875-1953)
Lee Strasberg (US ent./educ.; 1901-82)
Lee Tenghui (pres., Taiwan; 1923-)
Lee Trevino (golf; 1939-)
Lee Tsung Dao (Ch. physt.; 1926-)
Lee University, Washington and (VA)
Lee Van Cleef (ent.; 1925-89)
Lee, Brenda (ent.; 1944-)
Lee, Bruce (ent./martial arts; 1940-73)
Lee, Christopher (aka Lee Yuen Kam)(ent.; 1922-)
Lee, Fort (NJ)(city)
Lee, Fort (VA)(mil)
Lee, Francis Lightfoot (US pol.; 1734-97)
Lee, Gypsy Rose (b. Rose Louise Hovick)(ent.; 1914-70)
Lee, Henry "Light-Horse Harry" (US gen.; 1756-1818)
Lee, Manfred B(ennington)(pseud. Ellery Queen)(US writer; 1905-71)
Lee, Michele (ent.; 1942-)
Lee, Peggy (ent.; 1920-)
Lee, Pinky (b. Pinkus Leff)(ent.; 1908-93)
Lee, Regis & Kathie (TV show)
Lee, Robert E(dward)(US confed. gen.; 1807-70)
Lee, Spike (Shelton Jackson)(ent.; 1957-)
Lee, Stan (cartoonist, *Marvel Comics*; 1922-)
Leeds, England
Leekpai, Chuan (PM, Thailand)
Leeuwenhoek, Anton van (Dutch, father of microbiology; 1632-1723)
Leeward Islands (S. Pac.)
Leeward Islands, Lesser Antilles (Montserrat, Antigua, St. Christopher [St. Kitts]-Nevis, Barbuda, Anguilla, St. Martin, British Virgin Islands, U.S. Virgin Islands)
Leeza Gibbons (ent.)

Leeza, John and (TV show)
LeFaro, Scott (US jazz; 1936-61)
Left Bank (also Rive Gauche)(Paris)
Lefty (Robert Moses) Grove (baseball; 1900-75)
Legend™, Honda Acura (auto.)
Léger, Fernand (Fr. artist; 1881-1955)
Leggett & Platt/Hartex (US bus.)
L'eggs™ (hosiery)
L'eggs Products, Inc.
Leghari, Farooq (pres., Pak.)
Leghorn (chicken)
Leghorn, Foghorn (cartoon chara.)
Legion of Honor (Fr.)
Legion of Merit (US)
Legionnaire (member Amer. Legion)
Legionnaires' disease (also Legionnaires; also l.c.)
Lego™ (toys)
Legree, Simon (fict. chara., *Uncle Tom's Cabin*)
LeGuin, Ursula (US writer; 1929-)
Lehár, Franz (Hung. comp.; 1870-1948)
Lehmann, Lilli (Ger. opera; 1848-1929)
Lehmann, Lotte (Ger. opera; 1888-1976)
Lehrer News Hour, MacNeil, (TV show)
Lehrer, Jim (US news jour.; 1934-)
Leiber, Jerry (US comp.; 1933-)
Leibman, Ron (ent.; 1937-)
Leibnitz, Gottfried Wilhelm von, Baron (Ger. phil./math; 1646-1716)
Leibnitzianism (phil.)
Leica™ (camera)
Leica USA, Inc.
Leicester (cheese)
Leicester (sheep)
Leicester, England
Leicestershire (also Leicester)(county, Eng.)
Leif Ericsson (Norse expl.; c.1000)
Leifer, Carol (ent.; 1956-)
Leigh, Janet (ent.; 1927-)
Leigh, Jennifer Jason (ent.; 1958-)
Leigh, Mitch (US comp.; 1928-)
Leigh, Vivien (ent.; 1913-67)
Leighton, Margaret (ent.; 1922-76)
Leinsdorf, Erich (ent.; 1912-)
Leinster (province, Ir.)
Leipzig, Germany
Leland Stanford, A(masa)(US bus./finan./pol.; 1824-93)
LEM (lunar excursion module)
Lem, Stanislaw (Pol. writer; 1921-)
Lemaître, Georges Edouard (Belgium astron.; 1894-1966)
Leman, Lake (also Lake of Geneva)(Switz./Fr.)
LeMay, Curtis (Emerson)(US gen.; 1906-90)
Lemieux, Mario (hockey; 1965-)
Lemmon, Chris (ent.)
Lemmon, Jack (ent.; 1925-)
Lemnitzer, Lyman (US gen.; 1899-1988)

Proper Noun Speller

Lemon Jefferson, Blind (US jazz; 1897-1930)
Lemond, Greg (cyclist; 1961-)
Lemoore Naval Air Station (CA)
Lemuralia (ancient Roman rite)
Lena Horne (ent.; 1917-)
Lenape, Lenni (NAmer. Indians)(also Delaware)
Lender's™
Lender's Bagel B2akery (of Kraft, Inc.)(US bus.)
Lendl, Ivan (tennis; 1960-)
L'Enfant, Pierre Charles (Fr./US arch./eng.;
    1754-1825)
L'Engle, Madeleine (US writer; 1918-)
Lenin Library (Moscow)
Lenin Peak (Kyrgyzstan/Tajikistan)
Lenin, Vladimir Ilyich (Ulyanov)(USSR pol.;
    1870-1924)
Leningrad, Russia (now St. Petersburg)
Leninism (pol.)
Lennart Meri (pres., Estonia
Lenni Lenape (NAmer. Indians)(also Delaware)
Lennie Tristano (US jazz; 1919-78)
Lennie Wilkins (basketball; 1937-)
Lennon Sisters, the (pop music)
Lennon, John (Br. comp./ent.; 1940-80)
Lennon, Julian (ent.)
Lenox™
Lenox China, Inc.
Lenox Crystal, Inc.
Lenny Bruce (b. Leonard Alfred
    Schneider)(ent.; 1926-66)
Lenny Kravitz (ent.)
Leno, Jay (ent.; 1950-)
Lens Plus™ (eye care)
Lent (rel., period of fasting)
Lenya, Lotte (ent.; 1898-1981)
Lenz, Heinrich (Estonian physt.; 1804-65)
Lenz's law (physics)
Leo (zodiac; astron., lion)
Leo Carillo
Leo Delibes, C(lement) P(hilibert)(Fr. comp.;
    1836-91)
Leo Durocher (baseball; 1906-91)
Leo F. Buscaglia
Leo G. Carroll (ent.; 1892-1972)
Leo Gorcey (ent.; 1915-69)
Leo Minor (astron.; little lion)
Leo Robin (US lyricist; 1900-84)
Leo (Calvin) Rosten, (pseud. Leonard Q.
    Ross)(US humorist/sociol.)
Leo Szilard (US/Hung. physt.; 1898-1964)
Leo (Nikolaievich) Tolstoy, Count (Rus. writer;
    1828-1910)
Leominster, MA
Leon Ames (ent.; 1903-1993)
Léon Bakst (Rus. artist/designer; 1867-1924)
Léon Blum (Fr. pol.; 1872-1950)
Leon E. Panetta (US Chief of Staff; 1938-)
Léon Gambetta, (Fr. pol.; 1838-82)

Leon Jaworski (US atty.; 1905-82)
Leon Spinks (boxing; 1953-)
Léon Trotsky (b. Lev Davidovich
    Bronstein)(USSR pol.; 1879-1940)
Leon Uris (US writer; 1924-)
Léon Victor Auguste Bourgeois (Fr. pol.; 1851-
    1925)
Léon, Mexico
Léon, Nicaragua
Léon, (Juan) Ponce de (Sp. expl.; c1460-1521)
Léon, Spain
Leona Helmsley (US bus./hotel; c1920-)
Leonard Bernstein (US comp./cond.; 1918-90)
Leonard Bloomfield (US linguist; 1887-1949)
Leonard "Chico" Marx (ent.; 1886-1961)
Leonard Nimoy (ent.; 1931-)
Leonard Q. Ross (aka Leo [Calvin] Rosten)(US
    humorist/sociol.)
Leonard Ray Dawson (football; 1935-)
Leonard Roscoe Tanner, III (tennis; 1951-)
Leonard Sidney Woolf (Br. writer; 1880-1969)
Leonard Slatkin (US cond.; 1944-)
Leonard Wood, Fort, MO (mil.)
Leonard, Benny (Benjamin Leiner)(boxing;
    1896-1947)
Leonard, Elmore (US writer; 1925-)
Leonard, Sheldon (ent.; 1907-)
Leonard, Sugar Ray (boxing; 1956-)
Leonardo da Vinci (It. artist/scien.; 1452-1519)
Leonardo Fibonacci (It. math.; c1175-c1250)
Leoncavallo, Ruggiero (It. comp.; 1857-1919)
Leonhard Euler (Swiss math./physt.; 1707-83)
Leonid Ilyich Brezhnev (ex-pres., USSR; 1906-
    82)
Leonid Kizim (cosmo.)
Leonid Kravchuk (pres., Ukraine; 1934-)
Leonids meteor shower (Nov.)
Leonine Wall (Vatican)
Leonov, Aleksei (Arkhipovich)(cosmo., 1st to
    walk in space; 1934-)
Leontyne Price, (Mary)(opera; 1927-)
Leopold (Antoni Stanislaw) Stokowski (US
    cond.; 1882-1977)
Leopoldo Galtieri (ex-pres., Argentina; 1926-)
Leopoldville (now Kinshasa)
Lepisma (insect)
Leppard, Def (pop music)
Lepping, George (gov-gen., Solomon Islands)
Lepus (astron., hare)
Lerner & Loewe (US song writing team)
Lerner, Alan Jay (US lyricist; 1918-86)
Leroy (Robert) "Satchel" Paige (baseball; 1906-
    82)
Leroy Anderson (US comp.; 1908-75)
Leroy Kelly (football; 1942-)
LeRoy, Mervyn (ent.; 1900-87)
Les Aspin (ex-US Secy./Defense; 1938-)
Les Brown (ent.; 1912-)

Les Cayes, Haiti
Les Escaldes, Andorra
Les Fauves (also l.c.)(Fauvist artists)
Les Miserables (V. Hugo novel)
Les Paul & Mary Ford (ent.)
Les Paul (US inv./ent.; 1915-)
Les Sylphides (ballet)
Les Tremayne
LeSabre Roadmaster, Buick™ (auto.)
LeSabre, Buick™ (auto.)
Lesage, Alain-René (Fr. writer; 1668-1747)
Lesbos Island (now Lesvos)(Gr.)
Lescoulie, Jack
Leskovac, Yugoslavia
Lesley Ann Warren (ent.; 1946-)
Lesley J. McNair, Fort (DC)(mil.)
Lesley Stahl (US TV jour.; 1941-)
Leslie-Ann Down (ent.; 1954-)
Leslie Caron (Fr./US ent.; 1931-)
Leslie Fay, Inc.
Leslie Nielsen (ent.; 1926-)
Leslie Uggams (ent.; 1943-)
Leslie, Joan (ent.; 1925-)
Lesotho (Kingdom of)(formerly Basutoland)(S
    Afr.)
Lesseps, Ferdinand de, Vicomte (Fr. dipl./eng.;
    1805-94)
Lesser Antilles, West Indies (Aruba,
    Netherlands Antilles, Trinidad and Tobago,
    Windward Islands, Leeward Islands)
Lesser Dog (also Little Dog, Canis
    Minor)(astron.)
Lessing, Doris (May Taylor)(Br. writer; 1919-)
Lessing, Gotthold (Ephraim)(Ger. writer; 1729-
    81)
Lester (Raymond) Flatt (ent.; 1914-79)
Lester Maddox (ex-gov., GA)
Lester (Bowles) Pearson (ex-PM, Can.; 1897-
    1972)
Lester "Pres" (Willis) Young (US jazz; 1909-59)
Lesvos Island (formerly Lesbos)(Gr.)
Lethal Weapon (film)
Lethal Weapon 2 (film)
Lethal Weapon 3 (film)
Lethbridge, Alberta, Canada
Lethe (myth.)
Let's Make a Deal (TV show)
Letsie III (king, Lesotho
Letterkenny Army Depot (PA)(mil.)
Letterman, David (ent.; 1947-)
Letterman, Late Night With David (TV show)
Lettermen, the (pop music)
Letters, Doctor of (also D. Litt., Doctor
    Litterarum)
Leutze, Emanuel (US artist; 1816-68)
Leuven, Belgium (also Louvain)
Levant leather/morocco
Levant, Oscar (ent.; 1906-72)

LeVar Burton (also Levar)(ent.; 1957-)
Levene, Sam (ent.; 1905-80)
Lever Brothers Co., Inc. (us bus.)
Levertov, Denise (Br./US poet; 1923-)
Lévesque, René (ex-premier, Quebec, Can.;
    1922-87)
Levi P(arsons) Morton (ex-US VP; 1824-1920)
Levi Strauss (US bus.; c1829-1902)
Levi Strauss Co.
Levi (Isr. tribe)
Levi's™
Lévi-Strauss, Claude (Fr. anthrop.; 1908-1990)
Leviathan (rel.)
Levin, Carl M. (US cong.; 1934-)
Levin, Ira (US writer; 1929-)
Levine, David (cartoonist; 1926-)
Levine, James (ent.; 1943-)
Levine, Irving R. (US TV jour.)
Levinson, Barry (ent.; 1932-)
Levites (people)
Leviticus (rel.)
Levitt, Arthur, Jr. (Chair/SEC; 1931-)
Levittown, NY
Levolor™ blinds
Levolor, Inc.
Levon Ter-Petrosyan (pres., Armenia; 1943-)
Levuka, Fiji
Lévy-Bruhl, Lucien (Fr. phil.; 1857-1939)
Levy Mwanawasa (VP, Zambia)
Lew(is) Alcindor, Jr. (aka Kareem Abdul-
    Jabbar)(basketball; 1947-)
Lew Ayres (ent.; 1908-)
Lew Wasserman
Lewin, Kurt (US psych.; 1890-1947)
Lewis and Clark Expedition (St. Louis to Pac.;
    1804-06)
Lewis and the News, Huey (pop music)
Lewis Carroll (aka Charles Dodgson)(Br. writer/
    math.; 1832-98)
Lewis F(ranklin) Powell, Jr. (US jurist; 1907-)
Lewis Galoob, Inc.
Lewis Mumford (US writer/sociol.; 1895-1990)
Lewis structure/symbol (chem.)
Lewis, Anthony
Lewis, Sir (William) Arthur (Br. econ.; 1915-91)
Lewis, (Frederick) Carl(eton)(track; 1961-)
Lewis, Cecil Day (Ir. poet; 1904-72)
Lewis, C(live) S(taples)("Clive Hamilton")(Br.
    writer; 1898-1963)
Lewis, Daniel Day- (ent.; 1957-)
Lewis, Dawnn (ent.; 1960-)
Lewis, Emmanuel (ent.; 1971-)
Lewis, Jerry (b. Joseph Levitch)(ent.; 1926-)
Lewis, Jerry Lee (ent.; 1935-)
Lewis, Joe E. (ent.; 1902-71)
Lewis, John (US jazz; 1920-)
Lewis, John L(lewellyn)(US labor leader; 1880-
    1969)

Lewis, John R. (US cong.; 1940-)
Lewis, Lennox (boxing; 1965-)
Lewis, Mel (US jazz; 1929-90)
Lewis, Meriwether (US expl.; 1774-1809)
Lewis, Ramsey (US jazz)
Lewis, Reggie (basketball; 1966-93)
Lewis, Richard (ent.; 1947-)
Lewis, Robert Q. (ent.; 1920-91)
Lewis, Shari (ent.; 1934-)
Lewis, (Harry) Sinclair (US writer; 1885-1951)
Lewiston, ME
Lexington Blue Grass Army Depot (KY)
Lexington Herald-Leader (KY newspaper)
Lexington, Battle of (US hist.; 1775)
Lexington, KY, MA, NC
Lexis (compu. database, law)
Lexus (auto.)
Lexus SC300 (auto.)
Leyden jar (elec.)
L(yman) Frank Baum (US writer; 1856-1919)
L(eroy) Gordon Cooper, Jr. (astro.; 1927-)
Lhasa apso (dog)
Lhasa, Tibet, China
LH sedan, Chrysler (auto.)
Li (chem. sym., lithium)
Li Peng (PM, Ch.; 1928-)
Li (Tai) Po (Ch. poet; 705-62)
Li'l Abner (fict. chara.)
Liam Cosgrave (ex-PM, Ir.; 1920-)
Liam O'Flaherty (Ir. writer; 1897-1984)
Liaoning (province, Ch.)
Liaquat Ali Khan, (ex-PM, Pak.; 1895-1951)
Libbey™
Libbey Glass (US bus.)
Liber (It. myth.)
Liberace (b. Wladziu Valentino)(US pianist; 1919-87)
Liberal Party (Br. pol.; 1830-)
Liberal Party (US pol.; 1944-)
Liberal Party, Australian (Austl. pol.)
Liberal Republican Party (US pol.)
Liberation Army of Palestine (also Intifada)(est. 1987)
Liberia (Republic of)(W Afr.)
Libertarian Party (US pol.)
Liberty Bell (Philadelphia)
Liberty Bell 7 (also Mercury-Redstone 3)(1st US crewed space flight; May 5, 1961)
Liberty Bowl (college football)
Liberty Island (formerly Bedloe's or Bedloe Island)(NY)
Liberty Party (US pol.; 1840-48)
Liberty, Sons of (US hist.; 1765-66)
Liberty, Statue of (NYC)
Libra (zodiac; astron., balance)
Library of Alexandria (Eg.)
Library of Congress (DC)
Libreville, Gabon

Librium™ (med.)
Libya (Socialist People's Libyan Arab Jamahiriya)(N Afr.)
Libyan Desert (N Afr.)
Lichtenstein, Roy (US artist; 1923-)
Liddy, G. Gordon (US pol./Watergate)
Lidice, Czechoslovakia
Lie, Trygve H(alvdan)(Nor. pol./UN; 1896-1968)
Lieberman, Joseph I. (US cong.; 1942-)
Lieberman, Nancy
Liebermann, Max (Ger. artist; 1847-1935)
Liebfraumilch (wine)
Liebig condenser (chem.)
Liebig, Justus von, Baron (Ger. chem.; 1803-73)
Liechtenstein (Principality of)(W Eur.)
Liederkranz™ (cheese)
Liège (province, Belgium)
Liege, Belgium
Lien Chan (premier, Taiwan)
Liepaja, Lativa
Liepzig, Germany
Life (mag.)
Life Books, Time- (US bus.)
Life Guards (Br.)
Life of Riley, The (TV show, film)
Life With Father (play/film)
Lifebuoy™ (soap)
LifeSavers™
LifeSavers Co., Planters
Lifestyles of the Rich and Famous (TV show)
Lifetime (LIF)(cable TV)
Liggett, Fort Hunter (CA)(mil.)
Light-Horse Harry (Henry) Lee (US gen.; 1756-1818)
Light, City of (Paris)
Light, Judith (ent.; 1950-)
Light, San Antonio (TX newspaper)
Lightfoot, Gordon (ent.; 1938-)
Lightnin' (play/film)
Lightning, Tampa Bay (hockey team)
Lihue, HI
Lila Wallace (Acheson)(US publ.; 1889-1984)
Lilic, Zoran (pres., Yug.)
Lilith (myth.)
Liliuokalani (Lydia Kamekeha)(queen, Hawaii; 1838-1917)
Lille, France
Lillehammer, Norway
Lilli Lehmann (Ger. opera; 1848-1929)
Lilli Palmer (ent.; 1914-86)
Lillian Gish (ent.; 1895-1993)
Lillian (Florence) Hellman (US writer; 1905-84)
Lillian Russell (b. Helen Louise Leonard)(ent.; 1861-1922)
Lillian Vernon™
Lillian Vernon Corp.
Lillie Langtry ("the Jersey Lily")(b. Emily Charlotte le Breton)(Br. ent.; 1853-1929)

Lillie, Beatrice (ent.; 1894-1989)
Lilliput (fict. land, *Gulliver's Travels*)
Lilliputian (fict. charas., *Gulliver's Travels)*
Lilly (or Lyly, Lily), John (Br. writer; 1554?-1606)
Lilly & Company, Eli
Lilongwe, Malawi
Lilt™ (hair care)
Lily Pons (ent.; 1904-76)
Lily Tomlin (ent.; 1939-)
Lily (or Lyly, Lilly), John (Br. writer; 1554?-1606)
Lily(e), William (Br. scholar; c1468-1522)
Lima, OH
Lima, Peru
Limassol, Cyprus
Limbaugh, Rush (TV commentator)
Limbo (rel.)
Limburg (province, Belgium)
Limburg (province, Netherlands)
Limburger (also Limburg)(cheese)
Limehouse district (London)
Limelight
Limerick (county, Ir.)
Limited, Inc., The
Limoges china/ware
Limoges, France
Limón Dance Company, José
Limón, Costa Rica (also Puerto Limón)
Limón, José (Mex./US dancer; 1908-72)
Limousin (region, Fr.)
Limousine Liberal
Lina Wertmüller (It. ent.; 1926?-)
Lincoln Center for the Performing Arts
Lincoln-Douglas debates (US hist.; 1858)
Lincoln green (color)
Lincoln Journal (NE newspaper)
Lincoln Mark VIII
Lincoln Memorial (DC)
Lincoln-Mercury Continental (auto.)
Lincoln-Mercury Cougar (auto.)
Lincoln-Mercury Mark (auto.)
Lincoln-Mercury Sable (auto.)
Lincoln-Mercury Topaz (auto.)
Lincoln-Mercury Town Car (auto.)
Lincoln Monument (IL)
Lincoln Star (NE newspaper)
Lincoln Steffens, (Joseph)(US writer; 1866-1926)
Lincoln, Abraham (16th US pres.; 1809-65)
Lincoln, Benjamin (US mil./pol.; 1722-1810)
Lincoln, England
Lincoln, IL, NE, RI
Lincoln, Mary Todd (wife of A. Lincoln; 1818-82)
Lincoln, Robert Todd (US atty., A. Lincoln's son; 1843-1926)
Lincolnshire (county, Eng.)(also Lincoln)

Lind, Jenny (Johanna Maria Lind Goldschmidt, "The Swedish Nightingale")(ent.; 1820-87)
Linda Blair (ent.; 1959-)
Linda Bloodworth-Thomason (ent.)
Linda Darnell (ent.; 1921-65)
Linda Ellerbee
Linda Evans (ent.; 1942-)
Linda Fratianne (figure skating; 1960-)
Linda Gray (ent.; 1940-)
Linda Hamilton (ent.)
Linda Hunt (ent.; 1945-)
Linda Jezek (swimming; 1960-)
Linda Kozlowski (ent.)
Linda Lavin (ent.; 1937-)
Linda Myers (archery; 1947-)
Linda Ronstadt (ent.; 1946-)
Lindal Cedar™
Lindal Cedar Homes, Inc.
Lindbergh kidnapping
Lindbergh, Anne Spencer (Morrow)(US writer/aviator; 1906-)
Lindbergh, Charles A(ugustus)(US aviator; 1902-74)
Linden, Hal (ent.; 1931-)
Lindros, Eric (hockey; 1973-)
Lindsay™
Lindsay Boatbuilders, Mark (US bus.)
Lindsay Crouse (ent.; 1948-)
Lindsay International (US bus.)
Lindsay Olive Growers (US bus.)
Lindsay Wagner (ent.; 1949-)
Lindsay, John (Vliet)(ex-mayor, NYC; 1921-)
Lindsay, (Nicholas) Vachel (US poet; 1879-1931)
Lindy Hop (dance)(also l.c.)
Linehan, Kim (swimming; 1962-)
Lingala (lang.)
Lingayat (rel.)
Lingayata (rel.)
Linkletter, Art (ent.; 1912-)
Linn-Baker, Mark (ent.; 1953-)
Linotype™ (publ.)
Linus (fict. chara., *Peanuts*)
Linus (myth.)
Linus C(arl) Pauling (US chem.; 1901)
Linzer torte (pastry)
Lion-Hearted, Richard the (or Coeur de Lion, Richard I)(king, Eng.; 1157-99)
Lion King, The (film)
Lion, William the (king, Scot.; 1143-1214)
Lionel Barrymore (ent.; 1878-1954)
Lionel de Rothschild (Br. finan.; 1882-1942)
Lionel Hampton (US jazz; 1913-)
Lionel Nathan Rothschild, Baron de ("Lord Natty")(Br. finan./pol.; 1808-79)
Lionel Richie (ent.; 1950-)
Lionel Trilling (US writer/educ.; 1905-75)
Lions Club (US org.; est. 1917)

Lions, Detroit (football team)
Lions, Gulf of (S Fr.)
Lipari Islands (It.)
Lipchitz, Jacques (US sculptor; 1891-1973)
Lipizaner horse
Lippi, Filippo (or Filippino)(It. artist; 1457-1504)
Lippi, Fra Filippo (It. artist; 1406-69)
Lippmann, Walter (US jour.; 1889-1974)
Liptauer (cheese)
Lipton™ tea
Lipton, Inc., Thomas J.
Lipton, Peggy (ent.)
Lipton, Sir Thomas J(ohnstone)(Scot. bus., tea; 1850-1931)
Liquid Paper™
Liquid Paper Corp.
Liquid-plumr™
Liquori, Marty (runner; 1949-)
Lisa Bonet (ent.; 1967-)
Lisa Eichhorn (ent.; 1952-)
Lisa Gregory
Lisa Hartman (ent.; 1956-)
Lisa, Mona (aka *La Gioconda*)(da Vinci painting)
Lisbon, Portugal
Lisieux, St. Thérèse of (Fr. rel.; 1873-97)
Lissouba, Pascal (pres., Congo; 1931-)
Lister, Joseph, Baron (Br. phys., antiseptic surgery; 1827-1912)
Listerine™ (med.)
Listermint™ (med.)
Liston, Sonny (Charles)(boxing; 1933-71)
Liszt, Franz (Hung. comp.; 1811-86)
Literary Guild, The
Literary Magazine Review
Literature, Nobel Prize for
Lithgow, John (ent.; 1945-)
Lithuania (Republic of)(formerly part of USSR)(N Eur.)
Lithuanian (lang./people)
Little Anthony and the Imperials (pop music)
Little Bighorn, Battle of the (also Custer's Last Stand)(US/Sioux Indians; 1876)
Little Bo-Peep (fict. chara.)
Little Boy Blue (nursery rhyme)
Little Chickadee, My (film)
Little Corporal (Napoleon Bonaparte)
Little Dipper (also Ursa Minor)(astron.)
Little Dog (also Lesser Dog, Canis Minor)(astron.)
Little House on the Prairie (TV show)
Little Iodine (comic strip)
Little Jack Horner (nursery rhyme)
Little Jimmy Dickens (ent.)
Little John (fict. chara., *Robin Hood*)
Little King (comic strip)
Little League (baseball)

Little Leaguer (baseball)
Little Lord Fauntleroy (book by F. H. Burnett)
Little Lord Fauntleroy suit
Little Mermaid, The (film)
Little Miss Muffett (nursery rhyme)
Little Orphan Annie (fict. chara.)
Little Professor Book Centers, Inc.
Little Rascals (TV show)
Little Red Ridinghood (fairy tale)
Little Richard (b. Richard Penniman)(ent.; 1932-)
Little Rock Air Force Base (AR)(mil.)
Little Rock Democrat-Gazette (AR newspaper)
Little Rock, AR
Little Shop of Horrors (film; 1960, 1986)
Little Turtle, Chief (Michikinikwa)(Miami Indians; 1752?-1812)
Little Women (Meg, Jo, Beth & Amy March)(L.M. Alcott novel)
Little, Brown & Co., Inc.
Little, Chicken (fict. chara.)
Little, Cleavon (ent.; 1939-92)
Little, Floyd Douglas (football; 1942-)
Little, Lou (football; 1893-1979)
Little, Malcolm (aka Malcolm X)(US black-rights activist; 1926-65)
Little, Rich (ent.; 1938-)
Little, Stuart (E.B. White novel)
Littler, Gene (golf; 1930-)
Litton™
Litton Industries, Inc.
Liturgy of the Hours (also Divine Office)(rel.)
Litvinov, Maxim (USSR pol.; 1876-1951)
Liu Shaoqi (also Liu Shao-chi)(Ch. pol.; 1898?-1969?)
Liv Ullmann (ent.; 1938-)
Livarot (cheese)
Livermore Laboratory, Lawrence (nuclear research, CA)
Livermore, CA
Liverpool, England
Living Theatre (NYC/Eur.)
Livingston, Robert (US pol.; 1654-1728)
Livingston, Robert R. (US pol.; 1746-1813)
Livingstone, Dr. David (Scot. rel./expl. in Afr.; 1813-73)
Livingstone, (Sir Henry) Stanley and (Dr. David)
Livingstone, Zambia
Livonia, MI
Livy, Titus Livius (Roman hist.; 59 BC-AD 17
Liz Claiborne™ (clothing)
Liz Claiborne (US designer; 1929-)
Liz Claiborne, Inc.
Liz Smith (US jour.; 1923-)
Liza Minnelli (ent.; 1946-)
Lizabeth Scott (ent.; 1922-)
Lizzie A. Borden (US, tried/acquitted of ax

murders; 1860-1927)
Ljubljana, Slovenia
Lladró porcelain
Lladro USA, Ltd.
LL.B. (Legum Baccalaureus [Bachelor of Laws])
L. L. Bean™ (clothing)
L. L. Bean, Inc.
L. L. Cool (pop music)
LL.D. (Legum Doctor [Doctor of Laws])
Llewelyn I (king, Wales; 1173-1240)
Llewelyn II (king, Wales; c1225-1282)
LL.M. (Legum Magister [Master of Laws])
Lloyd Bentsen (US Secy./Treasury; 1921-)
Lloyd Bridges (ent.; 1913-)
Lloyd "Cowboy" Copas (ent.)
Lloyd Eisler (figure skating; 1964-)
Lloyd George, David (ex-PM, Br.; 1863-1945)
Lloyd M. Bucher, Commander (US mil.)
Lloyd Nolan (ent.; 1902-85)
Lloyd Price (ent.)
Lloyd Webber, Andrew (Br. comp.; 1948-)
Lloyd, Chris Evert- (tennis; 1954-)
Lloyd, Christopher (ent.; 1938-)
Lloyd, Emily (ent.; 1970-)
Lloyd, Harold (ent.; 1893-1971)
Lloyd's™
Lloyd's Electronics, Inc.
Lloyd's of London
LMT (local mean time)
LNG (liquefied natural gas)
Lobito, Angola
Lobos, Heitor Villa- (Brazilian comp.; 1881-1959)
lobster Newburg (food)
Loc, Tone (pop music)
Local Group (of galaxies)(astron.)
Loch Lomond (Scot. lake)
Loch Ness (lake, Scot.)
Loch Ness monster (Scot.)
Lochaber ax (Scot. weapon; 16th c)
Lochinvar (fict. chara., *Marmion*)
Lochner v. New York (US law; 1905)
Locke, David Ross (aka Petroleum V(esuvius) Nasby)(US humorist; 1833-88)
Locke, John (Br. phil.; 1632-1704)
Locke, Sondra (ent..; 1947-)
Lockhart, Gene (ent.; 1891-1957)
Lockhart, June (ent.; 1925-)
Lockheed Corp.
Locklear, Heather (ent.; 1961-)
Lockport, NY
Lodge, Henry Cabot (US pol.; 1850-1924)
Lodge, Henry Cabot, Jr. (US jour./pol.; 1902-85)
Lodi, CA, NJ
Lodi, Italy
Lodovico (or Ludovico) Carracci (It. artist; 1555-1619)
Lódz, Poland

Loesser, Frank (US comp.; 1910-69)
Loewe v. Lawler (US law; 1908)
Loewe, Frederick (US comp.; 1901-88)
Loewe, Lerner & (US song writing team)
Loews Corp.
Loft's Candies, Inc., Barricini/
Logan International Airport (Boston MA)
Logan, Inc., Jonathan
Logan, Joshua (US writer/ent.; 1908-88)
Logan, UT
Logan's Run (film; 1976)
Loggia, Robert (ent.; 1930-)
Loggins & Messina (pop music)
Loggins, Kenny (ent.; 1947-)
Lohengrin (Wagner opera)
Lohr Winery, J. (US bus.)
Loire River (Fr.)
Loire Valley (Fr. wine region)
Lois, Hi & (comic strip)
Lojze Peterle (Slovenian pol.)
Loki (myth.)
Lola Montez (ent.; 1818?-61)
Lolita (seductive young girl)
Lolita (V. Nabokov novel)
Lollobrigida, Gina (It. ent.; 1927-)
Lolo Falana (ent.; 1946-)
Loman, Willy (fict. chara., *Death of a Salesman*)
Lomb™, Bausch & (eye care)
Lomb, Inc., Bausch &
Lombard (banker/moneylender)
Lombard (people)
Lombard, Carole (b. Jane Alice Peters)(ent.; 1909-42)
Lombardi, Vince(nt Thomas)(football; 1913-70)
Lombardo, Guy (Albert)(ent.; 1902-77)
Lombardy (region, It.)
Lomé, Togo
Lomond, Loch (Scot. lake)
Lompoc, CA
Lomwe (lang./people)
Lon Chaney (ent.; 1883-1930)
Lon Chaney, Jr. (ent.; 1905-73)
London Bridge (now in AZ)
London broil
London Fog™ (raincoat)
London, England
London, Jack (John Griffith)(US writer; 1876-1916)
London, Julie (ent.; 1926-)
London, Ontario, Canada
London, Tower of (fortress; built 1078)
London, Treaty of (Br./Fr./Rus./It.; 1915)
Londonderry (county, NIre.)
Londonderry, Northern Ireland (now Derry)
Lone Ranger & Tonto (fict charas.)
Lone Star State (nickname, TX)
Lonette McKee (ent.; 1957-)
Long Beach Press-Telegram (CA newspaper)

Proper Noun Speller

Long Beach, CA, NY
Long Branch, NJ
Long Island Expressway (NYC)
Long Island iced tea (mixed drink)
Long Island Newsday (NY newspaper)
Long Island Sound (NY/CT)
Long Island, NY
Long John Silver's Seafood Shoppes (US bus.)
Long March (Ch. hist.; 1934-35)
Long Tom (WWII weapon)
Long, Huey P(ierce)("the Kingfish")(ex-gov., LA;
   1893-1935)
Long, Richard (ent.; 1927-77)
Long, Shelley (ent.; 1949-)
Longboat Key, FL
Longden, Johnny (horse racing; 1907-)
Longevity (mag.)
Longfellow, Henry Wadsworth (US poet; 1807-
   82)
Longford (county, Ir.)
Longhorn (cattle)
Longinus, Dionysius (Gr. critic; 1st c. AD)
Longmont, CO
Longs Drugs™
Longs Drug Stores, Inc.
Longstocking, Pippi (fict. chara.,
Longstreet, James (US gen.; 1821-1904)
Longueuil, Quebec, Canada
Longview, TX, WA
Loni Anderson (ent.; 1946-)
Look Who's Talking (film)
Look Who's Talking too (film)
Looking for Mr. Goodbar (film; 1977)
LOOM (Loyal Order of Moose)
Looney Tunes (cartoon)
Loos, Anita (US writer; 1888?-1981)
Lo/Ovral™ (med.)
Lopat, Eddie (baseball; 1918-92)
Lope (Félix) de Vega (Carpio)(Sp. writer; 1562-
   1635)
Lopez, Al (baseball; 1908-)
Lopez, Nancy (golf; 1957-)
Lopid™ (med.)
Lopressor™ (med.)
Lorado Taft (US sculptor; 1860-1936)
Lorain, OH
Lord & Taylor™
Lord & Taylor (US bus.)
Lord (God, Jesus)
Lord Baltimore (aka Sir George
   Calvert)(founded MD; 1606-75)
Lord Beaverbrook, Baron (aka William Maxwell
   Beaverbrook)(Brit. finan./pol.; 1879-1964)
Lord Byron (George Gordon)(Br. poet; 1788-
   1824)
Lord Fauntleroy suit, Little
Lord Fauntleroy, Little (book by F. H. Burnett)
Lord Greystoke (fict. chara., *Tarzan*)

Lord High Chancellor (Br.)(also Lord
   Chancellor)
Lord of hosts (God)
Lord of lords (Jesus Christ)
Lord of Misrule (former Christmas revelry
   director, Br.)
Lord of the Flies (W. Golding novel)
Lord of the Rings (J.R.R. Tolkien book)
Lord Peter Wimsey (fict. chara., D. Sayers)
Lord Tennyson, Alfred (Br. poet; 1809-92)
Lord, Jack (ent.; 1922-)
Lord's day, the (Sunday)
Lord's Prayer (also *Our Father, Paternoster*
   [*Pater Noster*])(prayer)
Lord's Supper (also Holy Communion,
   Eucharist)(rel.)
Lords, House of (Br. parliament)
Lords, Traci (ent.)
L'Oréal™
L'Oréal Cosmetics (US bus.)
L'Oréal Hair Care (US bus.)
Lorelei (Ger. folklore)
Loren, Sophia (b. Sophia Scicoloni)(It. ent.;
   1934-)
Lorena Bobbitt (US news)
Lorenz curve (econ.)
Lorenz Hart (US lyricist; 1895-1943)
Lorenzo de' Medici ("the Magnificent")(It. poet/
   pol.; 1449-92)
Lorenzo Ghiberti (It. sculptor; 1378-1455)
Lorenzo Lamas (ent.; 1958-)
Lorenzo, Frank
Loretta Lynn (Webb)(ent.; 1935-)
Loretta Swit (ent.; 1937-)
Loretta Young (ent.; 1913-)
Lorimar (US bus.)
Loring Air Force Base, ME (mil.)
Loring, Eugene (dancer/choreographer)
Loring, Gloria (ent.; 1946-)
Lorna Doone (R.D. Blackmore novel)
Lorna Luft (ent.)
Lorne Greene (ent.; 1915-87)
Lorrain, Claude (Fr. artist; 1600-82)
Lorraine (region, Fr.)
Lorraine Bracco (ent.; 1955-)
Lorraine Hansberry (US writer; 1930-65)
Lorraine, cross of
Lorraine, quiche
Lorre, Peter (b. Lázló Löwenstein)(ent.; 1904-
   64)
Lorus™ watch
Lorus (US bus.)
Los Alamos Scientific Laboratory (NM)
Los Alamos, NM
Los Angeleno (also Angeleno)(native of Los
   Angeles)
Los Angeles (mag.)
Los Angeles Basin

Los Angeles Clippers (basketball team)
Los Angeles County Museum
Los Angeles Dodgers (baseball team)
Los Angeles International Airport (CA)
Los Angeles Kings (hockey team)
Los Angeles Lakers (basketball team)
Los Angeles News (CA newspaper)
Los Angeles Raiders (football team)
Los Angeles Rams (football team)
Los Angeles Times (CA newspaper)
Los Angeles Times Book Review
Los Angeles, CA
Lost Colony (VA settlement; disappeared 1591)
Lost Generation, the (US lit.; 1920s)
Lot (rel.)
Lothario (also l.c.)(seducer/deceiver of women)
Lothian (region, Scot.)
Lotophagi (lotus-eaters)(myth.)
Lotos-Eaters, The (by Tennyson)
Lotrimin™ (med.)
Lott, Ronnie (football; 1959-)
Lott, Trent (US cong.; 1941-)
Lotta Crabtree (ent.; 1847-1924)
Lotte Lehmann (Ger. opera; 1888-1976)
Lotte Lenya (ent.; 1898-1981)
Lottery Case (also *Champion v. Ames*)(US law; 1903)
Lotus™ (auto.)
Lotus Development Corp.
Lotus 1-2-3™ (comp. software)
Lotus Sutra (rel.)
Lotus/Cars USA, Inc.
Lou(is Clark) Brock (baseball; 1939-)
Lou Costello (b. Louis Francis Cristillo)(ent.; 1906-59)
Lou Diamond Phillips (ent.; 1962-)
Lou Ferrigno (ent.)
Lou(is) Gehrig, (Henry)(baseball; 1903-41)
Lou Gehrig's disease (med.)
Lou Groza (football; 1924-)
Lou Little (football; 1893-1979)
Lou Rawls (ent.; 1936-)
Lou Reed (ent.; 1942-)
Loubomo, Congo
Loudon, Dorothy (ent.; 1933-)
Louella Parsons (US gossip columnist)
Louganis, Greg(ory)(US diver; 1960-)
Lough Neagh (lake, NIre.)
Louis (Rodolphe) Agassiz, (Jean)(Swiss nat.; 1807-73)
Louis-Antoine de Bougainville (Fr. nav.; 1729-1811)
Louis Antoine Godey (US publ.; 1804-78)
Louis "Satchmo" Armstrong (US jazz; 1900-71)
Louis Blanc, (Jean Joseph Charles)(Fr. socialist/hist.; 1811-82)
Louis Blériot (Fr. aviator; 1872-1936)
Louis B(urt) Mayer (ent.; 1885-1957)

Louis Bonaparte (bro. of Napoleon, king, Holland; 1778-1846)
Louis Botha (ex-PM, SAfr.; 1863-1919)
Louis Braille (Fr., blind inv. of Braille; 1809-52)
Louis (Dembitz) Brandeis (US jurist; 1856-1941)
Louis Calhern (ent.; 1895-1956)
Louis de Broglie (Fr. physt.; 1893-1987)
Louis de Frontenac (Fr./Can. gov.; 1620-98)
Louis(-Joseph) de (Montcalm-Gozon) Montcalm (Fr. mil.; 1712-59)
Louis de Rouvroy Saint-Simon, Duc de (Fr. mil./writer; 1675-1755)
Louis-Dreyfus, Julia (ent.; 1961-)
Louis Farrakhan (Islam/US rel.)
Louis Freeh (dir., FBI)
Louis Gossett, Jr. (ent.; 1936-)
Louis Harris (US pollster/writer; 1921-)
Louis Hector Berlioz (Fr. comp.; 1803-69)
Louis I ("the Pious)(Holy Roman emp.; 788-840)
Louis III ("the Child")(king, Ger.; 893-911)
Louis III (king, Fr.; 863-82)
Louis IV (d'Outremer)(king, Fr.; 921-54)
Louis Jacques Mande Daguerre (Fr. photo.; 1789-1851)
Louis Joliet (or Jolliet)(Fr./Can. expl.; 1645-1700)
Louis Jourdan (Fr. ent.; 1919-)
Louis Kahn (US arch.; 1901-74)
Louis (Dearborn) L'Amour (US writer; 1908-88)
Louis (Jean) Lumière (Fr. inv.; 1864-1948)
Louis Malle (Fr. ent.; 1932-)
Louis M. Martini Winery (US bus.)
Louis Moreau Gottschalk (US comp.; 1829-69)
Louis Mountbatten, Lord (Br. adm./earl; 1900-79)
Louis Nye (ent.)
Louis Pasteur (Fr. chem.; 1822-95)
Louis Philippe ("Philippe Egalité" "the Citizen King")(king, Fr.; 1773-1850)
Louis Prima (ent.; 1911-78)
Louis Quatorze style (Louis XIV, classic)
Louis Quinze style (Louis XV)(rococo)
Louis Rich™ (meats)
Louis Rich Co.
Louis S(eymour) B(azett) Leakey (Br. archaeol..; 1903-72)
Louis Seize style (Louis XVI, classic revival)
Louis S(tephen) St. Laurent (ex-PM, Can.;1882-1973)
Louis Stanton Auchincloss (US writer; 1917-)
Louis (Comfort) Tiffany (US artist/glassmaker; 1848-1933)
Louis Treize style (Louis XIII, baroque)
Louis VII (king, Fr.; c1120-80)
Louis Whitley Strieber
Louis X ("the Stubborn")(king, Fr.; 1289-1316)
Louis XI (king, Fr.; 1423-83)

Proper Noun Speller

Louis XII (king, Fr.; 1462-1515)
Louis XIII (king, Fr.; 1601-43)
Louis XIII style (Louis Treize, baroque)
Louis XIV ("the Sun King" "the Great")(king, Fr.; 1638-1715)
Louis XIV style (Louis Quatorze, classic)
Louis XV (king, Fr.; 1710-74)
Louis XV style (Louis Quinze, rococo)
Louis XVI (king, Fr.; 1754-93)
Louis XVI style (Louis Seize, classic revival)
Louis XVIII (king, Fr.; 1755-1824)
Louis, Joe (b. Joseph Louis Barrow)(boxing; 1914-81)
Louis, Morris (US artist; 1912-62)
Louis, Port (Mauritius)
Louisa May Alcott (US writer; 1832-88)
Louise Bourgeois (Fr./US sculptor; 1911-)
Louise Dresser (ent.; 1881-1965)
Louise Fletcher (ent.; 1936-)
Louise Lasser (ent.; 1939-)
Louise Mandrell (ent.)
Louise Nevelson (Rus./US sculptor; 1900-88)
Louise, Lake (Can.)
Louise, Marie (empress, Fr.; 1791-1847)
Louisiana (LA)
Louisiana French (Cajun)
Louisiana Purchase (US hist.; 1803)
Louisiana Territory
Louisville Courier-Journal (KY newspaper)
Louisville, KY
Lourdes, France
Lousma, Jack R(obert)(astro.; 1936-)
Louth (county, Ir.)
Louvain, Belgium (also Leuven)
L'Ouverture, François Toussaint (Haitian pol.; c1744-1803)
Louvre (Paris art museum)
Love and War (TV show)
Love at First Bite (film; 1979)
Love Connection (TV show)
Love Story (E. Segal's novel)
Love, American Style (TV show)
Lovecraft, H(oward) P(hillips)(US writer; 1890-1937)
Lovejoy, Frank (ent.; 1912-62)
Lovelace, Lady (aka Augusta Ada Byron)(Br. math./inv., compu.; 1815-52)
Lovelace, Richard (Br. poet; 1618-58)
Loveland, CO
Lovell, Sir (Alfred Charles) Bernard (Br. astron.; 1931-)
Lovell, James A, Jr. (astro.; 1928-)
Love's Baby Soft™
Love's Labour's Lost (Shakespeare comedy)
Lovin' Spoonful (pop music)
Loving (TV soap)
Loving v. Virginia (US law; 1967)
Lovis Corinth (Ger. artist; 1858-1925)

Lovitz, John (ent.; 1957-)
Low Church (rel.)
Low Countries (region, Eur.: Belgium/Netherlands/Luxembourg)
Low Sunday (also Quasimodo)(1st Sunday after Easter)
Low, Juliette (Gordon)(US, founded Girl Scouts; 1860-1927)
Lowe, Rob (ent.; 1964-)
Lowell National Historical Park (MA)
Lowell North (yachting; 1929-)
Lowell Weicker (CT gov.; 1931-)
Lowell, Amy (US poet; 1874-1925)
Lowell, James Russell (US poet/editor; 1819-91)
Lowell, MA
Lowell, Percival (US astron.; 1855-1916)
Lowell, Robert (US poet; 1917-77)
Lower California (also Baja California)
Lower Paleolithic period (early Old Stone Age; 200,000 to 2 million years ago)
Lower Saxony (state, Ger.)
Lowe's Companies, Inc.
Lowestoft porcelain
Lowestoft, England
Lowlands (Scot. area)
Lowry, Mike (WA gov.)
LOX (liquid oxygen)
Loxitane™ (med.)
Loy, Myrna (ent.; 1905-93)
Loyal Order of Moose
Loyola College (Baltimore)
Loyola University (New Orleans)
Loyola, St. Ignatius of (aka Iñigo de Oñez y Loyola)(Sp. rel.; 1491-1556)
Lozada, Gonzalo Sánchez de (pres., Bolivia)
LPG (liquefied petroleum gas)
LPM (lines per minute)
LPN (licensed practical nurse)
Lr (chem. sym., lawrencium)
L(afayette) Ron(ald) Hubbard (US writer/rel., Scientology; 1911-86)
L.S. (locus sigilli [the place of the seal])
LSAT (Law School Administration Test)
LSD (lysergic acid diethylamid, least significant digit)
LSS Holdings Corp.
Luanda, Angola (formerly Loanda)
Luang Prabang, Laos
Luann (cartoon chara.)
Luann Ryon (archery; 1953-)
Luanshya, Zambia
Luba-Lulua (also Chiluba)(lang.)
Luba-Shaba (lang.)
Lubango, Angola
Lubbers, Rudd (Rudolph Franz Marie)(PM, Netherlands; 1939-)
Lubbock Avalanche-Journal (TX newspaper)
Lubbock, TX

Lübeck, Germany
Lubitsch, Ernst (Ger. ent.; 1892-1947)
Lublin, Poland
Lubovitch, Lar (US dance; 1945-)
Lubriderm™ (skin care)
Lubu (lang.)
Lubumbashi, Zaire
Luby's Cafeterias, Inc.
Luca (d'Egidio di Ventura de') Signorelli (It. artist; c1445-1523)
Luca della Robbia (It. artist; 1400-82)
Lucan (aka Marcus Annaeus Lucanus)(Roman poet; 39-65)
Lucas Industries, Inc.
Lucas Samaras (US sculptor; 1936-)
Lucas, George W., Jr. (ent.; 1944-)
Lucci, Susan (ent.; 1948-)
Luce, Clare Boothe (US drama./dipl./pol.; 1903-87)
Luce, Henry Robinson (US publ.; 1898-1967)
Lucerne, Switzerland, (also Luzern)
Luci Baines Johnson (daughter, US pres.; 1947-)
Lucian (Gr. writer; c125-c190)
Luciano Pavarotti (It. opera; 1935-)
Luciano, Lucky (Salvatore)(US Mafia; 1899-1962)
Lucie Arnaz (ent.; 1951-)
Lucien Bonaparte (bro. of Napoleon, prince, Canino; 1775-1840)
Lucien Lévy-Bruhl (Fr. phil.; 1857-1939)
Lucientes, Francisco (José) de Goya y (Sp. artist; 1746-1828)
Lucifer (the devil)
Lucilius, Gaius (Roman poet; c180-c102 BC)
Lucille Ball (ent.; 1911-89)
Lucite™ (plastic)
Lucius Apuleius (Roman satirist/atty.; c124-c170 BC)
Lucius D. Clay (US gen.; 1897-1978)
Lucius Licinius Lucullus (Roman gen.; 110-56 BC)
Luckinbill, Laurence (ent.; 1934-)
Luckman, Sid (football; 1916-)
Lucknow, India
Lucky Charms™ (cereal)
Lucky (Salvatore) Luciano (US Mafia; 1899-1962)
Lucretia (legendary Roman heroine)
Lucretia (Coffin) Mott (US suffragist; 1793-1880)
Lucretius (Carus), Titus (Roman poet/phil.; c99-c55 BC)
Lucrezia Borgia (It., Duchess of Ferrara; 1480-1519)
Lucullus, Lucius Licinius (Roman gen.; 110-56 BC)
Lucy (fict. chara., *Peanuts*)

Lucy (skeletal remains of female hominid found in Ethiopia)
Lucy Show, The (TV show)
Lucy Stone (US suffragist; 1818-93)
Lucy Stoner (married woman who keeps maiden name)
Lüda, China (also Hüta)
Ludd, Ned (also Lludd, Nudd, King Ludd)(Welsh legend)
Ludden, Allen
Luden's, Inc.
Ludlum, Robert (US writer; 1927-)
Ludovico (or Lodovico) Carracci (It. artist; 1555-1619)
Ludovico Sforza ("The Moor")(It. pol.; 1451-1508)
Ludwig Boltzmann (Aus. physt.; 1844-1906)
Ludwig Erhard (ex-chanc., WGer.; 1897-1977)
Ludwig Mies van der Rohe (US arch.; 1886-1969)
Ludwig van Beethoven (Ger. comp.; 1770-1827)
Ludwig (Josef Johann) Wittgenstein (Aus. phil.; 1889-1951)
Ludwigshafen am Rhein, Germany
Luening, Otto (US comp.; 1900-)
Luft, Lorna (ent.)
Lufthansa German Airline
Luftwaffe (Ger. air force, WWI & WWII)
Lug (myth.)
Luganda (also Ganda)(lang.)
Lugansk, Ukraine
Lugar, Richard G(reen)(US cong.; 1932-)
Luger™ (pistol)
Lugosi, Bela (ent.; 1882-1956)
Luhya (lang./people)
Luigi Boccherini (It. comp.; 1743-1805)
Luigi Galvani (It. phys./physt.; 1737-98)
Luigi Nono (It. comp.; 1924-90)
Luigi Pirandello (It. writer; 1867-1936)
Luis Alberto Lacalle Herrera (pres. Uruguay; 1941-)
Luis de Gongora y Argote (Sp. writer; 1561-1627)
Luis Miquel Dominquin (Sp. matador; 1926-)
Luis Somozo (Debayle)(ex-pres., Nicaragua; 1922-67)
Luis Walter Alvarez (US physt.; 1911-88)
Luisa Tetrazzini (It. opera; 1874-1940)
Luka, Bosnia-Hercegovina
Lukas, J. Anthony
Luke Air Force Base, AZ (mil.)
Luke Appling (baseball; 1907-90)
Luke Hansard (Br. Parliament reporter; 1752-1828)
Luke Perry (ent.)
Luke Skywalker (fict. chara., *Star Wars*)
Luke, Cool Hand (film; 1967)
Luke, St. (rel.; 1st c. AD)

Luks, George (Benjamin)(US artist; 1867-1933)
Lull diagram (logic)
Lulu (ent.; 1948-)
Lum and Abner
Lumet, Sidney (ent.; 1924-)
Lumière, Auguste (Marie)(Fr. inv.; 1862-1954)
Lumière, Louis (Jean)(Fr. inv.; 1864-1948)
Lumina™, Chevrolet (auto.)
Lumina™ LS, Chevrolet (auto.)
Lumpenproletariat (lowest class, Marxism)
Lumumba, Patrice (Emergy)(ex-PM, Congo/Zaire; 1926-61)
Luna (myth.)
Luna (USSR uncrewed space probes)
Lunar Alps (mountains, the moon)
Lunar Excursion Module (LEM)
Lunar Orbiter (US uncrewed space probe)
Lunar Rover (also l.c.)(also lunar roving vehicle)
Lunceford, Jimmie (US jazz; 1902-47)
Lunch Bucket™ (meals)
Lunchables™ (snacks)
Lunden, Joan (US TV jour.; 1950-)
Lundgren, Dolph (ent.)
Lunik (USSR space probe)
Lunn teacake, Sally
Lunt, Alfred (ent.; 1892-1977)
Luo (lang./people)
Lupino, Ida (ent.; 1914-)
LuPone, Patti (ent.; 1949-)
Lupus (astron., wolf)
Luray Caverns (VA)
Lurex™ (metallic fabric)
Luri (lang.)
Lurie, Alison (US writer; 1926-)
Lusaka, Zambia
Lusitania, S.S. (Br. ship sunk by Ger.; 1915)
Lussac, Joseph (Louis) Gay- (Fr. chem./physt.; 1778-1850)
Luther Adler (ent.; 1903-84)
Luther Burbank (US horticulturist; 1849-1926)
Luther Vandross (ent.; 1951-)
Luther, Martin (Ger. rel./writer; 1483-1546)
Lutheran (rel.)
Lutheran Church (rel.)
Lutheranism (also Lutherism)(rel.)
Luvs™ (diapers)
Lu-Wang School (Ch. phil.)
Lux™ (soap)
Luxembourg (Grand Duchy of)(Eur.)
Luxembourg (province, Belgium)
Luxembourg, Luxembourg
Luxembourgish (lang.)
Luxor, Egypt (ancient ruins)
Luzern, Switzerland (also Lucerne)
Luzon (island, Philippines)
Lviv, Ukraine
Lwena (lang.)
LWM (low-water mark)

LWV (League of Women Voters)
Lyceum, the (Athens gymnasium where Aristotle taught)
Lycopodiophyta
Lycra™ (brand of spandex)
Lydia (ancient kingdom; 7th-6th c. BC)
Lydia E(stes) Pinkham (US bus.; 1819-83)
Lydia E. Pinkham's Vegetable Compound, Mrs. (med.)
Lydia Sokolova (Br. ballet; 1896-1974)
Lykes Brothers, Inc.
Lyle Menendez (US news)
Lyle Waggoner
Lyly (or Lily, Lilly), John (Br. writer; 1554?-1606)
Lyman Abbott (US rel.; 1835-1922)
Lyman Lemnitzer (US gen.; 1899-1988)
Lyme disease (tick-borne virus)
Lymon, Frankie (ent.)
Lyn Nofziger (US pol.)
Lynch & Co., Inc., Merrill (finan.)
Lynch, David (ent.; 1946-)
Lynch, Jack (John)(ex-PM, Ir.; 1917-)
Lynchburg, VA
Lynda Benglis
Lynda Bird Johnson Robb (daughter, US pres.; 1944-)
Lynda Carter (ent.; 1951-)
Lynde, Paul (ent.; 1926-82)
Lynden (Oscar) Pindling (ex-PM, Bahamas; 1930-)
Lyndon B(aines) Johnson (36th US pres.; 1908-73)
Lyndon B. Johnson National Historical Park (TX)
Lyndon B. Johnson Space Center (TX)
Lyndon H. LaRouche, Jr. (US pol./econ.; 1922-)
Lyndon, Barry (film; 1975)
Lynette "Squeaky" Fromme (US, shot Pres. Ford)
Lynn Anderson (ent.; 1947-)
Lynn Fontanne (ent.; 1887-1983)
Lynn Jeffrey (ent.; 1909-)
Lynn Johnston (cartoonist; *For Better or Worse*; 1947-)
Lynn Martin (US pol.; 1939)
Lynn Redgrave (ent.; 1943-)
Lynn Seymour (Can. ballet; 1939-)
Lynn Swann (football; 1952-)
Lynn, Diana (ent.; 1926-71)
Lynn, Frederic Michael (baseball; 1952-)
Lynn, Janet (figure skating; 1953-)
Lynn (Webb), Loretta (ent.; 1935-)
Lynn, MA
Lynx (astron., lynx)
Lynyrd Skynyrd (pop music)
Lyon, France
Lyondell Petrochemical Co.

Lyonel (Charles Adrian) Feininger (US artist; 1871-1956)
Lyonnesse (legendary Arthurian country)
Lyons, Council of
Lyons, France
Lyra (astron., lyre)
Lysander (Spartan gen.; 5th c BC)
Lysippus (also Lysippos)(Gr. sculptor; 4th c. BC)
Lysol™ (cleaner)
Lytell, Bert
Lytton Springs Winery (US bus.)
Lytton Strachey, (Giles)(Br. writer; 1880-1932)
Lyuben Berov (PM, Bulgaria)

M

MA (Massachusetts, Master of Arts)
Ma & Pa Kettle (fict. charas.)
Ma Bell (slang, AT&T)
Ma (Gertrude) Rainey (US jazz; 1886-1939)
Ma, Yo-Yo (US cellist; 1955-)
Maalox™ (med.)
Maaouya Ould Sidi Ahmed Taya (pres., Mauritania; 1943-)
Maastricht, the Netherlands (or Holland)
Mab, Queen (Ir./Eng. folklore)
Mabaruma
Mac Davis (ent.; 1956-)
Mac Maurice Wilkens (track; 1950-)
Mac, Fleetwood (pop music)
Macao (Port. province adjoining Ch.)
MacArthur, Douglas (US gen.; 1880-1964)
MacArthur, James (ent.; 1937-)
Macaulay Culkin (ent.; 1980-)
Macauley, Thomas B(abington), Baron (Br. hist./pol.; 1800-59)
Macbeth (king; Scot.; ?-1057)
Macbeth (Shakespeare play)
Macbeth, Lady (fict. chara., *Macbeth*)
Maccabee (also Hasmonaean)(rel.)
Macchio, Ralph (ent.; 1962-)
MacDiarmid, Hugh (b. Christopher Murray Grieve)(Scot. poet; 1892-1978)
MacDill Air Force Base, FL
Macdonald Carey (ent.; 1913-)
MacDonald, Jeanette (ent.; 1903-65)
Macdonald, Sir John Alexander (ex-PM, Can.; 1815-91)
MacDonald, John D. (US writer; 1916-86)
MacDonald, J(ames) Ramsay (ex-PM, Br.; 1866-1937)
Macdonald, Ross (aka Kenneth Millar)(US writer; 1915-)
MacDowell, Andie (ent.; 1958-)
Macduff, Lady (fict. chara., *Macbeth*)
Mace™ (also Chemical Mace)
Macedonia (republic. Yug.)(SE Eur.)
Macedonian (lang./people)
MacGraw, Ali (ent.; 1938-)
MacGyver (TV show)
Mach number (speed of a body/speed of sound ratio)
Mach, Ernst (Aus. physt./psych./phil.; 1838-1916)
Machel, Samora (ex-pres., Mozambique; 1933-86)
Machiavelli, Niccolo (di Bernardo)(It. pol./writer/phil.; 1469-1527)
Machiavellian deed (deceitful political manipulation)

Machu Picchu, Peru (Inca ruins)
Machungo, Mário da Graça (PM, Mozambique
MacInnes, Helen (Clark)(Scot. writer; 1907-85)
Macintosh™ Centris (compu.)
Macintosh™ computer
Macintosh Performa™ (compu.)
Mack Gordon (Pol./US lyricist; 1905-59)
Mack (Thomas) McLarty (US pol.; 1946-)
Mack Sennett (b. Michael Sinnott)(ent.; 1880-1960)
Mack Sennett Studios (old Hollywood)
Mack Trucks, Inc.
Mack, Connie (b. Cornelius McGillicuddy)(baseball; 1862-1956)
Mack, Connie, III (US cong.; 1940-)
Mack, Jillie
Macke, August (Ger. artist; 1887-1914)
MacKenzie Phillips (ent.; 1959-)
Mackenzie River (Can.)
Mackenzie, Alexander (ex-PM, Can.; 1822-92)
Mackenzie, Sir Alexander (Scot. expl.; 1764-1820)
MacKenzie, Gisele (ent.)
MacKenzie, Spuds (dog)
Mackey, John (football; 1941-)
Mackie, Bob
Mackinac, Straits of (Lake Huron/Lake Michigan)
Mackinaw blanket
Mackinaw boat
Mackinaw coat (also l.c.)
Mackintosh, Charles Rennie (Scot. arch.; 1868-1928)
MacLachlan, Kyle (ent.; 1960-)
MacLaine, Shirley (ent.; 1934-)
Maclean's (mag.)
MacLeish, Archibald (US poet; 1892-1982)
MacLeod, Gavin (ent.; 1930-)
Macmillan, (Maurice) Harold (ex-PM, Br.; 1895-1987)
MacMurray, Fred (ent.; 1908-91)
Macnee, Patrick (ent.; 1922-)
MacNeil, Cornell (ent.; 1922-)
MacNeil, Lehrer News Hour (TV show)
MacNelly, Jeff (cartoonist, *Shoe*; 1947-)
Macon (wine)
Macon Telegraph (GA newspaper)
Macon, GA
MacPherson struts (auto.)
MacRae, Gordon (ent.; 1921-86)
Macready, George (ent.; 1909-73)
MacUser (mag.)
Macworld (mag.)
Macy & Co., Inc., R. H.)
Macy, Bill (ent.; 1922-)
Macy's (department store)
Mad (mag.)
Mad Hatter, the (fict. chara., *Alice in*

Wonderland)
Mad Tea Party (*Alice in Wonderland*)
Madagascar (Democratic Republic of)(island, E Afr.)
Madalyn Murray O'Hair (US atheist/activist
Madame Bovary (G. Flaubert novel)
Madame Chiang Kai-shek (b. Soong Mei-ling)(Ch. lecturer/writer; 1898-)
Madame (Marie) Curie (Fr. physt., radium; 1867-1934)
Madame (Jeanne Bécu) du Barry (Comtesse, mistress, Louis XV; 1743-93)
Madame Helena Petrovna Blavatsky Hahn (Rus. theosophist; 1831-91)
Madame (Marie Grosholtz) Tussaud (Swiss wax modeler; 1760-1850)
Madame Tussaud's Exhibition (wax museum, London)
Madang, Papua New Guinea
MADD (Mothers Against Drunk Driving)
Madden, John (football/ent.; 1936-)
Maddox, Lester (ex-gov., GA)
Madeira (wine)
Madeira embroidery
Madeira Island(s)(region, Port.)
Madeira River (Brazil)
Madeira topaz
Madeleine Albright (US ambassador to U.N.; 1937-)
Madeleine L'Engle (US writer; 1918-)
Madeline Kahn (ent.; 1942-)
Madeline Manning (running; 1948-)
Mademoiselle (mag.)
Madhya Pradesh (state, India)
Madigan, Amy (ent.; 1957-)
Madison Avenue (NYC)
Madison Capital Times (WI newspaper)
Madison County, The Bridges of (R. J. Waller novel)
Madison Square Garden (NYC)
Madison State Journal (WI newspaper)
Madison, CT, IN, NJ, WI
Madison, Dolley (Payne Todd)(wife of ex-US pres.; 1768-1849)
Madison, James (4th US pres.; 1751-1836)
Madison, Marbury v. (US law; 1803)
Madlock, Bill (baseball; 1951-)
Madlyn Rhue (ent.; 1934-)
Madonna (b. Madonna Louise Veronica Ciccone)(ent.; 1958-)
Madonna lily (also Annunciation lily)
Madonna, the (also Holy Mother, Mary, Our Lady, Virgin Mary)(rel.)
Madras, India
Madrid, Spain
Madurese (lang.)
Madwoman of Chaillot, The (by J. Giraudoux)
Mae West (ent.; 1892?-1980)

Mae West (life jacket)
Maelstrom (hazardous whirlpool off Nor. coast)
Maestro™ (CAT system)
Maeterlinck, Count Maurice (Belgian writer; 1982-1947)
Mafeteng, Lesotho
Mafia (It. secret society)
Mafia don
Mafia princess
Mafioso
Magadha (ancient kingdom, India)
Magdalene, Mary (rel.; 1st c. AD)
Magdeburg, Germany
Magee, Patrick
Magellan (US uncrewed space probe)
Magellan, Ferdinand (Port. nav.; c1480-1521)
Magellan, Strait of (tip of SAmer.)
Magellanic clouds (astron.)
Magen David (also Star of David)(6 points, Jew. symbol)
Maggie and Jiggs (comic strip)
Maggie Smith (ent.; 1934-)
Magh (lang.)
Maghreb (name for NW Afr.)
Magi (also Wise Men of the East, Three Kings of the Orient, Three Wise Men)(rel.)
Magi (rel., the wise men)
Magic Chef™ (appliances)
Magic Chef, Inc.
Magic Johnson, (Earvin)(basketball; 1959-)
Magic Marker™
Magic Show, The (play)
Magic, Orlando (basketball team)
Magilla Gorilla (cartoon)
Magindanaon (lang.)
Maginot line (Fr. mil.)
Magna Carta (Br. hist.; 1215)
Magnani, Anna (ent.; 1908-73)
Magnavox™ (elec.)
Magnavox Co.
Magnificat (rel. song)
Magnificent Ambersons, The (B. Tarkington novel)
Magnin, I. (retail stores)
Magnolia State (nickname, MS)
Magnoliophyta (plant division)
Magnum, P.I. (TV show)
Magnus hitch (knot)
Magnus, Albertus, St. (also St. Albert the Great)(Ger. rel.; 1193-1280)
Magog, Gog and (rel.)
Magoo, Mr. (cartoon)
Magritte, René (Belgian artist; 1898-1967)
Magruder, Jeb Stuart (US pol./Watergate
Maguires, Molly (also Mollies)(US/Ir. secret society; c1854-77)
Maguires, The Molly (film; 1970)
Magyar (lang./people)

Mahabad, Azerbaijan
Mahabharata (rel.)
Mahadeva (rel.)
Mahakala (myth.)
Mahalia Jackson (US jazz; 1911-72)
Mahalapye, Botswana
Mahamadou Issoufou (PM, Niger)
Mahamane Ousmane (pres., Niger)
Mahan, Larry
Maharashtra (state, India)
Maharishi Mahesh Yogi (Hindu guru)
Mahathir bin Muhammad (PM, Malaysia; 1925-)
Mahatma Gandhi, (Mohandas K[aramchand])(Indian pol./pacifist; 1869-1948)
Mahavira, Vardhamana (legendary educ./rel.; ?-480? BC)
Mahayana Buddhism (rel.)
Mahdi (rel.)
Mahdi, Muhammad Ali (ex-pres., Somalia
Mahfouz, Naguib (Eg. writer; 1911-)
Mah-Jongg™ (game)
Mahler, Gustav (Aus. comp.; 1860-1911)
Mahmoud Zubi (PM, Syria
Mahmud I (sultan, Turk.; 1696-1754)
Mahmud II (sultan, Turk.; 1785-1839)
Mahoney, Breathless (fict. chara., *Dick Tracy*)
Mahovlich, Frank (Francis William)(hockey; 1938-)
Mahre, Phil(lip)(US skier; 1957)
Mahre, Steve(n)(US skier; 1957-)
Maid Marian (Robin Hood's sweetheart)
Maid of Orléans (also St. Joan of Arc, Jeanne d'Arc)(Fr. rel./mil.; 1412?-31)
Maidenform™ bra
Maidstone, England
Maiduguri, Nigeria
Mail Boxes Etc., USA (US bus.)
Mail, Charleston (WV newspaper)
Mailer, Norman (US writer; 1923-)
Mailgram™
Maillol, Aristide (Fr. sculptor; 1861-1944)
Maimonides, Moses (ben Maimon), Rabbi (aka RaMBaM)(Jew. rel./phil.; 1135-1204)
Main Street (central street of any town)
Main, Marjorie (ent.; 1890-1975)
Mainbocher (Main Rousseau Bocher)(US designer; 1891-1976)
Maine (ME)
Maine coon cat
Maine, to hell with Spain," "Remember the (Sp.-Amer. War; 1898)
Mairzy Doats (song)
Maitreya (also Mi-lo-fo, Miroku)(rel.)
Majali, Abd al-Salam al (PM, Jordan
Majerle, Dan (basketball; 1965-)
Majesty, Your (title)

Major Bowes' Original Amateur Hour
Major Dad (TV show)
Major Edward Bowes (ent.; 1874-1946)
Major M. J. Divine (also Father Divine)(b. George Baker)(US rel.; 1882-1965)
Major, John (PM, Br.; 1943-)
Major, Ursa (astron., great bear; part of Big Dipper)
Majorca (a Balearic island, Sp.)
Majors, Lee (ent.; 1940-)
Majuro, Marshall Islands
Makarios III (ex-pres., Cyprus; 1913-77)
Makarova, Natalia (Rus. ballet; 1940-)
Makassar (lang.)
Makeni, Sierra Leone
Maker (God)
Maktoum ibn Rashid al-Maktoum, Sheik (PM, UAE)
Makua (lang./people)
Malabo, Equatorial Guinea
Malacca (also Melaka)(state, Malaysia)
Malacca, Strait of (Indian Ocean/China Sea)
Malachi, or Malachy, or Malachias (rel.)
Malachy, St. (Irish rel.; 1095-1148)
Malaga (wine)
Malaga grapes
Málaga, Spain
Malagasy (lang./people)
Malamud, Bernard (US writer; 1914-86)
Malaprop, Mrs. (fict. chara, *The Rivals*; malapropism)
Malatya, Turkey
Malawi (Republic of)(SE Afr.)
Malawi, Lake (SE Afr.)
Malay (lang./people)
Malay Archipelago (islands, between Asia/Austl.)
Malay-Indonesian (lang./people)
Malay Peninsula (also Malaysia)
Malayalam (lang.)
Malayan-Indonesian (people)
Malayo-Polynesian (also Austronesian)(lang.)
Malaysia (also Malay Peninsula)
Malaysia (country, SE Afr.)
Malaysian Airline System (airline)
Malbin, Elaine (ent.; 1932-)
Malcolm Forbes (US publ.; 1919-90)
Malcolm-Jamal Warner (ent.; 1970-)
Malcolm Little (aka Malcolm X)(US black-rights activist; 1926-65)
Malcolm McDowell (ent.; 1943-)
Malcolm Muggeridge (Br. jour.; 1903-90)
Malcolm Muir (US publ.; 1885-1979)
Malcolm Wallop (US cong.; 1933-)
Malcolm X (b. Malcolm Little)(US black-rights activist; 1926-65)
Malden, Karl (ent.; 1913-)
Maldives (Republic of)(islands, N Indian Ocean)

Malé, Maldives
Malecela, John (PM, Tanzania)
Malek, Redha (PM, Algeria)
Malev Hungarian Airlines
Malevich, Kasimir (or Casimir)(Rus. artist;
  1878-1935)
Mali (Republic of)(NW Afr.)(formerly French
  Sudan)
Malibu, CA
Malietoa Tanumafili II (king/head of state,
  WSamoa
Maliki (Islamic law)
Malikites (rel.)
Malinke (lang./people)
Malinois (dog)
Malinowski, Bronislaw (Pol. anthrop.; 1884-
  1942)
Malkovich, John (ent.; 1953-)
Mallarmé, Stéphane (Fr. poet; 1842-98)
Malle, Louis (Fr. ent.; 1932-)
Malmaison (Napoleon I estate, Fr.)
Malmö, Sweden
Malmstrom Air Force Base, MT
Malone Story, The Bugsy (film; 1976)
Malone, Dorothy (ent.; 1925-)
Malone, Karl (basketball; 1963-)
Malone, Moses (basketball; 1955-)
Malory, Sir Thomas (Br. writer; c1400-71)
Malraux, André (Fr. writer; 1901-76)
Malta (Republic of)(island, Mediterranean Sea)
Maltese (dog, cat)
Maltese (lang.)
Maltese cross
Maltese Falcon, The (D. Hammett novel)
Malthus theory (population growth)
Malthus, Thomas R(obert)(Br. econ.; 1766-1834)
Malthusian (supporter, population theory)
Malthusian parameter (rate of population
  growth)
Malthusianism (population theory)
Malt-O-Meal™ (cereal)
Malval, Robert (Haitian pol.)
Mamaloni, Solomon (ex-PM, Soloman Islands;
  1943-)
Mamas and the Papas, the (pop music)
Mame, Auntie (play; film, 1958)
Mamet, David (US writer; 1947-)
Mamie (Doud) Eisenhower (wife of ex-US pres.;
  1896-1979)
Mamie Van Doren (ent.; 1933-)
Mammalia (biological class)
Mammon (rel.)
Mammoth Cave National Park (KY)
Mammoth Lakes, CA
M & M's™ (candy)
man Friday/girl Friday
Man From U.N.C.L.E. (TV show)
Man O'War (race horse)

Man of Galilee (Jesus)
Man of La Mancha (play)
Man of Sorrows (Jesus)
Man Ray (US artist; 1890-1976)
man of God (saint, clergyman, priest, etc.)
Man, Isle of (island, Irish Sea)
Man, Ivory Coast
Management and Budget, Office of (OMB)(US
  govt.)
Managua, Nicaragua
Manama, Bahrain (also Bahrain, Bahrain)
Manassas, VA
Manaus, Brazil
Mancha, Don Quixote de la (by Cervantes)
Mancha, La (district, Sp.)
Mancha, Man of La (play)
Manchester terrier (dog)
Manchester, CT, NH
Manchester, England
Manchester, Melissa (ent.; 1951-)
Manchester, William (US writer; 1922-)
Manchu (lang./people)
Manchu dynasty (Ch.; 1644-1912)
Manchu, Fu (fict. criminal)
Manchuria (NE region, Ch.)
Manchurian Candidate, The
Mancini, Henry (US comp.; 1924-94)
Mancini, Ray "Boom Boom" (boxing)
Manco Capac (legendary Inca ruler)
Mandalay, Myanmar
Mandan (NAmer. Indians)
Mandarin (lang.)
Mandarin Chinese (lang.)
Mande (lang./people)
Mandela, Nelson (Rolihlahla)(pres., SAfr.;
  1918-)
Mandela, Winnie (Nomzamo)(SAfr. pol./
  reformer; 1934-)
Mandell, Howie (ent.; 1955-)
Mandelstam, Osip ([Y]Emilevich)(Rus. poet;
  1891-1938?)
Mandingo (people)
Mandinka (lang./people)
Mandja (people)
Mandlikova, Hana (tennis; 1962-)
Mandrell, Barbara (ent.; 1948-)
Mandrell, Louise (ent.)
Mandy Patinkin (ent.; 1952-)
Manet, Édouard (Fr. artist; 1832-83)
Manfred B(ennington) Lee (pseud. Ellery
  Queen)(US writer; 1905-71)
Manganin™ (copper/manganese/nickel alloy)
Mangas Coloradas, Chief (Apache Indians;
  c1797-1863)
Mangione, Chuck (ent.; 1940-)
Manhattan (cocktail)
Manhattan (island, NYC borough)
Manhattan clam chowder

Manhattan Project (atomic bomb)
Manhattan Shirt Co., The
Manhattan Transfer, The (pop music)
Manicheanism (rel.)
Manifest Destiny (govt.)
Manila hemp/rope
Manila paper
Manila, Philippines
Manilow, Barry (ent.; 1946-)
Manipur (state, India)
Manitoba (province, Can.)
Manitoba, Lake (Can.)
Manjaca (people)
Mankiewicz, Joseph L(eo)(US ent./writer; 1909-93)
Manley, Michael (Norman)(ex-PM, Jamaica; 1924-)
Manley, Norman (ex-PM, Jamaica; 1892-1969)
Mann Act (also White Slave Traffic Act)(US hist.; 1910)
Mann, Barry (US comp.; 1939-)
Mann, Carol (golf; 1941-)
Mann, Herbie (US jazz; 1930-)
Mann, Horace (US pol./educ.; 1796-1859)
Mann, Murray Gell- (US physt.; 1929-)
Mann, Thomas (Ger. writer; 1875-1955)
Manne, Shelly
Mannerheim Line/line
Mannerheim, Carl Gustaf Emil von, Baron (Fin. gen./pol.; 1867-1951)
Mannerism (art style)
Mannheim School
Mannheim, Germany
Mannheim, Karl (Hung. sociol./hist.; 1893-1947)
Manning, Danny (basketball; 1966-)
Manning, Madeline (runner; 1948-)
Manning, Patrick A. M. (PM, Trinidad/Tobago; 1946-)
Mannington™ (flooring)
Mannington Mills, Inc.
Mannix (TV show)
Mann's Chinese Theater
Manoff, Dinah (ent.; 1958-)
Manor Care, Inc. (healthcare)
Manpower™
Manpower Temporary Services
Manpower, Inc.
Mansard roof
Mansard (or Mansart), (Nicolas) François (Fr. arch.; 1598-1666)
Mansfield, CT, OH
Mansfield, England
Mansfield, Jayne (ent.; 1932-67)
Mansfield, Katherine (Br. writer; 1888-1923)
Mansôa, Guinea-Bissau
Manson, Charles (US, mass murderer; 1934-)
Mansura, Egypt (also El Mansura)
Mantegna, Andrea (It. artist; 1431-1506)

Mantegna, Joe (ent.; 1947-)
Mantle, Mickey (Charles)(baseball; 1931-)
Mantoux test/technique (for TB)
Mantovani, Annunzio (ent.; 1905-80)
Mantua, Italy
Manu (myth.)
Manuel de Falla (Sp. comp.; 1876-1946)
Manuel Esquivel (PM, Belize; 1940-)
Manuel Luis Quezon y Molina (ex-pres. Phil.; 1878-1944)
Manuel (Antonio) Noriega (Morena), Gen. (ex-dictator, Panama; imprisoned for drug trafficking; 1938-)
Manuel Orantes (tennis; 1949-)
Manuel Santana (Martinez)(tennis; 1938-)
Manufacturers, National Association of (NAM)(est. 1895)
Manukau, New Zealand
Manx cat (also l.c.)
Manzanillo, Cuba
Manzini, Swaziland
Mao jacket
Mao Tse-tung (also Mao Zedong, Chairman Mao)(Ch. pol.; 1893-1976)
Maoism (pol. phil.)
Maori (lang./people)
Maple Leafs, Toronto (hockey team)
Maples, Marla (US, wife of D. Trump
Mapp v. Ohio (US law; 1961)
Mapplethorpe, Robert (US photo.; 1946-89)
Maputo, Mozambique (formerly Lourenço Marques)
Mara (rel.)
Maracaibo, Lake (Venezuela)
Maracaibo, Venezuela
Maradi, Niger
Marat, Jean Paul (Fr. pol.; 1743-93)
Marathi (lang.)
Marathon (ancient plain/village, Gr.)
Marathon, Battle of (Gr./Persia; 490 BC)
Maravich, Pistol Pete (Peter)(basketball; 1948-88)
Marble, Alice (tennis; 1913-90)
Marboro Books, Inc.
Marbury v. Madison (US law; 1803)
Marc Bazin (ex-PM, Haiti
Marc Chagall (Fr. artist; 1887-1985)
Marc Racicot (MT gov.)
Marc, Franz (Ger. artist; 1880-1916)
Marceau, Marcel (Fr. ent.; 1923-)
Marcel Breuer (US arch.; 1902-81)
Marcel Dionne (hockey; 1951-)
Marcel Duchamp (Fr. artist; 1887-1968)
Marcel Marceau (Fr. ent.; 1923-)
Marcel Proust (Fr. writer; 1871-1922)
Marcello Mastroianni (It. ent.; 1923-)
March Air Force Base, CA
March on Rome, the (It. hist.; 1922)

March, Fredric (ent.; 1897-1975)
Marchand, Nancy (ent.; 1928-)
Marche, Le (region, It.)
Marcia Jones Smoke (canoeing; 1941-)
Marciano, Rocky (b. Rocco Francis Marchegiano)(boxing; 1923-69)
Marco Polo (It. expl.; c1254-1324)
Marcolino José Carlos Moco (PM, Angola
Marconi, Guglielmo (It. eng./inv.; radio; 1874-1937)
Marcos, Ferdinand E(dralin)(ex-pres., Philippines; 1917-89)
Marcos, Imelda (Romualdez)(Phil. pol., wife of ex-pres; 1930-)
Marcus Annaeus Lucanus (aka Lucan)(Roman poet; 39-65)
Marcus Antonius (aka Mark Antony)(Roman gen.; 83?-30 BC)
Marcus Aurelius Antonius (b. Marcus Annius Verus)(emp., Rome; 121-180)
Marcus Cocceius Nerva (emp., Rome; c35-98)
Marcus Daly (US bus.; 1841-1900)
Marcus Garvey (Jamaican/US reformer; 1887-1940)
Marcus Junius Brutus (Roman pol., Caesar assassin; c78-42 BC)
Marcus Licinius Crassus (Roman gen.; c108-53 BC)
Marcus Tullius Cicero ("Tully")(Roman orator/ writer/pol.; 106-43 BC)
Marcus Vipsanius Agrippa (Roman mil./pol.; 63-12 BC)
Marcus Welby, M.D. (TV show)
Marcus™, Neiman- (retail)
Marcuse, Herbert (US phil.; 1898-1979)
Mardi Gras ("fat Tuesday")(festival)
Marduk (myth.)
Mare Imbrium (lunar sea)
Mare Island Naval Shipyard (CA)
Mare, Walter de la (Br. poet; 1873-1956)
Maren Seidler (track; 1962-)
Marengo, chicken (food)
Margaret (queen, Den.; 1353-1412)
Margaret (Rose)(princess, UK; 1930-)
Margaret Atwood (Can. writer; 1939-)
Margaret Bourke-White (US photo./writer; 1906-71)
Margaret Chase Smith (US pol.; 1897-)
Margaret Drabble (Br. writer; 1939-)
Margaret Fox (Can./US spiritualist; 1833-93)(and sister Katherine)
Margaret Fuller (US writer/reformer; 1810-50)
Margaret Leighton (ent.; 1922-76)
Margaret Maid of Norway (queen, Scot.; 1283-90)
Margaret Mead (US anthrop.; 1901-78)
Margaret Mitchell (US writer; 1900-49)
Margaret O'Brien (ent.; 1937-)

Margaret of Anjou (queen, Eng./wife of Henry VI; 1430-82)
Margaret of Austria (regent, Netherlands; 1480-1530)
Margaret of Navarre (also Margaret of Angoulême)(queen, Navarre; 1492-1549)
Margaret of Parma (Sp. regent, Netherlands; 1522-86)
Margaret of Valois (also Queen Margot)(Fr.; 1553-1615)
Margaret Rutherford, Dame (ent.; 1892-1972)
Margaret (Higgins) Sanger (US reformer; 1883-1966)
Margaret Smith Court (tennis; 1942-)
Margaret Sullavan (ent.; 1911-60)
Margaret (Hilda Roberts) Thatcher (ex-PM, Br.; 1925-)
Margaret Trudeau (Can., ex-wife of ex-PM)
Margaret Truman, (Mary)(daughter of ex-US pres.; 1924-)
Margaret Tudor (Eng., wife of James IV, Scot.; 1489-1541)
Margaret Whiting (ent.; 1924-)
Margarita (mixed drink)
Margaux (Fr. wine district)
Margaux Hemingway (ent.; 1955-)
Marge Champion (US dancer; 1923-)
Marge Piercy (US writer; 1936-)
Margery Daw
Margolin, Janet (ent.; 1943-)
Margot Fonteyn, Dame (ballet; 1919-91)
Margot Kidder (ent.; 1948-)
Margret, Ann- (Swed./US ent.; 1941-)
Margrethe II (queen, Den.; 1940-)
Maria Bueno (tennis; 1939-)
Maria Callas (ent.; 1923-77)
Maria Estela ("Isabel") Martínez de Perón (ex-pres., Argentina; 1931-)
Maria Goeppert Mayer (Ger./US physt.; 1906-72)
Maria Montessori (It. educ.; 1870-1952)
Maria Rilke, Rainer (Ger. poet; 1875-1926)
Maria Schell (ent.; 1926-)
Maria Shriver (US TV jour.; 1955-)
Maria Taglioni (It. ballet; 1804-84)
Maria Tallchief (US ballet; 1925-)
Maria Theresa (empress, Austria; 1717-80)
Maria Von Trapp, Baroness (b. Maria Augusta Kutschera)(Aus. singer; 1905-87)
Maria, Ave (also *Hail Mary*)(prayer)
Mariah Carey (ent.; 1970-)
Marian (or Mary Ann) Evans (pseud. George Eliot)(Br. writer; 1819-80)
Marian Anderson (ent.; 1902-1993)
Marian McPartland (US jazz; 1920-)
Marian Mercer (ent.; 1935-)
Marian, Maid (Robin Hood's sweetheart)
Mariana Islands (also Marianas)(NW Pac.)

Proper Noun Speller

Mariana Trench (deep depression, NW Pac.)
Marianne (Craig) Moore (US poet; 1887-1972)
Marichal, Juan (baseball; 1937-)
Marie (queen, Romania; 1875-1938)
Marie Antoinette (queen, Fr./wife of Louis XVI; 1755-93)
Marie Curie, Madame (Fr. physt., radium; 1867-1934)
Marie de' Medici (queen, Fr./wife of Henry IV; 1573-1642)
Marie Dressler (ent.; 1869-1934)
Marie Henri Beyle (aka Stendahl)(Fr. writer; 1783-1842)
Marie Ignace Augustine de Montijo Eugenie (empress, Fr.; 1826-1920)
Marie Louise (empress, Fr.; 1791-1847)
Marie Madeleine Pioche de la Vergne La Fayette (Comtesse de La Fayette)(Fr. writer; 1634-93)
Marie Osmond (ent.; 1959-)
Marie Rambert, Dame (b. Cyvia Rambam)(Br. ballet; 1888-1982)
Marie (Grosholtz) Tussaud, Madame (Anne) (Swiss wax modeler; 1760-1850)
Marie Wilson (ent.; 1917-72)
Marie, Rose (ent.; 1925-)
Mariel Hemingway (ent.; 1961-)
Marietta Corp., Martin
Marietta, GA, OH
Marietta, Naughty (play; film, 1935)
Mariette Hartley (ent.; 1940-)
Marigot, Dominica
Marilu Henner (ent.; 1952-)
Marilyn Cochran (skiing; 1950-)
Marilyn Horne (ent.; 1934)
Marilyn McCoo (ent.; 1943-)
Marilyn Monroe (b. Norma Jean Baker [or Mortenson])(ent.; 1926-62)
Marilyn Quayle (US atty, wife of ex-VP ; 1949-)
Marin, Cheech (ent.; 1946-)
Marin, John (US artist; 1870-1953)
Marina del Rey, CA
Marinaro, Ed
Marine Corps War Memorial, U.S. (also Iwo Jima)(VA)
Marine Corps, U.S. (US mil.)
Marine Fisheries Service, National (US govt. agcy.; est. 1970)
Mariner (US uncrewed space probes)
Mariners, Seattle (baseball team)
Marino, Dan (football; 1961-)
Mario (Gabriel) Andretti (auto racing; 1940-)
Mario da Graça Machungo (PM, Mozambique
Mário Lanza (opera; 1921-1959)
Mario Lemieux (hockey; 1965-)
Mario M(atthew) Cuomo (NY gov.; 1932-)
Mario Puzo (US writer; 1920-)
Mário (Alberto Nobre Lopes) Soares (pres.,

Port.; 1924-)
Marion Ross (ent.; 1928-)
Marion, Francis ("the Swamp Fox")(US mil/pol. c1732-95)
Marion, IN, OH
Maris, Roger (Eugene)(baseball; 1934-85)
Marisol (Escubar)(Venezuelan artist; 1930-)
Maritain, Jacques (Fr. phil.; 1882-1973)
Maritime Provinces (Can.: New Brunswick, Nova Scotia, Prince Edward Island)
Mariupol, Ukraine
Marjorie Kinnan Rawlings (US writer; 1896-1953)
Marjorie Main (ent.; 1890-1975)
Mark Antony (aka Marcus Antonius)(Roman gen.; 83?-30 BC)
Mark Clark (US gen.; 1896-1984)
Mark di Suvero (US artist; 1933-)
Mark Goodson (ent.; 1915-92)
Mark Hamill (ent.; 1951-)
Mark Harmon (ent.; 1951-)
Mark Hopkins Hotel (San Francisco)
Mark Lindsay Boatbuilders (US bus.)
Mark Linn-Baker (ent.; 1953-)
Mark Messier (hockey
Mark O. Hatfield (US cong.; 1922-)
Mark Rothko (Rus./US artist; 1903-70)
Mark Russell (ent.; 1932-)
Mark (Andrew) Spitz (swimming; 1950-)
Mark Taper Forum (in Los Angeles)
Mark Twain (aka Samuel Langhorne Clemens)(US writer; 1835-1910)
Mark VIII, Lincoln (auto.)
Mark, St. (b. John Mark)(rel.; 1st c AD)
Mark, Top of the (Mark Hopkins Hotel, San Francisco)
Markie Post (ent.; 1950-)
Marks and Spencer
Mark's Basilica, St. (Venice, It.)
Mark's fly, St. (insect)
Marla Gibbs (ent.; 1931-)
Marla Maples (US, wife of D. Trump)
Marlboro (cigarette)
Marlboro Man (Marlboro cigarettes)
Marlboro Music Festival
Marlborough, Duke of (aka John Churchill)(Br. mil.; 1650-1722)
Marlee Matlin (ent.; 1965-)
Marlene Dietrich (b. Maria Magdalene von Losch)(ent.; 1901-92)
Marley, Bob (Robert Nesta)(ent.; 1945-81)
Marley, the ghost of Jacob (fict. chara., *The Christmas Carol*)
Marlin Fitzwater (US pol.; 1942-)
Marlins, Florida (baseball team)
Marlo Thomas (ent.; 1943-)
Marlon Brando (ent.; 1924-)
Marlowe, Christopher (Br. writer; 1564-93)

Marlowe, Philip (fict. detective, R.T. Chandler)
Marmaduke (comic strip)
Marmara, Sea of (Turk.)
Marner, Silas (G. Eliot novel)
Maroilles (cheese)
Maronite (people)
Marple, Miss (fict. chara., A. Christie)
Marquesas Islands (Fr. Polynesia)
Marquette University (Milwaukee, WI)
Marquette, Jacques (Fr. expl./rel. in Amer.;
    1637-75)
Marquette, MI
Márquez, Felipe González (PM, Spain; 1942-)
Marquis de Lafayette (aka Marie Joseph
    Gilbert de Motier Lafayette)(Fr. mil./pol.;
    1757-1834)
Marquis de Sade (b. Donatien Alphonse
    François, Comte de Sade)(Fr. mil./writer;
    1740-1814)
Marquis of Queensberry rules (also
    Queensberry rules)(boxing)
Marquise de Pompadour (aka Jeanne
    Antoinette Poisson Le Normant
    d'Étioles)(mistress of Louis XV, Fr.; 1721-64)
Marrakesh, Morocco
Married...With Children (TV show)
Marriner, Neville (ent.; 1924-)
Marriott Corp.
Marriott Hotel(s)
Mars™ (candy)
Mars (planet, myth.)
Mars (US uncrewed space probes)
Mars brown (color)
Mars Observer (US uncrewed space probe)
Mars red (color)
Mars, Forrest E(dward)
Mars, Inc.
Marsala (wine)
Marsala, Sicily, Italy
Marsalis, Branford (ent.; 1960-)
Marsalis, Wynton (US jazz; 1961-)
Marsaxlokk, Malta
Marseillaise, La (Fr. anthem)
Marseille, France
Marsh Co., Abraham & Straus/Jordan
Marsh, Jean (ent.; 1934-)
Marsh, (Edith) Ngaio, Dame (NewZeal. writer;
    1899-1982)
Marsh, Reginald (US artist; 1898-1954)
Marsha Mason (ent.; 1942-)
Marshal Tito (b. Josip Broz)(ex-pres., Yug.;
    1892-1980)
Marshall Field (US merchant; 1834-1906)
Marshall Figure Salon, Gloria (US bus.)
Marshall Field's store
Marshall Islands (Republic of the)(W Pac.)
Marshall McLuhan, (Herbert)(Can. educ./
    writer; 1911-80)

Marshall Plan (also European Recovery
    Program)(after WWII)
Marshall Space Flight Center (AL)
Marshall Warren Nirenberg (US chem.; 1927-)
Marshall, E. G. (ent.; 1910)
Marshall, George C(atlett)(US gen.; 1880-1959)
Marshall, John (US jurist; 1755-1835)
Marshall, Penny (ent.; 1943-)
Marshall, Peter (ent.; 1927-)
Marshall, Thomas R(iley)(ex-US VP; 1854-1925)
Marshall, Thurgood (US jurist; 1908-93)
Marshall, TX
Marshallese (lang./people)
Mart Laar (PM, Estonia
Martello tower (mil.)(also l.c.)
Martens, Wilfried (ex-PM, Belgium; 1936-)
Martha and the Vandellas (pop music)
Martha Graham (US dancer/choreographer;
    1894-1991)
Martha Jane Burke (Calamity Jane)(US
    frontier heroine; c1852-1903)
Martha Plimpton
Martha Quinn (ent.; 1959-)
Martha Rae Watson (track; 1946-)
Martha Raye (ent.; 1916-)
Martha Rockwell (skiing; 1944-)
Martha Scott (ent.; 1914-)
Martha (Dandridge) Washington (wife of ex-US
    pres.; 1732-1802)
Martha White Foods, Inc.
Martha Wright (ent.; 1926-)
Martha's Vineyard (island, MA)
Marthinus (Wessels) Pretorius (SAfr. mil./pol.;
    1819-1901)
Marti, Jose (Julian)(Cuban pol./poet; 1853-95)
Martial (b. Marcus Valerius Martialis)(Roman
    poet; 41-104)
Martian
Martin Amerique, Inc., Remy
Martin Balsam (ent.; 1919-)
Martin Bormann (Ger. Nazi leader; 1900-45)
Martin Buber (Isr. phil.; 1878-1965)
Martin Frobisher, Sir (Br. nav./expl.; 1535-94)
Martin Gabel
Martin (or Meir) Kahan (Jew. activist; 1932-90)
Martin Landau (ent.; 1934-)
Martin Luther (Ger. rel./writer; 1483-1546)
Martin Luther King Day (Mon. closest to 1/15)
Martin Luther King, Jr., Rev. Dr. (US civil
    rights leader; 1929-68)
Martin Marietta Corp.
Martin Milner (ent.; 1927-)
Martin Mull (ent.; 1943-)
Martin Riessen (tennis; 1941-)
Martin Scorsese (ent.; 1942-)
Martin Sheen (ent.; 1940-)
Martin Short (ent.; 1950-)
Martin Van Buren (8th US pres.; 1782-1862)

Martin v. Hunter's Lessee (US law; 1816)

Martin, Billy (Alfred Manuel)(baseball; 1928-89)

Martin, Dean (ent.; 1917-)

Martin, Dick (ent.; 1923-)

Martin, Don (cartoonist, Mad magazine; 1931-)

Martin, Lynn (US pol.; 1939)

Martin, Mary (ent.; 1913-90)

Martin, Rick (Richard Lionel)(hockey; 1951-)

Martin, St. (Fr. rel.; c316-401)

Martin, Steve (ent.; 1945-)

Martin, Tony (ent.; 1913-)

Martina Arroyo (ent.; 1937-)

Martina Navratilova (tennis; 1956-)

Martindale-Hubbell

Martindale, Wink

Martinez, Bob (Robert)(US pol.; 1934-)

Martini & Prati Wines, Inc.

Martini & Rossi Asti Spumante™

Martini Winery, Louis M. (US bus.)

Martinique (Fr. island, West Indies)

Martinizing Dry Cleaning, One Hour (US bus.)

Martinmas (rel.)

Martin's Laugh-In, Rowan and (TV show)

Martin's Press, Inc., St.

Martins, Peter (US dancer; 1946-)

Martinsburg, WV

Martinsville, VA

Marty Feldman (ent.; 1933-82)

Marty Ingels

Marty Krofft

Marty Liquori (runner; 1949-)

Marty Robbins (ent.; 1925-82)

Martyr, St. Justin (It. rel.; 100?-165)

Marvel, Captain (comic strip)

Marvelettes, the (pop music)

Marvell, Andrew (Br. poet/satirist; 1621-78)

Marvelous Marvin Hagler (boxing; 1954-)

Marvin Gaye (ent.; 1939-84)

Marvin Hagler, Marvelous (boxing; 1954-)

Marvin Hamlisch (US comp.; 1944-)

Marvin Mitchelson (US atty.)

Marvin Windows & Doors (US bus.)

Marvin, Lee (ent.; 1924-87)

Marx Brothers (Chico, Harpo, Groucho, Gummo, Zeppo)

Marx Swimwear, Gilda (US bus.)

Marx, Arthur "Harpo" (ent.; 1888-1964)

Marx™, Gilda

Marx, Herbert "Zeppo" (ent.; 1901-79)

Marx, Julius "Groucho" (ent.; 1890-1977)

Marx, Karl (Heinrich)(Ger. phil.; 1818-83)

Marx, Leonard "Chico" (ent.; 1886-1961)

Marx, Milton "Gummo" (ent.; 1893-1977)

Marx, Richard

Marxism (phil.)

Mary (also the Madonna, Holy Mother, Our Lady, Virgin Mary)(rel.)

Mary Abigail Dodge (pseud. Gail Hamilton)(US writer; 1833-96)

Mary Ann (or Marian) Evans (pseud. George Eliot)(Br. writer; 1819-80)

Mary Astor (ent.; 1906-87)

Mary Baker Eddy (US, founder Christian Science; 1821-1910)

Mary Cassatt (US artist; 1845-1926)

Mary Decker Slaney (US runner; 1958-)

Mary Elizabeth Mapes Dodge (US writer/editor; 1831-1905)

Mary Elizabeth Mastrantonio (ent.; 1958-)

Mary Eugenia Charles (PM, Dominica; 1919-)

Mary Ford (ent.; 1928-77)

Mary Ford, Les Paul & (ent.)

Mary Frances Kennedy Fisher (M.F.K.)(US writer; 1909-92)

Mary Frann (ent.; 1943-)

Mary Gordon (US writer; 1949-)

Mary Gross

Mary Hart (ent.; 1951-)

Mary Higgins Clark (US writer; 1931-)

Mary I (also Mary Tudor, "Bloody Mary")(queen, Eng.; 1516-58)

Mary II (queen, Eng./Scot./Ir.; 1662-94)

Mary Jane (also maryjane)(slang, marijuana)

Mary Janes™ (candy sprinkles)

Mary Janes™ (shoes)

Mary Jo Kopechne (US, died at Chappaquiddick; 1941-69)

Mary Kay Cosmetics, Inc.

Mary Lamb (Br. writer; 1764-1847)

Mary (Douglas) Leakey (Br. archaeol..; 1913-)

Mary-le-Bow Church, St. (also Bow Church)(London)

Mary Lou Retton (US gymnast; 1968-)

Mary Lou Williams (US jazz; 1914-81)

Mary Magdalene (rel.; 1st c. AD)

Mary Martin (ent.; 1913-90)

Mary (Therese) McCarthy (US writer; 1912-89)

Mary (Ludwig Hays) McCauley ("Molly Pitcher")(US heroine; 1754-1832)

Mary McLeod Bethune (US educ./civil rights; 1875-1955)

Mary (Wortley) Montagu, Lady (aka Mary Pierrepont)(Br. writer; 1689-1762)

Mary of Burgundy (heiress of Charles the Bold; 1457-82)

Mary of Guise (queen to James V, Scot.; 1515-60)

Mary Pickford (b. Gladys Marie Smith)(ent.; 1893-1979)

Mary Poppins (P. Travers novel)

Mary Quant (Br. designer; 1934-)

Mary Roberts Rinehart (US writer; 1876-1958)

Mary Robinson (pres., Ir.; 1944-)

Mary Steenburgen (ent.; 1953-)

Mary Stolz

Mary Stuart (aka Mary, Queen of Scots)(queen, Scot.; 1542-87)
Mary Stuart Masterson (ent.; 1967-)
Mary Todd Lincoln (wife of A. Lincoln; 1818-82)
Mary Travers (ent.; 1936-)
Mary Tudor (also Mary I, "Bloody Mary")(queen, Eng.; 1516-58)
Mary Tyler Moore (ent.; 1937-)
Mary Wells (ent.; 1943-92)
Mary Wollstonecraft (Br. reformer; 1759-97)
Mary Wollstonecraft Shelley (Br. writer; 1797-1851)
Mary Worth (cartoon chara.)
Mary Wortley (Pierrepont) Montagu, Lady (Br. writer; 1689-1762)
Mary, Bloody (also Mary I, Mary Tudor)(queen, Eng.; 1516-58)
Mary, College of William and (VA)
Mary, Hail (also *Ave Maria*)(prayer)
Mary, Mary (play)
Mary, Queen of Scots (aka Mary Stuart)(queen, Scot.; 1542-87)
Mary, Typhoid (b. Mary Mallon)(Ir. cook, typhoid carrier; ?-1938)
Maryknoll Missioners (also Catholic Foreign Mission Society of America)(rel.)
Maryland (MD)
Maryland, McCulloch vs. (US law; 1819)
Masaccio (b. Tomaso [di Giovanni di Simone] Guidi)(It. artist; 1401-28)
Masada fortress (Isr. hist.; c70)
Masai (lang./people)
Masaka, Uganda
Masaki, Tanzania
Masako (Owada)(princess, Jap.; 1964-)
Masaryk, Jan (Garrigue)(Czech. pol.; 1886-1948)
Masaryk, Thomas G(arrigue)(ex-pres., Czech.; 1850-1937)
Masayoshi, Ohira (ex-PM, Jap.; 1910-80)
Mascagni, Pietro (It. comp.; 1863-1945)
Mascarenhas Monteiro, Antonio (pres., Cape Verde; 1944-)
Masco Corp., Inc.
Masefield, John (Br. poet; 1878-1967)
Maserati™
Maserati Automobiles, Inc.
Maserati, Ettore (It. bus./auto.; 1894-1990)
Maseru, Lesotho
M*A*S*H (TV show, film)
Mashburn, Jamal (basketball; 1972-)
Mashhad, Iran
Mashraq (E Mediterranean Arab countries: Egypt/Jordan/Lebanon/Sudan/Syria)
Masire, Quett (Ketumile Joni)(pres., Botswana; 1925-)
Masland™
Masland Carpets (US bus.)

Mason Adams (ent.; 1919-)
Mason City, IA
Mason-Dixon Line (between MD/PA, North/South)
Mason jar (also l.c.)
Mason, George (US pol.; 1725-92)
Mason, Jackie (b. Yacov Moshe Maza)(ent.; 1931-)
Mason, James (ent.; 1909-84)
Mason, John Landis (US inv.)
Mason, Marsha (ent.; 1942-)
Mason, Perry (fict. atty.)
Masonite™
Masonite Corp.
Mass (rel.)
Mass, Red (rel., Catholic blessing for legal profession)
Massachuset (NAmer. Indians)
Massachusetts (MA)
Massachusetts Bay (MA)
Massachusetts Bay Company (Br. co., founded Boston; 1630)
Massachusetts Institute of Technology (MIT)
Massacre of St. Bartholomew's Day (Fr. hist.; 1572)
Massapequa, NY
Massasoit, Chief (Wampanoag Indians, peace treaty with Pilgrims; c1590-1661)
Massawa, Eritrea
Massenet, Jules (Émile Frédéric)(Fr. comp.; 1842-1912)
Massengill™ (med.)
Massey, Raymond (ent.; 1896-1993)
Massey Co., Ltd., Caswell-
Massey-Ferguson, Inc.
Massif Central (plateau, Fr.)
Masson Vineyards, Paul (US bus.)
Masson™, Paul
Massys (or Matsys), Quentin (Flem. artist; 1466?-1530)
MAST (Military Anti-Shock Trousers)
Master of Arts (also M.A.)
Master of Science (also M.S.)
MasterCard™ (credit card)
Masterpiece Theatre (TV show)
Masters and Johnson, Drs. (sexual behavior study)
Masters Golf Tournament
Masters, Edgar Lee (US writer; 1869-1950)
Masters, Dr. William H(owell)(US phys./writer; 1915-)
Masterson, Bat (William Barclay)(US marshal; 1853-1921)
Masterson, Mary Stuart (ent.; 1967-)
Mastrantonio, Mary Elizabeth (ent.; 1958-)
Mastroianni, Marcello (It. ent.; 1923-)
Mastroianni, Umberto
Masur, Kurt (Ger. cond.; 1928-)

Mata Hari (b. Gertrud Margarete Zelle)(Dutch dancer, executed as spy by Fr.; 1876-1917)
Matabele (also Ndebele)(people)
Matadi, Zaire
Matamoros, Mexico
Match Light™ (charcoal)
Matchbox™
Matchbox Toys USA (US bus.)
Mathäus (or Matthias) Grünewald (Ger. artist; 1480-1528)
Mather Air Force Base, CA
Mather, Cotton (US rel.; 1663-1728)
Mather, Increase (US rel.; 1639-1723)
Matheson, Tim (ent.; 1947-)
Mathew B. Brady (US photo.; 1823?-96)
Mathews, Eddie (baseball; 1931-)
Mathews, Harlan (US cong.; 1927-)
Mathewson, Christy (Christopher)(baseball; 1880-1925)
Mathias, Bob (athlete; 1930-)
Mathis, Johnny (ent.; 1935-)
Matisse, Henri (Fr. artist; 1869-1954)
Matlin, Marlee (ent.; 1965-)
Matlock (TV show)
Mats Wilander (tennis)
Matson, Randy (shot putter; 1945-)
Matsuo, Bashö (aka Matsuo Munefusa)(Jap. poet, haiku; 1644-94)
Matsuoka, Yosuke (Jap. pol.; 1880-1946)
Matsys (or Massys), Quentin (Flem. artist; 1466?-1530)
Matt Biondi (swimming; 1965-)
Matt Dillon (ent.; 1964-)
Matt Dillon, Marshal (fict. chara., *Gunsmoke*)
Matt(hew Akbar) Groening (US cartoonist, *The Simpsons*; 1954-)
Mattel™ (toys)
Mattel, Inc.
Matterhorn (mountain peak, Alps)
Matthau, Walter (ent.; 1920-)
Matthew Arnold (Br. poet/critic; 1822-88)
Matthew Broderick (ent.; 1962-)
Matthew Bunker Ridgway (US gen.; 1895-)
Matthew Modine (ent.; 1959-)
Matthew Vassar (Br./US bus./educ.; 1792-1868)
Matthew Walker (knot)
Matthew, St. (rel.; 1st c. AD)
Matthias Corvinus (king, Hung.; 1440-90)
Matthias (or Mathäus) Grünewald (Ger. artist; 1480-1528)
Matthias, St. (chosen to replace Judas Iscariot)
Mattingly, Don (baseball; 1961-)
Mattingly, Thomas K. (astro.; 1936-)
Mature, Victor (ent.; 1916-)
Matuszak, John
Mau Mau (Kenyan mil. movement; 1952-60)
Maud Adams (Swed. ent.; 1945-)
Maud Land, Queen (region, Antarctica)

Maud Range, Queen (Antarctica)
Maude (TV show)
Maude Adams (b. Maude Kiskadden)(ent.; 1872-1953)
Maude, Harold and (film)
Maude, Micki & (film; 1984)
Maugham, W(illiam) Somerset (Br. writer; 1874-1965)
Maui (island, HI)
Maui (myth.)
Maui wowie (slang, Hawaiian marijuana)
Maui, HI
Mauldin, Bill (William Henry)(US writer/cartoonist; 1921-)
Maumoon Abdul Gayoom (pres., Maldives
Mauna Kea (dormant volcano, HI)
Mauna Loa (active volcano, HI)
Maundy Thursday (also Holy Thursday)(rel., Thursday before Easter)
Mauno (Henrik) Koivisto (pres., Fin.; 1923-)
Maupassant, (Henri René Albert) Guy de (Fr. writer; 1850-93)
Maureen Connolly ("Little Mo")(tennis; 1934-69)
Maureen McGovern (ent.; 1949-)
Maureen O'Hara (ent.; 1920-)
Maureen O'Sullivan (ent.; 1911-)
Maureen Stapleton (ent.; 1925-)
Mauriac, François (Fr. writer; 1885-1970)
Maurice Barrès (Fr. writer/pol.; 1862-1923)
Maurice Barrymore (ent.; 1848-1905)
Maurice B(razil) Prendergast (US artist; c1860-1924)
Maurice Chevalier (ent.; 1888-1972)
Maurice de Vlaminck (Fr. artist; 1876-1958)
Maurice Evans (ent.; 1901-89)
Maurice Maeterlinck, Count (Belgian writer; 1982-1947)
Maurice (Joseph) Ravel (Fr. comp.; 1875-1937)
Maurice (Joseph Henri) Richard ("the Rocket")(hockey; 1921-)
Maurice (Bernard) Sendak (US writer; 1928-)
Maurice Utrillo (Fr. artist; 1883-1955)
Maurier, Daphne Du (Br. writer; 1907-89)
Mauritania (Islamic Republic of)(NW Afr.)
Mauritius (Republic of)(island, Indian Ocean)
Maurois, André (aka Emile Herzog)(Fr. writer; 1885-1967)
Maury Povich (US TV jour.)
Maury Wills (baseball; 1932-)
Mauser™ (rifle/gun/pistol)
Mauser, Peter Paul (Ger. inv.; 1838-1914)
Mauser, Wilhelm (Ger. inv.; 1834-82)
Mausoleum at Halicarnassus (1 of 7 Wonders of the World)
Maverick (TV show)
Maverick, Bret (fict chara.; *Maverick*)
Mavericks, Dallas (basketball team)

Mawlid (rel.)
Max Abramovitz (US arch.; 1908-)
Max Baer (boxing; 1909-1959)
Max Baucus (US cong.; 1941-)
Max Beckmann (Ger. artist; 1884-1950)
Max Beerbohm, Sir (Br. critic/caricaturist;
    1872-1956)
Max Born (Ger. physt.; 1882-1970)
Max Delbruck (US biol.; 1907-81)
Max Ernst (Ger. artist; 1891-1976)
Max Factor™ (cosmetics)
Max Factor (US bus.; 1877-?)
Max Factor & Co.
Max Fleischer (US cartoonist, *Betty Boop,
    Popeye*; 1883-1972)
Max Gail (ent.; 1943-)
Max Headroom (fict. chara.)
Max Liebermann (Ger. artist; 1847-1935)
Max (Karl Ernst Ludwig) Planck (Ger. physt.;
    1858-1947)
Max Reinhardt (b. Max Goldmann)(ent.; 1873-
    1943)
Max Roach (US jazz; 1925-)
Max Schmeling (Ger. boxing; 1905-)
Max Shulman (US writer; 1919-88)
Max Von Sydow (Swed. ent.; 1929-)
Max Weber (Ger. sociol.; 1864-1920)
Max Weber (US artist; 1881-1961)
Max Wertheimer (Czech. psych./phil.; 1880-
    1943)
Maxell™
Maxell, Ltd., Hitachi-
Maxene Andrews (ent., Andrews Sisters; 1918-)
Maxfield Parrish, (Frederick)(US artist; 1870-
    1966)
Maxie Rosenbloom (boxing; 1904-76)
Maxim Gorky (or Gorki)(aka Aleksei
    Maksimovich Peshkov)(Rus. writer; 1868-
    1936)
Maxim Litvinov (USSR pol.; 1876-1951)
Maxim, Sir Hiram Stevens (US/Br. inv.; 1840-
    1916)
Maxima™, Nissan (auto.)
Maxime Carlot Korman (PM, Vanuatu)
Maximilian (emp., Mex.; 1832-67)
Maximilian I (Holy Roman emp.; 1459-1519)
Maximilian Schell (ent.; 1930-)
Maximilien (François Marie Isidore de)
    Robespierre (Fr. mil./pol.; 1758-94)
Maximus Verrucosus, Quintus Fabius
    ("Cunctator")(Roman pol./mil.; 275-03 BC)
Maxine Hong Kingston (US writer; 1940-)
Maxwell Air Force Base, AL
Maxwell Anderson (US writer; 1888-1959)
Maxwell Bodenheim (US writer; 1892-1954)
Maxwell Davenport Taylor (US gen.; 1901-87)
Maxwell House™ (coffee)
Maxwell House (US bus.)

Maxwell Smart (fict. TV chara.)
Maxwell, (Ian) Robert (b. Jan Ludvik
    Hock)(Czech./Br. publ.; 1923-91)
May apple (also Mayapple)(plant)
May beetle (also June bug, Junebug)
May Department Stores Co., The
May Day (May 1)
May queen
May wine
May, Elaine (ent.; 1932-)
Maya (CAmer. Indians)
Maya (lang./people)
Maya Angelou (US writer; 1928-)
Maya Mikhaylovna Plisetskaya (Rus. ballet;
    1925-)
Mayacamas Vineyards (US bus.)
Mayaguana, Bahamas
Mayagüez, Puerto Rico
Mayakovsky, Vladimir (Rus. writer; 1893-1930)
Mayan art (C Amer.; 200-900)
Mayan ruins
Mayaquiche (Guatemala Indians)
Maybeck, Bernard R. (US arch.; 1862-1957)
Maybelle Carter, "Mother" (ent.; 1909-78)
Maybelline™ (cosmetics)
Maybelline Co.
Mayberry R.F.D. (TV show)
Mayday (distress signal)
Mayer Foods Corp., Oscar
Mayer, Louis B(urt)(ent.; 1885-1957)
Mayer, Maria Goeppert (Ger./US physt.; 1906-
    72)
Mayer™, Oscar (meats)
Mayfair district (London)
Mayfield, Curtis (ent.; 1942-)
Mayflower (Pilgrim ship; 1620)
Mayflower Compact
Mayflower Transit, Inc.
Maynard Ferguson (ent.)
Maynard Smith, John (Br. biol.; 1920-)
Mayo (county, Ir.)
Mayo Clinic (med.)
Mayo, Virginia (ent.; 1920-)
Mayor of Casterbridge, The (Thomas Hardy
    novel)
Mayotte (a Comoro Island, Fr.)
Maypole (also l.c.)
Mayron, Melanie (ent.)
Mays, Kimberly (US news, switched at birth)
Mays, Willie (Howard)(baseball; 1931-)
Maytag™ (appliances)
Maytag Corp.
Maytag Co., The
Maytag repairman, the
Mayumi Moriyama
Mazandarani (lang.)
Mazar-i-Sharif, Afghanistan
Mazarin Bible (also Gutenberg Bible)

Gutenberg Bible (also Mazarin Bible)

Mazarin, Jules (b. Giulo Mazarini)(Fr. rel./pol.; 1602-61)

Mazatlán, Mexico

Mazda™ (auto.)

Mazda™ Miata (auto.)

Mazda™ Millenia (auto.)

Mazda Motors of America, Inc.

Mazda™ Protege

Mazdaism (also Zoroastrianism)(rel.)

Mazola™ (margarine/oil)

Mazowiecki, Tadeusz (ex-PM, Pol.; 1927-)

Mazursky, Paul (ent.; 1930-)

Mazzini, Giussepe (It. reformer; 1805-72)

MB (also mb)(megabyte)

MBA (Master of Business Administration)

Mba, Casimir Oye- (PM, Gabon

Mbabane, Swaziland

Mbala, Zambia

Mbale, Uganda

Mbandaka, Zaire

Mbasogo, Teodoro Obiang Nguema (pres., Equatorial Guinea; 1942-)

Mbilini, Prince (PM, Swaziland)

Mbini,Equatorial Guinea

Mboya, Tom (Kenyan pol.; 1930-69)

Mbundu (lang.)

MC (master of ceremonies, Marine Corps, Medical Corps)

McAdam, John Loudon (Scot. eng.; 1756-1836)

McAdoo, Bob (basketball; 1951-)

McAllen, TX

McAn Shoe Co., Thom

McArdle, Andrea (ent.; 1963-)

McAuliffe, Christa (US educ., *Challenger*; 1948-86)

McBridge, Patricia (ent.; 1942-)

McCain, John Stuart (US cong.; 1936-)

McCall Pattern Co.

McCall's (mag.)

McCall's Crochet Patterns (mag.)

McCall's Needlework (mag.)

McCallum, David (ent.; 1933-)

McCambridge, Mercedes (ent.; 1918-)

McCann, Specs

McCardle, Ex parte (US law; 1869)

McCarran International Airport (Las Vegas NV)

McCarthy, Andrew (ent.; 1963-)

McCarthy, Eugene (Joseph)(US pol.; 1916-)

McCarthy, Joe (Joseph Vincent)(baseball; 1887-1978)

McCarthy, Joseph R(aymond)(US pol.; 1908-57)

McCarthy, Kevin (ent.; 1914-)

McCarthy, Mary (Therese)(US writer; 1912-89)

McCarthyism (US hist.)

McCartney, (James) Paul (ent.; 1942-)

McCarver, Tim (ent.; 1941-)

McCauley, Mary (Ludwig Hays)("Molly Pitcher")(US heroine; 1754-1832)

McChord Air Force Base, WA

McClanahan, Rue (ent.; 1936-)

McClellan Air Force Base, CA

McClellan, Fort, AL (mil.)

McClellan, George B(rinton)(US gen.; 1826-85)

McClendon, Sarah

McClintock, Barbara (US geneticist; 1902-92)

McCloskey, Frank (US cong.; 1939-)

McClure, Doug (ent.; 1935-)

McClure, Sir Robert John le Mesurier (Br. expl.; 1807-73)

McClurg, Edie (ent.; 1951-)

McConnell Air Force Base, KS

McConnell, Mitch (US cong.; 1942-)

McCoo, Marilyn (ent.; 1943-)

McCormick™ (spices)

McCormick & Co., Inc.

McCormick harvester

McCormick, Cyrus (Hall)(US inv.; 1809-84)

McCovey, Willie (baseball; 1938-)

McCoy Feud, Hatfield- (opposite sides, Amer. Civil War)

McCoy Tyner (US jazz; 1938-)

McCoy, Fort (WI)

McCrea, Joel (ent.; 1905-90)

McCullers, Carson (Smith)(US writer; 1917-67)

McCulloch vs. Maryland (US law; 1819)

McCullough, Colleen (Austl. writer

McDaniel, Hattie (ent.; 1895-1952)

McDivitt, James A(lton)(astro.; 1929-)

McD.L.T ™ (McDonald's)

McDonald House, Ronald

McDonald, Lanny (hockey; 1953-)

McDonald, Ronald (fict. chara.)

McDonaldland™ cookies

McDonald's™

McDonald's Corp.

McDonnell Douglas Corp.

McDowall, Roddy (ent.; 1928-)

McDowell, Edward (US comp.; 1861-1908)

McDowell, Jack (baseball; 1966-)

McDowell, Malcolm (ent.; 1943-)

McDuck, Scrooge (cartoon chara.)

McEnroe, John (Patrick)(tennis; 1959-)

McEntire, Reba (ent.; 1954-)

M(aurits) C(ornelis) Escher (Dutch artist; 1902-72)

McFarland, Spanky (George)(ent.; 1928-93)

McFerrin, Bobby (ent.; 1950-)

McCabe & Mrs. Miller (film; 1971)

McGavin, Darren (ent.; 1922-)

McGee and Molly, Fibber (radio comedy)

McGee Corp., Kerr-

McGill University (Quebec, Can.)

McGill, James (Can. trader/finan.; 1744-1813)

McGillicuddy, Cornelius (aka Connie

Mack)(baseball; 1862-1956)
McGillis, Kelly (ent.; 1957-)
McGoohan, Patrick (ent.; 1928-)
McGovern, Elizabeth (ent.; 1961-)
McGovern, George S(tanley)(US pol.; 1922-)
McGovern, Maureen (ent.; 1949-)
McGowan, William G. (US bus.; 1928-92)
McGraw-Edison Co.
McGraw-Hill Book Co.
McGraw, Charles
McGraw, John (Joseph)(baseball; 1873-1934)
McGraw, Quick Draw (fict. chara.)
McGrew, The Shooting of Dan (R.W. Service
   ballad)
McGriff, Fred (baseball; 1963-)
McGuane, Thomas (US writer; 1939-)
McGuffey, William H(olmes)(US educ.; 1800-73)
McGuire Air Force Base, NJ
McGuire Sisters, The (pop music)
McGuire, Al (ent.; 1931-)
McGuire, Dorothy (ent.; 1919-)
McGwire, Mark (baseball; 1963-)
M. C. Hammer (b. Stanley Kirk Burrell)(ent.;
   1962-)
McHenry, Fort (MD)(*Star Spangled Banner*)
McHugh, Jimmy (US comp.; 1894-1969)
MCI Communications Corp.
McIlhenny Co. Tabasco™ sauce
McInerney, Jay
McIntire, John (ent.; 1907-91)
McIntosh (apple)
McIntyre, Joe (ent.; 1972-)
McKay, Jim (sports)
McKechnie, Donna (ent.; 1942-)
McKee, Lonette (ent.; 1957-)
McKeesport, PA
McKernan, John R., Jr. (ME gov.; 1948-)
McKim, Charles F(ollen)(US arch.; 1847-1909)
McKim, Charles M. (US arch.; 1920-)
McKinley National Park, Mount (now Denali
   National Park)(AK)
McKinley, Mount (also Denali)(AK)
McKinley, William (25th US pres.; 1843-1901)
McKinney, Helling v. (US law; 1993)
McKuen, Rod (US writer/comp.; 1933-)
McLaglen, Victor (ent.; 1907-71)
McLain, Dennis (baseball; 1944-)
McLarty, Mack (Thomas)(US pol.; 1946-)
McLaughlin Group (TV show)
McLaughlin's One on One (TV show)
McLean Stevenson (ent.; 1929-)
McLean, John (US jurist; 1785-1861)
McLuhan, (Herbert) Marshall (Can. educ./
   writer; 1911-80)
McMahon, Ed (ent.; 1923-)
McManus, George (US cartoonist, *Bringing Up
   Father*; 1884-1954)
McMillam Book Co., Inc.

McMillan, Kathy Laverne (track; 1957-)
McMurtry, Larry (Jeff)(US writer; 1936-)
McNair, Fort Lesley J., DC (mil.)
McNally World Atlas, Rand
McNamara, Robert (Strange)(US pol.; 1916-)
McNamara, Tank (cartoon chara,)
McNichol, Kristy (ent.; 1962-)
McPartland, Jimmy (US jazz; 1907-)
McPartland, Marian (US jazz; 1920-)
McPeak, Merrill A. (US mil./pol.)
McPhatter, Clyde (ent.)
McPherson, Aimee Semple (US rel.; 1890-1944)
McPherson, Fort, GA (mil.)
McQueen, Butterfly (ent.; 1911-)
McQueen, (Terrence) Steve(n)(ent.; 1930-80)
McRae, Carmen (ent.)
McRaney, Gerald (ent.; 1948-)
McWethy, John F.
McWherter, Ned R(ay)(TN gov.; 1930-)
MD (Maryland, Medicinae Doctor [Doctor of
   Medicine])
MD Magazine
ME (Maine)
Me and My Gal (play)
Me Decade (sociol.)
Mead™ (paper prods.)
Mead & Co., Inc., Dodd
Mead Corp., The
Mead Data General (compu. databases)
Mead Johnson & Co.
Mead, Lake (Hoover Dam, AZ/NV)
Mead, Margaret (US anthrop.; 1901-78)
Meade, Fort (MD)
Meade, George (Gordon)(US gen.; 1815-72)
Meade, George H. (US phil.; 1863-1931)
Meadows, Audrey (ent.; 1924-)
Meadows, Jayne (ent.; 1920-)
Mean (Joe) Greene (football; 1946-)
Means grass (also Johnson grass, Aleppo grass)
Meany, George (US labor leader; 1894-1980)
Meara, Anne (ent.; 1929-)
Meat Loaf (pop music)
Meath (county, Ir.)
Mecca, Saudi Arabia
Mecham, Evan (ex-gov, AZ;
Mechanix Illustrated (mag.)
Mechlin (lace)
Meciar, Vladimir (PM, Slovakia
Mecklenburg-Western Pomerania (state, Ger.)
Medal of Honor (also Congressional Medal of
   Honor)(mil.)
Medan, Indonesia
Medea (myth.)
Medellín cartel
Medellín, Colombia
Medfly (Mediterranean fruit fly)(also l.c.)
Medford, MA, OR
Medgar (Wiley) Evers (US civil rights leader;

1925-63)
Media General, Inc.
Medicaid (health insurance)(also l.c.)
Medicare (health insurance)(also l.c.)
Medici Chapel (also New Sacristy)(Florence, It.)
Medici collar (clothing)
Medici family (Florence, It.; 1434-1737)
Medici I, Cosimo de' (It., Duke of Florence; 1519-74)
Medici, Catherine de' (queen, Fr./wife of Henry II; 1518-89)
Medici, Cosimo de' (It. pol.; 1389-1464)
Medici, Lorenzo de' ("the Magnificent")(It. pol./ poet; 1449-92)
Medici, Marie de' (queen, Fr./wife of Henry IV; 1573-1642)
Medici, Piero de' (It. pol.; 1416-69)
Medicine Hat, Alberta, Canada
Medicine, Doctor of (also M.D., Medicinae Doctor)
Medicine, Nobel Prize for Physiology or
Medina, Saudi Arabia
Medis (compu. database, med.)
Mediterranean fruit fly (also Medfly, medfly)
Mediterranean Sea (between Eur./Afr./Asia)
Médoc (Fr. wine district)
Medtronic, Inc.
Medusa (myth.)
Medvedev, Vadim
Meeker, Ralph (ent.)
Meese, Edwin, III (US pol.; 1931-)
Meet the Press (TV show)
Meg Foster
Meg Ryan (ent.; 1963-)
Meg Tilly
Meghalaya (state, India)
Mehemet Ali (also Muhammad Ali)(Eg. pol./ mil.; 1769-1849)
Mehmed Emin Ali Pasha (Turk. leader; 1815-71)
Mehta, Zubin (India, cond.; 1936-)
Meier, Richard (US arch.; 1934-)
Meiji, Mutsuhito (Jap. emp.; 1852-1912)
Meiklejohn, Alexander (US educ.; 1872-1964)
Mein Kampf (Hitler's book/phil.)
Meineke™
Meineke Discount Muffler Shops, Inc.
Meir (or Martin) Kahan (Jew. activist; 1932-90)
Meir, Golda (also Goldie Mabovitch, Goldie Myerson)(ex-PM, Isr.; 1898-1978)
Meissen porcelain (also called Dresden china/ porcelain/ware)
Meissen, Germany
Meister Bräu™ (beer)
Meister Bräu, Inc.
Meistersinger (Ger. minstrels; 14th-16th c.)
Meithei (lang.)
Meknès, Morocco

Mekong Delta, Vietnam
Mekong River (SE Asia)
Meksi, Alexander (PM, Albania
Mel Allen (ent.; 1913-)
Mel Blanc (ent.; 1908-89)
Mel Brooks (b. Melvin Kaminsky)(ent.; 1926-)
Mel Carnahan (MO gov.)
Mel Ferrer (ent.; 1917-)
Mel Gibson (ent.; 1956-)
Mel Lewis (US jazz; 1929-90)
Mel Ott (baseball; 1909-58)
Mel Tillis (ent.; 1932-)
Mel Torme (ent.; 1925-)
Melaka (also Malacca)(state, Malaysia)
Melanchthon (b. Philipp Schwarzert)(Ger. rel.; 1497-1560)
Melanesia (islands, SW Pac.)
Melanesian (lang./people)
Melanesian-Polynesian (people)
Melanie Griffith (ent.; 1957-)
Melanie Klein (Aus. psych.; 1882-1960)
Melanie Mayron (ent.)
Melba Moore (ent.; 1945-)
Melba toast
Melba, Nellie, Dame (aka Helen Porter Mitchell)(Austl. opera; 1861-1931)
Melba, peach (also l.c.)
Melbourne Today (FL newspaper)
Melbourne, Australia
Melbourne, FL
Melcher, Terry (ent.)
Melchior (1 of Magi)
Melchior Ndadaye (ex-pres., Burundi; ?-1994)
Melchior, Lauritz (ent.; 1890-1973)
Melchite (rel.)
Meles Zenawi (pres., Ethiopia; 1955-)
Melina Mercouri (Gr. ent.; 1925-1994)
Melior (type style)
Melissa Gilbert (ent.; 1964-)
Melissa Manchester (ent.; 1951-)
Melissa Sue Anderson (ent.; 1962-)
Melitta™ (coffeemaker)
Melitta USA, Inc.
Mell Lazarus (cartoonist, *Momma, Miss Peach*; 1929-)
Mellaril™ (med.)
Mellencamp, John Cougar (ent.)
Mello, Fernando Collor de (ex-pres., Brazil; 1949-)
Mellon University, Carnegie- (PA)
Mellon, Andrew William (US finan./bus.; 1855-1937)
Melpomene (myth., muse)
Melrose Avenue (Los Angeles)
Melrose Place (TV show)
Melrose, FL, MA
Melrose, Scotland
Melvil Dewey (US librarian; 1851-1931)

Melville Corp.
Melville Weston Fuller (US jurist; 1833-1910)
Melville, Herman (US writer; 1819-91)
Melvin and Howard (film. 1980)
Melvin (Mouron) Belli (US atty.; 1907-)
Melvyn Douglas (ent.; 1901-81)
Memnon (myth.)
Memnon, Colossus of (ancient Eg. statue)
Memorial Day (formerly Decoration Day)(last
    Monday in May)
Memorial Stadium (Baltimore, MD)
Memphis (city, ancient Egypt)
Memphis Commerical Appeal (TN newspaper)
Memphis, TN
Menace, Dennis the (comic strip)
Menachem Begin (ex-PM, Isr.; 1913-92)
Menander (Gr. writer; 342-191 BC)
Mencius (also Mengtzu, Mengtse)(Ch. phil.;
    372?-289 BC)
Mencken, H(enry) L(ouis)(US writer/editor;
    1880-1956)
Mende (lang./people)
Mendel, Gregor J(ohann)(Aus. biol.; 1822-84)
Mendelism (also Mendel's law)(genetics)
Mendel's law (also Mendelism)(genetics)
Mendelssohn (-Bartholdy), (Jakob Ludwig)
    Felix (Ger. comp.; 1809-47)
Mendes, Chico (Filho Francisco)(Brazilian
    environ./labor leader; 1944-88)
Mendes, Sergio (ent.; 1941-)
Mendoza, Argentina
Menelaus, King (myth.)
Menem, Carlos (Saul)(pres., Argentina; 1935-)
Menendez, Erik (US news)
Menendez, Lyle (US news)
Mengele, Dr. Josef ("angel of death")(Ger. Nazi;
    ?-1979?)
Mengistu, Haile Mariam (ex-pres., Ethiopia;
    1937-)
Mengtse (also Mencius, Mengtzu)(Ch. phil.;
    372?-289 BC)
Ménière's disease/syndrome (med.)
Menjou, Adolphe (ent.; 1890-1963)
Menken, Alan (US comp.; 1950-)
Menlo Park, CA, NJ
Mennen Co., The
Menninger Clinic (psych.)(Topeka, KS)
Menninger Foundation for Psychiatric
    Education and Research
Menninger, Charles Frederick (US psych.;
    1862-1953)
Menninger, Karl A(ugustus)(US psych.; 1893-
    1990)
Menninger, William Claire (US psych.; 1899-
    1966)
Menno Simons (Dutch rel.; c1496-c1561)
Mennonite (rel.)
Mennonite Church

Mennonites (Amish, Dunkers, Plain
    People)(rel.)
Menorca (or Minorca) Island (Balearic Island,
    Mediterranean)
Menotti, Gian-Carlo (It./US comp.; 1911-)
Men's Fitness (mag.)
Men's Health (mag.)
Men's Journal (mag.)
Mensa (astron., table)
Mensa (high IQ group)
Mensk, Belarus (also Minsk)
Mentadent™ (med.)
Mentholatum™ rub (med.)
Menuhin, Sir Yehudi (Br. violinist; 1916-)
Menzies, Robert Gordon (ex-PM, Austl.; 1894-
    1978)
Meo (people)
Meow™ Mix (cat food)
Mephistopheles (also Mephisto)(the devil)
Mercalli scale (measures intensity of
    earthquake)
Mercator map projection (also Mercator's
    projection)
Mercator, Geradus (or Gerhardus)(aka Gerhard
    Kremer)(Flem. geographer; 1512-94)
Merce Cunningham (US dancer/choreographer;
    1919-)
Merced River (CA)
Mercedes McCambridge (ent.; 1918-)
Mercedes-Benz™ (auto.)
Mercedes-Benz™ C220 (auto.)
Mercedes-Benz™ C280 (auto.)
Mercedes-Benz™ E300 (auto.)
Mercedes-Benz™ E320 (auto.)
Mercedes-Benz™ E420 (auto.)
Mercedes-Benz™ E500 (auto.)
Mercedes-Benz™ 400E (auto.)
Mercedes-Benz™ S320 (auto.)
Mercedes-Benz™ S350 (auto.)
Mercedes-Benz™ S420 (auto.)
Mercedes-Benz™ S500 (auto.)
Mercedes-Benz™ S600 (auto.)
Mercedes-Benz™ SL320 (auto.)
Mercedes-Benz™ SL500 (auto.)
Mercedes-Benz™ SL600 (auto.)
Mercedes-Benz of North America, Inc.
Mercedes Ruehl
Mercer, Johnny (US lyricist; 1909-76)
Mercer, Marian (ent.; 1935-)
Merchant Marine Academy, U.S. (Kings Point,
    NY)
Merchant Marine, U.S. (US bus./mil.)
Merck & Co, Inc.
Merckx, Eddie ("the Cannibal")(Belgian cyclist;
    1945-)
Mercouri, Melina (Gr. ent.; 1925-1994)
Mercurochrome™ (med.)
Mercury (planet; myth.)

Mercury (US crewed space flights)
Mercury-Atlas (US crewed space flights)
Mercury-News, San Jose (CA newspaper)
Mercury-Redstone (US crewed space flights)
Mercury-Redstone 3 (also Liberty Bell 7)(1st US crewed space flight; May 5, 1961)
Mercury Villager, Ford (auto.)
Meredith Baxter (ent.; 1947-)
Meredith Corp.
Meredith Wilson (US comp.; 1902-84)
Meredith, Burgess (ent.; 1908-)
Meredith, George (Br. writer; 1828-1909)
Mergenthaler, Ottmar (Ger./US inv.; 1854-99)
Meri, Lennart (pres., Estonia
Mérida, Mexico
Meriden, CT
Meridian Naval Air Station (MS)
Meridian, MS
Mérimée, Prosper (Fr. writer; 1803-70)
Merina (people)
Merino (sheep)
Merino, José Francisco (VP, El Salvador
Merit, Legion of (US)
Meriwether Lewis (US expl.; 1774-1809)
Merkel, Una (ent.)
Merle Haggard (ent.; 1937-)
Merle Norman™
Merle Norman Cosmetics (US bus.)
Merle Norman Cosmetic Studios (US bus.)
Merle Oberon (ent.; 1911-79)
Merle Travis (ent.)
Merlin (legendary magician)
Merlin (Jay) Olsen (football/ent.; 1940-)
Merlot (grape)
Mermaid, The Little (film)
Merman, Ethel (ent.; 1908-84)
Merovingian dynasty (Fr.; 481-751)
Merriam-Webster Dictionary
Merriam-Webster, Inc.
Merriam-Webster's Collegiate™ Dictionary
Merrick, David (ent.; 1912-)
Merrie Melodies (cartoon)
Merrie Olde England
Merrill A. McPeak (US mil./pol.)
Merrill Lynch & Co., Inc. (finan.)
Merrill, Bob (US lyricist; 1921-)
Merrill, Charles E. (US finan.; 1885-1956)
Merrill, Dina (ent.; 1925-)
Merrill, Janice (track; 1962-)
Merrill, Robert (ent.; 1919-)
Merrill, Steve (NH gov.)
Merrimack v. Monitor (US hist.; 1862)
Merry Andrew (slang, adv. chara.)
Merryman, Ex parte (US law; 1861)
Mersey beat (pop music; mid-1960s)
Mersey River (Eng.)
Merseyside (county, Eng.)
Merthiolate™ (med.)

Merton, Thomas (US rel.; 1915-68)
Meru (lang.)
Merv Griffin (ent.; 1925-)
Mervyn LeRoy (ent.; 1900-87)
Merwyn Bogue (aka Ish Kabibble)(ent.; 1908-94
Mervyn's department store
Meryl Streep (ent.; 1949-)
Mesa Verde National Park (prehistoric ruins)(CO)
Mesa, AZ
Mesmer, Friedrich Anton (or Franz)(Ger. phys.; 1734-1815)
Mesolithic period (Middle Stone Age; 15,000 to 10,000 years ago)
Mesopotamia (ancient civilization, SW Asia)
Mesozoic era (225-65 million years ago)
Mesquite, TX
Messalina, Valeria (Roman empress; c22-48)
Messenia (ancient region, Gr.)
Messerschmitt plane (Ger. fighter aircraft, WWII)
Messerschmitt, Willy (Wilhelm)(Ger. airplane designer; 1898-1978)
Messiah (by Handel)
Messiah (rel. savior, Jesus)
Messick, Dale (cartoonist, *Brenda Starr*; 1906-)
Messier catalog/number/object (astron.)
Messier, Charles (Fr. astron.; 1730-1817)
Messier, Mark (hockey
Messina, Italy
Messina, Jim (ent.; 1947-)
Messina, Loggins & (pop music)
Messina, Strait of (channel, Mediterranean)
Mesta, Perle (US dipl.)
Metalious, Grace (US writer
Metallica (pop music)
Metamorphosis, The (Kafka)
Metamucil™ (laxative)
Metcalf, Laurie (ent.; 1955-)
Methedrine™ (med.)
Metheny, Pat(rick Bruce)(ent.; 1954-)
Method (style of acting)
Methodism (rel.)
Methodist (rel.)
Methodist Church (rel.)
Methodist University, Southern (SMU)(TX)
Methuselah (rel.; said to have lived 969 years)
Metis (myth.)
Metonic cycle (astron.)
Metrazol™
Metro™, Geo, Chevrolet (auto.)
Metrodome Stadium (Minneapolis, MN)
Metropolitan Community Church (rel.)
Metropolitan Home (mag.)
Metropolitan Life Insurance Co.
Metropolitan Museum of Art (NYC)
Metropolitan Opera Co.
Mets, New York (baseball team)

Metternich, Age of
Metternich, Clemens W(enzel) L(othar), Prince von (ex-chanc., Aus.; 1773-1859)
Metzenbaum, Howard M. (US cong.; 1917-)
Meursault wine
Meuse River (Eur.)
Mevacor™ (med.)
Mex, Tex- (lang., culture/food/music)
Mexicali, Mexico
Mexican bamboo (also Japanese knotweed)(plant)
Mexican bean beetle
Mexican coffee (mixed drink)
Mexican fruit fly/fruitfly
Mexican hairless (dog)
Mexican hat dance
Mexican stand-off
Mexican War (US/Mex.; 1846-48)
Mexicana Airlines (airline)
Mexico (United Mexican States)(CAmer.)
Mexico City, Mexico
Mexico, Gulf of (US/Mex.)
MexSp (abbrev. of Mexican-Spanish)
Meyer A(nselm) Rothschild (Ger. finan.; 1744-1812)
Meyer Guggenheim (US finan./bus.; 1828-1905)
Meyer Schapiro (US art hist.; 1904-)
Meyer, Deborah (swimming; 1952-)
Meyer, Joseph (US comp.; 1894-1987)
Meyerbeer, Giacomo (b. Jakob Liebmann Beer)(Ger. comp.; 1791-1864)
MFA (Master of Fine Arts)
M-14 (automatic rifle)
Mg (chem. sym., magnesium)
MGM Grand Hotel (Las Vegas)
MGM Records (US bus.)
MGM/UA (US bus.)
M. Grumbacher, Inc.
MGs, Booker T and the (pop music)
MH (Medal of Honor)
M. H. de Young Memorial Museum (San Francisco)
MI (Michigan, military intelligence)
MIA (also M.I.A.)(missing in action)
Mia Farrow (ent.; 1945-)
Miami (NAmer. Indians)
Miami Beach, FL
Miami Dolphins (football team)
Miami Heat (basketball team)
Miami Herald (FL newspaper)
Miami International Airport (FL)
Miami Sound Machine (pop music)
Miami Vice (TV show)
Miami, FL
Miao (lang.)
Miata, Mazda™ (auto.)
Micatin™ (med.)
Michael (king, Romania; 1921-)

Michael (William) Balfe (Ir. comp/ent.; 1808-70)
Michael Burton (swimming; 1947-)
Michael Caine (ent.; 1933-)
Michael Chang (tennis; 1972-)
Michael Cimino (US ent.; 1943-)
Michael Collins (astro.; 1930-)
Michael Constantine (ent.; 1927-)
Michael Crichton (US writer; 1942-)
Michael Donald Gallagher (skiing; 1941-)
Michael Douglas (ent.; 1944-)
Michael Eisner (US bus.; 1942-)
Michael Ellis DeBakey (US phys.; 1908-)
Michael Faraday (Br. chem./physt; 1791-1867)
Michael (or Mikhail) Fyodorovich Romanov (emp., Rus.; 1596-1645)
Michael Gross (ent.; 1947-)
Michael Harrington (US reformer/writer; 1928-89)
Michael "Mick" (Phillip) Jagger (ent.; 1943-)
Michael Jackson (ent.; 1958-)
Michael J. Fox (ent.; 1961-)
Michael "Mike" Jordan (basketball/baseball; 1963-)
Michael J. "Mike" Sullivan (WY gov.; 1939-)
Michael Keaton (ent.; 1951-)
Michael Landon (ent.; 1936-91)
Michael Learned (ent.; 1939-)
Michael (Norman) Manley (ex-PM, Jamaica; 1924-)
Michael Milken (US, "junk bond" king; 1946-)
Michael Moriarty (ent.; 1941-)
Michael Murphy (ent.; 1938-)
Michael Palin (ent.; 1943-)
Michael (Scudamore) Redgrave, Sir (ent.; 1908-85)
Michael Sarrazin (ent.)
Michael S. Dukakis (ex-gov., MA; 1933-)
Michael Spinks (boxing; 1956-)
Michael (Kemp) Tippett, Sir (Br. comp.; 1905-)
Michael Todd (ent.; 1909-58)
Michael Tucker (ent.; 1944-)
Michael Wigglesworth (US rel./writer; 1631-1705)
Michael Wilding (ent.; 1912-79)
Michael William Balfe (Ir. comp./singer; 1808-70)
Michael York (ent.; 1942-)
Michael, George (ent.. 1963-)
Michaelmas Day (rel.; Sept. 29)
Michaels, Al (ent.; 1944-)
Michal Kovac (pres., Slovakia
Michel (Eyquem) de Montaigne (Fr. writer; 1533-92)
Michel Ney (Fr. mil.; 1769-1815)
Michel, Robert H. (US pol.; 1923-)
Michelangelo Buonarroti (It. artist/poet; 1475-1564)
Michelangelo da Caravaggio (It. artist; 1573-

Proper Noun Speller

1610)
Michele Greene (ent.)
Michele Lee (ent.; 1942-)
Michelin™
Michelin Tire Corp.
Michelle Pfeiffer (ent.; 1957-)
Michelle Phillips (ent.; 1944-)
Michelob™ (beer)
Michelozzo Michelozzi (also Michelozzo di
     Bartolommeo)(It. sculptor/arch.; 1396-1472)
Michelson, Albert A(braham)(US physt.; 1852-
     1931)
Michener, James A(lbert)(US writer; 1907-)
Michigan (MI)
Michigan City, IN
Michigan, Lake (N central US)
Michikinikwa (aka Chief Little Turtle)(Miami
     Indians; 1752?-1812)
Mick (Michael Phillip) Jagger (ent.; 1943-)
Mickelson, George S. (ex-gov., SD; 1941-93)
Mickey Cohen
Mickey Finn (drugged drink)
Mickey Gilley (ent.; 1936-)
Mickey Kantor (US trade rep; 1939-)
Mickey (Charles) Mantle (baseball; 1931-)
Mickey Mouse (cartoon chara.)
Mickey Mouse (mag.)
Mickey Mouse Club (TV show)
Mickey Rooney (ent.; 1920-)
Mickey Rourke (ent.; 1953-)
Mickey Spillane (b. Frank Morrison
     Spillane)(US writer; 1918-)
Mickey (Mary Kathryn) Wright (golf; 1935-)
Micki & Maude (film; 1984)
Micmac (NAmer. Indians)
Micro-K Extencaps™ (med.)
Micronase™ (med.)
Micronesia (Federated States of)(islands, W
     Pac.)
Micronesian (people)
Microscopium (astron., microscope)
Microsoft™ (compu.)
Microsoft Corp.
Microsoft™ Excel (compu.)
Microsoft™ Word (compu.)
Microsoft™ Works (compu.)
Mid-Atlantic Ridge (ocean ridge)
Mid Glamorgan (county, Wales)
Midas International Corp.
Midas™ muffler
Midas touch
Midas, King (myth.)
Middle Ages (Eur. hist.; 5th-15th c.)
Middle America
Middle American Indians
Middle Atlantic States (US)(also Middle States)
Middle East (Asia/Africa)(also Mideast)
Middle English (lang.; c1050-1550)

Middle French
Middle Greek (also Medieval Greek)
Middle High German
Middle Irish
Middle Kingdom (Eg. hist.; c2040-1670 BC)(Ch.
     term for China until 1912)
Middle Latin (also Medieval Latin)
Middle Low German
Middle Paleolithic period (200,000-40,000 years
     ago)
Middle Path (rel.)
Middle Stone Age (Mesolithic period; 15,000 to
     10,000 years ago)
Middle Way (rel.)
Middle West (also Midwest)(N central US)
Middlesex (county, Eng.)
Middlesex, NJ
Middletown Record (NY newspaper)
Middletown Times Herald (NY newspaper)
Middletown, CT, NY, OH
Midgard serpent (myth.)
Midi-Pyrénées (region, Fr.)
Midianites (ancient people)
Midland, MI, TX
Midler, Bette (ent.; 1945-)
Midnight Cowboy (film; 1969)
Midnight, Captain (cartoon chara.)
Midol™ (med.)
Midori™ (liqueur)
Midori Ito (figure skating)
Midrash (rel.)
Midsummer Day (also St. John's Day)(June 24)
Midsummer-Night's Dream, A (Shakespeare
     play)
Midway Islands (N Pac.)
Midwest (also Middle West)(N central US)
Midwest City, OK
Midwest Express (airline)
Midwest Living (mag.)
Mien (lang.)
Mies van der Rohe, Ludwig (Ger./US arch.;
     1886-1969)
Mifflin Co., Houghton
Mifune Toshiro (Jap. actor; 1920-)
MIG jet fighter (also MiG, Mig)
Mighty Mouse (cartoon)
Miguel Angel Asturias (Guat. writer/dipl.; 1899-
     1974)
Miguel de Cervantes Saavedra (Sp. writer;
     1547-1616)
Miguel José Serra Junípero, Father (Sp. rel.;
     1713-84)
Miguel Trovoada (pres., São Tomé/Príncipe ;
     1936-)
Mikado, The (Gilbert and Sullivan)
Mikan, George (basketball; 1924-)
Mikasa Co.
Mike Bossy (hockey; 1957-)

Mike Connors (ent.; 1925-)
Mike Ditka (football
Mike Espy (US Secy./Agriculture; 1953-)
Mike Farrell (ent.; 1939-)
Mike Hammer (fict. chara., Mickey Spillane
  novels)
Mike (Michael) Jordan (basketball/baseball;
  1963-)
Mike Leavitt (UT gov.)
Mike Lowry (WA gov.)
Mike Myers (ent.; 1962-)
Mike Nichols (ent.; 1931-)
Mike Peters (cartoonist, *Mother Goose &
  Grimm*; 1943-)
Mike Powell (track; 1963-)
Mike Royko (US jour.)
Mike Schmidt (baseball; 1949-)
Mike (Michael J.) Sullivan (WY gov.; 1939-)
Mike (Michael Gerald) Tyson (boxing; 1966-)
Mike Wallace (US TV jour.; 1918-)
Mikhail Bakunin (Rus. pol.; 1814-76)
Mikhail Baryshnikov (Latvian/US dancer;
  1948-)
Mikhail Bulgakov (Rus. writer; 1891-1940)
Mikhail (or Michael) Fyodorovich Romanov
  (emp., Rus.; 1596-1645)
Mikhail Ivanovitch Glinka (Rus. comp.; 1804-
  57)
Mikhail (Larionovich) Kutuzov (Rus. mil.; 1745-
  1813)
Mikhail Mordkin (Rus. ballet; 1881-1944)
Mikhail S(ergeyevich) Gorbachev (ex-pres.; Rus.
  1931-)
Mikhail (Aleksandrovich) Sholokhov (Rus.
  writer; 1906-84)
Mikita, Stan (hockey; 1940-)
Miklos Nemeth (ex-PM, Hung.)
Miklos Rozsa (US comp.)
Mikoyan, Anastas (USSR pol.; 1895-1978)
Mikulski, Barbara A. (US cong.; 1936-)
Milan Kucan (pres., Slovenia)
Milan Panic (ex-PM, Yug.)
Milan point (lace)
Milan, Italy
Milan, Victor
Milano, Alyssa (ent.; 1972-)
Milanov, Zinka (Kunc)(Yug. opera; 1906-)
Milburn Stone (ent.; 1904-80)
Milburn, Rodney, Jr. (hurdler; 1950-)
Mildred Bailey (US jazz; 1907-51)
Mildred Natwick (ent.; 1908-)
Mildred Pierce (J.M. Cain novel)
Milenkovic, Stefan
Miles Davis (US jazz; 1926-91)
Miles Pharmaceuticals (US bus.)
Miles Standish (Br./Amer. settler/mil.; c1584-
  1656)
Miles, Sarah (ent.; 1941-)

Miles, Vera (ent.; 1929-)
Milford, CT, MA
Milhaud, Darius (Fr. comp.; 1892-1974)
Military Academy, U.S. (West Point, NY)(est.
  1802)
Military Channel, The (cable TV)
Milk-Bone™ (dog biscuits)
Milk Duds™ (candy)
Milk, Harvey (San Francisco pol., murdered)
Milken, Michael (US, "junk bond" king; 1946-)
Milky Way galaxy (astron.)
Milky Way™ (candy)
Mill, James (Scot. phil.; 1773-1836)
Mill, John Stuart (Br. phil./econ.; 1806-73)
Milland, Ray (ent.; 1905-86)
Millar, Kenneth (pseud. Ross Macdonald)(US
  writer; 1915-)
Millard Fillmore (13th US pres.; 1800-74)
Millay, Edna St. Vincent (US poet; 1892-1950)
Mille Fleur bantam (chicken)
Mille, Agnes De (US dancer/choreographer;
  1905-93)
Mille, Cecil B. De (ent.; 1881-1959)
Millenia, Mazda™ (auto.)
Millenial Church (also United Society of
  Believers in Christ's Second
  Coming[Appearing], Shakers)
Miller™ (beer)
Miller Brewing Co.
Miller Lite
Miller Story, The Glenn (film; 1954)
Miller, Ann (ent.; 1919-)
Miller, Arthur (US writer; 1915-)
Miller, Barney (TV show)
Miller, Cheryl (basketball; 1964-)
Miller, Daisy (Henry James novelette)
Miller, Dennis (ent.; 1953-)
Miller, Glenn (US jazz; 1904-44)
Miller, Henry (US writer; 1891-1980)
Miller, Inc., Herman (furniture)
Miller, Joe (familiar joke/book of jokes)
Miller, Johnny (golf; 1947-)
Miller, McCabe & Mrs. (film; 1971)
Miller, Mitch (ent.; 1911-)
Miller, Perry G. (US hist.; 1905-63)
Miller, Reggie (basketball; 1965-)
Miller, Robert "Bob" (NV gov.; 1945-)
Miller, Roger (ent.; 1936-92)
Miller, Shannon (gymnast; 1977-)
Miller, Walter D. (ex-SD gov.)
Miller, Zell (GA gov.; 1932-)
Millerand, Alexandre (ex-pres., Fr.; 1859-1943)
Miller's Outpost (store)
Millet, Jean François (Fr. artist; 1814-75)
Millett, Kate (US writer/feminist; 1934-)
Millicent Fenwick (US pol.; 1900-92)
Millie, Thoroughly Modern (film; 1967)
Milligan, Ex parte (US law; 1866)

Millikan, Robert A(ndrews)(US physt.; 1868-1953)
Millöcker, Karl
Mills Brothers, The (pop music)
Mills, Donna (ent.; 1942-)
Mills, Hayley (ent.)
Mills, John (ent.; 1908-)
Mills, Robert (US arch.; 1781-1855)
Mills, Wilbur D. (US pol.; 1910-92)
Millville, NJ
Milne, A(lan) A(lexander)(Br. writer; 1882-1956)
Milner, Martin (ent.; 1927-)
Milnes, Sherrill (ent.; 1935-)
Milo, Venus de (also *Venus of Melos, Aphrodite of Melos*)(Gr. statue; c.200 BC)
Mi-lo-fo (also Maitreya, Miroku)(rel.)
Milongo, André (ex-PM, Congo
Milos Forman (Czech. ent.; 1932-)
Milos, Greece (also Milo, Melos)(Venus de Milo found)
Milosevic, Slobodan (Serbian pol.; 1941-)
Milquetoast (a timid person)(also l.c.)
Milquetoast, Caspar (cartoon chara.)
Milsap, Ronnie (ent.; 1944-)
Milt Jackson (US jazz; 1923-)
Milton Ager (US comp.; 1893-1979)
Milton Berle ("Uncle Miltie")(ent.; 1908-)
Milton-Bradley™
Milton Bradley Co.
Milton Byron Babbitt (US comp.; 1916-)
Milton Caniff (cartoonist, *Terry & the Pirates, Steve Canyon*; 1907-88)
Milton Friedman (US econ.; 1912-_
Milton (Snavely) Hershey (US, founded chocolate co.; 1857-1945)
Milton "Gummo" Marx (ent.; 1893-1977)
Milton Obote, (Apollo)(ex-pres., Uganda; 1925-)
Milton, John (Br. poet; 1608-74)
Miltown™ (tranquilizer)
Milwaukee Brewers (baseball team)
Milwaukee Bucks (basketball team)
Milwaukee Journal (WI newspaper)
Milwaukee Sentinel (WI newspaper)
Milwaukee, WI
Milwaukee's Best™ (beer)
Mily Alexeyevich Balakirev (Rus. comp.; 1837-1910)
Mimas (Saturn moon, myth)
Mimeograph™
Mimetics™ (software)
Mindy, Mork and (TV show)
Minetics Corp.
Mimi Rogers (ent.)
Mimieux, Yvette (ent.)
Mimolette (cheese)
Min (lang.)
Mina (people)

Mina Sulman, Bahrain
Minamata disease (mercury poisoning)
Minamoto (also Genji)(Jap. hist.; 1192-1219)
Minangkabau (lang.)
Mindanao (island, Philippines)
Mindelo, Cape Verde
Mine Workers of America, United (UMWA)(union, est. 1890)
Mineo, Sal (ent.)
Minerva (myth.)
Miniver, Mrs. (film; 1942)
Ming dynasty (Ch. hist.; 1368-1644)
Ming porcelain
Mingo, Norman (cartoonist; 1896-1980)
Mingus, Charles (US jazz; 1922-79)
Minié ball (bullet; 19th c.)
Minimalism (art/music movement)(also l.c.)
Minita Gordon, (Elmira), Dame (gov-gen., Belize
Minneapolis-St. Paul International Airport (MN)
Minneapolis Star-Tribune (MN newspaper)
Minneapolis, MN
Minnehaha (fict. chara., Hiawatha's wife)
Minnelli, Liza (ent.; 1946-)
Minnelli, Vincente (ent.; 1910-86)
Minnesota (MN)
Minnesota Mining & Manufacturing Co. (3M)
Minnesota Multiphasic Personality Inventory (also MMPI)(psych.)
Minnesota North Stars (hockey team)
Minnesota Timberwolves (basketball team)
Minnesota Twins (baseball team)
Minnesota v. Dickerson (US law; 1993)
Minnesota Vikings (football team)
Minnesota, Near v. (US law; 1931-)
Minnie Maddern Fiske (ent.; 1865-1932)
Minnie Pearl (ent.; 1912-)
Minoan civilization (Crete; 3000-1100 BC)
Minolta™ (elec.)
Minor C. Keith (US bus.; 1848-1929)
Minor Prophets
Minor, Leo (astron.; little lion)
Minor, Ursa (astron., little/lesser bear; part of Little Dipper)
Minorca (chicken)
Minorca (or Menorca) Island (Balearic Island, Mediterranean)
Minoru Yamasaki (US arch,; 1912-86)
Minos, King (myth.)
Minot Air Force Station, ND
Minot, ND
Minotaur (myth.)
Minseito (Jap. pol. party)
Minsk, Belarus (also Mensk)
Mintoff, Dom(inic)(ex-PM, Malta; 1916-)
Minuit, Peter (Dutch admin. in Amer.; c1580-1638)

Minute Maid™ (juice)
Minute Man National Historical Park (MA)
Minuteman (US mil.; 1770s)(also US missile, mil. org.)
Minute™ rice
Minute Maid Foodservice Group (US bus.)
Miocene epoch (26-10 million years ago)
Miguel Trovoada (pres., São Tomé/Príncipe 1936-)
Miquelon, St. Pierre and (Fr. islands, Newfoundland)
Mir (USSR space station)
Mira variable (also Omicron Ceti)(astron.)
Mirabeau, Honoré Gabriel (Riqueti), Comte de (Fr. pol.; 1749-91)
Mirabella (mag.)
Miracle-Gro™ (agr.)
Miracle of Fátima
Miracle Whip™
Miracles, Smokey Robinson and the (pop music)
Miramax Films
Miranda (Uranus moon)
Miranda vs. Arizona (US law; 1966)
Miranda warnings (US law)
Miranda, Carmen (ent.; 1913-55)
Mirassou Vineyards (US bus.)
Mircea Snegur (pres., Moldova)
Miró, Joan (Sp. artist; 1893-1983)
Miroku (also Maitreya, Mi-lo-fo)(rel.)
Mirro™ (cookware)
MIRV (multiple independently targeted reentry vehicle)
Misanthrope, Le (Molière comedy)
Mischa Elman (ent.; 1891-1967)
Miserables, Les (V. Hugo novel)
Misere, Seychelles
Mishawaka, IN
Mishima Yukio (aka Hiraoka Kimitake)(Jap. writer; 1925-70)
Mishna(h) Law (also Oral)(rel.)
Miskolc, Hungary
Misrule, Lord of (former Christmas revelry director, Br.)
Miss America
Miss America Pageant, The
Miss Breck™ (hair care)
Miss Clairol™ (hair care)
Miss Daisy, Driving (film; 1989)
Miss Jean Brodie, The Prime of (film; 1969)
Miss Marple (fict. chara., A. Christie)
Miss Muffett, Little (nursery rhyme)
Miss Peach (comic strip)
Miss Piggy (Muppet)
Miss Right (slang)
Miss/Ms. Right (slang)
Miss Saigon (play)
Missing Persons (TV show)
Mission Viejo, CA

Mission, TX
Missionary Ridge, GA, TN
Mississauga, Ontario, Canada
Mississippi (MS)
Mississippi River (US, between Appalachian/ Rocky Mts.)
Mississippian period (345-320 million years ago)
Missoula, MT
Missouri (MO)
Missouri Compromise (US hist.; 1820-21)
Missouri River (central US)
Mister Roberts (film; 1955)
Mister Rogers' Neighborhood (TV show)
Mister Softee, Inc.
Mistral, Frédéric (Fr. poet; 1830-1914)
Mistral, Gabriela (aka Lucilla Godoy de Alcayaga)(Chilean poet; 1889-1957)
Misty Harbour™ (raincoat)
Misurata, Libya
Mita™
Mita Copystar America, Inc.
Mitch Leigh (US comp.; 1928-)
Mitch McConnell (US cong.; 1942-)
Mitch Miller (ent.; 1911-)
Mitch Snyder (US reformer/homeless; 1944-90)
Mitchell Parish (US comp.; 1901-)
Mitchell Systems, John Paul (US bus.)
Mitchell, Billy (US mil.; 1879-1936)
Mitchell, Cameron (ent.; 1918-)
Mitchell, Edgar D. (astro.)
Mitchell, George J. (US cong.; 1933-)
Mitchell, James (ent.; 1920-)
Mitchell, James (PM, St. Vincent/Grenadines)
Mitchell, James P(aul)(US bus./pol.; 1902-?)
Mitchell, John (US labor leader; 1870-1919)
Mitchell, John (Newton)(US pol./Watergate; 1913-88)
Mitchell, Joni (b. Roberta Joan Anderson)(ent.; 1943-)
Mitchell, Margaret (US writer; 1900-49)
Mitchell™, Paul (hair care)
Mitchell, Thomas (ent.; 1892-1962)
Mitchell, Wisconsin v. (US law; 1993)
Mitchelson, Marvin (US atty.)
Mitchum™ (anti-perspirant)
Mitchum, Robert (ent.; 1917-)
Mithraism (also Mithraicism)(rel.)
Mithras (myth.)
Mitsotakis, Constantine (ex-PM, Gr.; 1918-)
Mitsubishi™
Mitsubishi Electric Sales America, Inc.
Mitsubishi Fuso Truck of America, Inc.
Mitsubishi International Corp.
Mitsubishi Motor Sales of America, Inc.
Mitterrand, François (pres., Fr.; 1916-)
Mitty, The Secret Life of Walter (J. Thurber short story)

Mitzi Gaynor (ent.; 1930-)
Mix, Tom (Thomas Edwin)(ent.; 1880-1940)
Mixtec (Mex. Indians)
Miyazawa, Kiichi (ex-PM, Jap.; 1919-)
Mizoram (state, India)
Mizoyev, Akbar (Tajikistan pol.)
MJB Co.
MJB™ coffee
M. J. Divine, Major (also Father Divine)(b.
    George Baker)(US rel.; 1882-1965)
M. M. Kaye
MN (Minnesota)
Mn (chem. sym., manganese)
Mnemosyne (myth.)
MO (Missouri, money order)
Mo (chem. sym., molybdenum)
Mo Ti (also Mo-tze, Mo Tzu, Mo-tse, Mo
    Tse)(Ch. phil.; 5th c. BC)
Moab (ancient kingdom, Jordan)
Moabite (people)
Moabite Stone/stone (Moab hist.; 9th c. BC)
Moammar (or Moamer al, Muammar al)
    Khadafy (or Khaddhafi, Qaddafi, Gaddafi)
    (pres., Libya; 1942-)
Mobil™
Mobil Chemical Co.
Mobil Corp.
Mobil Oil Corp.
Mobile Press (AL newspaper)
Mobile Register (AL newspaper)
Mobile, AL
Möbius strip/band
Mobutu Sese Seko (Kuku Ngbendu wa
    Zabanga)(b. Joseph Désiré Mobutu)(pres.,
    Zaire; *Moby Dick* (by Herman Melville)
Moco, Marcolino José Carlos (PM, Angola)
Model A Ford (auto.)
Model T Ford (auto.)
Modena (pigeon)
Modena, Italy
Modern Bride (mag.)
Modern Electronics (mag.)
Modern English (also New English)(lang.)
Modern English, Early (lang.; c1550-1700)
Modern English, Late (lang.; c1700-present)
Modern Greek (also New Greek)
Modern Hebrew (also New Hebrew)
Modern Latin
Modern Maturity (mag.)
Modernism (art, rel.)
Modersohn-Becker, Paula (Ger. artist; 1867-
    1907)
Modest Petrovich Mussorgsky (Rus. comp.;
    1839-81)
Modesto Bee (CA newspaper)
Modesto, CA
Modigliani, Amedeo (It. artist; 1884-1920)
Modine, Matthew (ent.; 1959-)

Modjeska, Helena (ent.; 1844-1909)
Modoc (NAmer. Indians)
Modred (also Mordred)(King Arthur's killer)
Moe Howard (b. Moses Horwitz)(ent.; 1897-
    1975)
Moen (US bus.)
Moerae (also Moirai)(myth.)
Moët & Chandon champagne
Moffat, Donald (ent.; 1930-)
Moffo, Anna (ent.; 1927-)
Mogadishu, Somalia (also Mogadisho)
Mogae, Festus (VP, Botswana
Mogen (or Magen) David (also Star of David)
Mogen David™ (kosher foods)
Mogen David™ (wine)
Mogen David Wine Corp.
Mogilev, Belarus
Mogul art/architecture
Mogul Empire (dynasty, India; 1526-1857)
Mohammed (see Muhammad)
Mohammed Karim Lamrani (PM, Morocco
Mohammedanism (misnomer for Islam rel.)
Mohandas K(aramchand) "Mahatma" Gandhi
    (Indian pol./pacifist; 1869-1948)
Moharram (also Muharram)(rel.)
Mohave (also Mojave)(NAmer. Indians)
Mohave (or Mojave) Desert (S CA)
Mohawk (NAmer. Indians)
Mohawk Airlines
Mohawk Carpet Mills (US bus.)
Mohawk haircut (also l.c.)
Mohawk River (NY)
Mohegan (or Mohican)(NAmer. Indians)
Mohenjo-Daro (Pak. archeological site)
Mohican (or Mohegan)(NAmer. Indians)
Mohicans, The Last of the (J.F. Cooper novel)
Mohorovicic discontinuity (also Moho, M-
    discontinuity)(geol.)
Mohorovicic, Andrija (Yug. physt.; 1857-1936)
Mohs' scale (hardness of minerals)
Moi, Daniel arap (pres., Kenya; 1924-)
Moira (myth.)
Moira Shearer (ent.; 1926-)
Moirai (also Moerae)(myth.)
Moise K(apenda) Tshombe (ex-PM, Congo/Zaire;
    1919-69)
Moiseyev Dance Company
Mojave (or Mohave) Desert (S CA)
Mojave Indians (also Mohave)(AZ/CA)
Mokhehle, Ntsu (premier, Lesotho
Moldavia (now Moldova and Romania)
Moldavian (lang.)
Moldova (Republic of)(formerly part of USSR)(E
    central Eur.)
Moldovian (people)
Molière (b. Jean Baptiste Poquelin)(Fr. writer;
    1622-73)
Molina, Manuel Luis Quezon y (ex-pres.

Philippines; 1878-1944)

Molina, Rafael L. Trujillo (ex-pres., Dom Rep.; 1891-1961)

Molinaro, Al (ent.; 1919-)

Moline, IL

Molinism (rel.)

Molise (region, It.)

Molitor, Paul (baseball; 1956-)

Moll Flanders, The Fortunes and Misfortunes of the Famous (D. Defoe)

Moll, Richard (ent.; 1943-)

Mollet, Guy (Fr. pol.; 1905-75)

Mollicone, Joseph, Jr. (US bank scandal)

Mollie Parnis (US designer; 1905-92)

Mollweide (or homolographic) projection

Molly™ bolt (constr.)

Molly Maguires (also Mollies)(US/Ir. secret society; c1854-77)

Molly Maguires, The (film; 1970)

Molly McButter™ (food)

Molly Pitcher (b. Mary [Ludwig Hays] McCauley)(US heroine; 1754-1832)

Molly Ringwald (ent.; 1968-)

Molly Yard, (Mary Alexander)(ex-pres., NOW

Molly, Fibber McGee and (radio comedy)

Molnár, Ferenc (Hung. writer; 1878-1952)

Molokai (island, HI)

Molotov cocktail (homemade bomb)

Molotov, Vyacheslav M(ikhailovich)(ex-PM, Rus.; 1890-1986)

Moluccas (also Spice Islands)(Indonesia)

Mombasa, Kenya

Momma (comic strip)

Mommie Dearest (film; 1981)

Mommsen, Theodor (Ger. hist.; 1817-1903)

Mon-Khmer (lang.)

Mona Lisa (aka *La Gioconda*)(da Vinci painting)

Monaco (Principality of)(Eur.)

Monaco-Ville, Monaco

Monaco, Monaco

Monaghan (county, NIre.)

Mönchengladbach, Germany (formerly München-Gladbach)

Monck, George (Duke of Albemarle)(Br. mil./ pol.; 1608-70)

Monck's Regiment (Br. mil., now Coldstream Guards)

Moncton, New Brunswick, Canada

Mondale, Walter F(rederick) "Fritz" (US pol.; 1928-)

Mondavi Winery, Robert (US bus.)

Mondavi™, Robert

Monday Night Football, NFL (TV show)

Mondeo, Ford (auto.)

Mondrian, Piet (b. Pieter Cornelis Mondriaan)(Dutch artist; 1872-1944)

M-1 (or Garand) rifle (semiautomatic)

Monegasque (people)

Monet™ (jewelry)

Monet (US bus.)

Monet, Claude (Fr. artist; 1840-1926)

Monetgo Bay, Jamaica

Money (mag.)

Moneyline (TV show)

Moneysworth (mag.)

Mongar, Bhutan

Mongo (lang.)

Mongol (people)

Mongol (or Yüan) dynasty (Ch. ruling house; 1279-1368)

Mongol Empire (Rus./Ch. hist.; 1206-c1380)

Mongolia (State of)(formerly Outer Mongolia, People's Republic of Mongolia)(E central Asia)

Mongolia, Inner (NE Ch.)

Mongolia, Outer (now State of Mongolia)

Mongolian (lang./people)

Mongoloid (one of three major races of humans)

Mongoloid, or Mongolian idiot (now Down's syndrome)

Monica de Greiff

Monica Seles (tennis; 1973-)

Monica Vitti (ent.; 1931-)

Monistat™ 7 (med.)

Monitor, Merrimack v. (US hist.; 1862)

Monk, Art (football; 1957-)

Monk, Thelonious (Sphere)(US jazz; 1920-82)

Monkees, the (pop music)

Monmouth Beach, NJ

Monmouth, Battle of (US hist.; 1778)

Monmouth, Fort, NJ (mil.)

Monmouth, Geoffrey of (Br. writer/chronicler; c1100-54)

Mono Lake (CA)

Monoceros (astron., unicorn)

Monongahela River (PA/WV)

Monophysite (rel.)

Monopoly™ (game)

Monotheletism (also Monothelism)(rel.)

Monotype™ (graphics)

Monroe Auto Equipment Co.

Monroe Doctrine (US hist.; 1823)

Monroe™ shocks

Monroe, Fort, VA (mil.)

Monroe, James (5th US pres.; 1758-1831)

Monroe, LA

Monroe, Marilyn (b. Norma Jean Baker [or Mortenson])(ent.; 1926-62)

Monroe, Vaughn (ent.; 1911-73)

Monrovia, Liberia

Mons, Belgium

Monsanto Acrilan™ (carpet)

Monsanto Co.

Monseigneur (Fr. title)

Monsieur (Fr. for Mr.)

Monsignor (rel. title)
Mont Blanc (Alps, Fr./It.)
Mont-Royal, Quebec, Canada
Montagnais Indians/lang.)
Montagu, (Montague Francis) Ashley (Br./US
    anthrop.; 1905-)
Montagu, John (Earl of Sandwich)(Br. pol.;
    1718-92)
Montagu, Mary (Wortley), Lady (aka Mary
    Pierrepont)(Br. writer; 1689-1762)
Montague families, Capulet and (*Romeo and
    Juliet*)
Montague, Romeo (fict. chara., *Romeo & Juliet*)
Montaigne, Michel (Eyquem) de (Fr. writer;
    1533-92)
Montalban, Ricardo (ent.; 1920)
Montale, Eugenio (It. poet; 1896-1981)
Montana (MT)
Montana, Bob (cartoonist, *Archie*; 1920-75)
Montana, Joe (football; 1956-)
Montand, Yves (Fr. ent.; 1921-91)
Montauk (NAmer. Indians)
Montauk Point (NY)
Montcalm, Louis(-Joseph) de (Montcalm-
    Gozon)(Fr. mil.; 1712-59)
Monte Carlo method (statistics)
Monte Carlo, Monaco
Monte Cristo sandwich
Monte Cristo, Count of (by Dumas)
Montego Bay, Jamaica
Monteiro, Antonio Mascarenhas (pres., Cape
    Verde; 1944-)
Montel Williams (ent.)
Montelena Winery, Chateau (US bus.)
Monteil Paris (US bus.)
Montenegro (republic, Yug.)
Monterey Bay, CA
Monterey Jack (cheese)
Monterey Vineyard (US bus.)
Monterey, CA
Monterrey, Mexico
Montesquieu, Charles Louis (Fr. phil.; 1689-
    1755)
Montessori method/system/school (educ.)
Montessori, Maria (It. educ.; 1870-1952)
Monteverdi, Claudio (Giovanni Antonio)(It.
    comp.; 1567-1643)
Montevideo, Uruguay
Montez, Lola (ent.; 1818?-61)
Montezuma I (Aztec emp., Mex.; 1390?-1464?)
Montezuma II (Aztec emp., Mex.; 1466?-1520)
Montezuma's revenge (also Aztec two-
    step)(traveler's diarrhea)
Montgolfier, Jacques Étienne (Fr. hot-air
    balloonist; 1745-99)
Montgolfier, Joseph Michel (Fr. hot-air
    balloonist; 1740-1810)
Montgomery Advertiser (AL newspaper)

Montgomery Clift (ent.; 1920-66)
Montgomery Journal (AL newspaper)
Montgomery Ward™
Montgomery Ward & Co., Inc.
Montgomery Ward, Aaron (US bus.; 1843-1913)
Montgomery, AL, OH
Montgomery, Bernard Law (Br. mil.; 1887-
    1976)
Montgomery, Elizabeth (ent.; 1933-)
Montgomery, Jim (swimming; 1955-)
Montgomery, Robert (ent.; 1904-81)
Montgomery, Ruth (writer/psychic)
Montgomery, Wes (US jazz; 1925-68)
Monthan Air Force Base, Davis-, AZ (mil.)
Monticelli, Adolphe Joseph Thomas (Fr. artist;
    1824-86)
Monticello (T. Jefferson's home)(VA)
Monticello Carpet Mills (US bus.)
Montmartre (area, Paris)
Montparnasse (area, Paris)
Montpelier, VT
Montrachet cheese
Montrachet wine
Montreal Canadiens (hockey team)
Montreal Expos (baseball team)
Montreal-Nord, Quebec, Canada (also Montreal
    North)
Montreal, Quebec, Canada
Montreuil, France
Montreux International Jazz Festival
Montserrat (a Leeward island, Br. West Indies)
Monty Hall (ent.; 1925-)
Monty Python's Flying Circus (TV show)
Monty Woolley (ent.; 1888-1963)
Moody Air Force Base, GA
Moody Blues (pop music)
Moody, Dwight Lyman (US rel.; 1837-99)
Moody, Helen (Newington) Wills (tennis; 1906-)
Moody, Raymond
Moody, Ron (ent. 1924-)
Moog™ synthesizer (music)
Moog Electronics, Inc.
Moon Mulligan
Moon Mullins (comic strip)
Moon Unit Zappa (ent.)
Moon, Sun Myung, Rev. (Korean rel.; 1920-)
Moon, Warren (football; 1956-)
Moonie (follower of Rev. Moon, Unification
    Church; est. 1954)
Moonlighting (TV show)
Moor (people)
Moor of Venice, The Tragedy of Othello, The
    (Shakespeare play)
Moore & Co., Benjamin
Moore, Archie (boxing; 1913-)
Moore, Clayton (ent.; 1908-)
Moore, Clement C(lark)(US poet/educ.; 1779-
    1863)

Moore, Demi (ent.; 1962-)
Moore, Dudley (ent.; 1935-)
Moore, Garry (ent.; 1915-93)
Moore, George (Ir. writer; 1852-1933)
Moore, George E. (Br. phil.; 1873-1958)
Moore, George Foot (US rel.; 1851-1931)
Moore, Henry (Br. sculptor; 1898-1986)
Moore, John Bassett (US jurist; 1860-1947)
Moore, Marianne (Craig)(US poet; 1887-1972)
Moore, Mary Tyler (ent.; 1937-)
Moore, Melba (ent.; 1945-)
Moore, Roger (ent.; 1928-)
Moore, Terry (ent.; 1929-)
Moore, Thomas (Ir. poet; 1779-1852)
Moore, Victor (ent.; 1876-1962)
Moorehead, Agnes (ent.; 1906-74)
Moores, Dick (cartoonist, *Gasoline Alley*; 1909-86)
Moorhead, MN
Moorish arch (Sp.; 11-14th c.)
Moorish idol (fish)
Moors (people)
Moose Jaw, Saskatchewan, Canada
Moose, Loyal Order of (US org.)
Moosehead Lake (ME)
Mootsies Tootsies™ (shoes)
Mootsies Tootsies (US bus.)
Mop & Glo™ (floor cleaner)
Mopti, Mali
Moral Majority
Moran, Bugs (George)(US gangster)
Moráng, Nepal
Moranis, Rick (ent.; 1953-)
Morant, Breaker (film; 1979)
Moravia (regions, Czech.)
Moravian (rel.)
Moravian Church (also Renewed Church of the Brethren, Unitas Fratrum)
Mordecai (rel.)
Mordkin, Mikhail (Rus. ballet; 1881-1944)
Mordred (also Modred)(King Arthur's killer)
Mordvin (lang./people)
More (lang.)
More (cigarettes)
Moré, Hannah (Br. writer; 1745-1833)
More, Sir Thomas (Br. writer/pol.; 1478-1535)
Moreau, Dr. (fict. villain)
Moreau, Gustave (Fr. artist; 1826-98)
Moreau, Jeanne (Fr. ent.; 1928-)
Moreno Valley, CA
Moreno, Rita (ent.; 1931-)
Moresby, Port (Papua New Guinea)
Morey Amsterdam (ent.; 1914-)
Morgan (horse)
Morgan Fairchild (ent.; 1950-)
Morgan Freeman (ent.; 1937-)
Morgan le Fay (also Morgain le Fay)(King Arthur's fairy sister)

Morgan, Daniel (US mil.; 1736-1802)
Morgan, Dennis (ent.; 1910-)
Morgan, Harry (ent.; 1915-)
Morgan, Sir Henry (Welsh buccaneer in Amer.; 1635?-88)
Morgan, Joe (Leonard)(baseball; 1943-)
Morgan, John Hunt (US mil.; 1826-64)
Morgan, J(ohn) P(ierpont)(US finan.; 1837-1913)
Morgan, Thomas Hunt (US geneticist; 1866-1945)
Morgana, Fata (Arthurian)
Morgantown, WV
Morgenthau, Henry (US finan./dipl.; 1856-1946)
Morgenthau, Henry, Jr. (US publ./pol.; 1891-1967)
Moriarty, Michael (ent.; 1941-)
Moriarty, Professor (fict. chara., *Sherlock Holmes*)
Morihiro Hosokawa (PM, Jap.)
Morison, Samuel Eliot (US hist.; 1887-1976)
Morisot, Berthe (Fr. artist; 1841-95)
Morita, Pat (ent.; 1932-)
Moritz Chocolatier, St. (US bus.)
Moriyama, Mayumi
Mork and Mindy (TV show)
Morley Safer (US TV jour.; 1931-)
Morley, Christopher (Darlington)(US writer/editor; 1890-1957)
Morley, Robert (Br. ent.; 1908-92)
Mormon Church (also Latter-Day Saints, Church of Jesus Christ of the Latter-Day Saints)(rel.)
Mormon State (nickname, UT)
Mormon Tabernacle Choir
Mormon, Book of (rel.)
Mornay sauce (also l.c.)
Mornay, Rebecca De (ent.; 1962-)
Morning Call, Allentown (PA newspaper)
Morning News, Dallas (TX newspaper)
Moro, Aldo (ex-PM, It.; 1916-78)
Morocco (Kingdom of)(NW Afr.)
Morocco, Road to (film; 1942)
Moroni, Comoros
Morpheus (myth.)
Morphou, Cyprus
Morrall, Earl (football; 1934-)
Morrell™, John (meats)
Morrell & Co., John
Morrice, James Wilson (Can. artist; 1865-1924)
Morricone, Ennio (It. comp.; 1928-)
Morris Agency, Inc., William
Morris K. Udall (US pol.; 1922-)
Morris Louis (US artist; 1912-62)
Morris, Desmond (Br. writer; 1928-)
Morris, Gouverneur (US pol./dipl.; 1752-1816)
Morris, Greg (ent.; 1934-)
Morris, Inc., Philip

Morris, Robert (US pol./bus.; 1734-1806)
Morris, William (Br. designer; 1834-96)
Morris, Wright (US writer; 1910-)
Morrison, Jim (ent.; 1943-71)
Morrison, Toni (b. Chloe Anthony Wofford)(US
   writer; 1931-)
Morristown National Historical Park (NJ)
Morristown, NJ
Morro Bay, CA
Morrow, Rob (ent.; 1962-)
Morrow, Vic (ent.; 1932-82)
Mors (myth.)
Morse code (comm.)
Morse, Carlton E.
Morse, Robert (ent.; 1931-)
Morse, Samuel (Finley Breese)(US inv.,
   telegraph; 1791-1872)
Morse, Wayne (US pol.; 1900-74)
Mort Drucker (cartoonist, *Mad* magazine;
   1929-)
Mort Sahl (ent.; 1927)
Mort Walker (cartoonist; *Beetle Bailey*; 1923-)
Morte D'Arthur, Le (by T. Malory)
Mortgage Guarantee Insurance Corporation
   (also Maggie Mae)
Mortimer, John (Br. writer/atty.; 1923-)
Morton Dean
Morton Downey
Morton Downey, Jr.
Morton Gould (ent.; 1913-)
Morton International, Inc.
Morton™ salt
Morton, Craig L. (football; 1943-)
Morton, Gary
Morton, Jelly Roll (b. Ferdinand Joseph La
   Menthe)(US jazz; 1885-1941)
Morton, Joe (ent.; 1947-)
Morton, Levi P(arsons)(ex-US VP; 1824-1920)
Mosaic law (pertaining to Moses)
Mosconi, Wilie (billiards; 1913-)
Moscow Art Theater
Moscow mule (mixed drink)
Moscow, ID
Moscow, Russia
Moseley-Braun, Carol (US cong.; 1947-)
Moselle (wine)
Moser Proell, Annemarie (skiing; 1953-)
Moses (Hebrew rel.; c13th c BC)
Moses Lake, WA
Moses (ben Maimon) Maimonides, Rabbi (aka
   RaMBaM)(Jew. rel./phil.; 1135-1204)
Moses Malone (basketball; 1955-)
Moses, Ed(win Corley)(US track; 1955-)
Moses, Grandma (b. Anna Mary Robertson)(US
   artist; 1860-1961)
Moses, Law of (rel.)
Moses, William (ent.; 1959-)
Moshe Dayan (Isr. pol./gen.; 1915-81)

Moshi-Dagomba (people)
Moslem (see Muslim)
Mosquito Coast (area, CAmer.)
Moss Hart (US writer; 1904-61)
Moss Town, Bahamas
Mossadegh, Muhammad (ex-PM, Iran; 1880-
   1967)
Mössbauer effect (physics)
Mössbauer, Rudolf (Ger. physt.; 1929-)
Mossi (lang./people)
Mostar, Bosnia-Hercegovina
Mostel, Zero (Samuel Joel)(ent.; 1915-77)
Mosul, Iraq
Mot (myth.)
Motel 6, Inc.
Moten, Bennie (US jazz; 1894-1935)
Mother Cabrini (also St. Frances Xavier
   Cabrini)(US rel./reformer; 1850-1917)
Mother Earth News (mag.)
Mother Earth
Mother Goose (fict. author of fairy tales)
Mother Goose & Grimm (comic strip)
Mother Goose Tales (fairy tales, C. Perrault)
Mother Hubbard (fict. chara., nursery rhyme)
Mother Hubbard (loose gown; railroad engine)
Mother Jones (Mary Harris Jones)(US labor
   leader; 1830-1930)
Mother Jones (mag.)
Mother Lode (gold belt, CA)
Mother Maybelle Carter (ent.; 1909-78)
Mother Nature
Mother of God (rel.)
Mother Seton (also St. Elizabeth Ann [Bayley]
   Seton)(US rel.; 1774-1821)
Mother Superior (head nun of convent)
Mother Teresa (of Calcutta)(b. Agnes Gonxha
   Bojaxhiu)(Albanian rel.; 1910-)
Mother, Holy (also the Madonna, Mary, Our
   Lady, Virgin Mary)(rel.)
Mother, The Great (also The Great
   Goddess)(rel.)
Mother's Day (2nd Sunday in May)
Mothers Today (mag.)
Motherwell and Wishaw (Scot.)
Motherwell, Robert (Burns)(US artist; 1915-91)
Motley Crue (pop music)
Motor Boating & Sailing (mag.)
Motor Trend (mag.)
Motorland (mag.)
Motorola, Inc.
Motors Corp., General
Motown (nickname, Detroit, MI)
Motown Corp.
Motrin™ (med.)
Mott, Lucretia (Coffin)(US suffragist; 1793-
   1880)
Mott, Nevill Francis (Br. physt.; 1905-)
Motta, Jake La (boxing

Mottola, Tommy (ent.)
Mott's™
Mott's USA (US bus.)
Moulin Rouge (film; 1952)
Moulin Rouge (Paris dancehall)
Moulins, France
Moulmein, Myanmar
Mound Builders (Indians, NAmer.)
Moundou, Chad
Mounds™ (candy)
Moungar, Fidèle (PM, Chad
Mount Ararat (Turk.)(Noah's Ark landing)
Mount Baker-Snoqualmie National Forest (WA)
Mount Blackburn (AK)
Mount Clemens, MI
Mount Erebus (volcano, Antarctica)
Mt. Eden, Villa (US bus.)
Mt. Eden Vineyards (US bus.)
Mount Etna, (volcano, Sicily)
Mount Everest (highest mountain, Himalayas)
Mount Fairweather (AK)
Mount Fuji (also Fujiyama)(Jap. dormant
    volcano)
Mount Holyoke College (MA)
Mount Hopkins Observatory (now Fred
    Lawrence Whipple Observatory)(AZ)
Mount Kenya (also Kirinyaga)(extinct volcano)
Mount Kilimanjaro (Afr.)
Mount Kirinyaga (also Kenya)(extinct volcano)
Mount Kosciusko (Austl.)
Mount Laguna Air Force Station (CA)
Mount Lassen (also Lassen Peak)(CA volcano)
Mount McKinley (also Denali)(AK)
Mount McKinley National Park (now Denali
    National Park)(AK)
Mount Olivet (also Mount of Olives)(Jerusalem)
Mount Olympus (Gr.)
Mount Olympus (WA)
Mount Orizaba (also Citlaltepetl)(dormant
    volcano, Mex.)
Mount Palomar (CA)
Mount Parnassus (Gr.)
Mount Pearl, Newfoundland
Mount Pelée (volcano, Martinique)
Mount Pinatubo (active volcano; Philippines)
Mount Popocatépetl (volcano, Mex.)
Mount Rainier National Park (WA)
Mount Redoubt (active volcano, AK)
Mount Rushmore National Memorial (SD)
Mount Shasta (dormant volcano, CA)
Mount Sinai (NE Eg., Moses/10
    Commandments)
Mount St. Elias (mountain, AK/Can.)
Mount St. Helens (active volcano, WA)
Mount Suribachi (marine flag raising on Iwo
    Jima)
Mt. Veeder Winery (US bus.)
Mount Vernon (G. Washington's home)(VA)

Mount Vernon, NY
Mount Vesuvius (active volcano, It.)
Mount Whitney (CA)
Mount Zion (Jerusalem)
Mountain Dew™ (beverage)
Mountain Home Air Force Base, ID
Mountain Standard Time (also Mountain Time)
Mountain State (nickname, WV)
Mountain States
Mountbatten, Lord Louis (Br. adm./earl; 1900-
    79)
Mountbatten, Philip, Lt. (Duke of Edinburgh,
    Prince of the UK and NIre.; 1921-)
Mounted Police, Royal Canadian (RCMP,
    Mounties)(Can. police; est. 1873)
Mounties (Royal Canadian Mounted Police;
    1950-81)
Mourning, Alonzo (basketball; 1970-)
Mouse, Mickey (cartoon chara.)
Mouse, Mickey (mag.)
Mouse, Mighty (cartoon)
Mouskouri, Nana (ent.)
Movieline (mag.)
Movieola™ (film editing machine)
Moyers, Bill (US jour.; 1934-)
Moynihan, Daniel Patrick (US cong.; 1927-)
Mozambique (Republic of)(SE Afr.)
Mozambique Current (also Agulhas Current)
Mozart, Wolfgang Amadeus (Aus. comp.; 1756-
    91)
MP (military police, mounted police)
MPV (multi-purpose vehicle)
Mr. Belvedere (TV show)
Mr. Big (pop music)
Mr. Big (slang, man in charge)
Mr. Bill (fict. chara.)
Mr. Blackwell
Mr. Blandings Builds His Dream House (film;
    1948)
Mr. Bones (slang)
Mr. Bubble™ bubble bath
Mr. Charlie (Black slang, white man)
Mr. Chips, Goodbye, (film; 1939)
Mr. Clean (slang)
Mr. Clean™ (cleaner)
Mr. Coffee™
Mr. Coffee, Inc.
Mr. Cool (slang)
Mr. Ed (fict. horse)
Mr. Fixit (slang)
Mr. Frick (Werner) Groebli (ice skating; 1915-)
Mr. Goodbar™ (candy)
Mr. Goodbar, Looking for (film; 1977)
Mr. Goodwrench™
Mr. Hyde, The Strange Case of Dr. Jekyll and
    (by R.L. Stevenson)
Mr. Magoo (cartoon)
Mr. Nice Guy (slang)

Mr. Novak (TV show)
Mr. Right (slang)
Mr. Smith Goes to Washington (film; 1939)
Mr. Spock (fict. chara., *Star Trek*)
Mr. T (Lawrence Tero)(ent.; 1952-)
Mr. Tambo (slang)
Mr. Wizard's World (TV show)
Mrs. America
Mrs. Butterworth's™
Mrs. Columbo (TV show)
Mrs. Dash™
Mrs. Doubtfire (film)
Mrs. Fields, Inc.
Mrs. Malaprop (fict. chara, *The Rivals*; malapropism)
Mrs. Miller, McCabe & (film; 1971)
Mrs. Miniver (film; 1942)
Mrs. Muir, The Ghost and (film; 1947)
Mrs. Paul's™
Mrs. Paul's Kitchen (US bus.)
Mrs. Smith's (pies)
Mrs. Tiggy-Winkle, The Tale of (B. Potter story)
MS (Mississippi, multiple sclerosis)
Ms. (mag.)
MS-DOS (Microsoft Disc Operating System) (compu.)
MSG (monosodium glutamate)
Ms./Miss Right (slang)
M-16 (automatic rifle)
MST (Mountain Standard Time)
Mswati III (king, Swaziland; 1968-)
MT (Montana)
MTV Unplugged (TV show)
Muammar al (or Moamer al, Moammar) Khadafy (or Khaddhafi, Qaddafi, Gaddafi)(pres., Libya; 1942-)
Mubarak, Hosni (pres., Eqypt; 1928-)
Much Ado About Nothing (Shakespeare play)
Muda Hassanal Bolkiah, Sultan (PM, Brunei; 1946-)
Mudar Badran (ex-PM, Jordan)
Mudd, Roger (TV jour.; 1928-)
Muddy Waters (aka McKinley Morganfield)(ent.; 1915-83)
Mueller'™ (noodles)
Muenster cheese (also Munster, also l.c.)
Müeslix™ (cereal)
Muffets, The (
Muffett, Little Miss (nursery rhyme)
Mufulira, Zambia
Mugabe, Robert (Gabriel)(pres., Zimbabwe; 1925-)
Muggeridge, Malcolm (Br. jour.; 1903-90)
Muggs, J. Fred (TV chimp; c1952)
Muggsy Spanier (US jazz; 1906-67)
Mughal (also Mogul)(Muslim empire)
Muhajirun (rel.)
Muhammad ibn Abdullah (Arab, founded Islam; c570-632)
Muhammad Abdou (PM, Comoros
Muhammad Ali (also Mehemet Ali)(Eg. pol./ mil.; 1769-1849)
Muhammad Ali (b. Cassius Clay, Jr.)(boxing; 1942-)
Muhammad Ali Jinnah (India/Pak. pol.; 1876-1948)
Muhammad Farad Aidid (Somali gen.)
Muhammad II ("The Conqueror")(sultan, Turk.; 1432-81)
Muhammad Mossadegh (ex-PM, Iran; 1880-1967)
Muhammad Riza Pahlavi (shah, Iran; 1919-80)
Muhammad Zia ul-Haq ("President Zia")(ex-pres., Pak.; 1924-88)
Muhammad Ali Mahdi (ex-pres., Somalia
Muhammad, Elijah (b. Elijah Poole)(US rel.; 1897-1975)
Muhammad, Mahathir bin (PM, Malaysia; 1925-)
Muhammadanism (misnomer for Islam rel.)
Muharram (also Moharram)(rel.)
Muharraq, Bahrain
Muir Woods National Monument (CA)
Muir, John (US environ.; 1838-1914)
Muir, Malcolm (US publ.; 1885-1979)
Muir, The Ghost and Mrs. (film; 1947)
Mujaheddin (Islamic mil.)
Mujahedeen, Afghan (Islamic holy warriors)
Mujibur Rahman (aka Sheik Mujib)(ex-PM, Bangladesh; 1920-75)
Muk, Yon Hyong (ex-premier, NKorea
Mukalla, Yemen
Mukden (now Shenyang)
Muldaur, Diana (ent.; 1938-)
Muldoon, Sir Robert (David)(ex-PM, NewZeal.; 1921-92)
Mulgrew, Kate (ent.; 1955-)
Mulhare, Edward (ent.; 1923-)
Mülheim (an der Ruhr), Germany
Mulholland Drive (Los Angeles)
Mull, Martin (ent.; 1943-)
Müller counter, Geiger- (also Geiger counter)(detects radiation)
Muller v. Oregon (US law; 1908-)
Mulligan, Gerry (US jazz; 1927-)
Mulligan, Moon
Mulligan, Richard (ent.; 1932-)
Mullin, Chris (basketball; 1963-)
Mullins, Moon (comic strip)
Mulroney, Brian (ex-PM, Can.; 1939-)
Multan, Pakistan
Multigraph™ (graphics)
Multilith™ (graphics)
Mum™ (anti-perspirant)
Mumford, Lewis (US writer/sociol.; 1895-1990)
Munch, Edvard (Nor. artist; 1863-1944)

Munchausen syndrome (psych.)
München-Gladbach (now Mönchengladbach)
Muncie, IN
Munda (people)
Mundari (lang.)
Mundy, Carl E., Jr. (US gen.)
Munefusa, Matsuo (pseud. Bashö Matsuo)(Jap. poet, haiku; 1644-94)
Mungo, Van Lingo (baseball; 1911-85)
Muni, Paul (b. Muni Weisenfreund)(ent.; 1895-1967)
Munich Agreement/Pact (UK/Fr./Ger./It.; 1938)
Munich, Germany
Munn v. Illinois (US law; 1877)
Munro, Alice (Can. writer
Munro, H(ugh) H(ector)(pseud. Saki)(Br. writer; 1870-1916)
Munsel, Patrice (ent.; 1925-)
Munson, Ona (ent.)
Munson, Thurman (baseball; 1947-79)
Munster (province, Ir.)
Munster cheese (also Muenster)(also l.c.)
Münster, Germany
Munsters, The (TV show)
Muong (people)
Muppet Babies (cartoon)
Muppets, the (puppets)
Murakami, Haruki (Jap. writer; 1949-)
Murasaki, Shikibu, Lady (Jap. writer; c978-1031?)
Murat, Joachim (king, Naples; 1767-1815)
Murcia (region, Sp.)
Murder, Inc. (US prof. killers; 1930s)
Murder, She Wrote (TV show)
Murders in the Rue Morgue (film; 1971)
Murdoch, Iris (Br. writer; 1919-)
Murdoch, (Keith) Rupert (Austl. publ.; 1931-)
Murfreesboro, TN
Muriel Rukeyser (US poet; 1913-80)
Murillo, Bartolomé Estebán (Sp. artist; 1618-82)
Murine™ (med.)
Murine Co.
Murjani™ (clothes)
Murjani International (US bus.)
Murkowski, Frank H. (US cong.; 1933-)
Murmansk, Russia
Murnau, F(riedrich) W(ilhelm Plumpe)(Ger. ent.;1889-1931)
Murphy bed (stores in the wall)
Murphy Bed Co., Inc.
Murphy Brown (TV show)
Murphy, Audie (ent., war hero; 1924-71)
Murphy, Ben (ent.; 1942-)
Murphy, Calvin (basketball; 1948-)
Murphy, Dale (football; 1956-)
Murphy, Eddie (ent.; 1961-)
Murphy, George L. (US ent./pol.; 1902-92)

Murphy, Michael (ent.; 1938-)
Murphy, Turk (US jazz; 1915-87)
Murphy's Law
Murray cod (fish)
Murray Dance Studios, Arthur (US bus.)
Murray Gell-Mann (US physt.; 1929-)
Murray L. Barr (Can. phys.; 1908-)
Murray Perahia (US pianist; 1947-)
Murray River (Austl.)
Murray, Abraham, F. (ent.; 1939-)
Murray, Anne (ent.; 1945-)
Murray, Arthur (US dancer; 1896-1991)
Murray, Bill (ent.; 1950-)
Murray, Don (ent.; 1929-)
Murray, Ken (ent.; 1903-88)
Murray, Patty (US cong.; 1950-)
Murray, Philip (US labor leader; 1886-1952)
Murrow, Edward R(oscoe)(US TV jour.; 1908-65)
Musante, Tony (ent.; 1936-)
Musburger, Brent (ent.; 1939-)
Musca (astron., fly)
Muscadet (grape, wine)
Muscat (wine, grape)
Muscat, Oman (also Masqat)
Muscle Beach (Los Angeles)
Muscovite
Muscovy (also Grand Duchy of Muscovy)(founded c1271, Rus. empire)
Muscovy Company (also Russia Company)(Rus./ Eng. trading)
Muscovy duck (also musk duck)
Muses (myth., nine goddesses)
Museum of American Art, National (DC)
Museum of Fine Arts (Boston)
Museum of Modern Art (MOMA)(NYC)
Museveni, Yoweri Kaguta (pres., Uganda; 1945-)
Mushin, Nigeria
Musial, Stan(ley Frank)("Stan the Man")(baseball; 1920-)
Music Corp. of America (MCA)
Music Man, The (play)
Music Television (MTV)(cable TV)
Musician (mag.)
Muskegon, MI
Musicians, Three (by Picasso)
Musketeers, The Three (A. Dumas novel)
Musketeers, The Three (Athos, Porthos, Aramis)
Musketeers™, Three (candy bar)
Muskie, Edmund (US pol.; 1914-)
Muskogee, OK
Muskol™
Muslim (rel.)
Muslim Brotherhood (rel.)
Muslim League
Muslim, Shiite (rel.)

Muslim, Sunni (rel.)
Muslims, Black (also Nation of Islam)(rel.)
Musset, Alfred de (Fr. writer; 1810-57)
Mussolini, Benito (aka *Il Duce*)(ex-PM, It.;
    1883-1945)
Mussorgsky, Modest Petrovich (Rus. comp.;
    1839-81)
Mustang, Ford (auto.)
Mutalov, Abdul Hashim (PM, Uzbekistan)
Mutare, Zimbabwe
Muti, Riccardo (It. cond.; 1941-)
Mutiny on the Bounty (book, film)
Mutsamudu, Comoros
Mutsuhito Meiji (Jap. emp.; 1852-1912)
Mutt & Jeff (comic strip)
Mutual of Omaha Insurance Co.
Muybridge, Eadweard (aka Edward James
    Muggeridge)(US photo.; 1830-1904)
Muyinga, Burundi
Muzak™ (music)
Muzorewa, Abel (Tendekayi)(Zimbabwean pol./
    rel.; 1925-)
Mwanawasa, Levy (VP, Zambia)
Mwanza, Tanzania
Mwinyi, Ali Hassan (pres., Tanzania; 1925-)
MX missile (aka "Peacekeeper")
My Cousin Vinny (film; 1992)
My Fair Lady (play)
My Lai massacre (US/SViet.; 1968)
My Little Chickadee (film; 1940)
My Two Dads (TV show)
Myadec™ (multivitamins)
Myanmar (Union of)(formerly Burma)(SE Asia)
Mycelex™ (med.)
Mycenae (city, ancient Gr.)
Mycenaean civilization (Gr.; 4000-1000 BC)
Myer, Fort, VA (mil.)
Myers Rum Co., Ltd.
Myers Squibb Co., Bristol-
Myers, Fort (FL)(city)
Myers, Linda (archery; 1947-)
Myers, Mike (ent.; 1962-)
Myers, Russell (cartoonist, *Broom Hilda*; 1938-)
Myerson, Bess
Myers's rum
Mykonos Island, Greece (also Mikonos Island)
Mylanta™ (med.)
Mylanta-II™ (med.)
Mylar™ (polyester film)
Myrdal, Gunnar (Swed. econ.; 1898-1987)
Myrna Loy (ent.; 1905-93)
Myron (Gr. sculptor; c500-440 BC)
Myron Cohn (ent.; 1902-86
Myrtle Beach Air Force Base, SC
Myrtle Beach, SC
Mystic, CT
Mzuzu, Malawi

N

N (chem. sym., nitrogen)

N/A (not applicable)

Na (chem. sym., sodium)

NAACP (National Association for the Advancement of Colored People)(org. 1909)

Naas, Ireland

NAB (National Association of Broadcasters, naval air base)

Naber, John (swimming; 1956-)

NABET (National Association of Broadcast Employees and Technicians)

Nabis (Fr. art; 1889-99)

Nabisco™

Nabisco Brands, Inc.

Nabisco Foods (US bus.)

Nabisco, RJR (US bus.)

Nabokov, Vladimir (Vladomirovich)(Rus./US writer; 1899-1977)

Nabors, Jim (ent.; 1933-)

Nacio Herb Brown (US comp.; 1896-1964)

Nacogdoches, TX

Nader, Ralph (US atty./consumer advocate; 1934-)

Nadia Boulanger (Fr. cond./educ.; 1887-1979)

Nadia Comaneci (gymnast; 1961-)

Nadine Conner (ent.; 1913-)

NAFTA (North American Free Trade Agreement)(US/Can./Mex.; 1993)

Nagaland (state, India)

Nagari (also Devanagari)(alphabetic script)

Nagasaki, Japan (bombed in WWII; 8/9/45)

Nagel, Conrad (ent.; 1896-1970)

Nagorno-Karabakh (region, Azerbaijan)

Nagoya, Japan

Nagpur, India

Naguib Mahfouz (Eg. writer; 1911-)

Nagurski, Bronko (Bronislaw)(football; 1908-90)

Nagy, Ferenc (ex-PM, Hung.; 1903-)

Nagy, Imre (ex-PM, Hung.; c1895-1958)

Nagy, Ivan

Nahayan, Sheik Zaid bin Sultan al- (pres., UAE; 1918-)

Nahuatl (lang./people)

NAIA (National Association of Intercollegiate Athletics)

Nairobi, Kenya

Nair™ (hair remover)

Naish, J. Carroll (ent.; 1900-73)

Naismith, James (Can., inv. basketball; 1861-1939)

Najibullah, Ahmadzai (Afghan. pol.; 1947-)

Nakasone Yasuhiro (ex-PM, Jap.; 1917-)

Nakuru, Kenya

Nala (fict. chara., *The Lion King*)

Nalley™

Nalley's Fine Foods (US bus.)

NAM (National Association of Manufacturers)(est. 1895)

Nam Dinh, North Vietnam

Nama (people)

Namaliu, Rabbie (ex-PM, Papua New Guinea; 1947-)

Namangan, Uzbekistan

Namath, Joe (Joseph William)("Broadway Joe")(football; 1943-)

Namib Desert (Namibia)

Namibia (Republic of)(formerly South-West Africa)(SW Afr.)

Nampa, ID

Nampo, North Korea

Nampula, Mozambique

Namur (province, Belgium)

Namur, Belgium

Nana Mouskouri (ent.)

Nanaimo, British Columbia, Canada

Nanak (Ind. rel.; 1469-c1539)

Nance, Jim (football; 1943-92)

Nanchang, China

Nanchong, China (also Nanchung)

Nancy (comic strip)

Nancy Allen (ent.; 1949-)

Nancy Drew (fict. chara.)

Nancy Dussault (ent.; 1936-)

Nancy Kulp (ent.; 1921-91)

Nancy Landon Kassebaum (US cong.; 1932-)

Nancy Lieberman

Nancy Lopez (golf; 1957-)

Nancy Marchand (ent.; 1928-)

Nancy Reagan (b. Anne Francis Robbins, aka Nancy Davis)(wife of ex-US pres.; 1923-)

Nancy Richey Gunter (tennis; 1942-)

Nancy Walker (ent.; 1922-92)

Nancy Willard (writer/artist; 1936-)

Nancy Wilson (ent.; 1937-)

Nancy, France

Nanette Fabray (ent.; 1920-)

Nanjing, China (formerly Nanking)

Nanning, China

Nannygate (US hist.; 1993)

Nansen bottle (oceanographic instrument)

Nansen passport

Nansen, Fridtjof (Nor. expl; 1861-1930)

Nanterre, France

Nantes, Edict of (Fr. hist.; 1598)

Nantes, France

Nanticoke (NAmer. Indians)

Nanticoke Homes, Inc.

Nanticoke River (MD)

Nantucket Island (MA)

Nantucket Sound (MA)

Nantucket, MA

Naomi Judd (ent.; 1946-)

Napa (county, CA)
Napa Creek Winery (US bus.)
Napa Valley (CA wine region)
Napa Valley Wines (US bus.)
Napa Wine Cellars (US bus.)
Napa, CA
Napalese (people)
Naperville, IL
Napier, John (Scot. math.; 1550-1617)
Napier, New Zealand
Naples yellow (color)
Naples, FL
Naples, Italy (also Napoli)
Naples, Kingdom of (also Kingdom of the Two
  Sicilies)(S. It.)
Napoleon I (Napoleon Bonaparte, "the Little
  Corporal")(emp., Fr.; 1769-1821)
Napoleon II (François Charles Joseph
  Bonaparte)(titular king, Rome; 1811-32)
Napoleon III (Charles Louis-Napoleon
  Bonaparte)(emp., Fr.; 1808-73)
Napoleonic Code (also Code Napoléon)(Fr. law)
Napoleonic Wars (Eur. hist.; 1799-15)
Naprosyn™ (med.)
NARA (National Archives and Records
  Administration)(US govt. agcy.; est. 1984)
Nara, Japan
Naraka (rel.)
Narasimha Rao, P(amulaparti) V(enkata)(PM,
  India; 1921-)
Narayanganj, Bangladesh
Narbonne, France
Narcissus (myth.)
Narmada River (India)
Narragansett (NAmer. Indians)
Narragansett Bay (RI)
Narrows (strait, SE NYC)
Narrows Bridge, Verrazano- (NYC)
Naruhito (prince, Jap.)
Narva, Estonia
NASA (National Aeronautics and Space
  Administration)(US govt. agcy.; est. 1958)
Nasby, Petroleum V(esuvius)(pseud. David Ross
  Locke)(US humorist; 1833-88)
Nasca (also Nazca)(ancient Peru Indian culture)
Nash, Beau (Richard)(Br. dandy/gambler; 1674-
  1761
Nash, Ogden (US writer/humorist; 1902-71)
Nashe, Thomas (Br. writer; 1567-1601)
Nashua, NH
Nashville Banner (TN newspaper)
Nashville Network, The (TNN)(cable TV)
Nashville Now (TV show)
Nashville Tennessean (TN newspaper)
Nashville, TN
Nasik, India
Naskapi Indians/lang.)
Nasrin, Taslima (phys./writer)

Nassau, Germany
Nassau, the Bahamas
Nasser, Gamal Abdel (ex-pres., Eq.; 1918-70)
Nast, Conde (US publ.)
Nast, Thomas (US artist/cartoonist; 1840-1902)
Nastase, Ilie (tennis; 1946-)
Nastrond (myth.)
Nat "King" Cole (ent.; 1919-65)
Nat Turner (US slave/reformer; 1800-31)
Nat Turner, The Confessions of (W. Styron
  book)
Natal (province, SAfr.)
Natal, Brazil
Natalia Makarova (Rus. ballet; 1940-)
Natalie Cole (ent.; 1950-)
Natalie Wood (ent.; 1938-81)
NATAS (National Academy of Television Arts
  and Sciences, Emmy Awards)
Natasha (or Fataly) Badenov (fict. chara.)
Natchez (NAmer. Indians)
Natchez National Historical Park (MS)
Natchez Trace (road from Nashville TN to
  Natchez MS)
Natchez, MS
Natchitoches settlement (LA, 1st permanent
  settlement in LA Purchase)
Naté™, Jean (toiletries)
Naté, Inc., Jean
Nathan(iel) Bailey (Br. lexicographer; ?-1742)
Nathan Bedford Forrest (US gen.; 1821-77)
Nathan Hale (US mil.; 1755-76)
Nathan Mayer Rothschild (Ger./Br. finan.;
  1777-1836)
Nathan Mayer Rothschild, Sir (Br. pol./baron;
  1840-1915)
Nathan Strauss (Ger./US bus./finan.; 1848-
  1931)
Nathan, George Jean (US writer; 1882-1958)
Nathanael Greene (US mil.; 1742-86)
Nathanael West (aka Nathan Wallenstein
  Weinstein)(US writer; 1904-40)
Nathaniel Bacon (US colonial leader; 1647-76)
Nathaniel Currier (US lithographer; 1813-88)
Nathaniel Hawthorne (US writer; 1804-64)
Natick Research and Development Center (MA)
Natick, MA
Nation of Islam (also Black Muslims)(rel.)
Nation, Carrie (Amelia Moore)(US temperance
  leader; 1846-1911)
National Academy of Sciences (org.1863)
National Academy of Television Arts and
  Sciences (NATAS, Emmy Awards)
National Aeronautics and Space Administration
  (NASA)(US govt. agcy.; est. 1958)
National Air and Space Museum (Smithsonian,
  DC)
National Archives (DC)
National Archives and Records Administration

(NARA)(US govt. agcy.; est. 1984)

National Association for the Advancement of Colored People (NAACP)(org. 1909)

National Association of Broadcast Employees and Technicians (NABET)

National Association of Broadcasters (NAB)

National Association of Intercollegiate Athletics (NAIA)

National Association of Manufacturers (NAM)(est. 1895)

National Association of Real Estate Brokers

National Association of Realtors

National Association of Television and Radio Announcers (NATRA)

National Audubon Society (environ. org.)

National Ballet of Canada

National Baseball Hall of Fame and Museum (est. 1939, Cooperstown, NY)

National Basketball Association (NBA)

National Broadcasting Company (NBC)

National Bureau of Standards (NBS)(US govt. agcy.; est. 1901)

National Business Woman (mag.)

National Car Rental System, Inc.

National Christian Network

National Collegiate Athletic Association (NCAA)(est. 1906)

National Conference of Christians and Jews (est. 1928)

National Congress of Parents and Teachers (also National Parent-Teacher Association)(PTA)(est. 1897)

National Council of the Churches of Christ in the United States of America (est. 1950)

National Council on Alcoholism (org. 1944)

National Court Reporters Association (NCRA)

National Day (Ch., Sp., Viet.)

National Drug Control Policy, Office of (US govt.)

National Education Association of the United States (NEA)(est. 1906)

National Endowment for Democracy (US pol. agcy.)

National Endowment on (or for) the Arts and Humanities (US govt. agcy.; est. 1965)

National Enquirer (mag.)

National Examiner

National Football Conference (NFC)

National Football Foundation and Hall of Fame (NFFHF)(est. 1947)

National Football League (NFL)

National Gallery (London)

National Gallery of Art (Smithsonian, DC)

National Geographic (mag.)

National Geographic Explorer (TV show)

National Geographic Society (est. 1888)

National Governors' Association

National Guard of the United States (US mil.)

National Hockey League (NHL)

National Industrial Recovery Act (NIRA)(US law; 1933)

National Inquirer

National Institutes of Health (NIH)(US govt. agcy.; est. 1930)

National Invitation Tournament (NIT)(basketball)

National Labor Relations Act (NLRA)(US law; 1935)

National Labor Relations Board (NLRB)(US govt. agcy.; est. 1935)

National Labor Relations Board v. Jones and Laughlin Steel Co. (US law; 1937)

National Lampoon

National Lampoon's Animal House (film; 1978)

National League (baseball)

National League of Professional Baseball Clubs

National Marine Fisheries Service (US govt. agcy.; est. 1970)

National Medical Enterprises, Inc. (healthcare)

National Museum of American Art (Smithsonian, DC)

National Museum of American History (Smithsonian, DC)

National Museum of Natural History (Smithsonian, DC)

National Naval Medical Center (also Bethesda Naval Hospital??)(Bethesda, MD)

National Oceanic and Atmospheric Administration (NOAA)(US govt. agcy.; est. 1970)

National Organization for Women (NOW)

National Parent-Teacher Association (also National Congress of Parents and Teachers)(PTA)(est. 1897)

National Park Service (US govt. bureau)

National Party, Australian (Austl. pol.)

National Portrait Gallery (Smithsonian, DC)

National Public Radio (NPR)

National Red Cross, American (US relief agcy.; est. 1881)

National Republican Party (US pol.)

National Review (mag.)

National Rifle Association of America (NRA)

National Safety Council (est. 1913)

National Science Foundation (NSF)(US govt. agcy.; est. 1950)

National Security Council (NSC)(US govt. agcy.; est. 1947)

National Semiconductor Corp.

National Seurity Agency (NSA)(US govt.)

National Socialism (also Nazism)(Ger.)

National Socialist German Workers' Party (also Nazi Party)

National States Rights Party (US pol.)

National Theatre of Great Britain

National Transportation Safety Board (US govt.

agcy.; est. 1975)
National Unity Day (It.)
National Unity Party (US pol.)
National Urban League (org. 1910)
National Weather Service (US govt.; est.1870)
National Wildlife (mag.)
National Woman's Christian Temperance
   Union (WCTU)
National Zoological Park (Smithsonian, DC)
Nation's Business (mag.)
Nations, Commonwealth of
Nations, League of (internat'l govt. org.; 1920-)
Nations, United (internat'l org.; est. 1945)
Nationwide Insurance Co.
Natitingou, Benin
Native American (also American Indian)
Native Dancer (champion horse)
Nativity (rel.)
NATO (North Atlantic Treaty Organization)
NATRA (National Association of Television and
   Radio Announcers)
Natron, Lake (Tanzania)
Natural Bridges National Monument (UT)
Natural Health (mag.)
Natural History (mag.)
Naturalizer™ (shoes)
NaturalTouch™ (contact lenses)
Nature Made™ (vitamins)
Nature Valley™ (food)
Nature's Remedy™ (med.)
Natwick, Mildred (ent.; 1908-)
Natya, Bharat (dance, India)
Naugahyde™ (fabric)
Naugatuck, CT
Naughton, James (ent.; 1946-)
Naughty Marietta (play; film, 1935)
Naum Gabo (b. Naum Pevsner)(US sculptor;
   1890-1977)
Nauru (Republic of)(island, SW Pac.)
Nauruan (lang./people)
Nautilus™ (fitness)
Nautilus Industries
Nautilus Marine Engineering (US bus.)
Navajo (or Navaho) rug
Navajo (or Navaho)(NAmer. Indians)
Naval Academy, U.S. (Annapolis, MD)(est.
   1845)
Naval Jelly™
Naval Jelly Co., Inc.
Naval Medical Center, National (also Bethesda
   Naval Hospital??)(Bethesda, MD)
Naval Observatory (DC)
Navane™ (med.)
Navarone, The Guns of (film; 1961)
Navarra (also Navarre)(province, Sp.)
Navarra Vineyards (US bus.)
Navarre, Margaret of (also Margaret of
   Angoulême)(queen, Navarre; 1492-1549)

Navarro, Fats (Theodore)(US jazz; 1923-50)
Navigation Acts (Br. hist.; 17th-16th c.)
Navistar International Corp.
Navratilova, Martina (tennis; 1956-)
Navy Cross (mil.)
Navy, Department of the (US mil.)
Navy, U.S. (US mil.)
Nawaz Sharif (ex-PM, Pak.; 1948-)
Nazarbayev, Nursultan A. (pres., Kazakhstan;
   1940-)
Nazarene (rel.)
Nazarenes (grp. Ger. art.; 19th c.)
Nazareth, Israel
Nazarite (rel.)
Nazca (also Nasca)(ancient Peru Indian culture)
Nazi (Nazi Party member)
Nazi Party (also National Socialist German
   Workers' Party)
Nazism (also National Socialism)(Ger.)
Nb (chem. sym., niobium)
NBA (National Basketball Association)
NBC (National Broadcasting Company)
NBC News (TV show)
NBS (National Bureau of Standards)(US govt.
   agcy.; est. 1901)
NC (North Carolina)
NCAA (National Collegiate Athletic
   Association)(est. 1906)
N(ewel) C(onvers) Wyeth (US artist; 1882-1945)
ND (North Dakota)
Nd (chem. sym., neodymium)
Ndadaye, Melchior (ex-pres., Burundi; ?-1994)
NDE (near-death experience)
Ndebele (also Matabele)(people)
N'Djamena, Chad (also Ndjamena)
Ndola, Zambia
NE (Nebraska)
Ne (chem. sym., neon)
Ne Win (b. Maung Shu Maung)(ex-pres.,
   Myanmar; 1911-)
NEA Today (mag.)
Neagh, Lough (lake, NIre.)
Neal, Patricia (ent.; 1926-)
Nealon, Kevin (ent.; 1953-)
Neanderthal (*Homo sapiens neanderthalensis*)
   (lived 100,000 to 35,000 years ago)
Neapolitan (Naples citizen)
Neapolitan ice cream
Neapolitan mastiff (dog)
Near v. Minnesota (US law; 1931-)
Nebit-Dag, Turkmenistan
Nebraska (NE)
Nebraska Act/Bill, Kansas- (US hist.; 1854)
Nebuchadnezzar (or Nebuchadrezzar)(king,
   Babylonia; 604?-561? BC)
Nebula, Ring (astron.)
NEC Corp.
NEC Technologies, Inc.

Neckar River (Ger.)
Necker, Jacques (Fr. pol.; 1732-1804)
Ned Beatty (ent.; 1937-)
Ned Ludd (also Lludd, Nudd, King Ludd)(Welsh legend)
Ned R(ay) McWherter (TN gov.; 1930-)
Needham, MA
Needles, CA
Neenah, WI
Neet™ (hair remover)
Nefertiti (also Nefretete)(queen, Eg.; 14th c.)
Neff, Hildegarde (ent.)
Negev (also Negeb)(desert, Isr.)
Negombo, Sri Lanka
Negri, Pola (ent.; 1900-87)
Negro (also black, African American)(people)
Negro College Fund, United
Negroid (one of three major races of humans)
Negros (island, Philippines)
Nehemiah (rel.)
Nehemiah, Renaldo (track; 1959-)
Nehru jacket
Nehru, Jawaharlal (ex-PM, India; 1889-1964)
Neiafu, Tonga
Neijiang, China (also Neikiang, Nei-chaing)
Neil A(lden) Armstrong (astro., 1st to walk on moon; 1930-)
Neil Diamond (US comp./ent.; 1941-)
Neil Patrick Harris (ent.; 1973-)
Neil Sedaka (ent.; 1939-)
Neil Simon, (Marvin)(US writer; 1927-)
Neil Young (ent.; 1945-)
Neiman-Marcus™
Neiman-Marcus, Inc.
Neisse River (N central Eur.)
Nell (Eleanor) Gwyn (or Gwynne)(ent.; 1651-87)
Nellie Bly (Elizabeth Cochrane Seaman)(US jour./reformer; 1867-1922)
Nellie (Jacob Nelson) Fox (baseball; 1927-75)
Nellie Melba, Dame (aka Helen Porter Mitchell)(Austl. opera; 1861-1931)
Nellis Air Force Base, NV
Nelly (Leonie) Sachs (Ger. writer; 1891-1970)
Nelson A(ldrich) Rockefeller (ex-US VP; 1908-79)
Nelson Eddy (ent.; 1901-67)
Nelson (Rolihlahla) Mandela (pres., SAfr.; 1918-)
Nelson Riddle (US cond.; 1921-85)
Nelson River (Can.)
Nelson Wilmarth Aldrich (US finan./legislator; 1841-1915)
Nelson, Alice Dunbar-
Nelson, Byron (golf; 1911-)
Nelson, Cindy (skiing; 1955-)
Nelson, Craig T. (ent.; 1946-)
Nelson, E. Ben(jamin)(NE gov.; 1941-)
Nelson, Ed (ent.; 1928-)

Nelson, Harriet (Hilliard)(ent.; 1914-)
Nelson, Horatio, Viscount (Br. admiral; 1758-1805)
Nelson, Judd (ent.; 1959-)
Nelson, New Zealand
Nelson, Ozzie (ent.; 1906-75)
Nelson, Ozzie & Harriet (TV couple)
Nelson, Rick(y)(ent.; 1940-85)
Nelson, Tracy (ent.; 1963-)
Nelson, Willie (ent.; 1933-)
Nembutal™ (med.)
Nemean lion (myth.)
Nemerov, Howard (US writer; 1920-91)
Nemesis (myth.)
Nemeth, Miklos (ex-PM, Hung.)
Nemours & Co., E. I. du Pont de
Nemours, E(leuthere) I. du Pont de (US bus.; 1771-1834)
Nena, Jacob (VP, Micronesia
neo-Darwinism (evolution theory)
Neo-Synephrine™ (med.)
Neolithic period (New Stone Age; 10,000 to 4,500 years ago)
Neon, Chrysler Dodge/Plymouth (auto.)
Neoplatonism (phil.)
Neoptolemus (myth.)
Neosho River (KS)
Neosporin™ (med.)
Nepal (Kingdom of)(S Asia)
Nepalese (people)
Nepali (lang.)
Nephelococcygia (Aristophanes' utopia)
Nepos, Cornelius (Roman hist.; c100-c25 BC)
Neptune (planet; myth.)
Neptune, NJ
Nereid (Neptune moon; myth.)
Nereus (myth.)
Nero (b. Lucius Domitius Ahenobarbus, aka Nero Claudius Caesar Drusus Germanicus)(emp., Rome; 37-68)
Nero Germanicus, Tiberius Claudius Drusus (Claudius I)(emp., Rome; 10 BC-AD 54)
Nero (Caesar) Tiberius, Claudius (emp., Rome; 42 BC-AD 37)
Nero Wolfe (fict. detective)
Nero, Peter (US pianist; 1934-)
Neruda, Pablo (aka Neftali Ricardo Reyes y Basoalto)(Chilean poet; 1904-73)
Nerva, Marcus Cocceius (emp., Rome; c35-98)
Nervi, Pier Luigi (It. arch.; 1891-1979)
Nesbitt, Kathleen (ent.)
Nescafé™ (beverages)
Ness monster, Loch (Scot.)
Ness, Eliott (US FBI agent; 1902-57)
Ness, Loch (lake, Scot.)
Nesselrode mix (fruits/nuts, sauce)
Nestea™ (beverages)
Nestlé™

Nestlé™ Quik
Nestlé™ Toll House cookies
Nestle Beverage Co.
Nestlé Foods (US bus.)
Nestle USA (US bus.)
Nestor (myth.)
Netanya, Israel
Netherlands (Kingdom of the)(also Holland)(W
  Eur.)
Netherlands Antilles (West Indies)
Neto, Agostinho Antonio (ex-pres., Angola;
  1922-79)
Nets, New Jersey (basketball team)
Netzahualcóyotl, Mexico
Neuchâtel, Switzerland
Neufchâtel cheese
Neugebauer object, Becklin- (astro.)
Neuman, Alfred E. (fict. chara., *Mad*)
Neutra, Richard (Joseph)(US arch.; 1892-1970
Neutrogena™
Neutrogena Corp.
Neuwirth, Bebe (ent.)
Nevada (NV)
Nevelson, Louise (Rus./US sculptor; 1900-88)
Never-Never Land Peter Pan's)
Nevers, Ernie (football; 1903-76)
Neves, Brazil
Nevi'im (also Prophets)(rel.)
Nevil Shute (Br. writer/eng.; 1899-1960)
Nevill Francis Mott (Br. physt.; 1905-)
Neville Chamberlain (ex-PM, Br.; 1869-1940)
Neville Marriner (ent.; 1924-)
Nevins, Allan (US hist./educ.; 1890-1971)
Nevis, St. Christopher- (Federation of)(also St.
  Kitts-Nevis)(West Indies)
Nevis, St. Kitts- (officially Federation of St.
  Christopher-Nevis)(West Indies)
New Age (music)
New Age Journal (mag.)
New Albany, IN
New American Bible
New Amsterdam (now New York City)
New Atlantis (utopia, Sir Francis Bacon)
New Balance™
New Balance Athletic Shoes (US bus.)
New Bedford, MA
New Berlin, WI
New Bern, NC
New Britain Island (Papua New Guinea)
New Britain, CT
New Brunswick (province, Can.)
New Brunswick, NJ
New Caledonia (Fr. islands, S Pac.)
New Castle, IN, PA
New Choices for Retirement Living (mag.)
New Criticism (lit.)
New Cumberland Army Depot (PA)
New Deal (US hist./FDR; 1933)

New Delhi, India
New Democratic Party (NDP)(Can. pol.)
New England (region, NE US: CT/MA/ME/NH/
  RH/VT)
New England boiled dinner
New England clam chowder
New England Confederation
New England Journal of Medicine (mag.)
New England Patriots (football team)
New England Primer (18th c. schoolbook)
New England, United Colonies of (New England
  Confederation)(US his.)
New English (also Modern English)(lang.)
New English Bible
New Era, Lancaster (PA newspaper)
New Freedom™ (health)
New General Catalog (NGC)(astron.)
New Glasgow, Nova Scotia, Canada
New Granada (NW SAmer.)
New Guinea (island, SW Pac.)
New Guinea, Territory of (Papua New Guinea)
New Hampshire (NH)
New Hampshire chicken
New Harmony (utopian community, IN)
New Harmony, IN
New Haven Register (CT newspaper)
New Haven, CT
New Hebrides (now Vanuatu)
New Humanism (lit.)
New Iberia, LA
New Ireland (island, Papua New Guinea)
New Jersey (NJ)
New Jersey Devils (hockey team)
New Jersey Nets (basketball team)
New Jerusalem (heaven)
New Jerusalem, Church of the (also
  Swedenborgians)
New Kids on the Block (pop music)
New Kowloon, Hong Kong
New Left (pol.)
New London, CT
New Mexico (NM)
New Orleans lugger (boat)
New Orleans Saints (football team)
New Orleans Times-Picayune (LA newspaper)
New Orleans, Battle of (US/Br.; 1815)(Amer.
  Civil War; 1862)
New Orleans, LA
New Party (US pol.)
New Providence Island, Bahamas
New Providence, Bahamas
New Republic, The (mag.)
New Right (pol.)
New Rochelle, NY
New Sacristy (also Medici Chapel)(Florence, It.)
New Scotland Yard (Br. police)
New South Wales (state, Austl.)
New Stone Age (Neolithic period; 10,000 to

4,500 years ago)
New Testament (rel.)
New Thought (phil./rel.; mid 19th c.)
New Wave (Fr. lit.; 1950s)
New Wave (pop music; 1970s-)
New Westminster, British Columbia, Canada
New WKRP in Cincinnati (TV show)
New Woman (mag.)
New World (the Americas)
New Year's Day (January 1)
New Year's Eve (December 31)
New York (NY)
New York City Ballet (NYCB)
New York City, NY (NYC)
New York Daily News (NY newspaper)
New York fern (plant)
New York Giants (football team)
New York Islanders (hockey team)
New York Jets (football team)
New York Knicks (basketball team)
New York Life Insurance Co.
New York Magazine (mag.)
New York Mets (baseball team)
New York Post (NY newspaper)
New York Public Library (NYC)
New York Rangers (hockey team)
New York Review of Books, the
New York school (art; mid-20th c.)
New York Shakespeare Festival
New York steak (also New York strip)
New York Stock Exchange (also Big Board)
New York Times (NY newspaper)
New York Times Book Review
New York Times Co.
New York Times v. Sullivan (US law; 1964)
New York Yankees (baseball team)
New York, Gitlow v. (US law; 1925-)
New York, Lochner v. (US law; 1905)
New Yorker, Chrysler-Plymouth (auto.)
New Yorker, The (mag.)
New Zealand (SW Pac.)
Newark Air Force Station (OH)
Newark International Airport (NJ)
Newark Star-Ledger (NJ newspaper)
Newark, DE, NJ, OH
Newbery Award (children's lit.)
Newbery, John (Br. publ.; 1713-67)
Newburg (sauce)
Newburg, lobster (food)
Newburgh, NY
Newburyport, MA
Newcastle disease (birds/fowl)
Newcastle, Australia
Newcastle, Ontario, Canada
Newcastle, Thomas Pelham-Holles (ex-PM, Br.; 1693-1768)
Newcastle-under-Lyme, England
Newcastle-upon-Tyne, England (also

Newcastle)
Newcombe, John (tennis; 1943-)
Newell Convers Wyeth (US artist; 1882-1945)
Newfoundland (dog)
Newfoundland (province, Can.)
Newfoundland Time
Newgate prison (London; razed 1902)
Newhart, Bob (ent.; 1929-)
Newhouse, Donald E(dward)
Newhouse, Samuel I(rving), Jr. (US publ.; 1895-1979)
Newington, CT
Newley, Anthony (ent.; 1931-)
Newman, Barnett (US artist; 1905-70)
Newman, Edwin (US writer)
Newman, John H(enry)(Br. rel.; 1801-90)
Newman, Paul (ent.; 1925-)
Newman, Randy (ent.; 1943-)
Newmar, Julie
Newmarket, England
Newmarket, Ontario, Canada
Newport Beach, CA
Newport Jazz Festival (RI)
Newport News, VA
Newport, KY, RI
Newport, Wales
Newry, Northern Ireland
News & Free Press, Detroit (MI newspaper)
News & Observer, Raleigh (NC newspaper)
News & Record, Greensboro (NC newspaper)
News & World Report, U.S. (mag.)
News-Free Press, Chattanooga (TN newspaper)
News-Globe, Amarillo (TX newspaper)
News-Journal, Daytona Beach (FL newspaper)
News-Journal, Pensacola (FL newspaper)
News Journal, Wilmington (DE newspaper)
News-Leader, Springfield (MO newspaper)
News-Press, Fort Myers (FL newspaper)
News-Sentinel, Fort Wayne (IN newspaper)
News-Sentinel, Knoxville (TN newspaper)
News-Tribune, Duluth (MN newspaper)
News-Tribune, Tacoma (WA newspaper)
News, Anchorage (AK newspaper)
News, Bangor (ME newspaper)
News, Birmingham (AL newspaper)
News, Buffalo (NY newspaper)
News, Dayton (OH newspaper)
News, Detroit (MI newspaper)
News, Erie (PA newspaper)
News, Fort Lauderdale (FL newspaper)
News, Greenville (SC newspaper)
News, Harrisburg (PA newspaper)
News, Huntsville (AL newspaper)
News, Indianapolis (IN newspaper)
News, Lancaster (PA newspaper)
News, Los Angeles (CA newspaper)
News, Savannah (GA newspaper)
News, York (PA newspaper)

Newsday, Long Island (NY newspaper)
Newsnet (compu. database)
NewSport Television (cable TV)
Newsweek (mag.)
Newsweek, Inc.
Newt(on Leroy) Gingrich (US cong.; 1943-)
Newton-John, Olivia (ent.; 1947-)
Newton, Huey P. (US, cofounded Black
    Panthers; 1942-89)
Newton, IA, KS, MA
Newton, Sir Isaac (Br. physt./math., gravity;
    1642-1727)
Newton, Wayne (ent.; 1942-)
Newtonian physics
Newtonian reflector (astron.)
Newton's law(s) of motion (also Newtonian
    law)(physics)
Newton's rings (photo.)
Newtownabbey, Northern Ireland
Nexis (compu. database, news)
NeXt, Inc. (compu.)
Nexus Industries
Nexxus™ (hair care)
Nexxus Products Co.
Nexxus Products, Inc.
Ney, Michel (Fr. mil.; 1769-1815)
Nez Percé (NAmer. Indians)
Nez Percé National Historical Park (ID)
NFC (National Football Conference)
NFL (National Football League)
NFL Monday Night Football (TV show)
Ngaio Marsh, (Edith), Dame (NewZeal. writer;
    1899-1982)
Ngalops (people)
NGC (New General Catalog [astron.])
Ngo Dinh Diem (ex-pres., SViet.; 1901-63)
Ngozi, Burundi
Nguema, Francisco Macías (ex-pres., Equatorial
    Guinea; 1924-79)
Nguesso, Denis Sassou- (ex-pres., Congo; 1943-)
Ngugi wa Thiong'o (Kenyan writer; 1938-)
Ngulu (lang.)
Nguyen Van Thieu (ex-pres., SViet; 1923-)
Nguyen, Dustin
Ngwazi Hastings Kamuzu Banda (pres.,
    Malawi; 1902-)
NH (New Hampshire)
Nha Trang, Vietnam
NHL (National Hockey League)
Ni (chem. sym., nickel)
Niagara Falls, NY
Niagara Falls, Ontario, Canada
Niagara green (color)(also l.c.)
Niagara River (NY/Ontario)
Niamey, Niger
Niaux Cave (prehistoric paintings, Fr.)
Nibelung, The Ring of the (Richard Wagner
    tetralogy)

Nibelungenlied (13th c. Ger. epic poem)
Nibelungs (myth.)
Nicaea (ancient cities: now Iznik, Turk. and
    Nice, Fr.)
Nicaea, Council(s) of (also Nicene Council)(rel.;
    325)
Nicaea, Turkey (now Iznik)
Nicaragua (Republic of)(CAmer.)
Nicaraguan Revolution (1978-79)
Niccolo (di Bernardo) Machiavelli (It. pol./
    writer/phil.; 1469-1527)
Niccolo Paganini (It. comp.; 1782-1840)
Nice Guy, Mr. (slang)
Nice, France
Nicene Council (also Council(s) of Nicaea)(rel.;
    325)
Nicene Creed (rel.)
Nicéphore Soglo (pres., Benin; 1934-)
Nichelodeon (NIK)(cable TV)
Nicholas Biddle (US finan.; 1786-1844)
Nicholas Braithwaite (PM, Grenada; 1925-)
Nicholas Cage (ent.; 1964-)
Nicholas Copernicus (also Nicolaus)(Pol.
    astron.; 1473-1543)
Nicholas I (Nicolai Pavlovich)(emp., Rus.; 1796-
    1855)
Nicholas I, St. (Nicholas the Great)(pope; 800?-
    67)
Nicholas II (Nikolai Aleksandrovich)(emp.,
    Rus.; 1868-1918)
Nicholas III (Giovanni Gaetano Orsini)(It. pope;
    1210?-80)
Nicholas Murray Butler (US educ.; 1862-1947)
Nicholas Nickleby (C. Dickens novel)
Nicholas V (Tomaso Parentucelli)(It. pope;
    1397-1455)
Nicholas, Denise (ent.; 1944-)
Nicholas, Fayard (ent.; 1914-)
Nicholas, Harold (ent.; 1924-)
Nicholas, St. (also Santa Claus, Kriss Kringle)
Nicholo Amati (It. violin maker; 1596-1684)
Nichols, Mike (ent.; 1931-)
Nichols, Red (US jazz; 1905-65)
Nicholson, Ben (Br. artist; 1894-1982)
Nicholson, Jack (ent.; 1937-)
Nichrome™ (alloy)
Nick at Nite (TV)
Nick Carter (fict. detective)
Nick Faldo (golf; 1957-)
Nick Nolte (ent.; 1940-)
Nickelodeon (cable TV)
Nicklaus, Jack (William)(golf; 1940-)
Nickleby, Nicholas (C. Dickens novel)
Nickles, Donald Lee (US cong.; 1948-)
Nicks, Stevie (ent.; 1948-)
Nicobar Islands (Indian Ocean)
Nicodemus (rel.)
Nicol prism (physics/optics)

Nicola Pisano (It. artist; c1220-84)
Nicolae Ceausescu (ex-pres., Romania; 1918-89)
Nicolae Vacarolu (PM, Romania
Nicolai, (Carl) Otto (Ehrenfried)(Ger. comp.;
    1810-49)
Nicolas Poussin (Fr. artist; 1594-1665)
Nicolay (Andreyevich) Rimsky-Korsakov (Rus.
    comp.; 1844-1908)
Nicole Hollander (US cartoonist, *Sylvia*; 1939-)
Nicole Simpson (US news)
Nicosia, Cyprus
Nidre, Kol (rel.)
Niebuhr, Reinhold (US rel.; 1892-1971)
Niekro, Phil (baseball; 1939-)
Niels Henrik David Bohr (Dan. physt.; 1885-
    1962)
Nielsen Co., A. C. (TV ratings)
Nielsen, A. C. (US bus./ratings; 1897-1980)
Nielsen, Brigitte (ent.)
Nielsen, Carl August (Dan. comp.; 1865-1931)
Nielsen, Leslie (ent.; 1926-)
Niemeyer Soares Filho, Oscar (Brazilian arch.;
    1907-)
Niente Winery, Far (US bus.)
Nietzsche. Friedrich Wilhelm (Ger. phil.; 1844-
    1900)
Nieuw Amsterdam, Suriname
Nieuw Nickerie, Suriname
Nifleheim (also Niflheim)(myth.)
Nigel Bruce (ent.; 1895-1953)
Niger (Republic of)(NW Afr.)
Niger-Congo (langs.)
Niger River (W Afr.)
Nigeria (Federal Republic of)(W Afr.)
Night Court (TV show)
Night Journey (also al-Miraj)(rel.)
Nightingale, Florence (Br., founded modern
    nursing; 1820-1910)
Nightline (TV show)
Niigata, Japan
Niihua (island, HI)
Nijinsky, Vaslav (or Waslaw)(Rus. ballet; 1890-
    1950)
Nijmegen, Netherlands
Nike (myth.)
Nike™ (shoes)
Nike missile
Nike, Inc.
Nikica Valentic (PM, Croatia
Nikita S(ergeyevich) Khrushchev (ex-premier,
    USSR; 1894-1971)
Nikkei Average/Index
Nikko™
Nikko Audio (US bus.)
Nikko National Park (Jap.)
Nikko, Japan
Nikola Tesla (Croatia/US elec. eng.; 1856-1943)
Nikolaevich, Aleksandr (Alexander II)(emp.,

Rus.; 1818-81)
Nikolai A(leksandrovich) Bulganin (ex-PM
    USSR; 1895-1975)
Nikolai Bukharin (USSR, pol.; 1888-1938)
Nikolai (Vasilievich) Gogol (Rus. writer; 1809-
    52)
Nikolai Sokoloff (cond.)
Nikolay Viktorovich Podgorny (USSR pol.;
    1903-83)
Nikolayev, Andrian G(rigorievich)(cosmo.;
    1929-)
Nikolayev, Ukraine
Nikon™
Nikon, Inc.
Nikos Kazantzakis (Gr. writer; 1883?-1957)
Nile green (color)
Nile River (Eg.)
Niles, IL, OH
Nilo-Hamitic (lang.)
Nilote (lang./people)
Nilotic (lang./people)
Nilsson, Birgit (Swed., opera; 1918-)
Nimeiry, Gaafar Muhammad al- (ex-pres.,
    Sudan; 1930-)
Nîmes, France
Nimitz, Chester W(illiam)(US adm.; 1885-1966)
Nimoy, Leonard (ent.; 1931-)
Nimrod (great-grandson of Noah)
Nin, Anais (US writer; 1903-77)
Niña (C. Columbus ship; 1492)
Nina Blackwood
Nina Foch (ent.; 1924-)
Nina Ricci™
Nina Ricci Jewelry (US bus.)
Nina Simone (ent.; 1933-)
9 Lives™ (pet food)
Ninety-Five Theses (rel.)
Nineveh (ancient Assyrian capital)
Ning, Yang Chen (Ch. physt.; 1922-)
Ningbo, China (also Ning-po)
Ningxia (also Ningxia Hui)(region, Ch.)
Ninja™
Ninja Turtles (cartoon)
Ninja Turtles, Teenage Mutant (film, cartoon)
Nino Espinosa (baseball; 1953-88)
Niño, El (warm ocean current)
Ninotchka (film; 1939)
Nintendo™ (video games)
Nintendo Co. Ltd.
Nintendo of America, Inc.
Niobe (myth.)
Nipigon, Lake (Ontario, Can.)
Nipissing, Lake (Can.)
Nipon, Albert (clothing)
Nippon (Japanese for Japan)
Nippon Electric Co. (NEC)
Nippon Kogaku USA, Inc.
Nippon Steel Corp.

Nipponese (Japanese)
Nipsey Russell (ent.; 1924-)
Nirenberg, Marshall Warren (US chem.; 1927-)
Niro, Robert De (ent.; 1943-)
Nirvana (pop music)
Nis, Serbia
Nisan (also Nissan)(Jew. mo.)
Nisei (Amer. of Jap. descent)(also l.c.)
Nishapur, Iran
Nishinomiya, Japan
Nissan™ (auto.)
Nissan Altima™ (auto.)
Nissan™ Infiniti (auto.)
Nissan Maxima™ (auto.)
Nissan Motor Corp. USA.)
Nissan Quest™ (auto.)
Nissan™ Sentra (auto.)
Nissan™ Sentra SE-R (auto.)
Nissan™ Stanza
Nissan™ 300 ZX Turbo (auto.)
Nissen hut (also Quonset hut)
Nissin Foods USA Co., Inc.
Nita Barrow (gov-gen.; Barbados)
Niterói, Brazil
Nitty Gritty Dirt Band, The
Niue Island, New Zealand (also Savage Island)
Nivea™ (skin care)
Niven, David (ent.; 1909-83)
Nixon Cox, Tricia (Patricia)(daughter of ex-US
    pres.; 1946-)
Nixon Eisenhower, Julie (daughter of ex-US
    pres.; 1948-)
Nixon, Agnes
Nixon, Pat (b. Thelma Catherine Ryan)(wife of
    ex-US pres.; 1912-93)
Nixon, Richard Milhous (37th US pres.; 1913-
    94)
Nixon, U.S. v. (US law; 1974)
Niyazov, Saparmuryad (pres., Turkmenistan
Nizam (obsolete title, ruler of India)
Nizhny Novgorod, Russia (formerly Gorky)
Nizhny Tagil, Russia
Nizwa, Oman
NJ (New Jersey)
Njord (myth.)
N'Kayi, Congo
Nkole (lang.)
Nkomo, Joshua (Zimbabwean pol.; 1917-)
Nkongsamba, Cameroon
Nkrumah, Kwame (ex-pres., Ghana; 1909-72)
NLRB (National Labor Relations Board)
NM (New Mexico)
No (chem. sym., nobelium)
No (Jap. drama)
No nonsense™
No Nonsense Fashions, Inc.
No. 10 Downing Street (London)(PM residence)
No, Dr. (film; 1962)

Noah (rel.)
Noah Beery (ent.; 1884-1946)
Noah Beery, Jr. (ent.; 1913-)
Noah Webster (US lexicographer; 1758-1843)
Noah's Ark
Nob Hill (San Francisco)
Nobel Peace Prize
Nobel Prize for Chemistry
Nobel Prize for Literature
Nobel Prize for Physics
Nobel Prize for Physiology or Medicine
Nobel, Alfred B(ernhard)(Swed. chem./eng./
    finan.; 1833-96)
Noble Bookstores, Inc., Barnes &
Noble, James (ent.; 1922)
Noboru Takeshita (ex-PM, Jap.; 1924-)
Nod, land of (myth. land of sleep)
NoDoz™ (med.)
Noel (also Christmas, Xmas)(rel.)
Noel Coward, Sir (Br. writer/comp.; 1899-1973)
Nofzinger, Lyn (US pol.)
Nogales, AZ
Nogales, Mexico
Noguchi, Isamu (Jap./US artist; 1904-88)
Nolan Ryan (baseball; 1947-)
Nolan, Lloyd (ent.; 1902-85)
Noland, Kenneth (US artist; 1924-)
Nolde, Emil (b. Emil Hansen)(Ger. artist; 1867-
    1956)
Noll, Chuck (football; 1931-)
Nolte, Nick (ent.; 1940-)
Nome, AK
Nonesuch Records, Elektra/Asylum/ (US bus.)
Nono, Luigi (It. comp.; 1924-90)
Nonoxynol-9™ (spermicide)
Nonpartisan League (US pol. organ.; 1915-24)
noodles Romanoff
Noone, Peter (ent.; 1947-)
Noor (Mohammed) Hassanali (pres., Trinidad/
    Tobago)
Norbert Weiner (US math.; 1894-1964)
Norberto Costa Alegre (PM, Saõ Tomé/Príncipe)
Norcross, Inc.
Nord-Pas-de-Calais (region, Fr.)
Nordenskjöld, (Nils) Adolf Erik, Baron (Swed.
    expl.; 1832-1901)
Nordenskjöld, (Nils) Otto Gustaf (Swed. expl.;
    1869-1928)
Nordhausen, Germany
Nordic (people)
Nordic countries (Den./Fin./Iceland/Nor./Swed.)
Nordic Ski Imports, Inc.
NordicTrack™ (fitness)
NordicTrack, Inc.
Nordiques, Quebec (hockey team)
Nordstrom (US bus.)
Nordstrom store
Norelco™

Norelco Comsumer Products Co.
Norfolk (county, Eng.)
Norfolk Island (Austl.)
Norfolk Island pine
Norfolk jacket/coat
Norfolk Naval Air Station (VA)
Norfolk Naval Shipyard (VA)
Norfolk Southern Corp.
Norfolk terrier (dog)
Norfolk Virginian-Pilot (VA newspaper)
Norfolk, NE, VA
Norge™ (appliances)
Norge Co.
Noriega (Morena), Manuel (Antonio), Gen. (ex-
    dictator, Panama; imprisoned for drug
    trafficking; 1938-)
Noritake™ (china)
Noritake Co., Inc.
Norm Chomsky (US linguist; 1928-)
Norm Van Brocklin (football; 1926-83)
Norma (astron., square)
Norma Rae (film; 1979)
Norma Shearer (ent.; 1902-83)
Norma Talmadge (ent.; 1893-1957)
Normal, IL
Norman (people)
Norman architecture (Eur.; 12-13th c.)
Norman Bel Geddes (US designer; 1893-1958)
Norman Conquest (Eng. hist.; 1066)
Norman Cosmetics, Merle (US bus.)
Norman Cosmetic Studios, Merle (Merle
    Norman™ cosmetics)(US bus.)
Norman Cousins (US editor/writer; 1912-90)
Norman Dello Joio (US comp.; 1913-)
Norman Fell (ent. 1924-)
Norman French (lang.)
Norman Jewison (ent.; 1926-)
Norman Lear (ent.; 1922-)
Norman Mailer (US writer; 1923-)
Norman Manley (ex-PM, Jamaica; 1892-1969)
Norman Mingo (cartoonist; 1896-1980)
Norman M(attoon) Thomas (US pol.; 1884-1968)
Norman Rockwell (US artist; 1894-1978)
Norman Schwarzkopf, H., Jr. ("Stormin'
    Norman")(US gen.; 1934-)
Norman Vincent Peale, Rev. (US rel./writer;
    1898-93)
Norman, Greg(ory)(golf; 1955-)
Norman, Jessye (ent.; 1945-)
Norman™, Merle (cosmetics)
Norman, OK
Normandie, Basse- (region, Fr.)
Normandie, Haute- (region, Fr.)
Normandy (regions, Fr.)
Normandy campaign
Normandy landings (also D-Day)
Normandy, House of (Br. ruling family; 1066-
    1154)

Norodom Ranariddh (prince/co-PM, Cambodia
Norodom Sihanouk (king, Cambodia; 1922-)
Norplant™ (med.)
Norris, Chuck (ent.; 1940-)
Norris, Frank (US writer; 1870-1902)
Norris, George William (US pol.; 1861-1944)
Norris, Kathleen (Thompson)(US writer; 1880-
    1966)
Norristown, PA
Norrköping, Sweden
Norse (also Norseman)(ancient people)
Norse, Old (ancient lang.)
North America
North American Free Trade Agreement
    (NAFTA)(US/Can./Mex.; 1993)
North American Philips Co.
North American Rockwell Corp.
North American Soccer League (also NASL)
North Atlantic Current (also North Atlantic
    Drift)(warm ocean current)
North Atlantic Treaty (4/4/49)
North Atlantic Treaty Organization
    (NATO)(internat'l org.; est. 1949)
North Battleford, Saskatchewan, Canada
North Bay, Ontario, Canada
North Bergen, NJ
North Brabant (province, Netherlands)
North Cape (Nor.)
North Carolina (NC)
North Cascades National Park (WA)
North Charleston, SC
North Chicago, IL
North Dakota (ND)
North Dartmouth, MA
North Haven, CT
North Highlands, CA
North Holland (province, the Netherlands)
North Korea (Democratic People's Republic
    of)(E Asia)
North Las Vegas, NV
North Little Rock, AR
North Miami Beach, FL
North Miami, FL
North Olmsted, OH
North Platte River (W central US)
North Platte, NE
North Pole (northern point of Earth)
North Rhine-Westphalia (state, Ger.)
North Richland Hills, TX
North Sea (NW Eur.)
North Star (also Polaris, Polestar)(astron.)
North Star State (nickname, MN)
North Stars, Minnesota (hockey team)
North Tipperary (county, Ir.)
North Tonawanda, NY
North Vancouver, British Columbia, Canada
North-West Frontier Province (province, Pak.)
North Yemen (now part of Yemen)

North York, Ontario, Canada
North Yorkshire (county, Eng.)
North, Frederick (ex-PM, Br.; 1732-92)
North, Lowell (yachting; 1929-)
North, Oliver "Ollie", Lt. Col. (US mil./pol.; 1943-)
North, Sheree (ent.; 1933-)
Northampton, England
Northampton, MA
Northamptonshire (county, Eng.)
Northbrook, IL
Northeast Passage (Eur./Asia)
Northern Exposure (TV show)
Northern Hemisphere
Northern Ireland (part of the UK)
Northern Mariana Islands (Commonwealth of the)(Pac.)
Northern Rhodesia (now Zambia)
Northern Securities Co. v. U.S. (US law; 1904)
Northern Territory (territory, Austl.)
Northerner
Northglenn, CO
Northrop Corp.
Northumberland (county, Eng.)
Northumberland, John Dudley, Duke of (Br. pol.; c1502-53)
Northumbria (Anglo-Saxon kingdom; 6th-9th c.)
Northwest Airlines (airline)
Northwest Passage (AK/Can.)
Northwest Territories (territory, Can.)
Northwest Territory (US hist.: IL/IN/MI/MN/ OH/WI; 1783)
Northwestern Mutual Life™ (insurance)
Northwestern Mutual Life Insurance Co., The
Northwestern University (Chicago/Evanston, IL)
Norton Computing, Inc., Peter
Norton-Lambert Corp.
Norton Simon (US bus.; 1907-93)
Norton Simon Museum of Art (CA)
Norton Utilities™ (compu.)
Norton, Eleanor Holmes (US pol.; 1937-)
Norville, Deborah (US TV jour.; 1958-)
Norvo, Red (US jazz; 1908-)
Norwalk, CA, CT, OH
Norway (Kingdom of)(NW Eur.)
Norway maple (tree)
Norway pine
Norway rat
Norway spruce
Norwegian (lang./people)
Norwegian current
Norwegian elkhound (dog)
Norwegian Sea
Norwich terrier (dog)
Norwich, CT
Norwich, England
Norwood, MA, OH

Norworth, Jack (US lyricist; 1879-1959)
Nostradamus (b. Michel de Nostredame)(Fr. astrol./phys./seer; 1503-66)
Nostrand Reinhold Co., Inc., Van
Nosy/nosy Parker (slang, busybody)
Notre Dame Cathedral (also Notre Dame de Paris)
Notre Dame, The Hunchback of (by V. Hugo)
Notre Dame, University of (South Bend, IN)
Nottingham, England
Nottingham, Sheriff of (*Robin Hood*)
Nottinghamshire (also Notts)(county, Eng.)
Nouadhibou, Mauritania
Nouakchott, Mauritania
Nouhak Phoumsavan (pres., Laos; 1914-)
Nouméa, New Caledonia
Nova (also Nova Salmon)(smoked Pacific salmon)
Nova Iguaçu, Brazil
Nova Scotia (province, Can.)
Nova Scotia salmon
Novahistine™ (med.)
Novak, Kim (ent.; 1933-)
Novak, Mr. (TV show)
Novara, Italy
Novarro, Ramon (ent.; 1899-1968)
Novato, CA
Novaya Zemlya (islands, NW Russia)
Novell (US bus.)
Novello, Antonia
Novgorod, Russia
Novi Sad, Yugoslavia
Novocain™ (med.)
Novokuznetsk, Russia
Novosibirsk, Russia
NOW (National Organization for Women)
Nox (myth.)
Noxzema™ (skincare)
Noyce, Robert N. (US inv.; 1927-89)
Noyes, Alfred (Br. poet; 1880-1958)
Np (chem. sym., neptunium)
NPV (no par value)
NQB (no qualified bidders)
NRA (National Rifle Association)
NRC (Nuclear Regulatory Commission)
Nsanzimana, Sylvestre (ex-PM, Rwanda)
NSC (National Security Council)
NSF (non/not sufficient funds)
NTP (normal temperature and air pressure)
Ntsu Mokhehle (premier, Lesotho
Nu, U (Thakin)(ex-PM, Myanmar; 1907-)
Nuba (people)
Nubia (region, NE Afr.)
Nubian (lang./people)
Nubian Desert (NE Afr.)
Nubian goat
Nude Descending a Staircase (M. Duchamp painting)

Nuer (lang./people)
Nueva San Salvador, El Salvador
Nuevo Laredo, Mexico
Nuevo Léon (state, Mex.)
Nuggets, Denver (basketball team)
Nujoma, Sam (pres., Namibia; 1929-)
Nuku'alofa, Tonga
Numazu, Japan
Numbers, Book of (Bible)
Nung (lang.)
Nunn Bush™
Nunn-Bush Shoe Co.
Nunn, Sam(uel Augustus)(US cong.; 1938-)
Ñuñoa, Chile
Nupe (lang./people)
Nupercainal™ (med.)
Nuprin™ (med.)
Nuremberg Trials (Nazi war crimes)(1945-46)
Nuremberg, Germany
Nureyev, Rudolf (Rus. ballet; 1938-93)
Nurmi, Paavo (running; 1897-1973)
Nursultan A. Nazarbayev (pres., Kazakhstan;
   1940-)
Nut (myth.)
Nutcracker Suite, The (Tchaikovsky)
Nutley, NJ
Nutmeg State (nickname, CT)
Nutone (US bus.)
NutraSweet™
NutraSweet Co., The
Nutri/System™
Nutri/System, Inc. (US bus.)
Nutrition Corp., General (GNC)
Nutter Butter™ (cookies)
NV (Nevada)
NY (New York)
Nyad, Diana
Nyamwezi-Sukuma (lang.)
Nyanja (lang./people)
Nyasa, Lake (now Lake Malawi)
Nyasaland (now Malawi)
NYC (New York City)
Nye, Louis (ent.)
Nyerere, Julius (Kambarage)(ex-pres.,
   Tanzania; 1922-)
Nyers, Rezso (Hung. pol.; 1923-)
Nyíregyháza, Hungary
Nylint™
Nylint Toy Corp.
Nynex Corp. (also NYNEX)
NYPD Blue (TV show)
NyQuil™ (med.)
NYSE (New York Stock Exchange)
Nytol™ (med.)
Nyx (myth.)
Nzérékoré, Guinea

O (chem. sym., oxygen)
Oahu (island, HI)
Oak Forest, IL
Oak Lawn, IL
Oak Park, IL, MI
Oak Ridge Boys, The
Oak Ridge Vineyards (US bus.)
Oak Ridge, TN
Oakie, Jack (ent.; 1903-78)
Oakland Athletics (also Oakland A's)(baseball
    team)
Oakland Army Base (CA)
Oakland Tribune (CA newspaper)
Oakland, CA, NJ
Oakley, Annie (Phoebe Mozee)(ent./
    sharpshooter; 1860-1926)
Oakville, Ontario, Canada
OAPEC (Organization of Arab Petroleum
    Exporting Countries)(est.; 1968)
OAS (Organization of American States)(N/
    central/S Amer.; est.; 1948)
Oates, Hall & (pop music)
Oates, John (ent.; 1948-)
Oates, Joyce Carol (US writer; 1938-)
OAU (Organization of African Unity)(est. 1963)
Oaxaca, Mexico
o.b.™ (tampons)
Ob River (Rus.)
Obadiah (rel.)
Obata, Gyo (US arch.; 1923-)
OBE (out-of-body experience)
Obed Dlamini (ex-PM, Swaziland)
Oberammergau, Germany
Oberhausen, Germany
Oberlin College (OH)
Oberon (Uranus moon; myth.)
Oberon, Merle (ent.; 1911-79)
Obidos, Brazil
Óbidos, Portugal
Obie award (off Broadway)
Obock, Djibouti
Oboler, Arch
Obote, (Apollo) Milton (ex-pres., Uganda; 1925-)
O'Brien, Conan (ent.)
O'Brien, Dan (decathlon; 1966-)
O'Brien, Edmond (ent.; 1915-85)
O'Brien, Margaret (ent.; 1937-)
O'Brien, Pat (ent.; 1899-1983)
Observer-Times, Fayetteville (NC newspaper)
Observer, Charlotte (NC newspaper)
OC (officer commanding)
Ocala, FL
Ocasek, Ric (ent.)
O'Casey, Sean (Ir. writer; 1884-1964)

Occam, William of (Br. phil.; c1285-c1349)
Occam's razor (phil.)
Occident (Eur. + W. Hemisphere countries)
Occidental Petroleum Corp.
Occupational Safety and Health Administration
    (OSHA)(US govt. agcy.; est. 1970)
OCD (Office of Civil Defense)
Ocean City, MD, NJ
Ocean Spray™
Ocean Spray Cranberries, Inc.
Ocean State (nickname, RI)
Ocean, Billy (ent.; 1950-)
Oceania (collective name for Pac. islands)
Oceanic and Atmospheric Administration,
    National (NOAA)(US govt. agcy.; est. 1970)
Oceanic art
Oceanside, CA, NY
Oceanus (myth.)
O cedar Angler™ (broom)
Ochirbat, Punsalmaagiyn (pres., Mongolia;
    1943-)
Ocho Rios, Jamaica
Oconee National Forest (GA)
O'Connell, Daniel ("the Liberator")(Ir. pol.;
    1775-1847)
O'Connor, Carroll (ent.; 1924-)
O'Connor, Donald (ent.; 1925-)
O'Connor, (Mary) Flannery (US writer; 1925-
    64)
O'Connor, John (Joseph), Cardinal (US rel.;
    1920-)
O'Connor, Sandra Day (US jurist; 1930-)
O'Connor, Sinéad (ent.; 1967-)
O'Connor, Tay Pay (Thomas Power)(Ir. jour./
    pol.; 1848-1929)
OCR (optical character reader/recognition)
    (compu.)
OCS (Officer Candidate School)
Octans (astron., octant)
Octavia (Roman empress; c40-62)
Octavia (Roman, wife of M. Anthony; ?-11 BC)
Octavius, Gaius Julius Caesar (aka Caesar
    Augustus, Octavian)(1st Roman emp.; 63 BC-
    AD 14)
October Revolution (part of Russian Revolution;
    1917)
Octoberfest (also Oktoberfest)(Ger. beer
    festival)
Octopussy (film; 1983)
OD (overdose)
O'Day, Anita (US jazz; 1919-)
Odd Couple, The (film, TV show)
Odd Fellows, Independent Order of (fraternal
    society; est. 1918)
Oddsson, David (PM, Iceland
ODECA (Organization of Central American
    States)(est. 1951/1962)
Odense, Denmark

Oder (or Odra) River (N central Eur.)
Odessa, TX
Odessa, Ukraine
Odets, Clifford (US writer; 1906-63)
Odetta (b. Odetta Holmes)(ent.; 1930-)
Odilon Redon (Fr. artist; 1840-1916)
Odin (also Woden, Wotan, Wodan)(myth.)
Odio, Rodrigo Carazo
Odra (or Oder) River (N central Eur.)
Odysseus (fict. chara., Homer's *Odyssey, Illiad*)
Odyssey, the (by Homer)
OE (Old English)
OECD (Organization for Economic Cooperation
    & Development)
Oedipus (myth.)
Oedipus at Colonus (by Sophocles)
Oedipus complex (psych.)
Oedipus Rex (also *Oedipus Tyrannus*)(by
    Sophocles)
Oersted, Hans (Christian)(Dan. physt; 1777-
    1851)
Oerter, Al (discus thrower; 1936-)
Off Broadway (also off Broadway)(theater)
Off-Off Broadway (also off-off
    Broadway)(theater)
Offaly (county, Ir.)
Offenbach (am Main), Germany
Offenbach, Jacques (Levy)(Fr. comp.; 1819-80)
Office Act, Tenure of (US hist.; 1867)
Office Depot, Inc.
Office of Administration (US govt.)
Office of Economic Opportunity (OEC)(US
    govt.)
Office of High Commissioner for Refugees,
    United Nations (UNHCR)(est. 1951)
Office of Management and Budget (OMB)(US
    govt.)
Office of National Drug Control Policy, (US
    govt.)
Office of Personnel Management (OPM)(US
    govt. agcy.; est. 1979)
Office of Policy Development (US govt.)
Office of Science and Technology Policy (US
    govt.)
Office of the President and Vice President (US
    govt.)
Office of the U.S. Trade Representative (US
    govt.)
Offutt Air Force Base, NE
O'Flaherty, Liam (Ir. writer; 1897-1984)
Ogaden (region, Ethiopia)
Ogbomosho, Nigeria
Ogden Corp.
Ogden Nash (US writer/humorist; 1902-71)
Ogden, Gibbons v. (US law; 1924)
Ogden, UT
Ogdensburg, NY
Ogi, Adolf (pres., Switz.)

Ogilvy, David (US writer/adv.)
Oglethorpe, James E(dward)(Br. gen., founded
    Georgia; 1696-1785)
O'Grady, Sweet Rosie (film; 1943)
Ogun (state, Nigeria)
OH (Ohio)
Oh Boy!™ pizza
Oh Boy Corp.
Oh! Calcutta! (play)
Oh! Susanna (song)
O'Hair, Madalyn Murray (US atheist activist)
O'Hara, John (US writer; 1905-70)
O'Hara, Maureen (ent.; 1920-)
O'Hara, Scarlett (fict. chara., *Gone With the
    Wind*)
O'Hare International Airport (Chicago IL)
O Henry (aka William Sydney Porter)(US
    writer; 1862-1910)
O'Herlihy, Dan (ent.; 1919-)
Ohio (OH)
Ohio buckeye (tree)
Ohio River (E central US)
Ohio v. Akron Center for Reproductive Health
    (US law; 1983)
Ohio, Mapp v. (US law; 1961)
Ohira Masayoshi (ex-PM, Jap.; 1910-80)
Ohm, Georg (Simon)(Ger. physt.; 1789-1854)
Ohm's law (elec.)
O(rville) H(itchock) Platt (US pol.; 1827-1905)
Ohrid Lake (SE Eur.)
Ohsumi (Jap. space satellite)
Oil of Olay™ (skin care)
Oilers, Edmonton (hockey team)
Oilers, Houston (football team)
Oingo Boingo (pop music)
Oise River (W Eur.)
Oistins, Barbados
Oita, Japan
Ojai, CA
Ojibwa (also Chippewa)(NAmer. Indians)
O(renthal) J(ames) Simpson (football; 1947-)
OK (Oklahoma, oll korrect [all right])
OK Corral (Tombstone, AZ; gunfight; 1881)
O.K. Corral, Gunfight at the (film; 1957)
Oka River (W Russia)
Okayama, Japan
Okazaki, Japan
Okeechobee, FL
Okeechobee, Lake (FL)
O'Keefe, Dennis (ent.; 1908-68)
O'Keeffe, Georgia (US artist; 1887-1986)
Okefenokee Swamp (GA/FL)
Okhotsk, Sea of (N Pac.)
Okidata™
Okidata Corp.
Okie (slang)
Okinawa (island, Jap.)
Okker, Tom (tennis; 1944-)

Proper Noun Speller

Oklahoma (OK)
Oklahoma! (play/film)
Oklahoma City Oklahoman (OK newspaper)
Oklahoma City, OK
Oklahoma panhandle (formerly Territory of
　Cimarron)
Oklahoma, Ake v. (US law; 1985)
Oklahoman, Oklahoma City (OK newspaper)
Okmulgee, OK
Oksana Baiul (figure skating; 1978-)
Oktoberfest (also Octoberfest)(Ger. beer
　festival)
Olaf (or Olav) I (Tryggvesson)(king, Nor.; 969-
　1000)
Olaf (or Olav) II (Haraldsson)(St. Olaf)(king,
　Nor.; 995-1030)
Olaf (or Olav) III ("the Quiet")(king, Nor.; ?-
　1093)
Olaf (or Olav) V (b. Alexander Edward
　Christian Frederik of Glücksburg)(king, Nor.;
　1903-91)
Olajuwon, Hakeem (basketball; 1963-)
Olathe, KS
Olaus (or Ole) Roemer (Dan. astron.; 1644-
　1710)
Olay™, Oil of (skin care)
Olazabal, Jose Maria (golf; 1966-)
Olcott, Chauncey (US comp./ent.; 1860-1932)
Old Bailey (London criminal court)
Old Bay™ (seasoning)
Old Bay Co., Inc.
Old Colony State (nickname, MA)
Old Dominion (nickname, VA)
Old El Paso™
Old El Paso Foods Co.
Old English (also Anglo-Saxon)(lang.; c500-
　1050)
Old English (type style)
Old English Game (chicken)
Old English sheepdog
Old Faithful geyser (Yellowstone National
　Park)
Old Glory (also Stars and Stripes)(US flag)
Old-House Journal (mag.)
Old Ironsides (*Constitution, The*)(US naval
　ship)
Old Left (pol.)
Old Line State (nickname, MD)
Old Man River (Mississipi River)
Old Norse (ancient lang.)
Old North State (nickname, NC)
Old Pretender (aka James III, James [Francis]
　Edward Stuart)(Br. prince; 1688-1766)
Old Royal Observatory (London)(also Royal
　Greenwich Observatory)
Old Saybrook, CT
Old Scratch (the Devil)
Old Spice™ (men's cologne)

Old Stone Age (Paleolithic period; 2 million to
　15,000 years ago)
Old Testament (rel.)
Old Vic Theatre (also Royal Victoria
　Hall)(London)
Old World (Eur./Asia/Africa)
Old Yeller (F. Gipson novel)
Oldenburg, Claes (Thure)(US artist; 1929-)
Oldenburg, Germany
Oldfield cinquefoil (plant)
Oldfield, Barney (Berna Eli)(auto racing; 1878-
　1946)
Oldham, England
Olds, Ransom Eli (US bus./auto.; 1864-1950)
Oldsmobile Achieva™ (auto.)
Oldsmobile Calais (auto.)
Oldsmobile Ciera (auto.)
Oldsmobile Cutlass Supreme (auto.)
Oldsmobile Delta 88 (auto.)
Oldsmobile 88 (auto.)
Oldsmobile Toronado (auto.)
Olduvai Culture (500,000-2 million years ago)
Olduvai Gorge (archeo. site, Tanzania)
Ole (or Olaus) Roemer (Dan. astron.; 1644-
　1710)
O'Leary, Hazel R. (US Secy./Energy; 1937-)
Oleg Atkov (cosmo.)
Oleg Cassini (US designer; 1913-)
Oleg Cassini, Inc.
Olerud, John (baseball; 1968-)
O level (Br. educ., ordinary level)
Olga™ (clothing)
Olga Co.
Olga Korbut (Soviet gymnast; 1955-)
Olga Petrova
Oligocene epoch (38-26 million years ago)
Olin Corp.
Olin, Ken (ent.; 1954-)
Olinda, Brazil
Oliphant, Pat (US pol. cartoonist; 1935-)
Oliva, Tony (Pedro)(baseball; 1940-)
Olive Garden (US bus.)
Olive Oyl (fict. chara., *Popeye*)
Olive Schreiner (pseud. Ralph Iron)(SAfr.
　writer; 1855-1920)
Oliver Cromwell (Br. gen./pol.; 1599-1658)
Oliver Goldsmith (Br./Ir. writer; 1730?-74)
Oliver Hardy (ent.; 1892-1957)
Oliver "Ollie" North, Lt. Col. (US mil./pol.;
　1943-)
Oliver (Hazard) Perry (US mil.; 1785-1819)
Oliver Reed (ent.; 1938-)
Oliver Stone (ent.; 1946-)
Oliver Tambo (SAfr. pol.; 1917-93)
Oliver Twist (Dickens novel)
Oliver Wendell Holmes (US writer/phys.; 1809-
　94)
Oliver Wendell Holmes, Jr. (US jurist; 1841-

1935)

Oliver, King (Joseph)(US jazz; 1885-1938)
Oliver, Sy (US jazz; 1910-88)
Olives, Mount of (also Mt. Olivet)(Jerusalem)
Olivetti Corp.
Olivia Cole (ent.; 1942-)
Olivia De Havilland (ent.; 1916-)
Olivia Hussey (ent.)
Olivia Newton-John (ent.; 1947-)
Olivier, Sir Laurence (Kerr)(ent.; 1907-89)
Ollie, Kukla, Fran & (TV show)
Olmec (ancient Mex. Indians)
Olmos, Edward James (ent.; 1947-)
Olmsted v. U.S. (US law; 1928)
Olmsted, Frederick L(aw)(US landscaper; 1822-
    1903)
Olomouc, Czechoslovakia
Olsen, Merlin (Jay)(football/ent.; 1940-)
Olsten Corp.
Olsztyn, Poland
Olter, Bailey (pres., Micronesia)
Olvera Street (Los Angeles)
Olympia (ancient Gr. center)
Olympia Dukakis (ent.; 1931-)
Olympia oyster (also l.c.)
Olympia, WA
Olympiad (Gr., 4-year period between games)
Olympian (Gr. god; participant in games; native
    of Olympia)
Olympian Games (Gr.; 776 BC-AD 394)
Olympic Airways (airline)
Olympic Games (internat'l; 1896-)
Olympic Mountains (WA)
Olympic National Park (WA)
Olympic Peninsula (WA)
Olympics
Olympics, Summer
Olympics, Winter
Olympus (myth.)
Olympus™ (photo.)
Olympus, Mount (Gr.)
Olympus, Mount (WA)
Olympus Corp.
Om (rel.)
Omagh, Northern Ireland
Omaha (NAmer. Indians)
Omaha Steaks International (US bus.)
Omaha World-Herald (NE newspaper)
Omaha, NE
O'Malley, Walter (baseball exec.; 1903-79)
Oman (Sultanate of)(SW Asia)
Oman, Gulf of (Oman/Iran)
Omani Arab (people)
Omar (Islamic leader; c581-644)
Omar Abdel-Rahman, Sheik (Muslim rel.;
    1938-)
Omar Bongo, (Albert Bernard)(pres., Gabon;
    1935-)

Omar Hassan al-Bashir (PM, Sudan; 1944?-)
Omar Khayyám (Persian poet/math.; c1028-
    1122)
Omar Khayyám, The Rubáiyát of (book of
    verses)
Omar Nelson Bradley (US gen.; 1893-1981)
Omar Sharif (ent.; 1932-)
Omar Torrijos Herrera (Panamanian gen./pol.;
    1929-81)
Omarr, Sydney (astrol.)
OMB (Office of Management of Budget)(US
    govt.)
Omdurman, Sudan
Omega™
Omega Watch Corp.
Omicron Ceti (also Mira variable)(astron.)
Omisoka (Jap. New Year's Eve)
Omiya, Japan
Omni (mag.)
OmniCAT™ (CAT system)
Omni, Dodge (auto.)
Omnibus
Omniscient, the (God)
Omsk, Russia
Ona Munson (ent.)
Onassis, Aristotle Socrates (Gr. shipping
    magnate; 1900-75)
Onassis, Christina (Gr. heiress; 1951-88)
Onassis, Jacqueline "Jackie" Lee Bouvier
    Kennedy (US editor/photo.; wife of ex-US
    pres.; 1929-95)
Ondine (J. Genet play)
One-A-Day™ (med.)
One Day at a Time (TV show)
One Flew Over the Cuckoo's Nest (film; 1975)
One Hour Martinizing Dry Cleaning (US bus.)
101 Dalmatians
One Life to Live (TV soap)
O'Neal, Patrick (ent.; 1927-)
O'Neal, Ryan (ent.; 1941-)
O'Neal, Shaquille (basketball; 1972-)
O'Neal, Tatum (ent.; 1963-)
Onega, Lake (NW Russia)
Oneida (NAmer. Indians)
Oneida™ (silverware)
Oneida Community (NY rel. society; 1848)
Oneida Lake (NY)
Oneida, Ltd.
Oneida, NY
O'Neill, Ed (ent.; 1946-)
O'Neill, Eugene (Gladstone)(US writer; 1888-
    1953)
O'Neill, Jennifer (ent.; 1932-)
O'Neill, Tip (Thomas P.), Jr. (US pol.; 1912-
    1993)
Ong Teng Cheong (pres., Singapore)
Onitsha, Nigeria
Onkyo™ (stereo)

Onkyo USA Corp.
Online Access Guide
Ono, Yoko (ent.; 1933-)
Onondaga (NAmer. Indians)
Onondaga, Lake (NY)
Ontario (province, Can.)
Ontario, CA
Ontario, Lake (US/Can.)
Oort cloud (astron.)
Oort, Jan H(endrik)(Dutch astron.; 1900-92)
Oostende, Belgium (also Ostend)
Op Art (1960s)(also l.c.)
Opango, Jacques-Joachim Yhombi- (PM, Congo;
    1940-)
OPEC (Organization of Petroleum-Exporting
    Countries)(est. 1960)
Open Door policy
Operation Desert Shield (Gulf War; 1990-91)
Operation Desert Storm (Gulf War; 1991)
Operation Overlord (WWI Normandy invasion;
    6/6/44)
Ophelia (*Hamlet* chara.)
Ophiuchus (astron., serpent bearer)
Opium War, First (Br./Ch.; 1839-42)
Opium War, Second (Br./Ch.; 1856-60)
Opole (province, Pol.)
Opole, Poland
Oporto, Portugal (also Porto)
Oppenheimer, J(ulius) Robert (US physt.,
    atomic bomb; 1904-67)
Opper, Frederick Burr (cartoonist, *Happy
    Hooligan*; 1857-1937)
Oprah Winfrey (ent.; 1954-)
Opryland USA
Optima (type style)
Opus Dei (rel.)
OR (operating room, Oregon)
Oracle of Delphi (also Delphic oracle)(noted for
    ambiguous answers)
oracle of Apollo at Delphi
Oradea, Romania
Orajel™ (med.)
Oral-B™ (med.)
Oral Law (also Mishna[h])(rel.)
Oral Roberts (US rel.; 1918-)
Oran, Algeria (also Wahran)
Orange Bowl (college football)
Orange County Register (CA newspaper)
Orange Free State (province, SAfr.)
Orange River (S Afr.)
Orange Society (Ir.; est. 1795)
Orange Walk, Belize
Orange, CA, NJ, TX
Orange, House of (Br. ruling family; 1689-1702)
Orange, House of (royal family, Netherlands)
Orangemen (member, Orange Society)
Orantes, Manuel (tennis; 1949-)
Orbach, Jerry (ent.; 1935-)

Orbison, Roy (ent.; 1936-88)
ORC (Officers Reserve Corps)
Orcus (myth.)
Ord, Fort, CA (mil.)
Order of Lenin (Soviet award)
Order of Odd Fellows, Independent (fraternal
    society; est. 1918)
Order of Our Lady of Mercy (rel.)
Order of the Bath (Br. order of knighthood)
Order of the Purple Heart (US mil. metal)
Ordovician period (500-430 million years ago)
Ore-Ida™
Ore-Ida Foods, Inc.
Ore-Ida™ Tater Tots
Örebro, Sweden
Oregon (OR)
Oregon cedar (also Port Orford cedar)
Oregon fir (also Douglas fir)(tree)
Oregon grape (plant)
Oregon myrtle (also California laurel)
Oregon pine (tree)
Oregon Trail (from MO to OR; 1800s)
Oregon, Muller v. (US law; 1908-)
Oregonian, Portland (OR newspaper)
Orel Hershiser (baseball; 1958-)
Orël, Russia (also Oryol)
Orem, UT
Orenburg, Russia
Orense, Spain
Oreo™ (cookies)
Orestes (Euripides drama)
Orestes (myth.)
Orff, Carl (Ger. comp.; 1895-1982)
Organic Gardening (mag.)
Organization for Economic Cooperation and
    Development (OECD)(internat'l; est. 1961)
Organization for Women, National (NOW)
Organization of African Unity (OAU)(est. 1963)
Organization of American States (OAS)(N/
    central/S Amer.; est.; 1948)
Organization of Arab Petroleum Exporting
    Countries (OAPEC)(est.; 1968)
Organization of Central American States
    (ODECA)(est. 1951/1962)
Organization of Petroleum-Exporting Countries
    (OPEC)(est. 1960)
Oriental rug/carpet
Orientale basin (astron.)
O-ring (space shuttle gasket)
Orinoco River (SAmer.)
Orioles, Baltimore (baseball team)
Orion (astron., hunter; myth.)
Orion (US Navy plane)
Orion nebula (astron.)
Orion Pictures Corp.
Orionis, Beta (also Rigel)(astron.)
Orissa (state, India)
Oriya (lang.)

Orizaba, Mexico
Orizaba, Mount (also Citlaltepetl)(dormant
    volcano, Mex.)
Orkin Pest Control (US bus.)
Orkney Island(s)(Scot.)
Orlando and Dawn, Tony (pop music)
Orlando Gibbons (Br. comp.; 1583-1625)
Orlando International Airport (FL)
Orlando Magic (basketball team)
Orlando Sentinel (FL newspaper)
Orlando, FL
Orlando, Tony (ent.; 1944-)
Orléans, France
Orléans, Maid of (also St. Joan of Arc, Jeanne
    d'Arc)(Fr. rel./mil.; 1412?-31)
Orlon™ (fiber)
Orly, France
Ormandy, Eugene (US cond.; 1899-1985)
Ormazd (also Ormuzd, Ahura Mazda)(rel.)
Ormoc, Philippines
Ormuz (also Hormuz)(island, Iran)
Ormuz (or Hormuz), Strait of (Iran)
Ormuzd (also Ormazd, Ahura Mazda)(rel.)
Ornette Coleman (US jazz; 1930-)
Oromo (lang./people)
Orontes River (SW Asia)
O'Rourke, Heather (ent.; 1978-88)
Oroweat™
Oroweat Foods Co.
Orozco, José Clemente (Mex. artist; 1883-1949)
Orphan Annie, Little (fict. chara.)
Orpheus (myth.)
Orpheus (Stravinsky ballet)
Orphic Mysteries (also Orphism)(rel., ancient
    Gr.)
Orphism (rel./myth., ancient Gr.)
Orpington (chicken)
Orr, Bobby (Robert Gordon)(hockey; 1948-)
Orrin Grant Hatch (US cong.; 1934-)
Orser, Brian (figure skating)
Orsk, Russia
Orson Bean (ent.; 1928-)
Orson Welles, (George)(ent.; 1915-85)
Ortega™ (salsa/Mex. foods)
Ortega Saavedra, (José) Daniel (ex-pres.,
    Nicaragua; 1945-)
Orthodox (rel.)
Orthodox Christian (rel.)
Orthodox Church, Greek
Orthodox Eastern Church (also Eastern
    Orthodox Church)(rel.)
Orthodox Judaism
Ortho-Novum™ (med.)
Oruro, Bolivia
Orvieto (wine)
Orvieto, Italy
Orville Redenbacher™ (popcorn)
Orville Redenbacher (US bus.)

Orville Wright (US aviator/inv.; 1871-1948)
Orwell, George (aka Eric A[rthur] Blair)(Br.
    writer; 1903-50)
Ory, Kid (US jazz; 1886-1973)
Os (chem. sym., osmium)
Osage (NAmer. Indians)
Osage orange (tree)
Osage River (MO)
Osaka, Japan
Osasco, Brazil
Osbert Sacheverell Sitwell, Sir (Francis)(Br.
    writer; 1892-1969)
Osborne Computer Corp.
Osborne, John (James)(Br. writer; 1929-)
Osbourne, Ozzy (ent.; 1946-)
Os-Cal™ (calcium tablets)
Oscar (Academy Award statuette)
Oscar Arias Sanchez (ex-pres., Costa Rica;
    1941-)
Oscar de la Renta (US designer; 1932-)
Oscar de La Renta, Ltd.
Oscar Hammerstein (ent.; 1847-1919)
Oscar Hammerstein, II (US lyricist; 1895-1960)
Oscar Kokoschaka (Aus. artist; 1886-1980)
Oscar Levant (ent.; 1906-72)
Oscar Luigi Scalfaro (pres., It.)
Oscar Mayer™ (meats)
Oscar Mayer Foods Corp.
Oscar Niemeyer Soares Filho (Brazilian arch.;
    1907-)
Oscar Peterson (US jazz; 1925-)
Oscar Pettiford (US jazz; 1922-60)
Oscar Robertson (basketball; 1938-)
Oscar the Grouch (cartoon chara.)
Oscar (Fingal O'Flahertie Wills) Wilde (Ir.
    writer; 1854-1900)
Oscars (also Academy Awards)
Osceola National Forest
Osceola, Chief (Seminole Indians; 1800?-38)
OSG (Office of Secretary General [UN])
Osgood, Charles
Osh, Kyrgyzstan
OSHA (Occupational Safety and Health
    Administration)
Oshawa, Ontario, Canada
OshKosh™
OshKosh B'Gosh™
OshKosh B'Gosh, Inc.
Oshkosh, WI
Osho (or Shree) Rajneesh (aka Bhagwan)(b.
    Chaadra Mohan Jain)(Indian rel.; 1931-90)
Oshogbo, Nigeria
Osijek, Croatia
Osip ([Y]Emilevich) Mandelstam (Rus. poet;
    1891-1938?)
Osiris (myth.)
Oskar Straus (Aus. comp.; 1870-1954)
Oskar Werner

Oslin, K. T. (ent.; 1942-)
Oslo Fjord (or Fiord), Norway
Oslo, Norway
Osmond, Donny (ent.; 1958-)
Osmond, Marie (ent.; 1959-)
Osnabrück, Germany
O Sole Mio (song)
Osorno, Chile
Ossetian (people)
Ossie Davis (ent.; 1917-)
Ossig, Kaspar Schwenkfeld von (Ger. rel.; 1490-1561)
Ossining, NY
Ossip Zadkine (Rus. artist; 1890-1967)
Ostade, Adriaen van (Dutch artist; 1610-85)
Ostend Manifesto (US/Sp. re: Cuba; 1854)
Ostend, Belgium (also Oostende)
Oster Corp.
Oster Corp., Sunbeam
Osterizer™ blender
Ostpolitik (WGer. hist.; 1971-90)
Ostrava, Czechoslovakia
Ostrogoths (also East Goths)(ancient Germans)
Ostwald, Wilhelm (Ger. chem.; 1853-1932)
O'Sullivan, Maureen (ent.; 1911-)
Oswald Spengler (Ger. phil./hist.; 1880-1936)
Oswald, Lee Harvey (assassin of JFK; 1939-63)
Oswego River (NY)
Oswego tea (plant)
Oswego, Lake (OR)
Oswego, NY, OR
Otago (district, NewZeal.)
O Tannenbaum (Ger., Christmas tree)
O Tannenbaum (song)
OTB (off-track betting)
OTC (over-the-counter [stock trading])
OTEC (ocean thermal energy conversion)
Othello, The Moor of Venice, The Tragedy of (Shakespeare play)
Otis™
Otis Air Force Base, MA
Otis Elevator Co.
Otis Redding (ent.; 1941-67)
Otis Skinner (US writer/ent.; 1858-1942)
Otis, Elisha (Graves)(US inv., elevator; 1811-61)
O'Toole, Annette (ent.; 1953-)
O'Toole, Peter (ent.; 1932-)
Otsu, Japan
Ott, Mel (baseball; 1909-58)
Ottawa (NAmer. Indians)
Ottawa River (SE Can.)
Ottawa Senators (hockey team)
Ottawa, IL
Ottawa, Ontario, Canada
Ottmar Mergenthaler (Ger./US inv.; 1854-99)
Otto Dix (Ger. artist; 1891-1969)
Otto Graham (football; 1921-)

Otto Gustaf Nordenskjöld, (Nils)(Swed. expl.; 1869-1928)
Otto Hahn (Ger. chem.; 1879-1968)
Otto Klemperer (Ger. cond.; 1885-1973)
Otto Kruger (ent.; 1885-1974)
Otto Luening (US comp.; 1900-)
Otto (Ehrenfried) Nicolai, (Carl)(Ger. comp.; 1810-49)
Otto (Ludwig) Preminger (ent.; 1905-86)
Otto Soglow (US cartoonist, *Little King*; 1900-75)
Otto Stich (VP, Switz.)
Otto (Eduard Leopold) von Bismarck, Prince ("Iron Chancellor")(ex-chanc., Ger.; 1815-98)
Ottoman Empire (Turk.; 1300-1920)
Ottorino Respighi (It. comp.; 1879-1936)
Ottumwa, IA
Ouachita Mountains (S central US)
Ouachita River (S central US)
Ouagadougou, Burkina Faso (also Wagadugu)
Ouahran/Oran, Algeria
Ouattara, Alassane (PM, Ivory Coast
Oud, (Jacobus Johannes) Pieter (Dutch arch.; 1890-1963)
Ouedraogo, Youssouf (PM, Burkina Faso
Ouija™ board
Oujda, Morocco
Oulu, Finland
Our Father (also *Lord's Prayer, Paternoster [Pater Noster]*)(prayer)
Our Lady (also the Madonna, Holy Mother, Mary, Virgin Mary)(rel.)
Our Lady of Mercy, Order of (rel.)
Ouse River (also Great Ouse)(Eng.)
Outlaw Josey Wales, The (film; 1976)
Ousmane, Mahamane (pres., Niger
Outboard Marine Corp.
Outcault, Richard (US cartoonist, *Buster Brown*; 1863-1928)
Outdoor Life (mag.)
Outdoor Photographer (mag.)
Outer Hebrides (islands, W Scot.)
Outer Mongolia (now State of Mongolia)
Outlaw Josey Wales, The (film)
Outremont, Quebec, Canada
Outside (mag.)
Oval Office (US pres. office)
Ovaltine Food Products (US bus.)
Ovambo (people)
Overeaters Anonymous
Overijssel (province, Netherlands)
Overland Park, KS
Overlord, Operation (WWI Normandy invasion; 6/6/44)
Overton, Jayne Kennedy- (ent.; 1951-)
Oveta Culp Hobby (US publ./pol.; 1905-)
Ovett, Steve (track; 1955-)
Ovid (b. Publius Ovidius Naso)(Roman poet; 43

BC-AD 17)
Oviedo, Spain
Ovimbundu (people)
Owen K. Garriott (US physt./astro.; 1930-)
Owen, Robert (Br. phil./reformer; 1771-1858)
Owens-Corning Fiberglas Corp.
Owens-Illinois, Inc.
Owens, Buck (ent.; 1929-)
Owens, Jesse (James Cleveland)(track; 1913-80)
Owensboro, KY
Owsley (slang, LSD)
Owsley (b. Augustus Owsley Stanley, III)(US amateur chem./hallucinogens; fl. 1960s)
Oxbridge (Oxford and Cambridge, Br. universities)
Oxford bags (trousers)
Oxford Industries, Inc.
Oxford University (Eng.)
Oxford, England
Oxford, MS
Oxfordshire (county, Eng.)(also Oxon)
Oxmoor House, Inc.
Oxnard, CA
Oxus River (Amu Darya)(central Asia)
Oxy™ (med.)
Oxy5™ (med.)
Oxy10™ (med.)
Oye-Mba, Casimir (PM, Gabon
Oyl, Olive (fict. chara., *Popeye*)
Oyster Bay, NY
oysters Rockefeller
OZ™ (CAT system)
Oz (myth.)
Oz Munchkins
Oz, Frank (Muppet puppeteer; 1944-)
Oz, Land of
Oz, The Wizard of (by L.F. Baum)
Ozal, Turgut (ex-pres., Turk.; 1927-93)
Ozalid™ (photo.)
Ozark Mountains (also Ozarks)(central US)
Ozarks, Lake of the (MO)
Ozawa, Ichiro (Jap. writer)
Ozawa, Seiji (Jap./US cond.; 1935-)
Ozick, Cynthia (US writer; 1928-)
OZpc (CAT system)
Ozzie & Harriet Nelson (TV couple)
Ozzie Nelson (ent.; 1906-75)
Ozzy Osbourne (ent.; 1946-)

P

P (chem. sym., phosphorus)
PA (Pennsylvania, power of attorney, public-
    address system)
Paar, Jack (ent.; 1918-)
Paavo Nurmi (Olympic runner; 1897-1973)
PABA (para-aminobenzoic acid)
Pablo Casals (Sp. musician; 1876-1973)
Pablo Neruda (aka Neftali Ricardo Reyes y
    Basoalto)(Chilean poet; 1904-73)
Pablo (Ruiz y) Picasso (Sp. artist; 1881-1973)
Pabst Brewing Co.
PAC (political action committee)
Pace™
Pace Foods, Inc.
Pace, Darrell (archery; 1956-)
Pacers, Indiana (basketball team)
Pachelbel's Canon (J. Pachelbel music)
Pachelbel, Johann (Ger. comp.; 1653-1706)
Pachuca (de Soto), Mexico
Pacific Bell (comm.)
Pacific Coast Airline
Pacific Corp., Georgia-
Pacific Islanders (people)
Pacific Missile Test Center (CA)
Pacific Northwest
Pacific Ocean
Pacific Palisades (district, Los Angeles)
Pacific Rim National Park Reserve (Can.)
Pacific scandal (Can. hist.; 1873)
Pacific Standard Time (also Pacific Time)
Pacific Tea Co., Great Atlantic & (A&P Food
    Stores)
Pacific Telesis Group (phone. co.)
Pacific Time (also Pacific Standard Time)
Pacific War (Bolivia, Peru/Chile; 1879-83)
Pacific yew (tree)
Pacific, War of the (Chile/Bolivia, Peru; 1879-
    83)
Pacifica, CA
Pacificator, Great (also Great
    Compromiser)(Henry Clay)(US pol.; 1777-
    1852)
Pacino, Al(berto)(ent.; 1940-)
Packard Co., Hewlett- (HP)
Packer, Billy (ent.; 1940-)
Packers, Green Bay (football team)
Packwood, Bob (Robert William)(US cong.;
    1932-)
Pac-Man defense (econ.)
Padang, Indonesia
Paddington (area, Westminster, Eng.)
Paddy (slang, Irishman)
Paddy Chayefsky (US writer; 1923-81)
Paderborn, Germany

Paderewski, Ignace Jan (ex-PM, Pol./comp.;
    1860-1941)
Padre Island (Gulf of Mexico)
Padres, San Diego (baseball team)
Padua, Italy (also Padova)
Paducah, Duke of (aka Whitey [Edward
    Charles] Ford)(baseball; 1928-)
Paducah, KY
Paeniu, Bikenibeu (ex-PM, Tuvalu
Paganini, Niccolò (It. comp.; 1782-1840)
Page Boy™ (maternity clothes)
Page Boy Co., Inc.
Page, Geraldine (ent.; 1924-87)
Page, Hot Lips
Page, LaWanda (ent.; 1920-)
Page, Patti (ent.; 1927-)
Page, Robert Morris (US physt.; 1903-92)
PageMaker™, Aldus (compu.)
Pagliacci, I (R. Leoncavallo opera)
Pago Pago, American Samoa (formerly Pango
    Pango)
Pahang (state, Malaysia)
Pahlavi, Muhammad Riza (shah, Iran; 1919-80)
Pahlavi, Riza (shah, Iran; 1877-1944)
Paias Wingti (PM, Papua New Guinea; 1951-)
Paige, Janis (ent.; 1922-)
Paige, Satchel (Leroy Robert)(baseball; 1906-82)
Paine, Tom (Thomas)(US writer; 1737-1809)
PaineWebber Group, Inc.
PaineWebber, Inc.
Painted Desert, AZ
Painter, Sweatt v. (US law; 1950)
Paisley, Scotland (thread factories)
Paiute (or Piute)(NAmer. Indians)
Pakistan (Islamic Republic of)(S Asia)
Pakistan International Airlines
Pakistan wars, India-
Pakistani (people)
Pakse, Laos (also Pakxé)
Palace of Versailles (Fr.)
Paladin (TV show)
Palance, Jack (ent.; 1920-)
Palantine, IL
Palatinate, Rhineland- (state, Ger.)
Palatino (type style)
Palau (now Belau)
Palau Islands (W Pac.)
Palaung-Wa (lang.)
Palembang, Indonesia
Paleocene epoch (65-54 million years ago)
Paleolithic period (Old Stone Age; 2 million to
    15,000 years ago)
Paleozoic era (570-225 million years ago)
Palermo, Sicily (Italy)
Palestine (aka Holy Land, Canaan)(region, SW
    Asia)
Palestine Liberation Organization (PLO)(Arab,
    est. 1964)

Palestine National Liberation Movement (also al-Fatah)
Palestinian (people)
Palestrina, Giovanni P(ierluigi) da (It. comp.; c1525-94)
Paley, Grace (US writer; 1922-)
Paley, William (Br. rel.; 1743-1805)
Paley, William S. (US TV exec.; 1901-90)
Pali (lang.)
Pali Canon (also Tripitaka)(rel.)
Palin, Michael (ent.; 1943-)
Palisades Interstate Park (NJ/NY)
Pall Mall (cigarettes)
Pall Mall (London street famed for clubs)
Palladian style (arch.)
Palladian window (also Diocletian window)
Palladio, Andrea (It. arch.; 1508-80)
Palladium (myth.)
Pallas (astron.)
Pallas Athena (myth.)
Pallas's cat
Palm Beach, FL
Palm Springs, CA
Palm Sunday (Sunday before Easter)
Palma, Brian De (ent.; 1940)
Palma, Spain (also Palma de Mallorca)
Palmdale, CA
Palmer House (Chicago)
Palmer, AK, MA
Palmer, Arnold (Daniel)(golf; 1929-)
Palmer, Betsy (ent.; 1929-)
Palmer, James (Alvin)(baseball; 1945-)
Palmer, Jim (baseball; 1945-)
Palmer, John (McAuley)(US gen./pol.; 1817-1900)
Palmer, Lilli (ent.; 1914-86)
Palmer, Reginald (gov.-gen., Grenada
Palmerson, Henry John Temple, Viscount (ex-PM, Br.; 1784-1865)
Palmerston North, New Zealand
Palmetto State (nickname, SC)
Palmiro Togliatti (It. pol.; 1893-1964)
Palmolive™
Palmolive Co., Colgate-
Palmyra (also Tadmor)(ancient city, Syria)
Palmyra, NY
Palo Alto, CA
Paloma Picasso (US bus.; 1949-)
Paloma Picasso (US bus.)
Palomar Observatory (also Palomar Mountain Observatory)(CA)
Palomar, Mount (CA)
Palooka, Joe (comic strip)
Palos Verdes Estates, CA
Pam™ (cooking spray)
Pam Dawber (ent.; 1951-)
Pam Shriver (tennis; 1962-)
Pampangan (lang.)

Pampers™ (diapers)
Pamprin™ (med.)
Pan (myth.)
Pan Am™ (airline)
Pan Am Corp.
Pan American Day
Pan American Games
Pan-American Union (now Organization of American States)
Pan collar, Peter
Pan Industries, Peter
Pan, Peter (fict. chara.)
Pan, Peter (J. Barrie play)
Panadol™ (pain reliever)
PanAm Express (airline)
Panama (Republic of)(CAmer.)
Panama Canal (CAmer.)
Panama Canal Zone (CAmer.)
Panama City, FL
Panama City, Panama (also Panama, Panama)
Panama hat
Panama Jack™ (health)
Panama red (slang, marijuana from Panama)
Panasonic™ (elec.)
Panasonic Co.
Panay (island, Philippines)
Panay-Hiligaynon (lang.)
Pancaldi™ (shoes)
Pancaldi (US bus.)
Panchatantra (Sanskrit lit.; 4th c. BC)
Panchen Lama (Tibetan rel.; 1939-89)
Pancho (Richard Alonzo) Gonzalez (tennis; 1928-)
Pancho Villa (b. Doroteo Arango)(Mex. gen.; c1877-1923)
Pandaemonium (capital of hell in *Paradise Lost*)
Pandit (title of respect, India)
Pandit, Vijaya Lakshmi (dipl., India; 1900-90)
P and L (also P. and L., P.&L.)(profit and loss)
Pandora (myth.)
Pandora's box (myth.)
Panetta, Leon E. (US Chief of Staff; 1938-)
Panevezys, Lithuania
Pangai, Tonga
Pangasinan (lang.)
Pangloss (fict. chara., *Candide*)
Panhellenism
Panic, Milan (ex-PM, Yug.)
Panipat, India
Pankhurst, Emmeline (Goulden)(Br. suffragist; 1858-1928)
Panmunjom, Korea (also Panmunjon)(Korean War truce talks)
Pantages Theater (Los Angeles)
Pantagruel (F. Rabelais satire)
Pantaloon (also Pantalone)(fict. chara.)
Pantene™ (hair care)

Pantheon (temple, Rome)
Panthers, Carolina (football team)
Pantone Matching System™ (PMS)(colors/
    graphics)
Panyarachun, Anand (ex-PM, Thailand; 1933-)
Panza, Sancho (fict. chara., *Don Quixote*)
Paolo Soleri (US arch.; 1919-)
Paolo Uccello (b. Paolo di Dono)(It. artist; 1397-
    1475)
Paolo Veronese (It. artist; 1528-88)
Paolozzi, Eduardo (Br. sculptor; 1924-)
Pap smear/test (Papanicolaou test)(med.)
Papa Doc (François Duvalier)(ex-pres., Haiti;
    1907-71)
Papadopoulos, George (ex-pres., Gr.; 1919-)
Papago Indians/lang.)
Papal States (It.)
Papandreou, Andreas (George)(PM, Gr.; 1919-)
Papandreou, George (ex-PM, Gr.; 1888-1968)
Papas, Irene (ent.; 1926-)
Papas, the Mamas and the (pop music)
Papeete on Tahiti, French Polynesia
Papen, Franz von (Ger. pol.; 1879-1969)
Paper Mate™
Paper Mate Co., The
Paphos, Cyprus (Gk.)
Papillon (film; 1973)
Papp, Joseph (ent.; 1921-91)
Pappagallo™ (shoes)
Pappagallo (US bus.)
Papua New Guinea (SW Pac.)
Papua New Guinean (people)
Papuan (lang./people)
Paracel Islands (S Ch.)
Paracelsus, Philippus Aureolus (b.
    Theophrastus Bombastus von
    Hohenheim)(Swiss phys./chem.; 1493-1541)
Paraclete (Holy Spirit)
Parade (Sunday mag.)
Paradise (also Garden of Eden)(rel.)
Paradise Lost (Milton epic poem)
Paradise Regained (Milton epic poem)
Paraguay (Republic of)(SAmer.)
Parakou, Benin
Paramaribo, Suriname
Paramount Communications, Inc.
Paramount, CA
Paramount™
Paramount Pictures Corp.
Paramount Records (US bus.)
Paramus, NJ
Paraná, Argentina
Parcel Service™, United (UPS)
Parcheesi™ (game)
Parducci Winery, Ltd.
Parent-Teacher Association, National (also
    National Congress of Parents and
    Teachers)(PTA)(est. 1897)

Parent, Bernard Marcel (hockey; 1945-)
Parenting (mag.)
Parents (mag.)
Parents and Teachers, National Congress of
    (also National Parent-Teacher
    Association)(PTA)(est. 1897)
Pariah (rel., member of lowest caste)
Parian ware (porcelain)
Paris (myth.)
Paris green
Paris Opéra
Paris Pacts (1954)
Paris Peace Conference (1919)
Paris Review, The
Paris, France
Paris, plaster of (synthetic gypsum)
Paris, School/school of (art)
Paris, TN, TX
Paris, Treaty of (various peace treaties)
Paris, University of (aka Sorbonne)
Parish, Mitchell (US comp.; 1901-)
Parisian (people of Paris)
Parisienne (females of Paris)
Park Avenue (NYC)
Park Avenue, Buick™ (auto.)
Park Chung Hee (ex-pres., SKorea; 1917-79)
Park Service, National (US govt. bureau)
Park, (Douglas) Brad(ford)(hockey; 1948-)
Parkay™ (margarine)
Parke Bernet Gallery (NY art auction, now with
    Sotheby's)
Parke, Davis & Co.
Parker-Bowles, Camilla (Br. news)
Parker Brothers™ (games)
Parker Brothers (US bus.)
Parker Hannifin Corp.
Parker House Hotel (Boston)
Parker House (rolls)
Parker Stevenson (ent.; 1952-)
Parker, Bonnie (US criminal; 1911-34)
Parker, Charlie "Bird" (b. Charles Christopher
    Parker, Jr.)(US jazz; 1920-55)
Parker, Dorothy (Rothschild)(US writer; 1893-
    1967)
Parker, Eleanor (ent.; 1922-)
Parker, Fess (ent.; 1925-)
Parker, Jameson (ent.; 1947-)
Parker, Jean (ent.; 1912-)
Parker, Nosy/nosy (slang, busybody)
Parker, Sarah Jessica (ent.; 1965-)
Parkersburg, WV
Parkinson's disease
Parkinson's Law/law (work expands to fill the
    time allotted)
Parkman, Francis (US hist.; 1823-93)
Parks, Bert (ent.; 1914-92)
Parliament-Funkadelic (pop music)
Parliament, Houses of (Br. govt.)

Parma, Italy
Parma, Margaret of (Sp. regent, Netherlands; 1522-86)
Parma, OH
Parmesan cheese
Parnassian (lit.)
Parnassus, Mount (Gr.)
Parnell, Charles Stewart (Ir. pol.; 1846-91)
Parnis, Mollie (US designer; 1905-92)
Pärnu, Estonia
Paro Dzong, Bhutan
Paro, Bhutan
Parr, Catherine (6th wife of Henry VIII; 1512-48)
Parramatta, Australia
Parrish, (Frederick) Maxfield (US artist; 1870-1966)
Parry, Sir William Edward (Br. expl.; 1790-1855)
Parsee (also Parsi)(rel. community, India)
Parseghian, Ara (football; 1923-)
Parsifal, Sir (also Percivale)(Arthurian knight)
Parsons table
Parsons, Alan (ent.)
Parsons Project, Alan (pop music)
Parsons, Estelle (ent.; 1927-)
Parsons, Gram (ent.)
Parsons, Louella (US gossip columnist)
Parthenon (also Temple of Athena Parthenos, Gr.)
Parthia (ancient country, S Asia)
Parthian horsemen
Parthian shot
Parton, Dolly (ent.; 1946-)
Partridge Family, The (TV show)
Partridge, Eric (Honeywood)(Br. lexicographer; 1894-1979)
Party of God (also Hezbollah)(rel./mil.)
Parvati (also Anapurna, Annapurna, Devi)(myth.)
Pasadena, CA, TX
Pasadena Community Playhouse
Pasadena Tournament of Roses
Pasarell, Charles (tennis; 1944-)
Pasay, Philippines
Pascagoula, MS
Pascal (compu. lang.)
Pascal Lissouba (pres., Congo; 1931-)
Pascal, Blaise (Fr. phil./math.; 1623-62)
Pascal, Francine
Pascal's law/principle (physics)
Pascal's theorem (geometry)
Paschen's law (elect.)
Pasco, WA
Paseo, Toyota (auto.)
Pasha, Ali ("the Lion")(Turk. pol.; 1741-1822)
Pasha, Mehmed Emin Ali (Turk. pol.; 1815-71)
Pashto (also Pushtu)(lang.)

Paslode™ (power tools)
Paslode Co.
Paso (horse)
Pass, Joe (US jazz)
Passaic River (NJ)
Passaic, NJ
Passamaquoddy (NAmer. Indians)
Passamaquoddy Bay (ME/Can.)
Passat™, Volkswagen (auto.)
Passat™ GLX, Volkswagen (auto.)
Passion Sunday
Passion Week
Passiontide
Passos, John Dos (US writer; 1896-1970)
Passover (also Pesach)(rel.)
Pasternack, Josef A. (ent.; 1881-1940)
Pasternak, Boris (Leonidovich)(Rus. writer; 1890-1960)
Pasteur effect (med.)
Pasteur treatment (med.)
Pasteur, Louis (Fr. chem.; 1822-95)
Pasto, Colombia
Pat Benatar (ent.; 1953-)
Pat Boone (ent.; 1934-)
Pat Brown, (Edmund Gerald), Sr. (ex-gov., CA; 1905-)
Pat Buttram (ent.)
Pat Carroll (ent.; 1927-)
Pat Conroy (US writer; 1945-)
Pat(rick Floyd) Garrett, Sheriff (US sheriff, shot "Billy the Kid"; 1850-1908)
Pat Harrington, Jr. (ent.; 1929-)
Pat(rick Bruce) Metheny (ent.; 1954-)
Pat Morita (ent.; 1932-)
Pat Nixon (b. Thelma Catherine Ryan)(wife of ex-US pres.; 1912-93)
Pat O'Brien (ent.; 1899-1983)
Pat Oliphant (US pol. cartoonist; 1935-)
Pat Paulsen (US bus./ent.)
Pat Paulsen Vineyards (US bus.)
Pat (Marion Gordon) Robertson (US pol./rel.; 1930-)
Pat Sajak (ent.; 1947-)
Pat Summerall
Patagonia (region, Argentina)
Patan, Nepal (now Lalitpur)
Patasse, Ange (pres., Central African Republic)
Paternoster (or *Pater Noster*)(also *Lord's Prayer, Our Father*)(prayer)
Paterson, NJ
Pathan (people)
Pathé Journal (newsreel)
Pathé Gazette (newsreel)
Pathe, Charles (Fr. bus./films; 1863-1957)
Patiala, India
Patinkin, Mandy (ent.; 1952-)
Patna, India
Patras, Greece (also Patrái)

Patrice (Emergy) Lumumba (ex-PM, Congo/
  Zaire; 1926-61)
Patrice Munsel (ent.; 1925-)
Patricia Aburdene (US writer)
Patricia Busignani (captain-regent; San
  Marino)
Patricia Crowley (ent.)
Patricia Ireland (US, ex-pres. NOW; 1945-)
Patricia McBridge (ent.; 1942-)
Patricia Neal (ent.; 1926-)
Patricia (Scott) Schroeder (US cong.; 1940-)
Patricia Stevens International, Inc.
Patricio Aylwin Azócar (pres., Chile; 1918-)
Patrick Air Force Base, FL
Patrick A. M. Manning (PM, Trinidad/Tobago;
  1946-)
Patrick Campbell, Mrs. (aka Beatrice
  Tanner)(ent.; 1865-1940)
Patrick Duffy (ent. 1949-)
Patrick Ewing (basketball; 1962-)
Patrick Henry (US pol./orator; 1736-99)
Patrick J. Buchanan (US pol. commentator;
  1938-)
Patrick Leahy (US cong.; 1940-)
Patrick Macnee (ent.; 1922-)
Patrick Magee
Patrick Maynard Stuart Blackett, Baron (Br.
  physt.; 1897-1974)
Patrick McGoohan (ent.; 1928-)
Patrick Moynihan, Daniel (US cong.; 1927-)
Patrick O'Neal (ent.; 1927-)
Patrick Steptoe (US phys.; 1914-88)
Patrick Swayze (ent.; 1954-)
Patrick, St. (Ir. rel.; 389?-461?)
Patrick's Day, St. (3/17)
Patriot (antiaircraft missile)
Patriot-Ledger, Quincy (MA newspaper)
Patriot, Harrisburg (PA newspaper)
Patriots, New England (football team)
Patsayev, Viktor I(vanovich)(cosmo.; 1933-71)
Patsy Cline (ent.; 1932-63)
Patten, Dick Van (ent.; 1928-)
Patterson Air Force Base, Wright (OH)
Patterson, Floyd (boxing; 1935-)
Patterson, P(ercival) J. (PM, Jamaica; 1935-)
Patti Austin (ent.; 1948-)
Patti LaBelle (ent.; 1944-)
Patti LuPone (ent.; 1949-)
Patti Page (ent.; 1927-)
Patti Smith (ent.)
Patti, Adelina (It. opera; 1843-1919)
Patton, George S(mith)(US gen.; 1885-1945)
Patty Andrews (ent., Andrews Sisters; 1920-)
Patty (Patricia Jane) Berg (golf; 1918-)
Patty Duke Astin (ent.; 1946-)
Patty (Patricia) Hearst (US heiress, kidnapped/
  imprisoned; 1954-)
Patty Murray (US cong.; 1950-)

Patty, Sandi (ent.)
Pauguk (myth.)
Paul & Mary Ford, Les (ent.)
Paul Anka (Can./US comp./ent.; 1941-)
Paul A(nthony) Samuelson (US econ.; 1915-)
Paul A. Volcker (US econ.; 1927-)
Paul Azinger (golf
Paul Berg (US biol.; 1926-)
Paul Biya (pres., Cameroon; 1933-)
Paul Brown (football coach; 1908-91)
Paul "Bear" Bryant (football coach; 1913-83)
Paul Bunyan (& Babe the Blue Ox)(fict.
  lumberjack)
Paul Cézanne (Fr. artist; 1839-1906)
Paul Conrad (pol. cartoonist; 1924-)
Paul Coverdell (US cong.; 1939-)
Paul Delaroche (Fr. hist./artist; 1797-1856)
Paul Delvaux (Belgian artist; 1897-)
Paul Desmond (US jazz; 1924-77)
Paul Dessau (Ger. comp; 1894-1979)
Paul Douglas (ent.; 1907-59)
Paul Dukas (Fr. comp.; 1865-1935)
Paul Ehrlich (Ger. bacteriol.; 1854-1915)
Paul Francis Webster (US lyricist; 1907-84)
Paul (William) Gallico (US writer; 1897-1976)
Paul Gann (US reformer; 1912-89)
Paul Gauguin, (Eugène Henri)(Fr. artist; 1848-
  1903)
Paul Harvey (US news commentator; 1918-)
Paul Hawken (US bus./writer)
Paul Henri Spaak (Belgium pol.; 1899-1972)
Paul Hindemith (Ger./US comp.; 1895-1963)
Paul I (king, Gr.; 1901-64)
Paul III (b. Alessandro Farnese)(pope; 1468-
  1549)
Paul IV (b. Gian Pietro Carafa)(pope; 1476-
  1559)
Paul J. Weitz (astro.)
Paul Julius Reuter, Baron von (Ger. founded
  news agcy.; 1816-99)
Paul Junger Witt
Paul Keating (PM, Austl.; 1954-)
Paul Klee (Swiss artist; 1879-1940)
Paul Lynde (ent.; 1926-82)
Paul Masson™
Paul Masson Vineyards (US bus.)
Paul Mazursky (ent.; 1930-)
Paul McCartney, (James)(ent.; 1942-)
Paul Michael Glaser (ent.; 1942-)
Paul Mitchell™ (hair care)
Paul Mitchell Systems, John (US bus.)
Paul Molitor (baseball; 1956-)
Paul Muni (b. Muni Weisenfreund)(ent.; 1895-
  1967)
Paul Newman (ent.; 1925-)
Paul Prudhomme (US chef
Paul Revere (Amer. patriot/silversmith; 1735-
  1818)

Paul Revere and the Raiders (pop music)
Paul Reynaud (ex-PM, Fr.; 1878-1966)
Paul Robeson (ent.; 1898-1976)
Paul Rubens (pseud. Pee-Wee Herman)(ent.; 1952-)
Paul (Marvin) Rudolph (US arch.; 1918-)
Paul Scofield (ent.; 1922-)
Paul Sebastian, Inc.
Paul Shaffer (ent.; 1949-)
Paul Signac (Fr. artist; 1863-1935)
Paul Simon (ent.; 1942-)
Paul Simon (US cong.; 1928-)
Paul Sorvino (ent.; 1939-)
Paul S(pyros) Sarbanes (US cong.; 1933-)
Paul Stookey (ent.; 1937-)
Paul Terry (cartoonist, *Mighty Mouse*; 1887-1971)
Paul Theroux (US writer; 1941-)
Paul Tillich (US rel./phil.; 1886-1965)
Paul Tsongas (US pol.; 1941-)
Paul V (b. Camillo Borghese)(It., pope; 1552-1621)
Paul (Ambroise) Valéry (Fr. writer; 1871-1945)
Paul VI (b. Giovanni Battista Montini)(It., pope; 1897-1978)
Paul Wellstone (US cong.; 1944-)
Paul "Pops" Whiteman (US cond.; 1891-1967)
Paul Williams (ent.; 1940-)
Paul Winfield (ent.; 1941-)
Paul Zindel (US writer; 1936-)
Paul, Don Michael
Paul, Les (US inv./ent.; 1915-)
Paul, St. (rel.; c3-c67)
Paul, St. Vincent de (Fr. rel.; c1581-1660)
Paula Abdul (ent.; 1962-)
Paula Jones (US news)
Paula Modersohn-Becker (Ger. artist; 1867-1907)
Paula Poundstone (ent.)
Paula Prentiss (ent.; 1939-)
Paula Zahn (US TV jour.; 1956-)
Paulding, James Kirke (US writer/pol.; 1778-1860)
Paulette Goddard (ent.; 1905-90)
Pauley, (Margaret) Jane (US TV jour.; 1950-)
Pauli exclusion principle (physics)
Pauli, Wolfgang (Aus. physt.; 1900-58)
Paulina Porizkova (model)
Pauline Collins (ent.; 1940-)
Pauline Esther Friedman (pseud. Abigail Van Buren, "Dear Abby")(US advice columnist; 1918-)
Pauline Frederick (US radio/TV jour.; 1918-90)
Pauline Trigère (US designer; 1912-)
Pauline, The Perils of (film; 1947)
Pauling, Linus C(arl)(US chem.; 1901)
Paul's Kitchen, Mrs. (US bus.)
Paul's™, Mrs. (frozen fish)

Paulsen Vineyards, Pat (US bus.)
Paulsen, Pat (US bus./ent.)
Pavarotti, Luciano (It. opera; 1935-)
Pavel I. Belyayev (cosmo.; 1925-70)
Pavel R(omanovich) Popovich (cosmo.; 1930-)
Pavlov, Ivan (Petrovich)(Rus. physiol.; 1849-1936)
Pavlova, Anna (Rus. ballet; 1885-1931)
Pavlovich, Aleksandr (Alexander I)(emp., Rus.; 1777-1825)
Pavo (astron., peacock)
Pawlak, Waldemar (PM, Pol.)
Pawleys Island rope hammock
Pawnee (NAmer. Indians)
Pawtucket, RI
Pax (period of peace)
Pax Romana (peace imposed by strong nation on weaker one; e.g., ancient Rome over its dominions)
Paycheck, Johnny (ent.; 1941-)
Payette National Forest (ID)
Payette River (ID)
Pay Less Drug Stores Northwest, Inc.
Payless Car Rental System, Inc.
Payless Shoe Source (US bus.)
Payne-Gaposchkin, Cecilia Helena (Br./US astron.; 1900-79)
Payne, John (ent.; 1912-89)
Pays de la Loire (region, Fr.)
Paysandú, Uruguay
Payton, Walter (football; 1954-)
Paz Estenssoro, Victor (ex-pres., Bolivia; 1907-)
PBS (Public Broadcasting System)(TV)
PBS-TV
PBX (private branch exchange)
PC/Computing (mag.)
PC GlassBlock™
PC Magazine (mag.)
PC Today (mag.)
PC World (mag.)
PCB (polychlorinated biphenyl)
PCP (phenylcyclohexylpiperidine)
PCV (positive crankcase ventilation [valve])
PD (per diem, police department, postal district)
Pd (chem. sym., palladium)
PDQ (pretty damn quick)
P. D. Q. Bach (aka Peter Schickele)(ent.)
PE (physical education)
Peabo Bryson (ent.)
Peabody & Co., Inc., Kidder,
Peabody Radio and Television Awards, George Foster
Peabody, Elizabeth P. (US educ.; 1804-94)
Peabody, George (US bus./finan.; 1795-1869)
Peabody, MA
Peace Corps (US org.; est. 1961)
Peace Prize, Nobel

Peace River (W Can.)
Peace, Prince of (Jesus)
Peacemaker missile
Peach Bowl (college football)
Peach State (nickname, GA)
peach Melba (also l.c.)
Peach, Miss (comic strip)
Peachtree Doors, Inc.
Peachtree Softwear, Inc.
Peale, Charles Wilson (US artist; 1741-1827)
Peale, Norman Vincent, Rev. (US rel./writer; 1898-93)
Peale, Rembrandt (US artist; 1778-1860)
Peanut Factory™, The
Peanut Factory, Inc., The
Peanuts (comic strip)
pear William (liqueur)
Pearl (Mae) Bailey (US jazz singer; 1918-90)
Pearl Harbor, HI (WWII Jap. attack; 12/7/41)
Pearl Jam (pop music)
Pearl S(ydenstricker) Buck (US writer; 1892-1973)
Pearl, Minnie (ent.; 1912-)
Pearle Vision™
Pearle Vision, Inc.
Pearly Gates (entrance to heaven)
Pearson, Drew (US jour.; 1897-1969)
Pearson, Lester (Bowles)(ex-PM, Can.; 1897-1972)
Peary, Robert E(dwin)(US Arctic expl.; 1856-1920)
Pease Air Force Base, NH
Peavy, Queenie
Peck, Fletcher v. (US law; 1810)
Peck, George Wilbur (US writer; 1840-1916)
Peck, (Eldred) Gregory (ent.; 1916-)
Peckinpah, Sam (ent.; 1925-85)
Peck's Bad Boy (from G.W. Peck's newspaper stories)
Pecorino (cheese)
Pecos Bill (legendary cowboy)
Pecos National Historical Park (NM)
Pecos River (SW US)
Pecos, TX
Pécs, Hungary
Pedi (lang.)
Pedro Antonio de Alarcón (Sp. writer/pol.; 1833-91)
Pedro Juan Caballero, Paraguay
Pedroncelli Winery, J. (US bus.)
Peds™ (footwear)
Peds Products (US bus.)
Pee-Wee Herman (aka Paul Rubens)(ent.; 1952-)
Pee Wee King (US comp.)
Pee Wee (Harold) Reese (baseball; 1919-)
Pee Wee Russell (US jazz; 1906-69)
Pee-Wee's Big Adventure (film; 1985)

Pee-Wee's Playhouse (TV show)
Peekskill, NY
Peel, Emma
Peel, Sir Robert (ex-PM, Br.; 1788-1850)
Peeping Tom
Peer Gynt (H. Ibsen play)
Peer Gynt Suite (by E. Grieg)
Peerce, Jan (ent.; 1904-84)
Peete, Calvin (golf; 1943-)
Peg-Board™
Pegasus (astron., flying horse; myth.)
Peggy Cass (ent.; 1924-)
Peggy (Gale) Fleming (figure skating; 1948-)
Peggy Guggenheim (US finan.; 1898-1979)
Peggy Lee (ent.; 1920-)
Peggy Lipton (ent.)
Peggy Ryan (ent.; 1924-)
Peggy Sue Got Married (film; 1986)
Peggy Wood (ent.; 1892-1978)
Pegler, (James) Westbrook (US jour.; 1894-1969)
Pegu, Myanmar
Pei, I(eoh) M(ing)(US arch.; 1917-)
Pei-tsum, Hau (ex-PM, Taiwan)
Peipus, Lake (NE Eur.)
Peirce, Charles S(anders)(US physt./phil.; 1839-1914)
Pekalongan, Indonesia
Pekin, IL
Peking duck (also Beijing duck)
Peking Man (also Beijing man)(*Homo erectus*)
Peking, China (now Beijing)
Pekingese (Ch. dialect)
Pekingese (dog)
Pelagian (rel.)
Pelagianism (rel.)
Pelagius (Br. rel.; 360-420)
Pelasgian (ancient Gr. people)
Pelé (b. Edson Arantes do Nascimento)(Brazilian soccer; 1940-)
Pelée, Mount (volcano, Martinique)
Pelican Publishing Co.
Pelican State (nickname, LA)
Pell, Claiborne (US cong.; 1918-)
Pella™
Pella Windows & Doors (US bus.)
Peloponnese (also Peloponnesos)(Gr. peninsula)
Peloponnesian War (Athens/Sparta; 431-404 BC)
Peltier effect (elec./physics)
Peltier heat (physics)
Pembroke Pines, FL
Pen, Jean-Marie Le (Fr. pol.; 1928-)
Pena, Federico (US Secy./Trans.; 1947-)
Penaia Ganilau, Ratu Sir (pres., Fiji; 1918-)
Penang (also Pinang)(state, Malaysia)
Penang, Malaysia
Penates (myth.)

Pendaflex™ (files)
Penderecki, Krzysztof (Pol. comp.; 1933-)
Pendergrass, Teddy (ent.; 1950-)
Pendleton™
Pendleton blanket
Pendleton Woolen Mills (US bus.)
Pendleton, Terry (baseball; 1960-)
Pendragon, Uther (King Arthur's father)
Penelope (myth.)
Peng, Li (PM, Ch.; 1928-)
Penguin Inc., Viking
Penquin Records, Inc.
Penguins, Pittsburgh (hockey team)
Penn™ (tennis balls)
Penn Central Corp., The
Penn, Arthur (ent.; 1922-)
Penn, Sean (ent.; 1960-)
Penn, William (Br. Quaker, founded PA; 1644-1718)
Penney Co., J. C.
Penney, James C(ash)(US bus.; 1875-1971)
Pennine Alps (Switz./It.)
Pennine Chain (hills, N. Eng.)
Pennsauken, NJ
Pennsylvania (PA)
Pennsylvania Dutch (SE PA)
Pennsylvania State University Press, The (US bus.)
Pennsylvania, Prigg v. (US law; 1842)
Pennsylvanian period (upper Carboniferous period)
Penny Arcade (US bus.)
Penny Marshall (ent.; 1943-)
Penny Singleton (ent.)
Pennzoil™
Pennzoil Co.
Penobscot (NAmer. Indians)
Penobscot Bay (ME)
Penobscot River (ME)
Pensacola Naval Air Station (FL)
Pensacola News-Journal (FL newspaper)
Pensacola, FL
Pentagon Papers Case (US law; 1971)
Pentagon, The (VA)(US mil.)
Pentateuch (also Torah)(1st 5 books of Bible)
Pentax™
Pentax Corp.
Pentecost (also Whitsunday)(rel.)
Pentecostal Church(es)(rel.)
Pentecostalism (rel.)
Pentel™ pen
Pentel Co., Ltd.
Penthouse (mag.)
Pentium PC microprocessor chip (compu.)
Pentothal™ (also sodium pentothal)(med.)
Penzance, England
Penzance, The Pirates of (Gilbert & Sullivan operetta)

People™ Weekly (mag.)
People's Choice Awards, The
People's Court (TV show)
Peoples Drug Stores, Inc.
People's Party (also Populist Party)(US pol.; 1891-1908)
Peoria Journal Star (IL newspaper)
Peoria, AZ, IL
Pep Boys—Manny, Moe, & Jack (US bus.)
Pepe's Mexican Restaurant
Peppard, George (ent.; 1928-94)
Pepper, Art (US jazz; 1925-82)
Pepper, Claude (US pol.; 1901-89)
Pepper™, Dr (soda)
Pepperdine University (Los Angeles, CA)
Pepperell Mill Store, West Point- (US bus.)
Pepperidge Farm™
Pepperidge Farm, Inc.
Pepper/Seven-Up Cos., Dr
Pepper's Lonely Hearts Club Band, Sgt. (Beatles album)
Pepsi™
Pepsi-Cola™
Pepsi-Cola Co.
PepsiCo, Inc.
Pepsodent™ (toothpaste)
Pepto-Bismol™ (med.)
Pepys' Diary (by S. Pepys; London life; 1600s)
Pepys, Samuel (Br. writer; 1633-1703)
Pequot (NAmer. Indians)
Pequot War (Pequot/Br.; 1637)
Perahia, Murray (US pianist; 1947-)
Percheron draft horse (also Percheron Norman)
Percival Lowell (US astron.; 1855-1916)
Percivale, Sir (also Parsifal)(Arthurian knight)
Percocet™ (med.)
Percodan™ (med.)
Percogesic™ (med.)
Percy Bysshe Shelley (Br. poet; 1792-1822)
Percy Kilbride (ent.; 1888-1964)
Percy Wenrich (US comp.; 1887-1952)
Percy, Sir Henry (aka Hotspur)(Br. mil.; 1366-1403)
Perdue Farms (US bus.)
Père David's deer
Pereira, Columbia
Pereira, William (US arch.; 1909-85)
Perelman, S(idney) J(oseph)(US writer; 1904-79)
Peres, Shimon (ex-PM, Isr.; 1923-)
Pérez de Cuéllar, Javier (Peruvian/UN dipl.; 1920-)
Pérez, Carlos Andrés (ex-pres., Venezuela; 1922-)
Performa™, Macintosh (compu.)
Perga, Apollonius of (Gk. math.; c265-170 BC)
Pericles (Gr. pol.; c490-429 BC)
Pérignon, Curvée Dom (champagne)

Perilous, Siege (Arthurian)
Perils of Pauline, The (film; 1947)
Peripatetic (phil.)
Perkin Warbeck (Flem. pretender to Br. throne; 1474-99)
Perkins Co., Jackson &
Perkins Family Restaurant (US bus.)
Perkins, Carl (ent.; 1932-)
Perkins, Elizabeth (ent.; 1961-)
Perkins, Frances (US sociol.; 1882-1965)
Perkins™, Jackson & (plants/seeds)
Perkins, Tony (Anthony)(ent.; 1932-92)
Perle Mesta (US dipl.)
Perlman, Itzhak (Isr./US violinist; 1945-)
Perlman, Rhea (ent.; 1948-)
Perlman, Ron (ent.; 1950-)
Perm, Russia (formerly Molotov)
PermaSoft™
Permanent Court of Arbitration (internat'l court; est. 1899)
Permanent Court of International Justice, United Nations (also World Court)(est. 1945)
Permian period (280-225 million years ago)
Pernell Roberts (ent.; 1930-)
Pernod™ (liqueur)
Perón, Evita (b. Maria Eva Duarte)(Argentinian pol.; 1919-52)
Perón, Maria Estela ("Isabel") Martínez de (ex-pres., Argentina; 1931-)
Perón, Juan Domingo (ex-pres., Argentina; 1895-1974)
Perot, H. Ross (US bus./pol.; 1930-)
Perrault, Charles (Fr. writer; 1628-1703)
Perrier™ (water)
Perrier Group of America, The (US bus.)
Perrine, Valerie (ent.; 1943-)
Perrins, Inc., Lea &
Perry Como (ent.; 1912-)
Perry Drug Stores, Inc.
Perry Ellis™
Perry Ellis (designer)
Perry Ellis Sportswear, Inc.
Perry G. Miller (US hist.; 1905-63)
Perry King (ent.; 1948-)
Perry Mason (fict. atty.)
Perry, Gaylord (baseball; 1938-)
Perry, Jim (baseball; 1936-)
Perry, Luke (ent.)
Perry, Oliver (Hazard)(US mil.; 1785-1819)
Perseids meteor shower (astron.)
Persephone (also Proserpina)(myth.)
Persepolis (capital, ancient Persia)
Perseus (astron., hero; myth.)
Pershing, John J(oseph)("Blackjack")(US gen.; 1860-1948)
Persia (now Iran)
Persian (lang./people)
Persian berry (shrub)

Persian cat
Persian Empire (c539-c312 BC)
Persian Gulf (also Arabian Gulf)(SW Asia)
Persian Gulf States (Bahrain/Iran/Iraq/Kuwait/Oman/Qatar/Saudi Arabia/UAE)
Persian Gulf War (Kuwait, UN allies/Iraq; 1991)
Persian Gulf War syndrome (med.)
Persian knot (also Sehna knot)
Persian lamb
Persian (lang.)
Persian lilac
Persian melon
Persian red (color)
Persian rug/carpet
Persian violet
Persian walnut (also English walnut)
Persian War, Turko-
Persian wars (Gr./Persia; 499-449 BC)
Persius (aka Aulus Persius Flaccus)(Roman satirist; 34-62)
Personnel Management, Office of (OPM)(US govt. agcy.; est. 1979)
Perspex™ (constr.)
Pert/Plus™ (hair care)
Perth, Australia
Perth, Scotland
Peru (Republic of)(SAmer.)
Peru Current (formerly Humboldt Current)(cold ocean current)
Perugino, Pietro (de Cristoforo Vannucci)(It. artist; 1446-1523)
Peruvian perfume (slang, cocaine)
Pesach (also Passover)(rel.)
Pesci, Joe (ent.; 1943-)
Peshawar, Pakistan
Peshkov, Aleksei Maksimovich (pseud. Maxim Gorky [or Gorki])(Rus. writer; 1868-1936)
Pet, Inc.
PETA (People for the Ethical Treatment of Animals)
Petach Tikva, Israel
Petaluma, CA
Pete Maravich (basketball; 1948-88)
Pete 'N' Tillie (film; 1972)
Pete(r Edward) Rose (baseball; 1941-)
Pete (Alvin Ray) Rozelle (football exec.; 1926-)
Pete(r) R. Seeger (ent.; 1919-)
Pete V. Domenici (US cong.; 1932-)
Pete Wilson (CA gov.; 1933-)
Peter (or Pierre) Abelard (Fr. phil.; 1079-1142)
Peter Arno (aka Curtis Arnoux Peters)(cartoonist, *New Yorker*; 1904-68)
Peter Behrens (Ger. arch.; 1868-1940)
Peter Benchley (US writer; 1940-)
Peter Bogdanovich (ent.; 1939-)
Peter Boross (PM, Hung.)
Peter Boyle (ent.; 1933-)

Peter Carl Fabergé (Rus. jeweler; 1846-1920)
Peter Carruthers (figure skating)
Peter Cooper (US bus.; 1791-1883)
Peter Cushing (ent.; 1913-)
Peter Damian, St. (It. rel.; 1007-72)
Peter DeLuise
Peter De Vries (US writer; 1910-93)
Peter Falk (ent.; 1927-)
Peter Finch (ent.; 1916-77)
Peter Firth (ent.; 1953-)
Peter Fonda (ent.; 1939-)
Peter Frampton (ent.; 1950-)
Peter Gabriel (ent.; 1950-)
Peter Graves (ent.; 1926-)
Peter Gunn (TV show)
Peter Hall (Reginald Frederick)(Br. theater;
    1930-)
Peter Harrison (US arch.; 1716-75)
Peter I (Peter the Great)(ex-tzar, Rus.; 1672-
    1725)
Peter I(lyich) Tchaikovsky (Rus. comp.; 1840-
    93)
Peter Jennings (US TV jour.; 1938-)
Peter (or Piotr, Pyotr)(Alekseevich) Kropotkin,
    Prince (Rus. anarchist; 1842-1921)
Peter Lawford (ent.; 1923-84)
Peter Lind Hayes (ent.)
Peter Lorre (b. Lázló Löwenstein)(ent.; 1904-64)
Peter Marshall (ent.; 1927-)
Peter Martins (US dancer; 1946-)
Peter Maxwell Davies (Br. comp./cond.; 1934-)
Peter Minuit (Dutch admin. in Amer.; c1580-
    1638)
Peter Nero (US pianist; 1934-)
Peter Noone (ent.; 1947-)
Peter Norton Computing, Inc.
Peter O'Toole (ent.; 1932-)
Peter Pan (fict. chara.)
Peter Pan (J. Barrie play)
Peter Pan collar
Peter Pan Industries
Peter Pan™ peanut butter
Peter Paul Almond Joy™ (candy)
Peter Paul Cadbury Corp.
Peter Paul Mauser (Ger. inv.; 1838-1914)
Peter Paul Rubens (Flem. artist; 1577-1640)
Peter Piper (fict. chara.)
Peter Principle (econ./bus.)
Peter Rabbit (fict. chara.)
Peter Riegert (ent.; 1947-)
Peter (Mark) Roget (Br. phys./lexicographer,
    Roget's Thesaurus; 1779-1869)
Peter Schickele (pseud. P. D. Q. Bach)(ent.)
Peter Scolari (ent.; 1954-)
Peter Sellers (ent.; 1925-80)
Peter Serkin (US pianist; 1947-)
Peter Straub
Peter Strauss (ent.; 1947-)

Peter Stuyvesant (Dutch gov. of NY; 1592-1672)
Peter Taylor (US writer; 1917-)
Peter the Cruel (king, Castile/León; 1334-69)
Peter the Great (Peter I)(ex-tzar, Rus.; 1672-
    1725)
Peter Ueberroth (US bus./sports; 1937-)
Peter (Alexander) Ustinov, Sir (ent.; 1921-)
Peter Vidmar
Peter Weir (ent.; 1944-)
Peter Wimsey, Lord (fict. chara., D. Sayers)
Peter Yarrow (ent.; 1938-)
Peter, Paul and Mary (pop music)
Peter, St. (also Simon Peter)(rel.; ?-AD c64)
Peterbilt™
Peterbilt Motors Co.
Peterborough, England
Peterborough, Ontario, Canada
Peterle, Lojze (Slovenian pol.)
Peter's Church, St. (also St. Peter's
    Basilica)(Rome)
Peters, Bernadette (ent.; 1948-)
Peters, Brock (ent.; 1927-)
Peters, Curtis Arnoux (aka Peter
    Arno)(cartoonist, New Yorker; 1904-68)
Peters, Mike (cartoonist, Mother Goose &
    Grimm; 1943-)
Peters, Roberta (ent.; 1930-)
Petersburg, VA
Peterson, Cassandra (aka Elvira)(ent.; 1951-)
Peterson, Oscar (US jazz; 1925-)
Petit Trianon, Le (built for Mme de Pompadour
    by Louis XV)
Petit, Roland (Fr. ballet; 1924-)
Petition of Right (Br. hist.; 1628)
Petrarch (aka Francesco Petrarca)(It. poet;
    1304-74)
Petrarchan sonnet (also Italian sonnet)(lit.)
Petri dish (also l.c.)
Petrie Stores Corp.
Petrie, Sir (William Matthew) Flinders (Br.
    archaeol.; 1853-1942)
Petrified Forest National Park (AZ)
Petrified Forest, The (film)
Petrograd, Russia (now St. Petersburg)
Petroleum V(esuvius) Nasby (pseud. David Ross
    Locke)(US humorist; 1833-88)
Petroleum-Exporting Countries, Organization
    of (OPEC)(est. 1960)
Petronius, Gaius ("Arbiter Elegantiae")(Roman
    writer; ?-AD 66)
Petropavlovsk, Kazakhstan
Petrópolis, Brazil
Petrosyan, Levon Ter- (pres., Armenia; 1943-)
Petrova, Olga
Petruchio (fict. chara., Taming of the Shrew)
Pettiford, Oscar (US jazz; 1922-60)
Pettit, Bob (basketball; 1932-)
Petty and the Heartbreakers, Tom (pop music)

Petty, Richard (Lee)(auto racing; 1937-)
Petty, Tom (ent.; 1953-)
Petula Clark (ent.; 1932-)
Peugeot™ (auto.)
Peugeot Motors of America, Inc.
Peul (lang./people)
Pevsner, Antoine (Fr. artist; 1886-1962)
Peyton Place (G. Metalious novel)
Peyton Rous, (Francis)(US phys.; 1879-1970)
Pez Candy, Inc.
Pfaff™ sewing machine
Pfaff American Sales Corp.
Pfaltzgraff Co., Susquehanna
Pfeiffer, Michelle (ent.; 1957-)
Pfizer, Inc. (healthcare)
PGS (Professional Golfers Association)
P(ierre) G(ustave) T(outant) Beauregard (US
    gen.; 1818-93)
P(elham) G(renville) Wodehouse, Sir (US
    writer/humorist; 1881-1975)
Phaedo (by Plato)
Phaedra (myth.)
Phaethon (myth.)
Phalangist (Lebanese mil.)
Pham Van Dong (ex-PM, NViet.; 1906-)
Phan Dinh Khai (aka Le Duc Tho)(NViet pol.;
    1911-90)
Phanerozoic eon (most recent 570 million years)
Phantom of the Opera (play)
Pharaoh (Eg. title)
Pharaoh (or Pharaoh's) ant
Pharisees & Sadducees (opposing Hebrew grps;
    2nd c)
Phar Lap (film; 1983)
Phar Lap (race horse)
Pharmavite Corp.
Pharos lighthouse at Alexandria (1 of 7
    Wonders, Eg.)
Pheasant Ridge Winery (US bus.)
Phelps Vineyards, Joseph (US bus.)
Phenix City, AL
Phi Beta Kappa (honorary society; est. 1776)
Phi Beta Kappa key
Phidias (Gr. sculptor; c500-435 BC)
Phil Collins (ent.; 1951-)
Phil Donahue (ent.; 1935-)
Phil(ip Anthony) Esposito (hockey; 1942-)
Phil Everly (ent.; 1938-)
Phil Gramm (US cong.; 1942-)
Phil Harris (ent.; 1904-)
Phil(lip) Mahre (US skier; 1957)
Phil Niekro (baseball; 1939-)
Phil Rizzuto (baseball; 1918-)
Phil Silvers (ent.; 1912-85)
Phil Spitalny (cond.; 1890-1970)
Phil, Punxsutawney (groundhog)
Philadelphia and Reading Railroad
Philadelphia Daily News (PA newspaper)

Philadelphia Eagles (football team)
Philadelphia Flyers (hockey team)
Philadelphia Inquirer (PA newspaper)
Philadelphia lawyer
Philadelphia Museum of Art
Philadelphia Phillies (baseball team)
Philadelphia 76ers (basketball team)
Philadelphia, PA
Philbin, Regis (ent.)
Philip (Duke of Edinburgh, Prince of the UK,
    husband of Elizabeth II; 1921-)
Philip Barry (US writer; 1896-1949)
Philip Bosco (ent.; 1930-)
Philip Chesterfield, Lord (4th Earl of
    Chesterfield, Philip Dormer Stanhope)(Br.
    writer/pol.; 1694-1773)
Philip C(ortelyou) Johnson (US arch.; 1906-)
Philip D. Armour (US bus.; 1832-1901)
Philip Dormer Stanhope (4th Earl of
    Chesterfield, Lord Philip Chesterfield)(Br.
    writer/pol.; 1694-1773)
Philip II (king, Macedonia; 382-336 BC)
Philip II (king, Sp.; 1527-1598)
Philip II (Philip Augustus)(king, Fr.; 1165-
    1223)
Philip III (Philip the Bold)(king, Fr.; 1245-85)
Philip IV (Philip the Fair)(king, Fr.; 1268-1314)
Philip John Schuyler (US gen./pol.; 1733-1804)
Philip Kearny (US mil.; 1814-62)
Philip K. Wrigley (US bus., gum/baseball; 1895-
    1977)
Philip Larkin (Br. poet; 1922-85)
Philip Marlowe (fict. detective, R.T. Chandler)
Philip Michael Thomas (ent.; 1949-)
Philip Morris, Inc.
Philip Murray (US labor leader; 1886-1952)
Philip (Milton) Roth (US writer; 1933-)
Philip (Henry) Sheridan (US gen.; 1831-88)
Philip the Bold (Fr., duke, Burgundy; 1342-
    1404)
Philip the Bold (Philip III)(king, Fr.; 1245-85)
Philip the Fair (Philip IV)(king, Fr.; 1268-1314)
Philip the Good (Fr. duke, Burgundy; 1396-
    1467)
Philip the Tall (Philip V)(king, Fr.; c1294-1322)
Philip V (king, Sp.; 1683-1746)
Philip V (Philip the Tall)(king, Fr.; c1294-1322)
Philip VI (king, Fr.; 1293-1350)
Philip Weld (sailing; 1915-84)
Philipp Scheidemann (ex-chanc., Ger.; 1865-
    1939)
Philippe Junot
Philippe, Louis ("Philippe Egalité" "the Citizen
    King")(king, Fr.; 1773-1850)
Philippians (rel.)
Philippine Airlines (PAL)(airline)
Philippine mahogany (tree)
Philippines (Republic of the)(also Philippine

Islands)(SE Asia)

Philippus Aureolus Paracelsus (b. Theophrastus Bombastus von Hohenheim)(Swiss phys./chem.; 1493-1541)

Philips Co., North American

Philistine (ancient people)

Phillies, Philadelphia (baseball team)

Phillips curve (econ.)

Phillips head screw

Phillips™ Milk of Magnesia (med.)

Phillips Petroleum Co.

Phillips Screw Co.

Phillips™ screwdriver

Phillips 66 Co.

Phillips-Van Heusen Corp.

Phillips, Lou Diamond (ent.; 1962-)

Phillips, MacKenzie (ent.; 1959-)

Phillips, Michelle (ent.; 1944-)

Phillis Wheatley (Afr./US poet; 1753-84)

Philly Joe Jones (US jazz; 1923-85)

Philo Remington (US inv./bus.; 1816-89)

Philo T. Farnsworth (US physt./TV pioneer; 1906-71)

Philosophy, Doctor of (also Ph.D., doctorate)

pHisoDerm™ (med.)

Phnom Penh, Cambodia

Phobos (Mars' moon; myth., personification of fear)

Phobos Mission (USSR uncrewed space probes)

Phoebe (Saturn moon; myth.)

Phoebe Cates (ent.)

Phoebus (also Apollo)(myth., sun god)

Phoenicia (ancient Mediterranean kingdom; c1200-c332 BC)

Phoenician art

Phoenix (astron., phoenix/bird)

Phoenix (chicken)

Phoenix (US mil. missile)

Phoenix Cardinals (football team)

Phoenix Gazette (AZ newspaper)

Phoenix Republic (AZ newspaper)

Phoenix Suns (basketball team)

Phoenix, AZ

Phoenix, River (ent.; 1970-93)

Phomvihan, Kaysone (ex-PM, Laos; 1920-92)

Phone-Mate™

Phonemate, Inc.

Phonetic Alphabet, International (also IPA)

Photographic (mag.)

Photo-Mart (US bus.)

Photoshop™, Adobe (compu.)

Photostat™

Phoumsavan, Nouhak (pres., Laos; 1914-)

Phrenilin™ (med.)

Phrygian cap (headwear)

Phyfe, Duncan (Scot./US furniture maker; c1768-1854)

Phylicia Rashad (ent.; 1948-)

Phyllis (Stewart) Schlafly (US activist; 1924-)

Phyllis Diller (ent.; 1917-)

Physicians' Desk Reference™

Physics, Nobel Prize for

Physiology or Medicine, Nobel Prize for

Phytin™

Pia Zadora (ent.)

Piaf, Edith (b. Edith Giovanna Gassion)(Fr. ent.; 1915-63)

Picard, Jean (Fr. astron.; 1620-82)

Picard, Jean-Luc, Capt. (fict. chara., *Star Trek*)

Picardy (region, Fr.)

Picasso, Pablo (Ruiz y)(Sp. artist; 1881-1973)

Picasso, Paloma (US bus.; 1949-)

Picatinny Arsenal (NJ)

Piccadilly Circus (London)

Piccard, Auguste (Swiss physt.; 1884-1962)

Piccard, Jean Félix (Swiss chem./eng.; 1884-1963)

Piccone, Robin

Pickens, T. Boone

Pickering, Edward Charles (US astron./physt.; 1846-1919)

Pickering, William H(enry)(US astron.; 1858-1938)

Picket Fences (TV show)

Pickett, Cindy (ent.; 1947-)

Pickett, George E(dward)(US gen.; 1825-75)

Pickles, Christina

Pickford, Mary (b. Gladys Marie Smith)(ent.; 1893-1979)

Pickwick Papers, The (also *The Posthumous Papers of the Pickwick Club*)(C. Dickens novel)

Pickwick, Samuel (fict. chara., *Pickwick Papers*)

Pico Rivera, CA

Picone Hosiery, Evan- (US bus.)

Picone™, Evan

Picone, Inc., Evan-

Pictionary™ (game)

Pictor (astron., painter)

Picts (ancient Scots)

Picture of Dorian Gray, The (Oscar Wilde novel)

Picturephone™ (used briefly in 1960s)

Pidgeon, Walter (ent.; 1897-1984)

Pidgin English (also pidgin English)

Pidgin Sign Lang.

Pied Piper of Hamelin, The (by Robert Browning)

Piedmont (region, It.)

Piedmont Plateau (region, E. US)

Piedmont, Greenville (SC newspaper)

Pier I Imports, Inc.

Pier Luigi Nervi (It. arch.; 1891-1979)

Pierce Brosnan (ent.; 1953-)

Pierce, Fort, FL (city)

Pierce, Franklin (14th US pres.; 1804-69)

Pierce, Mildred (J.M. Cain novel)

Piercy, Marge (US writer; 1936-)
Piero de' Medici (It. pol.; 1416-69)
Piero della Francesca (It. artist; c1415-92)
Pierpont Morgan Library (NYC)
Pierre (or Peter) Abelard (Fr. phil.; 1079-1142)
Pierre Auguste Renoir (Fr. artist; 1841-1919)
Pierre Augustin Caron de Beaumarchais (Fr. writer; 1732-99)
Pierre Bérégovoy (ex-PM, France; 1925-)
Pierre Bonnard (Fr. artist; 1867-1947)
Pierre Boulez (Fr. comp./cond.; 1925-)
Pierre Buyoya, Maj. (ex-pres., Burundi; 1949?-)
Pierre Cardin (Fr. designer; 1922-)
Pierre Cecile Puvis de Chavannes (Fr. artist; 1824-98)
Pierre Charles L'Enfant (Fr./US arch./eng.; 1754-1825)
Pierre Curie (Fr. physt., radium; 1859-1906)
Pierre de Fermat (Fr. math.; 1601-65)
Pierre de Ronsard (Fr. poet; 1524-85)
Pierre Joseph Proudhon (Fr. phil.; 1809-65)
Pierre Laval (ex-PM, Fr.; 1883-1945)
Pierre-Paul Prud'hon (Fr. artist; 1758-1823)
Pierre Salinger
Pierre Samuel Du Pont (Fr. econ./pol.; 1739-1817)
Pierre Samuel du Pont (US bus.; 1870-?)
Pierre S(imon) Laplace (aka Marquis de Laplace)(Fr. astron./math.; 1749-1827)
Pierre (Elliott) Trudeau (ex-PM, Can.; 1919-)
Pierre, SD
Pierrefonds, Quebec, Canada
Piers Anthony
Piet Mondrian (b. Pieter Cornelis Mondriaan)(Dutch artist; 1872-1944)
Pieta (Michelangelo painting)
Pieter Brueghel, the Elder (also Breughel)(aka "Peasant Bruegel")(Flem. artist; 1525-69)
Pieter Brueghel, the Younger (also Breughel)(aka "Hell Bruegel")(Flem. artist; 1564-1638)
Pieter Oud, (Jacobus Johannes)(Dutch arch.; 1890-1963)
Pieter W. Botha (ex-pres., SAfr. pres.; 1916-)
Pieter Zeeman (Dutch physt.; 1865-1943)
Pietermaritzburg, South Africa
Pietism (rel.)
Pietro Belluschi (US arch.; 1899-?)
Pietro Mascagni (It. comp.; 1863-1945)
Pietro (de Cristoforo Vannucci) Perugino (It. artist; 1446-1523)
pig Latin
Pig, Porky (cartoon chara.)
Piggy, Miss (Muppet)
Piggledy, Higgledy- (play)
Piglet (Winnie-the-Pooh)
Pigs, Bay of (Cuban inlet, invasion)
Pik Kommunizma (also Communism

Peak)(formerly Mount Garmo, Mount Stalin)(Tajikisyan)
Pik-Nik™
Pik-Nik Foods, Inc.
Pike, James A(lbert), Bishop (US rel.; 1913-69)
Pike, Zebulon Montgomery (US expl./mil.; 1779-1813)
Pikes Peak (CO)
Pikesville, MD
Pilate, Pontius (Roman mil./pol.; 1st c. AD)
Pilgrim's Progress (J Bunyan allegory)
Pilgrims (also Pilgrim Fathers)(settled MA; 1620)
Pilipino (also Filipino)(lang.)
Pillars of Hercules (rocks/entrance, Strait of Gibralter)
Pillsbury™
Pillsbury Co., The
Pilobolus Dance Theater
Pilsener Bottling Co.
Pilsudski, Joseph (Pol. dictator; 1867-1935)
Piltdown man (anthrop. hoax)
Pima (NAmer. Indians)
Pimlico Race Course (Baltimore, MD)
Pinafore, H.M.S. (or The Lass that Loved a Sailor)(Gilbert/Sullivan opera)
Pinang (also Penang)(state, Malaysia)
Pinatubo, Mount (active volcano; Philippines)
Pincay, Laffit, Jr. (jockey; 1946-)
Pinchas Zuckerman (Isr. violinist/comp.; 1948-)
Pinchot, Bronson (ent.; 1959-)
Pinckney, Charles (US pol.; 1757-1824)
Pinckney, Charles Cotesworth (US pol.; 1746-1825)
Pinckney, Thomas (US pol.; 1750-1828)
Pindar (Gr. poet; c518-c438 BC)
Pindling, Lynden (Oscar)(ex-PM, Bahamas; 1930-)
Pine Bluff Arsenal (AR)
Pine Bluff, AR
Pine-Sol™ (cleaner)
Pine Tree State (nickname, ME)
Pinellas Park, FL
Ping-Pong™ (table tennis)
Pink Floyd (pop music)
Pink Panther Strikes Again, The (film; 1976)
Pink Panther, The (cartoon)
Pink Panther, The (film; 1964)
Pink Panther, The Return of the (film; 1975)
Pink Panther, The Revenge of the (film; 1978)
Pink Panther, Trail of the (film; 1982)
Pinkerton National Detective Agency
Pinkerton, Allan (US detective; 1819-84)
Pinkham, Lydia (Estes)(US bus.; 1819-83)
Pinkham's Vegetable Compound for "woman's weakness," Mrs. Lydia E. (med.)
Pinky Lee (b. Pinkus Leff)(ent.; 1908-93)
Pinocchio, The Adventures of (C. Collodi

fantasy)

Pinochet (Ugarte), Augusto (ex-pres., Chile; 1915-)

Pinot Blanc (grape, wine)

Pinot Chardonnay (wine)

Pinot Noir (grape, wine)(also l.c.)

Pinter, Harold (Br. writer; 1930-)

Pinto, Ford (auto.)

Pinyin (Ch. phonetic alphabet)

Pinza, Ezio (ent.; 1892-1957)

Pioneer™

Pioneer (US uncrewed space probes)

Pioneer Electronics USA, Inc.

Pioneer Press, St. Paul (MN newspaper)

Pioneer Venus (US uncrewed space probes)

Pioneers, Sons of the (music group)

Piotr (or Pyotr, Peter)(Alekseevich) Kropotkin, Prince (Rus. anarchist; 1842-1921)

PIP™

PIP Printing International (US bus.)

Piper Cherokee™

Piper Aircraft Corp.

Piper-Heidsieck™ champagne

Piper Laurie (ent.; 1932-)

Piper of Hamelin, The Pied (by Robert Browning)

Piper, Peter (fict. chara.)

Piper, Pied (fict. chara.)

Piper-Heidsieck™ (champagne)

Piper Sonoma (US bus.)

Pippen, Scottie (basketball; 1965-)

Pippi Longstocking (fict. chara.)

Pippin (play)

Pips, Gladys Knight & the (pop music)

Piraeus, Greece

Pirandello, Luigi (It. writer; 1867-1936)

Pirates of Penzance, The (Gilbert & Sullivan operetta)

Pirates, Pittsburgh (baseball team)

Pirates, Terry & the (comic strip)

Pisa, Council of (Roman Catholic Church; 1409)

Pisa, Italy

Pisa, Leaning Tower of (It.)

Pisanello, (b. Antonio Pisano)(It. artist; c1395-1455)

Pisano, Andrea (b. Andrea da Pontadera)(It. sculptor; c1290-c1349)

Pisano, Giovanni (It. artist; c1250-c1314)

Pisano, Nicola (It. artist; c1220-84)

Piscataway, NJ

Pisces (zodiac, astron., fish)

Piscis Austrinius (astron., southern fish)

Piscopo, Joe (ent.; 1951-)

Pismo Beach, CA

Pissarro, Camille (Jacob)(Fr. artist; 1830-1903)

Pistoia, Italy

Pistol Pete (Peter) Maravich (basketball; 1948-88)

Pistons, Detroit (basketball team)

Pitaka (rel.)

Pitaka, Abhidhamma (rel.)

Pitaka, Sutta (rel.)

Pitaka, Vinaya (rel.)

Pitcairn Island (Br. Polynesian island)

Pitcher, Molly (aka Mary [Ludwig Hays] McCauley)(US heroine; 1754-1832)

Pithecanthropus (anthrop.)

Pitkin, Walter

Pitman shorthand

Pitman, Sir Isaac (Br., inv. shorthand system; 1813-97)

Pitney-Bowes™ (office machines)

Pitney Bowes, Inc.

Pitocin™ (med.)

Pitot tube (fluid flow)

Pitot-static tube/system (taeronautics)

Pitt, William, the Elder (the "Great Commoner")(ex-PM, Br.; 1708-78)

Pitt, William, the Younger (ex-PM, Br.; 1759-1806)

Pitti Palace (It.)

Pitts, Zasu (ent.; 1898-1963)

Pittsburg Landing (also Battle of Shiloh)(US hist.; 1862)

Pittsburg, CA, KS

Pittsburgh Corning Corporation

Pittsburgh International Airport, Greater (PA)

Pittsburgh Penguins (hockey team)

Pittsburgh Pirates (baseball team)

Pittsburgh Post-Gazette (PA newspaper)

Pittsburgh Press (PA newspaper)

Pittsburgh Steelers (football team)

Pittsburgh Sun-Telegraph (PA newspaper)

Pittsburgh, PA

Pittsfield, MA

Piura, Peru

Pius II (b. Enea Silvio Piccolomini)(It., pope; 1405-64)

Pius IV (b. Giovanni Angelo Medici)(It., pope; 1499-1565)

Pius IX (b. Giovanni Maria Mastai-Ferretti)(It., pope; 1792-1878)

Pius V, St. (b. Antonio Ghislieri)(It., (pope; 1504-72)

Pius VI (b. Giovanni Angelo Braschi)(It., pope; 1717-99)

Pius VII (b. Luigi Barnaba Chiaramonti)(It., (pope; 1742-1823)

Pius X, St. (b. Giuseppe Melchiorre Sarto)(It. pope; 1835-1914)

Pius XI (b. Ambrogio Damiano Achille Ratti)(It., pope; 1857-1939)

Pius XII (b. Eugenio Pacelli)(It., pope; 1876-1958)

Pius, Antoninus (emp., Rome; AD 86-161)

Piute (NAmer. Indians)

Pizarro, Francisco (Sp. mil./expl.; 1475?-1541)
Pizza Hut™
Pizza Hut (US bus.)
Pizzetti, Ildebrando (It. comp./hist.; 1880-1968)
P(ercival) J. Patterson (PM, Jamaica; 1935-)
Place de la Concorde, (building/museum, Paris)
PKU (phenylketonuria)
Placentia, CA
Placid, Lake, NY
Placido Domingo (Sp. tenor; 1941-)
Plager, Barclay (hockey; 1941-88)
Plain Dealer, Cleveland (OH newspaper)
Plain of Jezreel (also Esdraelon Plain)(Isr.)
Plain People (Mennonites, Amish, Dunkers)(rel.)
Plainfield, NJ
Plains Indians (NAmer.)
Plains of Abraham, (Can.)
Plains, GA
Plainview, TX
Planck, Max (Karl Ernst Ludwig)(Ger. physt.; 1858-1947)
Planck's constant (physics)
Planck's (or Planck) radiation law/formula
Planet, Captain (TV show)
Planned Parenthood™
Planned Parenthood Federation of America, Inc. (aka Planned Parenthood-World Population)(US org; est. 1921)
Plano, TX
Plant, Robert (ent.; 1947-)
Plantabbs Corp.
Plantagenet (or Anjou), House of (Br. ruling family; 1154-1399)
Plantagenet, Richard (Duke of York)(Br. mil.; 1411-60)
Plantation walking horse (also Tennessee walking horse)
Plantation, FL
Plante, Jacques (hockey; 1929-86)
Planters™
Planters LifeSaver Co.
Plantin (type style)
plaster of Paris (synthetic gypsum)
Plasticine™ (modeling paste)
Plata, Rio de la (also River Plate)(SAmer.)
Plateau Indians
Plath, Sylvia (US writer; 1932-63)
Plato (Gr. phil.; c428-c347 BC)
Platonism (philosophy)
Platoon (film; 1986)
Platt Amendment (US hist.; 1901)
Platt/Hartex, Leggett & (US bus.)
Platt, O(rville) H(itchock)(US pol.; 1827-1905)
Platte River (NE)
Platte River, South (CO/NE)
Platters, the (pop music)
Plattsburgh Air Force Base, NY

Plautus, Titus Maccius (Roman writer; c254-c184 BC)
Plax™ (med.)
Play-Doh™
Playboy (mag.)
Playboy Enterprises, Inc.
Playboy of the Western World, The (John Millington Synge comedy)
Player, Gary (golf; 1935-)
Playgirl (mag.)
Playskool™ (toys)
Playskool Baby, Inc.
Playtex™
Playtex Apparel, Inc.
Plaza Hotel (NYC)
Plaza Suite (N. Simon play)
Pleiades (astron.; myth.)
Pleiku, Vietnam
Pleistocene epoch (2.5 million to 10,000 years ago)
Plekhanov, Georgi (Valentinovich)(Rus. phil., "Father of Russian Marxism"; 1857-1918)
Pleshette, Suzanne (ent.; 1937-)
Plessy v. Ferguson (US law; 1896)
Pleven, Bulgaria
Plexiglas™ (a plastic)
Pleasant Valley Wine Co.
Plimpton, George (US writer; 1927-)
Plimpton, Martha
Pliny the Elder (Gaius Plinius Secundus) (Roman scholar; 23-79)
Pliny the Younger (Gaius Plinius Caecilius Secundus)(Roman writer; 62-113)
Pliocene epoch (12-2.5 million years ago)
Pliofilm™
Plisetskaya, Maya Mikhaylovna (Rus. ballet; 1925-)
PLO (Palestine Liberation Organization)
Ploesti, Romania
Plott hound (dog)
Plough Corp., Schering-
Plovdiv, Bulgaria
P(amela) L. Travers (Austl. writer; 1906-)
Plum™, J. L. (clothing)
Plummer, Amanda (ent.; 1957-)
Plummer, Christopher (ent.; 1927-)
Plunkett, Jim (football; 1947-)
Plutarch (Gr. biographer; c46-120)
Pluto (planet; myth.)
Plutus (myth.)
Plymouth (auto.)
Plymouth Acclaim™ (auto.)
Plymouth Colony (Br. colony in MA; 1620)
Plymouth Company (Br. hist.; 1606-35)
Plymouth Grand Voyager LE (auto.)
Plymouth Horizon (auto.)
Plymouth Motor Co.
Plymouth Road Runner (auto.)

Plymouth Rock (chicken)
Plymouth Rock (Pilgrims landed)
Plymouth Sundance (auto.)
Plymouth Voyager (auto.)
Plymouth, CT, MA, MN
Plymouth, England
Plymouth, Montserrat
PM (also p.m.)(post meridiem, postmaster, prime minister)
PMG (paymaster general)
PMS (Pantone Matching System™)(colors/ graphics)
PMS (premenstrual syndrome)
PO (petty officer, post office [box])
Po (chem. sym., polonium)
Po River (It.)
Po, Li (Tai)(Ch. poet; 705-62)
POB (post office box)
Pocahontas (Rebecca Rolfe)(Amer. Indian heroine; c1595-1617)
Pocatello, ID
Poco (pop music)
Pocono Mountains (also Poconos)(PA)
Podgorica, Yugoslavia
Podgorny, Nikolay Viktorovich (USSR pol.; 1903-83)
Podunk (any small, isolated town)
Poe, Edgar Allan (US writer; 1809-49)
Pogo (comic strip)
Pogue, William (astro.)
Pohl, Frederik (US writer, sci-fi; 1919-)
Pohnpei, Micronesia
Pohnpeian (people)
Poincaré, Raymond (Nicolas Landry)(ex-pres., Fr.; 1860-1934)
Poindexter, Buster (ent.)
Poindexter, John F. (US pol.)
Poindexter, John M(arlan)(US adm.; 1936-)
Point Barrow, AK (northernmost point of US)
Point Mugu Nas, CA
point d'Alençon (also Alençon lace)
Pointe-a-Pitre, Guadeloupe
Pointe-aux-Trembles, Quebec, Canada (now part of Montreal)
Pointe-Claire, Quebec, Canada
Pointe-Noire, Congo
Pointillism (art)(also l.c.)
Poirot (TV show)
Poirot, Hercule (fict. detective, Agatha Christie)
Poison (pop music)
Poitier, Sidney (ent.; 1927-)
Poitou-Charentes (region, Fr.)
Pokhara, Nepal
Pol Pot (also Saloth Sar)(Cambodian pol.; 1925-)
Pola Negri (ent.; 1900-87)
Polack (slang)
Poland (Republic of)(E Eur.)

Polanski, Roman (ent.; 1933-)
Polaris (also North Star, Polestar)(astron.)
Polaroid™ camera
Polaroid Corp.
Pole (people)
Pole, North (N end of earth's axis)
Pole, South (S end of earth's axis)
Polestar (also North Star, Polaris)(astron.)
Polident™ (health)
Police Gazette
Police Story (TV show)
Police, the (pop music)
Policy Development, Office of (US govt.)
Polish (chicken)
Polish (lang./people)
Polish Airlines LOT
Polish Corridor (Pol. access to the Baltic)
Polish sausage
Politburo ("political bureau")(USSR)
Polk™
Polk Audio, Inc.
Polk, Fort, LA (mil.)
Polk, James Knox (11th US pres.; 1795-1849)
Pollack, Sydney (ent.; 1934-)
Pollenex™ (appliances)
Pollock v. Farmer's Loan and Trust Co. (US law; 1895)
Pollock, (Paul) Jackson (US artist; 1912-56)
Pollux, Castor and (astron.; myth., Gemini/ twins)
Polly Bergen (ent.; 1930-)
Pollyanna (E. Porter novel)
Pollyanna (foolishly optimistic person)
Polo, Marco (It. expl.; c1254-1324)
Polonius (*Hamlet* chara.)
Polo/Ralph Lauren Leathergoods (US bus.)
Poltava, Ukraine
Poltergeist (film; 1982)
Polybius (Gr. hist.; c200-c118 BC)
Polycarp, St. (Turk. rel.; 69?-155?)
Polyclitus (Gr. sculptor; 5th c. BC)
Polydorus (Gr. sculptor; 1st c. BC)
PolyGram Records, Inc.
Polyhymnia (myth.)
Polymox™ (med.)
Polynesia (islands, Pac.)
Polynesian (langs., people)
Polynesian, Malayo- (also Austronesian)(lang.)
Polynesian, Melanesian- (people)
Polyphemus (myth., Cyclops)
Polypodiophyta (ferns)
Polysporin™ (med.)
Pomerania (region, Pol.)
Pomeranian (dog)
Pomeranian (people)
Pomo Indians/lang.)
Pomona (myth.)
Pomona, CA

Pompadour, Marquise de (aka Jeanne Antoinette Poisson Le Normant d'Étioles)(mistress of Louis XV, Fr.; 1721-64)

Pompano Beach, FL

Pompeian red (also l.c.)(also dragon's blood)

Pompeii (ancient city, It.)

Pompey the Great (Gnaeus Pompeius Magnus)(Roman gen./pol.; 106-48 BC)

Pompidou, Georges (Jean Raymond)(ex-pres., Fr.; 1911-74)

Pomus, Jerome "Doc" (US comp.; 1925-91)

Ponce de León, (Juan)(Sp. expl.; c1460-1521)

Ponce, Puerto Rico

Ponchartrain, Lake (LA)

Ponchielli, Amilcare (It. comp.; 1834-86)

Ponderosa, Inc.

Pond's™ (skin care)

Pond's, Inc., Chesebrough-

pons Varolii (also l.c.)(brain nerve fibers)

Pons, Lily (ent.; 1904-76)

Pont de Nemours, E(leuthere) I. du (US bus.; 1771-1834)

Pont l'Évêque (cheese)

Pont Neuf bridge (Paris)

Pont Pharmaceuticals, du (US bus.)

Pont, E(leuthere) I. du (US bus.; 1771-1834)

Pont, Henry (Belin) du (US bus.; 1899-1970)

Pont, Samuel Francis du (US mil.; 1803-65)

Pont, Thomas Coleman du (US bus./pol.; 1863-1930)

Ponti, Carlo (It. ent.; 1913-)

Pontiac™ car

Pontiac™ Bonneville (auto.)

Pontiac™ Firebird (auto.)

Pontiac™ Grand Am (auto.)

Pontiac™ Grand Prix (auto.)

Pontiac™ Sunbird (auto.)

Pontiac™ Trans Am

Pontiac, Chief (Ottawa Indians; c1720-69)

Pontiac, IL, MI

Pontiac's Rebellion/Conspiracy (US hist.; 1763-66)

Pontianak, Indonesia

Pontius Pilate (Roman mil./pol.; 1st c. AD)

Pony Express (mail service; 1860-61)

Pony League (baseball)

Ponzi scheme/game (also Ponzi)(investment swindle)

Pooh Bah (also poobah)(

Pooh Corner, Welcome to (TV show)

Poole, England

Poona, India (also Pune)

Poor Richard's Almanac (by B. Franklin)

Pop Goes the Weasel (song)

Pop-Tarts™

Pop, Iggy (pop music)

Popayán, Colombia

Pope Air Force Base, NC

Pope Joan (card game)

Pope Valley Winery (US bus.)

Pope, Alexander (Br. poet; 1688-1744)

Pope, John Russell (US arch.; 1874-1937)

Popeye (cartoon)

Popeye Doyle

Popeye the sailor-man (cartoon chara.)

Popeye's Famous Fried Chicken & Biscuits, Inc.

Popocatépetl, Mount (volcano, Mex.)

Popovich, Pavel R(omanovich)(cosmo.; 1930-)

Poppins, Mary (P. Travers novel)

Popsicle™

Popular Mechanics (mag.)

Popular Photography (mag.)

Popular Science (mag.)

Populism (US hist.; late 19th c.)

Populist Party (also People's Party)(US pol.; 1891-1908)

Populist Party of America (US pol.)

Porch of the Caryatids (Gr., female figures used for columns)

Porcupine River (AK/Can.)

Porgy and Bess (Gershwin operetta)

Porizkova, Paulina (model)

Porky Pig (cartoon chara.)

Porsche™ (auto.)

Porsche Cars North America, Inc.

Porsche™ 911 (auto.)

Porsche™ 968 (auto.)

Porsche™ 928 GTS (auto.)

Porsche, Ferdinand (Ger. auto. eng.; 1875-1951)

Port Angeles, WA

Port Arthur, Ontario, Canada

Port Arthur, TX

Port-au-Prince, Haiti

Port Authority of New York and New Jersey

Port du Salut (also Port-Salut)(cheese)

Port Elizabeth, South Africa

Port Glaud, Seychelles

Port Harcourt, Nigeria

Port Huron, MI

Port Louis, Mauritius

Port Moresby, Papua New Guinea

Port-of-Spain, Trinidad

Port Richey, FL

Port Royal, Jamaica

Port Royal, SC

Port Said, Egypt

Port-Salut (also Port du Salut)(cheese)

Port Sudan, Sudan

Port Townsend, WA

Port-Vila, Vanatu

Porter Wagoner (ent.; 1927-)

Porter, Cole (US comp.; 1893-1964)

Porter, Katherine Anne (US writer; 1890-1980)

Porter, Sylvia F(eldman)(US finan. writer; 1914-91)

Porter, William Sydney (pseud. O Henry)(US

writer; 1862-1910)
Porterville, CA
Portinari de' Bardi, Beatrice (inspiration for Dante's Beatrice; 1266-90)
Portland Hoffa (ent.)
Portland Oregonian (OR newspaper)
Portland Press-Herald (ME newspaper)
Portland Telegram (ME newspaper)
Portland Trail Blazers (basketball team)
Portland, OR, ME, TX
Portman, John (US arch.; 1934-)
Portmeirion™
Portmeirion (US bus.)
Portnoy's Complaint (P. Roth novel)
Pôrto Alegre, Brazil
Porto Novo, Benin
Porto, Portugal (also Oporto)
Portobello Road market (London)
Portofino, Italy
Portsmouth Naval Shipyard (NH)
Portsmouth, Dominica
Portsmouth, England
Portsmouth, NH, OH, RI, VA
Portugal (Republic of)(SW Eur.)
Portuguese (lang./people)
Portuguese man-of-war (sea animal)
Portuguese water dog
Posadas, Argentina
Poseidon (myth.)
Poseidon Adventure, The (film; 1972)
Post™ (cereals)
Post & Courier, Charleston (SC newspaper)
Post Co., Washington
Post-Dispatch, St. Louis (MO newspaper)
Post Exchange™ (PX)(mil. store)(also l.c.)
Post-Gazette, Pittsburgh (PA newspaper)
Post-Herald, Birmingham (AL newspaper)
Post-Intelligencer, Seattle (WA newspaper)
Post-it™ notes
Post Standard, Syracuse (NY newspaper)
Post-Tribune, Gary (IN newspaper)
Post, Bridgeport (CT newspaper)
Post, Cincinnati (OH newspaper)
Post, Denver (CO newspaper)
Post, Emily (Price)(US writer, social etiquette; 1873?-1960)
Post, George Browne (US arch.; 1837-1913)
Post, Houston (TX newspaper)
Post, Laurens (Jan) Van der (SAfr. writer; 1906-)
Post, Markie (ent.; 1950-)
Post, New York (NY newspaper)
Post, Washington (DC newspaper)
Post, West Palm Beach (FL newspaper)
Post, Wiley (US aviator; 1899-1935)
Postal Service, U.S. (USPS)(US govt. agcy.; est. 1865)
Postman Always Rings Twice, The (J.M. Cain

novel)
Poston, Tom (ent.; 1927-)
Post Raisin Bran™ (cereal)
Pot, Pol (also Saloth Sar)(Cambodian pol.; 1925-)
Potawatomi (NAmer. Indians)
Potemkin village/Village (showy facade)
Potemkin, Grigory Aleksandrovich, Prince (Rus. pol.; 1739-91)
Potok, Chaim (US writer; 1929-)
Potomac River (DC/MD/VA/WV)
Potomac, MD
Potosí, Bolivia
Potsdam Conference (US/UK/USSR; 1945)
Potsdam, Germany
Potsdam, NY
Potter Stewart (US jurist; 1915-85)
Potter, (Helen) Beatrix (Br. writer/artist; 1866-1943)
Pott's disease
Potts, Annie (ent.)
Pottstown, PA
Potvin, Denis Charles (hockey; 1953-)
Poughkeepsie, NY
Pouilly-Fuissé (wine)
Pouilly-Fumé (wine)
Poul Nyrup Rasmussen (Dan. pol.)
Poul Schlüter (Dan. pol.; 1929-)
Poulenc, Francis (Jean Marcel)(Fr. comp.; 1899-1963)
Poulenc Rorer Consumer Pharmaceuticals, Rhone- (US bus.)
Pound, Ezra (Loomis)(US poet; 1885-1972)
Poundstone, Paula (ent.)
Poussaint, Alvin F. (ent.; 1934-)
Poussin, Nicolas (Fr. artist; 1594-1665)
Povich, Maury (US TV jour.)
POW (prisoner of war)
Powder Puff Derby
Powell, Adam Clayton, Jr. (US pol./rel.; 1908-72)
Powell, Boog (John)(baseball; 1941-)
Powell, Bud (US jazz; 1924-66)
Powell, Colin L(uther), Gen. (ex-chair., Joint Chiefs of Staff; 1937-)
Powell, Dick (ent.; 1904-63)
Powell, Eleanor (ent.; 1912-82)
Powell, Jane (ent.; 1928-)
Powell, John Wesley (US geol./ethnol.; 1834-1902)
Powell, Lake (AZ/UT)
Powell, Lewis F(ranklin), Jr. (US jurist; 1907-)
Powell, Mike (track; 1963-)
Powell, Sir Robert Baden- (Br. gen., founded Boy Scouts; 1857-1941)
Powell, William (ent.; 1892-1984)
Power, Tyrone (ent.; 1913-58)
Powers, Gary Francis (US mil.)

Powers, Hiram (US sculptor; 1805-73)
Powers, Stefanie (ent.; 1942-)
Powhatan (NAmer. Indians)
Poznan, Poland
PP (parcel post)
PPG Industries, Inc.
PR (public relations)
Prado (Madrid museum)
Praemium Imperiale (Imperial Prize)(Jap. art award)
Praetorian Guard (Roman bodyguards)
Prague, Czechoslovakia
Praia, Cape Verde
Prairie Provinces (Can.: Alberta, Manitoba, Saskatchewan)
Prairie State (nickname, IL)
Praise the Lord Network (PTL)(rel.)
Prati Wines, Inc., Martini &
Pravda (Rus. newspaper)
Praxiteles (Gr. sculptor; 400-330 BC)
Prayer, World Day of
Preakness (horse racing)
Preakness Stakes (horse racing)
Precambrian era (4.6 billion-570 million years ago)
Precambrian Shield (also Laurentian [or Canadian] Plateau/Shield)(Can.)
pre-Columbian (art/arch.; pre-16th c. AD)
Preemption Act (US hist.; 1841)
Prefontaine, Steve (Roland)(runner; 1951-75)
Prego™ (sauce)
Preliminary Scholastic Aptitude Test (also PSAT)
Premadasa, Ranasinghe (ex-pres., Sri Lanka; 1924-93)
Premarin™ (med.)
Premark International, Inc.
Premier Power™ (CAT system)
Premiere (mag.)
Preminger, Otto (Ludwig)(ent.; 1905-86)
Premium™ (saltines)
Prendergast, Maurice B(razil)(US artist; c1860-1924)
Prentice-Hall, Inc.
Prentiss, Paula (ent.; 1939-)
Preparation H™ (med.)
Pre-Raphaelite Brotherhood (PRB)(Br. art; 1848-53)
Pres (Lester Willis) Young (US jazz; 1909-59)
Presbyterian (rel.)
Presbyterian Church
Presbyterianism (rel.)
Prescott, William (Hickling)(US hist.; 1796-1859)
Preservation Hall Jazz Band
President and Vice President, Office of the (US govt.)
Presidential Medal of Freedom (US, highest civilian honor)
Presidents' Day
Presidio of San Francisco (US mil.)
Presidio, The (film; 1988)
Presley, Elvis (Aron)(ent.; 1935-77)
Presley, Priscilla (ent.; 1946-)
pre-Socratics (phil.)
Press & Sun-Bulletin, Binghamton (NY newspaper)
Press Association (Br. news org.; 1868)
Press-Democrat, Santa Rosa (CA newspaper)
Press-Enterprise, Riverside (CA newspaper)
Press-Gazette, Green Bay (WI newspaper)
Press-Herald, Portland (ME newspaper)
Press International, United (UPS)(US news org.; est. 1958)
Press-Telegram, Long Beach (CA newspaper)
Press, Asbury Park (NJ newspaper)
Press, Associated (AP)(US news org.; est. 1848)
Press, Atlantic City (NJ newspaper)
Press, Evansville (IN newspaper)
Press, Grand Rapids (MI newspaper)
Press, Mobile (AL newspaper)
Press, Pittsburgh (PA newspaper)
Press, Savannah (GA newspaper)
Presser, Jackie (US labor leader; 1927-88)
Pressler, Larry (US cong.; 1942-)
Prester John (legendary priest-king; 12th-16th c)
Preston Foster (ent.; 1901-70)
Preston Sturges (ent.; 1898-1959)
Preston, Billy (ent.; 1946-)
Preston, Robert (ent.; 1918-87)
Pretender, Old (aka James III, James [Francis] Edward Stuart)(Br. prince; 1688-1766)
Pretenders, the (pop music)
Pretoria, South Africa
Pretorius, Andries (SAfr. colonizer/mil.; 1799-1853)
Pretorius, Marthinus (Wessels)(SAfr. mil./pol.; 1819-1901)
Pretty Boy (Charles Arthur) Floyd (US bank robber; 1901-34)
Pretty Woman (film)
Prevention (mag.)
Previa, Toyota (auto.)
Previn, André (George)(US cond./comp.; 1929-)
Priam (myth.)
Priapus (myth.)
Price Co., The
Price is Right, The (TV show)
Price/Stern/Sloan Publishers, Inc.
Price Toys, Fisher- (US bus.)
Price Waterhouse
Price, George (Cadle)(ex-PM, Belize; 1919-)
Price, George (US cartoonist, *New Yorker*; 1901-)
Price, (Mary) Leontyne (opera; 1927-)

Price, Lloyd (ent.)
Price, Mark (basketball; 1964-)
Price, Nick (golf; 1957-)
Price, Ray (ent.; 1926-)
Price, Reynolds (US writer; 1933-)
Price, Vincent (ent.; 1911-93)
Pride and Prejudice (J. Austin novel)
Pride, Charlie (ent.; 1939-)
Priest, Judas (rock group)
Priestley, J(ohn) B(oynton)(Br. writer; 1894-1984)
Priestley, Jason (ent.; 1969-)
Priestley, Joseph (Br. chem./writer; 1733-1804)
Prigg v. Pennsylvania (US law; 1842)
Prijedor, Bosnia-Hercegovina
Prima, Louis (ent.; 1911-78)
Primatene™ (med.)
Prime of Miss Jean Brodie, The (film; 1969)
Primerica Corp.
PrimeTime Live (TV show)
Primitive Baptist
Primitive Friends
Primitive Methodist
Primo Carnera (boxing; 1907-67)
Prince (b. Prince Rogers Nelson)(ent.; 1960-)
Prince Albert (Br., husband of Queen Victoria; 1819-61)
Prince Albert (coat)
Prince Albert (prince, Monaco)
Prince Albert, Saskatchewan, Canada
Prince Andrew (Andrew Albert Christian Edward)(2nd son of Queen Elizabeth II; 1960-)
Prince and the Pauper, The (M. Twain novel)
Prince Caspian (by C.S. Lewis)
Prince Charles (Charles Philip Arthur George, Prince of Wales)(eldest son of Queen Elizabeth II; 1948-)
Prince Charming
Prince Edward (Edward Anthony Richard Louis, Prince of the UK)(3rd son of Queen Elizabeth II; 1964-)
Prince Edward Island (province, Can.)
Prince Hans Adam (head of state, Liechtenstein; 1945-)
Prince Mbilini (PM, Swaziland
Prince Naruhito (Jap.)
Prince Norodom Ranariddh (prince/PM, Cambodia)
Prince of Darkness (the Devil)
Prince of Peace (Jesus)
Prince of Wales (Prince Charles Philip Arthur George)(eldest son of Queen Elizabeth II; 1948-)
Prince Otto (Eduard Leopold) von Bismarck ("Iron Chancellor")(ex-chanc., Ger.; 1815-98)
Prince Rainier III (aka Rainier Louis Henri Maxence Bertrand de Grimaldi)(head of state, Monaco; 1923-)
Prince Rupert, British Columbia, Canada
Prince Valiant (comic strip)
Prince Valiant (hairstyle)
Prince von Bülow Bernhard (ex-chanc., Ger.; 1849-1929)
Prince William Sound (AK)
Prince, Bob (baseball announcer; 1917-85)
Princess Anne (Anne Elizabeth Alice Louise)(daughter of Queen Elizabeth II; 1950-)
Princess Beatrice (daughter of Prince Andrew and Sarah; 1988-)
Princess Diana (Princess of Wales, Lady Diana Spencer; 1961-)
Princess Caroline (princess, Monaco)
Princess Eugénie (daughter of Prince Andrew and Sarah; 1990-)
Princess Grace (b. Grace Patricia Kelly)(US actress; princess, Monaco; 1929-82)
Princess Margaret (Rose)(UK; 1930-)
Princess Masako (Owada)(Jap.; 1964-)
Princess Summerfall Winterspring (fict. chara., *Howdy Doody*)
Princeton University (NJ)
Princeton, NJ
Principal, Victoria (ent.)
Príncipe, São Tomé and (Democratic Republic of)(off W Afr. coast)
Pringles™ (chips)
Prinze, Freddie (ent.; 1954-77)
Priority Mail™ (USPS)
Priscilla Lane (ent.; 1917-)
Priscilla Presley (ent.; 1946-)
Pritikin diet
Privacy Act of 1974
Private Benjamin (film; 1980)
Prizm™ LSi, Geo (auto.)
Prizm™, Geo (auto.)
Prizzi's Honor (film; 1985)
Pro Bowl (football)
Probe GT, Ford (auto.)
Procardia™ (med.)
ProCAT™ (CAT system)
Procol Harum (pop music)
Proconsul (Afr. prehistoric ape skull)
Procrustean bed (sociology)
Procrustes (also Damastes)(myth.)
Procter & Gamble Co.
Procter, William C. (US bus., soap; 1862-1934)
Proctor Silex™ coffeemaker
Proctor-Silex, Inc., Hamilton Beach/
Procyon (also Alpha Canis Minoris)(astron.)
Prodigy (compu. database)
Product 19™, Kellogg's
Proell, Annemarie Moser (skiing; 1953-)
Professor Book Centers, Inc., Little
Professor Branestawm

Professor Moriarty (fict. chara., *Sherlock Holmes*)
Progressive-Conservative Party (Can. pol.)
Progressive Labor Party (Us pol.)
Progressive Party (US pol.)
Progressivism (US hist.; late 1800s, early 1900s)
Progresso™
Progresso Quality Foods (US bus.)
Prohibition (US history; 1920-33)
Prohibition Party (US pol.)
Project Head Start (also Head Start)(educ.)
Prokofiev, Sergei (Sergeyevich)(Rus. comp.; 1891-1953)
PROM (programmable read-only memory) (compu.)
Prometheus (myth.)
Promised Land (heaven)
Promised Land of Canaan (rel.)
Promises, Promises (play)
Promus Cos., Inc.
Prophet, The (by Kahlil Gibran)
Prophets (rel.)
Proscar™ (med.)
Prose Edda (also *Edda*)(Icelandic folk tales)
Proserpina (also Persephone)(myth.)
Prosky, Robert (ent.; 1930-)
Prosper Mérimée (Fr. writer; 1803-70)
Prospero (fict. chara., *The Tempest*)
Protagoras (Gr. phil.; 480?-411? BC)
Proterozoic period (2.5 billion-570 million years ago)
Protestant (rel.)
Protestant Reformation (also Reformation)(Eur. rel./hist.; 16th c.)
Protestant Union
Protestant work ethic
Protestantism (rel.)
Proteus (myth.)
Proton™ (elec.)
Proton Corp.
Protozoa (1-celled organisms)
Proudhon, Pierre Joseph (Fr. phil.; 1809-65)
Proust, Marcel (Fr. writer; 1871-1922)
Provence (region, Fr.)
Provence-Alpes-Côte d'Azur (region, Fr.)
Provençal (lang.)
Proventil™ (med.)
Provera™ (med.)
Proverbs, Book of (rel.)
Providence (rel.)
Providence Journal (RI newspaper)
Providence Journal-Bulletin (RI newspaper)
Providence, RI
Provincetown Players (MA/NYC; 1915-29)
Provincetown, MA
Provo, UT
Prowse, Juliet (ent.)

Proxima Centauri (astron.)
Proxmire, (Edward) William (US pol.; 1915-)
Prozac™ (med.)
Prudential Insurance Co. of America
Prud'hon, Pierre-Paul (Fr. artist; 1758-1823)
Prudhoe Bay (AK)
Prudhomme, Paul (US chef)
Prussia (state, Ger.)
Prussian blue (color)
Prussian collar (clothing)
Prussian red (color)
Prussian War, Austro- (also Seven Weeks' War); 1866)
Prussian War, Franco- (also Franco-German War)(Fr./Ger.-Prussia; 1870-71)
Pryce, Jonathan (ent.; 1947-)
Pryor, David Hampton (US cong.; 1934-)
Pryor, Richard (ent.; 1940-)
Przhevalsk, Kyrgyzstan
Przhevalski's horse
PS (postscript)
Psalms, (Book of)(also Psalter)(rel.)
Pseudepigrapha (re.)
Psilocybe (hallucinogenic mushroom)
PSRO (Professional Standards Review Organization)
PST (Pacific Standard Time)
Psyche (myth.)
Psyche knot
Psycho (film; 1960)
Psycho II (film; 1983)
Psycho III (film; 1986)
Psychology Today (mag.)
PT boat (US mil., patrol torpedo boat)
Pt (chem. sym., platinum)
PTA (Parent-Teacher Association)
Ptah (myth.)
P(hineas) T(aylor) Barnum (ent., circus; 1810-91)
PTL Club (Praise the Lord [J. Bakker])
Ptolemaic dynasty (Eg.; 323-30 BC)
Ptolemaic system (astron.)
Ptolemy (Claudius Ptolemaeus)(Eg. astron.; c100-170)
Ptolemy I (king, Eg.; c367-283 BC)
Ptolemy II (king, Eg.; 309-246 BC)
Ptolemy III (king, Eg.; 282?-221 BC)
Ptolemy V (king, Eg.; 210?-181 BC)
Ptolemy VI (king, Eg.; 186?-145 BC)
Ptolemy VII (king, Eg.; 184?-116 BC)
Ptolemy XIII (king, Eg.; 63-47 BC)
PT 109 (film; 1963)
Pu (chem. sym., plutonium)
Public Broadcasting System (PBS)(TV)
Public Enemy (pop music)
Public Works Administration (PWA)(US hist.; 1933-1943)
Public, John Q. (average US citizen)

Publishers Weekly (mag.)
Publius Cornelius Tacitus (Roman hist.; c55-c120)
Publix Super Markets, Inc.
Pucci Perfumes International, Inc., Emilio
Pucci, Emilio (It. designer; 1914-92)
Puccini, Giacomo (Antonio Domenico Michele Secondo Maria)(It. comp.; 1858-1924)
Puck (also Robin Goodfellow, Hobgoblin)(fict. chara, *A Midsummer Night's Dream*)
Puck of Pook's Hill (by Rudyard Kipling)
Puck, Wolfgang (chef)
Puckett and the Union Gap, Gary (pop music)
Puckett, Kirby (baseball; 1961-)
Puddleduck, Jemima
Puebla (de Zaragoza), Mexico
Pueblo (NAmer. Indians)
Pueblo, CO
Pueblo, U.S.S. (US ship./mil. incident, NKorea; 1968)
Puente, Tito (US jazz; 1923-)
Puerto Barrios, Guatemala
Puerto Cabello, Venezuela
Puerto Cabezas, Nicaragua
Puerto Cortés, Honduras
Puerto Limón, Costa Rica (also Limón)
Puerto Presidente Stroessner, Paraguay
Puerto Rico (Commonwealth of)(W Indies)
Puerto Sandino, Nicaragua
Puerto Vallarta, Mexico
Puget Sound (WA)
Puget Sound Naval Shipyard (WA)
Puglia (also Apulia)(region, It.)
Pulitzer, Joseph (US jour./publ./finan.; 1847-1911)
Pulitzer, Joseph, Jr. (US publ.; 1913-93)
Pulliam, Keshia Knight (ent.; 1979)
Pullman™ car (railroad sleeping/parlor car)
Pullman, George (Mortimer)(US inv./bus.; 1831-1901?)
Pulsar™
Pulsar Time, Inc.
Puma™ (sportswear)
Puma USA (US bus.)
Punakha, Bhutan
Punch-and-Judy show (Br. puppet show)
Punchinello (puppet show/chara.)
Pune, India (formerly Poona)
Punic Wars (Rome/Carthage; 264-241 BC, 218-201 BC, 149-146 BC)
Punisher, The (cartoon chara.)
Punjab (province, Pak.)
Punjab (state, India)
Punjabi (lang./people)
Punky Brewster (fict. chara.)
Punsalmaagiyn Ochirbat (pres., Mongolia; 1943-)
Punta Arenas, Chile

Punta Gorda, Belize
Punta Gorda, FL
Puntsagiyn Jasray (PM, Mongolia
Punxsutawney Phil (groundhog)
Punxsutawney, PA
Puppis (astron., stern/deck)
Purcell, Henry (Br. comp.; 1658?-95)
Purdue University (IN)
Pure Food and Drug Act (US hist.; 1906)
Pure Land Buddhism (rel.)
Purex Industries, Inc.
Purim (Jew. festival)
Purina™ (pet food)
Purina™ Cat Chow
Purina Co., Ralston
Purina™ Dog Chow
Purina™ Goat Chow
Puritan (rel.)
Puritan work ethic
Puritanism (rel.)
Purkinje, Johannes Evangelista (Czech. physiol.; 1787-1869)
Purkinje's cells/fibers (med.)
Purolator™
Purolator Products Co.
Purple Heart, Order of the (US mil. metal)
Purple Rose of Cairo, The (film; 1985)
Pusan, South Korea (also Busan)
Pushkin, Aleksandr (Sergeyevich)(Rus. writer; 1799-1837)
Pushtu (also Pashto)(lang.)
Putnam Publishing Group, The (US bus.)
Putt-Putt Golf Courses of America (US bus.)
Pu'uhonua o Honaunau National Historical Park (HI)
Puyallup (NAmer. Indians)
Puyallup, WA
Puzo, Mario (US writer; 1920-)
PVC (polyvinyl chloride)
P(amulaparti) V(enkata) Narasimha Rao (PM, India; 1921-)
PWA (Public Works Administration)
PX (post exchange, Post Exchange™)(mil. store)
Pygmalion (G.B. Shaw play)
Pygmalion (myth.)
Pygmy (people)
Pyle, Denver (ent.; 1920-)
Pyle, Ernest "Ernie" (US jour.; 1900-45)
Pyle, Gomer (fict. chara.)
Pym, John (Br. pol.; 1584-1643)
Pynchon, Thomas (US writer; 1937-)
Pyongyang, North Korea
Pyotr (or Piotr, Peter)(Alekseevich) Kropotkin, Prince (Rus. anarchist; 1842-1921)
Pyramid of Khufu (or Cheops), Great (Eg.)
Pyramid of Kafre (or Khafre)(Eg.)
Pyramus and Thisbe (myth.)
Pyrenees Mountains (Sp./Fr.)

Pyrenees, Great (dog)
Pyrex™
Pyrrhic victory (not worth winning)
Pyrrhus (king, Gr.; c318-272 BC)
Pyrrophyta (algae)
Pythagoras (Gr. phil./math.; c580-c500 BC)
Pythagorean theorem/scale (math.)
Pythian Games (ancient Gr.)
Pythias, Damon and (myth., loyal friendship)
Pythias, Knights of (US benevolent secret
    society; founded 1864)
Python (myth.)
Python's Flying Circus, Monty (TV show)
Pyxis (astron., compass)

Q (aka Sir Arthur [Thomas] Quiller-Couch)(Br. writer; 1863-1944)
Qaboos bin Said al-Said (sultan/PM, Oman; 1940-)
Qacentina/Constantine, Algeria
Qaddafi (or Khadafy, Khaddhafi, Gaddafi), Moammar (or Moamer al, Muammar al)(pres., Libya; 1942-)
Qaiwain (or Qaywayn), Umm al (state, UAE)
Qamdo, China
Q & A (question[s] and answer[s])
Qantas Airways, Ltd.
Qatar (State of)(Middle East)
Qattarah Depression (Eg.)
Qazvin (or Kazvin), Iran
QB (quarterback, qualified bidders)
QC (quality control)
Q clearance (highest nuclear security clearance)
Qin dynasty (also Ch'in)(Ch.; 221-206 BC)
Qing, Jiang (also Chiang Ching)(Ch. pol./widow of Mao Zedong; 1914-91)
Qingdao, China (also Tsingtao)
Qinghai (also Tsinghai)(province, Ch.)
Qiyama (rel.)
QM (quartermaster)
Qom, Iran (also Qum)
Qormi, Malta
QT (keep secret ["on the QT"])
Q-Tips™
Quaalude™ (sedative)
Quack Attack (cartoon)
Quad City Times, Davenport (IA newspaper)
Quadruple Alliance (Eur. hist.; 1718/1813/1834)
Quady Winery (US bus.)
Quaid, Dennis (ent.; 1954-)
Quaid, Randy (ent.; 1950-)
Quail Ridge Cellars & Vineyards (US bus.)
Quaker™ Oatmeal
Quaker Oats Co. The
Quaker State Corp.
Quaker State Oil Refining Corp.
Quakers (also [Religious] Society of Friends)(rel.)
Quakertown, PA
Quant, Mary (Br. designer; 1934-)
Quantico Marine Corps Development Command (VA)
Quantrill, William Clarke (US mil./outlaw; 1837-65)
Quantrill's Raiders (US Civil War guerrillas)
Quantum Leap (TV show)
Quapaw (NAmer. Indians)
Quargel (cheese)
Quarles, Francis (Br. poet; 1592-1644)

Quartermaster Corps (US mil.)
Quasar™ (elec.)
Quasar Co.
Quasimodo (also Low Sunday)(1st Sunday after Easter)
Quasimodo (fict. chara., *The Hunchback of Notre Dame*)
Quasimodo, Salvatore (It. poet; 1901-68)
Quaternary period (2.5 million years ago to present)
Quatre Bornes, Mauritius
Quattro™, Audi (auto.)
Quattrocento (It. art/lit.; 15th c.)
Quayle, (James) Dan(forth)(ex-US VP; 1947-)
Quayle, Marilyn (US atty., wife of ex-VP ; 1949-)
Que Que, Zimbabwe (also Kwekwe)
Quebec (province, Can.)
Quebec Nordiques (hockey team)
Quebec, Canada (province, Can.)
Quebec, Quebec, Canada
Quebecer (also Quebecker, Quebecois)(Quebec inhabitant)
Quechua (lang./people)
Queeg, Captain (fict. chara., *The Caine Mutiny*)
Queen (pop music)
Queen Anne style (arch./furn.; 1700-20)
Queen Anne's lace (flowering plant)
Queen Anne's War (Br./Fr. in Amer.; 1702-13)
Queen Beatrix (Wilhelmina Armgard)(queen, the Netherlands; 1938-)
Queen Charlotte Islands (Br. Columbia)
Queen Elizabeth II (Elizabeth Alexandra Mary Windsor)(queen, Eng./UK; 1926-)
Queen Elizabeth Islands (Can.)
Queen Margrethe II (queen, Den.; 1940-)
Queen Maud Land (region, Antarctica)
Queen Maud Range (mountains, Antarctica)
Queen of Hearts
Queen of Heaven (Virgin Mary)
Queen of Sheba (biblical, visited Solomon to test his wisdom)
Queen, Ellery (pseud. for US writers: Frederick Dannay, 1905-82; Manfred B. Lee, 1905-71)
Queenie Peavy
Queen's (or King's) Bench (Br. law)
Queen's (or King's) Counsel (Br. law)
queen's (or king's) English (correct English)
Queens (borough, NYC)
Queensberry rules (also Marquis of Queensberry rules)(boxing)
Queensberry, John Sholto Douglas (Marquis of Queensberry; 1844-1900)
Queensborough Bridge (NYC)
Queensland (state, Austl.)
Quentin Massys (or Matsys)(Flem. artist; 1466?-1530)
Querétaro, Mexico

Quesnay, Francois (Fr. econ.; 1694-1774)
Quest, Jonny (cartoon)
Quest™, Nissan (auto.)
Quett (Ketumile Joni) Masire (pres., Botswana; 1925-)
Quetta, Pakistan (also Kwatah)
Quetzalcoatl (myth.)
Quezaltenango, Guatemala
Quezon City, Philippines
Quezon y Molina, Manuel Luis (ex-pres. Philippines; 1878-1944)
quiche Lorraine
Quick Draw McGraw (fict. chara.)
Quicken™ (compu.)
Quickie™ (mop)
Quik Print™
Quik Print, Inc.
Quiller-Couch, Sir Arthur Thomas (aka "Q")(Br. writer; 1863-1944)
Quincy Jones (US jazz; 1933-)
Quincy Patriot-Ledger (MA newspaper)
Quincy, IL, MA
Quindlen, Anna (US jour.)
Quinn, Aidan (ent.; 1959-)
Quinn, Anthony (ent.; 1915-)
Quinn, Jane Bryant
Quinn, Martha (ent.; 1959-)
Quinn, Medicine Woman, Dr. (TV show)
Quintana Roo (state, Mex.)
Quintilian (Marcus Fabius Quintilianus)(Roman rhetorician; c35-c95)
Quintus Fabius Maximus Verrucosus ("Cunctator")(Roman pol./mil.; 275-03 BC)
Quisling, Vidkun (Nor. pol./traitor; 1887-1945)
Quito, Ecuador
Quivira, Gran (utopia)
Quixote de la Mancha, Don (by Cervantes)
Qum, Iran (also Qom)
Qumran (also Khirbet Qumran)(Dead Sea Scrolls site)
Quo Vadis (H. Sienkiewicz novel)
Quonset™ hut
Quran (also Koran)(rel.)
Quthing, Lesotho
QVC Network, Inc. (cable TV)

R

Ra (also Re)(Eg. sun god)
Ra (chem. sym., radium)
Ra (T. Heyerdahl raft used to cross Atl.; 1969-70)
Ra Expeditions (crossing Atl.; 1969-70)
Ra, Sun (b. Herman Blount)(US jazz; 1916-93)
Rabat, Morocco
Rabaul, Papua New Guinea
Rabb, Ellis (ent.; 1930-)
Rabbani, Burhanuddin (pres., Afghan.; 1940-)
Rabbie Namaliu (ex-PM, Papua New Guinea; 1947-)
Rabbinical Judaism (rel.)
Rabbit, Brer (fict. chara., *Uncle Remus*)
Rabbit, Peter (fict. chara.)
Rabbit?, Who Framed Roger (film)
Rabbitt, Eddie (ent.; 1941-)
Rabe, David (US writer; 1940-)
Rabelais, François (Fr. writer; 1495-1553)
Rabi, Isidor Isaac (US physt.; 1899-1988)
Rabin, Yitzhak (PM, Isr.; 1922-)
Rabindranath Tagore, Sir (Indian poet; 1861-1941)
Rabinowitz, Solomon (aka Shalom [or Sholom] Aleichem)(Yiddish writer; 1859-1916)
Rabuka, Sitiveni (PM, Fiji)
Rachel (Louise) Carson (US writer/biol.; 1907-64)
Rachel, Rachel (film; 1968)
Rachins, Alan (ent.; 1947-)
Rachmaninov, Sergei V(asilyevich)(Rus. comp./cond.; 1893-1943)
Racicot, Marc (MT gov.)
Racine, Jean (Baptiste)(Fr. writer; 1639-99)
Racine, WI
Radcliffe College (Cambridge, MA)
Radcliffe, Ann (Ward)(Br. writer; 1764-1823)
Raden Suharto (pres., Indonesia; 1921-)
Radford, VA
Radio City Music Hall (NYC)
Radio Corporation of America (RCA)
Radio Free Europe
Radio Liberty
Radio Shack (US bus.)
Radisson Hotels International (US bus.)
Radner, Gilda (ent.; 1946-89)
Radoje Kontic (premier; Yug.)
Radziwill, Princess Lee
Rae Dawn Chong (ent.; 1961-)
Rae, Charlotte (ent.; 1926-)
Rae, John (Scot. expl.; 1813-93)
Rae, Norma (film; 1979)
Rafael Angel Calderón Fournier (pres., Costa Rica; 1949-)

Rafael Angel Calderón Guardia (ex-pres., Costa Rica; 1900-71)
Rafael Leonardo Callejas (pres., Honduras; 1943-)
Rafael L. Trujillo Molina (ex-pres., Dom Rep.; 1891-1961)
Rafer Johnson (decathlon; 1935-)
Raffin, Deborah
Rafiq al-Hairi (PM, Lebanon)
Rafsanjani, Hojatolisiam Ali Akbar Hashemi (pres., Iran; 1934-)
Raft, George (ent.; 1895-1980)
Rage Against the Machine (pop music)
Raggedy Ann & Andy
Raggedy Ann doll
Raglan, FitzRoy (James Henry) Somerset, Baron (Br. gen., raglan sleeve; 1788-1855)
Ragnarök (also Götterdämmerung)(myth.)
Ragú™
Ragú Foods, Inc.
Rahal, Bobby
Rahman, Mujibur (aka Sheik Mujib)(ex-PM, Bangladesh; 1920-75)
Rahman, Sheik Omar Abdel- (Muslim rel.; 1938-)
Rahman, Tunku Abdul (ex-PM, Malaysia; 1903-90)
Rahman, Ziaur (ex-pres., Bangladesh; 1935-81)
Rahu (myth.)
Raid™ (bug killer)
Raiders of the Lost Ark (film; 1981)
Raiders, Los Angeles (football team)
Raiders, Paul Revere and the (pop music)
Rain Man (film)
Rainbow Bridge (UT)
Rainbow Bridge National Monument (UT)
Rainer Maria Rilke (Ger. poet; 1875-1926)
Rainer Werner Fassbinder (Ger. ent.; 1946-82)
Raines, Ella (ent.)
Rainey, Joseph Hayne (US pol.; 1832-87)
Rainey, Ma (Gertrude)(US jazz; 1886-1939)
Rainier III, Prince (aka Rainier Louis Henri Maxence Bertrand de Grimaldi)(head of state, Monaco; 1923-)
Rainier National Park, Mount (WA)
Rains, Claude (ent.; 1890-1967)
Rainy Lake (US/Can.)
Raisa (Maksimova Titorenko) Gorbachev (wife of ex-Rus. pres./educ.; 1934-)
Raisin Bran (cereal)
Raitt, Bonnie (ent.; 1949-)
Rajasthan (state, India)
Rajiv Gandhi (ex-PM, India; 1944-91)
Rajkot, India
Rajneesh, Shree (or Osho)(aka Bhagwan)(b. Chaadra Mohan Jain)(Indian rel.; 1931-90)
Rajshahi, Bangladesh (formerly Rampur Boalia)

Rakhmanov, Ali (acting pres., Tajikistan

Raleigh News & Observer (NC newspaper)

Raleigh, NC

Raleigh, Sir Walter (Br. expl./writer; 1552?-1618)

Ralph Adams Cram (US arch.; 1863-1942)

Ralph Bellamy (ent.; 1904-91)

Ralph Boston (jumper; 1939-)

Ralph David Abernathy (US rel./civil rights leader; 1926-90)

Ralph Edwards (ent.; 1913-)

Ralph Ellison (US writer; 1914-)

Ralph Houk (baseball; 1919-)

Ralph Iron (aka Olive Schreiner)(SAfr. writer; 1855-1920)

Ralph J. Bunche (US dipl.; 1904-71)

Ralph Kiner (baseball; 1922-)

Ralph Lauren™

Ralph Lauren (b. Ralph Lifshitz)(US designer; 1939-)

Ralph Lauren (US bus.)

Ralph Lauren Leathergoods, Polo/ (US bus.)

Ralph Macchio (ent.; 1962-)

Ralph Meeker (ent.)

Ralph Nader (US atty./consumer advocate; 1934-)

Ralph Roister Doister (N. Udall comedy)

Ralph T. Walker (US arch.; 1889-1973)

Ralph Vaughan Williams (Br. comp.; 1872-1958)

Ralph Waite (ent.; 1929-)

Ralph Waldo Emerson (US writer/phil.; 1803-82)

Ralston Purina Co.

Ralston, Dennis (tennis; 1942-)

Ralston, Esther (ent.; 1902-)

RAM (random access memory)(compu.)

RAM Laramie LT, Dodge (auto.)

RAM Laramie SLT, Dodge (auto.)

RAM Laramie ST, Dodge (auto.)

RAM, Dodge (auto.)

RAM Van, Dodge (auto.)

Rama (rel.)

Rama IX (b. Bhumibol Adulyadej)(king, Thailand; 1927-)

Ramada International Hotels & Resorts (US bus.)

Ramadan (Muslim holy month)

Ramaema, Elias , Col. (Lesotho, mil.)

Ramakrishna (Hindu rel./educ.; 1834-86)

Ramapithecus (anthrop.)

Ramaswamy Venkataraman (ex-pres., India)

Ramat Gan, Israel

Ramayana (Sanskrit epic)

Rambert, Marie, Dame (b. Cyvia Rambam)(Br. ballet; 1888-1982)

Rambo (film)

Ramcharger, Dodge (auto.)

Rameau, Jean Philippe (Fr. comp.; 1683-1764)

Ramey, Samuel (ent.; 1942-)

Ramiro de León Carpio (pres., Guat.)

Ramis, Harold (ent.)

Ramism (phil.)

Ramiz, Alia (ex-pres., Albania; 1925-)

Ramon Hnatyshyn (gov-gen., Can.)

Ramon Novarro (ent.; 1899-1968)

Ramón Velásquez (pres., Venezuela

Ramones, the (pop music)

Ramos gin fizz (mixed drink)

Ramos, Fidel V. (pres., Philippines; 1928-)

Rampal, Jean-Pierre (Fr. flutist; 1922-)

Rampur Boalia (now Rajshahi, Bangladesh)

Rams, Los Angeles (football team)

Ramses II (Eg. king; 13th c. BC)

Ramses III (Eg. king; 12th c. BC)

Ramsey Lewis (US jazz

Ramsgate, England

Ranariddh, Norodom (prince/co-PM, Cambodia)

Ranasinghe Premadasa (ex-pres., Sri Lanka; 1924-93)

Rancagua, Chile

Rancho Cordova, CA

Rancho Cucamonga, CA

Rancho Mirage, CA

Rancho Palos Verdes, CA

Rand International (US bus.)

Rand Co., Ingersoll-

Rand Corp., Sperry

Rand McNally & Co.

Rand McNally World Atlas

Rand, Ayn (US writer/phil.; 1905-82)

Rand, Remington

Rand, the (also Witwatersrand)(SAfr. gold mining area)

Randall, Tony (ent.; 1920-)

R & B (rhythm & blues)

R & D (research & development)

Randers, Denmark

Randolph Caldecott (Br. artist; 1846-86)

Randolph (Henry Spencer) Churchill, Lord (Br. pol., father of Winston; 1849-95)

Randolph Scott (ent.; 1898-1987)

Randolph, Edmund (Jennings)(US atty.; 1753-1813)

Randolph, John (ent.; 1915-)

Randolph, John (of Roanoke)(US pol.; 1773-1833)

Randolph, Joyce (ent. 1925-)

Randolph, MA

Random House Dictionary of the English Language, The

Random House, Inc.

R and R (or R & R)(rest and recreation, rest and recuperation, rock-'n'-roll, rock 'n' roll)

Randy Matson (shot putter; 1945-)

Randy Newman (ent.; 1943-)

Randy Quaid (ent.; 1950-)
Randy Travis (ent.; 1959-)
Range Rover™ (auto.)
Range Rover of North America, Inc.
Rangel, Charles (US pol.; 1930-)
Ranger (US uncrewed space probes)
Ranger & Tonto, Lone (fict charas.)
Ranger Boat Co.
Ranger Rick (mag.)
Ranger Rick's Nature Club
Ranger, Ford (auto.)
Rangers, New York (hockey team)
Rangers, Texas (baseball team)
Rangoon (now called Yangon)
Rangoon, Burma (now Yangon, Myanmar)
Ranil Wickremasinghe (PM, Sri Lanka)
Rankin, Jeannette (US pol.; 1880-1973)
Rankin, Judy (Torluemke)(golf; 1945-)
Ransom Eli Olds (US bus./auto.; 1864-1950)
Rantoul, IL
Rao, P(amulaparti) V(enkata) Narasimha (PM,
    India; 1921-)
Raoul Cédras, Lieut. Gen. (Haitian mil.)
Raoul Dufy (Fr. artist; 1877-1953)
Raoul Wallenberg (Swed. dipl.; 1912-47?)
Raoul Walsh (ent.; 1887-1980)
Raoult's law (chem.)
Rap Brown (b. Hubert Gerald Brown)(US
    activist; 1943-)
Rapa Nui (also Easter Island)(S Pac.)
Rape of the Sabine Women, (G. da Bologna
    sculpture, N. Poussin painting)
Raphael Sanzio (It. artist; 1483-1520)
Raphael, Sally Jessy (TV host)
Rapid City, SD
Rapidograph™ (graphic design)
RAPIDTEXT™ (text entry system)
RapidTEXT, Inc.
RapidWrite™ (text entry system)
Rappahannock River (VA)
Rapture, the (rel.)
Rapunzel (fict. chara.)
Raquel Welch (ent.; 1940-)
Ras al Khaimah (or Khaymah)(state, UAE)
Ras Asir (also Cape Guardafui)(cape, Somalia)
Rascals, Little (TV show)
Rascals, the (pop music)
Rashad, Ahmad (football)
Rashad, Phylicia (ent.; 1948-)
Raschi, Vic (baseball; 1919-88)
Rashid Al-Solh (ex-PM, Lebanon)
Rashomon (A. Ryunosuke short story)
Rasmussen, Knud Johan Victor (Dan. expl.;
    1879-1933)
Rasmussen, Poul Nyrup (Dan. pol.)
Rasputin, (Grigori Efimovich)(Rus. rel.; c1865-
    1916)
Rastafarian (rel.)

Rastafarianism (rel.)
RasterOps™ (compu.)
Ratelle, (Joseph Gilbert Yvon) Jean (hockey;
    1953-)
Rathbone, Basil (ent.; 1892-1967)
Rathenau, Walter (Ger. pol.; 1867-1922)
Rather, Dan (US TV jour.; 1931-)
Rather, The CBS Evening News With Dan (TV
    show)
Ratsiraka, Didier (ex-pres., Madagascar; 1936-)
Ratt (rock group)
Rattigan, Sir Terence (Mervyn)(Br. writer;
    1911-77)
Ratu Sir Penaia Ganilau (pres., Fiji; 1918-)
Ratzenberger, John (ent.; 1947-)
Rau, Santha Rama (Indian writer/astrol.;
    1923-)
Raul Julia (ent.; 1940-)
Rauschenberg, Robert (US artist; 1925-)
Ravana (myth.)
Rave™
Ravel, Maurice (Joseph)(Fr. comp.; 1875-1937)
Ravenna, Italy
Ravenna, OH
Ravi River (S Asia)
Ravi Shankar (comp., India; 1920-)
Ravony, Francisque (PM, Madagascar)
Rawhide (TV show)
Rawalpindi, Pakistan
Rawis, Betsy (Elizabeth Earle)(golf; 1928-)
Rawlings, Jerry (John)(pres., Ghana; 1947-)
Rawlings, Marjorie Kinnan (US writer; 1896-
    1953)
Rawls, Lou (ent.; 1936-)
Ray Bloch (ent.)
Ray Bolger (ent.; 1904-87)
Ray Bourque (hockey; 1960-)
Ray Bradbury (US writer, sci fi; 1920-)
Ray Brown (US jazz; 1926-)
Ray Charles (ent.; 1930-)
Ray Conniff (ent.; 1916-)
Ray Conniff Orchestra
Ray Ewry (Olympics; 1873-1937)
Ray(mond A.) Kroc (US bus., founded
    McDonald's; 1902-84)
Ray "Boom Boom" Mancini (boxing)
Ray Milland (ent.; 1905-86)
Ray Price (ent.; 1926-)
Ray Walston (ent.; 1924-)
Ray, Aldo (ent.; 1927-91)
Ray, James Earl (US, assassinated M.L. King;
    1929-)
Ray, John (Br. nat.; 1627-1705)
Ray, Johnnie (ent.; 1927-90)
Ray, Man (US artist; 1890-1976)
Rayburn, Sam(uel Taliaferro)(US pol.; 1882-
    1961)
Raye, Martha (ent.; 1916-)

Raymond Berry (football; 1933-)
Raymond Burr (ent.; 1917-93)
Raymond Chandler (US writer; 1888-1959)
Raymond Ditmars (US zool., writer; 1876-1942)
Raymond Duchamp-Villon (Fr. artist; 1876-1918)
Raymond Massey (ent.; 1896-1993)
Raymond Moody
Raymond (Nicolas Landry) Poincaré (ex-pres., Fr.; 1860-1934)
Raymond (Ames) Spruance (US mil.; 1886-1969)
Raymond Vineyard & Cellar (US bus.)
Raymond, Alex (cartoonist, *Flash Gordon, Jungle Jim*; 1909-56)
Raymond, Gene (ent.; 1908-)
Raynaud's disease
Rayovac Corp.
Raytheon Co.
Raytown, MO
Razaf, Andy (US lyricist; 1895-1973)
Razanamasy, Guy (Willy)(ex-PM, Madagascar)
Rb (chem. sym., rubidium)
R(ichard) Buckminster Fuller (US eng./arch.; 1895-1983)
RCA™
RCA Corp.
RCA Records (US bus.)
RCAF (Royal Canadian Air Force)
RCMP (Royal Canadian Mounted Police)
RCP (Royal College of Physicians)
RCS (Royal College of Surgeons)
RD (rural delivery)
RDA (recommended daily [or dietary] allowance)
R(onald) D(avid) Laing (Scot. psych./writer; 1927-89)
Re (also Ra)(Eg. sun god)
Re (chem. sym., rhenium)
Reach™ (health)
Reader's Digest (mag.)
Reader's Digest Association (publisher)
Reading Eagle (PA newspaper)
Reading Railroad, Philadelphia and
Reading Times (PA newspaper)
Reading, England
Reading, MA, OH, PA
Reagan, Nancy (b. Anne Francis Robbins, aka Nancy Davis)(wife of ex-US pres.; 1923-)
Reagan, Ronald (Wilson)(40th US pres.; 1911-)
Reaganomics (Reagan's economic policy)
Real Estate Brokers, National Association of
Real-Kill™ (pesticide)
Real Stories of the Highway Patrol (TV show)
ReaLemon™ juice
Realtor™
Realtors, National Association of
Reason, Age of (phil.)

Reason, The Age of (by Thomas Paine; 1794-96)
Reasoner, Harry (US TV jour.; 1923-91)
Reatta, Buick™ (auto.)
Reb, Johnny (Confederate soldier, southerner
Reba McEntire (ent.; 1954-)
Rebecca De Mornay (ent.; 1962-)
Rebecca of Sunnybrook Farm (film; 1938)
Rebecca West, Dame (b. Cicily Isabel Fairfield)(Br. writer; 1892-1983)
Recamier day bed
Récamier, Juliette (b. Jeanne Françoise Julie Adélaide Bernard)(Fr. society; 1777-1849)
Recife, Brazil
Recklinghausen, Germany
Reconstruction (US hist.; 1865-77)
Record-A-Call™
Record A Call (US bus.)
Record, Bergen County (NJ newspaper)
Record, Congressional (US Congress proceedings)
Record, Hackensack (NJ newspaper)
Record, Middletown (NY newspaper)
Record, York (PA newspaper)
Red Angus cattle
Red Army (USSR army until 1946)
Red (Arnold) Auerbach (basketball; 1917-)
Red Badge of Courage, The (Stephen Crane novel)
Red (Walter) Barber (ent.; 1908-92)
Red Bluff, CA
Red Buttons (ent.; 1919-)
Red Carpet™
Red Carpet Real Estate Services, Inc.
Red China (People's Republic of China)
Red Cloud, Chief (Sioux Indians; 1822-1909)
Red Crescent (functioning as Red Cross in Muslim countries)
Red Cross (internat'l relief agcy.; est. 1864)
Red Cross, American National (US relief agcy.; est. 1881)
Red Delicious (apple)
Red Foley (ent.; 1910-68)
Red Garland (US jazz; 1923-84)
Red (Harold) Grange (football; 1903-91)
Red (Charles Roger) Grooms (US artist; 1937-)
Red Hot Chili Peppers (pop music)
Red Jacket (Sagoyewatha)(Seneca Indian leader; c1756-1830)
Red (Leonard Patrick) Kelly (hockey; 1927-)
Red Light Bandit (Caryl Chessman)(US rapist; ?-1960)
Red Mass (rel., Catholic blessing for legal profession)
Red Nichols (US jazz; 1905-65)
Red No. 2 (dye banned by FDA as carcinogenic)
Red Norvo (US jazz; 1908-)
Red Ridinghood, Little (fairy tale)
Red River (of the North)(ND/MN/Can.)

Red River (S US)
Red River (SE Asia)
Red River Army Depot (TX)
Red River Rebellion (Can. hist.; 1869-70)
Red River Settlement (Can.)
Red Sea (NE Afr/SW Asia)
Red (Richard) Skelton (ent.; 1913-)
Red Sox, Boston (baseball team)
red Windsor (cheese)
Red Wing (Tantangamini)(Sioux leader; c1750-
c1825)
Red Wings, Detroit (hockey team)
Redbook (mag.)
Redd Foxx (ent.; 1922-91)
Reddi-wip™
Reddi-Wip, Inc.
Redding Products, Inc., Jheri
Redding, CA
Redding, Otis (ent.; 1941-67)
Reddy, Helen (ent.; 1941-)
Redeemer (Jesus Christ)
Redenbacher, Orville (US bus.)
Redenbacher™, Orville (popcorn)
Redfield, Robert (US anthrop.; 1897-1958)
Redford, (Charles) Robert (ent.; 1937-)
Redgrave, Lynn (ent.; 1943-)
Redgrave, Sir Michael (Scudamore)(ent.; 1908-
85)
Redgrave, Vanessa (ent.; 1937-)
Redha Malek (PM, Algeria)
Redken™ (hair care)
Redken Laboratories, Inc.
Redlands, CA
Redman, Don (US jazz; 1900-64)
Redmond, WA
Redon, Odilon (Fr. artist; 1840-1916)
Redondo Beach, CA
Redoubt, Mount (active volcano, AK)
Reds, Cincinnati (baseball team)
Redskins, Washington (football team)
Redstone 3, Mercury- (also Liberty Bell 7)(1st
US crewed space flight; May 5, 1961)
Redstone, Mercury- (US crewed space flights)
Redwood City, CA
Redwood National Park (CA)
Reebok™
Reebok International, Ltd.
Reed & Barton™
Reed & Barton Silversmiths (US bus.)
Reed Army Medical Center, Walter (DC)
Reed Show, The Donna (TV show)
Reed Smoot (US pol.; 1862-1941)
Reed, Andre (football; 1964-)
Reed, Sir Carol (Br. ent.; 1906-76)
Reed, Donna (ent.; 1921-86)
Reed, Ishmael (US writer; 1938-)
Reed, Jerry (ent.; 1937-)
Reed, Lou (ent.; 1942-)

Reed, Oliver (ent.; 1938-)
Reed, Rex (ent.; 1938-)
Reed, Robert (ent.; 1932-92)
Reed, Dr. Walter (US phys.; 1851-1902)
Reed, Willis (basketball; 1942-)
Reese Air Force Base, TX
Reese Finer Foods (US bus.)
Reese, Della (ent.; 1931-)
Reese, Pee Wee (Harold)(baseball; 1919-)
Reese's Peanut Butter Puffs™
Reese's Peanut Butter Cups™
Reese's Pieces™
Reeve, Christopher (ent.; 1952-)
Reeves, George (ent.; 1914-59)
Reeves, Jim (ent.)
Reeves, Keanu (ent.)
Reformation (also Protestant Reformation)(Eur.
rel./hist.; 16th c.)
Reformation Sunday (rel.)
Reformation, Catholic (also Counter
Reformation)(Eur. rel./hist.; 16th-17th c.)
Reformed Church in America
Regel's tripterygium (plant)
Régence style (Fr. furn.; early 18th c.)
Regency style (Br. arch./furn.; early 19th c.)
Regensburg, Germany
Regent's Park (London)
Regents of the University of California vs. Bakke
(US law; 1978)
Reggie Jackson (baseball; 1946-)
Reggie Lewis (basketball; 1966-93)
Reggio de Calabria, Italy
Reggio Nell'emilia, Italy
Regina Resnik (ent.; 1924-)
Regina, Saskatchewan, Canada
Reginald Denny (US news)
Reginald Denny (ent.; 1891-1967)
Reginald Gardiner
Reginald Marsh (US artist; 1898-1954)
Reginald Palmer (gov-gen., Grenada
Regis & Kathie Lee (TV show)
Regis Philbin (ent.)
Regis Toomey
Register-Guard, Eugene (OR newspaper)
Register Star, Rockford (IL newspaper)
Register, Des Moines (IA newspaper)
Register, Mobile (AL newspaper)
Register, New Haven (CT newspaper)
Register, Orange County (CA newspaper)
Regnier de Graaf (Dutch phys.; 1641-73)
Regular Army (US army maintained in both
peace and war)
Rehnquist, William H(ubbs)(US jurist; 1924-)
Rehoboam (king, Judah; 1st c. BC)
Rehoboth (Gebeit), Namibia
Rehoboth Beach, DE
Reich, First (Holy Roman Empire; 962-1806)
Reich, Robert (US Secy./Labor; 1946-)

Reich, Second (Ger. empire; 1871-1918)
Reich, Third (Nazi Germany; 1933-45)
Reich, Wilhelm (Aus. phys.; 1897-1957)
Reichstag (pre-WWII Ger. parliament)
Reichstag Fire (Ger. parliament bldg; 2/27/33)
Reid, Daphne Maxwell
Reid, Harry M. (US cong.; 1922-)
Reid, Tim (ent.; 1944-)
Reign of Terror (Fr. hist.; 1793-94)
Reiki (med.)
Reilly, Charles Nelson (ent.; 1931-)
Reims Cathedral (also Rheims)
Reims, France (also Rheims)
Reindeer Lake (W Can.)
Reiner, Carl (ent.; 1922-)
Reiner, Rob (ent.; 1945-)
Reinhardt, Django (US jazz; 1910-53)
Reinhardt, Max (b. Max Goldmann)(ent.; 1873-
    1943)
Reinhold Co., Inc., Van Nostrand
Reinhold Niebuhr (US rel.; 1892-1971)
Reinhold, Judge (ent.; 1956-)
Reinking, Ann (ent.; 1950-)
Reistertown, MD
Rejang (lang.)
Relafen™ (med.)
Religious Society of Friends (also Quakers,
    Society of Friends)(rel.)
REM (rapid eye movement)
Remarque, Erich Maria (Ger./US writer; 1898-
    1970)
Re/Max International, Inc.
Rembrandt™ (health)
Rembrandt Peale (US artist; 1778-1860)
Rembrandt (Harmenszoon) van Rijn (Dutch
    artist; 1606-69)
Remember the Maine, to hell with Spain" (Sp.-
    Amer. War; 1898)(put in quotes)
Remick, Lee (ent.; 1935-91)
Remington™
Remington Arms Co.
Remington Rand
Remington, Eliphalet (US inv./bus.; 1793-1861)
Remington, Frederic (US artist; 1861-1909)
Remington, Philo (US inv./bus.; 1816-89)
Remscheid, Germany
Remus, Romulus & (myth. twins raised by wolf/
    founded Rome)
Remus, Uncle (fict. narrator, J.C. Harris fables)
Remy Martin™ (cognac)
Remy Martin Amerique, Inc.
Renaissance (Eur. hist.; 1300-1600)
Renaissance (type style)
Renaissance art/arch. (Eur.; 1400-1600)
Renaissance man/woman
Renaldo Nehemiah (track; 1959-)
Renata Tebaldi (It. soprano; 1922-)
Renault™ (auto.)

Renault, Inc.
Rene Auberjonois (ent.; 1940-)
Rene Auguste Chouteau (US pioneer/fur trader;
    1749-1829)
Rene Descartes (Fr. phil.; 1596-1650)
Rene Enriquez (ent.; 1932-90)
Réne Felber (ex-pres., Switz.)
Rene Lalique (Fr. designer; 1860-1945)
Rene Lévesque (ex-premier, Quebec, Can.;
    1922-87)
Rene Magritte (Belgian artist; 1898-1967)
Rene, France-Albert (pres., Seychelles; 1935-)
Renfrew, Scotland
Rennes, France
Reno Gazette Journal (NV newspaper)
Reno, Janet (US atty. gen.; 1938-)
Reno, NV
Reno, Shaw v. (US law; 1993)
Renoir, Jean (Fr. ent./writer; 1894-1979)
Renoir, Pierre Auguste (Fr. artist; 1841-1919)
Rent-A-Wreck™
Rent-A-Wreck of America, Inc.
Renta, Ltd., Oscar de la
Renta, Oscar de la (US designer; 1932-)
Renuzit™
Renuzit Home Products, Inc.
Renwick, James, Jr. (US arch.; 1818-95)
REO Motor Car Co.
REO Speedwagon (pop music)
Replens™ (med.)
Repository, Canton (OH newspaper)
Republic Day (India)
Republic, Arizona (AZ newspaper)
Republic, Phoenix (AZ newspaper)
Republic, The (by Plato)
Republic, Third (Fr.; 1870-1940)
Republican Party (US pol.)
Republican River NE)
Republican, Springfield (MA newspaper)
Requiem (also Requiem Mass)(rel.)
Resch, Glenn "Chico" (hockey; 1948-)
Rescue 911 (TV show)
Reserve Officers Training Corps (ROTC)(US
    mil./educ.)
Resht, Iran
Resistencia, Argentina
Resnik, Regina (ent.; 1924-)
Resolve™ (cleaner)
Respect for the Aged Day (Jap.)
Respighi, Ottorino (It. comp.; 1879-1936)
Reston, James (Barrett)(US jour.; 1909-)
Reston, VA
Restoration (Br. hist.; 1660)
Restoration comedy (Br. theater; 1660+)
Restoril™ (med.)
Resurrection (rel.)
Retin-A™ (med.)
Retton, Mary Lou (US gymnast; 1968-)

Return of the Jedi (film)
Return of the Pink Panther, The (film; 1975)
Reuben Lucius "Rube" Goldberg (US cartoonist, *Boob McNutt*; 1883-1970)
Reuter, Paul Julius, Baron von (Ger., founded news agcy.; 1816-99)
Reuters (Br. news org.; est. 1851)
Reuther, Walter P(hilip)(US labor leader; 1907-70)
Revco, Inc.
Revelation (rel.)
Revenge of Frankenstein, The (film; 1958)
Revenge of the Pink Panther, The (film; 1978)
Revere and the Raiders, Paul (pop music)
Revere, MA
Revere, Paul (Amer. patriot/silversmith; 1735-1818)
Reverence, Your (title)
Reverend (rel. title)
Revereware™
Revere Ware, Inc.
Review-Journal, Las Vegas (NV newspaper)
Review of Books, the New York
Revised Standard Version (of the Bible)
Revised Version (of the Bible)
Revlon™
Revlon, Inc.
Revolution, American (also Revolutionary War; 1776-83)
Revolution, English (Eng. hist.; 1640-60)
Revolution, French (Fr. hist.; 1789-99)
Revolution, Russian (Rus. hist.; 1917)
Revolutionary Party, Socialist (Russian Populist Party; founded 1901)
Rex (cat)
Rex (Reginald Carey) Harrison (ent.; 1908-90)
Rex Reed (ent.; 1938-)
Rex Stout (US writer; 1886-1975)
Reye's syndrome (med.)
Reykjavík, Iceland
Reynard the Fox (medieval epic)
Reynaud, Paul (ex-PM, Fr.; 1878-1966)
Reynolds Aluminum Supply Co.
Reynolds™ foil
Reynolds Foods, Inc., R. J. (RJR Foods, Inc.)
Reynolds Metals Co.
Reynolds™ Plastic Wrap
Reynolds Wrap™
Reynolds Price (US writer; 1933-)
Reynolds Tobacco Co., R. J.)
Reynolds, Albert (PM, Ir.; 1932-)
Reynolds, Burt (ent.; 1936-)
Reynolds, Butch (Harry)(track; 1964-)
Reynolds, Debbie (ent.; 1932-)
Reynolds, Frank (US jour.; 1923-83)
Reynolds, Inc., Dean Witter
Reynolds, Sir Joshua (Br. artist; 1723-92)
Reynosa, Mexico

Rezso Nyers (Hung. pol.; 1923-)
RFD (rural free delivery)
Rh (chem. sym., rhodium)
Rh factor (also Rhesus factor)(med.)
Rh-negative (Rh-)(med.)
Rh-positive (Rh+)(med.)
Rhadamanthus (myth.)
Rhapsody in Blue (by G. Gershwin)
Rhea (Saturn moon; myth.)
Rhea Perlman (ent.; 1948-)
Rhee, Syngman (ex-pres., SKorea; 1875-1965)
Rheem Manufacturing Co.
Rheem™ water heater
Rheims Cathedral (also Reims)
Rheims, France (also Reims)
Rhesus factor (also Rh factor)(med.)
Rhett Butler (fict. chara., *Gone With the Wind*)
Rhiannon (myth.)
Rhine (wine)
Rhine River (Eur.)
Rhine, Joseph Banks (US psych.; 1895-1980)
Rhineland (region, Ger,)
Rhineland-Palatinate (state, Ger.)
R. H. Macy & Co., Inc.
Rhoda (TV show)
Rhode Island (RI)
Rhode Island bent (flowering plant, grass)
Rhode Island Red (chicken)
Rhode Island White (chicken)
Rhodes (Gr. island)
Rhodes scholar/scholarship
Rhodes, Apollonius of (Gk. poet; c220-180 BC)
Rhodes, Cecil (John)(Br./SAfr. pol., est. Rhodes scholarships; 1853-1902)
Rhodes, Colossus of (statue of Apollo, fell in 224 BC)
Rhodes, Greece
Rhodesia, Northern (now Zambia)
Rhodesia, Southern (now Zimbabwe)
Rhodesian man (extinct Pleistocene human)
Rhodesian ridgeback (also African lion hound)(dog)
Rhonda Fleming (ent.; 1923-)
Rhondda, Wales
Rhone (wine)
Rhône-Alpes (region, Fr.)
Rhone-Poulenc Rorer Consumer Pharmaceuticals (US bus.)
Rhône River (S Eur.)
Rhue, Madlyn (ent.; 1934-)
RI (Rhode Island)
Ribbentrop, Joachim von (Ger. Nazi pol.; 1893-1946)
Ribeirão Preto, Brazil
Ric Ocasek (ent.)
Ricardo Montalban (ent.; 1920)
Ricardo, David (Br. econ.; 1772-1823)
Riccardo Muti (It. cond.; 1941-)

Riccardo Zandonai (It. comp.; 1883-1944)
Ricci Jewelry, Nina (US bus.)
Ricci™, Nina
Rice-A-Roni™
Rice Krispies™ (cereal)
Rice University (Houston, TX)
Rice, Anne (US writer)
Rice, Donna (US news; 1958-)
Rice, Elmer (Leopold)(US writer; 1892-1967)
Rice, Jerry (football; 1962-)
Rice, Jim (baseball; 1953-)
Rich Co., Louis
Rich "Goose" Gossage (baseball; 1951-)
Rich Little (ent.; 1938-)
Rich, Buddy (US jazz; 1917-87)
Rich, Charlie (ent.; 1932-)
Rich, Frank
Rich, Ritchie (cartoon chara.)
Richard Adler (US comp.; 1921-)
Richard A. Gephardt (US cong.; 1941-)
Richard Aldington (Br. poet; 1892-1962)
Richard Anderson (ent.; 1926-)
Richard Arkwright, Sir (Br. inv.; 1732-92)
Richard Arlen (ent.; 1900-76)
Richard Attenborough, Sir (ent.; 1923-)
Richard Avedon (US photo.; 1923-)
Richard A. Whiting (US comp.; 1891-1938)
Richard Bach (US writer)
Richard Basehart (ent.; 1914-84)
Richard B. Cheney (US pol.; 1941-)
Richard Benjamin (ent.; 1938-)
Richard Boone (ent.; 1917-81)
Richard B(rinsley) Sheridan (Ir. writer/pol.;
    1751-1816)
Richard B. Shull (ent.; 1929-)
Richard Burbage (Br. Shakespearean actor;
    1567-1619)
Richard Burton (b. Richard Walter
    Jenkins)(ent.; 1925-84)
Richard "Dick" Button (figure skating, ent.;
    1929-)
Richard Chamberlain (ent.; 1935-)
Richard Conte (ent.; 1911-75)
Richard Craig Shelby (US cong.; 1934-)
Richard Crenna (ent.; 1926-)
Richard Dawson (ent.; 1932-)
Richard Dean Anderson (ent.; 1953-)
Richard Diebenkorn (US artist; 1922-93)
Richard D'Oyly Carte (Br. opera; 1844-1901)
Richard Dreyfuss (ent.; 1947-)
Richard Dysart (ent.; 1929-)
Richard E. Byrd, Adm. (US expl.; 1888-1957)
Richard (Phillips) Feynman (US physt.; 1918-
    88)
Richard F. Gordon, Jr. (astro.)
Richard Francis Burton, Sir (Br. expl.; 1821-90)
Richard (Jordan) Gatling (US inv.; 1818-1903)
Richard Gere (ent.; 1949-)

Richard G(reen) Lugar (US cong.; 1932-)
Richard Grenville (or Greynville), Sir (Br. mil.;
    1541-91)
Richard Harris (ent.; 1933-)
Richard H. Bryan (US cong.; 1937-)
Richard (McGarrah) Helms (US, CIA; 1913-)
Richard Henry Tawney (Br. hist.; 1880-1962)
Richard Howe, Earl (Br. mil.; 1726-99)
Richard I (the Lion-Hearted or Coeur de
    Lion)(king, Eng.; 1157-99)
Richard II (king, Eng.; 1367-1400)
Richard III (king, Eng.; 1452-85)
Richard Jaeckel (ent.; 1926-)
Richard Jordan (ent.; 1938-)
Richard Joseph Daley (ex-mayor, Chicago;
    1902-76)
Richard Kiley (ent.; 1922-)
Richard King (US rancher; 1825-85)
Richard LaClede Stockton (tennis; 1951-)
Richard Leakey (Br. archaeol..; 1944-)
Richard Le Gallienne (US/Br. writer; 1866-
    1947)
Richard Lewis (ent.; 1947-)
Richard Long (ent.; 1927-77)
Richard Lovelace (Br. poet; 1618-58)
Richard Marx
Richard M. Daley (Chicago mayor; 1942-)
Richard Meier (US arch.; 1934-)
Richard Milhous Nixon (37th US pres.; 1913-
    1994)
Richard M(entor) Johnson (ex-US VP; 1780-
    1850)
Richard Moll (ent.; 1943-)
Richard Mulligan (ent.; 1932-)
Richard (Joseph) Neutra (US arch.; 1892-1970)
Richard Outcault (US cartoonist, *Buster Brown*;
    1863-1928)
Richard (Lee) Petty (auto racing; 1937-)
Richard Plantagenet (Duke of York)(Br. mil.;
    1411-60)
Richard Pryor (ent.; 1940-)
Richard Riordan (Los Angeles mayor)
Richard (Charles) Rodgers (US comp.; 1902-79)
Richard "Dick" Scobee, (Francis)(astro.,
    Challenger; 1939-86)
Richard Simmons (ent.; 1948-)
Richard Speck (US mass murderer; 1942-91)
Richard Stahl (ent.; 1932-)
Richard Steele (Br. writer; 1672-1729)
Richard Stern (US writer; 1928-)
Richard (Georg) Strauss (Ger. comp./cond.;
    1864-1949)
Richard the Lion-Hearted (or Coeur de Lion,
    Richard I)(king, Eng.; 1157-99)
Richard Thomas (ent.; 1951-)
Richard Todd (ent.; 1919-)
Richard Upjohn (US arch.; 1802-78)
Richard von Krafft-Ebing, Baron (Ger. phys.;

1840-1902)
Richard von Weizsacker (pres., Ger.)
Richard (Wilhelm) Wagner (Ger. comp.; 1813-83)
Richard Widmark (ent.; 1914-)
Richard W. Riley (US Secy./Education; 1933-)
Richard W. Sears (US bus.; 1863-1914)
Richard, Keith (ent.; 1943-)
Richard, Little (b. Richard Penniman)(ent.; 1932-)
Richard, Maurice (Joseph Henri)("the Rocket")(hockey; 1921-)
Richards, Ann (TX gov.; 1933-)
Richards-Gebaur Air Force Base (MO)
Richardson-Vicks USA (US bus.)
Richardson, Bill (William)(US cong.; 1947-)
Richardson, Fort (AK)(mil.)
Richardson, Samuel (Br. writer; 1689-1761)
Richardson, TX
Richelieu, Armand Jean du Plessis, Duc de (Fr. rel.[cardinal]/pol.; 1585-1642)
Richey, Port (FL)
Richie Rich (cartoon chara.)
Richie, Lionel (ent.; 1950-)
Richland, WA
Richmond Times-Dispatch (VA newspaper)
Richmond, British Columbia, Canada
Richmond, CA, IN, KY, VA
Richmond, Mitch (basketball; 1965-)
Richter scale (measures magnitude of earthquake)
Richter, Charles Francis (US seismol.; 1900-85)
Rick (Richard) Barry (basketball; 1944-)
Rick James (ent.)
Rick (Richard Lionel) Martin (hockey; 1951-)
Rick Moranis (ent.; 1953-)
Rick(y) Nelson (ent.; 1940-85)
Rick Schroder (ent.; 1970-)
Rick Springfield (ent.; 1949-)
Rickenbacker Air Force Base (OH)
Rickenbacker, Eddie (Edward Vernon), Capt. (US aviator; 1890-1973)
Rickey Bell (football; 1949-84)
Rickey, (Wesley) Branch (baseball; 1881-1965)
Ricki Lake
Rickles, Don (ent.; 1926-)
Rickover, Hyman George, Adm. (US mil./A-bomb; 1900-86)
Ricoh™ copier
Ricoh Corp.
Ridder, Inc., Knight-
Riddle, Nelson (US cond.; 1921-85)
Ride, Sally K(irsten)(astro.; 1952-)
Ridge Vineyards, Inc.
Ridgemont High, Fast Times at (film; 1982)
Ridgway, Matthew Bunker (US gen.; 1895-93)
Ridley Scott (ent.; 1939-)
Riegert, Peter (ent.; 1947-)

Riegle, Donald W., Jr. (US cong.; 1938-)
Riemann integral/sphere/surface
Riemann, (Georg Friedrich) Bernhard (Ger. math.; 1826-66)
Riemannian geometry
Riesling (grape, wine)
Riesling, Johannisberg (wine)
Riesman, David (US sociol./writer; 1909-)
Riessen, Martin (tennis; 1941-)
Riff (lang./people)
Rifle Association of America, National (NRA)
Rifleman (TV show)
Rift Valley, (Great)(SW Asia/SE Afr.)
Riga, Latvia
Rigby, Cathy (gymnast)
Rigel (also Beta Orionis)(astron.)
Rigel Kentaurus (also Alpha Centauri)(astron.)
Rigg, Diana (ent.; 1938-)
Riggs, Bobby (tennis)
Right Guard™ (anti-perspirant)
Right Reverend (rel., form of address)
Right, Miss/Ms. (slang)
Right, Mr. (slang)
Right, Petition of (Br. hist.; 1628)
Righteous Brothers (pop music)
Rigney, William (baseball; 1918-)
Rigoletto (Verdi opera)
Rig-Veda (rel.)
Riis, Jacob (August)(US reformer; 1849-1914)
Rijeka, Croatia
Rijks Museum (also Ryks)(Amsterdam)
Rijn, Rembrandt (Harmenszoon) van (Dutch artist; 1606-69)
Riker, Commander William (fict. chara., *Star Trek*)
Riley, Fort, KS (mil.)
Riley, James Whitcomb (US poet; 1849-1916)
Riley, Jeannie C. (ent.; 1945-)
Riley, Pat (basketball; 1945-)
Riley, Richard W. (US Secy./Education; 1933-)
Riley, The Life of (TV show, film)
Rilke, Rainer Maria (Aus. poet; 1875-1926)
Rimbaud, (Jean Nicolas) Arthur (Fr. poet; 1854-91)
Rimini, Italy
Rimsky-Korsakov, Nicolay (Andreyevich)(Rus. comp.; 1844-1908)
Rin Tin Tin (dog)
Rin Tin Tin (TV show)
Rinehart, Mary Roberts (US writer; 1876-1958)
Ring(gold Wilmer) Lardner (US writer; 1885-1933)
Ring Nebula (astron.)
Ring of the Nibelung, The (Richard Wagner tetralogy)
Ringadoo, Veerasamy (Mauritian pol.)
Ringer's solution
Ringling Brothers and Barnum & Bailey Circus

Ringling Brothers Circus
Ringling, Charles (US circus; 1863-1926)
Ringo Starr (aka Richard Starkey)(ent.; 1940-)
Ringwald, Molly (ent.; 1968-)
Rio de Janeiro, Brazil (also Rio)
Rio de la Plata (also River Plate)(SAmer.)
Rio Grande River (also Río Bravo)(CO to Mex.)
Rio Grande, Brazil
Rio Rancho, NM
Riobamba, Ecuador
Rioja (wine)
Riopelle, Jean Paul (Can. artist; 1923-)
Riordan, Richard (Los Angeles mayor)
Riot Act (English law; 1715)
RIP (rest in peace)
Rip Torn (ent.; 1931-)
Rip Van Winkle (by W. Irving)
Ripken, Cal, Jr. (baseball; 1960-)
Ripley, Robert LeRoy (US cartoonist; 1894-?)
Ripley's Believe It or Not!
Ripper, Jack the (London murderer; 1888)
Risë Stevens (ent.; 1913-)
Rit™ (dye)
Rita Coolidge (ent.; 1945-)
Rita Dove (US poet
Rita Hayworth (ent.; 1918-87)
Rita Moreno (ent.; 1931-)
Ritalin™ (med.)
Ritchard, Cyril (ent.; 1898-1977)
Ritchie Valens (ent.)
Ritchie, Fort, MD (mil.)
RITE™ (text entry system)
Rite Aid Corp.
Rittenhouse, David (US astron./inv.; 1732-96)
Ritter, John (ent.; 1948-)
Ritter, Tex (Woodward Maurice)(ent.; 1907-74)
Ritter, Thelma (ent.; 1905-69)
Ritz-Carlton
Ritz Crackers™
Rive Gauche (also Left Bank)(Paris)
River Jordan (Pak.)
River Kwai, The Bridge on the (film; 1957)
River Phoenix (ent.; 1970-93)
River Styx (myth., underworld river)
Rivera, Chita (ent.; 1933-)
Rivera, Diego (Mex. artist; 1886-1957)
Rivera, (José) Fructuoso (ex-pres., Uruguay; 1784-1854)
Rivera, Geraldo (ent.; 1943-)
Rivera, José de (US sculptor; 1904-85)
Rivera, Uruguay
Rivers, Joan (ent.; 1933-)
Rivers, Johnny (ent.)
Rivers, Larry (b. Vitzroch Loiza Grossberg)(US artist; 1923-)
Riverside Church (NYC)
Riverside Press-Enterprise (CA newspaper)
Riverside, CA

Riveter, Rosie the (WWII symbol)
Riviera (Fr./It. Mediterranean coast)
Riviera Beach, FL
Riviera™, Buick (auto.)
Riyadh, Saudi Arabia
Riza Pahlavi (shah, Iran; 1877-1944)
Riza Pahlavi, Muhammad (shah, Iran; 1919-80)
Rizzo, Frank (ex-mayor, Phila.; 1921-91)
Rizzoli Bookstore
Rizzuto, Phil (baseball; 1918-)
R. James Woolsey (Director/CIA; 1941-)
R. J. Reynolds Foods, Inc. (RJR Foods, Inc.)
R. J. Reynolds Tobacco Co.
RJR Foods, Inc. (R. J. Reynolds Foods, Inc.)
RJR Nabisco (US bus.)
RKO Tape Corp.
RMA (Royal Military Academy)
RMC (Royal Military College)
RMS (Royal Mail Service, Royal Mail Ship)
RN (registered nurse, Royal Navy)
Rn (chem. sym. radon)
RNA (ribonucleic acid)
RNR (Royal Naval Reserve)
Roach Motel™
Roach, Hal (ent.; 1892-92)
Roach, Max (US jazz; 1925-)
Road & Track (mag.)
Road Runner, Plymouth™
Road to Morocco (film; 1942)
Road to Singapore (film; 1940)
Road to Utopia (film; 1946)
Road to Zanzibar (film; 1941)
Road Town, Tortola, British Virgin Islands
Roald Dahl (Br./US writer; 1916-90)
Roanoke Island, NC
Roanoke River (SE US)
Roanoke Times & World-News (VA newspaper)
Roanoke, VA
Roaring Twenties (also Roaring '20s)
Rob Lowe (ent.; 1964-)
Rob Morrow (ent.; 1962-)
Rob Reiner (ent.; 1945-)
Rob Roy (b. Robert MacGregor)(Scot. outlaw; 1671-1734)
Rob Roy (cocktail)
Rob Roy (W. Scott novel)
Robards, Jason, Jr. (ent.; 1922-)
Robb, Charles S. (US cong.; 1939-)
Robb, Lynda Bird Johnson (daughter of ex-US pres.; 1944-)
Robbe-Grillet, Alain (Fr. writer; 1922-)
Robbia, Andrea della (It. sculptor; 1437-1528)
Robbia, Luca della (It. artist; 1400-82)
Robbie Knievel
Robbin, Cock
Robbins, Harold (US writer; 1916-)
Robbins, Jerome (US ballet; 1918-)
Robbins, Marty (ent.; 1925-82)

Robbins, Tim (ent.; 1958-)
Robby Benson (ent.; 1955-)
Robert A(nson) Heinlein (US writer, sci-fi; 1907-88)
Robert Alda (ent.; 1914-86)
Robert Alexander Kennedy Runcie (Br. rel.; 1921-)
Robert Altman (ent.; 1925-)
Robert Altman (US atty.)
Robert Altman (US banker)
Robert A(ndrews) Millikan (US physt.; 1868-1953)
Robert Armbruster
Robert A(lphonso) Taft (US pol.; 1889-1953)
Robert Baden-Powell, Sir (Br. gen., founded Boy Scouts; 1857-1941)
Robert Benchley (US writer/humorist; 1889-1945)
Robert Bennett (US cong.; 1933-)
Robert Blake (ent.; 1933-)
Robert Blake, Adm. (Br. mil.; 1599-1657)
Robert Bosch Corp.
Robert Boyle (Br. physt./chem.; 1627-91)
Robert "Bobby" Breen (ent.)
Robert Brown (Scot. botanist; 1773-1858)
Robert Browning (Br. poet, husband of Elizabeth; 1812-89)
Robert Burns (Scot. poet; 1759-96)
Robert Carlyle Byrd (US cong.; 1917-)
Robert Casey (PA gov.; 1932-)
Robert Castlereagh (Br. pol.; 1769-1822)
Robert Cavelier La Salle, (René)(aka Sieur de La Salle)(Fr. expl.; 1643-87)
Robert Charles Gallo (US scien.; 1937-)
Robert Clive (Br. leader in India; 1725-74)
Robert Cochran (skiing; 1951-)
Robert Conrad (ent.; 1935-)
Robert Crichton (US writer; 1925-93)
Robert Crumb (cartoonist, underground; 1943-)
Robert C. Smith (US cong.; 1941-)
Robert Culp (ent.; 1930-)
Robert Cummings (ent.; 1908-90)
Robert De Niro (ent.; 1943-)
Robert Devereux (Earl of Essex)(Br. mil./pol.; 1566-1601)
Roberto DeVicenzo (golf; 1923-)
Robert "Bob" Dole (US cong.; 1923-)
Robert Downey, Jr. (ent.; 1965-)
Roberto Duran (boxing; 1951-)
Robert Duvall (ent.; 1931-)
Robert E(dward) Lee (US confed. gen.; 1807-70)
Robert Englund (ent.; 1948-)
Robert E(dwin) Peary (US Arctic expl.; 1856-1920)
Robert E. Rubin (Chair/Nat'l Econ Council; 1938-)
Robert Evans (ent.; 1930-)
Robert F(rancis) Kennedy (US pol.; 1925-68)

Robert Flaherty (ent.; 1884-1951)
Robert Foxworth (ent.; 1941-)
Robert (Lee) Frost (US poet; 1874-1963)
Robert Fulton (US gunsmith/artist/eng./inv. steamship; 1745-1815)
Robert F(erdinand) Wagner, Jr. (ex-mayor; NYC; 1910-1991)
Robert F(erdinand) Wagner, Sr. (US pol.; 1877-1953)
Robert Ginty (ent.; 1948-)
Robert Gordon Menzies (ex-PM, Austl.; 1894-1978)
Robert Goulet (ent.; 1933-)
Robert "Bob" Graham (US cong.; 1936-)
Robert (Ranke) Graves (Br. writer/hist.; 1895-1985)
Robert Guillaume (ent.; 1937-)
Robert Guiscard (Robert de Hauteville)(Norman /It. mil.; c1015-85)
Robert Hayes (ent.; 1947-)
Robert H. Goddard (US physt., father of modern rocketry; 1882-1945)
Robert H. Michel (US pol.; 1923-)
Robert Hooke (Br. physt./inv.; 1635-1703)
Robert "Bobby" James Fischer (US chess master; 1943-)
Robert "Bob" James Lee Hawke (ex-PM, Austl.; 1929-)
Robert James Waller (US writer
Robert Jemison Van de Graaff (US physt.; 1901-67)
Robert Joffrey (Abdullah Jaffa Bey Khan)(US ballet; 1930-88)
Robert John le Mesurier McClure, Sir (Br. expl.; 1807-73)
Robert Keenan Winery (US bus.)
Robert Klein (ent.; 1942-)
Robert Krups North America (US bus.)
Robert Lansing (ent.; 1928-)
Robert Lansing (US atty./pol.; 1864-1928)
Robert L. Crippen (astro.; 1937-)
Robert LeRoy Ripley (US cartoonist; 1894-?)
Robert Livingston (US pol.; 1654-1728)
Robert Loggia (ent.; 1930-)
Robert Louis (Balfour) Stevenson (Scot. writer; 1850-94)
Robert Lowell (US poet; 1917-77)
Robert Ludlum (US writer; 1927-)
Robert Malval (Haitian pol.)
Robert Mapplethorpe (US photo.; 1946-89)
Robert Marion La Follette (ex-gov., WI; 1855-1925)
Robert Marion La Follette, Jr. (US pol./publ., WI; 1895-1953)
Robert "Bob" Martinez (US pol.; 1934-)
Robert Maxwell, (Ian)(b. Jan Ludvik Hock)(Czech./Br. publ.; 1923-91)
Robert (Strange) McNamara (US pol.; 1916-)

Robert Merrill (ent.; 1919-)
Robert M. Gates (CIA Director; 1943-)
Robert "Bob" Miller (NV gov.; 1945-)
Robert Mills (US arch.; 1781-1855)
Robert Mitchum (ent.; 1917-)
Robert Mondavi™
Robert Mondavi Winery (US bus.)
Robert Montgomery (ent.; 1904-81)
Robert Morley (Br. ent.; 1908-92)
Robert Morris (US pol./bus.; 1734-1806)
Robert Morris Page (US physt.; 1903-92)
Robert Morse (ent.; 1931-)
Robert Moses "Lefty" Grove (baseball; 1900-75)
Robert (Burns) Motherwell (US artist; 1915-91)
Robert (Gabriel) Mugabe (pres., Zimbabwe;
    1925-)
Robert (David) Muldoon, Sir (ex-PM, NewZeal.;
    1921-92)
Robert N. Noyce (US inv.; 1927-89)
Robert of Courtenay (emp., Constantinople;
    13th c.)
Robert Oppenheimer, J(ulius)(US physt.,
    atomic bomb; 1904-67)
Robert Owen (Br. phil./reformer; 1771-1858)
Robert Peel, Sir (ex-PM, Br.; 1788-1850)
Robert Penn Warren (US writer; 1905-89)
Robert Plant (ent.; 1947-)
Robert Preston (ent.; 1918-87)
Robert Prosky (ent.; 1930-)
Robert Q. Lewis (ent.; 1920-91)
Robert Rauschenberg (US artist; 1925-)
Robert Redfield (US anthrop.; 1897-1958)
Robert Redford (Charles)(ent.; 1937-)
Robert Reed (ent.; 1932-1992)
Robert Reich (US Secy./Labor; 1946-)
Robert Richard Torrens, Sir (Br. pol. in Austl.;
    1814-84)
Robert R. Livingston (US pol.; 1746-1813)
Robert Rodale (US publ./organic gardening;
    1930-90)
Robert Ryan (ent.; 1909-73)
Robert Schuller (US rel.; 1926-)
Robert Schuman (Fr. 1886-1963)
Robert (Alexander) Schumann (Ger. comp.;
    1810-56)
Robert Shapiro (US atty.)
Robert Shaw (ent.; 1927-78)
Robert (Emmet) Sherwood (US writer; 1896-
    1955)
Robert S. Strauss (US dipl.; 1918-)
Robert Stack (ent.; 1919-)
Robert Stirling (Scot. rel./inv.; 1790-1878)
Robert Stone (US writer; 1937-)
Robert Taylor (ent.; 1911-69)
Robert Todd Lincoln (US atty., A. Lincoln's son;
    1843-1926)
Robert Townsend (ent.; 1957-)
Robert Trout

Robert Urich (ent.; 1940-)
Robert Vaughn (ent.; 1932-)
Robert Vesco (US finan./fugitive)
Robert Wagner (ent.; 1930-)
Robert Walden (ent.; 1943-)
Robert Walker (ent.; 1914-51)
Robert Walpole (Earl of Oxford)(Br. pol.; 1676-
    1745)
Robert W. Bunsen (Ger. chem., invented
    Bunsen burner; 1811-99)
Robert William Packwood (US cong.; 1932-)
Robert W(illiam) Service (Can. writer; 1874-
    1958)
Robert Young (ent.; 1907-)
Robert, Henry Martyn (US eng., wrote Robert's
    Rules of Order; 1837-1923)
Roberta Flack (ent.; 1939-)
Roberta Peters (ent.; 1930-)
Roberto Clemente (baseball; 1934-72)
Roberto Rossellini (It. ent.; 1906-77)
Robert's Rules of Order (parliamentary
    procedure; compiled 1876)
Roberts, Barbara (OR gov.; 1936-)
Roberts, Doris (ent.; 1929-)
Roberts, Eric (ent.; 1956-)
Roberts, Julia (ent.; 1967-)
Roberts, Mister (film; 1955)
Roberts, Oral (US rel.; 1918-)
Roberts, Pernell (ent.; 1930-)
Roberts, Tony (ent.; 1939-)
Robertson, Cliff (ent.; 1925-)
Robertson, Dale (ent.; 1923-)
Robertson, Oscar (basketball; 1938-)
Robertson, Pat (Marion Gordon)(US pol./rel.;
    1930-)
Robeson, Paul (ent.; 1898-1976)
Robespierre, Maximilien (François Marie
    Isidore de)(Fr. mil./pol.; 1758-94)
Robin and the Seven Hoods (film; 1964)
Robin Cook (writer)
Robin Givens (ent.; 1964-)
Robin Goodfellow (also Puck, Hobgoblin)(fict.
    chara, *A Midsummer Night's Dream*)
Robin Hood (legendary Eng. hero/outlaw; 13th-
    14th c.)
Robin Hood: Prince of Thieves (film)
Robin Hood's Merry Men
Robin Leach (ent.; 1941-)
Robin Piccone
Robin Strasser (ent.; 1945-)
Robin the Boy Wonder (fict. chara.)
Robin Williams (ent.; 1952-)
Robin, Christopher (fict. chara, *Winnie-the-
    Pooh*)
Robin, Leo (US lyricist; 1900-84)
Robinson and the Miracles, Smokey (pop music)
Robinson Crusoe (D. Defoe novel)
Robinson Jeffers, (John)(US writer; 1887-1962)

Robinson, Arnie (track; 1948-)

Robinson, Bill ("Bojangles")(US tap dancer; 1878-1949)

Robinson, Brooks (baseball; 1937-)

Robinson, Charles (ent.)

Robinson, Charles (US pol.; 1818-94)

Robinson, David (basketball; 1965-)

Robinson, Edward G. (ent.; 1893-1973)

Robinson, Edwin Arlington (US poet; 1869-1935)

Robinson, Frank (baseball; 1935-)

Robinson, Jackie (John Roosevelt)(baseball; 1919-72)

Robinson, James H. (US hist./educ.; 1863-1936)

Robinson, Larry (hockey; 1951-)

Robinson, Mary (pres., Ir.; 1944-)

Robinson, Smokey (William)(US comp.; 1940-)

Robinson, Sugar Ray (b. Walker Smith)(boxing; 1920-89)

Robinson, The Swiss Family (J. Wyss novel)

Robitaille, Luc (hockey; 1966-)

Robitussin™ (med.)

Robocop (film; 1987)

Robusti, Jacopo (aka Tintoretto)(It. artist; 1518-94)

Roche-Bobois (US bus.)

Roche limit (astron.)

Roche, Eugene (ent.; 1928-)

Roche, Kevin (US arch.; 1922-)

Rochefoucauld, François, Duc de La (Fr. writer; 1613-80)

Rochelle salt

"Rochester" Anderson, Eddie (ent.; 1905-77)

Rochester Democrat & Chronicle (NY newspaper)

Rochester Times-Union (NY newspaper)

Rochester, England

Rochester, MN, NH, NY

Rock and Roll Hall of Fame, The

Rock Cornish hen (also Rock Cornish game hen)

Rock Hill, SC

Rock Hudson (b. Roy Scherer, Jr.)(ent.; 1925-85)

Rock Island Arsenal (IL)

Rock Island, IL

Rock of Gibraltar (S coast of Sp.)

Rock Springs, WY

Rockefeller Center (NYC)

Rockefeller Foundation (est. 1913)

Rockefeller University (NYC)

Rockefeller, David (US finan.; 1915-)

Rockefeller, John D(avison)(US bus./finan.; 1839-1937)

Rockefeller, John D(avison), III (US finan.; 1906-78)

Rockefeller, John "Jay" D(avison), IV (US cong.; 1937-)

Rockefeller, John D(avison), Jr. (US bus./finan.; 1874-1960)

Rockefeller, Laurance S(pelman)(US bus./finan.; 1910-)

Rockefeller, Nelson A(ldrich)(ex-US VP; 1908-79)

Rockefeller, oysters

Rockefeller, William (US bus./finan.; 1841-1922)

Rockefeller, Winthrop (ex-gov., AR; 1912-73)

Rockets, Houston (basketball team)

Rockettes, the (ent.)

Rockford Files, The (TV show)

Rockford Register Star (IL newspaper)

Rockford, IL

Rockies, Colorado (baseball team)

Rockne, Knute (Kenneth)(football; 1888-1931)

Rockville, MD

Rockwell International Corp.

Rockwell Corp., North American

Rockwell, Martha (skiing; 1944-)

Rockwell, Norman (US artist; 1894-1978)

Rocky (film; 1976)

Rocky (Rocco Domenico) Colavito (baseball; 1933-)

Rocky Graziano (Thomas Rocco Barbella)(1919-90)

Rocky Horror Picture Show, The (film)

Rocky II (film; 1979)

Rocky III (film; 1982)

Rocky IV (film; 1985)

Rocky Marciano (b. Rocco Francis Marchegiano)(boxing; 1923-69)

Rocky Mount, NC

Rocky Mountain Arsenal (CO)

Rocky Mountain goat (also mountain goat)

Rocky Mountain National Park (CO)

Rocky Mountain News, Denver (CO newspaper)

Rocky Mountain sheep (also bighorn sheep)

Rocky Mountain spotted fever (med.)

Rocky Mountains (also Rockies)(W NAmer.)

Rocky V (film)

Rococo style (art/arch., Eur.; 18th c.)

Rod(ney Cline) Carew (baseball; 1945-)

Rod(rique) Gilbert (hockey; 1941-)

Rod(ney George) Laver (tennis; 1938-)

Rod McKuen (US writer/comp.; 1933-)

Rod Serling (ent.; 1924-75)

Rod Steiger (ent.; 1925-)

Rod Stewart (ent.; 1945-)

Rod Taylor (ent.; 1929-)

Rodale Press, Inc.

Rodale, Robert (US publ./organic gardening; 1930-90)

Roddenberry, Gene (Eugene Wesley)(writwe/producer, *Star Trek*; 1921-91)

Roddenbery Co., W. B.

Roddy McDowall (ent.; 1928-)

Rodeo Drive (in Beverly Hills)

Rodgers & Hart (comp./lyricist team)
Rodgers, Jimmy (ent.; 1933-)
Rodgers, Richard (Charles)(US comp.; 1902-79)
Rodham Clinton, Hillary (US atty.; wife of US pres.; 1947-)
Rodia, Simon (It. tile setter; 1875-1965)
Rodin, (François) Auguste (René)(Fr. sculptor; 1840-1917)
Rodman, Dennis (basketball; 1961-)
Rodney Crowell (ent.; 1950-)
Rodney Dangerfield (ent.; 1922-)
Rodney King (US news; 1965-)
Rodney Milburn, Jr. (hurdler; 1950-)
Rodolphe Kreutzer (Fr. comp.; 1766-1831)
Rodrigo Carazo Odio
Rodrigo Diaz de Bivar (also El Cid, el Campeador)(Sp. mil.; 1040-99)
Rodríguez, Andrés (ex-pres., Paraguay; 1923-)
Rodriquez, Johnny (ent.; 1951-)
Roe vs. Wade (US law; 1973)
Roebuck & Co., Sears
Roehm, Carolyne
Roemer, Olaus (or Ole)(Dan. astron.; 1644-1710)
Roentgen ray (also x-ray)
Roentgen, Wilhelm (Conrad)(Ger. physt., x-rays; 1845-1923)
Roethke, Theodore (US poet; 1908-1963)
Rogaine™ (med.)
Roger Bacon (Br. phil., scien.; 1214-94)
Roger Brooke Taney (US jurist; 1777-1864)
Roger Clemens (baseball; 1962-)
Roger de Coverly, Sir (dance)
Roger Ebert (US critic; 1942-)
Roger (Gilbert) Bannister, Sir (Brit, runner/phys.; 1929)
Roger Clinton (US pres.'s half-brother)
Roger (Eugene) Maris (baseball; 1934-85)
Roger Miller (ent.; 1936-92)
Roger Moore (ent.; 1928-)
Roger Mudd (TV jour.; 1928-)
Roger Rabbit?, Who Framed (film)
Roger (Huntington) Sessions (US comp.; 1896-1985)
Roger Sherman (US pol.; 1721-93)
Roger Staubach (football; 1942-)
Roger Vadim (ent.)
Roger Whittaker
Roger Williams (ent.)
Roger Williams (US rel.; c1603-83)
Roger, Jolly (the pirate flag)
Rogers Dry Lake, CA
Rogers Hornsby, (Rajah)(baseball; 1896-1963)
Rogers in the 21st Century, Buck (film; 1979)
Rogers' Neighborhood, Mister (TV show)
Rogers, Buck (fict. chara.)
Rogers, Carl R(ansom)(US psych.; 1902-87)
Rogers, Formfit (US bus.)

Rogers, Fred (ent.; 1928-)
Rogers, Ginger (ent.; 1911-)
Rogers, Kenny (ent.; 1938-)
Rogers, Mimi (ent.)
Rogers, Roy (b. Leonard Slye)(ent./cowboy; 1912-)
Rogers, Roy (nonalcoholic cocktail)
Rogers, Will(iam Penn Adair)(ent.; 1879-1935)
Roget, Peter (Mark)(Br. phys./lexicographer, *Roget's Thesaurus*;1779-1869)
Roget's Thesaurus (by Peter Mark Roget)
Rogier van der Weyden (Flem. artist; c1400-64)
Roh Tae Woo (ex-pres., SKorea; 1932-)
Rohe, Ludwig Mies van der (US arch.; 1886-1969)
Röhm, Ernst (Ger. Nazi; 1887-1934)
Rohmer, Sax (aka Arthur Sarsfield Ward)(Br. writer; 1886-1959)
Roister Doister, Ralph (Nicholas Udall comedy)
Rokina™ lens
Rokina International, Inc.
Rolaids™ (med.)
Roland (Eur. legendary hero; 8th c.)
Roland A. Wank (US arch.; 1898-1970)
Roland Barthes (Fr. critic; 1915-80)
Roland Petit (Fr. ballet; 1924-)
Roland, Chanson de (Fr. epic poem, *Song of Roland*)
Roland, Gilbert (ent.; 1905-)
Rolex™
Rolex Watch USA, Inc.
Rolfe, John (Br. colonist in VA, husband of Pocahontas; 1585-1622)
Rolfing™ (massage)
Rolfs™
Rolfs Leather Products (US bus.)
Rolland, Romain (Fr. writer; 1866-1944)
Rolle, Esther (ent.; 1933-)
Rollei™ (photo. equip.)
Rollei of America, Inc.
Roller Derby™ (roller skating)
Rollerblade™ (in-line skates)
Rolling Stone (mag.)
Rolling Stones, the (pop music)
Rollins, Sonny (Theodore Walter)(US jazz; 1929-)
Rolls-Royce™ (auto.)
Rolls-Royce™ Corniche (auto.)
Rolls-Royce Motors, Inc.
Rolodex™
Rolodex Corp.
ROM (read-only memory)(compu.)
Romain Rolland (Fr. writer; 1866-1944)
Roman alphabet (also Latin alphabet)
Roman art/arch. (ancient Rome; 4th c. BC-5th c. AD)
Roman brick
Roman calendar

Roman candle
Roman Catholic (rel.)
Roman Catholic Church (also Church of Rome)
Roman Catholicism (rel.)
Roman collar (also clerical collar)
Roman Curia (rel.)
Roman Empire (27 BC-5th c. AD)
Roman Gabriel (football; 1940-)
Roman Holiday (film)
Roman holiday (time of debauchery)
Roman law (ancient Rome)
Roman nose
Roman numerals (ancient Eur. number system, still used)
Roman Polanski (ent.; 1933-)
Roman sandal (footwear)
Roman senate
Roman wrestling, Greco-
Romana, Pax (peace imposed by strong nation on weaker one; e.g., ancient Rome over its dominions)
Romance Classics (cable TV)
Romance languages (Fr./It./Port./Romanian/Sp.)
Romancing the Stone (film; 1984)
Romanesque art/arch. (W Eur. arch.; 10th-12th c.)
Romania (SE Eur.)
Romanian (lang./people)
Romanoff and Juliet (film; 1961)
Romanoff, noodles
Romanov dynasty (Russian rulers; 1613-1917)
Romanov, Michael (or Mikhail) Fyodorovich (emp., Rus.; 1596-1645)
Romanticism (Eur./Amer. art, music, lit.; 19th c.)
Romany (lang./people)
Romberg, Sigmund (Hung. comp.; 1887-1951)
Rome (apple)
Rome, ancient (753 BC-AD 1453)
Rome, GA, NY
Rome, Georgia
Rome, Harold (US comp.; 1908-)
Rome, Italy
Rome, Sack of (capture by Goths/end of Roman Empire; 410 AD)
Rome, See of (also Holy See)(Vatican)
Rome, Seven Hills of
Rome, the March on (It. hist.; 1922)
Romeo and Juliet (Shakespeare play)
Romeo Montague (fict. chara., *Romeo & Juliet*)
Romer, Roy R. (CO gov.; 1928-)
Romero, Alfa (auto.)
Romero, Cesar (ent.; 1907-)
Rommel, Erwin (aka "Desert Fox")(Ger. gen. in NAfr.; 1891-1944)
Romney (sheep)
Romney, George (Br. artist; 1734-1802)
Romney, George (US pol./bus.; 1907-)

Romulus & Remus (myth. twins raised by wolf/founded Rome)
Romulus, MI
Ron B. Kitaj (US artist; 1932-)
Ron(ald Harmon) Brown (US Secy./Commerce; 1941-)
Ron Carter (US jazz; 1937-)
Ron Glass (ent.)
Ron Howard (ent.; 1953-)
Ron(ald) Hubbard, L(afayette)(US writer/rel., Scientology; 1911-86)
Ron Leibman (ent.; 1937-)
Ron Moody (ent. 1924-)
Ron Perlman (ent.; 1950-)
Ron Silver (ent.; 1946-)
Ron(ald) Ziegler (US pol.)
Rona Barrett (US gossip columnist)
Ronald Ames Guidry (baseball; 1950-)
Ronald Colman (ent.; 1891-1958)
Ronald E. Evans (astro.)
Ronald McDonald (fict. chara.)
Ronald McDonald House
Ronald (Wilson) Reagan (40th US pres.; 1911-)
Ronald Venetiaan (pres., Suriname; 1936-)
Rondônia (state, Brazil)
Ronettes, the (pop music)
Ronnie Milsap (ent.; 1944-)
Ronnie Ray Smith (sprinter; 1949-)
Ronny Cox (ent.; 1938-)
Rono, Harry (track; 1952-)
Ronsard, Pierre de (Fr. poet; 1524-85)
Ronstadt, Linda (ent.; 1946-)
Röntgen (or Röentgen), Wilhelm Konrad (Ger. physt.; 1845-1923)
Ronzoni™
Ronzoni Foods, Inc.
Rookie of the Year (baseball)
Roone Arledge (US TV exec.; 1931-)
Rooney, Andy (Andrew Aitken)(US TV jour.; 1919-)
Rooney, Art (football; 1901-88)
Rooney, Mickey (ent.; 1920-)
Roosa, Stuart A. (astro.; 1933-)
Roosevelt "Rosey" Grier (ent./football; 1932-)
Roosevelt Island (NY)
Roosevelt National Park, Theodore (ND)
Roosevelt, (Anna) Eleanor (wife of US pres., UN dipl.; 1884-1962)
Roosevelt, Franklin D(elano)(FDR)(32nd US pres.; 1882-1945)
Roosevelt, Franklin D(elano), Jr. (US pol.; 1914-88)
Roosevelt, Teddy (Theodore)(26th US pres.; 1858-1919)
Roosevelt's Rough Riders (US hist., Sp./Amer. War; 1898)
Rooster Cogburn (film; 1975)
Root, Elihu (US atty./pol.; 1845-1937)

Roots (A. Haley book)
Roper Poll
Roquefort (cheese)
Rorer Consumer Pharmaceuticals, Rhone-
    Poulenc (US bus.)
Rorschach test (inkblot psych. test)
Rory Calhoun (ent.; 1923-)
Rosa Bonheur (Maria Rosalie)(Fr. artist; 1822-
    99)
Rosa, Julius La (ent.)
Rosalind Russell (ent.; 1911-76)
Rosalyn Evette Bryant (track; 1956-)
Rosalynn Carter (wife of US pres.; 1927-)
Rosalynn Sumners (figure skating; 1964-)
Rosanna Arquette (ent.; 1959-)
Rosanne Cash (ent.; 1955-)
Rosario, Argentina
Rosarita™
Rosarita Mexican Foods Co.
Roscoe Lee Browne (ent.; 1925-)
Roscoe Tanner
Rose Bowl (CA)
Rose Bowl (college football)
Rose Kennedy (mother of ex-US pres.; 1890-)
Rose Marie (ent.; 1925-)
Rose Parade
Rose Schneiderman (US labor leader; 1884-
    1972)
Rose of Cairo, The Purple (film; 1985)
rose of Jericho (plant)
rose of Sharon (plant)
Rose, Audrey (film; 1977)
Rose, Axl (ent.)
Rose, Billy (ent.; 1899-1966)
Rose, Broadway Danny (film; 1984)
Rose, David (US comp.; 1910-90)
Rose, Jack (mixed drink)
Rose, Pete(r Edward)(baseball; 1941-)
Rose, Vincent (US comp.; 1880-1944)
Roseanne (TV show)
Roseanne (Barr) Arnold (ent.; 1952-)
Roseanne Roseannadanna (fict. chara.;
    Saturday Night Live)
Roseau, Dominica
Rosecomb bantam (chicken)
Rosemary Casals (tennis; 1948-)
Rosemary Clooney (ent.; 1928-)
Rosemary De Camp (ent.; 1910-)
Rosemary's Baby (film; 1968)
Rosenberg, Alfred (Ger. Nazi; 1893-1946)
Rosenberg, Ethel (Greenglass)(US, executed for
    treason; 1915-53
Rosenberg, Julius (US, executed for treason;
    1918-53)
Rosenbloom, Maxie (boxing; 1904-76)
Rosenblum Cellars, Inc.
Rosencrantz & Guildenstern (T. Stoppard play)
Roses, Guns 'N (pop music)

Roses, War of the (Eng. hist.; 1455-85)
Rosetta Stone/stone (Eg., hieroglyphics; from
    197 BC)
Roseville, MI, MN
Rosewall, Ken (tennis; 1934-)
Rosey (Roosevelt) Grier (ent./football; 1932-)
Rosh Hashanah (High Holy Day, Yom Kippur,
    High Holiday)
Rosicrucian Fraternity (phil./rel.)
Rosicrucians (internat'l phil./rel. order)
Rosie O'Grady, Sweet (film; 1943)
Rosie the Riveter (WWII symbol)
Rosolino, Frank (US jazz; 1926-78)
Ross Dependency (Antarctic)
Ross Ice Shelf (Antarctic)
Ross Island (Antarctic)
Ross Macdonald (aka Kenneth Millar)(US
    writer; 1915-)
Ross Perot, H. (US bus./pol.; 1930-)
Ross Sea (arm of Antarctic Ocean)
Ross, Betsy (Griscom)(made 1st US flag; 1752-
    1836)
Ross, Diana (ent.; 1944-)
Ross, Elisabeth Kübler- (Swiss/US phys./writer;
    1926-)
Ross, Sir James Clark (Br. expl.; 1800-62)
Ross, John (aka Coowescoowe)(Cherokee Indian
    chief; 1790-1866)
Ross, Sir John (Br. expl.; 1777-1856)
Ross, Katherine (ent.; 1942-)
Ross, Marion (ent.; 1928-)
Rossano Brazzi (It. ent.; 1916-)
Rossellini, Isabella (It. ent.; 1952-)
Rossellini, Roberto (It. ent.; 1906-77)
Rossellino, Antonio (It. sculptor; 1427-79)
Rossellino, Bernardo (It. arch./sculptor; 1409-
    64)
Rossetti, Christina (Georgina)(Br. poet; 1830-
    94)
Rossetti, Dante Gabriel (Br. poet/artist; 1828-
    82)
Rossi™, Carlo (wine)
Rossi Vineyards, Carlo (US bus.)
Rossignol™
Rossignol Ski Co, Inc.
Rossini, Gioacchino (Antonio)(It comp.; 1792-
    1868)
Rostand, Edmond (Fr. writer; 1868-1918)
Rosten, Leo (Calvin)(pseud. Leonard Q.
    Ross)(US humorist/sociol.)
Rostenkowski, Dan(iel)(US cong.; 1928-)
Rostock, Germany
Rostov-on-Don, Russia
Roswell, NM
Rotarian, The (mag.)
Rotary Club (bus./prof. club)
Rotary International (org. of bus./prof. clubs)
ROTC (Reserve Officers Training Corps)(US

mil./educ.)
Rote, Kyle (football; 1928-)
Roth, David Lee (ent.; 1955-)
Roth, Philip (Milton)(US writer; 1933-)
Roth, William Victor, Jr. (US cong.; 1921-)
Rothko, Mark (Rus./US artist; 1903-70)
Rothschild, Amschel Mayer (Ger. finan.; 1773-1855)
Rothschild, Anthony Gustav de (Br. finan.; 1887-1961)
Rothschild, Chateau Lafite- (Fr. wine)
Rothschild, Chateau Mouton- (Fr. wine)
Rothschild, James (Ger./Fr. finan.; 1792-1868)
Rothschild, Lionel de (Br. finan.; 1882-1942)
Rothschild, Lionel Nathan ("Lord Natty")(Br. finan./pol.; 1808-79)
Rothschild, Meyer A(nselm)(Ger. finan.; 1744-1812)
Rothschild, Nathan Mayer (Ger./Br. finan.; 1777-1836)
Rothschild, Sir Nathan Mayer (Br. pol./baron; 1840-1915)
Rothschild, Nathaniel Mayer Victor (Br. scien./pol./finan.; 1910-90)
Rothschild, Salomon (Ger./Aus. finan.; 1774-1855)
Rotisserie League (baseball)
Roto-Rooter™
Rotterdam, NY
Rotterdam, the Netherlands
Rottweiler (dog)
Rouault, Georges (Henri)(Fr. artist; 1871-1958)
Rouen (duck)
Rouen Cathedral
Rouen, France
Rough Riders, Roosevelt's (US hist., Sp./Amer. War; 1898)
Round Table, Knights of the (legendary King Arthur knights)
Roundhead (Br. hist.; 1640-60)
Round Hill Winery (US bus.)
Rourke, Mickey (ent.; 1953-)
Rous sarcoma (med.)
Rous, (Francis) Peyton (US phys.; 1879-1970)
Roush, Edd (baseball; 1893-1988)
Rousseau, Henri (Julien Félix)("Le Douanier")(Fr. artist; 1844-1910)
Rousseau, Jean Jacques (Fr. phil./writer; 1712-78
Rousseau, (Pierre Étienne) Theodore (Fr. artist; 1812-67)
Rovaniemi, Finland
Rover (astron.)
Rover, Lunar (also l.c.)(also lunar roving vehicle)
Rover™, Range (auto.)
Row Publishers, Inc., Harper &
Rowan and Martin's Laugh-In (TV show)

Rowan, Dan (ent.; 1922-87)
Rowlands, Gena (ent.; 1934-)
Rowse, A(lfred) L(eslie)(Br. hist.; 1903-)
Roxanne (film; 1987)
Roxy Music (pop music)
Roy (Claxton) Acuff (ent.; 1903-1992)
Roy Bean, "Judge" (US frontier; 1825?-1903)
Roy Campanella (baseball; 1921-93)
Roy Clark (ent.; 1933-)
Roy Eldridge (US jazz; 1911-89)
Roy Emerson (tennis; 1936-)
Roy Harris (US comp.; 1898-1979)
Roy Haynes (US jazz; 1926-)
Roy Lichtenstein (US artist; 1923-)
Roy Orbison (ent.; 1936-88)
Roy Rogers (b. Leonard Slye)(ent./cowboy; 1912-)
Roy Rogers (nonalcoholic cocktail)
Roy R. Romer (CO gov.; 1928-)
Roy Scheider (ent.; 1932-)
Roy Thinnes (ent.)
Roy Wilkins (US jour./reformer; 1901-81)
Roy, Rob (b. Robert MacGregor)(Scot. outlaw; 1671-1734)
Roy, Rob (cocktail)
Roy, Rob (W. Scott novel)
Royal Academy of Arts (Br. ; est. 1768)
Royal Air Maroc (airline)
Royal Ballet (formerly Sadler's Wells)(London)
Royal Canadian Mounted Police (RCMP, Mounties)(Can. police; est. 1873)
Royal Caribbean Cruise Line
Royal Copenhagen™
Royal Copenhagen Porcelain, Inc.
Royal Crown Cos., Inc.
Royal Danish Ballet
Royal Dutch Shell Group
Royal Greenwich Observatory (London)(also Old Royal Observatory)
Royal Guard, Yeomen of the, beefeaters)
Royal Highlanders (also Royal Highland Regiment, Black Watch)(Scot. mil.)
Royal Highness (title)
Royal Jordanian Airline (airline)
Royal Majesty (title)
Royal Nepal Airline
Royal Oak, MI
Royal Shakespeare Company (RSC)(Br. theater; est. 1961)
Royal Society (also Royal Society of London for the Advancement of Science; est. 1645)
Royal Victoria Hall (also Old Vic Theatre)(London)
Royal, Port (Jamaica)
Royal, Port (SC)
Royall Tyler (US writer; 1757-1826)
Royals, Kansas City (baseball team)
Royce Motors, Inc., Rolls-

Royce, (Frederick) Henry (Br. eng./Rolls-Royce; 1863-1933)

Royce, Josiah (US phil.; 1855-1916)

Royce™, Rolls- (auto.)

Royko, Mike (US jour.)

Roz Chast (cartoonist, *New Yorker*; 1954-)

Roz Ryan (ent.; 1951-)

Rozelle, Pete (Alvin Ray)(football exec.; 1926-)

Rozsa, Miklos (US comp.)

RPR (Registerd Professional Reporter)

RR (railroad)

R. R. Bowker Co.

R. R. Donnelley & Sons (US bus.)

RSVP (repondez s'il vous plait [please respond])

R2D2 (fict. chara., *Star Wars*)

Ru (chem. sym., ruthenium)

Ruanda (lang.)

Rubáiyát of Omar Khayyám, The (book of verses)

Rubbermaid™

Rubbermaid, Inc.

Rubbia, Carlo (It. physt.; 1934-)

Rubble, Barney (cartoon chara.)

Rube (Reuben Lucius) Goldberg (US cartoonist, *Boob McNutt*; 1883-1970)

Rube Goldberg (complex/impractical inventions)

Rubens, Paul (pseud. Pee-Wee Herman)(ent.; 1952-)

Rubens, Peter Paul (Flem. artist; 1577-1640)

Rubicon (ancient river dividing Italy/Gaul; 49 BC)

Rubicon, cross the (take an irrevocable step)

Rubik, Erno (Hung. arch. 1944-)

Rubik's Cube™ (puzzle)

Rubin, Robert E. (Chair/Nat'l Econ Council; 1938-)

Rubinstein, Anton (Grigoryevich)(Rus. pianist/comp.; 1829-94)

Rubinstein, Arthur (Pol./US pianist; 1887-1982)

Rubinstein, Helena (US bus.; 1871-1965)

Rubinstein, John (ent.; 1946-)

Ruby Dandridge

Ruby Dee (ent.; 1924-)

Ruby Keeler (ent.; 1909-93)

Ruby, Harry (US comp.; 1895-1974)

Ruby, Jack (US, murdered L.H. Oswald; 1911-67)

Rucker, Fort (AL)(mil.)

Rudd Weatherwax (Lassie's trainer)

Rudolf Bing, Sir (opera; 1902-)

Rudolf Diesel (Ger. eng.; 1858-1913)

Rudolf Friml (US comp.; 1879-1972)

Rudolf Hess, (Walther Richard)(Ger. Nazi; 1894-1987)

Rudolf Mössbauer (Ger. physt.; 1929-)

Rudolf Nureyev (Rus. ballet; 1938-1993)

Rudolf Serkin (US pianist; 1903-91)

Rudolf (Ludwig Carl) Virchow (Ger. pathol.; 1821-1902)

Rudolf von Laban (Hung. ballet; 1879-1958)

Rudolph Carnap (US phil.; 1891-1970)

Rudolph Dirks (cartoonist, *Katzenjammer Kids*; 1877-1968)

Rudolph "Rudd" Franz Marie Lubbers (PM, Netherlands; 1939-)

Rudolph Valentino (b. Rodolpho d'Antonguolla)(ent.; 1895-1926)

Rudolph W. Giuliani (NYC mayor

Rudolph, Paul (Marvin)(US arch.; 1918-)

Rudolph, Wilma (Glodean)(runner; 1940-)

Rudy Vallee (ent.; 1901-86)

Rudyard Kipling, (Joseph)(Br. writer; 1865-1936)

Rudy's Farm Co.

Rue McClanahan (ent.; 1936-)

Rue Morgue, The Murders in the (E.A. Poe story)

Ruehl, Mercedes

Ruffin, Edmund (US agriculturist; 1794-1865)

Rufino Tamayo (Mex. artist; 1899-1991)

RU486 (med.)

Rufus King (US pol.; 1755-1827)

Rufus, the Red (William II)(king, Eng.; c1056-1100)

Rugby & Soccer Supply (US bus.)

Rugby football (also l.c.)

Rugby School (Rugby, Eng., founded 1567)

Rugby shirt (also l.c.)

Rugby, England

Ruggell, Liechtenstein

Ruggiero Leoncavallo (It. comp.; 1857-1919)

Ruggles, Carl (US comp.; 1876-1971)

Ruggles, Charlie (Charles)(ent.; 1886-1970)

Ruhengeri, Rwanda

Ruhollah Khomenei, Ayatollah (Iran, rel.; 1900-89)

Ruhr River (Ger.)

Ruidoso, NM

Ruisdael, Jacob (Isaackszoon) van (Dutch artist; c1628-82)

Rukeyser, Muriel (US poet; 1913-80)

Rules of Order, Robert's (parliamentary procedure; compiled 1876)

Rumer Godden, (Margaret)(Br. writer; 1907-)

Rumpelstiltskin (fict. chara., *Grimms Fairy Tales*)

Run D.M.C. (pop music)

Runcie, Robert Alexander Kennedy (Br. rel.; 1921-)

Rundi (also Kirundi)(lang.)

Rundu, Namibia

Runner's World (mag.)

Runnymede (meadow on Thames River, near London)

Runyon, (Alfred) Damon (US writer/jour.; 1880-1946)

Rupert Brooke (Br. poet; 1887-1915)
Rupert Murdoch, (Keith)(Austl. publ.; 1931-)
Rupert, Prince (Br. mil.; 1619-82)
Rupert's Land (Can.)
Ruse, Bulgaria
Rush Limbaugh (TV commentator)
Rush, Barbara (ent.; 1930-)
Rush, Benjamin (US phys./writer; 1745-1813)
Rushdie, (Ahmed) Salman (Br. writer; 1947-)
Rushmore National Memorial, Mount (SD)
Rusk, (David) Dean (US pol.; 1909-)
Russ Columbo (ent.; 1908-34)
Russel Crouse (US writer; 1893-1966)
Russell Cave National Monument (AL)
Russell Corp.
Russell Feingold (US cong.; 1953-)
Russell L. Schweickart (astro.)
Russell Myers (cartoonist, *Broom Hilda*; 1938-)
Russell Sage (US finan.; 1816-1906)
Russell Stover Candies, Inc.
Russell terrier, Jack (dog)
Russell, Bertrand (Arthur William)(Br. phil./
    math.; 1872-1970)
Russell, Bill (basketball; 1934-)
Russell, Bill (US jazz; 1905-92)
Russell, Charles M. (US arch.; 1866-1926)
Russell, Charles T(aze)(US, rel./Jehovah's
    Witnesses; 1852-1916)
Russell, Gail (ent.; 1924-61)
Russell, George (US jazz; 1923-)
Russell, Jane (ent.; 1921-)
Russell, John (ex-PM, Br.; 1792-1878)
Russell, Ken (ent.; 1927-)
Russell, Kurt (ent.; 1951-)
Russell, Lillian (b. Helen Louise Leonard)(ent.;
    1861-1922)
Russell, Mark (ent.; 1932-)
Russell, Nipsey (ent.; 1924-)
Russell, Pee Wee (US jazz; 1906-69)
Russell, Rosalind (ent.; 1911-76)
Russell, Theresa (ent.; 1957-)
Russell's viper (snake)
Russia (Russian Federation; since
    1991)(formerly part of USSR)
Russia (USSR, Russian Empire; prior to 1991)
Russia Company (Rus./Eng. trading)
Russia Far East (formerly Soviet Far East)
Russian (lang./people)
Russian bank (card game)
Russian blouse
Russian Blue (formerly Archangel Blue)(cat)
Russian dressing
Russian Federation (also Russia)(N Asia/E
    Eur.)
Russian Information Telegraph Agency
    (RITA)(Rus. news agcy.)
Russian Orthodox (rel.)
Russian Orthodox Church

Russian owtchar (dog)
Russian Revolution (Rus. hist.; 1917)
Russian roulette
Russian Soviet Federated Socialist Republic
    (old Soviet Russia)
Russian Steppes, the (Rus. grasslands)
Russian thistle/tumbleweed (plant)
Russian wolfhound (now Borzoi)(dog)
Russo-Finnish War (Rus./Fin.; 1939-40)
Russo-Japanese War (Rus./Jap.; 1904-05)
Russo-Turkish Wars (Rus./Ottoman Turk.;
    17th-19th c.)
Rust-Oleum™
Rust-Oleum Corp.
Rustavi, Georgia
Rusty (Russell L.) Schweickart (astro.; 1935-)
Rusty (Daniel) Staub (baseball; 1944-)
Rutger Hauer (Neth. ent.; 1944-)
Rutgers University (NJ)
Rutgers University Press (US bus.)
Ruth Bader Ginsburg (US jurist; 1933-)
Ruth Benedict (US anthrop.; 1887-1948)
Ruth Buzzi (ent.; 1936-)
Ruth Draper (ent.; 1889-1956)
Ruth Etting (ent.)
Ruth Gordon (ent.; 1896-1985)
Ruth Hussey (ent.; 1914-)
Ruth Laredo (ent.; 1937-)
Ruth Montgomery (writer/psychic)
Ruth St. Denis (US dancer; 1877-1968)
Ruth Warrick (ent.; 1916-)
Ruth Westheimer, Dr. (b. Karola Ruth
    Siegal)(Ger./US sex therapist; 1928-)
Ruth, Babe (George Herman)(baseball; 1895-
    1948)
Rutherford atom/scattering
Rutherford B(irchard) Hayes (19th US pres.;
    1822-93)
Rutherford Hill Winery (US bus.)
Rutherford, Ann (ent.; 1920-)
Rutherford, Ernest, Baron (Br. physt.; 1871-
    1937)
Rutherford, Johnny (auto racing; 1938-)
Rutherford, Margaret, Dame (ent.; 1892-1972)
Rutland, VT
Rutledge, Ann (fianceé of Abraham Lincoln;
    1816-35)
Rutledge, Wiley Blount, Jr. (US jurist; 1894-
    1949)
Rutskoi, Alexander (Rus. pol.)
Ruttan, Susan (ent.; 1950-)
Rudd (Rudolph Franz Marie) Lubbers (PM,
    Netherlands; 1939-)
Rüütel, Arnold (ex-pres., Estonia
Ruysdael, Salomon van (Dutch artist; c1600-70)
RV (recreation vehicle)
R. Walter Cunningham (astro.; 1932-)
Rwanda (lang.)

Rwanda (Republic of)(central Afr.)

R. W. Frookie (US bus.)

Ryan O'Neal (ent.; 1941-)

Ryan White (US AIDS victim/activist; 1972-90)

Ryan, Irene (ent.; 1903-73)

Ryan, Meg (ent,; 1963-)

Ryan, Nolan (baseball; 1947-)

Ryan, Peggy (ent.; 1924-)

Ryan, Robert (ent.; 1909-73)

Ryan, Roz (ent.; 1951-)

Ryan, Thomas Fortune (US bus./finan.; 1851-1928)

Rybinsk, Russia

Rybnik, Poland

Rydell, Bobby (ent.; 1942-)

Ryder Cup (US/Eur. golf tournament)

Ryder Systems, Inc.

Ryder Truck Rental, Inc.

Ryder, Albert Pickham (US artist; 1847-1917)

Ryder, Winona (ent.; 1971-)

Rye House Plot (Br. hist.; 1683)

Ryks Museum (also Rijks)(Amsterdam)

Ryman Auditorium (Grand Ole Opry)

Ryon, Luann (archery; 1953-)

Ryukyu Islands (Jap.)

Ryun, Jim (James Ronald)(runner; 1947-)

Ryunosuke, Akutagawa (Jap. writer; 1892-1927)

Rzeszów, Poland

S

S (chem. sym., sulfur)
SA (Salvation Army)
Saab™ (auto.)
Saab 900™ (auto.)
Saab 900S™ (auto.)
Saab 9000™ (auto.)
Saab 9000CD™ (auto.)
Saab 9000CS™ (auto.)
Saab-Scania of America, Inc.
Saad al-Abdullah al-Salim al-Sabah, Sheik (PM, Kuwait)
Saadia ben Joseph (Jew. phil./scholar; 882-942)
Saadia ben Joseph al-Fayumi
Saale River (Ger.)
Saami (lang.)
Saanen (goat)
Saar River (Fr./Ger.)
Saarinen, (Gottlieb) Eliel (US arch.; 1873-1950)
Saarinen, Eero (US arch.; 1910-61)
Saarland (state, Ger.)
Saavedra, Miguel de Cervantes (Sp. writer; 1547-1616)
Saba (also Sheba)(ancient S Yemen)
Saba, the Netherlands Antilles
Sabah (state, Malaysia)
Sabah, Sheik Jaber al-Ahmad al-Jaber al- (emir, Kuwait; 1928-)
Sabah, Sheik Saad al-Abdullah al-Salim al- (PM, Kuwait
Sabatini, Gabriela (tennis; 1970-)
Sabbatai Zevi (Jew. rel.; 1626-76)
Sabbath (rel.)
Saberhagen, Bret (baseball; 1964-)
Sabres, Buffalo (hockey team)
Sabin vaccine (med.)
Sabin, Albert Bruce (US phys./microbiol.; 1906-93)
Sabine (ancient people, It.)
Sabine River (S central US)
Sabine Women, Rape of the (G. da Bologna sculpture, N. Poussin painting)
Sable, Lincoln-Mercury (auto.)
Sabrina (film; 1954)
SAC (Strategic Air Command)(US mil.)
Sac and Fox Indians (also Sauk)
Sacagawea (or Sacajawea)(US Indian, Lewis & Clark guide; 1787?-1812 or 1884)
Sacco-Vanzetti Case (Nicola & Bartolomeo)(MA murder trial; 1920-27)
Sacher torte (also Sachertorte)(also l.c)(dessert)
Sacheverell Sitwell, Sir (Br. writer; 1897-1988)
Sachs disease, Tay-
Sachs, Hans (Ger. writer; 1494-1576)
Sachs, Nelly (Leonie)(Ger. writer; 1891-1970)

Sack of Rome (capture by Goths/end of Roman Empire; 410 AD)
Sackville-West, Victoria Mary, Dame ("Vita")(Br. writer; 1892-1962)
Sacramento Bee (CA newspaper)
Sacramento Kings (basketball team)
Sacramento River (CA)
Sacramento Union (CA newspaper)
Sacramento, CA
Sacre-Coeur Church (Paris)
Sacred College of Cardinals (also College of Cardinals)(rel.)
Sacred Heart (heart of Jesus)
Sad Sack, The (comic strip)
Sada Thompson (ent.; 1929-)
Sadat, Anwar (el-)(ex-pres., Eg.; 1918-81)
SADD (Students Against Drunk Driving)
Saddam Hussein (al-Tikriti)(pres., Iraq; 1937-)
Sadducee (rel./pol.)
Sadducees, Pharisees & (opposing Hebrew grps; 2nd c)
Sade, Marquis de (b. Donatien Alphonse François, Comte de Sade)(Fr. mil./writer; 1740-1814)
Sadie Hawkins dance
Sadie Hawkins Day
Sadler's Wells Ballet (now Royal Ballet)(London)
Sadou Hayatou (ex-PM, Cameroon)
SAE (self-addressed envelope)
SAFECO™
SAFECO Corp.
SAFECO Insurance Co. of America
Safco Products Co.
Safeguard™ (soap)
Safer, Morley (US TV jour.; 1931-)
Saftee Glass Co., Inc.
Safety Council, National (est. 1913)
Safeway Stores, Inc.
Safire, William (US jour.; 1929-)
Sag Harbor
Sagan, Carl (Edward)(US astron./writer; 1934-)
Sagan, Françoise (b. Françoise Quoirez)(Fr. writer; 1935-)
Sage, Russell (US finan.; 1816-1906)
Sagebrush State (nickname, NV)
Saget, Bob (ent.; 1956-)
Saginaw, MI
Sagitta (astron., arrow)
Sagittarius (zodiac, astron., archer)
Sahara Desert (N Afr.)
Sahara Resorts
Sahel (region, Afr.)
Sahl, Mort (ent.; 1927)
Said Muhammad Djohar (pres., Comoros)
Said, Port (Egypt)
Said, Qaboos bin Said al- (sultan/PM, Oman; 1940-)

Saida, Lebanon (also Sayda, Sidon)
Saigon (now Ho Chi Minh City)
Saigon, Miss (play)
St. Agnes (Christian martyr; ?-304?)
St. Agnes's Eve (young woman may dream of future husband; 1/20)
St. Albans, Council of (Br. hist.)
St. Albans, England
St. Albans, VT
St. Albert the Great (also St. Albertus Magnus)(Ger. rel.; 1193-1280)
St. Ambrose (bishop of Milan; c340-397)
St. Andrew (patron saint of Scot.)
St. Andrew, Jamaica
St. Andrew's Cross/cross (X-shaped cross)
St. Andrews, Scotland
St. Anselm (archbishop of Canterbury; c1033-1109)
St. Anthony (Eg., founded monasticism; c251-356)
St. Anthony's Cross/cross (also tau cross)(T-shaped cross)
St. Anthony's fire (skin disease)
St. Athanasius (bishop of Alexandria; 298-373)
St. Augustine (1st archbishop of Canterbury; late 6th c.)
St. Augustine of Hippo (rel.; 354-430)
St. Augustine, FL
St. Barnabas ("fellow laborer")
St. Bartholomew (apostle)
St. Bartholomew's Day, Massacre of (Fr. hist.; 1572)
St. Bede ("the Venerable Bede")(Br. rel./hist.; c673-735)
St. Benedict (It., founded the Benedictines; c480-547)
St. Bernadette (aka Bernadette of Lourdes)(Fr.; 1844-79)
St. Bernard (dog)
St. Bonaventure (also Bonaventura)("the Seraphic Doctor")(It. rel./phil.; 1221-74)
St. Boniface (Br. rel. in Ger.; 680-754)
St. Cabrini Frances Xavier (also Mother Cabrini)(US theologian/reformer; 1850-1917)
St. Caius (also Gaius)(pope; ?-296)
St. Calixtus
St. Catherine of Siena (It. mystic; 1347-80)
St. Catharines, Ontario, Canada
St. Celestine I (pope; ?-432)
St. Celestine II (Guido del Castello)(pope; ?-1144)
St. Celestine III (Giacinto Bobone)(It. pope; 1106?-98)
St. Celestine IV (Gofredo Castiglioni)(It. pope; ?-1241)
St. Celestine V (Pietro di Murrone [or Morone])(pope; 1215-96)
Sainte-Chapelle (chapel, Paris)

Ste. Chapelle Winery, Inc.
St. Charles, MO
St. Christopher (patron saint of travelers
St. Christopher-Nevis (Federation of)(West Indies)
St. Clair Shores, MI
Saint Clair, Arthur (US gen.; 1736-1818)
St. Clair, Lake (US/Can.)
St. Clement Vineyards (US bus.)
St. Cloud, MN
St. Croix (US Virgin Island)
St. Cyprian (rel. in Africa; ?-258)
St. Denis, Ruth (US dancer; 1877-1968)
St. Dominic (Sp. rel, founded Dominican order; 1170-1221)
St. Elias National Park, Wrangell- (AK)
St. Elias, Mount (mountain, AK/Can.)
St. Elizabeth Ann (Bayley) Seton (also Mother Seton)(US rel.; 1774-1821)
St. Elmo's Fire (film; 1985)
St. Elmo's fire/light (visible electrical discharge)
Saint Emilion (Fr. wine district)
St. Eustatius, the Netherlands Antilles
Saint-Exupery, Antoine (Marie Roger) de (Fr. writer/aviator; 1900-44)
Sainte-Foy, Quebec, Canada
St. Frances Xavier Cabrini (also Mother Cabrini)(US rel./reformer; 1850-1917)
St. Francis of Assisi (It. rel., founded Franciscans; 1182-1226)
St. Francis Xavier (Francisco Javier)("the Apostle of the Indies")(Sp. rel.; 1506-52)
St. Gaius (also Caius)(pope; ?-296)
Saint-Gaudens, Augustus (US artist; 1848-1907)
St. George (by Donatello)
St. George (patron saint of Eng., legendary dragon slayer; ?-c303)
St. George's, Grenada
St. Gotthard (mountain, Switz.)
St. Gotthard Pass (Swiss Alps)
St. Gotthard Tunnel (Swiss Alps)
St. Gregory I ("the Great")(It., pope; c540-604)
St. Gregory II (It., pope; ?-731)
St. Gregory III (Syrian, pope; ?-741)
St. Gregory VII (aka Hildebrand)(It., pope; c1023-85)
St. Helena (Br. island[s], S Atl.)
St. Helens, Mount (active volcano, WA)
St. Hubert, Quebec, Canada
St. Ignatius of Loyola (aka (Iñigo de Oñez y Loyola)(Sp. rel.; 1491-1556)
St. Ives™
St. Ives Laboratories, Inc.
St. Jacques, coquilles (scallop dish)
St. James, Court of (Br. royal court)
St. James, Susan (ent.; 1946-)
St. Jean, Inc., Chateau

St. Joan of Arc (also Jeanne d'Arc, Maid of Orléans)(Fr. rel./mil.; 1412?-31)
St. John (US Virgin Island)
St. John River (ME/Can.)
St. John the Baptist (Judean rel.; c6 BC-AD 27)
St. John the Divine, Cathedral of (NYC)
St. John, Jill (ent.; 1940-)
St. John, New Brunswick, Canada
St. John's-bread (herb/spice, tree)
St. John's College (MD)
St. John's Day (also Midsummer Day)(June 24)
St. Johns River (FL)
St. John's University (NY)
Saint-John's-wort (plant)
St. Johns (or John's), Antigua and Barbuda
St. John's, Newfoundland, Canada
St. Joseph, MO
St. Jude (also St. Judas)(rel.; 1st c. AD)
St. Jude Children's Research Hospital
St. Justin Martyr (It. rel.; 100?-165)
St. Kitts-Nevis (officially Federation of St. Christopher-Nevis)(West Indies)
St.-Laurent SA, Yves (US bus.)
St. Laurent, French Guiana
St. Laurent, Louis S(tephen)(ex-PM, Can.; 1882-1973)
Saint-Laurent, Quebec, Canada
Saint-Laurent, Yves (Henri Donat Mathieu)(Fr. designer; 1936-)
St. Lawrence Islands National Park (Can.)
St. Lawrence River (NY/Can.)
St. Lawrence Seaway (NE US/SE Can.)
Saint-Léonard, Quebec, Canada
St. Louis Blues (hockey team)
St. Louis Cardinals (baseball team)
St. Louis International Airport, Lambert- (MO)
St. Louis Post-Dispatch (MO newspaper)
St. Louis, MO
Saint-Louis, Senegal
St. Louis, Spirit of (C. Lindbergh plane, transatlantic flight)
St. Lucia (island nation)(West Indies)
St. Luke (rel.; 1st c. AD)
St. Maarten, the Netherlands Antilles
St. Malachy (Irish rel.; 1095-1148)
St. Marcellin (cheese)
St. Mark (b. John Mark)(rel.; 1st c. AD)
St. Mark's Basilica (Venice, It.)
St. Mark's fly (insect)
St. Martin (Fr. rel.; c316-401)
St. Martin (island, Leeward Islands, West Indies)
St. Martin's Press, Inc.
St. Mary-le-Bow Church (also Bow Church)(London)
St. Mary's Honor Center c. Hicks (US law; 1993)
St. Matthew (aka Levi)(a tax collector)
St. Matthew (rel.; 1st c. AD)

St. Matthias (chosen to replace Judas Iscariot)
Ste. Michelle Vintners, Chateau (US bus.)
St. Moritz Chocolatier (US bus.)
St. Moritz, Switzerland
St. Nicholas (also Santa Claus, Kriss Kringle)
St. Nicholas I (Nicholas the Great)(pope; 800?-67)
St. Patrick (Ir. rel.; 389?-461?)
St. Patrick's Cathedral (NYC)
St. Patrick's Day (3/17)
St. Paul (rel.; c3-c67)
St. Paul International Airport, Minneapolis- (MN)
St. Paul Pioneer Press (MN newspaper)
St. Paul, MN
St. Peter (also Simon Peter)(rel.; ?-AD c64)
St. Peter Damian (It. rel.; 1007-72)
St. Peter's Church (also St. Peter's Basilica)(Rome)
St. Petersburg Times (FL newspaper)
St. Petersburg, FL
St. Petersburg, Russia (formerly Leningrad)
St. Pierre and Miquelon (Fr. islands, Newfoundland)
St. Polycarp (Turk. rel.; 69?-155?)
St. Regis-Sheraton Hotel (NYC)
Saint-Saëns, (Charles) Camille (Fr. comp.; 1835-1921)
St. Sebastian (Roman rel.; 3rd c.)
St. Siena, Catherine of (It. mystic; 1347-80)
Saint-Simon, Claude (Henri de Rouvoy), Comte de (Fr. phil.; 1760-1825)
Saint-Simon, Louis de Rouvroy, Duc de (Fr. mil./writer; 1675-1755)
Saint (or Santa) Sophia (also Hagia Sophia)(museum, Istanbul)
St. Stephen (1st Christian martyr; ?-AD 36?)
St. Teresa (of Ávila)(Sp. mystic; 1515-82)
St. Thérèse of Lisieux (Fr. rel.; 1873-97)
St. Thomas (US Virgin Island)
St. Thomas à Becket (Br. rel./pol.; 1118-70)
St. Thomas Aquinas ("the Angelic Doctor")(It. phil./rel.; 1225-74)
St. Thomas, Ontario, Canada
Saint-Tropez, France
St. Valentine (Roman rel.; ?-c270)
St. Valentine's Day (2/14)
St. Valentine's Day Massacre (US hist.; 1929)
St. Vincent and the Grenadines (island nation)(West Indies)
St. Vincent de Paul (Fr. rel.; 1576-1660)
St. Vincent Millay, Edna (US poet; 1892-1950)
St. Vitus (It. rel.; 3rd c.)
St. Vitus's(s) dance (nervous disorder)
St. Wenceslas (also "King Wenceslaus")(duke, Bohemia; 907-929)
Saint, Eva Marie (ent.; 1924-)
Saints, New Orleans (football team)

Proper Noun Speller

Saipan (island, Mariana Islands)
Saitoti, George (VP, Kenya
Sajak, Pat (ent.; 1947-)
Sakharov, Andrei Dmitrievich (Rus. physt.; 1921-89)
Saki (aka H[ector] H[ugh] Munro)(Br. writer; 1870-1916)
Sakigake (Jap. uncrewed space probe)
Sakrete™ (cement)
Sakrete, Inc.
Saks Fifth Avenue (US bus.)
Saks, Gene (ent.; 1921-)
Sakti (rel.)
Sal Mineo (ent.)
Sal-Rei, Cape Verde
Salacia (myth.)
Salalah, Oman
Salamanca, Spain
Salamis (island, Gr.)
Salazar, Alberto (track; 1958-)
Salazar, Antonio de O(liveira)(ex-PM, Port.; 1899-1970)
Sale of the Century (TV show)
Sale v. Haitian Centers Council (US law; 1993)
Saleh, Ali Abdullah (pres., Yemen)
Salem witchcraft trials (MA; 1692)
Salem, India
Salem, MA, OR, NH, VA, OH
Salerno, Anthony "Fat Tony" (US Mafia; 1912-92)
Salerno, Italy
Sales, Soupy (ent.; 1926-)
Sali Berisha (pres., Albania; 1944-)
Salic law (excludes inheritances to females; from 6th c.)
Salieri, Antonio (It. comp./cond.; 1750-1825)
Salim al-Sabah, Sheik Saad al-Abdullah al- (PM, Kuwait
Salina, KS
Salinan (NAmer. Indians)
Salinas de Gortari, Carlos (pres., Mex.; 1949-)
Salinas, CA
Salinger, J(erome) D(avid)(US writer; 1919-)
Salinger, Pierre
Salisbury Cathedral
Salisbury Plain, England (Stonehenge)
Salisbury steak
Salisbury, England
Salisbury, MD, NC
Salish (also Flathead)(NAmer. Indians)
Salk vaccine (polio)
Salk, Jonas (Edward)(US phys./biol.; 1914-)
Salk, Lee (US psych.; 1927-92)
Salle, (René) Robert Cavelier La (aka Sieur de La Salle)(Fr. expl.; 1643-87)
Sallie Mae (also Student Loan Marketing Association, SLMA)
Sallust (Gaius Sallustius Crispus)(Roman hist.; 86-34 BC)
Sally Field (ent.; 1946-)
Sally Hansen™ (cosmetics)
Sally Hansen (US bus.)
Sally Jessy Raphael (TV host)
Sally Kellerman (ent.; 1937-)
Sally K(irsten) Ride (astro.; 1952-)
Sally Lunn teacake
Sally Struthers (ent.; 1948-)
Salman Rushdie, (Ahmed)(Br. writer; 1947-)
Salmon P. Chase (US jurist; 1808-73)
Salmonella (bacteria)
Salome (danced for the head of John the Baptist; 1st c. AD)
Salomon Rothschild (Ger./Aus. finan.; 1774-1855)
Salomon van Ruysdael (Dutch artist; c1600-70)
Salon Selectives™ (hair care)
Salonen, Esa-Pekka
Saloth Sar (also Pol Pot)(Cambodian pol.; 1925-)
SALT (Strategic Arms Limitation Talks)(US/USSR; 1969-89)
Salt Lake City Tribune (UT newspaper)
Salt Lake City, UT
Salt River (AZ)
Salt River Bay National Historical Park (VI)
Salten, Felix (b. Siegmund Salzman)(Aus. writer; 1869-1945)
Salto, Uruguay
Salton Sea (CA lake)
Salton, Inc.
Salvador Dali (Sp. artist; 1904-89)
Salvador, Brazil (formerly Sao Salvador)
Salvador, El (Republic of)(CAmer.)
Salvador, San, Bahamas (also Watling Island)(1st Columbus landing?)
Salvador, San, El Salvador
Salvation Army (rel./charitable org.; est. 1865)
Salvatore Quasimodo (It. poet; 1901-68)
Salvatore Tonelli (captain-regent, San Marino)
Salween River (SE Asia)
Salyut (USSR crewed space flights)
Salzburg, Austria
Sam and Dave (pop music)
Sam Browne belt (mil. sword belt)
Sam Cooke (ent.; 1935-64)
Sam Donaldson (US TV jour.; 1934-)
Sam Elliot (ent.; 1944-)
Sam Ervin, Jr. (US pol.; 1896-1985)
Sam "Momo" Giancana (US gangster; 1908-75)
Sam "Lightnin'" Hopkins (US jazz; 1912-82)
Sam(uel) Houston (US gen./pol.; 1793-1863)
Sam (Robert Lee) Huff (football; 1934-)
Sam Jaffe (ent.; 1891-1984)
Sam Levene (ent.; 1905-80)
Sam Nujoma (pres., Namibia; 1929-)
Sam(uel Augustus) Nunn (US cong.; 1938-)

Sam Peckinpah (ent.; 1925-85)
Sam(uel Taliaferro) Rayburn (US pol.; 1882-1961)
Sam Shepard (US writer/ent.; 1943-)
Sam Slick (aka Thomas Chandler Haliburton)(Can. writer/judge/hist.; 1796-1865)
Sam(uel Jackson) "Slamming Sammy" Snead (golf; 1912-)
Sam Spade (fict. detective, D. Hammett)
Sam Spiegel (ent.; 1903-85)
Sam S. Shubert (US theater; 1876-1905)
Sam (Moore) Walton (US bus., Wal-Mart; 1918-92)
Sam Wanamaker (ent.; 1919-)
Sam Waterston (ent.; 1940-)
Sam, Kim Young (pres., SKorea; 1927-)
Sam, Uncle (nickname, US govt.)
Sama-Veda (rel.)
Samao National Park (Amer. Samoa)
Samoa Standard Time
Samara, Russia (formerly Kuybyshev)
Samaras, Lucas (US sculptor; 1936-)
Samaria (region, ancient Isr.)
Samaritan (ancient people)
Samarkand, Uzbekistan
Samarra, Great Mosque of
Samarra, Iraq
Samarrai, Ahmadal- (PM, Iraq)
Same Time, Next Year (play/film)
Samms, Emma (ent.; 1960-)
Sammy (Samuel Adrian) Baugh (football; 1914-)
Sammy Cahn (b. Samuel Cohen)(US lyricist; 1913-93)
Sammy Davis, Jr. (ent.; 1925-90)
Sammy Fain (US comp.; 1902-89)
Samoa (Independent State of Western)(SW Pac.)
Samoa (volcanic islands, SW Pac.)
Samoa, American (SW Pac.)
Samoan (lang./people)
Samora Machel (ex-pres., Mozambique; 1933-86)
Samoyed (dog)(also l.c.)
Samoyed (lang./people)
Samoyedic (lang.)
Sampras, Pete (tennis; 1971-)
Samson (Isr. hero; 11th c. BC)
Samson Agonistes (by J. Milton)
Samson & Delilah (rel.)
Samsonite Corp.
Samsonov, Aleksandr (Rus. mil.; 1859-1914)
Samsung™
Samsung Electronics America (US bus.)
Samuel Adams (US patriot; 1722-03)
Samuel Barber (US comp.; 1910-81)
Samuel Beckett (Ir. writer; 1906-89)
Samuel Butler (Br. writer; 1835-1902)

Samuel Coleridge-Taylor (Br. comp.; 1875-1912)
Samuel Colt (US gunsmith; 1814-62)
Samuel Cunard (Can., trans-Atl. navigation; 1787-1865)
Samuel de Champlain (Fr. expl.; c1567-1635)
Samuel Eliot Morison (US hist.; 1887-1976)
Samuel Francis du Pont (US mil.; 1803-65)
Samuel Goldwyn (b. Samuel Goldfish)(ent.; 1882-1974)
Samuel Gompers (US labor leader; 1850-1924)
Samuel Hinds (PM, Guyana
Samuel H. Kress (US bus.; 1863-1955)
Samuel H. Sheppard (US phys.; 1924-70)
Samuel I(rving) Newhouse, Jr. (US publ.; 1895-1979)
Samuel Johnson ("Dr. Johnson")(Br. lexicographer/writer; 1709-84)
Samuel Johnson (US educ.; 1696-1772)
Samuel Langhorne Clemens (pseud. Mark Twain)(US writer; 1835-1910)
Samuel L(ewis) Warner (ent.; 1887-1927)
Samuel (Finley Breese) Morse (US inv., telegraph; 1791-1872)
Samuel Pepys (Br. writer; 1633-1703)
Samuel Pickwick (fict. chara., *Pickwick Papers*)
Samuel Ramey (ent.; 1942-)
Samuel Richardson (Br. writer; 1689-1761)
Samuel Sewall (US judge, witch trials; 1652-1730)
Samuel Taylor Coleridge (Br. poet; 1772-1834)
Samuelson, Joan Benoit (Olympic marathon; 1957-)
Samuelson, Paul A(nthony)(US econ.; 1915-)
San Andreas fault (CA)
San Angelo, TX
San Antonio Express News (TX newspaper)
San Antonio Light (TX newspaper)
San Antonio Metropolitan Transit Authority, Garcia v. (US law; 1985)
San Antonio Missions National Historical Park (TX)
San Antonio Spurs (basketball team)
San Antonio, TX
San Bernardino Sun (CA newspaper)
San Bernardino, CA
San Bruno, CA
San Clemente, CA
San Cristóbal, Venezuela
San Diego Chargers (football team)
San Diego Padres (baseball team)
San Diego Union-Tribune (CA newspaper)
San Diego, CA
San Fernando Valley (CA)
San Fernando, Trinidad
San Francisco bomb (slang, cocaine/heroin/LSD)
San Francisco Chronicle (CA newspaper)
San Francisco Examiner (CA newspaper)
San Francisco 49ers (football team)

San Francisco Giants (baseball team)
San Francisco International Airport (CA)
San Francisco Maritime National Historical
    Park (CA)
San Francisco, CA
San Francisco, Presidio of (US mil.)
San Gabriel, CA
San Jacinto River (TX)
San Joaquin River (CA)
San Joaquin Valley
San Jose Mercury-News (CA newspaper)
San Jose Sharks (hockey team)
San Jose, CA
San José, Costa Rica
San Juan Capistrano, CA (swallows return
    annually: March 19)
San Juan Hill, Cuba (captured by US forces,
    Spanish-American War)
San Juan Island National Historical Park (WA)
San Juan, Argentina
San Juan, Puerto Rico
San Leandro, CA
San Luis Obispo, CA
San Luis Potosi, Mexico
San Luis Rey, The Bridge of (film; 1944)
San Marino (Republic of)(It.)
San Marino, CA
San Marino, San Marino
San Mateo, CA
San Miguel, El Salvador
San Miguelite, Panama
San Miquel de Tucuman, Argentina
San Pedro de Macorís, Dominican Republic
San Pedro Sula, Honduras
San-Pédro, Ivory Coast
San Quentin Prison (CA)
San Rafael, CA
San Remo, Italy
San Salvador, Bahamas (also Watling Island)
San Salvador, El Salvador
San Sebastian, Spain
Sana, Yemen (also Sana'a)
Sancerre (wine)
Sanchez, Oscar Arias (ex-pres., Costa Rica;
    1941-)
Sancho Panza (fict. chara., *Don Quixote*)
Sanctus (also *Tersanctus*)(rel.)
Sanctus bell (rung during Mass)
Sand, George (aka Amandine Aurore Lucie
    Dupin)(Fr. writer; 1804-76)
Sandburg, Carl (August)(US poet; 1878-1967)
Sandberg, Ryne (baseball; 1959-)
Sander Vanocur
Sanders Show, The Larry (TV show)
Sanders, Barry (football; 1968-)
Sanders, Deion (baseball, football; 1967-)
Sanders, George (ent.; 1906-72)
Sanders, Lawrence (US writer; 1920-)

Sanders, Summer (swimmer; 1972-)
Sanders, Wesberry v. (US law; 1964)
Sanderson, William (ent.; 1948-)
Sandi Patty (ent.)
Sandiego, Carmen (TV show)
Sandiford, Erskine Lloyd (PM, Barbados; 1937-)
Sandinista (member, Sandinist National
    Liberation Front, Nicaragua)
Sandino, Augusto César (Nicaraguan mil.;
    1893-1934)
S and L (savings and loan)
Sandra Bernhard (ent.; 1955-)
Sandra Boynton (US bus.)
Sandra Day O'Connor (US jurist; 1930-)
Sandra Dee (ent.; 1942-)
Sandra Haynie (golf; 1943-)
Sandro Botticelli (It. artist; 1444-1510)
Sandusky, OH
S & W™
S & W Fine Foods, Inc.
Sandrich, Jay
Sandwich Islands (now Hawaii)
Sandwich, Earl of (John Montagu)(Br. pol.;
    1718-92)
Sandy Dennis (ent.; 1937-92)
Sandy Duncan (ent.; 1946-)
Sandy (Sanford) Koufax (baseball; 1935-)
Sandy, Gary (ent.; 1945-)
Sandy, UT
Sanford and Son (TV show)
Sanford B. Dole (ex-gov., HI; 1844-1921)
Sanford, Isabel (ent.)
Sanforized™ (fabric treatment)
Sanger, Frederick (Br. biochem.; 1918-)
Sanger, Margaret (Higgins)(US reformer; 1883-
    1966)
Sangha (rel.)
Sangheli, Andrei (PM, Moldova)
Sangho (lang.)
Sangre de Cristo Mountains (NM/CO)
Sanhedrin (Jew. hist./govt.)
Sani Abacha (acting ruler, Nigeria
Sanibel Island, FL
Sanitas™
Sanitas Wallcoverings (US bus.)
Sanka™ (coffee)
Sankhya yoga (rel.)
Sanmarinese (people)
Sanskrit (lang.)
Sansom, Art (cartoonist, *The Born Loser*; 1920-
    91)
Sansovino, Andrea (It. sculptor; 1460-1529)
Sansovino, Jacopo (It. sculptor; 1486-1570)
Sansui™
Sansui Electronics Corp.
Sant'Angelo, Giorgio di
Santa (or Saint) Sophia (also Hagia
    Sophia)(museum, Istanbul)

Santa Ana winds (also Santa Anas)
Santa Ana, CA
Santa Ana, El Salvador
Santa Anita Derby
Santa Anita Park
Santa Anna, Antonio (López) de (ex-pres/gen., Mex.; 1795?-1876)
Santa Barbara Islands (CA)
Santa Barbara, CA
Santa Catalina, CA (also Catalina Island)
Santa Clara, CA
Santa Clara, Cuba
Santa Clarita, CA
Santa Claus (also St. Nicholas, Kriss Kringle)
Santa Cruz, Bolivia
Santa Cruz, CA
Santa Fe Opera (NM)
Santa Fe Pacific Corp.
Santa Fe Springs, CA (oil wells)
Santa Fe Trail (trade route, MO/NM; c1820-1880)
Santa Fe, Argentina
Santa Fe, NM
Santa Gertrudis (cattle)
Santa Maria, Brazil
Santa Maria, CA
Santa Marta, Colombia
Santa Monica, CA
Santa Rosa Press-Democrat (CA newspaper)
Santa Rosa, Argentina
Santa Rosa, CA
Santali (lang.)
Santana (pop music)
Santana, Carlos (ent.; 1947-)
Santana (Martinez), Manuel (tennis; 1938-)
Santander, Spain
Santayana, George (Sp./US writer/phil.; 1863-1952)
Santee River (SC)
Sant'Elia, Antonio (It. arch.; 1888-1916)
Santer, Jacques (PM, Luxembourg; 1937-)
Santeria (rel.)
Santha Rama Rau (Indian writer/astrol.; 1923-)
Santiago de Cuba, Cuba
Santiago de los Caballeros, Dominican Republic
Santiago, Chile
Santiago, Panama
Santini, The Great (film; 1980)
Santo Domingo, Dominican Republic
Santos-Dumont, Alberto (Fr. aviator; 1873-1932)
Santos, Brazil
Santos, José Eduardo dos (pres., Angola; 1942-)
Sanwa Bank, Ltd.
Sanyo™
Sanyo Electric Co., Inc.
Sanyo Fisher USA Corp.
São Domingos, Guinea-Bissau

São Paulo, Brazil
São Tomé and Príncipe (Democratic Republic of)(off W Afr. coast)
São Tomé, São Tomé and Príncipe
Saparmuryad, Niyazov, (pres., Turkmenistan
Sapir-Whorf hypothesis (linguistics)
Sapir, Edward (Ger./US anthrop.; 1884-1939)
Sappho (Gr. poet; c612-c580 BC)
Sapporo™
Sapporo, Japan
Sapporo Breweries, Ltd.
Sar, Saloth (also Pol Pot)(Cambodian pol.; 1925-)
Sara (people)
Sara Lee™
Sara Lee Corp.
Sara Teasdale (US poet; 1884-1933)
Saracen (people)
Saragossa, Spain (also Zaragoza)
Sarah (or Sara)(rel.)
Sarah Bernhardt (ent.; 1844-1923)
Sarah Caldwell (ent.; 1924-)
Sarah Churchill (Br., duchess of Marlboro; 1660-1744)
Sarah Margaret "Fergie" Ferguson (Br., Duchess of York; 1959-)
Sarah G. Blanding (US educ.; 1899-1985)
Sarah Jessica Parker (ent.; 1965-)
Sarah Lawrence College (NY)
Sarah McClendon
Sarah Miles (ent.; 1941-)
Sarah (Kemble) Siddons (ent.; 1755-1831)
Sarah (Lois) Vaughan (US jazz; 1924-90)
Sarajevo, Bosnia-Hercegovina
Sarakole (people)
Saran Wrap™
Saranac Lake, NY
Sarandon, Susan (ent.; 1946-)
Sarasota Herald-Tribune (FL newspaper)
Sarasota, FL
Sarasvati (myth.)
Saratoga National Historical Park (NY)
Saratoga Springs, NY
Saratoga Trunk (E. Ferber novel)
Saratoga trunk (luggage; 19th c.)
Saratoga, Battles of (US hist.; 1777)
Saratoga, CA
Saratov, Russia
Sarawak (state, Malaysia)
Sarazen, Gene (golf; 1902)
Sarbanes, Paul S(pyros)(US cong.; 1933-)
Sardinia (island, It.)
Sardi's restaurant
Sarelon™ (textile)
Sargasso Sea (N Atl.)
Sargent Shriver, (Robert), Jr. (US bus./pol.; 1915-)
Sargent, Dick (ent.)

Sargent, John Singer (US artist; 1856-1925)
Sargento™ (cheese)
Sarh, Chad
Sarkis, Elias (ex-pres., Lebanon)
Sarnath (archeol. site, India)
Sarnoff, David (US broadcasting pioneer, NBC; 1891-1971)
Sarnoff, Dorothy (ent.; 1917-)
Saroyan, William (US writer; 1908-81)
Sarrazin, Michael (ent.)
Sarto, Andrea del (It. artist; 1486-1530)
Sartre, Jean-Paul (Fr. phil./writer; 1905-80)
SAS (Scandinavian Airlines System)
SASE (self-addressed stamped envelope)
Saskatchewan (province, Can.)
Saskatoon, Saskatchewan, Canada
Sasquatch (also Big Foot or Bigfoot)
Sasser, James Ralph (US cong.; 1936-)
Sassoon, Beverly (US bus.)
Sassoon, Inc., Vidal
Sassoon™, Vidal (hair care)
Sassoon, Vidal (US bus.)
Sassou-Nguesso, Denis (ex-pres., Congo; 1943-)
Sassy (mag.)
SAT (Scholastic Aptitude Test, College Boards™)
Satan (the devil)
Satanic Verses, The (S. Rushdie novel)
Satanism (devil worship)
Satchel (Leroy Robert) Paige (baseball; 1906-82)
Satcitananda (rel.)
Satellite TV Week (mag.)
Satie, Erik (Alfred Leslie)(Fr. comp.; 1866-1925)
Sato, Eisaku (ex-PM, Jap.; 1901-75)
Satsuma vase/pottery
Satsuma, Japan
Sattui Winery, V. (US bus.)
Saturday Evening Post, The (mag.)
Saturday Night Fever (film)
Saturday Night Live (TV show)
Saturday-night special (cheap handgun)
Saturn™ (auto.)
Saturn (planet; myth.)
Saturn Corp.
Saturn rocket (US space program)
Saturn™ SW2 (auto.)
Saturn, Apollo- (US crewed space flights)
Saturn's rings (astron.)
Satyagraha (passive resistance)
Satyendranath Bose (Indian physt./chem./math.; 1894-1974)
Saud (king, Saudi Arabia; 1902-69)
Saud, Ibn (also Abdul-Azaz Ibn-Saud)(king, Saudi Arabia; 1880-1953)
Saudi Arabia (Kingdom of)(SW Asia)
Sauk and Fox Indians (also Sac)
Saul (king, Isr.; fl. 11th c BC)
Saul Baizerman

Saul Bellow (US writer; 1915-)
Saul Steinberg (US artist; 1914-)
Sault Ste. Marie Canals (also Soo Locks)(MI; Ontario, Can.)
Sault Ste. Marie, MI
Sault Ste. Marie, Ontario, Canada
Saunders Co., W. B.
Sausalito, CA
Sau-Sea™
Sau-Sea Foods, Inc.
Saussure, Ferdinand de (Swiss linguist; 1857-1913)
Sauterne (wine)(also l.c.)
Sauvignon (grape)
Sauvignon Blanc (grape, wine)
Savage, Fred (ent.; 1976-)
Savage's Station (Civil War battle, VA)
Savalas, Telly (ent.; 1924-94)
Savannah News (GA newspaper)
Savannah Press (GA newspaper)
Savannah™ (clothing)
Savannah, GA
Savannakhet, Laos
Savile Row cut (clothing)
Savimbi, Jonas (Angolan mil.; 1934-)
Savin™ copier
Savin Corp.
Savior (Jesus Christ)
Savitch, Jessica (Beth)(US TV jour.; 1947-83)
Savonarola (or Dante) chair
Savonarola, Girolamo (It. rel./reformer; 1452-98)
Sav-On-Drugs, Inc.
Savonnerie (carpet)
Savoy (area, Fr.)
Savoy cabbage
Sawyer, Amos (pres., Liberia)
Sawyer, Diane (US TV jour.; 1945-)
Sawyer, The Adventures of Tom (M. Twain novel)
Sawyer, Tom (fict. Mark Twain chara.)
Sawyer, Youngstown Sheet and Tube Co. v. (US law; 1952)
Sawzall (constr.)
Sax Rohmer (aka Arthur Sarsfield Ward)(Br. writer; 1886-1959)
Saxe-Coburg-Gotha, House of (Br. ruling family; 1901-10)
Saxon (people)
Saxon, John (ent.; 1935-)
Saxony (state, Ger.)
Sayers, Dorothy L(eigh)(Br. writer; 1893-1957)
Sayers, Gale (football; 1943-)
Sayles, John (ent.; 1950-)
Sayonara (film; 1957)
Say's law (econ.)
Sayyed Ali Khamenei, Ayatollah (Iran rel.; 1940-)

Sb (chem. sym., antimony)
SBA (Small Business Administration)
S-Blazer, Chevrolet™ (auto.)
SC (Security Council [UN], South Carolina)
Sc (chem. sym., scandium)
Scaggs, Boz (ent.; 1944-)
Scala, La (opera house, It.)
Scalfaro, Oscar Luigi (pres., It.)
Scalia, Antonin (US jurist; 1936-)
Scandinavian (lang./people)
Scandinavian (peninsula, NW Eur.)
Scandinavian Airlines System (SAS)
Scaramouche (fict. chara.)
Scaramouche (R. Sabatini novel)
Scarborough Fair (song)
Scarborough, Chuck (Charles)
Scarborough, England
Scarborough, ME
Scarborough, Ontario, Canada
Scarborough, Tobago
Scarlatti, (Giuseppe) Domenico (It. comp.; 1685-1757)
Scarlatti, (Pietro) Alessandro (Gaspare)(It. comp.; 1660-1725)
Scarlet Letter, The (Nathaniel Hawthorne novel)
Scarlet Pimpernel, The
Scarlet, Will (fict. chara., *Robin Hood*)
Scarlett O'Hara (fict. chara., *Gone With the Wind*)
Scarsdale Diet
Scarsdale, NY
SCAT (cat system)
Scatman Crothers (ent.; 1910-86)
Schaan, Liechtenstein
Schaap, Dick (US TV sports jour.)
Schaefer, George
Schaefer, Jack (US writer; 1908-91)
Schaefer, William Donald (MD gov.; 1921-)
Schafer, Edward T. (ND gov.)
Schallert, William (ent.; 1922-)
Schapiro, Meyer (US art hist.; 1904-)
Schary, Dore (US writer/ent./reformer; 1905-80)
Schechter v. U.S. (US law; 1935)
Scheduled Castes (also Harijans, formerly Untouchables)(India)
Scheherazade (fict. chara., *Arabian Nights*)
Scheherazade (Rimski-Korsakov symphony)
Scheib™, Earl (auto painting)
Scheib, Inc., Earl
Scheidemann, Philipp (ex-chanc., Ger.; 1865-1939)
Scheider, Roy (ent.; 1932-)
Schell, Maria (ent.; 1926-)
Schell, Maximilian (ent.; 1930-)
Schelling, Friedrich Wilhelm Joseph von (Ger. phil.; 1775-1854)
Schempp, Abington Township v. (US law; 1963-)

Schenck v. U.S. (US law; 1919)
Schenectady, NY
Schenkel, Chris (ent.; 1923-)
Schering-Plough Corp.
Schiaparelli, Elsa (Fr. designer; 1890-1973)
Schiaparelli, Giovanni (Virginio)(It. astron.; 1835-1910)
Schick™
Schick test (diphtheria immunity test)
Schick USA, Inc.
Schickele, Peter (pseud. P. D. Q. Bach)(ent.)
Schiele, Egon (Aus. artist; 1890-1918)
Schiff('s) reagent (aldehyde test)
Schildkraut, Joseph (ent.; 1895-1964)
Schiller, (Johann Christoph) Friedrich von (Ger. writer/hist.; 1759-1805)
Schindler's List (film)
Schirra, Wally (Walter Marty), Jr. (US astro.; 1923-)
Schism of the West (also the Great Schism)(rel.)
Schlafly, Phyllis (Stewart)(US activist; 1924-)
Schlatter, George (ent.)
Schlegel, August Wilhelm von (Ger. writer; 1767-1845)
Schlegel, Friedrich von (Ger. phil./writer; 1772-1829)
Schleiermacher, Friedrich (Ernst Daniel)(Ger. rel.; 1768-1834)
Schlemmer & Co., Inc., Hammacher,
Schlesinger, Arthur M(eier)(US hist.; 1888-1965)
Schlesinger, Arthur M(eier), Jr. (US hist.; 1917-)
Schleswig-Holstein (state, Ger.)
Schliemann, Heinrich (Ger. archaeol..; 1822-90)
Schlossberg, Caroline Kennedy (US atty., daughter of JFK; 1957-)
Schlumberger, Ltd.
Schlüter, Poul (Dan. pol.; 1929-)
Schmeling, Max (Ger. boxing; 1905-)
Schmid Laboratories (US bus.)
Schmidt telescope/reflector (astron.)
Schmidt, Helmut (Heinrich Waldemar)(ex-chanc., WGer.; 1918-)
Schmidt, Mike (baseball; 1949-)
Schmitt, Jack (Harrison Hahen)(US pol./astro.; 1935-)
Schneider, John (ent.; 1954-)
Schneiderman, Rose (US labor leader; 1884-1972)
Schoenberg, Arnold (Franz Walter)(Aus. comp.; 1874-1951)
Schofield Barracks (HI)(US mil.)
Schofield, John McAllister (US mil.; 1831-1906)
Scholastic Aptitude Test (SAT, College Boards™)
Schollander, Donald (swimming; 1946-)
Scholl's™, Dr.

School District of Abington Township v. Schempp (US law; 1963)

School of Athens (by Raphael)

School/school of Paris (art)

Schopenhauer, Arthur (Ger. phil.; 1788-1860)

Schorr, Daniel (US jour.; 1916-)

Schramsberg Vineyards Co.

Schreiber, Avery (ent.; 1935-)

Schreiner, Olive (pseud. Ralph Iron)(SAfr. writer; 1855-1920)

Schroder, Rick (ent.; 1970-)

Schrödinger, Erwin (Aus. physt.; 1887-1961)

Schrödinger's cat

Schroeder, Patricia (Scott)(US cong.; 1940-)

Schubert, Franz (Peter)(Aus. comp.; 1797-1828)

Schuller, Robert (US rel.; 1926-)

Schulman, A. (rubber/plastic products co.)

Schultz, Theodore W. (US econ.; 1902-)

Schulz, Charles M(onroe)(cartoonist, *Peanuts*; 1922-)

Schuman, Robert (ex-PM, Fr.; 1886-1963)

Schuman, William (Howard)(US comp.; 1910-92)

Schumann-Heink, Ernestine (opera; 1861-1936)

Schumann, Clara Josephine (Wieck)(Ger. pianist; 1819-96)

Schumann, Robert (Alexander)(Ger. comp.; 1810-56)

Schumpeter, Joseph (Alois)(US econ.; 1883-1950)

Schurz, Carl (Ger./US pol.; 1829-1906)

Schuschnigg, Kurt von (ex-chanc., Aus.; 1897-1977)

Schuster, Inc., Simon &

Schuyler Colfax (ex-US VP; 1823-85)

Schuyler, Philip John (US gen./pol.; 1733-1804)

Schuylkill River (PA)

Schwab, Charles M(ichael)(US bus.; 1862-1939)

Schwann cell (med.)

Schwann, Theodor (Ger. phys.; 1810-82)

Schwartz, Arthur (US comp.; 1900-84)

Schwarz Import, Ltd., F.A.O.)

Schwarzenegger, Arnold (ent.; 1947-)

Schwarzkopf, Elisabeth (Ger. opera; 1915-)

Schwarzkopf, H. Norman, Jr. ("Stormin' Norman")(US gen.; 1934-)

Schwarzschild radius (astron., physics)

Schweickart, Rusty (Russell L.)(astro.; 1935-)

Schweitzer, Dr. Albert (Ger. phys./phil./rel.; 1875-1965)

Schwenkfeld von Ossig, Kaspar (Ger. rel.; 1490-1561)

Schwenkfeldians (also Schwenkfelders)(rel.)

Schweppes™ (mixers)

Schweppes USA, Ltd.

Schwinger, Julian (Seymour)(US physt.; 1918-)

Schwinn™

Schwinn Bicycle Co.

Schwitters, Kurt (Ger. artist; 1887-1948)

Science and Technology Policy, Office of (US govt.)

Science Foundation, National (NSF)(US govt. agcy.; est. 1950)

Science, Doctor of (also Sc.D., Scientiae Doctor)

Sciences, National Academy of (org. 1863)

Scientific American (mag.)

Scientologist (rel.)

Scientology, Church of (rel.)

Scilla rock (now Scylla)(rock in Strait of Messina off coast of Italy)

Scilly, Cornwall and Isles of (county, Eng.)

S. C. Johnson & Son, Inc.

SCLC (Southern Christian Leadership Conference)

Scobee, Dick (Francis Richard)(astro., *Challenger*; 1939-86)

Scofield, Paul (ent.; 1922-)

Scolari, Peter (ent.; 1954-)

Scone, Scotland

Scone, Stone of (Scot. kings' coronation seat)

Scooby Doo (fict. chara.)

Scoop Fresh™ (cat litter)

Scopas (Gr. sculptor/arch.; fl. 4th c. BC)

Scope™ (mouthwash)

Scopes Trial (also Monkey Trial)(US, evolution; 1925)

Scopes, John T(homas)(US educ./evolution; 1901-70)

SCORE (Service Corps of Retired Executives)

Scoresby Sound (Greenland)

Scoresby, William (Br. expl.; 1789-1857)

Scorpio (zodiac, scorpion)

Scorpius (astron., scorpion)

Scorsese, Martin (ent.; 1942-)

Scot (or Scott), Jock (fishing)

Scotch and Soda (mixed drink)

Scotch Blackface (sheep)

Scotch broom (plant)

Scotch broth

Scotch collie (dog)

Scotch egg

Scotch Highland (cattle)

Scotch pine (tree)

Scotch™ tape

Scotch whiskey

Scotchgard™ (cleaner, protective coating)

Scotland (part of UK)

Scotland Yard, New (Br. police)

Scotland, Church of

Scotsman/Scotswoman

Scott Baio (ent.; 1961-)

Scott Bakula (ent.)

Scott Carpenter, M(alcolm)(astro.; 1925-)

Scott Case/Decision, Dred (US law, pro-slavery; 1856-57)

Scott Glenn (ent.; 1942-)

Scott Hamilton (figure skating; 1958-)
Scott Joplin (US jazz; 1868-1917)
Scott LeFaro (US jazz; 1936-61)
Scott Paper Co.
Scott, David R. (astro.)
Scott, Dred (US slave; 1795?-1858)
Scott, George C(ampbell)(ent.; 1927-)
Scott, Lizabeth (ent.; 1922-)
Scott, Martha (ent.; 1914-)
Scott, Randolph (ent.; 1898-1987)
Scott, Ridley (ent.; 1939-)
Scott, Sir Walter (Scot. writer; 1771-1832)
Scott, Willard (ent./meteor.)
Scott, Winfield ("Old Fuss and Feathers")(US gen.; 1786-1866)
Scott, Zachary (ent.; 1914-65)
Scotties™ (tissues)
Scottish (people)
Scottish deerhound (dog)
Scottish language
Scottish terrier (dog)(also Scotch terrier)
Scotts™ turf builder
Scottsboro Case (US law; 1931)
Scottsdale, AZ
ScotTowels™
Scoupe LS, Hyundai (auto.)
Scoupe Turbo, Hyundai (auto.)
Scoupe, Hyundai (auto.)
Scouting (mag.)
Scowcroft, Brent (US pol.; 1925-)
Scrabble™ (game)
Scranton Times (PA newspaper)
Scranton Tribune (PA newspaper)
Scranton, PA
Scratch (Satan)(also Old Scratch)
Scream, The (by Edvard Munch)
Scriabin, Alexander (Nikolayevich)(Rus. comp.; 1872-1915)
Scribe, (Augustin) Eugène (Fr. writer; 1791-1861)
Scriblerus Club (Br. lit. group; c1713-14)
Scribner, Charles, Jr. (US publ.)
Scribner, Charles, Sr. (US publ.)
Scribner's Sons, Charles (US bus.)
Scripps Co., E. W.
Scripps College (CA)
Scripps Institution of Oceanography (CA)
Scripps, Edward (Wyllis)(US publisher; 1854-1926)
Scripps, James Edmund (US publisher; 1835-1906)
Scripto Tokai Corp.
Scripture(s)(also Holy Scripture[s])(rel.)
Scrooge McDuck (cartoon chara.)
Scrooge, Ebenezer (fict. chara., *A Christmas Carol*)
Scruggs, Earl (ent.; 1924-)
Scud (Soviet missile)

Sculley, John (US bus.)
Scully, Vin (ent.; 1927-)
Sculptor (astron., sculptor)
Scutum (astron., shield)
Scylla and Charybdis (myth.)
Scylla rock (now Scilla)(off coast of It.)
Scyros (also Skiros, Skyros)(Gr. island)
Scythia (ancient region, Eur./Asia)
Scythians (ancient people)
SD (South Dakota)
SDI (Strategic Defense Initiative, Star Wars)(US mil.; 1983-)
Salvic languages
Se (chem. sym., selenium)
Sea Gull, The (A. Chekhov play)
Sea Islands (off coast of SC/GA/FL)
Sea of Galilee (also Lake Tiberias)(Isr.)
Sea of Japan (Jap./Pac.)
Sea of Marmara (Turk.)
Sea of Okhotsk (N Pac.)
Sea of Tranquility (also Mare Tranquillitatus)(dark plain on Moon)
Sea World
Sea World of Florida
Seabee (also See-Bee)(large, ocean-going vessel)
Seabees (construction battalions of US Navy)
Seaborg, Dr. Glenn T(heodore)(US chem./chair, AEC; 1912-)
Seagate Technology, Inc.
Seagram & Sons, Inc., Joseph E.
Seagram Beverage Co., The
Seagram Co., Ltd.
Seagram Distillers Co.
Seagram's™
Seagren, Bob (Robert Lloyd)(pole vaulter; 1946-)
Seagull, Jonathan Livingston (R. Bach novel)
Seahawk (US Navy helicopter)
Seahawks, Seattle (football team)
Sealab (Navy habitats for aquanauts)
Seale, Bobby (cofounded Black Panther Party)
Seal-O-Matic Manufacturing Co.
SEALS (Sea, Air, and Land Soldiers)(US mil.)
Sealtest™
Sealtest Foods (US bus.)
Sealy™ (mattress)
Sealy Posturepedic™ (mattress)
Sealy, Inc.
Sealyham terrier (dog)
Sean Connery (ent.; 1930-)
Sean O'Casey (Ir. writer; 1884-1964)
Sean Penn (ent.; 1960-)
Sears Tower (Chicago)(110 stories)
Sears, Richard W. (US bus.; 1863-1914)
Sears, Roebuck & Co.
Seasat (US space satellite)
Seashore test (music)
Seashore, Carl (US psych.; 1866-1949)

Seaside, CA
SEATO (Southeast Asia Treaty Organization) (1955-76)
Seattle Mariners (baseball team)
Seattle Post-Intelligencer (WA newspaper)
Seattle Seahawks (football team)
Seattle Slew (racehorse)
Seattle SuperSonics (basketball team)
Seattle Times (WA newspaper)
Seattle, Chief (also Seatlh)(Suquamish Indians; c1790-1866)
Seattle, WA
Seaver, Tom (baseball; 1944-)
Sebastian Cabot (ent.; 1918-77)
Sebastian Cabot (It. nav./expl.; 1474-1557)
Sebastian (Newbold) Coe (track; 1956-)
Sebastian, Inc., Paul
Sebastian, St. (Roman rel.; 3rd c.)
Sebastopol (goose)
Sebastopol, Crimea (also Sevastopol)
Seberg, Jean (ent.; 1938-79)
SEC (Securities and Exchange Commission)(US agcy.; est., 1934)
Secaucus, NJ
Secchi disk(s)(biology)
Secchi, Angelo (It. astron.; 1818-78)
Secession, War of (also American Civil War, War Between the States)(1861-65)
Seconal™ (sedative)
Second Coming (rel.)
Second Reich (Ger. empire; 1871-1918)
Second Temple (rel.)
Second Triumvirate (ancient Rome ruling board)
Second World War (also World War II, WWII)(1939-45)
Secret™ (anti-perspirant)
Secret Life of Walter Mitty, The (J. Thurber short story)
Secret Service, U.S. (US govt. agcy.; est. 1865)
Secretariat (of the UN)
Secretariat (racehorse)
Section Eight (also l.c.)(US Army discharge for unfitness/undesirable traits)
Securities and Exchange Commission (SEC)(US agcy.; est. 1934)
Security Council, National (NSC)(US govt. agcy.; est. 1947)
Security Council, United Nations
Sedaka, Neil (ent.; 1939-)
Seder (rel.)
Sedition Acts, Alien and (US hist.; 1798)
See-Bee (also Seabee)(large, ocean-going vessel)
See of Rome (also Holy See)(Vatican)
See, Holy (also See of Rome)(Vatican)
Seeger, Pete(r) R. (ent.; 1919-)
Seeing Eye dog (med.)
Seenu, Maldives

See's™
See's Candy Shop (US bus.)
Segal, Erich (US writer; 1937-)
Segal, George (ent.; 1934-)
Segal, George (US sculptor; 1924-)
Segar, Elzie C. (cartoonist, *Popeye*; 1894-1938)
Seger cone (ceramics)
Ségou, Mali
Segovia, Andrés (Sp. ent.; 1893-1987)
S. E. Hinton (US writer; 1948-)
Seidelman, Susan (ent.; 1952-)
Seidler, Maren (track; 1962-)
Seifert, Jaroslav (Czech. poet; 1902-86)
Seignoret, Clarence (Augustus)(pres., Dominica)
Seiji Ozawa (Jap./US cond.; 1935-)
Seiko Corp. of America
Seiko™ watch
Seine (river, Fr.)
Seinfeld (TV show)
Seinfeld, Jerry (ent.; 1954-)
Seingalt, Casanova de (also Giovanni Jacopo Casanova)(It. adventurer; 1725-98)
Seirra Leone (republic, W Afr.)
Seko (Kuku Ngbendu wa Zabanga), Mobutu Sese (b. Joseph Désiré Mobutu)(pres., Zaire; 1930-)
Sekondi-Takoradi, Ghana
Selassie, Haile (Ras [Prince] Tafari, "the Lion of Judah")(emp., Eth.; 1891-1975)
Seldane™ (med.)
Selective Service Act (US mil.; 1917)
Selene (myth.)
Seles, Monica (tennis; 1973-)
Self (mag.)
Selke, Frank (hockey; 1893-1985)
Selkirk, Alexander (Scot. sailor; 1676-1721)
Sellecca, Connie (ent.; 1955-)
Selleck, Tom (ent.; 1945-)
Sellers, Peter (ent.; 1925-80)
Selma Diamond (ent.; 1920-85)
Selma, AL, CA
Selsun Blue™ (med.)
Selznick, David O(liver)(ent.; 1902-65)
Semarang, Indonesia
Seminole (NAmer. Indians)
Semipalatinsk, Kazakhstan
Semite (people)
Semitic languages
Semyon (Konstantinovich) Timoshenko (USSR mil.; 1895-1970)
Sen, Hun (co-PM, Cambodia; 1950-)
Senate (of the U.S.)(US govt.)
Senate Finance Committee (US govt.)
Senators, Ottawa (hockey team)
Sendai, Japan
Sendak, Maurice (Bernard)(US writer; 1928-)
Seneca (lang.)

Seneca (Lucius Annaeus Seneca)(Roman phil./
    writer; 4 BC-AD 65)
Seneca (NAmer. Indians)
Seneca Army Depot (NY)(US mil.)
Seneca Falls, NY
Senegal (Republic of)(W Afr.)
Sennett Studios, Mack (old Hollywood)
Sennett, Mack (b. Michael Sinnott)(ent.; 1880-
    1960)
Sentinel, Milwaukee (WI newspaper)
Sentinel, Orlando (FL newspaper)
Sentra, Nissan™ (auto.)
Sentra SE-R, Nissan™ (auto.)
Senufo (lang./people)
Seoul, South Korea
Sephardim (Sp./Port. Jews)
Sepoy Rebellion/Mutiny (also Indian
    Mutiny)(India/Br.; 1857-58)
Septuagint (rel.)
Sequoia National Park (CA)
Sequoya, Chief (aka George Guess)(Cherokee
    Indians, scholar; c1766-1843)
Serafin, Barry (US TV jour.)
Serax™ (med.)
Serb (people)
Serbia (republic. Yug.)
Serbian (people)
Serbian Orthodox (rel.)
Serbo-Croatian (lang.)
Serbs (people)
Serekunda, Gambia
Serene Highness (title)
Serene Majesty (title)
Serengeti National Park (E Afr.)
Serengeti Plain (E Afr.)
Serenity™ pads
Serer (lang./people)
Seretse Khama (ex-pres., Botswana; 1921-80)
Serge (Sergei Alexandrovich) Koussevitsky
    (Rus. cond.; 1874-1951)
Sergeant Bilko (TV show)
Sergeant (Alvin Cullum) York (US mil.; 1887-
    1964)
Sergeant York (film; 1941)
Sergei (Pavlovich) Diaghilev (Rus. ballet; 1872-
    1929)
Sergei Mironovich Kirov (Rus. pol.; 1886-1934)
Sergei (Sergeyevich) Prokofiev (Rus. comp.;
    1891-1953)
Sergei Tereshchenko (PM, Kazakhstan
Sergei V(asilyevich) Rachmaninov (Rus. comp./
    cond.; 1893-1943)
Stanislavsky, Konstantin (Sergeivich)(Rus. ent.;
    1863-1938)
Sergio Franchi (ent.; 1933-90)
Sergio Mendes (ent.; 1941-)
Seria, Brunei
Series E bond (US Treasury)

Series H bond (US Treasury)
Serkin, Peter (US pianist; 1947-)
Serkin, Rudolf (US pianist; 1903-91)
Serling, Rod (ent.; 1924-75)
Sermon on the Mount (Jesus' Beatitudes)
Serowe, Botswana
Serpens (astron., serpent)
Serpico (film; 1973)
Serra Junípero, Miguel José, Father (Sp. rel.;
    1713-84)
Serrano ham
Serta™ (mattress)
Serta, Inc.
Service Cross, Distinguished (mil.)
Service Medal, Distinguished (mil.)
Service Merchandise, Inc.
Service Order, Distinguished (Br. mil.)
Service, Robert W(illiam)(Can. writer; 1874-
    1958)
ServiceMaster Co.
Servile Wars (Roman hist.; 1st-2nd c. BC)
Sesame Street (mag.)
Sesame Street (TV show)
Sesame Street Records (US bus.)
Sesotho (lang.)
Sessions, Roger (Huntington)(US comp.; 1896-
    1985)
Sessions, William S. (ex-dir./FBI; 1930-)
Sessue Hayakawa (ent.; 1890-1973)
Seth (rel.)
Seton Hall University (NJ)
Seton, Mother (also St. Elizabeth Ann [Bayley]
    Seton)(US rel.; 1774-1821)
Setswana (lang.)
Setúbal, Portugal
Seurat, Georges (Fr. artist; 1859-91)
Seurity Agency, National (NSA)(US govt.)
Seuss, Dr. (aka Theodore Seuss Geisel)(US
    writer/artist; 1904-91)
Sevareid, Eric (US TV jour.; 1913-92)
Sevastopol, Crimea (also Sebastopol)
Seven against Thebes (Aeschylus tragedy)
Seven and Seven (mixed drink)
Seven Cities of Cibola (utopia)
7-Eleven (US bus.)
Seven Hills of Rome
Seven Hills, City of (Rome)
Seven Sisters colleges (prestigious women
    colleges)
Seven-Up Cos., Dr Pepper/
Seven Weeks' War (also Austro-Prussian
    War)(1866)
Seven Wonders of the World
Seven Year Itch, The (film)
Seven Years' War (also French and Indian
    War)(Eur. hist.;1756-63)
Seventeen (mag.)
1776 (play)

Seventh-Day Adventist (rel.)
76ers, Philadelphia (basketball team)
Severini, Gino (It. artist; 1883-1966)
Severinsen, Doc (ent.; 1927-)
Severn bore (tidal wave)
Severn River (Wales/Eng.)
Seville Touring Sedan, Cadillac™ (auto.)
Seville, Cadillac™ (auto.)
Seville, Spain
Seville, The Barber of (Beaumarchais play, G. Rossini opera)
Sèvres porcelain/ware
Sèvres, France
Sew News (mag.)
Sewall, Samuel (US judge, witch trials; 1652-1730)
Seward Peninsula (AK)
Seward, William Henry (US pol.; 1801-72)
Seward's Folly/folly (also Alaska Purchase)($7.2 million; 1867)
Sewell, Anna (Br. writer; 1820-78)
Sewell, Joe (baseball; 1898-1990)
Sex Pistols (pop music)
Sextans (astron., sextant)
Sexton, Anne Harvey (US poet; 1928-74)
Seybou, Ali (ex-pres., Niger; 1940-)
Seychelles (Republic of)(islands, Indian Ocean)
Seyfert galaxy (astron.)
Seymour, Jane (ent.; 1951-)
Seymour, Jane (queen, Eng., 3rd wife of Henry VIII; 1509?-37)
Seymour, Lynn (Can. ballet; 1939-)
Sfax, Tunisia
Sforza, Carlo, Conte (It. pol./dipl.; 1873-1952)
Sforza, Francesco (It. pol.; 1401-66)
Sforza, Galeazzo Maria (It. pol.; 1444-76)
Sforza, Ludovico ("The Moor")(It. pol.; 1451-1508)
Sgt. Pepper's Lonely Hearts Club Band (Beatles album)
Shabbat (Jew. Sabbath)
Shabuoth (also Shavuoth)(rel.)
Shackelford, Ted (ent.; 1946-)
Shackleton, Sir Ernest (Henry)(Br. expl.; 1874-1922)
Shaddai (also Shadai)(rel.)
Shadow, Dodge (auto.)
Shafer Vineyards (US bus.)
Shaffer, Paul (ent.; 1949-)
Shafi'i (Islamic law)
Shafi'ites (rel.)
Shafter, Fort, HI (mil.)
Shagari, Alhaji Shehu (ex-pres., Nigeria; 1925-)
Shah, Rajah Azlan Muhibuddin (king, Malaysia)
Shahn, Ben(jamin)(US artist; 1898-1969)
Shake 'N Bake™ (food)
Shaker Heights, OH

Shaker, Sharif Zaid ibn (ex-PM, Jordan)
Shakers (also United Society of Believers in Christ's Second Coming[Appearing], Millenial Church)
Shakespeare Company, Royal (RSC)(Br. theater; est. 1961-)
Shakespeare, William (Br. writer; 1564-1616)
Shakespearean sonnet (also English sonnet, Elizabethan sonnet)
Shalala, Donna E. (US Secy./HHS; 1941-)
Shales, Tom (US TV critic; 1958-)
Shalimar™
Shalimar Accessories (US bus.)
Shalit, Gene (US critic)
Shalom (or Sholom) Aleichem (aka Solomon Rabinowitz)(Yiddish writer; 1859-1916)
Shalott, Lady of (Tennyson poem)
Shamir, Yitzhak (ex-PM, Isr.; 1915-)
Shamitoff Foods (US bus.)
Shamitoff's™
Shamu (whale)
Shamus (film; 1972)
Shan (lang./people)
Shandling, Garry (ent.; 1949-)
Shandong (province, Ch.)
Shandong Peninsula (Ch.)
Shandy, Tristram (L. Sterne novel)
Shane (film; 1953)
Shang dynasty (Ch. hist.; 1766-1122 BC)
Shanghai chicken
Shanghai, China
Shangkun, Yang (ex-pres., Ch.; 1907-)
Shangri-la (also Shangri-La)(utopia, from *Lost Horizon*)
Shankar Dayal Sharma (pres., India
Shankar, Ravi (comp., India; 1920-)
Shankar, Uday (dancer, India; 1900-77)
Shanker, Albert
Shannen Doherty (ent.)
Shannon International Airport (Ir.)
Shannon River (also River Shannon)(Ir.)
Shannon, Del (ent.; 1940-90)
Shantung silk (also l.c.)
Shanxi (province, Ch.)
Shaoqi, Liu (also Liu Shao-chi)(Ch. pol.; 1898?-1969?)
SHAPE (also Shape)(Supreme Headquarters Allied Powers, Eur.)
Shape (mag.)
Shapiro, Karl (Jay)(US poet/editor; 1913-)
Shapiro, Robert (US atty.)
Shapley, Harlow (US astron.; 1885-1972)
Shaquille O'Neal (basketball; 1972-)
Shar-Pei, Chinese (dog)
Sharchop (lang./people)
Shari Lewis (ent.; 1934-)
Shari, Ubangi- (now Central African Republic)
Sharif Zaid ibn Shaker (ex-PM, Jordan)

Sharif, Nawaz (ex-PM, Pak.; 1948-)
Sharif, Omar (ent.; 1932-)
Sharjah (state, UAE)
Sharkey, Jack (boxing)
Sharks, San Jose (hockey team)
Sharma, Shankar Dayal (pres., India
Sharon Gless (ent.; 1943-)
Sharon Pratt Kelly (DC mayor)
Sharon Stone (ent.)
Sharon Tate (Polanski)(ent.; 1943-69)
Sharon, Ariel (Isr. pol./mil.; 1928-)
Sharon, PA
Sharon, rose of (plant)
Sharp™
Sharp Electronics Corp.
Sharp, Becky (fict. chara., *Vanity Fair*)
Sharpe Army Depot (CA)(US mil.)
Sharpeville, South Africa
Shasta™
Shasta Beverages (US bus.)
Shasta daisy
Shasta, Mount (dormant volcano, CA)
Shastri, (Shri) Lal Bahadur (ex-PM, India;
    1904-66)
Shatalov, Vladimir A. (cosmo.; 1927-)
Shatner, William (ent.; 1931-)
Shatt-al-Arab River (Iraq)
Shavuoth (also Shabuoth)(rel.)
Shaw Air Force Base, SC (US mil.)
Shaw Industries, Inc.
Shaw v. Reno (US law; 1993)
Shaw, Artie (US jazz; 1910-)
Shaw, George Bernard (Ir. writer/critic; 1856-
    1950)
Shaw, Henry Wheeler (pseud. Josh Billings)(US
    humorist; 1818-85)
Shaw, Robert (ent.; 1927-78)
Shawnee (NAmer. Indians)
Shawnee, KS, OK
Shays' Rebellion (US hist.; 1786-87)
Shays, Daniel (US mil./pol.; 1747?-1825)
Shazam!
Shea Stadium (NYC)
Shea, John (ent.; 1949-)
Shean, Al (ent.)
Shean, (Ed) Gallagher & (Al)(ent.)
Shear Perfection (US bus.)
Shearer, Moira (ent.; 1926-)
Shearer, Norma (ent.; 1902-83)
Shearing, George (US jazz; 1919-)
Shearson Lehman Brothers, Inc.
Shearson Lehman Hutton Open
Sheba (also Saba)(ancient S Yemen)
Sheba, Queen of (biblical, visited Solomon to
    test his wisdom)
Shebat (also Shevat)(Jew. month)
Sheboygan, WI
Shecky Greene (ent.; 1926-)

Shedd's Food Products (US bus.)
Shedd's Spread™
Sheedy, Ally (ent.; 1962-)
Sheehan, Patty (golf; 1956-)
Sheehy, Gail (US writer)
Sheeler, Charles (US artist; 1883-1965)
Sheen, Charlie (ent.; 1965-)
Sheen, Fulton J(ohn), Bishop (US rel./writer/
    educ.; 1895-1979)
Sheen, Martin (ent.; 1940-)
Sheena Easton (ent.; 1959-)
Sheerness, England
Sheetrock™ (constr.)
Sheffield plate (copper/silver)
Sheffield, AL
Sheffield, England
Sheffield, Gary (baseball; 1968-)
Sheik™ (condoms)
Sheilah Graham (gossip columnist; 1904-88)
Sheila Young (speed skating; 1950-)
Shelby, Richard Craig (US cong.; 1934-)
Sheldon Leonard (ent.; 1907-)
Shell Oil Co.
Shelley Duvall (ent.; 1949-)
Shelley Duvall's Bedtime Stories (TV show)
Shelley Fabares (ent.; 1942-)
Shelley Long (ent.; 1949-)
Shelley Winters (ent.; 1922-)
Shelley, Mary Wollstonecraft (Br. writer; 1797-
    1851)
Shelley, Percy Bysshe (Br. poet; 1792-1822)
Shelly Berman (ent.; 1926-)
Shelly Manne
Shem-Tov, Baal (also Israel ben Eliezer)(Jew.
    rel.; c1700-60)
Shema (rel.)
Shemp Howard (b. Samuel Horwitz)(ent.; 1895-
    1955)
Shenandoah Mountains (VA/MD)
Shenandoah National Park (VA)
Shenandoah River (SE US)
Shenandoah Valley (VA)
Shenandoah, VA
Shenyang, China (formerly Mukden)
Shenzen (econ. community, S Ch.)
Sheol (hell)
Shepard, Alan B(artlett), Jr. (astro.; 1923-)
Shepard, Sam (US writer/ent.; 1943-)
Sheppard, Samuel H. (US phys.; 1924-70)
Shepherd, Cybill (ent.; 1949-)
Shepherd, Lee (auto racing; 1945-85)
Sheppard Air Force Base, TX (US mil.)
Sheraton Grand Hotel
Sheraton hotels
Sheraton Corp.
Sheraton, Thomas (Br. furniture designer;
    1751-1806)
Sherbrooke, Quebec, Canada

Shere Hite (US writer; 1942-)
Sheree North (ent.; 1933-)
Sheridan, Ann (ent.; 1915-67)
Sheridan, Fort (IL)(mil.)
Sheridan, Philip (Henry)(US gen.; 1831-88)
Sheridan, Richard B(rinsley)(Ir. writer/pol.; 1751-1816)
Sheridan, WY
Sheriff of Nottingham (*Robin Hood*)
Sherlock Holmes (fict. detective)
Sherman Antitrust Act (US hist.; 1890)
Sherman Edwards (US comp.; 1919-81)
Sherman Hemsley (ent.; 1938-)
Sherman Silver Purchase Act (US hist.; 1890)
Sherman, James S(choolcraft)(ex-US VP; 1855-1912)
Sherman, John (US pol.; 1823-1900)
Sherman, Roger (US pol.; 1721-93)
Sherman, TX
Sherman, William T(ecumseh)(US gen.; 1820-91)
Shero, Fred (hockey; 1945-90)
Sherpas (Himalayan mountaineers)
Sherrill Milnes (ent.; 1935-)
Sherrington, Sir Charles (Scott)(Br. physiol.; 1857-1952)
Sherry Lee Lansing
Sherwin-Williams Co.
Sherwood Anderson (US writer; 1876-1941)
Sherwood Forest (Nottinghamshire, Eng.; R. Hood's home)
Sherwood, Robert (Emmet)(US writer; 1896-1955)
Shetland Islands (Scot.)
Shetland pony
Shetland sheepdog (dog)
Shetland wool (fabric)
Shevardnadze, Eduard A. (pres., Georgia; 1928-)
Shevat (also Shebat)(Jew. month)
Shiba-Inu (dog)
Shield™ (soap)
Shields, Brooke (ent.; 1965-)
Shih Tzu (dog)
Shiite Muslim (also Shia)(rel., Islam)
Shik, Chung Won (ex-PM, SKorea)
Shikibu Murasaki, Lady (Jap. writer; c978-1031?)
Shikoku (island, Jap.)
Shilluk (lang.)
Shiloh (rel.)
Shiloh, Battle of (also Pittsburg Landing)(US hist.; 1862)
Shimon Peres (ex-PM, Isr.; 1923-)
Shinto (rel.)
Shintoism (rel.)
Shiraz, Iran
Shire (draft horse)

Shire, Talia (ent.; 1946-)
Shirelles, the (pop music)
Shires, the (Br. hunting counties)
Shirley Ann Grau (US writer; 1929-)
Shirley Babashoff (swimming; 1957-)
Shirley Bassey (ent.; 1937-)
Shirley Booth (ent.; 1907-92)
Shirley (Anita St. Hill) Chisholm (US pol.; 1924-)
Shirley Jackson (US writer; 1916-65)
Shirley Jones (ent.; 1934-)
Shirley MacLaine (ent.; 1934-)
Shirley Temple (non-alcoholic cocktail)
Shirley Temple Black (US ent./dipl.; 1928-)
Shirley Verrett (ent.; 1931-)
Shirley, Laverne & (TV show)
Shiseido™
Shiseido Cosmetics America, Ltd.
Shiva (also Siva)(Hindu god)
Shkodër, Albania (also Shkodra)
Shmuel Yosef Agnon (b. Samuel Josef Czaczkes)(Isr. writer; 1888-1970)
Shockley, Dr. William B(radford)(US physt.; 1910-89)
Shoe (comic strip)
Shoe Corp., Inc., U.S.
Shoemaker, Willie (William Lee)(US jockey; 1931-)
Shofar™
Shofar Kosher Foods, Inc.
Shogun (book, film)
Sholokhov, Mikhail (Aleksandrovich)(Rus. writer; 1905-84)
Sholom (or Shalom) Aleichem (aka Solomon Rabinowitz)(Yiddish writer; 1859-1916)
Shona (lang./people)
Shondells, Tommy James & the (pop music)
Shoney's (US bus.)
Shonin, Georgi S. (cosmo.)
Shoo-Fly Pie & Apple Pan Dowdy (song)
Shooting of Dan McGrew, The (R.W. Service ballad)
Shop 'Til You Drop (TV show)
Shop-Vac Corp.
Shopko Store
Shore, Dinah (ent.; 1917-94)
Shore, Eddie (hockey; 1902-85)
Short, Bobby (ent.; 1924-)
Short, Martin (ent.; 1950-)
Shorter, Frank (runner; 1947-)
Shorthorn (cattle)
Shoshone Falls (ID)
Shoshone National Forest (formerly Yellowstone Park Timber Reserve)
Shoshoni (also Shoshone)(NAmer. Indians)
Shostakovich, Dmitry (Dmitriyevich)(Rus. comp.; 1906-75)
Shotwell, James Thomson (Can/US hist.; 1874-

1965)
Shout™ (spot remover)
Show Me State (nickname, MO)
Shower to Shower™ (health)
Showtime (SHO)(cable TV)
Shredded Wheat Spoonsize™ (cereal)
Shredded Wheat, Nabisco™ (cereal)
Shree (or Osho) Rajneesh (aka Bhagwan)(b.
    Chaadra Mohan Jain)(Indian rel.; 1931-90)
Shreveport Times (LA newspaper)
Shreveport, LA
Shrew, The Taming of the (Shakespeare play)
Shriner (member of Ancient Arabic Order of
    Nobles of the Mystic Shrine)
Shriner, Herb (ent.)
Shriner, Wil
Shriver, (Robert) Sargent, Jr. (US bus./pol.;
    1915-)
Shriver, Eunice Kennedy (US, wife of pol.;
    1921-)
Shriver, Maria (US TV jour.; 1955-)
Shriver, Pam (tennis; 1962-)
Shropshire (county, Eng.)
Shropshire sheep
shroud of Turin (rel.)
Shrove Tuesday (also Mardi Gras)(rel.)
Shubert Alley (NYC)
Shubert Theater (NYC)
Shubert, Jacob J. (US theater; 1880-1963)
Shubert, Lee (US theater; 1875-1953)
Shubert, Sam S. (US theater; 1876-1905)
Shula, Don(ald Francis)(football; 1930-)
Shull, Richard B. (ent.; 1929-)
Shulman, Max (US writer; 1919-88)
Shultz, George P(ratt)(US pol.; 1920-)
Shushkevich, Stanislav S. (pres; Belarus
Shuster, Joe (cartoonist, *Superman*; 1914-92)
Shute, Nevil (Br. writer/eng.; 1899-1960)
Shwe, Than (head of state, Myanmar; 1933-)
Shylock (fict. moneylender, *Merchant of Venice*)
Si (chem. sym., silicon)
Si-Kiang River (also Xi Jiang)(Ch.)
Sialkot, Pakistan
Siam (now Thailand)
Siam (or Thailand), Gulf of
Siamese cat
Siamese fighting fish
Siamese twins
Sian, China (also Xian)
Siangtan, China (also Xiangtan)
Siauliai, Lithuania
Siba (fict. chara., *The Lion King*)
Sibelius, Jean (Julius Christian)(Fin. comp.;
    1865-1957)
Sibenik, Croatia
Siberia (region, N Asia)
Siberian husky (dog)
Siberian Railway, Trans- (>7,000 miles)

Sibomana, Adrien (ex-PM, Burundi)
Sica, Vittorio De (ent.; 1901-74)
Sichuan (also Szechwan)(province, Ch.)
Sichuan cuisine (also Szechwan)
Sicilian Vespers rebellion (It./Fr. hist.; 1282)
Siciliano, Angelo (aka Charles Atlas)(US body
    builder; 1894-1972)
Sicily, Italy (largest Mediterranean island)
Sickert, Walter Richard (Br. artist; 1860-1942)
Sid Caesar (ent.; 1922-)
Sid Krofft
Sid Luckman (football; 1916-)
Sid Vicious (ent.; 1957-79)
Sidamo (people)
Siddhartha, Gautama (Buddha)(Indian phil.,
    founded Buddhism; c563-c483 BC)
Siddons, Sarah (Kemble)(ent.; 1755-1831)
Sidewinder (missile)
Sidi Mohamed Ould Boubacar (PM, Mauritania
Sidney Bechet (US jazz; 1897-1959)
Sidney Catlett ("Big Sid")(US jazz; 1910-51)
Sidney Lanier (US poet; 1842-81)
Sidney Lumet (ent.; 1924-)
Sidney Poitier (ent.; 1927-)
Sidney (James) Webb (Br. reformer/writer;
    1859-1947)
Sidney, Sylvia (ent.; 1910-)
Sidon, Lebanon (also Sayda, Saida)
Sidonie Gabrielle Colette (Fr. writer; 1873-
    1954)
Sidqi, Atef (PM, Egypt)
SIDS (sudden infant death syndrome)
Siege of Yorktown (US hist.; 1781, 1862)
Siege Perilous (Arthurian)
Siegel, Benjamin "Bugsy"
Siegel, Jerry (cartoonist, *Superman*; 1914-)
Siegel, Joel
Siegfried (also Sigurd)(legendary Ger. hero;
    c700)
Siemaszko, Casey
Siemens Components, Inc.
Siemens Hearing Instruments, Inc.
Siena, Italy
Siena, St. Catherine of (It. mystic; 1347-80)
Sierra (mag.)
Sierra Club (conservation org.; est. 1892)
Sierra Club Books (US bus.)
Sierra Club Legal Defense Fund
Sierra Leone (Republic of)(W Afr.)
Sierra Madre (CO/WY mountain range)
Sierra Madre (Mex. mountain range)
Sierra Madre, CA
Sierra Nevada (CA mountain range)
Sierra Nevada (Sp. mountain range)
Sierra Vista Winery (US bus.)
Sigismund (Augustus) II (king, Pol.; 1520-72)
Sigismund (holy Roman emp,; 1368-1437)
Sigismund I ("The Old")(king, Pol.; 1467-1548)

Sigismund III (king, Pol.; 1566-1632)

Sigmund Freud (Aus. phys., founder of psychoanalysis; 1856-1939)

Sigmund Romberg (Hung. comp.; 1887-1951)

Sign (or sign) English

Signac, Paul (Fr. artist; 1863-1935)

Signal™ (mouthwash)

Signe Hasso (Swed. ent.; 1910-)

Signorelli, Luca (d'Egidio di Ventura de')(It. artist; c1445-1523)

Signoret, Simone (ent.; 1921-85)

Sigourney Weaver (ent.; 1949-)

Sigurd (also Siegfried)(legendary Ger. hero; c700)

Sihanouk, Norodom (king, Cambodia; 1922-)

S(amuel) I(chiye) Hayakawa (US educ./pol./ linguist; 1906-92)

Sikh (rel.)

Sikh Wars (India; 1845-49)

Sikhism (rel.)

Sikkim (state, India)

Sikking, James B. (ent.; 1934-)

Silas Marner (G. Eliot novel)

Silent Spring (R. Carson book)

Silent, William the (Dutch, Prince of Orange; 1533-84)

Silenus (myth.)

Silesia (region, Eur.)

Silex, Inc., Hamilton Beach/Proctor-

Silicon Valley (nickname, Santa Clara Co., CA)

Silius (Roman poet; c25-101)

Silivas, Daniela

Silkie (chicken)

Silkwood, Karen (US nuclear safety advocate)

Sill, Fort, OK (mil.)

Sills, Beverly (b. Belle Silverman)(US opera; 1929-)

Silurian period (430-395 million years ago)

Silva, Aníbal Cavaco (PM, Port.; 1939-)

Silver Spring, MD

Silver Springs, FL

Silver Star medal/Medal (mil.)

Silver State (nickname, NV)

Silver, Ron (ent.; 1946-)

Silverado Vineyards, The (US bus.)

Silverado™, Chevy (auto.)

Silverheels, Jay (ent.)

Silverman, Fred (ent.)

Silvers, Phil (ent.; 1912-85)

Silvester, Jay (discus thrower; 1937-)

Silvestre Siale Bileka (PM, Equatorial Guinea

Silvio Berlusconi (PM, It.)

Simi Valley (CA)

Simi Winery, Inc.

Simmel, George (Ger. sociol./phil.; 1858-1918)

Simmonds, Kennedy A(lphonse)(PM, St. Kitts-Nevis)

Simmons Beautyrest™ (mattress)

Simmons, Al (baseball; 1902-56)

Simmons, Gene (ent.; 1949-)

Simmons, Jean (ent.; 1929-)

Simmons, Richard (ent.; 1948-)

Simon & Schuster, Inc.

Simon Achidi Achu (PM, Cameroon)

Simon and Garfunkel (pop music)

Simon Bolivar ("El Libertador")(SAmer. pol.; 1783-1830)

Simon Guggenheim (US finan./bus.; 1867-1941)

Simon Le Bon (ent.; 1958-)

Simon Legree (fict. chara., *Uncle Tom's Cabin*)

Simon Museum of Art, Norton (CA)

Simon Peter (also St. Peter)(rel.; ?-AD c64)

Simon Rodia (It. tile setter; 1875-1965)

Simon Templar

Simon Wiesenthal (Aus. reformer; 1908-)

Simon, Carly (ent.; 1945-)

Simon, (Marvin) Neil (US writer; 1927-)

Simon, Norton (US bus.; 1907-93)

Simon, Paul (ent.; 1942-)

Simon, Paul (US cong.; 1928-)

Simon, Simple (nursery rhyme chara.)

Simon, St.

Simone de Beauvoir (Fr. writer; 1908-86)

Simone Signoret (ent.; 1921-85)

Simone, Nina (ent.; 1933-)

Simonides (Gr. poet; 556-c468 BC)

Simoniz™ (car wax)

Simoniz Co.

Simons, Menno (Dutch rel.; c1496-c1561)

Simple Simon (nursery rhyme chara.)

Simplesse™ (fat substitute)

Simplesse Co., The

Simplicity Pattern Co., Inc.

Simplon pass (Switz./It.)

Simpson, Alan K. (US cong.; 1931-)

Simpson, Bart (cartoon chara.)

Simpson, George Gaylord (US paleontol.; 1902-84)

Simpson, Nicole (US news)

Simpson, O(renthal) J(ames)(football; 1947-)

Simpson, Wallis "Wally" Warfield (Duchess of Windsor)(US socialite, m. Edward VIII; 1896-1986)

Simpsons, The (cartoon)

Sims, Billy (football; 1955-)

Sims, Zoot (US jazz; 1925-85)

Sinai Medical Center, Cedars-

Sinai Peninsula (Eg.)

Sinai, Mount (NE Eg.; Moses, 10 Commandments)

Sinanthropus (anthrop.)

Sinatra, Frank (Francis Albert)(ent.; 1915-)

Sinbad (ent.)

Sinbad the Sailor (also Sindbad)(fict. chara., *Arabian Nights)*

Sinclair Lewis, (Harry)(US writer; 1885-1951)

Sinclair, Upton (Beall)(US writer/reformer; 1878-1968)
Sinde bele (lang.)
Sindhi (lang./people)
Sine-Aid™ (med.)
Sinequan™ (med.)
Sinéad O'Connor (ent.; 1967-)
Sing Sing (state prison, NY)
Singapore (Republic of)(SE Asia)
Singapore Airlines, Ltd.
Singapore City, Singapore
Singapore sling (mixed drink)
Singapore, Road to (film; 1940)
Singer Co., The
Singer, Isaac B(ashevis)(Pol./US writer; 1904-91)
Singer, Isaac M(errit)(US, inv. sewing machine; 1811-75)
Singh, Vishwanath Pratap (ex-PM, India; 1931-)
Singhalese (also Sinhalese)(lang./people)
Singletary, Mike (football; 1958-)
Singleton, Penny (ent.)
Singleton, Zutty (US jazz; 1898-1975)
Sining, China (also Xining)
Sinkiang Uighur (also Xinjiang Uygur)(region, Ch.)
Sinn Fein (Ir. pol. party)
Sino-Japanese Wars (Jap./Ch.; 1894-95, 1931-45)
Sino-Soviet
Sino-Tibetan languages
Sinsiang, China (also Xinxiang)
Sinuiju, North Korea
Sinutab™ (med.)
Sioux (also Dakota)(NAmer. Indians)
Sioux City, IA
Sioux Falls, SD
Sioux State (nickname, ND)
Siphandon, Khamtai (PM, Laos; 1925-)
Sippie Wallace (ent.)
Siqueiros, David Alfaro (Mex. artist; 1896-1974)
Sir Bedivere (Arthurian knight)
Sir Bors (Arthurian knight)
Sir Galahad (Arthurian knight)
Sir Gawain (Arthurian knight)
Sir Percivale (also Parsifal)(Arthurian knight)
Sir Roger de Coverly (dance)
Sir Speedy™ (printing)
Sir Speedy, Inc.
Siren (myth.)
Sirhan B(ishara) Sirhan (assassinated R.F. Kennedy)
Sirica, John (US judge; 1904-92)
Sirimavo Bandaranaike (ex-PM, Sri Lanka; 1916-)
Sirius (astron., part of Canis Major [or Great Dog])

Siskel & Ebert (US critics)
Siskel, Gene (ent.; 1946-)
Sisler, George (Harold)(baseball; 1893-1973)
Sisley, Alfred (Fr. artist; 1840?-99)
Sisophon, Cambodia
Sissy Spacek (ent.; 1949-)
Sister (Elizabeth) Kenny (Austl. nurse; 1886-1952)
Sisters (TV show)
Sisters, The Lennon (pop music)
Sistine Chapel (Vatican)(Michelangelo frescoes)
Sisyphus (myth.)
Sitiveni Rabuka (PM, Fiji
Sitka National Historical Park (AK)
Sitka, AK
Sitting Bull, Chief (Tatanka Yotanka)(Sioux Indians; c1831-90)
Sitwell, Dame Edith (Br. writer; 1887-1964)
Sitwell, Sir (Francis) Osbert Sacheverell (Br. writer; 1892-1969)
Sitwell, Sir Sacheverell (Br. writer; 1897-1988)
Siuslaw National Forest
Siva (also Shiva)(Hindu god)
Sivan (Jew. month)
Six-Day War (Arab/Isr.; 1967)
Sixto Durán Bellén (pres., Ecuador; 1921-)
$64,000 Question (TV show)
60 Minutes (TV show)
Sizzler™
Sizzler Restaurants International (US bus.)
S(idney) J(oseph) Perelman (US writer; 1904-79)
Skeeter Davis (ent.)
Skelton, Red (Richard)(ent.; 1913-)
Skerritt, Tom (ent.; 1933-)
Skiing (mag.)
Skilcraft (US bus.)
Skilsaw (constr.)
Skinner box (psych.)
Skinner, B(urrhus) F(rederic)(US psych./writer; 1903-90)
Skinner, Cornelia Otis (US writer/ent.; 1901-79)
Skinner, Otis (US writer/ent.; 1858-1942)
Skin-So-Soft (skin care)
Skippy™ (peanut butter)
Skippy Homeier
Skiros (also Scyros, Skyros)(Gr. island)
Skjoldungs of Denmark, House of the (Br. ruling family; 1016-42)
Skokie, IL
Skopje, Macedonia
Skouras, Spyros (Panagiotes)(ent.; 1893-1971)
Skowron, Bill "Moose" (baseball; 1930-)
Sky Harbor International Airport (Phoenix AZ)
Skye (island, Scot.)
Skye terrier (dog)
Skylab (US space station)
Skylark, Buick™ (auto.)

Skyline Corp.
Skynyrd, Lynyrd (pop music)
Skyros (also Skiros, Scyros)(Gr. island)
Skywalker, Luke (fict. chara., *Star Wars*)
Skywest Airlines
Slade Gorton (US cong.; 1928-)
Slam Stewart (ent.)
Slaney, Mary Decker (US runner; 1958-)
Slatkin, Leonard (US cond.; 1944-)
Slaughter, Frank G. (US writer
Slav(ic)(lang./people)
Slave Coast (slavery traffic, W Afr.; 17th-19th
    c.)
Slayton, Donald Kent "Deke" (astro.; 1924-93)
Sleepinal™ (med.)
Sleeping Beauty (fict. chara.)
Sleeping Gypsy, The (Rousseau)
Sleuth (play/film)
Slezak, Erika (ent.; 1946-)
Slezak, Walter (ent.; 1902-83)
Slezevicius, Adolfas (PM, Lith.)
Slick, Grace (ent.; 1939-)
Slick, Sam (aka Thomas Chandler
    Haliburton)(Can. writer/judge/hist.; 1796-
    1865)
Slidell, John (US pol.; 1793-1871)
Slim Gaillard
slim Jim™
Slim Jim, Inc.
Sloan-Kettering Institute for Cancer Research
    (NYC)
Sloan Publishers, Inc., Price/Stern/
Sloan, Alfred Pritchard (US bus.; 1875-1966)
Sloan, John F(rench)(US artist; 1871-1951)
Slo-bid™ (med.)
Slobodan Milosevic (Serbian pol.; 1941-)
Slo-Phyllin™ (med.)
Slovak (lang./people)
Slovakia (Czech. republic)
Slovene (lang./people)
Slovenia (republic. Yug.)(SE Eur.)
Slovenian (lang.)
Slovo, Joe
Sly and the Family Stone (pop music)
Sm (chem. sym., samarium)
Small Business Administration (SBA)(US govt.
    agcy.; est. 1953)
SMART Yellow Pages™
Smart, Maxwell (fict. TV chara.)
SmartWriter™ (steno writer)
Smetana, Bedrich (Czech. comp.; 1824-84)
Smirnoff Beverage & Import Co.
Smirnoff, Yakov
Smith & Wesson (US bus.)
Smith College (MA)
Smith Corona™
Smith-Corona (US bus.)
Smith Goes to Washington, Mr. (film; 1939)

Smith, Adam (Br. econ.; 1723-90)
Smith, Alexis (ent.; 1921-)
Smith, Alfred E(manuel)(NY gov.; 1873-1944)
Smith, Allison (ent.; 1969-)
Smith, Barney, Harris Upham and Co.
Smith, Bessie (US jazz; 1894-1937)
Smith, Billy (hockey; 1950-)
Smith, Bruce (football; 1963-)
Smith, Bubba (Charles Aaron)(football; 1945-)
Smith, Buffalo Bob (ent.; 1917-)
Smith, Clarence "Pinetop" (US jazz; 1904-29)
Smith, David (Roland)(US sculptor; 1906-65)
Smith, Dean (basketball; 1931-)
Smith, Emmitt (football; 1969-)
Smith, Fort (AR)(city)
Smith, Hedrick (US writer; 1933-)
Smith, Howard K. (TV news jour.)
Smith, Ian (Douglas)(ex-PM, Rhodesia; 1919-)
Smith, Jaclyn (ent.; 1947-)
Smith, John (Br. colonist in Amer., Pocahontas;
    1580-1631)
Smith, John Maynard (Br. biol.; 1920-)
Smith, Joseph (US rel., founded Mormons;
    1805-44)
Smith, Kate (Kathryn)(ent.; 1909-86)
Smith, Keely (ent.; 1935-)
Smith, Lane
Smith, Liz (US jour.; 1923-)
Smith, Maggie (ent.; 1934-)
Smith, Margaret Chase (US pol.; 1897-)
Smith, Ozzie (baseball; 1954-)
Smith, Patti (ent.)
Smith, Robert C. (US cong.; 1941-)
Smith, Ronnie Ray (sprinter; 1949-)
Smith, Snuffy (cartoon chara.)
Smith, Stanley Roger (tennis; 1946-)
Smith, Thorne
Smith, Tommie (sprinter; 1944-)
Smith, Will (ent.; 1969-)
Smith, William Kennedy (US news)
Smith, Willie "The Lion" (US jazz; 1897-1973)
Smithereens, the (pop music)
Smithfield ham™
Smithfield Ham & Products Co., The
Smithfield, Ltd., Gwaltney of
SmithKline Beecham (US bus.)
Smithsonian (mag.)
Smithsonian Astrophysical Observatory (MA)
Smithsonian Environmental Research Center
    (MD)
Smithsonian Institution (DC)
Smithsonian Tropical Research Institute
    (Panama)
Smits, Jimmy (ent.; 1955-)
Smoke, Marcia Jones (canoeing; 1941-)
Smokey and the Bandit (film; 1977)
Smokey (William) Robinson (US comp.; 1940-)
Smokey Robinson and the Miracles (pop music)

Smokey the Bear (fict. chara.)

Smokey (Joseph) Wood (baseball; 1890-1985)

Smoky Mountains National Park, Great (NC/TN)

Smoky Mountains, Great (NC/TN)

Smoot Tariff Act, Hawley- (US hist.; 1930)

Smoot, Reed (US pol.; 1862-1941)

Smothers Brothers Comedy Hour (TV show)

Smothers, Dick (ent.; 1939-)

Smothers, Tom (ent.; 1937-)

Smucker Co., The J. M.

Smucker's™ (jams/jellies)

Smurf™ doll

Smurfs (TV show)

Smuts, Jan C(hristian)(ex-PM, SAfr.; 1870-1950)

Smyrna, Turkey (now Izmir)

Smyth, Ethel, Dame (Br. comp.; 1858-1944)

Smytington, Fife (AZ gov.; 1945-)

Sn (chem. sym., tin)

Snap-On Tools Corp.

S(amuel) N(athaniel) Behrman (US writer; 1893-1973)

Snead, Sam(uel Jackson) "Slamming Sammy" (golf; 1912-)

Snegur, Mircea (pres., Moldova)

Snell (van Royen), Willebrod (Dutch math./physt.; 1581-1626)

Snell's law (physics)

Sneva, Tom (auto racing; 1948-)

Snickers™ (candy)

Snider, Duke (Edwin)(baseball; 1926-)

Snipes, Wesley (ent.; 1962-)

Snodgrass, Carrie (ent.; 1946-)

Snodgrass, W(illiam) D(eWitt)(US poet; 1926-)

Snooks, Baby (fict. chara, radio)

Snooky Lanson (ent.; 1914-90)

Snoopy (fict. dog, *Peanuts*)

Snoqualmie Falls, WA

Snoqualmie Pass, WA

Snoqualmie, WA

Snow White (fict. chara.)

Snow, Baron C(harles) P(ercy)(Br. writer/physt.; 1905-80)

Snow, Hank (ent.; 1914-)

Snowdon, Earl of (Anthony Armstrong-Jones)(Br. photo.; 1930-)

Snowy™ bleach

Snowy Mountains (Austl. Alps)

Snuffy Jenkins

Snuffy Smith (cartoon chara.)

Snuggle™ (clothes softener)

Snyder, Jimmy "the Greek"

Snyder, Mitch (US reformer/homeless; 1944-90)

Snyder, Tom

Snyders, Frans (Flem. artist; 1579-1657)

Soap Box Derby™

Soap Opera Digest (mag.)

Soares, Mário (Alberto Nobre Lopes)(pres., Port.; 1924-)

SOB (son of a bitch)

Soccer League, North American (also NASL)

Social and Liberal Democrats (Br. pol. party)

Social/social Darwinism

Social Democratic Party (Br. pol. party; 1981-90)

Social Democrats (US pol. party)

Social Gospel movement (also l.c.)

Social Register™

Social Security Administration (SSA)(US govt. agcy.; est. 1946)

Socialist Labor Party (US pol.)

Socialist Party U.S.A. (US pol.)

Socialist Workers Party (US pol.)

Socialist Revolutionary Party (Russian Populist Party; founded 1901)

Society of Believers in Christ's Second Coming(Appearing), United (also Shakers, Millenial Church)

Society of Friends, (Religious)(also Quakers)(rel.)

Society of Jesus (Jesuits)(rel.)

Society, Royal (also Royal Society of London for the Advancement of Science; est. 1645)

Socks (US pres.'s cat)

Socorro, NM

Socrates (Gr. phil.; 469-399 BC)

Socratic method (phil./educ.)

Soddy, Frederick (Br. chem.; 1877-1956)

Sodium Pentothal™ (barbiturate)

Sodom and Gomorrah (ancient cities destroyed for wickedness)

Sofia, Bulgaria

Soft & Dri™ (anti-perspirant)

Soft Scrub™ (cleaner)

Softsoap™

Softsoap Enterprises, Inc.

Soglo, Nicéphore (pres., Benin; 1934-)

Soglow, Otto (US cartoonist, *Little King*; 1900-75)

SoHo (NYC)(also Soho)

Soho (London)

Sojourner Truth (US reformer; c1797-1883)

Sokodé, Togo

Sokoloff, Nikolai (cond.)

Sokolova, Lydia (Br. ballet; 1896-1974)

Sokolow, Anna (US dancer/choreographer; 1915-)

Sol (Roman sun god)

Sol Estes, Billy (US bus./scandal)

Sol, Armando Calderon (pres., El Salvador; 1948-)

Solarcaine™ (health)

Solarian™ (floor vinyl)

Solchiro Hondo (Jap. bus./auto.; 1907-91)

Soldier, Unknown (Arlington National

Cemetery [VA])
Soleri, Paolo (US arch.; 1919-)
Solh, Rashid Al- (ex-PM, Lebanon)
Solidarity (Pol. labor org.)
Solingen, Germany
Solo Cup Co.
Solo, Han (fict. chara., *Star Wars*)
Solomon (king, Isr.; fl. 10th c BC)
Solomon Islands (SW Pac.)
Solomon Mamaloni (ex-PM, Soloman Islands; 1943-)
Solomon Rabinowitz (pseud. Shalom (or Shalom) Aleichem)(Yiddish writer; 1859-1916)
Solomon R(obert) Guggenheim (US bus./finan.; 1861-1949)
Solomon R. Guggenheim Museum (NYC)
Solomon West Ridgeway Dias Bandaranaike (ex-PM, Sri Lanka; 1899-1959)
Solomon, Harold (tennis; 1952-)
Solomon, Knights of the Temple of (also Templar)(rel./mil. order; 1119-1307)
Solomon, Song of (also Song of Songs)(rel.)
Solomon's seal (plant)
Solon (Gr. pol.; c640-c560 BC)
Solovyov, Vladimir (Sergeyevich)(Rus. phil.; 1853-1900)
Solti, Sir Georg (Br. cond.; 1912-)
Solvang, CA
Solvay process (sodium carbonate)
Solvay, Ernest (Belgian chem.; 1838-1922)
Solyman (or Suleiman)("the Magnificent," "the Lawgiver")(sultan, Ottoman Empire; 1494-1566)
Solzhenitsyn, Alexander (or Aleksandr) Isayevich (Rus. writer; 1918-)
Somali (cat)
Somali (lang./people)
Somalia (Somali Democratic Republic)(NE Afr.)
Somaliland (region, E Afr.)
Somba (lang.)
Some Like it Hot (film)
Somers, Suzanne (ent.; 1946-)
Somerset (county, Eng.)
Somerset Maugham, W(illiam)(Br. writer; 1874-1965)
Somerset Raglan, FitzRoy (James Henry), Baron (Br. gen., raglan sleeve; 1788-1855)
Somerville, MA, NJ
Sominex™ (med.)
Sommer, Elke (ent.; 1940-)
Somnus (myth.)
Somoza (Debayle), Anastasio (ex-pres., Nicaragua; 1925-80)
Somoza (Debayle), Luis (ex-pres., Nicaragua; 1922-67)
Somoza (Garcia), Anastasio (ex-pres., Nicaragua; 1896-1956)

Son (Jesus)
Son of God (Jesus Christ)
Son of Man (Jesus Christ)
Sonata, Hyundai (auto.)
Sonata GL, Hyundai (auto.)
Sonata GLS, Hyundai (auto.)
Sondheim, Stephen (Joshua)(US comp./lyricist; 1930-)
Sondra Locke (ent.; 1947-)
Song of Roland (Fr. epic poem, *Chanson de Roland*)
Song of Solomon (also Song of Songs)(rel.)
Songhai Empire (NW Afr.; 8th-16th c.)
Songhua (also Sungari)(river, Ch.)
Sonja Henie (figure skating/ent.; 1912-69)
Sonny Bono (ent./pol.; 1935-)
Sonny Jurgensen (football; 1934-)
Sonny (Charles) Liston (boxing; 1933-71)
Sonny (Theodore Walter) Rollins (US jazz; 1929-)
Sonny Stitt (US jazz; 1924-82)
Sonny's Real Pit Bar-B-Q (US bus.)
Sonoma-Cutrer Vineyards (US bus.)
Sonoma Vineyards (US bus.)
Sonoma, Piper (US bus.)
Sonoma, Williams- (US bus.)
Sonora (state, Mex.)
Sons of Liberty (US hist.; 1765-66)
Sons of the Pioneers (music group)
Sontag, Susan (US writer; 1933-)
Sony™
Sony Corp. of America
Sony™ Walkman
Sooner State (nickname, OK)
Soon-Yi Farrow Previn (M. Farrow's daughter; 1971-)
SOP (standard operating procedure)
Sophia Loren (b. Sophia Scicoloni)(It. ent.; 1934-)
Sophia, Saint (or Santa)(also Hagia Sophia)(museum, Istanbul)
Sophie Tucker (b. Sophie Abruza)(ent.; 1884-1966)
Sophie's Choice (W. Styron novel)
Sophists (ancient Gr. teachers/scholars)
Sophocles (Gr. drama.; c496-406 BC)
Sopwith Camel biplane
Sopwith, Sir Thomas (Br. aircraft designer; 1888-1989)
Sorbian (lang.)
Sorbonne (University of Paris)
Sören (or Søren) Kierkegaard (Dan. phil.; 1813-55)
Sorrell Booke (ent.; 1930-)
Sorrento, Italy
Sorrows, Man of (Jesus)
Sorvino, Paul (ent.; 1939-)
SOS (save our ship [distress signal])

Soss Manufacturing Co.
Sosuke, Uno (ex-PM, Jap.; 1922-)
Sotheby's auction house
Sothern, Ann (ent.; 1909-)
Sotho (lang./people)
Soto, Hernando (or Fernando) de (Sp. expl.;
c1496-1542)
Soul, David (ent.; 1943-)
Sound of Music, The (play/film)
Soundesign Corp.
Soundesign™ radio
Soupy Sales (ent.; 1926-)
Sousa, John Philip (US comp.; 1854-1932)
Sousse, Tunisia
Soussous (people)
Souter, David H(ackett)(US jurist; 1939-)
South Africa (Republic of)
South Africa, Union of (now Republic of South
Africa)
South African Airways (airline)
South African War (also Boer War)(Boers/Br.;
1899-1902)
South America
South American Indians
South Australia (state, Austl.)
South Bend Tribune (IN newspaper)
South Bend, IN
South Carolina (SC)
South China Sea (also China Sea)(off SE Asia)
South Dakota (SD)
South Dartmouth, MA
South Gate, CA
South Korea (Republic of Korea)(E Asia)
South Lake Tahoe, CA
South Orkney Islands
South Pacific (play; film, 1958)
South Platte River (CO/NE)
South Pole (S end of earth's axis)
South Sea Bubble (Br. hist.; 1720)
South Seas
South Tipperary (county, Ir.)
South-West Africa (now Namibia)
South Weymouth Naval Air Station (MA)
South Yemen (now part of Yemen)
South, the (US region)
Southampton, England
Southampton, NY
Southeast Asia (region, Asia)
Southeast Asia Treaty Organization
(SEATO)(1954-77)
Southern Alps (NewZeal.)
Southern Bell™
Southern Cone Common Market (Argentina/
Brazil/Paraguay/Uruguay; 1991-)
Southern Cross (also Stars and
Bars)(Confederate flag)
Southern Hemisphere
Southern Illinois University Press (US bus.)

Southern Living (mag.)
Southern Methodist University (SMU)(TX)
Southern Rhodesia (now Zimbabwe)
Southern Triangle (astron., Triangulum
Australe)
Southern Yemen (now Yemen)
Southerner
Southfield, MI
Southgate, MI
Southhampton, Earl of (Henry Wriothesley)(Br.
scholar; 1573-1624)
Southside Johnny and the Asbury Jukes (pop
music)
Southwest Airlines Co.
Southwestern Bell Corp. (phone co.)
Southwestern Indians
Soutine, Chaim (Fr. artist; 1893-1943)
Souverain, Chateau (US bus.)
Soviet Far East (now Russia Far East)
Soviet Socialist Republics, Union of
(USSR)(disbanded 1991)
Soviet Union (also Union of Soviet Socialist
Republics, USSR)(disbanded 1991)
Soviet, Sino-
Sow, Abdoulaye Sekou (PM, Mali)
Soweto, South Africa (*South West Township*)
Soyinka, Wole (Nigerian writer; 1934-)
Soylent Green (film; 1973)
Soyuz (USSR crewed space flights)
Spaak, Paul Henri (Belgium pol.; 1899-1972)
Spaatz, Carl (US mil.; 1891-1974)
Space Age (also l.c.)
Spacek, Sissy (ent.; 1949-)
Spacelab (space station)
Spacemaster Home Products (US bus.)
Spacesaver Corp.
Spacey, Kevin (ent.; 1960-)
Spackle™ (constr.)
Spade Cooley (ent.)
Spade, Sam (fict. detective, D. Hammett)
Spader, James (ent.; 1960-)
Spahn, Warren (Edward)(baseball; 1921-)
Spain (SW Eur.)
Spalding™
Spalding Sports Worldwide (US bus.)
Spalding, Albert (Goodwill)(baseball; 1850-
1915)
Spam™
Span™, Spic & (cleaner)
Spaniard
Spanier, Muggsy (US jazz; 1906-67)
Spanish (lang./people)
Spanish American War (Sp./US; 1898)
Spanish Armada (Invincible Armada)(fleet of
ships; 1588)
Spanish Civil War (1936-39)
Spanish fly (aphrodisiac)
Spanish Guinea (now Equatorial Guinea)

Spanish Inquisition
Spanish mackerel (fish)
Spanish Main (Caribbean/N SAmer.; 16th-17th c.)
Spanish moss (air plant)
Spanish ocher (color)
Spanish onion
Spanish paprika
Spanish rice
Spanish Steps (Rome)
Spanish Town, Jamaica
Spanish Wells, the Bahamas
Spanky (George) McFarland (ent.; 1928-93)
Spano, Joe (ent.; 1946-)
Spar (also SPAR)(women's U.S. Coast Guard reserve; WWII)
Sparkletts™
Sparkletts Water Co.
Sparks, NV
Sparky (George) Anderson (baseball; 1934-)
Sparta (also Lacedaemon)(ancient Gr.)
Spartacists (also Spartacus Party)(Ger. hist.; early 1900's)
Spartacus (Thracian slave/gladiator; ?-73 BC)
Spartacus (film; 1960)
Spartanburg, SC
SPCA (Society for the Prevention of Cruelty to Animals)
SPCC (Society for the Prevention of Cruelty to Children)
Speaker of the House (US govt.)
Speaker, Tris(tram)(baseball; 1888-1958)
Special Astrophysical Observatory (USSR)
Special Forces (also Green Berets)(US mil.)
Special K™ (cereal)
Special Olympics (for handicapped)
Speck, Richard (US mass murderer; 1942-91)
Specs McCann
Specter, J. Arlen (US cong.; 1930-)
Speed Queen (US bus.)
Speed Stick™ (deodorant)
Speedee Oil Change and Tune-Up (US bus.)
Speedo™ (sportswear)
Speedo America (US bus.)
Speedy Transmission Centers (US bus.)
Speer, Albert (Ger. arch./Nazi pol.; 1905-81)
Speightstown, Barbados
Speke, John Hanning (Br. expl. in Afr.; 1827-64)
Spelling, Aaron (ent.; 1928-)
Spelling, Tori (ent.)
Spencer (steak)
Spencer-Churchill, Baroness Clementine (wife of ex-Br. PM; 1885-1977)
Spencer Davis Group (pop music)
Spencer Gifts, Inc.
Spencer Tracy (US ent.; 1900-67)
Spencer, Brian (hockey; 1949-88)

Spencer, John (ent.; 1946-)
Spencer's, Inc.
Spengler, Oswald (Ger. phil./hist.; 1880-1936)
Spenser, Edmund (Br. poet; 1552-99)
Sperry Rand Corp.
Sperry Univac (US bus.)
Sperry, Elmer Ambrose (US eng./inv.; 1860-1930)
Spetznaz (mil.)
Sphinx (myth.)
Sphinx, the Great (Eg.; c2500 BC)
Spic and Span™ (cleaner)
Spice Islands™ (seasoning)
Spice Islands (also Moluccas)(Indonesia)
Spider-Man, The Amazing (cartoon chara.)
Spider Woman, Kiss of the (film; 1985)
Spider, Alfa Romero™ (auto.)
Spiegel catalog
Spiegel, Inc.
Spiegel, Der (*The Mirror,* Ger. news mag.)
Spiegel, Sam (ent.; 1903-85)
Spiegelman, Art (cartoonist; 1948-)
Spielberg, Steven (ent./writer; 1947-)
Spike (Shelton Jackson) Lee (ent.; 1957-)
Spike Jones (ent.; 1911-1965)
Spillane, Mickey (b. Frank Morrison Spillane)(US writer; 1918-)
Spin (mag.)
Spinks, Leon (boxing; 1953-)
Spinks, Michael (boxing; 1956-)
Spinoza, Benedict de (also Baruch)(Dutch phil.; 1632-77)
Spirit (Holy Spirit)
Spirit of St. Louis (Charles Lindbergh plane, transatlantic flight)
Spirit, Dodge (auto.)
Spiro T(heodore) Agnew (ex-US VP; 1918-)
Spitz, Mark (Andrew)(US swimmer; 1950-)
Split, Croatia
Spitalny, Phil (cond.; 1890-1970)
Spivak, Charlie
Spivak, Lawrence (ent.; 1900-)
Spivey, Victoria
Spock, Dr. Benjamin (McLane)(US phys./educ.; 1903-)
Spock, Mr. (fict. chara., *Star Trek*)
Spode china™ (also Spode ware)
Spode, Josiah (Br. potter, father; 1733-97)
Spode, Josiah (Br. potter, son; 1754-1827)
Spokane Spokesman-Review (WA newspaper)
Spokane, WA
Spokesman-Review, Spokane (WA newspaper)
Spoleto Festival (also Festival of the Two Worlds)(It. and SC)
Spoon River Anthology (by Edgar Lee Masters)
Spooner, William Archibald, Rev. (spoonerism)
Sport (mag.)
Sporting News, The (mag.)

Sports Afield (mag.)
Sports Illustrated (mag.)
Sports Illustrated for Kids (mag.)
Sportside™, Chevy (auto.)
Spotsylvania, PA
Sprachgefühl (linguistics)
Spray'n Wash™ (stain remover)
Spring Air™
Spring Air Bedding, Inc.
Spring Bank Holiday (Br.)
Spring Byington (ent.; 1893-1971)
Spring Valley™ (vitamins)
Springdale, AR
Springer, Jerry
Springfield News-Leader (MO newspaper)
Springfield Republican (MA newspaper)
Springfield rifle
Springfield State Journal-Register (IL
   newspaper)
Springfield Union News (MA newspaper)
Springfield Union-News (MA newspaper)
Springfield, Buffalo (pop music)
Springfield, Dusty (ent.; 1939-)
Springfield, IL, MA, MO, OH, OR, PA, TN, VT
Springfield, Rick (ent.; 1949-)
Springsteen, Bruce (ent.; 1949-)
Sprint™
Sprint Communications Co.
Sprint Corp.
Sprite™
Spruance, Raymond (Ames)(US mil.; 1886-
   1969)
Spruce Goose (plane)
Spud Chandler (baseball; 1907-90)
Spuds MacKenzie (dog)
Spurs, San Antonio (basketball team)
Sputnik (USSR space satellite, world's 1st)
Spy (mag.)
Spyri, Johanna (Swiss writer; 1827-1901)
Spyros (Panagiotes) Skouras (ent.; 1893-1971)
Square One Television (TV show)
Squaw Valley, CA
Squeaky (Lynette) Fromme (US, shot Pres.
   Ford)
Squeeze (pop music)
Squibb Co., Bristol-Myers
Squirrel Nutkin
Sr (chem. sym., strontium)
Sranantonga (lang.)
Sri Lanka (Democratic Socialist Republic
   of)(formerly Ceylon)(island, Indian Ocean)
SRO (standing room only)
SS (Schutzstaffel [mil. unit, Nazi party], social
   security)
SSA (Social Security Administration)
S.S. *Andrea Doria* (steamship, sank 1956)
S.S. *Lusitania* (Br. ship sunk by Ger.; 1915)
SSS (Selective Service System)

SST (supersonic transport)
S.S. *Titanic* (Br. luxury liner; sunk 1912)
Stabler, Kenneth (football; 1945-)
Stack, Robert (ent.; 1919)
Stacy Keach (ent.; 1941-)
Stade, Frederica Von (ent.; 1945-)
Stafford Cripps, Sir (Br. pol.; 1889-1952)
Stafford, Jim
Stafford, Jo (ent.; 1918-)
Stafford, Thomas P. (astro.)
Staffordshire (also Stafford)(county, Eng.)
Staffordshire bull terrier (dog)
Stagg, Amos Alonzo (football; 1862-1965)
Stag's Leap Wine Cellars (US bus.)
Stahl, Lesley (US TV jour.; 1941-)
Stahl, Richard (ent.; 1932-)
StairMaster (US bus.)
Stalin, Joseph (b. Iosif Vissarionovich
   Dzhugashvili)(ex-dictator, USSR; 1879-1953)
Stalingrad (now Volgograd)
Stallone, Sylvester "Sly" (ent.; 1946-)
Stamford, CT
Stamos, John (ent.; 1963-)
Stamp Act (Br./US hist.; 1765)
Stamp Act Congress (US hist.; 1765)
Stan Drake (cartoonist)
Stan Freberg
Stan(ley) Getz (US jazz; 1927-91)
Stan Kenton (US jazz; 1912-79)
Stan Laurel (b. Arthur Stanley Jefferson)(ent.;
   1890-1965)
Stan Lee (cartoonist, *Marvel Comics*; 1922-)
Stan Mikita (hockey; 1940-)
Stan(ley Frank) Musial ("Stan the
   Man")(baseball; 1920-)
Standard & Poor's Corp.
Standard Book Number, International (ISBN)
Standard Oil Co.
Standard Oil Co. of California
Standard Oil Co. of New Jersey
Standard Oil Co. of Indiana
Standard Oil Co. of New Jersey, et al. v. U.S.
   (US law; 1911)
Standardbred (also American trotter)(horse)
Standards, National Bureau of (NBS)(US govt.
   agcy.; est. 1901)
Standish, Miles (Br./Amer. settler/mil.; c1584-
   1656)
Stanford-Binet test (intelligence test)
Stanford Linear Accelerator Center (CA)
Stanford University (CA)
Stanford White (US arch.; 1853-1906)
Stanford, A(masa) Leland (US bus./finan./pol.;
   1824-93)
Stang, Arnold (ent.; 1925-)
Stanhome, Inc.
Stanhope, Philip Dormer (4th Earl of
   Chesterfield, Lord Philip Chesterfield)(Br.

writer/pol.; 1694-1773)
Stanislaus James (gov-gen., St. Lucia)
Stanislaus National Forest
Stanislav S. Shushkevich (pres; Belarus
Stanislavsky, Konstantin (Sergeivich)(Rus. ent.;
  1863-1938)
Stanislaw Lem (Pol. writer; 1921-)
Stanley and (Dr. David) Livingstone, (Sir
  Henry)
Stanley-Bostitch Inc.,
Stanley Cup (ice hockey)
Stanley Dancer (harness racing; 1927-)
Stanley Donen (ent.; 1924-)
Stanley Elkin (US writer; 1930-)
Stanley Kramer (ent.; 1913-)
Stanley Kubrick (ent.; 1928-)
Stanley Roger Smith (tennis; 1946-)
Stanley Steemer™
Stanley Steemer Carpet Cleaner (US bus.)
Stanley Works (US bus.)
Stanley, Sir Henry M(orton)(aka John
  Rowlands)(Br. jour./expl.; 1841-1904)
Stanley, Kim (ent.; 1925-)
Stanton, Edwin M(cMasters)(US mil./pol.; 1814-
  69)
Stanton, Elizabeth Cady (US suffragist; 1815-
  1902)
Stanton, Harry Dean (ent.; 1926-)
Stanwyck, Barbara (ent.; 1907-90)
Stanza, Nissan™ (auto)
Stapleton International Airport (Denver CO)
Stapleton, Jean (ent.; 1923-)
Stapleton, Maureen (ent.; 1925-)
Star (mag.)
Star-Bulletin, Honolulu (HI newspaper)
Star Chamber, Court of (Br. hist.; 1487-1641)
Star-Ledger, Newark (NJ newspaper)
Star of Bethlehem
Star-of-Bethlehem (plant)
Star of David (also Magen David)(6 points, Jew.
  symbol)
Star Search (TV show)
Star-Spangled Banner, The (US national
  anthem by Francis Scott Key)
Star-Telegram, Fort Worth (TX newspaper)
Star Trek (TV show)
Star Trek: Deep Space Nine (TV show)
Star Trek II: The Wrath of Khan (film; 1982)
Star Trek III: The Search for Spock (film; 1984)
Star Trek IV: The Voyage Home (film; 1986)
Star Trek: The Motion Picture (film; 1979))
Star Trek: The Next Generation (TV show)
Star-Tribune, Minneapolis (MN newspaper)
Star Wars (film; 1977)
Star Wars (Strategic Defense Initiative,
  SDI)(US mil.;1983-)
Star, Indianapolis (IN newspaper)
Star, Kansas City (MO newspaper)

Star, Lincoln (NE newspaper)
Starfire™, Buick (auto.)
Stargell, Willie (baseball; 1941-)
Stark, Koo (Br. news)
Starkist™ tuna
StarKist Foods, Inc.
Starr, Bart (football; 1934-)
Starr, Belle (b. Myra Belle Shirley)(US outlaw;
  1848-89)
Starr, Brenda (comic strip)
Starr, Ringo (aka Richard Starkey)(ent.; 1940-)
Starry Night, The (Vincent van Gogh)
Stars and Bars (also Southern
  Cross)(Confederate flag)
Stars and Stripes (also Old Glory)(US flag)
START (Strategic Arms Reduction Talks)(US/
  USSR; 1982-)
Stash™
Stash Tea Co.
Stassen, Harold (Edward)(US pol.; 1907-)
State Farm Insurance™
State Journal-Register, Springfield (IL
  newspaper)
State-Journal, Lansing (MI newspaper)
State Journal, Madison (WI newspaper)
State of the Union message/address (US govt.)
State, Columbia (SC newspaper)
State, Department of (US govt.)
Staten Island (borough, NYC)
Staten Island Advance (NY newspaper)
Stater Brothers, Inc.
States, War Between the (also War of
  Secession, American Civil War)(1861-65)
Stations of the Cross (rel.)
Statius (Roman poet; c45-c96)
Statler Brothers, The
Statler Hotel
Statue of Liberty (NYC)
Statue of Liberty play (football)
Staub, Rusty (Daniel)(baseball; 1944-)
Staubach, Roger (football; 1942-)
Stavanger, Norway
Stayfree™ (health)
Stead, Christina (Austl. writer; 1903-83)
steak Diane
Steamboat Springs, CO
Stedman's Medical Dictionary
Steed, John
Steel Workers of America, United
  (USWA)(union; est. 1942)
Steel, Danielle (writer)
Steelcase™ (office furniture)
Steelcase, Inc.
Steele, Sir Richard (Br. writer; 1672-1729)
Steelers, Pittsburgh (football team)
Steely Dan (pop music)
Steen, Jan (Havickszoon)(Dutch artist; 1626-79)
Steenburgen, Mary (ent.; 1953-)

Stefan Edberg (tennis; 1966-)
Stefan Milenkovic
Stefan Wyszynski, Cardinal (Pol. rel.; 1901-81)
Stefanie Powers (ent.; 1942-)
Steffens, (Joseph) Lincoln (US writer; 1866-1926)
Steffi (Stephanie Maria) Graf (tennis; 1969-)
Stegner, Wallace (US writer; 1909-93)
Steichen, Edward (US photo.; 1879-1973)
Steig, William (cartoonist, *New Yorker*; 1907-)
Steiger, Janet D. (Chair/FTC; 1939-)
Steiger, Rod (ent.; 1925-)
Stein, Clarence S. (US arch.; 1882-1975)
Stein, Gertrude (US writer; 1874-1946)
Steinbeck, John (Ernst)(US writer; 1902-68)
Steinberg, Saul (US artist; 1914-)
Steinbrenner, George (Michael), III (US bus./baseball; 1930-)
Steinem, Gloria (US jour./feminist; 1934-)
Steinkraus, William C. (equestrian; 1925-)
Steinmetz, Charles P(roteus)(Ger./US eng.; 1865-1923)
Steinway & Sons (US bus.)
Steinway Musical Properties, Inc.
Steinway piano
Steinway, Henry Engelhard (b. Steinweg)(US piano manufacturer; 1797-1871)
Stelazine™ (med.)
Stella Adler (US acting teacher; 1901-1992)
Stella Dallas (film; 1937)
Stella D'oro Biscuit Co., Inc.
Stella Stevens (ent.; 1936-)
Stella, Frank (US artist; 1936-)
Sten gun
Stendahl (aka Marie Henri Beyle)(Fr. writer; 1783-1842)
StenEd™
Stenerud, Jan (football; 1942-)
Stengel, Casey (Charles)(baseball; 1890-1975)
Stenmark, Ingemar (skiing; 1956-)
StenoCAT by Gigatron (US bus.)
StenoCAT™ (CAT system)
Stenograph™
Stenograph Corp.
StenoRam ULTRA™ (steno writer)
StenoRAM™ (stenowriter)
Stenotype Educational Products, Inc. (StenEd™)
Stenovations (US bus.)
Stenoware, Inc.
Stentura™ (steno writer)
Steny Hamilton Hoyer (US cong.; 1939-)
Step Saver™ (cleaner)
Stepford Wives (film)
Stephane Grappelli (US jazz; 1908-)
Stéphane Mallarmé (Fr. poet; 1842-98)
Stephanie Zimbalist (ent.; 1956-)
Stephen A. Douglas (US pol./orator; 1813-61)

Stephen Biko (b. Stephen Bantu)(SAfr. civil rights leader; 1946-77)
Stephen Breyer (US jurist; 1939-)
Stephen Collins Foster (US comp.; 1826-64)
Stephen Coonts (US writer)
Stephen Crane (US writer; 1871-1900)
Stephen Decatur (US mil.; 1779-1820)
Stephen Fuller Austin (Texas colonizer; 1793-1836)
Stephen Girard (US finan.; 1750-1831)
Stephen (William) Hawking (Br. physt./math./writer; 1942-)
Stephen Jay Gould (US paleontol./writer; 1941-)
Stephen J. Cannell (ent.; 1942-)
Stephen (Watts) Kearny (US mil.; 1794-1848)
Stephen King (US writer; 1947-)
Stephen Lang (ent.; 1952-)
Stephen (Butler) Leacock (Can. writer/humorist; 1868-1944)
Stephen (Joshua) Sondheim (US comp./lyricist; 1930-)
Stephen Stills (ent.; 1945-)
Stephen Vincent Benét (US writer; 1898-1943)
Stephen Wozniak (US bus./inv./compu.; 1950-)
Stephen, St. (1st Christian martyr; ?-AD 36?)
Stephens, Darren (fict. chara., *Bewitched*)
Stephens, James (ent.; 1951-)
Stephens, James (Ir. writer; 1882-1950)
Stepin Fetchit (ent.; 1898-1985)
Steppenwolf (pop music)
Steppes, the Russian (Rus. grasslands)
Steptoe, Patrick (US phys.; 1914-88)
Sterapred™ (med.)
Stereo Review (mag.)
Sterling Drug, Inc.
Sterling Hayden (ent.)
Sterling Heights, MI
Sterling Holloway (ent.; 1905-1992)
Sterling Optical (US bus.)
Sterling Vineyards (US bus.)
Stern/Sloan Publishers, Inc., Price/
Stern, David J. (basketball; 1942-)
Stern, Howard (ent.; 1954-)
Stern, Isaac (Rus. violinist; 1920-)
Stern, Richard (US writer; 1928-)
Sterne, Laurence (Ir. writer; 1713-68)
Sternhagen, Frances (ent.; 1930-)
Stetson, John B(atterson)(US bus.; 1830-1906)
Stetson™ (cologne)
Stetson™ (hat)
Stetson Hat Co., Inc.
Stettinius, Edward R., Jr. (US bus./pol.; 1900-49)
Steuben glass™
Steuben Glass (US bus.)
Steuben, Friedrich Wilhelm (Ludolf Gerhard Augustin) von, Baron (Prussian/US gen.; 1730-94)

Steubenville, OH
Steve Allen (ent.; 1921-)
Steve Canyon (comic strip)
Steve(n Norman) Carlton (baseball; 1944-)
Steve Cauthen (jockey)
Steve Ditko (cartoonist, *Spider-Man*; 1927-)
Steve Forrest (ent.; 1924-)
Steve Garvey (baseball; 1948-)
Steve Guttenberg (ent.; 1958-)
Steve(n) Jobs (US bus./compu.; 1955-)
Steve Kanaly (ent.; 1946-)
Steve Kroft
Steve Lawrence (ent.; 1935-)
Steve(n) Mahre (US skier; 1957-)
Steve Martin (ent.; 1945-)
Steve(n) McQueen, (Terrence)(ent.; 1930-80)
Steve Merrill (NH gov.)
Steve Ovett (track; 1955-)
Steve (Roland) Prefontaine (runner; 1951-75)
Steve Winwood (ent.; 1948-)
Steven Bochco (ent.; 1943-)
Steven Halpern
Steven Spielberg (ent./writer; 1947-)
Steven Wright (ent.; 1955-)
Stevens International, Inc., Patricia
Stevens, Andrew (ent.; 1955-)
Stevens, Cat (ent.; 1948-)
Stevens, Connie (ent.; 1938-)
Stevens, Inger (ent.; 1934-70)
Stevens, John Paul (US jurist; 1920-)
Stevens, Risë (ent.; 1913-)
Stevens, Stella (ent.; 1936-)
Stevens, Ted (US cong.; 1923-)
Stevens, Wallace (US poet; 1879-1955)
Stevenson, Adlai E(wing)(ex-US VP; 1835-1914)
Stevenson, Adlai E(wing), II (US pol./IL gov.;
    1900-65)
Stevenson, Adlai E(wing), III (US pol.; 1930-)
Stevenson, McLean (ent.; 1929-)
Stevenson, Parker (ent.; 1952-)
Stevenson, Robert Louis (Balfour)(Scot. writer;
    1850-94)
Stevie Nicks (ent.; 1948-)
Stevie Ray Vaughan (ent.; 1956-90)
Stevie Wonder (b. Steveland Judkins
    Morris)(ent.; 1950-)
Stewart Granger, (James)(ent.; 1913-93)
Stewart, Dave (baseball; 1957-)
Stewart, Jackie (auto racing; 1939-)
Stewart, James "Jimmy" (ent.; 1908-)
Stewart, Potter (US jurist; 1915-85)
Stewart, Rod (ent.; 1945-)
Stewart, Slam (ent.)
Stich, Otto (VP, Switz.)
Stick*Free (gum)
Stick Ups™ (air freshener)
Stieff™, Kirk-
Stieff Co., Kirk

Stieglitz, Alfred (US photo.; 1864-1946)
Stiers, David Ogden (ent.; 1942-)
Stijl, de (Dutch art, early 20th c.)
Stiller, Jerry (ent.; 1929-)
Stills, Stephen (ent.; 1945-)
Stillson wrench™ (constr.)
Stillwater, OK, MN
Stilton cheese
Stilwell, Joseph W(arren)("Vinegar Joe")(US
    gen.; 1883-1946)
Stimson Doctrine (US denouncement of
    Japanese invasion of Manchuria)
Stimson, Henry L(ewis)(US pol.; 1867-1950)
Sting (b. Gordon Sumner)(ent.; 1951-)
Stinger (antiaircraft missile)
Stirling engine
Stirling, Robert (Scot. rel./inv.; 1790-1878)
Stitt, Sonny (US jazz; 1924-82)
Stock Market Crash (US; 10/24/29)
Stockard Channing (ent.; 1944-)
Stockhausen, Karlheinz (Ger. comp.; 1928-)
Stockholm, Sweden
Stockton, CA
Stockton, Frank (Francis Richard)(US writer;
    1834-1902)
Stockton, John (basketball; 1962-)
Stockton, Richard LaClede (tennis; 1951-)
Stockwell, Dean (ent.; 1936-)
Stoicism (phil.)
Stoke-on-Trent, England (also Stoke-upon-
    Trent)
Stokely USA, Inc.
Stoker, Bram (Abraham)(Br. writer; 1847-1912)
Stokes respiration, Cheyne- (med.)
Stokowski, Leopold (Antoni Stanislaw)(US
    cond.; 1882-1977)
Stolojan, Theodor (ex-PM, Romania)
Stoltz, Eric (ent.; 1961-)
Stolz, Mary
Stone Age (2 million to 4,500 years ago)
Stone Age, Middle (Mesolithic period; 15,000 to
    10,000 years ago)
Stone Age, New (Neolithic period; 10,000 to
    4,500 years ago)
Stone Age, Old (Paleolithic period; 2 million to
    15,000 years ago)
Stone Mill Winery, Inc.
Stone Mountain Memorial (GA)
Stone of Scone (Scot. kings' coronation seat)
Stone, Edward Durell (US arch.; 1902-75)
Stone, Harlan Fiske (US jurist; 1872-1946)
Stone, I. F. (US jour.; 1908-89)
Stone, Irving (US writer; 1903-89)
Stone, Lucy (US suffragist; 1818-93)
Stone, Milburn (ent.; 1904-80)
Stone, Oliver (ent./writer; 1946-)
Stone, Robert (US writer; 1937-)
Stone, Sharon (ent.)

Stonehenge (Salisbury Plain, Eng.)(monument; c2500 BC)

Stoner, Lucy (married woman who keeps maiden name)

Stones, Dwight Edwin (track; 1953-)

Stonewall Jackson (ent.)

Stonewall (Thomas Jonathan) Jackson (US gen.; 1824-63)

Stony Hill Vineyard (US bus.)

Stony Point, NY

Stony Ridge Winery (US bus.)

Stooges, Three (Curly, Moe, Larry)

Stookey, Paul (ent.; 1937-)

Stoppard, Tom (b. Thomas Straussler)(Br. writer; 1937-)

Storch, Larry (ent.; 1923-)

Storey, David Malcolm (Br. writer; 1933-)

Storm, Gale (ent.; 1922-)

Story Vineyard (US bus.)

Story, Fort (VA)(mil.)

Story, Joseph (US jurist; 1779-1845)

Storybook Mountain Vineyards (US bus.)

Stossel, John

Stouffer Foods Corp.

Stouffer Hotels & Resorts (US bus.)

Stouffer's™ frozen food

Stouffer's Lean Cuisine™

Stout, Rex (US writer; 1886-1975)

Stove Top™ dressing

Stover Candies, Inc., Russell

Stow-A-Way Industries

Stowaway Sports Industries, Inc.

Stowe, Harriet Beecher (US writer/abolitionist; 1811-96)

STP (standard temperature and pressure)

STP Corp.

Strabo (Gr. hist./geographer; c63 BC-AD 21)

Strachey, (Giles) Lytton (Br. writer; 1880-1932)

Stradella, Alessandro (It. comp.; 1642-82)

Stradivarius violin

Stradivarius, Antonius (also Antonio Stradivari)(It. violin maker; 1644-1737)

Straight, Beatrice (ent.; 1918-)

Strait of Belle Isle (Labrador/Newfoundland)

Strait of Dover (Eng./Fr.)

Strait of Gibralter (NAfr./Sp.)

Strait of Hormuz (or Ormuz)(Iran)

Strait of Juan de Fuca (also Juan de Fuca Strait)(WA/Can.)

Strait of Magellan (tip of SAmer.)

Strait of Malacca (Indian Ocean/China Sea)

Strait of Messina (channel, Mediterranean)

Strait of Ormuz (or Hormuz)(Iran)

Strait, George (ent.; 1952-)

Straits of Mackinac (Lake Huron/Lake Michigan)

Straits Settlements (Br. colony, SE Asia; 1867-1946)

Strange, Curtis (golf)

Strangelove: or, How I Learned to Stop Worrying and Love the Bomb, Dr. (film; 1964)

Strasberg, Lee (US ent./educ.; 1901-82)

Strasberg, Susan (ent.)

Strasbourg, France

Strasky, Jan (ex-PM, Czech.)

Strasser, Robin (ent.; 1945-)

Strasser, Valentine (pres., Sierra Leone

Strategic Air Command (SAC)(US mil.)

Strategic Arms Limitation Talks (SALT)(US/USSR; 1969-89)

Strategic Arms Reduction Talks (START)(US/USSR; 1982-)

Strategic Defense Initiative (SDI, Star Wars)(US mil.;1983-)

Stratemeyer, Edward (US writer; 1862-1930)

Stratford, CT

Stratford-on-Avon, England (also Stratford-upon-Avon)(Shakespeare home)

Stratford, Ontario, Canada

Strathclyde (region, Scot.)

Strathmore Paper Co.

Straub, Peter

Straus/Jordan Marsh Co., Abraham &

Straus, Nathan (Ger./US bus./finan.; 1848-1931)

Straus, Oskar (Aus. comp.; 1870-1954)

Strauss Co., Levi

Strauss, Claude Lévi- (Fr. anthrop.; 1908-1990)

Strauss, Franz Joseph (WGer. pol.; 1915-88)

Strauss, Johann (the Elder)(Aus.comp./cond.; 1804-49)

Strauss, Johann (the Younger)("The Waltz King")(Aus. comp.; 1825-99)

Strauss, Josef (Aus. comp.; 1827-70)

Strauss, Levi (US bus.; c1829-1902)

Strauss, Peter (ent.; 1947-)

Strauss, Richard (Georg)(Ger. comp./cond.; 1864-1949)

Strauss, Robert S. (US dipl.; 1918-)

Stravinsky, Igor F(ederovich)(Rus./US comp.; 1882-1971)

Strawberry, Darryl (baseball; 1962-)

Strawbridge & Clothier (US bus.)

Strayhorn, Billy (US jazz; 1915-67)

Streep, Meryl (ent.; 1949-)

Strega (liqueur)

Streicher, Julius (Ger. Nazi/publ.; 1885-1946)

Streisand, Barbra (ent.; 1942-)

Stresemann, Gustav (ex-chanc., Ger.; 1878-1929)

Stresstabs™ (med.)

Stri-Dex™ (med.)

Stride Rite™ (shoes)

Stride Rite Corp.

Strieber, Louis Whitley

Strindberg, (Johan) August (Swed. writer;

1849-1912)
Stripes, Stars and (also Old Glory)(US flag)
Stritch, Elaine (ent.; 1926-)
Stroessner, Alfredo (ex-pres., Paraguay; 1912-)
Stroganoff, beef (also beef stroganoff)
Stroh Brewery Co., The
Stroh's™
Stroheim, Erich Von (ent.; 1885-1957)
Strom Thurmond, J(ames)(US cong.; 1902-)
Stromboli Island (active volcano, It.)
Strouse, Charles (US comp.; 1928-)
Struthers, Sally (ent.; 1948-)
Stuart A. Roosa (astro.; 1933-)
Stuart Hall Co., Inc.
Stuart Little (E.B. White novel)
Stuart Symington (US pol.; 1901-88)
Stuart, Charles Edward (aka the Young
  Pretender, Bonnie Prince Charles [or
  Charlie])(prince, Br.; 1720-88)
Stuart, Gilbert (Charles)(US artist; 1755-1828)
Stuart, House of (Br. ruling family; 1603-49,
  1660-88, 1702-14)
Stuart, J(ames) E(well) B(rown)(US mil.; 1833-
  64)
Stuart, James (Francis) Edward ("Old
  Pretender")(prince, Br.; 1688-1766)
Stuart, Mary (aka Mary, Queen of Scots)(queen,
  Scot.; 1542-87)
Stubby Kaye
Stuckey's Corp.
Stubbs, George (Br. artist; 1724-1806)
Studebaker (auto.)
Studebaker-Packard Corp.
Studebaker, Clement (US bus.; 1831-1901)
Student Loan Marketing Association (also
  SLMA, Sallie Mae)
Studs Terkel (US writer; 1912-)
Stunt Dawgs (cartoon)
Sturbridge, MA
Sturgeon, Theodore (aka Edward Hamilton
  Waldo (US writer; 1918-35)
Sturges, John (ent.; 1910-92)
Sturges, Preston (ent.; 1898-1959)
Sturm und Drang (Storm and Stress)(Ger. lit.;
  18th c.)
Stuttgart Ballet
Stuttgart, Germany
Stutz Bearcat (auto.)
Stutz Motor Car Co. of America
Stuyvesant, Bedford- (Brooklyn neighborhood)
Stuyvesant, Peter (Dutch gov. of NY; 1592-
  1672)
Styne, Jule (Br./US comp.; 1905-)
Styrofoam™
Styron, William (Clark), Jr. (US writer; 1925-)
Styx (myth. underground river)
Styx (pop music)
Suárez González, Adolfo (ex-PM, Sp.; 1933-)

Suave™ (hair care)
Subaru™ (auto.)
Subaru™ Legacy (auto.)
Subaru of America, Inc.
Subaru™ SVX (auto.)
Subotica, Serbia
Success (mag.)
Success™ (rice)
Suchocka, Hanna (ex-PM, Pol.)
Suckling, Sir John (Br. poet; 1609-42)
Sucre, Bolivia
Sucrets™ (med.)
Sudafed™ (med.)
Sudan (Democratic Republic of)(NE Afr.)
Sudan, French (now Republic of Mali)(NW Afr.)
Sudan, Port (Sudan)
Sudanic tribal (lang.)
Sudanic tribes
Sudbury Consumer Products, Inc.
Sudbury, MA
Sudbury, Ontario, Canada
SueBee™ (honey)
Suetonius (Gaius Suetonius
  Tranquillus)(Roman hist.; c69-c140)
Suez Canal (Eg.)
Suez Crisis (mil.; 1956)
Suez, Egypt
Suez, Gulf of (Eg.)
Suffolk (county, Eng.)
Suffolk draft horse
Suffolk sheep
Suffolk, VA
Sufi (rel.)
Sufism (rel.)
Sugar Babies (play)
Sugar Bowl (college football)
Sugar Daddy
Sugar Loaf Mountain (Rio de Janeiro, Brazil)
Sugar Ray Leonard (boxing; 1956-)
Sugar Ray Robinson (b. Walker Smith)(boxing;
  1920-89)
Suharto, Raden (pres., Indonesia; 1921-)
Sui dynasty (Ch. hist.; 589-618)
Suisei (Jap. uncrewed space probe)
Suisse (Fr. for Switz.)
Suk, Josef (Czech. comp.; 1874-1935)
Sukarno, Achmed (ex-pres., Indonesia; 1901-70)
Sukhumi, Georgia
Sukkoth (also Feast of Tabernacles)(rel.)
Sukkur, Pakistan
Sukuma, Nyamwezi- (lang.)
Sulawesi (formerly Celebes)(Indonesian island)
Suleiman (or Solyman)("the Magnificent," "the
  Lawgiver")(sultan, Ottoman Empire; 1494-
  1566)
Suleyman Demirel (PM, Turk.; 1924-)
Sullavan, Margaret (ent.; 1911-60)
Sullivan, Sir Arthur S(eymour)(Br. comp.; 1842-

1900)
Sullivan, Barry (ent.; 1912-94)
Sullivan, Ed(ward Vincent)(ent.; 1902-74)
Sullivan, Francis L. (ent.; 1903-56)
Sullivan, Gilbert & (created comic operas)
Sullivan, Gordon R. (US mil.)
Sullivan, Harry Stack (US psych.; 1892-1949)
Sullivan, John (US mil./pol.; 1740-95)
Sullivan, John L(awrence)(boxing; 1858-1918)
Sullivan, Kathleen (ent.)
Sullivan, Mike (Michael J.)(WY gov.; 1939-)
Sullivan, New York Times v. (US law; 1964)
Sullivan, Susan (ent.; 1944-)
Sullivanian theory (psych.)
Sully, Thomas (US artist; 1783-1872)
Sultan (chicken)
Sultan of Brunei (Muda Hassanal Bolkiah
    Mu'izzaddin Waddaulah)
Sulu Archipelago (volcanic islands, SW
    Philippines)
Sulu Sea (E of Philippines)
Sulzberger, Arthur Hays (US publ.; 1881-1968)
Sulzberger, Arthur Ochs (US publ.; 1926-)
Sulzberger, Iphigene Ochs (US publ.; 1883-
    1990)
Sumac, Yma (Peru. ent.; 1927-)
Sumatra (chicken)
Sumatra (island, Indonesia)
Sumer (ancient country, SW Asia)
Sumerian (lang.)
Sumerian civilization (SW Asia; c3500BC)
Sumgait, Azerbaijan
Summer Olympics (also Summer Games)
Summer, Donna (ent.; 1948-)
Summerall, Pat
Summerfall Winterspring, Princess (fict. chara.,
    Howdy Doody)
Summerhill (Eng. school)
Summer's Eve™ douche
Sumner Locke Elliott
Sumner, Charles (US pol.; 1811-74)
Sumners, Rosalynn (figure skating; 1964-)
Sumter, Fort, SC (fort)
Sumter, SC
Sun Belt (also Sunbelt, also l.c.)(S/SW US)
Sun Company, Inc.
Sun-Diamond Growers of California (US bus.)
Sun-Lite, Inc.
Sun-Maid Growers of California (US bus.)
Sun Microsystems™
Sun Microsystems, Inc.
Sun Myung Moon, Rev. (Korean rel.; 1920-)
Sun Oil Co.
Sun Ra (b. Herman Blount)(US jazz; 1916-93)
Sun-Sentinel, Fort Lauderdale (FL newspaper)
Sun-Telegraph, Pittsburgh (PA newspaper)
Sun-Times, Chicago (IL newspaper)
Sun Valley, ID

Sun Yat-sen (Ch. pol./mil.; 1866-1925)
Sun, Baltimore (MD newspaper)
Sun, Gainesville (FL newspaper)
Sun, Las Vegas (NV newspaper)
Sun, San Bernardino (CA newspaper)
Sun, Toronto (Can. newspaper)
Sun, Vancouver (Can. newspaper)
Sunapee trout (fish)
Sunbeam™
Sunbeam Appliance Co.
Sunbeam Oster Corp.
Sunbelt (S US)
Sunbird, Pontiac™ (auto.)
Sunburst Fruit Juices (US bus.)
Sundance Kid, Butch Cassidy and the (film;
    1969)
Sundance: The Early Days, Butch and (film;
    1979)
Sundance, Plymouth (auto.)
Sundanese (lang./people)
*Sunday Afternoon on the Island of La Grande
    Jatte, A* (by Seurat)
Sunday best/clothes
Sunday drive
Sunday-go-to-meeting clothes
Sunday Mirror (Br. newspaper)
Sunday Night Movie, CBS (TV show)
Sunday punch (knockout punch)
Sunday school (also Sabbath school)(rel.)
Sunday, Billy (William Ashley)(US rel.; 1862-
    1935)
Sunday, Bloody (Rus. hist, 1905; NIre. hist.,
    1972)
Sundlun, Bruce G. (RI gov.; 1920-)
Sundown Vitamins, Inc.
Sunflower State (nickname, KS)
Sung dynasty (Ch. hist.; 960-1280)
Sung, Kim Il (pres., NKorea; 1912-)
Sungari (also Songhua)(river, Ch.)
Sunkist™
Sunkist Growers, Inc.
Sunni Muslim (rel.)
Sunnites (rel.)
Sunny Delight™ (drink)
Sunny (Martha) von Bulow (US news)
Sunnyvale, CA
Sunray Products (US bus.)
Sunrise, FL
Suns, Phoenix (basketball team)
Sunset (mag.)
Sunset Magazine & Books (US bus.)
Sunshine Krispy™ (crackers)
Sunshine Network (SUN)(cable TV)
Sunshine State (nickname, FL)
Sunshine State (nickname, SD)
Sunsweet™ prunes
Sununu, John H. (US pol.; 1939-)
Sunyata (rel.)

Super Bowl (football)
Super 8 Motels, Inc.
Super Glue™
Superboy (cartoon chara.)
Supercuts™
Supercuts (US bus.)
Superdome, the (New Orleans)
Superfund (US govt.)
Supergirl (cartoon chara.)
Superior, Lake (US/Can.)
Superior, Mother (head nun of convent)
Superior, WI
Superman (fict. chara.)
Superman (film, TV show, comics)
Superman II (film)
Superman III (film)
Superman IV (film)
SuperSonics, Seattle (basketball team)
Supper, Last (rel.)
Supper, Lord's (also Holy Communion,
    Eucharist)(rel.)
Supper, The Last (da Vinci)
Supra, Toyota (auto.)
Suprematism (Rus. art; 1913-18)(also l.c.)
Supreme Being (God)
Supreme Council (also Supreme Soviet)(former
    USSR govt.)
Supreme Court, U.S. (also High Court)
Supreme Soviet (also Supreme Council)(former
    USSR govt.)
Supremes, the (pop music)
Sur, Lebanon (site of ancient port of Tyre)
Surabaya, Indonesia
Surat Huseynov (PM, Azerbaijan
Sure & Natural™ (health)
Surgeon General (of the US)
Surgeon General's Report (smoking)
Suribachi, Mount (marine flag raising on Iwo
    Jima)
Surinam toad
Suriname (Republic of)(also Surinam)(formerly
    Dutch Guiana)(N SAmer.)
Surrealism (art, lit.; mid 1990s)(also l.c.)
Surrey (county, Eng.)
Surveyor (US uncrewed space probes)
Surya (myth.)
Susan Anspach (ent.; 1939-)
Susan Anton (ent.; 1950-)
Susan B(rownell) Anthony (US reformer/
    suffragist; 1820-1906)
Susan Cheever (US writer)
Susan Clark (ent.; 1940-)
Susan Dey (ent.; 1952-)
Susan Faludi (US writer)
Susan Hayward (ent.; 1917-75)
Susan Isaacs
Susan Lucci (ent.; 1948-)
Susan Maxwell Berning (golf; 1941-)

Susan Ruttan (ent.; 1950-)
Susan St. James (ent.; 1946-)
Susan Sarandon (ent.; 1946-)
Susan Seidelman (ent.; 1952-)
Susan Sontag (US writer; 1933-)
Susan Strasberg (ent.)
Susan Sullivan (ent.; 1944-)
Susann, Jacqueline (US writer; 1921-74)
Susanna, Oh! (song)
Susannah York (ent.; 1942-)
Susquehanna Pfaltzgraff Co.
Susquehanna River (MD/PA/NY)
Susquehanna University (PA)
Susquehanna, PA
Sussex cattle
Sussex chicken
Sussex spaniel (dog)
Sussex, East (county, Eng.)
Sussex, West (county, Eng.)
Susskind, David (ent.; 1920-)
Sustrisno, Try (VP, Indonesia)
Susu (people)
Sutherland, Donald (ent.; 1934-)
Sutherland, Graham (Vivian)(Br. artist; 1903-
    80)
Sutherland, Joan, Dame (opera; 1926-)
Sutherland, Kiefer (ent.; 1966-)
Sutra, Kama (also Kamasutra)(Indian/Sanskrit
    treatise on love)
Sutra, Lotus (rel.)
Sutta Pitaka (rel.)
Sutter Home Winery, Inc.
Sutter, John A(ugustus)(US pioneer, gold; 1803-
    80)
Sutter's Mill, CA (gold discovered; 1848)
Sutton, Don(ald Howard)(baseball; 1945-)
Sutton, Willie (US bank robber; 1901-80)
Suva, Fiji
Suvero, Mark di (US artist; 1933-)
Suwannee River (also Swanee)(GA/FL)
Suzanne Pleshette (ent.; 1937-)
Suzanne Somers (ent.; 1946-)
Suzanne Vega
Suzette, crepes (also l.c.)
Suzuki Harunobu (Jap. artist; 1725-70)
Suzuki Samurai (auto.)
Suzuki of America Automotive Corp.
Suzuki Zenko (ex-PM, Jap; 1911-)
Suzuki, Daisetz Teitaro (Jap. rel.; 1870-1966)
Suzy Wong
Svengali (dominating fict. chara., *Trilby*)
Sverdlovsk (now Ekaterinburg)
Svetlana (Iosifovna) Alliluyeva, (daughter of J.
    Stalin; 1927-)
Svetovid (myth.)
Swabia (region, Ger.)
Swabian League (Ger. hist.; 14th-15th c.)
Swaggart, Jimmy, Rev. (US rel.)

Swahili (also Kiswahili)(lang.)
SWAK (sealed with a kiss)
Swakopmund, Namibia
Swammerdam, Jan (Dutch biol./nat.; 1637-80)
Swamp Fox, the (Francis Marion)(US mil./pol. c1732-95)
Swan, John (premier, Bermuda)
Swann vs. Charlotte-Mecklenburg County Board of Education (US law; 1971)
Swann, Lynn (football; 1952-)
Swansea, MA
Swansea, Wales
Swanson™ frozen foods
Swanson, Gloria (b. Gloria Josephine Mae Svenson)(ent.; 1899-1983)
Swarthmore College (PA)
Swarthout, Gladys (US opera; 1904-69)
S.W.A.T. team (also SWAT)(Special Weapons and Tactics)(law enforcement)
Swatch™
Swatch Watch USA (US bus.)
Swayze, John Cameron (US TV jour.)
Swayze, Patrick (ent.; 1954-)
Swazi (lang./people)
Swaziland (Kingdom of)(SE Afr.)
Sweatt v. Painter (US law; 1950)
Sweden (Kingdom of)(N Eur.)
Swedenborg, Emanuel (Swed. phil./rel.; 1688-1772)
Swedenborgians (also Church of the New Jerusalem)
Swedes (people)
Swedish (lang./people)
Swedish massage (med.)
Swedish turnip (rutabaga)
Sweeney Todd (play)
Sweet 'N Low™
Sweet Home, OR
Sweet Rosie O'Grady (film; 1943)
Sweetheart Cup Co., Inc.
Sweetwater, TX
Swift and Co. v. U.S. (US law; 1905)
Swift-Eckrich, Armour (US bus.)
Swift, Gustavus (US pioneer meat packer; 1839-1903)
Swift, Jonathan (b. Isaac Bickerstaff)(Br. writer; 1667-1745)
Swift, Kay (US comp.; 1908-93)
Swigart, John L., Jr (astro.)
Swinburne, Algernon (Charles)(Br. poet; 1837-1909)
Swingline stapler
Swingline, Inc.
Swiss (people)
Swiss account (econ.)
Swiss Alps
Swiss army knife™
Swiss chard (plant)

Swiss cheese
Swiss Colony Stores, Inc.
Swiss Family Robinson, The (J. Wyss novel)
Swiss Guards (Swiss guards of the pope)
Swiss Miss™ (pudding)
Swiss steak
Swissair (airline)
Swit, Loretta (ent.; 1937-)
Switzerland (Swiss Confederation)(W Eur.)
Swoosie Kurtz (ent.; 1944-)
Swope, Gerard (US bus./econ.; 1872-1957)
Sword/sword of Damocles
Sy Barry (cartoonist
Sy Oliver (US jazz; 1910-88)
Sybarite (wealthy inhabitant, ancient Sybaris)(also l.c.)
Sybil Thorndike, (Agnes), Dame (ent.; 1882-1976)
Sycamore Creek Vineyards (US bus.)
Sydenham, Thomas (Br. phys.; 1624-89)
Sydenham's chorea (med.)
Sydney Boehm
Sydney Greenstreet (ent.; 1879-1954)
Sydney Omarr (astrol.)
Sydney Pollack (ent.; 1934-)
Sydney silky (dog)
Sydney, New South Wales, Australia
Sydney, Nova Scotia, Canada
Sydow, Max Von (Swed. ent.; 1929-)
Sylphide, La (ballet)
Sylphides, Les (ballet)
Sylva, Buddy De (US lyricist; 1895-1950)
Sylvaner (wine)
Sylvania™ (light bulb)
Sylvania Electric Products, Inc.
Sylvester "Sly" Stallone (ent.; 1946-)
Sylvester the Cat (cartoon chara.)
Sylvestre Nsanzimana (ex-PM, Rwanda)
Sylvia (comic strip)
Sylvia Plath (US writer; 1932-63)
Sylvia F(eldman) Porter (US finan. writer; 1914-91)
Sylvia Sidney (ent.; 1910-)
Sylvia Syms (ent.; 1918-92)
Sylvie Kinigi (PM, Burundi)
Symbionese Liberation Army (US urban guerrillas; early '70s)
Symbolism (Fr. art/lit.; late 19th c.)
Symington, Stuart (US pol.; 1901-88)
Symmetrel™ (med.)
Symphonie Fantastique (by H. Berlioz)
Syms, Sylvia (ent.; 1918-92)
Syms Corp.
Synanon (place, therapy)
Syncom (US space satellite)
Syndecrete™ (constr.)
Synge, John M(illington)(Ir. writer; 1871-1909)
Syngman Rhee (ex-pres., SKorea; 1875-1965)

Synoptic Gospels (rel.)
Synthroid™ (med.)
Syr Darya River (W central Asia)
Syracuse Herald-American (NY newspaper)
Syracuse Herald-Journal (NY newspaper)
Syracuse Post Standard (NY newspaper)
Syracuse watch glass (chem.)
Syracuse, Italy
Syracuse, NY
Syria (Syrian Arab Republic)(SW Asia)
Syriac language
Syrian bear
Syrinx (myth.)
System of Units, International (also SI,
    Système Internationale d'Unités)
Szczecin, Poland
Szechwan (also Sichuan)(province, Ch.)
Szechwan cuisine (also Sichuan)
Szeged, Hungary
Szell, George (US cond.; 1897-1970)
Szilard, Leo (US/Hung. physt.; 1898-1964)

T

T, Mr. (Lawrence Tero)(ent.; 1952-)
Ta (chem. sym., tantalum)
Taal, the (lang.)
Tabasco (state, Mex.)
Tabasco™ sauce
Tabernacles, Feast of (also Sukkoth)(rel.)
Tabone, Vincent (Censu)(pres., Malta
Tabriz (Pers. rug)
Tabriz, Iran
TACA International Airlines
T account (econ.)
Tacitus, Publius Cornelius (Roman hist.; c55-c120)
Taco Bell™ restaurant
Taco Bell, Inc.
Tacoma News-Tribune (WA newspaper)
Tacoma, WA
TacoTime™ restaurant
Taco Time International, Inc.
Tadd Dameron (US jazz; 1917-65)
Tadeusz Mazowiecki (ex-PM, Pol.; 1927-)
Tadjoura, Gulf of (Djibouti)
Tadmor (also Palmyra)(ancient city, Syria)
Tadjik (also Tajik, Tadzhik)(lang./people)
Taegu, South Korea
Taejon, South Korea
Taft, Lorado (US sculptor; 1860-1936)
Taft, Robert A(lphonso)(US pol.; 1889-1953)
Taft, William Howard (27th US pres.; 1857-1930)
Taft-Hartley Act (Labor-Management Relations Act of 1947)
Tagalog (lang./people)
Tagamet™ (med.)
Taglioni, Maria (It. ballet; 1804-84)
Tagore, Sir Rabindranath (Indian poet; 1861-1941)
Tahiti (island, Fr. Polynesia)
Tahitian (lang./people)
Tahoe, Lake (CA/NV)
Tahoua, Niger
Tai (lang./people)
Taichung, Taiwan
Taif, Saudi Arabia
Tailhook Association (Navy/Marine pilot assoc.)
Tailhook sex scandal (US news)
Tainan, Taiwan
Taine, Hippolyte (Adolphe)(Fr. hist.; 1828-93)
Taipei, Taiwan (also Taibei)
Taiping Rebellion (Ch. hist.; 1850-64)
Taiwan (lang.)
Taiwan (Republic of China)(also Formosa)(E Asia)
Taiwanese (people)

Taiyuan, China
Taj Mahal (mausoleum, India)
Tajik (also Tadjik, Tadzhik)(lang./people)
Tajikistan (Republic of)(formerly part of USSR)(central Asia)
Takei, George (ent.)
Takeshita, Noboru (ex-PM, Jap.; 1924-)
Talbot, J(ames) Thomas
Talbot, William Henry Fox (Br. photo.; 1800-77)
Talbot's™ (clothing)
Talbots, Inc.
Tale of Mrs. Tiggy-Winkle, The (B. Potter story)
Tales From the Crypt (TV show, comic book)
Tales of Hoffmann, The (Jacques Offenbach opera)
Talia Shire (ent.; 1946-)
Taliesen West (F. L. Wright)
Talking Heads (pop music)
Tall, Philip the (Philip V)(king, Fr.; c1294-1322)
Talladega National Forest
Tallahassee Democrat (FL newspaper)
Tallahassee, FL
Tallchief, Maria (US ballet; 1925-)
Talleyrand(-Périgord), Charles (Maurice) de (Fr. pol.; 1754-1838)
Tallinn, Estonia
Tallis, Thomas (Br. comp.; c1510-85)
Tallulah Bankhead (ent.; 1902-68)
Talmadge, Constance (ent.)
Talmadge, Norma (ent.; 1893-1957)
Talmud, the (rel.)
Talwin™ (med.)
Tamale, Ghana
Tamara Karsavina (Rus. ballet; 1885-1978)
Tamayo, Rufino (Mex. artist; 1899-1991)
Tambo, Mr. (slang)
Tambo, Oliver (SAfr. pol.; 1917-93)
Tambrands, Inc.
Tamburlaine (also Tamerlane)(Mongol mil.; 1336-1405)
Tamden Computers (US bus.)
Tamil (lang./people)
Taming of the Shrew, The (Shakespeare play)
Tamirat Layne (PM, Ethiopia)
Tamiroff, Akim (ent.; 1899-1972)
Tammany bosses (US hist.)
Tammany Hall (US pol. hist.; 1800-1930s)
Tammany Society (also Columbian Order of NYC)
Tammuz (Jew. month; myth.)
Tammy Faye (LaValley) Bakker (ex-wife of Jim Bakker)
Tammy Grimes (ent.; 1934-)
Tammy Wynette (ent.; 1942-)
Tampa Bay Buccaneers (football team)
Tampa Bay Lightning (hockey team)
Tampa Times (FL newspaper)
Tampa Tribune (FL newspaper)

Tampa, FL
Tampax™ (tampons)
Tampax, Inc.
Tampere, Finland
Tampico, Mexico
Tamuning, Guam
Tan, Amy (US writer)
Tanaka, Kakuei (ex-PM, Jap.; 1918-93)
Tandem™
Tandem Computers, Inc.
Tandjungpriok, Indonesia
Tandy™ (compu.)
Tandy Corp.
Tandy, Jessica (ent.; 1909-)
Taney, Roger Brooke (US jurist; 1777-1864)
T'ang (or Tang) dynasty (Ch. hist.; 618-907)
Tanga, Tanzania
Tanganyika, Lake (E Afr.)
Tangier, Morocco
Tangier, VA
Tanglewood Festival (MA)
Tangshan, China
Tanguay, Eva (ent.; 1878-1947)
Tanguy, Yves (Fr. artist; 1900-55)
Tannenbaum, O (Ger., Christmas tree)
Tannenbaum, O (song)
Tanner, Beatrice (aka Mrs. Patrick
    Campbell)(ent.; 1865-1940)
Tanner, Leonard Roscoe, III (tennis; 1951-)
Tanner, Roscoe
Tannhäuser (Ger. poet; 13th c.)
Tannhäuser (R. Wagner opera)
Tansu Ciller (PM, Turk.)
Tantalus (myth.)
Tantra (rel.)
Tanumafili II, Malietoa (king/head of state, W
    Samoa)
Tanya Tucker (ent.; 1958-)
Tanzania (United Republic of)(E Afr.)
Tao-te Ching (rel.)
Taoism (rel.)
Taoist (rel.)
Taos, NM
Tappan™ (appliances)
Tappan Co., The
Tara (hill, Ir.)
Tara (plantation, *Gone With the Wind*)
Tarascan (SAmer. Indians)
Tarawa atoll (central Pac.)
Tarawa, Kiribati
Tar-baby (fict. chara.)
Tarbell, Ida Minerva (US writer; 1857-1944)
Targa™ car radio
Targa Accessories, Inc.
Target™ (stores)
Tar Heel State (nickname, NC)
Tarif, Sheik Amin (Islamic rel.; 1898-1993)
Tarkenton, Fran(cis Asbury)(football; 1940-)

Tarkett, Inc.
Tarkington, (Newton) Booth (US writer; 1869-
    1946)
Tarnower, Herman (US phys., Scarsdale Diet;
    1911-80)
Tarpon Springs, FL
Tarrytown, NY
Tarsus, Turkey
Tartar (also Tatar)(people)
Tartabull, Danny (baseball; 1962-)
Tartarstan (E Russia)
Tartarus (myth., lowest region of Hades)
Tartikoff, Brandon (ent.; 1949-)
Tartu, Estonia
Tartuffe, Le (Molière comedy)
Tarzan (fict. chara.)
Tarzan of the Apes (by Edgar Rice Burroughs)
Tarzan, The Ape Man (film; 1932, 1981)
Tasaday (people)
Tashkent, Uzbekistan
Taslima Nasrin (phys./writer)
Tasman Sea (S Pac.)
Tasman, Abel Janszoon (Dutch expl./nav.;
    1603?-59)
Tasmania (state, Austl.)
Tasmanian devil (marsupial)
Tass (Telegrafnoye Agentstvo Sovyetskovo
    Soyuza)(Rus. news agcy.)
Tass, ITAR- (Rus. news org.)
Tasso, Torquato (It. poet; 1544-95)
Tastee-Freez International, Inc.
Taster's Choice™ (coffee)
Tastykake™
Tastykake, Inc.
Tatanka Yotanka (Chief Sitting Bull)(Sioux
    Indians; c1831-90)
Tatar (also Tartar)(people)
Tate Co., Ashton-
Tate Gallery (London)
Tate (Polanski), Sharon (ent.; 1943-69)
Tatiana Troyanos (ent.; 1938-)
Tatiana™ perfume
Tatum O'Neal (ent.; 1963-)
Tatum, Art(hur)(US jazz; 1910-56)
Tatum, Edward Lawrie (US biochem.; 1909-75)
Tatum, Goose (Reece)(basketball)
Tatung™ (compu.)
Tatung Co. of America, Inc.
Taufa'ahau Tupou IV (king, Tonga; 1918-)
Taupin, Bernie (lyricist)
Taurus (zodiac, astron., bull)
Taurus, Ford (auto.)
Taussig, Frank W. (US econ./educ.; 1859-1940)
Taussig, Helen Brooke (US phys.; 1898-1986)
Tavist-D™ (med.)
Tawney, Richard Henry (Br. hist.; 1880-1962)
Taxco, Mexico
Tay Pay (Thomas Power) O'Connor (Ir. jour./

pol.; 1848-1929)
Tay-Sachs disease
Taya, Maaouya Ould Sidi Ahmed (pres., Mauritania; 1943-)
Tayback, Vic (b. Victor Tabback)(ent.; 1930-90)
Taylor Wine Co., Inc. The
Taylor, A(lan) J(ohn) P(ercivale)(Br. hist.; 1906-89)
Taylor, Ann (designer)
Taylor, (James) Bayard (US jour.; 1825-78)
Taylor, Billy (US jazz; 1921-)
Taylor, Cecil (US jazz; 1933-)
Taylor, Deems (US comp.; 1885-1966)
Taylor, Elizabeth (Rosemond)(ent.; 1932-)
Taylor, Frederick Winslow (US inv.; 1856-1915)
Taylor, James (ent.; 1948-)
Taylor, Lawrence (football; 1959-)
Taylor, Lord & (US bus.)
Taylor, Maxwell Davenport (US gen.; 1901-87)
Taylor, Peter (US writer; 1917-)
Taylor, Robert (ent.; 1911-69)
Taylor, Rod (ent.; 1929-)
Taylor, Samuel Coleridge- (Br. comp.; 1875-1912)
Taylor, Zachary ("Old Rough and Ready")(12th US pres.; 1784-1850)
Taystee™
Taystee Bakeries (US bus.)
TB (tuberculosis)
Tb (chem. sym., terbium)
TBA (to be announced)
T-bar (also tee)(constr.)
Tbilisi, Georgia (formerly Tiflis)
T-bill (Treasury bill)
T-Bird (Thunderbird™)(auto.)
T-bone steak
T. Boone Pickens
TBS SuperStation (TBS)(cable TV)
Tc (chem. sym., technetium)
Tchaikovsky, Peter I(lyich)(Rus. comp.; 1840-93)
TD (touchdown)
Te (chem. sym., tellurium)
Teach, Edward (also Thatch, Thach, Blackbeard)(pirate; ?-1718)
Teachers Insurance and Annuity Association fo America
Teagarden, Jack (Weldon John)(US jazz; 1905-64)
Teamsters Union (International Brotherhood of Teamsters, Chauffeurs, Warehousemen, and Helpers of America)(trade union; est. 1903)
Teaneck, NJ
Teannaki, Teatao (pres., Kiribati)
Teapot Dome scandal (US hist.; 1920s)
Teasdale, Sara (US poet; 1884-1933)
Teatao Teannaki (pres., Kiribati)
Tebaldi, Renata (It. soprano; 1922-)

Tebbetts, Birdie (George R.)(baseball; 1914-)
Tebet (also Tevet)(Jew. month)
T cell (also T lymphocyte)(med)
Technicolor™ (color process)
Technics (US bus.)
Tecumseh Chief (also Tecumtha)(Shawnee Indians; 1768-1813)
Ted & Alice, Bob & Carol & (film; 1969)
Ted Bundy (US serial killer; ?-1989)
Ted Danson (ent.; 1947-)
Ted DeCorsia
Ted Healy (b. Charles Earnest Nash)(ent.; 1896-1937)
Ted (Edward James) Hughes (Br. poet; 1930-)
Ted (Edward Moore) Kennedy (US cong.; 1932-)
Ted Key (cartoonist, *Hazel*; 1912-)
Ted Kluszeewski (baseball; 1924-88)
Ted Knight (ent.; 1923-86)
Ted Koppel (US TV jour.; 1940-)
Ted (Thaddeus John) Kwalik (football; 1947-)
Ted Shackelford (ent.; 1946-)
Ted Stevens (US cong.; 1923-)
Ted Turner (US bus./media; 1938-)
Ted (Theodore Samuel) Williams (baseball; 1918-)
Teddy Pendergrass (ent.; 1950-)
Teddy (Theodore) Roosevelt (26th US pres.; 1858-1919)
Teddy Wilson (US jazz; 1912-86)
Teen (mag.)
Teenage Mutant Ninja Turtles (film, cartoon)
Teflon™ (nonstick plastic)
Tegrin™ (med.)
Tegucigalpa, Honduras
Tehachapi Mountains (CA)
Tehachapi, CA
Tehran Conference (FDR/Churchill/Stalin; 1943)
Tehran, Iran (also Teheran)
Teicher, Ferrante & (US piano duet)
Teke (lang./people)
Tektronix, Inc.
Tel Aviv, Israel (also Tel Aviv-Jaffa)
T(homas) E(dward) Lawrence (of Arabia)(Br. mil.; 1888-1935)
Teledyne Water Pik (US bus.)
Teledyne, Inc.
Telegram Gazette, Worcester (MA newspaper)
Telegram, Portland (ME newspaper)
Telegraph, Macon (GA newspaper)
Telegraph, Worcester (MA newspaper)
Telemann, Georg Philipp (Ger. comp.; 1681-1767)
Teleme (cheese)
Telephoto™ (comm.)
TelePrompTer™
Telescopium (astron., telescope)
Teletype™

Proper Noun Speller

Teletype Corp.

Television and Radio Announcers, National Association of (also NATRA)

Television Arts and Sciences, National Academy of (NATAS, Emmy Awards)

Television Food Network (cable TV)

Telex (comm.)(also l.c.)

Telex Corp., The

Tell, William (legendary Swiss patriot; 14th c.)

Teller, Dr. Edward (US physt., A-bomb/H-bomb; 1908-)

Telluride, CO

Telly Savalas (ent.; 1924-94)

Telstar (US space satellite)

Telugu (lang./people)

Tema, Ghana

Temne (lang./people)

Tempe, AZ

Tempest, The (Shakespeare play)

Tempestt Bledsoe (ent.; 1973-)

Templar (Knights of the Temple of Solomon)(rel./mil. order; 1119-1307)

Templar, Simon

Temple Black, Shirley (US ent./dipl.; 1928-)

Temple of Amen (or Amon)(Karnak, Eg.; built 13th-20th c. BC)

Temple of Artemis at Ephesus (also Artemision)

Temple of Athena (Gr.)

Temple of Athena Nike (Gr.)

Temple of Athena Parthenos (also Parthenon, Gr.)

Temple of Jerusalem (rel.)

Temple of Solomon, Knights of the (also Templar)(rel./mil. order; 1119-1307)

Temple University (PA)

Temple, Shirley (non-alcoholic cocktail)

Temple, TX

temples of Karnak (Eg., built 21st-1st c. BC)

Tempo, Ford (auto.)

Temptations, the (pop music)

Tempter (Satan)

Temuco, Chile

Ten Commandments (also Decalog[ue])(rel.)

Ten Years' War (Cuba/Sp.; 1868-78)

Tenderloin district (city district noted for corruption)

Tenerife (Canary island)

Tenerife (lace)

Teng Hsiao-ping (also Deng Xiaoping)(Ch. pol.; 1904-)

Tenghui, Lee (pres., Taiwan; 1923-)

Tenneco, Inc.

Tennessee (TN)

Tennessee Ernie Ford (ent.; 1919-91)

Tennessee River (SE US)

Tennessee Valley Authority (TVA)(US govt. corp.; est. 1933)

Tennessee Valley Authority, Ashwander v. (US law; 1936)

Tennessee walking horse (also Plantation walking horse)

Tennessee (Thomas Lanier) Williams (US writer; 1914-83)

Tennessean, Nashville (TN newspaper)

Tenniel, Sir John, (Br. artist; 1820-1914)

Tennille, Captain & (Daryl & Toni)(pop music)

Tennille, Toni (ent.; 1943-)

Tennis (mag.)

Tennyson, Alfred, Lord (Br. poet; 1809-92)

Tenormin™ (med.)

Tenuate™ (med.)

Tenure of Office Act (US hist.; 1867)

Teodoro Obiang Nguema Mbasogo (pres., Equatorial Guinea; 1942-)

Teotihuacán (ancient Mex. city)

Tepe Gawra, Iraq (archeological site)

Terbrugghen, Hendrick (Dutch artist; 1588-1629)

Tercel, Toyota (auto.)

Terence (Mervyn) Rattigan, Sir (Br. writer; 1911-77)

Terence (Roman drama.; 185-c159 BC)

Terence Trent D'Arby (ent.; 1962-)

Teresa (of Ávila), St. (Sp. mystic; 1515-82)

Teresa (of Calcutta), Mother (b. Agnes Gonxha Bojaxhiu)(Albanian rel.; 1910-)

Teresa Brewer (ent.; 1931-)

Teresa Wright (ent.; 1918-)

Tereshchenko, Sergei (PM, Kazakhstan)

Tereshkova, Valentina (Vladimirovna)(cosmo., 1st woman in space; 1937-)

Teri Garr (ent.; 1945-)

Terkel, Studs (US writer; 1912-)

Termagant (myth.)

Terminator, The (film)

Terminator 2: Judgment Day (film)

Terminix International, Inc.

Ter-Petrosyan, Levon (pres., Armenia; 1943-)

Terpsichore (myth.)

Terramycin™ (med.)

Terre Haute, IN

Terror, Reign of (Fr. hist.; 1793-94)

Terry & the Pirates (comic strip)

Terry Bradshaw (football; 1948-)

Terry Drinkwater

Terry E. Branstad (IA gov.; 1946-)

Terry Melcher (ent.)

Terry Moore (ent.; 1929-)

Terry-Thomas (b. Thomas Terry Hoar Stevens)(ent.; 1912-90)

Terry (Terence Hardy) Waite (Br. rel., hostage; 1939-)

Terry, Dame Ellen (Alicia)(ent.; 1847-1928)

Terry, Paul (cartoonist, *Mighty Mouse*; 1887-1971)

Tersanctus (also *Sanctus*)(rel.)

Tertiary period (65-2.5 million years ago)
Terylene™ (polyester fiber)
Tesh, John (ent.)
Tesla coil/transformer (elec.)
Tesla, Nikola (Croatia/US elec.eng.; 1856-1943)
Tess Harper (ent.; 1950-)
Tess of the D'Urbervilles (T. Hardy novel)
Test Ban Treaty (US/USSR/UK; 1963)
Tet (Viet. holiday)
Tet Offensive (Viet.; 1968)
Tethys (Saturn moon; myth.)
Teton Range (Rocky Mts., WY)
Tetrazzini, Luisa (It. opera; 1874-1940)
Tetrazzini, chicken (food)
Teutonic Knights (Knights of the Teutonic
    Order)(Ger. mil./rel.; est. 1190)
Tevet (also Tebet)(Jew. month)
Tex Avery (cartoonist, *Bugs Bunny, Porky Pig,
    Daffy Duck*; 1908-80)
Tex-Mex (culture/food/lang./music)
Tex (Woodward Maurice) Ritter (ent.; 1907-74)
Texaco, Inc.
Texarkana Gazette (AR newspaper)
Texarkana, AR, TX
Texas (TX)
Texas Instruments, Inc.
Texas leaguer (baseball)
Texas Longhorn/longhorn (cattle)
Texas Monthly (mag.)
Texas Rangers (baseball team)
Texas Rangers (law enforcement corps; est.
    1835)
Texas two-step (dance)
Texas v. White (US law; 1869)
Texasware (US bus.)
Texsport (US bus.)
Textron, Inc.
Teyateyaneng, Lesotho
T formation (football)
TGIF (thank God it's Friday)
T-group (psych.)
Th (chem. sym., thorium)
Thackeray, William Makepeace (Br. writer;
    1811-63)
Thad Cochran (US cong.; 1937-)
Thad Jones (US jazz; 1923-86)
Thai (lang./people)
Thai Airways International (airline)
Thai cuisine
Thai stick (slang, marijuana from Thailand)
Thailand (Kingdom of)(formerly Siam)(SE Asia)
Thailand (or Siam), Gulf of
Thalberg, Irving (Grant)(ent.; 1899-1936)
Thales (Gr. phil.; c634-c546 BC)
Thalia (myth.)
Thames River (Eng.)
Than Shwe (head of state, Myanmar; 1933-)
Thanatos (myth.)

Thang, Ton Duc (ex-pres., NViet.; 1888-1980)
Thani, Sheik Khalifa ibn Hamad al- (emir,
    Qatar; 1932-)
Thanksgiving Day (US)
Thant, U (Burmese dipl./UN; 1909-74)
Tharp, Twyla (US dancer; 1941-)
Tharsis ridge (astron.)
Thatch (or Thach)(aka Edward Teach,
    Blackbeard)(pirate; ?-1718)
Thatcher, Margaret (Hilda Roberts)(ex-PM, Br.;
    1925-)
Thaves, Bob (cartoonist, *Frank and Ernest*;
    1924-)
The Hague, Netherlands
Thebes (cities, ancient Gr., ancient Eg.)
Thebes, Seven against (Aeschylus tragedy)
Theismann, Joe (football; 1946-)
Thelma Ritter (ent.; 1905-69)
Thelonious (Sphere) Monk (US jazz; 1920-82)
Themis (myth.)
Themistocles (Gr. pol./mil.; 527?-460? BC)
Theo van Doesburg (Dutch artist/writer; 1883-
    1931)
Theocritus (Gr. poet; c310-c250 BC)
Theodor Mommsen (Ger. hist.; 1817-1903)
Theodor Schwann (Ger. phys.; 1810-82)
Theodor Stolojan (ex-PM, Romania)
Theodore Dreiser (US writer; 1871-1945)
Theodore H. White (US jour.; 1915-86)
Theodore N. Vail (US bus.; 1845-1920)
Theodore Roethke (US poet; 1908-1963)
Theodore "Teddy" Roosevelt (26th US pres.;
    1858-1919)
Theodore Roosevelt National Park (ND)
Theodore Rousseau, (Pierre Étienne)(Fr. artist;
    1812-67)
Theodore Seuss Geisel (pseud. Dr. Seuss)(US
    writer/artist; 1904-91)
Theodore Sturgeon (aka Edward Hamilton
    Waldo (US writer; 1918-85)
Theodore W. Schultz (US econ.; 1902-)
Theo-Dur™ (med.)
Theognis (Gr. poet; fl. 6th c. BC)
Theology, Doctor of (also D.Th., D.Theol.)
Theophrastus (Gr. phil.; c372-c287 BC)
Theosophical Society (mystical rel.)
Theosophy (rel.)
TheraFlu™ (med.)
Theragran™ (med.)
Theragran-M™ (med.)
Theravada Buddhism (rel.)
Theresa Russell (ent.; 1957-)
Theresa, Maria (empress, Austria; 1717-80)
Thérèse of Lisieux, St. (Fr. rel.; 1873-97)
Thermodor™
Thermador/Waste King (US bus.)
Thermofax™
Thermos™

Theroux, Paul (US writer; 1941-)
Theseus (myth.)
Thespis (Gr. poet; 6th c. BC)
Thessalonians (rel.)
Thessaloniki, Greece
Thessaly (region, Gr.)
Thiam, Habib (PM, Senegal)
Thicke, Alan (ent.; 1947-)
Thiès, Senegal
Thieu, Nguyen Van (ex-pres., SViet; 1923-)
Thimbu, Bhutan (also Thimphu)
Thinnes, Roy (ent.)
Thinsulate™ (fabric)
Thiokol™ (synthetic rubber)
Thiong'o, Ngugi wa (Kenyan writer; 1938-)
Third of May, 1808 (by Goya)
Third Reich (Nazi Germany; 1933-45)
Third Republic (Fr.; 1870-1940)
Third World (less developed nations)
Thirteen Colonies (original US states)
Thirty Years' War (Eur.; 1618-48)
Thirtysomething (TV show)
This is Your Life (TV show)
This Morning (TV show)
This Week (TV show)
This Week with David Brinkley (TV show)
Thisbe, Pyramus and (myth.)
Thívai, Greece (formerly Thebes)
Tho, Le Duc (aka Phan Dinh Khai)(NViet pol.;
    1911-90)
Thoeni, Gustavo (skiing; 1951-)
Thom McAn Shoe Co.
Thomas à Becket, St. (Br. rel./pol.; 1118-70)
Thomas A. Dooley (US phys.; 1927-61)
Thomas A(ndrews) Hendricks (ex-US VP; 1819-
    85)
Thomas à Kempis (Gr. rel.; c1380-1471)
Thomas Alva Edison (US inv.; 1847-1931)
Thomas Ambroise (Fr. comp.; 1811-96)
Thomas Andrew Daschle (US cong.; 1947-)
Thomas Aquinas, St. ("the Angelic Doctor")(It.
    phil./rel.; 1225-74)
Thomas Bailey Aldrich (US writer; 1836-1907)
Thomas Barnardo (Br. reformer; 1845-1905)
Thomas Beecham, Sir (Br. cond.; 1879-1961)
Thomas Berger (US writer; 1924-)
Thomas B(abington) Macauley, Baron (Br. hist./
    pol.; 1800-59)
Thomas Bodley, Sir (Br. scholar/dipl., founded
    Bodleian Library; 1545-1613)
Thomas Bowdler (Shakespeare editor; 1754-
    1825)
Thomas Carew (Br. poet; 1595?-?)
Thomas Carlyle (Scot. hist.; 1795-1881)
Thomas C. Durant (US indust/finan.; 1820-85)
Thomas Chandler Haliburton (pseud. Sam
    Slick)(Can. writer/judge/hist.; 1796-1865)
Thomas Chatterton (Br. poet; 1752-70)

Thomas Chippendale (Br. furniture designer;
    c1718-79)
Thomas Cole (US artist; 1801-48)
Thomas Coleman du Pont (US bus./pol.; 1863-
    1930)
Thomas Cook (Br. travel agent; 1808-92)
Thomas Cranmer (Br. rel./writer; 1489-1556)
Thomas Decker (or Dekker)(Br. writer; 1572?-
    1632?)
Thomas Eakins (US artist; 1844-1916)
Thomas E(dmund) Dewey (ex-gov., NY; 1902-
    71)
Thomas™ English muffins
Thomas Fortune Ryan (US bus./finan.; 1851-
    1928)
Thomas Gage (Br. gen./colonial gov.; 1721-87)
Thomas Gainsborough (Br. artist; 1727-88)
Thomas Gallaudet (US rel./educ. for the deaf;
    1822-1902)
Thomas G(arrigue) Masaryk (ex-pres., Czech.;
    1850-1937)
Thomas Graham (Scot. chem.; 1805-69)
Thomas Gray (Br. poet; 1716-71)
Thomas Gresham, Sir (Br. finan.; 1519?-79)
Thomas Hardy (Br. writer; 1840-1928)
Thomas Hart Benton (US artist; 1889-1975)
Thomas Hart Benton (US pol.; 1782-1858)
Thomas Hastings (US arch.; 1860-1929)
Thomas Hearns ("Hit Man")(boxing)
Thomas Hobbes (Br. writer/phil.; 1588-1679)
Thomas Hobson (Br. bus.; 1544-1631)
Thomas Hopkins Gallaudet (US educ. for the
    deaf; 1787-1851)
Thomas Hunt Morgan (US geneticist; 1866-
    1945)
Thomas Jefferson (3rd US pres.; 1743-1826)
Thomas Jefferson Memorial (DC)
Thomas J. Lipton, Inc.
Thomas J(ohnstone) Lipton, Sir (Scot. bus., tea;
    1850-1931)
Thomas Jonathan "Stonewall" Jackson (US
    gen.; 1824-63)
Thomas J(ohn) Watson (US bus.; 1874-1956)
Thomas J(ohn) Watson, Jr. (US bus.; 1914-93)
Thomas (Michael) Keneally (Austl. writer;
    1935-)
Thomas Kennerly, Jr. (pseud. Tom Wolfe)(US
    writer; 1931-)
Thomas Kid (or Kyd)(Br. writer; c1557-95)
Thomas Klestil (pres., Austria; 1932-)
Thomas K. Mattingly (astro.; 1936-)
Thomas Lawrence, Sir (Br. artist; 1769-1830)
Thomas Malory, Sir (Br. writer; c1400-71)
Thomas Mann (Ger. writer; 1875-1955)
Thomas McGuane (US writer; 1939-)
Thomas "Mack" McLarty (US pol.; 1946-)
Thomas Merton (US rel.; 1915-68)
Thomas Mitchell (ent.; 1892-1962)

Thomas Moore (Ir. poet; 1779-1852)
Thomas More, Sir (Br. writer/pol.; 1478-1535)
Thomas Nashe (Br. writer; 1567-1601)
Thomas Nast (US artist/cartoonist; 1840-1902)
Thomas "Tom" Paine (US writer; 1737-1809)
Thomas Pelham-Holles Newcastle (ex-PM, Br.; 1693-1768)
Thomas Pinckney (US pol.; 1750-1828)
Thomas P. "Tip" O'Neill, Jr. (US pol.; 1912-1993)
Thomas Power "Tay Pay" O'Connor (Ir. jour./pol.; 1848-1929)
Thomas P. Stafford (astro.)
Thomas Pynchon (US writer; 1937-)
Thomas R. Harkin (US cong.; 1939-)
Thomas R(obert) Malthus (Br. econ.; 1766-1834)
Thomas R(iley) Marshall (ex-US VP; 1854-1925)
Thomas S. Foley (US cong.; 1929-)
Thomas Sheraton (Br. furniture designer; 1751-1806)
Thomas Sopwith, Sir (Br. aircraft designer; 1888-1989)
Thomas Sully (US artist; 1783-1872)
Thomas Sydenham (Br. phys.; 1624-89)
Thomas Tallis (Br. comp.; c1510-85)
Thomas "Fats" Waller (US comp./US jazz; 1904-43)
Thomas (Clayton) Wolfe (US writer; 1900-38)
Thomas Wolsey, Cardinal (Br. rel./pol.; 1475-1530)
Thomas, Clarence (US jurist; 1948-)
Thomas, Danny (ent.; 1912-91)
Thomas, Debi (figure skating)
Thomas, Derrick (football; 1967-)
Thomas, doubting
Thomas, Dylan (Marlais)(Welsh poet; 1914-53)
Thomas, Frank (baseball; 1968-)
Thomas, George H(enry)(US mil.; 1816-70)
Thomas, Isiah (basketball; 1961-)
Thomas, Jay (ent.)
Thomas, Marlo (ent.; 1943-)
Thomas. Norman M(attoon)(US pol.; 1884-1968)
Thomas, Philip Michael (ent.; 1949-)
Thomas, Richard (ent.; 1951-)
Thomas, Terry- (b. Thomas Terry Hoar Stevens)(ent.; 1912-90)
Thomas, Thurman (football; 1966-)
Thomason, Harry (ent.)
Thomason, Linda Bloodworth- (ent.)
Thomasville Furniture Industries, Inc.
Thomism (phil.)
Thompson & Formby, Inc.
Thompson seedless grapes
Thompson submachine gun (also Tommy gun)
Thompson, David (basketball; 1954-)
Thompson, Emma (ent.; 1959-)
Thompson, James Walter (US bus.; 1847-1928)
Thompson, John (basketball; 1941-)

Thompson, John Taliaferro (US mil./inv.; 1860-1940)
Thompson, Hunter S. (US jour.; 1939-)
Thompson, Lea (ent.; 1961-)
Thompson, Sada (ent.; 1929-)
Thompson, Tommy G. (WI gov.; 1941-)
Thomson effect, Joule- (thermodynamics)
Thomson Newspapers Holding, Inc. (Can.)
Thomson, Sir J(oseph) J(ohn)(Br. physt.; 1856-1940)
Thomson, Kenneth R(oy)
Thor (myth)
Thor Heyerdahl (Nor. expl./anthrop.; 1914-)
Thorazine™ (med.)
Thoreau, Henry David (US writer/phil./nat.; 1817-62)
Thorndike, (Agnes) Sybil, Dame (ent.; 1882-1976)
Thorne Smith
Thornton (Niven) Wilder (US writer; 1897-1975)
Thoroughbred (horse)
Thoroughly Modern Millie (film; 1967)
Thorpe, Jim (James Francis)(athlete; 1888-1953)
Thorstein B(unde) Veblen (US econ.; 1857-1929)
Thoth (myth.)
Thousand and One Nights, The (also *Arabian Nights, The Arabian Nights' Entertainments*)(myth.)
Thousand Island dressing
Thousand Islands (St. Lawrence River, US/Can.)
Thousand Oaks, CA
Thrace (ancient empire, SE Eur.)
Three Dog Night (pop music)
Three Emperors' League (Aus.-Hung./Ger./Rus.; 1872)
Three Faces of Eve, The (film; 1957)
Three Kingdoms period (Korean hist.; began 3rd c.)
Three Kings of the Orient (also Wise Men of the East, Magi, Three Wise Men)(rel.)
3M (Minnesota Mining & Manufacturing Co.)(US bus.)
Three Men and a Baby (film)
Three Mile Island (PA)(nuclear accident; 1979)
Three Musicians (by Picasso)
Three Musketeers, The (A. Dumas novel)
Three Musketeers, The (Athos, Porthos, Aramis)
three R's, the (reading, 'riting, 'rithmetic)
Three Stooges (Curly, Moe, Larry)
Three Suns, The
321 Contact (mag.)
Three Wise Men (also Wise Men of the East, Magi, Three Kings of the Orient)(rel.)
Three's Company (TV show)

Thrift Drug Co.
Thrifty™
Thrifty Rent-A-Car System, Inc.
Thucydides (Gr. hist.; c455-c400 BC)
Thugs (former sect of murders/robbers, India)
Thule (northernmost land)
Thule, Greenland
Thumb Tom, Gen. (aka Charles Sherwood
    Stratton)(US circus midget; 1838-83)
Thumb, Tom (folklore)
Thumbelina (cartoon)
Thunder Bay, Ontario, Canada
Thunderbird™, Ford (also T-Bird)(auto.)
Thurber, James (Grover)(US writer/humorist;
    1894-1961)
Thurgood Marshall (US jurist; 1908-93)
Thuringia (former state, Ger.)
Thurman Munson (baseball; 1947-79)
Thurmond, J(ames) Strom (US cong.; 1902-)
Thutmose I, II, III (Eg. kings; 1524-1450 BC)
T(erence) H(anbury) White (Br. writer; 1906-64)
Ti (chem. sym., titanium)
Ti, Mo (also Mo-tze, Mo Tzu, Mo-tse, Mo
    Tse)(Ch. phil.; 5th c. BC)
Tiahuanacu (also Tiahuanaco)(pre-Incan
    culture)
Tiananmen Square (Beijing, Ch.)
Tianjin, China (formerly Tientsin)
Tibbett, Lawrence (Mervil)(ent.; 1896-1960)
Tibbs, Casey
Tiber River (It.)
Tiberius Claudius Drusus Nero Germanicus
    (Claudius I)(emp., Rome; 10 BC-AD 54)
Tiberius, Claudius Nero (Caesar)(emp., Rome;
    42 BC-AD 37)
Tibet (SW Ch.)
Tibetan (lang./people)
Tibetan Book of the Dead, The (rel.)
Tibetan Buddhism
Tibetan languages, Sino-
Tibetan mastiff (dog)
Tibetan spaniel (dog)
Tibetan terrier (dog)
Tibullus (Roman poet; c55-19 BC)
Tic Tac Dough (TV show)
Ticketmaster Corp.
Ticonderoga (ship, nuclear accident off Jap.
    coast; 1965)
Ticonderoga, Fort (NY)(fort)
Ticonderoga, NY
Tide™ (detergent)
Tiegs, Cheryl (model/ent.; 1947-)
Tientsin (rug)
Tientsin, China (also Tianjin)
Tiepolo ceiling
Tiepolo, Giovanni Battista (It. artist; 1696-
    1770)
Tierney, Gene (ent.; 1920-91)

Tierra del Fuego (island grp., Chile/Argentina)
Tiffany (ent.; 1971-)
Tiffany & Co.
Tiffany Chin
Tiffany lamp
Tiffany, Charles Lewis (US bus.; 1912-1902)
Tiffany, Louis (Comfort)(US artist/glassmaker;
    1848-1933)
Tiffany's, Breakfast at (film; 1961)
Tiflis (now Tbilisi)
Tiger Moth airplanes
Tiger? The Lady or the (F.R. Stockton short
    story)
Tigers, Detroit (baseball team)
Tigger (fict. chara., *Winnie-the-Pooh*)
Tiggy-Winkle, The Tale of Mrs. (B. Potter story)
Tigré (lang./people)
Tigré (region, Ethiopia)
Tigrinya (lang.)
Tigris River (Tur./Iraq)
Tiit, Vahl (ex-PM, Estonia)
Tijuana Brass, Herb Alpert and The (pop
    music)
Tijuana, Mexico
Tiki, Kon- (myth.)
Tiki, Kon (T. Heyerdahl raft used to cross Pac.;
    1947)
Tilden, Big Bill (William Tatem), Jr. (tennis;
    1893-1953)
Till Eulenspiegel (Ger. legend/practical jokes;
    14th c.)
Tillamook cheese
Tillamook, OR
Tillich, Paul (US rel./phil.; 1886-1965)
Tillis, Mel (ent.; 1932-)
Tilly, Meg
Tilsit cheese
Tilton, Charlene (ent.)
Tilzer, Albert von (US comp.; 1878-1956)
Tilzer, Harry von (US comp.; 1872-1946)
Tim Allen (b. Timothy Allen Dick)(ent.)
Tim Conway (ent.; 1933-)
Tim Matheson (ent.; 1947-)
Tim McCarver (ent.; 1941-)
Tim Reid (ent.; 1944-)
Tim Robbins (ent.; 1958-)
Tim, Tiny (ent.; 1923-)
Timakata, Fred (pres., Vanuatu)
Timberwolves, Minnesota (basketball team)
Timbuktu, Mali (also Tombouctou)
Time (mag.)
Time Trax (TV show)
Time Warner, Inc.
Time, Inc.
Time-Life Books (US bus.)
Time Life Libraries, Inc.
Time Life, Inc.
Time Warner Communications, Inc.

Times & World-News, Roanoke (VA newspaper)
Times Book Review, New York
Times-Dispatch, Richmond (VA newspaper)
Times Herald, Middletown (NY newspaper)
Times Mirror Co., The
Times-Picayune, New Orleans (LA newspaper)
Times Roman (type style)
Times Square (NYC)
Times-Union, Albany (NY newspaper)
Times-Union, Jacksonville (FL newspaper)
Times-Union, Rochester (NY newspaper)
Times, Cape Cod (MA newspaper)
Times, Chattanooga (TN newspaper)
Times, El Paso (TX newspaper)
Times, Erie (PA newspaper)
Times, Huntsville (AL newspaper)
Times, Lake County (IN newspaper)
Times, Los Angeles (CA newspaper)
Times, New York (NY newspaper)
Times, Reading (PA newspaper)
Times, Scranton (PA newspaper)
Times, Seattle (WA newspaper)
Times, Shreveport (LA newspaper)
Times, St. Petersburg (FL newspaper)
Times, Tampa (FL newspaper)
Times, Washington (DC newspaper)
Timex Corp.
Timisoara, Romania
Timon (Gr. phil.; c320-c230 BC)
Timon of Athens (by Shakespeare)
Timoshenko, Semyon (Konstantinovich)(USSR
    mil.; 1895-1970)
Timothy Bottoms (ent.; 1951-)
Timothy Busfield (ent.; 1957-)
Timothy Dalton (ent.; 1944-)
Timothy Daly (ent.; 1958-)
Timothy Hutton (ent.; 1960-)
Timothy Leary (US educ./writer; 1920-)
Timurids dynasty (founded by Tamerlane [or
    Timur], Tartar conqueror)
Tin Pan Alley (district where pop music is
    published, esp. NYC)
Tina Turner (ent.; 1938-)
Tina Yothers
Tinactin™ (med.)
Tinker, Grant (ent.; 1926-)
Tinkertoy™
Tinseltown (Hollywood)
Tintoretto, Il ('the little dyer')(b. Jacopo
    Robusti)(It. artist; 1518-94)
Tiny Tim (ent.; 1923-)
Tiny Tim Cratchit (fict. chara., A Christmas
    Carol)
Tiny Toons (cartoon)
Tiomkin, Dimitri (Rus./US comp.; 1899-)
Tip (Thomas P.) O'Neill, Jr. (US pol.; 1912-
    1993)
Tippecanoe (nickname, Wm. Henry Harrison)

Tippecanoe River (IN)
Tippecanoe, Battle of (US hist.; 1811)
Tipperary, North (county, Ir.)
Tipperary, South (county, Ir.)
Tippett, Sir Michael (Kemp)(Br. comp.; 1905-)
Tippi Hedren (ent.)
Tippy's Taco House, Inc.
Tirana, Albania (also Tiranë)
Tiraspol, Moldova
Tire, General (US bus.)
Tiro (US space satellite)
Tirolean (also Tyrolean, Tyrolese,
    Tirolese)(clothing style, people)
Tirpitz, Alfred von (Ger. mil.; 1849-1930)
Tirthankara (rel.)
Tisarana (rel.)
Tishri (Jew. month)
Tissot, J(ames) J(oseph Jacques)(Fr. artist;
    1836-1902)
Titan (Saturn moon; myth.)
Titan (US uncrewed space probe)
Titan crane (films)
Titan rocket (US space program)
Titania (queen of fairyland, Midsummer Night's
    Dream)
Titania (Uranus moon)
Titanic, S.S. (Br. luxury liner; sunk 1912)
Titian (b. Tiziano Vecellio)(It. artist; c1477-
    1576)
Titicaca, Lake (SAmer.)
Tito Puente (US jazz; 1923-)
Tito, Marshal (Josip Broz)(ex-pres., Yug.; 1892-
    1980)
Titograd, Yugoslavia
Titov, Gherman (or Herman)
    S(tepanovich)(cosmo.; 1935-)
Tittle, Y(elberton) A(braham)(football; 1926-)
Titus Andronicus (Shakespeare play)
Titus Flavius Sabinus Vespasian(us)(Roman
    emp.; AD 9-79)
Titus Livius Livy (Roman hist.; 59 BC-AD 17)
Titus Lucretius (Carus)(Roman poet/phil.; c99-
    c55 BC)
Titus Maccius Plautus (Roman writer; c254-
    c184 BC)
Titus, Arch of (statue)
Titusville, FL, PA
Tivoli Gardens (It.)
Tivoli, Italy
Tizard, Catherine (gov-gen., NewZeal.)
Tl (chem. sym., thallium)
Tlaloc (myth.)
TLC (tender, loving care)
Tlingit (NAmer Indians)
TM (trademark, transcendental meditation)
Tm (chem. sym., thulium)
TN (Tennessee)
TNT (trinitrotoluene)(explosive)

Proper Noun Speller

Toad of Toad Hall
Toamasina, Madagascar
Toaripi Lauti (gov-gen., Tuvalu
Toastmaster, Inc.
Toastmaster, The (mag.)
Tobacco Road (E. Caldwell novel)
Tobago (Republic of Trinidad and)(West Indies)
Tobias Wolff (US writer; 1945-)
Tobin, James (US econ.; 1918-)
Tobruk, Libya
Toby Belch, Sir (fict, chara., *Twelfth Night*)
Tocqueville, Alexis (Charles Henri Maurice
    Clérel) de (Fr. hist.; 1805-59)
Today™ (med.)
Today (TV show)
Today, Melbourne (FL newspaper)
Today, USA (newspaper)
Todd, Michael (ent.; 1909-58)
Todd, Richard (ent.; 1919-)
Todd, Sweeney (play)
Todor Zhivkov (ex-pres.; Bulgaria; 1911-)
Toffler, Alvin (US sociol./writer writer; 1928-)
Tofilau Eti Alesana (PM, WSamoa)
Tofranil™ (med.)
Tofutti (US bus.)
Toggenburg (goat)
Togliatti, Palmiro (It. pol.; 1893-1964)
Togo (Republic of)(W Afr)
Togo Heihachiro, Marquis (Jap. mil.; 1847-
    1934)
Tojo Hideki (ex-PM, Jap.; 1884-1948)
Tokai Corp., Scripto
Tokaj, Hungary (also Tokay)
Tokay (grape, wine)
Tokelau Islands (NewZeal.)
Tokina Optical Corp.
Toklas, Alice B. (US writer; 1877-1967)
Tokugawa (Jap. shogun family; 1603-1867)
Tokushima, Japan
Tokyo, Japan
Toledo Blade (OH newspaper)
Toledo, OH
Toledo, Spain
Toliary, Madagascar
Tolkien, J(ohn) R(onald) R(euel)(Br. writer/
    educ.; 1892-1973)
Toll House™ (chocolate chips)
Tolstoy, Leo (Nikolaievich), Count (Rus. writer;
    1828-1910)
Toltec (Mex. Indians)
Tom and Jerry (cartoon)
Tom and Jerry (cocktail)
Tom Batiuk (cartoonist)
Tom Berenger (ent.; 1950-)
Tom Bosley (ent.; 1927-)
Tom Bradley (ex-mayor, Los Angeles, CA;
    1917-)
Tom Brokaw (US TV jour.; 1940-)

Tom Carper (DE gov.)
Tom Carvel (Ger./US bus.; 1908-90)
Tom Clancy (Ir. ent.; 1923-90)
Tom Clancy (US writer; 1947-)
Tom Collins (mixed drink)
Tom Conti (Scot. ent.; 1941-)
Tom Courtenay (ent.; 1937-)
Tom Cruise (b. Thomas Cruise Mapother,
    IV)(ent.; 1962-)
Tom Dooley (song)
Tom Ewell (ent.; 1909-)
Tom Fogarty (ent.; 1942-90)
Tom Hanks (ent.; 1956-)
Tom (Thomas E.) Hayden (US pol.; 1941-)
Tom Hulce (ent.; 1953-)
Tom Jarriel (TV jour.)
Tom Jones (ent.; 1940-)
Tom Landry (football; 1924-)
Tom Mboya (Kenyan pol.; 1930-69)
Tom (Thomas Edwin) Mix (ent.; 1880-1940)
Tom Okker (tennis; 1944-)
Tom (Thomas) Paine (US writer; 1737-1809)
Tom Petty (ent.; 1953-)
Tom Petty and the Heartbreakers (pop music)
Tom Poston (ent.; 1927-)
Tom Sawyer (fict. Mark Twain chara.)
Tom Sawyer, The Adventures of (M. Twain
    novel)
Tom Seaver (baseball; 1944-)
Tom Selleck (ent.; 1945-)
Tom Shales (US TV critic; 1958-)
Tom Skerritt (ent.; 1933-)
Tom Smothers (ent.; 1937-)
Tom Sneva (auto racing; 1948-)
Tom Snyder
Tom Stoppard (b. Thomas Straussler)(Br.
    writer; 1937-)
Tom T. Hall (ent.; 1936-)
Tom Thumb (folklore)
Tom Thumb, Gen. (aka Charles Sherwood
    Stratton)(US circus midget; 1838-83)
Tom Waits (ent.)
Tom Watson (golf; 1949-)
Tom Weiskopf (golf; 1942-)
Tom Wilson (cartoonist, *Ziggy*; 1931-)
Tom Wolfe (aka Thomas Kennerly, Jr.)(US
    writer; 1931-)
Tom Wopat
Tom, Dick, and Harry (the ordinary person)
Tom, Long (WWII weapon)
Tom, Peeping
Tom, Uncle (fict. chara., *Uncle Tom's Cabin*;
    slang, subservient black)
Tomba, Alberto (skiing; 1966-)
Tombouctou, Mali (also Timbuktu)
Tombstone, AZ
Tomlin, Lily (ent.; 1939-)
Tommie Smith (sprinter; 1944-)

Tommaso Guidi (Masaccio)(It. artist; 1401-28?
Tommy (Br. slang, army private)
Tommy Aaron (baseball; 1939-84)
Tommy Atkins (slang, Br. army private)
Tommy (Thomas) Chong (ent.; 1938-)
Tommy Dorsey (US cond.; 1905-56)
Tommy G. Thompson (WI gov.; 1941-)
Tommy gun (also Thompson submachine gun)
Tommy James & the Shondells (pop music)
Tommy Lasorda (baseball/ent.; 1927-)
Tommy Lee Jones (ent.; 1946-)
Tommy Mottola (ent.)
Tommy Tune (ent.; 1939-)
Tompkins, Daniel D. (ex-US VP; 1774-1825)
Tom's Cabin, Uncle (H.B. Stowe novel)
Tomsk, Siberia
Ton Duc Thang (ex-pres., NViet; 1888-1980)
Tone Loc (pop music)
Tone, Franchot (ent.; 1903-68)
Tonelli, Salvatore (captain-regent, San Marino)
Tong, Goh Chok (PM, Singapore; 1941-)
Tonga (Kingdom of)(also Friendly Islands)(SW Pac.)
Tongan (lang./people)
Toni Morrison (b. Chloe Anthony Wofford)(US writer; 1931-)
Toni Tennille (ent.; 1943-)
Tonight (TV show)
Tonight Show with Jay Leno, The (TV show)
Tonight Show, The (TV show)
Tonkin Gulf (also Gulf of Tonkin)(Viet./Ch.)
Tonkin Gulf resolution (US hist.; 1964)
Tonto, Lone Ranger & (fict charas.)
Tony Award (theater)
Tony Bennett (ent.; 1926-)
Tony Conigliaro (baseball; 1945-90)
Tony Curtis (ent.; 1925-)
Tony Danza (ent.; 1950-)
Tony Dorsett (football; 1954-)
Tony (Anthony) Francisco (ent.; 1928-)
Tony Gwynn (baseball; 1960-)
Tony Martin (ent.; 1913-)
Tony Musante (ent.; 1936-)
Tony (Pedro) Oliva (baseball; 1940-)
Tony Orlando (ent.; 1944-)
Tony Orlando and Dawn (pop music)
Tony (Anthony) Perkins (ent.; 1932-92)
Tony Randall (ent.; 1920-)
Tony Roberts (ent.; 1939-)
Tonya Harding (figure skating)
Tooele Army Depot (UT)(US mil.)
Toomey, William (decathlon; 1939-)
Toomey, Regis
Toonerville trolley (dilapidated train/trolley)
Tootsie (film; 1982)
Tootsie Pop™ (candy)
Tootsie Roll™ (candy)
Tootsie Roll Industries, Inc,

Toowoomba, Queensland, Australia
Top Forty (also Top 40, top forty)
Top Gun (film)
Top of the Mark (Mark Hopkins Hotel, San Francisco)
Top-Sider™ (shoe)
Topaz, Lincoln-Mercury (auto.)
Topeka, KS
Tophet(h)(place of punishment after death)
Topol (toothpaste)
Toradol™ (med.)
Torah (also Pentateuch)(1st 5 books of Bible)
Torch Song Trilogy (play)
Tori Spelling (ent.)
Tormak, Kyrgyzstan
Torme, Mel (ent.; 1925-)
Torn, Rip (ent.; 1931-)
Toro Co., The
Toronado, Oldsmobile (auto.)
Toronto Blue Jays (baseball team)
Toronto Globe & Mail (Can. newspaper)
Toronto Maple Leafs (hockey team)
Toronto Sun (Can. newspaper)
Toronto, Ontario, Canada
Torquato Tasso (It. poet; 1544-95)
Torrance, CA
Torremolinos, Spain
Torrens Act (Austl. hist.; 1857)
Torrens, Sir Robert Richard (Br. pol. in Austl.; 1814-84)
Torrey pine (tree)
Torrid Zone (also Tropical Zone, Tropics)(between tropics of Cancer and Capricorn)
Torrijos Herrera, Omar (Panamanian gen./pol.; 1929-81)
Tors, Ivan
Tortilla Flat (John Steinbeck novel)
Tortola (Br. Virgin Island)
Tortuga (island, Haiti)
Torvill, Jayne (figure skating)
Tory Party (Br. pol. party; c1680-1830)
Tosca (Giacomo Puccini opera)
Toscanini, Arturo (It. cond.; 1867-1957)
Toshiba™
Toshiba American Information Systems, Inc.
Toshiba America, Inc.
Toshiki, Kaifu (ex-PM, Jap.; 1931-)
Toshiro, Mifune (Jap. actor; 1920-)
Tostitos™
Totally Different Pauly (TV show)
Totie Fields (ent.; 1931-78)
Totino's Pizza Co.
Toto (dog, *Wizard of Oz*)
Toucouleur (people)
Tough, Dave (US jazz; 1908-48)
Toulouse (goose)
Toulouse-Lautrec, Henri (Marie Raymond) de

(Fr. artist; 1864-1901)

Toulouse, France

Tour de France (Fr. bicycle race)

Toure, Amadou Toumani (ex-pres., Mali)

Tourette's syndrome/disease

Touring America (mag.)

Tournament of Roses Parade

Tours, France

Tov, Baal Shem- (also Israel ben Eliezer)(Jew. rel.; c1700-60)

Tovah Feldshuh (ent.; 1952-)

Tower Books

Tower of Babel (Babylon, different languages)

Tower of London (fortress; built 1078)

Tower Records/Video

Tower, John G. (US pol.; 1926-91)

Towle Manufacturing Co.

Town & Country (mag.)

Town & County, Chrysler (auto.)

Town Car, Lincoln-Mercury (auto.)

Townes, Charles Hard (US physt./educ.; 1915-)

Townsend plan (pension plan, never enacted)

Townsend, Francis E(verett)(US phys./ reformer; 1867-1960)

Townsend, Port (WA)

Townsend, Robert (ent.; 1957-)

Townshend Acts (Br./Amer. hist.; 1767)

Townshend Charles (Br. pol., Townshend Acts; 1725-67)

Townshend, Charles, Viscount ("Turnip")(Br. pol./agr.; 1675-1738)

Townshend, George, Marquis (Br. mil.; 1724-1807)

Townsville, Queensland, Australia

Towson, MD

Toynbee, Arnold (Joseph)(Br. hist.; 1889-1975)

Toyota (auto.)

Toyota Camry (auto.)

Toyota Camry Wagon (auto.)

Toyota Celica (auto.)

Toyota Corolla (auto.)

Toyota Land Cruiser (auto.)

Toyota Motor Sales USA, Inc.

Toyota MR2 (auto.)

Toyota Paseo (auto.)

Toyota Previa (auto.)

Toyota Supra (auto.)

Toyota T100 (auto.)

Toyota Tercel (auto.)

Toys "R" Us (US bus.)

Trabzon, Turkey (also Trebizond)

Tracey Ullman (ent.; 1959-)

Tracker™, Chevrolet Geo (auto.)

Tracy Austin (tennis; 1962-)

Tracy Caulkins (swimming; 1963-)

Tracy Chapman (ent.; 1964-)

Tracy Keenan Wynn

Tracy Nelson (ent.; 1963-)

Tracy, Dick (fict. chara.)

Tracy, Spencer (US ent.; 1900-67)

Trade Representative, Office of the U.S. (US govt.)

Trade Unions Congress (TUC)(Br.)

Trader Vic's (restaurant)

Trader Vic's Food Products, Inc.

Trafalgar Square (London)

Trafalgar, Battle of (Eng./Fr.-Sp.; 1805)

Traffic (pop music)

Tragedy of Othello, The Moor of Venice, The (Shakespeare play)

Trail Blazers, Portland (basketball team)

Trail of the Pink Panther (film; 1982)

Trailblazer (US bus.)

Trailways™ bus

Trakehner (horse)

Tralee, Ireland

Trane™ (air conditioner)

Tranquility, Sea of (also Mare Tranquillitatus)(dark plain on Moon)

Trans African Airline

Trans-Alaskan Pipeline (oil transport; 1977-)

Trans Am, Pontiac™ (auto.)

Trans-Amazonian Highway (also Transamazonica)(Brazil; 1970-)

Trans-Siberian Railway (>7,000 miles)

Trans World Airlines, Inc. (TWA)

Transamerica Corp.

Transamerica Pyramid

Transbrasil Airlines

Transjordan (area, Jordan)

Transportation Safety Board, National (US govt. agcy.; est. 1975)

Transportation, Department of (DOT)(US govt.)

Transvaal, South Africa

Transylvania (region, Romania)

Transylvanian Alps

Tranxene™ (med.)

Trapp Family Singers

Trapp, Baroness Maria Von (b. Maria Augusta Kutschera)(Aus. singer; 1905-87)

Trapper John, M.D. (TV show)

Trapper Keeper™ notebook

Trappist (monk/nun order; est. 1664)

Trappist cheese (also Gethsemane cheese)

Traubel, Helen (US opera; 1903-72)

Travanti, Daniel J. (ent.; 1940-)

Travel & Leisure (mag.)

Travel Holiday (mag.)

Travelers Aid Association of America (est. 1917)

Travelers Corp.

Travelodge International, Inc.

Travers, Mary (ent.; 1936-)

Travers, P(amela) L. (Austl. writer; 1906-)

Traviata, La (G. Verdi opera)

Travis Air Force Base, CA (US mil.)

Travis, Merle (ent.)

Travis, Randy (ent.; 1959-)
Travolta, John (ent.; 1954-)
Treacher, Arthur (ent.; 1894-1975)
Treacher's Fish & Chips, Arthur (US bus.)
Treadway Hotels & Resorts (US bus.)
Treasure Island (R. L. Stevenson novel)
Treasure Island Naval Station (CA)
Treasure Island, FL, TN
Treasure State (nickname, MT)
Treasurer of the United States
Treasury, Department of the (US govt.)
Treat Williams (ent.; 1951-)
Treaty of Amiens (Br. & Fr./Sp./Batavia; 1802)
Treaty of Cambrai (Rome/Fr.; 1529)
Treaty of Ghent (US/Br.; 1814)
Treaty of Guadalupe Hidalgo (ended Mexican
    War; 1848)
Treaty of London (Br./Fr./Rus./It.; 1915)
Treaty of Paris (various peace treaties)
Treaty of Versailles (Allies/Ger.; 1919)
Trebek, Alex (ent.; 1940-)
Trebizond Empire (c1204-1461)
Trebizond, Turkey (also Trabzon)
Treblinka (Nazi concentration camp, Pol.)
Tree of Life, Inc.
Tree Top, Inc.
Tree, Ellen (Kean)(ent.; 1806-80)
Tree, Sir Herbert (b. Herbert Beerbohm)(ent.;
    1853-1917)
Treeing Walker coonhound (dog)
Trekkie (*Star Trek* fan)
Tremayne, Les
Trenary, Jill
Trent Affair (Br./US; 1861)
Trent Lott (US cong.; 1941-)
Trent River (Eng.)
Trent, Council of (rel. hist.; 1545-63)
Trenton Times (NJ newspaper)
Trenton, MI, NJ
Trenton, Ontario, Canada
Trentonian (NJ newspaper)
Trevelyan, Sir George (Otto)(Br. hist.; 1838-
    1928)
Trevelyan, George Macaulay (Br. hist.; 1876-
    1962)
Trevi Fountain (Rome)
Trevino, Lee (golf; 1939-)
Trevor, Claire (ent.; 1909-)
Triad (Ch. secret society; est. AD 36)
Triaminicin™ (med.)
Triaminicol™ (med.)
Triaminic™ (med.)
Triangle Shirtwaist Factory fire (NYC)(lead to
    labor reform; 1911)
Triangulum (astron., triangle)
Triangulum Australe (astron., Southern
    Triangle)
Trianon, Le Petit (built for Mme. de Pompadour

by Louis XV)
Triassic period (225-195 million years ago)
Triavil™ (med.)
TriBeCa (NYC)(also Tribeca)
Tribes of Israel
Triborough Bridge (NYC)
Tribune Co.
Tribune-Review, Greensburg (PA newspaper)
Tribune, Albuquerque (NM newspaper)
Tribune, Chicago (IL newspaper)
Tribune, Oakland (CA newspaper)
Tribune, Salt Lake City (UT newspaper)
Tribune, Scranton (PA newspaper)
Tribune, South Bend (IN newspaper)
Tribune, Tampa (FL newspaper)
Tricia (Patricia) Nixon Cox (daughter of ex-US
    pres.; 1946-)
Trident (US nuclear missile)
Trident™ gum
Trier (wine glass)
Trier, Germany
Trieste, Italy
Trifari (US bus.)
Trigère, Pauline (US designer; 1912-)
Trigger (Roy Rogers' horse)
Trillin, Calvin (US writer; 1935-)
Trilling, Lionel (US writer/educ.; 1905-75)
Trimox™ (med.)
Trimurti (rel.)
Trincomalee, Sri Lanka
Trinidad and Tobago (Republic of)(West Indies)
Trinity College (Dublin, Ir.)
Trinity Industries, Inc.
Trinity Sunday (Sunday after Pentecost)(rel.)
Trinity, the (also Holy Trinity)(Father, Son,
    Holy Ghost/Spirit)(rel.)
Triphasil™ (med.)
Tripitaka (also Pali Canon)(rel.)
Triple Alliance (Eur. hist.; various countries/
    dates)
Triple Crown (baseball)
Triple Crown (horse racing)
Triple Entente (Br./Fr./Rus.; 1907-17)
Tripoli, Lebanon
Tripoli, Libya
Tripolitan War (US/Tripoli; 1801-5)
Tris(tram) Speaker (baseball; 1888-1958)
Triscuit™, Nabisco (crackers)
Tristan and Isolde (also Tristam, Iseult)(Celtic
    legend)
Tristan da Cunha (Br. volcanic islands, S Atl.)
Tristano, Lennie (US jazz; 1919-78)
Tristesse, Bonjour (F. Sagan novel)
Tristram Shandy (Laurence Sterne novel)
Triton (Neptune moon; myth.)
Triumvirate, First/Second (ancient Rome ruling
    board)
Trivandrum, India

Trivial Pursuit™ (game)
Trix™ cereal
Troilus and Cressida (Shakespeare play)
Trois-Rivières, Quebec, Canada (Three Rivers)
Trojan™ (condom)
Trojan Horse (myth.)
Trojan War (Asia Minor; mid 13th c. BC)
Trojan Women, The (Euripides tragedy)
Troll Magazine (mag.)
Trollope, Anthony (Br. writer; 1815-82)
Trombe wall (constr.)
Troncoso, Carlos A. Morales (VP, Dom Rep.)
Trondheim, Norway
Tropic of Cancer (H. Miller novel)
tropic of Cancer (23°27' N of equator)
Tropic of Capricorn (H. Miller novel)
tropic of Capricorn (23°27' S of equator)
Tropical Zone (also Tropics, Torrid
    Zone)(between tropics of Cancer and
    Capricorn)
Trotsky, Léon (b. Lev Davidovich
    Bronstein)(USSR pol.; 1879-1940)
Trotskyism (pol. phil.)
Trottier, Bryan (hockey; 1956-)
Trout, Robert
Trovatore, Il (Verdi opera)
Trovoada, Miguel (pres., São Tomé/Príncipe ;
    1936-)
Trower, Robin (ent.)
Troy (ancient city, Asia Minor)
Troy-Bilt™ (garden equip.)
Troy Donahue (ent.; 1936-)
Troy, AL, MI, NY, OH
Troyanos, Tatiana (ent.; 1938-)
Truckee, CA
Trudeau, Garry (Can./US cartoonist,
    Doonesbury; 1948-)
Trudeau, Margaret (Can., ex-wife of ex-PM)
Trudeau, Pierre (Elliott)(ex-PM, Can.; 1919-)
True Grit (film)
True Story (mag.)
True Story Plus (mag.)
Truex, Ernest (ent.; 1890-1973)
Truffaut, François (Fr. ent.; 1932-84)
Trujillo, César Gaviria (pres., Colombia; 1947-)
Trujillo, Peru
Trukese (people)
Truman Bradley
Truman Capote (US writer; 1924-84)
Truman Doctrine (US hist.; 1947)
Truman, Bess (Wallace)(wife of ex-US pres.;
    1885-1982)
Truman, Harry S (33rd US pres.; 1884-1972)
Truman, (Mary) Margaret (daughter of ex-US
    pres.; 1924-)
Trumbull, John (US artist; 1756-1843)
Trumbull, John (US poet/atty.; 1750-1831)
Trumbull, Jonathan (US pol.; 1710-85)

Trump, Donald J.(US bus.; 1946-)
Trump, Ivana (US, ex-wife of D. Trump)
Truro, Nova Scotia, Canada
Trustees of Dartmouth College v. Woodward
    (US law; 1819)
Truth or Consequences (radio/TV show)
Truth or Consequences, NM
Truth, Sojourner (US reformer; c1797-1883)
TRW, Inc.
Try Sustrisno (VP, Indonesia)
Trygve H(alvdan) Lie (Nor. pol./UN; 1896-1968)
Tse, Mo (also Mo Ti, Mo-tze, Mo Tzu, Mo-
    tse)(Ch. phil.; 5th c. BC)
T(homas) S(terns) Eliot (US/Br. poet; 1888-
    1965)
Tse-tung, Mao (also Mao Zedong, Chairman
    Mao)(Ch. pol.; 1893-1976)
T-shirt (also tee shirt, tee, T)
Tshisekedi, Etienne (premier, Zaire
Tshombe, Moise K(apenda)(ex-PM, Congo/Zaire;
    1919-69)
Tsimshian (NAmer. Indians)
Tsinghai (also Qinghai)(province, Ch.)
Tsingtao, China (also Qingdao)
Tsongas, Paul (US pol.; 1941-)
T square (T-shaped ruler)
T-stop (hockey, photo.)
T-strap (shoe)
Tsuen Wan, Hong Kong
Tswana (lang./people)
Tu Fu (Ch. poet; 710-770)
Tuareg (people)
Tuatha Dé Danann (myth.)
Tubb, Ernest (ent.)
Tubman, Harriet (b. Araminta Ross)(US
    reformer; c1820-1913)
Tuborg™ beer
Tucana (astron., toucan)
Tuchman, Barbara W(ertheim)(US writer/hist.;
    1912-89)
Tuck, Friar (fict. chara., *Robin Hood*)
Tucker, Forrest (ent.; 1919-86)
Tucker, Jim Guy (AR gov.)
Tucker, Michael (ent.; 1944-)
Tucker, Sophie (b. Sophie Abruza)(ent.; 1884-
    1966)
Tucker, Tanya (ent.; 1958-)
Tucson Citizen (AZ newspaper)
Tucson Star (AZ newspaper)
Tucson, AZ
Tucuman, Argentina
Tucumcari, NM
Tudjman, Franjo (pres., Croatia; 1922-)
Tudor style (art/arch.; 1485-1603)
Tudor, House of (Br. ruling family; 1485-1603)
Tudor, Margaret (Eng., wife of James IV, Scot.;
    1489-1541)
Tudor, Mary (also Mary I, "Bloody

Mary")(queen, Eng.; 1516-58)
Tuesday Weld (ent.; 1943-)
Tuftex Industries
Tugboat Annie
Tuileries Gardens (Paris)
Tuinal™ (barbiturate)
Tukulor (lang./people)
Tulane University (New Orleans, LA)
Tull, Jethro (Br. agr.; 1674-1741)
Tull, Jethro (pop music)
Tulsa World (OK newspaper)
Tulsa, OK
Tultex Apparel Group (US bus.)
Tumacacori National Historical Park (AZ)
Tumbling Tumbleweeds (song)
Tums™ (med.)
Tums E-X™ (med.)
Tumwater, WA
Tunbridge Wells, England
Tune, Tommy (ent.; 1939-)
Tunis, Tunisia
Tunisia (Republic of)(N Afr.)
Tunku Abdul Rahman (ex-PM, Malaysia; 1903-90)
Tunney, Gene (b. James Joseph Tunney)(boxing; 1898-1978)
Tupelo, MS
Tupou IV, Taufa'ahau (king, Tonga; 1918-)
Tupperware™
Tupperware Co.
Tupperware party
Turandot (G. Puccini opera)
TurboCAT™ (CAT system)
Turgenev, Ivan (Sergeievich)(Rus. writer; 1818-83)
Turgut Ozal (ex-pres., Turk.; 1927-93)
Turin, Italy
Turin, shroud of (rel.)
Turk (horse)
Turk (lang./people)
Turk Murphy (US jazz; 1915-87)
Turken (chicken)
Turkey (Republic of)(SE Eur./SW Asia)
Turkic (lang.)
Turkish (lang./people)
Turkish bath
Turkish delight (also Turkish paste)(candy)
Turkish skirt
Turkish swimming (cat)
Turkish tobacco
Turkish towel (also l.c.)
Turkish van (cat)
Turkish Wars, Russo- (Rus./Ottoman Turk.; 17th-19th c.)
Turkman (also Turkoman)(lang./people)
Turkmenistan (Republic of)(formerly part of USSR)(central Asia)
Turko-Persian war

Turkoman (also Turkman)(lang./people)
Turkoman (rug)
Turk's-head (knot)
Turks and Caicos Islands (Br. West Indies)
Turku, Finland
Turner Broadcasting System, Inc.
Turner Network Television (TNT)(cable TV)
Turner, Big Joe (ent.; 1911-85)
Turner, Frederick J(ackson)(US hist./educ.; 1861-1932)
Turner, Ike (ent.; 1931-)
Turner, Janine (ent.; 1962-)
Turner, J(oseph) M(allord) W(illiam)(Br. artist; 1774-1851)
Turner, John (Napier)(ex-PM, Can.; 1929-)
Turner, Kathleen (ent.; 1954-)
Turner, Lana (ent.; 1920-)
Turner, Nat (US slave/reformer; 1800-31)
Turner, Ted (US bus./media; 1938-)
Turner, The Confessions of Nat (W. Styron book)
Turner, Tina (ent.; 1938-)
Turner's syndrome (genetics)
Turpin, Ben (ent.; 1874-1940)
Turpin, Dick (Richard)(Br. highwayman; 1706-39)
Tursenbek Chyngyshev (PM, Kyrgyzstan)
Turtle Wax, Inc.
Turturro, John (ent.; 1967-)
Tuscaloosa, AL
Tuscan column (arch.)
Tuscany (region, It.)
Tuscarora (NAmer. Indians)
Tuskegee National Forest
Tuskegee University (AL)
Tussaud, Madame (Anne) Marie (Grosholtz)(Swiss wax modeler; 1760-1850)
Tussaud's Exhibition, Madame (wax museum, London)
Tussy Cosmetics, Inc.
Tut, King (Tutankhamen)(king, Eg.; 1343-25 BC)
Tutong, Brunei
Tuttle, Frank
Tutu, Desmond (Mpilo)(SAfr. rel.; 1931-)
Tutume, Botswana
Tuvalu (South West Pac. State of)(W Pac.)
Tuvaluan (lang.)
Tuzla, Bosnia-Hercegovina
TVA (Tennessee Valley Authority)
Tver, Russia (formerly Kalinin)
TV Guide (mag.)
TWA™ (Trans World Airlines™)
Twa (people)
Twagiramungu, Faustin (PM, Rwanda
Twain, Mark (aka Samuel Langhorne Clemens)(US writer; 1835-1910)
Tweed Ring (corrupt NYC politicians)

Tweed, William M(arcy)("Boss Tweed")(US pol.;
    1823-78)
Tweedledum & Tweedledee (2 almost identical
    people/things)
Twelfth Day (12 days after Christmas [Jan. 6],
    Epiphany)
Twelfth Night (rel.)
Twelfth Night, Or What You Will (Shakespeare
    play)
Twelve, the (12 apostles chosen by Christ)
Twelve Tables, Law of the (Roman law; est.
    451-50 BC)
Twelve Tribes (rel.)
Twenties, Roaring (also Roaring '20s)
20th Century-Fox Film Co.
20th Century-Fox Record Corp.
20th Century Plastics Co.
20/20 (TV show)
Twentynine Palms, CA
Twiggy (aka Leslie Hornby)(model; 1946-)
Twilight of the Gods (also
    Götterdämmerung)(Ger. myth.)
Twilight Zone (TV show, film)
Twin Cities (Minneapolis & St. Paul, MI)
Twin Falls, ID
Twin Peaks (TV show)
Twinkies™
Twins, Minnesota (baseball team)
Twist, Oliver (Dickens novel)
Twisted Sister (pop music)
Twittering Machine (by Klee)
Twitty, Conway (ent.; 1933-93)
Twix™ candy
Two Gentlemen of Verona, The (Shakespeare
    play)
2 Live Crew (pop music)
Two Sicilies (former kingdom, Sicily and S.
    Italy)
2001: A Space Odyssey (film; 1968)
Twyla Tharp (US dancer; 1941-)
TX (Texas)
Ty(rus Raymond) Cobb (baseball; 1886-1961)
Tyana, Apollonius of (Gr. phil.; 1st c. AD)
Tyche (myth.)
Tyco™ (toys)
Tyco Industries, Inc.
Tylenol™ (med.)
Tyler, Anne (US writer; 1941-)
Tyler, John (10th US pres.; 1790-1862)
Tyler, Royall (US writer; 1757-1826)
Tyler, TX
Tyler, Wat (Walter)(Br. rebel; ?-1381)
Tyne Daly (ent.; 1947-)
Tyner, McCoy (US jazz; 1938-)
Type A personality
Type B personality
Typhoid Mary (b. Mary Mallon)(Ir. cook,
    typhoid carrier; ?-1938)

Typhon (myth.)
Tyre, Apollonius of (fict. Gr. hero)
Tyre, Lebanon
Tyrian purple (color)
Tyrol, Austria (also Tirol)
Tyrolean (also Tirolean, Tyrolese,
    Tirolese)(clothing style, people)
Tyrone (William) Guthrie, Sir (Br. ent.; 1900-
    71)
Tyrone Power (ent.; 1913-58)
Tyrrhenian Sea (arm, Mediterranean)
Tyson™
Tyson Foods, Inc.
Tyson, Cicely (ent.; 1933-)
Tyson, Laura D'Andrea (Chair/Council Econ.
    Advisers; 1947-)
Tyson, Mike (Michael Gerald)(boxing; 1966-)
Tyus, Wyomia (track; 1945-)
Tzekung, China (also Zigong)
Tzu, Mo (also Mo-tze, Mo Ti, Mo-tse, Mo
    Tse)(Ch. phil.; 5th c. BC)

U

UAE (United Arab Emirates)
UAL Corp.
UAW (United Automobile Workers)
Ubangi River (central Afr.)
Ubangi-Shari (now Central African Republic)
Übermensch (Ger., superman)
U-boat
U bolt
UCC (Uniform Commercial Code)
Uccello, Paolo (b. Paolo di Dono)(It. artist; 1397-1475)
Udall, Morris K. (US pol.; 1922-)
Uday Shankar (dancer, India; 1900-77)
Udon Thani, Thailand
Ueberroth, Peter (US bus./sports; 1937-)
Uecker, Bob ("Mr. Baseball")(ent.; 1935-)
Uffizi Gallery (Florence, It.)
Uffizi Palace (Florence, It.)
UFO (unidentified flying object)
Uganda (Republic of)(E Afr.)
Ugarte, Augusto Pinochet (ex-pres., Chile; 1915-)
Uggams, Leslie (ent.; 1943-)
Ugly American
Ugly Duckling Rent-A-Car (US bus.)
U-Haul™
UHF (ultrahigh frequency)
Uhuru (US space satellite)
Uigur (people)
Uitzilopochtli (also Huitzilopochtli)(myth.)
Ukraine (E central Eur.)(formerly part of USSR)
Ukrainian (lang./people)
Ukrainian Catholic (rel.)
ul-Adha, Eid (Muslim festival)
Ulan Bator, Mongolia (also Ulaanbaatar)
Ulbricht, Walter (Ger. pol.; 1893-1873)
ul-Fitr, Eid (Muslim festival)
ul-Haq, Muhammad Zia ("President Zia")(ex-pres., Pak.; 1924-88)
Ullman, Tracey (ent.; 1959-)
Ullmann, Liv (ent.; 1938-)
Ulmanis, Guntis (pres., Latvia
Ulrich (or Huldreich) Zwingli (Swiss rel.; 1484-1531)
Ulster (area, NIre.; province, Ir.)
Ultra/brite™ (toothpaste)
Ultra Downy™ (clothers softener)
Ultra Slim Fast™
Ultrasuede™ (synthetic leather)
Ulysses (J. Joyce novel)
Ulysses S(impson) Grant (18th US pres.; 1822-85)
Ulysses, king of Ithaca (also Odysseus)(myth.)

Umar Arteh Ghalib (ex-PM, Somalia)
Umberto Boccioni (It. artist; 1882-1916)
Umberto Giordano (It. comp.; 1867-1948)
Umberto Mastroianni
Umbrella Tree, Under the (TV show)
Umbriel (astron.)
Umm al Qaiwain (or Qaywayn)(UAE)
UN (United Nations)
Un-American Activities, House Committee on (HUAC)(US govt. comm.; 1938-75)
Una Merkel (ent.)
Uncle Remus (fict. narrator, J.C. Harris fables)
Uncle Sam (nickname, US govt.)
Uncle Tom (fict. chara., *Uncle Tom's Cabin*; slang, subservient black)
Uncle Tom's Cabin (H.B. Stowe novel)
Uncle Vanya (A. Chekhov play)
UNCTAD (United Nations Conference on Trade and Development)(est. 1964)
Under the Umbrella Tree (TV show)
Under the Yum Yum Tree (film; 1963)
Underground Railroad (US hist., for escaping slaves)
Underwood™
Underwood Deviled Ham™
Underwood, Blair (ent.)
Underwood's Fine Foods (US bus.)
Underwriters Laboratories, Inc.
UNDP (United Nations Development Program)(est. 1965)
UNESCO (United Nations Educational, Scientific, and Cultural Organization)(est. 1945)
UNHCR (United Nations Office of High Commissioner for Refugees)(est. 1951)
Uniate Church
Unicap™ (med.)
Unicap M™ (med.)
Unicap Sr.™ (med.)
Unicap T™ (med.)
UNICEF (United Nations Children's Fund, formerly United Nations International Children's Emergency Fund)(est. 1946)
UNIDO (United Nations Industrial Development Organization)(est. 1966)
Unifax™ (UPI wire service)
Unification Church (also Moonies; est. 1954)
Unilever PLC (US bus.)
Union Carbide Corp.
Union Gap, Gary Puckett and the (pop music)
Union Jack (Br. flag)
Union News, Springfield (MA newspaper)
Union of South Africa (now Republic of South Africa)
Union of Soviet Socialist Republics (USSR)(disbanded 1991)
Union Pacific Corp.
Union-Tribune, San Diego (CA newspaper)

Union, Sacramento (CA newspaper)
Uniroyal Chemical Co., Inc.
Uniroyal Goodrich Tire Co.
Unisom™ (med.)
Unisys Corp.
UNITAR (United Nations Institute for Training and Research)(est. 1963)
Unitarian Universalist Association (rel.)
Unitarianism (rel.)
Unitas, Johnny (John Constantine)(football; 1933-)
United Airlines
United Arab Emirates (UAE)(SW Asia)
United Arab Republic (Egypt/Syria; 1958-61)
United Artists Corp. (UA)(film co.)
United Automobile Workers of America (UAW)(union, est. 1935)
United Brethren in Christ, Church of the
United Church of Canada
United Church of Christ
United Colonies of New England (New England Confederation)(US his.)
United Kingdom (of Great Britain and Northern Ireland)(Eng./Scot./Wales/ NIre.)(UK)(NW Eur.)
United Methodist Church
United Mine Workers of America (UMWA)(union, est. 1890)
United Nations (internat'l org.; est. 1945)
United Nations Children's Fund (UNICEF)(formerly United Nations International Children's Emergency Fund)(est. 1946)
United Nations Conference on Environment and Development (Earth Summit)(June 1992)
United Nations Conference on Trade and Development (UNCTAD)(est. 1964)
United Nations Day
United Nations Development Program (UNDP)(est. 1965)
United Nations Educational, Scientific, and Cultural Organization (UNESCO)(est. 1945)
United Nations Industrial Development Organization (UNIDO)(est. 1966)
United Nations Institute for Training and Research (UNITAR)(est. 1963)
United Nations Office of High Commissioner for Refugees (UNHCR)(est. 1951)
United Nations Permanent Court of International Justice (World Court)(est. 1945)
United Nations Security Council
United Negro College Fund
United Parcel Service™ (UPS)
United Press International (UPI)(US news org..; est. 1958)
United Service Organizations, Inc. (USO)(est.

1941)
United Society of Believers in Christ's Second Coming(Appearing)(also Shakers, Millenial Church)
United States (U.S., US)
United States Air Force (US mil.)
United States Air Force Academy (Colorado Springs, CO)(est. 1954)
United States Army (US mil.)
United States Coast Guard (US mil.)
United States Coast Guard Academy (New London, CT)(est. 1876)
United States Department of Agriculture (USDA)
United States District Court (USDC)(US law)
United States Geological Survey (USGS)
United States Information Agency (USIA)
United States Marine Corps (US mil.)
United States Merchant Marine (US bus./mil.)
United States Merchant Marine Academy (Kings Point, NY)
United States Military Academy (West Point, NY)(est. 1802)
United States Naval Academy (Annapolis, MD)(est. 1845)
United States Navy (US mil.)
United States of America (USA, U.S.A.)
United States Postal Service (USPS)
United Steel Workers of America (USWA)(union; est. 1942)
United Technologies Corp.
United Van Lines, Inc.
United Way (charitable org.; est. 1918)
Univac, Sperry (US bus.)
Univar Corp.
Univers (type style)
Universal City Studios (US bus.)
Universal Foods Corp.
Universal Pictures (US bus.)
Universal Product Code (also UPC)
Universal Studios (US bus.)
Universalism (rel.)
Universal machines (med.)
University of California Press (US bus.)
University of Chicago Press (US bus.)
University of Illinois Press (US bus.)
University of Michigan Press (US bus.)
University of Missouri Press (US bus.)
University of Nebraska Press (US bus.)
University of New Mexico Press (US bus.)
University of Notre Dame (South Bend, IN)
University of Oklahoma Press (US bus.)
University of Paris (aka Sorbonne)
University of Tennessee Press (US bus.)
University of Utah Press (US bus.)
Unix (compu.)
Unknown Soldier (Arlington National Cemetery [VA])

Uno Sosuke (ex-PM, Jap; 1922-)
Unocal Corp.
Unser, Al (auto racing; 1939-)
Unser, Al, Jr. (auto racing; 1962-)
Unser, Bobby (auto racing; 1934-)
Unsinkable Molly Brown, The (film; 1964)
Unsolved Mysteries (TV show)
Untouchables (TV show, film)
U (Thakin) Nu (ex-PM, Myanmar; 1907-)
Upanishads (rel.)
UPC (Universal Product Code)
Updike, John (Hoyer)(US writer; 1932-)
UPI (United Press International)
UPI Cable News
UPI Radio Network
Upjohn Co.
Upjohn, Richard (US arch.; 1802-78)
Upland, CA
Upper Volta (now Burkina Faso)
Uppsala, Sweden
UPS (United Parcel Service)
Upson board™ (constr.)
Upton (Beall) Sinclair (US writer/reformer; 1878-1968)
Uptown Comedy Club (TV show)
Ur (ancient city, Mesopotamia)
Ural Mountains (Eur./Asia)
Ural River (Eur./Asia)
Urania (myth.)
Uranus (planet; myth.)
Urban Cowboy (film; 1980)
Urban League, National (org. 1910)
Urbana, IL
Urdu (lang./people)
Uri Geller
Uriah Heep (villain, *David Copperfield*)
Urich, Robert (ent.; 1940-)
Uris, Leon (US writer; 1924-)
Ursa Major (astron., great bear; part of Big Dipper)
Ursa Minor (astron., little/lesser bear; part of Little Dipper)
Ursula Andress (Swiss ent.; 1936-)
Ursula LeGuin (US writer; 1929-)
Uruguay (Republic of)(S Amer.)
US (also U.S., United States)
US (mag.)
U.S. (also US, United States)
U.S. Air Force (US mil.)
U.S. Air Force Academy (Colorado Springs, CO) (est. 1954)
U.S. Army (US mil.)
U.S. Coast Guard (US mil.)
U.S. Coast Guard Academy (New London, CT) (est. 1876)
U.S. Department of Agriculture (USDA)
U.S. District Court (USDC)(US law)
U.S. Geological Survey (USGS)

U.S. Gulf States (AL/FL/LA/MS/TX)
U.S. Information Agency (USIA)
U.S. Marine Corps (US mil.)
U.S. Marine Corps War Memorial (also Iwo Jima Memorial)(VA)
U.S. Merchant Marine (US bus./mil.)
U.S. Merchant Marine Academy (Kings Point, NY)
U.S. Military Academy (West Point, NY)(est. 1802)
U.S. Naval Academy (Annapolis, MD)(est. 1845)
U.S. Navy (US mil.)
U.S. News & World Report (mag.)
U.S. Pharmacopoeia (USP)
U.S. Postal Service (USPS)(US govt. agcy.; est. 1865)
U.S. Shoe Corp., Inc.
U.S. Steel Group, USX- (US bus.)
U.S. Trade Representative, Office of the (US govt.)
U.S. v. American Tobacco Co. (US law; 1911)
U.S. v. Butler (US law; 1936)
U.S. v. Classic (US law; 1941)
U.S. v. Darby Lumber Co. (US law; 1941)
U.S. v. Dixon (US law; 1993)
U.S. v. E. C. Knight Co. (US law; 1895)
U.S. v. Gouveja (US law; 1984)
U.S. v. Nixon (US law; 1974)
U.S. West, Inc.
U.S., Abrams v. (US law; 1919)
U.S., Addyston Pipe and Steel Co. v. (US law; 1899)
U.S,. Austin v. (US law; 1993)
U.S., Dennis et al v. (US law; 1951)
U.S., Heart of Atlanta Motel, Inc. v. (US law; 1964)
U.S., Hylton v. (US law; 1796)
U.S., Korematsu v. (US law; 1944)
U.S., Northern Securities Co. v. (US law; 1904)
U.S., Olmsted v. (US law; 1928)
U.S., Schechter v. (US law; 1935)
U.S., Schenck v. (US law; 1919)
U.S., Standard Oil Co. of New Jersey, et al. v. (US law; 1911)
U.S., Swift and Co. v. (US law; 1905)
USA (also U.S.A., United States of America)
U.S.A. (also USA, United States of America)
USA Network (USA)(cable TV)
USA Today (newspaper)
USA Today Crosswords (mag.)
USAF (United States Air Force)
USAir Group, Inc.
USAir, Inc. (airline)
USCG (United States Coast Guard)
USDA (United States Department of Agriculture)
USES (United States Employment Service)
USGS (United States Geological Survey)

Usher, The Fall of the House of (E.A. Poe short
   story)
Ushuaia, Argentina
USIA (United States Information Agency)
USM (United States Mail, United States Mint)
USMC (United States Marine Corps)
USN (United States Navy)
USNG (United States National Guard)
USO (United Service Organizations, Inc.)(est.
   1941)
USP (United States Pharmacopoeia)
USPS (United States Postal Service)
USS (United States Senate, United States Ship)
U.S.S. *Chesapeake*
U.S.S. *Pueblo* (US ship./mil. incident, NKorea;
   1968)
U.S.S. *Vincennes* (US ship/mil. incident, Iran;
   1987)
USSR (Union of Soviet Socialist Republics)
   (disbanded 1991)
UST, Inc.
Ustinov, Sir Peter (Alexander)(ent.; 1921-)
USX-U.S. Steel Group (US bus.)
UT (Utah)
Utah (UT)
Utah Jazz (basketball team)
Ute (NAmer. Indians)
Uteem, Cassam (pres., Mauritius
U Thant (Burmese dipl./UN; 1909-74)
Uther Pendragon (King Arthur's father)
Utica (ancient city, N Afr.)
Utica, NY
Utilicare (utility assistance, low-income elderly)
Utley, Garrick
Utopia (imaginary, ideal land)
Utopia (T. More book)
Utopia, Road to (film; 1946)
Utrecht, Netherlands
Utrillo, Maurice (Fr. artist; 1883-1955)
U-turn
U2 (pop music)
U-2 (US spy plane)
UV (ultraviolet)
Uxmal (ancient city, Mex.)
Uzbek (lang./people)
Uzbekistan (Republic of)(formerly part of
   USSR)(central Asia)
Uzi submachine gun

V

V (chem. sym., vanadium)
VA (Virginia)
Vacarolu, Nicolae (PM, Romania)
Vacaville, CA
Vaccaro, Brenda (ent.; 1939-)
Vachel Lindsay, (Nicholas)(US poet; 1879-1931)
Vacherin (cheese)
Václav Havel (pres./writer, Czech; 1936-)
Václav Klaus (PM, Czech; 1941-)
Vader, Darth (fict. chara., *Star Wars*)
Vadim Medvedev
Vadim, Roger (ent.)
Vaduz, Liechtenstein
Vaea, Baron (PM, Tonga)
Vahl Tiit (ex-PM, Estonia)
Vail, CO
Vail, Theodore N. (US bus.; 1845-1920)
Val Bisoglio (ent.; 1926-)
Val Dufour (ent.; 1927-)
Val Wine Co., Ltd., The Clos du
Valachi Papers, The (film; 1972)
Valdepeas (wine)
Valdez, AK
Valdez, Exxon (US tanker, oil spill; 1989)
Valdis Birkavs (PM, Latvia)
Valdosta, GA
Vale, Jerry (ent.; 1931-)
Valencia oranges
Valencia, CA
Valencia, Spain
Valencia, Venezuela
Valencian (people)
Valenciennes (lace)
Valenciennes, France
Valens, Ritchie (ent.)
Valenti, Jack (US writer; 1921-)
Valentic, Nikica (PM, Croatia)
Valentin (Vitalyevich) Lebedev (cosmo.; 1942-)
Valentina (Vladimirovna) Tereshkova (cosmo., 1st woman in space; 1937-)
Valentine Strasser (pres., Sierra Leone)
Valentine, St. (Roman rel.; ?-c270)
Valentine's Day, St. (2/14)
Valentino, Rudolph (b. Rodolpho Guglielmi)(ent.; 1895-1926)
Valenzuela, Fernando (baseball; 1960-)
Valera, Eamon de (ex-PM/pres., Ir.; 1882-1975)
Valeri Brumel (jumper; 1942-)
Valeria Messalina (Roman empress; c22-48)
Valerie Bertinelli (ent.; 1960-)
Valerie Harper (ent.; 1940-)
Valerie Perrine (ent.; 1943-)
Valéry F. Bykovsky (cosmo.; 1934-)
Valéry Giscard d'Estaing (ex-pres., Fr.; 1926-)

Valéry N(ikolayevich) Kubasov (cosmo.; 1935-)
Valéry, Paul (Ambroise)(Fr. writer; 1871-1945)
Valhalla (myth.)
Valiant, Prince (comic strip)
Valium™ (med.)
Valjean, Jean (fict. chara., *Les Miserables*)
Valkyrie (myth.)
Vallee, Rudy (ent.; 1901-86)
Vallejo, CA
Valletta, Malta
Valley Forge (PA)
Valley Forge National Historical Park (PA)
Valli, Frankie (ent.; 1937-)
Valli, June
Valois, Margaret of (also Queen Margot)(Fr.; 1553-1615)
Valparaíso, Chile
Valparaiso, IN
Valpolicella (wine)
Valsalva maneuver (med., trans.)
Value™ Rent-A-Car
Valvoline™
Valvoline Instant Oil Change (US bus.)
Van Allen radiation belts (regions surrounding earth)
Van Allsburg, Chris (US writer/artist; 1949-)
van Alstyne, Egbert (US comp.; 1882-1951)
Van Ark, Joan (ent.; 1943-)
van Beethoven, Ludwig (Ger. comp.; 1770-1827)
Van Brocklin, Norm (football; 1926-83)
Van Buren, Abigail (Dear Abby)(b. Pauline Esther Friedman)(US advice columnist; 1918-)
Van Buren, Martin (8th US pres.; 1782-1862)
Van Camp Sea Food Co., Inc.
Van Camp's Beanee Weenee
Van Cleef & Arpels™
Van Cleef & Arpels, Inc.
Van Cleef, Lee (ent.; 1925-89)
Van Cliburn (Harvey Lavan Cliburn, Jr.)(ent.; 1934-)
Van Conversion, Inc.
Van Damme, Jean-Claude (ent.)
Van de Graaff generator (also electrostatic generator)
Van de Graaff, Robert Jemison (US physt.; 1901-67)
Van de Kamp's Frozen Foods (US bus.)
Van der Post, Laurens (Jan)(SAfr. writer; 1906-)
van der Rohe, Ludwig Mies (US arch.; 1886-1969)
van der Weyden, Rogier (Flem. artist; c1400-64)
van Doesburg, Theo (Dutch artist/writer; 1883-1931)
Van Dong, Pham (ex-PM, NViet.; 1906-)
Van Doren, Charles (US educ./TV scandal)
Van Doren, Mamie (ent.; 1933-)

Van Druten, John (William)(US writer; 1901-57)

van Dyck, Sir Anthony (Flem. artist; 1599-1641)

Van Dyke, Dick (ent.; 1925-)

Van Dyke, Jerry (ent.; 1931-)

van Eyck, Hubert (or Huybrecht)(Flem. artist; 1366-1426)

van Eyck, Jan (Flem. artist; 1385?-1441?)

Van Fleet, Jo (ent.; 1922-)

van Gogh, Vincent (Dutch artist; 1853-90)

Van Halen, Eddie (ent.; 1957-)

Van Heflin (ent.; 1910-71)

Van Heusen Corp., Phillips-

Van Heusen, Jimmy (James)(US comp.; 1913-90)

Van Houten & Zoon, Inc., C. J.)

Van Impe, Jack (TV show)

Van Johnson (ent.; 1916-)

van Leeuwenhoek, Anton (Dutch, father of microbiology; 1632-1723)

Van Lingo Mungo (baseball; 1911-85)

Van Nostrand Reinhold Co., Inc.

Van Nuys, CA

van Ostade, Adriaen (Dutch artist; 1610-85)

Van Patten, Dick (ent.; 1928-)

van Rijn, Rembrandt (Harmenszoon)(Dutch artist; 1606-69)

van Ruisdael, Jacob (Isaackszoon)(Dutch artist; c1628-82

van Ruysdael, Salomon (Dutch artist; c1600-70)

Van Slyke, Andy (baseball; 1960-)

Van Thieu, Nguyen (ex-pres., SViet; 1923-)

Von Trapp, Baroness Maria (b. Maria Augusta Kutschera)(Aus. singer; 1905-87)

Van Vogt, A(lfred) E(lton)(US writer; 1912-)

Van Winkle, Rip (by W. Irving)

Van Wyck Brooks (US hist.; 1886-1963)

Vance Air Force Base, OK

Vance Brand (astro.; 1931-)

Vance, Cyrus R(oberts)(US pol.; 1917-)

Vance, Vivian (ent.; 1911-79)

Vancouver Canucks (hockey team)

Vancouver Island (Can.)

Vancouver Sun (Can. newspaper)

Vancouver, British Columbia, Canada

Vancouver, WA

Vandellas, Martha and the (pop music)

Vandenberg Air Force Base, CA

Vandenberg, Arthur H(endrick)(US pol.; 1884-1951)

Vanderbilt University (TN)

Vanderbilt, Amy (US writer/manners)

Vanderbilt, Cornelius (US bus./finan.; 1794-1877)

Vanderbilt, Cornelius (US bus./finan.; 1843-99)

Vanderbilt™, Gloria (perfume/clothing)

Vanderbilt, Gloria (US bus.)

Vanderbilt, William Henry (US bus./finan.; 1821-85)

Vanderbilt's Complete Book of Etiquette, Amy

Vanderlyn, John (US artist; 1775-1852)

Vandross, Luther (ent.; 1951-)

Vandyke (beard)(also l.c.)

Vandyke brown (also Cassel brown, Cassel earth)(color)

Vandyke collar

Vanessa Harwood

Vanessa Redgrave (ent.; 1937-)

Vanessa Williams (ent.; 1963-)

Vanguard (US space satellite)

Vanir (myth.)

Vanity Fair (mag.)

Vanna White (ent.; 1957-)

Vannevar Bush (US eng.; 1890-1974)

Vanocur, Sander

Vanquish™ (med.)

Vanuatu (Republic of)(SW Pac.)

Vanya, Uncle (A. Chekhov play)

Vanzetti Case, Sacco- (Nicola & Bartolomeo)(MA murder trial; 1920-27)

VAR (visual-aural range)

Varathane™ (constr.)

Varden, Dolly (clothing style)

Varden, Dolly (fict. chara.)

Vardhamana Mahavira (legendary educ./rel.; ?-480? BC)

Vargas, Virgilio Barco (ex-pres., Columbia; 1921-)

Varig Brazilian Airlines

Varna, Bulgaria

Varolii, pons (also l.c.)(brain nerve fibers)

Varona, Donna De

Vasco da Gama (Port. nav.; c1460-1524)

Vasco Núñez de Balboa (Sp. expl., discovered Pac.; 1475-1519)

Vaseline™ (med.)

Vaseline Intensive Care™

Vasili (or Wassily, Vasily) Kandinsky (Rus. artist; 1866-1944)

Vaslav (or Waslaw) Nijinsky (Rus. ballet; 1890-1950)

Vasotec™ (med.)

Vassar College (NY)

Vassar, Matthew (Br./US bus./educ.; 1792-1868)

Vassilou, George (ex-pres., Cyprus; 1931-)

Västeras, Sweden

Vatican (govt. of the pope)

Vatican City (The Holy See)(independent state in Rome)

Vatican Councils (rel. hist.; 1869-70, 1962-65)

Vatican Library (Rome)

Vatican Palace (also Vatican)(pope's residence)

Vaughan Williams, Ralph (Br. comp.; 1872-1958)

Vaughan, Sarah (Lois)(US jazz; 1924-90)

Vaughan, Stevie Ray (ent.; 1956-90)
Vaughn Monroe (ent.; 1911-73)
Vaughn, Robert (ent.; 1932-)
Vaxholm, Sweden
VC (vice chairman, vice consul, Victoria Cross, Viet Cong)
VCR (videocassette recorder)
VD (venereal disease)
V-Day (Victory Day)
VDT (video display terminal)(compu.)
VDU (video display unit)
Veblen, Thorstein B(unde)(US econ.; 1857-1929)
Veda(s)(sacred Hindu books)
Veda, Atharva- (rel.)
Veda, Rig- (rel.)
Veda, Sama- (rel.)
Veda, Yajur- (rel.)
Vedanta Society (rel.)
V-E Day (WWII Allies victory in Eur.; 5/8/45)
Veerasamy Ringadoo (Mauritian pol.)
Vega (USSR uncrewed space probes)
Vega (Carpio), Lope (Félix) de (Sp. writer; 1562-1635)
Vegetarian Times (mag.)
Veiga, Carlos (PM, Cape Verde)
Vega, Chevrolet™ (auto.)
Vega, Suzanne
V8™ (juice)
Vela (astron., sail)
Velázquez, Diego (Rodríguez de Silva y)(Sp. artist; 1599-1660)
Velásquez, Ramón (pres., Venezuela)
Velcro™
Velcro USA, Inc.
Velox™ (graphic design)
Velux™ (windows)
Velveeta™ (cheese)
Velvet Underground, the (pop music)
Venatici, Canes (astron., hunting dogs)
Venera (USSR uncrewed space probes)
Venerable Bede, the (aka St. Bede)(Br. rel./hist.; c673-735)
Venetiaan, Ronald (pres., Suriname; 1936-)
Venetian blue (color)
Venetian cloth (fabric)
Venetian lamp
Venetian point (lace)
Venetian red (color)
Venezuela (Republic of)(N SAmer.)
Venice, CA, FL
Venice, Italy
Venizelos, Eleutherios (Gr. pol.; 1864-1936)
Venkataraman, Ramaswamy (ex-pres., India
Venn diagram (math.)
Ventarama Skylight Corp.
Ventolin™ (med.)
Ventspils, Latvia
Ventura, CA

Venus (planet; myth.)
Venus de Milo (also *Venus of Melos, Aphrodite of Melos*)(Gr. statue; c200 BC)
Venus('s) flytrap (plant)
Venuta, Benay (ent.; 1911-)
Venuti, Joe (US jazz; 1904-78)
Vera-Ellen (ent.; 1926-81)
Vera Miles (ent.; 1929-)
Vera Sportswear (US bus.)
Veracruz, Mexico
Verbatim Corp.
Verdi, Giuseppe (Fortunino Francesco)(It. comp.; 1813-1901)
Verdi Travelwear (US bus.)
Verdon, Gwen (ent.; 1925-)
Verdun, France
Verdun, Quebec, Canada
Vere C(ornwall) Bird (PM, Antigua and Barbuda)
Vereen, Ben (ent.; 1946-)
Vergil (Publius Vergilius Maro)(also Virgil)(Roman poet; 70-19 BC)
Vermeer, Jan (Dutch artist; 1632-75)
Vermont (VT)
Verne, Jules (Fr. writer; 1828-1905)
Vernon Castle (US dancer; 1887-1918)
Vernon Corp., Lillian
Vernon Duke (US comp.; 1903-69)
Vernon, Mount (G. Washington's home)(VA)
Vero Beach, FL
Verona, Italy
Verona, NJ
Veronese, Paolo (It. artist; 1528-88)
Veronica Hamel (ent.; 1943-)
Veronica Lake (ent.; 1919-73)
Verrazano-Narrows Bridge (NYC)
Verrett, Shirley (ent.; 1931-)
Verrocchio, Andrea del (b. Andrea di Michele di Francesco di Cioni)(It. artist; 1435-88)
Verrucosus, Quintus Fabius Maximus ("Cunctator")(Roman pol./mil.; 275-03 BC)
Versailles, France
Versailles, Palace of (Fr.)
Versailles, Treaty of (Allies/Ger.; 1919)
Vesco, Robert (US finan./fugitive)
Vespasian(us), Titus Flavius Sabinus (Roman emp.; AD 9-79)
Vespa™ motor scooter
Vespucius, Americus (also Amerigo Vespucci)(It. nav./expl.; 1451?-1512)
Vesta (astron.; myth.)
Vesuvius, Mount (active volcano, It.)
Veterans Administration (now Department of Veterans Affairs)
Veterans Affairs, Department of (US govt.)
Veterans Day (formerly Armistice Day)
Veterans of Foreign Wars of the United States (VFW)(est. 1899)

Proper Noun Speller

VF Corp.
VFR (visual flight rules)
VFW (Veterans of Foreign Wars)
VHF (very high frequency)
VHS (video home system)
VI (Virgin Islands)
Viadent™
Viadent, Inc.
Vic Damone (ent.; 1928-)
Vic Dickenson (US jazz; 1906-84)
Vic Fazio (US cong.; 1942-)
Vic Morrow (ent.; 1932-82)
Vic Raschi (baseball; 1919-88)
Vic Tayback (b. Victor Tabback)(ent.; 1930-90)
Vic Theatre, Old (also Royal Victoria
    Hall)(London)
Vicar of (Jesus) Christ (pope)
Vicara™ (fiber)
Vicente Aleixandre (Sp. poet; 1898-1984)
Vicenza, Italy
Vichy government (WWII regime; 1940-44)
Vichy Springs Mineral Water Corp.
Vichy, France (health resort)
Vicious, Sid (ent.; 1957-79)
Vickers Petroleum Corp.
Vickers, Jon (ent.; 1926-)
Vicki! (TV show)
Vicki Lawrence (ent.; 1949-)
Vicks™
Vicks USA, Richardson- (US bus.)
Vicks VapoRub™ (med.)
Vicksburg, Campaign of (US hist.; 1862-63)
Vicksburg, MS
Vico, Giovanni (Battista)(It. hist./phil.; 1668-
    1744)
Vicodin™ (med.)
Victor Borge (Dan./US ent./musician; 1909-)
Victor Hasselblad, Inc.
Victor Herbert (Ir./US comp./cond.; 1859-1924)
Victor (Marie) Hugo (Fr. writer; 1802-85)
Victor Hugo Cárdenas (VP, Bolivia
Victor Jory (ent.; 1902-82)
Victor Mature (ent.; 1916-)
Victor McLaglen (ent.; 1907-71)
Victor Milan
Victor Moore (ent.; 1876-1962)
Victor Paz Estenssoro (ex-pres., Bolivia; 1907-)
Victor/Victoria (film; 1982)
Victoria (mag.)
Victoria (myth.)
Victoria (b. Alexandrina Victoria)(queen, UK;
    1819-1901
Victoria (state, Austl.)
Victoria & Albert Museum (London)
Victoria Claflin Woodhull (US publ./reformer;
    1838-1927)
Victoria Cross (Br. mil. award)
Victoria Falls (Afr.)

Victoria Hall, Royal (also Old Vic
    Theatre)(London)
Victoria Jackson (ent.; 1959-)
Victoria Mary Sackville-West, Dame
    ("Vita")(Br. writer; 1892-1962)
Victoria Principal (ent.)
Victoria Spivey
Victoria, British Columbia, Canada
Victoria, Guadalupe (b. Manuel Félix
    Fernández)(ex-pres., Mex.; 1789-1843)
Victoria, Hong Kong (also Hong Kong City)
Victoria, Lake (Afr.)
Victoria, Seychelles
Victoria, TX
Victorian style (arch./lit.; mid- to late 19th c.)
Victoria's Secret (US bus.)
Victory Garden, The (TV show)
Vida Blue (baseball; 1949-)
Vidal Sassoon™
Vidal Sassoon (US bus.)
Vidal Sassoon, Inc.
Vidal, Gore (US writer/critic; 1925-)
Video (mag.)
Video Hits One (VH-1)
Vidkun Quisling (Nor. pol./traitor; 1887-1945)
Vidmar, Peter
Vidor, King (Wallis)(ent.; 1895-1982)
Vieira, João Bernardo (pres., Guinea-Bissau;
    1939-)
Vienna sausage
Vienna Sausage Manufacturing Co.
Vienna, Austria
Vienna, Congress of (Eur. hist.; 1814-15)
Vienna, VA, WV
Vientiane, Laos
Vietcong (National Front for the Liberation of
    SViet.; 1960-75?)
Vietminh (Vietnam Independence League;
    1941-54?)
Vietnam (Socialist Republic of)(SE Asia)
Vietnam War (NViet./SViet.; 1954-75. US
    involvement; 1964-75)
Vietnam War Memorial
Vietnamese (lang./people)
Vietnamization (US mil. policy, Vietnam War)
Vigdís Finnbogadóttir (pres., Iceland; 1930-)
Vigo, Spain
Vigoda, Abe (ent.; 1921-)
Vijaya Lakshmi Pandit (dipl., India; 1900-90)
Viking (ancient Scandinavian sea warrior)
Viking (US uncrewed space probes)
Viking Penguin Inc.
Vikings, Minnesota (football team)
Vikki Carr (ent.; 1941-)
Viktor I(vanovich) Patsayev (cosmo.; 1933-71)
Viktor S. Chemomyrdin (PM, Rus.)
Viktor V(asilyevich) Gorbatko (cosmo.; 1934-)
Vila, Efate, Vanuatu

Vilas, Guillermo (tennis; 1952-)

Villa-Lobos, Heitor (Brazilian comp.; 1881-1959)

Villa Mt. Eden (US bus.)

Villa, Pancho (Villa, Francisco, b. Doroteo Arango)(Mex. gen.; c1877-1923)

Village Voice

Villanonva, PA

Villanova University (PA)

Villechaize, Herve (ent.; 1943-93)

Villeroy & Boch™

Villeroy & Boch Tableware, Ltd.

Villon, François (Fr. poet; 1431-65?)

Villon, Jacques (b. Gaston Duchamp)(Fr. artist; 1875-1963)

Villon, Raymond Duchamp- (Fr. artist; 1876-1918)

Vilnius, Lithuania

Vin Scully (ent.; 1927-)

Viña del Mar, Chile

Vinaya Pitaka (rel.)

Vince(nt Thomas) Lombardi (football; 1913-70)

Vincennes, France

Vincennes, IN

Vincennes, U.S.S. (US ship/mil. incident, Iran; 1987)

Vincent and the Grenadines, St. (island nation)(West Indies)

Vincent de Paul, St. (Fr. rel.; c1581-1660)

Vincent d'Indy, (Paul Marie Théodore)(Fr. comp.; 1851-1931)

Vincent Foster, Jr. (US pol.; ?-1993)

Vincent Gardenia (ent.; 1921-92)

Vincent Millay, Edna St. (US poet; 1892-1950)

Vincent Price (ent.; 1911-93)

Vincent Rose (US comp.; 1880-1944)

Vincent (Censu) Tabone (pres., Malta

Vincent van Gogh (Dutch artist; 1853-90)

Vincent Youmans (US comp.; 1898-1946)

Vincent, Gene (ent.; 1935-71)

Vincent, Jan-Michael (ent.; 1944-)

Vincente Minnelli (ent.; 1910-86)

Vincenzo Bellini (It. comp.; 1801-35)

Vinci, Leonardo da (It. artist/scien.; 1452-1519)

Vindicator, Youngstown (OH newspaper)

Vineland, NJ

Vinny, My Cousin (film; 1992)

Vinton, Bobby (ent.; 1935-)

Vinylite™ (constr.)

Viola, Frank (baseball; 1960-)

Violeta Barrios de Chamorro (pres., Nicaragua; 1939-)

Viper, Dodge (auto.)

Virchow, Rudolf (Ludwig Carl)(Ger. pathol.; 1821-1902)

Viren, Lasse (track; 1949-)

Virgil (Publius Vergilius Maro)(also Vergil)(Roman poet; 70-19 BC)

Virgil I. "Gus" Grissom (astro.; 1926-67)

Virgilio Barco Vargas (ex-pres., Columbia; 1921-)

Virgilio Godoy (VP, Nicaragua

Virgin Gorda (Br. Virgin Island)

Virgin Islands National Park (St. John Island)

Virgin Islands, British (West Indies)

Virgin Islands, U.S. (West Indies)

Virgin Mary (also the Madonna, Holy Mother, Mary, Our Lady)(rel.)

Virginia (VA)

Virginia Beach, VA

Virginia City, NV

Virginia Company (Br. colonization cos. in Amer.; 1606)

Virginia creeper (plant)

Virginia Dare (1st Eng. child born in Amer.; ,1587-?)

Virginia deer (white-tailed deer)

Virginia E(shelman) Johnson, Dr. (US psych.,Masters & Johnson; 1925-)

Virginia fence (also Virginia rail fence, snake fence)

Virginia Graham (ent.; 1912-)

Virginia ham

Virginia Mayo (ent.; 1920-)

Virginia pepperwood (plant)

Virginia reel (dance)

Virginia Resolutions, Kentucky and (US hist.; 1798)

Virginia tobacco

Virginia Wade (tennis; 1945-)

Virginia (Stephen) Woolf, (Adeline)(Br. writer; 1882-1941)

Virginia Woolf?, Who's Afraid of (film; 1966)

Virginia, Loving v. (US law; 1967)

Virgo (astron., zodiac, virgin/maiden)

Visa™ (credit card)

Visalia, CA

Vishnu (rel.)

Vishwanath Pratap Singh (ex-PM, India; 1931-)

Visigoth (people)

Visine™ (med.)

Vision 486™ (CAT system/writer)

Vision TSi, Eagle (auto.)

VISTA (Volunteers in Service to America)

Vitale, Dick (ent.; 1940-)

Vitalis™ (hair tonic)

Vitas Gerulaitis (tennis; 1954-)

Vitebsk, Belarus

Viterbo, Italy

Vito Genovese (US Mafia; 1898-1969)

Vitold Fokin (Ukrainian pol.)

Vitruvius (Pollio), (Marcus)(Roman arch.; 1st c. BC)

Vittadini, Adrienne (clothing)

Vittel/USA (US bus.)

Vitti, Monica (ent.; 1931-)

Vittorio De Sica (ent.; 1901-74)
Vittorio Gassman (ent.; 1922-)
Vitus'(s) dance, St. (nervous disorder)
Vitus, St. (It. rel.; 3rd c.)
Viva™ paper towels
Viva Zapata! (film)
Vivactil™ (med.)
Vivaldi, Antonio (Lucio)(It. comp.; 1678-1741)
Vivarin™ (med.)
Vivian Blaine (ent.; 1921-)
Vivian Vance (ent.; 1911-79)
Vivien Leigh (ent.; 1913-67)
Vivienne Della Chiesa (ent.; 1920-)
Vivitar Corp.
Vizsla (dog)
V-J Day (WWII Allies victory over Japan; 8/15/45)
Vlaams (lang.)
Vladimir A. Shatalov (cosmo.; 1927-)
Vladimir Ashkenazy (Rus. pianist/cond.; 1937-)
Vladimir Feltsman (Rus. pianist; 1952-)
Vladimir Horowitz (Rus./US pianist; 1904-89)
Vladimir Ilyich (Ulyanov) Lenin (USSR leader; 1870-1924)
Vladimir Mayakovsky (Rus. writer; 1893-1930)
Vladimir Meciar (PM, Slovakia)
Vladimir M(ikhalovich) Komarov (cosmo.; 1927-67)
Vladimir (Vladomirovich) Nabokov (Rus./US writer; 1899-1977)
Vladimir (Sergeyevich) Solovyov (Rus. phil.; 1853-1900)
Vladimir (Kosma) Zworykin ("Father of Television")(Rus./US physt./eng./inv.; 1889-1982)
Vladimir, Russia
Vladislav N. Volkov (cosmo.)
Vladivostok, Russia
Vlaminck, Maurice de (Fr. artist; 1876-1958)
Vlasic™
Vlasic Foods, Inc.
VLF (very low frequency)
Vlore, Albania
VMD (Foctor of Veterinary Medicine)
V neck (clothing)
Vo Chi Cong (ex-pres., Viet.)
Vo Van Kiet (PM, Viet.)
VO5™ (hair care)
Vogt, A(lfred) E(lton) Van (US writer; 1912-)
Vogue (mag.)
Vogue Pattern Service (US bus.)
Voice of America (US broadcasting service)
Voice of the Turtle, The (play/film)
Voight, Jon (ent.; 1938-)
Voinovich, George (OH gov.; 1936-)
Voit™
Voit Sports, Inc.
Vojvodina (province, Yug.)

Vol, Frank De
Volans (astron., flying fish)
Volcker, Paul A. (US econ.; 1927-)
Volga River (Eur.)
Volgograd, Russia (formerly Stalingrad)
Volkov, Vladislav N. (cosmo.)
Volkswagen™ (auto.)(also Bug, Beetle, VW)
Volkswagen Cabrio™ (auto.)
Volkswagen Corrado™ (auto.)
Volkswagen EuroVan™ (auto.)
Volkswagen Jetta™ (auto.)
Volkswagen Jetta™ GL (auto.)
Volkswagen of America, Inc.
Volkswagen Passat™ (auto.)
Volkswagen™ Rabbit (auto.)
Volkswagenwerke
Volpone (B. Jonson play)
Volstead Act (Prohibition; 1919)
Volstead, Andrew (US pol.; 1860-1947)
Volsunga Saga (also *Volsungasaga*)(myth.)
Volta River (Ghana)
Volta, Alessandro, Count (It. physt.; 1745-1827)
Voltaic languages
Voltaire (b. Françoise Marie Arouet)(Fr. phil./writer; (1694-1778)
Voltaren™ (med.)
Volunteer State (nickname, TN)
Volvo (auto.)
Volvo GM Heavy Truck Corp.
Volvo North America Corp.
Volyanov, Boris V. (cosmo.)
von Behring, Emil (Ger. bacteriol.; 1854-1917)
von Bismarck, Otto (Eduard Leopold), Prince ("Iron Chancellor")(ex-chanc., Ger.; 1815-98)
von Blücher, Gebhard (Ger. gen.; 1742-1819)
von Braun, Werner (or Wernher)(Ger./US eng.; 1912-77)
von Bülow, Bernhard, Prince (ex-chanc., Ger.; 1849-1929)
von Bulow, Claus (US news)
von Bulow, Sunny (Martha)(US news)
von Clausewitz, Karl (Ger. mil.; 1780-1831)
von Dohnányi, Ernst (or Ernö)(Hung. pianist/comp.; 1877-1960)
von Flotow, Friedrich (Ger. comp.; 1812-83)
von Fraunhofer, Joseph (Ger. optician/physt.; 1787-1826)
von Furstenberg, Diane (US bus.)
von Furstenberg Importing Co., Diane
von Gluck, Christoph W(illibald)(Ger. comp.; 1714-87)
von Goethe, Johann Wolfgang (Ger. writer/phil.; 1749-1852)
von Humboldt, (Friedrich Heinrich) Alexander, Baron (Ger. expl.; 1769-1859)
von Karajan, Herbert (Aus. cond.; 1908-)
von Kluck, Alexander (Ger. gen.; 1846-1934)
von Krafft-Ebing, Richard, Baron (Ger. phys.;

1840-1902)

von Laban, Rudolf (Hung. ballet; 1879-1958)

von Leibnitz, Gottfried Wilhelm, Baron (Ger. phil./math; 1646-1716)

von Liebig, Justus, Baron (Ger. chem.; 1803-73)

von Mannerheim, Carl Gustaf Emil, Baron (Fin. gen./pol.; 1867-1951)

von Ossig, Kaspar Schwenkfeld (Ger. rel.; 1490-1561)

von Papen, Franz (Ger. pol.; 1879-1969)

von Ribbentrop, Joachim (Ger. Nazi pol.; 1893-1946)

Von Ryan's Express (film; 1965)

von Schelling, Friedrich Wilhelm Joseph (Ger. phil.; 1775-1854)

von Schiller, (Johann Christoph) Friedrich (Ger. writer/hist.; 1759-1805)

von Schlegel, August Wilhelm (Ger. writer; 1767-1845)

von Schlegel, Friedrich (Ger. phil./writer; 1772-1829)

von Schuschnigg, Kurt (ex-chanc., Aus.; 1897-1977)

Von Stade, Frederica (ent.; 1945-)

von Steuben, Friedrich Wilhelm (Ludolf Gerhard Augustin), Baron (Prussian/US gen.; 1730-94)

Von Stroheim, Erich (ent.; 1885-1957)

Von Sydow, Max (Swed. ent.; 1929-)

von Tilzer, Albert (US comp.; 1878-1956)

von Tilzer, Harry (US comp.; 1872-1946)

von Tirpitz, Alfred (Ger. mil.; 1849-1930)

von Trapp family (singers)

von Wassermann, August (Ger. phys./bacteriol.; 1866-1925)

von Weber, Carl Maria (Friedrich Ernst), Baron (Ger. comp.; 1786-1826)

von Weizsacker, Richard (pres., Ger.)

Von Zell, Harry (ent.; 1906-81)

von Zeppelin, Ferdinand Graf, Count (Ger. mil./aeronaut; 1838-1917)

V1, V2 (Ger. flying bombs; WWII)

Vonnegut, Kurt, Jr. (US writer; 1922-)

Vorlage (Ger., skiing)

Voskhod (USSR crewed space flights)

Vostok (USSR crewed space flights)

Voto, Bernard A. De (US hist.; 1897-1955)

Vouvray (wine)

Voyager (US uncrewed space probes)

Voyager, Plymouth (auto.)

Voyageurs National Park (MN)

VP (vice president)

Vranitzky, Franz (chanc., Aus.; 1937-)

Vreeland, Diana (Fr./US editor/designer; 1903-89)

Vries, Hugo De (Dutch botanist; 1848-1935)

Vries, Peter De (US writer; 1910-93)

VS (veterinary surgeon)

V. Sattui Winery (US bus.)

VT (variable time, Vermont)

Vuarnet-France (US bus.)

Vuillard, (Jean) Édouard (Fr. artist; 1868-1940)

Vukovar, Croatia

Vulcan (mil. weapon)

Vulcan (myth.)

Vulgar Latin

Vulgate (rel.)

Vulpecula (astron., fox)

VU/TEXT (compu. database)

Vyacheslav F. Kebich, (PM, Belarus)

Vyacheslav M(ikhailovich) Molotov (ex-PM, Rus.; 1890-1986)

Vyatka, Russia (formerly Kirov)

Vytautas Landsbergis (ex-pres., Lith.; 1932-)

W

W (chem. sym., tungsten)
WA (Washington)
Wabash (railroad slang)
Wabash Cannonball (A.P. Carter song)
Wabash River (central US)
Wabash, IN
WAC (Women's Army Corps)
Waco, TX
Waddaulah, Muda Hassanal Bolkiah
    Mu'izzaddin (sultan, Brunei)
Wade Boggs (baseball; 1958-)
Wade-Giles system (Eng. representation of Ch.)
Wade, Benjamin Franklin (US pol.; 1800-78)
Wade, Roe vs. (US law; 1973)
Wade, Virginia (tennis; 1945-)
Wadi Medani, Sudan
WAF (Women in the Air Force)
Waffle House, Inc.
Wagadugu, Burkina Faso (also Ouagadougou)
Wages and Hours Act (also Fair Labor
    Standards Act; 1938)
Waggoner, Lyle
Wagnalls Corp., Funk &
Wagnalls, Adam Willis (US publ.; 1843-1924)
Wagner, (John Peter) Honus (baseball; 1867-
    1955)
Wagner, Lindsay (ent.; 1949-)
Wagner, Richard (Wilhelm)(Ger. comp.; 1813-
    83)
Wagner, Robert (ent.; 1930-)
Wagner, Robert F(erdinand), Jr. (ex-mayor,
    NYC; 1910-1991)
Wagner, Robert F(erdinand), Sr. (US pol.; 1877-
    1953)
Wagoner, Porter (ent.; 1927-)
Wahabi (rel.)
Wahl, Ken (ent. 1956-)
Wahlberg, Donnie (ent.; 1969-)
Wahran, Algeria
Waihee, John D., III (HI gov.; 1946-)
Waikiki Beach (Honolulu, HI)
Wailing Wall (also Western
    Wall)(Jerusalem)(rel.)
Waimea, HI
Wain, Bea (ent.; 1917-)
Wainwright, Fort (AK)(mil.)
Wainwright, Gideon v. (US law; 1963)
Wainwright, Jonathan M(ayhew)(US gen.;
    1883-1953)
Waipahu, HI
Waite, Ralph (ent.; 1929-)
Waite, Terry (Terence Hardy)(Br. rel., hostage;
    1939-)
Waiting for Godot (S. Beckett play)

Waits, Tom (ent.)
Waitz, Grete (Andersen)(runner; 1953-)
Wake Forest, NC
Wake Island (US air base, central Pac.)
Wakefield, Dick (baseball; 1921-85)
Wakefield, England
Wakefield, MA, VA
Walcott, Jersey Joe (b. Arnold Raymond
    Cream)(boxing; 1914-)
Waldemar, Pawlak (PM, Pol.)
Walden Pond (MA)(Thoreau's inspiration)
Walden, Robert (ent.; 1943-)
Waldenbooks
Waldheim, Kurt (ex-pres., Aus./UN dipl.; 1918-)
Waldorf salad
Waldorf-Astoria Hotel (NYC)
Waler (horse)
Wales (Principality of)(part of UK)
Wales Conference (hockey)
Wales, Prince of (Prince Charles Philip Arthur
    George)(eldest son of Queen Elizabeth II;
    1948-)
Wales, The Outlaw Josey (film; 1976)
Walesa, Lech (pres., Pol.; 1943-)
Walgreen Co.
Walgreen, Charles R. (US bus.; 1873-1939)
Walhalla (also Valhalla, Walhall,
    Valhall)(myth.)
Walken, Christopher (ent.; 1943-)
Walker & Sons, Inc., Hiram
Walker, Alice (US writer; 1944-)
Walker, Jimmy (James John)(ex-mayor, NYC;
    1881-1946)
Walker™, Johnnie (whiskey)
Walker, Larry (baseball; 1966-)
Walker, Matthew (knot)
Walker, Mort (cartoonist; *Beetle Bailey*; 1923-)
Walker, Nancy (ent.; 1922-92)
Walker, Ralph T. (US arch.; 1889-1973)
Walker, Robert (ent.; 1914-51)
Walkman™ (music)
Wall of China, Great (1,450 miles; built 214 BC)
Wall Street (NYC)(US financial center)
Wall Street Journal (newspaper)
Walla Walla, WA
Wallace Beery (ent.; 1889-1949)
Wallace K. Harrison (US arch.; 1895-1981)
Wallace Stegner (US writer; 1909-93)
Wallace Stevens (US poet; 1879-1955)
Wallace, Alfred Russel (Br. nat.; 1823-1913)
Wallace, DeWitt (US publ.; 1889-1981)
Wallace, George C(orley)(ex-gov., AL; 1919-)
Wallace, Henry A(gard)(ex-US VP; 1888-1965)
Wallace, Irving (US writer; 1916-90)
Wallace, Lila (Acheson)(US publ.; 1889-1984)
Wallace, Mike (US TV jour.; 1918-)
Wallace, Sippie (ent.)
Wallach, Eli (ent.; 1915-)

Wallawalla (NAmer. Indians)
Wallbanger, Harvey (mixed drink)
Wallenberg, Raoul (Swed. dipl.; 1912-47?)
Wallenda, Karl (Ger. circus; 1905-78)
Waller, Fats (Thomas Wright)(US comp./jazz; 1904-43)
Waller, Robert James (US writer)
Wallis and Futuna Islands (SW Pac.)
Wallis "Wally" Warfield Simpson (Duchess of Windsor)(US socialite, m. Edward VIII; 1896-1986)
Wallis, Hal (Harold Brent)(ent.; 1899-1986)
Walloon (lang./people)
Wallop, Malcolm (US cong.; 1933-)
Wally Cox (ent.; 1924-73)
Wally (Walter J.) Hickel (AK gov.; 1919-)
Wally (Walter Marty) Schirra, Jr. (US astro.; 1923-)
Wal-Mart™
Wal-Mart Stores, Inc.
Walnut Creek, CA
Walpole, Horace (Horatio)(Earl of Oxford)(Br. writer; 1717-97)
Walpole, Robert (Earl of Oxford)(Br. pol.; 1676-1745)
Walpurgis Night (May 1)
Walsh, Adam (football; 1902-85)
Walsh, Bill (football; 1931-)
Walsh, Raoul (ent.; 1887-1980)
Walston, Ray (ent.; 1924-)
Walt Disney Co., The
Walt(er) Elias Disney (US bus./ent.; 1901-66)
Walt Frazier (basketball; 1945-)
Walt Kelly (cartoonist, *Pogo*; 1913-73)
Walt(er) Whitman (US poet; 1819-92)
Walter Alston (baseball; 1911-84)
Walter Annenberg (US publ./finan.; 1908-)
Walter Bagehot (Br. econ./jour.; 1826-77)
Walter Brennan (ent.; 1894-1974)
Walter Camp (football; 1859-1925)
Walter Corp., Jim
Walter Cronkite (US TV jour.; 1916-)
Walter Cunningham, R. (astro.; 1932-)
Walter de la Mare (Br. poet; 1873-1956)
Walter D. Miller (ex-SD gov.)
Walter Donaldson (US comp.; 1893-1947)
Walter F. Kerr (US writer/critic; 1913-)
Walter F(rederick) "Fritz" Mondale (US pol.; 1928-)
Walter F(rancis) White (US reformer; 1893-1955)
Walter (Adolf) Gropius (US arch.; 1883-1969)
Walter Hagen (golf; 1892-1969)
Walter Houser Brattain (US physt./inv.; 1902-87)
Walter Huston (ent.; 1884-1950)
Walter (Perry) "Big Train" Johnson (baseball; 1887-1946)

Walter Koenig
Walter Lantz (cartoonist, *Woody Woodpecker*; 1900-)
Walter Lippmann (US jour.; 1889-1974)
Walter L. Jacobs (US bus.; 1898-1985)
Walter Matthau (ent.; 1920-)
Walter Mitty, The Secret Life of (J. Thurber short story)
Walter O'Malley (baseball exec.; 1903-79)
Walter Payton (football; 1954-)
Walter P(ercy) Chrysler (US car bus.; 1875-1940)
Walter Pidgeon (ent.; 1897-1984)
Walter Pitkin
Walter P(hilip) Reuther (US labor leader; 1907-70)
Walter P. Webb (US hist.; 1888-1963)
Walter Raleigh, Sir (Br. expl./writer; 1552?-1618)
Walter Rathenau (Ger. pol.; 1867-1922)
Walter Reed Army Medical Center (DC)
Walter Reed, Dr. (US phys.; 1851-1902)
Walter Richard Sickert (Br. artist; 1860-1942)
Walter Scott, Sir (Scot. writer; 1771-1832)
Walter Slezak (ent.; 1902-83)
Walter Ulbricht (Ger. pol.; 1893-1873)
Walter Wanger
Walter Winchell (US newscaster; 1897-1972)
Walter, Jessica (ent.; 1944-)
Walters, Barbara (US TV jour.; 1931-)
Walters, David (OK gov.; 1951-)
Walton Beach, Fort (FL)(city)
Walton, Bill (basketball; 1952-)
Walton, Izaak (Br. writer; 1593-1683)
Walton, Sam (Moore)(US bus./Wal-Mart; 1918-92)
Walton, Sir William (Turner)(Br. comp.; 1902-83)
Waltons, The (TV show)
Wambaugh, Joseph (US writer; 1937-)
Wanamaker, Inc., John
Wanamaker, John (US bus.; 1838-1922)
Wanamaker, Sam (ent.; 1919-)
Wanamaker's (department store)
Wandering Jew (legendary Jew condemned to wander)
wandering Jew (plant)
Wanderjahr (Ger., year of travel)
Wang An-Shih (Ch. pol.; 1021-86)
Wang Laboratories, Inc.
Wang School, Lu- (Ch. phil.)
Wang Wei (Ch. poet/artist; 699-759)
Wang, An (Ch./US inv./bus.; 1920-90)
Wangchuk, Jigme Singye (king, Bhutan
Wanger, Walter
Wank, Roland A. (US arch.; 1898-1970)
Wankel engine (auto.)
Wankel, Felix (Ger., inv.; 1902-88)

Wapner, Judge Joseph (*People's Court*)
War Between the States (also American Civil War, War of Secession)(1861-65)
War of 1812 (US/Br.; 1812-15)
War of Jenkin's Ear (Br./Sp.; 1739-41)
War of Secession (also American Civil War, War Between the States)(1861-65)
War of the Nations (also World War I, First World War, Great War)(1914-18)
War of the Pacific (Chile/Bolivia, Peru; 1879-83)
War of the Roses (Eng. hist.; 1455-85)
War Powers Act (US hist.; 1973)
War, Department of (US govt.)
Warbeck, Perkin (Flem. pretender to Br. throne; 1474-99)
Ward Bond (ent.; 1903-60)
Ward, Aaron Montgomery (US bus.; 1843-1913)
Ward, Fred (ent.; 1943-)
Warden, Jack (ent.; 1920-)
Warfield, William (ent.; 1920-)
Warhol, Andy (b. Andrew Warhola)(US artist; 1927-87)
Waring Products (US bus.)
Waring, Fred M. (US cond., designed Waring blender; 1900-84)
Warner Books (US bus.)
Warner Brothers, Inc. (film co.)
Warner Brothers Records, Inc. (film co.)
Warner Cable Corp.
Warner Communications, Inc., Time
Warner-Lambert Co.
Warner, Albert (ent.; 1884-1967)
Warner, Harry M(orris)(ent.; 1881-1958)
Warner, Inc., Time
Warner, Jack L(eonard)(ent.; 1892-1978)
Warner, John W. (US cong.; 1927-)
Warner, Malcolm-Jamal (ent.; 1970-)
Warner, Samuel L(ewis)(ent.; 1887-1927)
Warren Beatty (ent.; 1937-)
Warren Berlinger (ent.; 1937-)
Warren Bridge, Charles River Bridge v. (US law; 1837)
Warren Christopher (US Secy./State; 1925-)
Warren Commission (US hist.; 1963-64)
Warren ("Baby") Dodds (US jazz; 1898-1959)
Warren Earl Burger (US jurist; 1907-)
Warren G(amaliel) Harding (29th US pres.; 1865-1923)
Warren Giles (baseball exec.; 1896-1979)
Warren Report (US hist.; 1964)
Warren (Edward) Spahn (baseball; 1921-)
Warren, Earl (US jurist; 1891-1974)
Warren, Harry (US comp.; 1893-1981)
Warren, Lesley Ann (ent.; 1946-)
Warren, MI, OH
Warren, Robert Penn (US writer; 1905-89)
Warri, Nigeria
Warrick, Ruth (ent.; 1916-)

Warriors, Golden State (basketball team)
Warsaw Pact (also Warsaw Treaty Organization)(USSR/E Eur.; 1955-91)
Warsaw, IN
Warsaw, Poland
Warwick, Dionne (ent.; 1941-)
Warwick, England
Warwick, RI
Warwickshire (county, Eng.)
Wasatch Range (ID/UT)
Washington (WA)
Washington Allston (US artist; 1779-1843)
Washington and Lee University (VA)
Washington Bullets (basketball team)
Washington Capitals (hockey team)
Washington Irving (US writer/hist.; 1783-1859)
Washington Journalism Review
Washington Monument (DC)
Washington pie
Washington Post (DC newspaper)
Washington Post Co.
Washington Redskins (football team)
Washington thorn (tree)
Washington Times (DC newspaper)
Washington, Booker T(aliaferro)(US educ./reformer; 1856-1915)
Washington, DC (District of Columbia, US capital)
Washington, Denzel (ent.; 1954-)
Washington, Dinah (ent.; 1924-63)
Washington, George (1st US pres.; 1732-99)
Washington, Martha (Dandridge)(wife of ex-US pres.; 1732-1802)
Washingtonia (tree)
Washingtonian (mag.)
Washington's Birthday (February 22)
Waslaw (or Vaslav) Nijinsky (Rus. ballet; 1890-1950)
Wasmosy, Juan Carlos (pres., Paraguay; 1942-)
WASP (white Anglo-Saxon protestant)
Wassail (mixed drink)
Wasserman, Lew
Wassermann test/reaction (for syphilis)
Wassermann, August von (Ger. phys./bacteriol.; 1866-1925)
Wassily (or Vasili, Vasily) Kandinsky (Rus. artist; 1866-1944)
Waste King, Thermador/ (US bus.)
Wat (Walter) Tyler (Br. rebel; ?-1381)
Water Pik™
Waterbury, CT
Waterfield, Bob (football; 1921-83)
Waterford glass/crystal
Waterford Glass, Inc.
Waterford, CT
Waterford, Ireland
Watergate (US hist.; 1972-74)
Watergate Hotel/apartments (DC)

Waterloo Bridge (film)
Waterloo, Battle of (Napoleon's defeat; 1815)
Waterloo, Belgium
Waterloo, IA
Waterloo, Ontario, Canada
Waterman, Willard (ent.)
Waters, Ethel (ent.; 1900-77)
Waters, Muddy (aka McKinley Morganfield)(ent.; 1915-83)
Watership Down (R. Adams novel)
Waterston, Sam (ent.; 1940-)
Watertown, MA, NY, SD
Waterville, ME
Watervliet Arsenal (NY)
Watervliet, NY
Watkins, Carlene (ent.; 1952-)
W. Atlee Burpee Co.
Watley, Jody
Watling Island, Bahamas (also San Salvador)
WATS (Wide Area Telecommunications Service) (comm.)
Watson-Crick model (3-D structure of DNA)
Watson, Dr. (fict. chara. w/Sherlock Holmes)
Watson, James Dewey (US biol.; 1928-)
Watson, Martha Rae (track; 1946-)
Watson, Thomas J(ohn)(US bus.; 1874-1956)
Watson, Thomas J(ohn), Jr. (US bus.; 1914-93)
Watson, Tom (golf; 1949-)
Watt, James E. (Scot. eng./inv.; 1736-1819)
Watt, James G. (US pol.)
Watteau back (clothing)
Watteau hat
Watteau, Jean Antoine (Fr. artist; 1684-1721)
Watterson, Bill (cartoonist, *Calvin and Hobbes*; 1958-)
Wattleton, Faye (US reformer; 1943-)
Watts riots (Los Angeles; 1965)
Watts, George Frederic (Bt. artist; 1817-1904)
Watusi (people)
Waugh, Evelyn (Arthur St. John)(Br. writer; 1903-66)
Waukegan, IL
Waukesha, WI
Wausau Paper Mills Co.
Wausau, WI
Wauwatosa, WI
Wavell, Archibald (Percival)(Br. mil.; 1883-1950)
Waves (also WAVES)(Women's Reserve, US Navy)
Waxman, Franz
Way, Middle (rel.)
Wayans, Damon (ent.; 1960-)
Wayans, Keenan Ivory (ent.; 1958-)
Waylon Jennings (ent.; 1937-)
Wayne Gretzky (hockey; 1961-)
Wayne L. Hays (US pol.; 1912-89)
Wayne Morse (US pol.; 1900-74)

Wayne Newton (ent.; 1942-)
Wayne State University (MI)
Wayne, Anthony (Mad Anthony)(US gen.; 1745-96)
Wayne, Bruce (ent.)
Wayne, David (ent.; 1914-)
Wayne, Fort (IN)(city)
Wayne, John (b. Marion Michael Morrison, aka "the Duke")(ent.; 1907-79)
Wayne's World (film; 1992)
Ways and Means Committee, House (US govt.)
W. B. Roddenbery Co., Inc. (Roddenbery's)
W. B. Saunders Co.
W(illiam) B(utler) Yeats (Ir. writer; 1865-1939)
WCC (World Council of Churches)
W. C. Fields (b. William Claude Dukenfield)(ent.; 1880-1946)
W(illiam) C(hristopher) Handy (US jazz; 1873-1958)
WCTU (Woman's Christian Temperance Union)
W(illiam) D(eWitt) Snodgrass (US poet; 1926-)
Wealthy apple
Weather Channel, The (cable TV)
Weather Service, National (US govt.; est.1870)
Weatherwax, Rudd (Lassie's trainer)
Weaver, Charlie (aka Cliff Arquette)(ent.; 1905-74)
Weaver, Dennis (ent.; 1924-)
Weaver, Doodles
Weaver, Earl (baseball; 1930-)
Weaver, Fritz (ent.; 1926-)
Weaver, Sigourney (ent.; 1949-)
Webb Hotels, Del (US bus.)
Webb, (Martha) Beatrice (Potter)(Br. reformer/writer; 1858-1943)
Webb, Chick (US jazz; 1902-39)
Webb, Clifton (ent.; 1891-1966)
Webb, Jack (ent.; 1920-82)
Webb, Jimmy (US comp.; 1946-)
Webb, Sidney (James)(Br. reformer/writer; 1859-1947)
Webb, Walter P. (US hist.; 1888-1963)
Webber, Andrew Lloyd (Br. comp.; 1948-)
Webber, Chris (basketball; 1973-)
W(illiam) E(dward) B(urghardt) Du Bois (US educ./writer, NAACP; 1868-1963)
Weber Food Products Co.
Weber, Carl Maria (Friedrich Ernst) von, Baron (Ger. comp.; 1786-1826)
Weber, Max (Ger. econ./hist.; 1864-1920)
Weber, Max (US artist; 1881-1961)
Webster Dictionary, Merriam-
Webster, Alex (football; 1931-)
Webster, Ben (US jazz; 1909-73)
Webster, Daniel (US orator/pol.; 1782-1852)
Webster, Noah (US lexicographer; 1758-1843)
Webster, Paul Francis (US lyricist; 1907-84)
Webster's New World Dictionary of American

English

Wechsler Scales (intelligence tests)
Weddell Sea (S Atl.)
Wedgwood blue (color)
Wedgwood™ china
Wedgewood USA, Inc.
Wedgwood, Josiah (Br. potter; 1730-95)
Wedtech scandal (US news; mid-1980s)
Wee Kim Wee (ex-pres., Singapore; 1914-)
Wee Willie Winkie (fict. chara.)
Wee, Wee Kim (ex-pres., Singapore; 1914-)
Weeb Ewbank (football; 1907-)
Weed Eater, Inc.
Weed, CA
Week in Review (TV show)
Weeki Wachee Springs (FL)
Wegener, Alfred L(othar)(Ger. meteor.; 1880-
    1930)
Wei, Wang (Ch. poet/artist; 699-759)
Weibel Vineyards (US bus.)
Weicker, Lowell (CT gov.; 1931-)
Weight Watchers™
Weight Watchers International, Inc.
Weight Watchers Magazine
Weil, Cynthia (US comp.; 1937-)
Weill, Kurt (Julian)(Ger./US comp.; 1900-50)
Weimar Republic (Ger. hist.; 1919-33)
Weimar, Germany
Weimaraner (dog)
Weinberg principle/law/distribution, Hardy-
    (genetics)
Weinberger, Caspar "Cap" W(illard)(US pol.;
    1917-)
Weiner, Norbert (US math.; 1894-1964)
Weir, Peter (ent.; 1944-)
Weis Markets, Inc.
Weiskopf, Tom (golf; 1942-)
Weiss, George (baseball exec.; 1895-1972)
Weissmuller, Johnny (Peter John)(US
    swimmer/ent.; 1903-84)
Weitz, Bruce (ent.; 1943-)
Weitz, Paul J. (astro.)
Weizman, Ezer (pres., Isr.; 1924-)
Weizmann, Chaim (ex-pres., Isr.; 1874-1952)
Weizsacker, Richard von (pres., Ger.)
Welby, M.D., Marcus (TV show)
Welch Foods, Inc.
Welch, Raquel (ent.; 1940-)
Welcome Back, Kotter (TV show)
Welcome to Pooh Corner (TV show)
Welcome Wagon (to welcome newcomers)
Weld, Philip (sailing; 1915-84)
Weld, William F. (MA gov.; 1945-)
Weldon Roberts Rubber Co.
Welk, Lawrence (US cond.; 1903-92)
Welland Ship Canal (Lake Erie/Lake Ontario)
Welles, (George) Orson (ent.; 1915-85)
Welles, Gideon (US pol./jour.; 1802-78)

Wellesley College (MA)
Wellesley, Arthur (Duke of Wellington)(Br. mil.;
    1769-1852)
Wellesley, MA
Wellington boots (also l.c.)
Wellington, beef
Wellington, (Arthur Wellesley), Duke of (Br.
    mil.; 1769-1852)
Wellington, New Zealand
Wells Fargo & Co.
Wells Fargo Bank
Wells, H(erbert) G(eorge)(Br. writer; 1866-1946)
Wells, Kitty (ent.; 1919-)
Wells, Mary (ent.; 1943-92)
Wellstone, Paul (US cong.; 1944-)
Welsh (lang./people)
Welsh cob (pony)
Welsh corgi (dog)
Welsh pony
Welsh rabbit (also Welsh rarebit)(cheese dish)
Welsh springer spaniel (dog)
Welsh terrier (dog)
Weltanschauung (Ger., world-view)
Well-Tempered Clavier (by Johann S. Bach)
Weltgeist (Ger., spirit of the times)
Weltschmerz (also l.c.)(Ger., world-pain,
    sentimental pessimism)
Welty, Eudora (US writer; 1909-)
Wembley (district, London)
Wenatchee National Forest
Wenceslas (emp., Rome; king, Ger./Bohemia;
    1361-1419)
Wenceslas, Good King (also Wenceslaus)(song)
Wenceslas, St. (also "King Wenceslaus")(duke,
    Bohemia; 907-929)
Wendell Corey (ent.; 1914-68)
Wendell Hampton Ford (US cong.; 1924-)
Wendell L(ewis) Willkie (US pol.; 1892-1944)
Wendt, George (ent.; 1948-)
Wendy Hiller, Dame (ent.; 1912-)
Wendy's International, Inc.
Wendy's™ restaurant
Wenrich, Percy (US comp.; 1887-1952)
Wensleydale (cheese)
Wente Brothers (US bus.)
Wenzel, Hanni
Werner Carl Heisenberg (Ger. physt.; 1901-76)
Werner Herzog (Ger. ent.; 1942-)
Werner Klemperer (Ger. ent.; 1919-)
Werner (or Wernher) von Braun (Ger./US eng.;
    1912-77)
Werner, Oskar
Wertheimer, Max (Czech. psych./phil.; 1880-
    1943)
Werther's™ Original (candy)
Wertmüller, Lina (It. ent.; 1926?-)
Wes Craven
Wes Montgomery (US jazz; 1925-68)

Wesberry v. Sanders (US law; 1964)
Wesley Crusher, Ensign (fict. chara., *Star Trek*)
Wesley Snipes (ent.; 1962-)
Wesley, John (Br. rel., founded Methodism; 1703-91)
Wesleyan College (GA)
Wesleyan University (CT)
Wessex (Eng. kingdom; 6th-9th c.)
Wesson Fire Arms Co.
Wesson, Inc., Hunt-
West Bank (of Jordan River)(disputed area, SW Asia)
West Bend Co., The
West Bengal (state, India)
West Bromwich, England
West Chester, PA
West Flanders (province, Belgium)
West Germany (now part of Germany)
West Hartford, CT
West Haven, CT
West Highland (cattle)
West Highland white terrier (dog)
West Indian (people)
West Indies (Bahamas, Greater Antilles, Lesser Antilles)
West Jordan, UT
West Orange, NJ
West Pakistan (now Republic of Pakistan)
West Palm Beach Post (FL newspaper)
West Palm Beach, FL
West Point (fort., NY)
West Point-Pepperell Mill Store (US bus.)
West Point, US Military Academy at (NY)
West Siberian Plain (region, Siberia)
West Side Story (film; 1961)
West Sussex (county, Eng.)
West Valley City, UT
West Virginia (WV)
West Virginia State Board of Education v. Barnette (US law; 1943)
West, American (west of Mississippi River)
West, Benjamin (US artist; 1738-1820)
West, Dottie (ent.; 1932-91)
West, Jerry (basketball; 1938-)
West, Jessamyn (US writer; 1903-84)
West, Mae (ent.; 1892-1980)
West, Mae (life jacket)
West, Nathanael (aka Nathan Wallenstein Weinstein)(US writer; 1904-40)
West, Rebecca, Dame (b. Cicily Isabel Fairfield)(Br. writer; 1892-1983)
West, Dame Victoria Mary Sackville- ("Vita") (Br. writer; 1892-1962)
WestAir Airlines
Westbrook Pegler, (James)(US jour.; 1894-1969)
Westchester, NY, IL
Westclox (US bus.)
Westerlies (winds)

Western Australia (state, Austl.)
Western Auto Supply (US bus.)
Western blot (med.)
Western Conference (basketball)
Western Hemisphere
Western saddle (also stock saddle)
Western Samoa (Independent State of)(SW Pac.)
Western Tsin (or Chin) dynasty (also Chin)(Ch.; 265-316)
Western Union™ (comm.)
Western Union Corp.
Western Wall (also Wailing Wall)(Jerusalem) (rel.)
Westerner
Westfalia (Volkswagen van)
Westheimer, Dr. Ruth (b. Karola Ruth Siegal) (Ger./US sex therapist; 1928-)
Westin hotels
Westinghouse™ (appliances)
Westinghouse break (rr.)
Westinghouse Electric Corp.
Westinghouse, George (US bus.; 1846-1914)
Westlake, Donald E. (US writer; 1933-)
Westlaw (compu. database, law)
Westminster Abbey (also Collegiate Church of St. Peter)(London)
Westminster Palace (Houses of Parliament)(London)
Westminster, CA, CO
Westmoreland, William (Childs)(US gen.; 1914-)
Weston, Jack (ent.; 1924-)
Westover Air Force Base, MA
Westphalia (region, Ger.)
Westphalian ham
Westvaco Corp.
Westworld (film; 1973)
Wet 'n' Wild™ (cosmetics)
Wexford (county, Ir.)
Weyden, Rogier van der (Flem. artist; c1400-64)
Weyerhaeuser Co.
Weyerhaeuser™ lumber
Weymouth, MA
Wff'n Proof Learning Games Associates (US bus.)
Whalers, Hartford (hockey team)
Wharton, Edith (Newbold Jones)(US writer; 1862-1937)
Whatever Happened to Baby Jane? (film; 1962)
What's Happening!! (TV show)
What's Happening Now!! (TV show)
What's My Line? (TV show)
W. H. Auden (Br. poet; 1907-73)
Wheaties™ cereal
Wheatley, Phillis (Afr./US poet; 1753-84)
Wheaton, IL, MD
Wheaton, Wil

Wheatstone bridge (elect.)
Wheel of Fortune (TV show)
wheel of Fortune (gambling)
Wheeler Air Force Base, HI
Wheeler, William A(lmon)(ex-US VP; 1819-87)
Wheeling, IL, WV
Whidbey Island Naval Air Station (WA)
Whiffenpoof Song, The
Whig Party (UK/US hist.)
Whipple Observatory, (Fred Lawrence)(AZ)
Whipple, Fred Lawrence (US astron.; 1906-)
Whirlpool™ (appliances)
Whirlpool Corp.
Whiskas™ cat food
Whiskey Rebellion (US hist.; 1794)
Whiskey Ring (US hist./scandal)
Whistler, James (Abbott) McNeill (US artist; 1834-1903)
Whitaker, Pernell (boxing; 1964-)
Whitchurch-Stouffville, Ontario, Canada
White Castle Systems, Inc.
White Christmas (song)
White Foods, Inc., Martha
White Friar (Carmelite friar)
White House, the (also Executive Mansion)(US pres. residence)(DC)
White Leghorn (chicken)
White Plains, NY
White Rain™ (hair care)
White Russian (cocktail)
White Sands Missile Range, NM
White Slave Traffic Act (also Mann Act)(US hist.; 1910)
White Sox, Chicago (baseball team)
White, Betty (ent.; 1922-)
White, Bill
White, Byron R(aymond)("Whizzer")(US jurist; 1917-)
White, Devon (baseball; 1962-)
White, E(lwyn) B(rooks)(US writer; 1899-1985)
White, Edward H(iggins), II (astro., 1st Amer. to walk in space; 1930-67)
White, Jesse (ent.; 1919-)
White, Margaret Bourke- (US photo./writer; 1906-71)
White, Reggie (football; 1961-)
White, Ryan (US AIDS victim/activist; 1972-90)
White, Stanford (US arch.; 1853-1906)
White, Texas v. (US law; 1869)
White, T(erence) H(anbury)(Br. writer; 1906-64)
White, Theodore H. (US jour.; 1915-86)
White, Vanna (ent.; 1957-)
White, Walter F(rancis)(US reformer; 1893-1955)
White, Willye B. (jumper; 1936-)
Whitechapel district (London)
Whitefriars district (London)
Whitehall Palace (London)

Whitehead, Alfred North (Br. phil./math.; 1861-1947)
Whitehorse, Yukon Territory, Canada
Whiteman Air Force Base, MO
Whiteman, Paul ("Pops")(US cond.; 1891-1967)
Whitesnake (pop music)
Whitewater (US pol. scandal; 1994)
Whitey (Edward Charles) Ford ("Duke of Paducah")(baseball; 1928-)
Whiting Field Naval Air Station, FL
Whiting, Margaret (ent.; 1924-)
Whiting, Richard A. (US comp.; 1891-1938)
Whitman Corp.
Whitman, Walt(er)(US poet; 1819-92)
Whitmore, James (ent.; 1921-)
Whitney Houston (ent.; 1963-)
Whitney Museum of American Art (NYC)
Whitney M(oore) Young, Jr. (US reformer; 1921-71)
Whitney v. California (US law; 1927)
Whitney, Eli (US inv./bus.; 1765-1825)
Whitney, John Hay (US publ./finan.; 1905-82)
Whitney, Mount (CA)
Whitsunday (also Pentecost)(rel.)
Whittaker, Roger
Whittier, CA
Whittier, John Greenleaf (US poet/jour.; 1807-92)
Whitworth, Kathy (golf; 1939-)
WHO (World Health Organization [UN])
Who Framed Roger Rabbit? (film)
Who, the (pop music)
Whoopi Goldberg (b. Karen Johnson)(ent.; 1950-)
Who's Afraid of Virginia Woolf? (film; 1966)
Who's the Boss (TV show)
Whyte classification (rr.)
WI (West Indies, Wisconsin)
WIA (wounded in action)
Wichita (NAmer. Indians)
Wichita Eagle (KS newspaper)
Wichita Falls, TX
Wichita, KS
Wickes Cos., Inc.
Wicklow (county, Ir.)
Wickremasinghe, Ranil (PM, Sri Lanka)
Wicks 'N Sticks (US bus.)
Wide Area Telecommunications Service (also WATS)(comm.)
Wideman, John Edgar (US writer; 1941-)
Widing, Juha (hockey; 1948-85)
Widmark, Richard (ent.; 1914-)
Wiener schnitzel (veal dish)
Wienerschnitzel International, Inc.
Wiesbaden, Germany
Wiesel, Elie(zer)(US writer/reformer; 1928-)
Wiesenthal, Simon (Aus. reformer; 1908-)
Wiest, Dianne (ent.; 1948-)

Wiffle Ball, Inc., The
Wigglesworth, Michael (US rel./writer; 1631-1705)
Wight, Isle of (island/county, Eng.)
Wigwam Mills, Inc.
Wijetunge, Dingiri Banda (pres., Sri Lanka)
Wil Shriner
Wil Wheaton
Wilander, Mats (tennis)
Wilberforce, William (Br. reformer; 1759-1833)
Wilbur D. Mills (US pol.; 1910-92)
Wilbur Wright (US aviator/inv.; 1867-1912)
Wilcox, Ella Wheeler (US poet; 1850-1919)
Wild Bill Davison (US jazz; 1906-89)
Wild Bill (James Butler) Hickok (US frontier/law; 1837-76)
Wild Eights (also Crazy Eights)(card game)
Wild Kingdom (TV show)
Wild West (also old West)
Wild, Wild West, The (TV show)
Wilde, Brandon De (ent.; 1942-72)
Wilde, Cornel (ent; 1915-89)
Wilde, Oscar (Fingal O'Flahertie Wills)(Ir. writer; 1854-1900)
Wilder, Billy (Samuel)(ent./writer; 1906-)
Wilder, (Lawrence) Douglas (ex-gov., VA; 1931-)
Wilder, Gene (ent.; 1935-)
Wilder, Laura Ingalls (US writer; 1867-1957)
Wilder, Thornton (Niven)(US writer; 1897-1975)
Wilderness of Zin
Wilderness Road (route for settlers of old West)
Wilderness, Battle of the (US hist.; 1864)
Wilding, Michael (ent.; 1912-79)
Wiley Blount Rutledge, Jr. (US jurist; 1894-1949)
Wiley Post (US aviator; 1899-1935)
Wilford Brimley (ent.; 1934-)
Wilfredo Lam (Cuban artist; 1902-82)
Wilfried Martens (ex-PM, Belgium; 1936-)
Wilhelm Friedemann Bach (Ger. comp.; 1710-84)
Wilhelm (Karl) Grimm (Ger. writer/linguist; 1786-1859)
Wilhelm Mauser (Ger. inv.; 1834-82)
Wilhelm Ostwald (Ger. chem.; 1853-1932)
Wilhelm Reich (Aus. phys.; 1897-1957)
Wilhelm (Conrad) Roentgen (Ger. physt., x-rays; 1845-1923)
Wilhelmina I (Wilhelmina Helena Pauline Maria [of Orange-Nassau])(queen, Netherlands; 1880-1962)
Wilhelmshaven, Germany
Wilie Mosconi (billiards; 1913-)
Wilkens, Mac Maurice (track; 1950-)
Wilkes-Barre, PA
Wilkins, Domique (basketball; 1960-)
Wilkins, Lennie (basketball; 1937-)

Wilkins, Roy (US jour./reformer; 1901-81)
Wilkinson Sword, Inc.
Wilkinson, Bud (football; 1916-)
Will & Baumer Candle Co., Inc.
Will Durant (US hist.; 1885-1981)
Will Geer (ent.; 1902-78)
Will K. Kellogg (US bus.; 1860-1951)
Will(iam Penn Adair) Rogers (ent.; 1879-1935)
Will Scarlet (fict. chara., *Robin Hood*)
Will Smith (ent.; 1969-)
Will, George (US jour.; 1941-)
Willa (Sibert) Cather (US writer; 1873-1947)
Willamette Industries, Inc.
Willamette National Forest
Willamette River (OR)
Willard Scott (ent./meteor.)
Willard Waterman (ent.)
Willard, Archibald M. (US artist; 1836-1918)
Willard, Emma (Hart)(US educ.; 1787-1870)
Willard, Frances E(lizabeth Caroline)(US educ./reformer; 1839-98)
Willard, Frank (cartoonist, *Moon Mullins*; 1893-1958)
Willard, Nancy (writer/artist; 1936-)
Willebrod Snell (Dutch math./physt.; 1581-1626)
Willem Dafoe (ent.; 1955-)
Willem de Kooning (US artist; 1904-)
Willemstad, Netherlands Antilles
Willi Baumeister (Ger. artist; 1889-1955)
William A. Anders (astro.; 1933-)
William and Mary, College of (VA)
William Atherton (ent.; 1947-)
William A(lmon) Wheeler (ex-US VP; 1819-87)
William Baffin (Br. nav.; 1584-1622)
William Baldwin (ent.; 1963-)
William Barclay "Bat" Masterson (US marshal; 1853-1921)
William Baziotes (US artist; 1912-63)
William Beebe, (Charles)(US nat./expl./writer; 1877-1962)
William Bendix (ent.; 1906-64)
William Blackstone, Sir (Br. jurist; 1723-80)
William Blake (Br. poet/artist; 1757-1827)
William Bligh (Br. captain, H.M.S. *Bounty*; 1754-1817)
William Booth ("General Booth")(Br., founded Salvation Army; 1829-1912)
William Boyd (ent.; 1898-1972)
William Bradford (1st gov., Pilgrim colony; 1590-1657)
William Brewster (Br., Pilgrim leader; 1567-1644)
William B(radford) Shockley, Dr. (US physt.; 1910-89)
William Butler Yeats (Ir. writer; 1865-1939)
William Byrd (Br. comp.; 1543-1623)
William Carlos Williams (US poet; 1883-1963)

William Caslon (Br. typographer; 1692-1766)
William Caxton (1st English printer; c1422-91)
William C. Bullitt (US dipl.; 1891-1967)
William C. Durant (US bus./auto.; 1861-1947)
William C. Gargas (US phys.; 1854-1920)
William Chambers, Sir (Br. arch.; 1723-96)
William Christopher (ent.; 1932-)
William Claire Menninger (US psych.; 1899-1966)
William Clarke Quantrill (US mil./outlaw; 1837-65)
William Colgate (US bus.; 1783-1857)
William Congreve (Br. writer; 1670-1729)
William Conrad (ent.; 1920-)
William C. Procter (US bus./soap; 1862-1934)
William Cowper (Br. judge; 1665?-1723)
William Cowper (Br. phys.; 1666-1709)
William Cowper (Br. poet; 1731-1800)
William Crookes, Sir (Br. physt./chem.; 1832-1919)
William C. Steinkraus (equestrian; 1925-)
William Cullen Bryant (US poet/jour.; 1794-1878)
William Daniel Leahy (US adm.; 1875-1959)
William Daniels (ent.; 1927-)_
William Demarest (ent.; 1892-1983)
William Devane (ent.; 1937-)
William Donald Schaefer (MD gov.; 1921-)
William Dudley Haywood (US labor leader; 1869-1928)
William E. Borah (US pol.; 1865-1940)
William Edward Parry, Sir (Br. expl.; 1790-1855)
William E(wart) Gladstone (ex-PM, Br.; 1809-98)
William Ellery Channing (US rel.; 1780-1842)
William Faulkner (US writer; 1897-1962)
William F. Buckley, Jr. (US editor/writer; 1925-)
William F(rederick) Cody, (Buffalo Bill)(Amer. scout/ent.; 1846-1917)
William F(rederick) Halsey (US mil.; 1882-1959)
William Foxwell Albright (US archaeol..; 1891-1971)
William Franklin "Billy" Graham, Rev. (US rel.; 1918-)
William Frawley (ent.; 1887-1966)
William Friedkin (ent.; 1939-)
William F. Weld (MA gov.; 1945-)
William Gaddis (US writer; 1922-)
William George Fargo (US bus.; 1818-81)
William George Hayden (gov-gen., Austl.)
William Gilbert, Sir (Br. physt./phys.; 1540-1603)
William (James) Glackens (US artist; 1870-1938)
William G. McGowan (US bus.; 1928-92)

William (Gerald) Golding (US writer; 1912-93)
William Goldman (US writer; 1931-)
William Green (US labor leader; 1873-1952)
William Gregg (US bus.; 1800-67)
William Harrison Ainsworth (Br. writer; 1805-82)
William Harvey (Br. phys.; 1578-1657)
William Haughton (harness racing; 1923-86)
William Henry Bonney ("Billy the Kid")(US outlaw; 1859-81)
William Henry Bragg, Sir (Br. physt.; 1862-1942)
William Henry Fox Talbot (Br. photo.; 1800-77)
William Henry Harrison (9th US pres.; 1773-1841)
William Henry "Bill" Mauldin (US writer/cartoonist; 1921-)
William Henry Seward (US pol.; 1801-72)
William Henry Vanderbilt (US bus./finan.; 1821-85)
William Hill Winery (US bus.)
William H(owell) Masters, Dr. (US phys./writer; 1915-)
William H(olmes) McGuffey (US educ.; 1800-73)
William Hogarth (Br. artist; 1697-1764)
William Howard Taft (27th US pres.; 1857-1930)
William Howe, Sir (Br. mil.; 1729-1814)
William H(enry) Pickering (US astron.; 1858-1938)
William H(ubbs) Rehnquist (US jurist; 1924-)
William Hurt (ent.; 1950-)
William I (b. Friedrich Wilhelm Viktor Albert)(emp., Ger.; 1859-1941)
William I (b. Willem Frederik)(king, Netherlands; 1772-1843)
William I (the Conqueror)(king, Eng.; 1027-87)
William II (b. Wilhelm Friedrich Ludwig)(emp., Ger.; 1797-1888)
William II (b. Willem Frederik George Lodewijk)(king, Netherlands; 1792-1849)
William II (Rufus, the Red)(king, Eng.; c1056-1100)
William III (b. Willem Alexander Paul Frederik Lodewijk)(king, Netherlands; 1817-90)
William III (of Orange)(king, Br./Ir.; 1650-1702)
William (Motter) Inge (US writer; 1913-73)
William (Ralph) Inge (Br. rel.; 1860-1954)
William IV (king, Br./Ir.; 1765-1837)
William James (US phil./psych.; 1842-1910)
William Janklow (SD gov.)
William J(oseph) Brennan, Jr. (US jurist; 1906-)
William J. Casey (ex-dir./FBI; 1914-87)
William Jefferson Clinton ("Bill")(42nd US Pres.; 1946-)
William Jenner (Br. phys.; 1815-98)
William Jennings Bryan (US pol./orator; 1860-

1925)
William Katt (ent.)
William Kennedy (US writer; 1928-)
William Kennedy Smith (US news)
William Kidd (aka Captain Kidd)(Scot. pirate; 1645?-1701)
William Kunstler (US atty.; 1919-)
William Lawrence Bragg, Sir (Br. physt.; 1890-1971)
William Lily(e)(Br. scholar; c1468-1522)
William Lloyd Garrison (US reformer; 1805-79)
William Lyon Mackenzie King (ex-PM, Can.; 1874-1950)
William Makepeace Thackeray (Br. writer; 1811-63)
William Manchester (US writer; 1922-)
William Maxwell Beaverbrook, Baron (aka Lord Beaverbrook)(Br. finan./pol.; 1879-1964)
William McKinley (25th US pres.; 1843-1901)
William M. Gaines (US publ.; 1922-92)
William Morris (Br. designer; 1834-96)
William Morris Agency, Inc.
William Moses (ent.; 1959-)
William M(arcy) Tweed ("Boss Tweed")(US pol.; 1823-78)
William O(rville) Douglas (US jurist; 1898-1980)
William of Occam (Br. phil.; c1285-c1349)
William of Orange (William III)(king, Br./Ir.; 1650-1702)
William Paley (Br. rel.; 1743-1805)
William Penn (Br. Quaker, founded PA; 1644-1718)
William Pereira (US arch.; 1909-85)
William Philip Arthur Louis (eldest son of Prince Charles & Princess Diana)
William Pitt, the Elder (the "Great Commoner") (ex-PM, Br.; 1708-78)
William Pitt, the Younger (ex-PM, Br.; 1759-1806)
William Pogue (astro.)
William Powell (ent.; 1892-1984)
William (Hickling) Prescott (US hist.; 1796-1859)
William Proxmire, (Edward)(US pol.; 1915-)
William Randolph Hearst (US publ.; 1863-1951)
William Randolph Hearst, Jr. (US publ.; 1908-93)
William "Bill" Richardson (US cong.; 1947-)
William Rigney (baseball; 1918-)
William R. Higgins (US mil.)
William Riker, Commander (fict. chara., *Star Trek*)
William R(ufus De Vane) King (ex.US VP; 1786-1853)
William Rockefeller (US bus./finan.; 1841-1922)
William Safire (US jour.; 1929-)
William Sanderson (ent.; 1948-)

William Saroyan (US writer; 1908-81)
William Schallert (ent.; 1922-)
William (Howard) Schuman (US comp.; 1910-92)
William S. Cohen (US cong.; 1940-)
William Scoresby (Br. expl.; 1789-1857)
William Shakespeare (Br. writer; 1564-1616)
William S(hakespeare) Hart (ent.; 1870?-1946)
William Shatner (ent.; 1931-)
William S. Knudsen (US bus.; 1879-1848)
William S. Paley (US TV exec.; 1901-90)
William S. Sessions (ex-dir./FBI; 1930-)
William Steig (cartoonist, *New Yorker*; 1907-)
William (Clark) Styron, Jr. (US writer; 1925-)
William Sydney Porter (pseud. O Henry)(US writer; 1862-1910)
William Tell (legendary Swiss patriot; 14th c.)
William the Conqueror (William I)(king, Eng.; 1027-87)
William the Lion (king, Scot.; 1143-1214)
William the Silent (Dutch, Prince of Orange; 1533-84)
William Thomas Cosgrave (Ir. pol.; 1880-1965)
William Thomson Kelvin, Lord (Br. physt./ math.; 1824-1907)
William (Tatem) "Big Bill" Tilden, Jr. (tennis; 1893-1953)
William Toomey (decathlon; 1939-)
William T(ecumseh) Sherman (US gen.; 1820-91)
William Victor Roth, Jr. (US cong.; 1921-)
William (Turner) Walton, Sir (Br. comp.; 1902-83)
William Warfield (ent.; 1920-)
William (Childs) Westmoreland (US gen.; 1914-)
William Wilberforce (Br. reformer; 1759-1833)
William Windom (ent.; 1923-)
William Wordsworth (Br. poet; 1770-1850)
William Wrigley, Jr. (US bus., gum/baseball; 1861-1932)
William Wrigley, Jr. Co.
William Wurster (US arch.; 1895-1973)
William Wyndham Grenville, Baron (Br. pol.; 1759-1834)
William, pear (liqueur)
Williams Co., Sherwin-
Williams-Sonoma (US bus.)
Williams, Andy (ent.; 1930-)
Williams, Billy Dee (ent.; 1937-)
Williams, Charles "Cootie" (US jazz; 1908-85)
Williams, Cindy (ent.; 1947-)
Williams, Del (football; 1945-84)
Williams, Dick (baseball; 1929-)
Williams, Edward Bennett (US atty.; 1920-88)
Williams, Esther (ent., swimmer; 1923-)
Williams, Gunther Gebel-
Williams, Guy (ent.; 1924-89)

Williams, Hal (ent.; 1938-)
Williams, Hank (ent.; 1923-53)
Williams, Hank, Jr. (ent.; 1939-)
Williams, JoBeth (ent.; 1953-)
Williams, Joe (ent.; 1918-)
Williams, John (US comp./cond.; 1932-)
Williams, Mary Lou (US jazz; 1914-81)
Williams, Matt (baseball; 1965-)
Williams, Mitch (baseball; 1964-)
Williams, Montel (ent.)
Williams, Paul (ent.; 1940-)
Williams, Ralph Vaughan (Br. comp.; 1872-
    1958)
Williams, Robin (ent.; 1952-)
Williams, Roger (ent.)
Williams, Roger (US rel.; c1603-83)
Williams, Ted (Theodore Samuel)(baseball;
    1918-)
Williams, Tennessee (Thomas Lanier)(US
    writer; 1914-83)
Williams, Treat (ent.; 1951-)
Williams, Vanessa (ent.; 1963-)
Williams, William Carlos (US poet; 1883-1963)
Williamsburg, VA
Williamsport, PA
Willie Davenport (track; 1943-)
Willie (Howard) Mays (baseball; 1931-)
Willie McCovey (baseball; 1938-)
Willie Nelson (ent.; 1933-)
Willie (William Lee) Shoemaker (US jockey;
    1931-)
Willie "The Lion" Smith (US jazz; 1897-1973)
Willie Stargell (baseball; 1941-)
Willie Sutton (US bank robber; 1901-80)
Willie Winkie, Wee (fict. chara.)
Willis Reed (basketball; 1942-)
Willis, Bruce (ent.; 1955-)
Willkie, Wendell L(ewis)(US pol.; 1892-1944)
Wills, Chill (ent.; 1903-78)
Wills (Moody), Helen Newington (tennis; 1906-)
Wills, Maury (baseball; 1932-)
Willy (Herbert Ernst Karl Frahm) Brandt (ex-
    chanc., WGer.; 1913-92)
Willy Loman (fict. chara., *Death of a Salesman*)
Willy (Wilhelm) Messerschmitt (Ger. airplane
    designer; 1898-1978)
Willy Wonka Brands (US bus.)
Willy, Chilly (cartoon chara.)
Willye B. White (jumper; 1936-)
Wilma (Glodean) Rudolph (runner; 1940-)
Wilmington News Journal (DE newspaper)
Wilmington, DE, MA, NC, OH
Wilmot Proviso (US hist.; 1846)
Wilson Sporting Goods Co.
Wilson, August (US writer; 1945-)
Wilson, Brian (ent.; 1942-)
Wilson, Demond (ent.; 1946-)
Wilson, Edmund (US writer/critic; 1895-1972)

Wilson, Edward O. (US zool.; 1929-)
Wilson, Elizabeth (ent.; 1925-)
Wilson, Flip (ent.; 1933-)
Wilson, Gahan (US cartoonist; 1930-)
Wilson, Sir (James) Harold (ex-PM, Br.; 1916-)
Wilson, Henry (ex-US VP; 1812-75)
Wilson, Jackie (ent.)
Wilson, Lanford (US writer; 1937-)
Wilson, Marie (ent.; 1917-72)
Wilson, Meredith (US comp.; 1902-84)
Wilson, Nancy (ent.; 1937-)
Wilson, Pete (CA gov.; 1933-)
Wilson, Teddy (US jazz; 1912-86)
Wilson, Tom (cartoonist, *Ziggy*; 1931-)
Wilson, (Thomas) Woodrow (28th US pres.;
    1856-1924)
Wilt (Norman) Chamberlain (Wilt the
    Stilt)(basketball; 1936-)
Wilton (carpet)
Wilton Corp.
Wilton Industries, Inc.
Wiltshire (county, Eng.)
Wimbledon (tennis, London)
Wimsey, Lord Peter (fict. chara., D. Sayers)
Win, Ne (b. Maung Shu Maung)(ex-pres.,
    Myanmar; 1911-)
Winchell, Walter (US newscaster; 1897-1972)
Winchester Cathedral (Eng.)
Winchester drive/disk (compu.)
Winchester™ rifle
Winchester, England
Winchester, MA, VA
Wind Cave National Park (SD)
Wind in the Willows, The (by K. Grahame)
Wind Song™ (perfume)
Windbreaker™ (jacket)
Windemere Press, Inc.
Windermere, Lake (Eng.)
Windex™ (cleaner)
Windhoek, Namibia
Winding, Kai (US jazz; 1922-83)
Windmere™ (appliances)
Windmere Corp.
Windom, William (ent.; 1923-)
Window Rock, AZ
Windows™ (compu.)
Windows Computer Magazine (mag.)
Windscale (now Sellafield)(Cumbria,
    Eng.)(nuclear accident; 1957)
Windsor Castle (residence, Br. royalty)
Windsor chair
Windsor knot
Windsor tie
Windsor Vineyards & Great River Winery (US
    bus.)
Windsor, CT
Windsor, Duchess of (Wallis "Wally" Warfield
    Simpson)(US socialite, m. Edward VIII; 1896-

1986)

Windsor, Duke of (Edward VIII)(abdicated Br. throne; 1894-1972)

Windsor, England (officially Windsor and Maidenhead)

Windsor, House of (Br. ruling family; 1910-present)

Windsor, Ontario, Canada

Windward Islands, Lesser Antilles (Grenada, Barbados, St. Vincent, St. Lucia, Martinque, Dominica, Guadeloupe)

Windward Passage (channel, Haiti/Cuba)

Windy City (Chicago)

Winesap (apple)

Winfield Scott ("Old Fuss and Feathers")(US gen.; 1786-1866)

Winfield, Dave (baseball; 1951-)

Winfield, Paul (ent.; 1941-)

Winfrey, Oprah (ent.; 1954-)

Wing, Red (Tantangamini)(Sioux leader; c1750-c1825)

Winger, Debra (ent.; 1955-)

Wings (TV show)

Wingti, Paias (PM, Papua New Guinea; 1951-)

Winkerbean, Funky (comic strip)

Winkie, Wee Willie (fict. chara.)

Winkle, The Tale of Mrs. Tiggy- (B. Potter story)

Winkle, Rip Van (by W. Irving)

Winkler, Henry (ent.; 1945-)

Winn-Dixie Stores, Inc.

Winnebago (NAmer. Indians)

Winnebago Industries, Inc.

Winnebago™ RV

Winnebago, Lake (WI)

Winnemucca, NV

Winnetka, IL

Winnie (Nomzamo) Mandela (SAfr. pol./reformer; 1934-)

Winnie-the-Pooh (A. A. Milne children's stories)

Winnipeg (Can. river)

Winnipeg Free Press

Winnipeg Jets (hockey team)

Winnipeg, Lake (Can.)

Winnipeg, Manitoba, Canada

Winona Ryder (ent.; 1971-)

Winslow Homer (US artist; 1836-1910)

Winslow, AZ

Winston (Leonard Spencer) Churchill, Sir (ex-PM, Br.; 1874-1965)

Winston Churchill (US writer; 1871-1947)

Winston-Salem, NC

Winston-Salem Journal (NC newspaper)

Winston, Harry (US bus./diamonds

Winston, Inc., Harry

Winter Haven, FL

Winter King, the (Frederick V)(king, Bohemia for one winter; 1596-1632)

Winter of Our Discontent, The (J. Steinbeck novel)

Winter Olympics

Winter Park, FL

Winter's Tale, The (Shakespeare play)

Winters, Jonathan (ent.; 1925-)

Winters, Shelley (ent.; 1922-)

Winthrop Rockefeller (ex-gov., AR; 1912-73)

Winthrop, John (Br./Amer., ex-gov., MA; 1588-1649)

Winthrop, John (ex-gov., CT; 1606-76)

Winthrop, John (or Fitz-John)(ex-gov., CT; 1638-1707)

Winthrop, John (US astron./math./physt.; 1714-79)

Winwood, Steve (ent.; 1948-)

Wirephoto™ (comm.)

Wisconsin (WI)

Wisconsin Cheese (US bus.)

Wisconsin v. Mitchell (US law; 1993)

Wise Foods (US bus.)

Wise Men of the East (also Magi, Three Kings of the Orient, Three Wise Men)(rel.)

Wisk™ detergent

Witches of Eastwick, The (film; 1987)

Wite-Out Products, Inc.

Withers, Jane (ent.; 1926-)

Witherspoon, John (US rel.; 1723-94)

Witness Protection Program (US govt.)

Witt, James Lee (Dir./Fed Emergency Mgmt Agy; 1944-)

Witt, Katarina (Ger. figure skating; 1965-)

Witt, Paul Junger

Witter Reynolds, Inc., Dean

Wittgenstein, Ludwig (Josef Johann)(Aus. phil.; 1889-1951)

Witwatersrand (also the Rand)(SAfr. gold mining area)

Wiz, The (play/film)

Wizard™ (air freshener)

Wizard of Id (comic strip)

Wizard of Oz, The (by L.F. Baum)

Wizard's World, Mr. (TV show)

WKRP in Cincinnati (TV show)

W(enzel) L(othar) Metternich, Clemens (Prince von Metternich)(ex-chanc., Aus.; 1773-1859)

WO (warrant officer)

Wobblies (members Industrial Workers of the World)

Wobegon, Lake (fict. town, G. Keillor)

Wodan (also Woden, Odin, Wotan)(myth.)

Wodehouse, Sir P(elham) G(renville)(US writer/humorist; 1881-1975)

Woden (also Odin, Wotan, Wodan)(myth.)

Wofford, Harris (US cong.; 1926-)

Wojceich Jaruzelski (ex-pres., Pol.; 1923-)

Wojtyla, Karol (Pope John Paul II)(Pol. pope; 1920-)

Wole Soyinka (Nigerian writer; 1934-)

Wolf-Ferrari, Ermanno (It. comp.; 1876-1948)

Wolf Trap Farm Park for the Performing Arts (VA)

Wolf, Burt (US chef/writer)

Wolf, Hugo (Aus. comp.; 1860-1903)

Wolfe, Billy De (ent.; 1907-74)

Wolfe, Nero (fict. detective)

Wolfe, Thomas (Clayton)(US writer; 1900-38)

Wolfe, Tom (b. Thomas Kennerly Wolfe, Jr.)(US writer; 1931-)

Wolff Industries, Inc.

Wolff Shoe Co.

Wolff, Tobias (US writer; 1945-)

Wolfgang Amadeus Mozart (Aus. comp.; 1756-91)

Wolfgang Pauli (Aus. physt.; 1900-58)

Wolfgang Puck (chef)

Wolfman Jack (disc jockey, *American Graffiti*)

Wollongong, New South Wales, Australia

Wollstonecraft, Mary (Br. reformer; 1759-97)

Wolof (lang./people)

Wolper, David L. (ent.)

Wolsey, Thomas, Cardinal (Br. rel./pol.; 1475-1530)

Wolverine (cartoon chara.)

Wolverine State (nickname, MI)

Wolverine World Wide Corp.

Woman's Christian Temperance Union, National (WCTU)

Woman's Day (mag.)

Woman's World (mag.)

Women Voters, League of

Women's Army Corps (WAC)(US mil.; est. 1942)

Women's Wear Daily (trade paper/garment industry)

Wonder Bar Products, Inc.

Wonder State (nickname, AR)

Wonder Woman (comic, TV show)

Wonder Years, The (TV show)

Wonder, Stevie (b. Steveland Judkins Morris)(ent.; 1950-)

Wong, Suzy

Wonka Brands, Willy (US bus.)

Wonsan, North Korea

Woo, Roh Tae (ex-pres., SKorea; 1932-)

Wood Reading Dynamics, Evelyn (US bus.)

Wood, Danny (ent.; 1969-)

Wood, Fort Leonard (MO)(mil.)

Wood, Grant (US artist; 1891-1942)

Wood, Kimba (US atty.)

Wood, Natalie (ent.; 1938-81)

Wood, Peggy (ent.; 1892-1978)

Wood, Smokey (Joseph)(baseball; 1890-1985)

Woodard, Alfre (ent.; 1953-)

Wooden, John R. (basketball; 1910-)

Woodhead, Cynthia (swimming; 1964-)

Woodhouse, Barbara (Br. dog trainer)

Woodhull, Victoria Claflin (US publ./reformer; 1838-1927)

Woodiwiss, Kathleen (writer)

Woodpecker, Woody (cartoon)

Woodrow Wilson, (Thomas)(28th US pres.; 1856-1924)

Woods Hole Oceanographic Institution (MA)

Woods, James (ent.; 1947-)

Woods, Lake of the (Ontario, Can.)

Woodstock Festival (also Woodstock Music & Art Fair)(NY rock festival; 1969)

Woodstock, NY

Woodward & Bernstein (Watergate reporters)

Woodward, Bob (US jour.; 1943-)

Woodward, Edward (ent.; 1930-)

Woodward, Joanne (ent.; 1930-)

Woodward, Trustees of Dartmouth College v. (US law; 1819)

Woody Allen (b. Allen Stewart Konigsberg)(ent.; 1935-)

Woody (Woodrow Wilson) Guthrie (ent.; 1912-67)

Woody Hayes (football; 1913-87)

Woody Harrelson (ent.; 1961-)

Woody Woodpecker (cartoon)

Woolco™ (stores)

Woolery, Chuck (ent.)

Woolf, Leonard Sidney (Br. writer; 1880-1969)

Woolf, (Adeline) Virginia (Stephen)(Br. writer; 1882-1941)

Woolf?, Who's Afraid of Virginia (film; 1966)

Woolite™ (soap)

Woollcott, Alexander (US writer; 1887-1943)

Woolley, Monty (ent.; 1888-1963)

Woolsey, R. James (Director/CIA; 1941-)

Woolworth Building (NYC)

Woolworth Co., F. W.

Woolworth, Frank W(infield)(US bus.; 1852-1919)

Woolworth's™ (stores)

Woonsocket, RI

Wopat, Tom

Worcester china/porcelain (also Royal Worcester)

Worcester Telegram Gazette (MA newspaper)

Worcester Telegraph (MA newspaper)

Worcester, England

Worcester, MA

Worcestershire sauce

Word of God, the

Word, Microsoft™ (compu.)

Worden, Alfred M. (astro.; 1932-)

WordPerfect™ (compu.)

WordPerfect Corp.

WordStar™ (compu.)

WordStar International, Inc.

Wordsworth, Dorothy (Br. writer; 1771-1855)

Wordsworth, William (Br. poet; 1770-1850)

Worf, Lieutenant (fict. chara., *Star Trek*)

Workbasket, The (mag.)
Workbench (mag.)
Working Mother (mag.)
Working Woman (mag.)
Works Projects Administration (WPA)(also
    Works Progress Administration)(US hist;
    1935-43)
World According to Garp, The (J. Irving novel)
World Bank (International Bank for
    Reconstruction and Development)(UN; est.
    1945)
World Council of Churches (WCC)(est. 1945)
World Court (also United Nations Permanent
    Court of International Justice)(est. 1945)
World Cup (soccer)
World Day of Prayer
World Ecology Report (mag.)
World Health Day (UN)
World Health Organization (WHO)(UN; est.
    1946)
World-Herald, Omaha (NE newspaper)
World Intellectual Property Organization
    (WIPO)(UN; est. 1974)
World Meteorological Organization (WMO)(UN;
    est. 1947)
World Savings & Loan Association
World Series (baseball)
World Trade Center (NYC)
World War I (also WWI, First World War)(1914-
    18)
World War I Allies (chiefly Fr., Br., Rus., US)
World War I Central Powers (Ger., Aus-Hung.,
    Turk.)
World War II (also WWII, Second World War)
    (1939-45)
World War II Allies (chiefly Br., US, USSR,
    Ch.)
World War II Axis Powers (Ger., Jap., It.)
World Wide Fund for Nature (WWF)(formerly
    World Wildlife Fund)(est. 1961)
World, Third (less developed nations)
Worldwatch Institute
Worley, Jo Anne (ent.)
Worms, Diet of (rel. hist.; 1521)
Worms, Germany
Worship, Your (title)
Worth, Fort (TX)(city)
Worth, Mary (cartoon chara.)
Worthy, James (basketball; 1961-)
Wotan (also Woden, Odin, Wodan)(myth.)
Wottle, David James (runner; 1950-)
Wouk, Herman (US writer; 1915-)
Woulff bottle (chem.)
Wounded Knee (SD)(US Army/Sioux conflict;
    1890)
Wozniak, Stephen (US bus./inv./compu.; 1950-)
WPA (Works Projects Administration)
WPM (also wpm)(words per minute)

WRAC (Women's Royal Army Corps)
WRAF (Women's Royal Air Force)
Wrangell-St. Elias National Park (AK)
Wrangler Co.
Wrather, Jack
Wray, Fay (ent.; 1907-)
Wreck of the Hesperus, The (by. H.W.
    Longfellow)
Wren, Sir Christopher (Br. arch./astron./math.;
    1632-1723)
Wrexham, Wales
W. R. Grace & Co.
Wright brothers (Wilbur & Orville)
Wright Morris (US writer; 1910-)
Wright Patterson Air Force Base, OH
Wright, Frank Lloyd (US arch.; 1867-1959)
Wright, Martha (ent.; 1926-)
Wright, Mickey (Mary Kathryn)(golf; 1935-)
Wright, Orville (US aviator/inv.; 1871-1948)
Wright, Steven (ent.; 1955-)
Wright, Teresa (ent.; 1918-)
Wright, Wilbur (US aviator/inv.; 1867-1912)
Wrigley Field (Chicago)
Wrigley, Philip K. (US bus., gum/baseball;
    1895-1977)
Wrigley, Jr. Co., William
Wrigley, William, Jr. (US bus., gum/baseball;
    1861-1932)
Wrigley's™ gum
Wrinkle in Time, A (book)
Wriothesley, Henry (Earl of Southhampton)(Br.
    scholar; 1573-1624)
Writer, The (mag.)
Writer's Digest (mag.)
Wroclaw, Poland
W(illiam) S(chwenck) Gilbert (Br. writer; 1836-
    1911)
W(illiam) Somerset Maugham (Br. writer; 1874-
    1965)
Wu (lang.)
Wuhan, China (also Han Cities)
Wuppertal, Germany
Wurlitzer™
Wurlitzer Co., The
Wurster, William (US arch.; 1895-1973)
Wurtsmith Air Force Base, MI
Wuthering Heights (E. Brontë novel)
WV (West Virginia)
WWI (World War I, First World War)(1914-18)
WWII (World War II, Second World War)(1939-
    45)
WY (Wyoming)
Wyandotte (chicken)
Wyandotte, MI
Wyatt (Berry Stapp) Earp (US frontier; 1848-
    1929)
Wyatt, Jane (ent.; 1911-)
Wycliffe, John (Br. rel.; c1320-84)

Wyeth, Andrew N(ewell)(US artist; 1917-)
Wyeth, James Browning (US artist; 1946-)
Wyeth, N(ewel) C(onvers)(US artist; 1882-1945)
Wylie, Elinor (US poet; 1885-1928)
Wyman, Jane (ent.; 1914-)
Wynette, Tammy (ent.; 1942-)
Wynken, Blynken & Nod (E. Field poem)
Wynn, Ed (ent.; 1886-1966)
Wynn, Keenan (ent.; 1916-86)
Wynn, Tracy Keenan
Wynonna Judd (ent.; 1964-)
Wynton Marsalis (US jazz; 1961-)
Wyomia Tyus (track; 1945-)
Wyoming (WY)
WYSIWYG (compu., what you see is what you
    get)
Wyss, Johann David (Swiss writer; 1743-1818)
Wyss, Johann Rudolf (Swiss writer; 1782-1830)
Wyszynski, Stefan, Cardinal (Pol. rel.; 1901-81)
Wythe, George (US jurist; 1726-1806)

X

X, Malcolm (b. Malcolm Little)(US black-rights activist; 1926-65)
X-Acto™ knife
X-Acto, Inc.
Xanadu (film; 1980)
Xanadu (legendary utopian city)
Xanax™ (med.)
Xantac™ (med.)
Xanthippe (wife of Socrates; late 5th c BC)(ill-tempered)
Xavier Cugat (Sp./US cond.; 1920-90)
Xavier, Francis, St. (Francisco Javier)("the Apostle of the Indies")(Sp. rel.; 1506-52)
X chromosome (med.)
Xe (chem. sym., xenon)
XEC5™ (CAT system)
XEC-2001™ (CAT system)
Xenocrates (Gr. phil.; 396-14 BC)
Xenophanes (Gr. phil./poet; c570-c480 BC)
Xenophon (Gr. hist.; c434-c355 BC)
Xerox™ (copiers)
Xerox Corp.
Xerxes I (king, Persia; c519-465 BC)
X-Files, The (TV show)
Xhosa (lang./people)
Xi Jiang River (also Si-Kiang)(Ch.)
Xia dynasty (also Hsia)(Ch.; 2205-1766 BC)
Xian, China (also Sian)
Xiang (lang.)
Xiangtan, China (also Siangtan)
Xiaoping, Deng (also Teng Hsiao-ping)(Ch. pol.; 1904-)
Xingú (region, Brazil)
Xining, China (also Sining)
Xinjiang Uygur (also Sinkiang Uighur)(region, Ch.)
Xinxiang, China (also Sinsiang)
Xipe (myth.)
Xmas (abbrev., Christmas)
X-Men, The (cartoon charas.)
Xochipilli (myth.)
Xscribe Corp.
Xylocaine™ (med.)
XYZ Affair (US hist.; 1797-98)

Y

Y (chem. sym., yttrium)
Yaacov Agam (Isr. artist; 1928-)
Yablonski, Joseph A. (US labor leader; ?-1969)
Yaga, Baba (myth. monster, eats children)
Yahoo (fict. chara./race, *Gulliver's Travels*) (lower case as lout, yokel)
Yahtzee (game)
Yahweh (Jehovah)(rel.)
Yajur-Veda (rel.)
Yakima (NAmer. Indians)
Yakima, WA
Yakov Smirnoff
Yakovlev, Aleksandr N. (Rus. pol.)
Yakovlev, Aleksandr S. (Rus. airplane designer; 1905-89)
Yakut (people)
Yale University (CT)
Yale, Elihu (US bus./finan.; 1649-1721)
Yalta Conference (Churchill [UK]/Roosevelt [US]/Stalin [USSR]; 1945)
Yalta, Crimea
Yalu River (Korea/Ch.)(also Amnok)
Yama (Hindu god of the dead)
Yamaguchi, Kristi (figure skating; 1971-)
Yamaha Corp. of America
Yamaha Motor Corp. USA
Yamasaki, Minoru (US arch,; 1912-86)
Yamoussoukro, Ivory Coast
Yanbu al-Bahr, Saudi Arabia
Yancey, Jimmy (US jazz; 1894-1951)
Yang Shangkun (ex-pres., Ch.; 1907-)
Yang, Chen Ning (Ch./US physt.; 1922-)
Yang, Lee and (Ch. physicists)
Yangon, Myanmar (formerly Rangoon)
Yangtze Kiang River (also Chang Jiang)(Ch/)
Yankee (US northerner)
Yankee Doodle (song)
Yankee Doodle Dandy (song; film, 1942)
Yankee screwdriver™ (constr.)
Yankee Stadium (Bronx, NY)
Yankees, New York (baseball team)
Yankovic, Weird Al
Yanomano (also Yanomama)(lang./people)
Yao (lang./people)
Yaoundé, Cameroon
Yaphet Kotto (ent.; 1937-)
Yaqui River (Mex.)
Yaqui Indians/lang.)
Yarborough (card game term)
Yarborough, Barton
Yarborough, (William) Cal(eb)(auto racing; 1939-)
Yarborough, Glenn (ent.; 1930-)
Yarbro, Chelsea Quinn

Yard, (Mary Alexander) Molly (ex-pres., NOW)
Yardbirds, the (pop music)
Yardley of London, Inc.
Yaren, Nauru
Yarrow, Peter (ent.; 1938-)
Yasmin (Aga) Khan, Princess
Yassir Arafat (also Yasser)(PLO Chairman;
   1929-)
Yastrzemski, Carl (baseball; 1939-)
Yasuhiro, Nakasone (ex-PM, Jap.; 1917-)
Y(elberton) A(braham) Tittle (football; 1926-)
Yat-sen, Sun (Ch. pol./mil.; 1866-1925)
Yawkey, Jean R. (US bus./baseball; 1908-92)
Yazoo River (MS)
Yb (chem. sym., ytterbium)
Yeager, Chuck (Charles Elwood), Col. (US
   aviator; 1923-)
Yeats, W(illiam) B(utler)(Ir. writer; 1865-1939)
Yegorov, Boris B. (cosmo.; 1937-)
Yehudi Menuhin, Sir (Br. violinist; 1916-)
Yeliseyev, Aleksei (cosmo.; 1934-)
Yellen, Jack (US lyricist; 1892-1991)
Yeller, Old (F. Gipson novel)
Yellow Brick Road
Yellow Christ (by Gauguin)
Yellow Pages™
Yellow River (also Huang He)(Ch.)
Yellow Sea (also Huang Hai)(Ch./Korea)
Yellowknife, Northwest Territories, Canada
Yellowstone Falls (Yellowstone Nat'l Park)
Yellowstone Lake (Yellowstone Nat'l Park)
Yellowstone National Park (ID/MT/WY)
Yellowstone River (W US)
Yeltsin, Boris (Nikolayevich)(pres., Rus.; 1931-)
Yemen (Republic of)(SW Asia)
Yemen Airways
Yemen, North (now part of Yemen)
Yemen, South (now part of Yemen)
Yemenites (people)
Yenisei River (Rus.)
Yentl (film; 1983)
Yerby, Frank (US writer; 1916-92)
Yerevan, Armenia
YES™ (clothing)
Yes (pop music)
Yes Clothing Co.
Yevgeny Aleksandrovich Yevtushenko (Rus.
   poet; 1933-)
Yevgeny V(asilyevich) Khrunov (cosmo.; 1933-)
Yevtushenko, Yevgeny Aleksandrovich (Rus.
   poet; 1933-)
Yggdrasil (myth.)
Yhombi-Opango, Jacques-Joachim (PM, Congo;
   1940-)
Yi (lang./people)
Yichun (province, Ch.)
Yiddish (lang.)
Yield House, Inc.

Yip (E. Y.) Harburg (US lyricist; 1898-1981)
Yitzhak Rabin (PM, Isr.; 1922-)
Yitzhak Shamir (ex-PM, Isr.; 1915-)
YM (mag.)
Yma Sumac (Peru. ent.; 1927-)
YMCA (Young Men's Christian Association)
YMHA (Young Men's Hebrew Association)
Yoakam, Dwight (ent.)
Yogi & Friends (cartoon)
Yogi Bear (cartoon)
Yogi Bear Bunch (cartoon)
Yogi Bear's Jellystone Park Camp-Resort (US
   bus.)
Yogi (Lawrence Peter) Berra (baseball; 1925-)
Yogi, Maharishi Mahesh (Hindu guru)
Yoko Ono (ent.; 1933-)
Yokohama, Japan
Yom Kippur (Day of Atonement)(rel.)
Yom Kippur War (Eg., Syria/Isr.; 1973)
Yon Hyong Muk (ex-premier, NKorea)
Yonkers, NY
Yoo-Hoo Chocolate Beverage Corp.
Yoplait™ yogurt
Yoplait USA, Inc.
York Candies (US bus.)
York Dispatch (PA newspaper)
York News (PA newspaper)
York Record (PA newspaper)
York, Dick (ent.; 1929-92)
York, England
York, House of (Br. ruling family; 1461-70,
   1471-85)
York, Michael (ent.; 1942-)
York, Ontario, Canada
York, PA
York, Sergeant (Alvin Cullum)(US mil.; 1887-
   1964)
York, Susannah (ent.; 1942-)
Yorkin, Bud (ent.)
Yorkshire chair (also Derbyshire chair)
Yorkshire dresser
Yorkshire ham/hog
Yorkshire pudding
Yorkshire terrier (dog)
Yorktown Naval Weapons Station (VA)
Yorktown, Siege of (US hist.; 1781, 1862)
Yoruba (lang./people)
Yosemite Falls (Yosemite Nat'l Park)
Yosemite National Park (CA)
Yosuke Matsuoka (Jap. pol.; 1880-1946)
Yotanka, Tatanka (Chief Sitting Bull)(Sioux
   Indians; c1831-90)
Yothers, Tina
You Bet Your Life (radio/TV show)
You Can't Do That on Television (TV show)
You Can't Go Home Again (T. Wolfe novel)
Youmans, Vincent (US comp.; 1898-1946)
Young and Rubicom, Inc.

Young and the Restless (TV soap)
Young Frankenstein (film; 1974)
Young Memorial Museum, M. H. de (San Francisco)
Young Men's Christian Association (YMCA)(est. 1844)
Young Riders, The (TV show)
Young Turk (young rebel)
Young Women's Christian Association (YMCA)(est. 1855)
Young, Alan (ent.; 1919-)
Young, Andrew Jackson, Jr. (US dipl./pol.; 1932-)
Young, Art (pol. cartoonist; 1866-1943)
Young, Brigham (US rel./Mormon; 1801-77)
Young, Burt (ent.; 1940-)
Young, Chic (cartoonist, *Blondie*; 1901-73)
Young, Coleman (Detroit mayor; 1918-)
Young, Cy (Denton True)(baseball; 1867-1955)
Young, Dean (cartoonist)
Young, Gig (ent.; 1913-78)
Young, Inc., Ernst &
Young, John W(atts)(astro.; 1930-)
Young, Karen
Young, Loretta (ent.; 1913-)
Young, Neil (ent.; 1945-)
Young, Pres (Lester Willis)(US jazz; 1909-59)
Young, Robert (ent.; 1907-)
Young, Sheila (speed skating; 1950-)
Young, Steve (football; 1961-)
Young, Whitney M(oore), Jr. (US reformer; 1921-71)
Younger, (Thomas) Cole(man)(US outlaw; 1844-1916)
Youngstown Sheet and Tube Co. v. Sawyer (US law; 1952)
Youngstown Vindicator (OH newspaper)
Youngstown, OH
Your Cheatin' Heart (H. Williams song)
Your Eminence (title)
Your Excellency (title)
Your Grace (title)
Your Highness (title)
Your Holiness (title)
Your Honor (title)
Your Majesty (title)
Your Money (mag.)
Your Reverence (title)
Your Worship (title)
Youssouf Ouedraogo (PM, Burkina Faso)
Yoweri Kaguta Museveni (pres., Uganda; 1945-)
Yo-Yo Ma (US cellist; 1955-)
Ypsilanti, MI
Yüan (or Mongol) dynasty (Ch. ruling house; 1279-1368)
Yuban™ coffee
Yucatán (state, Mex.)
Yucatán peninsula (CAmer.)

Yue (lang.)
Yuga, Kali- (rel.)
Yugo™ car
Yugoslavia (Federal Republic of)(SE Eur.)
Yukio, Mishima (aka Hiraoka Kimitake)(Jap. writer; 1925-70)
Yukon River (NAmer.)
Yukon Territory (Can.)
Yukon, Fort (AK)(city)
Yul Brynner (ent.; 1915-85)
Yuma Indians
Yuma Proving Ground (AZ)
Yuma, AZ
Yum Yum Tree, Under the (film; 1963)
Yunnan (province, Ch.)
Yuppie
Yuri A(lexeyevich) Gagarin (cosmo.; 1st to orbit space; 1934-68)
Yuri Andropov (ex-pres., Rus.; 1914-84)
Yvan Serge Cournoyer (hockey; 1943-)
Yves Montand (Fr. ent.; 1921-91)
Yves (Henri Donat Mathieu) Saint-Laurent (Fr. designer; 1936-)
Yves St.-Laurent SA (US bus.)
Yves Tanguy (Fr. artist; 1900-55)
Yvette Mimieux (ent.)
Yvonne DeCarlo (ent.; 1922-)
YWCA (Young Women's Christian Association)
YWHA (Young Women's Hebrew Association)
Yzerman, Steve (hockey; 1965-)

Z

Zabanga, Mobutu Sese Seko Kuku Ngbendu wa (b. Joseph Désiré Mobutu)(pres., Zaire; 1930-)¡
Zabrze, Poland (also Hindenburg)
Zaca Mesa Winery (US bus.)
Zacatecas purple (slang, Mexican purple marijuana)
Zachary Scott (ent.; 1914-65)
Zachary Taylor ("Old Rough and Ready")(12th US pres.; 1784-1850)
Zack's Famous Frozen Yogurt, Inc.
Zacky Foods Co.
Zadar, Croatia
Zadkine, Ossip (Rus. artist; 1890-1967)
Zadora, Pia (ent.)
Zafy, Albert (pres., Madagascar; 1927?-)
Zagreb, Croatia
Zagros Mountains (Iran)
Zaharias, Babe (Mildred) Didrikson (US athlete; 1914-56)
Zahn, Paula (US TV jour.; 1956-)
Zaid bin Sultan al-Nahayan, Sheik (pres., UAE; 1918-)
Zaire (Republic of)(central Afr.)
Zambezi River (Afr.)
Zambia (Republic of)(formerly Northern Rhodesia)(S central Afr.)
Zambia Airways
Zamboanga, Philippines
Zamboni machine (hockey)
Zamfir
Zamora, Jaime Paz (ex-pres., Bolivia
Zandonai, Riccardo (It. comp.; 1883-1944)
Zane Grey (US writer; 1875-1939)
Zanesville, OH
Zantac™ (med.)
Zanuck, Darryl F(rancis)(ent.; 1902-79)
Zanzibar, Road to (film; 1941)
Zanzibar, Tanzania
Zapata, Emiliano (Mex. mil./agr.; c1879-1919)
Zaporozhye, Ukraine
Zapotec (Mex. Indians)
Zappa, Dweezil (ent.)
Zappa, Moon Unit (ent.)
Zappa, Frank (ent.; 1940-1993)
Zaragoza, Spain (also Saragossa)
Zarathustra (also Zoroaster)(Persian rel./educ.; 6th c. BC)
Zaria, Nigeria
Zarqa, Jordan
Zasu Pitts (ent.; 1898-1963)
Zayak, Elaine (US figure skating; 1965-)
ZCMI Department Store
Zealot (rel.)

Zebulon Montgomery Pike (US expl./mil.; 1779-1813)
Zechariah (rel.)
Zedekiah (king, Judah; 6th c. BC)
Zedong, Mao (also Mao Tse-tung, Chairman Mao)(Ch. pol.; 1893-1976)
Zeebrugge, Belgium
Zeeland (province, Netherlands)
Zeeman effect/splitting (optics)
Zeeman, Pieter (Dutch physt.; 1865-1943)
Zeffirelli, Franco (ent.; 1923-)
Zeist, Netherlands
Zeitgeist (Ger., spirit of the time)
Zelig (film; 1983)
Zell Miller (GA gov.; 1932-)
Zell, Harry Von (ent.; 1906-81)
Zellerbach (US bus.)
Zemin, Jiang (pres., Ch.; 1926-)
Zen Buddhism (rel.)
Zena Enterprises, Inc.
Zenawi, Meles (pres., Ethiopia; 1955-)
Zend-Avesta (rel.)
Zener cards (ESP)
Zener diode (elec.)
Zenica, Bosnia-Hercegovina
Zenith™
Zenith Electronics Corp.
Zenko, Suzuki (ex-PM, Jap; 1911-)
Zeno of Citium (Gr. phil.; late 4th early 3rd c. BC)
Zeno of Elea (Gr. phil./math.; c490-430 BC)
Zephyr Hills Water Co.
Zephyrus (myth.)
Zeppelin, Ferdinand von, Graf (Ger. mil./ aeronaut; 1838-1917)
Zeppelin, Graf (Ger. airship)
Zeppelin, Led (pop music)
Zeppo (Herbert) Marx (ent.; 1901-79)
Zerbe, Anthony (ent.; 1936-)
Zermatt, Switzerland
Zero (Samuel Joel) Mostel (ent.; 1915-77)
Zeron Group
Zest™ soap
Zeus (myth.)
Zeus (sculpture by Phidias, 1 of 7 Wonders)
Zevi, Sabbatai (Jew. rel.; 1626-76)
Zhangjiakou, China (also Changchiakow)
Zhao Ziyang (Ch. pol.; 1918-)
Zhejiang (also Chekiang)(province, Ch.)
Zhelev, Zhelyu (pres., Bulgaria; 1936-)
Zhelyu Zhelev (pres., Bulgaria; 1936-)
Zhengzhou, China (also Chengchow)
Zhivago, Doctor (B. Pasternak novel)
Zhivkov, Todor (ex-pres.; Bulgaria; 1911-)
Zhou Enlai (also Chou En-Lai)(ex-PM, Ch.; 1898-1976)
Zhuang (lang./people)
Zhukov, Georgi (Konstantinovich)(USSR mil.;

1895-1974)

Zia ul-Haq, Muhammad ("President Zia")(ex-pres., Pak.; 1924-88)

Zia, Begum Khaleda (PM, Bangladesh; 1944-)

Ziaur Rahman (ex-pres., Bangladesh; 1935-81)

Ziegfeld Follies, The

Ziegfeld, Flo(renz)(ent.; 1869-1932)

Ziegler, Ron(ald)(US pol.)

Ziggy (cartoon)

Ziggy Elman

Zigong, China (also Tzekung)

Zimbabwe (Republic of)(formerly Rhodesia)(S central Afr.)

Zimbalist, Efrem, Jr. (ent.; 1923-)

Zimbalist, Efrem, Sr. (US violinist/comp.; 1889-1985)

Zimbalist, Stephanie (ent.; 1956-)

Zimmer, Kim

Zindel, Paul (US writer; 1936-)

Zinder, Niger

Zine el-Abidine Ben Ali (pres., Tunisia; 1936-)

Zinka (Kunc) Milanov (Yug. opera; 1906-)

Zinnermann, Fred(erick)(ent.; 1907-)

Zinsser, Hans (US bacteriol.; 1878-1940)

Zion National Park (UT)

Zion, Mount (Jerusalem)

Zionism (Jew. pol. movement)

Zip-a-dee-doo-dah (song)

ZIP Code™

ZIP + 4™

Ziploc™ (storage bags)

Zippo Manufacturing Co.

Ziyang, Zhao (Ch. pol.; 1918-)

Zn (chem. sym., zinc)

Zoë Baird (US atty.)

Zoeller, Fuzzy (golf)

Zog I (b. Ahmed Bey Zogu)(king, Albania; 1895-1961)

Zohar (rel.)

Zola Budd (SAfr. athlete; 1966-)

Zola, Émile (Édouard Charles Antoine)(Fr. writer; 1840-1902)

Zoltán Kodály (Hung. comp.; 1882-1967)

Zomba, Malawi

Zona Gale (US writer; 1874-1938)

Zond (Soviet space probes)

Zoot Sims (US jazz; 1925-85)

Zorach v. Clausen (US law; 1952)

Zoran Lilic (pres., Yug.)

Zorba the Greek (film; 1964)

Zorn, Anders (Leonhard)(Swed. artist; 1860-1920)

Zoroaster (also Zarathustra)(Persian rel./educ.; 6th c. BC)

Zoroastrianism (also Mazdaism)(rel.)

Zorro (TV show)

Zorro, the Glade Blade (film; 1981)

Zouave (also l.c.)(mil.)

Zouave jacket

Zouérate, Mauritania

Z particle (phys.)

ZPG (zero population growth)

Zr (chem. sym., zirconium)

Zrenjanin, Yugoslavia

Zsa Zsa Gabor (ent.; ?-)

Zubi, Mahmoud (PM, Syria

Zubin Mehta (India, cond.; 1936-)

Zuckerman Unbound (P. Roth novel)

Zuckerman, Pinchas (Isr. violinist/comp.; 1948-)

Zuider Zee (former sea inlet, Holland)

Zukor, Adolph (ent.; 1873-1976)

Zulfikar Ali Bhutto (ex-pres/PM, Pak.; 1928-79)

Zulu (lang./people)

Zululand (region, SAfr.)

Zumwalt, Elmo, III (US adm.)

Zuni (NAmer Indians)

Zuni (pueblo, NM)

Zuni-Cibola National Historical Park (NM)

Zürich, Switzerland

Zutty Singleton (US jazz; 1898-1975)

Zviad Gamsakhurdia (ex-pres., Georgia

Zwickau, Germany

Zwingli, Huldreich (or Ulrich)(Swiss rel.; 1484-1531)

Zwinglianism (rel.)

Zwolle, Netherlands

Zworykin, Vladimir (Kosma)("Father of Television")(Rus./US physt./eng./inv.; 1889-1982)

ZZ Top (pop music)